THE BEST
237 BUSINESS SCHOOLS

THE BEST
237 BUSINESS SCHOOLS

2006 EDITION

Nedda Gilbert
and the Staff
of The Princeton Review

Random House, Inc.
New York
www.PrincetonReview.com

The Princeton Review, Inc.
2315 Broadway
New York, NY 10024
E-mail: bookeditor@review.com

ISBN: 0-375-76500-X

Editorial Director: Robert Franek
Production Editor: Christine LaRubio
Production Manager: Scott Harris
Account Manager: David Soto
Editor: Lisa Marie Rovito

Manufactured in the United States of America.

9 8 7 6 5 4 3 2 1

2006 Edition

ACKNOWLEDGMENTS

This book absolutely would not have been possible without the help of my husband, Paul. With each edition of this guide, his insights and support have been invaluable—this book continues to be as much his as it is mine. That said, I also need to thank my eleven-year-old daughter, Kaela, and her seven-year-old sister, Lexi, for enduring all my time immersed in this project.

A big thanks goes to Tom Meltzer and Anna Weinberg for their smart and savvy profile writing. The following people were also instrumental in the completion of this book: Scott Harris, Christine LaRubio, Lisa Marie Rovito, Erik Olson, David Soto, Ben Zelevansky, Steven Aglione, Sarah Kruchko, and Jeff Adams for putting all the pieces together; the sales staff at The Princeton Review, Tore Erickson and Josh Escott; Robert Franek and Young Shin, as well as Alicia Ernst and John Katzman, for giving me the chance to write this book; and to the folks at Random House, who helped this project reach fruition.

Thanks go to Kristin Hansen (Tuck '01) and Matt Camp (Tuck '02), and to Ramona Payne and all the folks at The Diversity Pipeline Alliance. I am also grateful for the unique insights provided by Cathy Crane-Moley, Stanford Graduate School of Business Class of '92, and by Patricia Melnikoff and Chiara Perry, Harvard Business School, Class of '92; Caroline Grossman, University of Chicago Graduate School of Business, Class of '03; Sara Weiss, MIT Sloan School of Management, Class of '04; and Stephen Hazelton, MIT Sloan School of Management, Class of '05. Thanks are also due to the business school folks who went far out of their way to provide essential information. They continue to make this book relevant and vital.

Linda Baldwin, Director of Admissions, The Anderson School, UCLA

Derek Bolton, Assistant Dean and Director of Admissions, Stanford University School of Business

Eileen Chang, Associate Director of Admissions, Harvard Business School

Allan Friedman, Director of Communications and Public Relations, University of Chicago

Wendy Hansen, Associate Director of Admissions, Stanford Business School

Stacey Kole, Deputy Dean for the full-time MBA Program and clinical professor of Economics, University of Chicago Graduate School of Business

Steven Lubrano, Assistant Dean and Director the MBA Program, Tuck School of Business

Rose Martinelli, former Director of Admissions and Financial Aid, The Wharton School MBA Program

Jon McLaughlin, Assistant MBA Admissions Director, Sloan School of Management, MIT

Julia Min, Director of MBA Admissions, Stern School of Business at New York University

Jeanne Wilt, Assistant Dean of Admissions and Career Development, Michigan

ACKNOWLEDGMENTS

CONTENTS

INTRODUCTION

A RETURN TO OUR ROOTS

Over the past 12 years, The Princeton Review has annually published a guide to business schools. For the early editions of the guide, we collected opinion surveys from thousands of students at a select group of graduate business schools as well as school statistics from school administrators that include enrollment and demographic figures, tuition, and the average GMAT scores of entering students. We used the students' opinions to craft descriptive narratives of the schools they attended and reported the statistics in the sidebars of those narratives.

Beginning with the 2001 edition of the guide, we discontinued collecting opinion surveys from students and writing narrative descriptions of the schools; instead we focused solely on collecting and reporting school statistics. While we were able to report statistics for many more business schools in the new guide's format (the last [2000] edition of the guide with narrative descriptions profiled only 80 schools, and the first edition of the statistics-only guide profiled 372 schools), we learned over the next few years that readers are interested in more than just school-reported statistics. They want to read what the experts—current graduate business school students—have to say about the experiences of today's graduate business student. They want from-the-horse's-mouth accounts of what's great (*and* what's not) at each school.

So last year we decided to reintroduce the student survey-driven descriptive narrative, offering students a more intimate look at the inner workings of each school.

We also brought back several top 10 lists that rank the profiled schools according to various metrics (more on the rankings later). You'll find these rankings on page 67.

Taken together, we believe that these candid student opinions, school statistics, and rankings provide a unique and helpful resource to help you decide what business schools to apply to. But let us stress that we hope that this book will not be the *only* resource you turn to when making this expensive (both in terms of time and treasure) decision. Do additional research on the Internet and in newspapers, magazines, and other periodicals. Talk to admissions officers and current students at the programs that interest you. If at all possible, visit the campuses you are seriously considering. But treat the advice of all these resources (including ours) as you would treat advice from anyone regarding any situation: as input that reflects the values and opinions of others as you *form your own opinion*.

TWO TYPES OF ENTRIES

For each of the 237 business schools in this book, you will find one of two possible types of entries: a two-page profile with lots of descriptive text and statistics, or a straight statistical listing. Our descriptive profiles are driven primarily by 1) comments business students provide in response to open-ended questions on our student survey and 2) our own statistical analysis of student responses to the many multiple-choice questions on the survey. While many business students complete a survey unsolicited by us at http://survey.review.com, in the vast majority of cases we rely on business school administrators to get the word out about our survey to their students. In the ideal scenario, the business school administration sends a Princeton Review-authored e-mail to all business students with an embedded link to our survey website (again, http://survey.review.com). If for some reason there are restrictions that prevent the administration from contacting the entire graduate business school student body on behalf of an outside party, they often help us find other ways to notify students of the fact that we are seeking their opinions such as advertising in business student publications or posting on business student community websites. In almost all cases, when the administration is cooperative, we are able to collect opinions from a sufficient number of students to produce an accurate descriptive profile and ratings of its business school.

There is a group of business school administrators, however, that doesn't agree with us that current business school student opinions presented in descriptive profile and rankings formats are useful to prospective business school students. Administrators at the many AACSB-accredited business schools not appearing with two-page descriptive profiles are a part of this group. They either ignored our multiple attempts to contact them in order to request their assistance in notifying their students about our survey, or they simply refused to work with us at all. And while we would like to be able to write a descriptive profile on each of these many schools anyway, we won't do so with minimal business student opinion.

So if you are a prospective business school student and would like to read current business student opinion about schools that do not appear with a two-page descriptive profile, contact the schools and communicate this desire to them. (We include contact information in each of the business school data listings.) If you are a current business student at one of the many AACSB-accredited business schools without a two-page descriptive profile, please don't send us angry letters; instead, go to http://survey.review.com, complete a survey about your school, and tell all of your fellow students to do the same.

You will find statistics for business schools whose administrators were willing to report their school statistics to us but unwilling to allow us to survey their students under the school's name in the section of the book entitled "Business School Data Listings."

One more thing to note about different entries: The majority of our various rankings are based wholly or partly on student feedback to our survey. Only one top ten ranking, The Toughest to Get Into, is based on school-reported statistics alone. So while *any* of the 448 schools listed in the book may appear on that list, *only those schools with two-page descriptive profiles will appear on all other rankings lists.*

BUT SOME THINGS NEVER CHANGE

Admission to the business school of your choice, especially if your choice is among the most selective programs, will require your absolute best shot. One way to improve your chances is to make sure you apply to schools that are a good fit—and the comments provided by students in our descriptive profiles will provide more insight into the personality of each school than its glossy view book.

In addition, you'll find plenty of useful information in Part I of this book on how to get in to business school and what to expect once you arrive. You'll find out what criteria are used to evaluate applicants and who decides your fate. You will also hear directly from admissions officers what dooms an application and how to ace the interview. We've even interviewed deans at several of the top schools to share with you their take on recent events, including trends in business, b-school applications, recruitment, and placement.

Again, it is our hope that you will consult our profiles as a resource when choosing a list of schools that suit your academic and social needs, and that our advice is helpful to you during the application process. Good luck!

HOW WE PRODUCE THIS BOOK

In August 1999, we published *The Best 80 Business Schools, 2000 Edition*. By the time the 2001 edition of the guide was published, we had shifted our focus from student opinion-driven profiles of a select number of schools to more data-driven profiles of every graduate business school accredited by the AACSB. Although we continue to present readers with data from all 414 accredited graduate b-schools, we have reintroduced the student survey-based descriptive profile. In order to clarify our position, intent, and methodology, we've created a series of questions and answers regarding the collection of data and the production of our descriptive profiles.

How do we choose which b-schools to survey and profile? And why do some competitive schools have only a data listing?

Any business school that is AACSB-accredited and offers a Master of Business Administration degree may have a data listing included in the book, as long as that school provides us with a sufficient amount of school-specific data. In addition, this year we offered an opportunity to assist us in collecting online business student surveys to each of those accredited schools where the primary language of instruction is English.

Some schools were unable to solicit surveys from their students via e-mail due to restrictive privacy policies; others simply chose not to participate. Schools that declined to work with us to survey their students remain in the book, although they do not have a descriptive profile. A school with only a data listing does not suggest that the school is less competitive or compelling; we only separated these profile types into two sections for easier reference. If you're not sure where to find information on a school in which you're interested, you can refer to our alphabetical b-school listing in the back of the book.

There is no fee to be included in this book. If you're an administrator at an accredited business school and would like to have your school included, please send an e-mail to surveysupport@review.com.

What's the AACSB, and by what standards are schools accredited?

The AACSB stands for the Association to Advance Collegiate Schools of Business. In April 2003, the AACSB made some significant changes to its standards for accreditation. In fact, the actual number of standards went from 41 to 21. Some of the changes in accreditation include a shift from requiring a certain number of full-time faculty members with doctorates to a focus on teacher participation. Schools may employ more part-time faculty members if they are actively involved in the students' business education. The onus of both the development of a unique curriculum and the evaluation of the success of that curriculum will fall on each b-school, and schools will be reviewed by the association every five years instead of every ten. As a result of the changes in accreditation standards, a number of schools have been newly accredited or re-accredited.

How were the student surveys collected?

Back in fall 2004, we contacted admissions officers at all accredited graduate b-schools and requested that they help us survey their students by distributing our Princeton Review-authored survey message to the student body via e-mail. The survey message explained the purpose of the survey and contained a link to our online business student survey. We had a phenomenal response from students—at least ten percent of full-time students responded at almost all institutions we surveyed; at many schools, we scored responses from as many as one-third or one-half of the student body—and nearly all students in a few cases.

The surveys are made up of 79 multiple-choice questions and 7 free-response questions, covering 5 sections: About Yourself, Students, Academics, Careers, and Quality of Life. Students may complete the secure online survey at any time and may save their survey responses, returning later, until the survey is complete and ready for submission. Students sign in to the online survey using their school-issued .edu e-mail address to ensure that their response is attributed to the correct school, and the respondent certifies before submission that he or she is indeed a current student enrolled in said program. In addition, an automated message is sent to this address once the student has submitted the survey, and they must click on a link in the e-mail message in order to validate their survey. We also offered a paper version of the survey to a few schools that were unable to e-mail their students regarding our online survey.

We use the resulting responses to craft descriptive profiles that are representative of the respondents' feelings toward the b-school they attend. Although we concede that well-written and/or humorous comments are favored for inclusion, they would never be used unless they best stated what numerous students have told us.

What about the ranking lists and ratings?

When we decided to bring the enclosed student opinion-driven resources back into the fold, we updated our online survey and reconsidered all ranking lists. You will find that only a few of the rankings in this year's book resemble our b-school rankings of yester-year. We've done our best to include only those topics most vital to success in business school, and we have added a few brand new lists that you will find timely and relevant.

We offer several ranking lists on a variety of considerations, from academic experience, to career expectations, to the atmosphere for women and minority students. It must be noted, however, that none of these lists purports to rank the business schools by their overall quality. Nor should any combination of the categories we've chosen be construed as representing the raw ingredients for such a ranking. We have made no attempt to gauge the "prestige" of these schools, and we wonder whether we could accurately do so even if we tried. What we have done, however, is presented a number of lists using information from two very large databases—one of statistical information collected from business schools and another of subjective data gathered via our survey of 11,000 business students at 237 AACSB-accredited business schools. We do believe that there is a right business school for you, and that our rankings, when used in conjunction of our profile of each school, will help you select the best schools to apply to.

We have also added five ratings to the book this year: Admissions Selectivity, Academic Experience, Career, Professors Interesting, and Professors Accessible. These ratings are based on student survey responses and/or institutionally reported data. An Admissions Selectivity Rating has been assigned to each of the accredited institutions included herewith, but the other four ratings are assigned only to those schools that have a descriptive profile in the book; therefore, these four ratings are to be used to compare the surveyed institutions within this edition of the book only. (We explain what factors are considered in each rating in the following section.)

What do the schools have to say about all this?

Our contact at each school is kept abreast of the profile's status throughout the production process. After having established a contact through whom we are able to reach online student respondents, we get to work writing our profiles and crunching the data. Once these have been poured into profile pages, we send a copy of the school's profile to our contact via e-mail and "snail mail." We request that the administrator review the data and comments included in the profile, and we invite corrections and suggestions to any inaccurate data or text that is considered misrepresentative of overall student opinion. With this information in hand, we revisit survey responses and investigate any such claims.

We are aware that a general distaste for rankings permeates the business school community, and that top schools have recently backed down from providing necessary data for such calculations. We agree that overall rankings that decide the "best" school overall are not-so-helpful to students, and that they may be tainted by the desire of school administrators to propel their schools into the upper echelon of revered business institutions in terms of reputation, without taking the necessary measures to actually increase the quality of the school. This is why the meat of our book is the schools' descriptive profiles, which are meant to showcase each school's unique personality. The ranking lists are simply used as reference points for students looking for a particular attribute in a prospective b-school. We don't claim to be the final word on what school has the best MBA program in the country—it's nearly impossible to determine. We simply relay the messages that the students at each school are sending us, and we are clear about how our rankings are determined.

HOW THIS BOOK IS ORGANIZED

This book is packed with information about business schools, and we want to make sure you know how to find what you're looking for. So here's a breakdown of the book's main parts.

Part I includes a few chapters to give you an idea of what to expect at business school and how to put together a winning application.

Part II has our b-school ranking lists. Of the 12 lists, 7 are based entirely on student survey responses; 1 is based solely on institutionally-reported data; and 4 are based on a combination of survey responses and statistical information. Along with each list, you will find information about which survey questions or statistical factors were used to calculate the rankings.

Part III contains profiles of all AACSB-accredited graduate schools with MBA programs divided into two sections: those with descriptive profiles, based on student surveys, and those with only a statistical listing.

Part III-A: Business School Descriptive Profiles
Please see the sample descriptive profile below

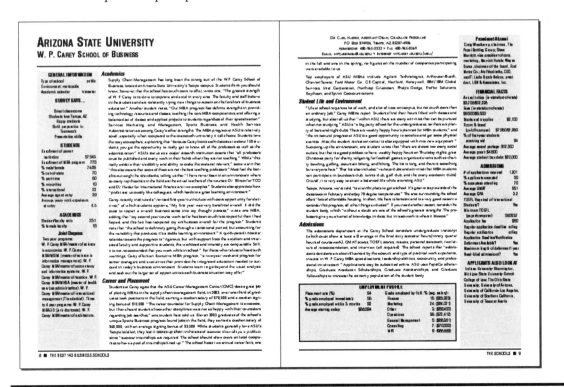

Each two-page spread is made up of 8 major components. At the top of each page, you'll find the name of the business school, along with the name of an admissions contact and his or her address, phone number, fax number, if applicable, and e-mail address. This section also includes the b-school's website address. There are two sidebars (the narrow columns on the outer edge of each page) that contain information reported by the schools through the Business Data Set (BDS) and some student survey data as well. The Survey Says reflects areas where students at each school feel the strongest; there are 9 different possible results. We also offer an Employment Profile for each school, which is also made up of statistical information from the BDS. The main body of the profile contains Academics, Placement and Recruiting, Student/Campus Life, and Admissions. Each is based on student survey responses and may call upon statistical data where necessary. Read on for more info on each individual part.

THE SIDEBARS

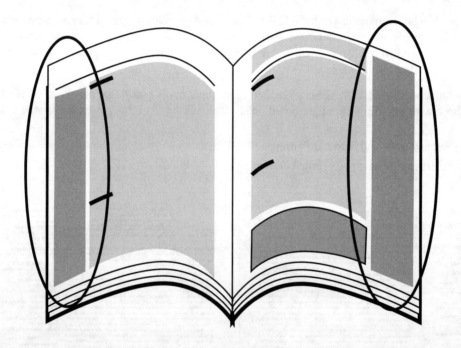

All information in the sidebars falls under the following categories: General Information, Academics, Financial Facts, and Admissions. Please note that not every category will appear for every school; in some cases the information is not reported or not applicable. These are the same data fields that are reported for those schools listed in Part III-B: Business School Data Listings, save for 4 of the 5 ratings, which appear only in the descriptive profiles.

Here is what each heading tells you.

General Information

Type of school

Public or private school

Affiliation

Any religious order with which the school is affiliated

Environment

Whether the campus is located in a metropolis, city, town, village, or rural setting

Academic Calendar

Whether the school schedule runs according to trimesters, semesters, quarters, or another calendar type like a 4-1-4 (4 month semester - 1 month interim term - 4 month semester)

Schedule

From the full-time only MBAs to part-time and evening programs

SURVEY SAYS

Survey Says gives you an at-a-glance look at what students are most in agreement about at their school. You'll find up to six results per school. Three will reflect the top three subject areas as indicated by responses to the following question:

How well your school has prepared you in the following areas:

Marketing

Finance

Accounting

General management

Operations

Teamwork

Communication/Interpersonal skills

Presentation skills

Quantitative skills

Computer skills

Doing business in a global economy

Entrepreneurial studies

In addition, Survey Says may include (up to) three things from the following list that students at were most in agreement about:

- Students like Hometown, State. Based on level of agreement with the statement, "I like the town where my school is located."

- Friendly students. Based on level of agreement with the statement, "Your business school classmates are friendly."

- Good social scene. Based on level of agreement with the statement, "Your business school classmates have active social lives."

- Good peer network. Based on level of agreement with the statement, "Your business school classmates are the type of people you want to network with after graduation."

- Cutting edge classes. Based on responses to the question, "How well has your school integrated new business trends and practices into course offerings?"

- Helpful alumni. Based on responses to the question, "How helpful have alumni been in assisting you in your job search?"

- Happy students. Based on level of agreement with the statement, "Overall, I am happy here."

- Smart classrooms. Based on level of agreement with the statement, "Classroom facilities are equipped with computer/multimedia resources."

Students

Enrollment of parent institution

Total number of undergraduate and graduate students enrolled in parent institution program

Enrollment of MBA program

Total number of students enrolled in MBA programs at the business school, including both full- and part-time programs

"% male/female" through "% international"

Items based on demographic information about b-school students as reported by the schools

Average age at entry

The average age of incoming first-year MBA students

Average years work experience at entry

The average years of work experience for incoming first-year MBA students

Academics

Academic Experience Rating

This rating measures the quality of the learning environment. Each school is given a score between 60 and 99. Factors taken into consideration include GMAT scores and undergraduate grades of enrolled students; percent accepted; percent enrolled; student: faculty ratio; and student survey questions pertaining to faculty, fellow students, and realization of academic expectations. This rating is intended to be used only to compare those schools within this edition of the book whose students completed our business student survey.

Please note that if a 60* Academic Experience Rating appears for any school, it means that the school didn't report all the rating's underlying data points by our deadline, so we were unable to calculate an accurate rating. In such cases, the reader is advised to follow up with the school about specific measures this rating takes into account.

Please also note that many foreign institutions use a grading system that is different from the standard U.S. GPA; as a result, we approximated their Admissions Selectivity and Academic Ratings, indicating this with a † following the rating.

Student/Faculty Ratio

The ratio of full-time graduate instructional faculty members to all enrolled MBA students

Professors Interesting Rating

Based on the answers given by students to the survey question, "Overall, how good are your professors as teachers?" Ratings fall between 60 and 99. This rating is intended to be used to compare those schools within this edition of the book whose students completed our business student survey.

Professors Accessible Rating

Based on the answers given by students to the survey question, "How accessible are your professors outside of the classroom?" Ratings fall between 60 and 99. This rating is intended to be used to compare those schools within this edition of the book whose students completed our business student survey.

% female faculty

Percent of graduate business faculty in the 2004–2005 academic year who were women

% minority faculty

Percent of graduate business faculty in the 2004–2005 academic year who were members of minority groups

Joint Degrees

A list of joint degrees offered by the business school. See Decoding Degrees on page 519 for the full name of each degree.

Prominent Alumni

School administrators may submit the name, title, and company of up to five prominent alumni.

Financial Facts

Please note that we rely on foreign institutions to convert financial figures into U.S. dollars. Please check with any foreign schools you are considering for up-to-date figures and conversion rates.

"Tuition (in-state/out-of-state)" and "Fees (in-state/out-of-state)"

In-state and out-of-state tuition and fees per academic year. At state-supported public schools, in-state tuition and fees are likely to be significantly lower than out-of-state expenses.

Books and supplies

Estimated cost of books and supplies for one academic year

Room and board

Cost of room and board on campus per academic year, and estimate of off-campus living expenses for this time period

"% of students receiving aid" through "% of students receiving grants"

Percent of students receiving aid, then specifically those receiving grants and loans. These numbers reflect the percentage of all enrolled MBA students that receive financial aid, regardless of whether or not they applied for financial aid or for specific aid types. Likewise, the second figure, "% of first year students receiving aid" takes into account all first-year MBA students, regardless of whether they applied for financial aid or specific aid types.

Average award package

For students who received financial aid, this is the average award amount.

Average grant

For students who received grants, this is the average amount of grant money awarded.

Average student loan debt

The average dollar amount of outstanding educational MBA loans per graduate (class of 2003) at the time of graduation

Admissions

Admissions Selectivity Rating

This rating measures the competitiveness of the school's admissions. Factors taken into consideration include the average GMAT score and undergraduate GPA of the first-year class, the percent of students accepted, and the percent of applicants who are accepted and ultimately enroll. No student survey data is used in this calculation. Ratings fall between 60 and 99. This rating is intended to be used to compare all schools within this edition of the book, regardless of whether their students completed our business student survey.

Please note that if a 60* Admissions Selectivity Rating appears for any school, it means that the school did not report all of the rating's underlying data points by our deadline, so we were unable to calculate an accurate rating. In such cases, the reader is advised to follow up with the school about specific measures this rating takes into account.

Please also note that many foreign institutions use a grading system that is different from the standard U.S. GPA; as a result, we approximated their Admissions Selectivity and Academic Ratings, indicating this with a † next to the rating.

of applications received

The total number of applications received for any and all MBA programs at the school

% applicants accepted

The percentage of applicants to which the school offered admission

% acceptees attending

Of those accepted students, the percentage of those who enrolled.

Average GMAT

The average GMAT score for the first-year class

Average GPA

The average undergraduate GPA of the first year class, reported on a 4-point scale

TOEFL required of international applicants?

For those international students interested in applying, the b-school reports whether the Test of English as a Foreign Language (TOEFL) is required.

Minimum TOEFL (paper/computer)

The minimum TOEFL score necessary for consideration. We list acceptable scores for both the paper and computer versions of the test.

Application fee

The amount it costs to file an application with the school

"Regular application deadline" and "Regular notification deadline"

This regular application deadline reflects the date by which all materials must be postmarked; the notification date tells you when you can expect to hear back.

Application Deadline/Notification; Round 1, Round 2, etc.

The corresponding dates for those business schools that have multiple application deadlines. The application date generally refers to the postmark deadline.

"Early decision program?" and "ED deadline/notification"

If a school offers an early decision option, we'll tell you when early decision apps are due to be postmarked, and when you'll be notified of the school's decision.

"Deferment available?" and "Maximum length of deferment"

Some schools allow accepted students to defer enrollment for a year or more, while others require students who postpone attendance to re-apply.

Transfer students accepted?

Whether or not students are accepted from other MBA programs

Non-fall admissions?

Some business schools may allow students to matriculate at the beginning of each semester, while for others, the invitation to attend stipulates that fall attendance is mandatory.

Need-blind admissions?

Whether or not the school considers applications without regard to the candidate's financial need

Applicants also look at

The school reports that students applying to their school are also known to apply to a short list of other schools.

EMPLOYMENT PROFILE

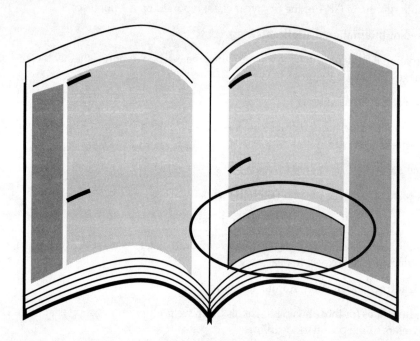

Career Rating

Taking into account both student survey responses and statistical data, this rating measures the confidence students have in their school's ability to lead them to fruitful employment opportunities, as well as the school's own record of having done so. Factors taken into consideration include the average starting salary and percent of students employed at graduation from the Business Data Set and questions from the student survey, assessing the efforts of the placement office, the quality of recruiting companies, level of preparation, and opportunities for off-campus projects, internships, and mentorships. Ratings fall between 60 and 99. This rating is intended to be used to compare those schools within this edition of the book whose students completed our business student survey.

* Please note that if a 60* Career Rating appears for any school, it means that the school did not report all of the rating's underlying data points by our deadline, so we were unable to calculate an accurate rating. In such cases, the reader is advised to follow up with the school about specific measures this rating takes into account.

Placement Rate (%)

Indicates how many students (or what percentage of them anyway) of the graduating class of 2003 were eventually placed in jobs, as tracked by the career services or career placement office.

# of companies recruiting on campus

The number of companies seeking recruits on campus each year

% grads employed immediately

This reflects the percentage of MBA grads who already had a job by the time they graduated from business school.

% grads employed within six months

This reflects the percentage of MBA grads in the class of 2003 who earned a job within 6 months of graduation.

Average starting salary

Average starting salary of all 2004 graduates

Grads employed by field (avg. salary)

Reflects the distribution of 2004 graduates across many different industries and company types.

Descriptive Profile

Each school's descriptive profile is made up of four sections which highlight those qualities that characterize the school as a unique institution. *Academics* covers students' opinions on the quality of professors, curriculum, special or noteworthy programs, the administration, and anything else academic in nature. *Career and Placement* deals with the school's efforts to secure internships and jobs for its current students and graduates; information about alumni assistance and popular recruiters of MBAs at the school may also be included. In *Student Life and Environment*, you'll find out how students balance work and play and whether they find it manageable; often, you'll also find reviews of the school's facilities as well. Finally, the *Admissions* section describes the admissions committee is looking for in potential students.

All quotes in these sections are taken from students' essay responses to our survey. We choose quotes based on the accuracy with which they reflect our overall survey results.

Part III-B: Business School Data Listings

This section contains all of the statistical info that is presented alongside the descriptive profile and is described starting on page 5. Each school in this section will receive an Admissions Selectivity rating but will not receive the other 3 ratings, the Survey Says, or a descriptive profile.

Part IV: School Says

Part IV offers more detailed information about particular business schools authored by the schools themselves. The business schools included in this section pay a small fee for this space. These schools also have descriptive profiles or data listings in Part III.

Everything Else

Following Part IV, we offer a small section of profiles of b-schools who may pay a small fee for inclusion. Next is a section entitled *Decoding Degrees* that will help you make sense of the myriad degree abbreviations you'll see listed in the book. You'll then find the indexes—alphabetical by school name, and then by location. Finally, you'll have an opportunity to learn more about our author Nedda Gilbert.

Enjoy and good luck!

PART I
ALL ABOUT BUSINESS SCHOOL

CHAPTER 1

THIS ISN'T YOUR FATHER'S (OR MOTHER'S) B-SCHOOL ANYMORE

THE NEW MBA CLASS: FEWER, YOUNGER, AND WORKING WHILE THEY LEARN

The MBA has always been seen as a golden passport, the trip ticket to romance and riches. The destination: career acceleration, power networks and recruiters, elite employers, and of course, generous paychecks.

But not everyone wants to make the trip. Several factors will always impact on the popularity of the MBA: 1) the state of the economy—interest in getting the MBA has generally waxed and waned with economic times; 2) trends and favorable or unfavorable press—in the 1980s, a rash of insider trading scandals in which MBAs were ensnared made the degree look smarmy and other graduate programs, notably law and medicine, look more appealing; 3) the immediacy of good professional opportunities—the collapse of the dot-com boom, followed by the severe retrenchment of traditional MBA destinations (such as investment banks and consulting firms) in a depressed economy, has left many current MBAs stranded; and 4) recruiter demand for newly minted MBAs—do employers see the skill sets of today's MBAs bringing measurable value to their companies?

THE CONTINUING B-SCHOOL SLUMP: INTEREST AND APPLICATIONS SLIDE

It appears that more would-be managers are sticking it out and climbing the ladder in the workforce instead of turning to business schools to earn that resume-boosting MBA. According to the Graduate Management Admissions Council (GMAC), applications at business schools for 2004 were down overall by somewhere in the range of 15 percent–35 percent. In almost half of the programs surveyed in the most recent poll, there was a reported drop in applications of 20 percent or more. This is the second year in a row for which a decline has been reported.

A STRONGER ECONOMY + A HEFTY PRICE TAG = SCARING STUDENTS AWAY

The weak economy of the past few years has been behind the wheel in driving MBA unpopularity. Concerns about the lingering effects of the recession have made the once-golden MBA an unsure investment. In an already tight job market, fewer students wanted to take on the opportunity costs of leaving their current jobs, paying a hefty sum for tuition, and still having to scramble for a job after they graduate. The numbers do tell: B-school has lost its appeal as a safe haven from turbulent times, much less a straight-shot pathway to guaranteed riches.

Finally, the economy appears to be recovering. But application numbers are still less than stellar and the hiring of new MBAs has not fully rebounded. One note of difference: at top-brand schools, the picture is much rosier. Placement rates are fast returning to pre-September 11 levels.

YOUNGER MINDS

Although growing applicant pools may make admission seem more competitive, there are now some unrecognized opportunities for candidates with less than the traditional two to four years of work experience to make a strong case for admittance.

Interest in turning to b-school after September 11 reinforced a small but notable trend toward re-thinking rigid admittance standards on work experience. Many schools had already begun to assess their emphasis on work experience as the be-all and end-all.

Admissions officers at large benchmark schools such as Stanford say that at their respective institutions this trend pre-dates the economic downturn. Derek Bolton, director of admissions at Stanford notes, "The pendulum has gone too far in one direction in terms of the number of younger candidates applying to b-school. It has not kept pace with the overall pace of applicants. We want more young applicants applying. The goal is to bring the average age down in the next couple of years."

"What's driving this is the willingness on the part of the b-schools to not be rigidly fixed on what's right for someone. We may not always be the best judge of when the best time is for a candidate to go to b-school," continues Bolton.

Wharton's former Director of Admissions Rose Martinelli observed "a shift in that we became more tuned in to when students are ready in their leadership, professional, and personal development. We see so many nontraditional students that we don't want to have rules on when they can apply. We don't want to miss out on fabulous applicants because they don't think they can get in."

"When the applicant pool continues to get older and older, then we're closing out younger applicants who are on a fast track." Martinelli continues, "Why should we wait? Why should they wait? We want to catch the human element in the application process."

"Heading into the 2005 application filing period, this perspective continues to hold true. Echoes University of Chicago's Stacey Kole, "The pendulum had swung too far in terms of the type of student who should be admitted and when. Now schools are correcting that and experimenting, taking less experienced candidates. We believe that this experimentation is a good thing."

The Draw of The Part-Time Program

Ironically, even as the economy appears to be in an upswing, many young adults are choosing to brave a newly robust job market over emersing themselves in the uncertainty—and those high costs—of a professional school like business or even law. Because part-time and executive education programs have not suffered the decline that full-time programs have, pundits say that the future of b-school may lie in those programs that offer more flexible part-time opportunities, allowing students to get the degree without making a full-time commitment. In fact, Stacey Kole, Deputy Dean for the full-time MBA Program and Clinical Professor of Economics, University of Chicago Graduate School of Business states, "There is this tendency to think of the MBA as a full-time-only product. But schools like Chicago offer MBA programs in the evening, on weekends, and in executive program formats. For us, whether the student matriculates in our part-time or full-time program, the process is exactly the same. Ours is the same degree only delivered in full-time, part-time, and weekend formats with different scheduling options. Chicago GSB offers individuals interested in an MBA considerable flexibility in how they pursue their education."

Kole continues, "Part-time and executive programs are now providing more of the outside-the-classroom, extracurricular experience that did not exist 10 years ago. For example, they are offering student-led clubs, speakers, and recruiter events that historically were the exclusive domain of full-time programs. This is one explanation for why part-time programs are looking like better substitutes for a full-time program." Flexibility is not the only draw.

There may be more to the story, too. Because they may be less likely to be in committed relationships or have families, younger students are more active, generous alumni, and b-schools can't afford to ignore the market that these younger students represent. Despite the heightened competition, candidates with less experience are increasingly being deemed worthy of a coveted b-school seat.

PAYBACK TIME

The MBA, particularly at the top schools, continues to pay out high dividends to grads. Even during these uncertain times, recent MBA graduates reported a surge in salary of over 35 percent at graduation. That's a hefty return on investment. But the degree doesn't come with any promises. The world of business requires some risk, as many MBA wannabes found out several years go: You can enter a business school program at the height of the economy only to graduate when things are dismal. But you can also enter b-school at low tide then watch as the job market swells and employers are fighting over the newest and brightest MBA grads, including you.

FOREIGN MBA STUDENTS: THE NEW REALITY

Opportunities to study or work abroad during an MBA program are considered highly relevant. Likewise, international enrollment at U.S. business schools has always been a priority. At some schools, the percentage of foreign students has been sky-high, anywhere from 30 to 40 percent. Of course, that was before the new screening and tracking processes for international applicants went into effect.

Previously, our position was clear: International students represent a win-win proposition for both U.S. business schools and the foreign industries that send them here. American business schools prize the global perspective and diversity international students bring into the classroom and community; foreign businesses operating in a global economy desire expertise in U.S. business practices which are becoming the international standard.

Unfortunately, due to international security issues, this informal but critical partnership faces greater challenges. These have come primarily in the form of increased scrutiny. In fact, stricter U. S. visa restrictions are cited as the number-one reason for the slowing of international applicants to U.S. MBA programs. According to GMAC, in 2004, this resulted in a significant decrease in foreign applications for over 70% of MBA programs.

The big change for foreign students is a double whammy. First, they must slog through tougher rules and procedures for obtaining and maintaining a visa under the United States Citizenship and Immigration Services (USCIS). The snags can be considerable—and that's just getting in.

Many foreign students feel that even if they are successful in obtaining a student visa, they will face an even tougher battle after they graduate: trying to get a work visa. That puts them back to square one. Though armed with an American MBA, they often find themselves looking for work in their home country—from which they may originally have wanted a professional out.

Foreign Students: Getting In

As of January 2003, U.S. institutions must comply with the Student and Exchange Visitor Information System, or SEVIS, which tracks foreign students and exchange visitors, as well as some foreign professors. While there is hope that SEVIS will prevent potential terrorists from slipping through the cracks, critics fear that the intensified scrutiny drives away many foreign applicants. The system causes major delays in obtaining a student visa and leaving or re-entering the country. In addition, compliance with SEVIS requires the staff of international student offices to perform a great deal of data entry, detracting from the face-time advisors can spend with foreign students.

For the foreseeable future, students wishing to obtain a visa will not be able to escape the shadow of world events, but they should not be deterred. Most business schools stand firm on their commitment to foreign applicants throughout the entire process.

In fact, Don Martin, Director of Admissions at the renowned University of Chicago notes that the number of international students enrolled at Chicago has remained constant. Martin says, "We have made no change in terms of our desire and commitment to enroll foreign students. This world will never go back to what it was before it became a global village. For the sake of diversity and the perspective international students bring to the table, or for understanding foreign business culture, we need to have people who represent that world in every sense of that word."

Martin does agree that for foreign MBA students intending to study on American soil, "The journey of enrolling them is going to be more challenging. A part of that is tied into the changes the U.S. government has imposed on getting visas. Some applicants will need to take another year for the paperwork." But most notably, he sees different forces at play in the shrinking foreign MBA market, namely, the competition U.S. schools are feeling from business schools abroad. Continues Martin, "The issue influencing more international business students away from U.S. business schools is the large amount of European, Australian, and Latin American business schools that heretofore I would not have thought would have had as much pull as they did. These business schools have become more visible and prominent. They are being ranked by the large news organizations and magazines. So I would say American business schools still want international students, but the ability to recruit and draw them here to us, will be difficult against this new competition."

To those applying for a visa, Wharton's Director of Admissions Rose Martinelli offers this advice: "Emphasize plans to return home, [not] plans to immigrate to the United States." If a visa is denied, many schools will defer admission and hold that student's spot until the visa is obtained. Sums up Martinelli: "It may take a little longer for students from some countries to get their visas. But decisions here are not made based on whether they got a visa or not. Decisions are made based on what they'll do at our school and on the contributions they'll make."

Of course, all this is subject to change, perhaps even by the time of this book's publication. Non-U.S. citizens should visit the USCIS website (http://uscis.gov) for the latest information on student visas.

Foreign Students: Getting a Job

Just when a foreign student is ready to reap the rewards of their hard-won business degree, they hit another roadblock. And this one's a brick wall: an unforgiving and limited job market fueled not just by a new wartime security, but rather by a new nationalism.

Historically, foreign students have always had a tougher time than their American counterparts in trying to get that first job out of b-school. That's because of the hassle of sponsoring a foreigner on a visa, rigid immigration rules, and other cultural and relocation issues. Nonetheless, for grads of the top schools, there has always been a pot of gold waiting at the end of that long journey. That pot of gold has meant the opportunity to embark on an entirely new career and life—to be sponsored by a U.S. company, on U.S. soil, with post-MBA pay scales that supersede those of their home countries and launch them on a high-earnings career path.

Since September 11, the environment in the United States has changed, and the home-field advantage of American MBAs is even greater. Simply put, U.S. companies have been reluctant to offer a foreign MBA a plush job over an American MBA who is equally talented and qualified. The result is that foreign hires have been more limited to hard-to-fill positions, to employment in their locations abroad, or to positions in the student's home country. Many MBA recruiters won't even offer an international student an interview.

As for companies shrinking their foreign MBA hires down to bare bones, as we've said many times before, and Don Martin concurs, where you go to school matters. He explains, "Some companies have changed their hiring strategies. Fewer overall international students are being hired, but not at our school. Companies typically will drop down from their list of 10 schools they go to, to a much smaller number of programs. In a high percentage, we've remained on their lists. We are seeing 90 percent of our international students placed in internships and going on to full-time hires."

The result of the shrinking job market for most foreign students, is that business schools have begun to cut back on the number of applicants admitted, and this has made it even tougher to get accepted. Many schools have begun to be upfront about the limited career opportunities on U.S. soil for foreigners. Indeed, this will soon be compounded by a reduction of more than 50 percent in the number or work visas the government issues annually to employees sponsored by their company.

But as the economy heats up and MBA hiring begins to rebound, it is possible that recruiters, particularly Wall Street and the top-flight consulting firms, will once again open their doors to whomever is most qualified, foreign or not. History, it should be remembered, shows us that the top jobs always go to the most capable applicants. This next cycle should be no different than the preceding cycles. Talent still rules.

In the meantime, buyers beware: an MBA is not the passport to riches it once was for foreign applicants. International students should think twice about the costs of pursuing a degree that may only deliver them back into the hands of their home countries saddled with the debts, but not the benefit, of an MBA education.

THE CONTINUING RELEVANCE OF BUSINESS SCHOOL

The MBA is such an attractive option because it *does* confer huge value on the recipient. Business schools know how to keep pace with the rapidly changing face of business. After all, that's *their* business, so you're never really out of the game. In fact, if you look at the nation's top business programs, you'll find exciting innovations in curriculum that reflect all that's new and relevant. This includes unique opportunities for teamwork, internships, and laboratory simulations that replicate real-world, real-time business scenarios.

The integration of these real-world experiences into the basics produces better-trained, more well-rounded managers, as graduates are more adept at discerning the correlation between principle and reality. Even so, a turn from fad courses in search of business knowledge that is more widely applicable and more relevant long-term has caused a strong return to fundamentals.

BACKPEDALING TO THE BASICS

Many top schools are reviving the old classics: it's back to basics. Both schools and students now have enough of a perspective to look back at the frenzy of the last business cycle and understand that enduring values are rooted in a solid foundation. Gone is the frothy demand for trendy courses on e-commerce and other hype-driven topics. Just three years ago, a class at Stanford on the principles of Internet marketing was oversubscribed. Last year, only two people signed up for it.

So here's a sampler of the back-to-basics you'll get at b-school: an in-depth immersion in all of the key functional areas of an organization: marketing, management, sales, finance, operations, logistics, and so on. And you'll look at these areas across dozens of industries and organizational types, from start-ups to Fortune 500 companies.

But the renewed focus on basics doesn't mean that you'll find yourself shorted on current events. Expect plenty of case study debate on corporate governance and the Enron debacle, and expect the themes of global perspective and technological competence to permeate many programs. You'll also find classes and seminars on leadership gaining popularity. "We're seeing a resurgence of leadership courses as students seek out professions and business models that are other-oriented," notes Stanford's Bolton. "This may be a new generation. But these are students who look at business as a positive force in the world, a more noble calling."

SURVIVOR POWER

Once you have your MBA, you can expect to hit the ground running. You'll start off your post b-school career with a load of contacts that you will periodically leverage over your career. Many graduates use the degree to embark on entirely new career paths than those that brought them to the school; consultants become bankers, entrepreneurs become consultants, marketers become financiers, and so on. The MBA has and will continue to be a terrific opportunity to reinvent oneself.

"An MBA is unlike any other professional degree because the breadth of knowledge poises you for a multitude of career choices," says Julia Min, Director of MBA Admissions for NYU Stern School of Business. "You can be an investment banker, yet two years from that point, segue into nonprofit work. You can move from banking to corporate finance, to a venture-capital proposition, to ultimately having an entrepreneurial experience. So it's a credential that allows you the flexibility to explore different industries; it's a long-term investment that will give you the tools to transition if you want to."

"What's wonderful about the MBA is that it provides fundamental skills that you can use whenever and wherever you need them," champions Martinelli. "I'm a cheerleader for the nontraditional because I feel the MBA is such a fundamental tool. It offers an ability to enter the business world and link passion with functionality."

"For example, for folks who want to go into public service or nonprofit, even the arts industry, they're very narrow fields. You need the passion and vision to be successful in them. But often credibility is undermined when you don't understand the business world's perspective," states Martinelli.

"You've got to know that industry if you're going to make it viable for the future. But you have to be able to know how to talk to the business world in order to get those investments to make it happen. And that's one of the reasons why an MBA is so valuable. It bestows credibility in the marketplace and helps us maintain these organizations in a world that doesn't often respect passion over the bottom line," she continues.

The big question remains: Will your MBA get you the job you want when you graduate? Despite the recent economic downturn, hundreds of companies continue to visit and recruit from business school campuses, (though they may have reduced their hires). This is because recruiters exist in a symbiotic relationship with business schools. Companies that depend on business school talent can ill afford to bypass campus recruiting for fear that when their hiring needs increase again, the school or students will be less receptive to their offers. Employers need to maintain their strong presence. They need to know that they'll have top picks when the good times return. Thus, MBA programs remain one of the most effective means to get oneself in front of recruiters and senior managers from the most desirable companies. And while that may not grant you "immunity" from an economy of up and downs, it will absolutely improve you survivor power.

COMPETITION HAS EASED UP

With an economic recovery at hand (and hopefully well underway by the time this book hits shelves), the chance to dive into any number of secure, well-paying jobs will lure a percentage of professionals away from the MBA. After years of struggling through economic hardship, a decent paycheck from the pocket of a newly strong labor market may seem the best bet. And it's no doubt that risk-averse individuals would prefer the stability of a secure job to what might-be, could-be, or should-be two years down the road—even with an MBA in hand. This may keep the applicant pool smaller.

Additionally, the continued absence of foreign applicants, who at many schools comprised well over 20 percent of students, will keep applications down, too. Other factors include the fact that there are currently smaller percentages of people in the country who are in the typical age bracket of business school applicants.

Lastly, the increased interest in part-time MBA programs may continue to drive the decline in full-time business school applications.

What does all of this mean? Basically this: If you have a handsome application and you plan on applying to the most competitive programs this year, you may find yourself met with welcoming arms.

As the Song Goes...Money, Money, Money, Money...

But don't go buying the flashy car to go with that flashy degree quite yet. It needs to be said that, after several years of a slump, there could actually be a surge in this upcoming applicant pool that would correspond with improvements in the economy. Recruiters are once again storming the top business schools as hiring slowly returns to healthy levels. At programs like Chicago, Harvard, and Stanford, six-figure salaries and signing bonuses of $10,000-plus are still the norm. That's why it's important to remember that the MBA from the right school can deliver an immediate and hefty return on investment. According to the Graduate Management Admission Council Global MBA Graduate Survey of 2004, respondents reported an annual (mean) salary of $56,499 before entering business school and a (mean) salary of $76,147 in their first job out. Data is not yet in on the class of 2005, but early reports suggest an even greater salary leap.

Another trend worth noting: Although applications are down overall at b-schools, that doesn't mean the quality of applicants has suffered. Notes Chicago's Kole, "Our applications are of high quality, and applicants appear to be quite focused with regard to why they seek an advanced degree. Whether they are career switchers or planning to resume their career path, those applicants who present a compelling story for why they want to be here, leave a stronger impression with the admissions committee."

Top schools are always going to have people knocking at their doors. And the possibility that business school applications in general could once again rise means you'll still want to be competitive. The long process starts with developing a solid application strategy and applying to a diverse portfolio of schools.

Let Us Help You Decide

There are many factors to consider when deciding whether or not to pursue an MBA, and we'll help you make that decision in the following chapters. We'll also tell you a bit about each school in our profiles and prepare you for further research into the schools on your list. We've worked hard to provide you with thorough information on every angle of the MBA, but you don't have to take our word for it—see for yourself. Stanford's Bolton advises future applicants, "Start early. Visit as many schools as you can, because it's very hard to differentiate among programs from websites, books, and marketing materials. You need to get a feeling from walking down the halls."

After you decide to go, finding the right program can be extremely difficult. Bolton explains, "Applicants really have to dig beneath the programs they're looking at to determine what's going to make them happy. A lot of people wind up going to the wrong school. A lot of external factors contribute to that. People shouldn't worry about justifying the decision to others, but to themselves."

Making the Decision to Go

The next step for you may be b-school. Indeed, armed with an MBA you may journey far. But the success of your trip and the direction you take will depend on knowing exactly why you're going to b-school and just what you'll be getting out of it.

The most critical questions you need to ask yourself are the following: Do you really want a career in business? What do you want the MBA to do for you? Are you looking to gain credibility, accelerate your development, or move into a new job or industry? Perhaps you're looking to start your own business, and entrepreneurial study will be important.

Knowing what you want doesn't just affect your decision to go, it also affects your candidacy; admissions committees favor applicants who have clear goals and objectives. Moreover, once at school, students who know what they want make the most of their two years. If you're uncertain about your goals, opportunities for career development—such as networking, mentoring, student clubs, and recruiter events—are squandered.

You also need to find a school that fits your individual needs. Consider the personal and financial costs. This may be the single biggest investment of your life. How much salary will you forego by leaving the workforce? What will the tuition be? How will you pay for it? If you have a family, spouse, or significant other, how will getting your MBA affect them?

If you do have a spouse, you may choose a program that involves partners in campus life. If status is your top priority, you should simply choose the most prestigious school you can get into.

The MBA presents many opportunities but no guarantees. As with any opportunity, you must make the most of it. Whether you go to a first-tier school or to a part-time program close to home, you'll acquire the skills that can jump-start your career. But your success will have more to do with you than with the piece of paper your MBA is printed on.

CHAPTER 2
WHAT B-SCHOOL IS REALLY LIKE

AN ACADEMIC PERSPECTIVE

The objective of all MBA programs is to prepare students for a professional career in business. One business school puts it this way:

Graduates should be all of the following:

1. Able to think and reason independently, creatively, and analytically

2. Skilled in the use of quantitative techniques

3. Literate in the use of software applications as management tools

4. Knowledgeable about the world's management issues and problems

5. Willing to work in and successfully cope with conditions of uncertainty, risk, and change

6. Astute decision makers

7. Ethically and socially responsible

8. Able to manage in an increasingly global environment

9. Proficient in utilizing technology as a mode of doing business

Sound like a tall order? Possibly. But this level of expectation is what business school is all about.

Nearly all MBA programs feature a core curriculum that focuses on the major disciplines of business: finance, management, accounting, marketing, manufacturing, decision sciences, economics, and organizational behavior. Unless your school allows you to place out of them, these courses are mandatory. Core courses provide broad functional knowledge in one discipline. To illustrate, a core marketing course covers pricing, segmentation, communications, product-line planning, and implementation. Electives provide a narrow focus that deepen the area of study. For example, a marketing elective might be entirely devoted to pricing.

Students sometimes question the need for such a comprehensive core program, but the functional areas of a real business are not parallel lines. All departments of a business affect each other every day. For example, an MBA in a manufacturing job might be asked by a financial controller why the company's product has become unprofitable to produce. Without an understanding of how product costs are accounted for, this MBA wouldn't know how to respond to a critical and legitimate request.

At most schools, the first term or year is devoted to a rigid core curriculum. Some schools allow first-years to take core courses side by side with electives. Still others have come up with an entirely new way of covering the basics, integrating the core courses into one cross-functional learning experience, which may also include sessions on topics such as globalization, ethics, and managing diversity. Half-year to year-long courses are team-taught by professors who see you through all disciplines.

TEACHING METHODOLOGY

Business schools employ two basic teaching methods: case study and lecture. Usually, they employ some combination of the two. The most popular is the case study approach. Students are presented with either real or hypothetical business scenarios and are asked to analyze them. This method provides concrete situations (rather than abstractions) that require mastery of a wide range of skills. Students often find case studies exciting because they can engage in spirited discussions about possible solutions to given business problems and because they get an opportunity to apply newly acquired business knowledge.

On the other hand, lecturing is a teaching method in which—you guessed it—the professor speaks to the class and the class listens. The efficacy of the lecture method depends entirely on the professor. If the professor is compelling, you'll probably get a lot out of the class. If the professor is boring, you probably won't listen, which isn't necessarily a big deal since many professors make their class notes available on computer disc or in the library.

THE CLASSROOM EXPERIENCE

Professors teaching case methodology often begin class with a "cold call." A randomly selected student opens the class with an analysis of the case and makes recommendations for solutions. The cold call forces you to be prepared and to think on your feet.

No doubt, a cold call can be intimidating. But unlike law school, b-school professors don't use the Socratic Method to torture you, testing your thinking with a pounding cross-examination. They're training managers, not trial lawyers. At worst, particularly if you're unprepared, a professor will abruptly dismiss your contribution.

Alternatively, professors ask for a volunteer to open a case, particularly someone who has had real industry experience with the issues. After the opening, the discussion is broadened to include the whole class. Everyone tries to get in a good comment, particularly if class participation counts heavily toward the grade. "Chip shots"—unenlightened, just-say-anything-to-get-credit comments—are common. So are "air hogs," students who go on and on because they like nothing more than to hear themselves pontificate.

Depending on the school, class discussions can degenerate into wars of ego rather than ideas. But for the most part, debates are kept constructive and civilized. Students are competitive, but not offensively so, and learn to make their points succinctly and persuasively.

A Glossary of Insider Lingo

B-school students, graduates, and professors—like most close-knit, somewhat solipsistic groups—seem to speak their own weird language. Here's a sampler of MBA jargon (with English translations):

Admissions Mistake: How each student perceives him or herself until getting first-year grades back from midterms.

Air Hogs: Students who monopolize classroom discussion and love to hear themselves speak.

B2B: "Business to Business"—a company that sells not to retail consumers, but to other enterprises. With the renewed focus on more traditional industries, this now stands for "Back to Basics."

B2C: "Business to Consumer"—a company that sells primarily to individual retail consumers. As with the above joke about B2B, business students occasionally say this really means "Back to Consulting."

Back of the Envelope: A quick analysis of numbers, as if scribbled on the back of an envelope.

Benchmarking: Comparing a company to others in the industry.

Burn Rate: Amount of cash a money-losing company consumes during a period of time.

Case Study Method: Popular teaching method that uses real-life business cases for analysis.

Cold Call: Unexpected, often dreaded request by the professor to open a case discussion.

Chip Shot: Vacant and often cheesy comments used not to truly benefit class discussion, but rather to get credit for participation.

Cycle Time: How fast you can turn something around.

Deliverable: Your end product.

Four Ps: Elements of a marketing strategy: Price, Promotion, Place, Product.

Fume Date: Date the company will run out of cash reserves.

Functional Areas: The basic disciplines of business (e.g., finance, marketing, R&D).

HP12-C: A calculator that works nothing like a regular one, used by finance types when they don't have Excel handy.

Lingo Bingo: A furtive game of Bingo whereby he who "wins" must work a decided upon, often trite phrase (see "chip shot") into the class discussion. For example: "I didn't actually read the case last night, but the protagonist is two beers short of a six-pack." The winner also earns a prize and the admiration of classmates.

Low Hanging Fruit: Tasks or goals that are most easy to achieve (consultant jargon).

Monitize: To turn an idea into a moneymaking scheme.

Net Net: End result.

Power Nap: Quick, intense, in-class recharge for the continually sleep deprived.

Power Tool: Someone who does all the work and sits in the front row of the class with his or her hand up.

Pre-enrollment Courses: Commonly known as MBA summer camp—quantitative courses to get the numerically challenged up to speed.

Pro Forma: Financial presentation of hypothetical events, such as projected earnings.

Quant Jock: A numerical athlete who is happiest crunching numbers.

Rule of Three: You should not talk more than three times in any given class, but you should participate at least once over the course of three classes.

Run the Numbers: Analyze quantitatively.

Shrimp Boy: A student who comes to a corporate event just to scarf down the food.

Skydeck: Refers to the back row of the classroom, usually when it's amphitheater style.

Slice and Dice: Running all kinds of quantitative analysis on a set of numbers.

Soft Skills: Conflict resolution, teamwork, negotiation, oral and written communication.

Take-aways: The key points of a lecture or meeting that participants should remember.

The Five Forces: Michael Porter's model for analyzing the strategic attractiveness of an industry.

Three Cs: The primary forces considered in marketing: Customer, Competition, Company.

Value-Based Decision Making: Values and ethics as part of the practice of business.

YOUR FIRST YEAR

The first six months of b-school can be daunting. You're unfamiliar with the subjects. There's a tremendous amount of work to do. And when you least have the skills to do so, there's pressure to stay with the pack. All of this produces anxiety and a tendency to over-prepare. Eventually, students learn shortcuts and settle into a routine, but until then much of the first year is just plain tough. The programs usually pack more learning into the first term than they do into each of the remaining terms. For the schools to teach the core curriculum (which accounts for as much as 70 percent of learning) in a limited time, an intensive pace is considered necessary. Much of the second year will be spent on gaining proficiency in your area of expertise and on searching for a job.

The good news is that the schools recognize how tough the first year can be. During the early part of the program, they anchor students socially by placing them in small sections, sometimes called "cohorts." You take many or all of your classes with your section-mates. Sectioning encourages the formation of personal and working relationships and can help make a large program feel like a school within a school.

Because so much has to be accomplished in so little time, getting an MBA is like living in fast-forward. This is especially true of the job search. No sooner are you in the program than recruiters for summer jobs show up, which tends to divert students from their studies. First-years aggressively pursue summer positions, which are linked with the promise of a permanent job offer if the summer goes well. At some schools, the recruiting period begins as early as October, at others in January or February.

A DAY IN THE LIFE

Matt Camp, First Year
Tuck School of Business, Dartmouth College

7:00 A.M.: Get dressed. Out of the door by 7:45 A.M. to head to the campus dining hall for breakfast. If I have time, I'll grab the *Financial Times* and *The Wall Street Journal* and gloss over the front page. Today, I have an informal get-to-know-you-better a meeting with marketing professor over breakfast.

8:30 A.M.: Core class in Corporate Finance. Grab any seat in a tiered classroom set-up. I'm usually in the middle toward the side. If possible, the front row stays empty.

10:00 A.M.: Go to e-mail kiosk on campus and check messages. Hang out or do a quick run to the library to read more of the *Times*.

10:30 A.M.: Macroeconomics lecture/case study class. Again, no assigned seating. Expect cold calls on case. Cold calls are not terrifying. Professors are supportive, not out to embarrass you. Class discussion is lively, with a mix of people offering their view.

Noon: Back to the cafeteria. Tuck may be one of the few schools where everyone eats together at the same place. There isn't much in town, and you're tight on time, so it doesn't make sense to go back home or elsewhere. It's crowded, so I look for friends, but basically grab a seat anywhere at one of the large tables that seat six to seven. Professors, administrators, and students all eat at the same place. Food is above average.

1:15 P.M.: Classes are over for the day. From this point here, I begin to start homework; there's a lot of work to do. I can go to a study room on campus, but they get booked up pretty quickly for groups, so I head to the library. The majority of the people are doing work for tomorrow. It's rare to have someone working on a project that's due the following week. It's pretty much day-to-day.

4:00 P.M.: I head off to one of the scheduled sports I've signed up for. Today it's soccer, played about one mile from campus. I drive; friends hitch a ride with me. This is a big international scene, mostly men, but there's a small group of women too. It's definitely a game we play hard, but in a very congenial way.

6:00 P.M.: Head back to campus. I'm hungry. It's off to the dining hall again. Most first-years live in dorms, so home cooking is not an option. Almost all second-years live off-campus, so they head back for a home-cooked meal. Cafeteria is not crowded; I may eat alone.

7:00 P.M.: Head home for a quick shower and change. The night is just beginning.

7:30 P.M.: Meet with study group at school to flesh out rest of work that needs to be done in preparation for tomorrow's classes.

11:00 P.M.: Students and their wives/husbands or partners head out to play ice hockey at one of the two rinks here. Wives/husbands and partners play. Because there are different levels, there are different games going on for different skill levels. It's a lot of fun.

Midnight: Time to go and celebrate either a hard game or a sore butt, but everyone goes to get some wings and a beer. There are only two bars on campus, and they close at 1:00 A.M. so we head to one of them.

1:00 A.M.: After the bar closes, people head home.

1:15 A.M.: Exhausted, I go to bed. No TV. I've forgotten what that is.

Your Second Year

Relax, the second year is easier. By now, students know what's important and what's not. Second-years work more efficiently than first-years. Academic anxiety is no longer a factor. Having mastered the broad-based core curriculum, students now enjoy taking electives and developing an area of specialization.

Anxiety in the second year has more to do with the arduous task of finding a job. For some lucky students, a summer position has yielded a full-time offer. But even those students often go through the whole recruiting grind anyway because they don't want to cut off any opportunities prematurely.

Most MBAs leave school with a full-time offer. Sometimes it's their only offer. Sometimes it's not their dream job, which may be why most grads change jobs after just two years. One student summed up the whole two-year academic/recruiting process like this: "The first-year students collapse in the winter quarter because of on-campus recruiting. The second-years collapse academically in the first quarter of their second year because it's so competitive to get a good job. And when a second-year does get a job, he or she forgets about class entirely. That's why pass/fail was invented."

A DAY IN THE LIFE

KRISTIN HANSEN, SECOND-YEAR

Tuck School of Business, Dartmouth College

9:00 A.M.: Wake-up (my first class is at 10:30 A.M.) and finish work for Monday classes.

10:15 A.M.: Ride my bike to campus for 10:30 A.M. class.

10:30 A.M.: Head to International Economics class, an elective. I have only three classes this semester, my last. Prior to this I had four and a half classes each term. I front-loaded so I would have a light last semester. Grab a yogurt and juice on way in. Eat in class. We discuss a currency crisis case.

Noon: Head to study room to plug my personal computer into one of the many networked connections on campus to check e-mail. Finish work for next class.

1:00 P.M.: Grab a quick lunch in the dining hall. Will bring it to eat during class.

1:15 P.M.: Managerial Decision Making class, another elective. Today is the very last class that second-years will have at Tuck; we're off to graduation! Our professor brings in strawberries and champagne to celebrate. We all hang out and toast each other. This obviously doesn't happen everyday, but this is just the kind of thing a Tuck professor would do.

2:45 P.M.: I'm one of four Tuck social chairpersons, so I use this time to send e-mails to my co-chairs about the upcoming chili cook-off and farm party. Then I send a message to the school regarding other social events for the weekend. I get an e-mail from the New York office of CS First Boston, with whom I've accepted a job offer, with a calendar of the dates for my private client-services training.

3:00 P.M.: Go for a run, swim, or bike.

5:00 P.M.: Head home to shower and change. Usually I'd make dinner at home and eat, but tonight, I'm heading out to a social event. So I relax a bit and do an hour of preparation for the next day. On Monday, Tuesday, and Wednesday nights, the workload is heavier.

7:00 P.M.: Off to a Turkey Fry Dinner. This is a meal that will be prepared by my two economics professors. They donated this "dinner" for the charity student auction. Friends of mine bid on it and won. Each of eight bidders gets to bring a guest, and I'm one of the guests. The professors are hosting this at one of their homes. Basically, they're taking three large turkeys and fry-o-lating them.

8:30 P.M.: We all head out to an open mic night, led by the same two economics professors that hosted the Turkey Fry. It's held at a local bar. Anyone in the audience can get onstage and perform. I'm a member of the Tuck band, so I get up on stage with my acoustic guitar and play various folk and bluegrass songs. This is a great warm-up for the Open Mic night at Tuck.

10:45 P.M.: We head out for Pub Night in downtown Hanover.

1:00 A.M.: The bar closes, so we head to "The End Zone," one of the second-year houses close to campus. All the second-year houses are named; these are names that have been passed down from generation to generation. On a typical Thursday night at Tuck, a small number of students will stay out until 3:00 A.M. I'm usually one of them.

3:00 A.M.: I walk home. My house, called "Girls in the Hood," is just a ten-minute stroll away. I may grab a 3:00 A.M. snack. Then, I quickly fall asleep, exhausted.

Life Outside of Class

Business school is more than academics and a big-bucks job. A spirited community provides ample opportunity for social interaction, extracurricular activity, and career development.

Much of campus life revolves around student-run clubs. There are groups for just about every career interest and social need—from "MBAs for a Greener America" to the "Small Business Club." There's even a group for significant others on most campuses. The clubs are a great way to meet classmates with similar interests and to get in on the social scene. They might have a reputation for throwing the best black-tie balls, pizza-and-keg events, and professional mixers. During orientation week, these clubs aggressively market themselves to first-years.

Various socially responsible projects are also popular on campus. An emphasis on volunteer work is part of the overall trend toward good citizenship. Perhaps to counter the greed of the 1980s, "giving back" is the b-school style of the moment. There is usually a wide range of options—from tutoring in an inner-city school to working in a soup kitchen to renovating public buildings.

Still another way to get involved is to work on a school committee. Here you might serve on a task force designed to improve student quality of life. Or you might work in the admissions office and interview prospective students.

For those with more creative urges there are always the old standbys: extracurriculars such as the school paper, yearbook, or school play. At some schools, the latter takes the form of the b-school follies and is a highlight of the year. Like the student clubs, these are a great way to get to know your fellow students.

Finally, you can play on intramural sports teams or attend the numerous informal get-togethers, dinner parties, and group trips. There are also plenty of regularly scheduled pub nights, just in case you thought your beer-guzzling days were over.

Most former MBA students say that going to b-school was the best decision they ever made. That's primarily because of nonacademic experiences. Make the most of your classes, but take the time to get involved and enjoy yourself.

Chapter 3

Palm Pilots and Power Breakfasts: What Does an MBA Offer?

NUTS-AND-BOLTS BUSINESS SKILLS

Graduate business schools teach the applied science of business. The best business schools combine the latest academic theories with pragmatic concepts, hands-on experience, and real-world solutions.

B-schools also teach the analytical skills used to make complicated business decisions. You learn how to define the critical issues, apply analytical techniques, develop the criteria for decisions, and make decisions after evaluating their impact on other variables.

After two years, you're ready to market a box of cereal. Or prepare a valuation of the cereal company's worth. You'll speak the language of business. You'll know the tools of the trade. Your expertise will extend to many areas and industries. In short, you will have acquired the skills that open doors.

ACCESS TO RECRUITERS, ENTRÉE TO NEW FIELDS

Applicants tend to place great emphasis on "incoming" and "outgoing" statistics. First they ask, "Will I get in?" Then they ask, "Will I get a job?"

Obviously, the first is largely dependent on how selective the school is and the quality of your credentials. The latter question can almost assuredly be answered in the positive, "Yes, you will."

But the real question is: How many—and what kind—of offers will you receive? Again, that is dependent on the appeal of the school to recruiters (which is a readily available statistic you can get from each school) and the particular industry you elect to pursue. For example, investment banks and consulting firms are always going to come to the schools for formal recruiting periods, whereas more off-the-beaten-path choices will possibly require you to go off campus in search of opportunity.

It's Good to Be Wanted, It's Great to Be Paid

According to many top schools, recruiter appetite for new grads is up. The latest figures suggest a strong market for newly minted MBAs. This comes after several years of depressed interest where the immediate economic value of the MBA was in question.

As we reported in Chapter 1, the average return on investment for business school grads in 2004 was an impressive 35 percent increase in annual salary. According to the Graduate Management Council, the before and after picture looks something like this: Average entering salary: roughly $56,000. Average first job out of school salary: $79,000. Presumably, starting salaries will continue to increase as the economy improves.

The majority of top grads receive a generous relocation package too. Indeed, if you were fortunate enough to have spent the summer between your first and second year at a consulting company, then you will, in all likelihood, also receive a "rebate" on your tuition. These companies often pick up a student's second-year tuition bill. The best package, however, goes to those MBA students who worked at the firm before b-school. These lucky capitalists often get their whole tuition paid for.

GETTING THE MBA FOR THE LONG RUN

Although MBA hiring appears to be on an upswing, going to business school still requires you to take a bit of a gamble. Leaner years make business school a riskier proposition. The nation appears to be heading out of what has been a lingering recession, but economic factors are always unpredictable. Furthermore, the world has witnessed great political turmoil. All of these factors can quickly and negatively impact the job market for newly minted MBAs.

So as you make plans to go to b-school, you need to accept that there is some risk that the labor market won't greet you with open arms at graduation. Consider the plight of MBAs from just three years ago: when they entered b-school, the economy was roaring ahead. The immediate future looked exceptionally bright. Most MBAs probably thought that once they got in, they had it made, and they looked forward to generous starting salaries and bonuses. Few probably anticipated that tough times could hit so dramatically.

But that's just the point. Good times and bad times cycle in and out. Fortunately, it looks as though we are cycling into a good time. Many economic experts agree that the economy is looking up and the markets will continue to improve. This means traditional hirers of MBAs, such as the investment banks and consulting firms may once again be wooing many a b-school grad. Still, it's hard to know when all of the recruiters who typically hire MBAs will feel comfortable again about bringing their hiring levels back up to what they were before the downturn.

The best way to consider the value of the degree is by focusing on its long-lasting benefits. "When people come here for their MBA, they talk about retooling for their life. They think about the long term and recognize that there are some short term hurdles," says Rose Martinelli, director of admissions at the Wharton School. "Just out of business school, this is the very first job in a long career. This is really about building blocks and going for the long run. You may have to work harder to find a job now, but building your career is a lifelong process." The MBA gives you the tools, networking, and polish to meaningfully enhance your long-term prospects and earning potential.

"There is real opportunity here. The opportunity right now is to pursue your passion and perhaps not your wallet," continues Martinelli. "We're seeing more of an equalization in salary. Those high-paying jobs in finance, investment banking, and consulting are fewer and harder to find. So here you have an opportunity for a job with a true learning experience rather than one that just pays a lot. More people are going into nonprofit and government and making contributions back to the community."

BRAND POWER COUNTS

Of course, there is great variability with placement rates and starting salaries among schools. The MBA does not swap your tuition bill for a guarantee that you'll get rich quick. As we've noted, it is at the best schools— those that have the greatest prestige and global recognition—where the strongest recovery is taking place. It's brand power at work. Even in an uncertain economy, top schools will continue to produce in-demand MBAs for the marketplace.

Branded schools tend to have an extensive history with big recruiting companies because the schools are a steady source of exceptional talent. As the economy stabilizes and hiring creeps up again, recruiters are naturally going to orient themselves at the top-brand schools.

At the University of Chicago, Deputy Dean Stacey Kole notes: "Recruiting activity is up, in the order of 20 percent. Hiring activity has really skyrocketed. I think that companies are feeling more comfortable that the economy is in good shape and are resuming their pre-September 11th hiring patterns. We had thousands of interviews available for our grads."

At less prominent schools, the picture may not be quite as optimistic. It is important to consider placement rates, and the list of companies that typically recruit on campus, at any school you are considering.

GETTING A JOB

For most would-be MBAs, b-school represents a fresh beginning—either in their current profession or in an entirely different industry. Whatever promise the degree holds for you, it's wise to question what the return on your investment will be.

As with starting salary, several factors affect job placement. School reputation and ties to industries and employers are important. At the top programs, the lists of recruiters read like a "Who's Who" of American companies. These schools not only attract the greatest volume of recruiters, but consistently get the attention of those considered "blue chip."

Not to be overlooked are lesser-known, regional schools that often have the strongest relationships with local employers and industries. Some b-schools (many of them state universities) are regarded by both academicians and employers as number one in their respective regions. In other words, as far as the local business community is concerned, these programs offer as much prestige and pull as a nationally ranked program.

Student clubs also play a big part in getting a job because they extend the recruiting efforts at many schools. They host a variety of events that allow you to meet leading business people, so that you can learn about their industries and their specific companies. Most important, these clubs are very effective at bringing in recruiters and other interested parties that do not recruit through traditional mainstream channels. For example, the high-tech, international, and entertainment student clubs provide career opportunities not available through the front door.

Your background and experiences also affect your success in securing a position. Important factors are academic specialization, academic standing, prior work experience, and intangibles such as your personal fit with the company. These days, what you did before b-school is particularly important; it helps establish credibility and gives you an edge in competing for a position in a specific field. For those using b-school to switch careers to a new industry, it's helpful if something on your resume ties your interest to the new profession. It's smart to secure a summer job in the new area.

Finally, persistence and initiative are critical factors in the job search. Since the beginning of this decade, many fast tracks have been narrowed. Increasingly, even at the best schools, finding a job requires off-campus recruiting efforts and ferreting out the hidden jobs.

A RETURN ON YOUR INVESTMENT

Not everyone measures their return on investment from business school with a dollar amount. (See, the interview at the end of this chapter as one example.) We've heard many b-school grads explain that the fundamental skills, the network of people, and the proper environment in which to formulate their long-term career path were the most valuable things they wanted to get back from their MBA programs—and that in doing so, considered the experience a success, regardless of their starting salary at graduation.

But for those who are anxious to start paying back those school loans, it's important to note that the industry in which you are hired can strongly affect your job prospects. Traditionally heavy hirers such as investment banking and consulting companies continue to lead the salary pack. Historically these sectors have offered the highest starting salaries and sign on bonuses, gravitating to the name-brand schools. At Chicago, Kole notes, "We saw tremendous activity in consulting, investment banking, investment management, and in leadership development programs. We are up in all of these areas, but most significantly in management consulting."

Also impacting your placement outlook is the geographic location of the school. Regional powerhouses such as Rutgers University in New Jersey may hold great sway at nearby, national employers such as Johnson & Johnson and Warner Lambert/Pfizer, providing graduates of those programs a unique competitive advantage. Although these companies reach out far and wide to recruit everywhere, a homegrown MBA may catch their attention and hold greater appeal.

As always, prioritize your criteria for school selection. Research whom the top-hirers are at any school you are considering. If you know what field you are interested in, look at how well a particular business school's track record is in finding jobs for their graduates in that industry. To cement the relationships between school and recruiter, companies often foster a partnership with the school that includes sponsoring academic projects and internships, and hosting school club functions and informational cocktail hour events.

You may indeed be accepted at one of the nation's most prestigious schools, but if they lack real access to the type of industry you desire, you are better off elsewhere.

FRIENDS WHO ARE GOING PLACES, ALUMNI WHO ARE ALREADY THERE

Most students say that the best part about b-school is meeting classmates with whom they share common goals and interests. Many students claim that the "single greatest resource is each other." Not surprisingly, with so many bright and ambitious people cocooned in one place, b-school can be the time of your life. It presents numerous professional and social opportunities. It can be where you find future customers, business partners, and mentors. It can also be where you establish lifelong friendships. And after graduation, these classmates form an enduring network of contacts and professional assistance.

Alumni are also an important part of the b-school experience. While professors teach business theory and practice, alumni provide insight into the real business world. When you're ready to interview, they can provide advice on how to get hired by the companies recruiting at your school. In some cases, they help secure the interview and shepherd you through the hiring process.

B-schools love to boast about the influence of their alumni network. To be sure, some are very powerful. But this varies from institution to institution. At the very least, alumni will help you get your foot in the door. A resume sent to an alum at a given company, instead of to "Sir or Madam" in the personnel department, has a much better chance of being noticed and acted on.

After you graduate, the network continues to grow. Regional alumni clubs and alumni publications keep you plugged in to the network with class notes detailing who's doing what, where, and with whom.

Throughout your career, an active alumni relations department can give you continued support. Post-MBA executive education series, fund-raising events, and continued job-placement efforts are all resources you can draw on for years to come.

In the interview below, a recent grad's professor is responsible for the connections that will help him start his own business overseas.

STEPHEN HAZELTON, MIT SLOAN SCHOOL OF MANAGEMENT, CLASS OF 2005

Stephen: I think we spoke about you adding something to your interview about how incredible Sloan's access is to the entrepreneurial world/venture capital world is.

So my question might be (which would follow your answer about meeting the professor who introduced you to the Vietnam venture capitalist), "Specifically, how else did Sloan provide you with access to the real world of opportunity?" I can change that question, and I welcome you to help me out here with that.

Q: What made you decide to get the MBA and go to the MIT Sloan School of Business?

A: There are probably three different reasons why I went to school. First, there were skills I needed to learn. Examples of key courses I took include Entrepreneurial Finance, which will be very relevant for me in the coming months when I begin to negotiate with investors; Law for the Entrepreneur which was practical and relevant; Negotiations was another—whether it is for life in general or business—and Accounting—that's a very standard course, but it was an area in which I did not have much experience. So, the curriculum was a big draw for me.

The second draw was MIT Sloan's strong focus on entrepreneurship. If you look at the world of entrepreneurship on a map, the two hotspots are Silicon Valley and Route 128, (a highway in the Boston area where most start ups and venture capital firms are located.) I wanted to be in that community and understand and have access to it. Finally, I wanted to meet and learn from my classmates, given their diverse backgrounds.

Q: Now as you approach graduation, has the MBA performed for you in the way you thought it would?

A: I wanted to pursue entrepreneurship internationally. I have a background in Latin American markets, and for me the MBA has been highly relevant. The way I gauge that is how the MBA helped me with what I'm going to be doing after school, which is starting a business focused on financial services- in Vietnam. A professor of mine went out of her way to put me in touch with a venture capitalist in Hanoi and things went on from there. This investor has a network in Vietnam and is going to support me both financially and otherwise; without this it would be a bit daunting to take a shot on my own.

Had I not gone to MIT Sloan and gotten to know this professor I'm not sure all this would have happened. So the MBA has been highly relevant because what I'm going to be doing is a direct result of my attending MIT Sloan.

Q: Specifically, how else did MIT Sloan provide you with real exposure and access?

A: Because of MIT's rich tradition in entrepreneurship, we get a lot of interest from that community. We have numerous opportunities to build business plans, receive feedback, pitch to investors and learn from successful entrepreneurs that come to campus. It's a really special environment.

Another unique way is the popular course, Global Entrepreneurship Lab. Students in the course spend the month of January working with a start-up in emerging markets around the world. Companies host students and provide a view into how entrepreneurship is done in, for instance, Brazil or China.

Q: What were you doing before business school?

A: I was working for a non-profit called Endeavor. Its mission is to promote entrepreneurship in emerging markets. They're in Africa and South America. My focusł was on South America; I lived in Chile for a while and helped restart the local office there.

Q: Does it matter where you go to school?

A: In my case it definitely did.

Q: What advice would you give to today's applicant?

A: Make sure you understand why you want to go business school and what you want to get out of it. I would advise someone attending a program to use that two-year window to assess what they really are passionate about rather than pursue some of the fast-track careers by default.

Q: What do you mean by fast-track career by default?

A: Just because a company comes to campus to recruit doesn't mean it's necessarily right for you. I would consider those opportunities. But I think some people go into that track without considering other options. Consider other options based on your interests as well.

Q: If you had to do it all over again would you do anything differently?

A: I would apply to fewer schools. I applied to four. I would have applied to two b-schools because what I was looking for was at MIT Sloan and Stanford.

Q; How do you measure return on investment?

A: First off, I should say that I have a fellowship from Sloan that covers almost all of my tuition. I think that gives me a little bit of a different perspective. The flip side is I have the average debt that others do in my living expenses. So I invested a fair amount of my own money, alhtough I will not have those huge tuition bills to pay off.

I think some people look at the MBA payoff based on what kind of job will they get that's well regarded or pays them better than what they were making before business school. I don't. I don't look at education as a financial thing. It's a lifelong thing. I feel very closely connected to MIT and will come back here for support for the rest of my career.

As for money, I will be making very little money starting my own business.

It's true, a business education costs a lot of money, but it should not be a financial decision.

I want to add that I'm an immigrant to this country. The MBA is a wonderful way for an immigrant to assimilate into the business world.

Q: How would you describe your experience with your peers at Sloan?

A: In going into any situation where there are relationships to be made, I'm a quality versus quantity type of person. So I've made some really great friends here—people I will keep in touch with for the rest of my life. It's what I expected and hoped for.

CHAPTER 4

ADMISSIONS

PREPARING TO BE A SUCCESSFUL APPLICANT

GET GOOD GRADES

If you're still in school, concentrate on getting good grades. A high GPA says you've got not only brains, but also discipline. It shows the admissions committee you have what you need to make it through the program. If you're applying directly from college or have limited job experience, your grades will matter even more. The admissions committee will have little else on which to evaluate you.

It's especially important that you do well in courses such as economics, statistics, and calculus. Success in these courses is more meaningful than success in classes like "Monday Night at the Movies" film appreciation. Of course, English is also important; b-schools want students who communicate well.

STRENGTHEN MATH SKILLS

Number-crunching is an inescapable part of b-school. If your work experience has failed to develop your quantitative skills, take an accounting or statistics course for credit at a local college or b-school. If you have a liberal arts background and did poorly in math, or got a low GMAT math score, this is especially important. Getting a decent grade will go a long way toward convincing the admissions committee you can manage the quantitative challenges of the program.

WORK FOR A FEW YEARS—BUT NOT TOO MANY

Business schools have traditionally favored applicants who have worked full-time for several years. There are three primary reasons for this: 1) With experience comes maturity; 2) You're more likely to know what you want out of the program; 3) Your experience enables you to bring real-work perspectives to the classroom. Because business school is designed for you to learn from your classmates, each student's contribution is important.

Until recently, b-schools preferred to admit only those students with two to five years of work experience. The rationale was that at two years you have worked enough to be able to make a solid contribution, while beyond four or five, you might be too advanced in your career to appreciate the program fully. However, as we noted earlier in this book, there is a new trend among top schools toward admitting "younger" applicants—that is, candidates with limited work experience as well as those straight from college.

Depending on the schools to which you're applying and the strength of your resume of accomplishments, you may not need full-time, professional work experience. Of course, there's a catch: The younger you are, the harder you'll have to work to supply supporting evidence for your case as a qualified applicant. Be prepared to convince admissions committees that you've already done some incredible things, especially if you're hailing straight from college.

If you've targeted top-flight schools like Wharton, Columbia, or Stanford, applying fresh out of college is still a long shot. While your chances of gaining admission with little work experience have improved, your best shot is still to err on the conservative side and get a year or two of some professional experience under your belt.

If you're not interested in the big league or you plan on attending a local program, the number of years you should work before applying may vary. Research the admissions requirements at your target school. There's no doubt the MBA will jumpstart your career and have long-lasting effects on your business (and perhaps personal) outlook. If you're not ready to face the real world after college, plenty of solid b-schools will welcome you to another two years of academia.

There is one caveat to this advice, however. If your grades are weak, consider working at least three years before applying. The more professional success you have, the greater the likelihood that admissions committees will overlook your GPA.

LET YOUR JOB WORK FOR YOU

Many companies encourage employees to go to b-school. Some of these companies have close ties to a favored b-school and produce well-qualified applicants. If their employees are going to the kinds of schools you want to get into, these may be smart places to work.

Other companies, such as investment banks, feature training programs, at the end of which trainees go to b-school or leave the company. These programs hire undergraduates right out of school. They're known for producing solid, highly skilled applicants. Moreover, they're full of well-connected alumni who may write influential letters of recommendation.

Happily, the opposite tactic—working in an industry that generates few applicants—can be equally effective. Admissions officers look for students from underrepresented professions. Applicants from biotechnology, health care, not-for-profit, and even the Peace Corps are viewed favorably.

One way to set yourself apart is to have had two entirely different professional experiences before business school. For example, if you worked in finance, your next job might be in a different field, like marketing. Supplementing quantitative work with qualitative experiences demonstrates versatility.

Finally, what you do in your job is important. Seek out opportunities to distinguish yourself. Even if your responsibilities are limited, exceed the expectations of the position. B-schools are looking for leaders.

MARCH FROM THE MILITARY

A surprising number of b-school students hail from the military (although the armed forces probably had commanders in mind, not CEOs, when they designed their regimen). Military officers know how to be managers because they've held command positions. And they know how to lead a team under the most difficult of circumstances.

Because most have traveled all over the world, they also know how to work with people from different cultures. As a result, they're ideally suited to learn alongside students with diverse backgrounds and perspectives. B-schools with a global focus are particularly attracted to such experience.

The decision to enlist in the military is a very personal one. However, if you've thought of joining those few good men and women, this may be as effective a means of preparing for b-school as more traditional avenues.

CHECK OUT THOSE ESSAY QUESTIONS NOW

You're worried you don't have interesting stories to tell. Or you just don't know what to write. What do you do?

Ideally, several months before your application is due, you should read the essay questions and begin to think about your answers. Could you describe an ethical dilemma at work? Are you involved in anything outside the office (or classroom)? If not, now is the time to do something about it. While this may seem contrived, it's preferable to sitting down to write the application and finding you have to scrape for or, even worse, manufacture situations.

Use the essay questions as a framework for your personal and professional activities. Look back over your business calendar, and see if you can find some meaty experiences for the essays in your work life. Keep your eyes open for a situation that involves questionable ethics. And if all you do is work, work, work, get involved in activities that round out your background. In other words, get a life.

Get involved in community-based activities. Some possibilities are being a big brother/big sister, tutoring in a literacy program, or initiating a recycling project. Demonstrating a concern for others looks good to admissions committees, and hey, it's good for your soul, too.

It's also important to seek out leadership experiences. B-schools are looking for individuals who can manage groups. Volunteer to chair a professional committee or run for an office in a club. It's a wide-open world; you can pick from any number of activities. The bottom line is this: The extracurriculars you select can show that you are mature, multifaceted, and appealing.

We don't mean to sound cynical. Obviously, the best applications do nothing more than describe your true, heartfelt interests and show off your sparkling personality. We're not suggesting you try to guess which activity will win the hearts of admissions directors and then mold yourself accordingly. Instead, think of projects and activities you care about, that maybe you haven't gotten around to acting on, and act on them now!

Pick Your Recommenders Carefully

By the time you apply to business school, you shouldn't have to scramble for recommendations. Like the material for your essays, sources for recommendations should be considered long before the application is due.

How do you get great recommendations? Obviously, good work is a prerequisite. Whom you ask is equally important. Bosses who know you well will recommend you on both a personal and professional level. They can provide specific examples of your accomplishments, skills, and character. Additionally, they can convey a high level of interest in your candidacy.

There's also the issue of trust. B-school recommendations are made in confidence; you probably won't see exactly what's been written about you. Choose someone you can trust to deliver the kind of recommendation that will push you over the top. A casual acquaintance may fail you by writing an adequate, yet mostly humdrum letter.

Cultivate relationships that yield glowing recommendations. Former and current professors, employers, clients, and managers are all good choices. An equally impressive recommendation can come from someone who has observed you in a worthwhile extracurricular activity.

We said before you won't see *exactly* what's being written about you, but that doesn't mean you should just hand a blank piece of paper to your recommender. Left to their own devices, recommenders may create a portrait that leaves out your best features. You need to prep them on what to write. Remind them of those projects or activities in which you achieved some success. You might also discuss the total picture of yourself that you are trying to create. The recommendation should reinforce what you're saying about yourself in your essays.

About "Big Shot" recommendations: Don't bother. Getting some professional golfer who's a friend of your dad's to write you a recommendation will do you no good if he doesn't know you very well, even if he is "president of the universe." Don't try to fudge your application—let people who really know you and your work tell the honest, believable, and impressive truth.

PREPARE FOR THE GRADUATE MANAGEMENT ADMISSION TEST (GMAT)

Most b-schools require you to take the GMAT. The GMAT is now a three-and-a-half-hour computer adaptive test (CAT) with multiple-choice math and verbal sections as well as an essay section. It's the kind of test you hate to take and schools love to require.

Why is the GMAT required? B-schools believe it measures your verbal and quantitative skills and predicts success in the MBA program. Some think this is a bunch of hooey, but most schools weigh your GMAT scores heavily in the admissions decision. If nothing else, it gives the school a quantitative tool to compare you with other applicants.

The test begins with the Analytical Writing Assessment (AWA) containing two essays questions. In the past, all questions that have appeared on the official GMAT have been drawn from a list of about 150 topics that appear in *The Official Guide to the GMAT* (published by the Educational Testing Service). Review that list and you'll have a pretty good idea of what to expect from the AWA. You will have 30 minutes to write each essay. By the way, you will be required to type your essay at the computer. Depending on how rusty your typing skills are, you may want to consider a bit of practice.

Next comes the multiple-choice section which has two parts: a seventy-five-minute math section and a seventy-five-minute verbal section. The math section includes problem-solving questions (e.g., "Train A leaves Baltimore at 6:32 A.M. . . .") and data-sufficiency questions. Data-sufficiency questions require you to determine whether you have been given enough information to solve a particular math problem. The good news about these types of questions is that you don't actually have to solve the problem; the bad news is that these questions can be very tricky. The verbal section tests reading skills (reading comprehension), grammar (sentence correction), and logic (critical reasoning).

For those unfamiliar with CAT exams, here's a brief overview of how they work: On multiple-choice sections, the computer starts by asking a question of medium difficulty. If you answer it correctly, the computer asks you a question that is slightly more difficult than the previous question. If you answer incorrectly, the computer asks a slightly easier question next. The test continues this way until you have answered enough questions that it can make an accurate (or so they say) assessment of your performance and assign you a score.

Most people feel they have no control over the GMAT. They dread it as the potential bomb in their application. But relax; you have more control than you think. You can take a test-preparation course to review the math and verbal material, learn test-taking strategies, and build your confidence. Test-prep courses can be highly effective. The Princeton Review offers what we think is the best GMAT course available. Even better, it offers two options for online preparation in addition to the traditional classroom course and one-on-one tutoring. Another option is to take a look at our book *Cracking the GMAT CAT*, which reviews all the subjects and covers all the tips you would learn in one of our courses.

How many times should you take the GMAT? More than once if you didn't ace it on the first try. But watch out: Multiple scores that fall in the same range make you look unprepared. Don't take the test more than once if you don't expect a decent increase, and don't even think of taking it the first time without serious preparation. Limiting your GMAT attempts to two is best. Three tries are okay if there were unusual circumstances or if you really need another shot at it. If you take it more than three times, the admissions committee will think you have an unhealthy obsession. A final note: If you submit more than one score, most schools will take the highest.

If you don't have math courses on your college transcript or numbers-oriented work experience, it's especially important to get a solid score on the quantitative section. There's a lot of math between you and the MBA.

HOW THE ADMISSIONS CRITERIA ARE WEIGHTED

Although admissions requirements vary among business schools, most rely on the following criteria: GMAT score, college GPA, work experience, your essays, letters of recommendation (academic and/or professional), an interview with an admissions representative, and your extracurriculars. The first four are generally the most heavily weighted. The more competitive the school, the less room there is for weakness in any area. Any component out of sync, such as a weak GMAT score, is potentially harmful.

Happily, the admissions process at business school is one where great emphasis is placed on getting to know you as a person. The essay component is the element that allows the schools to do just that. Your essays can refute weaknesses, fill in gaps, and in general, charmingly persuade an admissions board you've got the right stuff. They are the single most important criteria in business school admissions.

But as we've just said, they're not the only criteria. All pieces of your application must come together to form a cohesive whole. It is the *entire application* that determines whether you win admission.

ANTICIPATE AND COORDINATE

The application process is very time-consuming, so anticipating what you need to accomplish within the admissions time frame is critical. To make the best use of our advice, you should first contact each of the programs on your personal list of schools. Their standards and criteria for admission may vary, and you'll need to follow their specific guidelines. Please note that the less competitive a school is, the more easily you may be able to breeze through (or completely omit) the rigorous requirements we identify as crucial in the application process for the top programs.

In addition, business school applicants are often overwhelmed by how much they have to do to complete not only one, but several applications. Proper management of the process is essential, since there are so many factors to coordinate in each application.

You'll have to prep for the GMAT, then actually take the test, round up some writers for your recommendations, follow up with those chosen to write recommendations, make sure the recommendations are mailed in on time, have your college transcript sent, and finally, write the essays. Of course, some schools require an interview as well. What makes all of this particularly challenging is that many applicants have to fit this in among the demands of a full-time job.

We know that it takes a supreme force of will to complete even one application. As grad school applications go, a top business school's is pretty daunting. So if you don't stay focused on the details and deadlines, you may drop the ball.

There are many common and incredibly embarrassing mistakes you can avoid with prudent early planning. They include allowing your recommendation writers to miss the deadline, submitting an application full of typos and grammatical errors, sending one school an essay intended for another, or forgetting to change the school name when using the same essay for several applications. Applicants who wind up cramming for the GMAT or squeezing their essay writing into several all-nighters seriously shortchange themselves.

APPLY EARLY

The best advice is plan early and apply early. The former diminishes the likelihood of an accidental omission or a missed deadline. The latter increases your chances of acceptance.

The filing period ranges anywhere from six to eight months. The earlier you apply, the better your chances. There are a number of reasons for this:

First, there's plenty of space available early on. As the application deadline nears, spaces fill up. The majority of applicants don't apply until the later months because of procrastination or unavoidable delays. As the deadline draws close, the greatest number of applicants compete for the fewest number of spaces.

Second, in the beginning, admissions officers have little clue about how selective they can be. They haven't reviewed enough applications to determine the competitiveness of the pool. An early application may be judged more on its own merit than how it stacks up against others. This is in your favor if the pool turns out to be unusually competitive. Above all, admissions officers like to lock their classes in early; they can't be certain they'll get their normal supply of applicants. Admissions decisions may be more generous at this time.

Third, by getting your application in early you're showing a strong interest. The admissions committee is likely to view you as someone keen on going to their school.

To be sure, some admissions officers report that the first batch of applications tend to be from candidates with strong qualifications, confident of acceptance. In this case, you might not be the very first one on line; but closer to the front is still better than lost in the heap of last-minute hopefuls.

Of course, if applications are down that year at all b-schools or—thanks to the latest drop in its ranking—at the one to which you are applying, then filing later means you can benefit from admissions officers desperately filling spaces. But this is risky business, especially since the rankings don't come out until the spring.

Conversely, if the school to which you are applying was recently ranked number one or two, applying early may make only a marginal difference. Swings in the rankings from year to year send school applications soaring and sagging. From beginning to end, a newly crowned number-one or two school will be flooded with applications. Regardless, do not put in your application until you are satisfied that it is the best you can make it. Once a school has passed on your application, it will not reconsider you until the following year.

ROUNDS VS. ROLLING ADMISSIONS

Applications are processed in one of two ways: rounds or rolling admissions. Schools that use rounds divide the filing period into three or so timed cycles. Applications are batched into the round in which they are received and reviewed in competition with others in that round. A list of a b-school's round dates can be obtained by contacting their admissions office if they employ this method. Applications to schools with rolling admissions are reviewed on an ongoing basis as they are received.

GMAT AND GPA

The GMAT and GPA are used in two ways. First, they're "success indicators" for the academic work you'll have to slog through if admitted—will you have the brainpower to succeed in the program? Second, they're used as benchmarks to compare each applicant to other applicants within the pool. At the more selective schools, you'll need a higher score and average to stay in the game.

The Educational Testing Service (ETS) administers the GMAT. You'll need to register to take the exam by calling 800-GMAT-NOW (800-462-8669) or by registering online at www.mba.com. Many applicants take the exam more than once to improve their scores. Test preparation is also an option for boosting your numbers—call 800-2Review (800-273-8439) for more information about The Princeton Review's GMAT courses.

Your college transcript is a major factor in the strength of your candidacy. Some schools focus more closely on the junior- and senior-year grades than the overall GPA, and most consider the reputation of your college and the difficulty of your course selections. A transcript loaded with offerings like "Environmental Appreciation" and "The Child in You" won't be valued as highly as one packed with calculus and history classes.

The Essays

Admissions committees consider the essays the clincher, the swing vote on the "admit/deny" issue. Essays offer the most substance about who you really are. The GMAT and GPA reveal little about you, only that you won't crash and burn. Your work history provides a record of performance and justifies your stated desire to study business. But the essays tie all the pieces of the application together and create a summary of your experiences, skills, background, and beliefs.

The essays do more than give answers to questions. They create thumbnail psychological profiles. Depending on how you answer a question or what you present, you reveal yourself in any number of ways—creative, witty, open-minded, articulate, mature—to name a few. Likewise, your essay can reveal a negative side, such as arrogance, sloppiness, or an inability to think and write clearly.

For more in-depth information about essays, including samples from successful applicants, check out *Business School Essays That Made a Difference* at www.princetonreview.com/mba/bookstore.asp.

Letters of Recommendation

Letters of recommendation act as a reality check. Admissions committees expect them to support and reinforce what they're seeing in the rest of your application. When the information doesn't match up with the picture you've painted, it makes you look bad. Because you won't see the recommendation (it's sent in "blind"), you won't even know there's a problem. This can mean the end of your candidacy.

That's why you need to take extreme care in selecting your references.

Scan each application for guidelines on choosing your references—business schools typically request an academic or professional reference. The academic reference should be someone who can evaluate your performance in an academic environment. It's better to ask an instructor, teacher's aide, or mentor who knew you well than a famous professor who barely knew your name.

The same holds true for your professional reference. Seek out individuals who can evaluate your performance on many levels. The reference will be far more credible. Finding the right person to write your professional reference, however, can be trickier. You may not wish to reveal to your boss early on that you plan on leaving, and if the dynamics of your relationship are not ideal (hey, it happens once in a while), he or she might not make an appropriate reference. If this is the case, seek out a boss at a former job or someone who was your supervisor at your current job but has since moved to another organization. Avoid friends, colleagues, and clients as references unless the school explicitly says its okay.

Advise your writers on themes and qualities you highlighted in your application. Suggest that they include real-life examples of your performance to illustrate their points. In other words, script the recommendation as best you can. Your boss, even if he or she is your biggest fan, may not know what your recommendation should include.

A great recommendation is rarely enough to save a weak application from doom. But it might push a borderline case over to the "admit" pile. Mediocre recommendations can be damaging; an application that is strong in all other areas now has a weakness, an inconsistency.

A final warning on this topic: Procrastination is common here. Micromanage your references so that each recommendation arrives on time! If need be, provide packaging for an overnight letter, have your reference seal it up, and then ship it out yourself.

THE INTERVIEW

Not all business schools attach equal value to the interview. For some, it's an essential screening tool. For others, it's used to make a final decision on those caught somewhere between "admit" and "reject." Some schools may encourage, but not require, the interview. Others make it informative, with little connection to the admissions decision.

Like the letters of recommendation, an interview may serve as a reality check to reinforce the total picture. It may also be used to fill in the blanks, particularly in borderline cases.

If an interview is offered, take it. In person, you may be an entirely more compelling candidate. You can further address weaknesses or bring dull essays to life. Most important, you can display the kinds of qualities—enthusiasm, sense of humor, maturity—that often fill in the blanks and positively sway an admissions decision.

Act quickly to schedule your interview. Admissions departments often lack the time and staff to interview every candidate who walks through their doors. You don't want your application decision delayed by several months (and placed in a more competitive round or pool) because your interview was scheduled late in the filing period.

A great interview can tip the scale in the "admit" direction. How do you know if it was great? You were calm and focused. You expressed yourself and your ideas clearly. Your interviewer invited you to go rock climbing with him next weekend. (Okay, let's just say you developed a solid personal rapport with the interviewer.)

A mediocre interview may not have much impact, unless your application is hanging on by a thread. In such a case, the person you're talking to (harsh as it may seem) is probably looking for a reason not to admit you, rather than a reason to let you in. If you feel your application may be in that hazy, marginal area, try to be extra-inspired in your interview.

Approach this meeting as you would a job interview. Dress and act the part of a professional. But at the same time, remember: You're being sized up as a person in all of your dimensions. Avoid acting stiff or like a stuffed shirt. Limit your use of business jargon. Be personable. Gear yourself up for an enjoyable conversation where you may discuss your hobbies or recent cross-country trip. Talk about your passions or any areas in which you have achieved excellence—even something like gourmet cooking. Just avoid stunt-like gimmicks (we don't advise you to pull out a platter of peppercorn pâté sautéed in anchovy sauce). The idea is to get the interviewer thinking of you as someone who will contribute greatly to the quality of campus life. Try to be your witty, charming, natural self.

CHAPTER 5

QUOTAS, RECRUITMENT, AND DIVERSITY

B-schools don't have to operate under quotas—governmental or otherwise. However, they probably try harder than most corporations to recruit diverse groups of people. Just as the modern business world has become global and multicultural, so too have b-schools. They must not only teach diversity in the classroom but also make it a reality in their campus population and, if possible, faculty.

Schools that have a diverse student body tend to be proud of it. They tout their success in profiles that demographically slice and dice the previous year's class by gender, race, and geographic and international residency. Prospective students can review this data and compare the diversity of the schools they've applied to.

But such diversity doesn't come naturally from the demographics of the applicant pool. Admissions committees have to work hard at it. In some cases, enrollment is encouraged with generous financial aid packages and scholarships.

While they don't have quotas per se, they do target groups for admission, seeking a demographic balance in many areas. Have they admitted enough women, minorities, foreign students, marketing strategists, and liberal arts majors? Are different parts of the country represented?

As we've said before, the best b-schools tend to attract top talent, students, and recruiters to their campus. Women and minorities are the most sought-after groups targeted for admission. So it's no surprise that programs that report higher-than-average female and minority enrollments tend to be among the very best.

AN INITIATIVE FOR MINORITIES

Some schools report higher minority enrollments than others, so our advice is consistent: you need to thoroughly research the program you've set your sights on. Consider your goals. Do you simply want to attend the most prestigious program? How will social factors impact your goals and experiences on campus?

As you explore the schools in this book, you'll find that one program is especially noteworthy for its unfaltering commitment to diversity. Unsurprisingly, it is the University of Michigan, which recently won the Outstanding Educational Institution of the Year Award from the National Black MBA Association (NBMBA). This award is presented to an institution that has made the greatest contribution toward encouraging African Americans to enter the field of business.

We don't want to single out just one school, as most business schools aspire to diversify their programs. It's the number of minorities applying to business school that has remained consistently low.

An initiative of the Graduate Management Admissions Council called The Diversity Pipeline Alliance (www.diversitypipeline.org) was formed to reverse this trend and increase the number of African Americans, Hispanic Americans, and Native Americans pursuing a business career. Much like the initiative for women, this organization plans a powerful marketing campaign with a pro-business career message for students from middle school to graduate school. It offers information on current opportunities for mentorships, internships, and financial assistance and provides an impressive roster of member organizations, services, and educational opportunities.

Minority enrollment at business schools is still quite low, so in all likelihood, you will not experience the dramatic upward shift in b-school demographics in the near future that initiatives like the Diversity Pipeline Alliance hope to influence. However, by recognizing the disparity between the minority presence in the U.S. and minority involvement in business education and practice, we are working toward a solution.

As you make up your mind about where you want to go, know that the scenario is positive and that new infrastructures exist to support your business career.

FEMALE APPEAL: BUSINESS SCHOOLS GET UP TO SPEED

If you've toured the campus and classrooms of a business school, you may have noticed something: On average, roughly 70 percent of any given MBA program's students are male. While this may make a nice pool of dating prospects for the women who are enrolled, it's not something business schools are happy with—far from it! In fact, it's something they are working to change as quickly as they can.

Top-flight schools typically see higher female enrollment, in part because of all they offer, but also because, just as males do, women want to benefit from the status of an elite school. Stanford, for example, had a 26 percent female enrollment 10 years ago; now, women make up 38 percent of the class of 2004. While 38 percent may not match the 50 percent male-to-female ratio at other grad schools, closing the MBA gap is only a matter of time.

SCHOOL INITIATIVES

How can we be sure? One reason is that getting women enthused about a career in business is a sky-high priority at business schools across the country these days. To wit, many business schools have launched their own women-only outreach and recruiting events. New York University's Stern School aptly calls its initiative "Opening Doors for Women." Sessions are generally held in the fall in cities nationwide and are offered through the admissions offices. Receptions like this one aim to dispel myths, address the perceived lack of role models, and help women make informed decisions.

Stanford's events, says Wendy Hansen, Associate Director of Admissions at the Stanford Business School, "focus on the educational experience, but also on the unique types of issues women have, such as: how does getting the MBA fit in with having a family or having a spouse? How do I make this experience fit in with my life?"

Julia Minn, Director of Admissions at Stern, says attendees often find comfort in numbers, "Roughly 400 women attend our events. Seeing such a large presence of women is empowering. They realize they're not in this alone, that there are other women around like them." Eileen Chang, Associate Director of Admissions at the Harvard Business School notes Harvard's attendees are similarly impacted: "Women may come in skeptical and curious. But they come out energized that the MBA is a real opportunity for them."

If all this sounds like good public relations, it is. Schools want to get the word out: MBAs offer women viable opportunities. But if the business schools are talking the talk, they're also walking the walk. There's nothing superficial about this campaign. Bit by bit, the MBA landscape for women is changing.

Opportunities begin even before the first day of class. At Stanford, admitted women are treated to one-on-one admit-lunches with female alum. Once an admit gets to campus, they find MBA life is chock-full of student-run women and management programs, support groups, retreats, executive conferences, mentoring programs, and other dedicated resources for women-only.

For many years now, most business programs have had an on-campus Partners Club for spouses and significant others—a benefit to both female and male students. Newcomers to the business-school scene now include groups like The Parents Club and Biz Kids where students can find family-oriented classmates and activities. Perhaps the most symbolic gesture of the increasing influence of women in business school is Stanford's provision of a private nursing room for MBA-moms and their babies in their main classroom facility.

MORE FLEXIBILITY AND MAKING IT WORK

Of course, there's still room for improvement. A continuing problem at business schools is a lack of coursework and case study material featuring women leaders. Likewise, there is an absence of female professors on the academic scene.

Apart from these lingering issues, business schools continue to tackle the particular issues women face. Still not sure it's for you? The late starting age can be a turn-off. But even here, there are new options and opportunities to consider.

If you are stressed out from trying to have it all and have written off getting an MBA, new early-initiative programs might make you pause and reconsider your decision. Harvard and Stanford have developed an early career track that aims to minimize the importance of the biological clock in a prospective applicant's decision to pursue an MBA. Other schools are likely to follow suit.

The early career track offers a solution that is as simple as it is practical: admit women (and men) to the MBA program either straight out of college or with just a few years of work experience. Chang says, "We're hoping that this spurs more women to come to Harvard Business School when they realize they can attain this degree earlier. This gives them a bigger window in which to achieve their professional and personal goals. One might argue that at a younger age, you have fewer ties. As you go further into your career, by nature of many things, you loose that flexibility."

Beginning a business career earlier eliminates the immediate problem of timing. But what happens down the road? While it helps to remove one timing issue, it can't indefinitely postpone the balancing act that shadows many women's careers. It's hard to rationalize the opportunity costs of the MBA knowing the investment might be forsaken when tough choices have to be made.

To this, business schools blame misconceptions about the utility of the MBA. They feel that many women underestimate the broad reach of the degree. The MBA is not just for hard-core careers like banking and finance, but also for not-for-profit work, less high-stress industries such as consumer goods, and leadership positions in a wide range of fields.

Further, says Hansen, "There is a tremendous amount of flexibility in a general management degree. The MBA positions you much more effectively to make an impact wherever you fall at different points in your life. It gives you the tools and framework to apply those skills at different levels and in different intensities. For example, women can rise to a partner level or a senior leadership position and then scale back to a different role within the organization. They can also scale back to part-time work." In other words, the investment doesn't have to be forsaken, it might instead be redirected.

There's no doubt the return on investment (that's ROI for business speak) for the MBA is high. Six-figure salaries and sign-on bonuses that pay you back your MBA tuition are hard to beat (and unlike medical, veterinary, and law school grads, you won't have malpractice premiums eating into your take-home pay). Ironically, the cost of getting to this point has, thus far, simply been too high for women. But times are a-changin'. If you've thought business school might be right for you, keep investigating—you might be right.

WHERE ARE THE WOMEN IN MBA PROGRAMS?

Are you a professional woman in her mid-to-late twenties? Do you see graduate school in your future? During these tough times, you might envision yourself back on campus sooner rather than later. Downturns do tend to fuel grad school applications. After all, what better place to wait out the economy and avoid the gaping pit of joblessness?

Grad school can be a cure-all for many ills: It can jump-start or redirect a stubbornly off-track career; it can give you a place to hang out while you figure out what you want to be when you grow up (law school, a three-year degree, offers an even longer alternative); and it can transform your personal life as you vault into a new career. Even in uncertain times there is certainty in knowing that after two years in school you can emerge reborn as a professional with a spanking new identity, prescribed career track, and a solid alumni network.

Despite the huge appeal of graduate school, be it as an escape from bad times or as your true, chosen path, MBA programs have remained a problematic choice for many women. Female enrollment at law, medical, and veterinary schools now hovers at, or near, the 50 percent mark. So what's up with business schools? Why has female enrollment at business schools stagnated around 30 percent?

Even during the best of times, business schools have struggled to attract women. Is it because of the unique challenges women face in building and sustaining their careers over a lifetime of choices, both professional and personal, or is there another reason? Clearly an MBA presents many opportunities, but, for women, do these opportunities outweigh any potential upset to their already delicate balancing acts?

THINKING OF FAMILY

Let's start with biology—as in biological clocks. Since a prerequisite for admission to many business programs is prior work experience, business school students typically start a bit older than their law or med school counterparts do. In fact, the average starting age for full-time MBA students is 28. This means that by the time graduation rolls around, MBA students are heading into their thirties—a prime time for marriage and children. For some women, that timing couldn't be worse.

Newly minted MBAs are just starting to reap the rewards of their business school investments by scoring brand new, mid-to-senior level jobs. With these jobs come ever-greater demands and time pressures. But, for many, the pressure to have a personal life is just as great. Those kinds of competing priorities are the very headaches women hope to avoid. Making matters worse, MBA jobs at the senior level can vault women into a culture that may still be dominated by old-school thinking (translation: men) and a culture that, perhaps, may be less tolerant of balancing work commitments with family.

But the whole entanglement begins long before business school graduation. Again, because MBA students tend to be older, many women have to factor a partner or children into the graduate school decision, especially if it involves relinquishing a paycheck and/or relocation. But here comes a potential double standard: Husbands and boyfriends, especially those with careers, are often less willing to relocate on their female partner's behalf, than vice versa.

NO URGENT MATTER

Another reason business school enrollment for women may be low is that an MBA is not a barrier to entry nor is it a requirement for success in business. In addition, it isn't a rite of passage in many fields that appeal to high numbers of women: marketing, publishing, fashion, and teaching. By contrast, notes Eileen Chang, Associate Director of Admissions at the Harvard Business School, "If your objective is to be a lawyer or doctor, you simply can't practice without the requisite degree. Business school is fundamentally different because the career path is one where the MBA can put you on any number of tracks—be it banking, accounting, or management—but doesn't require a credential." Between the lack of required degree for business and the late starting age to enter a program, some women perceive a high opportunity cost for the MBA.

FEAR OF MATH?

Why more women aren't pursuing The MBA is a question the business schools have been asking themselves for years. Some hard answers came in the form of a recent study by University of Michigan's Business School Center for the Education of Women and the Catalyst Foundation. The following issues were identified as key obstacles to business school for women: the MBA is still seen as a male domain; there is a lack of support from employers; a lack of career opportunity and flexibility; a lack of access to powerful business networks and role models; and a perception that b-school is overloaded with math.

On the math issue, according to the schools, math fears are just that—fears. Harvard's Chang observes, "Maybe historically, math was considered a hurdle. But we see so many women who have strong skills coming from fields that are quantitative, such as banking and engineering, that I think the math fears are almost a myth. But this is a myth we want to work against. We want applicants to know they can handle the math."

Julia Min, Director of Admissions at New York University's Stern School of Business, concurs, "The math phobia may be unfounded to a certain degree, and still it's a perception that has been long-lasting. Women come here and perform extremely well."

But if you're frightened by math, you need to know that a business school education does require a basic command of the subject. "You do need to be comfortable with numbers," advises Wendy Hansen, Associate Director of Admissions at the Stanford Business School. She continues, "The strongest MBA programs are going to be rigorous in math. Knowing how to influence and lead an organization requires understanding the language of business, which includes accounting and finance."

Still, prospective MBAs with a math-phobia need not panic; most programs will work with students who lack the necessary math background. "At Stanford, we have a pre-term program of courses before classes begin to get students up to speed," says Hansen, "We also encourage people to take quantitative courses before they come to our school to develop their skills."

If your math fears are not so easily assuaged, concerns about a persistent Old Boys Network might be. While female enrollment at Stanford was stuck at 26 percent 10 years ago, for the class of 2004, it has climbed to 38 percent. Some people feel those numbers are still not high enough. In response to this, Hansen notes, "Women may say, I don't see the masses of female role models doing what I want to do. That is going to change slowly. But it is going to change. We have to reach a point where those in school reach a place where they are out in the world having an impact."

OUR ADVICE

Look at the number of female MBA students attending your targeted school and evaluate whether you would feel comfortable there. Research the number and range of student organizations for women only and speak with female MBAs about school life.

WHERE ARE THEY NOW?

It takes a monumental leap of faith to go to business school—to take two years out of your professional life, go to zero income, and drop $60,000 or more on tuition. By contrast, making the decision to go to medical or law school is more straightforward. Of the three so-called primary professions—business, medicine, and law—business is the only one you can pursue without a degree. In fact, you can become highly successful (and may already be) without an MBA. So how do you decide?

Perhaps the best way to assess the value of the MBA is to talk to the people who have already gone through the program and can reflect on the experience and the credential. Over the next several pages, you'll find a series of interviews with women who have graduated with an MBA. Their graduation dates range from 1992 to 2004, but their common thread lies in how valuable each of them found their advanced degree to be. Each of the women came from different backgrounds, went to different schools, were hoping for different things from their b-school experiences, and took different approaches to their career paths. Here, they share their choices, advice, and what they might change if they were to do it all again.

We begin with Cathy Crane-Moley, an outstanding MBA with the talent, passion, and drive that have made her one of America's most successful businesswomen. In fact, Entelos, Inc., which Cathy co-founded in 1996, has recently been named one of the 13 coolest companies in the nation by *Fortune* magazine.

Ten years out, Crane-Moley is the co-founder and senior vice-president of strategy, Entelos, Inc. and former chief financial officer and head of corporate development.

CATHY CRANE-MOLEY, STANFORD GRADUATE SCHOOL OF BUSINESS, CLASS OF '92

Q: Cathy, as a newly minted MBA, what were your thoughts on what the degree could do for you?

A: At that point in time, I didn't have a 10-plus-year horizon in my view. My thoughts were more about the immediate future of my career. I was a molecular biology major as an undergrad. I had worked in sales and in the field and had a big passion for health care. So that's really why I went to get an MBA, to follow through on my passion and vision for a business career in the health care sector.

Q: How did you target Stanford as the school that would deliver on that vision?

A: That's an interesting question. I lived in Virginia at the time and I did a lot of research on schools. I had a number of goals, some of which changed once I got to business school, but one of the goals was to go to a top school—which Stanford is. And I was really interested in somehow combining international business and entrepreneurship, so another goal was to find an environment that would support my exposure to that. So I applied to Stanford and Harvard and Wharton and all the types of schools that would have recruiters coming on campus from an international background. I chose Stanford as the best environment for my combined vision.

Q: What was it about Stanford that fit with your career aspirations in particular?

A: What I really wanted from the MBA was to have the credibility to go build a company in health care. I had an expectation that business school would help me be a better businessperson in science. My goal was to be able to tie together the business and science and pursue a business career in biotechnology health care.

When I went to Stanford I was pretty nervous because all these investment bankers and consultants were using intimidating terms like "run the numbers." When I got to business school I learned that it just meant 2 + 2. So for me it was really about learning a whole new language. Every domain has it's own jargon and half the battle is learning the language. Business isn't rocket science. It has some very pragmatic, practical, and even intuitive components to it. So putting a language to it was a critical step for me.

Q: Did you use Stanford's formal on-campus recruiting to get your first job or did you have to do a one-of-a-kind type of job search?

A: I did a little bit of both. The [formalized] on-campus recruiting I did was more for the sake of exposure. Mostly, I created my own job search, which touches on the MBA and [the] important[ance] [of] the school's networks. The Stanford community was pivotal to my getting the job. There is no question that if I hadn't come out of Stanford, I would not have had the job I had.

Q: Why?

A: A couple of things. Right out of school, I became an entrepreneur-in-residence at the Mayfield Fund, a venture firm on Sand Hill Road [one of the most nationally prominent addresses for ventures funding]. The combination of my background and MBA was a big plus, but mostly getting my foot in the door was the result of befriending a wonderful woman who was from Stanford's Class of '87. She became a really strong mentor and made endless introductions in the venture community for me. She is now a dear friend of mine and was instrumental in my soul-searching.

Until 1995, when we merged with a public company. Then I started my current company with my four co-founders in 1996, which is also in the biotechnology sector.

Q: It sounds as though the Stanford networks were invaluable to this first experience out. What about this next stage?

A: Absolutely invaluable. Not just because of the connections—that's one component—but in your own brainstorming about what you want to be in your life.

At business school, you are surrounded by people who have done everything. There were people in my environment that had been entrepreneurs, venture capitalists, investment bankers, and international marketers at pharmaceutical companies. There were incredibly helpful connected professors and alumni. It was all at your fingertips as you were solidifying your own vision.

Q: I'm guessing that you would advise students beginning their MBA studies to think hard about why they're there and to take advantage of all the opportunities?

A: Absolutely. What can happen is that it's easy to do it [pursue the opportunities], but it's also easy not to do it.

Stanford is a classic example. It's in such a beautiful location and people want to experience California; you can easily be distracted. But this is two years when anyone will return your call. You have heads of state, heads of corporations visiting, people in the nonprofit area showing up. And all you have to do is get on your bike and ride over there.

The other thing is, there are people who have come from a particular background, like investment banking and consulting, who know they intend to return to those careers after business school. But even if that is your goal, you still should use the two years to check everything out. You should use the two years to get more exposure and think about long term.

Q: It's clear the networking opportunities were critical to your future career developments, but how important would you say actual content learning at school was?

A: It actually was. But you'll see differences depending on people's backgrounds. For my husband, who was an undergrad at Wharton (I met him at Stanford), he could do corporate finance with his eyes closed. But for me, a molecular biology major as an undergrad, I had never taken business classes, so the academic training was critical. Take corporate finance, for example. I cannot imagine anyone being in the business world without formal corporate finance. Our strategy classes, entrepreneurial classes, small business classes were all great for me. Anything like cost accounting [or some of the options theory, I could have done without. But the pragmatic fundamentals gave me the tools to build two businesses from nothing.

Q: How was being a woman at Stanford?

A: It was wonderful. The quality of people, male and female, was superb. I believe we have a ratio of 33 percent female. We had strong women and we did great. I never noticed any sort of difference in abilities based on gender.

Q: Was the business school environment intimidating?

A: I didn't think so. I felt very inspired by the people around me.

Q: What advice do you have for someone thinking about going to business school now?

A: I think it comes back to the theme we've already touched on: make the most of the community that you can, way over and above what the classes offer. Business school is a very unique opportunity— live it while you are there.

CHIARA PERRY, HARVARD BUSINESS SCHOOL, CLASS OF '92
SENIOR PRICING ANALYST, A DIVISION OF UNITED TECHNOLOGIES

Q: In 1992 the nation was in a recession. Jobs, even for Harvard b-school grads, were scarce. What was your mindset coming out of the program?

A: Well, I was fortunate in that I had a job in place before graduating. And I was thinking about the opportunities and challenges I'd face in that position. The company that made me the offer was part of United Technologies, and they had come on campus looking for MBAs. I was really happy to already have the offer by graduation so I didn't have to worry about looking for some great job over the summer.

It's true that in 1992 the economy wasn't in great shape, so many people were heading into graduation without an offer yet. I had a lot of things going on in my life at that time: I got married and moved a thousand miles away from the east coast to the middle of the Midwest [Indiana].

In terms of my expectations about the degree, I think they were that it put me into an elevated position and salary compared to the people I would be working with at my new job.

Q: Given your job offer, were you happy with what the MBA did for you?

A: Oh, absolutely. The company was excited to have hired me, and I was excited to work for them. I still work for the same company in the same location.

Q: To what do you attribute having stayed with the same company for so long?

A: I think it's several things. It's a great place to work. They treat their employees really well. And I don't like to play the sexist card, but it's a wonderful company to work for if you're a woman. My husband and I also really love Bloomington, Indiana. We have two children, and this is a great place to raise a family. So it's been several factors, including having children come into the equation. I only work three days a week now, but I have a professional position.

Q: Switching subjects, what kind of person is ideally suited for an MBA?

A: I think the type of person that benefits from the MBA is someone who wants to learn a lot, but also realizes that this isn't rocket science. Yes, there are challenging courses, and I learned a tremendous amount when I was at school. But I thought it was hard because of the overwhelming amount of work, the perceived competitiveness within the class, at least the first year. It wasn't necessarily hard academically. There was only one class I felt a bit overwhelmed by. Mostly, I pretty much felt, "Oh, I can do this."

So, back to your question. Someone who can go into a business school program with the attitude that this is a good thing to have, that you're going to challenge yourself and expand your expertise is going to benefit the most. It's great if you can do it full-time because you can really devote yourself to the program and figure out what you want to do with your life.

Q: So how important is it to go to a really good school?

A: I think it is important because people look at the school you've gone to and are impressed with you. And I have to be honest, that will make you feel good. People will say, "Oh my gosh, you went to Harvard!" In a social setting, when people ask me where I went to school, I almost hesitate, because I know there will be this big reaction, especially out here in the Midwest. Not very many people out here went to Harvard.

Right out of business school, I felt, you know, if this job doesn't work, I can go almost anywhere I want with this degree. I know that sounds kind of arrogant but I knew that with my business experience before I went to Harvard, and now with my MBA, I could take a risk. I could come out to this small town in the Midwest and if I needed to, I could leave and be okay.

Even ten years later, I think that's still true. A Harvard MBA certainly is helpful when you're trying to move to the next place or job. I don't think I can go anywhere I want now, because I've taken a little curve in my career track to be with my children. I've been working part time for three years now, three days a week. But the MBA from Harvard is going to be very helpful if we decide to leave.

Q: What, specifically?

A: The part-time schedule. Going back to full-time.

Q: Do you ever anticipate re-entering the workforce as a full-time person or leaving your job? And if so, how do you think the opportunities will be enhanced with the MBA?

A: It's actually good you ask that question, because right now I'm grappling with that. Our factory is moving all of its manufacturing to Mexico. And so the question is, what will happen to the office staff? Will we go, have some role, or be laid off? That's an unanswered question right now.

Because we'd like to stay in the area, my husband and I have been thinking about different things I can do. So the MBA will be very beneficial as I face these issues.

Q: What else did you get out of the two years you were at school?

A: I met a lot of wonderfully diverse and interesting people. Many people were like Wall Street–Harvard–back to Wall Street, or consulting–Harvard–back to consulting. Or people were switching careers. There were people who had been in the Peace Corps, done public not-for-profit work, or come from the military. So from that perspective, it was just wonderful to meet all those incredible people.

And how many smart people can you put in a room? I mean students were just incredibly bright. It was impressive and added tremendously to the classes.

Q: As you have passed the ten-year mark, how do you feel about the value of your business school training?

A: I absolutely still utilize it. I still think back on cases and situations and examples that I use to resolve issues going on in work. For example, we are moving some aspect of the business to Mexico, and I can remember that I did a case on that. Plus, with this colleague of mine who is currently getting his MBA, we'll chat even more about some of those issues from class.

But looking back, I can still remember comments I made in class, and my teachers and the classes themselves. It was a very valuable, memorable time in my life. But it wasn't always pleasant . . .

Q: Why wasn't it pleasant?

A: The first year class set-up and the overwhelming desire to make value-added comments was an immense amount of pressure on me. I mean I'm probably obsessive, but I even think of comments now!

Q: Someone reading this book might not understand what this comment thing is all about.

A: Comments you made to contribute to classroom discussion which, depending on the class, counted toward your grade. Comments could almost define the class—coming up with comments to be brilliant, or prove yourself to the others. I remember I was always second-guessing what I said in class. I could have said it better, or I could have said it a different way, that kind of thing.

Q: Looking back, if you could do anything differently, what would it be?

A: Well, probably I would do a little better at networking and then keeping in touch with section mates, because I may need to call them at some point. I think if you have those networks in place, it's not really calling to ask for a job, it's talking about your situation, and then those people know what's going on and may be able to let you know about an opportunity.

Having been at the same job for more than ten years, and being out in the Midwest, I'm a little less connected to the pipeline of, "Hey, do you need someone like me at your company?" And that goes both ways. You know, time is a problem, and when kids come along, things change greatly. It's just hard to fit everything in.

Q: Summing up, what advice do you have for someone reading this book?

A: The MBA gives you an extra couple of years to go and figure out what you want to do. I liken it to what college does for you, but this is your second breath. And it's a very valuable one. I recommend you go full time, so you can really focus.

"Over a decade ago, I sat in a classroom and discussed for 90 minutes how to approach a crisis. Somehow that exercise of analyzing and debating potential scenarios left an impression on me that helped me years later. . . I was told by several people that I would understand the true value of my MBA after 10 years. I would say that is mostly true."

Q: Patty, what kind of opportunities were you looking for post-MBA?

A: I was looking for an opportunity with a consumer-oriented company that sold goods and services. I was seeking product management, marketing, or strategic planning opportunities.

I was interested in working for a large multinational company, so I interviewed with companies like Disney and Sara Lee Corporation.

Q: Did they come on campus?

A: Yes they did.

Q: So you relied heavily on on-campus recruiters?

A: Very heavily. My second year I attended quite a few corporate presentations from different sectors: technology, packaged goods, and so forth.

At that time, we had the opportunity to attend recruiting presentations and the weekly Q&A sessions with well-known business leaders that are part of the second-year general management course. So by going to the more general presentations and learning about the companies or going to specific recruiting presentations, I actually came across quite a varied group of organizations.

Q: What was your summer position between your first and second year?

A: I participated in a fellowship in Eastern Europe. I worked with a group that was consulting with factories in Poland that were at risk of going out of business. It was 1991, so it was right after the fall of the communist system in Poland and there were a number of state-run factories and businesses that were in a state of collapse.

Q: How did you find your way to Poland?

A: I had worked previously with two of the founders of a consulting practice in Poland.

Q: You learned of this opportunity for a fellowship in Poland at Harvard? How did you unearth that?

A: Actually, it was a formalized program of doing nonprofit work. There were a number of HBS students who participated in the program.

I had to complete an application that explained the nature of the nonprofit work, and upon my return, I was required to write a summary report.

Q: Why did you seek out this particular opportunity in Europe for your summer job? A lot of MBAs expect that summer job to be the one that leads to a final job offer.

A: I'm always looking for interesting experiences in my life. I wanted to work overseas. I figured I probably wouldn't end up living my life in Eastern Europe, and so it was a unique opportunity at the time.

Q: How relevant were the things you learned at business school for your first job out?

A: I probably learned more basic analytical, communication, and process management skills from my experience at Bain & Co. My HBS education helped me to understand many of the big-picture issues facing the corporation.

Q: What did you learn at business school?

A: (Long pause) I can tell you more about how business school helps me today than how it helped me then. [Several people told me] that I would understand the true value of my MBA after 10 years. I would say that is mostly true.

In the short term however, I did find that the finance courses I took helped me in my first job. I chose to take several finance courses at HBS because I wanted to develop a more in-depth understanding of that area. I did not plan on working in finance post-HBS, and I didn't think I would ever have another opportunity to learn about it.

Ten years out, it's all about the leadership and people issues. For example, my company was facing a potential product recall recently. I found myself drawing upon the case we studied on the Tylenol recall at J&J. I asked myself, what were the big picture decisions they had to make? How fast? How serious? What is the potential damage? What is the action plan and how will we communicate it? Being able to draw from that exposure to a crisis management situation was very helpful. Over a decade ago, I sat in a classroom and discussed for 90 minutes how to approach a crisis. Somehow that exercise of analyzing and debating potential scenarios left an impression on me that helped me years later.

Q: If there were anything you could go back and do differently at business school what would it be?

A: I would take more of those organizational behavior classes that I laughed at.

Q: Because?

A: Oh you know, power, "group norms," and other people issues. None of those issues seemed that important to me at the time. I was still focused on mastering my knowledge in academic disciplines.

Q: Did you all laugh at them?

A: I don't think we valued those courses as much as other courses in the curriculum. But now I see the value, having managed so many people. In the second year, I might have taken more leadership courses and those organizational behavior courses.

Q: Do you think it was more intimidating for you to go to business school as a woman?

A: No. But I think I had to work harder in certain ways earlier on to establish myself as a credible voice in the class. Somehow I felt that if a woman was perceived to be too harsh or too focused, there was a natural tendency not to like her. And so I do think that women have to work harder at finding their place and fitting in.

Q: Overall would you say business school is an intimidating place?

A: No. I enjoyed it. I made great friends at HBS. I think the first week is terrifying for everyone, but overall, no.

Q: What would you say to someone who said, should I get my MBA today?

A: I think it depends on their circumstances. If they're very successful in business already and they are financially secure, I'm not sure business school is necessary. I meet incredible business people all the time who don't have MBAs.

But I think if you're younger in your career, or you're trying to make a career change, or you've found yourself limited, then I think it's a wonderful opportunity to go for two years and get the MBA.

Q: Do you think you went at the right time for the right reasons?

A: Absolutely. I was 25. It was perfect for a young woman with three years of business experience post-college, with my objectives, to go and get the MBA from the very best school I could.

CAROLINE GROSSMAN, UNIVERSITY OF CHICAGO GRADUATE SCHOOL OF BUSINESS, CLASS OF 2003
SENIOR ASSOCIATE BRAND MANAGER, KRAFT

Q: Did you have a specific career path in mind, or an industry you wanted to gain entry to in deciding to get your MBA?

A: My interests were fairly broad. I wanted to gain general management experience. So I was thinking about using the MBA to pursue either general management or consulting.

Q: What did you do before business school?

A: I worked as a teacher for three years, both abroad and in inner-city schools, and then worked in program management at an education non-profit. I had a liberal arts background.

Q: So this was a big career change for you. What made you decide to switch gears?

A: Although I liked the social service mission of the jobs I was doing, I wasn't fulfilled by the specific job functions in those positions. I wanted to go to business school to get to a place where I could be satisfied by and challenged by the actual work. When I thought about the kinds of work I liked most, I realized it was strategic thinking and project leadership. That pointed me toward business and the MBA.

Q: So, how did you wind up at Kraft?

A: I had an internship there in the summer between my first and second years. Now I'm working in a brand management position, and at Kraft, this offers me a perfect mix of marketing and general business management experiences. Brand Managers at Kraft have profit and loss responsibility in addition to setting the strategic vision for the business. Ultimately, they are responsible for achieving the business results on their brand. As my first job out of business school, it has very much met my needs.

Q: What was your sense of the value of the degree around graduation, and now, one and a half years later?

A: My MBA facilitated a major job transition. I had access to this specific opportunity through on-campus recruiting, and my coursework and extracurricular activities helped prepare me to do the job. I feel very pleased to have landed where I have, and I certainly needed the MBA to get started in this direction. I felt pretty confident that coming out of Chicago I would have the tool kit I needed for the job I was going to be doing.

Q: **In what ways is the MBA relevant and not relevant in today's world?**

A: The MBA opens a lot of doors. It allows a candidate access to companies to which one otherwise might not have access. The MBA is a ticket to a conversation with those organizations. Mind you, the ticket is only to a conversation—the job you have to get yourself. There are some companies who simply won't look at someone who does not have the MBA; it's a prerequisite.

I have to add that most of one's career is built in the workplace, not in the classroom. But school sets you up for success. You're creating a foundation of knowledge, as well as the strategic frameworks that you'll need to process all of the learning once you're in the workplace. For a very short time after business school, perhaps you could perform in my kind of job without the MBA. But over time, for strategy, decision-making, and being able to truly lead, the MBA will be highly relevant.

Q: **What advice would you give those considering leaving the workforce for an MBA?**

A: Be ready to hit the ground running because the job search process begins day one. Do some thinking about what you want to do with your career before you get to campus so you can focus your career exploration at school once you arrive.

Q: **How do you measure return on investment for the MBA?**

A: I was looking to make a major career switch, so my reasons for going to business school were very straightforward. Because I came from the teaching field, and am now in a position at a leading consumer goods company, I would have to say I am completely satisfied with the return on my investment.

But I think this will vary depending on the type of job you left behind. It will also depend on where you land after the MBA and the extent to which that new position meets your goal. The more introspection you have about that you are looking for, the greater your return on investment.

I also measure ROI (return on investment) in terms of long- and short-term returns. At Chicago, I learned a lot of frameworks for making business decisions, which will help me in the long run. And in the short run, I acquired the skills and knowledge I needed to hit the ground running at work.

Q: **How important is it where you go to school?**

A: I think it's very important. You should ask yourself what it is that you want to get out of the experience and then consider what the school offers and if it's a good fit.

In my case, I wanted a lens for looking at business challenges and problems. Because I had a liberal arts background, I was looking for quantitative rigor to balance that out, and wanted to be sure that I'd be somewhere I could master business fundamentals. Chicago gave me that. The economics courses, in particular, really helped frame my thinking, and it was in the Marketing course that I learned the basis of what I do everyday at work.

You might also consider the regional location of the schools you're looking at. In certain industries, such as consulting and investment banking, firms interview at many business schools then place hires in different offices nationally. But other companies tend to recruit in the geographic region in which they are based.

Q: If you could go back in time, is there anything you would do differently with your time at Chicago?

A: I'm not one for regrets. I had a balanced experience at Chicago. I had a leadership position in a student organization, and was a member of a couple of others, which helped me. I built a strong network, which facilitated the career transition I was looking for. I learned a lot, and I had a good time. What more could I ask for?

I think the key to achieving this level of satisfaction with business school is picking your mandatories (for me, a career transition) and balance. There is so much to do that you can't do everything to the fullest, so you have to either focus or do a little of everything. The latter approach was a good fit for me.

SARA WEISS, MIT SLOAN SCHOOL OF MANAGEMENT, CLASS OF 2004

Q: What were your reasons for going to b-school?

A: I was looking for a career change. At the time, I wanted to become an energy trader. In fact, in my b-school essays I wrote about how I wanted to work for Enron. And then within three days of submitting my last application, Enron just imploded.

Q: Isn't that a little unusual, having a specific company to work for in mind?

A: Yes, it is. But Enron was unique in the role that they played in this field. That is why I had so specifically targeted the company. In the end, I wound up working in the financial market, which naturally is very different from the energy markets. But a lot of the attributes and experiences I was looking for in a job, I found in the financial markets.

Q: What were you doing before business school?

A: I was doing management consulting. I did process design and systems implementation for electric utilities. This is why I first got interested in energy-related fields.

Q: So how was the MBA going to advance your career? It sounds like you already had a strong career path and future.

A: I had a strong career path in consulting, but I didn't find myself fulfilled by that job. By the time I arrived at Sloan, I knew what I was looking for. It was something more dynamic and fast-paced. I wanted something where I had more control over my career path. I was looking for a job where I had immediately measurable results versus consulting, where you do these projects and you never really know if the project was successful until many years later.

It was really my Sloan classmates who helped me find my new focus. The community at Sloan is extremely supportive, and people are very willing to share their experiences and offer insight to each other. When I got to Sloan, I immediately knew that I had joined an incredible network. The students back each other up and help each other out. Without my peers, I would not have been able to find my focus so quickly or make such a successful transition.

Q: How did you feel about the value of the MBA as graduation approached?

A: I was able to look back and pinpoint several things I had gotten out of the MBA. First, I learned about finance, accounting, and other disciplines, which was the content I needed to start my new job. More importantly, I developed tremendously as a person. In a lot of ways, I became more level-headed in my decision-making and I fine-tuned my skills as a professional. I think I just came out as a better package. I looked back right after I graduated and thought, "Wow, this is a huge transformation I've undergone in these two years."

But probably the most important thing I got out of business school is a network of incredible friends. I really got to know my classmates well, because we spent so much time together doing a wide range of activities inside and outside the classroom. My Sloan friends are closer to me than my college friends. Not only are they valued friends, but they are also people I will turn to for career support for the rest of my life.

Q: How, if at all, has your perception of the value of the degree changed?

A: I definitely feel the value. I absolutely use the finance content I learned directly in my job. Even the classes I thought were useless at the time, such as the organizational behavior classes, the touchy-feely classes, I have found those extraordinarily relevant.

Q: Why is that?

A: In my current job, I have many different layers of colleagues and clients. The dynamics of the teams I work with and am expected to perform with are complicated. So all of that stuff about how people interact with each other, require motivation, ownership, etc, I'm using all of that.

Q: Does it matter where you get your MBA?

A: Yes, of course. But it matters more what you decide to get out of it. A program is only as good as what you decide to invest in it and in turn what you take away from it.

Q: Do you notice a difference among graduates of different programs?

A: Yes, in their soft skills. For example, anyone can learn textbook accounting. Just about every business program has accounting courses and most schools will require you to take at least one. But not every school has a community that is team-oriented or is involved in projects with the local business community. Not every school provides students with presentation experience. Students in programs that support class participation learn to express themselves eloquently on the fly.

Q: In what ways is the MBA relevant and not relevant in today's world?

A: I think that everything you learn in business school can also be learned in the real world. I don't think there is anything new. You just learn it faster, better, and have more fun doing it in a full-time MBA program. That makes it ultimately relevant and yet completely unnecessary. Nobody ever needs an MBA, but it's a huge leg up. The MBA gives you a much more focused and concentrated experience. The magic of it is in the environment and the people.

Q: How do you measure return on investment?

A: Personally, I actually don't measure my experience in terms of return on investment. I believe very strongly that education is worth its cost, as long as you give it your all, so you don't just spend all this money and cut class. Some people I know look at it differently. They measure the opportunity cost in dollars and ensure for themselves that they will make back those dollars. I think those people are missing a big piece of what is most important about business school. The real value isn't measurable.

Q: What advice would you give to today's applicants?

A: Try to do as much thinking as you can (even if it's in abstract terms), before you do your applications. Think about what is important to you, what you're looking for, what's missing from your life today, and who you want to be in the future. You don't need to know specifically what your next steps are. But the more focused you are, the more you are prepared to take advantage of what business school has to offer.

Q: If you had to do b-school all over again, what would you do differently?

A: I would study less. I would stress less. I would join more extracurricular clubs unrelated to my chosen career path. I would definitely throw that cocktail party on my roof deck in Beacon Hill, something that I never got around to doing. And I would take a class at Harvard's Kennedy School. There. That's my list.

Chapter 6

Money Matters

How Much Will It Cost?

The Truth

To say that business school is an expensive endeavor is an understatement. In fact, to really gauge how expensive business school is, you need to look not only at your tuition costs and living expenses, but also at the opportunity cost of foregoing a salary for the length of your program. Think about it: You'll have a net outflow of money.

But keep in mind that, unlike law school or medical school, business school is just a two-year program. And once those two years are over, you can expect to reap the rewards of your increased market value. Unfortunately, business school differs from law school and medical school in a much less desirable way as well—there are serious limitations on the amount of money available through scholarships and grants. Most of you will be limited to loans, and lots of them.

Try not to get too upset about borrowing the money for business school; think of it as an investment in yourself. But, like all investments, it should be carefully thought out and discussed with everyone (spouse, partner, etc.) concerned. This is especially important for those of you considering business school. You need a law degree to practice law, and a medical degree to practice medicine, but a business degree is not required to work in business. That said, certain professional opportunities may be tougher to pursue without an MBA on your resume.

The Cost of B-School

So get out some paper, a pencil, and a calculator, and figure out how much it will cost you to attend school. What should you include? Your opportunity cost (lost income) and your cost of attending b-school (tuition and fees). One more thing: For a more accurate assessment of your investment, you should figure taxes into the equation by dividing tuition cost by .65 (this assumes taxes of about 35 percent). Why? Because in order to pay tuition of $25,000, you would have to make a pre-tax income of about $38,500. If you are lucky enough to have a source of aid that does not require repayment, such as a grant, scholarship, or wealthy benefactor, subtract that amount from the cost of attending b-school.

For example, if you currently make $50,000 and plan to attend a business school that costs $25,000 per year, your investment would be approximately $177,000.

$(50,000 \times 2) + [(25,000 \times 2)/.65] = 177,000$

Now say you receive an annual grant of $5,000. Your investment would now be approximately $161,500.

$(50,000 \times 2) + [(20,000 \times 2)/.65] = 161,500$

How Long Will It Take You to Recoup Your Investment?

To estimate this figure, you first need to estimate your expected salary increase post-MBA. Check out the average starting salaries for graduates of the programs you are looking at and adjust upward/downward based on the industry you plan to enter. Subtract your current salary from your expected salary and you'll get your expected salary increase.

Once you complete the step above, divide your investment (tuition and fees plus lost income) by your expected salary increase, and then add 2 (the length of a full-time MBA program). If you are contemplating a one-year MBA program, just add 1.

Going back to the example above, if your pre-MBA salary is $50,000 and you expect to make $75,000 when you graduate, your expected salary increase is $25,000 (a 50 percent increase). Let's assume you did not receive a grant and that your investment will be about $177,000.

$(177,000/25,000) + 2 = 9.08$

It will take you approximately nine years to earn back your investment.

Keep in mind, these are approximations and don't take into account annual raises, inflation, and so on. But it is interesting, isn't it?

While business school is an expensive proposition, the financial rewards of having your MBA can be immensely lucrative as we discussed before. You won't be forced into bankruptcy if you finance it correctly. There are tried-and-true ways to reduce your initial costs, finance the costs on the horizon, and manage the debt you'll leave school with—all without selling your soul to the highest bidder.

Comparison Shopping

While cost shouldn't be the first thing on your mind when you are choosing a school, depending on your goals in getting an MBA, it might be fairly high on your list. Private schools aren't the only business schools. Many state schools have fantastic reputations. Regional schools may be more generous with financial aid. Tuition costs will vary widely between public and private schools, especially if you qualify as an in-state student. Keep in mind, however, that salary gains tend to be less dramatic at more regional schools.

HOW DO I FUND MY MBA?

The short answer: loans. Unless your company is underwriting your MBA, or you're able to pay your way in cash, you'll be financing your two years of business school through a portfolio of loans. Loans typically come in one of two forms: federal and private. Only a few of you will be lucky enough to qualify for, and get, grants and scholarships.

Anyone with reasonably good credit, regardless of financial need, can borrow money for business school. If you have financial need, you will probably be eligible for some type of financial aid if you meet the following basic qualifications:

- You are a United States citizen or a permanent U.S. resident.

- You are registered for Selective Service if you are a male, or you have documentation to prove that you are exempt.

- You are not in default on student loans already.

- You don't have a horrendous credit history.

International applicants to business school should take note: Most U.S. business schools will require all international students to pay in full or show proof that they will be able to pay the entire cost of the MBA prior to beginning the MBA program.

FEDERAL LOANS

The federal government funds federal loan programs. Federal loans are usually the "first resort" for borrowers because many are subsidized by the federal government and offer generous interest rates. Some do not begin charging you interest until after you complete your degree. Most federal loans are need-based, but some higher interest federal loans are available regardless of financial circumstances. Your business school's financial aid office will determine what your need is, if any.

PRIVATE LOANS

Don't think private loans are available only from banks. There are programs that exist for the express purpose of lending money to business students. These loans are expensive and interest accumulates during your studies. You will also be responsible for many extra charges (guarantees and insurance fees).

ALTERNATIVE SOURCES OF FUNDING

We've already mentioned these in one form or other, but they are worthy of a bit more attention.

The first alternative is sponsorship of your employer or educational reimbursement. Not all companies treat this the same way, but if you are able to get your employer to kick in a portion of the cost, you are better off than before. But beware, this benefit also comes with strings attached. Most companies that pay for your MBA will require a commitment of several years upon graduation. If you renege, you could be liable for the full cost of your education. Others will require that you attend business school part time, which you may or may not want to do. Often, part-time students are ineligible to participate in on-campus recruiting efforts to the same extent as full-time students.

Educational reimbursement can come in another form as well. Some companies will provide sign-on bonuses to new MBAs that will cover the cost of a year's tuition. This is a fantastic development from the years of a robust economy, but it is by no means a guarantee during tougher times. Don't assume that you will have this option open to you just because it has been a common occurrence in past years.

The other "alternative" source of funding is a financial gift from family or another source. Either you have a resource that is willing and able to fund all or part of your MBA, or you don't. If you do, be thankful.

APPLYING FOR FINANCIAL AID

In order to become eligible for financial aid of any kind, you will need to complete the Free Application for Federal Student Aid, also known as the FAFSA. You complete and submit this form after January 1 of the year in which you plan to enter business school. You should aim to complete and submit this form as soon as possible after the first of the year to avoid any potential delays. The FAFSA is available from a school's financial aid office. You can also download the form directly from the website of the U.S. Department of Education at www.fafsa.ed.gov. A third option is to use the FAFSA Express software (also downloadable from the website) and transmit the application electronically.

It is important to note that the form requires information from your federal income tax returns. Plan to file your taxes early that year.

In addition to the FAFSA form, most schools will have their own financial aid form that you will be required to complete and submit. These often have their own deadlines, so it is wise to keep careful track of all the forms you must complete and all their respective deadlines. Yes, it's a lot of paperwork, but get over it. You'll be much happier when the tuition bill arrives.

LOAN SPECIFICS

GUIDE TO FEDERAL LOANS

Stafford Loans

Stafford loans require you to complete the FAFSA form in order to qualify. These are very desirable loans because they offer low-interest rates capped at 8.25 percent and are federally guaranteed. There is a limit to how much you can borrow in this program. The maximum amount per year you may borrow as a graduate student is $18,500, $10,000 of which must be unsubsidized loans. The maximum amount you may borrow in total is $138,500 (only $65,500 of this may be in subsidized loans). The aggregate amount includes any Stafford loans you may have from your undergraduate or other graduate studies. One caveat: At the time of this writing, the Higher Ed Act is under review for reauthorization; loan limits may be affected.

The loans come in two types: subsidized and unsubsidized. Subsidized loans are need-based as determined by your business school. They do not charge interest while you are in school or in authorized deferment period (such as the first six months after graduation). This cost is picked up by the government (hence the name "subsidized"). Repayment begins at that time. Unsubsidized loans are not need-based and do charge interest from the time of disbursement to the time of full repayment. You can pay the interest while you are in school or opt for capitalization, in which case the interest is added to the principal. You will pay more in the long run if you choose capitalization. Interest payments may be tax deductible, so be sure to check. The standard repayment period for both is ten years.

You will pay a small origination and guarantee fee for each loan, but this is not an out-of-pocket expense. It is simply deducted from the loan amount. Some schools will allow you to borrow the money under the Stafford program directly from them, while others will require you to borrow from a bank. For more information on federal loans, call the Federal Student Aid Information Center at 1-800-433-3243.

Perkins Loans

Perkins loans are available to graduate students who demonstrate exceptional financial need. The financial aid office will determine your eligibility for a Perkins Loan. If you qualify for a Perkins Loan as part of your financial aid package, take it. The loans are made by the schools and are repaid to the schools, although the federal government provides a large portion of the funds. You can borrow up to $6,000 for each year of graduate study up to a total of $40,000 (this includes any money borrowed under this program during undergraduate study). The interest rates on this loan are low, usually 5 percent. There are no fees attached. The grace period is nine months upon graduation.

PRIVATE/COMMERCIAL LOANS

This is expensive territory. Not only are interest rates high, but terms are also quite different from those found with federal loans. You may not be able to defer payment of interest or principal until after graduation. Origination and guarantee fees are also much higher since these loans are unsecured. After all, banks and other specialized lenders exist to loan money to folks like you, and unlike the federal government, want to make money doing it. If you go this route, shop around diligently. Think of it as good practice for your post-MBA executive career.

Below we list some of the more well-known and well-respected institutions that provide financial assistance for graduate and professional school. Keep in mind that most programs require the borrower to be attending an approved graduate program at least part-time. If you choose to investigate loans outside of the educational market, such as a personal line of credit, credit card, or a loan against an insurance plan, be aware that these can be quite costly.

The Access Group, Business Access Loan

Website: www.accessgroup.org

Phone: 1-800-282-1550

The Education Resources Institute (TERI) PEP Program

Website: www.teri.org.

Citibank CitiAssist® Loan

Website: http://studentloan.citibank.com

Phone: 1-800-692-8200

Nellie Mae EXCEL Grad Loan

Website: www.nelliemae.com

Phone: 1-800-FOR-TUITION

Sallie Mae MBA Loans

Website: www.salliemae.com

Phone: 1-888-2SALLIE (272-5543)

SCHOLARSHIPS AND GRANTS

The usual sources for this type of funding are alumni groups and civic organizations. This funding is limited, and actual awards tend to be small. Even if you benefited from generous scholarship funding as an undergraduate, it would be unwise to assume you'll have the same experience as a graduate student. But do investigate. You never know what's out there. Schools will frequently list any scholarships and grants that are available at the back of their financial aid catalog.

For more information about financing your business school education, check out *Paying for Graduate School Without Going Broke*, available in our online bookstore at www.princetonreview.com/mba/bookstore.asp.

PART II
SCHOOLS RANKED BY CATEGORY

On the following pages you will find eleven top ten lists of business schools ranked according to various metrics. As we noted earlier, none of these lists purports to rank the business schools by their overall quality. Nor should any combination of the categories we've chosen be construed as representing the raw ingredients for such a ranking. We have made no attempt to gauge the "prestige" of these schools, and we wonder whether we could accurately do so even if we tried. What we have done, however, is presented a number of lists using information from two very large databases—one of statistical information collected from business schools, and another of subjective data gathered via our survey of 11,000 business students at 143 business schools.

Ten of the ranking lists are based partly or wholly on opinions collected through our business student survey. The only schools that may appear in these lists are the 143 business schools from which we were able to collect a sufficient number of student surveys to accurately represent the student experience in our various ratings and descriptive profiles.

One of the rankings, Toughest to Get Into, incorporates *only* admissions statistics reported to us by the business schools. Therefore, any business school appearing in this edition of the guide, whether we collected student surveys from it or not, may appear on this list.

Under the title of each list is an explanation of what criteria the ranking is based on. For explanations of many of the individual rankings components, turn to the "How This Book is Organized" Section, on page 4.

It's worth repeating: there is no one best business school in America. There is a best business school for you. By using these rankings in conjunction with the descriptive profiles and data listings in subsequent sections of this book, we hope that you will begin to identify the attributes of a business school that are important to you, as well as those schools that can best help you to achieve your personal and professional goals.

Please note that in an effort to avoid comparing apples to oranges, we have not placed any international business schools on any of our rankings lists.

The top schools in each category appear in descending order.

TOUGHEST TO GET INTO

BASED ON THE ADMISSIONS SELECTIVITY RATING (SEE PAGE 10 FOR EXPLANATION)

1. Harvard University
2. Stanford University
3. University of Pennsylvania
4. Massachusetts Institute of Technology
5. Columbia University
6. University of California-Berkeley
7. Northwestern University
8. University of California—Los Angeles
9. New York University
10. Dartmouth College

BEST CAREER PROSPECTS

BASED ON THE CAREER RATING (SEE PAGE 12 FOR EXPLANATION)

1. Stanford University
2. Harvard University
3. University of California—Berkeley
4. Duke University
5. Columbia University
6. New York University
7. The University of Chicago
8. University of California-Los Angeles
9. Dartmouth College
10. University of Michigan

BEST OVERALL ACADEMIC EXPERIENCE

BASED ON THE ACADEMIC EXPERIENCE RATING (SEE PAGE 8 FOR EXPLANATION)

1. Massachusetts Institute of Technology
2. Dartmouth College
3. New York University
4. University of California-Los Angeles
5. Yale University
6. University of Massachusetts Amherst
7. Northwestern University
8. Stanford University
9. Harvard University
10. University of California—Berkeley

BEST PROFESSORS

BASED ON THE PROFESSORS INTERESTING AND PROFESSORS ACCESSIBLE RATINGS (SEE PAGE 9 FOR EXPLANATIONS)

1. Indiana University
2. University of Virginia
3. Acton MBA in Entrepreneurship
4. University of Massachusetts Amherst
5. University of Alabama—Tuscaloosa
6. Duke University
7. Washington University in St. Louis
8. College of William and Mary
9. Southern Methodist University
10. Harvard University

MOST COMPETITIVE STUDENTS

Based on student assessment of how competitive classmates are, how heavy the workload is, and the perceived academic pressure

1. Acton MBA in Entrepreneurship
2. University of Rochester
3. Rensselaer Polytechnic Institute
4. Purdue University
5. Howard University
6. Rice University
7. Bowling Green State University
8. University of Arkansas—Fayetteville
9. Clarkson University
10. Texas A&M University

BEST CAMPUS ENVIRONMENT

Based on student assessment of the safety, attractiveness and location of the school

1. Emory University
2. University of California—Los Angeles
3. Boston College
4. Stanford University
5. Dartmouth College
6. University of North Carolina at Chapel Hill
7. University of Utah
8. Pepperdine University
9. Loyola Marymount University
10. University of Denver

MOST FAMILY FRIENDLY

Based on student assessment of: how happy married students are, how many students have children, how helpful the business school is to students with children, and how much the school does for the spouses of students

1. Brigham Young University
2. Dartmouth College
3. Stetson University
4. Stanford University
5. Harvard University
6. Duke University
7. Thunderbird
8. Naval Postgraduate School
9. Cornell University
10. Northwestern University

BEST CAMPUS FACILITIES

Based on student assessment of the quality of classroom, library and gym facilities

1. Stetson University
2. Texas Christian University (TCU)
3. Indiana University
4. University of Alabama—Tuscaloosa
5. University of Georgia
6. University of Virginia
7. University of Oregon
8. Harvard University
9. University of California—Berkeley
10. University of Connecticut

BEST ADMINISTERED

*BASED ON STUDENT ASSESSMENT OF HOW SMOOTHLY THE SCHOOL IS RUN, AND THE
EASE WITH WHICH STUDENTS CAN GET INTO REQUIRED AND POPULAR COURSES*

1. Elon University

2. Colorado State University

3. Washington University in St. Louis

4. Seattle Pacific University

5. Texas A&M University

6. West Virginia University

7. Villanova University

8. University of Alabama-Tuscaloosa

9. Valparaiso University

10. Emory University

GREATEST OPPORTUNITY FOR MINORITY STUDENTS

*BASED ON THE PERCENT OF STUDENTS FROM MINORITIES, THE PERCENT OF FACULTY
FROM MINORITIES, AND STUDENT ASSESSMENT OF RESOURCES FOR MINORITY STUDENTS,
HOW SUPPORTIVE THE CULTURE IS OF MINORITY STUDENTS, AND WHETHER FELLOW
STUDENTS ARE ETHNICALLY AND RACIALLY DIVERSE*

1. Howard University

2. Texas A&M International University

3. San Francisco State University

4. American University

5. Thunderbird

6. The University of Texas at San Antonio

7. Barry University

8. Loyola Marymount University

9. University of San Francisco

10. University of Maryland—College Park

GREATEST OPPORTUNITY FOR WOMEN

*BASED ON THE PERCENT OF STUDENTS WHO ARE FEMALE, THE PERCENT OF FACULTY WHO
ARE FEMALE, AND STUDENT ASSESSMENT OF: RESOURCES FOR FEMALE STUDENTS, HOW
SUPPORTIVE THE CULTURE IS OF FEMALE STUDENTS, WHETHER THE BUSINESS SCHOOL
OFFERS COURSEWORK FOR WOMEN ENTREPRENEURS, AND WHETHER CASE STUDY
MATERIALS FOR CLASSES PROPORTIONATELY REFLECT WOMEN IN BUSINESS*

1. Babson College

2. University of California—Berkeley

3. Worcester Polytechnic Institute

4. Cornell University

5. Duke University

6. Stanford University

7. Rice University

8. University of California, Davis

9. Texas Christian University (TCU)

10. University of California—Los Angeles

PART III-A
BUSINESS SCHOOL
DESCRIPTIVE PROFILES

ACTON MBA IN ENTREPRENEURSHIP
HARDIN SIMMONS UNIVERSITY

GENERAL INFORMATION
Type of school   private
Affiliation   American Baptist
Academic calendar   August–April

SURVEY SAYS...
Friendly students
Happy students
Smart classrooms
Solid preparation in:
Entrepreneurial studies

STUDENTS
Enrollment of parent
  institution   2,200
Enrollment of MBA program   14
% male/female   79/21
% minorities   7
Average age at entry   28
Average years work experience
  at entry   6

ACADEMICS
Academic Experience Rating   90
Student/faculty ratio   1:1
Profs interesting rating   99
Profs accessible rating   85
% female faculty   15

Academics

An MBA from Acton stands out in many ways, but primarily among those ways is the experience in entrepreneurship that it offers. Students are pushed, pulled, bullied, and coddled in an extremely intense nine-month program, but at the end, most of them feel they come out with the skills they need to launch their own businesses or to help others launch theirs. As one student puts it, "the 80 to 90 hours per week that are described are real. It requires that much time. If you want clubs and day care and society, go to UT. If you want a cut-and-dry, no-nonsense business education, go with an Acton MBA."

Acton professors are "highly successful entrepreneurs who teach the keys to business success [by] using the Socratic Methods and expecting a high workload to be accomplished every week." Because Acton recognizes that every student is also a customer, feedback on teacher performance is relied upon heavily. One student reports, "We have no tenured faculty. The professor(s) who are ranked at the bottom by the students must take a semester off to audit other professors. If they fail to improve when they come back, they're asked to leave." For the most part, however, "they work hard and [students] must work even harder to keep pace and push [them]selves to learn the lessons that are not commonly taught in most business schools in America today."

Students move through the program in a cohort of "highly talented students that have been handpicked by [the] admissions committee; students will come to rely upon each other in a profound way." During the first semester, students take five case-based courses. Three of these are the sales, operations, and counting courses, which are also known as the tools courses. During the second semester, students take four classes that "dig more deeply into the four phases of the lifecycle of a business covered in the entrepreneurial process." These courses are opportunity analysis, gathering resources and launch, growth and harvest. One class that some consider the most important of all is "Life of Meaning," in which students learn how to think about their business careers in broader and longer terms—about the impact a job will have on their lives, not just their income.

What students find most exciting about the curriculum, however, is how case-focused it is. During their time in the program, students are confronted with more than "250 challenging case dilemmas." Students boast that "the case-based style of learning is the nearly exclusive approach used in this program, which [they] find exceptional. The real-world experience of the professors has also been vital to [their] experience." And others call Acton's program an "intense learning experience for those who like the complete immersion technique."

Nota Bene: At the time we were going to print, Acton was in talks about, but had not yet applied for, accreditation from the Association to Advance Collegiate Schools of Business (AACSB).

TRACY BALBOA, DIRECTOR OF ENROLLMENT
515 CONGRESS AVENUE, SUITE 1875, AUSTIN, TX 78701 UNITED STATES
PHONE: 512-703-1232 • FAX: 512-495-9480
E-MAIL: TBALBOA@ACTONMBA.ORG • WEBSITE: WWW.ACTONMBA.ORG

Career and Placement

Unlike many b-schools, Acton's career resource center doesn't send out millions of resumes each year. Instead, students are encouraged to focus on specific jobs at specific companies that could help them achieve their long-term goals. According to the school's website, "once a professor is convinced that a student has made a considered choice, the professor will call that employer to make a personal introduction."

Companies who have accepted Acton students in the past include 3M, Goldman Sachs, Merrill Lynch, American Airlines, AT&T Wireless Services, IBM, Microsoft, BP, Newgistics, and Salion.

Student Life and Environment

Some students go out of their way to emphasize that "while this is the most fun [they've] ever had, the only thing [students] will be doing is case prep and analysis, individually and with your classmates. There is no time for *anything* else. [Students] will not be able to shop, socialize, etc. This is 100 percent immersion." Still, one part of becoming a successful entrepreneur is learning "how to manage our time for studies, health, and family." And most students agree that there is no better place to learn this than Acton. "This program is focused on learning how to start and operate businesses, and the goal is to put you under enough pressure to give you that experience while managing your schedule."

Admissions

Most students will agree that, "if you are not willing to give all you can for nine months solid, then please, don't apply." Overall, Acton students have an average GMAT score of 610 and an average undergraduate GPA of 3.2. Approximately 25 percent of the students have 10 years or more of full-time work experience, and 33 percent had less than three years of work experience. Students who studied at a college level in a language other than English are required to take the TOEFL. A minimum score of 550 is required on that exam.

FINANCIAL FACTS

Annual tuition	$31,000
% of students receiving aid	43
% of students receiving loans	43

ADMISSIONS

Admissions Selectivity Rating	**79**
# of applications received	26
% applicants accepted	77
% acceptees attending	70
Average GMAT	610
Average GPA	3.2
TOEFL Required of International Students?	Yes
Application fee	$50
International application fee	$50
Regular application deadline	Rolling
Regular notification	Rolling
Application Deadline/Notification	
Round 1:	11/15 / 12/15
Round 2:	1/15 / 2/15
Round 3:	3/15 / 4/15
Round 4:	4/15 / 5/15

EMPLOYMENT PROFILE

		Grads employed by field	%: avg. salary
Career Rating	74	Finance	15: $120,000
% grads employed immediately	70	Marketing	8: $60,000
Average starting salary	$70,000	Operations	8: $40,000
		Consulting	12: $80,000
		Entrepreneurship	12: $50,000
		General Management	19: $70,000
		Other	14: $60,000
		Internet/New Media	4: $120,000
		Non-profit	8: $50,000

ALFRED UNIVERSITY
COLLEGE OF BUSINESS

GENERAL INFORMATION
Type of school   private

SURVEY SAYS...
Friendly students
Good peer network
Happy students
Solid preparation in:
General management
Teamwork

ACADEMICS
Academic Experience Rating   **67**
Student/faculty ratio   2:1
Profs interesting rating   72
Profs accessible rating   86

Academics

If you're looking for an intimate MBA experience, you can hardly top the one offered at Alfred University: This program serves a population of 60 graduate students, only 15 of whom attend full-time. The result is a program with a "family atmosphere in which the school cares about the individual." As one student told us, "The greatest strength of Alfred University is its size. The classes are between 10 and 20 people, and the interaction is incredible. One really feels a part of the class discussions." The school is especially strong in entrepreneurial studies, an area abetted by the university's Center for Family Business and Entrepreneurial Leadership, a research center.

Professors at Alfred have the time to go the extra mile for students, and they do it by "making sure that the students are comprehending the course material [and] not just completing assignments. They are very personable with everyone and encourage one-on-one meetings." Students also appreciate that "professors here are very diverse and have experiences [in other countries] ranging from Japan to Tunisia."

With no crowd to fight, Alfred students have a better chance to shine. One student writes, "One professor liked a paper I wrote for his class. He offered to coauthor another paper with me and pursue getting it published. These opportunities are so valuable to me and something I would never have expected." Another student was able to land an assistantship in which she "helped plan an international business conference in Ecuador." She says, "Not only did I get great experience working on this project, but I was also able to travel to Ecuador and participate in the conference. It was one of the best experiences I've ever had." One student sums up, "The personal relationship with faculty and administrators open a lot of doors that would normally slam shut in your face at other schools. It's these personal relationships that nurture change, improvement, and downright fantastic opportunities."

Of course, a small school can only offer students so much; many agree that "a larger variety of curriculum would bring a great deal of value to the students." Even so, they regard their MBA experience as extremely positive. They approve of the school's "active learning" strategies, which emphasize teamwork, case studies, simulations, and field experience (usually gained through an internship). They also love the administration's dedication to the program. "They are constantly striving to improve the program and the school. As a result, I have found the program challenging, rewarding, and enriching," explains one student.

Career and Placement

All Alfred students receive career services through the Robert R. McComsey Career Development Center. The office provides one-on-one counseling sessions; workshops in interviewing, resume writing, and networking; a career library with online and conventional print resources; and annual job fairs. The school boasts a 100 percent placement rate for its MBAs. Students point out, however, that Alfred's remote location complicates their search for jobs and internships. One MBA candidate explains, "Outside internships and projects are more difficult to obtain due to the university's rural location. However, the administration is undertaking maneuvers to expand local, as well as international, opportunities with particular focus on MBA students."

Prominent employers of Alfred MBAs include Alstom, AOL Communications, Avantt Consulting, LLC, Met Life/New England Financial, General Electric, and Eli Lilly, A-Citynet, Corning Inc., Dresser Rand, Nestle Co., NYSEG, Toro Energy, Walmart.

CATHLEEN JOHNSON, COORDINATOR OF GRADUATE ADMISSIONS
OFFICE OF GRADUATE ADMISSIONS, ALUMNI HALL, SAXON DRIVE, ALFRED, NY 14802 U.S.
PHONE: 800-541-9229 • FAX: 607-871-2198
E-MAIL: GRADINQUIRY@ALFRED.EDU • WEBSITE: WWW.BUSINESS.ALFRED.EDU/MBA.HTML

FINANCIAL FACTS

Annual tuition	$28,450
Fees	$810
Books and supplies	$850
Room & board (on/off-campus)	$9,200/$8,200

ADMISSIONS

Admissions Selectivity Rating	**60***
Average GMAT	534
Average GPA	3.1
Minimum TOEFL (paper/computer)	590/243
Application fee	$50

Student Life and Environment

Alfred, New York, is a quiet, rural town with few distractions, and accordingly, student life centers on campus. The university is a community of about 2,500 students, including 250 business undergrads and 60 MBAs, making it large enough to support all manner of activity. One student explains, "Basically, if you can dream it up, you can do it at Alfred. I became an entrepreneur through all of Alfred's clubs and organizations long before I looked into a business degree. The MBA program has helped me hone my skills and expand my horizons by giving me valuable insight. I have become very empowered and am eager to take on a whole slew of projects and tasks to make a difference in the world—and if it helps me earn a living, too, all the better." One resident director adds, "I know that there are many activities on and around campus. It is up to the residents to take the initiative and join in."

Alfred's infrastructure includes "plenty of computers and good Internet bandwidth, [but] the recreational facilities aren't the best, and the library needs help. Fortunately, a large renovation and expansion project is slated to start very soon, which could be the largest project for the university within the last few decades. Renovations to both facilities will address shortcomings of the university, greatly enhance the campus, and benefit students." Alfred's sixteen Division III intercollegiate teams provide entertainment, as does the popular intramural sports program. The school's divisions of music, theater, and dance frequently hold performances. Alfred also has an active visual-arts community; it houses one of the best ceramic-arts programs in the country.

The village of Alfred has a year-round population of 1,000, and surrounding towns are not much larger. The city of Rochester is only 80 miles away, with Buffalo only a little farther down the road. Bring a four-wheel drive vehicle with good snow tires.

Admissions

Applicants must provide the school with official copies of undergraduate transcripts, GMAT scores, TOEFL scores (for international students whose first language is not English), a personal statement, and letters of recommendation (preferably from former employers or professors). Previous work experience is not required. An interview is optional.

EMPLOYMENT PROFILE	
Career Rating	**67**
% grads employed immediately	100
Average starting salary	$39,000

AMERICAN UNIVERSITY
KOGOD SCHOOL OF BUSINESS

Academics

Founded in 1955, Kogod School of Business at American University was the first business school in Washington, DC. With only about 200 full-time students at a time, intimacy and friendliness is the name of the game. Students, for the most part, "have been impressed by almost every faculty member [they've] come into contact with. They are very open to questions and help outside of the classroom." Not only do professors aggressively push their "open door" policy, but administrators get top marks for helpfulness as well. As one student puts it, "it is a very good sign that most of the students have become personal friends with the administration staff." Students appreciate the responsiveness of the majority of the staff and say that, though "Kogod School of Business is still growing and expanding, [they appreciate that] students and professors are pushing the boundaries of what is possible."

Aside from the basic MBA, Kogod offers two joint degrees: an MBA/MA in international studies and a JD/MBA. They also offer an MS in taxation, an MS in information technology management, and an MS in management. According to students, "The academic strengths are corporate finance and international management, [and the school has] great professors in international business, finance, and IT." Most students greatly appreciate the emphasis the school places on "the use and impact of technology in business today and in the future."

More than half of the curriculum's credits are occupied by core courses: accounting concepts and applications, managerial economics, financial management, applied managerial statistics, organizational behavior and human resources management, and marketing management. The rest of the course load is taken up by "advanced breadth" electives in courses like manager in the international economy; applied production and operations management; business, ethics, and society; and business law.

In the spirit of international cooperation, Kogod offers a study-abroad program with the University of Paris—Dauphine in France. As one student says, "Kogod has done well to remain on the cutting edge of international business but still needs to clarify in which direction certain programs and projects will go."

Career and Placement

Unlike many students of other schools, Kogod students seem more or less satisfied with the work done by their Graduate Career Services department. As one says, a great benefit of studying at Kogod is the "interaction with so many experienced businessmen from over 70 nations allows the students to build the communications skills and contacts needed for future success." Most students agree that the school would benefit if it would "involve more alumni [and work harder on] networking events with other schools and professionals." Despite this, most students point out that Kogod provides "a lot of different clubs and events that help the students to become involved and increase networking opportunities."

Companies like Accenture, Citibank, Ernst & Young, MCI Worldcom, NASDAQ, and World Bank (among many others) all have a recruiting presence on campus, and students generally place well out of the program. Marketing and sales jobs were the most common, with positions in finance and accounting coming in second place. The mean starting package (including bonus) was $71,117 for 2003, with those who chose to work in the nonprofit sector earning the highest average salary at $85,000.

SONDRA SMITH, DIRECTOR OF GRADUATE ADMISSIONS AND FINANCIAL AID
4400 MASSACHUSETTS AVENUE NORTHWEST, WASHINGTON, DC 20016-8044 UNITED STATES
PHONE: 202-885-1913 • FAX: 202-885-1078
E-MAIL: KOGODMBA@AMERICAN.EDU • WEBSITE: WWW.KOGOD.AMERICAN.EDU

Student Life and Environment

Situated on 84 acres of land in one of DC's most attractive residential neighborhoods, Kogod School of Business earns rave reviews from its students for physical environs. They brag that Kogod's "biggest asset [is that] it is in Washington, DC. The opportunities are endless, being in such an international city. It's nice that the campus is in northern DC, though, because you feel like you're on a campus instead of in the heart of downtown." Others agree, adding, "the school has a very international flavor in both its studies and its social activities." Others praise the "great location [and] excellent technology." The Kogod building itself is both wireless and state-of-the-art. Students mostly appreciate the facilities, but some complain that the "size of the school building is too small to support a much larger student population."

The Graduate Business Association sponsors intramural sports (from soccer and golf to football and bicycling), and pickup games and informal competition is common on the wide green lawns of American University's quad. Students say that the university "has been good at providing a wide range of activities for students; however, amenities and study space is sparse and not a real priority." Other students say that, despite the heavy workload, "the full-time students have a very close and active social life. It is not uncommon for the majority of the class to head down to Adam's Morgan or Georgetown for the night."

American University provides a free shuttle bus from the campus to the DC Metro and runs a van service that runs to Capitol Hill, Dupont Circle, and Georgetown. The city bus also makes stops on campus. Though students are eager to point out that the campus caters to "many students from different countries," others counter that they would "like to see more racial diversity. There is already a lot of cultural diversity."

Admissions

In the fall of 2003, the average undergraduate GPA at Kogod was 3.14, and the average GMAT was 590. Forty-nine different countries were represented in the student body, and 60 percent of the student body was male. The average number of years of work experience was five, and in total, there were 478 part- and full-time students enrolled. A minimum TOEFL score of 600 (paper based) or 250 (computer-based) is required for provisional acceptance.

FINANCIAL FACTS

Annual tuition	$25,766
Fees	$300
Books and supplies	$800
Room & board (on/off-campus)	$9,676/$12,000
% of students receiving grants	25

ADMISSIONS

Admissions Selectivity Rating	78
# of applications received	485
% applicants accepted	57
% acceptees attending	42
Average GMAT	570
Range of GMAT	530-610
Average GPA	3.04
TOEFL Required of International Students?	Yes
Minimum TOEFL (paper/computer)	600/250
Application fee	$75
International application fee	$75
Regular application deadline	Rolling
Regular notification	Rolling
Deferment Available?	Yes
Maximum length of deferment	1 year
Transfer students accepted?	Yes

Transfer application policy: Transfer students must meet the same requirements as non-transfer students. Nine credits may be transferred into the program from an AACSB accredited MBA program.

Non-fall admissions?	Yes
Need-blind admissions?	Yes

APPLICANTS ALSO LOOK AT

Georgetown University, The George Washington University, University of Maryland—College Park.

EMPLOYMENT PROFILE

Career Rating	70	Grads employed by field	%: avg. salary
Placement rate (%)	54	Finance	29: $66,780
% grads employed immediately	31	Human Resources	2: $64,000
Average starting salary	$64,264	Marketing	9: $55,250
		MIS	5: $90,000
		Operations	2: $60,000
		Consulting	19: $50,571
		General Management	10: $67,250
		Other	24: $68,056

APPALACHIAN STATE UNIVERSITY
WALKER COLLEGE OF BUSINESS

Academics

The nascent graduate business program at Appalachian State University's Walker College of Business offers a select few students "what is probably the most reasonably priced graduate program in the state—incredible bargain." At present, fewer than 20 students are enrolled in the program, which offers a conventional MBA, an MS in accounting, and graduate certificate programs in finance, human-resource management, and information systems. Housed in the same hall as the university's mainframe computer, the MBA program puts computers to good use, employing computer simulations and computer analysis as well as computer-aided instruction in the classroom.

First-year studies at Walker commence with MBA Enrichment, a required program that includes "orientation sessions, workshops, a team-building outdoor experience, and social time for students to get acquainted." The freshman curriculum is entirely prescribed and is designed to "provide students with a broad foundation of knowledge." Students must complete an internship or international experience between their first and second years. Second-year studies consist of five required courses and five electives. Instruction at Walker incorporates case study, group discussion, role playing, guest-led seminars, field projects, team projects, and individual presentations. Students tell us that the Walker approach consists of "lots of work: You have to read and study a lot, [and] you get to learn! With so many assignments and reading, we are turning ourselves into sources of knowledge."

MBAs tell us that faculty members "are very well prepared; they have both the academic and professional experience that makes their teaching valuable. Academic quality is one of the greatest strengths of the school." They warn, however, that the program has a few kinks to iron out. One student warns, "Organization and overall program direction are currently being reassessed and will be better defined and articulated by next year. Once the restructuring has had time to develop, the MBA program will be one of the best buys in the state for the money."

Career and Placement

ASU's MBA program is much too small to support its own Career Services Office; students must use the school's Career Development Center, which serves all ASU enrollees. The office offers a variety of career-prep classes in interviewing, resume writing, networking, cover letters, and job hunting. It also sponsors career fairs and provides online support including links to job boards and major-related resources.

Students recognize the limitations of their situation. They approvingly report, "The school has a good relationship with alumni and companies in nearby Charlotte, the second-largest financial mecca in the U.S.," but concede that that's not always enough. One student writes, "They need to do more to help students get internships and job positions. They do have departments and people that guide us and show us what steps we should take, but they should also have more agreements with some companies for sending students every year for internships." Companies most likely to hire Walker grads include Bank of America, BB&T, Duke Energy, IBM, Lowe's Companies, MDI, Murray Supply, North Carolina State University, Regeneron Pharmaceuticals, Rubbermaid Newell, Wachovia, and Wake Tech.

ANNA BASNIGHT, ADMISSIONS CONTACT
ASU BOX 32068, BOONE, NC 28608-2068 UNITED STATES
PHONE: 828-262-2130 • FAX: 828-262-2709
E-MAIL: BASNIGHTAL@APPSTATE.EDU • WEBSITE: WWW.BUSINESS.APPSTATE.EDU

Student Life and Environment

Unlike most MBA programs, Walker does not support much of an extracurricular scene; with its tiny student body, it can barely populate one club, let alone several. Accordingly, "most people pursue their own personal hobbies during their spare time. Being near the Blue Ridge Parkway and several ski slopes, a lot of people are involved in outdoor activities." As one student puts it, "If you like nature, long winters, and small, close-knit groups of friends, then you should look into ASU. And if you like skiing, you're golden."

On the other hand, "when you want to have some night life, there is almost none." That's because "[hometown] Boone is a very small town. It has several movie theaters, including one that is $1.50," but not much else to offer. As one student explains it, "This is a beautiful place, meant for studying." Fortunately, the university community at large (which numbers over 15,000 students) offers up many forms of diversion, including ASU's 18 intercollegiate athletic teams. The university houses several museums and is host to numerous performing-arts series.

When students crave a more urban environment, they road-trip to either Asheville or Winston-Salem; each is just under a two-hour drive from campus. Lexington, NC, is also only two hours away. It's not a huge city, but it is home to arguably the best barbecue in the state (and thus, from a Tar Heel perspective, the best barbecue in the world).

Admissions

Applications to the Walker MBA program are processed by the admissions office at the Cratis D. Williams Graduate School. Prospective students must submit GMAT scores, an undergraduate transcript, letters of recommendation, a resume (at least one year of work experience is required), and two essays. An interview is strongly recommended but not required. Applicants must have completed at least one undergraduate class in each of the following areas: calculus, microeconomics, and statistics (summer courses in these subjects are offered for applicants who do not meet this requirement). Students should arrive with a working knowledge of Microsoft Excel®, Word®, and PowerPoint®.

The school uses a formula to set minimum admissions requirements. The formula is (GPA x 200) + GMAT = admissions score; GPA is tallied based only on the final 60 hours of undergraduate course work. An admissions score of at least 1050 is required but does not guarantee admission. Application materials must arrive no later than 3/1; admission is for the fall term only.

FINANCIAL FACTS

Annual tuition (in-state/out-of-state)	$1,668/$11,177
Fees	$1,361
Books and supplies	$1,200
Room & board	$4,082
Average grant	$1,000

ADMISSIONS

Admissions Selectivity Rating	**65**
# of applications received	24
% applicants accepted	92
% acceptees attending	64
Average GMAT	512
Range of GMAT	440-560
Average GPA	3.36
TOEFL Required of International Students?	Yes
Minimum TOEFL (paper/computer)	550/233
Application fee	$35
Regular application deadline	3/1
Regular notification	3/31
Deferment Available?	Yes
Maximum length of deferment	1 year
Transfer students accepted?	Yes
Transfer application policy: Up to six hours of graduate credit may be transferred for equivalent courses completed with at least grade of B.	
Need-blind admissions?	Yes

APPLICANTS ALSO LOOK AT

North Carolina State University, University of North Carolina at Chapel Hill, University of North Carolina at Greensboro, Western Carolina University.

ARIZONA STATE UNIVERSITY
W. P. CAREY SCHOOL OF BUSINESS

Academics

Supply Chain Management has long been the strong suit of the W. P. Carey School of Business, located on Arizona State University's Tempe campus. Students think you should know, however, that the school has much more to offer; wrote one, "The greatest strength of W. P. Carey is its drive to improve and excel in every area. The faculty and staff believe in the students and are constantly trying new things to remain on the forefront of business education." Another student notes, "Our MBA program has definite strengths in providing technology resources and classes, teaching the core MBA competencies, and offering a balanced set of classes and applied projects to students regardless of their specialization." Services marketing and management, sports business, and health services administration are among Carey's other strengths. The MBA program at ASU is relatively small, especially when compared with the mammoth university it calls home. Students love the cozy atmosphere, explaining that "because Carey limits each class size to about 150 students, you get the opportunity to really get to know all of the professors as well as the administration." ASU's status as a major research institution means that "all professors must be published and many work in their fields when they are not teaching." While "this really adds to their credibility and ability to make the material relevant," some warn that "this also means that some of them are not the best teaching professors." Most feel the benefits outweigh the drawbacks, telling us that "[they] have never been in an environment where so many top theorists in the field are the actual teachers of the courses. Dr. Ellram for TCO and Dr. Nadari for international finance are two examples." Students also appreciate how "profs treat [them] mostly like colleagues, which leads to a great learning environment."

Carey recently instituted a "revised first-year curriculum with more opportunity for electives," of which students approve. One student says, "My first year was very beneficial overall. It did the most to impart an overall business sense into my thought process. My second year course work so far has been much less impactful than I had hoped, and this fact has tempered my enthusiasm overall for the program." Students note that "the school is definitely going through a transitional period, but accounting for the variability that produces, it's a stable learning environment." A quick-paced trimester calendar means the program is "rigorous, but with support from the excellent and interested faculty and supportive students, the workload and intensity are conquerable. Still, it is not recommended that you work while in school." For students who refuse to heed such warnings, Carey offers an executive MBA program, "a two-year weekend program for senior managers and executives that provides the integrated education needed to succeed in today's business environment. Students learn to go beyond the usual analysis and seek out the larger set of opportunities each business situation may offer."

Career and Placement

Students at Carey agree that the W. P. Carey School Career Management Center (CMC) does a great job of placing MBAs in the supply-chain management field; in 2003, over one-third of graduates took positions in the field, earning a median salary of $70,500 and a median signing bonus of $10,000. "The career counselor for Supply Chain Management is awesome, but I have heard students from other disciplines were not as happy with their counselors regarding job searches," one student told us. Eleven 2003 graduates of the school's unique sports business program found jobs in the field; they earned a median salary of $60,000, with an average signing bonus of $3,500. While students generally love ASU's Tempe location, they feel it comes up short in the area of summer internships, a problem since "summer internships are required. The school should draw more on local companies to have a pool of internships lined up." The school hosts two annual

Dr. Gerry Keim, Associate Dean, W. P. Carey MBA
PO Box 874906, Tempe, AZ 85287-4906 United States
Phone: 480-965-3332 • Fax: 480-965-8569
E-mail: wpcareymba@asu.edu • Website: http://wpcarey.asu.edu/mba

career fairs, one in the fall and one in the spring; no figures on the number of companies participating were available to us.

Top employers of W. P. Carey MBAs include Agilent Technologies, Anheuser-Busch, ChevronTexaco, Ford Motor Co., GE Capital, Hartford, Honeywell, IBM/IBM Global Services, Intel Corporation, Northrop Grumman, Phelps Dodge, ProNet Solutions, Raytheon, and Sprint Communications.

Student Life and Environment

"Life at school requires a lot of work and a lot of time on campus, but not much more than an ordinary job," Carey MBAs report. Students find their hours filled with classes and studying, but also tell us that "within ASU, there are many activities that can be pursued when not studying." ASU is "a big party school for the undergraduates, so there are plenty of bars and nightclubs. There are weekly happy hours planned for MBA students," and "the intramural program at ASU is a good opportunity to socialize and get some physical exercise. Also, the student recreation center is equipped with nice new equipment." Summing up the environment, one student wrote that "there are almost too many social outlets, but that is a good problem to have: weekly happy hours on Thursday nights, a great Christmas party for charity, tailgating for football games, organized events such as charity bowling, golfing, mountain biking, and hiking. The list is long, and there is something for everyone here." That list also includes "various clubs and activities that MBA students can participate in (outdoors club, tennis club, golf club, and the many academic clubs). Overall, it is very easy to attain a balanced life while attending ASU."

Tempe, Arizona, we're told, "is a terrific place to go to school. It's great to step outside of the classroom in February and enjoy 70-degree temperatures." The area surrounding the school offers "lots of affordable housing. In short, life here is fantastic and is a very good reason to consider this program, all other things excluded." If you need another reason, consider the student body, which "without a doubt are one of the school's greatest strengths. The professors give you a kernel of knowledge in class, but teamwork is where it blooms."

Admissions

The admissions department at the Carey School considers undergraduate transcripts (which must show at least a B average in the final 60-semester-hours/90-quarter-hours of course work), GMAT scores, TOEFL scores, resume, personal statement, two letters of recommendation, and interview (all required). The school reports that "admission decisions are also influenced by the amount and type of practical work experience, interest in W. P. Carey MBA specializations, leadership abilities, community, and professional involvement." Applications may be submitted online. ASU uses PepsiCo scholarships, graduate academic scholarships, graduate assistantships, and graduate fellowships to increase the minority population of the student body.

Prominent Alumni

Craig Weatherup, Chairman, The Pepsi Bottling Group; Steve Marriott, Vice President of Corp. Marketing, Marriott Hotels; Wayne Doran, Chairman of the Board, Ford Motor Co.; George Schreiber, CEO, SEMCO ENERGY, Inc.; Jack Furst, Partner, Hicks, Muse, Tate & Furst, Inc..

FINANCIAL FACTS

Annual tuition (in-state/out-of-state)	$5,038/$13,558
Fees	$9,500
Books and supplies	$2,100
Room & board	$7,960
% of students receiving aid	95
% of students receiving loans	83
% of students receiving grants	21
Average award package	$15,622
Average grant	$9,074
Average student loan debt	$31,245

ADMISSIONS

Admissions Selectivity Rating	95
# of applications received	1170
% applicants accepted	42
% acceptees attending	89
Average GMAT	649
Range of GMAT	590-683
Average GPA	3.4
TOEFL Required of International Students?	Yes
Minimum TOEFL (paper/computer)	580/237
Application fee	$50
International application fee	$50
Regular application deadline	Rolling
Regular notification	Rolling
Deferment Available?	Yes
Maximum length of deferment	1 year
Non-fall admissions?	Yes
Need-blind admissions?	Yes

APPLICANTS ALSO LOOK AT

Indiana University, Michigan State University, The Ohio State University, The University of Texas at Austin, University of Arizona, University of California-Los Angeles, University of Southern California.

EMPLOYMENT PROFILE				
Career Rating	86	Grads employed by field	%:	avg. salary
Placement rate (%)	92	Finance	25:	$76,529
% grads employed immediately	58	Marketing	17:	$69,417
Average starting salary	$70,843	MIS	7:	$74,166
		Operations	26:	$71,522
		Consulting	11:	$63,556
		General Management	9:	$58,820
		Other	5:	$74,000

AUBURN UNIVERSITY
COLLEGE OF BUSINESS

Academics

Students seeking an MBA from Auburn University can follow one of three curriculum models: The traditional on-campus model; the new, increasingly popular distance model, called the Outreach Program, which allows students to fulfill most of the obligations toward their degrees from the comfort of their own homes (students must attend one five-day case analysis during their final fall semester, but otherwise never need to visit campus); and the executive MBA program (EMBA), which requires five one-week residencies over a two year period, with the larger portion of instruction coming via Internet and CD technologies. The distance program offers concentrations in finance, health care administration, human resource development, management information systems, technology management, marketing, and production/operations management. The full-time program offers all of these, plus concentrations in agribusiness, economic development, and sports management. The EMBA offers specializations in technology management and health care administration.

Full-time students warn that "It can be too much of a course load in the first semester, an absolute killer!" However, they appreciate how "everything is organized" so that "students take the same classes, [meaning that] getting the right courses is not a problem," and also recognize other benefits of this curricular approach; one student explains, "This degree has taught me as much about life as it did business. You get to see the synergistic effect of these lessons when you reach the end of the curriculum." The workload and the design of the program "encourage us to work as a team, and participate in class. This provides us an opportunity to realize what we are strong at, and what we are not so strong at." One shortcoming of the program is that "the different course offerings at Auburn are limited. Currently, Auburn is working towards expanding the concentrations in which MBA students can focus."

Students tell us that "The atmosphere is the best aspect of Auburn. The academics are great and the faculty and administration are excellent, but that's just a part of...the MBA program at Auburn University. Auburn will prepare you inside and outside of the classroom to be successful. [It's] a choice that you'll never regret." Another student agrees, "The courses have been great, but the...extra training and development in things such as leadership and impression management have really made the program stand out." The program is challenging, but an administration that "is extremely helpful and always available to help with questions and problems" and professors who "treat us with respect and...as professionals" help students shoulder the load.

Career and Placement

Auburn's Careers Services Office handles career counseling and recruitment services for MBAs. The office provides one-on-one counseling, seminars, workshops, and a career library; it also organizes career expos and on-campus recruiting events. Students approve, telling us that "over a hundred companies recruit on campus every semester" and touting "a huge alumni base with which to network. The alumni are a great strength of this school." Employers who often hire Auburn MBAs include AmSouth Bank, Colonial Bank, Home Depot, Total Systems, and Wal-Mart.

MR. J. DON FLOWERS, DIRECTOR MBA ADMISSIONS & OPERATIONS
415 WEST MAGNOLIA AVENUE, SUITE 503, LOWDER BUSINESS BUILDING, AUBURN, AL 36849 U.S.
PHONE: 334-844-4060 • FAX: 334-844-2964
E-MAIL: MBAINFO@AUBURN.EDU • WEBSITE: WWW.MBA.BUSINESS.AUBURN.EDU

Student Life and Environment

"There is more to Auburn than an MBA program," students at this large, southern university remind us. "The school has quality sports teams and multitudes of other activities that allow you to really enjoy your time here." The town of Auburn itself is a source of pride and comfort for many MBAs; "There isn't a better college town in the country," writes a typical student, pointing out that "football season is always exciting and game days present a great tailgating atmosphere. The night life is good as well, with a good number of bars close to campus." With its "smaller-town atmosphere with plenty of things to do and people to meet," Auburn "can provide something to appeal to everybody," but especially to those who "like sweet tea, chicken fingers, and football."

Auburn's full-time MBA program "offers numerous opportunities for students to meet people and network. In addition to social events, the MBA program has an established mentor program that pairs first-year students with second-year students." Students note that "the way the program is structured, you can't help but know everyone in the on-campus MBA program, which creates a cohesive group that can be drawn on for help." Accordingly, MBA students note that they "all stick together and are willing to help each other out with studying and doing projects. Nobody is going to stab you in the back to get a better grade. We try to lift each other up."

Auburn MBAs evince "Southern hospitality in full force" by not only "tailgating, playing intramurals, and barhopping together," but also by "getting very involved in the community through volunteer organizations." It's "a very diverse group with different backgrounds. Some are married with children; some are international; some are business people; some are engineering; some have years of work experience; some came straight from undergrad. Anyone of any age could fit in at Auburn because the students are so diverse."

Admissions

All applicants to the Auburn MBA program must submit official transcripts for all postsecondary academic work, an official GMAT score report, three letters of recommendation, a completed application to the graduate school, and a completed application to the MBA program, including a signed copy of the MBA Code of Ethics and Responsibilities. Work experience and a personal interview are both encouraged, but neither is required. International students whose first language is not English must also submit TOEFL scores. Undergraduate-level competency in accounting, calculus, economics, finance, management, marketing, and statistics are all prerequisites to starting the Auburn MBA program. Students lacking appropriate undergraduate credentials may purchase the corresponding courses on CD, and must subsequently pass a competency exam in each course prior to commencing work on the MBA. In an effort to boost the population of underrepresented students, Auburn makes recruiting trips to minority campuses.

FINANCIAL FACTS

Annual tuition (in-state/out-of-state)	$4,610/$13,830
Fees	$218
Books and supplies	$900
Room & board	$6,686
% of students receiving aid	65
% of first-year students receiving aid	78
% of students receiving grants	25
Average award package	$6,115
Average grant	$1,200
Average student loan debt	$14,665

ADMISSIONS

Admissions Selectivity Rating	82
# of applications received	134
% applicants accepted	60
% acceptees attending	62
Average GMAT	587
Range of GMAT	540-610
Average GPA	3.2
TOEFL Required of International Students?	Yes
Minimum TOEFL (paper/computer)	550/213
Application fee	$25
International application fee	$50
Regular application deadline	3/1
Regular notification	4/1
Deferment Available?	Yes
Maximum length of deferment	1 year
Transfer students accepted?	Yes
Transfer application policy: AACSB schools only. Case-by-case basis and elective courses only. Limit of 12 credit hours (electives) accepted as transfer.	
Need-blind admissions?	Yes

EMPLOYMENT PROFILE

Career Rating	79	Grads employed by field	%: avg. salary
Placement rate (%)	64	Finance	35: $49,075
# of companies recruiting on-campus	100	Marketing	15: $48,925
% grads employed immediately	37	MIS	8: $59,600
Average starting salary	$51,500	Operations	15: $55,250
		Consulting	12: $54,833
		General Management	15: $47,400

AUBURN UNIVERSITY—MONTGOMERY
SCHOOL OF BUSINESS

GENERAL INFORMATION
Type of school   public
Environment   city

SURVEY SAYS...
Friendly students
Happy students
Solid preparation in:
General management
Teamwork
Communication/interpersonal skills
Presentation skills

STUDENTS
Enrollment of parent
  institution   6,206
Enrollment of MBA program   240
% male/female   45/55
% minorities   10

ACADEMICS
Academic Experience Rating   62
Student/faculty ratio   20:1
Profs interesting rating   75
Profs accessible rating   66
% female faculty   25
% minority faculty   10

Academics

The AACSB-accredited MBA program at Auburn University Montgomery is designed for part-time students; in fact, any student wishing to exceed a course load of nine hours per semester must first receive approval from the dean of the School of Business. Students in this program appreciate how "course offerings cater to students' work schedules" by meeting during convenient evening hours.

The MBA program at AUM is divided into three parts. The first is called the Basic Program, consisting of 11 half-term courses covering business concepts typically taught at the undergraduate level (accounting, management, marketing, business law, microeconomics, macroeconomics, operations management, statistics, MIS, and finance). Students who can demonstrate sufficient background in these areas may petition to be exempted from some or all of these requirements. The second part of the program is the Business Core, a seven-course set of classes covering such integrative concepts as managerial applications of accounting information and synergistic organizational strategy (the latter is a capstone course), as well as such essential functions as marketing, data analysis, and managing personnel. The program concludes with either three or four electives, depending on whether the student chooses a general MBA or a specialization. Specializations are offered in contract management, economics, finance, global business management, information systems, management of information technology, management, and marketing.

AUM MBAs brag that "the teachers are great and enjoy what they do," although some feel that some classes rely too heavily on lectures and that "profs could try to involve students more in the classroom and encourage more interaction." Many also agree that the program "would benefit from more offerings in high-tech and computer-related fields." Comprehensive exit exams are required of all students who complete the program with a GPA below 3.25. Comprehensive exams may be taken no more than three times.

Career and Placement

The Career Development Center (CDC) at AUM serves all university students and alumni. The office maintains a library of career-related material, including documents tracking salary and hiring trends around the region, state, country, and world. Career counseling services are available, as are job fairs, seminars, and workshops in interviewing, job hunting, and resume and cover-letter writing. Students agree that the CDC's services are adequate, though on many students' wish lists are "better career advice and job placement" options. The office arranges internships and recruiting events for qualifying MBA students.

Student Life and Environment

AUM MBAs are typically "commuters who attend mostly for education and do not contribute much to the university outside of classes." There are "lots of military" here as well as a large number of international students. Most students "are in their 20s or 30s and hold full-time jobs. Many have spouses and children" who take up what little free time they have. As a result, "social life isn't huge here, but that's great; there are no distractions!" notes one student. International students occasionally recreate through "a club called ISA (International Students Association), which helps new foreign students get together and socialize as well as share their culture with others, through banquets."

SHARON JONES, ADMISSION SPECIALIST
PO BOX 244023 MONTGOMERY, AL 36124 UNITED STATES
PHONE: 334-244-3623 • FAX: 334-244-3927
E-MAIL: VJONES1@MAIL.AUM.EDU • WEBSITE: WWW.AUM.EDU

Montgomery is a midsize southern city well known for its integral part in the civil rights movement. The population of the city is about evenly split between whites and blacks, with small Hispanic, Native American, and Asian populations accounting for a small minority. The city is home to the Alabama Shakespeare Festival, a year-round enterprise that mounts a dozen or more productions and draws over 300,000 visitors annually. Another major attraction is the minor-league baseball team, Montgomery Biscuits, the AA affiliate of the Tampa Bay Devil Rays. And no Montgomery summer is complete without City Stages, a three-day outdoor music festival that in recent years has attracted such headliners as Ralph Stanley, P-Funk, Al Green, Kid Rock, Jurassic 5, and Shelby Lynne. The all-day event closes a good portion of the downtown area to traffic.

Admissions

Applicants to the AUM MBA program must submit official transcripts for all previous post-secondary academic work, official GMAT score reports, and a completed application form. The screening committee may request an interview, typically in the case of borderline candidates; otherwise, interviews are not required. The admissions committee applies an undisclosed mathematical formula to applicants' GPA and GMAT, using the formula results and other considerations in reaching its decision. International applicants must meet all of the above requirements and must also provide certified English translations of any academic transcripts not in English and a course-by-course evaluation of undergraduate work "by a recognized, expert service in the field of foreign credential evaluations and international admissions." Applicants whose first language is not English must submit TOEFL scores. Candidates may be admitted conditionally pending completion of prerequisite undergraduate-level classes in business.

FINANCIAL FACTS

Annual tuition (in-state/out-of-state)	$4,563/$13,689
Books and supplies	$1,500
Average grant	$3,000

ADMISSIONS

Admissions Selectivity Rating	**65**
# of applications received	109
% applicants accepted	89
% acceptees attending	90
Average GMAT	500
Average GPA	2.9
TOEFL Required of International Students?	Yes
Minimum TOEFL (paper)	500
Application fee	$25
Regular application deadline	Rolling
Regular notification	Rolling
Non-fall admissions?	Yes
Need-blind admissions?	Yes

EMPLOYMENT PROFILE

Career Rating	**61**
% grads employed immediately	95
Average starting salary	$37,000

BABSON COLLEGE
F. W. OLIN GRADUATE SCHOOL OF BUSINESS

GENERAL INFORMATION

Type of school	private
Environment	village
Academic calendar	semester

SURVEY SAYS...
Friendly students
Smart classrooms
Solid preparation in:
General management
Teamwork
Presentation skills
Entrepreneurial studies

STUDENTS

Enrollment of parent institution	3,342
Enrollment of MBA program	1,625
% male/female	71/29
% out-of-state	43
% part-time	74
% minorities	14
% international	39
Average age at entry	29
Average years work experience at entry	5.7

ACADEMICS

Academic Experience Rating	**89**
Student/faculty ratio	14:1
Profs interesting rating	93
Profs accessible rating	95
% female faculty	32
% minority faculty	11

Prominent Alumni

Robert Davis, Founder, Lycos; Venture Partner, Highland Capital; Mark Holowesko, President, Templeton Holdings Ltd; Akio Toyoda, Managing Director Toyota Motor Group; Michael Smith, Chairman and CEO, Hughes Electronics; Win Priem, Retired President & CEO, Korn/Ferry International Inc.

Academics

Babson's MBA program has many virtues to recommend it, and if you give students enough time, they'll get around to mentioning all of them. Invariably, however, the first two things they mention—usually one right after the other—are the school's excellent entrepreneurship program and its fully integrated first-year core curriculum. Nearly everyone we surveyed seemed to regard these two aspects of the program as the ones that make Babson a world-class business school.

Entrepreneurship has long been Babson's top discipline; one student writes, "It's the access to top-notch professorial talent that makes this program number one. Bob Rosenberg, the former CEO of Dunkin' Donuts, who grew the company from 13 stores to 3,000, is my franchising professor. And now he'll take my phone call for consultations and advice. How cool is that?" Babson's reputation in this field means the program attracts students who "seem to have the same type of personality, and they are all encouraged to look at things in a new, different light." One MBA explains, "Babson students don't go and generally become partners in huge companies, but they [start] companies and have good qualities of life." The school also boasts strong departments in marketing, finance (applied investments), high tech, and consulting.

Before students can specialize, however, they must first complete the demanding core curriculum. One student explains, "The first-year mod program is very integrated, and all the professors work very closely to provide cross-functional case work. Finance, marketing, accounting, entrepreneurship, ethics—all integrated each day." Another student adds, "Babson's integrative curriculum has been a highlight of my experience. We would have classes on current events such as Enron, taught by both accounting and ethics professors. It really gives a different perspective to the learning." First year also includes a year-long consulting project that "brings MBA students directly into contact with the 'real world,' instead of viewing reality from behind tempered glass, as is true of the case method. Also, you work with the same team for the entire year, so teamwork is very important." The core is so integral to the Babson experience that it is even integrated into the part-time evening program.

Students warn that Babson really piles on the work. "It's overwhelming," writes one student, "I realize that there just isn't enough time to cover a lot of materials within the limited time we have, but I sometimes question the strategy of the administration to overload us. We learn about so much that we usually have a hard time remembering what was learned last week." When the going gets rough, students can seek out their professors for help; they're "completely accessible, to the point of being willing to open their own Rolodexes to students."

Career and Placement

Students in the past have expressed frustration over the Career Development Office. One MBA student mentioned last year that "the career services office could stand to be improved but I think it is an area of top priority right now. There is a struggle with maintaining the focus on entrepreneurship and recruiting big-name companies to campus. I don't think that it has to be mutually exclusive." Since we last surveyed Babson MBAs, the redesign of the Career Development Office has been completed, involving the creation of a new approach that centers on relationship management within the industry. The school reports that in 2005, both students and recruiters seem to be responding favorably to these recent improvements. Babson students benefit from an alumni network more than 10,000 strong. About 140 companies recruit on campus each year; about 80 come seeking summer interns.

KATE KLEPPER, DEAN OF GRADUATE ADMISSIONS
OLIN HALL BABSON PARK, WELLESLEY, MA 02457-0310 UNITED STATES
PHONE: 781-239-4317 • FAX: 781-239-4194
E-MAIL: MBAADMISSION@BABSON.EDU • WEBSITE: WWW.BABSON.EDU/MBA

Top employers of Babson MBAs include Adventis; A.T. Kearney; Bank of America; Bose Corporation; Boston Scientific Corporation; EMC Corporation; Fidelity Capital; Fidelity Investments; Genuity; The Hartford; IBM; International Data Corporation (IDC); Liberty Mutual; Merill Lynch; Our Group; Philips Medical Systems; PricewaterhouseCoopers; Staples, Inc.; and Strategic Pricing Group, Inc.

Student Life and Environment

For full-time, two-year students (the school also offers an accelerated one-year program, a hybrid learning program, and a part-time evening program), the Babson experience is actually two distinct experiences: an intensive, community-oriented first year, and a much-less-communal second year. The first-year workload and the emphasis on team-work means students are together nearly 24/7. The second year, on the other hand, "is all about taking the skills learned in the first, where we are trained as financial analysts and business consultants, and applying them to what you want to learn and develop."

Social opportunities are available, however. The school sponsors family events for married students. One such student reports, "My husband is welcome to partner's events, which are held frequently. My husband and I socialize with other couples (and single students) from the program. We celebrate each other's children's birthdays and celebrate one another's successes. This is a very close-knit, supportive, and caring community. I couldn't be happier." There's also "a regular Thursday night at Roger's Pub, and at least one or two other Boston social nights a week. With only 150 students per class, you get to know everyone in your class well." The fact that hometown Wellesley is a dry town actually helps matters, since it corrals students into Roger's (the campus bar). Wellesley, "a beautiful suburb, [is conveniently located to] allow easy access to Boston and all its resources for social activity."

Admissions

A completed Babson application includes official copies of all undergraduate and graduate transcripts, GMAT scores, two letters of recommendation (from supervisors at current or former jobs), essays, TOEFL scores (non-native English speakers), and a resume or curriculum vitae. The admissions committee looks at all of these and notes that "admissions decisions are also influenced by the candidate's fit with Babson's team orientation, modular curriculum, entrepreneurial focus, and global mind-set." Interviews, while not required, are "an important part of the admission process."

FINANCIAL FACTS

Annual tuition	$29,900
Books and supplies	$1,964
Room & board	$15,780
% of students receiving aid	68
% of first-year students receiving aid	66
% of students receiving loans	50
% of students receiving grants	46
Average award package	$20,104
Average grant	$17,280
Average student loan debt	$60,731

ADMISSIONS

Admissions Selectivity Rating	85
# of applications received	610
% applicants accepted	59
% acceptees attending	45
Average GMAT	630
Range of GMAT	580-680
Average GPA	3.2
TOEFL Required of International Students?	Yes
Minimum TOEFL (paper/computer)	600/250
Application fee	$100
Regular application deadline	4/15
Regular notification	5/31
Application Deadline/Notification	
Round 1:	11/30 / 2/15
Round 2:	1/31 / 3/31
Round 3:	3/15 / 4/30
Round 4:	4/15 / 5/31
Deferment Available?	Yes
Maximum length of deferment	1 year
Transfer students accepted?	Yes
Transfer application policy: We accept transfer credit from an AACSB accredited program into our Evening MBA program.	
Non-fall admissions?	Yes
Need-blind admissions?	Yes

APPLICANTS ALSO LOOK AT

Boston College, Boston University, Dartmouth College, Harvard University, Massachusetts Institute of Technology, New York University, Northwestern University.

EMPLOYMENT PROFILE

Career Rating	85	Grads employed by field	%: avg. salary
Placement rate (%)	100	Finance	25: $73,547
# of companies recruiting on-campus	137	Marketing	25: $69,155
% grads employed immediately	53	Operations	4: $55,375
Average starting salary	$76,300	Consulting	13: $81,353
		Entrepreneurship	17: $70,774
		General Management	14: $71,059
		Other	2

BARRY UNIVERSITY
ANDREAS SCHOOL OF BUSINESS

GENERAL INFORMATION
Type of school	private
Affiliation	Roman Catholic
Academic calendar	all year

SURVEY SAYS...
Friendly students
Cutting edge classes
Happy students
Solid preparation in:
Teamwork
Communication/interpersonal skills
Presentation skills

STUDENTS
Enrollment of parent institution	9,207
Enrollment of MBA program	101
% male/female	46/54
% part-time	63
% minorities	27
% international	59

ACADEMICS
Academic Experience Rating	**82**
Student/faculty ratio	9:1
Profs interesting rating	84
Profs accessible rating	86
% female faculty	27
% minority faculty	41

Joint Degrees
Master of Science in Human
Resources Development/MBA
Master of Science in Sport
Management/MBA
Master of Science in Nursing/MBA
Doctor of Podiatric Medicine/MBA

Academics

Besides offering all of the advantages of a small, private school, the Andreas School of Business at Barry University manages to offer a surprising number of custom-tailored options to meet the needs and goals of its student body. Part-timers, who make up about two-thirds of the student body here, can choose between evening classes (on both the main campus and the Coral Springs campus) or the Saturday MBA Program. Full-time students can complete their program of study at the main campus. All students can opt for dual degrees in Human Resource Development, Nursing, Podiatry, and Sports Management: the last is an especially popular option, cited by a number of MBAs as their primary reason for choosing Barry. Besides a General MBA, Andreas also offers a full complement of areas of specialization, with options including accounting, e-commerce, finance, health services administration, international business, management, MIS, and marketing. Besides the MBA, the School of Business also offers a Master of Science in Accounting (MSA) and a Master of Science in Management (MSM).

All told, Barry provides choices that are typically available only at larger universities. Yet this program is relatively pint-sized, to the great advantage of its MBAs. One, such MBA explains, "Because the business school is small, you get the benefit of personalized attention. The administrators and class coordinators know your name, and professors can always make time for you to visit them." Another agrees, "No other school would give you such personal attention. Several of my classes have had fewer than 10 students, and the professor tailors the material to fit our schedules and individual ambitions. And because there's such close contact, it's easy to build relationships with professors. I even was able to collaborate with one professor on writing a business case that will appear in a textbook supplement."

Andreas classes "are designed to challenge students in several ways. One is the explanation of theories; others include the implementation of practical assignments or case studies." In keeping with the school's Catholic worldview, many courses "promote social responsibility." The school's religious affiliation also helps it attract international students, whose presence "truly prepares students for working with many different types of people in many different contexts."

Career and Placement

Andreas's MBAs receive career assistance through the Career and Counseling Center, which serves the university at large. A program of 80 mostly part-timers can't expect a dedicated career office, students concede, and one student tells us, "While job placement efforts could certainly be improved, I, like most Barry MBAs, have a job already, so I'm not really worried about the post-graduation job hunt, and that might be why Barry doesn't bring more companies to campus and be more aggressive in job placement. But for those students who do need to find work after school, Barry isn't equipped to be the kind of resource they really need." International students are among those who feel most strongly that these services must be improved. However, the school has recently hired a full-time Career Services Director, and the office does offer the bonus of ongoing placement for graduates and alumni of the School of Business at their request.

Jose J. Poza Jr., Marketing Director
11300 Northeast 2nd Avenue, Miami Shores, FL 33161 United States
Phone: 305-899-3535 • Fax: 305-892-6412
E-mail: jpoza@mail.barry.edu • Website: www.barry.edu/business

Student Life and Environment

For MBA students, Barry is "mostly a commuter school, so most MBA students are on campus in the evenings or weekends. As a result, there is not much extracurricular life. Not that that's necessarily a bad thing; as one student observes, "Barry is tranquil and laid back, the ideal place for a person who would get overwhelmed by a high-stress, back-stabbing MBA program. The MBA school is also made for people already working full-time." The school offers "limited clubs," and didn't even have a graduate business association until students took the initiative to form one. Those who truly desire a higher level of involvement can find it here, though. One student explains, "I have made myself get involved. I am a former student-athlete, currently a residence assistant as well as a graduate assistant. So my life has been great here. There is potential for everyone if you look for it."

"There is a vast cultural diversity within the university" and the MBA program at Barry. "It is delightful to see the peace that exists among classmates." Students "are very willing to help one another. There are always study groups, and in every class all students have each others' phone numbers, e-mails, etc. so that we can discuss the class when we need to." One MBA notes, "Learning in a cohort group has been the number one reason my MBA experience at Barry has been so successful. We've bonded as classmates, collaborated on projects, and built friendships that will extend beyond our MBA studies. In general, Barry MBA students are culturally diverse, unfailingly nice and, since most work full-time while going to school, eager to use their degree to move up the career ladder."

Barry is located in Miami Shores, a central location offering easy access to the entire Miami metropolitan area. The area surrounding the campus offers access to the beach, and plenty of shopping, dining, and housing.

Admissions

The admissions committee at Barry University looks closely at the following components of the application: undergraduate GPA; GMAT scores; quality of undergraduate curriculum; personal essay; two letters of reference; and TOEFL scores (for non-native English speakers). All of the following are prerequisites to MBA study: 6 credit hours of introductory accounting; 6 credit hours of macro and microeconomics; 3 credit hours of algebra or precalculus; 3 credit hours of statistics; 3 credit hours of introductory computer skills; 3 credit hours of finance; 3 credit hours of management; 3 credit hours of operations management; and 3 credit hours of marketing. Students may demonstrate competency in any of these areas through undergraduate work or, in some cases, CLEP testing.

FINANCIAL FACTS

Fall tuition	$24,660
Books and supplies	$1,500
Room & board	$13,000
% of students receiving aid	76
% of students receiving loans	43
% of students receiving grants	61
Average award package	$11,662
Average grant	$1,782

ADMISSIONS

Admissions Selectivity Rating	80
# of applications received	176
% applicants accepted	30
% acceptees attending	65
Average GMAT	474
Range of GMAT	400-680
Average GPA	3.12
TOEFL Required of International Students?	Yes
Minimum TOEFL (paper/computer)	550/213
Application fee	$30
International application fee	$30
Regular application deadline	Rolling
Regular notification	Rolling
Deferment Available?	Yes
Maximum length of deferment	1 year
Transfer students accepted?	Yes
Transfer application policy: Up to six transfer credits	
Non-fall admissions?	Yes

BARUCH COLLEGE—CITY UNIVERSITY OF NEW YORK
ZICKLIN SCHOOL OF BUSINESS

Academics

"Finance and accounting are known to be great subjects to study" at Baruch College's Zicklin School of Business, an MBA program that offers full-time study but caters primarily to the flex-time student. Baruch offers students three program options: a conventional full-time honors cohort-based MBA program (about 105 students), an Accelerated Part-Time Program (APT) that is less selective than the honors program but also a cohort program scheduled to allow graduation in just over two years (about 130 students), and a Flex-Time program that allows students to study toward the MBA degree at either a full- or part-time pace, switching back and forth as their work and study needs dictate(about 1000 students).

Historically, Zicklin is known for its strengths in finance and accounting; study in finance, we're told, is enhanced by "an in-house financial trading floor with Bloomberg and Reuters" as well as the proximity of many finance bigwigs. ("There are a lot of top executives who have attended at least one [CUNY school], if not Baruch in particular," students explain, "and our administration and professors are always pulling in these types of people for guest lectures and panel discussions.") MBAs also love Baruch's "great fieldwork class, current topics in business, where each semester teams of students go on-site to a firm to solve a problem." Offerings in general management, operations, and entrepreneurship are also strong, if not as widely recognized. Professors are a mixed bag; one MBA writes, "The great teachers are committed to their students (no teaching assistants here), knowledgeable, always prepared with relevant new material, and an enthusiasm for the subject that is outstanding and contagious. The bad ones are set in their ways, not interested in the problems of the students, boring, and out-of-date." Some students happily report that the administration "is extremely concerned about quality of teaching, is taking drastic steps to improve the school's rating, and is proactively involved in all activities of the school."

Zicklin's facilities, "located in downtown Manhattan in a new, modern 14-story building, are equipped for multimedia integration." Undergraduates roam most of the building, but the top floor is reserved for MBAs, who love the new digs, praising the "ultra-comfortable, interactive classrooms with great audiovisual capability" and the "high-tech wireless Internet connectivity" available to them. Their only complaint is that "space is at a premium, and at times a good place to study is hard to find, be that with a group using a whiteboard or just somewhere quiet to read." Most head across the street to Baruch's award winning library to read and meet with study groups. A "good collection of online databases" helps students muddle through their case studies.

Career and Placement

MBAs praise the "big efforts on career management for the students" at Zicklin; these efforts include a variety of workshops stressing the keys to successful interviewing, resume presentation, networking, and follow-up. Events held throughout the school year are designed to capitalize on alumni relations by bringing big-name grads back to campus; Baruch's Manhattan location looms large in this endeavor. The school maintains its own job-posting board; students can also access job postings at monstertrak.com.

Nearly half of Baruch's MBAs wind up in accounting and finance. Top employers include Citigroup, Deloitte & Touche, Ernst & Young, HSBC, and PricewaterhouseCoopers. Average starting salaries range from $56,400 (accounting) to $81,300 (general management). The vast majority of grads remain in the Mid-Atlantic region, although some find employment overseas. MBAs note that "Baruch is historically an accounting school, and this is reflected in the companies that recruit here and what positions they recruit for."

Student Life and Environment

"Since most students live scattered throughout New York City, the Bronx, Manhattan, Brooklyn, and Queens," students note that the Zicklin campus "lacks the typical college campus feel. However, our school is located in the heart of New York City. There are many bars and great restaurants nearby. We have a standing Thursday night engagement at one of a few bars that are close by, and we get pretty good attendance." During the school day, MBAs keep "busy with classes, a lot of guest lectures, group assignments, and exams. Students gain the most from their school experience through working together, in formal groups and informal groups." The school's location, "in a neighborhood called Murray Hill, which has been locally renamed to 'Curry Hill' because of the plethora of amazingly great Indian restaurants nearby," places students just a few miles north of the city's famous Financial District.

Zicklin MBAs praise their fellow students as "one of the school's greatest strengths. The quality and diversity of students has been the best part of b-school. We have galvanized as a group and work hard for each other more so than for our professors' approval." They'd be even closer if they had the opportunity to live together, but unfortunately nearby housing is in very short supply. "I wish the school would look into providing housing/accommodation help," students complain.

Admissions

Baruch requires applicants to submit the following: undergraduate and graduate transcripts, GMAT scores, letters of recommendation, personal statement, and history of work experience. International students must submit TOEFL and TWE scores unless they have completed undergraduate work in the United States. The school stresses that "over 50 percent of Zicklin's full-time MBA and MS students are international, and the level of English proficiency of applicants whose native language is not English is an important admission criterion. [TOEFL/TWE] scores, along with the GMAT Verbal and Analytical Writing scores, are the primary indicators of English proficiency. They help determine not only who is offered admission but also whether or not admitted applicants are required to take advanced business English and other remedial English courses at Baruch before they begin their master's program." The school has no specific programs to promote minority recruitment, noting that "City University of New York affiliation and unusually low tuition rates make us well known to these groups."

FINANCIAL FACTS

Annual tuition (in-state/out-of-state)	$7,500/$15,800
Fees	$218
Books and supplies	$1,000
Room & Board	$16,500
% of students receiving aid	84
% of first-year students receiving aid	82
% of students receiving loans	24
% of students receiving grants	57
Average award package	$9,000
Average grant	$4,000
Average student loan debt	$15,000

ADMISSIONS

Admissions Selectivity Rating	81
# of applications received	1068
% applicants accepted	64
% acceptees attending	57
Average GMAT	591
Range of GMAT	550-640
Average GPA	3.3
TOEFL Required of International Students?	Yes
Minimum TOEFL (paper/computer)	590/243
Application fee	$125
International application fee	$125
Regular application deadline	4/30
Regular notification	6/15
Deferment Available?	Yes
Maximum length of deferment	1 year
Transfer students accepted?	Yes
Transfer application policy: Same application process as all applicants; up to 12 credits from an AACSB-accredited institution may be transferred	
Non-fall admissions?	Yes
Need-blind admissions?	Yes

APPLICANTS ALSO LOOK AT

Columbia University, Fordham University, Hofstra University, New York University, Pace University, Rutgers—The State University of New Jersey, St. John's University.

EMPLOYMENT PROFILE

Career Rating	76	Grads employed by field	%: avg. salary
Placement rate (%)	83	Accounting	29: $56,400
% grads employed immediately	52	Finance	21: $68,250
Average starting salary	$61,430	Marketing	21: $59,929
		Consulting	6: $34,700
		General Management	9: $81,333
		Other	11: $50,242

BAYLOR UNIVERSITY
HANKAMER SCHOOL OF BUSINESS

Academics

A unique lockstep curriculum and an accelerated calendar (three semesters plus one summer semester constitutes the entire program, which can be completed in 16 months) distinguish the MBA program at Baylor University, a Baptist school south of Dallas. Students at Hankamer take all core courses as a single unit, a process that fosters camaraderie and teamwork; the approach also integrates the major disciplines (economics, accounting, marketing, finance, management, and quantitative business analysis) to foster an interdisciplinary approach to business problem-solving. MBAs love the "emphasis on understanding how each subject area fits with other subject areas," telling us that "the lockstep curriculum is a good way to remind me of the knowledge I learned in previous semesters and integrate everything in between the semesters."

Another distinctive feature of the Hankamer MBA is the Focus Firm Project, in which students work with executives of a chosen firm to address core problems at the company. According to the school, "The focus-firm approach to learning provides real-time delivery of theoretical applications, technological advances, global awareness, functional integration, and team-centered learning." In the spring of 2004, Baylor students worked with Chili's Too restaurants to help develop a brand strategy for the chain. MBAs tell us the program "positively separates Baylor from other MBA programs."

Baylor's program is small, meaning that "you have to come to every class prepared if you want to get good grades. Professors really know you." It also means lots of opportunities to show your stuff. One MBA reports, "In my first semester, I had over 30 presentations, most of which were in [a] team setting. Teamwork and presentation skills are really stressed here." Professors are "extremely accessible and willing to spend time with the students." And many students find them "very receptive to new ideas and differences of opinion." Although others temper this observation, pointing out that "Baylor is Baptist, and it affects the overall thinking of teachers [and] faculty. It is good when it comes to moral practice, which is so important in business, but it gets annoying sometimes, especially if you come from a different culture."

Career and Placement

Baylor's MBA program offers career services through its central Baylor University Career Services Office. The office provides support in contacting alumni, career-development workshops, and access to the BearTRAK job database. The office also matches the resumes of current students and job-seeking alumni to positions posted through both BearTRAK and Monstertrak and contacts students when appropriate positions arise. Job fairs and similar events are organized for the university at large but not specifically for the MBA program. Students in the past have agreed that the Career Services Office "needs a lot of help." Currently they do not do much, but the administration has shown they are committed to building it." Fortunately, the school has taken this to heart and is making significant improvements to their career services efforts, reflected in their internships and placement statistics which in May 2005, reached an all time high.

Companies that most frequently hire Baylor MBAs include Accenture, Alltel, AT&T, Bank One, Cap Gemini, Conoco, Continental Airlines, Deloitte Touche Tomahtsu, Dynegy, ExxonMobil, HBK Investments, H.E.B. Grocery, IBM, Intecap, JP Morgan Chase, Lockheed Martin, Microsoft, Raytheon, Shell, Southwest Airlines, SBC Communications, Sprint, Tivoli, Tucker Alan, TXU, and VHA Inc. Two-thirds of Baylor grads remain in the Southwest Central region for work; about one in six find positions outside the country.

LAURIE WILSON, DIRECTOR, MBA ADMISSIONS
ONE BEAR PLACE #98013, 1311 SOUTH 5TH STREET, WACO, TX 76798-8013 UNITED STATES
PHONE: 254-710-3718 • FAX: 254-710-1066
E-MAIL: MBA_INFO@BAYLOR.EDU • WEBSITE: WWW.BAYLOR.EDU/MBA

Location and Environment

Hanmaker is located on Baylor's "huge, quite scenic campus [with] numerous resources, including an excellent gym/Student Life Center and a wide variety of intramurals." There's "a lot of construction going on here: new academic buildings, new dorms, garages, etc. It all makes you feel like you are a part of something really big and going forward." Much of that forward movement has already taken place at Hanmaker, which occupies "one of the newest buildings on the Baylor campus." The facility "features wireless networking, seminar-style classrooms, a seventy-five-seat video-conferencing room and the Graduate Center [to] maximize discussion and interaction between students and faculty." Students can use their laptops to hook into the wireless network anywhere on campus.

MBAs tell us that Baylor is "a great place to go to school. There are plenty of opportunities for social interaction with other students. Everyone is generally very friendly." The Graduate Business Association "does an excellent job of planning social and career events for students and faculty, [with] a doughnut hour every Wednesday, during which all the MBA students and faculty meet and talk, as well as mixer dinners and other activities several times per semester." A word of caution for those with families, though; "Life is geared towards the singles, with little emphasis for those who are married with children. Outside activities focus on sports, parties, and general fun. This works well for the majority of students who are single or just married." Also, extracurricular time at Baylor is limited by the demands of the curriculum. One student explains, "Life is very busy and fast paced due to five-week core courses. These courses are short and packed with action. You cannot afford to get behind even for a very short time."

Hometown Waco is in the proverbial heart of Texas. While it is within 150 miles of four major metropolitan areas (Dallas, Austin, San Antonio, and Houston), Waco itself "is a small town that does not have a good public transportation system, especially to and from Dallas. It would be good if the university could provide some transportation service between Baylor and Dallas."

Admissions

Applicants to Baylor must provide the school GMAT (and TOEFL, when appropriate) scores, undergraduate transcripts, three essays (all examine aspects of whether the applicant is a good "fit" with Baylor's MBA program), letters of recommendation, and a current resume. An interview is optional. Evidence of leadership skills and community service is also considered. While applicants need not have majored in a business-related discipline as undergraduates, those who did not must complete the Integrated Management Seminar, "a unique one-semester seminar that satisfies all business prerequisites. It is offered for students without previous business training."

FINANCIAL FACTS

Annual tuition	$17,900
Fees	$2,591
Books and supplies	$8,000
Room & board	$10,000
% of students receiving aid	80
% of first-year students receiving aid	80
Average grant	$17,425

ADMISSIONS

Admissions Selectivity Rating	**84**
# of applications received	126
% applicants accepted	56
% acceptees attending	67
Average GMAT	595
Range of GMAT	540-640
Average GPA	3.1
TOEFL Required of International Students?	Yes
Minimum TOEFL (paper/computer)	600/250
Application fee	$50
International application fee	$50
Regular application deadline	6/15
Regular notification	Rolling
Deferment Available?	Yes
Maximum length of deferment	1 year
Transfer students accepted?	Yes
Transfer application policy: A student who has been admitted to a graduate program at another university and who desires admission to Baylor must present a transcript that presents the student's active, satisfactory work toward the same degree. Only 6 hrs may be transferred into the program.	
Non-fall admissions?	Yes
Need-blind admissions?	Yes

APPLICANTS ALSO LOOK AT
Babson College, Rice University, South Texas College of Law, Southern Methodist University, Texas Christian University (TCU), The University of Texas at Arlington, The University of Texas at Dallas.

EMPLOYMENT PROFILE

Career Rating	78	Grads employed by field	%: avg. salary
Placement rate (%)	90	Finance	30: $40,750
% grads employed immediately	48	Human Resources	5: $37,000
Average starting salary	$51,600	Marketing	15: $68,500
		MIS	5: $57,500
		Operations	2
		Consulting	5: $84,500
		General Management	25: $70,000
		Other	13: $50,000

BELMONT UNIVERSITY
THE JACK C. MASSEY GRADUATE SCHOOL OF BUSINESS

Academics

"Flexible scheduling combined with the real-world experiences of the students and professors really make Massey an excellent school for adults that work full-time," students at this Nashville b-school tell us, tidily summarizing the key attractions of this predominantly part-time program. While Massey is home to a few full-timers, the MBA and MACC programs are designed to accommodate part-time students; all classes are held in long evening sessions.

Massey operates on an unusual five-term calendar. Both the fall and spring semesters are divided into one 10-week and one 5-week term; classes meet once a week during the 10-week term and twice a week during the 5-week term. A 10-week summer semester rounds out the school year. Both the short and long sessions pack a lot of information into a relatively short period. As a result, "the overall academic experience at Belmont is challenging, although not so challenging that it's intimidating." One student notes, "Class material is not watered-down in an attempt to make the MBA easy to obtain. The school expects a commitment and that is what it takes to complete the program." Easing the challenge is the fact that "Belmont offers a comfortable atmosphere where students are friendly with one another. Everyone wants to succeed, but I have never encountered the cutthroats that you hear about when MBA programs are mentioned."

Students especially appreciate Massey's "practical curriculum [that] places a strong emphasis on learning through practical applications, case studies, and teamwork." One student observes, "This approach mimics the real world quite well. I believe that because of this approach, I will be able to easily apply what I have learned. I am already seeing a change in my decision-making process at work." MBAs also tell us that "the school has a commitment not only to the development of business knowledge, but also to the development of a business mentality and the nonacademic skills required for career success in our chosen field." Professors "prepare material beyond the textbook to increase students' overall experiences," which explains why students feel "the school's greatest strength is the faculty. Professors take pride in delivering their lectures so that students not only know but [also] understand the material being covered and can apply these business skills in their own careers." Students are especially sanguine about Massey's offerings in accountancy, entrepreneurship, and finance. The school also draws on its location in Music City to offer a number of electives focusing on the music biz.

Career and Placement

Career Services at Belmont are provided by an office "solely dedicated to business students." Because most MBAs are part-time students with full-time jobs, this office naturally focuses most of its efforts on Belmont's undergraduates, causing one student to observe that "it would be nice to see a staff member who understands our needs help MBA students. Right now the undergraduate business and MBA programs share the same office and staff." The school reports that the office provides MBAs, MACCs, and alumni with "a wide range of resources to assist in conducting a job search or managing your current career. And this service is free and available to all Belmont MBAs—for life!" The school also claims a "powerful" alumni network that is over 1,000 strong. One student writes, "Out of all alumni, there are about 800 who work in the area. That is a large networking and recruiting base. The alumni are active participants in the school in testimonials at informationals and in recruiting students for employment."

TONYA HOLLIN, ADMISSIONS ASSISTANT
1900 BELMONT BOULEVARD, NASHVILLE, TN 37212 UNITED STATES
PHONE: 615-460-6480 • FAX: 615-460-6353
E-MAIL: MASSEYADMISSIONS@MAIL.BELMONT.EDU • WEBSITE: MASSEY.BELMONT.EDU

Top employers of Massey MBAs include Bridgestone/Firestone, Caterpillar Financial, Deloitte Touche Tohmatsu, Ernst & Young, and Hospital Corporation of America.

Student Life and Environment

The MBA program at Belmont is populated by "students who primarily work full-time and go to classes at night. It's very difficult with that schedule and family responsibilities to get involved with social activities." Not that the school isn't trying; students report, "currently, we are trying to involve students outside of classes. We are organizing community service activities and events after class. We have gotten good numbers at these events, so we will continue with more of them." Among these events are "various professional-development programs and lectures series. These, plus the personal attention you receive from professors and administrators, provide all students [with] the experience of a full-time MBA program."

The Massey program requires a good deal of teamwork; "most students try to work as efficiently and constructively as they can, especially in regard to group projects and presentations." One proud student comments that the "team-based environment tends to extend outside of the classroom. We are in a night program, but the friendships we have made definitely extend outside of the school walls. Our program is very time-consuming, but there is a strong sense of accomplishment amongst the students. The time definitely is worth it!" Off-campus opportunities are plentiful. One student explains, "Being in Nashville, an entertainment city, there is no shortage of things to do. It's not uncommon to go grab a drink or see a band after class. Everyone makes friends pretty fast."

Admissions

Massey considers all of the following components of an application for both the MBA and MACC programs: undergraduate and (if applicable) graduate transcripts, GMAT scores, letters of recommendation, personal statement, and a resume demonstrating a minimum of two years of post-baccalaureate professional experience. The school also looks for evidence of a student's "commitment to be involved and contribute to the learning experience of fellow students." Special programs to improve minority/disadvantaged recruitment include partnership programs with Fisk University and Meharry Medical College.

FINANCIAL FACTS

Annual tuition	$18,600
Fees	$600
Books and supplies	$750
% of students receiving aid	67
% of first-year students receiving aid	67
% of students receiving loans	54
% of students receiving grants	22
Average award package	$15,173
Average grant	$4,805

ADMISSIONS

Admissions Selectivity Rating	73
# of applications received	55
% applicants accepted	75
% acceptees attending	83
Average GMAT	515
Range of GMAT	460-560
Average GPA	3.14
TOEFL Required of International Students?	Yes
Minimum TOEFL (paper/computer)	550/213
Application fee	$50
International application fee	$50
Regular application deadline	7/1
Regular notification	7/1
Deferment Available?	Yes
Maximum length of deferment	1 year
Transfer students accepted?	Yes
Transfer application policy: Application process is the same for all students; up to 6 hours from an accredited university may be applied to program of study.	
Non-fall admissions?	Yes
Need-blind admissions?	Yes

APPLICANTS ALSO LOOK AT

Middle Tennessee State University, University of Tennessee, Vanderbilt University.

EMPLOYMENT PROFILE

Career Rating	80	Grads employed by field:	%
Placement rate (%)	98	Accounting	22
% grads employed immediately	88	Finance	11
Average starting salary	$52,500	Human Resources	2
		Marketing	5
		MIS	2
		Operations	9
		Consulting	3
		General Management	5
		Other	17

Bentley College
The Elkin B. McCallum Graduate School of Business

Academics

"Bentley College's strengths are found in the integration of technology and business," business students tell us, confirming the school's reputations as one of the nation's most wired campuses. The school's state-of-the-art facilities, with "IT infrastructure second to none, [allow Bentley to pursue] work centered where business disciplines such as marketing, finance, and accounting intersect with technology." Coupled with the school's technology focus is its dedication to "constant re-evaluation of curriculum [in order to adapt it to] our diverse business climate."

The curriculum, of course, lies at the heart of the Bentley experience, and students love it. "While all the bells and whistles that come with an MBA program are important (and Bentley has them all)," one student tells us, "The actual program itself is what we are all here for. More specifically, I am referring to the strong applicability of all of my classes to real-world issues and challenges, the breadth of business disciplines from which to choose, the strength of all of my fellow students, the highly engaging lectures, and the staggering level of IT infrastructure throughout our whole campus." While Bentley's reputation relies primarily on its finance programs, students tell us that other disciplines are equally strong, if not as widely celebrated. Students are particularly proud of the school's "tremendous Business Ethics Office and Center for Marketing Technology."

Students rave that Bentley professors "have real-world experience that they combine with cutting-edge curriculums to deliver a top-quality product." Most instructors "establish a very close relationship with the students, not only academically but personally, which helps in the development of the students throughout the program"; another fact that students appreciate. One student writes, "I did my undergraduate degree at a large university, and the difference is striking. I find the faculty extremely supportive. I really get the feeling that they understand they must make larger investments in us to ensure our success, and they do it without hesitation. There are established lines of communication for the students to voice our opinions on class structure and curriculum, and the feedback/changes are immediate." Students say the administration "is also very involved in the graduate community and cares a lot about the students."

Career and Placement

The Graduate Center for Career Services (GCCS) at Bentley recently introduced a new training program called the Career Management Series (CMS); this eight-module program is designed "to assist McCallum graduate students in developing skills that will allow them to compete more effectively in the marketplace." Modules are fine-tuned by degree program, meaning that students in marketing attend different sessions than do students in financial planning or accounting. GCCS' Career Development Workshop Series supplements the training, offering sessions on preparation for case consulting, interviewing, salary negotiation, creativity, and leadership.

Bentley hosts two career fairs, one each semester, and over the course of the school year approximately 250 recruiting opportunities are posted for graduate students. Students have access to a number of online resources, including MonsterTrak. Companies interviewing the greatest number of Bentley graduate students include Booz Allen; Deloitte Touche; EMC Corporation; FedEx; Fidelity; Gillette; IBM; Intel; Johnson & Johnson; KPMG; PricewaterhouseCoopers LLP; Raytheon; Staples, Inc.; State Street Corporation; Teradyne, Inc; and Verizon.

Student Life and Environment

Bentley students form a solid, supportive community that MBAs truly appreciate. "There are always people around working in teams, and there is a camaraderie that makes it easy to stop and talk," students tell us. One student writes, "We are all very interested in learning from each others' experiences, our current jobs, and even what we have recently read in publication. We work hard, and we help each other through open and honest feedback. We all agree to be here to learn about our strengths as well as our weaknesses, and these bitter pills are much better when administered by people who care about you." Students often meet for meals through the school's Lunch Connections and Dinner Connections series; each allows students to interact in a casual and convenient on-campus locale.

The student body's closeness is apparent in the "tons of student organizations and social activities" that Bentley students enjoy together. MBAs report, "The academic clubs are outstanding. They are student-run and continuously bring top-notch CEOs and senior management to campus for lectures, career panel sessions, etc. In addition, they plan such great events as trips to the New York Stock Exchange, investment trading contests, and alumni networking parties." Some groups are major-related (Graduate Finance Association, Graduate Marketing Organization, Graduate Information Systems Association), while others are professional groups (Society for the Advancement of Management, National Association of Black Accountants).

Students praise the "beautiful and peaceful campus" of Bentley and especially enjoy the facilities at the Dana Athletic Center. If you crave an urban environment, the "bustle of Boston" is only 10 miles east.

Admissions

Bentley applicants must provide GMAT scores, an undergraduate transcript, two letters of recommendation, three essays (two required topics and a final essay answering one of three supplied questions), and a TOEFL score, when appropriate. Interviews are required for the daytime MBA only; they are recommended for all other programs. The admissions office reviews the entire application in an attempt to assess an applicant's academic potential, commitment to career, fit with the school and other admitted students, and the quality of prior work experience (a minimum of two years' work experience is strongly recommended).

FINANCIAL FACTS

Annual tuition	$21,024
Fees	$300
Books and supplies	$1,020
Room & board	$11,570
% of students receiving aid	26
% of first-year students receiving aid	46
% of students receiving loans	28
% of students receiving grants	14
Average award package	$16,269
Average grant	$11,971
Average student loan debt	$40,469

ADMISSIONS

Admissions Selectivity Rating	74
# of applications received	391
% applicants accepted	75
% acceptees attending	49
Average GMAT	545
Range of GMAT	490-590
Average GPA	3.53
TOEFL Required of International Students?	Yes
Minimum TOEFL (paper/computer)	600/250
Application fee	$50
International application fee	$50
Regular application deadline	6/1
Regular notification	Rolling
Deferment Available?	Yes
Maximum length of deferment	1 year
Transfer students accepted?	Yes
Transfer application policy: Up to 7 Business Fundamentals core courses will be accepted subject to meeting criteria (minimum 3.0 grade; less than 5 years old; course equivalency; from accredited school). No electives will be accepted.	
Non-fall admissions?	Yes
Need-blind admissions?	Yes

EMPLOYMENT PROFILE

		Grads employed by field	%: avg. salary
Career Rating	90		
Placement rate (%)	96	Accounting	7: $82,500
# of companies recruiting on-campus	138	Finance	11: $80,000
% grads employed immediately	58	Marketing	4: $47,500
Average starting salary	$79,000	MIS	19: $70,400
		Operations	4: $62,500
		Other	7: $82,500

BINGHAMTON UNIVERSITY—STATE UNIVERSITY OF NEW YORK
SCHOOL OF MANAGEMENT

GENERAL INFORMATION
Type of school	public
Environment	town
Academic calendar	2 semesters

SURVEY SAYS...
Friendly students
Happy students
Smart classrooms
Solid preparation in:
Teamwork
Presentation skills

STUDENTS
Enrollment of parent institution	13,860
Enrollment of MBA program	111
% male/female	59/41
% out-of-state	2
% part-time	12
% international	59
Average age at entry	24
Average years work experience at entry	2

ACADEMICS
Academic Experience Rating	73
Student/faculty ratio	6:1
Profs interesting rating	61
Profs accessible rating	74
% female faculty	18
% minority faculty	1

Joint Degrees
Watson (School of Engineering)/
MBA Fast Track: 5 years
Harpur (College of Arts &
Sciences)/MBA Fast Track: 5 years

Prominent Alumni
CFO, Electronic Data Systems;
Executive Director Information
Systems, Morgan Stanley, Dean
Witter; Director of International
Operations, Doran Precision
Systems; President, New York
Electric and Gas; CFO, Electronic
Data Systems.

Academics

The School of Management at SUNY Binghamton (Binghamton University to the locals) piggybacks on the university's "world renowned Center for Leadership Studies" to offer a highly regarded concentration in HRM/consulting and leadership. Finance is another strong area at SOM; the Journal of Finance recently ranked the faculty twenty-third out of 330 finance departments in terms of research productivity per faculty member. MBAs here also speak highly of Binghamton's accounting program.

That's not a bad trifecta for a program as small as this one (fewer than 130 MBAs attend, most full-time); the presence of a large research university with a big undergraduate business program certainly helps a lot here. Despite their high profile as research heavy-weights, professors earn praise for being "very approachable. Many prefer to be on a first-name basis with students [and] are available for hours each day and very willing to work with students. They can be flexible with workload if there is a week with an inordinate amount of projects due and/or tests." As at many research-intensive institutions, not all are great teachers. "Most present their ideas clearly, some less so diplomatically," offers one MBA.

Students especially appreciate that "the SOM is constantly trying to improve. That means administrators are open to student suggestions and they support students as much as they can in academics and job searching." One MBA observes, "Everyone, including the Dean and Associate Dean, has an open-door policy." MBAs are less enthusiastic about the pervasiveness of team-based study throughout the curriculum. One student laments, "So many of my international colleagues are dependent on my assistance for understanding the basic information being presented in class that it greatly hampers my ability to learn as an individual."

Despite this drawback, most here feel that this same "diversity (of interests and backgrounds) among students and faculty" is actually one of Binghamton's strengths. Best of all, it's an MBA that can be acquired for the proverbial song. As one student explains, "Considering the price of an MBA here, you get a great education for your money!"

Career and Placement

Like most small programs, Binghamton lacks a powerhouse Career Development Center; it's simply too hard to attract lots of recruiters to a campus this remote to interview so few MBAs. The office does what it can, offering counseling services, career workshops, resume-development services, resume-referral services, a career-resource library, and access to the alumni network.

Top employers of Binghamton MBAs include Ernst & Young, Estée Lauder, Wal-Mart, Canon, American Express, BAE Systems, State Street Corp., KPMG, and First Capital. About two-thirds of all graduates remain in the Mid-Atlantic states or New England. Approximately one in eight lands a job overseas.

Student Life and Environment

Binghamton MBAs "focus heavily on academics. One MBA says, "Many of us are teaching as well as pursuing our own degree. For many of us, there is little time for clubs or other activities." Which works out just fine, since there aren't many, anyway. The program is simply too small to sustain much in the way of MBA-specific extracurricular clubs. The university at large, however, is another matter. It's home to "many under-graduate-organized clubs (over 250) that accept any student as a member." One MBA explains, "Because Binghamton has such a large undergraduate population, there are

ALESIA WHEELER-WADE, ASST. DIRECTOR MBA/MS PROGRAM
SCHOOL OF MANAGEMENT, BINGHAMTON, NY 13902 UNITED STATES
PHONE: 607-777-2317 • FAX: 607-777-4872
E-MAIL: SOMADVIS@BINGHAMTON.EDU • WEBSITE: SOM.BINGHAMTON.EDU

clubs for many activities, sports, intellectual interests, and nationalities. If you're out-doorsy, this is a great place to be." So long as you own a raincoat, that is. As one MBA warns, "The weather is very overcast and it rains a lot," making "the town seem worn down and lethargic."

Indeed, students agree that hometown Binghamton "doesn't have much going on, but it's a quiet, inexpensive place to concentrate on studies. And the graduate student population is large and diverse, providing opportunities to meet people." On another positive note, "The areas surrounding campus are very safe" and the downtown area has "a number of college bars." There's also an "excellent transportation system run by students (grad and undergrad) that specifically targets the off-campus locations where most students live. It also provides jobs for students." For those so inclined, "the athletic facilities on campus are very nice, and very useable to every student."

Binghamton's "enthusiastic, outgoing, very diverse" student body includes a sizeable aggregation of international students who "share what they have learned through life experience." Most here "are very studious and competitive," which "fosters an intellectually stimulating environment." They're not cutthroat, however. They "enjoy commiserating with each other over [their] workloads" and when it comes down to it are "more cooperative than competitive, which helps create a friendly learning environment for everyone."

Admissions

Applicants to the Binghamton MBA program must submit two copies of official undergraduate transcripts for all college work, two letters of recommendation, a personal statement, and GMAT scores. Work experience, while preferred, is not required. Additionally, international students must submit a certified statement of financial responsibility and TOEFL scores (minimum acceptable paper-and-pencil score is 580).

To attract minority applicants, the School of Management offers the Clifford D. Clark Graduate Fellowship Program for Underrepresented Minority Students. According to the school, "These fellowships are granted to students entering both masters and doctoral degree programs and carry stipends of between $6,800 and $12,750 (depending on discipline) for the academic year plus a full-tuition scholarship. Renewals or graduate assistantships may be awarded in subsequent years, depending upon availability of funds."

FINANCIAL FACTS

Annual tuition (in-state/out-of-state)	$7,100/$11,340
Fees	$867
Books and supplies	$1,500
Room & board	$5,000
% of students receiving aid	50
% of first-year students receiving aid	40
% of students receiving loans	27
% of students receiving grants	31
Average award package	$8,275
Average grant	$8,275
Average student loan debt	$26,929

ADMISSIONS

Admissions Selectivity Rating	82
# of applications received	273
% applicants accepted	65
% acceptees attending	41
Average GMAT	615
Range of GMAT	580-640
Average GPA	3.32
TOEFL Required of International Students?	Yes
Minimum TOEFL (paper/computer)	580/237
Application fee	$55
Regular application deadline	3/15
Regular notification	Rolling
Deferment Available?	Yes
Maximum length of deferment	1 year
Need-blind admissions?	Yes

APPLICANTS ALSO LOOK AT

Albany Law School, Baruch College/CUNY, Syracuse University, SUNY at Buffalo.

EMPLOYMENT PROFILE			
Career Rating	71	**Grads employed by field**	**%: avg. salary**
# of companies recruiting on-campus	100	Accounting	3: $53,000
% grads employed immediately	22	Finance	19: $58,000
Average starting salary	$60,929	Marketing	6: $43,000
		Operations	9: $78,667
		Consulting	6: $62,500

BOSTON COLLEGE
CARROLL SCHOOL OF MANAGEMENT

GENERAL INFORMATION
Type of school	private
Affiliation	Roman Catholic-Jesuit
Environment	city
Academic calendar	semester

SURVEY SAYS...
Students love Chestnut Hill, MA
Friendly students
Good peer network
Solid preparation in:
Teamwork
Communication/interpersonal skills

STUDENTS
Enrollment of parent institution	14,379
Enrollment of MBA program	663
% male/female	65/35
% part-time	71
% minorities	10
% international	26
Average age at entry	28
Average years work experience at entry	4.70

ACADEMICS
Academic Experience Rating	**94**
Student/faculty ratio	13:1
Profs interesting rating	93
Profs accessible rating	94

Joint Degrees
MBA/MSF: 2 years
MBA/JD: 4 years
MBA/MSW: 3 years
MBA/MSN: 3-4 years
MBA/MS Biology, Geology, Geophysics: 3 years
MBA/MA Math, Slavic Studies, Russian, Linguistics: 3 years

Academics

For a first-year MBA student at the Carroll School, starting out "is one of the toughest experiences I have ever had, and it was just what I wanted out of a program. Long hours and challenging courses translated into a terrific learning experience." As one student says, "I've learned more in seven weeks than I did in four years of college."

Boston College strives for a "unique partnership between students and faculty with an innovative curriculum." In the first year of full-time enrollment, students take almost all core courses designed to enhance technical skills. But they also participate in the MBA Business Plan Competition, in which teams of first years compete for the best plan for a new business venture. In the second year, however, there are only four required courses (Parts III and IV of management practice, "Strategic Management and Management Information Systems, and Social Issues in Management and Global Competitiveness"). The rest are electives chosen with specialization and career paths in mind.

The finance department is proudly touted as a great strength of the program, and most students agree, "Finance professors are some of the best in the country." The pride is justified, but that can sometimes come at a cost to other departments, especially when it comes to electives, which "could be more diverse." "The majority of them are focused around finance" complains one student, and many feel that "the excellence of the finance and accounting programs should be mirrored in the others."

Though the administration of late has been "somewhat in transition," they offer an executive lecture series "that includes such industry leaders as the president of Dell, CTO of Microsoft, and many other senior executives." Still, most students agree that the administration could stand to work on its communication with students.

Career and Recruiting

The alumni network is acknowledged by most students as one of Carroll's greatest strengths. Because of the deep commitment to community-building while on campus, alumni often leave Boston College fiercely loyal to the school and especially the MBA program. The MBA student government sponsors tailgates for home football games, and it's not uncommon to see "alumni, faculty, and students alike mingle before and after the game." These are people who know the value of keeping in touch. "I'm working as well my second year, and my coworkers still are talking to my IT professor, networking," one student says.

If this loyalty has a downside, it's that career services might rely too heavily on it. Many students think that the Career Services Department could "always improve, especially in current times." Many complain that job opportunities are too often limited to the Northeast, where many alumni end up. "Boston College is too focused on the Northeast region and financial positions and sometimes neglects other opportunities for students."

Still, job placement is high. Students get ample opportunity to work with alumni, and a program during the first year has all first-year full-time MBAs consulting directly with a company through the MBA Consulting Project. Representatives from companies like Dell, GE, and Southwest Airlines have all been a presence on campus. Overall, most students agree that they've "never been so certain that [their] experience, academic and otherwise, would be relevant to [their] future success."

SHELLEY CONLEY, DIRECTOR OF GRADUATE MANAGEMENT ENROLLMENT
FULTON HALL 315, CHESTNUT HILL, MA 02467 UNITED STATES
PHONE: 617-552-3920 • FAX: 617-552-8078
E-MAIL: BCMBA@BC.EDU • WEBSITE: WWW.BC.EDU/MBA/

Student Life and Environment

In order to survive in a small, rigorous environment, MBA students at Boston College tend to bond quickly. Rather than foster cutthroat competition, Carroll students have learned to pull together. All 100 students are "genuinely interested in learning and making sure that [their] peers are learning." People "emphasize the importance of working with each other and getting to know everybody." One student says, "In only a year and half, we've formed friendships that will last for our entire lives. We've seen our peers through weddings, the births of children, and the deaths and sicknesses of parents. It's rare to find a MBA program with a culture that supports a balance between competition/ambition and compassion."

With a campus just a T ride away from Boston center, the cultural life exceeds that of many institutions. City living is, as always, a plus for most of the MBA students at BC. "The other day," one student explains, "I sat and listened to a jazz band play the opening of an African American Art Exhibit. It was great. The night after, I met with almost my entire program at a local bar." For students of the Carroll School, social life is very much a part of academic life. With the newly revamped Fulton Hall serving as the social and academic center of the program, students have newer and better facilities in which to study and socialize, and they marvel at the "truly well-rounded nature of the community: extending from an incredible alumni network to vibrant art offerings to intense academic demands." Still, the tailgating parties, the winter social, spring formal, and "Thirsty Thursdays" (a weekly pub crawl) rate high on everyone's to-do list. "The emphasis is on excelling in all pursuits, none to the exclusion of the other (whether that means cutting loose at an Irish pub or contributing deep preparation to a class discussion or helping local kids do their biology homework)." Students "know how to balance the academic rigors with the right amount of social activity, whether that be going to the pub, intramurals, or other social events. The work gets done, but not at the expense of personal needs."

Admissions

At Boston College, "the depth and breadth of academic, cultural, and professional experiences" are all considered when admitting new MBA students. The average GMAT score of an admitted full-time MBA student was 661, and the average GPA was 3.3. Many incoming students had worked between three and five years before applying for the MBA, and the average class boasts a wide variety of undergraduate majors: humanities and social sciences are refreshingly well-represented. TOEFL scores are required of those students for whom English is not their first language, and the minimum score required for admission is 600 or an equivalent computer-based score of 250. Scholarships are awarded on the basis of academic merit.

FINANCIAL FACTS

Annual tuition	$29,100
Fees	$150
Books and supplies	$1,500
% of first-year students receiving aid	79
Average grant	$17,191

ADMISSIONS

Admissions Selectivity Rating	95
# of applications received	709
% applicants accepted	30
% acceptees attending	47
Average GMAT	653
Range of GMAT	590-720
Average GPA	3.31
TOEFL Required of International Students?	Yes
Minimum TOEFL (paper/computer)	600/250
Application fee	$100
International application fee	$100
Regular application deadline	3/15
Regular notification	5/1
Application Deadline/Notification	
Round 1:	11/15 / 1/15
Round 2:	2/15 / 4/15
Round 3:	3/15 / 5/01
Transfer students accepted?	Yes
Transfer application policy: 4 courses are accepted (with a grade of B or higher) from other AACSB MBA Programs.	
Need-blind admissions?	Yes

APPLICANTS ALSO LOOK AT

Babson College, Boston University, Georgetown University, Harvard University, Massachusetts Institute of Technology, New York University, Northeastern University.

EMPLOYMENT PROFILE

Career Rating	85	Grads employed by field	%: avg. salary
Placement rate (%)	78	Finance	18: $70,000
% grads employed immediately	57	Human Resources	1: NR
Average starting salary	$69,219	Marketing	12: $60,464
		MIS	1: NR
		Operations	5: $67,600
		Consulting	5: $88,000
		General Management	1: NR
		Other	55: $70,136
		Non-profit	2: NR

BOSTON UNIVERSITY
SCHOOL OF MANAGEMENT

Academics

At Boston University School of Management, most students agree that the greatest strength is the faculty. Said to be "very accessible," professors often "go out to local bars with students." While research is a responsibility of all faculty members, "their focus is on teaching. Bad professors don't stay long." Teachers "pay due deference to the theoretical but place a strong emphasis on practical application of the knowledge they impart." The first year consists of mainly core courses, usually taught by department chairs who are "recognizable and well-respected leaders in their fields." The advantage of a pre-determined course schedule is that BU's administration can coordinate assignments and course materials in all of the classes. This means learning exactly "what you need to know from one class just in time to do the project in another class. It also results in a very choreographed, jam-packed schedule of projects." In addition to a strong core schedule, Boston University offers over 100 elective courses designed to focus studies on a specific kind of management or business. But occupying pride of place in Boston University's school of management is the joint MS/MBA program. It's the only program of its kind currently being offered in the world. The program, which can be completed in just 21 months, offers advanced degrees in both business management and information systems. According to BU's website, the program is designed to respond "to the digital revolution's impact on organizations, fusing a traditional management curriculum with expertise about the IT systems that have fundamentally changed business strategies and operations." And, according to one student, "although the MS/MBA program has a technology focus, the learnings definitely have larger management and business strategy implications." Despite the strengths of the MS/MBA program, or *because* of them, some students feel that "the administration's focus on the MS/MBA program also seems to turn some students off. Other full-time MBAs feel left out of this 'signature' degree."

Each class of about 60, which the students call "cohorts," is divided into teams of five. Teams are carefully chosen and are meant to represent the same kind of diversity a student could expect to find in the workplace. Working with a mix of genders, cultures, experience, and age, the teams foster the development of communication and diplomacy. And it's a good thing: Each year teams prepare a case for a student-sponsored competition. Teams present their case analysis to a panel of judges made up of faculty members and professionals from the corporate world. One student says, "I usually hate working in a team. But I have learned a lot about how to work in one and efficiently complete projects." The only drawback of the team system, for some students, is that "the student population tends to be fragmented among cohort lines. Students within the same cohort are very likely to keep in contact after graduation. However, I cannot say for certain that intercohort relationships have the same level of depth." Others complain that "strict adherence to the cohort system reduces schedule flexibility and seems of little educational value. The same goals may be achieved, in my view, through group projects." Another much-lauded program is the Public and Nonprofit Management Program. Designed for students who hope to use business management skills to address humanitarian and governmental concerns, the program is "an incredible strength" of the school.

Career and Placement

Although many students would like to see more businesses pursuing their employment —after all, "who can ever have enough companies coming to their school?"—recruiters from Akamai, Deloitte Touche Tohmatsu, Ernst & Young, Johnson & Johnson, JP Morgan Chase & Co., and a number of other major companies all have a strong presence on campus. Despite some complaints that the career center is "still weak," 75 percent of the

HAYDEN ESTRADA, ASSISTANT DEAN FOR GRADUATE ADMISSIONS
595 COMMONWEALTH AVENUE, BOSTON, MA 02215 UNITED STATES
PHONE: 617-353-2670 • FAX: 617-353-7368
E-MAIL: MBA@BU.EDU • WEBSITE: WWW.MANAGEMENT.BU.EDU

graduate class of 2002 was employed within three months of their graduation. And with a significantly increased career-center staff, BU is "gradually beginning to attract companies that in the past only looked in Cambridge."

The public and nonprofit management program has its own director and a "strong alumni database." This is "very helpful in setting up internships and informational interviews." One of the major events sponsored by the public/nonprofit program, Link Day, in which students meet for one day with nonprofits, academics, and local professionals to analyze a specific problem facing a nonprofit organization, also offers valuable networking opportunities.

Student Life and Environment

Located just around the corner from Fenway Park, Boston University's School of Management combines a "big-city feel," with many of the comforts of a small community. "Extremely convenient to public transportation and the city," the school offers countless cultural and social opportunities, and "a great Boston Harbor cruise and a fun spring gala every year. Social life is as diverse as the city." Other social events featured include an MBA soccer tournament and regular beers with professors. According to one student, "BU's second-greatest strength is the tight-knit community it develops. This leads to a strong alumni network, which is key to achieving career success." The downside of the big-city feel, for most students, is cost. Since housing in Boston (as in most urban areas) is dear, many would like to see more options for graduate student housing.

With about 30 percent of the class consisting of international students, many MBAs-to-be celebrate the diversity of the student population. "In every class we get such a broad perspective, and there are always students familiar with what (or which country) we are discussing." The Rafik B. Hariri Building for BU's School of Management: is "beautiful and very high tech—maybe the best b-school campus in the country." With dataports from every seat, five computer labs, a lecture hall that seats 375, an in-house management library and its own Starbucks, the Management School's building is "technologically at the forefront of the industry."

Admissions

Often enrolling about 150 students a year, Boston University looks for students who can demonstrate "both academic and professional success." In 2003, about 80 percent of the GMAT scores fell between 600 and 710. The average undergraduate GPA was 3.15. Many incoming students had about five years of full-time, post-graduate work experience before they applied for the MBA. TOEFL scores are required of those students for whom English is not the first language, and the minimum required score is 250.

EMPLOYMENT PROFILE	
Career Rating	82
% grads employed immediately	71
Average starting salary	$78,299

FINANCIAL FACTS

Annual tuition	$29,988
Fees	$364
Books and supplies	$1,344
Room & board	$10,540
% of students receiving aid	63
% of first-year students receiving aid	80
% of students receiving loans	50
% of students receiving grants	53
Average award package	$28,814
Average grant	$17,163

ADMISSIONS

Admissions Selectivity Rating	87
# of applications received	703
% applicants accepted	51
% acceptees attending	44
Average GMAT	637
Range of GMAT	640-690
Average GPA	3.21
TOEFL Required of International Students?	Yes
Minimum TOEFL (paper/computer)	600/250
Application fee	$125
Regular application deadline	2/15
Regular notification	4/1
Application Deadline/Notification	
Round 1:	12/1 / 2/1
Round 2:	1/5 / 3/1
Round 3:	2/15 / 4/1
Round 4:	4/1 / 5/15
Deferment Available?	Yes
Maximum length of deferment	1 year
Transfer students accepted?	Yes
Transfer application policy: Classes must be AACSB-accredited.	
Need-blind admissions?	Yes

APPLICANTS ALSO LOOK AT

Babson College, Boston College, Case Western Reserve University, Duke University, Georgetown University, New York University.

BOWLING GREEN STATE UNIVERSITY
COLLEGE OF BUSINESS ADMINISTRATION

Academics

For students wishing to fast-track their business careers, the MBA program at the College of Business Administration at Bowling Green State University provides an excellent opportunity. BGSU's general MBA program can be completed in 14 months, even by students without an undergraduate degree in business; a specialization (currently available in accounting, finance, or management information systems) can be added with only an additional semester's work.

"Academics are intensive, as expected of an MBA program," students tell us. One student explains, "When I started BGSU, I thought it would be a piece of cake for me. But I soon realized that the professors were serious about their work and expectations and settled for nothing but the best. To my dismay, all the fun and frolic I thought I would experience went down the drain. I have to spend many, many hours studying and preparing for classes and tests." Despite the rigors of the curriculum, most students find the program manageable, including those with no previous business education. One such MBA student explains, "Having no business background, I found that professors' accessibility outside the classroom and readiness to assist in learning were of great importance to my success in BGSU MBA program."

BGSU professors are a mixed bag. One student notes, "Some are outstanding, while some are just okay. Few are terrible. Most are willing to help outside the classroom and encourage questions. The program is pretty well laid out for students." The curriculum puts a heavy emphasis on group projects and teamwork, creating an *esprit de corps* that permeates not only the student body but also the faculty and administration. One student writes, "Everyone here works together as a team! The professors, administrative staff, and students all want us to see our goal of graduating with MBAs."

The College of Business' full-time program features "a leadership assessment and development component consisting of a series of workshops. The workshops lead students through an ongoing process of reflection and self-discovery so that each obtains a better understanding of his or herself in relation to a desired management career." Students find the workshops helpful in their career development. They also appreciate "Professional Development Sessions on Fridays, where [they] meet with industry leaders and interact with them in a professional and mentorship atmosphere."

Career and Placement

To assist BGSU students in their job searches, the College of Business offers "a series of co-curricular professional-development seminars, covering topics such as oral presentation and report writing, team facilitation, effective negotiations, career planning, and organizational politics." Career services are provided through the university's Career Center, which serves all undergraduates and graduates. The school's remote location and small student body dissuade many large companies from recruiting on campus, students tell us.

Top employers of BGSU MBAs in recent years include American Express, American Greetings, Ernst & Young, Marathon Ashland, National City Corporation, Nationwide Insurance, Owens Corning, Plante & Moran, Progressive Insurance, and State Farm Insurance. The school reports that over half its graduates find their first job outside the United States.

Student Life and Environment

Students at BGSU tell us that "the graduate students' cohort is very internationally diverse, which gives the opportunity to enjoy different cultures and languages." This

Carmen Castro-Rivera, Director, Graduate Studies in Business
369 Business Administration Building, Bowling Green, OH 43403 United States
Phone: 419-372-2488 • Fax: 419-372-2875
E-mail: mba-info@cba.bgsu.edu • Website: www.bgsumba.com

FINANCIAL FACTS

Annual tuition (in-state/out-of-state)	$12,174/$10,440
Fees	$1,188
Books and supplies	$1,000
Room & Board	$5,800
% of students receiving grants	97
Average grant	$23,942

assertion is borne out by that statistics. About one-third of the MBAs are international students; they represent 16 countries. The school also notes that "across all programs, students range in age from 22 to 52, with an average of 29. The average work experience of full-time, part-time, and executive students is 3, 6, and 10 years, respectively, but work experience is not required of full-time or part-time students."

On a campus of nearly 20,000 students, the College of Business facility is home to "a smaller community of professors, business students, and equipment where it is extremely easy to locate resources. Classrooms and a computer lab are located on the main floor and professors, and more computer labs are located upstairs. At BGSU, time is not wasted locating resources." MBAs also appreciate how "BGSU provides numerous locations for dining, studying, relaxing, and socially interacting with other students. The Bowen-Thompson Student Union is a one-stop central place to do these things." They also tell us that "there are lots of extracurricular activities and opportunities available at the school," including plenty of clubs and organizations. The Business Club, for one, "has social activities ranging from guest speakers to having beers at the local bar. Sometimes we even invite our professors." Others are dedicated to the various international communities within the student body.

While no one would mistake Bowling Green for a megalopolis, students find the town charming. It's "a quiet town with not many distractions, so it's a good environment to study. The university is the city for the most part." Students extol the "low prices, very cheap places to live off campus, [and the fact that] more than anything, it's safe." BGSU's location provides "easy access to Chicago, Cleveland, Detroit, [and] Toledo, a large city, is only 15 to 20 [minutes] away." The chief drawback? "The weather may be a bit harsh during winter. If you don't mind the cold, it's a nice place to be."

Admissions

The College of Business Administration notes on its website that "some schools require business experience for admission. BGSU does not. The full-time program is designed for students who will be new to their chosen fields." Prior work experience is a factor in the assignment of assistantships, however. Applicants must submit an official transcript from each college or university attended, GMAT scores, a current resume, two letters of recommendation, and a personal statement; interviews are optional and can be conducted in person or by telephone. International students must also provide the school with TOEFL scores if their native language is not English. BGSU undertakes Project Search to aid underrepresented and disadvantaged students; the program "recruits students for University graduate programs (primarily full-time) and then coordinates an array of services designed to lead these students from enrollment through graduation."

ADMISSIONS

Admissions Selectivity Rating	78
# of applications received	111
% applicants accepted	60
% acceptees attending	75
Average GMAT	536
Range of GMAT	340-690
Average GPA	3.3
TOEFL Required of International Students?	Yes
Minimum TOEFL (paper/computer)	550/213
Application fee	$30
International application fee	$30
Regular application deadline	Rolling
Regular notification	Rolling
Deferment Available?	Yes
Maximum length of deferment	1 year
Transfer students accepted?	Yes
Transfer application policy: Students in the MBA programs (full-time, evening, and executive) are limited to a maximum of six graduate credit hours of transfer credit from AACSB accredited institutions. See website for specific regulations regarding transfer students.	
Non-fall admissions?	Yes
Need-blind admissions?	Yes

EMPLOYMENT PROFILE

Career Rating	**60***
# of companies recruiting on-campus	300

BRIGHAM YOUNG UNIVERSITY (UTAH)
MARRIOTT SCHOOL OF MANAGEMENT

Academics

The MBA program at Brigham Young's Marriott School of Management "provides a success-oriented environment that also promotes students' finding an elusive work-life balance," report students at this full-time-only Utah institution. At Marriott, "the coursework is intense but manageable, and professors are almost always available for private consultations with students who are experiencing difficulties or who simply want to discuss applications of concepts that go beyond the scope of the course."

Students love the finance and accounting tracks at Marriott, reporting that "many big companies come to recruit good accounting students." Organizational behavior/human resources is also "a well-developed track." Marriott is home to three career training centers: the Rollins Center for eBusiness, the Center for Entrepreneurship, and the Center for International Business Education and Research (CIBER), which offers an International Management Certificate. The school has also recently added the H. Taylor Peery Institute of Financial Services to enhance its already solid finance program.

Across the curriculum, students praise their "extremely impressive professors, nearly all of whom come from a top-five school." Professors here "push you to your edge, but are very willing to lend a hand when you're slipping." While "most of them have extensive real-world and consulting experience, not all professors are recognized experts in their academic fields. This is primarily a teaching university." For the most part, students are glad to receive "a practical education that might not be possible from a pure 'academic' professor," but some wonder whether "the school could benefit from recruiting and retaining more top-talent professors."

With a first year that requires the completion of 33 credits, students quickly learn "how to prioritize," a skill they acquire "by being overwhelmed with work." The second year is not quite as rigorous, as students are given much more freedom to pursue electives and fields of specialization (here termed 'tracks'). Students appreciate the "academic rigor balanced by charity for the individual" as well as the "religious and ethical emphasis" of the curriculum. They also boast that "tuition is amazingly low." (Note that rates are slightly higher for non-LDS members.)

Career and Placement

Career services at Marriott are provided by the Steven and Georgia White Business Career Center, which are described in school brochures as "the focal point for the school's placement, internship, and field study efforts." Facilities include a reference library, interview rooms, a large presentation room, and an eRecruiting system. School materials identify nearly 100 companies that recruit at the Marriott School.

Employers most likely to hire Marriott MBAs include American Express, Cigna, Daimler Chrysler, Dell, DOW Chemical, Ernst & Young, Ford Motor Company, Gap, Inc., General Electric, General Mills, Hewlett-Packard, Hollywood Entertainment, Honeywell, IBM, Intel, Nutraceutical, Payless Shoes, Partners Group, Procter & Gamble, Union Pacific, U.S. Department of Agriculture, and Yellow Freight.

Student Life and Environment

The typical Marriott MBA student "is married, has at least one child, and has three years of work experience. He or she is very smart, competitive, socially active, team-oriented, and religious." (BYU is affiliated with The Church of Jesus Christ of Latter-day Saints, as are, in one student's estimate, 80 percent of students here.) They are also typically "a bit older than usual business school students, and they serve in the community more." It is important to note that "the ethical standards at BYU are extremely high." Religious life imposes many restrictions that students outside the faith may find surprising. Indeed, "students have many lifestyle limitations." These include abstaining from consumption of alcohol and coffee.

For those comfortable in "such an un-diverse place," students agree that "there is no better program in the world for students with families. The MBA spouses' association is the most active group on campus and provides unparalleled support" for family members of MBA students. In their leisure time, students enjoy "plenty of activities, many of them multi-cultural, including Asian, Polynesian, Latino-American festivals." There are also lots of opportunities for outdoor activities. Students boast of the school's proximity to "the Wasatch Front," a natural retreat that "offers an excellent opportunity to enjoy life outside the classroom." Students remind us, however, that "you won't see much of the 'beers on Friday after class happening'" here.

The Marriott MBA program is housed in the Tanner Building, "a great place to eat, socialize, get to know each other, and bond—but not a great place to do work. The study rooms ought to be quiet, well-lit, have an Internet jack (the wireless fails sometimes), and a power outlet. Power outlets come at a premium if you want one, so it's best to bring your own power strip to share." Students would like to see these problems remedied by the addition of new study areas.

Admissions

A completed application to the Marriott MBA program includes an application form, personal essays, an official GMAT score report, official transcripts for all post-secondary academic work, three letters of recommendation (one academic, two professional), an honor code commitment form, and a personal statement of intent. An interview is required; the school contacts applicants who have cleared initial screening to set up an interview appointment. International students must submit all of the above and must also provide financial disclosure forms and, if appropriate, TOEFL scores. A minimum of two years of full-time, post-undergraduate professional experience is required, but management experience is strongly preferred. Personal attributes are also considered; the school "values applicants who exemplify a sense of directedness and a commitment to the principles of the restored gospel of Jesus Christ," according to the school's brochure.

FINANCIAL FACTS

Annual tuition	$7,160
Fees	$60
Books and supplies	$1,700
Room & board (on/off-campus)	$7,741/$8,286
% of students receiving aid	76
% of first-year students receiving aid	92
% of students receiving loans	36
% of students receiving grants	66
Average award package	$7,791
Average grant	$5,371
Average student loan debt	$10,578

ADMISSIONS

Admissions Selectivity Rating	90
# of applications received	346
% applicants accepted	54
% acceptees attending	66
Average GMAT	653
Range of GMAT	620-690
Average GPA	3.53
TOEFL Required of International Students?	Yes
Minimum TOEFL (paper/computer)	590/240
Application fee	$50
International application fee	$50
Regular application deadline	3/1
Regular notification	Rolling
Application Deadline/Notification	
Round 1:	1/15 / 2/28
Round 2:	3/1 / 4/30
Early decision program?	Yes
ED Deadline/Notification	1/15 / 2/28
Deferment Available?	Yes
Maximum length of deferment	2 years
Transfer students accepted?	Yes
Transfer application policy: Up tp 15 credit hours of grad-level courses can be a, no pass/fail grades, minimum grade of B.	
Need-blind admissions?	Yes

EMPLOYMENT PROFILE

Career Rating	89	Grads employed by field	%: avg. salary
Placement rate (%)	82	Finance	46: $72,217
% grads employed immediately	67	Human Resources	13: $61,036
Average starting salary	$69,402	Marketing	11: $73,143
		Operations	6: $55,963
		General Management	16: $67,091
		Other	8: $66,200

BUTLER UNIVERSITY
COLLEGE OF BUSINESS ADMINISTRATION

GENERAL INFORMATION

Type of school	private
Environment	metropolis
Academic calendar	semester

SURVEY SAYS...

Students love Indianapolis, IN
Friendly students
Happy students
Smart classrooms
Solid preparation in:
Teamwork

STUDENTS

Enrollment of parent institution	4,415
Enrollment of MBA program	228
% male/female	75/25
% part-time	93
% minorities	4
% international	23
Average age at entry	28
Average years work experience at entry	3

ACADEMICS

Academic Experience Rating	**82**
Student/faculty ratio	20:1
Profs interesting rating	81
Profs accessible rating	80
% female faculty	32
% minority faculty	17
Joint Degrees	

PharmD/MBA: 6 years full-time to completion.

Academics

Butler's predominantly part-time MBA program provides students with "a specialized focus on today's management trends and issues [that] is ideal for early- and mid-career professionals." Students praise its "ability to cater to adult working professionals." They go on to tell us that "the program is very flexible, allowing students to choose their own schedules and take courses, for up to five years if necessary." In order to accommodate its overbooked MBAs, Butler's program eschews lockstep curricular organization; instead, it offers "a customized program in business administration [with] an individual path to graduation prepared for each incoming student based on his or her academic background." Because the program is tailored to each incoming student's needs and acquired experience, "the length of time it will take to get an MBA here depends on the total number of credit hours required in each student's individual path to graduation and how many courses are taken per semester."

Butler offers concentration in four areas: finance, marketing, international business, and leadership. Students especially love the last, bragging that "the leadership concentration is awesome." They also praise school's "focus on soft people skills. I don't think you get this in many MBA programs." One student comented that "the quality of technical courses such as accounting and finance could improve [and] a better selection of classes overall" would help. Despite this, most of the students we surveyed would agree with one who wrote, "My overall experience at Butler has been tremendous. I will and do recommend Butler to anyone pursuing an MBA."

That's because MBAs at Butler are in near-universal agreement about the excellence of Butler's faculty. Professors "tie together theory and real-world practices [with] experience, intelligence, and wisdom, [offering] a good blend of academic and professional insight. Many of them serve as consultants for top firms." Perhaps most important to this crop of students is that the professors "are understanding about the pressures of working full-time and also going to graduate school, along with family responsibilities. They are willing to make time to meet with students and try to make class as fun as possible." Similarly, "the administration is always asking how well the program is preparing the students for the future. It continually evaluates the course offerings and considers changes while being sensitive to those who are mid-way through when changes occur." There's one final ingredient in the Butler mix: "the broad array of students' interests and work experiences. The background of the student population is a real asset. Most are out there working in the real world and can offer insightful thinking and examples."

Career and Placement

Career services for Butler MBAs are handled through the Center of Career Planning and Development, which serves the university at large. The school does not hold an active role in seeking jobs for its students for the understandable reason that the vast majority of its students already have them. As one student told us, "There basically is no placement office for graduate programs."

Students who aren't Butler MBAs do have access to the university's career facilities, however. Butler's few full-timers can use the office to find internships; companies employing Butler interns in recent years include Deloitte & Touche Tohmatsu, Ernst & Young, Indiana Outdoor Advertising, Merrill Lynch, Met Life, and Prescient Information Systems. The office also offers counseling in interviewing, resume-building, and dining etiquette, as well as access to Internet-based job search tools.

STEPHANIE JUDGE, DIRECTOR OF MARKETING
4600 SUNSET AVENUE, INDIANAPOLIS, IN 46208-3485 UNITED STATES
PHONE: 317-940-9221 • FAX: 317-940-9455
E-MAIL: MBA@BUTLER.EDU • WEBSITE: WWW.BUTLER.EDU/CBA/MBA

Location and Environment

Butler's largely part-time student body spends little time on campus once schoolwork is done. As one student explains, "Since the overwhelming majority of students are in school part-time and employed full-time, most people have their lives outside of school and get together only for class, group projects, and study groups (which are very common)." The few full-timers "are mostly from outside the country," we're told. Despite the dearth of social opportunities, students feel they know each other well enough to endorse their classmates. "They are very open and friendly, creating a pleasant environment," writes one MBA. Another notes, "The student body population is small enough to have smaller, more personal classes, which is beneficial in getting to know fellow classmates and creating an atmosphere of togetherness."

Although most students are too busy to take advantage of them, "many activities are offered to the students and faculty at Butler, [including] plenty of social activities and events aimed at improving the program." The school hosts "lots of business leaders as guest speakers, networking breakfasts, and an MBA club [to help students] not only learn but also network with fellow classmates." Butler's men's basketball team is popular with some students, who find time in their busy schedules to attend home games.

The Butler campus is a homey environment, students tell us. One student writes, "After a long day of work and class, I enjoy walking out to my car and hearing the music students practicing through open windows in the building across the way. I also love the traditional campus environment. I can find a parking space right outside my building after work, and I feel safe walking to my car. Also, the buildings are well-equipped and clean." They also tell us that "the campus is beautiful [and that] Indianapolis is a wonderful city" offering both fine entertainment and exciting business opportunities.

Admissions

The Butler admissions department "takes a very holistic approach when looking at applicants. [They] consider undergraduate record, GMAT score, work experience, and letters of recommendation. Admittance to the program is more personalized than a standardized minimum score on the GMAT." TOEFL scores are required of students whose native language is not English. The school accepts online applications, accessible at the school's website; the school waives the application fee for students who apply online.

FINANCIAL FACTS

Annual tuition	$7,500
Books and supplies	$650

ADMISSIONS

Admissions Selectivity Rating	86
# of applications received	136
% applicants accepted	40
% acceptees attending	87
Average GMAT	550
Average GPA	3.2
TOEFL Required of International Students?	Yes
Minimum TOEFL (paper/computer)	550/213
Application fee	$0
Regular application deadline	7/15
Regular notification	8/10
Deferment Available?	Yes
Maximum length of deferment	1 year
Transfer students accepted?	Yes
Transfer application policy: Up to 9 credit hours, pending approval.	
Non-fall admissions?	Yes

APPLICANTS ALSO LOOK AT

Indiana University, Indiana University—Purdue University Indianapolis.

EMPLOYMENT PROFILE	
Career Rating	76
% grads employed immediately	93
Average starting salary	$70,000

CALIFORNIA STATE POLYTECHNIC AT SAN LUIS OBISPO
ORFALEA COLLEGE OF BUSINESS

GENERAL INFORMATION
Type of school	public
Environment	town
Academic calendar	quarter

SURVEY SAYS...
Students love San Luis Obispo, CA
Friendly students
Happy students
Smart classrooms
Solid preparation in:
Teamwork
Communication/interpersonal skills

STUDENTS
Enrollment of parent institution	18,800
Enrollment of MBA program	97
% male/female	61/39
% out-of-state	20
% part-time	10
% minorities	10
% international	8
Average age at entry	27
Average years work experience at entry	3

ACADEMICS
Academic Experience Rating	**77**
Student/faculty ratio	25:1
Profs interesting rating	83
Profs accessible rating	79
% female faculty	20
% minority faculty	20

Joint Degrees
MBA/MS in Engineering Management
MBA/MS in Computer Science
MBA/MS in Electrical Engineering
MBA/MS in Mechanical Engineering
MBA/MS in Industrial and Technical Studies
MBA/MS in Industrial Engineering
MBA/MS in Civil and Environmental Engineering
Various additional dual degree options are available.

Academics

"Learn by doing" is the educational philosophy of the Orfalea College of Business at Cal Poly San Luis Obispo, and students tell us that it's a philosophy adhered to throughout the graduate business program. The program focuses strongly on the technological aspects of business. One student reports, "The learn-by-doing philosophy here is true. This school really teaches you to get into the nitty-gritty of how things work in the real world." Another student adds, "The learn-by-doing philosophy gives us a functional knowledge that will be essential in our jobs. We have a hands-on learning environment that includes great labs and really tough courses."

Cal Poly offers specializations in agribusiness, general management, and graphic communication; a master's of science in industrial and technical studies; and "blended programs" in architectural management and landscape architectural management. Also offered are dual-degree programs. Dual degrees are popular for those with an undergraduate degree in such areas as engineering, industrial technology, and agribusiness.

The Cal Poly MBA program is a 60–64 unit program that provides students who are willing to commit to a rigorous schedule of prescribed courses the option to complete the program in just over 10 months. A traditional MBA model for those not pursing this accelerated option and/or simultaneously pursuing dual degrees is also offered. Several specifically developed elective courses have been added to the curriculum including Commercial Development of Innovative Technologies, Effective Communication Skills for Managers and a transformational two-and-a-half week "Doing Business in Asia" business study tour to the People's Republic of China.

While students love the curriculum, most feel that "Cal Poly's strongest asset is the professors. They are enthusiastic and very knowledgeable about their subjects." They also create a "casual atmosphere that is very conducive to learning and sharing ideas," which students appreciate; they attribute this atmosphere in part to "classes that are very small (some less then 10 people) so the interaction level is high. I feel I know all my professors very well. Lots of classroom participation, lots of group interaction." The administration, has at many large state schools, "is very disorganized in terms of records and paperwork. Administrative operations definitely need to improve."

Career and Placement

The Career Services Office at Cal Poly SLO offers students assistance with job searches and career planning through workshops, counseling sessions, job fairs, and online databases and resume books. MBAs tell us, "Students generally find employment before graduation," in large part because the school feeds the region's tech-heavy businesses. Even so, some students feel the office could do a better job, and say the school "needs to create more connections with Bay Area companies." Approximately 300 companies recruit on campus during the year; about 25 travel to the school to recruit summer interns.

Companies most likely to recruit Orfalea MBAs include Agilent Technology; Amgen, Inc.; Deloitte Consulting; IBM; Lawrence Livermore Labs; Northrop Grumman; Pacific Gas & Electric; and Sun MicroSystems.

Student Life and Environment

Students refer lovingly to the pace at Cal Poly Sal Luis Obispo as "the SLO life," describing it as "a good combination of hard work and fun. The vibe is quite casual." MBAs enjoy "a small-town atmosphere, which makes it easy to socialize on a regular basis.

CHRIS CARR, ASSOCIATE DEAN OF GRADUATE PROGRAMS
1 GRAND AVENUE, OCOB SAN LUIS, OBISPO, CA 93407 UNITED STATES
PHONE: 805-756-2637 • FAX: 805-756-0110
E-MAIL: MBA@CALPOLY.EDU • WEBSITE: HTTP://MBA.CALPOLY.EDU

Many of us have become good friends and spend most of our free time with each other." With "lots of social activities, [SLO is] a very comfortable, close-knit community. It's away from big cities; however, it is close enough for easy interviews and contacts." Students appreciate "the diversity of subcultures on campus (the university at large has substantial Asian and Hispanic populations), which provides a neat experience."

The town San Luis Obispo, MBAs brag, "is a beautiful, nearly idyllic place on the central coast of California. The climate is magnificent year-round." One student mentions that SLO "is near the beach and the mountains, so there is a lot of recreation available at all times throughout the year, and most people here enjoy the chance to relax outdoors often." The town also "has great character in its immediate surroundings, as well as traditions such as Thursday night Farmer's Market, which are a lot of fun. All of these enhance the entire education experience and make the town and college unique to other schools."

Orfalea MBAs enjoy "brand-new facilities including a great recreation center and performing-arts center." The school also has a "nice-size campus and a great gym, [as well as] beautiful surroundings [and] a friendly student body." No wonder students tell us that "Cal Poly is a wonderful school. It's a lot of work, but the MBA program does a lot to make you sure you are still having fun."

Admissions

Admissions at the Orfalea College of Business consider all of the following components of a student's application: GMAT score (minimum 530 required), TOEFL score (where applicable), undergraduate transcript (demonstrating at least a 2.5 GPA for the final two full years of undergraduate study), two letters of recommendation, and a supplemental application. Interviews are optional. While admission is "primarily based on GPA and GMAT achievement, some candidates who receive low scores may be evaluated based on additional factors such as work experience, statement of purpose, and letters of recommendation." The school also notes that work experience (three years) is desired, but not required.

Prominent Alumni

Robert Rowell, President, Golden State Warriors; Linda Ozawa Olds, Founder, Jamba Juice; Bill Swanson, Chairman & CEO, Raytheon Company; Burt Rutan, Pres., Scaled Composites, designer SpaceShipOne; Gary Bloom, CEO, Veritas.

FINANCIAL FACTS

Annual tuition (in-state/out-of-state)	$4,827/$15,675
Books and supplies	$1,260
Room & board	$7,938
% of students receiving aid	45
% of first-year students receiving aid	25
% of students receiving loans	45
% of students receiving grants	5
Average award package	$11,080
Average grant	$2,073

ADMISSIONS

Admissions Selectivity Rating	86
# of applications received	166
% applicants accepted	40
% acceptees attending	74
Average GMAT	590
Range of GMAT	560-620
Average GPA	3.2
TOEFL Required of International Students?	Yes
Minimum TOEFL (paper/computer)	550/213
Application fee	$55
International application fee	$55
Regular application deadline	7/1
Regular notification	Rolling
Deferment Available?	Yes
Maximum length of deferment	2 years
Transfer students accepted?	Yes
Transfer application policy: Up to 8 units are transferable.	
Need-blind admissions?	Yes

APPLICANTS ALSO LOOK AT

San Diego State University, San Francisco State University, San Jose State University, University of California—Berkeley, University of California—Davis, University of California—Irvine, University of California—Los Angeles.

EMPLOYMENT PROFILE

Career Rating	**87**
Placement rate (%)	100
# of companies recruiting on-campus	300
% grads employed immediately	70
Average starting salary	$68,000

CALIFORNIA STATE UNIVERSITY—CHICO
COLLEGE OF BUSINESS

GENERAL INFORMATION
Type of school	public
Environment	village
Academic calendar	semester

SURVEY SAYS...
Students love Chico, CA
Friendly students
Smart classrooms
Solid preparation in:
Finance
Teamwork
Presentation skills
Computer skills

STUDENTS
Enrollment of parent institution	14,000
Enrollment of MBA program	65
% male/female	65/35
% part-time	30
% international	43
Average age at entry	27
Average years work experience at entry	3

ACADEMICS
Academic Experience Rating	**63**
Student/faculty ratio	35:1
Profs interesting rating	61
Profs accessible rating	61
% female faculty	20

Joint Degrees
MBA/MIS: 2 years

Prominent Alumni
Prabhakar Kalavacharla, Managing Partner, KPMG; Ed Byers, Managing Partner, Deloitte & Touche; Masayuki Ishizaki, Managing Partner, Accenture; Bill Bales, CFO, Sierra Nevada Brewing Company.

Academics

Many students choose California State University—Chico for its "emphasis on cutting-edge information system knowledge and technologies," citing "their focus on IT, the future of business," as a primary reason for choosing to enroll in the program. Chico was the first school to participate in the SAP University Alliance Program, which trains students in software that manages and integrates information in a corporate business setting. College of Business students also publish an annual magazine, *Link*, dedicated to business and technology issues. Students tell us that they also enjoy excellent industry contacts through the teaching staff, internship office, and career services.

Chico stands out for its "outstanding achievement teaching MIS," though students report that the quality of instruction is generally very high. "Small classes mean good opportunity for individual attention from teachers," and applied learning is a foundation of the program. Coursework emphasizes "tons of teamwork and presentation" and "most business professors choose the hands-on approach in teaching and are open-minded to suggestions and ideas." However, while students are highly satisfied with the instruction in modern topics such as e-commerce and technology, they warn that more traditional subjects do not always receive the attention they might at more conventional business schools. Students admit that "professors range from excellent to to-be-avoided," and that "instruction in finance is weak."

The College of Business at Chico "is geared toward MBA students who did not have business undergrad," and therefore the curriculum comprises a broad base of courses in accounting, finance, management, international business, technology, and e-commerce. For students with extensive professional experience or who pursued an undergraduate degree in business, the curriculum provides a worthy examination of these concepts, but such students tells us that "the workload is moderate" and easy to balance alongside full-time employment. In the words of a second year student, "Coming from industry, the workload is not that difficult to manage." Those entering the program with a less intensive business background, however—particularly for those with less technology know-how—find the program rather challenging; writes one such student, "I was not prepared in computers for my accounting BS, so it's been a little overwhelming." As the curriculum is broad-based, with the exception of the technology focus, students at Chico may design a moderately focused business education. Chico does not offer concentrations in special areas of study, nor highly focused electives in certain industries or topics.

As part of the California State school system, Chico has been affected by the state's widely publicized budget cuts. As a result, the school is "sometimes a bit of a logistical nightmare." In addition, facilities and resources do not always meet student needs. For example, "the library is hardly ever open and closes early" and "the cash-strapped school needs updated computers for some labs."

Career & Placement

Chico graduates tend to find work in a fairly wide range of industries. In an average year, students from the graduate and undergraduate programs find work in over 250 different companies. When interviewing for jobs, Chico students notice that "this school is appreciated by industry," especially in the high tech sector. In particular, employers seek Chico grads for their strong knowledge of computers and technology, and students agree that "the unique curriculum helps a lot in job hunting."

SANDY JENSEN, ADVISER, BUSINESS GRADUATE PROGRAMS
CHICO 041, WEST LST & ORANGE STREET CHICO, CA 95929 UNITED STATES
PHONE: 530-898-4425 • FAX: 530-898-5889
E-MAIL: SJENSEN@CSUCHICO.EDU • WEBSITE: WWW.COB.CSUCHICO.EDU

According to Chico's administration, 80 percent of recruiters rate the Chico State curriculum as outstanding or above average compared with other universities at which they recruit. In recent years, the following companies—among others—came to recruit at Chico State: Andersen Consulting, Anixter, Bank of America, Chevron, Deloitte & Touche, Ernst & Young, First Interstate Bank, Hewlett Packard, Intel, Paine Webber, PriceWaterhouseCoopers, Sears, System Integrators, Tandem Computers, Wal-Mart, and Wallace Computer Services.

Student Life & Environment

The undergraduate college at Chico is known throughout California as something of a "party school," and while "most graduate students are not socially active," they say the outgoing vibe definitely rubs off on the business school community. At Chico, you won't see frowns, complaints, or negative competition. By all accounts, Chico is a "friendly environment with lots of happy students and professors." An MBA student writes, "The college environment—both people and campus—makes the experience here unforgettable." Drawing students from Northern California and across the world, the student body is very "culturally diverse," with a "vastly international student base." In general, the international students attend classes full time, whereas the majority of California residents "are returning-to-school, working adults" who hold full or part-time jobs while pursuing their business degree.

Located in idyllic Northern California, hometown Chico is an excellent place to study, as it is "laid back, small, safe, and affordable." In addition to its excellent atmosphere, Chico is well placed for anyone hoping to work in the greater Northern California region, drawing students from the local community, the San Francisco Bay Area, and Sacramento.

Admissions

To apply to Chico's graduate program in business, you must submit a completed application, an application fee, a statement of purpose, three letters of recommendation, and GMAT scores. The minimum acceptable GMAT score is the 50th percentile. There is no minimum work requirement to apply to Chico State, and students are accepted from every undergraduate major.

FINANCIAL FACTS

Annual tuition (in-state/out-of-state)	$3,600/$9,600
Books and supplies	$1,200
Room & board	$9,500
% of students receiving aid	65
% of first-year students receiving aid	50
% of students receiving loans	65
% of students receiving grants	10
Average award package	$10,000
Average grant	$1,000

ADMISSIONS

Admissions Selectivity Rating	80
# of applications received	75
% applicants accepted	56
% acceptees attending	52
Average GMAT	560
Range of GMAT	540-710
Average GPA	3.3
TOEFL Required of International Students?	Yes
Minimum TOEFL (paper/computer)	550/213
Application fee	$55
International application fee	$55
Regular application deadline	Rolling
Regular notification	Rolling
Deferment Available?	Yes
Maximum length of deferment	1 year
Transfer students accepted?	Yes
Transfer application policy: Must meet our admissions criteria	
Non-fall admissions?	Yes
Need-blind admissions?	Yes

APPLICANTS ALSO LOOK AT

California State University—Sacramento, San Francisco State University.

EMPLOYMENT PROFILE

		Grads employed by field	%: avg. salary
Career Rating	77	Accounting	10: $58,000
Placement rate (%)	90	Finance	2: $55,000
# of companies recruiting on-campus	350	MIS	70: $60,000
% grads employed immediately	80	Consulting	10: $65,000
Average starting salary	$60,000	General Management	1: $55,000
		Other	5: $55,000
		Internet/New Media	2: $55,000

CALIFORNIA STATE UNIVERSITY—FULLERTON
GRADUATE SCHOOL OF BUSINESS

Academics

The Graduate School of Business at California State University—Fullerton offers "one of only four accredited accounting programs in the state" as well as "a good selection of specializations [at] approximately one-fifth the cost of other MBA programs in the area (UCI, USC, UCLA, Pepperdine)." Students appreciate these assets, as well as the school's "flexible, non-lockstep" curriculum that allows the completely part-time student body to wedge an MBA program into their hectic lives.

CSUF offers three MBA options: the Generalist Plan, the Specialist Plan, and the International Business MBA. The Generalist Plan is designed for students with little or no undergraduate background in business. The program begins with a nine-course foundation sequence (up to three courses can be waived based on equivalent undergraduate work). Students then proceed through seven subject-specific advanced seminars (six prescribed, one elective), a comprehensive capstone course, and a concluding written project or oral examinations. Students with no business background are relieved to find that the program brings them up to speed. One student currently following the foundation sequence writes, "The professors are very helpful and knowledgeable, as well as approachable, which is truly appreciated." MBAs here warn, however, that "the program is long. It could take close to four years to complete on a part-time basis." They also note that "the program allows only elective course for Generalist program. I would prefer the option to have more."

CSFU's Specialist Plan allows students to develop a concentration in accounting, business economics, finance, e-commerce, entrepreneurship, management, management science/information systems, or marketing. The program commences with a 10-course foundation sequence (some or all courses can be waived based on equivalent undergraduate work), then proceeds to six advanced seminars. Students then choose four concentration-related electives before concluding the program with a comprehensive capstone course, and a concluding written project or oral examinations. Students praise this "well-structured program that allows flexibility yet covers all relevant topics," singling out the accounting and finance offerings as "outstanding."

The third option at CSFU is the International Business MBA, which consists of the 10-course foundation sequence (some or all courses can be waived based on equivalent undergraduate work), five advanced seminars, five concentration courses, the comprehensive capstone course, and the concluding written project or oral examinations.

Students in all programs agree that "the faculty consistently challenge us, but make sure we learn the material." Students go on to say that "the academic experience is very beneficial because there is a lot of interaction between students and professors." They also tell us that "the school could improve with some technology . . . like more wireless Internet access, which is limited to a few buildings on campus." For the convenience of those in the south Orange County region, CSUF offers slightly modified versions of the Generalist and Specialist MBA programs at a facility near the Irvine Spectrum.

Career and Placement

The Cal State Fullerton Career Planning and Placement Center provides career services to MBAs at both the Fullerton and Irvine Spectrum locations. Services include walk-in counseling, interview tips, resume review, and job databases. Students may continue to utilize these facilities for up to one year after they graduate for a $25 fee.

Student Life and Environment

Don't expect much hand-holding from the folks who run the CSUF MBA program. One student observes, "The school could do a better job in partnering and treating the graduate business students like the professionals that we are, and less like numbers.... Except for the milk and cookies that arriving MBA candidates get at the orientation, there are absolutely no mixers hosted by the school whatsoever. It's very clear from the beginning: you're on your own." Not that it matters much to most students, who "tend to work full-time and are not heavily involved in school life." One student explains, "I don't spend much time at school except when there is a group meeting and going to class." But the feeling is that "while I am there, I do enjoy the campus and the people." Students point out, "Some group-project efforts are challenging due to people's schedules and geographic locations. Overall, we always seem to work it out." Students respect each other's schedules and tell us, "These are great people that I love to hang out with."

The MBA program at Fullerton "has a diverse culture, which is great. The students and professors come from a wide variety of countries, backgrounds, and beliefs which makes the experience even better." Additionally, "almost all MBA students have full-time careers—this is vital for the exchange of ideas." Overall, students tend to be on the youngish side. One student speculates, "Most are in their late twenties or early thirties." The "large international population [includes] a big percentage of Asian nationals."

Admissions

Cal State Fullerton requires the following of all applicants to its MBA program: an "acceptable bachelor's degree from an appropriately accredited institution," with a minimum GPA of 2.5 for the final two years of undergraduate work; GMAT scores reflecting placement in the top 50 percent on the verbal, analytical, and quantitative sections of the exam; a completed background sheet that includes a summary of academic and professional experience and a personal essay; and demonstrated proficiency in calculus and introductory-level computer programming. International students whose first language is not English must score a minimum 570 on the TOEFL paper-and-pencil exam.

FINANCIAL FACTS

Annual tuition (in-state/out-of-state)	$0/$6,768
Fees	$2,726
Books and supplies	$810
Room & board (on/off-campus)	$9,056/$10,810
% of students receiving aid	52
% of first-year students receiving aid	18
% of students receiving loans	37
% of students receiving grants	15
Average award package	$6,738
Average grant	$1,772
Average student loan debt	$15,404

ADMISSIONS

Admissions Selectivity Rating	**82**
# of applications received	528
% applicants accepted	34
% acceptees attending	46
Average GMAT	522
Average GPA	3.28
TOEFL Required of International Students?	Yes
Minimum TOEFL (paper/computer)	570/230
Application fee	$55
International application fee	$55
Regular application deadline	Rolling
Regular notification	Rolling
Transfer students accepted?	Yes
Transfer application policy: Students must apply as a new student and courses will be evaluted	
Non-fall admissions?	Yes

EMPLOYMENT PROFILE

Career Rating	**70**
# of companies recruiting on-campus	208
Average starting salary	$62,666

CALIFORNIA STATE UNIVERSITY—LONG BEACH
COLLEGE OF BUSINESS ADMINISTRATION

GENERAL INFORMATION
Type of school | public
Environment | city
Academic calendar | semester

SURVEY SAYS...
Students love Long Beach, CA
Friendly students
Happy students
Smart classrooms
Solid preparation in:
Presentation skills

STUDENTS
Enrollment of parent
  institution | 33,000
Enrollment of MBA program | 310
% male/female | 58/42
% out-of-state | 1
% part-time | 70
% minorities | 15
% international | 30
Average age at entry | 28
Average years work experience
  at entry | 5

ACADEMICS
Academic Experience Rating | 79
Student/faculty ratio | 25:1
Profs interesting rating | 65
Profs accessible rating | 76

Academics

The College of Business Administration at California State University—Long Beach—the "best business school in the California State University system," according to some students here—offers five different MBA programs for the convenience of its students. Most popular among the different options is the Evening MBA, a self-paced program that can be pursued either full- or part-time. Evening classes meet during the week with a curriculum that includes prerequisite courses (which can be waived for students with undergraduate business degrees), core courses, electives (three in one area must be completed for an area of concentration), and a capstone course. Concentrations are offered in information systems, finance, human resources, marketing, general management, .accounting, and health care.

Those looking for a more traditional, cohort-based MBA program in a part-time setting will appreciate the Fully Employed MBA (FEMBA) program, a 23-month sequence of four 10-week sessions per year, scheduled on Saturdays for the convenience of full-time workers. FEMBA combines the benefits of a lockstep curriculum and the team-based learning inherent in the cohort system with the expedience of weekend classes. All books and materials are included in the price of the FEMBA program—another plus for those who hate unpleasant surprises.

CSULB also offers three smaller, more specialized MBA programs: the Corporate MBA Program for Boeing, available only to qualified Boeing employees; the Fully Employed MBA Program for Municipal and Public Agency Managers, which focuses on business skills and concepts useful in government and education; and a one-year Accelerated MBA, a full-time program for students anxious to jump-start their business careers.

Students typically choose CSULB for its low tuition rates, which translate into an excellent ROI. One student writes, "It was the best investment, when you take into account the tuition, the flexible schedule of classes, and the time it generally takes to complete the MBA program." Once admitted, students also enjoy "perfect class sizes that allow all students to contribute to discussions" and professors who "usually come from the private sector and teach more from 'real-world' experience than from theory." Professors here "take an interest in seeing you succeed." Some also describe "a light workload," which could be viewed as plus or a minus, depending on what a particular student wants from the program.

Career and Placement

CSULB's Career Development Center provides counseling and placement services for all students at the university. The office coordinates career fairs and manages online job postings through BeachLINK, a database accessible only to those with CSULB accounts and passwords. Students report that "the school has a great networking program through mentors in local business."

Student Life and Environment

There are "many different countries represented, including Saudi Arabia and China" in CSULB's student body. One MBA observes, "I rarely have had access to such people before. It is great to meet them in an intellectual environment, which offers a contrast to information provided by the media." Students here are "friendly for the most part and very goal-oriented." In classes, "there seems to be a good mix of married and single students ranging from mid-20s to mid-40s. Some have children, but most don't. Most everyone works at least part-time, if not full-time [because] very few come from a privileged background." One student comments, "I am an older student (48), but found that my age didn't matter as much as I thought it would."

The campus offers "plenty of places to eat" and "is very accommodating of wonderful group meetings and other opportunities to meet fellow students." On the down side, "because this is mostly a commuter campus, there is little or no after-school socializing." Students report that the campus itself "is beautiful and big enough to keep you in shape walking from place to place." Overall, students experience a "very laid-back atmosphere" on campus and point out that despite this, "everyone is still constantly focused on the tasks at hand."

Admissions

Undergraduate GPA and GMAT score are the most important factors in admissions decisions at CSULB. The school requires a minimum GPA of 2.75 for the applicants' final two years worth of undergraduate credits (either the final 60 semester credits or the final 90 quarter credits). In addition, applicants earn a minimum score of 490 on the GMAT, with a "good balance between the quantitative and verbal sections" and an analytical writing score of at least 3.0. Letters of recommendation, a personal essay, and a resume are also considered in the admissions process. The school notes that "work experience and computer experience are recommended" of all applicants.

FINANCIAL FACTS

Annual tuition (in-state/out-of-state)	$0/$7,896
Fees (in-state/out-of-state)	$1,822/$3,164

ADMISSIONS

Admissions Selectivity Rating	**91**
# of applications received	298
% applicants accepted	85
% acceptees attending	79
Average GMAT	560
Range of GMAT	480-710
Average GPA	3.3
TOEFL Required of International Students?	Yes
Minimum TOEFL (paper/computer)	550/213
Application fee	$55
Regular application deadline	3/30
Regular notification	5/1
Deferment Available?	Yes
Maximum length of deferment	1 semester
Transfer students accepted?	Yes
Transfer application policy: Transfer students must meet our regular admissions criteria.	
Non-fall admissions?	Yes

APPLICANTS ALSO LOOK AT

California State University—Fullerton, California State University—Los Angeles, Pepperdine University, University of California-Irvine.

CALIFORNIA STATE UNIVERSITY—SAN BERNARDINO
COLLEGE OF BUSINESS AND PUBLIC ADMINISTRATION

GENERAL INFORMATION
Type of school	public
Environment	city
Academic calendar	quarter

SURVEY SAYS...
Administration
Friendly students
Happy students
Smart classrooms
Solid preparation in:
Presentation skills
Quantitative skills

STUDENTS
Enrollment of parent institution	16,927
Enrollment of MBA program	314
% male/female	57/43
% out-of-state	1
% part-time	33
% minorities	8
% international	46
Average age at entry	29
Average years work experience at entry	4

ACADEMICS
Academic Experience Rating	**73**
Student/faculty ratio	20:1
Profs interesting rating	89
Profs accessible rating	80
% female faculty	17
% minority faculty	6

Joint Degrees
Claremont Graduate University (CGU) has an articulate PhD program in Information Science with CSUSB's MBA Program. As many as 54 CSUSB quarter units can be counted towards your PhD at CGU.

Academics

The MBA program at California State University—San Bernardino is "designed for the working professional," with most classes meeting twice weekly in the evenings. Students appreciate the flexibility of the program, and also love the way the school "beats the brush establishing student demand for a course. Courses are added when people respond in numbers that they need, and others are deleted based on this same criteria." Best of all, they love the "excellent return on investment" this low-priced program offers. CSUSB operates on a quarterly academic schedule. The MBA program requires 48 quarter units consisting of: seven core courses (accounting, financial theory, information management, organization theory, global corporate strategy, marketing, and operations); and five electives in one of seven concentrations (accounting, finance, entrepreneurship, information management, management, marketing management, and operations management). In addition, all students must create a portfolio of coursework, to be reviewed by faculty, and must complete either a comprehensive project or pass a comprehensive written examination in their area of concentration.

Students speak highly of CSUSB's program in operations management, where "students have competed against better-known schools and kick their butts. The small class size and attention to students serves CSUSB well." They also praise the finance and entrepreneurship programs. The latter is strengthened by the College of Business' Inland Empire Center for Entrepreneurship, a research center that promotes entrepreneurship in the surrounding area. Students report that faculty in all areas "seek to challenge the students, and they are more interested in learning rather than quantitative exam scores. They act as facilitators rather than dictators, and that is very motivating." Students also tell us that their "professors are real people who genuinely care about your academic and professional goals. Most professors have 'real-life' business experience and are not entrenched in academia."

CSUSB offers other strengths as well. The computer labs "are open extended hours and 99 percent of the stuff works." With more than 400 computer workstations in the b-school facility, students generally have an easy time getting a workstation when they need one. The administration "does a satisfactory job considering the state financial mess." Finally, "the outside-of-class opportunities are very diverse." One student reports, "During my time at CSUSB I took an internship that allowed me face time with the CFO and vice president of a Fortune 500 company."

Career and Placement

The Career Development Center at CSUSB serves all students at the university—undergraduate and graduate. Counselors there offer workshops in interviewing, resume writing, and job search strategies. The office arranges on-campus interviews and alumni meet-and-greets, and also maintains a database of job listings. A few students feel that "there needs to be more interaction between the school and alumni and businesses in the area to develop more school programs and help students with job placement," but the school's newly-form Business Alliance group should help. Employers likely to hire CSUSB MBAs include Arrowhead Credit Union, GE Transportation, Enterprise Rent-a-Car, American Express Financial, ESRI, Arthur Anderson, FEMA, Wells Fargo, and almost all the regional accounting firms, banks, and credit unions.

Student Life and Environment

The College of Business and Public Administration is located in the 10-year-old Jack H. Brown Hall, a modern facility that suits the needs of the program. Students describe the campus as "a little oasis in San Bernardino. You drive on a smog-filled freeway, and sud-

909-880-5703, Director of Admissions and Recruitment
5500 University Parkway, San Bernardino, CA 92407 United States
Phone: 909-880-5703 • Fax: 909-880-7582
E-mail: mba@csusb.edu • Website: www.csusb.edu

denly you see this open landscape in front of you. It is a pleasure walking around on a safe campus when the sun is shining, with the snow-covered mountains as the scenic backdrop." They also regard it as a "quiet, good place to do research because there are not a lot of recreation parks around."

Campus life is available for those with time to enjoy it. One student says, "There are many professional organizations open to MBA students. I belong to The Council of Logistics Management (CLM), Society for Human Resource Management (SHRM), and the American Production and Inventory Control Society (APICS). Our student organizations have visited operations such as Home Depot's cross-dock facility and Unilever's distribution center. The school even provided funding for all the student members of APICS who wished to attend the 2004 International Conference in San Diego." Most students, though, "do not live on or near campus. They are locally employed and attend school during the evenings." This group rarely has time for anything other than class, study, and group work.

CSUSB's student body "is split between a large contingent of foreign students and the rest, who are generally from the Inland Empire. Many students just continued their undergraduate studies and therefore lack any significant experience in the business work environment." The student body also includes "accomplished professionals returning to gain a competitive advantage over their peers due to changing market conditions." Students get along well, as one describes it: "My fellow students are an interesting diverse group of people that have many experiences different from my own. They are what makes the environment relaxed yet professional all at the same time." Approximately "one-quarter to one-third of students live on campus or in apartments just off campus," with the rest commuting.

Admissions

Applicants to the CSUSB MBA program must first apply for admission to the university, which requires a baccalaureate with a GPA of at least 2.5 for the final two years of undergraduate work. Students clearing this hurdle may then apply for admission to the MBA program. Applicants must submit two sets of official transcripts for all post-secondary academic work; an official GMAT score report; and a personal statement. Three letters of recommendation are recommended but are technically optional. International students must additionally provide an Affidavit of Financial Support and TOEFL scores. The minimum requirement for admission to the program is a formula score of 1050 under the formula [(undergraduate GPA × 200) + GMAT score], with a minimum GMAT score of 470 and a minimum GPA of 2.5. No student may begin MBA work without having earned at least a C grade in the following undergraduate courses or their equivalent at another accredited institution: financial accounting I and II; microeconomics; macroeconomics; business finance; corporate finance; information management; business law; management and organization behavior; expository writing for administration; strategic management; marketing principles; business statistics; and principles of supply chain management.

FINANCIAL FACTS

Fees	$3,500 plus $226 per unit
Books and supplies	$1,500
Room & board (on/off-campus)	$9,000/$12,000
% of students receiving aid	33
% of first-year students receiving aid	33
% of students receiving loans	33
Average award package	$6,625

ADMISSIONS

Admissions Selectivity Rating	73
# of applications received	249
% applicants accepted	67
% acceptees attending	56
Average GMAT	530
Range of GMAT	470-610
Average GPA	3.25
TOEFL Required of International Students?	Yes
Minimum TOEFL (paper/computer)	550/213
Application fee	$55
International application fee	$55
Regular application deadline	7/1
Regular notification	9/1
Early decision program?	Yes
ED Deadline/Notification	2/1 / 6/1
Deferment Available?	Yes
Maximum length of deferment	1 year
Transfer students accepted?	Yes
Transfer application policy: Only three graduate courses may be transferred into the MBA program from approved U.S. Universities.	
Non-fall admissions?	Yes
Need-blind admissions?	Yes

APPLICANTS ALSO LOOK AT

California State Polytechnic University—Pomona, California State University—Fullerton, California State University—Los Angeles, University of California-Riverside.

EMPLOYMENT PROFILE

Career Rating	71

CARNEGIE MELLON UNIVERSITY
TEPPER SCHOOL OF BUSINESS

GENERAL INFORMATION
Type of school	private
Environment	metropolis
Academic calendar	mini semester

SURVEY SAYS...
Cutting edge classes
Smart classrooms
Solid preparation in:
Finance
Teamwork
Quantitative skills

STUDENTS
Enrollment of parent institution	9,800
Enrollment of MBA program	661
% male/female	79/21
% part-time	41
% minorities	5
% international	26
Average age at entry	28
Average years work experience at entry	4.5

ACADEMICS
Academic Experience Rating	**92**
Student/faculty ratio	5:1
Profs interesting rating	81
Profs accessible rating	86
% female faculty	16
% minority faculty	15

Joint Degrees
MBA/JD: 3-4 years; MBA/Computational Finance: 2.5 years; MBA/Software Engineering: 2.5 years; MBA/Environmental Engineering: 2 years; MBA/Civil Engineering: 2 years.

Academics

Carnegie Mellon's Tepper School of Business prides itself on the lengths to which it goes "to fully integrate course curriculum throughout the campus community." The school's unique "cross-campus curriculum builds industry depth in tandem with business fundamentals," according to the school. The result is "a borderless b-school [that can quickly adapt to incorporate] emerging and high-growth industries." Students praise the approach, telling us it facilitates "opportunities to start technology-related companies with cross-campus collaboration."

Students caution that Carnegie Mellon's MBA program has a heavy quantitative emphasis, which translates into an often-burdensome workload. The upside is that it "leaves you with a skill set few other business schools can match." Students tell us that the curriculum is designed to "combine the deep quant skills into practical understanding and intuition throughout all course work." It also means that the school has an unusually large population of engineers and computer scientists. Throughout the two-year program, "team and group work is stressed heavily, and there is a stress on effective communication." Also, "independent research projects are common."

By all accounts, the faculty at Tepper is stellar. The school touts its professors by reporting that they "are consistently represented among the highest scoring ratings for Intellectual Capital reviews, attesting to their worldwide recognition for innovative research, peer reviewed published papers, global consulting network as well as government and association appointments." MBAs agree, telling us, "The professors here are definitely leaders in their fields, such as Alan Meltzer in economics or Joel Stern in finance. They are all on the cutting edge of research, and they do a nice job of integrating their work into the classroom." Even better, they're "engaging and accessible outside of class." Students agree that "the academic side of this school is its real strength" and single out operations, IT, and finance as the best of the group.

About the only sore spot with students is the facility dedicated to their program. MBAs grouse, "We have too many students for too small a building. We need more study rooms for group study, more and bigger lockers, [and] more bathrooms. We need a dedicated lounge, not just an extension to the food court." Also, one student notes, "The building infrastructure has been allowed to fall apart."

Career and Placement

Carnegie Mellon's Career Opportunities Center (COC) supplies a range of services to MBAs, including workshops on job-seeking skills and strategies, career panel presentations, counseling, mock interviews, resume review, career fairs, and alumni networking. The school maintains facilities to allow telerecruiting, which is important because "it's always a struggle to get employers to Pittsburgh. It's an unfortunate situation that is currently being approached in creative ways."

Top employers of Tepper MBAs include: Alcoa, Bank of America, Capital One, Deutsche Bank, Alex Brown, Goldman Sachs, Honeywell, IBM, McKinsey & Co., National City Corporation, PNC Bank, and Samsung Electronics. The school places 13 percent of its graduates outside the country; at least another 30 percent are placed with U.S. companies well outside Carnegie Mellon's geographic region.

LAURIE STEWART, EXECUTIVE DIRECTOR OF MASTERS ADMISSIONS
TEPPER SCHOOL OF BUSINESS, 5000 FORBES AVENUE, PITTSBURGH, PA 15213 UNITED STATES
PHONE: 412-268-2272 • FAX: 412-268-4209
E-MAIL: MBA-ADMISSIONS@ANDREW.CMU.EDU • WEBSITE: WWW.TEPPER.CMU.EDU

Student Life and Environment

Carnegie Mellon MBAs "are always very busy" with course work, especially during their first two semesters, which are "very, very intense, with five core classes at a time." Second year "offers some more opportunities for socializing." All students try to find time for "the regular Thursday night bar crawl and free beer and food at school at 5 P.M. every Friday." Students tell us, "Social committee parties are also very well attended." Most events are open "not only to students of the MBA program but also to their friends, family, and spouses." Social life is made somewhat more manageable by the size of the school. As one student explains, "I enjoy very much being at a medium-sized school. You get to know most of the people, and you develop life-lasting friendships. Even though students work hard, you can always find someone to chat and relax [with]."

The program is also home to some 20-odd student clubs, ranging from professional and minority interest clubs to those with extracurricular foci, such as the golf club, the wine club, and the roadrunners club. Tepper MBAs somehow find time to publish a weekly newsletter, the whimsical *Robber Barons* (whose motto is "All the news that fits, we print").

Although its many assets are hardly a secret to residents, Pittsburgh often surprises out-of-towners who arrive expecting a decrepit steel town. MBAs tell us, "Pittsburgh is a better town that I ever expected. Full of culture and entertainment, it is not the steel town of old." The city has enjoyed a renaissance over the past decade and is now home to "great cultural [and] music opportunities for a mid-sized city. There's lots of interesting development being done around Pittsburgh." Students are especially partial to the "great local bars" where they often run into people just like themselves; "young professionals in Pittsburgh are a small, tight-knit group," students report.

Admissions

Carnegie Mellon requires the following of MBA applicants: undergraduate transcripts (and graduate transcripts, if applicable), GMAT scores, TOEFL scores (for students whose native language is not English), two letters of recommendation, essays, and a resume/employment record. Post-undergraduate work experience is not required, although "candidates with post-undergraduate professional experience have, everything else equal, a better chance for admission." Most of those admitted to the program arrive with two to eight years of work experience. Minority recruiting is facilitated through Connections Weekend, a conference for prospective minority students (usually occurring in December) and through participation in the Consortium for Graduate Study and Management.

Prominent Alumni

Jim Swartz, Founding Partner, Accel Partners; David Tepper, President and Founder, Appaloosa Management L.P.; Pam Zilly, Senior Managing Director, The Blackstone Group; David Coulter, Chairman, West Coast Region, JP Morgan Chase & Co.; Yoshiaki Fujimori, President & CEO, GE (General Electric) Asia Pacific.

FINANCIAL FACTS

Annual tuition	$38,800
Fees	$394
Books and supplies	$4,650
Room & board	$12,755
% of students receiving aid	65
% of first-year students receiving aid	58
% of students receiving loans	65
% of students receiving grants	69
Average award package	$45,000
Average grant	$6,465
Average student loan debt	$56,592

ADMISSIONS

Admissions Selectivity Rating	96
# of applications received	1194
% applicants accepted	28
% acceptees attending	45
Average GMAT	691
Range of GMAT	660-720
Average GPA	3.3
TOEFL Required of International Students?	Yes
Minimum TOEFL (paper/computer)	600/250
Application fee	$100
International application fee	$100
Regular application deadline	3/21
Regular notification	5/2
Application Deadline/Notification	
Round 1:	11/15 / 1/17
Round 2:	1/10 / 3/14
Round 3:	3/21 / 5/2
Round 4:	5/2 / 6/6
Need-blind admissions?	Yes

APPLICANTS ALSO LOOK AT

Cornell University, Massachusetts Institute of Technology, New York University, Northwestern University, University of Chicago, University of Michigan, University of Pennsylvania.

EMPLOYMENT PROFILE			
Career Rating	89	Grads employed by field	%: avg. salary
Placement rate (%)	92	Finance	35: $82,812
% grads employed immediately	67	Marketing	16: $74,913
Average starting salary	$82,185	MIS	4: $82,143
		Operations	7: $76,583
		Strategic Planning	6: $80,812
		Consulting	23: $92,467
		General Management	6: $71,372
		Other	3: $59,246

CASE WESTERN RESERVE UNIVERSITY
WEATHERHEAD SCHOOL OF MANAGEMENT

GENERAL INFORMATION
Type of school	private
Environment	metropolis
Academic calendar	semester

SURVEY SAYS...
Happy students
Smart classrooms
Solid preparation in:
Teamwork
Communication/interpersonal skills

STUDENTS
Enrollment of parent institution	11,118
Enrollment of MBA program	739
% male/female	62/38
% out-of-state	69
% part time	37
% minorities	9
% international	37
Average age at entry	27
Average years work experience at entry	5

ACADEMICS
Academic Experience Rating	**88**
Student/faculty ratio	11:1
Profs interesting rating	85
Profs accessible rating	88
% female faculty	20
% minority faculty	5

Joint Degrees
MBA/JD: 4 yrs; MBA/MD: 5 yrs; MBA/MS in Nursing: 2.5 yrs; Master in nonprofit organizations/JD: 4 yrs; Master in Nonprofit/MA: 2.5 yrs; MBA/Master of Science in Social Aministration: 2.5 yrs; MBA/Master of International Management: 2.5 yrs; Master of Accountancy/MBA: 2 yrs; MBA/Master of Public Health: 2.5 yrs

Prominent Alumni
John Breen, CEO (ret.) Sherwin Williams; Clayton Deutsch, Managing Partner, McKinsey & Co., Chicago; David Daberko, Chairman and CEO, National city Bank; John Neff, CEO (ret.) Vanguard Fund; Joseph Sabatini, Managing Director, JPMorganChase.

Academics

"The greatest strengths at Weatherhead," MBAs in Case Western Reserve's b-school explain, "are innovation, commitment, and energy. This school is continuously looking for ways to stand out and be recognized, and they have done an excellent job." A "beautiful new building" with "great infrastructure—a wired building and multimedia classrooms, LAN, and wireless networks"—plays a role in Weatherhead's forward-thinking approach, but it's the curriculum and the professors who teach it that truly occupy center stage. A focus on organizational behavior, "a field in which Weatherhead is a world leader," helps define the Weatherhead way. One MBA explains, "All the current research has shown that effective organizations have resonant leaders. I believe Case's program is unique in that they incorporate this training into their management degree." However, this approach has its critics; one student complains, "The school's curriculum is dominated by organization behavior thought, often to the detriment of the more conventional business school courses. The school aims to be 'unique,' for better and for worse." But many of the MBAs approve enthusiastically. Students also speak highly of Weatherhead's offerings in finance and entrepreneurship.

Students are even more united in their praise of Weatherhead's faculty. One MBA writes, "Professors are the top in their field. The organizational behavior, entrepreneurship, and marketing faculty are all on the boards of *Fortune* 500 companies and bring a real-life experience to the table at each class. Many faculty have written 'the book' on their subject matters or contributed to another's book." Because "Weatherhead is smaller than many of the top business schools, [it] allows for a great deal of interaction. I see my professors around the building, and they are always very friendly and happy to chat." Administrators are also "wholly committed to the students. There is an energy that flows through the building, and it is contagious." Curriculum highlights include the Second Year Action Learning Project, "a great consulting opportunity for graduate business students to assist local companies with real issues." Teamwork and group projects are emphasized throughout the two-year program.

Career and Placement

All on-campus interviews, information sessions, referrals, and resume books are processed through Weatherhead's e-Recruiting system (known as WeRS); students may check the WeRS website to keep abreast of all special events including club events and activities (career services are handled through the Career and Student Life Center). The school holds Career Expos in both the fall and spring terms. While some students feel that "the Career and Student Life Center is a great resource for everything from mock interviews, resume review, and job leads," others complain that "the career office has been largely unhelpful." One MBA notes, "In my experience, [they] focus too much on grooming the students and not enough on attracting quality companies to campus." Another MBA reconciles these disparate views by explaining that "the career services office is working hard to make improvements and be proactive in the face of a down economy. [However], they have a ways to go and need to focus on their ability to coordinate and stay on top of things."

Major employers of Case Western MBAs include American Greetings, Eaton Corporation, Emerson Electric, Honeywell, Johnson Controls, Johnson & Johnson, Progressive Corporation, and Samsung. Starting salaries range from just below $53,000 (marketing) to just below $80,000 (operations). About two-thirds of all graduates remain in the Midwest when they start their careers; a little over 10 percent head overseas.

KEITH AUER, DIRECTOR OF ADMISSIONS
160 PETER B. LEWIS BUILDING, 10900 EUCLID AVENUE, CLEVELAND, OH 44106-7235 U.S.
PHONE: 216-368-2030 • FAX: 216-368-5548
E-MAIL: MBA.ADMISSION@WEATHERHEAD.CWRU.EDU • WEBSITE: WWW.WEATHERHEAD.CWRU.EDU

Student Life and Environment

Weatherhead's home is "a new building designed by Frank Gehry. The libraries and resources are tremendous, and the classroom and study facilities are state-of-the-art." One part-time student writes, "The accessibility to the latest media and technology is incredible—in fact, it's better than my company's!" The school goes to great lengths to create homey touches, which students appreciate. One student reports, "On Wednesdays, they hire music students from the Cleveland Institute of Music to play chamber music in the open foyer, which is absolutely beautiful. Nothing can compare to the feeling I have when I enter this amazingly beautiful building, hear classical music echoing through the halls, and prepare for my classes!"

Wednesday isn't the only special day at Weatherhead. Thursdays bring an event called Business Casual, "which is a chance to get something to eat and relax. Once a month the Business Casuals take on an international flair and are hosted by a different ethnic group, such as the Latin American students, [who include] salsa dancing [at the event]." At other times, "there's beer and food provided. It's enjoyable because it give us a chance to relax and socialize with our peers." Students say that throughout the week, "life is very dynamic inside the school. There are a lot of events, group of interest meetings, snacks offered for late classes—a real city inside the city, except that you know everyone!" Most students are active in a number of clubs. One MBA explains, "Course work is heavy, but it would be completely manageable if so many people weren't involved with other campus activities like clubs, speakers, events, and projects." Weatherhead MBAs are proud of the diversity of their student body. "The fact that there are more than 25 states of the United States and more than 30 countries from across the world represented, teaches you to work in a very diverse environment," one student writes. Another student adds, "I feel like I have to bring a passport when I go to class; we are truly an international school." Hometown Cleveland, we're assured, "is very underrated. There are tons [of things] to do here."

Admissions

Prospective Weatherhead students must submit undergraduate transcripts, a GMAT score, two letters of recommendation, four essay responses to questions provided by the school, and a current resume. International students must also provide TOEFL scores and a statement of financial responsibility. Interviews are conducted only at the request of the Admission Committee. The committee pays close attention to "diversity of work and/or educational experience; demonstrated leadership abilities; and demonstrated community involvement." Minority recruitment is facilitated by "on-campus scholars weekends and networking with minority professional associations and Weatherhead alumni. [Also,] referrals from minority alumni are given an application-fee waiver." The school notes that applicants improve their chances of admission by applying during the early admission rounds.

FINANCIAL FACTS

Annual tuition	$29,040
Fees	$874
Books and supplies	$1,300
Room & board (on/off-campus)	$13,100/$14,024
% of students receiving aid	80
% of first-year students receiving aid	80
% of students receiving loans	47
% of students receiving grants	80
Average award package	$23,200
Average grant	$13,900
Average student loan debt	$37,400

ADMISSIONS

Admissions Selectivity Rating	88
# of applications received	340
% applicants accepted	49
% acceptees attending	60
Average GMAT	615
Range of GMAT	500-710
Average GPA	3.16
TOEFL Required of International Students?	Yes
Minimum TOEFL (paper/computer)	600/250
Application fee	$50
International application fee	$50
Regular application deadline	3/1
Regular notification	4/1
Application Deadline/Notification	
Round 1:	11/30 / 1/15
Round 2:	1/31 / 2/28
Round 3:	3/1 / 4/15
Round 4:	3/1 / 6/1
Transfer students accepted?	Yes
Transfer application policy: Maximum number of transferable credits is 6 semester hours from an AASCB-accredited program.	
Non-fall admissions?	Yes
Need-blind admissions?	Yes

APPLICANTS ALSO LOOK AT

The Ohio State University, University of Michigan, University of Notre Dame, University of Pittsburgh, University of Virginia, Vanderbilt University, Washington University in St. Louis.

EMPLOYMENT PROFILE

Career Rating	84	Grads employed by field	%: avg. salary
Placement rate (%)	83	Finance	25: $73,250
% grads employed immediately	62	Marketing	22: $64,022
Average starting salary	$68,158	Operations	9: $66,111
		Consulting	5: $70,000
		Other	5: $62,790

Catholic University of Leuven & Ghent U.
Vlerick Leuven Gent Management School

GENERAL INFORMATION
Type of school	public
Academic calendar	2004/5

SURVEY SAYS...
Students love Leuven, VB
Friendly students
Solid preparation in:
Entrepreneurial studies

STUDENTS
Enrollment of parent institution	30,000
Enrollment of MBA program	250
% male/female	75/25
% out-of-state	10
% part-time	80
% minorities	100
% international	86
Average age at entry	31
Average years work experience at entry	7

ACADEMICS
Academic Experience Rating	**87**
Student/faculty ratio	4:1
Profs interesting rating	66
Profs accessible rating	64
% female faculty	25
% minority faculty	100

Prominent Alumni
Frank Meysman, CEO Sara Lee; Roger Chua, COO Banking; Bill Bygrave, Professor Author; Lutgart Van Den Berghe, Corporate Governance; Sophie Manigart, Entrepreneurial Finance.

Academics

Executive development programs are huge at Vlerick Leuven Gent: the Belgian b-school hosts over 3,000 managers in its open-enrollment seminars and company-specific programs, but the school is also home to a growing MBA program, one whose stature around the world is also growing. The school currently offers a full-time English language MBA at its Leuven campus, a part-time Dutch language MBA at its Ghent campus, and a part-time English language MBA at both campuses. The full-time general MBA can be completed in one year, as can masters degrees in marketing and financial management; an MBA in financial services takes two years to complete. In total, about 250 students pursue MBAs at VLG.

Vlerick Leuven Gent was founded in 1953 by Professor Andre Vlerick; over the years it has developed associations with Ghent University and the Katholieke Universiteit Leuven, and today it serves as the autonomous management school of these prestigious universities, the two largest in Belgium. Association with these two more established schools provides a solid research base; the school's autonomy allows it to "build strong ties with the business community" and "enables it to respond to the development needs of this community in an optimal way," according to the school's brochure. As one student observes, "The fact that the school is backed up by two recognized universities is apparent. It benefits greatly from its location and the support and research of its two parent universities."

MBA programs at Vlerick Leuven Gent maintain "a strong international focus" derived not only from the curriculum but also from the student body. One student writes, "The basic strength of this program is the dual academic-practical approach. On the one hand, the academic orientation of the professors builds a solid knowledge foundation, while on the other, the experiences of the rest of the multicultural group enrich the whole educational experience." Students tell us that "professors and academics show a lot of respect for the audience, are extremely knowledgeable, and have in many cases extensive personal activity in the fields of management they are covering." MBAs here especially enjoy "the specialization seminars in entrepreneurship and doing business in Europe." Many students feel, however, that "the international MBA could use more international faculty. Most teachers are from Belgium." Students also report that "the workload is extremely heavy," but add that the benefits of the program—good value in a major economic center of the European Union—outweigh any shortfalls.

Career and Placement

The Career Services Office (CSO) at Vlerick Leuven Gent organizes regular career events on campus; the office also coordinates multi-campus events and online recruiting. In an effort to keep pace with the internationalization of the school's curriculum and student body, the CSO has spent the last few years developing business contacts throughout the world to supplement its already strong base of Belgian businesses. The CSO also offers counseling services and advice on resume-writing, interviewing, searching for jobs, and salary negotiation. According to the school's website, "The intention (of the CSO's efforts) is to develop a career management program that throughout the entire year will operate as an integral part of the various courses, with presentations, interactive workshops, and networking events." The office also plans to develop "a life-long career guidance program, whereby alumni of Vlerick Leuven Gent Management School will become even more deeply involved in activities organized by the CSO." Students tell us these efforts are working, praising the "great alumni network."

CHARLOTTE DE VOLDER, PROGRAMME COORDINATOR
VLAMINGENSTRAAT 83, 3000 LEUVEN, REEP 1, 9000 GENT, VB 3000 BELGIUM
PHONE: 001-32-16-32-35-89 • FAX: 001-32-16-32-35-81
E-MAIL: MBA@VLERICK.BE • WEBSITE: WWW.VLERICK.COM

Student Life and Environment

Full-time students at Vlerick Leuven Gent experience a nonstop academic grind. Reports one student, "Life in school starts every day (including exams period, studying for the exams, most of weekends) at 9:00 P.M. and ends at 12:00 A.M. After that, individual work at home is usually required. In this frame, the quality of life can't be good. But then again, this is a commitment well known before the enrollment, so its consistency is remarkable. I personally face time problems and issues with domestic tasks (laundry, house cleaning, nutrition). I skipped visiting my home country at Christmas to catch up with the material I needed to know…and this is the situation that I face [at] Easter." Some here manage to squeeze in some free time; they describe "an excellent lifestyle in the very small and safe student town of Leuven, with lots of social, sports, and cultural activities." One student notes, "Belgium is a beer-drinker's paradise. Need I say more?"

Students "represent every continent, which makes participating in the group a very interesting learning experience." They are "active social animals and real team players, and students are very much diversified in professional and academic experience and competencies."

Admissions

Admission to the Vlerick Leuven Gent Management School requires an undergraduate degree from an institution "recognized by the relevant authorities of the home country." Work experience "is beneficial but not required." Other admissions requirements depend on the method of application; students may choose the 'distance procedure' or the 'on-campus assessment procedure.' Both require a completed application, a resume, a copy of one's passport, and official copies of all post-secondary transcripts and diplomas. The distance procedure requires, in addition, an official GMAT score report, an official TOEFL score report (students whose native language is English are exempted from this requirement), two letters of recommendation, and a personal statement. On-campus assessment "requires your attendance at one of [the school's] in-house admission tests, which consist of an analytical test, a written comprehension test and two personal interviews (a motivation interview and a management potential/knowledge interview)."

FINANCIAL FACTS

Annual tuition	$15,000
Room & board (on/off-campus)	$8,000/$10,000
% of students receiving aid	10
% of first-year students receiving aid	10
% of students receiving grants	10
Average award package	$20,000
Average grant	$4,000
Average student loan debt	$10,000

ADMISSIONS

Admissions Selectivity Rating	94
# of applications received	300
% applicants accepted	34
% acceptees attending	50
Average GMAT	636
Range of GMAT	600-650
Average GPA	3.5
TOEFL Required of International Students?	Yes
Minimum TOEFL (paper/computer)	/255
Application fee	$50
International application fee	$50
Regular application deadline	6/30
Regular notification	7/14
Application Deadline/Notification	
Round 1:	1/22 / 2/1
Round 2:	3/24 / 4/1
Round 3:	6/30 / 7/14
Deferment Available?	Yes
Maximum length of deferment	1 year
Need-blind admissions?	Yes

APPLICANTS ALSO LOOK AT

Erasmus University, ESADE, HEC School of Management, IMD(International Institute for Management Development), INSEAD.

EMPLOYMENT PROFILE			
Career Rating	87	Grads employed by field %: avg. salary	
Placement rate (%)	100	Accounting	10: NR
# of companies recruiting on-campus	50	Finance	15: NR
% grads employed immediately	35	Marketing	10: NR
Average starting salary	$93,000	Strategic Planning	5: NR
		Consulting	15: NR
		Entrepreneurship	20: NR
		General Management	10: NR
		Venture Capital	5: NR
		Internet/New Media	5: NR
		Non-profit	5: NR

CHAPMAN UNIVERSITY
THE GEORGE L. ARGYROS SCHOOL OF BUSINESS AND ECONOMICS

Academics

"Chapman may be a small private university, but don't underestimate the quality here. Chapman is as good as, if not better than, many of the larger universities in the U.S.," MBAs in this Orange County program tell us. One student writes, "It was not a surprise to us to see Chapman listed among 'the hidden gems' in the *Washington Post*."

Chapman's MBA program—which can be completed on either a part-time or full-time basis–loads students up with core requirements. A whopping 33 of the 52 credits necessary for graduation are devoted to the core here. Students applaud the core's "strong foundation in concepts needed for today's business" and especially its "focus on business ethics as well as typical business topics." Some here, though, "wish the school allowed [them] to devote more time to majors and concentrations, as other business schools do." Chapman currently offers both general business degrees and degrees with an emphasis in business economics, finance, entrepreneurship, management, marketing, or international business. Students tell us that "the greatest strengths of [their] business school is in economics and international business." The school adds that the "four research centers represent the strength of the school: The Anderson Center for Economic Research, the Center for Real Estate, the Ralph Leatherby Center for Entrepreneurship and Ethics, and the Walter Schmid Center for International Business." Chapman also offers an Executive MBA program.

Chapman profs "are very accessible outside of class, and they help you to understand ideas or concepts not fully understood during class time. During projects they are helpful in steering you to the right path to get more justifiable solutions." Several students comment that they "would like to see more international faculty at Chapman." One writes, "The whole world is now heading towards globalization. To have international faculty come and teach at Chapman would open entirely new perspectives. This will strengthen Chapman's International Business program even more." Even those who see room for improvement, though, report satisfaction with the school. One MBA explains, "This program is as rigorous as top programs, but, unlike at other larger universities, you won't get lost here at Chapman. Not only do the faculty and staff know you by name, but you'll also build a strong bond with the faculty, staff, and other students even after you have graduated, resulting in global networking."

Career and Placement

Chapman's Career Development Center provides services—including job fairs, counseling, workshops, and online databases—to the entire student body of the university. Students wish there were "more activities geared toward MBA students. The only job fair I've heard of consisted of mail order businesses and UPS. What if you don't want to work there? A professional career fair would be nice, or a job board/placement office dedicated solely to the business school." Students also bemoan the fact that "there is little communication with the school's alumni." Recognizing the need for improvement in this area, the school's administration is offering "Hands-On Career Assistance" to new full-time students, starting in the fall of 2005. Additionally, the university is unveiling a state of the art alumni database, which promises to significantly increase networking activity between students and alumni.

Student Life and Environment

Chapman University has an enrollment of approximately 5,100 just under one-third of which represents graduate students. The business program is relatively small, with just over 140 prospective MBAs, most attending part-time. The MBA population here is "a

DEBRA GONDA, ASSOCIATE DIRECTOR
BECKMAN HALL;ONE UNIVERSITY DRIVE, ORANGE, CA 92866 UNITED STATES
PHONE: 877-CHAP-MBA • FAX: 714-997-6757
E-MAIL: MBA@CHAPMAN.EDU • WEBSITE: WWW.CHAPMAN.EDU/ARGYROS/

FINANCIAL FACTS

Annual tuition	$18,360
Books and supplies	$1,600
Average grant	$3,500

good mix, with some really smart and experienced students, and others who are book smart, funny, nice, friendly, and helpful." Students' ages "run from early 20s to 40s. Ethnic backgrounds and nationalities vary too, as well as types and degree of work experience. The gender mix is about 50–50." MBAs describe "a good, competitive yet friendly atmosphere with students. Everyone pushes fellow students to do better and go that extra mile, and not just to get a good grade but to understand the material."

Because "Chapman is a commuter school, most people don't relocate to take classes, and not many people are looking for additional friends. Between work, school, and the friends we already have, it doesn't leave much time for classmates." The school does plan occasional events for MBAs, though. One student writes, "The business school usually hosts a get-together event two to three times a semester, whether it's just an hour of eating pizza, sipping coffee, and chatting with the dean, associated deans, and faculty, or a soccer match between the faculty and the business students. Even though each of these events usually doesn't last longer than two hours, these types of activities have helped created a strong bond among the students, faculty, and staff." The school also hosts "a Distinguished Speaker series, where someone comes in and talks about their experiences and [students] get free dinner," as well as a dinner program in which students have the opportunity to share a meal and a conversation with highly respected members of Orange County and Southern California. Students appreciate that "the campus is located in a very nice area, and has extremely good on-campus facilities, considering the small overall size of the school."

Admissions

The admissions office factors "academic performance, leadership ability, work experience, and communication skills" into each of its decisions. The school requires a minimum GPA of 2.5 for the applicants' final two years worth of undergraduate credits (either the final 60 semester credits or the final 90 quarter credits). All applications must include an official GMAT score report, sealed copies of official transcripts for all post-secondary academic work, two letters of recommendation "from individuals familiar with the applicant's academic or professional abilities," and a completed application with a personal statement "explaining why the applicant is interested in pursuing a graduate degree at Chapman." Two years of business-related work experience is preferred. International applicants must "submit a certified statement demonstrating financial ability to cover all education and living expenses for the full period of time for which the student is applying, [and] all international students, except those from countries where English is the primary language, must take the TOEFL examination and achieve a score of 550 or higher on the paper-based test (or 213 on the computerized version)." Admission to the Executive MBA program requires at least seven years of professional experience and a one-on-one on-campus interview.

ADMISSIONS

Admissions Selectivity Rating	74
# of applications received	109
% applicants accepted	60
% acceptees attending	54
Average GMAT	520
Average GPA	3.1
TOEFL Required of International Students?	Yes
Minimum TOEFL (paper/computer)	550/213
Application fee	$40
International application fee	$40
Regular application deadline	7/1
Regular notification	Rolling
Deferment Available?	Yes
Maximum length of deferment	1 year
Transfer students accepted?	Yes
Transfer application policy: Transfer up to six units of course work	
Non-fall admissions?	Yes
Need-blind admissions?	Yes

APPLICANTS ALSO LOOK AT

California State University—Fullerton, Pepperdine University, University of California—Irvine, University of Southern California.

EMPLOYMENT PROFILE

Career Rating	60*
# of companies recruiting on-campus	40
% grads employed within three months	70

THE CHINESE UNIVERSITY OF HONG KONG
FACULTY OF BUSINESS ADMINISTRATION

GENERAL INFORMATION

Type of school	public
Academic calendar	2004-2005

SURVEY SAYS...

Students love Shatin, NT,
Friendly students
Happy students
Smart classrooms
Solid preparation in:
Teamwork

STUDENTS

Enrollment of parent institution	16,263
Enrollment of MBA program	394
% male/female	67/33
% part-time	86
% international	75
Average age at entry	28
Average years work experience at entry	5

ACADEMICS

Academic Experience Rating	**85**
Student/faculty ratio	4:1
Profs interesting rating	70
Profs accessible rating	75
% female faculty	18

Joint Degrees

Reciprocal Recognition of credits program with HEC, France (2 years in total - 1 year at CUMBA and 1 year at HEC)

Prominent Alumni

Irving Koo, Gp Mkg & Corp Relations Dir, CLP Holdings; Rebecca Lai, Permanent Sec for Civil Services, HKSARG; Roger Luk, Managing Dir & Deputy Chief Exe, Hang Seng Bank; Tat-lun Ng, Managing Dir, Energizer Co. Inc.; Joseph Pang, Exe Dir & Deputy Chief Exe, Bank of East Asia Ltd.

Academics

China, it can be said without fear of contradiction, has one of the world's fastest growing economies, and opportunities abound there for the savvy businessperson. The various MBA programs at the Chinese University of Hong Kong offer a foot in the door for students interested in those opportunities. As one of the region's older MBA programs, CUHK has a deep and loyal alumni network set to help newly minted MBAs make their mark in Asia. Even more to students' advantage, the school has a solid reputation in the region; *Asia Inc.* magazine has named the CUMBA program the best in the Asian Pacific for three consecutive years (2002–2004).

A broad range of options are available at CUHK. Besides its full-time and part-time MBA, the school offers more specific MBAs in finance and health care as well as its One MBA Global Executive MBA Program, a truly international degree conferred jointly by the program's five participating programs (which are spread across four continents).

Students report that the CUMBA teaching method has "adopted quite a lot of the U.S. university systems. A large proportion of professors got their PhDs in the U.S., so their teaching styles are quite open-minded. Plus, they all know that lecturing is not their only function. They understand how to guide the students in their thinking and encourage class discussions." Instruction styles include "lots of case studies as well as in-class exercises and discussion. The faculty brings their experiences to the classroom, giving the material real-world application and making theories relevant to students." MBAs reap the best of American and local approaches; "Some professors coming from the U.S. have relatively more international business experiences, while local professors have extensive local business exposure," one MBA student explains. The international student body, we're told, "brings a scope of ideas to our study. Courses in HR, marketing, and global business wouldn't be nearly as interesting without such a range of viewpoints in the classroom. With professors facilitating discussion, the students really bring so much to the learning process."

CUHK administrators "are very interested in the quality of the education we are receiving," notes one student. "They are always interested in students feedback about professors, classes, and courses we would like to see in the future." Students no doubt tell administrators how much they love the school's mentoring program. One happy student reports, "Through the mentorship program, I have the opportunity to get to know my 'big brother' (who works in a senior position of a top investment house) and learn from his wisdom and experience both personally and professionally."

Career and Placement

Students give good marks to the Chinese University's Career Planning and Development Centre, which provides career services to CUMBAs. They save their highest praise, however, for the university's alumni network, explaining that "CUMBA has the longest history in HK as well as in Asia. That's why our large alumni network is a key strength of the school." Graduates who wish to remain in Hong Kong or China "will find a lot of support here," while students happily discover that "alumni act as mentors for students and give students an alternative to professors for feedback and help in locating jobs, networking with business professionals in the area, and giving guidance in making career choices. This is a great help to students, especially those from outside Hong Kong."

Major employers of CUMBAs include ABN AMRO Bank; The Boston Consulting Group; CalTEX Companies (Greater China), Ltd.; Citibank; Credit Suisse First Boston (HK), Ltd.; Dah Sing Bank; DBS Kwong On Bank; Deloitte Consulting; Goldman Sachs; Grey Advertising (HK); HKSAR Government; Hong Kong & China Gas Company, Ltd.;

HSBC; JPMorgan Chase; KPMG; Mass Transit Railway Corporation; Merrill Lynch (Asia), Ltd.; Nestle (HK), Ltd.; and UBS Warburg.

Student Life and Environment

The student body at CUHK comes from "a good mix of all types of backgrounds, including age, career, and country of origin." MBAs brag that they "are quite an international family. Through group projects and assignments, we have learned how to cooperate with classmates from different backgrounds and countries as well as how to allocate resources effectively through teamwork." Local students pitch in to help internationals adjust to life in Hong Kong. One helpful local student reports, "As we have a lot of nonlocal students (from countries such as the U.S., Canada, France, Japan, Korea, China, and India), we always organize activities outside campus such as camping, hiking, or eating Hong Kong–style food. As a local student, I like to bring the Hong Kong culture to [nonlocal students], and at the same time, I can learn their culture as well."

The CUHK curriculum places a heavy load on students, so students find themselves "spending quite a lot of time on team projects outside class." Extracurricular life also includes career-related activities such as "meeting local business leaders through executive talks." Students "also organize firm visits so that [they] have more connections to the business community." Despite their many school responsibilities, most MBAs still find time for occasional fun. Students report, "Sometimes the MBA Students Association will hold some extracurricular activities like a Halloween party, a boat cruise, football games, or karaoke." They also point out, however, that "with such a small program, student clubs and other activities are not so easy to organize."

CUHK's "beautiful campus [is] very spacious, with many trees and recreational infrastructure. This atmosphere is excellent for studying and living." Facilities are also top-notch; students tell us, "The learning infrastructure is excellent. We have wireless broadband network in every classroom, canteen, and building. We have numerous computer laboratories (30 to 50 computers in each room), four university libraries, and sufficient hostels for us." When students want to leave campus, they find that "transportation is excellent. We could take a bus/mini-bus/subway/train, and it's about 10 minutes to town."

Admissions

The MBA program at the Chinese University of Hong Kong requires applicants to submit undergraduate transcripts (except in extraordinary circumstances, a minimum B average is required), GMAT scores, personal essays, and letters of recommendation. An interview, which can be conducted by telephone, is required. English proficiency (as demonstrated by TOEFL scores, for non-native English speakers) is also required. Work experience is "preferable" but not required. Applicants to the part-time and executive MBA programs must have at least three years of work experience.

FINANCIAL FACTS	
Annual tuition	$22,212
Books and supplies	$10,974
Room & board	$3,000
Average grant	$3,367

ADMISSIONS	
Admissions Selectivity Rating	85
# of applications received	707
% applicants accepted	68
% acceptees attending	71
Average GMAT	641
Average GPA	3.3
Application fee	$25
International application fee	$25
Regular application deadline	2/28
Regular notification	4/30
Deferment Available?	Yes
Maximum length of deferment	1 year
Need-blind admissions?	Yes

EMPLOYMENT PROFILE			
Career Rating	81	Grads employed by field:	
Placement rate (%)	95	Accounting	14
% grads employed immediately	50	Finance	25
Average starting salary	$59,470	Marketing	13
		Operations	2
		Consulting	20
		Other	26

THE CITADEL
THE CITADEL SCHOOL OF BUSINESS ADMINISTRATION

Academics

The Citadel offers "the only AACSB accredited program in Charleston" as well as "a reasonably priced degree"—two features that attract the school's predominantly part-time student body.

The Citadel MBA is a 48-hour program consisting of 24 hours of basic required courses, 12 hours of advanced required courses, and 12 hours of electives. Students who have successfully completed equivalent courses at the undergraduate or graduate level may be permitted to waive some or all of the basic required courses. In order to qualify, students must have completed the work within the previous five years. Electives may be used to develop concentrations in health care administration, hospitality/tourism, or international business. The Citadel also offers two joint degrees: a PharmD/MBA and an MD/MBA.

Students report, "Citadel professors seem incredibly committed to their craft. Most have been at it for decades yet bring verve and enthusiasm to each class." Students appreciate that "professors understand that most of us work over 40 hours per week. They spread out the course load so we can manage it more easily." This spirit of accommodation permeates the entire school. One student writes, "I have found that at any point in my academic career in the Citadel's business school that I have been able to approach all administrators and faculty with ease. Overall, the business school has a family feel, and everyone is looking out for your best interest." In the realm of improvements, some students would like to see the school offer a wider range of electives, and some feel that the faculty needs to be broadened. One student explains, "Many of the core courses are taught by the same professor (i.e., one professor teaches all business law courses, another teaches all the marketing courses, etc.). For someone like me, who has no business background, it seems we receive a very narrow view of the business world."

Career and Placement

The Citadel Career Center provides career services to all students on the Citadel campus. The office provides counseling services; workshops in interviewing, resume building, and job search strategies; career fairs; online job databases; and on-campus recruiting and interviewing. However, much of the office's work is geared toward serving the school's much-larger undergraduate population rather than MBAs and others enrolled in the College of Graduate and Professional Studies.

Student Life and Environment

Citadel MBAs are typically "hard-working individuals juggling full-time jobs, a family, and classes at night." Even so, many try to make time to participate in the school's popular mentoring program, in which "interested students are paired with someone in the community who works or worked in the student's desired career field." The program capitalizes on the fact that "there are many successful retirees in the area who are interested in advising students," but also includes "many accomplished business professionals still working in the field. The program gives the student real insight into that profession rather than the candy-coated version that someone who has never worked in that profession may give."

Students here enjoy other extracurricular options as well. "As part of the Leadership Forum, guest speakers from all over the country come to the Citadel to share their experiences with students," we're told. Plus "the MBA Association is instrumental in developing relationships among students and professors. It's great organization to be a part

FINANCIAL FACTS

Annual tuition (in-state/out-of-state)
$6,522/$15,918

of." Students also find time in their busy schedules for "occasional social gatherings throughout the year. They range from beers at the local tavern to sit-down dinners in five-star restaurants."

Citadel MBAs "are extremely motivated and resourceful. Everyone greets each other with that wonderful Charleston charm." Commenting on the student body, one student notes that it is "ethnically diverse, in that 10 to 15 percent of my classmates are from other countries and cultures such as Africa, the Middle East, Europe, Asia, and South America." Students "attend classes during the evening either on campus or at a centralized city location called the Low Country Graduate Center. Unlike most undergraduate classes, the students really want to be there and are always eager to participate in class discussions." As one student says, "I only go at night, but I really enjoy the beautiful, quiet campus that's full of diversity and a willingness to learn."

Admissions

Students may apply for admission to the Citadel School of Business Administration for the fall, spring, or summer term. Applicants must submit all of the following materials: a completed application form with application fee; sealed copies of official transcripts for all post-secondary work (transcripts representing work completed outside the U.S. should be translated and evaluated by an academic credential evaluation organization recognized by the Citadel); a sealed official copy of the GMAT score report (a minimum score of 400 is required); two letters of reference from undergraduate professors, business associates, and/or supervisors in government or military service; a resume; and two short personal essays. International students whose first language is not English are required to submit official TOEFL score reports (a minimum score of 550 is required). The school may request an applicant to submit to an interview; otherwise, interviews are not required. The school offers provisional admission to some candidates; provisional status remains in effect until the student has completed all basic courses with a GPA of at least 3.0.

ADMISSIONS

Admissions Selectivity Rating	**68**
TOEFL Required of International Students?	Yes
Minimum TOEFL (paper)	550
Application fee	$25
Regular application deadline	8/1
Regular notification	On or after 8/1
Transfer students accepted?	Yes
Transfer application policy: A maximum of six hours credit for graduate courses from an accredited institution (including consortia and AACSB-accredited institutions) may be approved for transfer.	
Non-fall admissions?	Yes
Need-blind admissions?	Yes

CLAREMONT GRADUATE UNIVERSITY
THE PETER F. DRUCKER AND MASATOSHI ITO GRADUATE SCHOOL OF MANAGEMENT

GENERAL INFORMATION
Type of school	private
Environment	village
Academic calendar	semester

SURVEY SAYS...
Friendly students
Happy students
Smart classrooms
Solid preparation in:
General management
Teamwork

STUDENTS
Enrollment of parent institution	2,038
Enrollment of MBA program	180
% male/female	69/31
% out-of-state	10
% part-time	24
% minorities	26
% international	20
Average age at entry	34
Average years work experience at entry	5

ACADEMICS
Academic Experience Rating	85
Student/faculty ratio	12:1
Profs interesting rating	84
Profs accessible rating	88
% female faculty	15

Joint Degrees
Dual-degree programs in human resources, biosciences, information sciences, economics, education, psychology, public policy, and by special arrangement in other disciplines.

Prominent Alumni
Charles Emery, Senior VP & CEO, Blue Cross Blue Shield NJ; Stephen Rountree, President & CEO Disney Music Center; Rajiv Dutta, Chief Financial Officer, eBay, Inc.; Colin Forkner, CEO & Vice Chairman, Pacific Coast National Bank; Brian Mulvaney, Exec. Vice President, Aramark Corporation; Karen Miggins, Executive Director, NAVAIR Weapons Division, China Lake, CA

Academics

"The Drucker name and philosophy—that management is a liberal art—is the greatest strength" of the b-school residing among the Claremont Consortium of Colleges in Claremont, California. Peter F. Drucker's groundbreaking insights into management have appeared in such prestigious publications as the *Harvard Business Review,* and they inform the entire curriculum at his namesake institution. As one MBA put it, "The greatest strength of the school is its orientation toward management rather than toward business. Management is a discipline taught at this school through the wisdom of Peter Drucker, perhaps the most prolific and perceptive observer of trends and management practices of the past century."

Consistent with Drucker's approach, "the school's academic strength is with the traditionally 'softer' skills. The classes in leadership, strategy, organizational behavior, morality and leadership, and Drucker-on-Management are outstanding." Drucker's global perspective necessitates an interdisciplinary approach; "accounting, organizational behavior, and strategy are connected to each other."

Drucker's relatively small size does pose some problems for students. One student explains, "Small schools have small-school problems. We need more classes and more professors to teach those classes." The school is too small to maintain full departments in all disciplines, necessitating the hiring of part-time or adjunct professors, who tend to be less accomplished and less popular with students. Permanent faculty, on the other hand, "are immediately accessible, and many are recognized leaders in venture finance, corporate governance, strategy, cost management, etc." Access to the Claremont Consortium means students "can take some classes other departments, such as HRD, economics, psychology, biology, and education" and even develop their own dual degrees.

Career and Placement

Drucker's career services are handled through the Claremont Graduate University Office of Career Management. According to the school's website, the office provides "structure and services, including counseling and specific workshops, to help students focus their search, to target appropriate employers, to implement their job search strategies, and to build skills in self-marketing." While students don't like that the onus is on them to look for a job, and many feel that career services "needs a lot of improvement," Drucker grads are generally successful in landing positions soon after graduation; over half are employed before they even receive their sheepskin. Top hiring companies include Accenture, Boeing, Deloitte Touche Tohmatsu, Deutsche Bank, Jet Propulsion Laboratory, Johnson & Johnson, Marsh & MacLellan, Northop Grumman, PricewaterhouseCoopers, Rainbird, and Trust Company of the West. A robust 35 percent of Drucker MBAs gain employment outside the U.S.

Location and Environment

"Life at Drucker is school, school, school, and a little playing on the side," students tell us, noting that theirs is not an especially cohesive student body. One MBA explains, "There are three groups of students at Drucker: (1) people who work part-time and spend little time at the school outside of class, (2) international students who keep to themselves largely, and (3) a small group of full-time students who spend large amounts of time at school. The three groups co-exist, but do not interact too often outside of class, resulting in a school culture that lacks strong cohesion." Yet, despite this, students say their peers are "generally very friendly" and that here, "everyone knows your name."

MARIAESTELLA L. CUARA, RECRUITING & ADMISSIONS COORDINATOR
1021 NORTH DARTMOUTH AVENUE, CLAREMONT, CA 91711 UNITED STATES
PHONE: 909-607-7811 • FAX: 909-607-9104
E-MAIL: DRUCKER@CGU.EDU • WEBSITE: WWW.DRUCKER.CGU.EDU

The school's premium location helps make up for any lack of social life within the Drucker universe. Claremont is "one hour from the beach, 45 minutes from downtown Los Angeles, 40 minutes from skiing, and 20 minutes from great golf. Because there are so many activities around here, we can do many things during the two years." Claremont is also "very conducive to weekend getaways. Last semester I took weekend trips with fellow students to San Francisco, San Diego, Las Vegas, and Palm Springs. There is also something incredible about being within an hour of the beach, the mountains, or the desert." The location also allows for "network opportunities with other Southern CA MBA programs (USC, UCLA, UCI, and Pepperdine)." The town of Claremont itself is "laid back and mellow" and excellent for studying.

Claremont Graduate University is part of the Claremont Consortium, which includes five undergraduate colleges (Claremont McKenna, with its exceptional economics department; Harvey Mudd, an excellent engineering school; all-female Scripps College; Pomona College; and Pitzer) and the Keck Graduate Institute, "which is very popular and gaining industry recognition in leaps and bounds for its research and quality of students who are management-oriented scientists." MBAs tell us that "intellectually, there are a lot of opportunities here for stimulation between events offered at Drucker, events offered by the other colleges at CGU, and events offered by the other schools that comprise the Claremont Consortium."

Admissions

Drucker's admissions committee "evaluates the whole individual rather than focusing on any single area." It considers GMAT scores, college transcript, three letters of recommendation, a personal statement (in 2004, the statement prompt asked students to identify what they would contribute to the school, and also to recount a previous ethical dilemma and their solution), and "leadership potential as indicated by experience (resume) and/or references." Interviews are required of all applicants by invitation. Minority recruitment is facilitated through "the Albrecht Endowed Fellowship, awarded to students who demonstrate academic and professional potential and financial need; other minority funding sources are available."

FINANCIAL FACTS

Annual tuition	$37,614
Fees	$250
Books and supplies	$1,500
Room & board (on/off-campus)	$12,000/$13,000
% of students receiving aid	67
% of first-year students receiving aid	54
Average award package	$15,000
Average grant	$6,800
Average student loan debt	$42,686

ADMISSIONS

Admissions Selectivity Rating	86
# of applications received	200
% applicants accepted	50
% acceptees attending	68
Average GMAT	600
Range of GMAT	555-640
Average GPA	3.2
TOEFL Required of International Students?	Yes
Minimum TOEFL (paper/computer)	600/250
Application fee	$55
International application fee	$55
Regular application deadline	Rolling
Regular notification	Rolling
Deferment Available?	Yes
Maximum length of deferment	2 semesters
Transfer students accepted?	Yes
Transfer application policy: The maximum number of transferable credits is 10 units.	
Non-fall admissions?	Yes
Need-blind admissions?	Yes

APPLICANTS ALSO LOOK AT

Pepperdine University, University of California—Irvine, University of California—Los Angeles, University of Southern California

EMPLOYMENT PROFILE

Career Rating	71	Grads employed by field	%: avg. salary
# of companies recruiting on-campus	84	Finance	24
% grads employed immediately	52	Human Resources	4
Average starting salary	$68,857	Marketing	33
		MIS	5
		Operations	5
		Consulting	12
		General Management	4
		Venture Capital	4
		Other	4
		Non-profit	5

CLARK UNIVERSITY
GRADUATE SCHOOL OF MANAGEMENT

GENERAL INFORMATION
Type of school	private
Environment	city
Academic calendar	semester

SURVEY SAYS...
Friendly students
Happy students
Smart classrooms
Solid preparation in:
Teamwork
Communication/interpersonal skills
Doing business in a global economy

STUDENTS
Enrollment of parent institution	3,115
Enrollment of MBA program	317
% male/female	57/43
% part-time	49
% minorities	5
% international	70
Average age at entry	27
Average years work experience at entry	4.50

ACADEMICS
Academic Experience Rating	**66**
Student/faculty ratio	14:1
Profs interesting rating	72
Profs accessible rating	80

Academics

A small MBA program with a strong finance department, Clark University's Graduate School of Management combines intimacy with the resources of a major university. Students approve, telling us that "the smaller size of the program is really a plus. As a student, you do not feel like a number or a dollar sign. Faculty actually know who you are and where your interests are." The small classes also mean that "students are able to initiate and put into action new ideas. Entrepreneurs and self-starters can really excel here."

Clark's professors "are wonderful. Their main focus is not lecturing and leaving once the class is over, but rather making sure everyone is understanding [the material]. They encourage questions to be asked throughout the class and will gladly provide outside classroom help for those who request it." The administration "is also quite helpful. They will go out of their way to help with questions or problems." Students approve of Clark's general philosophy regarding the academic grind, telling us that "Clark is a reality school. It's not a place where people expect the impossible just because it will be a learning experience or are unwilling to help you out for the same reason. The entire school is a team, working to prepare every graduate for excellence in the future. If you work hard and get things done as required and on time and are communicating with whomever is necessary, then people are willing to help you and problem-solve when you need it."

Of course, small programs also have their drawbacks, such as "too few elective courses" and relatively slow tech upgrades. Some students also feel "The business school is very isolated, and it would be better to integrate the other graduate schools on campus with our own." Despite these drawbacks, though, most students are satisfied; as one student puts it, "I am confident I will leave here with the tools necessary to succeed in my chosen field."

Career and Placement

Clark University's Career Center trains MBAs in "the career development process of matching skills, interests, and values to career fields and occupations" and teaches students job-research skills, resume-writing techniques, and interviewing dos and don'ts through a series of seminars and mock interviews. Clark's website notes that the Graduate School of Management is "a small business school focused on individual students [that is] able to adapt to your career goals whether you are planning a mid-career change or are in the early stages of launching your professional life."

Companies that most often hire Clark MBAs include Anheuser-Busch; Bloomberg, L.P.; Deutsche Bank; EMC; Fallon Health Care System; the Federal Reserve Bank; KPMG; Lucent Technologies; Priceline.com; and the Worcester Art Museum. Many Clark MBAs go on to jobs outside the country, most likely due to the high number of full-time international MBAs.

Student Life and Environment

With a huge international student population, Clark's Graduate School of Management offers students a useful "diversity of different cultures. The different perspectives on business and ethics are very valuable. I feel especially for American citizens that many good lessons are learned in and out of the classroom." As one student explains, "In times when globalization is one of the main features of modern business, the impact of the

PATRICIA TOLLO, DIRECTOR OF ADMISSION,GRADUATE SCHOOL OF MANAGEMEN
950 MAIN STREET, WORCESTER, MA 01610 UNITED STATES
PHONE: 508-793-7406 • FAX: 508-793-8822
E-MAIL: CLARKMBA@CLARKU.EDU • WEBSITE: WWW.CLARKU.EDU/GSOM

diverse student community on future business leaders cannot be overestimated." The school highlights its diversity by sponsoring a variety of international dinners throughout the school year.

The dinners are just one of many activities that fill Clark MBAs' extracurricular schedules. The school "has a terrific student council that plans social activities for MBA students. The events are very popular" and quite numerous. One student recounts, "in the fall we went on two hiking trips, had a Halloween Party, attended professional sports games, went to Six Flags Amusement park, and went on ski trips, just to name a few. This spring already planned are whitewater rafting, a trip to Boston to see the Blue Man Group, a Harlem Globetrotters basketball game, a Red Sox game, an end-of-the-year banquet, and more hiking and skiing trips. There's a lot to do, if someone is willing to participate." As if that weren't enough, MBAs are "also having private parties and casual get-togethers on their own." As one MBA sums up, "This school [focuses on] more than just study. [It includes] students' lives, friendships, interesting work, and joy."

Business-related extracurriculars, however, are a little harder to come by; many MBAs complain that the school needs "more business clubs [and] more visits from business leaders who aren't alumni." Some MBAs see the student body as another shortcoming; while they appreciate the international influence, they think that many of their classmates lack the necessary experience to contribute in the classroom. "The school should consider admitting only students with a minimum of two years' of work experience to enhance class quality," is how one MBA put it. Another MBA notes, "The students are quite immature. Many of them are fifth-year students [i.e., BA/MBA dual-degree students] who are earning a grad degree for free."

Clark's campus earns high marks. MBAs describe it as "attractive and well maintained. The classrooms are comfortable and conducive to learning." Worcester, on the other hand, "is not up to par, and social life is limited to our immediate neighborhood."

Admissions

Clark offers applicants an unusual option: The school accepts either the GMAT or the GRE, to add diversity to the applicant pool. The program, Clark's website notes, benefits from "the fresh perspective that liberal arts and social science undergraduates bring to our classroom." All applicants must also submit an undergraduate transcript, a personal statement, two letters of recommendation, TOEFL scores (for international applicants) and a resume. Interviews are optional. The standardized-test requirement is automatically waived for any applicant holding a PhD, MD, or JD.

FINANCIAL FACTS

Annual tuition	$18,130
Fees	$695
Books and supplies	$800
Room & board (on/off-campus)	$8,400/$9,000
% of students receiving aid	35
% of first-year students receiving aid	32
% of students receiving grants	35
Average award package	$7,600
Average grant	$6,700

ADMISSIONS

Admissions Selectivity Rating	68
# of applications received	275
% applicants accepted	83
% acceptees attending	42
Average GMAT	542
Average GPA	3.12
TOEFL Required of International Students?	Yes
Minimum TOEFL (paper/computer)	550/213
Application fee	$50
International application fee	$50
Regular application deadline	6/1
Regular notification	Rolling
Deferment Available?	Yes
Maximum length of deferment	1 year
Transfer students accepted?	Yes
Transfer application policy: A maximum of two courses may be transferred into the program. Courses must have been taken at an AACSB accredited school. Additional courses taken on the graduate level may be applicable to course waivers.	
Non-fall admissions?	Yes
Need-blind admissions?	Yes

APPLICANTS ALSO LOOK AT

Babson College, Bentley College, Boston University, Northeastern University, Rochester Institute of Technology, Suffolk University.

EMPLOYMENT PROFILE

Career Rating	81
Placement rate (%)	95

CLARKSON UNIVERSITY
SCHOOL OF BUSINESS

Academics

Clarkson University is best known for its fine engineering programs, so it should come as no surprise that the focus at Clarkson University School of Business is on developing business acumen in engineers. Students recognize what makes their school special, telling us, "Clarkson's academic record is outstanding. It is a competitive engineering school with a growing business program." The curriculum stresses a creative approach to problem-solving typically associated with advanced engineers; as one student puts it, "The program's greatest strength is its emphasis on quality of work and its ability to get you to see beyond the surface of a particular subject or problem. Clarkson has made me a better strategic thinker." The school's "strong industry connections [and] good reputation in the technology world" are particularly valuable to those seeking to break into the business side of engineering.

Clarkson MBAs are anxious to get their degrees and move on, and the school's accelerated one-year program suits their needs perfectly. One MBA writes, "The one-year program is perfect in that it is economically sound and academically challenging." Another student adds, "The workload is intense, [with] a strong stress on the team-based experience." Students feel that "the group-work emphasis will help in future employment. And the fast pace and large workload proves [their] ability to work under pressure."

Two "Focus Weeks" shuffled into the academic calendar help slow the breakneck pace. In the fall semester, it's L.E.A.D Week, a leadership development program that uses videotaped simulations designed to help MBAs "develop meta-competencies in giving and receiving performance-related feedback." Springtime brings Perspectives Week, during which alumni return to campus to deliver speeches and provide networking opportunities. Student teams make presentations to panels of professors and alumni during this program.

Clarkson MBAs praise the faculty, reporting that "professors are incredibly concerned with student progress. They are very accessible outside the classroom and more than willing to start up conversations in the middle of a hallway with any student." However, "they will not tell you the way to succeed. All they will do is guide you in your search to find success." In this way, "the faculty at Clarkson treat their students as equals," which MBAs appreciate.

Career and Placement

Clarkson MBAs receive career services from the university's Career Center, which serves all students at the university. The Center schedules career fairs each semester (which draw between 80 and 90 recruiting companies), helps students contact Clarkson's alumni network, and provides students with access to the online job database MonsterTrak. MBAs give the office mixed reviews, telling us, "Clarkson gets many companies to the career fair; however, most are engineering firms. They could try to get more business-related type firms." Some students praise the "many helpful resources such as e-recruiting" provided.

Clarkson MBAs most frequently find work with Accenture, Cooper Industries, Frito-Lay, GE, Household International, IBM, Knowledge Systems and Research, Northwestern Mutual, Texas Instruments, and Whiting-Turner. About three-quarters remain in the region after graduation.

BRENDA KOZSAN, ASSOCIATE DIRECTOR OF GRADUATE PROGRAMS
CU BOX 5770, POTSDAM, NY 13699 UNITED STATES
PHONE: 315-268-6613 • FAX: 315-268-3810
E-MAIL: BUSGRAD@CLARKSON.EDU • WEBSITE: WWW.CLARKSON.EDU/BUSINESS/GRADUATE

Student Life and Environment

Clarkson's predominantly full-time student body tell us that there's a predictable rhythm to their school days. "In the MBA program, you are generally on campus from 8 AM until 6 or 7 PM. There is a lot of work and a lot of meetings to attend with group members," explains one student. Students needn't brave the rugged Potsdam winters during the day because "all classes are taken in one single building." The b-school facility "is very business-like. There are multiple computer labs as well as student lounges to relax. Multiple 'Learning Development Labs' are available for students to work quietly in throughout each day. It feels more like entering a business than classrooms. It helps one become more productive."

Potsdam, of course, is hardly a bustling metropolis. The closest large city is Ottawa, which lies approximately 90 miles and one international border to the north. Students warn that "it is cold for most of the year [and that] there are only about three bars in town, which are shared with a local SUNY school. Unless you skate or enjoy winter sports, there isn't much else in Potsdam to do." Another MBA puts it more bluntly: "The night life is terrible here in Potsdam, NY. There is really nothing to do here."

Some students, however, manage to see the glass as half-full instead of half-empty. One optimist reports that "a vast diversity of sports, intramurals, and clubs allow students to keep busy outside of class and to socialize with their peers. A vast majority of the students are involved in an activity of one sort or another." Fortunately for all, Clarkson's accelerated one-year program keeps most students too busy to worry about what type of fun they are, or are not, missing. Students work hard all week long and through much of the weekend as well. One MBA explains, "Weekends are spent doing work all day long. You go out with friends one night a week on the weekend; that's about it."

Admissions

The admissions department at Clarkson University requires that applicants submit an undergraduate transcript, GMAT scores, TOEFL scores, and a Test of Spoken English (TSE) (for international students whose native language is not English; the TSE can be administered via telephone), a detailed resume, two one-page essays on assigned topics (both autobiographical), and three letters of reference. Awards of merit-based scholarships are determined during the admissions process; no separate application is required. Those requiring foundation course work prior to commencing their MBAs "may enroll in the courses at Clarkson before entering the advanced MBA program. For students doing graduate work at another university, they are allowed to transfer in nine credit hours of graduate work."

FINANCIAL FACTS

Annual tuition	$28,105
Fees	$215
Books and supplies	$2,000
Room & board	$7,000
% of students receiving aid	85
% of first-year students receiving aid	85
% of students receiving loans	75
% of students receiving grants	85
Average award package	$7,000
Average grant	$5,000
Average student loan debt	$29,920

ADMISSIONS

Admissions Selectivity Rating	79
# of applications received	155
% applicants accepted	55
% acceptees attending	81
Average GMAT	528
Range of GMAT	460-590
Average GPA	3.3
TOEFL Required of International Students?	Yes
Minimum TOEFL (paper/computer)	600/250
Application fee	$25
International application fee	$35
Regular application deadline	Rolling
Regular notification	Rolling
Deferment Available?	Yes
Maximum length of deferment	1 year
Transfer students accepted?	Yes

Transfer application policy: Graduate students who need to complete foundation coursework may eoll in the courses at Clarkson before entering the advanced MBA program. For students doing graduate work at another university, they are allowed to transfer in up to 9 credit hours of graduate work.

Non-fall admissions?	Yes
Need-blind admissions?	Yes

APPLICANTS ALSO LOOK AT

Binghamton University—State University of New York, Rensselaer Polytechnic Institute, Rochester Institute of Technology, Syracuse University, University of Rochester.

EMPLOYMENT PROFILE

Career Rating	77	Grads employed by field	%: avg. salary
Placement rate (%)	90	Finance	4: $62,500
# of companies recruiting on-campus	85	Marketing	13: $49,000
% grads employed immediately	48	MIS	10: $56,667
Average starting salary	$57,000	Operations	4: $57,000
		Consulting	35: $54,722
		General Management	16: $53,500
		Other	8: $48,903

THE COLLEGE OF WILLIAM & MARY
SCHOOL OF BUSINESS ADMINISTRATION

Academics

In a small community like the College of William & Mary's School of Business Administration, it's no surprise that students consider their fellow scholars and faculty members their most valuable commodity. "The professors are class acts," says one MBA. "They know their subject matter and always make themselves available for further help." Another student adds, "Their energy is mind-boggling."

An already-intimate experience is made even more so through the teams into which first-year students are divided. Teams are designed to be diverse and aim to reflect varying strengths and the realities of today's workplace. As the school's website states, "as in today's corporate culture, your first-year team must work together to succeed." And cooperation begins with an outdoor obstacle course on the first day of orientation. Something's working, though, because throughout the two-year program, students tend to work with one another instead of against. "The environment is supportive and not as competitive as I assume other schools to be," says one student. "From the first day of class, we were told that we were not each other's competition—every other MBA from every other program was. I dig that." Another student says, "The atmosphere isn't set-up for competition. I don't know who's at the top of my class, and frankly I don't care. Nor have I talked to anyone that does."

On one hand, electives aren't an option until the spring semester of the first year, at which point students select two six-week electives designed to prepare them for their summer internships. On the other hand, the key word for the second year is "focus." The School of Business Administration expects its students to choose targeted, advanced-level electives with a specific career in mind. Though in this year electives span seven major categories—accounting, finance and economics, marketing, information technology, operations and quantitative methods, organizational behavior and human resource management, and the environment of business—many students feel "the number of electives is a bit limited."

One oft-touted program at William & Mary is the Executive Partners mentoring program. One student says, "Williamsburg is a popular retirement location for senior executives, and many of them want to give back to the school. They mentor students, help with networking, and provide valuable input during projects." The retired executives work on a volunteer basis, and there are about 100 of them available to students at any given point.

As one student says, "William & Mary is very focused on providing its students with international business experience through short, intensive visits and exchange programs." In addition to hosting a student body which is about 40 percent international, William & Mary has an exchange program with Otto Beisheim Graduate School in Koblenz, Germany (for summer or semester-long programs) and a briefer program in Paris (summer only).

Career and Placement

Unfortunately, career services appears to be the department which most students target as needing the most work. One student says, "There's not a big variety of companies recruiting on campus; it's hard to get internship placement due to the school small-town location." New direction, however, may improve the quality, and several students have

KATHY WILLIAMS PATTISON, DIRECTOR, MBA ADMISSIONS
PO BOX 8795, WILLIAMSBURG, VA 23187 UNITED STATES
PHONE: 757-221-2900 • FAX: 757-221-2958
E-MAIL: ADMISSIONS@BUSINESS.WM.EDU • WEBSITE: HTTP://MBA.WM.EDU

high hopes. "I expect it will be much stronger next year," says one. In the past, however, students have compensated for the weakness of career services by getting involved in the Executive Partners mentoring program. Contact with retired executives has enabled many students to get jobs or internships at big-name firms.

Student Life and Admissions

William & Mary has the unusual luck of being located in tiny historic Williamsburg, not far from the metropolitan area of Washington, DC. Students rave about the "breathtaking scenery" and the comforts of living in a small town. In such a town, students are "intimately involved in the community and feel accepted by most of the residents." Others agree, adding, "You do not feel like a number here." But even the quaint beauty of historic Williamsburg "can get old in a hurry. Clearly, there's a lack of places to hang out in this town." One of the most popular, however, is Green Leafe, a bar across the street from the business school, where students often meet on Thursday evenings to relax and kick off a three-day weekend of studying. Though some chafe at the small size of the town, most students agree, "This environment does have many benefits. It allows students to focus on their studies and also get to know their fellow classmates." In addition, with over 20 different countries represented on the business-administration school campus (ranging from Belarus to Thailand, from China to Peru), William & Mary isn't quite the provincial backwater some outsiders would claim.

One weakness on which the school is working on is the facilities. Parking is limited, and "we don't have lockers, classrooms are packed, and we often are forced to drive to a satellite campus, which is 30 minutes away," one student reports. Still, the school is raising funds for a new business-school building, which will "provide better facilities for current students (i.e., more study rooms) and attract more applicants to the school."

Admissions

At William & Mary, admissions look for students who can display a "wide range of academic fields and professional experiences [and] who demonstrate strong leadership skills and have clear professional goals." Only about 70 to 80 students meet these qualifications each year, and 43 percent of those are international students. The range of GMAT scores for accepted applicants in 2004 was 500 to 730, and the average was 593. Foreign students who have worked in the U.S. for two or more years (full-time) or who have received a degree at an English-speaking university are not required to submit TOEFL scores. For those who did take it, though, the average score for the computer-based test was 263 and 623 for the paper-based test.

FINANCIAL FACTS

Annual tuition (in-state/out-of-state)	$15,266/$27,938
Books and supplies	$1,500
Room & board	$8,330
% of students receiving aid	70
% of first-year students receiving aid	62
% of students receiving loans	39
% of students receiving grants	23
Average award package	$21,012
Average grant	$7,935
Average student loan debt	$23,150

ADMISSIONS

Admissions Selectivity Rating	74
# of applications received	249
% applicants accepted	68
% acceptees attending	36
Average GMAT	593
Range of GMAT	500-730
TOEFL Required of International Students?	Yes
Minimum TOEFL (paper/computer)	600/250
Application fee	$100
International application fee	$100
Regular application deadline	3/15
Regular notification	Rolling
Application Deadline	
Round 1:	11/15
Round 2:	1/15
Round 3:	3/15
Round 4:	5/15
Early decision program?	Yes
ED Deadline/Notification	11/15 / 1/1
Deferment Available?	Yes
Maximum length of deferment	1 year
Need-blind admissions?	Yes

APPLICANTS ALSO LOOK AT

Georgetown University, University of Maryland—College Park, University of North Carolina at Chapel Hill, University of Virginia, Vanderbilt University, Wake Forest University—Full-time MBA Program.

EMPLOYMENT PROFILE

		Grads employed by field	%: avg. salary
Career Rating	76		
Placement rate (%)	72	Finance	46: $69,238
% grads employed immediately	46	Marketing	16: $69,125
% grads employed within three months	72	Consulting	26: $77,364
Average starting salary	$72,185	Global Management	8: $71,875

COLORADO STATE UNIVERSITY
COLLEGE OF BUSINESS

GENERAL INFORMATION
Type of school   public
Environment   city
Academic calendar   August-May

SURVEY SAYS...
Friendly students
Good peer network
Cutting edge classes
Happy students
Solid preparation in:
Teamwork

STUDENTS
Enrollment of parent
  institution   25,042
Enrollment of MBA program   399
% male/female   61/39
% out-of-state   27
% part-time   100
% minorities   11
Average age at entry   36
Average years work experience
  at entry   12

ACADEMICS
Academic Experience Rating   88
Student/faculty ratio   30:1
Profs interesting rating   90
Profs accessible rating   82
% female faculty   34

Academics

A distance learning leader, Colorado State University has consistently endeavored to deliver one of the best distance-learning MBAs in the country. Its efforts seem to have paid off. Students in the program agree that "the CSU School of Business is an innovator in distance-learning techniques; it has worked the kinks out both academically and operationally." The school also offers a part-time evening MBA program. Both the evening and the distance-learning MBA are "comprehensive lock-step programs" that are identical in content.

Here's how the CSU MBA works: part-time MBAs attend classes on campus once a week per course taken. (Students on the two-year plan take two classes per semester, as well as those on the four-year plan.) Classes are taped, burned to DVD, and sent to students in the distance-learning program. Distance learners tell us that their program "seems less 'distancy' because of the recorded lectures on DVD and the fact that we have the identical pace and curriculum as the on-campus students." Students in both programs keep in touch with their professors and each other through Embanet, a communications software product that allows professors to post assignments and students to complete projects in a virtual meeting space. One student writes, "The program requires extensive use of work teams in a virtual environment, which is 100 percent what a graduate will likely experience in today's business world, because most coworkers will be located in another building, state, time zone, or country."

Whether they complete the program on campus or at home, students enjoy a curriculum that "is not just theory, but very heavy on application. What is taught has immediate applications at my job." comments one working student. CSU professors "are tough and require a heavy workload," but they are also "understanding of the demands on part-time students" and can be "flexible with emergencies." They "teach cutting-edge theory and practice" and are informed by their own experience in the business world. "All professors have worked or are currently working in the industry they are teaching us about. The adjunct professors are also well qualified and put a tremendous amount of time into the students." Accounting, economics, and finance are reportedly the faculty's strongest areas. Perhaps the greatest drawback of the program is that it offers only a general MBA. One student explains, "The school does not offer electives, only core courses." Nearly all students here agree that CSU's strengths far outweigh its weaknesses, however; sums up one MBA, "The school is very ambitious and works hard to create a program that really serves the business students. It is an outstanding program."

Career and Placement

The part-time nature of CSU's MBA program is designed for working professionals, who comprise the vast majority of the student body. The school maintains a Career Center Liaison to coordinate activities between the College of Business and the university's Career Center, but the responsibilities of this office are primarily aimed at serving undergraduates. This doesn't have much of an impact on MBAs, however, since most CSU MBAs already have good jobs with such powerhouses as Agilent, Argen, Celestica, Colgate-Palmolive, ConAgra, FedEx, Hewlett-Packard, Honeywell, MCI WorldCom, National Textiles, the Parson Group, Siemens, Sun Microsystems, UPS, and Wells Fargo Bank.

RACHEL STOLL, GRADUATE ADMISSIONS COORDINATOR
160 ROCKWELL HALL, FORT COLLINS, CO 80523-1201 UNITED STATES
PHONE: 970-491-3704 • FAX: 970-491-2348
E-MAIL: RACHEL.STOLL@COLOSTATE.EDU • WEBSITE: WWW.BIZ.COLOSTATE.EDU

FINANCIAL FACTS

Annual tuition (in-state/out-of-state)	
	$8,100/$1,900
Books and supplies	$1,800

ADMISSIONS

Admissions Selectivity Rating	87
# of applications received	222
% applicants accepted	60
% acceptees attending	88
Average GMAT	640
Average GPA	3.2
TOEFL Required of	
International Students?	Yes
Minimum TOEFL	
(paper/computer)	565/227
Application fee	$50
Regular application deadline	7/15
Regular notification	Rolling
Deferment Available?	Yes
Maximum length of	
deferment	1 year
Transfer students accepted?	Yes
Transfer application policy: No	
transfer credits are accepted.	
Non-fall admissions?	Yes
Need-blind admissions?	Yes

Student Life and Environment

Nestled in the foothills of the Rockies "with a beautiful view," Colorado State University "is a thriving, vibrant community" of 24,000 students, 1,550 faculty, and numerous administrators and employees. The school offers "great access to many academic and social venues, and a pleasant campus atmosphere that supports learning." Taking advantage of these proves "a little tough for older students. Within the MBA program, people are juggling so many balls that they hardly have time to partake." Those who can manage a few free moments enjoy and appreciate the "strong clubs and activities [and] plenty of intramural sports." Many distance students "never visit the campus at all," however.

Among the on-campus student body, "work experiences vary from vet students to engineers in high-tech companies to nurses and general mangers at Fortune 100 companies." One MBA writes, "There are even some students who work for not-for-profit firms, which adds yet another level of interest to class discussions and the overall quality of the program at Colorado State University." One student notes, however, that "the program does attract a lot of professional engineers. I wish there were more variety in terms of work experience." A solid mix of international MBAs includes "students from Asia, Latin America, and Canada." Distance learners come "from all types of backgrounds and from all over the place." The average age of students is around 35, and the typical CSU student has about 10 to 15 years of work experience.

Admissions

CSU admits on-campus MBAs in the fall only; distance learners are admitted for either the fall or the spring semester. All applicants must submit a completed application form, a resume, a cover letter, an official GMAT score report, two copies of official transcripts for all post-secondary academic work, and three recommendations. Applicants whose native language is not English must also submit an official TOEFL score report. According to the school's website, CSU looks to "select a richly diverse set of students with various undergraduate degrees and professional experiences. Additional requirements include a minimum of four years post-undergraduate professional work experience, Previous academic performance, GMAT scores, work experience and recommendations are some of the factors considered. In addition, the applicant's personal cover letter should reflect carefully considered reasons for pursuing a business degree at the master's level." Applicants with GPAs below 3.0 must include a letter explaining the circumstances under which they received such grades.

EMPLOYMENT PROFILE	
Career Rating	60*
Placement rate (%)	95

COLUMBIA UNIVERSITY
COLUMBIA BUSINESS SCHOOL

Academics

"No other school offers the same caliber of professors, students, varied curriculum, work-life balance, dedication to the local community, and connections and exposure to both the for-profit and nonprofit worlds" as does Columbia, graduate business students at this New York City stalwart tell us. A high-profile program in America's highest-profile city, Columbia offers the kind of MBA program where "it is an everyday occurrence to see a New York Times real estate article in which your professor is quoted, learn from a Nobel Prize-winning economist, and attend lectures given by CEOs from Fortune 100 companies."

Columbia "excels across academic programs," with solid offerings in finance, marketing, real estate, and management. Students are especially enthusiastic about the unique Social Enterprise program, which places social impact on equal footing with the bottom line; the program provides excellent training for those interested in government or the nonprofit sector. Students also single out the Media program, another unusual offering; the program benefits heavily from the concentration of media outlets in and around New York City.

Columbia's core curriculum occupies most of a student's first year, accounting for 45 percent of credits required for the degree. Students agree that the core is the school's weakest aspect; while appreciating the integrated design of the core, many here feel its execution could be better. One student writes, "With the core, the faculty are either extremely talented or extremely poor. There's little consistency and no middle ground. Core professors are generally not as good at teaching the 'soft courses.'" Things improve as students move on to electives, where "at least 80 percent of the professors fall into the 'fully committed' and 'engaging' categories." Through both years of the program, "Students are amazingly respectful of each other in the classroom setting and offer real-world experience that enriches every lesson plan." Students also appreciate that "the administration is responsive and attentive to the needs of the student body, and tremendously supportive of career and community-service activities."

Career and Placement

The MBA Career Services Office (CSO) at Columbia benefits from a propitious location in the financial capital of the world. The office helps students coordinate internship and employment searches and also provides "a range of complementary resources..., from intimate workshops on interviewing and presentation skills to a five-part course on different aspects of the job," according to the School's website. The CSO also draws from the region's many business leaders for lectures, seminars, and panel discussions. The School reports that "Hundreds of employers actively recruit at Columbia Business School each year, conducting thousands of on-campus interviews and numerous corporate presentations. Columbia also receives thousands of job postings for off-campus full-time and intern positions."

Nearly half the class of 2004 landed in the finance sector, and basically all graduates enjoyed handsome starting salaries. Top employers include: American Express; Bank of America; Booz Allen Hamilton; Citigroup; Deutsche Bank; Goldman, Sachs & Company, Inc.; McKinsey & Company; JPMorgan Chase; Lehman Brothers; and Morgan Stanley.

LINDA MEEHAN, ASSISTANT DEAN FOR ADMISSIONS
3022 BROADWAY, URIS HALL, ROOM 216, NEW YORK, NY 10027 UNITED STATES
PHONE: 212-854-1961 • FAX: 212-662-6754
E-MAIL: APPLY@CLAVEN.GSB.COLUMBIA.EDU • WEBSITE: WWW.GSB.COLUMBIA.EDU

Student Life and Environment

Life at the Columbia Business School is busy, with "a diversity of clubs across all interest areas that, if anything, provide too many options." Then, of course, there's New York City, with its fabulous cultural outlets, world-class eateries, and endless selection of entertainment options. Observes one student, "Since a lot of students are coming from the city, they have lives outside of just the school social scene, which for me is good. We are in New York City so I think it is important to take advantage of that." Sums up another, "Columbia offers its students the greatest work-life balance. We work hard, party hard, volunteer our time in the community, explore New York City, and easily maintain groups of friends both within and outside the business school."

Columbia's campus is located in Morningside Heights, directly north of Manhattan's Upper West Side. The once run-down neighborhood has undergone quite a makeover in the last decade and is now a much more fashionable and expensive address. The enclosed campus runs eight city blocks, small by any standards other than New York's but absolutely expansive compared to, say, NYU. The b-school facilities "don't have enough space, but they're addressing that." Everyone agrees that Columbia's gym "is just terrible;" most prefer jogging in nearby Riverside Park to working out at the gym.

The student body here is "extremely diverse and interesting, international and helpful." The program's high degree of selectiveness ensures that all are accomplished, motivated, and talented. One MBA writes, "The students at Columbia are some of the most well rounded, worldly, tolerant, intelligent, self-motivated, and fun people I've ever met. Beyond all of Columbia's amazing attributes, the students may be the biggest draw to the business school."

Admissions

So you want to be a Columbia MBA? So do a lot of people, making Columbia one of the hardest graduate business schools to gain admission to. In selecting applicants for admission, the school reports that "By design, efforts are made to admit students who add different perspectives to the learning experience. In this way, students are continually learning from the diverse professional experiences and cultural/geographical backgrounds of their classmates. Columbia Business School has also maintained, through a concerted strategic effort, one of the highest enrollments of women and underrepresented minorities among top business schools. In addition, the Office of Admissions, in conjunction with the School's Black Business Students Association, Hispanic Business Association, and African American Alumni Association, sponsors information sessions and receptions for prospective students."

FINANCIAL FACTS

Annual tuition	$36,296
Fees	$2,479
Books and supplies	$1,134
Room & board	$17,820
% of students receiving aid	71

ADMISSIONS

Admissions Selectivity Rating	99
# of applications received	4,871
% applicants accepted	15
% acceptees attending	71
Average GMAT	709
Range of GMAT	660-760
Average GPA	3.4
TOEFL Required of International Students?	Yes
Application fee	$215
International application fee	$215
Regular application deadline	4/20
Regular notification	Rolling
Early decision program?	Yes
ED Deadline/Notification	10/15 / 12/30
Non-fall admissions?	Yes
Need-blind admissions?	Yes

APPLICANTS ALSO LOOK AT

Harvard University, Stanford University, University of Pennsylvania.

EMPLOYMENT PROFILE			
Career Rating	97	Grads employed by field	%: avg. salary
Placement rate (%)	90	Accounting	1: $125,000
% grads employed immediately	79	Finance	44: $125,267
Average starting salary	$143,682	Human Resources	1: $105,000
		Marketing	10: $94,231
		Strategic Planning	2: $113,675
		Consulting	21: $129,273
		Entrepreneurship	4: $158,167
		General Management	3: $116,200
		Venture Capital	2: $192,456
		Other	8: $109,861
		Non-profit	2: $68,046

Concordia University
John Molson School of Business

Academics

Students looking for "a family-like atmosphere with an emphasis on practice and real world cases" should consider the MBA program at Concordia University's John Molson School of Business. Here, students receive a solid general education in business principles as well as the opportunity to specialize in accounting, finance, international business, aviation management, investment management, e-business, portfolio management, non-profit, and sport administration. Molson operates on a fast-paced, trimester academic calendar. Classes, given in English only, are scheduled in both daytime and evening time slots on Mondays through Thursdays "to accommodate both the part-time and full-time student body." Summer classes are offered in the evenings only.

With approximately 300 MBAs (split nearly evenly among full-timers and part-timers), Molson can provide each student with whatever he/she needs to maximize his/her education. One MBA notes, "The greatest strength of the school is its cooperative spirit in the administration, faculty, placement center, and fellow students. Whenever you are looking for something or trying to accomplish something, people here have a can-do attitude." Students agree that at Molson "you are not just a number, but a person. Everything is more personal here."

One of the high points of the school's academic year is the International Case Competition, held on campus and billed as "the only truly global case competition in the world." Molson students love it and bemoan only the fact that not everyone can participate. "The school should offer the incredible training that the case competition team gets to everyone," writes one student. "That boot camp-intense training is like putting your MBA skills into overdrive." The Concordia Small Business Consulting Bureau offers students another opportunity to flex their business muscles while helping local businesses fine tune their business plans and reach new consumers.

Molson MBAs praise the curricular mix of "practical and hands-on education with academics, rather than solely case studies or theories," and give their professors high marks, reporting that they "are keen and sharp with a sense of humor and realism about today's challenges. The professors are tough, and we'll do even better when we graduate because of it." Students are less sanguine about the facilities, which "are old and not very comfortable," but point out that "new facilities are under construction and should be ready by 2006–07."

Career and Placement

The Career Placement Centre at John Molson serves both undergraduates and graduates. In fact, "The career center has only recently started to give graduate student-specific seminars," reports one MBA, "but there is still not a different career center for MBAs." The office provides the standard complement of career counseling, guest lectures, mock interviews, job postings, seminars in networking, resume writing, and salary negotiation. Students generally agree it's not enough, complaining about both the number and quality of positions available.

Employers who most frequently hire Molson MBAs include Royal Bank, Bombardier, Air Canada, Merck Frosst, Novartis, TD Bank, Eicon Networks, Cap Gemini, Ernst & Young, and Concordia University, but not, oddly, the Molson Brewery.

LISSA MATYAS, ASSISTANT DIRECTOR
1455 DE MAISONNEUVE BOULEVARD WEST, GM 710 MONTREAL, QC H3G 1M8 CANADA
PHONE: 514-848-2717 • FAX: 514-848-2816
E-MAIL: MBA@JMSB.CONCORDIA.CA • WEBSITE: WWW.JOHNMOLSON.CONCORDIA.CA

Student Life and Environment

Molson MBAs have opportunities to get involved beyond the classroom, as "there is a minimum of one social activity a month (and up to three per month) for students to relax and have fun, such as a Halloween dance, pub night, an apple-picking trip, or wine-tasting. In addition, sports skills such as golf lessons or intro to scuba lessons and other sports are also offered." There are also "plenty of professional extracurricular activities to take part in, [such as] business leaders who are brought in from the community to share their experiences, past and present, [but] it seems like there is a core of 40 students who are active in everything (i.e., making the most out of their MBA) while the remainder only attend class."

The Molson campus "is in downtown Montreal, an amazing city in which to live, and off-campus living is great." As a bonus, Montreal is a major player in international finance, pharmaceutical research, and aerospace development, providing lots of internship and placement opportunities for MBAs. The urban setting means that "the campus is not that attractive, but there are lots of possibilities to socialize outside of school. The student life is influenced by the Montreal lifestyle . . . it is not just work." Students complain that the campus "is lacking in open space where the students can sit down together, and the graduate lounge is often overcrowded," but they expect that the new b-school facility will remedy these problems.

"'Multicultural diversity' is the best way to describe what makes the difference in the Concordia MBA program," writes one student, alluding to the UN-style mix that constitutes the Molson student body. About one-third of the students are Canadian; nearly as many are Chinese, and as many again hail from Europe. American students typically make up about three percent of the student body. One MBA opines, "The value of the program is greatly enhanced by the cumulative experiences of people coming from all parts of the world. Since people from Montreal are accustomed to this international environment, one feels really welcome here." Students tend to be "intellectually nimble, trustworthy, and respectful, with diverse professional experiences and a willingness to work cooperatively."

Admissions

Concordia admissions officers seek students with "real-world work experience, strong academic backgrounds, clear career objectives, and a commitment to excellence." Applicants must meet the following minimum requirements: undergraduate GPA of 3.0; two years of full-time work experience; a GMAT score of 600; and, for international students, a TOEFL score of 600 (paper-and-pencil) or 250 (computer-based). Career/leadership potential, level of maturity, communication skills, and how closely the student's goals match the program's are also weighed. Complete applications include a personal essay, a resume, official undergraduate transcripts, at least two letters of recommendation, and test scores.

FINANCIAL FACTS

Annual tuition (in-state/out-of-state)	$1,668/$12,500
Fees (in-state/out-of-state)	$945/$1,000
Books and supplies	$1,000
Room & board (on/off-campus)	$10,000/$11,000
% of students receiving aid	15
% of first-year students receiving aid	15
Average award package	$8,000
Average grant	$9,000

ADMISSIONS

Admissions Selectivity Rating	95
# of applications received	323
% applicants accepted	33
% acceptees attending	49
Average GMAT	662
Range of GMAT	620-690
Average GPA	3.3
TOEFL Required of International Students?	Yes
Minimum TOEFL (paper/computer)	600/250
Application fee	$50
International application fee	$50
Regular application deadline	Rolling
Regular notification	Rolling
Early decision program?	Yes
Deferment Available?	Yes
Maximum length of deferment	1 year
Transfer students accepted?	Yes
Transfer application policy: Applicants may be eligible for advanced standing.	
Non-fall admissions?	Yes
Need-blind admissions?	Yes

APPLICANTS ALSO LOOK AT

McGill University, Queen's University, University of Toronto, University of Western Ontario.

EMPLOYMENT PROFILE	
Career Rating	74
Placement rate (%)	86
% grads employed immediately	41
Average starting salary	$61,427

CORNELL UNIVERSITY
THE JOHNSON GRADUATE SCHOOL OF MANAGEMENT

GENERAL INFORMATION

Type of school	private
Environment	town
Academic calendar	semester

SURVEY SAYS...

Friendly students
Good peer network
Happy students
Smart classrooms
Solid preparation in:
Finance
Teamwork

STUDENTS

Enrollment of parent institution	21,026
Enrollment of MBA program	544
% male/female	72/28
% out-of-state	9
% minorities	6
% international	25
Average age at entry	27
Average years work experience at entry	5

ACADEMICS

Academic Experience Rating	96
Student/faculty ratio	6:1
Profs interesting rating	89
Profs accessible rating	99
% female faculty	22
% minority faculty	21

Joint Degrees

MBA/MILR: 2-3 years
MBA/MEng: 2-3 years
MBA/MA Asian Studies: 3 years
MBA/JD: 4 years
MBA/MPS-RE: 3 years

Prominent Alumni

Jim Morgan '63, Chairman of Applied Materials; Richard Marin '76, Chairman and CEO of Bear Stearns Asset Management; H. Fisk Johnson '84, Chairman of S.C. Johnson and Son.

Academics

Students claim with justified pride that the Johnson School of Management at Cornell University is and always has been a student-focused school. The administration is quick to respond to student suggestions, and "the top five administrators (deans) attend the student-council meetings each week to listen to student feedback and take action items." Academics are "challenging but grounded in reality," and students agree that there is little of the back-stabbing that may go on in other schools. "We are not cutthroat competitors trying to get the best grade we can. We are all successful people, coming together in this challenging and diverse environment to network, learn, and further ourselves as leaders for the business world." As one student points out, "All top business schools have great professors and great programs; this one provides an atmosphere of camaraderie and friendship. No other school could offer me that." Still, though the school's community values cooperation and teamwork, "in no way are Cornell MBAs pushovers—we can bring a competitive fight to anyone!"

Among the most unique features of the Johnson School are the voluntary immersion courses taken by students in the spring semester of their first year. According to the school's website, in these courses, "immersion—learning curriculum replaces lecture—and case-based training with integrated, experiential, reality-based learning." Students in immersion courses are asked to solve real business problems in real-world time and are then "evaluated as they would be on the job." The courses "provide a challenge in whatever field you're in, so that you will be well-equipped to handle the pressures of the summer internship." On one hand, immersion courses are among the most popular and do indeed often result in summer internships. "Some recruiters have said this is the primary reason they come to this school to recruit." On the other hand, "choosing an immersion forces you to pick your career rather quickly—perhaps too quickly if you don't know what you want to do just yet."

One benefit of being a part of such a large university is the access students have to other departments. Prospective MBAs brag about the "excellent contact [they have with] other Cornell schools—like the engineering and the hotel schools!" Working with other departments, students can often customize their immersion courses. One student says, "I was interested in real estate and was able to take courses from Cornell's Hotel School, City and Regional Planning Program, and program in real estate."

Career and Placement

Some students feel that Cornell's somewhat remote location prevents companies from visiting, especially in the middle of an Ithaca winter—"cold!"—but the Career Management Center has tried its hardest to make up for that. In 2003 they hired "four corporate jets to fly recruiters from major cities to Ithaca for the day, which resulted in a significant number of summer internships and full-time jobs." Still, some students feel the center could be working harder. "The diversity of companies recruiting on campus could be improved, [and] more high-level speakers could be brought to campus to discuss timely business issues." Others point out that "while top companies from various industries come on campus to recruit, if a student wants to do something outside the norm, it is extremely difficult. A person looking to enter the investment-banking field will have no problem, but if you want investment management, the Career Services Department is lacking."

Nonetheless, the Career Management Center reported that, after graduation, "80 percent of the members of the Class of 2003 who were seeking full-time positions had received at least one offer." And 90 percent of the salaries for those graduates of the class of 2003

Ms. Natalie Grinblatt, Director, Office of Admissions and Financial Aid
111 Sage Hall, Ithaca, New York 14853, NY 14853 United States
Phone: 607-255-4526 • Fax: 607-255-0065
E-mail: mba@cornell.edu • Website: www.johnson.cornell.edu

who were hired fell between $60,000 and $103,000.

Another boon to the program is the strong alumni network. According to most students, the alumni are "in many fields in high positions, and the school brings them back periodically to give inspiring talks. Cornell and Johnson School alumni are extremely helpful—they go out of their way to get involved in career planning and job search."

Student Life and Environment

Located approximately three hours north of New York City, Cornell University is situated in beautiful Ithaca, New York, "a remote place, but a lovely one. The lake and trees provide for a beautiful backdrop in fall." A town of about 30,000, Ithaca is "a bit off the beaten path, but there is a surprisingly high number of outstanding restaurants (thanks to the hotel school)." The small size and the distance from major cities is a drawback for some, but most students, particularly those who've come with families, agree that, though "we might not have as many social options as students in major cities, we definitely have as much fun—we just create it ourselves!" Clubs and teams abound on a campus of about 20,000: "We have a club for everything," students say, "from health care to operations management and from hockey to singing," and there's a happy hour every Thursday.

Unfortunately, what they lack in size, they sometimes also lack in diversity: "Our location and size require that we put forth a more formal effort than schools in large cities, and we should probably do even more to attract candidates from underrepresented groups." On the other hand, their Office of Women and Minorities in Business is largely agreed to be "outstanding in their ability to nurture and support minorities and women in the program, as well as prospective students."

Sage Hall, the main building for the school, is the envy of other departments on campus. Over 100 years old, the building was completely gutted in 1996 and rebuilt "with the latest and greatest technology (wireless in whole building and stadium seating/wireless/LAN connections in classrooms)," while still retaining the beauty of the original structure.

Admissions

According to its admissions office, students admitted to the Johnson School are "not only intelligent and highly professional but can bring a fresh perspective and energy to their interactions with faculty and peers. In addition to a clear record of academic and professional achievement, we value independent thinking, teamwork, and interpersonal skills." All applicants are required to take the GMAT, and those for whom English is not their native language are required to take the TOEFL exam. Prior work experience is strongly recommended.

FINANCIAL FACTS

Annual tuition	$36,350
Fees	$62
Books and supplies	$1,100
Room & board	$9,500
% of students receiving aid	75
% of first-year students receiving aid	77
% of students receiving loans	65
% of students receiving grants	30
Average award package	$39,300
Average grant	$24,000
Average student loan debt	$66,500

ADMISSIONS

Admissions Selectivity Rating	94
# of applications received	1,827
% applicants accepted	36
% acceptees attending	47
Average GMAT	673
Range of GMAT	600-730
Average GPA	3.26
TOEFL Required of International Students?	Yes
Minimum TOEFL (paper/computer)	600/250
Application fee	$180
International application fee	$180
Regular application deadline	3/15
Regular notification	5/31
Application Deadline/Notification	
Round 1:	11/15 / 1/31
Round 2:	1/15 / 3/31
Round 3:	3/15 / 5/31
Round 4:	3/1 / 4/30
Early decision program?	Yes
ED Deadline/Notification	10/15 / 12/15
Non-fall admissions?	Yes
Need-blind admissions?	Yes

APPLICANTS ALSO LOOK AT

Columbia University, Dartmouth College, Harvard University, University of Michigan, University of Pennsylvania.

EMPLOYMENT PROFILE

Career Rating	92	Grads employed by field	%: avg. salary
Placement rate (%)	83	Finance	36: $87,373
% grads employed immediately	64	Marketing	25: $85,896
Average starting salary	$87,831	MIS	1: $97,000
		Operations	2: $81,200
		Consulting	15: $92,686
		General Management	17: $88,615
		Other	4: $79,178

CRANFIELD UNIVERSITY
CRANFIELD SCHOOL OF MANAGEMENT

GENERAL INFORMATION
Type of school	public
Academic calendar	year long

SURVEY SAYS...
Friendly students
Happy students
Solid preparation in:
General management
Teamwork
Communication/interpersonal skills
Presentation skills

STUDENTS
Enrollment of parent institution	
Enrollment of MBA program	205
% male/female	82/18
% part-time	39
% international	60
Average age at entry	31
Average years work experience at entry	8

ACADEMICS
Academic Experience Rating	92
Student/faculty ratio	3:1
Profs interesting rating	94
Profs accessible rating	89
% female faculty	27

Prominent Alumni
Ted Tuppen, CEO Enterprise Inns; Nigel Doughty, CEO Doughty Hanson; John McFarlane, CEO ANZ Banking Grp; Steven Crawshaw, CEO Bradford & Bingley; Michael Wemms, Chairman House of Fraser.

Academics

The Cranfield approach to business education, MBAs at the school tell us, stresses "application rather than pure theory and teamwork rather than individual reward." This intensive program, "is very demanding due to the condensed nature of the course (it covers a traditional U.S. two-year syllabus in 11 months)." It cuts right to the heart of the matter by "focusing on the personal and professional skills that business leaders need. Teamwork, communication, and presentation skills are crucial to the Cranfield experience." As one MBA puts it, "The academic experience at Cranfield is so much more than just a series of business classes. It is a lifestyle and leadership-development course."

Students heap praise on practically every discipline offered at Cranfield, from accounting to finance to supply-chain management. They love that all areas "focus on practical and applied learning, with teaching provided by leading consultants in their field." Professors, "almost all of whom are great teachers with industry experience, which brings real meaning to the case studies and the learning," push students to their limits. As one MBA explains, "We are actively encouraged to do things and to get out of our comfort zone, and I believe that our personal communication and networking skills will be superior as a result."

Cranfield MBAs often work in "learning teams," attacking case studies in three-day cycles; teams start preparing Wednesday's cases on Monday or Thursday's cases on Tuesday, for example. Teams must produce group reports, which earn a single grade for each member; therefore, individuals must work through their differences to present a report that satisfies everyone in the group. This "team approach to assignments teaches us to respect diversity," students tell us. One student explains, "The emphasis on teamwork means that you have to develop good interpersonal skills very quickly." Students also note that "the fact that students have significant work experience (more than seven years on average) helps."

Because of the curriculum's breakneck pace, "the main issue is being able to humanly process all the material!" The reward for all the hard work is "knowing you will be prepared for life after Cranfield." One student analogizes, "Being at Cranfield is like sky diving. It's risky, expensive, and scares the living hell out of you just before you make the leap. But once you have jumped, it's an exhilarating roller coaster of a ride, and I have the feeling that it will all be over too soon and that I will want to do it again."

Career and Placement

Cranfield's careers office supports its MBAs with a variety of services, including a yearbook (distributed to hundreds of recruiters, the book contains all graduates' short resumes), on-campus recruiting events, and career-preparatory workshops. Students can use the careers office to access employer databases, self-assessment instruments, and alumni. This last is considered most valuable by the MBAs we spoke with. One typical survey respondent lauded the "incredible alumni help," reporting, "I contacted several in jobs with a high level of responsibility and mostly received answers within 24 hours!" Students are not entirely sold on the office's efficacy; however, many wish for "a greater diversity of recruiting companies on campus." One student writes, "We need more proactive support by the career center in order to compete with other famous schools located in big cities, especially because this school is not located in a big city." Companies recruiting on the Cranfield campus include Accenture, American Express, Atkins, Bank of Luxembourg, Booz Allen Hamilton, Eli Lilly and Company, General Motors, KPMG, Marconi, Pfizer, Pharmacia, Sir Robert McAlpine Ltd., and Tesco.

Student Life and Environment

Cranfield University "is located in a quiet village, creating a close community where

EILEEN FISHER, ADMISSIONS EXECUTIVE
CRANFIELD SCHOOL OF MANAGEMENT, CRANFIELD, BEDFORD, MK43 0AL ENGLAND
PHONE: 011-440-1234 754431 • FAX: 011-440-1234 752439
E-MAIL: MBAADMISSIONS@CRANFIELD.AC.UK • WEBSITE: WWW.CRANFIELDMBA.INFO

most students live in houses and flats." This isolated locale—"it takes 20 minutes to drive to the nearest supermarket"—means that students must rely on one another for entertainment. Fortunately, "there is no dearth of social events, which more than makes up for the school being in a bit of wilderness." Students tell us, "There are many social activities and opportunities to network with other business schools, such as Oxford, London Business School, Cambridge, and others [as well as tons of] clubs for different sports activities like badminton, basketball, cricket, football, motor sports, scuba diving, sailing, or rugby and others for dancing, jujitsu, or yoga."

Students especially appreciate Cranfield's family-friendly atmosphere, telling us that extracurricular activities "are inclusive of the diverse student population, partners, and families." One MBA notes, "My wife enjoys socializing with other partners, attending the dancing club, and other sports activities such as touch rugby and badminton. My two kids enjoy playing in the safe school playground. They also enjoy [the] various activities arranged by school or student clubs."

There are drawbacks to Cranfield's remote location, of course. Students warn, "You need a car, as public transport in rural England is not great." They also complain that "there are very few options to eat on campus and very little access to options off-campus. Restaurants on campus are closed by 7:30 P.M., further reducing the options for hard-working students."

Cranfield's diverse student body is "a real eye-opener that helps us understand different viewpoints," MBAs tell us, as well as an excellent source of food and entertainment. One student reports, "We recently had international week, with presentations and food given by students from over 10 countries. Our Diwali festival celebration was attended by over 350 people—and there are only 136 students on the course!" Students interact constantly due to the curricular emphasis on teamwork; every term, students "are split into teams consisting of six or seven persons, all mostly of different nationalities."

Admissions

Applicants to Cranfield are required to submit the following to the school's admissions department: undergraduate transcript, GMAT scores, TOEFL scores (for ESL students), a resume demonstrating a minimum of three years' full-time work experience, letters of recommendation, personal essays, and an interview. The school notes that it is possible for applicants lacking undergraduate degrees to gain entrance to the MBA program; such students, however, "all have considerably more than the minimum requirement of three years' work experience" and are required to "prove to the Admissions Board that [they] can cope with the academic side of the work by achieving a GMAT score of 600 or more."

FINANCIAL FACTS

Annual tuition	$46,900
Books and supplies	$938
Room & board	$6,700
% of first-year students receiving aid	18
Average grant	$19,500

ADMISSIONS

Admissions Selectivity Rating	83
# of applications received	348
% applicants accepted	63
% acceptees attending	58
Average GMAT	660
Range of GMAT	630-730
TOEFL Required of International Students?	Yes
Minimum TOEFL (paper/computer)	600/250
Application fee	$140
Regular application deadline	Rolling
Regular notification	Rolling
Deferment Available?	Yes
Maximum length of deferment	2 years

APPLICANTS ALSO LOOK AT

INSEAD, University of Cambridge, University of London, University of Manchester, University of Oxford, University of Warwick.

EMPLOYMENT PROFILE

Career Rating	91	Grads employed by field	%: avg. salary
# of companies recruiting on-campus	60	Accounting	2: $75,340
% grads employed immediately	36	Finance	12: $150,680
Average starting salary	$111,660	Marketing	9: $88,520
		Operations	3: $117,720
		Strategic Planning	12: $94,930
		Consulting	24: $116,750
		General Management	15: $142,670
		Other	20: $101,710
		Non-profit	3: $75,340

DARTMOUTH COLLEGE
TUCK SCHOOL OF BUSINESS

GENERAL INFORMATION
Type of school	private
Environment	village
Academic calendar	quarters

SURVEY SAYS...
Friendly students
Good peer network
Happy students
Smart classrooms
Solid preparation in:
General management
Teamwork
Communication/interpersonal skills

STUDENTS
Enrollment of parent institution	5,700
Enrollment of MBA program	503
% male/female	75/25
% out-of-state	96
% minorities	18
% international	31
Average age at entry	28
Average years work experience at entry	5

ACADEMICS
Academic Experience Rating	**99**
Student/faculty ratio	9:1
Profs interesting rating	95
Profs accessible rating	97
% female faculty	19
% minority faculty	18

Joint Degrees
Tuck offers dual and joint-degree programs and other creative curricular options. Tuck partners with the Fletcher School of Law and Diplomacy at Tufts University, Kennedy School of Government at Harvard University, Vermont Law School, Dartmouth's Thayer School of Engineering, and Dartmouth Medical School.

Academics

Founded in 1900, Tuck School of Business at Dartmouth was the first graduate school of business in the country. And today, in the New England town of Hanover, New Hampshire, the school honors its tradition of excellence and continues to attract the very best to its campus. Students brag that they "have the opportunity to have lunch, dinner, and office hours with top executives on a daily basis." In addition,"faculty who come to Tuck are here to teach, which really differentiates Tuck from other top schools where visiting executives or adjunct faculty are primarily doing the instruction."

The first year is comprised of core courses, one elective, and projects, and at the beginning of each year, the class is divided into study groups of four or five. The school selects the groups for "diversity of experience," and students are "wowed" by the cooperation that they feel "fosters a culture of excellence without being competitive, overbearing, or arrogant." Other students agree, and add that "teamwork is important at Tuck, which is fantastic." The new curriculum also offers the Leadership Forum with specific training and coaching on building leadership skills.

The second year at Tuck consists of electives. In this year, students are offered the opportunity to develop courses of independent studies and are encouraged to pursue field studies. General management is Tuck's forte, and students recognize and applaud this: "Specialization is not Tuck's focus. General management is—and that is what the school excels at." Other students point out that with general management as its focus, the school becomes a "consulting and banking feeder school, with great connections to the top firms."

For students hoping to work on a joint degree, while escaping the busy city atmosphere, Tuck has partnered with the Fletcher School of Law and Diplomacy at Tufts University, the Kennedy School of Government at Harvard University, Thayer School of Engineering at Dartmouth College, Dartmouth Medical School, and Vermont Law School. Tuck has recently expanded international business opportunities, as well as increased recognition outside of the United States; international exchange programs are also offered with schools in Japan, Germany, England, Spain, and Chile. The curriculum also includes specific training and coaching on leadership skills.

A common complaint in the past years has been the rapid increase in the number of students and the relatively static status of the school's faculty and facilities. "The school is currently growing enrollment," one student complained, "but I do not see a commensurate increase in resources such as housing and teaching." Fortunately, the school seems to be addressing this by pointing out that it is not currently growing enrollment and instead is adding faculty before students.

Career and Placement

Alumni cooperation amazes most students at Tuck, who have reported exceptional cooperation from alumni at every level of the business sector. "Admission to the school," one student says, "is a lifelong pass to a 'secret society' that starts the day you matriculate." According to the school, annual alumni giving is as high as 62 percent—higher than any business school in the country. For the Tuckies, though, they easily explain, "There's a reason why Tuck alums are known to be so loyal and helpful: They loved their time here."

The administration has worked hard to bring executives and recruiters to campus, and once they arrive they tend to spend at least a full day with students. In addition, most students feel that the "geographical diversity" of companies that recruit on campus is insufficient: Another student says, "The career office is East Coast–focused and apparently is unaware that large sections of the United States exist, let alone the rest of the world." In order to combat the potential isolation of the location, "administrators put forth great efforts to bring CEOs and business leaders to campus."

If there's anything that the career office has not been slow to recognize, however, is the value of preparation. Several students report that they "started reviewing resumes and preparing for [their] internship search during orientation—before classes even started."

Student Life and Environment

Students at Tuck describe the student body as "a unique group of urban sophisticates in a rural setting." Lest you're thinking *Green Acres*, know that most students agree that in Hanover, life is "idyllic," not dull. "Unlike the schools in big cities, I can leave my laptop anywhere," one student says. "It sounds trivial, but it's been important to feel that I am in a safe environment, both among my peers and in the community." Students agree and add that "half [of] the first-years live on-campus, so there is a very tight feeling of community." Students will also find natural beauty and resources abound.

Those students enrolled at Tuck describe a "real family feel," and this may be due to the fact that of the approximately 240 full-time MBA students per class, almost half are married. Luckily, most students agree that "Tuck does a great job integrating spouses into the mix." Spouses and partners are welcome at all events and even some classes, and the program has even made room for "Tiny Tuckies" (children of students).

Some find the male-to-female ratio discouraging—in 2003, only about 25 percent of MBA were female, but Tuck has been working on outreach efforts to female student perspectives and is projecting a 5 percent increase in the female student body by 2006. Students also complain about insufficient on-campus housing. However, the close-knit community atmosphere at Tuck receives high praise as one student explains, "The "TPs" (Tuck Partners), "Tiny Tuckies" (children) and "TCs" (Tuck Canines) are fully part of the community. Family member are invited to every non-academic event and some TPs have been allowed to sit in on classes." Still, in the end, most Tuckies agree that "if you want a city or variety, go somewhere else. If you want intense learning and a somewhat conformist camaraderie, go to Tuck."

Admissions

The average GMAT score of an admitted Tuck MBA student was 704, and the average GPA was 3.4. All incoming students had worked full-time prior to applying for the MBA, and the average class boasts a wide variety of undergraduate majors. TOEFL scores are required of those students for whom English is not the first language, and the minimum score required for admission is a 600 or an equivalent computer-based score of 250. Both need-based and merit scholarships are awarded.

EMPLOYMENT PROFILE	
Career Rating	95
Placement rate (%)	95
% grads employed immediately	75
Average starting salary	$131,000

FINANCIAL FACTS

Annual tuition	$36,390
Fees	$245
Books and supplies	$5,180
Room & board (on/off-campus)	$9,265/$9,845
% of students receiving aid	78
% of first-year students receiving aid	80
% of students receiving loans	74
% of students receiving grants	31
Average award package	$35,300
Average grant	$13,840
Average student loan debt	$69,050

ADMISSIONS

Admissions Selectivity Rating	97
# of applications received	1716
% applicants accepted	27
% acceptees attending	58
Average GMAT	704
Average GPA	3.4
TOEFL Required of International Students?	Yes
Application fee	$210
International application fee	$210
Regular application deadline	4/18
Regular notification	5/16
Application Deadline/Notification	
Round 1:	10/18 / 12/17
Round 2:	12/01 / 2/15
Round 3:	1/17 / 3/17
Round 4:	4/18 / 5/16
Early decision program?	Yes
ED Deadline/Notification	10/18 / 12/17
Deferment Available?	Yes
Maximum length of deferment	Case by case basis
Need-blind admissions?	Yes

APPLICANTS ALSO LOOK AT

Columbia University, Harvard University, Northwestern University, Stanford University, University of Pennsylvania.

DREXEL UNIVERSITY
LeBow College of Business

GENERAL INFORMATION
Type of school	private
Environment	metropolis
Academic calendar	quarter

SURVEY SAYS...
Students love Philadelphia, PA
Friendly students
Happy students
Smart classrooms
Solid preparation in:
Teamwork
Presentation skills

STUDENTS
Enrollment of parent institution	
Enrollment of MBA program	858
% male/female	60/40
% part-time	71
% minorities	14
% international	29
Average age at entry	30

ACADEMICS
Academic Experience Rating	**80**
Student/faculty ratio	16:1
Profs interesting rating	76
Profs accessible rating	72
% female faculty	26
% minority faculty	29
Joint Degrees	
MBA/MS: 1-3 years	

Academics

Drexel University's LeBow College of Business offers a variety of MBA options, all designed to maximize the time students devote to their studies. At the top of the list is the one-year MBA, an intensive full-time program that offers an MBA degree in half the usual time. Then there's the professional MBA, for busy professionals seeking a part-time degree; two types of online MBAs, one traditional, the other tech-focused; the GVC MBA, which offers residents of the Great Valley region a mixture of online and off-campus courses; and the executive MBA, for students with at least five years professional experience. There is also the LeBow Evening Accelerated Drexel (LEAD) MBA and Two-Year MBA. The MBA curriculum integrates leadership and ethics, industry perspectives and technology management.

Drexel has long been known as a fine tech and engineering school, so it should come as no surprise that the LeBow curriculum "stresses technology at every level, from class lectures to student presentations to learning modes. We are even required to take a class on technology's effect in the business world," says one student. As a result of this focus, "the majority of the faculty is up on all of the latest information and communications technologies, which is a rarity at more traditional, nontech-focused MBA programs." The school really flashes its tech chops with its "flexible and high-quality Techno MBA Online program, which enables me to take classes from anywhere I wish, even when traveling on business for my job," says one busy MBA.

The LeBow faculty offers an "excellent mix of experienced academia with entrepreneurial professors." Students tell us "The quality of the professors, particularly in the areas of quantitative studies (finance, statistics, decision sciences) is very high" and point out that "Wharton is across the street, and some of their professors also teach at Drexel." Students who attend the majority of their classes on campus note, "Most professors are very accessible and truly care about their students. You get a very high degree of personal attention at Drexel, particularly in the one-year MBA program." They also appreciate that "the technology is great. It's a WiFi campus, with great audio/visual in classrooms and work areas."

Other LeBow assets include the school's Laurence A. Baiada Center for Entrepreneurship in Technology, which "provides workshops facilitated by professionals with real-world experience. They show how the concepts taught in class are applied to real-world experiences." Students praise the availability of online classes at LeBow, although they wish the school would make the classes available to all students; they are currently available primarily to students in the online MBA programs.

Career and Placement

The Office of MBA Career Services is a new office at LeBow since 2003. The staff provides students with "extensive career counseling and customized job-search resources through a series of workshops, self-assessment counseling, and formal employer networking activities." Students agree that the office meets these obligations, but they also feel that "Career Services looks at the job-search process from a very high level and takes a 'one-size-fits-all' approach. Career Services at Drexel is very good for students with little or no experience. For those of us with significant experience (5 or 10-plus) years, it isn't much help." Many also feel that the school could do a better job of attracting on-campus recruiters. "We need to improve Career Services so that students have a chance with top companies," says one student.

Student Life and Environment

Drexel "is primarily a 'commuter' school located in the city of Philadelphia. Most MBA students live off campus and commute at least a half an hour to school." Accordingly, "if

ANNA SEREFEAS, GRADUATE ADMISSIONS AND RECRUITMENT
3141 CHESTNUT STREET, 105 MATHESON HALL, PHILADELPHIA, PA 19104-2875 UNITED STATES
PHONE: 215-895-0592 • FAX: 215-895-1012
E-MAIL: AS326@DREXEL.EDU • WEBSITE: WWW.LEBOW.DREXEL.EDU/

you are looking for a sense of community, then do not choose Drexel. I was looking for a quality education in a compressed time frame—community wasn't important to me," one MBA says. Nor is it to most of the students at LeBow; like this respondent, they are most interested in squeezing their MBAs into already-hectic schedules. Even most of those who visit the campus "really only attend classes. We use the library when we have to meet with other students but do not spend much time on the campus." Those who study online or who attend satellite classrooms have even less interaction with one another.

In an effort to foster some sense of community, LeBow students recently formed an MBA Association. "It tries, but it's still new," students tell us, adding that it's worth the effort to join clubs and make connections with fellow classmates. One MBA writes, "Life is all about the people you meet and making the effort. The people in the program are generally great—you just need to make an effort to meet them. You can usually meet people at the New Deck Tavern, just off campus. Join the MBA Association and be active. It really helps you meet new people and provides networking opportunities."

Fortunately, for those with the time and inclination for a social life, Drexel is located in one of America's great cities, Philadelphia. Students agree, "One of Drexel's strong points is its location. Philly is between New York and Washington, DC, and there are many companies within this area, which makes networking much easier. This also allows students to have a wider variety of companies to choose from for internships (they can still take classes part-time and work)." The school itself is "located in a very social area (with bars, restaurants, [and] entertainment)," although a word of caution: It is not located too terribly far from some of Philly's more crime-plagued neighborhoods.

Admissions

According to the admissions committee at LeBow, "Successful applicants possess intellectual curiosity, strong analytical ability, effective communication skills, and well-defined areas of academic interest that are connected to their future career goals." Full-time post-baccalaureate professional experience is not required for admission, although it is "strongly recommended." Applicants must provide the admissions committee with official copies of all college and university transcripts, GMAT scores, TOEFL scores (where applicable), letters of recommendation; a personal statement, and a resume. An interview is optional.

FINANCIAL FACTS

Annual tuition	$45,000
Books and supplies	$15,000

ADMISSIONS

Admissions Selectivity Rating	86
# of applications received	770
% applicants accepted	43
% acceptees attending	22
Average GMAT	590
Average GPA	3.25
TOEFL Required of International Students?	Yes
Minimum TOEFL (paper/computer)	600/250
Application fee	$50
International application fee	$50
Regular application deadline	
Regular notification	Rolling
Early decision program?	Yes
ED Deadline/Notification	10/1; 12/1; 1/1
Deferment Available?	Yes
Maximum length of deferment	1 year
Transfer students accepted?	Yes
Transfer application policy: Must apply for the professional MBA and be in good academic standing at current institution.	
Non-fall admissions?	Yes
Need-blind admissions?	Yes

EMPLOYMENT PROFILE

Career Rating	72	Grads employed by field	%: avg. salary
% grads employed immediately	45	Finance	43: $55,000
Average starting salary	$57,710	Human Resources	4: $68,000
		Marketing	14: $61,000
		Operations	18: $58,600
		Consulting	7: $50,500
		General Management	7: $65,000
		Other	7

DUKE UNIVERSITY
FUQUA SCHOOL OF BUSINESS

GENERAL INFORMATION
Type of school	private
Environment	city
Academic calendar	terms

SURVEY SAYS...
Friendly students
Good social scene
Good peer network
Happy students
Smart classrooms
Solid preparation in:
Teamwork

STUDENTS
Enrollment of parent institution	11,929
Enrollment of MBA program	1,331
% male/female	70/30
% minorities	18
% international	29
Average age at entry	29
Average years work experience at entry	5

ACADEMICS
Academic Experience Rating	**97**
Student/faculty ratio	11:1
Profs interesting rating	96
Profs accessible rating	98
% female faculty	23
% minority faculty	2

Joint Degrees
MBA/JD: 4 years; MBA/Master of Public Policy: 2-3 years; MBA/Master of Forestry: 2-3 years; MBA/Master of Environmental Management: 3 years; MBA/MS Engineering: 2-3 years; MBA/MD: 5 years; MBA/MSN in Nursing: 2-3 years

Academics

Student involvement—not just in academics, but in all facets of extracurricular life—is the hallmark of the MBA program at Duke's Fuqua School of Business. Students here use the term "Team Fuqua" to sum up the collaborative spirit that binds MBAs, professors, and administration at this high-profile southern university. "Classes are broken into sections, and Fuqua weaves the team concept into those sections' cultures from day one." It all starts with the Integrative Learning Experience, an orientation-cum-Outward Bound experience. It continues with the core curriculum, "taught as a mixture of case- and lecture-based learning," with a "heavy emphasis on teamwork and projects."

Fuqua terms are "rapid-paced," lasting only six weeks (classes meet in two two-hour sessions weekly). The curriculum "emphasizes leadership and communication skills," with outstanding offerings in marketing, finance, and health management. Students describe the program as "well-balanced, with strength in many areas," and boast that it "allows [them] to explore many different options." One MBA student says that the professors are "leaders in their fields. They are engaged in the class, and they are highly passionate about their subjects. It's hard to imagine a professor making basic accounting enjoyable, but my professor has me loving the class because of his energy and passion."

Students and administrators are also on the same team at Duke. "Fuqua is exceptionally responsive to student feedback, and any issue is resolved quickly." For example, "Duke University has made a specific point in the last two years to get its top professors back into teaching core courses after some weakness two years ago in student reviews of core classes. They have been successful, and it has made the core course offerings very strong." Duke MBAs are deeply involved in nearly all aspects of managing the program, which they describe as "almost completely student-run. Almost any event you attend—whether career, speaker, social, or otherwise—is devised, organized, and marketed by students."

Duke also offers three Executive MBA options: an MBA Weekend Program that meets alternate weekends in Durham; an MBA Global Program that combines distance-learning and international in-classroom residencies; and the MBA Cross Continent Program that combines week-long international residencies and distance learning. The Global Program requires a minimum of ten years professional experience; the Cross Continent Program is designed for less experienced managers.

Career and Placement

The Career Management Center at Fuqua works with students throughout their tenure to enhance their networking skills and improve their resumes. Many, however, feel that the office is the weak link in the program, complaining that it "needs more talent, maybe more ex-MBA-types who can communicate with companies better." One student notes, "The career center has a lot of tools available to the students, but they are not rolled out well. There are opportunities for assistance—such as mentors and career fellows—that are not well advertised to students, and thus are underused resources." On the bright side, "the career center has recently taken a huge step forward," and the "small alumni base [is] phenomenally loyal. Alums bend over backward to help students find jobs and offer career wisdom. In fact, it is pretty common for alums to spend several hours on the phone each week with current students." The recent addition of a new Career services director and additional staff, as well as the creation of the CMC Channel should help to open up opportunities, as well as enhance communication and between the office and students.

Employers most likely to hire Fuqua MBAs include Johnson & Johnson; IBM; American Express; Kraft Food; Citigroup; Deloitte Consulting; Bank of America; Bear Sterns; DuPont; and Eli Lilly & Associates.

Liz M. Riley, Assistant Dean and Director of Admissions
1 Towerview Drive, Durham, NC 27708-0104 United States
Phone: 919-660-7705 • Fax: 919-681-8026
E-mail: admissions-info@fuqua.duke.edu • Website: www.fuqua.duke.edu

Student Life and Environment

Duke offers "excellent health care and leadership resources." The Team Fuqua spirit pervades all aspects of life at Duke, including extracurricular activities. On Fuqua Fridays, the school "provides free food, beer, and wine to all Fuqua students, faculty, and their families." One happy student writes, "It's great to see everyone outside of the classroom, and to meet people's wives, husbands, and kids." MBAs also enjoy "regular cultural events," such as "two International Food Festivals each year, International Week, Asian Festival, Latin American/South American events, and events with European business leaders." Students "arrange an annual MBA Games event at which many top-tier business schools compete." The school uses the "monies raised to help the North Carolina Special Olympics athletes to compete." Despite their busy schedules, students also find time to collaborate on FuquaVision, an SNL-like parody of life at Fuqua produced "at least once per term. The films are a riot and really show the initiative of students here."

Basketball fanatics could hardly find a happier home, nor could golf enthusiasts; the Duke course is the best of many excellent local facilities available to Duke students. Students point out that "the weather here is great, and the area is outstanding for families." Hometown Durham, although small, "has tons of great restaurants and more to do than most people think." It also offers easy access to Raleigh and Chapel Hill; together the three cities form North Carolina's Triangle region, which offers a decent (if sprawling) approximation of urban amenities. One student sums up, "With 800 like-minded classmates around, a great climate, awesome natural resources, and (Chapel Hill's) Franklin Street only a short drive away, there is plenty to do. The culture and people are great, and school will suck up any ounce of time you give it."

Admissions

Applicants to the Fuqua MBA Program must provide the Admissions Department with a one-page business resume, three essays (describe your work experience; describe your career goals; explain what you will contribute to the Fuqua Program), official GMAT scores, official transcripts for all post-secondary academic work, and two recommendations. An interview, though not required, is "strongly encouraged." International students must also provide official TOEFL scores if English is not their first language. To promote recruitment of underrepresented students, Duke conducts MBA Workshops for Minority Applicants, participates in "aggressive minority scholarship programs with partners including the Toigo Foundation," and hosts the Leadership Education and Development (LEAD) Summer Business Institute. The Weekend Executive MBA "prefers" at least five years of professional experience; the Global Executive MBA requires a minimum of ten years' professional experience; the Cross Continent Executive MBA requires three to nine years' experience.

FINANCIAL FACTS

Annual tuition	$35,450
Fees	$1,349
Books and supplies	$1,600
Room and board	$13,300
% of students receiving aid	82
% of first-year students receiving aid	81
% of students receiving loans	75
% of students receiving grants	37
Average award package	$62,468
Average grant	$18,202
Average student loan debt	$66,415

ADMISSIONS

Admissions Selectivity Rating	95
# of applications received	2,367
% applicants accepted	38
% acceptees attending	45
Average GMAT	705
Range of GMAT	690-730
Average GPA	3.4
TOEFL Required of International Students?	Yes
Minimum TOEFL (paper/computer)	600/250
Application fee	$175
International application fee	$175
Regular application deadline	2/5
Regular notification	3/5
Application Deadline/Notification	
Round 1:	11/1 / 12/16
Round 2:	1/3 / 2/17
Round 3:	2/1 / 3/24
Round 4:	3/15 / 5/12
Deferment Available?	Yes
Maximum length of deferment	1 year
Need-blind admissions?	Yes

EMPLOYMENT PROFILE

Career Rating	98	Grads employed by field	%: avg. salary
Placement rate (%)	96	Finance	38: $83,206
# of companies recruiting on-campus	142	Marketing	27: $79,426
% grads employed immediately	77	Operations	2: $80,167
Average starting salary	$84,255	Strategic Planning	4: $92,100
		Consulting	13: $96,924
		General Management	11: $85,069
		Other	2: $79,711
		Non-profit	3: $70,500

DUQUESNE UNIVERSITY
JOHN F. DONAHUE GRADUATE SCHOOL OF BUSINESS

Academics

"Duquesne is very up-to-date with current business practices, research, and ethics," students at the John F. Donahue Graduate School of Business tell us. Among the distinctive curricular features at this prestigious Pittsburgh university is the "great emphasis on understanding the value chain of a company and how all functions interact within the entire enterprise value chain." Donahue even requires a course in the subject: understanding the value chain is designed to give MBAs unique insight into "how business disciplines work together as a process to create value for customers, employees, and shareholders," according to the school catalog.

The concept that business is a process requiring interdisciplinary analysis is stressed repeatedly throughout the MBA program, which consists of nine core courses and five electives. Students lacking sufficient undergraduate coursework in business are typically required to take some or all of an additional nine-course complement of pre-MBA knowledge and skills-related classes. The Donahue School offers a whopping 14 areas of concentration: accounting, business ethics, electronic business, entrepreneurship, environmental management, finance, health care management, human resource management, information systems management, international business, marketing, supply chain management, and taxation. Students may also opt for a general MBA without specialization. Students in our survey singled out offerings in accounting, business ethics, and finance for praise.

Duquesne faculty members "are easily approachable and always available for students outside of class," not only at the downtown campus but also at satellite locations. One student explains, "I am attending school part-time at a satellite campus, yet still we have full, tenured, and even department-heading professors who drive out of their way to instruct us." Profs are also "very professional and knowledgeable about their fields." One student writes, "Most professors are able to provide real-life examples, experiences, and issues. It is not just 'academic perspectives' that only exist in the classroom. Most topics we cover are solutions that could be implemented in a practical setting."

Career and Placement

Duquesne's Career Services Office provides placement and counseling services to all of the university's undergraduate and graduate students. Yet students are "disappointed with the career services program," which they complain "does not do a good job of recruiting potential employers outside of the Pittsburgh region." Some feel the school's top priority should be "to better integrate the students in social/networking situations, and to involve its alumni to assist students as career mentors." Others think the focus should be on marketing. One student comments, "This is a great school, and I think we should take the time to submit the paperwork that needs to get done to rank us as one of the top business schools in the country by those 'Top B-Schools' lists. With greater visibility, more companies would recruit at Duquesne, which would improve our post-graduate job placement rates, which don't seem to be very strong."

Employers most likely to hire Donohue MBAs include the Mellon Financial Corporation, Management Science Associates, PNC Corporation, U.S. Steel Corporation, Mine Safety Appliance Corporation, Alcoa, Deloitte and Touche, Federal Express Ground, and the H. J. Heinz Corporation

PATRICIA MOORE, ASSISTANT DIRECTOR
600 FORBES AVENUE, PITTSBURGH, PA 15282 UNITED STATES
PHONE: 412-396-6276 • FAX: 412-396-1726
E-MAIL: GRAD-BUS@DUQ.EDU • WEBSITE: WWW.BUS.DUQ.EDU/GRAD/

Student Life and Environment

"The MBA program at Duquesne is really a part-time program," students here explain, with "most of the classes held at night. As a result, you are removed from the rest of the campus." MBAs point out, "Student social clubs do exist, but participation is low due to most students' part-time status. Full-time students do integrate during the day." These full-timers, who make up about 20 percent of the student body, participate in the "many clubs and activities available," which include "MBA happy hours, pizza sessions with speakers, and a Halloween party with a bus trip." The faculty "is very willing to help students establish and advise student organizations."

Students here also enjoy the campus's "modern and well-constructed gym facilities, [the] nice coffee shops and food on campus, [and] the overall safe environment." Because the school is located downtown, students are "not far from professional sports activities. You can walk to Penguins hockey games in five minutes and to Pirates and Steelers games in just a little more." Pittsburgh, most here agree, "is a great city for universities. There is a wealth of knowledge in the area." One student challenges, "For those people who have never been to Pittsburgh, I think they would be surprised as to how great a city it is. It has grown beyond its dark, Steel City image." Students from warmer climes should take note that winters in Pittsburgh are long, cold, and snowy.

"The age range of students is very mixed" at Duquesne. Students observe that "some have just earned their undergraduate degrees, some took a few years off to work, and others are married with kids and coming back to school after many years in the work force." Quite a few are "middle to upper managers with backgrounds in engineering and manufacturing." Because of "a great international program, [there are] many international students, mostly from Latin America, Eastern Europe, China, and Africa. The diversity adds a lot to classes, as does hearing about the experiences of international classmates."

Admissions

All applicants to the Donahue MBA program must submit official transcripts for all post-secondary academic work, an official GMAT score report, two letters of recommendation, and an autobiographical statement. International students must also submit official TOEFL scores. Work experience is not a prerequisite to entering the program.

FINANCIAL FACTS

Annual tuition	$16,767
Fees	$1,593
Books and supplies	$2,500
Room & board (on-campus)	$7,170
% of students receiving aid	70
% of first-year students receiving aid	70
% of students receiving grants	27
Average grant	$16,767

ADMISSIONS

Admissions Selectivity Rating	70
# of applications received	201
% applicants accepted	76
% acceptees attending	64
Average GMAT	510
Average GPA	3.1
TOEFL Required of International Students?	Yes
Minimum TOEFL (paper/computer)	550/213
Application fee	$50
International application fee	$50
Regular application deadline	6/1
Regular notification	7/1
Deferment Available?	Yes
Maximum length of deferment	1 year
Transfer students accepted?	Yes
Transfer application policy: Will accept up to 15 transfer credits from an accredited college or university.	
Non-fall admissions?	Yes
Need-blind admissions?	Yes

APPLICANTS ALSO LOOK AT

Carnegie Mellon, University of Pittsburgh.

EMPLOYMENT PROFILE

Career Rating	73
Placement rate (%)	90
# of companies recruiting on-campus	155
% grads employed immediately	95
Average starting salary	$55,000

EAST CAROLINA UNIVERSITY
COLLEGE OF BUSINESS

Academics

"The greatest strengths of East Carolina University are the many excellent programs that are available, and the fact that most of them are nationally accredited programs," explain students at this state university about 90 miles east of Raleigh. Students also appreciate the availability of online classes that are "better than [they] would have imagined. The professors are computer savvy so you notice little difference between online and a classroom setting."

The ECU MBA is designed to meet the needs of both business and non-business undergraduates. It can also accommodate those without professional experience as well as those who have worked in business, though the school "strongly encourages" those without professional experience "to obtain career-related experience while earning their MBA." Depending on the student's background, the MBA program requires between 10 and 20 courses. For a quick return on investment, the curriculum can be completed in as little as one year by a full-time student with a strong undergraduate background in business.

ECU's MBA program starts with 10 core courses covering material traditionally covered in undergraduate business programs. Some or all of these classes may be waived. Waiver decisions are made on a student-by-student and course-by-course basis. In order for a waiver to be granted the university requires a minimum grade of B in equivalent undergraduate courses. The core makes up the first half of the program; the second half consists of 10 business breadth courses, seven required and three electives. Elective choices are limited; only 15 are offered at any given time, with elective selection rotating on an annual basis. Those seeking a concentration must take four courses in their chosen area of specialization. ECU offers concentrations in development and environmental planning, health care management, international management, MIS, and school business management. Most students devote their three breadth electives to their specialization, and therefore need complete only one additional course. Approximately 15 percent of ECU MBAs choose a specialization.

Students here applaud "the helpfulness of the instructors," whom they regard as "demanding and, at the same time, willing to do anything for everyone in order to do excellently." One student notes, "Our instructors may not currently be industry leaders, but they have amazing and successful (i.e., enviable) past careers and seem to be here as volunteers to help the future." Another says, "I took away something important from each of them." ECU administrators "do a great job of improving the quality of resources and courses to stay current with business trends."

Career and Placement

Career services are provided to ECU MBAs by the Student Professional Development Office, a division of the Academic Affairs Office. The office provides Recruiting resources, sponsors on-campus job fairs, organizes seminars and classroom presentations on job search skills, and offers one-on-one counseling and other advising resources.

Len Rhodes, Assistant Dean for Graduate Programs
3203 Bate Building, Greenville, NC 27858-4353 United States
Phone: 252-328-6970 • Fax: 252-328-2106
E-mail: gradbus@mail.ecu.edu • Website: www.business.ecu.edu/grad

Student Life and Environment

Many MBAs at ECU describe a collegiate atmosphere both on campus and within their program, lauding the "good parties [and] excellent sports teams, especially the football team, which receives a lot of support from students. [They] all love to go out and tailgate before the games." Students also keep busy in more grown-up pursuits. One student explains, "We're active in business projects to help local businesses, which is a great way to find local opportunities and learn along the way. Many MBA students are involved with something else at the school, like film, international house, physics, hospital, etc. Many MBAs also volunteer building websites, analysis, and at the hospital." Students also recommend the campus's Ledonia Wright Culture Center, which "holds interesting events that are fun to go to."

Hometown Greenville is conveniently located less than two hours from both Raleigh and the North Carolina shore. There's not a lot of big business in the immediate area, however, and students warn that the crime rate here is relatively high.

Students in the MBA program describe themselves as "very open and friendly, and always willing to help you try to understand something or explain a problem you might have in a particular subject." There are "many international students from Asian countries and Africa," with most of the domestic students originating from the eastern part of the state. Many students here are freshly minted college grads, meaning that they don't bring a whole lot in the way of real-world experience to their graduate business classes.

Admissions

To be considered for admission to the MBA program at ECU, applicants must score at least 950 under the formula [(undergraduate GPA × 200) + GMAT score], with a minimum GMAT score of 400. Students who received their undergraduate degrees less than a year before their projected starting date for the MBA program, must achieve a score of 950 with a minimum GMAT score of 450. However, if their undergraduate GPA was at least 3.5, they must score at least 400 on the GMAT. Applicants must submit official copies of all post-secondary academic transcripts, and official GMAT score reports. International students must exceed the formula-score requirements indicated above by 50 points and must also provide official TOEFL score reports.

FINANCIAL FACTS

Annual tuition (in-state/out-of-state)	$3,536/$13,852
Books and supplies	$500

ADMISSIONS

Admissions Selectivity Rating	**67**
# of applications received	330
% applicants accepted	82
% acceptees attending	74
Average GMAT	498
Average GPA	3.11
TOEFL Required of International Students?	Yes
Minimum TOEFL (paper/computer)	550/213
Application fee	$50
International application fee	$50
Regular application deadline	Rolling
Regular notification	Rolling
Deferment Available?	Yes
Maximum length of deferment	1 year
Transfer students accepted?	Yes
Transfer application policy: Maximum of 9 semester credit hours from AACSB accredited institution accepted	
Non-fall admissions?	Yes
Need-blind admissions?	Yes

EAST TENNESSEE STATE UNIVERSITY
COLLEGE OF BUSINESS AND TECHNOLOGY

GENERAL INFORMATION
Type of school	public
Environment	town
Academic calendar	semester

SURVEY SAYS...
Smart classrooms
Solid preparation in:
Teamwork
Communication/interpersonal skills
Presentation skills

STUDENTS
Enrollment of parent institution	12,000
Enrollment of MBA program	113
% male/female	55/45
% out-of-state	10
% part-time	75
% minorities	10
% international	10
Average age at entry	28
Average years work experience at entry	3

ACADEMICS
Academic Experience Rating	**72**
Student/faculty ratio	7:1
Profs interesting rating	65
Profs accessible rating	81
% female faculty	10

Prominent Alumni
Pal Barger, Food Services.

Academics

There aren't many choices at the College of Business and Technology at East Tennessee State University—the small program maintains only three business and four technology departments (accounting, economics/finance—urban studies, management/marketing)—but for those who are interested in a general purpose business degree, ETSU delivers. In addition to the traditional MBA, the school also offers an MAcc (master's of accounting), an MPA (master's of public administration), and a graduate certificate in business administration for "those who seek a basic understanding of business administration but who may not be able to make the commitment of time, effort, and money required to seek a master's degree."

MBAs at ETSU feel that "the administration and faculty here are very student-oriented. Most have set times when they are available outside of class; others excel and really go the extra mile both in class presentation and in their availability to those students that require extra instruction." Professors are regarded as "very knowledgeable in their fields, and many of them are widely recognized as great scholars." One student writes, "Most of them have a work background that can lead to some very good discussions in class, and [the professors present] the applications of the concepts in the real world through their stories." Faculty members are also "easy to work with and understanding about personal matters that can arise."

Some students feel that the program could raise its standards. One MBA mentions that "it teaches to a very low level. Many of the courses are easier than AP-level high-school courses. It seems as if the school is afraid to challenge its students for fear of decreased enrollment. In multiple classes we have touched on a subject that is 'too complex for this program.'" Others see the situation somewhat differently, telling us, "They do a very good job on getting the student prepared with the knowledge that is needed in the workplace, but there is just so much that can be taught in the classroom setting, and the true learning from the classroom is applied to the jobs that are obtained after school." Part of the problem lies in the student body; most have full-time jobs in addition to school responsibilities, leaving them overextended. One student warns, "Group work here is a big problem. In 10 out of 13 classes, I have been required to be in a group. Most likely you have one or two people who do not participate in the group, leaving the workload for the other two or three people. Those individuals who do not participate always get the same grade." On a positive note, students love that "the school is large enough to offer remote learning facilities, and classes are generally available at convenient times for working adults."

Career and Placement

The Career Placement and Internship Services Office at East Tennessee University serves the school's entire undergraduate and graduate student body. The office hosts recruitment visits from various companies, sponsors and participates in career fairs, maintains online job boards and resume books, and offers counseling in interview skills, job search, career match, and resume writing. In the spring of 2004, on-campus recruiters included New York Life, Norfolk Southern, Wachovia, and Wells Fargo. Students are aware that "Johnson City is a small town, which limits the amount of recruiting that is done on campus." Even so, many "believe that [the] school could improve by really showing students what is available out there and helping them find jobs when they get done. It is there right now [at the Career Placement and Internship Services Office], but a student really has to push to find it."

Student Life and Environment

East Tennessee State University is located in Johnson City, a small Appalachian city close to both the North Carolina and Virginia borders. The surrounding area, dubbed the

DRIVE MARTHA POINTER, DIRECTOR OF GRADUATE STUDIES
PO BOX 70699 JOHNSON CITY, TN 37614 UNITED STATES
PHONE: 423-439-5314 • FAX: 423-439-5274
E-MAIL: BUSINESS@BUSINESS.ETSU.EDU • WEBSITE: WWW.ETSU.EDU/GRADSTUD/INDEX.HTM

Tri-Cities region, also includes Bristol and Kingsport; the charming town of Abingdon, Virginia, is also not too far afield. The area is an outdoor enthusiast's paradise, offering plenty of opportunities for hiking, climbing, skiing, and nature walks. The Tri-Cities area is a rising force in the health-care industry, with a developing biotech industry that could bring big players to the region.

With 11,000 students (about 2,000 of whom are graduate students), the ETSU campus has the population to support a busy social scene. MBAs report, "There is a very good social scene, with Thursday nights being the night that most students go out to the clubs. There are not a lot of clubs in the area, but there are many places that one can go and have a beer if they so choose." Students try to find time to support their men's basketball them, the ETSU Bucs, which in the 2003–2004 year, won its second consecutive trip to "the Big Dance" (that's the NCAA Tournament to the uninitiated).

ETSU has expanded in recent years, adding several new buildings including a fitness center (students love the "new, fully equipped athletic facility"). Not all MBAs take the time to enjoy the ETSU campus, however; they note that "the school is a high commuter school. This leads to a low participation level in on-campus clubs" and other activities. Those who do participate recommend the school's several national honor societies. One student touts "the university organization called 'President's Pride.' Through this organization, I am able to socialize with other students, faculty, administrators, and [members of the] community by volunteering for university/community functions."

Through its Adult, Commuter, and Transfer Services (ACTS) Office, ETSU assists its many nontraditional students in adapting to student life. ACTS staff advise students on the nuts and bolts of registration, direct them to the campus's various tutoring services, and help parents find child-care services. This last one can be a problem for MBAs, who typically attend evening classes. One such student comments, "I have a 15-month old, and I have tried to get some type of care for my child so I can study or attend group meetings, and I have had no luck. This has been the most frustrating part of my school experience."

Admissions

Applications to the College of Business and Technology at East Tennessee State University are considered on a rolling basis. Applicants must submit the following to the Graduate Admissions Office: official copies of transcripts for all undergraduate and graduate work, standardized test scores (GMAT for the MBA or MAcc, GRE for the MPA), TOEFL scores (where applicable; minimum score 550), a personal statement, letters of recommendation, and a resume. Applicants to the MPA program must have a minimum undergraduate GPA of 3.0. All applicants are presumed to be competent with computers and math literate through calculus.

FINANCIAL FACTS

Annual tuition (in-state/out-of-state)	$4,276/$12,208
Fees	$630
Books and supplies	$1,000
Room & board (on/off-campus)	$3,500/$7,000
% of students receiving aid	25
% of first-year students receiving aid	25
% of students receiving grants	25
Average award package	$6,000
Average grant	$6,000
Average student loan debt	$5,000

ADMISSIONS

Admissions Selectivity Rating	73
# of applications received	70
% applicants accepted	77
% acceptees attending	85
Average GMAT	530
Range of GMAT	450-700
Average GPA	3.2
TOEFL Required of International Students?	Yes
Minimum TOEFL (paper/computer)	550/213
Application fee	$25
International application fee	$35
Regular application deadline	6/4
Regular notification	Rolling
Deferment Available?	Yes
Maximum length of deferment	1 year
Transfer students accepted?	Yes
Transfer application policy: Up to 9 approved hours may be accepted.	
Non-fall admissions?	Yes

APPLICANTS ALSO LOOK AT

University of Tennessee, Virginia Polytechnic Institute and State University.

EMPLOYMENT PROFILE

Career Rating	61	Grads employed by field	%: avg. salary
Placement rate (%)	70	Accounting	20: $40,000
# of companies recruiting on-campus	25	Human Resources	10: $25,000
% grads employed immediately	70	Marketing	10: $35,000
Average starting salary	$35,000	Entrepreneurship	10: $35,000
		General Management	50: $30,000

EASTERN MICHIGAN UNIVERSITY
COLLEGE OF BUSINESS

GENERAL INFORMATION
Type of school	public
Environment	city
Academic calendar	semester

SURVEY SAYS...
Happy students
Smart classrooms
Solid preparation in:
General management
Teamwork
Communication/interpersonal skills
Presentation skills

STUDENTS
Enrollment of parent institution	24,000
Enrollment of MBA program	504
% male/female	47/53
% part-time	77
% minorities	11
% international	23
Average age at entry	30
Average years work experience at entry	4

ACADEMICS
Academic Experience Rating	68
Student/faculty ratio	21:1
Profs interesting rating	72
Profs accessible rating	62
% female faculty	40
% minority faculty	27

Prominent Alumni
Raymond Lombardi, CEO/Deloitte & Touche; James Webb, Aon Risk Services; Joseph Chrzanowski, Executive Director/GM; Laurie Bohlen, VP, Field Marketing/Dominos Pizza; Michael Procida, Executive Director of HR/Ford.

Academics

With its "ability to pull professionals from the different industries located in the southeastern Michigan area [and] an excellent location for jobs," the College of Business at Eastern Michigan University offers "an awesome MBA" to aspiring area businesspeople. The program is designed to fast-track students to their desired degrees; students with undergraduate degrees in business can conceivably complete the program with as few as 36 semester hours (others will require 57 to 63 semester hours). The program is offered during weekday evenings at the Ypsilanti campus; on Saturdays in Livonia, in order to accommodate students with full-time jobs.

The EMU curriculum, the school states, offers "a broad understanding of business functions, including the relationship of business to society as a whole and the impact of legal forces on business" in the following areas: computer information systems, e-business, entrepreneurship, enterprise business intelligence, finance, human-resource management, international business, nonprofit management, and supply-chain management. The school offers specialized degrees in all these areas and a general MBA, as well as further specialized graduate certificates in accounting, human resources, information systems, and organizational development. Throughout the program "an international perspective is provided."

Students praise a wide range of EMU offerings, touting the "excellent entrepreneur services, [the] very demanding but great management professors," and the faculty in finance, computer information, and supply-chain management. Students warn that instructors can occasionally plow through material at breakneck pace. Students say the professors sometimes "need to know that students are not as good as [the professors] are, and they need to come down to the student level to teach." All MBAs are impressed with the fact that "the professors are approachable and easy to talk to. They help as much as they can," even going the extra mile to meet with students whose jobs and family obligations make get-togethers difficult.

Career and Placement

The Career Services Center of Eastern Michigan University assists all EMU students, graduate and undergraduate, in their efforts to "plan a career, develop job-search skills, obtain student employment while attending college, and secure a job upon graduation. Most services are also available to EMU alumni." The office offers walk-in advising, a candidate-referral service, and several job fairs over the course of the school year.

All told, about 40 companies visit campus to recruit EMU MBAs every year. Major employers of EMU MBAs include American Sun Roof, Bank One, Com Share, Compuware, Creative Solutions, Deloitte Touche Tohmatsu, Ford Motor, General Motors, Johnson Controls, Masco Corp, Pfizer Inc., Visteon Corporation, and Yakaki. Average starting salaries of EMU grads range from $32,000 (nonprofit sector) to $61,500 (marketing), with most categories falling into the high $40K to low $50K range.

Student Life and Environment

EMU works hard to serve its varied student body. Residents and singles find much to do within the MBA community. One student writes, "Beside my classes, I attend weekly meetings of various student groups and participate in events organized by these groups. I spend time at our library where I do my research using the excellent computer labs, books, and journals. Students often come together outside of the campus and spend quality time together." MBAs agree that "there are a number of organizations/clubs and activities that anyone can join. There are postings for many activities all year long." The

Dawn Malone, Assistant Dean, Graduate programs
4004 Owen, Ypsilanti, MI 48197 United States
Phone: 734-487-4444 • Fax: 734-483-1316
E-mail: cob.graduate@emich.edu • Website: www.cob.emich.edu/gr/

FINANCIAL FACTS

Annual tuition (in-state/out-of-state)	
	$4,547/$9,205
Fees	$1,400
Books and supplies	$900
Room & board	$7,700
Average grant	$1,000

school's many part-timers and students with families find amenities tailored to their needs as well. Another student writes, "There is childcare service and early childhood programs for students with children. Family housing is available for those who need it. Overall, everything at this school is excellent." The Department of Safety provides a "SEEUS" walking- and mobile-escort service for extra on-campus security after dark.

That's good, since Ypsilanti is an urban environment with a traditionally high crime rate. Students report that "the crime in the city has improved, but there are still occasional incidents near campus," but hasten to add that SEEUS and other campus security measures ensure a "safe and friendly environment" on campus. A sizeable part of the university's population (approximately 24,000) lives "on or near the immediate campus [in] typical lower-income student housing off-campus or typical student dorms/apartments on-campus." MBA students, however, are primarily commuters; as one student writes, "It is more-or-less a commuter campus, and the students spend a lot more time off campus than on." MBAs appreciate the school's proximity to Ann Arbor and Detroit; both cities are seen as major assets in their search for work.

Students praise EMU's capacity to attract "a nontraditional student body with a wealth of real-life business experience." The MBA program draws a large international population, representing 32 countries in all. Also, an unusually large proportion of the student body is female.

Admissions

EMU's admissions office requires applicants to earn a degree from a regionally accredited college and submit transcripts from undergraduate institutions, GMAT scores, TOEFL scores (when appropriate), essays, and a resume. To gain admission, students must demonstrate an undergraduate GPA of at least 2.5 or a GPA of at least 2.75 for the final two years of undergraduate course work and a GMAT score of at least 450, as well as letters of recommendation; an interview is optional. Conditional admission may be granted to students whose undergraduate GPA or GMAT score is lower than the graduate business school normally considers acceptable, but shows promise of success in the program by other means. Applicants lacking the "required common body of knowledge that each student must complete before enrolling" must take EMU's 500-level foundation courses.

ADMISSIONS

Admissions Selectivity Rating	69
# of applications received	284
% applicants accepted	77
% acceptees attending	46
Average GMAT	500
Range of GMAT	390-585
Average GPA	3.6
TOEFL Required of	
International Students?	Yes
Minimum TOEFL	
(paper/computer)	500/213
Application fee	$35
International application fee	$35
Regular application deadline	5/15
Regular notification	6/15
Application Deadline	
Round 1:	5/15
Round 2:	11/1
Round 3:	3/15
Round 4:	4/15
Deferment Available?	Yes
Maximum length of	
deferment	1 year
Transfer students accepted?	Yes
Transfer application policy: 6 credits	
may be accepted upon approval.	
Non-fall admissions?	Yes
Need-blind admissions?	Yes

APPLICANTS ALSO LOOK AT

Central Michigan University, Michigan State University, Oakland University, University of Michigan, University of Michigan—Dearborn, Wayne State University, Western Michigan University.

EMPLOYMENT PROFILE

Career Rating	66	Grads employed by field	%: avg. salary
# of companies recruiting on-campus	42	Accounting	10: $48,000
% grads employed immediately	95	Finance	9: $44,500
Average starting salary	$50,050	Human Resources	8: $40,400
		Marketing	15: $61,500
		MIS	8: $44,500
		Operations	16: $52,600
		Consulting	7: $49,600
		General Management	18: $57,500
		Global Management	5: $50,500
		Other	1: $50,000
		Non-profit	3: $32,000

EASTERN WASHINGTON UNIVERSITY
COLLEGE OF BUSINESS AND PUBLIC ADMINISTRATION

GENERAL INFORMATION
Type of school	public
Environment	city
Academic calendar	quarter

SURVEY SAYS...
Students love Cheney, WA
Friendly students
Happy students
Smart classrooms
Solid preparation in:
Teamwork

STUDENTS
Enrollment of parent institution	9,700
Enrollment of MBA program	123
% male/female	53/47
% out-of-state	8
% part-time	39
% minorities	9
% international	23
Average age at entry	26
Average years work experience at entry	5

ACADEMICS
Academic Experience Rating	**61**
Student/faculty ratio	20:1
Profs interesting rating	63
Profs accessible rating	67
% female faculty	46

Joint Degrees
MBA/MPA: 2 years

Academics

Eastern Washington University offers an MBA that's "cheaper than that offered by other local schools" (namely Gonzaga University) and can be completed in just one year by the extremely diligent. Thanks to the school's active Center for Entrepreneurial Studies, entrepreneurship is among the standout disciplines here. Students praise the school's offerings in healthcare administration as well, lauding the "great certificate program to accompany the MBA that gives great versatility and unprecedented access in seminar format to professionals active in our community's healthcare industry."

EWU's MBA program is one of the few anywhere "taught by faculty from more than one department." Instructors here are drawn not only from the Department of Management but also from the Departments of Accounting and Information Systems, ensuring students the opportunity to develop "a unique and interdisciplinary business expertise." Because the business facility also houses the school's Public Administration Program, EWU students have the option to combine an MBA with an MPA.

The EWU MBA consists of 49 credit hours. Core courses constitute 33 hours of required work; electives take up the remaining 16 hours. Foundation courses can add up to an additional 32 hours of required coursework, and many or all of these courses can be waived for students with relatively recent undergraduate business degrees. Because EWU operates on a quarterly academic calendar, students who place out of foundation courses may complete the program in one year by taking 10+ credits per semester. Some here feel that "quarters are too short to learn anything" and that "classes spanning two quarters (i.e., with a part I and part II) would be beneficial." Others would like to see "a greater variety of electives offered" as well as "concentrations in areas such as marketing, project management, leadership management, finance, and technology." It should be noted, both of these problem areas are typical of smaller programs. In the asset column, students love "the great evening schedule with convenient hours for working professionals" and praise the "excellent group of well-rounded professionals staff[ing] the program. They are welcoming when you drop by their offices to ask for assistance or guidance."

Career and Placement

The Office of Career Services provides counseling and placement services for the entire EWU student body. The office organizes occasional career fairs and posts notices for other career fairs held in the area. In addition, the office hosts on-campus interviews and other recruitment events and maintains an online placement files service, which provides students' resumes, letters of recommendation, and other documents to prospective employers. Most of Career Services' efforts are directed at the school's substantial undergraduate population. MBAs feel that the school "could definitely improve career services and offer students more opportunities to interact with potential employers."

Cynthia Parker, Secretary Senior
668 North Riverpoint Blvd., Suite A, Spokane, WA 99202-1660
Phone: 509-359-2285 • Fax: 509-358-2267
E-mail: cparker@mail.ewu.edu • Website: www.ewu.edu/x1032.xml

Student Life and Environment

The smallish, predominantly part-time MBA program at EWU consists of "many working professionals and/or students with adequate business experience, [with] a number of younger, less experienced students from Asia" thrown into the mix. The size and part-time nature of the program is not conducive to a cohesive student community. Further exacerbating the situation is the fact that "there's really no organized method of creating social networks with fellow students available. Some students do go out after class to discuss politics, school, etc. all the same, but it's not under the auspices of the school." Students don't even get to tap into the culture of EWU's main campus, since the MBA program "is located on a satellite campus in downtown Spokane, 20 miles from the main campus." While the location can inhibit extracurricular life, it does have the advantage of convenience for those students who work in the downtown area.

Classes convene at the Riverpoint Higher Education Park, located on the banks of the Spokane River. The facility is home to EWU's College of Business and Public Administration, a boon to those seeking a dual degree in those two fields. Riverpoint houses a 200-seat auditorium and a number of state-of-the-art classrooms.

Admissions

Eastern Washington University requires all the following materials from applicants to its MBA program: two copies of the completed application for admission to a graduate program; two copies of official transcripts for all post-secondary academic work; and an official GMAT score report no more than five years old. The MBA program director reserves the right to require additional information. International applicants must provide all of the above materials as well as an official TOEFL score report (if their first language is not English; students must score 580 for admission to the MBA program, 525 to be considered for pre-MBA foundation course work). EWU requires a minimum undergraduate GPA of 3.0 and a minimum GMAT score of 450. The school's website notes, "All students who graduate from the MBA program should have some practical work experience. The majority of students who are accepted into the program are working professionals and meet this requirement. For those students who enter the program lacking professional work experience, an internship should be part of the student's MBA program. Up to four credits earned while in an internship may be used for MBA elective credit."

FINANCIAL FACTS

Annual tuition (in-state/out-of-state)	$7,696/$15,800
Fees	$75
Books and supplies	$1,500
Room & board (on/off-campus)	$6,900/$12,000

ADMISSIONS

Admissions Selectivity Rating	70
# of applications received	137
% applicants accepted	72
% acceptees attending	56
Average GMAT	498
Range of GMAT	420-600
Average GPA	3.14
TOEFL Required of International Students?	Yes
Minimum TOEFL (paper/computer)	580/237
Application fee	$35
International application fee	$35
Regular application deadline	1/1
Regular notification	1/1
Deferment Available?	Yes
Maximum length of deferment	1 year
Transfer students accepted?	Yes
Transfer application policy: We will accept up to 12 transfer credits.	
Non-fall admissions?	Yes
Need-blind admissions?	Yes

EMPLOYMENT PROFILE

Career Rating	72
Placement rate (%)	80

ELON UNIVERSITY
MARTHA AND SPENCER LOVE SCHOOL OF BUSINESS

Academics

Flexible scheduling, an affordable degree, and a "focus on leadership and soft-skill development" earn the praises of MBA students at Elon, a premier regional university in North Carolina's Triad region. Nearly all the part-timers here work full-time in addition to fulfilling their academic responsibilities, so students understandably demand convenience in their program. Elon delivers, scheduling all classes once a week in the evenings (6 P.M. to 8:50 P.M., Monday through Thursday) during the spring and fall semesters, classes during the accelerated January and summer terms meet twice a week. Since the school doesn't have lock-step sequencing, "students can choose the courses they feel fit with their current schedules and time tables." As a result, many finish the program in as brief a period as 21 months—on average, students take approximately two years to complete the program.

Elon MBAs can also earn their degrees without putting a significant dent in their bank accounts. One student explains, "What binds most students is the desire to have a strong, valued-added education at a reasonable expense." Many here feel that "the marginal benefits received at schools with higher tuitions aren't worth the extra costs." For the 2004–2005 academic year, courses cost $1,113 each, and students were able to complete their degrees for just under $15,000.

MBAs here praise the "alternative teaching styles and small class sizes." The curriculum "stresses community and teamwork. We do many projects together. The school does not curve the grades in a way such that a portion of the class makes an F; therefore, we all try to work together and not fight for the top position." True to its historic connection to the United Church of Christ, "Elon is as much concerned with producing ethical, trust-worthy, and successful leaders as it is with developing students' academic performance." Professors here "are very accessible and actively engage students to improve both the learning experience and the program overall. There is a tremendous opportunity to tailor class projects to individual interests, which enhances the level of enthusiasm and discussion."

Career and Placement

Career placement services are provided by Elon's Career Development Office, which serves all students in the university. Services offered specifically for MBAs include a battery of self-assessment tools, faculty advising, and seminars with area business leaders. (Through the Legends of Business program, students have met with and learned from Knight Kiplinger, editor-in-chief of the *Kiplinger Letter*; J. Richard Munro, Former Chairman and CEO of Time Warner; and Edward N. Ney, former ambassador to Canada and former Chairman, President and CEO of Young and Rubicam, Inc.) The Love School Board of Advisors meets regularly to work with the administration and faculty to ensure that the program is relevant to the needs of organizations.

Elon MBAs work for some of the area's top employers, including AstraZeneca Pharmaceuticals, Blue Cross & Blue Shield of North Carolina, Cisco Systems, Duke Energy, GE Capital, GlaxoSmithKline, IBM, LabCorp, Lucent Technologies, Procter & Gamble, UNC Hospitals, Wachovia, and Wake Med.

ARTHUR W. FADDE, DIRECTOR OF GRADUATE ADMISSIONS
100 CAMPUS DRIVE, 2750 CAMPUS BOX, ELON, NC 27244 UNITED STATES
PHONE: 800-334-8448 EXT. 3 • FAX: 336-278-7699
E-MAIL: GRADADM@ELON.EDU • WEBSITE: WWW.ELON.EDU/MBA

Student Life and Environment

While students do "study together and occasionally socialize outside of class, most of [them] are older, working, and have active lives apart from the school." Because "the school draws from a large geographic area, it's somewhat hard to mingle with classmates outside of class."

Despite the lack of a "life at school," Elon students sing the praises of their classmates, whom they regard as "an extended family. Students accept each other for who they are and are more than willing to help each other grow and develop in the program." One MBA notes, "I've worked in groups with many strong opinions stemming from a depth of experience and awareness of current events and trends. Many personalities lean towards leadership, and there is a good diversity in both culture and professional background." The student body spans "a wide range of ages, with experienced students helping to educate the less experienced, and the less experienced often assisting the older ones with new perspectives."

Facilities at Elon are undergoing a major upgrade with construction on the Ernest A. Koury Sr. Business Center. The facility, which will house both the undergraduate and graduate business programs, will include the Read Finance Center, computer and research labs, a digital theater, and a variety of classroom designs to suit Elon's nationally recognized style of engaged learning.

Elon's central North Carolina location makes it well situated to serve the Triad region, which includes the Greensboro, High Point, and the Winston–Salem metropolitan areas. As a destination, Elon is notable mostly for its proximity to fine dining in Durham, Chapel Hill, and Greensboro; great barbecue in Lexington; the state's best zoo in Asheboro; and some of the finest golf courses in the nation.

Admissions

The Elon MBA requires a minimum of two years professional experience for all applicants. A completed application must include three letters of recommendation (two from work supervisors), official transcripts from all post-secondary schools attended, and GMAT scores. Students whose native language is not English must also submit TOEFL scores (minimum 550 written, 213 computer). Applicants must exceed a score of 1000 under the formula [(undergraduate GPA $\times$ 200) + GMAT score], and must also have a minimum GMAT score of 470. Undergraduate classes in financial accounting, management, microeconomics, and statistics are required foundationa; courses in the MBA program. Students may begin in August or January; applications are assessed on a rolling basis.

FINANCIAL FACTS

Annual tuition $371 per credit hour

ADMISSIONS

Admissions Selectivity Rating	71
# of applications received	69
% applicants accepted	81
% acceptees attending	84
Average GMAT	524
Range of GMAT	480-560
Average GPA	3.2
Minimum TOEFL (paper/computer)	550/213
Application fee	$35
International application fee	$35
Regular application deadline	Rolling
Regular notification	Rolling
Deferment Available?	Yes
Maximum length of deferment	1 year
Transfer students accepted?	Yes
Transfer application policy: A student may transfer up to 9 semester hours of credit from another accredited graduate school.	
Non-fall admissions?	Yes
Need-blind admissions?	Yes

APPLICANTS ALSO LOOK AT

North Carolina State University, University of North Carolina at Greensboro, Wake Forest University—Winston-Salem.

EMPLOYMENT PROFILE			
Career Rating	60*	Grads employed by field:	
# of companies recruiting on-campus	50	Accounting	8
% grads employed immediately	100	Finance	10
		Human Resources	5
		Marketing	17
		MIS	12
		Operations	22
		Consulting	3
		Entrepreneurship	3
		General Management	5
		Other	7
		Non-profit	8

EMORY UNIVERSITY
GOIZUETA BUSINESS SCHOOL

GENERAL INFORMATION
Type of school	private
Environment	metropolis
Academic calendar	semester

SURVEY SAYS...
Students love Atlanta, GA
Friendly students
Good peer network
Happy students
Smart classrooms
Solid preparation in:
Teamwork
Communication/interpersonal skills
Presentation skills

STUDENTS
Enrollment of parent institution	11,781
Enrollment of MBA program	677
% male/female	71/29
% out-of-state	55
% part-time	18
% minorities	18
% international	24
Average age at entry	28
Average years work experience at entry	5

ACADEMICS
Academic Experience Rating	**93**
Student/faculty ratio	5:1
Profs interesting rating	83
Profs accessible rating	95
% female faculty	28
% minority faculty	19

Joint Degrees
MBA/JD: 4 years
MBA/MPH: 2-3 years
MBA/MDiv: 4 years

Prominent Alumni
Alan Lacy, MBA, CEO, Sears;
Michael Golden, EMBA, Vice
Chairman & SVP, New York Times
Company; Charles Jenkins Jr., BBA,
MBA,CEO, Publix Super Markets,
Inc.; C. Scott Mayfield, EMBA,
President, Mayfield Dairy Farms,
Inc.; Andrew Conway, MBA,
Managing Director, Credit Suisse
First Boston.

Academics

Named after the one-time CEO of the Coca-Cola Company, the Goizueta (pronounced "goy-SWET-uh") Business School at Emory University shares its namesake's penchant for innovative change. Students report favorably that their school "is constantly striving to improve Goizueta. Administrators often ask for our feedback. If we want something to change, we provide our suggestions and a plan to change it, and it's changed. They want to give us the best experience possible." Another MBA adds, "On numerous occasions, projects or proposals generated by students have been adopted by the MBA program. Specifically, several courses have been created by students (they designed the curriculum and interviewed candidates to teach it). If a student is willing to take on the responsibility of addressing a need and taking the solution from paper to fruition, he or she finds the administration to be an excellent partner in the process."

Students appreciate Goizueta's customer-friendly approach, but that's hardly the school's only asset. Goizueta MBAs also benefit from the school's Atlanta locale, which puts them in the neighborhood of many of the nation's largest companies. The strength of Atlanta's business community feeds the faculty and the guest-speaker roster; as one student puts it, "Professors do a great job of bringing business leaders into the classroom. They take full advantage of Atlanta's business connections." Students love Goizueta's finance program; marketing, strategy/entrepreneurship, and consulting are also reportedly strong. Goizueta offers students a fair amount of flexibility, allowing two-year MBAs eleven electives to supplement core courses and other requirements. Core courses "are extremely rigorous and challenging, [some students feel that] there could be more electives to choose from," but the courses that are available are largely excellent. Professors earn high marks for accessibility. One student reports, "I met one-on-one with every one of my professors first semester, and they were all so supportive and willing to give me extra help. Last semester, I had met with my managerial accounting professor a few times throughout the semester and had spent a few hours with her before the final. She came up to me in the middle of the final to see how I was doing and to boost my confidence by reminding me that I was extremely prepared for the test and that I would do great!" Students also love the "fantastic facilities," telling us that "the wireless network in the building makes it easy to be connected."

Career and Placement

The Career Management Center (CMC) at Goizueta "has made tremendous strides over the past three years, but there is still room for improvement. The staff is focused on bringing companies to campus, but could perhaps focus more on cultivating stronger relationships with businesses in the Atlanta community." Many students feel that the office's shortcomings result more from a weak economy than from any lack of effort or expertise on its part. Recruitment efforts are enhanced by the fact that over 700 of the U.S.'s *Fortune* 1000 companies have headquarters in Atlanta. Employers who most frequently hire Goizueta MBAs include Bright House, CHEP International, Citigroup, Delta Air Lines, Earthlink, Eastman Kodak, GE Capital, Honeywell, IBM, ING, Kimberly Clark, NCR, PricewaterhouseCoopers, Procter & Gamble, The Gallup Organization, The Home Depot, Trammell Crow, Turner Broadcasting, and Wachovia. About three-fifths of Goizueta MBAs remain in the South Atlantic region; approximately 1 in 10 finds work outside the United States.

Student Life and Environment

Students love the tight community formed within the Goizueta MBA program. As one student explains, "Life at Goizueta is terrific. I know all of the 160+ members of my two-year MBA class and approximately half of the first year and one-year MBA students via

Julie R. Barefoot, Associate Dean and Director of MBA Admissions
1300 Clifton Road, Atlanta, GA 30322 United States
Phone: 404-727-6311 • Fax: 404-727-4612
E-mail: Admissions@bus.emory.edu • Website: www.goizueta.emory.edu

the Finance Club and other activities. I believe that this is the reason there exists such a pleasant atmosphere at school; without sounding too corny, it really becomes like an extended family." Another student agrees, "We have such a tight network that most people know everybody. You can walk through our common areas and always see people working together on a project, someone helping someone with his resume, someone helping someone with her finance homework. Even when we are not working on assigned team projects, we are always working in teams for something—to help someone with a resume, a cover letter, or an interview. Whatever it is, we work as a team." Students tell us, "The familial atmosphere among students is facilitated to a large degree by the administration. Activities such as student orientation (ropes course, sky diving), three-week international business modules in January, and frequent student get-togethers provide a wealth of opportunities for the students to socialize with one another." Regular program-wide rendezvous include kegs in the courtyard every Thursday ("since there are no classes on Fridays," and bagels every Monday and Wednesday morning. There are "constant gatherings in people's homes, including a weekly poker game, [and, at the end of the fall semester,] a school-wide, *Family Feud*–style event. It gives a great break prior to final exams." All contribute to the especially strong sense of community at Goizueta.

Because it is a relatively small program, Goizueta "offers a large number of leadership positions in the school, particularly in proportion to the number of students. If you want to get involved, you can. There's something for everyone." MBAs tell us that they are "extremely busy. While a fair portion of this can be attributed to class work, there are also a tremendous number of activities that are run by students. These activities range from case competitions to speaker panels to charity events to intramural sports; everyone is involved in something." Then, of course, there's Atlanta, which offers "great restaurants and concerts, as well as major league baseball, hockey, football, and basketball games."

Admissions

Applicants to the Goizueta MBA program must submit undergraduate transcripts (course work should demonstrate solid analytical and/or quantitative skills; one semester of college-level statistics is required), GMAT scores, TOEFL scores (international students), a resume (applicants are required to have "several years of full-time work experience"), two letters of recommendation, and essays. An interview is strongly recommended but is not required. Minority recruitment efforts include participation in the Consortium of Graduate Study in Management, Management for Tomorrow (MLT), and the Forte Foundation. Additionally, the school reports that it hosts 'Inside Goizueta: A Conference for Prospective Minority Students' and attends the National Black MBA and National Society for Hispanic MBA conferences.

FINANCIAL FACTS

Annual tuition	$32,096
Fees	$422
Books and supplies	$1,900
% of students receiving aid	82
% of first-year students receiving aid	74
% of students receiving loans	57
% of students receiving grants	60
Average award package	$31,542
Average grant	$17,815
Average student loan debt	$54,404

ADMISSIONS

Admissions Selectivity Rating	94
# of applications received	1080
% applicants accepted	37
% acceptees attending	39
Average GMAT	680
Range of GMAT	650-710
Average GPA	3.4
TOEFL Required of International Students?	Yes
Minimum TOEFL (paper/computer)	600/250
Application fee	$140
International application fee	$140
Regular application deadline	3/15
Regular notification	Rolling
Deferment Available?	Yes
Maximum length of deferment	1 year
Need-blind admissions?	Yes

APPLICANTS ALSO LOOK AT

Duke University, New York University, Northwestern University, University of Michigan, University of North Carolina at Chapel Hill, University of Pennsylvania, University of Virginia.

EMPLOYMENT PROFILE

Career Rating	93	Grads employed by field	%: avg. salary
% grads employed immediately	74	Finance	33: $78,248
Average starting salary	$85,734	Marketing	24: $76,109
		Operations	4: $76,000
		Consulting	21: $89,252
		General Management	4: $74,938
		Other	14: $81,497

ESADE BUSINESS SCHOOL

Academics

Students at the prestigious ESADE Business School in Barcelona have two full-time MBA options: an 18-month program geared toward students seeking an international dual degree as well as students with nonbusiness backgrounds; and a one-year program designed for highly experienced students seeking a career boost or a fresh start as international entrepreneurs. Both are bilingual programs (but courses in the one-year program are conducted primarily in English). ESADE also offers a part-time program, taught primarily in Spanish, to local students.

Students report that "ESADE places emphasis is on teamwork and collaborative learning." They go on to say, "The workload is significant, but always manageable." The teamwork focus means "half of the learning is done among students through interactions, arguments, and negotiations. These are the skills you will never learn by simply sitting in the classroom, even with the greatest professors teaching you the greatest classes ever." Leadership is also stressed in the "cutting-edge" LEAD (Leadership Assessment and Development) program, in which student groups undertake a challenging business simulation, and then review a videotape of their work to analyze which roles were taken by each group member and how successfully each member utilized leadership skills in performing his or her role.

Professors at ESADE sometimes make courses too "heavily lecture-oriented," and some "don't speak good English," but generally professors earn praise for "knowing exactly the material and subjects of the other courses" and for being "accessible after class." Furthermore, students say, "Since class size is small, you can approach professors very casually, and they are friendly and helpful." Students are especially impressed with the marketing program, and they also tell us, "ESADE has one of the best language programs in Europe, which is very important in an International MBA." The administration is very responsive to student input. One MBA writes," It is not uncommon for student suggestions or proposals to change school policy. In this sense, students feel very respected and important at ESADE."

ESADE offers a dual degree MBA in conjunction with four prestigious U.S. MBA-granting institutions and four equally prestigious Latin American schools; those who complete the program receive degrees from both ESADE and the participating American school.

Career and Placement

ESADE's Career Services office "has only gotten properly started the last couple of years and is not up to par by standards of U.S. schools," observes one American exchange student. However, MBAs report that "the department has made strong improvements in the last few years. There is still room to grow, especially in the connection between employers and students, but they are on their way. They are improving, and this effort must be recognized." Although the school claims contact with more than 1,500 employers, a few students still feel that "ESADE could improve recruiting efforts to companies based in the U.S." and "abroad." The office hosts on-campus forums, recruiting events, corporate presentations, networking and alumni events, workshops, and seminars. It also maintains a Career Resources Center with hard-copy and electronic databases and other reference materials.

Employers most likely to hire ESADE MBAs include Novartis, Citigroup, Bayer, PWC, L'Oreal, General Electric, BBVA, Accenture, Nike, Deloitte & Touche, Intel, Danone, Dupont, and KPMG.

NURIA GUILERA, MBA MARKETING AND ADMISSIONS DIRECTOR
AVENUE D'ESPLUGUES, 92-96 BARCELONA, 08034 SPAIN
PHONE: 011-34-934-952-088 • FAX: 011-34-934-953-828
E-MAIL: MBA@ESADE.EDU • WEBSITE: WWW.ESADE.EDU

FINANCIAL FACTS

Annual tuition	$29,575
Books and supplies	$200
% of first-year students receiving aid	40
Average grant	$18,474

ADMISSIONS

Admissions Selectivity Rating	**85**
# of applications received	281
% applicants accepted	63
% acceptees attending	45
Average GMAT	630
Range of GMAT	600-700
Average GPA	3.5
TOEFL Required of International Students?	Yes
Minimum TOEFL (paper/computer)	600/250
Application fee	$100
International application fee	$100
Regular application deadline	6/30
Regular notification	Rolling
Deferment Available?	Yes
Maximum length of deferment	1 year
Non-fall admissions?	Yes
Need-blind admissions?	Yes

Student Life and Environment

"ESADE is a well-balanced school," and it features "individual activities as well as team-work opportunities." While the workload can be demanding, "there is always time to go and have a beer with your friends." Many students enjoy spending each morning "with a cup of café con leche on the sunny terrace of the school overlooking Barcelona." Whether working or playing, ESADE MBAs enjoy a convivial atmosphere. One student comments, "People are very friendly. Even though we may work a lot, social life is very important. I don't see ESADE as an MBA factory like many other business schools, but more like a place to live a once-in-a-lifetime experience."

ESADE "doesn't provide accommodations for students, but the school has an agency that will find you the living space you want. This city is unbeatable and very, very safe." Barcelona, which students call "a very attractive city that has a great social and cultural life," is home to world-renowned art galleries and museums, concert halls, theaters, and international athletic events—not to mention the trippy architectural masterpieces by Antonio Gaudí. It's also a port city and one of the great economic centers of southern Europe.

ESADE's student body is "very diverse, interactive, friendly, creative, and dynamic." One student reports, "My academic team of seven students (which works together the entire first year) has people from Greece, Spain, Puerto Rico, France, Canada, the U.S., and Japan. In terms of business background: corporate finance in a blue-chip company, stock trading in a brokerage, marketing in IT, marketing in biotech, managing a theme park, operations/logistics in the automobile industry, and operations/logistics in meat production. It's a very diverse group." Students go on to say this school "is a very team-oriented and supportive culture and people form very personal and strong relationships."

Admissions

Applicants to the 18-month full-time MBA program must have a minimum of two years' full-time work experience. Applicants to the one-year full-time MBA program must have at least five years of full-time work experience and an undergraduate degree in business or economics (candidates with engineering or mathematics degrees are evaluated in the light of their business experience). Completed applications must include: official transcripts for all undergraduate work, official GMAT and English proficiency scores (ESADE offers its own English proficiency exam), two letters of recommendation, and an application form. Interviews are conducted at the school's request only; all admitted students are interviewed prior to admission. According to the school's website, "Aspects taken into account during the admission process include: the candidate's intellectual abilities; professional potential; maturity; motivation; and ability to work as part of a team."

EMPLOYMENT PROFILE

Career Rating	88	Grads employed by field:	
Placement rate (%)	95	Finance	16
% grads employed immediately	74	Marketing	23
Average starting salary	$72,093	Consulting	23
		General Management	34
		Other	3
		Non-profit	1

ESSEC BUSINESS SCHOOL
THE ESSEC MBA PROGRAM

GENERAL INFORMATION
Type of school   private
Academic calendar   trimester

SURVEY SAYS...
Good social scene
Happy students
Solid preparation in:
Teamwork

STUDENTS
Enrollment of parent
  institution
Enrollment of MBA program   1,834
% male/female   52/48
Average age at entry   23
Average years work experience
  at entry   1

ACADEMICS
Academic Experience Rating   89
Student/faculty ratio   19:1
Profs interesting rating   75
Profs accessible rating   73
% female faculty   23
Joint Degrees
ESSEC-Mannheim double-degree
MBA, ESSEC-Nanyang
Technological University double-
degree MBA, ESSEC-Guanghua
School of Management double-
degree MBA, ESSEC-Seoul National
University (double-degree MBA or
ESSEC MBA + Seoul MA in
International Relations). ESSEC-TEC
double-degree MBA. European MBA
with ESSEC, Mannheim U. and
Warwick University.
Prominent Alumni
Gilles Pelisson, CEO, Bougues
Telecom; Dominique Reiniche,
President Europe, Coca Cola;
Christian Balmes, Chairman & CEO,
Shell France; Patrick Cescau,
Chairman, Unilever; Jean-Louis
Petitbon, Managing Director, Egon
Zehnder Int'l France.

Academics

ESSEC advertises its program as a "flexible, integrative MBA," and students confirm that this French business school adheres to truth-in-advertising principles. As per flexibility, "students choose all the courses they attempt. It's the first school in France that decided to follow a process like that. It's great because you don't spend your time in courses that don't interest you." The integrative aspect comes through 18 months of required internships (which can be waived for students with equivalent post-baccalaureate professional experience) and optional apprenticeships.

ESSEC MBAs "are allowed to choose their own classes and professional experiences. Each student is tutored by a resident teacher who provides advice and insights; by alternating periods in school and interning with companies, ESSEC students gain much maturity and understanding of the stakes of their future careers." One student explains, "Everything is flexible, as long as we stay within the criteria needed to graduate, from the number of courses per day, per week, per quarter, per semester, the lengths of each internship and other professional experience, to the choice of courses or the way to fulfill our required international content." ESSEC MBAs can meet this requirement through study abroad at an ESSEC partner school, a dual degree at one of five international schools, or an internship or humanitarian mission abroad.

The ESSEC curriculum is broad, offering over 200 electives each term, so "you can be a generalist or become really specialized in a particular domain." Students report that "for a business school, ESSEC is really aware of new concerns like ethics and sustainable development, and it tries to make the students aware of what happens in the world economy nowadays." MBAs warn, "You have to be responsible and define your own goals, and the course attribution system is somehow complicated, but the administration is outstanding: they make this complex system work smoothly, deal with the high flexibility, answer your questions, and always try to improve our school, making it the most innovative in France." All students work with a mentor "who follows you and helps you throughout your scholarly half of the program."

ESSEC professors are often "top executives in French companies and are thus experts of the evolutions of the techniques used in the fields in which they teach." Others are well-known in research circles. ESSEC's strengths include such uncommon areas as international hospitality management, luxury brand management, agrifood and agribusiness management, sports marketing, and ethics and biotechnology.

Career and Placement

The Office of Corporate/Student Relations at ESSEC Business School keeps busy by handling the 8,000+ internship offers that pour into the school each year. In addition, the office provides one-on-one counseling; organizes on-campus recruitment, company visits, and job fairs; and manages the school's large apprenticeship program (under which students work for an area company for two years while simultaneously continuing their studies at ESSEC). Each year 220 employers visit the campus to recruit MBAs for full-time work; another 700 offer internship positions.

Employers who most frequently hire ESSEC graduates include Accenture, BNP Paribas, Danone, Deloitte Touche Tohmatsu, Deutsche Bank, EDF-GDF, L'Oréal, Michelin, Pfizer, Pinault Printemps Redoute, PricewaterhouseCoopers, Procter & Gamble, Renault, Societe Generale, and 3 Suisses International.

Mr. Philippe Regimbart, Director of Admissions
Avenue Bernard Hirsch, B.P. 50105 Cergy-Pontoise, 95021 France
Phone: 011-33-1-3443-3095 • Fax: 011-33-1-3443-3111
E-mail: merizio@essec.fr • Website: www.essec.edu

Student Life and Environment

ESSEC "has a very good feeling of appartenance (belonging), [forged in part by the] many school clubs which easily bring people together." One MBA notes, "The number of associations in this business school enables you to do any activities you ever dreamed of, from sky-diving to bartending, or any others. The associations and clubs are really numerous and different, encompassing sports (sailing, football, basketball, tennis, golf), culture (theatre, poetry, cinema, photography), and economics and politics. Any student can create a new association, and the administration helps us."

"Most students spend a lot of time on campus, [which] will become a lot nicer: Heavy construction work is on its way, both for the school and for the student housing." Students note that the campus is relatively large by French standards," and that "new amenities will happily be built in the coming years to modernize the old-looking main buildings from the 1970s!" While some complain that "the location is unfortunately outside the capital," others like their hometown of Cergy Pontoise, "a suburb in the northwest of Paris. Cergy is 30 minutes away by tube from the center of Paris, and the train station is just near the school. Cergy Pontoise is quite a big city (150,000 people) with all facilities (supermarkets, many different shops for all types of shopping). So you do not have to go into Paris all the time if you do not want to. Last but not least, living in Cergy Pontoise is very nice because you can have quite a cheap flat, and you are at the same time very close to the center of Paris with a straight tube line. It is perfect!"

The ESSEC student body represents 63 countries; nearly half its students are women. Most MBAs are young. According to one student, "There are very few students who are married or have children because the average age is 22 to 23."

Admissions

ESSEC requires the following of international applicants to its MBA program: official copies of all undergraduate and graduate transcripts; TOEFL, GMAT or TAGE/MAGE (the French equivalent of the GMAT) scores; letters of recommendation; a personal statement; and a resume. According to the school's website, "A minimum of 18 months of validated professional experience is required, but students with insufficient experience may enroll if admitted and carry out this work requirement during their ESSEC MBA program in periods of internship. In such cases, the program will be prolonged and may last longer than two years."

FINANCIAL FACTS

Annual tuition	$10,709
Books and supplies	$565
Room & board (on/off-campus)	$7,500/$11,260
% of students receiving aid	36
% of first-year students receiving aid	33
% of students receiving grants	12
Average award package	$5,822
Average grant	$4,225
Average student loan debt	$25,422

ADMISSIONS

Admissions Selectivity Rating	**97**
# of applications received	4,686
% applicants accepted	19
% acceptees attending	61
Average GMAT	670
Range of GMAT	600-780
TOEFL Required of International Students?	Yes
Minimum TOEFL (paper/computer)	600/230
Application fee	$195
International application fee	$195
Regular application deadline	3/1
Regular notification	6/4
Deferment Available?	Yes
Maximum length of deferment	1 year
Need-blind admissions?	Yes

APPLICANTS ALSO LOOK AT

E.M. LYON, ESCP-EAP European School of Management, HEC School of Management.

EMPLOYMENT PROFILE			
Career Rating	**81**	Grads employed by field:	
Placement rate (%)	77	Accounting	8
# of companies recruiting on-campus	220	Finance	11
% grads employed immediately	43	Human Resources	2
Average starting salary	$49,014	Marketing	30
		MIS	2
		Operations	6
		Consulting	32
		General Management	3
		Other	6

FAIRFIELD UNIVERSITY
THE DOLAN SCHOOL OF BUSINESS

GENERAL INFORMATION
Type of school   private
Affiliation   Roman Catholic-Jesuit
Environment   town
Academic calendar   semester

SURVEY SAYS...
Students love Fairfield, CT
Friendly students
Happy students
Smart classrooms
Solid preparation in:
Teamwork

STUDENTS
Enrollment of parent
  institution   5,154
Enrollment of MBA program   191
% male/female   91/9
% part-time   88
% minorities   5
% international   17
Average age at entry   29
Average years work experience
  at entry   6

ACADEMICS
Academic Experience Rating   69
Student/faculty ratio   23:1
Profs interesting rating   75
Profs accessible rating   72
% female faculty   36
% minority faculty   2
Prominent Alumni
Drive E. Gerald Corrigan, Managing
Director, Goldman, Sachs & Co.;
Joseph Berardino, CEO Andersen;
Robert Murphy, Jr., Senior V.P., The
Walt Disney Company Foundation;
Christopher McCormick, President
& CEO, LL Bean, Inc.; Drive Francis
Tedesco, President, Medical College
of Georgia.

Academics

"Jesuit tenets" guide instruction at the Dolan School of Business, a small, mostly part-time program at Fairfield University that boasts "a fine finance program." Dolan offers graduates an MBA (part-time and full-time), an MS in finance, and a one-year MBA in accounting. Qualified professionals may enroll in certificate programs for advanced study in accounting, finance, human resource management, information systems & operations management, international business, marketing, and taxation here.

The Dolan MBA curriculum is divided into three components: core courses, breadth courses, and elective specialization or concentration courses. Core classes count toward the graduate degree; they are meant to be functional areas of deficiency in students' academic business backgrounds, and some or all can be waived for students who successfully completed undergraduate courses in the areas these classes cover. Breadth courses account for 18 credits toward the degree and cover important concepts in accounting, finance, information systems, management, business ethics, and marketing. The remainder of the curriculum consists of 12 credits of concentration courses (concentrations are available in accounting, finance, human resource management, information systems and operations, general management, international business, marketing, and taxation), an additional three elective credits, and a three-credit capstone course in global competitive strategy.

The One-Year MBA in accounting is open to undergraduates in accounting from all undergraduate institutions. Pursued full-time, this program "leads to the MBA and fulfills requirements to sit for the uniform CPA examination" in 12 to 15 months.

Dolan students praise their "very accessible and helpful faculty," telling us that "professors' enthusiasm contributes a lot to the learning experience. The coursework is current and interesting." Courses are held between 7:00 and 10 P.M. on weekday evenings for the convenience of employed students; a limited number of weekend courses are also available.

Career and Placement

The Dolan MBA program is a small, predominantly part-time program in which most students already have careers; a number of students actually attend at their employers' expense. This situation creates a relatively small demand for career services within the program; students seeking such services must use the Career Planning Center, which serves the entire student body of the university. The Dolan Graduate Business Association, run by students, is probably the most aggressive advocate for career services within the program. Professors and alumni are also regarded as valuable resources for those seeking internships or careers.

Employers most likely to hire Dolan MBAs include American Skandia, Bayer Corporation, Cendant Corporation, The Common Fund, Gartner, General Electric, People's Bank, Pitney Bowes, Pfizer, UBS Warburg, Unilever, and United Technologies.

DR. DANA A. WILKIE, ASSISTANT DEAN/DIRECTOR OF GRADUATE PROGRAMS
1073 NORTH BENSON ROAD, FAIRFIELD, CT 06824 UNITED STATES
PHONE: 203-254-4000 • FAX: 203-254-4029
E-MAIL: DLAURIA@MAIL.FAIRFIELD.EDU • WEBSITE: WWW.FAIRFIELD.EDU/MBA

Student Life and Environment

The Dolan School of Business is housed in a 70,000 square foot facility that includes a 150-seat amphitheater, a wireless computer network, two high-tech computer labs, eight breakout rooms for meetings and projects, and numerous classrooms and offices. Classrooms are equipped to accommodate all up-to-date teaching technologies. Students here praise the "informal, relaxed atmosphere" and "safe campus" that makes the "heavy workload" a little easier to handle. Most agree that extracurricular life is minimal, and that there's "not much for MBAs to do here on campus except go to class."

Dolan students benefit from the school's location near New York City. Nearly fifty Fortune 500 companies are headquartered within 50 miles of the school; a little further afield (in New York City itself and lower Westchester County, all within an hour from campus) approximately one hundred Fortune 500 companies maintain significant presences. Fairfield County is home to the greatest concentration of U.S. headquarters for foreign multinationals; many of these firms work with the university to provide experiential learning opportunities.

Admissions

Applications may be submitted to Dolan via mail or the Internet. Applications are processed on a rolling basis, and students may commence the program in any term. The Admissions Committee considers applicants' post-secondary academic records, GMAT scores, two letters of recommendation, and resume or other self-evaluation of work experience. In general, applicants are expected to have achieved a minimum undergraduate GPA of 3.00 and a score of at least 500 on the GMAT. International students from non-English speaking countries must submit TOEFL scores (a minimum score of 550 is required). Applicants to the one-year MBA program in accounting and taxation must meet all the above criteria and must also provide a statement of certification from his/her accounting department faculty and a letter of recommendation from either a former employer or a faculty member outside the discipline of accounting. This program is open only to students who hold, or are in the process of earning, an undergraduate degree in accounting. All entering students in all programs must demonstrate proficiency in microeconomics, macroeconomics, calculus, and statistics. Successful completion of undergraduate work in these areas is the most common way of demonstrating proficiency.

FINANCIAL FACTS

Annual tuition	$22,000
Fees	$100
Books and supplies	$1,000

ADMISSIONS

Admissions Selectivity Rating	**76**
# of applications received	72
% applicants accepted	78
% acceptees attending	100
Average GMAT	550
Range of GMAT	490-650
Average GPA	3.2
TOEFL Required of International Students?	Yes
Minimum TOEFL (paper/computer)	550/213
Application fee	$55
International application fee	$55
Regular application deadline	Rolling
Regular notification	Rolling
Deferment Available?	Yes
Maximum length of deferment	1 year
Transfer students accepted?	Yes
Transfer application policy: 6 credits or Jesuit University Transfer Program.	
Non-fall admissions?	Yes

APPLICANTS ALSO LOOK AT

Pace University, Quinnipiac University, University of Connecticut.

EMPLOYMENT PROFILE	
Career Rating	**60***
% grads employed immediately	98

FLORIDA ATLANTIC UNIVERSITY
COLLEGE OF BUSINESS

GENERAL INFORMATION
Type of school   public
Environment   city
Academic calendar   semesters

SURVEY SAYS...
Friendly students
Solid preparation in:
Teamwork
Communication/interpersonal skills
Presentation skills

STUDENTS
Enrollment of parent institution	25,383
Enrollment of MBA program	490
% male/female	56/44
% part-time	72
% minorities	29
Average age at entry	31
Average years work experience at entry	6.5

ACADEMICS
Academic Experience Rating	**79**
Student/faculty ratio	14:1
Profs interesting rating	89
Profs accessible rating	81
% female faculty	30

Academics

A wide variety of programs and an equally wide variety of class sites distinguish the MBA programs at Florida Atlantic University's College of Business. Local students are drawn here by the price and convenience; those from farther away come for such distinctive programs as the MBA in Sports Management, which is "one of a handful of such programs in the country that is AACSB accredited," or the Masters of Forensic Accounting—"the oldest program in the nation and one of the few available online. Others come for the MBA in Accounting "whose students rank among the top ten in CPA Exam passage rates," or the MS in International Business program through which "many students go to Spain and Brazil."

FAU offers MBA classes online as well as on its campuses in Boca Raton, Jupiter, Port Saint Lucie, and two sites in Fort Lauderdale. While students appreciate that "the multiple campuses allows the school to draw students from a wide geographic area," some complain that "the school does not offer a full curriculum at any single location, so you frequently have to drive between campuses that range from 20 to 60 miles apart. Also, courses aren't always offered in the same order as the curriculum requires they are taken." MBAs' praise for the distance-learning program is more unequivocal; they love its convenience and describe it as "a good value." Writes one participant, "For those of us in distance learning, the professors are very accommodating and available. I am very pleased with distance delivery."

Students here tell us that FAU professors "are recognized leaders in industry." Several "do consulting, expert-witness, or law-enforcement work outside of the classroom," while others "are solid professors from northern schools that have come to retire in South Florida." Reports one student, "Many of my professors have outstanding multidisciplinary knowledge and easiness in sharing it with the students." But another explains, "I come from a top 20 undergraduate school, so I've been disappointed in the ambition of some of the students, but the professors make up for that." Students also tell us that "classes are challenging and involved, and the cases are from real-world scenarios." As at many state schools, the administration "is a nightmare—not at all user-friendly."

Career and Placement

FAU's College of Business houses the Career Resources and Alumni Relations Center to provide undergraduates and graduate business students with "invaluable guidance with interviewing skills, resume preparation, locating employment opportunities, and locating internships." The office also compiles student resumes on a CD-ROM to be distributed to South Florida businesses. Graduate students have exclusive access to the Job Connection, an Internet-based notification system that alerts them to job postings that match their qualifications. FAU participates in a statewide job fair held in the autumn.

Student Life and Environment

FAU attracts students from "a variety of different backgrounds both in business and culture," with "many coming from fields other than business, such as healthcare, law, and government." There are also a number of freshly minted undergrads in the program. This "diversity of the student body gives students a chance to share different job experiences and look at the business world from many perspectives." International students appreciate that "colleagues are friendly and helpful, which is extremely important for those of us who are separated from family and friends. During my MBA program I have made many friends and I am sure that even after graduation I will be able to maintain good relationships with many of my colleagues."

FREDRICK TAYLOR, GRADUATE ADVISOR
MASTERS STUDIES, FW 101, 777 GLADES ROAD, BOCA RATON, FL 33431 UNITED STATES
PHONE: 561-297-3650 • FAX: 561-297-1315
E-MAIL: MBA@FAU.EDU • WEBSITE: WWW.BUSINESS.FAU.EDU

Because so many MBAs are part-time students with full-time jobs, "there is virtually no social activity on campus. It is a great school for students who are married, have children, or are already pursuing a career." Explains one student, "The students are focused on getting home after class, since most have been working all day before class. The interaction is limited to what is necessary to get the work done, mostly. People are generally nice, but not very sociable unless they are part of some special group, like sports management or the like." Full-time students enjoy more opportunities to participate in the university community, and they take advantage of them. Writes one, "The university gives all students a chance to participate in sport events, concerts, charity actions, religious organization, and minority clubs. FAU also offers free access to self-defense classes, fitness classes, a gym, and a swimming pool."

Admissions

Admission to a FAU MBA program requires the following: an undergraduate degree with a GPA of at least 3.0 (on a four-point scale) for the final 60 semester hours of undergraduate course work from an accredited institution; and a score of at least 500 on the GMAT, earned within the previous five years. In addition to the above qualifications, international students whose first language is not English must also submit official score reports indicating a score of at least 600 on the TOEFL and at least 250 on the Test of Spoken English (TSE). All international applicants must submit Certification of Financial Responsibility and must provide translation and accredited evaluation of their undergraduate transcripts (the latter is necessary only if a grading system other than the American system was used at the degree-granting institution). For all applicants, letters of recommendation, a resume, an interview, and a personal statement are all optional. After undergraduate record and standardized test scores, work history is the most important factor in admissions decisions.

FINANCIAL FACTS

Annual tuition (in-state/out-of-state)	$5,571/$20,868
Books and supplies	$1,200

ADMISSIONS

Admissions Selectivity Rating	77
# of applications received	457
% applicants accepted	59
% acceptees attending	62
Average GMAT	525
Range of GMAT	474-568
Average GPA	3.3
TOEFL Required of International Students?	Yes
Minimum TOEFL (paper/computer)	600/250
Application fee	$30
International application fee	$30
Regular application deadline	7/1
Regular notification	Rolling
Deferment Available?	Yes
Maximum length of deferment	1 year
Non-fall admissions?	Yes
Need-blind admissions?	Yes

APPLICANTS ALSO LOOK AT

Florida International University, Florida State University, Miami University, University of Central Florida, University of Florida, University of South Florida.

EMPLOYMENT PROFILE	
Career Rating	73
Placement rate (%)	95
# of companies recruiting on-campus	101
Average starting salary	$39,000

FLORIDA GULF COAST UNIVERSITY
COLLEGE OF BUSINESS

GENERAL INFORMATION
Type of school   public
Academic calendar   semester

SURVEY SAYS...
Friendly students
Happy students
Solid preparation in:
Teamwork

ACADEMICS
Academic Experience Rating   62
Profs interesting rating   88
Profs accessible rating   85

Academics

Pragmatic concerns—location, affordability, convenience, and the ability to earn a degree quickly—motivate most who select the MBA program at Florida Gulf Coast University, a relatively new institution located two hours' south of Tampa Bay. This predominantly part-time program, which pursues "a clear mission to incorporate the global, national, and local business environment into the curriculum of our specific classes," represents a real bargain for native Floridians who, thanks to a well-developed distance learning program, can benefit no matter where they live in the state.

FGCU was established in 1997, which means that "the school has new facilities with technology in most classrooms," a major plus in today's tech-driven business world. One student writes, "Technological savvy is important, and we maximize and leverage our position as a new school with new equipment to aid learning, communication, and feedback." The school has quickly developed a reputation among Sunshine State natives. as one put it, "I chose this school because I know that FGCU is going to be the next big university in Florida, and I want to be part of it."

The FGCU MBA "emphasizes the application of analytical, technical, and behavioral tools to solve organizational problems," with "a focus on teamwork and team building so students frequently work closely together." The program consists of 24 hours of foundation courses, 21 hours of core courses, and 9 hours of concentration courses. Students with solid business backgrounds or college transcripts deep in business courses may have some or all of their foundation courses waived. Concentrations are available in finance, general management, marketing, or information systems. Or, students may choose to design their own interdisciplinary concentration.

MBAs praise the faculty at FGCU, telling us that professors "are very helpful. They bring a lot of experience and tips with them to the class." One MBA observes, "The generally small size of the program makes the professors very available." Students also appreciate that "FGCU has made a big commitment to online access, not only in distance learning but in having nearly all services online–registration, submitting homework (even for traditional classroom classes), the bookstore, class chat rooms, class-specific e-mail, etc." Although there are still a few bugs in the system, "time should help all of the programs and the campus to become more well-rounded. For being such a new school, FGCU should be commended for where they are now."

Career and Placement

All career services at Florida Gulf Coast University are provided by the school's Career Development Services Office, which assists undergraduates and graduate students in all areas. The office sponsors a variety of events throughout the year, including workshops, seminars, on-campus recruiting visits, and a career fair.

Because the school is relatively new—FGCU welcomed its first students in 1997—its alumni network is in the early stages of development with a major campaign underway to network alum. One student writes, "Over time I hope the university gets more national recognition to reward the staff for their efforts. As alumni become distributed through the national work force, I hope for more national corporations to recruit from our student ranks."

ANA HILL, ADMISSIONS-REGISTRAR OFFICER-GRADUATE ADMISSIONS
10501 FGCU BOULEVARD SOUTH, FORT MYERS, FL 33965 UNITED STATES
PHONE: 888-889-1095 • FAX: 239-590-7894
E-MAIL: GRADUATE@FGCU.EDU • WEBSITE: WWW.FGCU.EDU

Student Life and Environment

FGCU's location, "15 minutes from the Gulf of Mexico (Bonita Springs or Fort Myers Beach) in the center of a cypress swamp filled with wildlife," is regarded as one of the school's greatest assets." Students say "You can't beat the quality of life in southwest Florida. It's still a fairly small town in a beautiful part of the country where it's warm and green all year with great beaches." Better still, the region is "a major growth area, with exciting opportunities for employment in the near future."

FGCU is growing right along with its surroundings; "During the past four years the student population has doubled at FGCU. There have been a number of buildings added," students report. While FGCU "is too young to have a major college sports presence, [the] student athletics program has excellent student athletes who are also great in academics." Greek life "is beginning to become established," and those who live on campus enjoy dorms "located on a lake with water sports (sailing, kayaking, and canoeing). There are always activities available either to the general population or through clubs."

Most students here, however, don't have much time for such diversions. Those who actually attend classes on campus—the school also serves a sizeable distance-learning population—generally work full-time. Many have family obligations too, leaving little (make that, zero) time for extracurriculars. One MBA explains, "Other than being in class, there really is no campus life for MBA students, as we all have regular full-time jobs, families, and we live scattered around the area in our own homes. Additionally, many of the classes are offered online, so sometimes your 'classmates' might be located in other countries. As for on-campus classes, the students are friendly and laid back (this is southwest Florida after all!). But we all go our separate ways to our 'real' lives, home, and our families when class is over." FGCU MBAs "range from students who have just graduated from an undergraduate program to those who have been in the workforce for over 20 years." The types of professions in which these students work range from accounting and real estate to law and the service industry.

Admissions

Admission to the MBA program at FGCU is based on a combination of undergraduate GPA and GMAT scores. To be considered, applicants must have either (1) a minimum GPA of 3.0 for their final 60 credit hours of undergraduate work; (2) a minimum GMAT score of 500; or (3) a formula score of at least 1050 under the formula [(undergraduate GPA + 200) + GMAT score], with a minimum GMAT score of at least 400. International students must also submit TOEFL scores (minimum 550 written, 213 computerized). Students may apply for admission to either the fall or spring semester. Students may complete a maximum of nine credit hours of graduate level courses before gaining official admission to the program.

FINANCIAL FACTS

Annual tuition (in-state/out-of-state)
$2,634/$10,088

ADMISSIONS

Admissions Selectivity Rating	60*
Application fee	$30
Regular application deadline	6/15
Non-fall admissions?	Yes

FLORIDA STATE UNIVERSITY
COLLEGE OF BUSINESS

Academics

"Florida State University's MBA program is comparatively small," which students tell us "has many advantages." Reports one student, "Every person within the admissions and administrative offices knows each student's name and a little about each person. We say 'hello' in the halls and their doors are never closed. They assist each student not only with academic affairs and support, but also with personal issues if needed." The small size of the program also means that "professors are easily accessible to help with any questions or concerns that may arise. The size of the program also allows them to act on their concern for the progress of the students." On the downside, "as a smaller program, they don't receive much national recognition."

For most of the school's current students, national recognition is not their main concern, anyway. They are mostly local and predominantly part-time, looking to advance in jobs they already hold or make an upward move within the local job market. What students here generally want most is affordability, convenience, and a solid reputation within the state. FSU scores big on all three counts. A low, in-state tuition suits most MBAs' budgets, while a selection of part-time and full-time options presents an unusually wide range of choices for a program of this size. This all adds up to make an "MBA program that is a hidden treasure waiting to be discovered." Both the full-time program and the part-time program on the main campus in Tallahassee offer concentrations in finance, global entrepreneurship, and marketing and supply chain management. Part-time programs at branch campuses, "though completely served by the faculty of the main campus, offer only general MBAs. There is no real area of concentration offered because electives are inconsistent." The school also offers an online MBA that students can complete "from anywhere in the world." The online program allows for a general MBA, as well as concentrations in hospitality administration and real estate finance and analysis.

Career and Placement

Even though FSU's MBA program is small and largely part-time, the school maintains a separate career services office for graduate students in business. It also sponsors a mentoring program that "connects protégés with mentors who can share their experience and wisdom concerning general business leadership skills, professional success factors, management skills, team building, and communication skills," according to the school's website. Students feel the school could "improve its efforts to help students find internships and attract recruiting companies that specifically target MBAs."

Employers most likely to hire FSU MBAs include Raytheon, Harris, and BB&T. The school reports that 33 percent of its graduates find work in operations (avg. salary $70,000), 25 percent find work in finance ($42,500), and 17 percent in marketing ($51,250).

Student Life and Environment

Students love FSU's "amazing, beautiful campus" with its "enthusiastic students and diligent professors." They also love hometown Tallahassee, which they describe as "a small town, but big enough to have malls and good restaurants. It's also close to the beach, which is great." Those interested in government careers should find plenty to interest them here, as "Tallahassee is a very political city with thousands of state employees, providing a unique opportunity to take advantage of many state employment positions."

RONALD G. MOTTER, COORDINATOR, MASTERS PROGRAMS ADMISSIONS
GRADUATE OFFICE, COLLEGE OF BUSINESS, FSU, TALLAHASSEE, FL 32306-1110 UNITED STATES
PHONE: 850-644-6458 • FAX: 850-644-0588
E-MAIL: GRADPROG@COB.FSU.EDU • WEBSITE: WWW.COB.FSU.EDU

The mostly part-time students here "usually attend evening classes twice a week and meet with small groups outside of class whenever we can. That's about it for campus involvement." Full-timers get more involved in the life of the university, which of course includes "outstanding athletics programs. The FSU football and baseball teams are constantly in the national championship race, so it makes for a very exciting sports atmosphere." One student writes, "The best time is during football season when students can get to know each other at tailgates and other events." Another claims that for students here, "the nightlife is second to none. There's nothing like going to Bullwinkle's after a tough exam!"

FSU MBAs tell us the school runs "a smooth operation" all around. They enjoy "a friendly atmosphere that allows for positive group cohesiveness during teamwork exercises." Students benefit from each others' "diverse backgrounds. We have people who have just graduated from undergraduate programs, people returning to school after a few years of work experience, and people with previous experience in the military. Overall, we have a very tight-knit group of students." Students speculate that their classmates have, "on average, about five years of work experience."

Admissions

The Admissions Office at Florida State University requires all of the following from applicants to its MBA program: official copies of transcripts for all post-secondary academic work; an official GMAT score report; three letters of recommendation from former professors and/or employers; a resume; and a personal statement. Students must have proficiency working with PCs. International students whose first language is not English must also submit an official score report for the TOEFL (minimum score of 600 paper-based test or 250 computer-based test required). All test scores must be no more than five years old. The school lists the following programs designed to increase recruitment of underrepresented and disadvantaged students: the FAMU Feeder Program, FAMU Graduate & Professional Days, GradQuest, MBA Advantage, Minority Student Orientation Program, Leslie Wilson Assistantships, the Delores Auzenne Minority Fellowship, and the University Fellowship.

FINANCIAL FACTS

Annual tuition (in-state/out-of-state)	$9,407/$35,264
Books and supplies	$5,750
Room & board (on/off-campus)	$13,000/$15,000
Average award package	$10,000
Average grant	$2,500

ADMISSIONS

Admissions Selectivity Rating	84
# of applications received	104
% applicants accepted	49
% acceptees attending	84
Average GMAT	553
Average GPA	3.3
TOEFL Required of International Students?	Yes
Minimum TOEFL (paper/computer)	600/250
Application fee	$30
International application fee	$30
Regular application deadline	2/1
Regular notification	Rolling
Deferment Available?	Yes
Maximum length of deferment	1 year
Transfer students accepted?	Yes
Transfer application policy: Transfer applicants must complete the same application process as all other applicants.	
Non-fall admissions?	Yes
Need-blind admissions?	Yes

APPLICANTS ALSO LOOK AT

University of Florida, University of North Florida, University of South Florida.

EMPLOYMENT PROFILE

Career Rating	70	Grads employed by field	%: avg. salary
Placement rate (%)	44	Finance	25: $42,500
# of companies recruiting on-campus	20	Marketing	17: $51,250
% grads employed immediately	30	Operations	33: $70,000
Average starting salary	$61,989	General Management	8
		Other	17: $75,200

FRANCIS MARION UNIVERSITY
SCHOOL OF BUSINESS

GENERAL INFORMATION

Type of school	public
Environment	rural
Academic calendar	semester

SURVEY SAYS...

Friendly students
Happy students
Solid preparation in:
Teamwork
Presentation skills
Quantitative skills

STUDENTS

Enrollment of parent institution	3,947
Enrollment of MBA program	61
% male/female	49/51
% part-time	95
% minorities	20
% international	7
Average age at entry	29

ACADEMICS

Academic Experience Rating	**61**
Student/faculty ratio	3:1
Profs interesting rating	71
Profs accessible rating	63

Academics

The School of Business at South Carolina's Francis Marion University offers a "convenient" MBA program "scheduled in the evening to accommodate working students." Since FMU is a state school, it does so at a price that doesn't break the bank.

This small school—one of the smallest state universities to earn AACSB accreditation, according to the university view book—affords "plenty of good one-on-one time with teachers" to its almost exclusively part-time student body. FMU offers both a general MBA and an MBA with a concentration in Health Management. The former is designed to serve the general business population of the Pee Dee region and beyond; the latter is directed toward individuals currently employed in the health care field and/or those with backgrounds in health care. The Health Management Degree is delivered to FMU students through online classes and resources."

All FMU MBAs must complete courses in accounting for management control, managerial economics, financial theory and applications, management science and statistics, marketing, and finance. Students in the general MBA program must also complete classes in financial accounting, information systems, international business, production management, entrepreneurship, and strategic management. Students pursuing a health concentration must also complete classes in health policy, health economics, health care delivery systems, financial management for health care organizations, and health law and risk management. Students in health management may also take three hours of elective coursework. At the conclusion of the program, students must pass comprehensive final examinations covering 10 of 12 functions.

MBAs tell us that the program meets their needs, although some feel that "there is too much busy work" and others complain that "some classes are too easy, more suitable to undergraduates than MBAs." One student suggests, "Tailor the program to the real jobs graduates will get." Many also feel that "the school needs to offer more and a wider variety of MBA classes." Most, however, tell us that the convenience and cost of the degree are strong positives.

Career and Placement

FMU's MBA program is too small to support career services dedicated exclusively to its students. MBAs receive career assistance from the university's Office of Career Development, which serves undergraduates and graduates in all divisions. Students here also benefit from an active Alumni Association, whose newest chapter is the MBA Alumni Chapter.

BEN KYER, DIRECTOR
BOX 100547 FLORENCE, SC 29501-0547 UNITED STATES
PHONE: 843-661-1436 • FAX: 843-661-1432
E-MAIL: ALPHA1@FMARION.EDU • WEBSITE: HTTP://ALPHA1.FMARION.EDU/~MBA/

Student Life and Environment

Life in the FMU MBA program "can be hectic," especially toward the end of the semester. "It seems like all projects and exams are due at the same time," writes one student. Most students are "intelligent and hardworking…professional adults trying to obtain a common goal" while juggling careers and family obligations along with their academic responsibilities. As a result, few participate in extracurricular activities.

To enhance campus life, FMU hosts regular artists and lecture series. The school also houses an art gallery that displays student and faculty work as well as traveling exhibitions, film series, a planetarium and observatory, concerts, and festivals. FMU's Patriots compete in Division II of the NCAA. Popular spectator sports include basketball, soccer, men's baseball, women's softball, and women's volleyball.

FMU is located just outside of Florence, SC, a city of 33,000 that offers movie theaters, malls, restaurants, a symphony orchestra, and professional hockey (the Pee Dee Pride skate in the East Coast Hockey League). The city is located at the intersections of I-95 and I-20, making travel in all four cardinal directions a snap. Columbia, Charleston, Myrtle Beach, and Fayetteville, NC, are all within 100 miles.

Admissions

Applicants to the FMU MBA program must submit a completed application; official transcripts for all post-secondary academic work, in a sealed envelope addressed to the applicant from the awarding school; official GMAT scores; two letters of recommendation; and a personal statement of purpose. All materials must be delivered to the school in a single envelope or package. In addition, international applicants must submit official TOEFL scores and a Confidential Financial Statement form demonstrating their ability to pay all expenses related to an FMU MBA. All successful applicants meet the following minimum guidelines: a score greater than 950 under the formula [(undergraduate GPA × 200) + GMAT score] or a score greater than 1000 under the formula [(GPA for final 60 hours of undergraduates work × 200) + GMAT score]. Applicants with non-business undergraduate degrees are generally required to complete the business foundation sequence prior to beginning work on their MBA. The sequence is an 18-hour, eight course curriculum covering the basics of accounting, economics, statistics, business law, management, information systems, finance, and marketing. Students with undergraduate business degrees typically have this requirement waived.

FINANCIAL FACTS

Annual tuition (in-state/out-of-state)	$3,460/$6,920
Fees	$60
Books and supplies	$600
% of students receiving aid	8
Average grant	$1,000

ADMISSIONS

Admissions Selectivity Rating	61
# of applications received	33
% applicants accepted	85
% acceptees attending	93
Average GMAT	400
Average GPA	3.0
TOEFL Required of International Students?	Yes
Minimum TOEFL (paper/computer)	550/213
Application fee	$25
Regular application deadline	Rolling
Regular notification	Rolling
Deferment Available?	Yes

EMPLOYMENT PROFILE

Career Rating	74
Placement rate (%)	95
# of companies recruiting on-campus	100

THE GEORGE WASHINGTON UNIVERSITY
SCHOOL OF BUSINESS

Academics

It would be difficult to overestimate the impact George Washington's DC address has on the university's School of Business. It influences everything from the curriculum (especially strong in international business) to the extraordinary quality of the faculty to the "incredible speakers who 'stop by' while they're in town" (recent visitors included Colin Powell, Warren Buffett, and Sumner Redstone). It allows the school to forge "a strong relationship with the government and nonprofit organizations [and to] allow access to DC VIPs and great internships," all of which help students mold their future careers while still in the program. As one student put it, "One of the greatest strengths of GW is its location in downtown DC. It allows you to network with numerous employers without practically having to leave the campus. It allowed me also to combine my second-year full-time studies with working at the World Bank (it was just a five-minute commute from school to work)."

Of course, the School of Business is much more than just a fashionable address. The school boasts a broad variety of excellent tracks; besides the aforementioned international business, operational management, accounting, entrepreneurship, and management science offerings are all considered first-rate. Students proudly note, "There are several unique concentrations that are excellent, such as tourism, environmental policy, and public policy." The school encourages students to explore and even create these off-the-beaten-path disciplines. One MBA explains, "I am in a unique concentration (environmental policy and management), and instead of viewing me as 'the strange one,' the faculty and students embrace this nontraditional business pursuit." Throughout the curriculum, there is a "strong emphasis on teamwork [that] makes learning much more efficient, effective, and enjoyable." One student writes, "We learn how to work in teams and how to make teams function and perform toward our goals. That's a really great asset because now when I am working I feel that I can have any project done regardless of the deadline pressure and diversity of team composition." Team projects also help students get through the "very heavy [workload, which is so demanding that] it's a matter of figuring out the 'need to get done' versus the 'nice to get done.'" One student explains, "Some of the professors give us [a] really hard time in class, but at the end we could not believe how much we have learned." GW's faculty is "very internationally oriented, originates from various parts of the world, participates in think-tanks, committees, [and] sometimes act as consultants."

Career and Placement

GW is well-connected throughout our nation's capital and does an excellent job of bringing DC-area recruiters to campus. This suits many students perfectly; some, however, complain that "the school definitely needs to do a better job of bringing in firms who are looking to recruit outside of the DC area. Many of the students are looking to work outside of DC, and there is almost no chance to get a job outside of DC through the school."

GW's F. David Fowler Graduate Career Center does provide students with the tools they need to search for jobs on their own, including access to various e-recruiting databases and alumni contacts. While most graduates remain in the DC area after graduation, about one in five finds work overseas. Top employers of GW grads include BB&T Corporation, Bearing Point, Corporate Executive Board, Cushman & Wakefield, General Services Administration, Johnson & Johnson, KPMG, Science Applications International Corporation, and World Bank Group.

Student Life and Environment

"The greatest strength of the George Washington full-time MBA program is its size," students tell us, pointing out that "the classes are small and intimate and by the end of the

TRACY WIDMAN, DIRECTOR, DATA AND ENROLLMENT MANAGEMENT
710 21ST STREET, NW, SUITE 206, WASHINGTON, DC 20052 UNITED STATES
PHONE: 202-994-5536 • FAX: 202-994-2286
E-MAIL: MBAFT@GWU.EDU • WEBSITE: WWW.BUSINESS.GWU.EDU/

first semester, you know everyone! No one gets lost in the shuffle like in larger pro-grams." First-year students form an especially tight group because "the first year is all done in cohorts. You are assigned to a group of five students that you perform all work with in all classes your first year. This was a great experience, and I learned a lot from working with my group. These groups facilitate teamwork and communication. As an added bonus, there is not a high level of cutthroat competition" notes one MBA. During the second year, "there is no fixed study team anymore; however, most professors include one assignment (project, case, presentation) to be done with other students."

Students also get together for various social and extracurricular functions. The program "has happy hours once every week that are a good time for students to meet each other and have fun." The MBA Association "is very involved in getting everyone involved in different types of events, [including] date parties, formals, and informal events like din-ner parties, cocktail parties, and movies. Professors often join us at social events," stu-dents say. To keep students up-to-date, "the MBA Association sends out 'Monday Mail' weekly; it gives an overview of activities during the week (sports, cultural, community), and IPO (Informal Public Outing), which takes place each Thursday in a different bar in the area." The school as a whole strives "to make sure that people are not always study-oriented, but also social-oriented and community-oriented."

Even without a heavy workload and a crammed-full extracurricular schedule, students could busy themselves by enjoying the major metropolis GW calls home. The school "has an excellent location in the heart of Washington, DC. It has a lot of connections with the business community, which also plays a part in class activities." Students note that the "extremely accessible public transportation [make it easy for them to attend cultural events and] a variety of seminars all over the city." The school is building a "new, state-of-the-art facility" for the business school, which should open in the Spring of 2006. Students say it will be "a wonderful improvement." The student body is "a diverse mix of international students and a fair amount of women. The students are interested in international and global business issues, and a significant number of students may pur-sue careers in nonprofit and government. Most of the students are young."

Admissions

The admissions office at the School of Business requires applicants to submit under-graduate transcripts, GMAT scores, TOEFL scores (for non-native English speakers), two recommendations, an interview, a resume, and a personal statement (for the 2004–2005 year, the prompt asked students to describe their goals in pursuing an MBA). In its quest to ensure diversity in its student body, the GWU admissions office takes country of ori-gin into account when making its decisions.

FINANCIAL FACTS

Annual tuition	$23,652
Books and supplies	$2,480
Room & board	$14,598
% of students receiving aid	75
% of first-year students receiving aid	40
% of students receiving loans	50
% of students receiving grants	40
Average award package	$25,000
Average grant	$10,000
Average student loan debt	$42,254

ADMISSIONS

Admissions Selectivity Rating	83
# of applications received	777
% applicants accepted	71
% acceptees attending	49
Average GMAT	630
Range of GMAT	570-710
Average GPA	3.6
TOEFL Required of International Students?	Yes
Minimum TOEFL (paper/computer)	600/250
Application fee	$60
International application fee	$60
Regular application deadline	4/1
Regular notification	Rolling
Transfer students accepted?	Yes
Transfer application policy: Standard application procedures.	
Non-fall admissions?	Yes
Need-blind admissions?	Yes

APPLICANTS ALSO LOOK AT

Boston College, Boston University, Georgetown University, New York University, Thunderbird, University of Maryland, College Park, Vanderbilt University.

EMPLOYMENT PROFILE

Career Rating	78	Grads employed by field	%: avg. salary
Placement rate (%)	60	Finance	29: $60,556
# of companies recruiting on-campus	59	Marketing	24: $58,640
% grads employed immediately	60	Operations	7: $77,500
Average starting salary	$67,966	Consulting	22: $59,625
		General Management	11: $68,750
		Non-profit	7: $46,000

GEORGETOWN UNIVERSITY
MCDONOUGH SCHOOL OF BUSINESS

GENERAL INFORMATION
Type of school	private
Affiliation	Roman Catholic-Jesuit
Environment	metropolis
Academic calendar	module

SURVEY SAYS...
Students love Washington, DC
Friendly students
Happy students
Solid preparation in:
Teamwork

STUDENTS
Enrollment of parent institution	12,000
Enrollment of MBA program	510
% male/female	69/31
% minorities	8
% international	39
Average age at entry	28
Average years work experience at entry	5.17

ACADEMICS
Academic Experience Rating	**88**
Student/faculty ratio	8:1
Profs interesting rating	84
Profs accessible rating	86
% female faculty	23
% minority faculty	14

Joint Degrees
MBA/MSFS: 3 years; MBA/MA Physics: 3 years; MBA/JD: 4 years MBA/MPP: 3 years; MBA/MD: 5 years; MBA/PhD in Physics: 5 years

Academics

The fact that the McDonough School of Business at Georgetown University is a young program is a point of considerable pride with most of its MBA students. With "only 20 years as a program, [it has] experienced many growing pains," but students note, "We are a top-30 business school!" Despite its youth, the school lays claim to "truly remarkable, distinguished professors that make time to be sociable after class" and a friendly, helpful bunch of students who make time to help study and party. According to students, this is thanks to an extremely responsive administration and "a great program that is never satisfied with the status quo."

McDonough's MBA program is a two-year, full-time program. Students don't take majors or concentrations, as the program is designed for general management. As a general-management program, an MBA from McDonough is ideal for students with backgrounds in the liberal arts, science, or with technical undergraduate degrees. All courses in the fall of the first semester are core requirements, but in the second semester, students are invited to take three electives. The program runs in a module system that breaks the semesters up. Students say it's "great for cramming many subjects into a short amount of time. The problem is that we have midterms or finals every three weeks." Others say that modules, combined with the "heavy core course load, leaves very little time for lively current topic debate."

Just as in the undergraduate program, a major strength of Georgetown's MBA program is the international focus of the education. Students proudly boast of their school's "international presence with a great mix of cultures." Students agree, "The large percentage of international students and internationally focused classes help prepare students for working in a global economy." International students, of course, also bring in valuable and "diverse perspectives and opinions." In the second year of the program, students are required to participate in a one-week project in a country with emerging business markets. "Also," says one student, "the link to Georgetown University's School of Foreign Service and the location in Washington, DC, means that there are always interesting things going on linked to international business." In addition, the school's prime location means that students experience "many visits by important statesmen and opportunities to meet them."

With the department's approval, MBA students are welcome to take elective courses outside of the business department. Students at McDonough often opt to take electives in the School of Foreign Service, the Government Department, and the Public Policy Program—all strong programs in their own right. Students appreciate it and say that "access to Georgetown's other schools is one of its key strengths."

McDonough also offers joint degrees with the Graduate Public Policy Program (MBA/MPP), the Law Center (JD/MBA), the School of Foreign Service (MBA/MSFS), the Medical School (MD/MBA), and the Graduate School (MBA/MA Physics, MBA/PhD Physics).

MONICA GRAY, DIRECTOR OF ADMISSIONS
BOX 571148, WASHINGTON, DC 20057-1148 UNITED STATES
PHONE: 202-687-4200 • FAX: 202-687-7809
E-MAIL: MBA@GEORGETOWN.EDU • WEBSITE: WWW.MBA.GEORGETOWN.EDU

Career and Placement

Most students agree that McDonough's Career Management Center could step up its efforts a little, but then "career management is always an issue with students [at many campuses]." On the other hand, the alumni network is outstanding. Graduates of the McDonough program seem to be able to rely not just on fellow MBA alums, but anyone who went to Georgetown. As one student says, "Alumni of the school are very loyal to the school." Being Georgetown, of course, there's also a very "strong international alumni network" in place, and the projects and competitions in which students participate internationally have led to numerous internships and employment offers.

Student Life and Environment

Most McDonough students agree that you can't beat the nation's capital for location. "DC is a great city with its finger on the pulse of the nation." And Georgetown, located slightly outside of the bustling metropolis's center, is situated on "one of the most beautiful campuses [students have] ever seen." Life in the city, obviously, offers students a variety of options for social and cultural life. In addition, "the university offers a variety of speakers, guest lecturers, and events. The most difficult task is managing your time appropriately so that you can take advantage of all Georgetown has to offer."

Because 35 percent of all students entering the McDonough School are international students, diversity is something students come to expect and enjoy. Indeed, students claim to be able to "go out for drinks with a half-dozen students and realize that six different countries are represented in [their] party." Countries represented range from Trinidad/Tobago to Switzerland.

Though most students agree that McDonough's facilities leave something to be desired, the program is working feverishly to remedy that and have just broken ground for a new, high tech facility, which they aim to complete in 2008.

Admissions

The average GMAT score of an admitted full-time MBA student at McDonough was 661, and the average GPA was 3.3. Most incoming students had worked between three and five years before applying for the MBA, and at least two years of full-time work experience is generally recommended. TOEFL scores are required of those students for whom English is not their first language, unless they've obtained a degree from an English-speaking institution of higher education. The minimum required TOEFL score is 600 for the written test and 250 for the computer-based test. Merit-based scholarships are awarded, and the school considers every student admitted to the program for scholarships.

FINANCIAL FACTS

Annual tuition	$33,960
Fees	$2,030
Books and supplies	$2,088
% of students receiving aid	76
% of first-year students receiving aid	38
% of students receiving loans	80
% of students receiving grants	26
Average award package	$40,000
Average grant	$10,000
Average student loan debt	$58,000

ADMISSIONS

Admissions Selectivity Rating	92
# of applications received	1582
% applicants accepted	41
% acceptees attending	40
Average GMAT	662
Range of GMAT	610-710
Average GPA	3.3
TOEFL Required of International Students?	Yes
Minimum TOEFL (paper/computer)	600/250
Application fee	$125
International application fee	$125
Regular application deadline	2/10
Regular notification	3/30
Application Deadline—Notification	
Round 1:	12/2—1/26
Round 2:	2/10—3/30
Round 3:	4/21—5/25
Need-blind admissions?	Yes

EMPLOYMENT PROFILE			
Career Rating	84	Grads employed by field	%: avg. salary
Placement rate (%)	88	Finance	34: $76,531
# of companies recruiting on-campus	100	Marketing	25: $75,585
Average starting salary	$77,861	MIS	1: $90,000
		Operations	4: $79,000
		Consulting	20: $76,531
		General Management	7: $84,045
		Other	9: $81,153

GEORGIA INSTITUTE OF TECHNOLOGY
COLLEGE OF MANAGEMENT

GENERAL INFORMATION
Type of school   public
Environment   metropolis
Academic calendar   semester

SURVEY SAYS...
Students love Atlanta, GA
Friendly students
Good peer network
Happy students
Smart classrooms
Solid preparation in:
Accounting
Quantitative skills

STUDENTS
Enrollment of parent
  institution   15,576
Enrollment of MBA program   167
% male/female   75/25
% out-of-state   45
% minorities   19
% international   32
Average age at entry   27
Average years work experience
  at entry   4

ACADEMICS
Academic Experience Rating   89
Profs interesting rating   80
Profs accessible rating   85
% female faculty   15
Joint Degrees
Dual degree programs with any
Masters or PhD degree at Georgia
Tech.

Academics

"There is no better business-school deal in the country than Georgia Tech," MBA students at the College of Management tell us, an assertion that's true especially for Georgia residents; their total two-year bill amounts to a small fraction of what they're likely to earn after graduation. Despite the College of Management's low tuition and fees, Georgia Tech hardly skimps on its offerings. The school's new home, Technology Square, is a $53 million multipurpose facility that, according to the school, "brings the College of Management together in the same location with Georgia Tech's programmatic centers for improving the economy of the state of Georgia, nurturing high tech business ventures, and spreading knowledge all over the world via distance learning." Making a good deal even better is the fact that "at least half of the students have assistantships where they work within the business school or at Georgia Tech, receiving a full scholarship plus $6,000-a-year stipend."

As one would expect at a tech school, the College of Management maintains a "sharp technical focus." One student notes, "The student body is heavily weighted towards engineers, so there is a strong quantitative bias. Poets will find it challenging, but not impossible, to keep up with all the math." About half the student body majored in engineering or computer science in undergraduate school; a little less than one-third earned baccalaureate degrees in business.

In part because of the emphasis on quantitative analysis, "the workload is heavy, but fair." One MBA explains, "Georgia Tech as a whole cultivates a tough academic image, and the business school in general does its best to uphold that tradition. Final grades are distributed as you would expect in an MBA program, but there is a lot of sweating until the curve is applied." Those seeking an extra challenge can pursue a dual degree, combining the MBA with any master's or PhD degree offered at the university.

Professors defy the tech-school stereotype of the incomprehensible, research-driven geek; on the contrary, they are "excellent and extremely accessible outside of class, [offering] lots of personal attention." Students say, "They care about how we are doing and seem open to our feedback." Similarly, administrators are "student-friendly and open to feedback, and [they're] forever looking for ways to improve." About the only complaint students register concerns the school's national reputation. A typical MBA writes, "This program is absolutely wonderful, but too few people know about it at all. [The College of Management] needs to do a much, much better job of getting the word out."

Career and Placement

Unique among the various schools that comprise Georgia Tech, the College of Management maintains its own distinct Career Development Office. A two-day career fair, held each fall, is among the major annual on-campus recruiting events, drawing more than 300 companies to visit the campus. Four smaller career fairs are scattered across the calendar. The school also participates in a 15-member MBA consortium that organizes events in Atlanta, New York, and on the West Coast; the consortium helps attract companies that might not visit the Georgia Tech campus due to the relatively small size of the MBA program. Students give the Career Development Office high marks, telling us, "The career center has been incredibly active in making sure every student is able to find internships or jobs in the coming summer."

Tech grads often head overseas for their first jobs; one in five is employed outside the U.S. after graduation. Approximately 60 percent remain in the Southeast. Top employers include Assurant Group, BellSouth, Caterpillar, Coca-Cola Company, Dell, Disney,

Earthlink, Ernst & Young, GE Supply, Georgia Pacific Corporation, McKesson, NASD, Philip Morris, Southern Company, and United Parcel Service.

Student Life and Environment

The College of Management's new digs are in a "great new location on campus, right in the middle of an area of town on the rise." The "brand-new incredible facility [features not only the requisite] plasma screens, video-conferencing, and computers [but also] a Starbucks and Barnes & Noble just downstairs, so there's no falling asleep or staying out of touch with the rest of the world." The school's Atlanta location is unquestionably an asset. Students tell us, "Atlanta is a great city to live in," as it offers great internship and job opportunities. "I have been working on several real-life projects for world-class companies based in Atlanta," notes an MBA. The city also "contributes a great deal to the social life here. There's always a bunch of activities going on."

The Georgia Tech campus is almost as hopping as the city surrounding it. Students report, "There are great opportunities to get more involved with the school and help shape the direction of the program during your two years here and beyond. The staff regularly conducts town halls and lunch meetings to make sure the students are getting their needs met." Students also say, "Study groups, classes, social meets, guest speakers, and presentations and research [help fill the days, as do] intramurals and intercollegiate athletics [and] mixers with surrounding schools (Emory and GSU) and lots of clubs; everyone is involved in a club."

MBA students "really enjoy the diversity of the student body, with its high percentage of international students." Many opine, "The student body is a bit more experienced and mature than other campuses, which was one of the reasons I chose to come here."

Admissions

Georgia Tech reviews all application materials carefully; those materials must include undergraduate transcripts, GMAT scores, TOEFL scores (when required), letters of recommendation, personal essays, and work history. Applicants must have completed study in calculus prior to enrollment. The school "strongly recommends [that applicants] have a familiarity with probability concepts prior to beginning the MBA program." It also points out that "full-time work experience greatly enhances your application and the quality of learning you receive in the MBA program. More than 95 percent of [the school's] most recent class had worked full-time prior to admission." Georgia Tech's MBA program is full-time, and admission is for the fall semester only. Minority recruitment is enhanced through "FOCUS programs on campus, information sessions, Regent's Opportunity Scholarships, and minority student outreach."

FINANCIAL FACTS

Annual tuition (in-state/out-of-state)	$6,420/$22,950
Books and supplies	$1,400
Room & board	$12,000
% of students receiving grants	30
Average grant	$6,000
Average student loan debt	$16,000

ADMISSIONS

Admissions Selectivity Rating	94
# of applications received	316
% applicants accepted	37
% acceptees attending	55
Average GMAT	655
Range of GMAT	600-700
Average GPA	3.43
TOEFL Required of International Students?	Yes
Minimum TOEFL (paper/computer)	600/250
Application fee	$50
International application fee	$50
Regular application deadline	3/15
Regular notification	Rolling
Deferment Available?	Yes
Maximum length of deferment	1 year
Need-blind admissions?	Yes

APPLICANTS ALSO LOOK AT

Emory University, Indiana University, Purdue University, University of Georgia, University of Maryland—College Park, University of North Carolina at Chapel Hill, Vanderbilt University.

EMPLOYMENT PROFILE

Career Rating	83	Grads employed by field	%: avg. salary
Placement rate (%)	92	Accounting	9: $43,417
% grads employed immediately	51	Finance	24: $67,116
Average starting salary	$68,297	Marketing	13: $63,985
		MIS	15: $76,644
		Operations	27: $71,100
		General Management	12: $80,000

Georgia Southern University
College of Business Administration

Academics

The College of Business Administration at Georgia Southern University serves a predominately local student population with a general MBA, as well as MBAs with concentrations in accounting, health services administration, information systems, and international business. A Master of Accounting Degree is also available, and students in our survey speak especially highly of the accountancy programs.

Less than half of Georgia Southern's MBAs are full-time students; others attend part-time, usually on top of a full-time work schedule. Well aware of this noble act, the school works hard to accommodate the varied lifestyles of its students. One part-timer writes, "The administration at Georgia Southern has been very helpful. My schedule has been hectic, but they have worked with me to graduate in a timely manner." Many of the full-timers are students who "got their BAs here and just stuck around." One such student explains, "I completed my undergraduate degree at Georgia Southern, and when the MBA program started a concentration in Information Systems, I took the opportunity to continue my education in a field that I am very interested in."

Convenience, cost, and comfort are the three main reasons so many undergraduates choose to remain on at GSU. One student writes "I love the faculty here. Because Georgia Southern is a teaching institution, the professors are very accessible and willing to help. They have time to work with students and to teach classes." Another notes, "There's no academic Darwinism here, no weed-out courses. Unlike other schools, GSU professors support and assist students, and seem genuinely interested in their success." Students also appreciate "that the quality of the courses offered is equivalent to those at larger business schools, but there is no 'big school mindset.'" One drawback students point out is that "there are sometimes difficulties getting into classes. This is due to a sudden boom in business school students. Currently, the student/professor ratio is fairly high."

Full-time students attend classes at GSU's Statesboro campuses. Part-timers may attend classes in Statesboro or Savannah, or they may participate in the distance-learning program by attending classes in Brunswick. A Web-exclusive collaborative MBA is offered in conjunction with five other schools in the University of Georgia system.

Career and Placement

Georgia Southern's small MBA program is served by a satellite office of the university's central Career Services Office. Many career-oriented events, such as workshops and recruitment events, serve the university at large rather than business students exclusively. According to the school's website, the COBA Satellite Office houses "literature on academic majors, career information...handouts and other resources to help prepare you for professional employment and graduate school."

Nearly 100 employers visit the Georgia Southern campus each year. Top employers of graduating MBAs include: Gulfstream Aerospace, Inc.; Memorial Medical Hospital; Great Dane Trucking, Inc.; and Sun Trust Bank.

Student Life and Environment

GSU's MBA program boasts "a highly diverse" student body. Students tell us that they "vary widely in terms of race, sex, and culture. Most are working in a related business field, but there are also students who have recently completed their undergraduate degrees and have no related experience to contribute. They range in ages between 23 and 53." More than 10 percent of the student body is international.

Dr. Michael McDonald, Graduate Program Director
PO Box 8154, Statesboro, GA 30460-8154 United States
Phone: 912-681-5767 • Fax: 912-681-0740
E-mail: gradschool@georgiasouthern.edu • Website: coba.georgiasouthern.edu/mba

With a small student body (and an even smaller full-time population), GSU lacks the makings of an active extracurricular scene. Even so, one student reports that "There are many different functions and activities to attend. For example, this year I attended an evening dinner that was directed at teaching students how to maintain etiquette in a professional setting. There were different companies that sponsored tables and either one or two representatives would also participate at each table." The school also hosts major-related organizations. Students tell us they feel "a lot of pressure from the faculty to achieve and to remain active in school-sponsored events. There are incentives (positive and negative) that encourage participation."

Hometown Statesboro "is a small town in southeast Georgia where the college and Wal-Mart are pretty much all that's going on. Because GSU is the attraction in Statesboro, life here is all about studying and working. Most people go to Savannah or Atlanta on weekends." At least it's good to know that "the area surrounding the campus is primarily geared toward serving the needs of students, producing a 'college town' atmosphere. The facilities provided (gyms, computer labs, student center, etc.) are of a quality usually only seen at much larger schools."

Admissions

Admission to the Georgia Southern MBA program is determined through the application of the formula [(undergraduate GPA × 200) + GMAT score]. A score of at least 1000 ensures admission. Applicants may receive provisional admission with a score between 950 and 1000, with an undergraduate GPA of at least 2.80, or with a GMAT score of at least 470.

An alternate formula applies to students who do not qualify under the formula above but who excelled during their final two years of undergraduate work. This formula, called the upper-level formula, is [(undergraduate GPA for final 60 semester hours × 200) + GMAT score]. A score of at least 1050 qualifies. Students who have not taken the GMAT may also gain admission if their undergraduate GPA is at least 3.25, or their GPA for their final 60 semester hours is at least 3.5. Students in this category must submit an acceptable GMAT score by the time they complete their second graduate-level course.

FINANCIAL FACTS

Annual tuition (in-state/out-of-state)	$2,786/$11,146
Fees	$700
Books and supplies	$700
Room & board (on/off-campus)	$6,000/$2,500
% of students receiving aid	94
% of first-year students receiving aid	91
% of students receiving loans	49
% of students receiving grants	67
Average award package	$9,256
Average grant	$5,209
Average student loan debt	$22,280

ADMISSIONS

Admissions Selectivity Rating	65
# of applications received	111
% applicants accepted	84
% acceptees attending	74
Average GMAT	479
Range of GMAT	420-530
Average GPA	3.26
TOEFL Required of International Students?	Yes
Minimum TOEFL (paper/computer)	530/213
Application fee	$30
International application fee	$30
Regular application deadline	6/1
Regular notification	7/1
Deferment Available?	Yes
Maximum length of deferment	1 year
Transfer students accepted?	Yes
Transfer application policy: No more than 6 semester hours of graduate credit may be transferred to a graduate program at Georgia Southern. Only grades of B or higher will be accepted for transfer.	
Non-fall admissions?	Yes
Need-blind admissions?	Yes

APPLICANTS ALSO LOOK AT

Georgia State University, Kennesaw State University, University of Georgia.

EMPLOYMENT PROFILE	
Career Rating	60*
# of companies recruiting on-campus	95

GEORGIA STATE UNIVERSITY
J. MACK ROBINSON COLLEGE OF BUSINESS

GENERAL INFORMATION
Type of school	public
Academic calendar	semester

SURVEY SAYS...
Students love Atlanta, GA
Friendly students
Happy students
Smart classrooms

STUDENTS
Enrollment of parent institution	27,000
Enrollment of MBA program	1,380
% male/female	64/36
% out-of-state	26
% part-time	86
% minorities	9
% international	30
Average age at entry	30
Average years work experience at entry	7

ACADEMICS
Academic Experience Rating	**83**
Student/faculty ratio	23:1
Profs interesting rating	89
Profs accessible rating	87
% female faculty	31
% minority faculty	13

Joint Degrees
MBA/JD: 2-8 years
MBA/MHA: 2-5 years
Global Partners MBA will commence in the fall of 2005 with our partners at Sorbonne University in Paris and the COPPEAD in Rio de Janeiro.

Prominent Alumni
James E. Copeland, Deloitte & Touche/Tomats; A.W. Bill Dahlberg, Chairman of Mirant; Kenneth Lewis, Chairman & CEO of Bank of America; Richard H. Lenny, Chairman/Hershey Foods; Mackey McDonald, Chairman, President & CEO of VF Corp.

Academics

Georgia State University offers three types of MBAs through its J. Mack Robinson College of Business: the Flexible MBA, a full-time or part-time program that allows students to begin during any semester and to schedule classes around other obligations; the Global Partners MBA, a full-time, 14-month program that includes six-week residencies in Paris and Rio, a two-week residency in China, three days in Washington DC, and the remaining time in Atlanta and at an internship or field-experiment site; and the Executive MBA, an 18-month, lockstep, Friday-and-Saturday program focusing on international business and leadership. The Executive MBA program is open only to applicants with at least seven years of work experience and a minimum of five years at the management level.

In all programs, students report that "professors at GSU are highly qualified. Many of them either work or have worked outside academia, giving them a much fuller understanding of business and the pressures students face. Additionally, the professors seem to be enthusiastic about teaching. They seem to genuinely enjoy class and stimulate class discussions." Notes one student, "The top-quality instructors have enabled me to quickly turn business theory into real-world results for my employer." Students are especially high on the finance program, which they tell us is "super hard, but super good!" Programs in accounting and actuarial science also receive MBAs' praise. In all disciplines, students report that "the workload is challenging, but it all is very relevant," although a few students complain that "some of the case studies seem a little dated." In the best classes, professors "really focus on drawing course work right out of the *Wall Street Journal*. The professor never even touched the textbook. It was great, but I understand why everyone doesn't do it; it's a lot of additional work for the professor."

Career and Placement

The Office of Graduate Career Management (GCM) at GSU offers a full range of services, including career advising, career workshops, the career leader self-assessment service, assistance with internships, resume review, resume referral, alumni contacts, a career library, recruitment events, on-campus interviews, and online job databases. While students "would like to see some bigger names recruiting on campus, especially in banking," most agree that the GCM does a solid job serving a large clientele.

In 2004, the top 10 recruiters of GSU MBAs were: BB&T; Chick-fil-A; ChoicePoint; Cox Communications; GE Power Systems; KPMG, LLP; PricewaterhouseCoopers; Radiant Systems; Reznick, Fedder & Silverman; and Wachovia. Three-tenths of recent graduates found work in accounting (avg. starting salary $58,000). About one in four found work in finance ($55,000); one in six was employed in marketing ($51,500).

Student Life and Environment

The MBAs at Georgia State are "mostly older students with more work experience. Many have families. All are very intelligent and hard-working." Most attend part-time while working full-time jobs and are "very willing to share job experiences that relate to classroom material. They talk a lot in class, which is helpful." "Many are international students," all of them full-timers. Because most students have substantial obligations outside school, "there is no real sense of a student body here. It's every wo/man for her/himself." Writes one student, "I wish there is something that we could do to make life more communal, but given that so many attendees work, this is difficult. This is one of the drawbacks from going to part-time school. If I could do it over, I may have quit

NAOMI LEADER, ASSISTANT TO THE DIRECTOR
PO BOX 3988, ATLANTA, GA 30302-3988 UNITED STATES
PHONE: 404-463-4568 • FAX: 404-651-2721
E-MAIL: MASTERSADMISSIONS@GSU.EDU • WEBSITE: ROBINSON.GSU.EDU

work and gone to school full-time. But on other hand, I have continually been able to apply, in real-time, the things that I learn in school to my work. In retrospect, [this experience] has probably reinforced this work more than anything."

Students love hometown Atlanta, which "offers great resources" both for career opportunities and for fine living. The city is home to a number of *Fortune* 500 companies, including Coca Cola, Home Depot, and Delta Airlines. On campus, GSU's MBA Centers "are immaculate and well thought out in terms of their design to facilitate class discussion and student/teacher interaction."

Admissions

Applicants to GSU MBA programs must submit all of the following materials to the Office of Admissions: official copies of transcripts for all post-secondary academic work; an official GMAT score report; a resume (at least two years of full-time professional experience is preferred); and two personal essays. Letters of recommendation are not required but are considered for those candidates who submit them. International students must submit, in addition to the above materials, evidence of sufficient financial resources to fund their MBA studies; an independent evaluation of all academic transcripts for work completed abroad; and, for students whose first language is not English, an official score report for the TOEFL. International students are required to carry a full-time course load.

FINANCIAL FACTS

Annual tuition (in-state/out-of-state)	$4,544/$18,176
Fees	$786
Books and supplies	$1,000
Room & board (on/off-campus)	$8,976/$8,876
% of students receiving aid	20
% of first-year students receiving aid	20
% of students receiving loans	20
Average award package	$13,758
Average student loan debt	$29,640

ADMISSIONS

Admissions Selectivity Rating	89
# of applications received	585
% applicants accepted	50
% acceptees attending	67
Average GMAT	620
Range of GMAT	580-660
Average GPA	3.3
TOEFL Required of International Students?	Yes
Minimum TOEFL (paper/computer)	610/255
Application fee	$50
International application fee	$50
Regular application deadline	5/1
Regular notification	6/15
Deferment Available?	Yes
Maximum length of deferment	1 year
Non-fall admissions?	Yes
Need-blind admissions?	Yes

APPLICANTS ALSO LOOK AT

Baruch College/City University of New York, Clark Atlanta University, Emory University, Georgia Institute of Technology, Kennesaw State University, University of Florida, University of Georgia,

EMPLOYMENT PROFILE

Career Rating	65	**Grads employed by field**	**%: avg. salary**
Placement rate (%)	35	Accounting	30: $58,000
% grads employed immediately	60	Finance	27: $55,000
Average starting salary	$55,033	Human Resources	6: $40,500
		Marketing	16: $51,500
		MIS	6: $62,500
		Consulting	8: $50,500
		Other	7: $67,233

GONZAGA UNIVERSITY
SCHOOL OF BUSINESS ADMINISTRATION

Academics

With its "Jesuit tradition in which ethics are strongly emphasized," Gonzaga University serves up a solid AACSB-accredited MBA to its predominantly full-time student body. Accounting is among the school's strongest areas, as "Gonzaga has an excellent reputation for preparing students to take the CPA exam, of which the pass rate among Gonzaga students is high." Number-crunchers here may opt for an MAcc, an MBA with a concentration in accounting, or a combined MBA/MAcc. Gonzaga offers concentrations in finance, management information systems, and marketing. Students may also opt to design an individualized concentration.

Gonzaga's MBA curriculum consists of 22 credits in core courses (11 two-credit classes) and 11 credits in electives, through which students may develop a concentration if they so desire. Students who did not major in business as undergraduates are typically required to complete a series of foundation requirements prior to beginning work on their MBA. Overall, students appreciate the program's "very integrated approach [and the] accessible teachers who are friendly and intelligent and have created a great learning environment." For the most part, students report that they find the professors and administration members "wonderful to work with." Some, however, complain about a "heavy emphasis on examination-based measurement. It can be too much like the undergraduate experience. There is little emphasis on writing papers and research, and thus little opportunity for creativity."

The MBA respondents to our survey see improvements on the horizon, however, referring to some of the problems they encounter as mere "growing pains." One explains: "The administration of the university and the business school are both very forward-thinking. Both have been expanding and upgrading the programs at the school. I know that I am at a school that is continuing to grow and gain in national prominence."

Career and Placement

The Gonzaga Career Center and the School of Business Administration staff and faculty provide career counseling and placement services to MBAs here, including career 301 seminars covering self-assessment, career planning, resume writing, and conducting a successful job search; mock interviews and interview critiques; on-campus recruiting and interviewing; a career resources library; alumni events; and internship placement assistance. Some would like to see "more internship" opportunities, but students have few complaints.

Employers of Gonzaga business graduates include Accenture, Bank of America, Boeing, Empire Health, Ernst & Young, KPMG, Nordstrom Corporate, Merril Lynch, Microsoft, Nike, Pitney Bowes, Potlatch, Washington Trust, and the Wells Fargo Bank.

STACEY CHATMAN, GRADUATE PROGRAMS SPECIALIST FOR ADMISSIONS
502 EAST BOONE AVENUE, SPOKANE, WA 99528-0009 UNITED STATES
PHONE: 509-324-4622 • FAX: 509-323-5811
E-MAIL: CHATMAN@JEPSON.GONZAGA.EDU • WEBSITE: WWW.JEPSON.GONZAGA.EDU/GRADUATE

Student Life and Environment

"There are two types of MBA students at GU." There are "those who graduated from GU as an undergrad; most of these students are straight out of the undergrad program. There are also those who are new to the university; most of them have work experience and are a few years older than the students who have their undergrad degree from GU." In general, "Students here are friendly and intelligent." There are a fair number of international MBAs, including "students from places like Nepal, China, the Ukraine, the UK, India, Lebanon, and Latin America." Women make up just under one-third of the student body. (One female respondent would like to see the school place a "greater emphasis on women in business.") Students call their fellow MBAs "warm, intelligent, [and] hardworking" and are quick to sing the praises of the "friendly" atmosphere at GU.

"Life at GU is awesome" for those who spend time around campus (though part-timers generally don't, as many work full-time). "There are all sorts of activities and club sports for students to participate in (including Young Republicans and Young Democrats clubs, philosophy clubs, business clubs, and sports teams in hockey, lacrosse, and much more)." Gonzaga's nationally ranked men's basketball team is the source of much GU student pride. One MBA writes, "Basketball season is awesome. Going to the games is fun, and it builds camaraderie within the student body." While "the curriculum is challenging, there is still plenty of free time to work or enjoy life outside of school," a fact of GU life that students appreciate. While a few report that they opted to pursue their degrees at GU because of the "Jesuit educator emphasis," most don't comment at all on the school's religious affiliation.

Admissions

Applicants to the MBA program at Gonzaga must submit two official copies of all post-secondary academic transcripts, official GMAT scores, two letters of recommendation, a professional resume, and a completed application. International students must also submit official TOEFL scores (if English is not their first language) and a financial declaration form. Work experience is not required, "although the majority of students who enter the program have 4 or 5 years prior work experience." A minimum GMAT score of 500 is strongly preferred by the Admissions Committee.

FINANCIAL FACTS

Annual tuition	$11,100
Fees	$50
Books and supplies	$600
% of first-year students receiving aid	90
Average grant	$7,000

ADMISSIONS

Admissions Selectivity Rating	77
# of applications received	212
% applicants accepted	63
% acceptees attending	67
Average GMAT	540
Range of GMAT	480-600
Average GPA	3.3
TOEFL Required of International Students?	Yes
Minimum TOEFL (paper/computer)	600/250
Application fee	$45
International application fee	$45
Regular application deadline	Rolling
Regular notification	Rolling
Deferment Available?	Yes
Maximum length of deferment	3 years
Transfer students accepted?	Yes
Transfer application policy: Transcripts are evaluated to ensure that desired learning objectives have been fulfilled.	
Non-fall admissions?	Yes

EMPLOYMENT PROFILE

Career Rating	78
Placement rate (%)	92
# of companies recruiting on-campus	55
% grads employed immediately	56
Average starting salary	$55,000

GRADUATE COLLEGE OF UNION UNIVERSITY
SCHOOL OF MANAGEMENT

GENERAL INFORMATION

Type of school	private
Environment	town
Academic calendar	trimester

SURVEY SAYS...
Friendly students
Smart classrooms
Solid preparation in:
Teamwork
Presentation skills

STUDENTS

Enrollment of parent institution	494
Enrollment of MBA program	231
% male/female	60/40
% out-of-state	4
% part-time	47
% minorities	30
% international	10
Average age at entry	25
Average years work experience at entry	3

ACADEMICS

Academic Experience Rating	61
Student/faculty ratio	15:1
Profs interesting rating	63
Profs accessible rating	70
% female faculty	38
% minority faculty	9

Joint Degrees
MBA/JD: 4 years; BA/BS-MBA
(Accelerated MBA): 5 years;
PharmD/MS or MBA: 6 years

Prominent Alumni
Michael Keegan, President-M&T
Bank, Albany, NY; Wayne
McDougall, DFO-MapInfo, Troy, NY;
James Mandell, President-Boston
Children's Hospital; James Figge,
Medical Director CDPHP-HMO
Albany, NY.

Academics

The School of Management at the Graduate College of Union University offers both a conventional MBA and a unique MBA in Healthcare Management. The former focuses on all areas of general management with an emphasis on global business; the latter "prepares graduates for management positions in health-service delivery organizations (for example, hospitals, managed care organizations, group practices, long-term care) and in related organizations (for example, consulting, government, corporate benefits)," according to the school's website.

MBA students at the Graduate College benefit from small classes (the average class size is 17). Classes meet in the evening to accommodate part-time students, who make up roughly half the student population. A conventional MBA consists of 10 core courses and 10 advanced. The core includes a capstone course and standard surveys of core business skills (including accounting, statistics, and finance) as well as such unique classes as "Managing Ethically in a Global Environment" and "Managing People and Teams in organizations." Students choose courses from any of the following elective areas to establish a concentration: finance, economics, marketing, operations/management science, and international business. The program typically takes a full-time student two years to complete; part-timers generally complete it in four years.

The Graduate College's MBA in Healthcare Management emphasizes both theory and practice; that's why the academic curriculum is supplemented with a mandatory internship, typically completed between the first and second years of the program. Because of the specialized nature of the degree, only two electives are allowed in this program; the other 18 courses are required. The 10 required courses mirror the conventional MBA core. The other 8, which include such subjects as "Health Systems Marketing and Planning," "Structural Dynamics in Health Systems," and "Legal Aspects of Health Care," are specific to the health administration program.

Graduate College MBAs can pursue joint degrees in law or pharmacy; a five-year BA/MBA option is quite popular because it allows students to pursue an MBA without first accumulating several years of experience. Students appreciate that "teachers are all very enthusiastic and interested in our learning program" and "are, for the most part, always available to talk, whether it be class-related or not." The administration is reportedly "outstandingly friendly and service-oriented," and "tuition is reasonable."

Career and Placement

MBA Career Services operates in conjunction with Union's Becker Career Center to provide internship opportunities, mentoring programs, and job-search guidance. Approximately 25 companies visit the college to recruit graduating MBAs; about 30 companies recruit summer interns. Students say that the career center is "great for internships but not for careers."

Top employers of the Graduate College MBAs include General Electric, IBM, KPMG, Lehman Brothers, and PricewaterhouseCoopers. Nearly all MBAs remain in and around the New York State area after graduation.

Student Life and Environment

The Graduate College's student body is "diverse in age, race, citizenship, occupation, and career goals. Students are friendly and team-oriented." The MBA program is an unusual mix of the very young and the much older; there are "lots of five-year under-grads, and nontraditional students generally return after a long time in the workforce. There aren't a whole lot of young professionals here." Students report that, unlike many MBA programs, "minority and female students are very common and thus are very well supported." There are roughly one in five students that are international students.

The Graduate College is located near Albany, New York, in the town of Schenectady. Sperling's Best Places recently ranked the Albany-Schenectady area the least stressful city among America's top 100 metropolitan areas. The area is home to many schools that together bring a total of 55,000 students to the region every school year. The Graduate College is located on the Union College campus which covers 100 acres and houses a substantial library, several new classroom and laboratory facilities, an arts center, and a student center with a 3,000-seat hockey arena and rink.

Admissions

In evaluating MBA applications, the Graduate College of Union University reviews academic records, stated career goals, letters of recommendation, and standardized test scores (GMAT for all applicants, plus TOEFL for international students). Admissions officers also use the application to assess applicants' stated career goals and their fit with both the program and the university community. The Graduate College generally requires an undergraduate GPA of 3.0; the average full-time student typically enters with a higher undergraduate GPA. Applications are assessed on a rolling basis with admissions decisions delivered within two weeks of receipt of the completed application.

FINANCIAL FACTS

Annual tuition	$19,200
Fees	$150
Books and supplies	$1,200
Room & Board	$8,800
% of students receiving aid	61
% of first-year students receiving aid	75
% of students receiving loans	42
% of students receiving grants	30
Average award package	$14,868
Average grant	$5,750
Average student loan debt	$29,387

ADMISSIONS

Admissions Selectivity Rating	70
# of applications received	79
% applicants accepted	94
% acceptees attending	72
Average GMAT	545
Range of GMAT	470-680
Average GPA	3.3
TOEFL Required of International Students?	Yes
Minimum TOEFL (paper/computer)	550/213
Application fee	$60
International application fee	$60
Regular application deadline	Rolling
Regular notification	Rolling
Deferment Available?	Yes
Maximum length of deferment	1 year
Transfer students accepted?	Yes
Transfer application policy: Will accept up to 8 courses (20 required).	
Non-fall admissions?	Yes
Need-blind admissions?	Yes

APPLICANTS ALSO LOOK AT

Albany Law School, Rensselaer Polytechnic Institute.

EMPLOYMENT PROFILE

Career Rating	73	**Grads employed by field**	**%: avg. salary**
Placement rate (%)	90	Accounting	6: NR
# of companies recruiting on-campus	25	Finance	29: NR
% grads employed immediately	42	Marketing	9: NR
Average starting salary	$58,600	MIS	3: NR
		Operations	6: NR
		Consulting	5: NR
		General Management	11: NR
		Other	17: NR
		Non-profit	14: NR

GRAND VALLEY STATE UNIVERSITY
SEIDMAN COLLEGE OF BUSINESS

Academics

With a newly renovated campus, state-of-the-art facilities, and a solid regional reputation, the Grand Valley State University MBA program has quite a lot to offer its working-professional student body. MBAs here appreciate what they have, bragging that "technologically, the campus has no equal when it comes to wireless Internet access and computer resource availability." They also praise the "affordability" and "flexibility" of the program as well as the "quality of instruction."

Most students are part-timers, and thus take advantage of the aforementioned flexible scheduling options, which include evening and weekend courses delivered in seven- or 14-week modules. Students wishing to fast-track can complete the program in as few as 16 months. Most students here are from the area, and as a result, many are familiar with the local business leaders who "work with the school and take interest in the curriculum being offered. Their input also lends real-world examples to classroom material and theory." Students' work experiences similarly enrich the classroom experience.

Seidman professors "are often active in the business world, maintaining the edge to pass on to the students." Their involvement with more than 400 local and national companies generates opportunities for students to work on projects in area organizations under the supervision of the faculty and establish "connections with the West Michigan business community." One MBA reports, "I have had accounting instructors who were former Securities and Exchange Commission executives. My global competitiveness class was taught by a former director of the World Bank. My auditing professor was an adjunct professor who also happened to be a Partner at BDO Seidman. Overall, of the 11 classes taken to earn my MBA, nine were taught by PhDs and two of those PhDs were also CPAs." Many students single out faculty in finance and accounting for praise; of the latter, they note, "The Seidman School of Business has always had a very high pass rate on the CPA exam. I was able to pass in two attempts after having been out of school for a number of years and then brushing up through the Becker Review. The accounting courses definitely gave me a good background to draw from."

Career and Placement

Career placement and counseling services are provided through the university's Career Services Office, which offers a variety of online resources, seminars and workshops, individual counseling services, and recruitment events. "The Business School office has been incredible in supporting student goals," and someone is "always available."

Student Life and Environment

The Seidman MBA program is housed in the DeVos Center on GVSU's downtown Grand Rapids campus, which students tell us is "nearly new and maintained with incredible focus and attention." Assets include "beautiful courtyards and facilities to accommodate a person who wants to relax, [and a] great new high-tech library." Although a few express past parking woes, some also praise the "new parking garage with lots of spots." The DeVos Center also features "many open gathering spaces, which increase the experiences of interacting with other students inside and outside of the business school," as well as "great technology, with free wireless Internet for laptops and PDAs." Students report that "classrooms are all up-to-date with equipment and lighting," and mention that they "are invited to use the technology for presentations and lectures during many activities."

CLAUDIA BAJEMA, GRADUATE BUSINESS PROGRAMS DIRECTOR
401 WEST FULTON, GRAND RAPIDS, MI 49504 UNITED STATES
PHONE: 616-331-7400 • FAX: 616-331-7389
E-MAIL: GO2GVMBA@GVSU.EDU • WEBSITE: WWW.GVSU.EDU/BUSINESS

MBAs enjoy "strong ties with the balance of the university to keep students in touch with the rest of college life." Students tell us, "Strong athletic programs also serve as an avenue to bring students together for a common, energetic experience" Even so, most students here spend little extracurricular time on campus. One Explains; "The MBA program is pretty nonsocial, as most people are working full-time. The undergrad campus has a more active life." Some would like to see more of "a community for graduate students," while others are happy with the status quo.

"GVSU pulls from a fairly wide geographic area for business graduate students, and many commute 40 minutes to an hour for classes and library use. With strong family commitments, many students return home after class, but there is networking between students that live in similar areas which is very helpful." The post-work environment can be very comforting as "occasionally a portion of the class will gather at a local establishment following class or an exam." Students represent "a diverse base coming from various sectors, including teaching, accounting, health sciences, engineering, and law. The students have strong ties, ranging from local, small businesses to international conglomerates, located here in the area." They are "career-oriented, driven, experienced people who are often balancing an active family, social, and business life."

Admissions

Completed applications to the Grand Valley State MBA program include official transcripts for all previous post-secondary academic work, an essay describing the applicant's goals and objectives, GMAT scores, and, for non-native English speakers, TOEFL scores. Students who have previously completed graduate programs may apply for a waiver of the GMAT requirement. Students who have not previously completed coursework in core business disciplines may be admitted to the program conditionally, pending completion of foundation courses in financial and managerial accounting, data analysis, finance, business law, macro- and micro-economics, marketing, and operations. Students can place out of foundation courses through school-administered examinations. In its efforts to attract underrepresented students, GVSU offers scholarships for African American and Hispanic students.

FINANCIAL FACTS

Annual tuition (in-state/out-of-state)	$4,968/$10,800
Fees	$30
Books and supplies	$1,500
Room & board (on/off-campus)	$6,500/$5,000
% of students receiving aid	26
Average grant	$4,360

ADMISSIONS

Admissions Selectivity Rating	**75**
# of applications received	105
% applicants accepted	85
% acceptees attending	93
Average GMAT	564
Range of GMAT	520-680
Average GPA	3.3
TOEFL Required of International Students?	Yes
Minimum TOEFL (paper/computer)	550/213
Application fee	$30
International application fee	$30
Regular application deadline	8/1
Regular notification	Rolling
Deferment Available?	Yes
Maximum length of deferment	1 year
Transfer students accepted?	Yes
Transfer application policy: Students may transfer up to 9 credits with B or better at discretion of program director.	
Non-fall admissions?	Yes
Need-blind admissions?	Yes

APPLICANTS ALSO LOOK AT
Western Michigan University.

EMPLOYMENT PROFILE

		Grads employed by field: %	
Career Rating	**60***	**Grads employed by field: %**	
% grads employed immediately	93	Accounting	13
		Finance	13
		Human Resources	3
		Marketing	10
		Operations	10
		Strategic Planning	10
		Consulting	10
		Entrepreneurship	10
		General Management	10
		Global Management	10
		Quantitative	1

HARVARD UNIVERSITY
HARVARD BUSINESS SCHOOL

Academics

A "tried and true General Management focus with no concentrations or majors and no published GPAs," a "pedagogical approach that relies strongly on the case method," and most of all "a reputation as the best business program in the country" make Harvard Business School one of the top prizes in the MBA admissions sweepstakes. Applicants lucky enough to gain admission here rarely decide to go elsewhere.

The School's full-time-only program is relatively large; approximately 900 students enter the program each year. Students tell us that, "Despite its large size, the school feels surprisingly small" thanks to a combination of factors. First is an administration that "could be a role model for any enterprise. This place is very well run." Second is the subdivision of classes into smaller sections of 90 students, who together attack approximately 500 case studies during their two years here. Finally, there's a faculty that "is obviously committed to excelling at teaching and developing relationships with the students. Each faculty member loves being here, regardless of whether they are a superstar or not, and that makes a difference. Faculty guide discussion well and enliven the classroom."

The case method predominates at Harvard; explains one student, "I sit in my section of 90 students every day and debate business topics. My section mates come from all walks of life and all of them are incredibly successful. I prepare my 13 cases per week so that I can contribute to this environment." Students love the approach, although they point out that "the case method is not as great for quantitative courses such as finance." Numerous field-study classes supplement the program, especially during the second year, which is devoted to elective study. School wide initiative—combinations of interdisciplinary classes, field study, contests, and club work—encourage research and provide added focus in the areas of social enterprise, entrepreneurship, global issues, and leadership.

Ultimately, though, HBS' strength resides in the quality of its instructors. Notes one student, "HBS is one of the few schools where a large part of the professor's evaluation is based on classroom teaching. The professors at HBS are wonderful teachers and take great interest in their students." As one first-year puts it, "If first semester is representative of the whole experience, I'll be a happy grad. My accounting professor managed to make accounting my favorite class (seems unimaginable!), and I'll definitely take whatever he teaches during the second year of elective courses."

Career and Placement

Harvard Business School hardly needs a Career Development Center, any more than Rolls Royce needs salesmen to move its cars. The school maintains a robust career services office all the same, providing a full range of counseling and internship- and career-placement services. Over 800 companies pay recruiting visits to the HBS campus each year in search of full-time hires; another 400 come looking for summer interns. Nearly half of all MBAs remain on the east coast after graduation, about half of whom take jobs in New York City. Twenty percent find international placements; half work in Europe and about a quarter work in Asia.

Student Life and Environment

Life at HBS "is as hectic as you want it to be." One student writes, "My life is pretty much moving along at breakneck speed. I wouldn't want it any other way because the school offers an incredible amount and array of activities, from volunteer consulting to running conferences." Because Harvard University is a magnet for innovative and prestigious thinkers in all disciplines, "This place is like a candy story for a five-year old; you want

FINANCIAL FACTS

Annual tuition	$35,600
% of students receiving aid	66

ADMISSIONS

Admissions Selectivity Rating	99
# of applications received	8,512
% applicants accepted	12
Average GMAT	708
Average GPA	3.6
TOEFL Required of International Students?	Yes
Minimum TOEFL (paper/computer)	610/253
Application fee	$200
Application Deadline/Notification	
Round 1:	10/16 / 1/21
Round 2:	1/8 / 3/31
Round 3:	3/11 / 5/12
Need-blind admissions?	Yes

to eat a lot more than what's good for you. You can spend all your time on studies, lectures from academics/politicians from all over the world, visiting business leaders, conferences, sports, or the night life. A 60-hour day would be appropriate."

Students generally manage to find the time to enjoy "a very social and outgoing environment" at HBS. Writes one married student, "Most weekends my husband and I have a choice: the 'college scene' where we can hit up the Harvard or Central Square bars with the singles, or the 'married scene' where we have dinner, play goofy board games, and drink with our 'couple friends.' Either can be a great escape from the other, and both are always a lot of fun!" Close relationship are easy to forge here, as "the section system means you have 89 close friends in the program, which makes learning and being here fun. It also means in the business world there will always be 89 incredibly smart, connected people who will go to bat for me no matter what."

The population of this program is, unsurprisingly, exceptional. As one MBA explains, "The quality of people here is unlike anything I've experienced. For the first time in my adult life, I'm surrounded by people whose interests and abilities fascinate and inspire me. All religions, nationalities, cultures, and sexual orientations exist here, happily, and together. I think Boston cultivates this kind of 'meshing of all thoughts' in such a way that everyone is comfortable, and everyone learns. The city and the school are both comfortable in their own skins, and the students take on that characteristic here."

Admissions

Applicants to Harvard Business School must submit a "complete HBS application portfolio, including personal essays, academics transcripts, and three letters of recommendation." In addition, students must provide scores from the GMAT, and applicants from non-English speaking countries must submit scores for either the TOEFL or the IELTS (scores must be no more than two years old). Applications must be submitted online. Academic ability, leadership experience, and unique personal characteristics all figure prominently into the admissions decision. The school's viewbook notes that "Because our MBA curriculum is fast-paced and rigorously analytical, we strongly encourage all applicants to complete introductory courses in quantitative subjects such as accounting, finance, and economics before coming to HBS. For some candidates, we may make admission contingent upon their completing such courses before they enroll." Good luck!

EMPLOYMENT PROFILE

		Grads employed by field	%: avg. salary
Career Rating	99	Finance	27: $85,000
# of companies recruiting on-campus	803	Consulting	20: $105,000
% grads employed immediately	88	Entrepreneurship	9: $100,000
Average starting salary	$90,000	General Management	8: $95,000
		Venture Capital	12: $120,000
		Internet/New Media	23
		Non-profit	1: $80,000

HEC Montreal
MBA Program

GENERAL INFORMATION
Type of school   public

SURVEY SAYS...
Students love Montreal, QC
Friendly students
Happy students
Smart classrooms
Solid preparation in:
Teamwork

STUDENTS
Enrollment of parent
  institution
Enrollment of MBA program   475
% male/female   70/30
% part-time   64
% international   50
Average age at entry   31
Average years work experience
  at entry   6

ACADEMICS
Academic Experience Rating   **81**
Student/faculty ratio   7:1
Profs interesting rating   78
Profs accessible rating   80
% female faculty   25
Prominent Alumni
Mr. Louis Couillard, MBA '91,
President, Pfizer France; Mr. Thierry
Vandal, MBA '95, President, Hydro-
Quebec; Ms. Lucienne Robillard,
MBA 84, President of the Queen's
Privy Council for Canada; Ms.
Marie-Claude Peyrache, MBA '73,
Group Exec. Director, France
Telecom; Mr. Louis Roquet, MBA
'73, President and COO, Desjardins
Venture Capital.

Academics

HEC Montreal, the "little school that could," has truly ascended the ranks of international MBA programs in recent years. A relatively obscure school until the 1990s, HEC Montreal launched a curriculum overhaul midway through the decade that yielded dramatic results: within a decade, the school had become the first North American institution to earn accreditation from EQUIS (the European Foundation for Management Development), AMBA (the Association of MBAs of the United Kingdom), and AACSB International.

HEC Montreal offers both a full-time and a part-time MBA program. International students are eligible for the full-time program only; this program, aptly named 'the Intensive MBA,' "is really a full two-year program condensed into 54 weeks. If you are motivated and disciplined, then you will succeed in this environment." Students warn that "it is very intensive and there is a solid workload throughout the program, with very few breaks in between." Cohort-based education and an emphasis on team projects helps students develop an esprit de corps to weather the program's challenges; explains one MBA, "We, all 180 students, take all the same classes for the first six months, which makes for great understanding amongst ourselves. We all know what the others are going through regarding workload and projects." While most here praise the full-time program, a few complain that "Sometimes the pace is a bit too fast and we don't have time to sit back and reflect on what we've learned. Also, the pace does not allow much time for extra-curricular seminars." Students may choose between French-only instruction and English-only instruction; roughly 60 percent of students opt for the English-only program.

The part-time program at HEC Montreal, called the MBA in Action, takes three years to complete. The curricula for the full-time and part-time programs are virtually identical; the major difference is that part-time students are exempted from the requirement to complete a field project. Part-timers warn that "occasionally we get professors who are low-level outsiders rather than the mostly experienced professors who teach the entire full-time program, and some of them are not such great teachers." They also point out that the program's team-learning format is hampered by the fact that "lots of students drop out or don't show up for meetings because of work obligations. Not enough effort is put into restoring team spirit when that happens." Students in both programs agree that the school "makes good use of classroom technology" and that "teaching methods tend to be very participative and pragmatic."

Career and Placement

The HEC Montreal Career Centre provides career and placement services to undergraduates, graduates, and alumni. According to the school viewbook, "The Centre is well known for its personalized approach, and provides constant support for students as well as recent and past graduates: helping them prepare for interviews and draw up their résumés, providing information on the labor market, job-search strategies, conducting psychometric assessments (academic guidance and skills profiling), and career planning, assessment and redirection."

Companies that recruit on campus include Bank of Canada, Bombardier Inc., Canadian National, CDP Caisse de dépôt et placement du Québec, Crédit Commercial de France, Deloitte Consulting, Johnson & Johnson, KPMG, Merrill Lynch, National Bank, Peugot, Procter & Gamble, Scotiabank, and the Toronto Stock Exchange.

IVANA.BONADUCE@HEC.CA, STUDENT ADVISOR
3000 CHEMIN DE LA COTE STE-CATHERINE, MONTREAL, QC H3T 2A7 CANADA
PHONE: 514-340-6957 • FAX: 514-340-5640
E-MAIL: MBA@HEC.CA • WEBSITE: WWW.HEC.CA

FINANCIAL FACTS

Annual tuition (in-state/out-of-state)	
	$6,200/$14,800
Books and supplies	$3,000
Room & board	$12,000
Average grant	$3,800

ADMISSIONS

Admissions Selectivity Rating	77
# of applications received	391
% applicants accepted	67
% acceptees attending	67
Average GMAT	600
TOEFL Required of International Students?	Yes
Minimum TOEFL (paper/computer)	600/250
Application fee	$50
International application fee	$50
Regular application deadline	4/1
Regular notification	5/15
International application deadline	2/15
International application notification	4/1

Student Life and Environment

The MBA program at HEC Montreal is "very well located in Montreal, near the subway with access to all the Université de Montreal complex for other classes, if wanted." Facilities include "a new building that is aesthetically very nice, with lots of services for students," and "the biggest business library on campus." Students appreciate that the School is situated on "a nice, open space and that everything you need—food, lodging, subway, sports—is available on site." The gym facilities, students tell us, "are considered to be the best in Montreal."

For both full-time and part-time students, "the compressed six-week course terms (including exam period) makes the work pace fast and heavy," so "there is not necessarily a lot of time for social activities. However, the student association does try very hard to coordinate activities for" students, including "cinq à sept happy hours, a Quebec tradition that is alive and well at HEC Montreal. Every other Thursday, the student association takes over the campus lounge and we blow off a little steam! The parties are so much fun that the undergraduates try to sneak in, no doubt attracted by the dancing on the bars!" One student observes, "Our MBA association aims to involve all students in deciding what types of activities are provided. They concentrate on providing social activities that encourage the integration of English and French speaking students, as well as the international student community of HEC Montreal. Events such as the Magic of the Lanterns in the Botanical Gardens and an International Pot-Luck dinner are perfect ways of opening up cultural barriers and introducing a broader, more international environment, where students are encouraged to share experiences and learn from each other."

Admissions

Applicants to HEC Montreal must hold a baccalaureate earned "with a satisfactory average." Students must also demonstrate "at least two years of relevant full-time work experience" subsequent to completing undergraduate study. Applications must also include an official score report for the GMAT and two letters of recommendation (at least one from an employer). Non-native English speakers applying to the English-only program must pass the HECTOPE business English test (administered by HEC Montreal) or submit scores for either the TOEFL or IELTS. Non-native French speakers applying to the French-only program must complete the Test de français international (an ETS-administered exam). Applicants who are not citizens of Canada must obtain a certificat d'acceptation du Québec (C.A.Q.) and a document attesting to their right to reside in Canada (Student Authorization or Ministerial Permit). The school recommends that accepted students apply for these documents as soon as they receive confirmation of their admission to the program.

EMPLOYMENT PROFILE			
Career Rating	83	Grads employed by field %: avg. salary	
Placement rate (%)	90	Finance	14: $59,000
% grads employed immediately	14	Marketing	22: $49,500
Average starting salary	$54,500	MIS	8: $75,250
		Operations	6: $41,500
		Consulting	21: $54,265
		General Management	14: $63,500
		Other	15: $43,200

HEC SCHOOL OF MANAGEMENT—PARIS
HEC MBA PROGRAM

GENERAL INFORMATION
Type of school   public
Academic calendar   quarter

SURVEY SAYS...
Friendly students
Good peer network
Happy students
Solid preparation in:
Teamwork
Communication/interpersonal skills
Presentation skills

STUDENTS
Enrollment of parent
   institution   2,700
Enrollment of MBA program   201
% male/female   72/28
% international   80
Average age at entry   30
Average years work experience
   at entry   6

ACADEMICS
Academic Experience Rating   95
Student/faculty ratio   4:1
Profs interesting rating   80
Profs accessible rating   73
% female faculty   15

Joint Degrees
8 Double-degree programs are
available as an option. These
include NYU, LSE, The Fletcher
School of Law and Diplomacy,
Chinese U of Hongkong, FGV
(Brazil), ITESM (Mexico), UTDT
(Argentina) and PUC (Chile). Study
periods vary between programs.

Prominent Alumni
Sidney Taurel, President & CEO, Eli
Lilly & Co; Fumiaki Maeda,
Managing Director, Mitsubishi Bank;
Daniel Bernard, CEO, Carrefour;
Pierre Danon, COD, Cap Gemini;
Pascal Cagni, VP, Apple.

Academics

"The sense of community [and] the focus on creating international mangers [are] amazing" at the HEC School of Management, whose full-time, 16-month MBA program is offered in both an English-only and bilingual format. Because of its generalist approach, the HEC MBA "enables students to understand and participate in all functions of a business." Students tell us that "there is heavy emphasis on general skills as well as the human, personal interactions that are necessary in order to be successful in business, particularly in a multicultural and multilingual environment." Arithmophobes, take note: "Because it focuses on creating general management skills, the school does not focus on developing in-depth quantitative skills."

At HEC, "teamwork is stressed among the students, faculty, and administration to build a memorable MBA family, [especially] during the early phases of the program. The latter part of the course is more individual." The classroom atmosphere, students agree, is convivial. Students report, "The academic workload and class schedule are challenging but workable" and appreciate the duration of the program, which "is neither too short nor too long."

HEC instructors are "a diversified group of professors, with differing talents and competencies. The differentiation in styles and backgrounds is as apparent in the faculty as in the student body, which adds to the international experience of adapting to new cultures and environments." Students note, "Open communication and willingness to cooperate is a strong forte among all faculty, [and] professors' contacts in the business community make the classroom interactive." HEC's name carries considerable weight in Europe, allowing the school to "attract excellent speakers." One student writes, "During my 15 months of class, HEC had the pleasure of welcoming the Prime Minister, some of his team of ministers, and CEOs of global and French companies (Airbus, Nissan, Renault, Dassault)."

Of course, the school's location also means that the school has "a French public-service-type administration," which catches more than a few foreign students off-guard. American students, in particular, have little patience for the "completely rigid, bureaucratic, and inefficient structure [that] needs to be completely overhauled." Some, however, see a silver lining to this dark cloud: "The advantage is that you get a much better understanding of French society than you would if there was a non-French-style administration."

Career and Placement

The Career Development Office at HEC provides counseling services, workshops, and seminars in job-search skills and interview techniques, access to online self-assessment instruments, contact to the school's 25,000+ alumni worldwide, four major job fairs per year, and "privileged access to firms actively supporting HEC." The office sponsors regular corporate presentations and recruitment programs that bring over 200 employers to campus each year. Thirty-eight percent of all non-European members of the class of 2004 found employment in Europe; 88 percent found positions "of international scope." Nearly half used their degree to change both the sector and function of their careers.

Students see both strengths and weaknesses in the career office. One writes, "If you want to work in France, the name of HEC will help you for life. This is a fantastic networking opportunity in France, and it is growing on the international scale." However, many feel that career services are "currently too focused on French companies or French divisions of international companies. Efforts need to be made to improve the relationship with other international companies." Employers most likely to hire HEC MBAs include Barclays Capital; BT Retail; Hilti; Johnson & Johnson; L'Oréal; Michelin; Nestlé; and Société Générale.

Student Life and Environment

The first term at HEC is grueling, students tell us, and during that initial period, "life centers around the campus and the MBA building. Students are getting involved in one or two extracurriculars that are important to them, but it is difficult to get involved in much more because of the workload." Things ease up afterwards, allowing students a little more time to enjoy all that the campus and Paris have to offer. Throughout the school year, "there are never two days without an event organized by one of the clubs, either a professional club or sports club." Every Wednesday night brings "Happy Hour at the Piano Bar, a chilled-out bar with wood floors, glass walls that overlook campus, candles, and good beer." Beer? Not for everyone. Many here "love kicking back after a hard day's work and enjoying a glass of Bordeaux."

HEC "offers the advantage of being part of a larger institution and as such is not insulated within its own self-absorbed environment," which students appreciate. They also praise the campus, which is "located in a beautiful forest, not far from Versailles and Paris." The 250-acre campus provides plenty of space to kick the soccer ball (i.e. football) around. The campus also features tennis courts, basketball courts, a climbing wall, and a nine-hole golf course. The proximity to Paris "adds a cultural and artistic flavor to the experience."

HEC's student body is 80 percent international, representing over 40 countries. The setting is "incredibly international [and] intellectually stimulating. Everyone has unique and insightful insights into not just business, but politics, society, and culture."

Admissions

HEC requires the following of applicants: an electronically filed application form; official undergraduate transcripts, transcripts for all graduate work; GMAT scores (and TOEFL scores, where appropriate); two letters of recommendation; four passport-size photos and a copy of one's passport or birth certificate; and the application fee. An interview is required as its results are given serious consideration in the admissions decision. The school's literature states, "The admissions process for the HEC MBA Program is a rigorous one. The MBA experience is an interactive one, and each participant is called upon to contribute to the learning process through his or her personal and professional experience." As a result, past academic, professional, and personal experience are all important factors. The ability to perform well in teamwork situations is also considered essential.

FINANCIAL FACTS

Annual tuition	$46,000
Books and supplies	$1,100
Room & board (on/off-campus)	
	$15,000/$20,000
% of students receiving aid	70
% of students receiving loans	60
% of students receiving grants	33
Average grant	$9,000

ADMISSIONS

Admissions Selectivity Rating	97
# of applications received	888
% applicants accepted	21
% acceptees attending	58
Average GMAT	660
Range of GMAT	590-750
Average GPA	NA
TOEFL Required of International Students?	Yes
Minimum TOEFL (paper/computer)	600/250
Application fee	$100
International application fee	$100
Sept. intake application deadline	4/29
Sept. intake notification	6/3
Jan. intake application deadline	4/11
Jan. intake notification	8/12
Deferment Available?	Yes
Maximum length of deferment	1 year
Non-fall admissions?	Yes
Need-blind admissions?	Yes

APPLICANTS ALSO LOOK AT

INSEAD, LBS.

EMPLOYMENT PROFILE

Career Rating	90	Grads employed by field	%: avg. salary
Placement rate (%)	88	Finance	24: $94,850
# of companies recruiting on-campus	210	Marketing	18: $90,203
Average starting salary	$100,568	MIS	1
		Operations	4
		Consulting	9: $100,450
		General Management	18: $102,314
		Global Management	20: $96,660
		Other	4

HHL—Leipzig Graduate School of Management

Academics

HHL, the Leipzig Graduate School of Management, offers German and international business students an appealing mix of a well-established name and modern innovation. Founded in 1898, HHL is the oldest business school in Germany, and its students benefit from its deserved reputation as a solid training ground for European managers. The MBA program, however, is relatively new, having only graduated its first class in 2001. Because the program is still in its nascent stages, students tell us, "It is striving to achieve more in the global ranking, so they really make an effort, as opposed to many established schools that expect their reputation to work for them." Since the program runs its course in a scant 15 months, it also appeals to the cost-conscious and to those in a hurry to climb the corporate ladder of success.

The HHL curriculum is divided into three categories. Core courses cover the basics in economics, quantitative skills, and IT; this segment of the program is particularly well-suited to the German students "whose prior academic training was not focused on business but rather was in the natural sciences, humanities, or social sciences" and whom the Admissions Office targets. Specialization courses in accounting, finance, marketing, business organization, and strategy allow students to hone a particular skill set. Students tell us that specializations in finance, marketing, and strategy "are the tops, especially finance and marketing with very well-known professors who publish a lot in their field and are on boards of corporations." Application courses in such areas as e-commerce, innovation management, and corporate-government relations keep students abreast of contemporary issues in the business world.

HHL professors "can be contacted almost 24 hours a day," and "those who are comfortable with English can even be fun in classes." Some students complain, "Most professors are visiting, which makes life harder," especially when their tenure is brief. One frustrated MBA queried, "A two-week finance course? That is unbelievable, plus impossible to learn anything from such a course." The administration "is practically invisible, which is great. They are there when you need them, but normally they don't mess up," note students. Internships, study abroad, and independent study options are all available. A high-quality education at a reasonable price is sited by students as one of the main reasons they chose the school.

Career and Placement

HHL MBAs report with satisfaction that "one of the big strengths of this program is its excellent contact to companies. Almost all top companies in consulting, banking, and industry come for presentation and recruiting. Companies react surprisingly positively when saying that you are from our school." One student comments, "Concerning placement, there is a huge database of direct contact people. Rather than applying over a 'website' one can contact people or alumni. This helps to stay away from the crowd that applies over recruiting websites of companies."

According to HHL, the school "has a record of placing graduates with prominent international firms-including Arthur Andersen, BASF, Bayer, Bertelsmann, Booz Allen & Hamilton, Boston Consulting Group, Daimler-Chrysler, Deutsche Bank, Ernst & Young, Ford, Henkel, Kirch-Gruppe, KPMG, McKinsey, Nestlé, Procter & Gamble, Siemens, and Volkswagen-as well as with many German 'Mittelstand' companies." Other companies that recruit on campus include A.T. Kearney, Accenture, Allianz AG, BMW, Citibank, FairAd, Goldman Sachs, Horváth & Partner, Lufthansa Cargo, OnVista, Porsche, Sachsen LB, and Wellington.

PETRA SPANKA, EXECUTIVE DIRECTOR
JAHNALLEE 59, LEIPZIG, 04109 GERMANY
PHONE: 01149341-9851-734 • FAX: 01149341-9851-731
E-MAIL: PETRA.SPANKA@MBA.HHL.DE • WEBSITE: WWW.HHL.DE

FINANCIAL FACTS

Annual tuition	$20,800
Books and supplies	$300
Room & board	$7,500
Average grant	$100,000

ADMISSIONS

Admissions Selectivity Rating	91
# of applications received	100
% applicants accepted	40
% acceptees attending	72
Average GMAT	600
Range of GMAT	550-750
Average GPA	3.5
TOEFL Required of International Students?	Yes
Minimum TOEFL (paper/computer)	600/250
Regular application deadline	6/1
Regular notification	7/1
Application Deadline/Notification	
Round 1:	4/1 / 5/1
Round 2:	5/1 / 6/1
Round 3:	6/1 / 7/1
Deferment Available?	Yes
Maximum length of deferment	1 year
Transfer students accepted?	Yes
Transfer application policy: Coursework and examinations in an economic degree program at another university or college of equal status is admissable pending review.	
Need-blind admissions?	Yes

Student Life and Environment

An accelerated academic schedule at HHL means that "life is somewhat focused on the courses. There is a lot of pre-work and post-work to do for almost all courses. Most courses integrate a high amount of applied case studies and group work. In some weeks/months the balance of studying and doing other things is bad (i.e., a lot of studying)." One student notes, "Classes in finance are especially tough, but teach a lot that you need later in respective jobs." Even so, there is some time leftover to socialize. One MBA writes, "The school organizes a lot of parties and integrates in social life staff (i.e., professors) and students. The professors and students are almost on a friendship level and they help the students where they can."

Many students were attracted to the school because it represents "a somewhat wild mixture of nations, ages, and backgrounds," with about one third hailing from Germany and the rest "from different countries in Asia, South and North America, Europe, etc. Also, they have different working experiences; some of them are business men, some are engineers. Some worked for law firms, some served in the Navy as IT engineers." What they all share in common is that they "are ready to help, ready to work, and ready to party." As one student observes, "They are very interesting and challenging to work with. I can't imagine better fellow students!"

Leipzig is "a great town [with] a long academic record [and] many sports facilities," students tell us. Bach and Schumann put this ancient trade center on the musical map, and their traditions are carried on today in the city's many concert halls, theaters, cafés and cabarets, jazz clubs, and discos. The city is conveniently located for travel to and from Berlin, Dresden, and Weimar, as well as to major Czech and Polish cities.

Admissions

All applicants to HHL's MBA program must submit GMAT scores (according to the school, students with scores of at least 650 "are more likely to be offered admission than applicants with lower scores"), proof of undergraduate degree and transcripts, two recommendations, a resume, and a completed application. Non-native English speakers must also submit proof of English proficiency. HHL accepts TOEFL scores to fulfill this requirement; it mandates a minimum score of 600 on the paper-and-pencil version or 250 on the computer-based exam. The admissions committee convenes once a month to consider all completed applications, at which point it decides either to accept, reject, or waitlist each candidate.

EMPLOYMENT PROFILE

Career Rating	84	Grads employed by field	%
Placement rate (%)	95	Accounting	3
# of companies recruiting on-campus	37	Finance	3
% grads employed immediately	85	Human Resources	5
Average starting salary	$55,000	Marketing	12
		MIS	5
		Operations	12
		Consulting	12
		Communications	7
		Entrepreneurship	5
		General Management	12
		Global Management	5
		Other	5
		Internet/New Media	12

HOFSTRA UNIVERSITY
FRANK G. ZARB SCHOOL OF BUSINESS

GENERAL INFORMATION
Type of school	private
Environment	city
Academic calendar	4-1-4

SURVEY SAYS...
Smart classrooms
Solid preparation in:
Teamwork
Presentation skills

STUDENTS
Enrollment of parent institution	12,999
Enrollment of MBA program	390
% male/female	66/34
% out-of-state	6
% part-time	65
% minorities	15
% international	20
Average age at entry	26
Average years work experience at entry	2.5

ACADEMICS
Academic Experience Rating	**72**
Student/faculty ratio	8:1
Profs interesting rating	63
Profs accessible rating	69
% female faculty	19
% minority faculty	23

Joint Degrees
MBA/JD: 4 years

Prominent Alumni
Frank G. Zarb, Senior Advisor & Managing Dir., Hellman & Friedman; Salvatore F. Sodano, Chairman & CEO, American Stock Exchange; James Campbell, President & CEO, GE Consumer & Industrial Americas; Patrick J. Purcell, President & Publisher, Herald Media; Donna Iucolano, CEO North America, International Masters Publisher.

Academics

Business grad students come to Hofstra seeking "a state-of-the-art education at an accessible price," and most leave feeling they've accomplished their goal. The Zarb School, students report, "is on the cutting edge of technology—almost all classrooms have a computer at every desk." A world of research awaits students, as the library "provides off-campus access to 34 business-specific databases, including Lexis/Nexis services."

Zarb students may choose from a variety of degree options: an MBA, an MS, a four-year combined JD/MBA program, and an executive MBA (EMBA) for those already deeply immersed in the working world. Students tell us, "If you hope to have managerial position, you should go for an MBA because you will learn from each field of business," but those interested in marketing should consider the MS "since you have to take a lot of marketing classes, many more than MBA students even if their concentration is marketing. You will learn a lot about this specific field."

Hofstra's finance program earns the highest praise from students. They tell us, "Finance professors are cutting edge, often pulling together a curriculum not found in textbooks, incorporating tools developed and used in the field." Throughout all disciplines, instructors "are, to a person, accomplished and well-recognized leaders in the business realm. The body of instructors is truly unparalleled in terms of experience and ability." They are also readily accessible; "many of them have open-door policies," one MBA reports.

Perhaps Hofstra's greatest asset, however, is its location. As one student put it, "Although the school is not as well-known as Harvard, the great strength of Hofstra is the location. Because we have New York City very close to us, we can benefit a lot from it. There are so many more job opportunities here than any other cities, and Hofstra is pretty well-known for people in New York. Also we can benefit a lot socially being here. Since networking is a very important factor, if you are an ambitious business student, you might happen to bump into someone at a restaurant and end up networking with him or her—and who knows? You might get a job!"

Career and Placement

Hofstra maintains an MBA career center seperate from the university career center, which provides advisement, networking, and career development plans. Fortunately, Hofstra's proximity to New York City—and to numerous businesses headquartered on Long Island—makes students' search for employment easier than at many business schools. Over 300 employers pay recruiting visits to the Hofstra campus each year; about half as many come to Hofstra seeking summer interns. Top employers include Arrow Electronics, Inc.; Citibank; Computer Associates; Deloitte Touche Tohmatsu; Deutsche Bank; Ernst & Young; JP Morgan Chase; Pall Corporation; PricewaterhouseCoopers; and North Shore, LIJ Health Systems, Hain Celestial, KPMG, Integrated Business Systems, Quest Diagnostics and Henry Schein.

Marketing and finance claim the majority of Hofstra MBAs. Average starting salaries range from $53,667 (accounting) to over $100,000 (consulting). In 2004, the average starting salary in finance was $66,800; in marketing, the average starting salary was $68,692. Over 90 percent find work in the Northeast region.

CAROL DRUMMER, DEAN FOR GRADUATE ADMISSIONS
126 HOFSTRA UNIVERSITY, 105 MEMORIAL HALL, HEMPSTEAD, NY 11549 UNITED STATES
PHONE: 866-472-3463 • FAX: 516-463-4664
E-MAIL: GRADSTUDENT@HOFSTRA.EDU • WEBSITE: WWW.HOFSTRA.EDU / ACADEMICS / BUSINESS

Student Life and Environment

Hofstra's "safe, friendly, [and] gorgeous [campus boasts] great facilities, including a wonderful library, laboratories, and gym." The campus is home to "a lot of social events, and the school offers transportation to the Nassau Veterans Memorial Coliseum," home to the New York Islanders, concerts, and major trade shows. Students are less excited about the school's hometown of Hempstead but consider the school's location a plus overall. One MBA explains, "Although the school is located [in] not-too-nice [of a] neighborhood, we can easily go to Manhattan (New York City) by taking the Long Island Railroad. We can go there on weekends and have fun, which is a very good way of removing stress and forgetting about school for just a little while. I truly believe that New York City is one of the most exciting cities in the world, and having it very close to the school is the biggest advantage of students of Hofstra, both socially and academically." The location also "offers students the opportunity to live among the suburbs of New York City, [placing them in] the hub of the business world" without having to endure big-city crowds and expenses.

Most graduate students "are very friendly, helpful, and driven, as well as pretty active in student associations, of which there are plenty." Clubs and organizations include the International MBA/MS Association, Graduate Women in Business, the Hofstra Investment Banking Association, and the Hofstra Business Consulting Group. If there's a knock on the student body, it is that it's "overwhelmingly part-time, comprising working professionals. Students tend not to engage themselves in thorough discussion and analysis of presented material. It is understandably difficult to work a full day and then contribute to a class at night, but if one desires a quality education, then it is a necessity."

Admissions

Applicants to Hofstra's graduate business programs must submit an official undergraduate transcript, GMAT scores, letters of recommendation, a personal statement, and a resume; students whose first language is not English must submit TOEFL scores. Admissions decisions are "also influenced by evidence of leadership, communication skills, [and performance on the] analytical writing assessment of GMAT," the school tells us. The admissions department also reports that "special consideration in the application process is given to minority students from disadvantaged backgrounds." Hofstra makes no undergraduate curricular requirements of its MBA students, no major precludes admission to the school, and no specific courses are required prior to admission. Applicants to the MS program in accounting or taxation must hold an undergraduate degree in accounting. Applicants to the EMBA program must document a minimum of seven years' work experience.

FINANCIAL FACTS

Annual tuition	$16,200
Fees	$920
Books and supplies	$3,000
Room & board (on/off-campus)	$8,590/$10,175
% of students receiving aid	47
% of first-year students receiving aid	55
% of students receiving loans	38
% of students receiving grants	18
Average award package	$14,691
Average grant	$4,566
Average student loan debt	$25,809

ADMISSIONS

Admissions Selectivity Rating	78
# of applications received	348
% applicants accepted	48
% acceptees attending	51
Average GMAT	519
Range of GMAT	470-560
Average GPA	3.2
TOEFL Required of International Students?	Yes
Application fee	$60
International application fee	$60
Regular application deadline	Rolling
Regular notification	Rolling
Deferment Available?	Yes
Maximum length of deferment	1 year
Transfer students accepted?	Yes
Transfer application policy: Number of transferable credits is limited to a maximum of 9 credits.	
Non-fall admissions?	Yes
Need-blind admissions?	Yes

APPLICANTS ALSO LOOK AT

Baruch College—City University of New York, New York University, Pace University, St. John's University.

EMPLOYMENT PROFILE

Career Rating	82	Grads employed by field	%: avg. salary
Placement rate (%)	86	Accounting	18: $53,667
# of companies recruiting on-campus	406	Finance	30: $66,800
% grads employed immediately	75	Marketing	26: $68,692
Average starting salary	$67,170	MIS	6: $93,167
		Consulting	4: $105,000
		General Management	10: $56,000
		Other	6: $63,333

HONG KONG U. OF SCIENCE AND TECHNOLOGY
HKUST BUSINESS SCHOOL

Academics

"You can't learn about a region from a distance. You need to experience it personally." So say the international students drawn to the MBA program at the Hong Kong University of Science and Technology; they come here looking for "easy access to the Chinese culture for Western students," and they know that this is the place to get it. One MBA writes, "There is no way a school in Europe or the U.S. could teach you about this region as well as HKUST can. There is no other school in Asia that can touch it in that respect." Another agrees, "HKUST has the best Chinese faculty in the world catering to business in China."

Full-time students can choose from two curricular options at HKUST: a 12-month option that minimizes the student's time away from work, and a 16-month option that allows for participation in exchange programs with one of 49 overseas business schools. The school also offers a part-time MBA. Students tell us that "the finance faculty is top-notch, as it needs to be for a financial center of the world like Hong Kong," and that "the school is also excellent in accounting and IT." Consulting, strategy, and marketing reportedly "could be stronger." The faculty has strong credentials One MBA reports, "It's a very strong research faculty who present their findings at the international level. They are also, for the most part, very capable of imparting with their insights in a compelling and engaging manner."

MBAs also praise the program's "emphasis on teamwork, [the] good balance of practical case-based teaching and theory" in the classroom, and a curricular structure that ensures students are prepared to participate in class. "There are compulsory assignments to hand-in before class, which is good to force students to prepare for class and also arrive on time. The professors also count participation towards the grade, so students are encouraged to raise questions."

HKUST is also home to a part-time MBA program, which takes two years to complete. Part-time students complete the same required courses as do full-timers but have fewer elective options; the school admits about 120 part-timers each year, dividing them into two cohorts of 60. The program is scheduled "to meet the special needs of working professionals and managers."

Career and Placement

HKUST maintains a dedicated MBA Career Development Office for its graduate students in business. The office offers career counseling, a variety of self-assessment tools, workshops in job-search and interview skills, recruiting events, internships, resume books, and job listings. Students feel that they need closer relationships or partnerships with companies, especially large companies in mainland China and other important countries or cities outside Hong Kong." MBAs also tell us that "this is still a young program," which they see as both an impediment and an asset. "Our alumni network is still relatively small; however, there is no doubt that the people we are studying with are the future of China and this region. So it's a small network, but a very useful one indeed," writes one student.

Employers who most frequently hire HKUST MBAs include UBS, Morgan Stanley, FedEx, Citibank, HSBC, Schroders, Emerson Electric Co., and McKinsey & Company. Just under half of HKUST grads wind up in the finance sector.

Student Life and Environment

Full-time students at HKUST constitute "a small group with around 50 students, yet with diversity in both culture background and working experience. We are friendly, helpful, active, and full of creative ideas!" Students come here from all around the world as one student reports, "The range of nationalities present spans from Thai, Korean, Israeli, Indian, and Filipino to New Zealander, Swiss, Irish, French, and Canadian." There are a lot of students from mainland China here; international students appreciate how "their background provides invaluable input into the program."

The HKUST campus "on a hill overlooking the ocean [is] an oasis that is only 20 minutes by MTR from the heart of the central business district." Students enjoy "numerous activities after class. Every Friday noon, students, faculty, and some staff of MBA office will have a self-service lunch together. It is a small family atmosphere, and we chat with each other casually. After the lunch, there will be a country presentation by one or a group of students from a certain country." Students spend leisure time together too, "hiking the trails beside the sea, boating, enjoying night life on the famous bar street of Hong Kong, attending concerts, [or] shopping." One MBA writes, "School life cycles between periods of intense work and pure fun."

Students love Hong Kong, "a very international city" of seven million. As one MBA puts it, "Hong Kong is Asia's world city. If you don't have a life here, you just don't have a life." The "nightlife, food, entertainment are all world-class," the city is "super-safe," and the "public transportation is excellent." The school's location "is convenient to visit the Hong Kong stock exchange or other big companies. You are even able to do some field study in mainland China."

Admissions

HKUST expects all applicants to hold "a good bachelor degree from a recognized university" and to have strong GMAT scores, full-time work experience (at least three years for the part-time program, at least one year for the full-time program), and to be proficient in English. All applicants must provide two letters of reference along with official copies of their transcripts and GMAT score reports. Students whose first language is not English must also provide TOEFL scores. An interview, scheduled at the school's behest, is required prior to admission; it can be conducted by telephone if a face-to-face interview is impractical. The online application is "strongly advised" by the school "for data accuracy and convenience of data update."

FINANCIAL FACTS

Annual tuition	$26,000
Books and supplies	$8,700
Room & board (on/off-campus)	
	$3,100/$6,200
Average grant	$5,420

ADMISSIONS

Admissions Selectivity Rating	90
# of applications received	241
% applicants accepted	34
% acceptees attending	60
Average GMAT	620
Range of GMAT	580-660
Application fee	$64
International application fee	$64
Regular application deadline	3/15
Regular notification	5/30
Application Deadline/Notification	
Round 1:	12/15 / 2/28
Round 2:	3/15 / 05/30
Deferment Available?	Yes
Maximum length of	
deferment	1 year

EMPLOYMENT PROFILE

Career Rating	72	Grads employed by field	%: avg. salary
Placement rate (%)	100	Accounting	7: $39,500
# of companies recruiting on-campus	120	Finance	25: $38,500
% grads employed immediately	51	Marketing	14: $37,500
Average starting salary	$40,500	Strategic Planning	10: $32,500
		Consulting	17: $43,500
		Communications	5: $40,000
		Global Management	10: $36,500
		Other	12: $55,500

HOWARD UNIVERSITY
SCHOOL OF BUSINESS

GENERAL INFORMATION

Type of school	private
Academic calendar	semester

SURVEY SAYS...
Friendly students
Solid preparation in:
Teamwork
Presentation skills

STUDENTS

Enrollment of parent institution	10,866
Enrollment of MBA program	105
% male/female	52/48
% out-of-state	30
% part-time	32
% minorities	54
% international	34
Average age at entry	28
Average years work experience at entry	3

ACADEMICS

Academic Experience Rating	**84**
Student/faculty ratio	4:1
Profs interesting rating	80
Profs accessible rating	84
% female faculty	22
% minority faculty	89

Joint Degrees
MBA/JD: 4 years
BBA/MBA Accounting: 5 years
BSE/MBA Engineering: 5.5-6 years

Prominent Alumni
Rodney E. Thomas, CEO, Thomas & Herbert Consulting, LLC; Kerry L. Nelson, Sr. VP, Nonprofit Foundations, Northern Trust.

Academics

One of the few primarily African American universities in the country, Howard University also boasts the oldest fully accredited business school in the Washington, DC, area. And pride in the legacy of both the university and their business school program really pulls the community together. As one student puts it, "What is lovely about Howard University is the easy access to professors and the close relations the students have with their professors. They not only impart their knowledge but also treat the students like family." Students find a sense of cooperative spirit in their classmates as well, despite the rigors of academic life. According to one student, "My classmates are the best. You [can] always borrow someone's notes or text to catch up on if you're falling behind. That, to me, is the ultimate MBA experience: having a group of people you enjoy working with and who are willing to work with you." Another student points out that, with such a small, friendly group of people, Howard's greatest strength is its "ability to personalize the education and tend to the individual needs of a smaller student body."

Along with huge amounts of time spent on studying, Howard students also attend case competitions and conferences all over the country and are often particularly involved in the National Black MBA Association, which provides scholarships, funding, and counseling to prospective MBAs. Howard students are regularly awarded scholarships—often at a higher rate than other institutions—and greatly benefit from these networking opportunities. As one student says, "Throughout my tenure at Howard, I have been involved in more than 10 case competitions. The cases cover a broad spectrum of topics. From these experiences, I have acquired valuable research skills that I have used later both in my courses at school and in my internships in corporate America."

In 2000, in response to current business trends and needs, Howard added a supply chain management concentration to their basic MBA program, and it has quickly become one of the program's greatest strengths. Students point out Howard's "very strong supply chain and finance concentrations, [these departments often draw] prominent individuals to Howard to teach. If one is fortunate enough, he or she may get into the respective class. It is good to know that some people still see the potential at the school." Still, some are disappointed that these two departments seem to stand alone. "The finance department seems to be the only department that has involvement from the graduate level. All other organizations and activities are centered around undergraduates."

Career and Placement

Like so many students, Howard University's prospective MBAs place "exposure to *Fortune* 500 companies and executives of those companies" high at the top of their wish list and would like to see the career-resource center doing more to facilitate those meetings. In fact, complaints about job placement are fairly frequent. Still, among the top recruiters at Howard were Ariba, Citigroup, Dell, Eaton, IBM, Intel, K + MG, PWC, Tyco, and UTC. Other students do claim that the school's "great relationship with major employers results in very high job placement." And in 2004, the mean base salary for graduating MBAs was $72,786, not including bonuses and other compensation.

Students would also like to see a "stronger alumni network" and think that "administration and recruitment efforts" could be kicked up a notch. Students would also like to see more "alumni involvement and endowments" and think the school has a long way to go to make that happen.

Verna K. Supel, Associate Director
2600 Sixth Street Northwest, Suite 236, Washington, DC 20059 United States
Phone: 202-806-1725 • Fax: 202-986-4435 • E-mail: MBA_bschool@howard.edu
Website: www.bschool.howard.edu/Programs/MBA/index.html

Student Life and Environment

Though Howard benefits from its Washington, DC, location and lovely historic campus, most students say that, with their schoolwork, they have little time to enjoy the world around them. As one student puts it, "Life at my school does not extend very much beyond academics, and even if it did, "by the time I finish all my schoolwork, all I want to do is sleep. I have no extra energy left over for much of a social life," relates another MBA.

Despite the rigorous schedule, students agree that Howard "definitely exudes a sense of family." Many graduate students live on-campus and point out that "the university administration does a good job in ensuring the security of both the students and their property. A nonresident cannot get into the dorms unless signed in by a resident who is held responsible for any visitors in his or her name." Others, however, complain that "campus housing is just as expensive as off-campus housing, which leads many people to move farther away and commute. Howard really needs to provide more housing at lower costs."

Admissions

At Howard University's School of Business, the entering class of 2004 had a mean GPA of 3.1, and the mean GMAT score was 518; 64 percent of the incoming students were African American, and 34 percent were African and Caribbean. In addition, 48 percent of the incoming students were female, 34 percent were international, 97 percent of the incoming students had some post-graduate work, and the average amount of post-graduate work was three years. Student with an undergraduate degree in business equaled 39 percent, but 19 percent had majored in the humanities.

FINANCIAL FACTS

Annual tuition	$13,270
Fees	$805
Books and supplies	$2,000
Room & board (on/off-campus)	$10,000/$15,000
% of students receiving aid	90
% of first-year students receiving aid	88
% of students receiving loans	54
% of students receiving grants	76
Average award package	$22,623
Average grant	$14,887
Average student loan debt	$28,877

ADMISSIONS

Admissions Selectivity Rating	86
# of applications received	320
% applicants accepted	25
% acceptees attending	70
Average GMAT	518
Range of GMAT	480-550
Average GPA	3.1
TOEFL Required of International Students?	Yes
Minimum TOEFL (paper/computer)	550/213
Application fee	$65
International application fee	$65
Regular application deadline	4/1
Regular notification	5/1
Application Deadline/Notification	
Round 1:	11/15 / 1/1
Round 2:	2/1 / 3/1
Round 3:	4/1 / 5/1
Early decision program?	Yes
ED Deadline/Notification	
Fall (Full-time MBA) - 11/15 / 1/1	
Deferment Available?	Yes
Maximum length of deferment	2 semesters
Transfer students accepted?	Yes
Transfer application policy: Must meet Howard's MBA Program Admission Criteria; can only transfer a maximum of 6.0 credit hours from an AACSB-accredited Graduate Business Program.	
Non-fall admissions?	Yes
Need-blind admissions?	Yes

APPLICANTS ALSO LOOK AT

American U, Clark Atlanta U, George Mason U, Georgetown U, The George Washington U, U of Maryland—College Park.

EMPLOYMENT PROFILE

Career Rating	88	Grads employed by field	%: avg. salary
Placement rate (%)	89	Accounting	7: $57,250
# of companies recruiting on-campus	55	Finance	32: $81,000
% grads employed immediately	60	Human Resources	3: $65,000
Average starting salary	$72,786	Marketing	19: $66,333
		Operations	23: $73,857
		Consulting	9: $68,500
		General Management	7: $79,250

ILLINOIS INSTITUTE OF TECHNOLOGY
STUART GRADUATE SCHOOL OF BUSINESS

GENERAL INFORMATION
Type of school	private
Environment	metropolis
Academic calendar	quarters

SURVEY SAYS...
Students love Chicago, IL
Happy students
Smart classrooms

STUDENTS
Enrollment of parent institution	6,378
Enrollment of MBA program	167
% male/female	72/28
% part-time	37
% minorities	3
% international	83

ACADEMICS
Academic Experience Rating	**69**
Student/faculty ratio	15:1
Profs interesting rating	80
Profs accessible rating	79
% female faculty	8

Joint Degrees
MBA/JD: 4-6 years
MBA/MS: 2-3 years
JD/MS Environmental Management:
3-5 years

Prominent Alumni
Robert Growney, President and
COO, Motorola; John Calamos,
Pres., Chief Inv. Off., FnDrive,
Calamos Asset Mgmt.; Ajva
Taulananda, President, TelecomASIA
Corp.; Carl Spetzler, Chairman, Fndr,
Strategic Decisions Group; Les
Jezuit, President, Quixote Corp.

Academics

The Stuart Graduate School of Business at Chicago's Illinois Institute of Technology recognizes the diverse needs of its student body and works hard to accommodate them all. Those looking to expedite their MBAs, for example, can enroll in the school's full-time program; about one-third of the students here do just that. Those who want to pursue their degrees contemporaneously with their careers have a number of part-time options, including the lock-step "two-year part-time fast-track MBA" (offered at the school's Rice Campus in Wheaton) and the "customizable world-class MBA." Classes are scheduled during weekdays, evenings, and weekends for the convenience of all of Stuart's constituencies. All MBA programs consist of a minimum of 16 classes; specialization is available in all but the fast-track program and requires an additional four classes.

IIT is a world-class research institution, and, not surprisingly, Stuart MBAs benefit from the presence of the high-powered academics here. Three research centers—the Center for Financial Markets, the Chicago Geospatial Exchange, and the Center for Sustainable Enterprise—offer unique options to adventurous MBAs. There is even an optional specialization in sustainable enterprise that trains students "to identify, develop, communicate, and help implement practical and equitable business strategies that advance the ecological sustainability of the Chicago area while fostering current and future economic viability." Stuart was recently ranked among the world's leaders in incorporating environmental management.

Many here, however, prefer more traditional fare. Stuart MBAs laud the school's entrepreneurship program as well as offerings in finance and marketing. Some extol the advantages conferred by the presence of a healthcare concentration, and quite a few full-timers take advantage of dual-degree programs in law or public administration. Throughout the curriculum, students praise "the use of technology and real-life examples, and the application of business problems." Stuart professors "are always willing to help and provide out-of-the-classroom tutorials and further explanations," plus "their experience and techniques are outstanding." Similarly, administrators "are extremely helpful and go out of their way to get to know each student personally and help anyone." With IIT's small cohorts, "there is no crowding in the libraries, computer labs, etc. And, we get to learn a lot from group discussions." For many, though, "the school's greatest strength is its strategic location. It is because of its location that we are able to get internships and other opportunities to work." About the only weakness here, students tell us, is that "the school's image needs to be improved. The rankings need improvement and people need to know about IIT a lot more."

Career and Placement

The Office of Career Services at the Stuart MBA program provides students with one-on-one career counseling, workshops in interviewing and resume preparation, and research on companies and opportunities appropriate to each student's goals. A self-assessment, conducted as students enter the program, helps the office tailor its services to the individual needs of each MBA. The university at large conducts career fairs through its Career Development Center.

Employers who most frequently hire Stuart MBAs include Bank One, Northern Trust, Bank of America, ABN-Amro, Lucent Technologies, JP Morgan, Navistar, Johnson & Johnson, Capitol One, Vankampen, US EPA, Reuters, Cantor Fitzgerald, McLagan Partners, Motorola, Inc., and Akamal Trading. About half of all Stuart MBAs remain in the Midwest after graduation; most of the rest head to one of the two coasts.

AMANDA SCHONFELD, ASSOCIATE DIRECTOR OF ADMISSIONS
565 WEST ADAMS STREET, CHICAGO, IL 60661 UNITED STATES
PHONE: 312-906-6521 • FAX: 312-906-6549
E-MAIL: ADMISSIONS@STUART.IIT.EDU • WEBSITE: WWW.STUART.IIT.EDU

Student Life and Environment

IIT's main MBA programs are located "in a separate building in downtown Chicago. That building houses law and business school students only, so there isn't much activity there really, just serious-looking students walking to and fro. The main campus has more life, and there is a free shuttle to transport you between campuses. I appreciate the peace and quiet of our building, though. It's very easy to find a nook to study in without constant interference," remarks one student. MBAs participate in "lots of study groups. We also have socials every Wednesday, and students often go out into town in small groups." Despite these opportunities, many here feel that they "need more organizations, activities, a bigger career center, and more seminars and activities with others outside the school (i.e. businesses, other universities, etc.)."

The student body includes many who have considerable work experience, as well as "a lot of diversity in terms of nationality and occupation." One student observes, "The diverse population aids in creating a learning experience unlike any other. Students learn as much (if not more) outside the classroom than in the classroom, just by interacting with everyone around them." When they can find the time, students love to take advantage of "the world's biggest financial city," which also offers plenty in the way of culture, entertainment, fine dining, and nightlife. Again, it comes back to location. "Stuart is located near the Chicago loop in the midst of big-name business companies allowing for excellent networking and job opportunities. It's also very close to public transportation."

Admissions

The IIT Stuart Graduate School of Business requires applicants to submit GMAT scores, official undergraduate transcripts for all schools attended, two letters of recommendation from people "who can attest to your academic or professional qualifications," two required essays (personal statement and career goals) with the option to submit additional essays (describe a difficult challenge you have faced, describe your ideal company), and a resume. International students must also submit TOEFL scores no more than two years old. Undergraduate transcripts in languages other than English must be accompanied by an English translation.

FINANCIAL FACTS

Annual tuition	$19,000
Books and supplies	$890
Room & board (on/off-campus)	$6,631/$13,866
% of students receiving aid	32
% of first-year students receiving aid	39
% of students receiving loans	17
Average award package	$14,142
Average grant	$10,000
Average student loan debt	$39,577

ADMISSIONS

Admissions Selectivity Rating	**70**
# of applications received	284
% applicants accepted	78
% acceptees attending	23
Average GMAT	568
Range of GMAT	490-650
Average GPA	3.0
TOEFL Required of International Students?	Yes
Minimum TOEFL (paper/computer)	600/250
Application fee	$75
International application fee	$75
Regular application deadline	8/15
Regular notification	Rolling
Deferment Available?	Yes
Maximum length of deferment	1 year
Transfer students accepted?	Yes
Transfer application policy: With advisor approval may transfer up to 4 core courses and 2 elective courses.	
Non-fall admissions?	Yes
Need-blind admissions?	Yes

EMPLOYMENT PROFILE

Career Rating	78	Grads employed by field	%: avg. salary
Placement rate (%)	95	Finance	19: $65,000
# of companies recruiting on-campus	60	Marketing	19: $60,000
% grads employed immediately	12	MIS	33: $60,000
Average starting salary	$62,780	Operations	11: $55,000
		Other	18: $58,000

IMD INTERNATIONAL

GENERAL INFORMATION

Type of school	private
Academic calendar	Jan–Nov

SURVEY SAYS...

Friendly students
Good peer network
Smart classrooms
Solid preparation in:
Teamwork
Communication/interpersonal skills

STUDENTS

Enrollment of MBA program	87
% male/female	78/22
% international	98
Average age at entry	31
Average years work experience at entry	7

ACADEMICS

Academic Experience Rating	**96**
Student/faculty ratio	2:1
Profs interesting rating	79
Profs accessible rating	76
% female faculty	5

Prominent Alumni

Mr Nick Shreiber, CEO, Tetra Pak Group; Mr Kjeld Kristiansen, President, LEGO Group; Mr Juergen Fischer, President EMEA, Hilton International; Ms Carol Flaton, Managing Director, Credit Suisse First Boston; Mr Mark Cornell, CEO, Champagne Krug SA.

Academics

A highly selective one-year MBA program with a strong focus on leadership skills, the IMD MBA is an "intense" but "worthwhile" program in which "the development of leadership and team skills in a demanding environment gets everyone ready for the real world beyond the MBA program." Students appreciate the "real-world, real-learning" focus at IMD, where "classes feel more practical than academic, which is suitable for the average student, who is 31 years old with seven years of work experience."

IMD starts its program in January with a five-month sequence called Building Blocks. It is the toughest part of the program, students tell us, in which "14-hour days are the norm [and] just about everything is done in teams that work under high time pressure. This brings out all the colors of team members very quickly, so you learn much about people and teamwork, even those of us already experienced with it." MBAs warn that the "class and teams are expected to self-manage their priorities and meet all program goals." The school does a good job of selecting students who can handle these responsibilities; as one MBA explains, "We receive a ton of information in a short period of time, and it works because the students and faculty are both up for the challenge to be the best."

The second portion of the MBA program commences in June, when students engage in networking exercises, complete entrepreneurship and consulting projects, and prepare for a field-learning experience in the rebuilding nation of Bosnia-Herzegovina. After a summer break, students return to undertake long-term (two months) international consulting projects, then return to school for electives and a weeklong leadership program. With so many strands to coordinate, it's fortunate that "this school is run in the traditional Swiss way; in other words, like clockwork. Everything is very structured and it works, (although it can, at times, be perceived as inflexible)."

IMD professors "bring many real-life situations into the classroom and share with us the latest thinking." Students report approvingly that "there is no tenure for the faculty, which makes people listen to the feedback from the MBA class. This is taken very seriously." Students only wish the school were better known in the U.S.; one student remarks, "We are not very well known outside of Europe, and there needs to be work done to raise the awareness of IMD."

Career and Placement

Career Development Services at IMD are provided by the school's career services team, faculty members, a corporate development team that "works closely with IMD clients to solve their corporate development needs through IMD public and in-company programs," a "learning network" of 150 affiliated international companies, and alumni. Self-assessment, individual counseling, workshops, and on-campus recruiting are all available to IMD MBAs. Employers most likely to hire IMD graduates include J.M. Huber Corporation, Medtronic, Philip Morris, GE Capital, Shell International, Novartis International AG, McKinsey & Company, Indesit Company, and the Samsung Global Strategy Group.

Student Life and Environment

IMD's MBA program is intensive. One student warns, "The first six months are like bootcamp: classes eight hours a day, six days a week, and group work another six hours a day minimum. Everything is closed when we are free, so there is very little interaction with the city during the first semester of work." Fortunately, "that first semester is not just all about working hard. The bonds and friendships you develop here last a lifetime, and the alumni networks are a great testament to that." Also, "it gets a bit better the last five months, [when] life changes dramatically" and travel becomes an integral part of the program. Students first take a one-week Discovery Expedition to Bosnia-Herzegovina, then "become consultants to international companies for two months. This involves extensive traveling for most and exciting exposure."

Because of the nature of the program, students see precious little of hometown Lausanne, but when they can get out they find a small, lovely European city that provides ready access to Lac Léman and the mountains. Geneva is close by to provide big-city diversions and access to international banks and corporations, government agencies, and NGOs.

The "small group of 90 students [at IMD] enables MBAs to really get to know each and every one of the participants in the program very well. Also, the student environment promotes a real sense of shared purpose and makes people actively contribute not only to courses but also in extracurricular activities." Students are competitive, but in a healthy way— "competition is between teams, not individuals"—and appreciate that "you will never find arrogant know-alls in this program, despite the high level of experience students have. You will find brilliant people with an exceptional sense of curiosity to learn from your experiences. The strict selection convinces everyone that each student is here for a reason." Thirty-eight nationalities are represented within the student body, bringing a "wide diversity of student backgrounds from a cultural and nationality point of view as well as work experiences, which bring great value during discussions."

Admissions

"The admission process is probably the longest and toughest among all the top business schools," students at IMD tell us, and they may well be right. The first stage of the application process is pretty standard: applicants send in an application, personal essay, official transcripts, GMAT scores, three letters of recommendation, and a resume (showing a minimum three years' professional experience that includes "some international exposure"). The next stage, though, is unusually rigorous; it's a by-invitation-only interview day that includes not only a personal interview with an admissions committee member but also an impromptu presentation and a case-study discussion with a group of other interviewees. The school uses this multistage review process to cull from its applicant pool a group of 90 students who are not only bright, accomplished, and innovative but who also demonstrate both leadership potential and strong interpersonal skills.

FINANCIAL FACTS

Annual tuition	$45,600
Fees	$16,600
Room & board	$14,900
% of students receiving aid	32
% of students receiving loans	29
% of students receiving grants	13
Average award package	$36,720
Average grant	$24,845

ADMISSIONS

Admissions Selectivity Rating	90
# of applications received	400
% applicants accepted	28
% acceptees attending	79
Average GMAT	675
Range of GMAT	630-710
Application fee	$260
International application fee	$260
Regular application deadline	9/1
Regular notification	Rolling
Application Deadline	
Round 1:	4/1
Round 2:	6/1
Round 3:	8/1
Round 4:	9/1
Non-fall admissions?	Yes
Need-blind admissions?	Yes

APPLICANTS ALSO LOOK AT
Columbia University, Harvard University, IESE Business School, INSEAD, Stanford University, University of London, University of Pennsylvania.

EMPLOYMENT PROFILE

Career Rating	94	**Grads employed by field %: avg. salary**	
Placement rate (%)	100	Finance	12: $121,000
# of companies recruiting on-campus	45	Consulting	12: $113,000
% grads employed immediately	85	Other	76: $120,000
Average starting salary	$119,000		

INDIANA UNIVERSITY—BLOOMINGTON
KELLEY SCHOOL OF BUSINESS

GENERAL INFORMATION

Type of school	public
Environment	town
Academic calendar	semester

SURVEY SAYS...
Happy students
Smart classrooms
Solid preparation in:
Marketing
Teamwork
Quantitative skills

STUDENTS

Enrollment of parent institution	37,821
Enrollment of MBA program	767
% male/female	74/26
% out-of-state	44
% part-time	0
% minorities	14
% international	29
Average age at entry	28
Average years work experience at entry	5

ACADEMICS

Academic Experience Rating	**95**
Student/faculty ratio	23:1
Profs interesting rating	99
Profs accessible rating	99
% female faculty	26
% minority faculty	14

Joint Degrees
MBA/JD: 4 years
MBA/MA (area studies): 3 years
MBA/MA (telecommunications): 3 years

Prominent Alumni
John T. Chambers, MBA '76, President and CEO, Cisco Systems, Inc.; Phillip Francis, MBA '71, Chairman & CEO, PETSMART, Inc; Jeff M. Fettig, MBA '81, Chairman and CEO, Whirlpool Corporation; Hideo Ito, MBA '77, Chairman, CEO Toshiba; Bradley Alford, MBA '80, President & CEO, Nestle Brands Co.

Academics

Blue-chip offerings in marketing, finance, and general management distinguish the Kelley School of Business at Indiana University—Bloomington, a highly regarded MBA program boasting a stellar faculty, a first-class facility, and an innovative integrated core curriculum. Of the last, students tell us, "The integrated core curriculum is seamless. A mix of 8 professors come in and out of class during the 15-week core, and the timing is perfect. For example, soon after we learn about regressions in quant, we apply those skills in finance to forecast betas and in marketing research. Everything is like that." One MBA writes, "I can't imagine the amount of time that goes into organizing that many professors and their related subjects into one smooth 15-week class that covers the core business competencies." It's a heady sequence, students warn. One student who has been through the core explains, "Initially, it can be overwhelming, but the beauty of it is that it all comes together at the end."

Kelley professors are a distinguished lot. As one student observes, "The first thing that I noticed was that all of my first-year professors had written top-selling books for their academic field. Soon after attending classes I realized that these were the best professors I had ever had." Another student notes, "Most have served on multiple boards and advised companies like Microsoft, Owens, the Dallas Mavericks, and the Pentagon, [and better still,] they're our friends. They get to know us outside the classroom and really want to help us reach our personal goals. They care about us as people, too." Students love how "the faculty and administration take an active role outside the classroom, advising student clubs and organizations, participating in charitable events, and contributing to students' professional endeavors by taking the time to review resumes, conduct mock interviews, and actively networking with their professional contacts to help students succeed in their lives after graduation."

Kelley is housed in a "brand-new, state-of-the-art facility [that is] simply amazing. Every classroom has projectors, document cameras, an audio/video system, wireless and hard-wire connections, teleprompters, and video cameras to tape class for online replay." MBAs have access to "approximately 30 breakout rooms for team meetings, a trading room with many Bloomberg terminals, a student lounge with a big-screen TV, vending machines, and places to reheat meals. All students have lockers and access to changing rooms for interviews." Students especially appreciate that "the classrooms are available to the students 24 hours a day." No wonder MBAs agree that "the Kelley School of Business building is fabulous."

Students also love Kelley's academies, "an integral feature of the Kelley MBA program [that blends] advanced course work, sector-focused experiences, special projects, field trips, industry speakers, and direct involvement with the senior practitioners on their advisory boards." One student tells us, "The dedication by a professor to focus on a specific set of students that are actively interested in a specific area is unusual and extremely effective."

Career and Placement

IU's Graduate Career Services Office does a good job of bringing both regional and national companies to campus, but students feel that "not enough effort is made to bring new companies to campus. The office heavily focuses in brand management and corporate finance. If you are pursuing a career in other fields, you must conduct your own independent off-campus job search." Some students optimistically note, "Career services is improving by moving from focusing mostly on a stable of on-campus recruiters to

James Holmen, Director of Admissions and Financial Aid
1275 East Tenth Street, Suite 2010, Bloomington, IN 47405-1703 United States
Phone: 812-855-8006 • Fax: 812-855-9039
E-mail: mbaoffice@indiana.edu • Website: www.kelley.indiana.edu/mba

more progressive career development methods," such as e-recruiting. Students are also helped by the fact that "the faculty actively works with the students to find jobs/internships."

In 2003, companies most likely to hire Kelley MBAs (in descending order of number of hires) were Lilly, Bristol Meyers Squibb/Mead Johnson, Procter & Gamble, Brown and Williamson Tobacco, Kraft Foods, Whirlpool Corporation, Johnson & Johnson/Ethicon/DePuy, Banc of America Securities, and Intel. Nearly two-thirds of all graduates found work in the manufacturing sector; about one in five was employed in the financial services sector. The average hiring bonus for all 2003 MBAs was slightly over $12,000.

Student Life and Environment

Life in Bloomington, MBAs report, "is wonderful. It is a small, safe town and community where you have the opportunity to see peers and professors/administrators at local restaurants and grocery stores." Bloomington offers "a surprising number of great ethnic restaurants: Afghan, Chinese, Thai, Indian, Korean, and Japanese [as well as] many sports bars that offer such things as half-priced martini nights."

Kelley students benefit greatly from the greater Indiana University. One student reports, "The School of Music and School of Theatre and Arts give outstanding performances. Many Broadway and high-profile performers come to the school. There is no shortage of things to do." Many MBAs attend IU basketball games religiously, and we're told that athletic events and intramural sports in general are very popular. While students appreciate all that IU offers, they are also pleased that they "have [their] own separate building away from undergrads. This is important for a Big Ten school," where at least some of the undergrads are more interested in a good time than in getting work done.

Kelley's student body demonstrates "ethnic and professional diversity, which really enhances your view of both the business and cultural world. Students are very concerned with the well-being of their classmates and the program. This is illustrated by the deep commitment students make beyond their academic pursuits to lead professional clubs and extracurricular activities that enrich not only their fellow classmates but the community as well."

Admissions

IU evaluates potential MBAs on the basis of their previous academic record, GMAT scores, work experience (most successful applicants have at least two years of relevant work experience), record of leadership, two letters of reference, and essays. Applicants are expected to be familiar with algebra, statistics, and the functions of a spreadsheet. "For some majors, a working knowledge of calculus is important," the school notes. IU is a member of the Consortium for Graduate Study in Management, "which offers substantial support to underrepresented minority students."

FINANCIAL FACTS

Annual tuition (in-state/out-of-state)	$12,826/$25,652
Fees	$1,091
Books and supplies	$1,900
Room & board	$8,750
% of students receiving aid	95
% of first-year students receiving aid	95
% of students receiving loans	90
% of students receiving grants	45
Average award package	$25,500
Average grant	$13,800
Average student loan debt	$33,500

ADMISSIONS

Admissions Selectivity Rating	93
# of applications received	1,221
% applicants accepted	33
% acceptees attending	48
Average GMAT	644
Range of GMAT	610-680
Average GPA	3.3
TOEFL Required of International Students?	Yes
Minimum TOEFL (paper/computer)	600/250
Application fee	$75
International application fee	$75
Regular application deadline	3/1
Regular notification	4/30
Application Deadline	
Round 1:	11/15
Round 2:	1/15
Round 3:	3/1
Round 4:	4/15
Deferment Available?	Yes
Maximum length of deferment	1 year
Need-blind admissions?	Yes

APPLICANTS ALSO LOOK AT

The University of Texas at Austin, University of Michigan, University of North Carolina at Chapel Hill, Vanderbilt University, Washington University in St. Louis.

EMPLOYMENT PROFILE

Career Rating	86	Grads employed by field	%: avg. salary
Placement rate (%)	78	Finance	36: $77,627
% grads employed immediately	56	Human Resources	3: $69,877
Average starting salary	$76,866	Marketing	38: $75,230
		MIS	1: $30,000
		Operations	2: $80,750
		Consulting	14: $82,391
		General Management	5: $76,500

INDIANA UNIVERSITY KOKOMO
SCHOOL OF BUSINESS

GENERAL INFORMATION
Type of school	public
Environment	village
Academic calendar	semester

SURVEY SAYS...
Students love Kokomo, IN
Happy students

STUDENTS
Enrollment of parent institution	2,796
Enrollment of MBA program	92
% male/female	63/37
% part-time	98
% minorities	13
% international	7
Average years work experience at entry	8

ACADEMICS
Academic Experience Rating	71
Student/faculty ratio	15:1
Profs interesting rating	81
Profs accessible rating	99
% female faculty	40
% minority faculty	20

Academics

The almost-exclusively part-time, local student body of the MBA program at Indiana University Kokomo love the convenience, the affordability, and the prestige of their graduate business program. A public school that is one of only a dozen AACSB-accredited MBA programs in the state of Indiana, Kokomo represents the best option for business people seeking an affordable career advancement opportunity in and around this city of 50,000.

IU Kokomo's program is "attuned to the regional industry base" of north-central Indiana but is also flexible enough to "foster effective management of resources in diverse organizational units and settings." Students tell us that the program is well designed "to meet the overall aspirations of the employees of the local companies," which they appreciate. Because nearly all its students work full-time, the program offers flexible scheduling. All required classes are held during the week in the evening hours; electives are offered either during the day or in the evenings. Classes are alternately offered in 8- and 16-week formats, accommodating both those in a hurry to complete coursework and those who wish to learn at a (somewhat) less frantic pace. In either format, "MBA classes emphasize frequent presentations and assignments, so the pace of classes is hectic and challenging." Except for a capstone course, classes may be taken in any order, another accommodation to the convenience of IU's busy students. Part-time students generally complete the 30-credit program in four years.

Students love the IU faculty, which is comprised of many "active researchers published in peer-review journals," some of whom also happen to be "excellent instructors with teaching awards." One MBA writes, "We have an excellent group of professionals who constantly strive to improve themselves and their students by seeking new challenges." Most profs "are extremely knowledgeable and very eager to help students and offer advice or guidance, [and they] are understanding of working students, especially when work requires us to travel." MBAs also appreciate how Kokomo's smaller campus "offers an intimate learning environment."

There are also drawbacks to a small program on a small campus, MBAs note. Many feel that they "need more diverse business classes. The school needs to offer more electives and concentration areas." One MBA opines, "More major choices like finance and accounting and IT in the MBA would be welcome. Also, the school needs to offer electives on entrepreneurship. Right now it's only available as an independent study." Also on students' wish list remain "opportunities to work with local companies and industries and participate on projects with them."

NIRANJAN PATI, DEAN OF THE SCHOOL OF BUSINESS
PO BOX 9003, KOKOMO, IN 46904-9003 UNITED STATES
PHONE: 765-455-9465 • FAX: 765-455-9348 • E-MAIL: MBADIRECTOR@IUK.EDU
WEBSITE: WWW.IUK.EDU/ACADEMIC_PROGRAM/BUSINESS/INDEX.HTML

Career and Placement

IU Kokomo does not aggressively promote its career services for MBA students. Because most students in the program "are employed full-time in positions of responsibility," few actually require placement services or career counseling, and those who do generally rely on the assistance of their professors. MBAs may take advantage of the university's Office of Career Services, which maintains job boards, a Career Library and Resource Center, and online career-related databases. Those actively seeking work complain that "the quality of on-campus recruiting employers, the placement facilities, and the connections to alumni and businesses in the community all need improvement."

Kokomo MBAs are "a very diverse group with a wide range of industry backgrounds." Their employers include DaimlerChrysler, Delphi Delco, First National Bank, First Source Bank, Star Financial Bank, General Motors, Haynes International, Howard Community Hospital, St. Joseph Hospital, Subaru-Isuzu, and other smaller local businesses. Students regard their peers as "friendly, and more importantly, they submit assignments [on] time and are well prepared for tests. They value teamwork."

Student Life and Environment

"There's not much to do on campus" at IU Kokomo, which provides "a good learning environment [but] no social aspects." The situation doesn't bother most MBAs, who barely have time for their classes and study groups, much less extracurricular activity. The school offers childcare services, which students greatly appreciate.

Admissions

Admission to the MBA program at IU Kokomo requires a bachelor's degree from an accredited college or university (business major not required); a completed application to the program; a personal statement; and official transcripts for all post-secondary academic work. Most applicants must also submit GMAT scores; those already holding graduate degrees from accredited institutions, however, are exempted from this requirement. An admission index (AI) of at least 1000 under the formula [(undergraduate GPA × 200) + GMAT score] is required of all applicants who submit GMAT scores. Successful completion of undergraduate-level courses in calculus, statistics and composition, and a background in microcomputer applications are prerequisites to beginning the MBA program, however these courses can be completed after admission to the program. International applicants must meet the aforementioned requirements and must also submit TOEFL scores. The school reports that "admission decisions are based on an overall assessment of the applicant's academic capability, professional achievement, and potential. The MBA program admits students for fall, spring, and summer semesters."

FINANCIAL FACTS

Annual tuition (in-state/out-of-state)	$4,206/$9,619
Fees	$235
Books and supplies	$800

ADMISSIONS

Admissions Selectivity Rating	68
# of applications received	29
% applicants accepted	97
% acceptees attending	100
Average GMAT	519
Average GPA	3.3
TOEFL Required of International Students?	Yes
Minimum TOEFL (paper/computer)	550/213
Application fee	$40
International application fee	$60
Regular application deadline	8/1
Regular notification	Rolling
Deferment Available?	Yes
Non-fall admissions?	Yes
Need-blind admissions?	Yes

EMPLOYMENT PROFILE	
Career Rating	80
Placement rate (%)	100
% grads employed immediately	100

INDIANA UNIVERSITY OF PENNSYLVANIA
EBERLY COLLEGE OF BUSINESS AND INFORMATION TECHNOLOGY

GENERAL INFORMATION

Type of school	public
Academic calendar	semester

SURVEY SAYS...
Friendly students
Good social scene
Smart classrooms
Solid preparation in:
Teamwork

STUDENTS

Enrollment of parent institution	13,868
Enrollment of MBA program	136
% male/female	62/38
% out-of-state	79
% part-time	21
% minorities	6
% international	65
Average age at entry	26

ACADEMICS

Academic Experience Rating	**69**
Student/faculty ratio	12:1
Profs interesting rating	64
Profs accessible rating	74
% female faculty	24
% minority faculty	27

Academics

Eberly College of Business at Indiana University in Pennsylvania features a fully AACSB accredited general MBA that lays a strong foundation in basic management skills. There are several areas of concentration available, including accounting, finance, management, management information systems, and marketing. Though it is not a large program, students appreciate that "Eberly College of Business [is not only] nice and modern, [but] the class sizes are just right and the professors, for the most part, are great." Another student adds, "The smaller classrooms are my favorite part. You can get to know the professor on a name-to-name basis."

There are only eight required courses for the MBA: managerial economics, managerial accounting, marketing management, organizational analysis, management information systems, financial management, quantitative methods, and business policy. The other three courses are electives and can be selected from any of the following areas: marketing, management, business statistics, management information systems, international business, accounting, management, or finance. Students are also permitted to count an internship toward their elective credit. Graduate-level courses outside of the business-school curriculum are also permitted, and in the past, students have opted to study in such diverse areas as labor relations, economics, and public affairs. Some students argue that Eberly's "greatest strength is its marketing department."

According to students, one of the school's greatest strengths is its faculty. As one student puts it, "Our professors are very passionate about their careers, and this passion is displayed in the classroom. I think this passion is absorbed by us and transferred into maybe a slight interest in the subject." Students appreciate how "the university tries to facilitate a relationship between students with diverse backgrounds."

Career and Placement

Eberly students are mostly enthusiastic about the efforts of their career center. According to one, "There are actually conventions in school where marketing companies come and talk to the graduating students. Many companies choose IUP graduates. This is a great way to network and get a job interview." Others point out numerous networking opportunities. One student mentions, "IUP holds Business Day every year where you can network with current and past students. There are numerous job fairs we can attend. We have a business-networking event every year at homecoming and then again for the business days." In a small town with few distractions, most students learn the value of bonding with their classmates as well, forging future networking opportunities, and feel confident that these bonds and their education will serve them well once they graduate.

Student Life and Environment

Though the name is confusing, Eberly is not, in fact, a dual-state school. Nestled in the Allegheny foothills, Eberly is located in Indiana, Pennsylvania, a small town about an hour northeast of Pittsburgh. Because of the size of the town (about 30,000), the campus of Indiana University is ranked among the five safest campuses in the United States (for campuses housing 5,000 students or more). Despite the small size, Eberly promises that students don't lack entertainment. According to their website, "You'll be able to attend any of more than 200 cultural and entertainment events each year; choose from some 200 recognized clubs, activities, and organizations (including one of the country's finest marching bands); and enjoy the fun and the excitement of successful varsity, intramural, and club sports programs." And students, though somewhat grudgingly, admit that there are perks to living in a small town. One MBA lists the vast amount of things to do,

KRISH KRISHNAN, DRIVE
101 STRIGHT HALL, 210 SOUTH 10TH STREET, INDIANA, PA 15705-1081 UNITED STATES
PHONE: 724-357-2222 • FAX: 724-357-4862
E-MAIL: GRADUATE_ADMISSIONS@IUP.EDU • WEBSITE: WWW.EBERLY.IUP.EDU

"There are movies at the downtown theatre for $4, and that includes admission, popcorn, and drinks. We have lots of places to eat; a few nice places to shop. We are within an hour of Pittsburgh, and a group on campus sells tickets for bus tours to NYC and DC. There are plenty of other activities to keep yourself busy." In addition, "IUP also has a co-op recreational park that people can go to for free and throw a Frisbee® in the acres and acres of ground, hike on trails, go sledding or tubing on the hills, rent sleds, or sit in the lodge. It's fun here!" remarks another student. And in spite of the location of the school, "we get a wide range of students from many cities. Diversity is not bad, [even though] we could become a more diverse school."

Being somewhat isolated, students have to make their own fun. Sororities and fraternities abound, and, according to some students, Indiana University is "well-known as a party school." According to most MBAs, "The social aspect of this school is great. Once the kids get out into the real world and get a job, their social skills will be really good for working in groups." The $10 million Eberly College of Business complex has been around since 1996, but students aren't complaining and seem to agree with the school's claim that the building houses "teaching-intensive, state-of-the-art technology, [and is] designed with students in mind." The building "features a 500-seat auditorium, two 24 hour computer labs, large-screen television monitors, and a fiber-optics network throughout the complex." As one student puts it, "The student union is a few years new, and the exercise facility is superb. It's a great place to blow off steam before a huge test."

The only thing to watch out for, it seems, is the weather. One somewhat diplomatic student points out that "the weather in this part of the state isn't the best. We have a lot of cold, cloudy, and rainy/snowy days. An umbrella is your best friend."

Admissions

Eberly's student body is 65 percent international, and 22 different countries are represented; 35 percent of the students have some prior work experience in business, and 25 percent are still working full-time while pursuing their MBA. Though Eberly has no minimum GMAT or TOEFL scores, they do prefer that applicants score above 500 on the GMATs and above 550 on the TOEFL exam. TOEFL scores are required of those students for whom English is not their native language. There is no minimum GPA: Applicants who have a GPA lower than 2.6 who have still scored above 500 on the GMAT will be considered by Eberly's Board of Admissions.

FINANCIAL FACTS

Annual tuition (in-state/out-of-state)	$2,759/$4,415
Fees (in-state/out-of-state)	$471/$496
Books and supplies	$800
Room & board	$4,702
Average grant	$5,240

ADMISSIONS

Admissions Selectivity Rating	**70**
# of applications received	144
% applicants accepted	73
% acceptees attending	39
Average GMAT	530
Average GPA	3.2
TOEFL Required of International Students?	Yes
Minimum TOEFL (paper/computer)	523/193
Application fee	$30
International application fee	$30
Regular application deadline	7/30
Regular notification	Rolling
Deferment Available?	Yes
Maximum length of deferment	1 year
Transfer students accepted?	Yes
Transfer application policy: Written request for transfer required of transfer applicants. Maximum of six credits transfer.	
Non-fall admissions?	Yes
Need-blind admissions?	Yes

EMPLOYMENT PROFILE

Career Rating	**65**
Placement rate (%)	68
Average starting salary	$41,116

INDIANA UNIVERSITY SOUTHEAST
SCHOOL OF BUSINESS

GENERAL INFORMATION
Type of school   public
Environment   small town
Academic calendar   semester

SURVEY SAYS...
Friendly students
Cutting edge classes
Happy students
Smart classrooms

STUDENTS
Enrollment of parent
   institution   6,410
Enrollment of MBA program   222
% male/female   64/36
% part-time   98

ACADEMICS
Academic Experience Rating   **71**
Student/faculty ratio   11:1
Profs interesting rating   83
Profs accessible rating   74
Joint Degrees
MBA/MSF: 3-4 years (plus foundation course work)

Academics

The MBA program at Indiana University Southeast is designed to be a part-time program; students must petition the MBA Policies Committee to take more than the normal course load of six credit hours per semester and three credit hours per each of two summer sessions. That suits most students here fine. They're largely a full-time working, part-time degree-seeking group ready to put in at least two years' work to earn their degrees.

IUS's MBA curriculum is divided into four phases. The first "emphasizes the development and mastery of the fundamental tools of decision-making," while the second focuses on communication skills, ethical issues, and functioning within the business environment. The third phase consists of advanced courses as well as an integrative class in decision-making; the fourth includes of a strategic management class and two electives. Students with non-business undergraduate degrees typically must complete up to eight foundation classes before beginning their MBA work. Some students tell us that "coursework doesn't seem to 'build' and there are no academic concentrations, which is a major disappointment." Most, however, focus on the positives, which include "good technology integration into curriculum,…small classes that can be very attractive to someone wanting more one-on-one interaction with their professor, [and the] challenging workload."

A community service requirement of 20 hours "in projects such as volunteering for Big Brothers/Big Sisters, providing tax assistance to the elderly or disadvantaged, or participating in a United Way agency" is a unique aspect of this program. "Services such as directing or participating in a community cleanup sponsored by the Rotary Club or chairing a church clothing drive for the needy are acceptable projects because they serve a need of the greater community." Once students have completed their service, they must submit a one- to two-page summary of their role in the experience to the MBA director.

Career and Placement

The Office of Career Services and Placement at IUS serves all undergraduate and graduate students at the school. It offers all the standard services: "opportunities for career exploration, clarification, and professional growth, thereby increasing career awareness, instilling personal confidence, providing enhanced employment opportunities, and encouraging [students and alumni] to achieve their personal and professional career-related goals"—in other words, counseling, job fairs, workshops, and online job boards. MBAs here would like to see "better networking and job search opportunities. Because nearly every student already has a job, there is not much in the way of recruitment or networking through the school."

Student Life and Environment

IUS "is a commuter campus," so "students come to class and leave." Classes are also offered at an off-campus site in Jeffersonville, IN at the IU Southeast Graduate Center; this is very convenient for students who are coming in from nearby Louisville, KY. A typical student writes, "I tend to go straight to my class, which meets once a week, am engaged in it for three hours, then go right home. I have a family at home, and it is my preference to not participate in the limited school activities." Those limited activities include "various meetings to help students network with other students, teaching staff, and other business professionals." Some here feel "more clubs and/or activities geared specifically toward MBA students would be nice."

GENE BECKMAN, DIRECTOR OF GRADUATE BUSINESS PROGRAMS
HILLSIDE HALL 117, 4201 GRANT LINE ROAD, NEW ALBANY, IN 47150 UNITED STATES
PHONE: 812-941-2364 • FAX: 812-941-2581
E-MAIL: IUSMBA@IUS.EDU • WEBSITE: WWW.IUS.EDU/MBA/

The IUS curriculum requires some teamwork, and fortunately "there are many locations available to meet with groups or teams." The school also boasts "a brand-new, state-of-the-art library that is almost completed, which will offer many more meeting rooms and high-tech equipment available for student use."

MBAs at IUS are a "diverse group. Some students are younger and the MBA program represents an extension of their undergraduate degree, while others have been in the work force for at least ten years prior to returning to the classroom." One MBA writes, "The diversity (minority, work experience, life experience) in the student population is what contributes so much to the academic excellence at the school. Students learn from each other." The preponderance of professionals here means students are "generally more cooperative, as the vast majority hold full-time jobs and competition is really a non-factor."

Admissions

Completed applications to the IUS MBA program must include an official GMAT score report, official copies of all undergraduate transcripts, and a resume. The school uses the following formula to evaluate candidates: [(undergraduate GPA × 200) + GMAT score], IUS looks for candidates with a formula score of at least 1050, with GMAT scores of at least 470. Students with undergraduate degrees in business are likely to place out of some or all of the school's eight foundation courses in business; all other admitted students must complete these foundation courses before beginning work on the actual MBA.

FINANCIAL FACTS
Annual tuition (in-state/out-of-state)
$225/$506 per credit

ADMISSIONS
Admissions Selectivity Rating	**70**
# of applications received	111
% applicants accepted	86
% acceptees attending	83
Average GMAT	525
Average GPA	3.2
TOEFL Required of International Students?	Yes
Minimum TOEFL (paper/computer)	550/213
Application fee	$35
International application fee	$55
Regular application deadline	Rolling
Regular notification	Rolling
Deferment Available?	Yes
Maximum length of deferment	indefinite
Transfer students accepted?	Yes

Transfer application policy: Students may transfer a maximum of 6 graduate credit hours (with no grades below B) from another AACSB-accredited MBA program to count toward the 36 credit hour MBA curriculum at IU Southeast. Students may request that graduate credit not meeting this criterion be reviewed for transfer approval. The final disposition of all transfer course work is determined by the Graduate Business Policies Committee.

Non-fall admissions?	Yes
Need-blind admissions?	Yes

INSEAD

Academics

To some INSEAD MBAs, their school is "the only truly international MBA" available. With two campuses located halfway around the globe from each other—one in Singapore, the other outside Paris—and the option to study at both during the "very accelerated" one-year program offered here, INSEAD truly has an advantage over other pretenders to the title. A student body "from all over the world, with no nationality represented by more than 10 percent of the intake" in any give term, further bolsters INSEAD's claim to primacy. Students may apply to either INSEAD campus; more than half choose to take their core requirements in one location, and then travel to the other for at least one of the curriculum's three elective segments. Exchange with Wharton is also available during the fourth and fifth segments of the curriculum. The program begins with two, two-month core sequences covering basic business principles and functional skills. The final three two-month segments include courses in global and IT management issues plus 10 electives. Students tell us that the program "is really well designed. It is probably the most dynamic and innovative school in the world." While some say "it's too intensive, with not enough time to digest sufficiently before graduation," others tell us "it suits [our] ambitions perfectly. We learn fast and there is never a lull, but the workload is manageable and [we]'ve learned a great deal that I think [we] can apply directly." INSEAD professors are "a mix of stars and some clouds of dust. The stars can make a lecture blow your mind, while the clouds of dust can leave you stranded in a boring space. Fortunately there are more stars." Reports an exchange student from Wharton, "INSEAD professors are much better prepared for classes–evident in the depth of material covered in the allotted time–than professors I had at Wharton." Students identify consulting, finance, and entrepreneurship as the faculty's strongest areas. INSEAD's administration is a tale of two campuses—or, more accurately, a tale of two countries. Explains one student, "In France, the day-to-day administration is poor, as is the IT. The country is not efficient, nor particularly friendly." In Singapore, on the other hand, "The administration is extremely efficient. Everyone knows your name–the food servers, the office personnel, sometimes even the receptionist. The campus has about 100 students and it is very intimate." Basically, "the Singapore campus runs like a Ferrari while the Fontainebleau campus runs like a Peugeot."

Career and Placement

INSEAD maintains Career Management Services (CMS) offices on both its European and Asia campuses. The offices promote students to employers around the globe while providing MBAs with one-on-one counseling and coaching, job search strategies, and on-campus recruiting events. Students generally feel that "CMS could improve. The school has a great record of top companies coming on campus, and the alumni network is very efficient, but sometimes INSEAD CMS could be more proactive in connecting students with companies who are not on-campus recruiters." Students in Asia complain that "the CMS is not yet connected to all major Asian companies here in Singapore," but they also point out that "additional resources recently allotted to CMS here is a good start." An "alumni network so huge you find them wherever you go [is] extremely accessible and supportive." Employers most likely to hire INSEAD MBAs include McKinsey & Company; American Express; Booz Allen Hamilton; General Electric; the Boston Consulting Group; Johnson & Johnson; Bain & Company; A.T. Kearney; Honeywell; and Royal Dutch Shell.

Student Life and Environment

Dealing with "a one-year program that leaves everyone fully focused on school life" means "life at school is very hectic" for students on both INSEAD campuses. The school mandates some fun time by declaring about 15 "National Weeks" per school year, during which "each

FINANCIAL FACTS

Annual tuition	$57,000
Books and supplies	$30,000
% of first-year students receiving aid	50
Average grant	$15,000

ADMISSIONS

Admissions Selectivity Rating	60*
Average GMAT	704
Average GPA	4
TOEFL Required of International Students?	Yes
Minimum TOEFL (paper/computer)	620/260
Application fee	$250
Regular application deadline	3/23
Regular notification	6/24
Application Deadline/Notification	
Round 1:	3/23 / 6/24
Round 2:	5/18 / 9/9
Round 3:	6/29 / 10/14
Non-fall admissions?	Yes
Need-blind admissions?	Yes

country 'owns' a specific week and activities are organized around a country theme. Students are given specific names related to the country and the professors use them, which make interactions really funny. One of my friends was called Albert Einstein all through German Week." Students also participate in "twenty or so different clubs. The school is MBA-only, so clubs are all with MBAs. This puts pressure on MBAs to organize clubs in an already hectic year, but it also means that the networking with your classmates is that much better." When they can find time, students in Fontainebleau organize small group dinners or "blowout parties in elegant French country chateaus with professional DJs, dancers, and always an open bar." Students experience "good French cuisine, good wine, enjoyable social activities, a great forest, and the pleasure of living in a nice and typical French town." Coming along with the territory is a "bureaucracy and inefficiency impossible to experience elsewhere." Students organize "fewer activities in Singapore but more group travel and barbecues. Indeed, most participants tend to stay in the same two buildings near the campus," which is "fabulous" with its "modern facilities," and is contrasted by escapes to Bali or Thailand. INSEAD students "are definitely the greatest asset at the school," according to their peers. One explains, "You will not find a more international group at any school in the world. I've been to other schools that boast an 'international' student body. That usually means the occasional token Asian. Here you have equal numbers of Chinese, Indians, French, Brits, Americans, etc. To top it off, every one of those people is from the top of their respective classes before coming here." Even though, "students are graded on a forced z-curve, so there are people who will fail a class," INSEAD MBAs "are helpful to each other and most tend to do fine." One student says, "This year has been truly unforgettable—I would recommend the program to anyone who wants to meet talented, fantastic people from literally every corner of the world."

Admissions

INSEAD has two intake points, in September and January. Students may apply to begin the program at either time; application is online only. All applicants must provide a personal profile, resume, five personal essays, two recommendations attesting to leadership potential and management capacity, a photograph, an official GMAT score report, and official transcripts for all post-secondary academic work. In addition, all students must enter the program with proficiency in English and a second language. Non-native English speakers may submit results from the TOEFL, TOEIC, CPE, or IELTS. English speakers must provide certification of a second language. A third commercially useful language (sorry, no Latin!) is required to graduate. While language instruction is available through INSEAD, the intensity of the MBA program is such that the school recommends students get a start on their third language before the program begins. While most admitted students have "several years of meaningful professional experience and demonstrate clear management potential," work experience is not a hard-and-fast prerequisite to admission. The applicant's choice of campus is not taken into account in the admission decision; however, placement at one's campus of choice is not fully guaranteed.

EMPLOYMENT PROFILE

Career Rating	89	Grads employed by field:	
Placement rate (%)	70	Finance	21
# of companies recruiting on-campus	84	Marketing	12
% grads employed immediately	70	Operations	4
Average starting salary	$106,043	Strategic Planning	10
		Consulting	38
		General Management	10
		Other	5

IONA COLLEGE
HAGAN SCHOOL OF BUSINESS

GENERAL INFORMATION
Type of school	private
Affiliation	Roman Catholic
Environment	town
Academic calendar	trimester

SURVEY SAYS...
Happy students
Smart classrooms
Solid preparation in:
Teamwork
Communication/interpersonal skills
Presentation skills
Doing business in a global economy

STUDENTS
Enrollment of parent institution	4,329
Enrollment of MBA program	372
% male/female	67/33
% out-of-state	22
% part-time	89
% minorities	9
% international	5
Average age at entry	30
Average years work experience at entry	5

ACADEMICS
Academic Experience Rating	78
Student/faculty ratio	5:1
Profs interesting rating	86
Profs accessible rating	71
% female faculty	22

Prominent Alumni
Alfred F. Kelly, Jr, President Consumer Card Services, American Express; Catherine R. Kinney, Group Executive VP, New York Stock Exchange; Don Mc Lean, Singer/Song Writer; Alberto Vilar, President/Founder, Amerindo Investment Advisors; Robert V. LaPenta, President and CFO, L3 Communications.

Academics

Flexibility and convenience are among the top selling points of the Hagan School of Business MBA at Iona College. Hagan's student body is drawn largely from the ranks of full-time professionals seeking a career boost. The school delivers what students seek through concentrated classes (usually meeting one evening per week, for three hours), a trimester schedule that allows students to receive their degrees more quickly, and a limited number of distance-learning courses per trimester (usually six or seven). Students enjoy the accelerated academic calendar saying, "It keeps us involved in school all year long. Since many of the students are working, it makes sense not to have a long winter break. We can continue to progress in the MBA program and not waste six or eight weeks around the holidays."

For its few full-timers, Hagan also offers a nice campus in a location convenient to job seekers. AT&T, Bell Atlantic, IBM, Kraft Foods, Inc., Lederle Laboratories, MasterCard, PepsiCo, and a number of large banks, brokerage houses and insurance firms all make their homes in surrounding Westchester and Rockland counties. Students approvingly report, "The school has a good relationship with several large companies. They just moved their Pearl River campus into a professional building, which I feel helps make it more attractive to professional students." One student points out that "Wyeth Pharmaceutical has a relationship with Hagan School of Business in which professors teach MBA level courses on-site. This creates a great atmosphere, as all of the students taking classes on-site at Wyeth are Wyeth employees, with common interests."

Hagan takes a practical approach to business education; classes "deal with many real-world situations, and through my course work I feel better prepared to handle them. Many of the situations covered in class have been discussed through the eyes of my fellow classmates, and it is great to get their perspectives since they have lived through these situations," one student says. Professors also bring a lot of professional experience to the table as they "are not professors from the 'ivory tower' but professional, successful business people who are sharing their knowledge. It is wonderful to be able to apply theoretical concepts to real-life examples with their help." One student points out many positive aspects, saying, "[Hagan] puts great emphasis on presentation and teamwork skills, and I believe by repetition, one can become better in these crucial areas of everyday business. I know it has definitely helped me in my managerial position."

Hagan offers concentrations in management, human-resource management, financial management, marketing, and information and decision-technology management.

Career and Placement

The Career Services Office at Iona College serves MBAs with counseling services, job listings, Internet-based job databases and resume books, resume and cover letter workshops and critiques, mock interviews, and tests to assess students' interests and strengths. Forty-two businesses and organizations attended Iona's 2003 Fall Career and Internships Expo; they included the American Red Cross, Country Bank, Fleet Boston, New York Life, Northwestern Mutual, and PepsiCo. Over the course of the year, approximately 100 recruiters visit the Iona campus. Career Services are important to only some of Iona's MBAs; many are part-time students with full-time employers that pay part or all of their tuition.

Tara Feller, Director of MBA Admissions
715 North Avenue New Rochelle, NY 10801 United States
Phone: 914-633-2288 • Fax: 914-637-7720
E-mail: hagan@iona.edu • Website: www.iona.edu/hagan

Student Life and Environment

"The majority of students at Hagan work full-time jobs along with taking classes," students tell us, meaning that "between work and classes, there isn't much time for [much] else." Many take classes at one of Iona's satellite campuses, where they see even less of one other than do MBAs on the main campus. One student observes, "[They] show up for class and go home. There isn't much of a student life involved. That is not a criticism of the school, it's just the way it is for a part-time graduate program at a campus that is removed from the college scene of their main campus in New Rochelle."

Hagan's student body features "a good mix of the ages of students. The experience levels of students greatly differ, but that makes the classes more interesting." Some students feel that Iona needs to be a bit more selective in its admissions. One such MBA writes, "I think most students are there for the right reasons and work hard, but I believe by interviewing prospects, they could weed out many of the unmotivated students. Some seem to come back immediately after graduating from undergraduate school only because they have nothing better to do, and I think an interview would help to eliminate these students."

There are a few full-timers on Iona's New Rochelle campus. They tell us that they enjoy "a very friendly atmosphere. There are always students on or around campus. There are activities and social events coordinated by the school to help people meet each other." They also appreciate that "school facilities and resources are easily accessible to students. There is a welcoming and warm feeling on campus." However, "the school doesn't offer many clubs at the graduate level. They should also host or refer people to more networking events." One MBA agrees, "There could be more networking and social events for students in the MBA program. I would like to be able to meet more students outside of class in a social setting, but it is difficult with students who do not live on or close to campus. More networking events for MBA students would bring classmates together who have never met one another."

Admissions

Applications to Hagan must include official transcripts from each undergraduate and graduate institution attended, a GMAT score report, two letters of recommendation, a personal statement, and a resume. International students must also provide TOEFL scores, WES, and a cash-support affidavit. Interviews are optional; work experience is not required, although "many students do have considerable work experience." Applications are processed and admissions decisions made on a rolling basis. Applications remain valid for one year.

FINANCIAL FACTS

Annual tuition	$15,660
Fees	$195
% of students receiving aid	60
% of first-year students receiving aid	78
% of students receiving loans	36
% of students receiving grants	48
Average award package	$10,525
Average grant	$2,941
Average student loan debt	$20,051

ADMISSIONS

Admissions Selectivity Rating	73
# of applications received	129
% applicants accepted	73
% acceptees attending	88
Average GMAT	514
Range of GMAT	450-550
Average GPA	3.2
TOEFL Required of International Students?	Yes
Minimum TOEFL (paper/computer)	550/213
Application fee	$50
International application fee	$50
Regular application deadline	Rolling
Regular notification	Rolling
Deferment Available?	Yes
Maximum length of deferment	1 year
Transfer students accepted?	Yes
Transfer application policy: Max of 6 upper-level credits accepted. 30 credit minimum required to earn a degree at Iona.	
Non-fall admissions?	Yes
Need-blind admissions?	Yes

APPLICANTS ALSO LOOK AT

Alliant International University, Fordham University, Pace University.

EMPLOYMENT PROFILE

Career Rating	**60***
# of companies recruiting on-campus	145

JACKSONVILLE STATE UNIVERSITY
COLLEGE OF COMMERCE AND BUSINESS ADMINISTRATION

GENERAL INFORMATION

Type of school	public
Environment	village

SURVEY SAYS...
Friendly students
Happy students
Smart classrooms
Solid preparation in:
Finance
General management
Teamwork
Communication/interpersonal skills

STUDENTS

Enrollment of parent institution	8,900
Enrollment of MBA program	100
% male/female	50/50
% out-of-state	10
% part-time	70
% minorities	10
% international	75
Average age at entry	37
Average years work experience at entry	5

ACADEMICS

Academic Experience Rating	**61**
Student/faculty ratio	15:1
Profs interesting rating	64
Profs accessible rating	64
% female faculty	33

Academics

The College of Commerce and Business Administration at Jacksonville State University offers a small, predominantly part-time AACSB-accredited MBA program that students praise for its convenience, affordability, and "personalized attention." The school serves the city of Jacksonville and the eastern Alabama region.

JSU offers both full-time and part-time MBA tracks. JSU's undergraduate program generally provides the majority of full-time students, as most continue directly from their bachelor's degree on to earn their master's. The part-time program is the almost-exclusive domain of area residents "who are working full-time and trying to get ahead in their careers by getting an MBA."

A sequence of foundation courses makes the JSU MBA available to everyone, even students with no previous academic experience in business. The eight-course foundation track covers business organization and administration, statistics; principles of financial accounting; macroeconomics; business; finance; business law and ethics; operations and technology; and marketing. Students with undergraduate coursework in these areas may place out of the courses and begin immediately on degree-related coursework, which consists of 10 courses: seven required courses, one organization class chosen from a group of three, one international business class chosen from a group of three, and an elective. Students may choose to pursue a concentration in accounting, which requires an additional six hours of coursework.

All candidates for a master's degree at JSU must pass comprehensive oral examinations at the end of their program, which some here find stressful and unnecessary. "I do not agree with the oral exams policy. If instructors believe that a student knows the material and that student makes the grade on exams and projects, that should be sufficient," writes one student. Otherwise, students generally express satisfaction with the program, praising the school's administration ("It has a good vision and is focused") and the "well-read, detail-oriented, and dedicated" professors who "have good experience in the fields in which they teach." While most here applaud the school's efforts to provide distance-education options, they also anxiously await the day when the school works the bugs out of the system. One MBA warns, "The school often puts too many students in the distance-learning classes. Also, we lose 20 minutes on average per class due to technical difficulties."

Career and Placement

JSU's Office of Career Placement Services is oriented primarily toward serving the school's undergraduate programs, although it also offers services to graduate students and alumni. The office coordinates career fairs, referrals, on-campus job interviews, and job listings. It also maintains a reference room, conducts mock interviews, and offers workshops in resume writing. Students can sign up for an e-mail service that notifies them whenever new jobs are posted with the school. Individual career counseling is offered through the Office of Counseling and Career Services.

Drive Jean Pugliese, Associate Dean
700 Pelham Road N Jacksonville, AL 36265 United States
Phone: 256-782-5329 • Fax: 256-782-5321
E-mail: pugliese@jsucc.jsu.edu • Website: www.jsu.edu

Student Life and Environment

Students describe their peers as "academically curious, energized, competitive, and sociable." While "there are a lot of activities from student organizations Monday to Thursday" available to MBAs on the FSU campus, most students are "way too busy balancing personal lives (jobs, spouses, kids, volunteer work, church) and school to worry about clubs!" Once Friday rolls around, "most residents go home, and the campus is a ghost town on weekends." The school could "improve school spirit and attendance at schools activities" but so many students only have time to be on campus for class, that the point might be moot.

JSU is the largest employer in Jacksonville, an eastern Alabama town of approximately 8,000. Other major employers in the area include the Anniston Army Depot, the Regional Medical Center, and a number of manufacturing and distribution concerns. Jacksonville is less than 100 miles from Atlanta and Birmingham.

Admissions

Applicants to the JSU MBA program must meet one of the following minimum requirements to be considered for unconditional admission: a score of at least 950 under the formula [(undergraduate GPA × 200) + GMAT score]; or, a score of at least 1000 under the formula [(undergraduate GPA for final 64 hours of coursework taken toward undergraduate degree × 200) + GMAT score]. Scores of 850 (entire undergraduate GPA) or 900 (final 64 hours) are sufficient to qualify students for conditional admission. Students admitted conditionally must earn a GPA of at least 3.0 for their first 12 hours of graduate coursework and must complete the coursework within a time frame established by the Graduate Committee. All applicants must first seek admission to the College of Graduate Studies; only after gaining admission to the college are they admitted to a particular program. Applicants must then provide the college of Graduate Studies with official copies of all post-secondary academic transcripts and three Graduate Reference forms completed by people who can assess the applicant's potential for success in the MBA program. Applicants whose native language is not English must provide an official TOEFL score report.

FINANCIAL FACTS

Annual tuition (in-state/out-of-state)	$2,940/$5,880
Books and supplies	$1,500
Average grant	$1,000

ADMISSIONS

Admissions Selectivity Rating	**62**
# of applications received	40
% applicants accepted	80
% acceptees attending	78
Average GMAT	470
Range of GMAT	250-650
Average GPA	2.7
TOEFL Required of International Students?	Yes
Minimum TOEFL (paper/computer)	500/173
Application fee	$20
International application fee	$20
Regular application deadline	6/30
Regular notification	7/31
Transfer students accepted?	Yes
Transfer application policy: 6 hours of approved courses with grade of A or B.	
Non-fall admissions?	Yes
Need-blind admissions?	Yes

Career Rating	**61***
Placement rate (%)	10

JOHN CARROLL UNIVERSITY
THE BOLER SCHOOL OF BUSINESS

GENERAL INFORMATION
Type of school	private
Affiliation	Roman Catholic-Jesuit
Environment	village
Academic calendar	semesters

SURVEY SAYS...
Students love University Heights, OH
Friendly students
Helpful alumni
Happy students
Smart classrooms
Solid preparation in:
Communication/interpersonal skills

STUDENTS
Enrollment of parent institution	4,101
Enrollment of MBA program	207
% male/female	55/45
% part-time	93
% minorities	2
Average age at entry	27
Average years work experience at entry	3

ACADEMICS
Academic Experience Rating	**70**
Student/faculty ratio	16:1
Profs interesting rating	78
Profs accessible rating	82
% female faculty	25
% minority faculty	1

Joint Degrees
Communications Management: 2-3 years

Academics

Accountancy is the strongest area at the Boler School of Business at John Carroll University, a Jesuit institution on the outskirts of Cleveland. One JCU student reports, "The people in this program are predominantly accounting students. The emphasis in many of the classes, even non-accounting classes, has a strong focus on accounting." Through the Accountancy Department, students can receive either an MBA with a concentration in accountancy or an MSAcc. Beyond this specialization, Boler also offers MBA concentrations in finance, marketing, human resource management, and international business.

Designed to meet the needs of part-time students, the Boler MBA offers a great degree of "flexibility of scheduling." Students may proceed through the program at their own pace, taking as few as one or as many as five courses per term (the latter option allows students with undergraduate business degrees to graduate in one year). Boler's membership in the 23-school Jesuit MBA network also affords students who relocate mid-program the opportunity to transfer all their credits to a Jesuit MBA program in or near their new hometown.

The Boler MBA is divided into four blocks. The first block consists of eight foundation courses, some or all of which can be waived on the basis of undergraduate academic achievement. Required courses covering fundamental business functions constitute the second block. The third block consists of three electives, one of which must be among a group of international business classes. The final block consists of two integrative courses covering business ethics and corporate strategic management. The school's Jesuit foundations ensure that ethics are stressed throughout the curriculum.

MBAs at Boler report that "the greatest strength of JCU is its culture. The students, faculty, staff, and administrators are all friendly and helpful. The focus is always on developing the whole person though academics and ethics discussions." Instructor access is the subject of much praise. One student writes, "I didn't think I would be able to meet and speak with my professors with the same frequency as my undergraduate experiences, but every time I've requested to meet or speak with one of my professors, it has always been a smooth process." Professors "are able to bring experience as well as theory to their classes [and] are very well known in their fields—in many cases considered experts." Some MBAs here feel that the school "needs to develop more concentrations and focus the program toward those concentrations" in order "to become more competitive with leading business schools." Campus technology also needs an upgrade, students report.

Career and Placement

Boler MBAs seeking career guidance and placement services may use the Center for Career Services, which attends to the needs of the entire university population. Services provided include online job and resume posting, counseling, and interview scheduling. The office also functions as a clearinghouse for alumni network contacts and employer inquiries. An annual business-related job fair, open to both graduates and undergraduates in the business school, draws more than 90 recruiters to the campus.

GAYLE BRUNO-GANNON, ASSISTANT TO THE DEAN ADMISSIONS AND RECRUITING
20700 NORTH PARK BOULEVARD, UNIVERSITY HEIGHTS, OH 44118-4581 UNITED STATES
PHONE: 216-397-1970 • FAX: 216-397-1728
E-MAIL: GGANNON@JCU.EDU • WEBSITE: HTTP://BSOB.JCU.EDU/GRADBUSINESS

Student Life and Environment

Because "about half the MBA students have jobs and are extremely busy; a good portion are married; [and] most students here attend part-time and only come to campus for class once a week, it is more difficult to bond here than it would be in a full-time program, and most people are mainly focused on their lives/jobs outside of school." School thus functions as "a complement to that life." Some wish the school offered "more graduate student activities, clubs, and more opportunities for career planning, mentoring, and meeting with successful alumni." They see the formation of a Graduate Student Association, which "is working on developing a graduate student life and addressing graduate student issues," as a step in the right direction.

The "hard-working, busy professionals" who populate most of the part-time ranks stand in stark contrast to the majority of full-timers, who "have just completed their undergraduate degrees and have no relevant real-world work experience." Some feel that "the school caters to these students a great deal; the classes are more like advanced undergraduate classes rather than graduate classes for working professionals." Others approve of both the pacing and the classroom mix, telling us that their peers "come from a variety of academic and work backgrounds. Many are entry-level and mid-level management. The program is somewhat competitive, but not a cutthroat environment."

Admissions

Applicants to John Carroll University's MBA program must provide the school's admissions department with a completed graduate school application form, an official GMAT score report, official transcripts for all post-secondary academic work, at least one letter of recommendation, a resume, and a statement of purpose essay titled, "Graduate business education: Enabling me to achieve my personal goals and become a leader." International students must also provide TOEFL scores, appropriate financial documentation, and, when applicable, an English translation of all documents submitted in a language other than English. Academic record and GMAT scores are the most important factors in the admissions decision; letters of recommendation, the essay, and work experience are also considered important. According to the school's website, previous work experience "is not required, but having professional experience provides a frame of reference for classroom discussion, and is therefore encouraged."

FINANCIAL FACTS

Annual tuition	$14,274
Books and supplies	$800
% of students receiving aid	46
% of first-year students receiving aid	25
% of students receiving loans	61
% of students receiving grants	21
Average award package	$5,300
Average grant	$5,300

ADMISSIONS

Admissions Selectivity Rating	71
# of applications received	74
% applicants accepted	88
% acceptees attending	49
Average GMAT	540
Range of GMAT	450-640
Average GPA	3.2
TOEFL Required of International Students?	Yes
Minimum TOEFL (paper/computer)	550/213
Application fee	$25
International application fee	$35
Regular application deadline	Rolling
Regular notification	Rolling
Deferment Available?	Yes
Maximum length of deferment	1 year
Transfer students accepted?	Yes
Transfer application policy: Applicants from members of the network of MBA Programs at Jesuit Universities and Colleges, will have all credits transferred. Otherwise, applicantions are reviewed on a case-by-case basis.	
Non-fall admissions?	Yes
Need-blind admissions?	Yes

APPLICANTS ALSO LOOK AT

Case Western Reserve University, Cleveland State University.

EMPLOYMENT PROFILE	
Career Rating	**82**
Placement rate (%)	80
# of companies recruiting on-campus	347

KENNESAW STATE UNIVERSITY
MICHAEL J. COLES COLLEGE OF BUSINESS

GENERAL INFORMATION

Type of school	public
Environment	city
Academic calendar	semester

SURVEY SAYS...

Students love Kennesaw, GA
Helpful alumni
Happy students
Smart classrooms
Solid preparation in:
Teamwork
Communication/interpersonal skills

STUDENTS

Enrollment of parent institution	17,961
Enrollment of MBA program	471
% male/female	60/40
% out-of-state	22
% part-time	72
% minorities	32
% international	22
Average age at entry	31
Average years work experience at entry	9

ACADEMICS

Academic Experience Rating	**73**
Student/faculty ratio	13:1
Profs interesting rating	81
Profs accessible rating	68
% female faculty	35
% minority faculty	12

Academics

Prospective MBAs at the Michael J. Coles College of Business at Kennesaw State University may choose from three program options: the Career Growth MBA, a traditional on-campus MBA program scheduled for the convenience of its predominantly part-time student body; a WebMBA, which allows more experienced students to complete the degree in 18 months with only a single visit to campus (the rest of the program can be completed from home); and an MBA for Experienced Professionals, an 18-month Executive MBA program in which classes meet one weekend per month. Coles also offers a Master of Accounting (MAcc) degree.

Students in the Career Growth MBA program, the most popular of the options, appreciate the "flexibility it gives students who work full-time" and the "excellent curriculum that lets you choose from courses that are actually applicable to your career." Professors here "are knowledgeable and supportive [and] have extensive experience in their fields. They usually have more than one graduate degree and are very involved in the business community in Atlanta." One MBA tells us, "Never have I experienced such a committed group of individuals." Some students complain that "there are many excellent classes in the catalog. However, most are rarely offered." But most focus on positive aspects of the program. One student sums up, "The challenge of this program has shown me what I'm truly made of! I've done things that I never would have dreamed of doing. As a result, I have a tremendous amount of confidence in my personal ability. This experience has and will open hundreds of doors, not just in the workplace, but most importantly, in my mind."

Career and Placement

KSU's Career Services Center coordinates a number of events and provides a range of services to the school's graduate business students. Events and services include career fairs, internship fairs, a statewide job fair, and ongoing on-campus interviews, as well as OwlTRAK, an online job- and resume-posting database. The CSC regularly updates its website to keep students informed of upcoming events.

In addition, KSU has contracted Advanced Career Development, Inc. (ACDI) to provide students with assessments and counseling services, access to exclusive databases, and resume, cover letter, and career-planning counseling. (Call it outsourcing if you like.) Students give the service good marks, and especially like the fact that the services are provided at no additional cost to them.

Student Life and Environment

With over 18,000 students, Kennesaw State is the third-largest school in the University System of Georgia. Located just 20 miles northwest of downtown Atlanta, KSU is conveniently located to benefit from the wealth of the big city. The school draws faculty and guest lecturers from the metropolitan area and full-time students find it easier to secure meaningful internships because of the city's many opportunities.

The Coles school is located in the Burruss Building, a modern business facility complete with tiered and traditional classrooms, seminar rooms, meeting areas, and networked computer labs. All classrooms are equipped to accommodate modern presentation technology. Burruss is also the site of the Tetley Lectures, an endowed series that regularly brings business leaders to campus to lecture and interact with Coles students.

STEVEN KING, ASSISTANT DIRECTOR
1000 CHASTAIN ROAD, #0132, KENNESAW, GA 30144 UNITED STATES
PHONE: 770-420-4377 • FAX: 770-420-4435
E-MAIL: KSUGRAD@KENNESAW.EDU • WEBSITE: HTTP://COLES.KENNESAW.EDU/GBO

Most Coles MBAs are part-time students with jobs and families, and accordingly, most "show up, do [their] work, discuss some issues with classmates, and head home." To accommodate these students, "classes are mainly at night. The people here are friendly; it is not a competitive program at all since people are usually already employed." A "significant number of foreign students adds to [the] diverse mix," though students detect "a couple of distinct groups of students. There is one group of people who have plenty of work experience and are building upon this. The other group has little work experience and doesn't add as much to group activities. The first group seems to be taking harder classes and harder professors to learn more from this experience. The second group targets less challenging professors just to get out." Full-time students report "a diverse environment that is set up to promote interaction between students. There are many activities designed to bring the school together. The athletics give the school the national recognition that they deserve."

Admissions

Applicants to all graduate business programs at Kennesaw State must submit the following to the Office of Graduate Admissions: a completed application (hard copy or on line); one official transcript for each school attended, including the school that awarded the baccalaureate (a minimum undergraduate GPA of 2.8 is required for admission); and an official report of GMAT score (a minimum score of 500 is required). In addition, international applicants must also provide TOEFL scores (if their native language is not English); a sponsor letter; a bank letter certifying sufficient support funds; a copy of a valid passport; an evaluation of all transcripts for academic work completed outside the U.S.; and proof of immigrant status. The Graduate Business Office reserves the right to request, in addition, a resume, statement of objectives, and two letters of recommendation from all candidates. At least two years of full-time professional business experience is strongly preferred for candidates to all programs.

FINANCIAL FACTS

Annual tuition (in-state/out-of-state)	$1,393/$5,573
Fees	$676
Books and supplies	$1,050

ADMISSIONS

Admissions Selectivity Rating	74
# of applications received	193
% applicants accepted	65
% acceptees attending	74
Average GMAT	510
Range of GMAT	480-550
Average GPA	3.2
TOEFL Required of International Students?	Yes
Minimum TOEFL (paper/computer)	550/213
Application fee	$30
International application fee	$30
Regular application deadline	Rolling
Regular notification	Rolling
Deferment Available?	Yes
Maximum length of deferment	1 year
Transfer students accepted?	Yes
Transfer application policy: Transfer credit from AACSB international accredited universities is possible. Limits and restrictions apply.	
Non-fall admissions?	Yes
Need-blind admissions?	Yes

APPLICANTS ALSO LOOK AT

Georgia State University.

EMPLOYMENT PROFILE

Career Rating	61
# of companies recruiting on-campus	68
% grads employed immediately	97

KENT STATE UNIVERSITY
COLLEGE OF BUSINESS ADMINISTRATION & GRADUATE SCHOOL OF MANAGEMENT

Academics

The Graduate School of Management at Kent State University offers both a full-time MBA and a part-time Professional MBA, with the ratio of part-time students to full-time students being roughly two to one. The school also offers three dual-degree options (in conjunction with the Nursing Program, the Library Science Program), as well as opportunities to study abroad. Finally, the Kent State GSM offers an Executive MBA to candidates with the prerequisite amount of work experience and the support of their employers.

A Kent State MBA requires between 39 and 54 hours of coursework. It can be completed by a full-time student in 15 months, though many students take two years to finish. The number of required credits depends upon the student's undergraduate work in business. A core course can be waived, for example, for students who have previously taken two undergraduate courses or one graduate course in the core subject and earned a grade of B or better. The entire core curriculum consists of 30 credit hours of classwork; the remainder of the program is made up of executive modules, integrative management courses, and electives. The school offers concentrations in accounting, finance, human resource management, information systems, international business, and marketing.

Students here tell us that the majority of professors "are very passionate about their fields." Most have deep real-world experience. They are "also lawyers and business people and everything else, so they know what it's like to have a heavy workload, and they demand excellence without letting the class get so stuffy that you don't want to be there." Some excel at "incorporating new computer-based learning tools and keeping up with technology," although they can be stymied in their efforts by the resources of the university. "Many of the classrooms are not equipped with multimedia connections, and some professors still rely on overheads instead of PowerPoint presentations," one student warns. Students here do appreciate that the "tutoring possibilities are fabulous."

Career and Placement

The Kent State Career Services Center provides "comprehensive employment search services" for the GSM graduate students, as well as workshops in interviewing, resume writing, and job search strategies. The CSC posts employment opportunities and coordinates on-campus interviews, and the office reports that approximately 500 employers visit the campus to hire for business and government positions each year.

Employers most likely to hire Kent State MBAs include Ernst and Young, Progressive Insurance, Key Bank, Little Tikes, Jo-Ann Stores Inc., Summa Health System, FedEx Systems, The Timken Company, and Diebold Inc.

LOUISE DITCHEY, DIRECTOR, MASTER'S PROGRAMS
PO BOX 5190 KENT, OH 44242-0001 UNITED STATES
PHONE: 330-672-2282 • FAX: 330-672-7303
E-MAIL: GRADBUS@BSA3.KENT.EDU • WEBSITE: WWW.BUSINESS.KENT.EDU/GRAD

Student Life and Environment

Kent State is a large university where "there is always something going on, whether it is a sports event or a speaker on campus. Kent gives its students many opportunities to get out of their rooms and meet people." Many agree that the school is "very large but very friendly." Full-time students here tend to be either international students or recent undergraduates. In either case, they are typically closer in age to undergraduates than to the older part-time students in their program, and they are more likely to enjoy collegiate recreation. Many work out regularly, taking advantage of "the 52,000 square foot student recreation center, which houses an enormous weightlifting facility and cardio machines. There is a three-story rock wall, a one-sixth mile indoor track, racquetball courts, basketball courts, volleyball courts, and badminton courts. It is the best part of campus."

Students report that Kent has "a beautiful campus" with "nice dorms" but that its "classrooms are older and not aesthetically pleasing or comfortable. The rooms are too hot in the winter and cold in the summer. The chairs are connected to the tables and when you move yours, you may move your neighbor as well." Commuters appreciate that "if you have a night class, you have the opportunity to have a member of campus security walk you to your class. Also, the bus system here is very helpful."

Kent's part-time students are typically "blue-collar managers or individuals working in small- to medium-size manufacturing and financial institutions. Most are married with children." It is "harder for those students to make time for the group projects that teachers frequently assign," we're told, which sometimes creates tension between the "older, non-traditional students" and the younger ones with fewer outside commitments. But, for the most part, full-time and part-time students get along well here. International students "are from so many different countries and walks of life, it gives an extremely diverse learning environment. Everyone learns from one another's experiences."

Admissions

Applicants to the MBA program at Kent State must provide the school with official transcripts from all post-secondary institutions attended; an official GMAT score report; a resume; letters of recommendation (three for the full-time program, two for the Professional MBA program); and a personal statement. International students must additionally provide TOEFL scores (if English is not their native language) and must complete an International Student Application to the school.

FINANCIAL FACTS

Annual tuition (in-state/out-of-state)	$7,980/$14,992
Books and supplies	$1,000
Room & board (on/off-campus)	$5,960/$5,675
% of students receiving aid	35
% of first-year students receiving aid	25
Average award package	$14,480

ADMISSIONS

Admissions Selectivity Rating	72
# of applications received	127
% applicants accepted	76
% acceptees attending	48
Average GMAT	540
Range of GMAT	450-660
Average GPA	3.4
TOEFL Required of International Students?	Yes
Minimum TOEFL (paper/computer)	550/213
Application fee	$30
International application fee	$30
Regular application deadline	4/1
Regular notification	4/15
Deferment Available?	Yes
Maximum length of deferment	1 year
Transfer students accepted?	Yes
Transfer application policy: Must be from AASCB accredited program and less than 6 years old by the time Kent degree is conferred; 12 credit hours maximum; must be approved by the graduate committee and dean.	
Non-fall admissions?	Yes
Need-blind admissions?	Yes

APPLICANTS ALSO LOOK AT

Bowling Green State University, Case Western Reserve University, Cleveland State University, John Carroll University, The Ohio State University, The University of Akron, Youngstown State University.

EMPLOYMENT PROFILE

		Grads employed by field:	
Career Rating	68	Accounting	23
Placement rate (%)	85	Human Resources	8
# of companies recruiting on-campus	95	Marketing	15
Average starting salary	$37,900	MIS	15
		Operations	4
		Consulting	8
		Other	12

LAMAR UNIVERSITY
COLLEGE OF BUSINESS

GENERAL INFORMATION
Type of school | public
Environment | village
Academic calendar | semester

SURVEY SAYS...
Friendly students
Good social scene
Happy students
Smart classrooms
Solid preparation in:
Communication/interpersonal skills
Presentation skills
Computer skills

STUDENTS
Enrollment of parent
  institution | 10,804
Enrollment of MBA program | 81
% male/female | 56/44
% out-of-state | 35
% part-time | 36
% minorities | 6
% international | 27
Average age at entry | 25
Average years work experience
  at entry | 3

ACADEMICS
Academic Experience Rating | 61
Student/faculty ratio | 14:1
Profs interesting rating | 72
Profs accessible rating | 64
% female faculty | 30
% minority faculty | 10
Joint Degrees
MSN in Administration: 2-3 years

Academics

Texans seeking an affordable MBA in a cozy atmosphere would do well to consider the College of Business at Lamar University, a public institution in Beaumont (about 90 miles east of Houston). This program of fewer than 100 students "has made great improvements in recent years," students tell us. One student reports, "I've only seen things get better since I arrived. The quality of a business degree here is improving rapidly as compared with other schools, and Lamar is becoming a true leader in a business education." The size of the program translates into "a student-teacher ratio that is somewhat smaller than it is at other colleges. The quality of our education is competitive despite the size, and we are at a distinct advantage of having one-on-one assistance with professors."

Students can receive a Lamar MBA in short order. Those with undergraduate business degrees, for example, can place out of some or all first-year courses, allowing them to procure their degrees in a year's time. In addition, "there are mini-sessions and summer sessions, which allow students to pick up extra classes in a short amount of time. These sessions are very beneficial." Management and marketing offers the largest number of courses at Lamar; the school also offers courses in economics and finance, information systems and analysis, and accounting and business law. Lamar is home to the Institute for Entrepreneurial Studies and the Small Business Development Center.

Lamar professors are well-loved by the MBAs, who tell us that "for the most part, all the professors are wonderful. They are all educated and have work experience in the field in which they are teaching, [and] the majority are willing to take extra time to help you with your questions." Professors' willingness to work with both individuals and groups of students, MBAs tell us, "reflects the prioritization the faculty gives students and teaching." Advisors are similarly "very nice and helpful." The pace of the curriculum can be slow at times, due in part to some students' lack of background in business studies. One student complains, "The school seriously needs to raise the admission standards. My school's relaxed admission policy lowers my overall learning experience."

Career and Placement

All career services for Lamar MBAs are provided by the university's Career Center; apart from contacts provided by professors, there are few career services offered at Lamar that specifically serve MBAs. The office conducts school-wide job fairs (including recruitment events geared specifically toward minorities), interviewing and resume-building workshops, one-on-one counseling, and online job databases.

Students warn that "the Career Center has limited resources. There aren't many companies that come to the Lamar campus to recruit students, and job-placement programs for business undergrads and grad students need to be improved." A February 2004 report in *The Beaumont Enterprise* confirms this assessment, pointing out that the number of companies attending Lamar's Spring Career Expo has declined by two-thirds in the past five years. Students can, however, access a wide range of companies by attending the Houston Area Consortium of Career Centers Texas Job Fair, held annually at the University of Houston.

SANDY DRANE, GRADUATE ADMISSIONS OFFICE
PO BOX L0078 BEAUMONT, TX 77710 UNITED STATES
PHONE: 409-880-8356 • FAX: 409-880-8414
E-MAIL: DRANESL@HAL.LAMAR.EDU • WEBSITE: WWW.LAMAR.EDU

Student Life and Environment

With fewer than 100 students and a largely part-time population, Lamar's MBA program is "fairly small. Also, unlike most schools, Lamar University is mostly composed of students that commute to and from school. Even though a large living facility has been set-up for students, most students live off of campus. The overall mood of the university is distant." Most students agree, "There is not much life on campus besides the occasional party."

The neighborhood surrounding the school offers little help, as "Lamar University is in a somewhat run-down area of town. Fortunately, the campus police department and City of Beaumont P.D. do a very good job of providing a secure environment for students, staff, and visitors." It is not, however, an area that encourages students to hang out in their free time. As one student puts it, "The area around the campus does not reflect the growing university population. There's not much for students."

That's not to say one can't get involved at Lamar; it just requires more than the usual amount of effort. One go-getter explains, "I've been involved on campus in some of the clubs as well as attending classes. There are all sorts of opportunities. I've participated in the choir and gone to all types of extracurricular events: Deaf events, art shows, literary events, musical concerts, and performances."

Students feel that Lamar is making efforts to upgrade campus life by "providing the opportunity of a social life through student organizations and activities, newly constructed living quarters, and exceptional eating facilities." Furthermore, "Lamar University is currently making great strides to improve not only the physical appearance of the campus but also bring the classrooms up to modern standards with new multimedia equipment."

Admissions

Lamar University requires all applicants to provide GMAT scores, undergraduate transcripts, and TOEFL scores (for students whose native language is not English). An interview, letters of recommendation, personal statement, resume, and evidence of computer experience are all recommended but not required; all are taken into account in rendering an admissions decision. The school applies two formulae combining GPA and GMAT scores to set minimum admissions standards; see the school's website for details. In all instances, a minimum GMAT score of 450 is required for unconditional admission; students with scores between 400 and 450 qualify for conditional admission, pending completion of nine hours of course work with at least a 3.0 GPA.

FINANCIAL FACTS

Annual tuition (in-state/out-of-state)	$2,142/$6,786
Fees	$819
Books and supplies	$1,000
Room & board (on/off-campus)	$5,104/$4,000
% of students receiving aid	30
% of first-year students receiving aid	10
% of students receiving grants	30
Average grant	$7,000

ADMISSIONS

Admissions Selectivity Rating	69
# of applications received	44
% applicants accepted	80
% acceptees attending	69
Average GMAT	488
Range of GMAT	450-560
Average GPA	3.6
TOEFL Required of International Students?	Yes
Minimum TOEFL (paper/computer)	525/200
Application fee	$20
International application fee	$75
Regular application deadline	5/1
Regular notification	Rolling
Deferment Available?	Yes
Maximum length of deferment	1 year
Non-fall admissions?	Yes
Need-blind admissions?	Yes

EMPLOYMENT PROFILE

Career Rating	64
Placement rate (%)	80
Average starting salary	$45,000

LONG ISLAND UNIVERSITY—CW POST CAMPUS
COLLEGE OF MANAGEMENT

GENERAL INFORMATION
Type of school	private
Academic calendar	trimester

SURVEY SAYS...
Students love Brookville, NY
Friendly students
Smart classrooms
Solid preparation in:
Teamwork

STUDENTS
Enrollment of parent institution	31,000
Enrollment of MBA program	370
% male/female	63/37
% part-time	87
% minorities	2
Average age at entry	28
Average years work experience at entry	4

ACADEMICS
Academic Experience Rating	**69**
Student/faculty ratio	18:1
Profs interesting rating	78
Profs accessible rating	62
% female faculty	8

Joint Degrees
MBA/JD: 4-5 years

Academics

One of only two AACSB-accredited MBA programs on Long Island (the other is Hofstra, located in nearby Hempstead), the College of Management at Long Island University— CW Post Campus serves the area's sizeable population by providing a prestigious graduate degree accessible to full-timers and part-timers alike.

The vast majority of graduate students here are part-timers, attending classes in the evenings and/or on Saturdays. The College offers two part-time programs to satisfy these students' needs: the Campus MBA, with classes that meet weekly Monday through Thursday (there are two time slots for classes each night: 6:40 to 8:30 P.M., and 8:40 to 10:30 P.M.); and the Saturday MBA, which features intensive five-week classes (meeting from 9 A.M. to 3:30 P.M.) to allow students with the requisite undergraduate background in business to earn their degrees in 15 to 23 months. Students in the Campus MBA program may supplement their curricula with Saturday classes.

Full-time students may also enroll in the Campus MBA, or they may opt for the Accelerated International MBA. The latter, a 36-credit program "particularly suited for students who have majored in business administration at the undergraduate level," sends students to London for one semester and to Paris for a summer term; the entire program is completed in one year (students spend the fall semester on the CW Post campus).

Students here extol the "excellent academic experience" and "professors who understand and are willing to accommodate students." Students complain that "the school should offer a wider range of elective courses" and wish that it would "allow independent study to better accommodate students' interests and their graduation timeframes." All students here may supplement their degrees by combining four 700-level electives to earn an advanced certificate in any of the following areas: accounting and taxation, finance, international business, management, management information systems, and marketing.

Career and Placement

The Office of Professional Experience & Career Planning at CW Post handles counseling and placement responsibilities for all students. The office provides self-assessment diagnostics, career counseling, resume and job-search advisement, mock interviews, job fairs, recruiting events, and online databases. An MBA Association supplements these services by "helping students network with each other and exchange ideas and information helpful for career advancement in our competitive business world," according to the College's MBA Bulletin.

BETH CARSON, DIRECTOR OF GRADUATE AND INTERNATIONAL ADMISSIONS
720 NORTHERN BOULEVARD, BROOKVILLE, NY 11548 UNITED STATES
PHONE: 516-299-3952 • FAX: 516-299-2418
E-MAIL: BETH.CARSON@LIU.EDU • WEBSITE: WWW.LIU.EDU/POSTMBA

Student Life and Environment

Unlike most New York area schools, the Post campus of LIU boasts a "beautiful campus" spread out across 300+ acres of prime real estate. Twenty acres of the campus are devoted to an arboretum; the entire campus is heavily wooded, with over 4,000 trees that include some of the largest trees on Long Island. Students love the campus but warn that "it's hard to find many buildings the first few times on campus because it's so big" and that "there is definitely a parking problem around the most heavily used buildings."

College of Management facilities include "an excellent library and computer labs." Students appreciate that the school "is willing to spend the money necessary to upgrade facilities and classrooms, which as a result, tend to be in great shape." Unfortunately, "The resources are not geared toward returning adult students, so things like the bookstore hours and campus facilities are not open when we're usually here." The part-timers who make up the majority of the student body note that "this is a commuter school, so there are very few clubs or activities geared toward graduate students, especially those of us who work. There is the occasional function during business hours, but many of us can't make it to them."

Post's "extremely friendly and helpful" MBA students include many students hit by the nation's recent economic woes; "There are a number of students who are here because they were not able to get a job after graduation," explains one student. Others "are working toward getting another job." Overall, "there is a range of experience levels, from significant work experience to none at all."

Admissions

Prerequisites to admission to the Post MBA include competence in business communications, mathematics, and computers, as demonstrated through undergraduate work, successful completion of a related workshop, or successful completion of a waiver exam. All applicants must submit a completed application form, an official GMAT score report, two copies of official transcripts for all post-secondary academic work, a resume, a personal essay explaining one's purpose in pursuing an MBA, and two letters of recommendation. Students whose first language is not English must also submit official results for the TOEFL (minimum score of 527 on the paper-based test, 197 on the computer-based test); students who completed undergraduate degrees from institutions that teach primarily in English are exempted from this requirement.

FINANCIAL FACTS

Annual tuition	$12,690
Fees	$900
Books and supplies	$1,500
Room & board (on/off-campus)	$8,800/$5,800
% of students receiving aid	80
% of students receiving loans	80
% of students receiving grants	2
Average award package	$8,500
Average grant	$3,000

ADMISSIONS

Admissions Selectivity Rating	76
# of applications received	335
% applicants accepted	51
% acceptees attending	82
Average GMAT	487
Range of GMAT	420-690
Average GPA	3
TOEFL Required of International Students?	Yes
Minimum TOEFL (paper/computer)	527/197
Application fee	$30
International application fee	$30
Regular application deadline	8/5
Regular notification	7/5
Deferment Available?	Yes
Maximum length of deferment	1 year
Transfer students accepted?	Yes
Transfer application policy: Maximum of 6 credits within the last five years, grades of B or better. AACSB accredited School.	
Non-fall admissions?	Yes
Need-blind admissions?	Yes

APPLICANTS ALSO LOOK AT

Hofstra University, St. John's University.

EMPLOYMENT PROFILE

Career Rating	60*
# of companies recruiting on-campus	65

LOUISIANA STATE UNIVERSITY
E.J. OURSO COLLEGE OF BUSINESS ADMINISTRATION

GENERAL INFORMATION
Type of school	public
Environment	metropolis
Academic calendar	August–May

SURVEY SAYS...
Friendly students
Happy students
Smart classrooms
Solid preparation in:
Teamwork
Communication/interpersonal skills
Presentation skills

STUDENTS
Enrollment of parent institution	31,481
Enrollment of MBA program	140
% male/female	72/28
% out-of-state	18
% minorities	14
% international	18
Average age at entry	24
Average years work experience at entry	2

ACADEMICS
Academic Experience Rating	**90**
Student/faculty ratio	9:1
Profs interesting rating	80
Profs accessible rating	82
% female faculty	6

Joint Degrees
Dual MBA/JD: 4 years

Prominent Alumni
Harry Hawkes, Executive VP and CEO of Hearst-Argyle Television; D. Martin, Managing director of EnCap Ivestments,LLC; Kerry Chauvin, Chairman and CEO of Gulf Island Fabrication, LA; Clifford J. Neese, President and CEO of Neese Industries, Inc.; Markham Mcknight, President and CEO of Wright & Percy Insurance Agn.

Academics

A "world-renowned internal audit program, very intense and real-world driven," and a great football team are two of the main attractions of the Flores MBA Program at the E.J. Ourso College of Business Administration—and not necessarily in that order. Sure, students here take their schoolwork and careers very seriously, but there's something about the school's location in Baton Rouge that reminds MBAs there's more to life than case studies and presentations. They get the job done here, and they do it well, but they also remember to save time to enjoy the gorgeous campus, the accommodating hometown, the darn good food, and their convivial classmates.

Although the marquee feature at Ourso is the internal audit program—its graduates have won the International CIA Student High Achievement Award on the Certified Internal Auditor Examination eleven times in the last fourteen years—the school is hardly a one-trick pony. Other standouts include the entrepreneur program ("consistently one of the top in the nation") and a solid concentration in real estate. All students here must complete "a strong core curriculum" that provides "a good academic foundation, but without the cutthroat competition that I think could be harmful to the learning environment," writes one MBA. Another notes, "The combination of case studies and current event discussions that have been integrated into the coursework provide the chance to see exactly how the lessons from lectures and text are implemented in today's fluid business environment."

Professors "really try to connect in-class concepts with real world application. Also, students are exposed to professional panels, presentations by industry leaders, and in-state trips to prominent businesses. And trips to foreign countries are offered for international business classes." Students also love the administration, praising it as "second to none. They provide students with a place to go if they need to resolve a problem or just have someone to speak to." "The only drawback here is the brick-and-mortar facilities, [which] are old and deteriorating."

Career and Placement

Flores MBAs are served in their career pursuits by a number of offices and programs, including the LSU Career Services Center, the MBA Internship Program, the Center for Internal Audit Placement Services, and the school's MBA specialization advisers.

Of 68 graduating members of the class of 2003, 41 had full-time employment at commencement. Eighteen MBAs found work at Fortune 500 companies (Altria Group, Inc; Chevron; Eli Lilly; Entergy Corporation; ExxonMobil; Fed Ex; Hartford Financial Services; IBM; International Paper; Lockheed Martin; Schering-Plough;The Shaw Group; and Wal-Mart). Employers that most consistently hire the greatest number of Flores MBAs include Accenture, Chevron, Deloitte & Touche, Entergy Corporation, ExxonMobil, Ernst & Young, Eli Lilly, FedEx, IBM, KPMG Peat Marwick, Lockheed Martin, LSU PricewaterhouseCoopers, and Shell. Nearly 350 companies recruit for full-time employees each year on the LSU campus; just over 100 seek summer interns here.

Student Life and Environment

You'd be hard pressed to find an MBA student here who will badmouth the quality of life at LSU. Students praise the "great social scene," the campus ("one of the most attractive available"), and the "many clubs and organizations that one can join, so that there is always some type of activity going on for the general school public." One student reports, "The MBA association is always having a gathering or some service activity. The

Kathleen Bosworth, Associate Director, Flores MBA Programs
3170 CEBA Building, Baton Rouge, LA 70803 United States
Phone: 225-578-8867 • Fax: 225-578-2421
E-mail: busmba@lsu.edu • Website: www.bus.lsu.edu/mba

FINANCIAL FACTS

Annual tuition (in-state/out-of-state)	
	$8,275/$16,575
Books and supplies	$1,500
Room & board	$5,800

students are always getting together for trips to the bar after a particularly tough day at school." Extracurricular life peaks during the fall, when football dominates the entire campus. One MBA explains, "No matter where you're at on campus or what's going on in your classes or life, you can't ignore the electricity of what's happening each Saturday night. You have to fight the RV's to park for class...on Thursday! Anticipating the Golden Band from Tigerland marching through campus, watching the games at Death Valley...there's nothing like it."

Students also love hometown Baton Rouge, where "there are lots of places to go out, from the Chimes, with a beer menu of over 120 [varieties], to multiple dance clubs around town. The downtown area is beginning to see more life brought to it, which adds more flavor to the mix." Even the pigskin-averse can't resist the allure of "walking through campus amongst the newly bloomed azaleas, under the stately oaks that have adorned the banks of the Mississippi for over 200 years. Friends and professors alike stroll down Highland Road, just a few miles from plantations as old as sugar, all the while getting an education that anyone would be proud of."

The "true Southern ladies and gentlemen" who attend LSU "take advantage of the opportunity to socialize during and after class. This small class size has ultimately allowed us to become a close-knit class," notes one MBA. The class includes "quite a few highly technical engineers, because of the proximity to large oil refineries" and some other professionals. However "the majority do not have work experience, and this means there are strong differences between the objectives that everyone has. Married students and older students with more work experience tend to have better focus toward their career objectives."

Admissions

Admissions Selectivity Rating	92
# of applications received	270
% applicants accepted	37
% acceptees attending	73
Average GMAT	606
Range of GMAT	590-630
Average GPA	3.4
TOEFL Required of International Students?	Yes
Minimum TOEFL (paper/computer)	550/213
Application fee	$25
International application fee	$25
Regular application deadline	5/15
Regular notification	Rolling
Early decision program?	Yes
ED Deadline/Notification	9/15 / 12/15

All applicants to Flores must submit a complete set of undergraduate transcripts (minimum 3.0 GPA required), GMAT scores, letters of recommendation, a personal statement, and a resume of extracurricular activities. An interview is required but previous work experience, while preferred, is not. Admissions officers study the application for evidence of "community work, demonstrated leadership potential, career direction and purpose, personal qualities and interpersonal skills, and academic performance and promise." International applicants must also submit the TOEFL (minimum score: 550 written, 213 computer-based). All students must have completed an introductory calculus course and an introductory accounting course prior to commencing work on their MBAs.

Career Rating	84	Grads employed by field %: avg. salary	
Placement rate (%)	100	Accounting	38: $45,125
# of companies recruiting on-campus	346	Finance	37: $45,125
% grads employed immediately	68	Marketing	7: $42,000
Average starting salary	$48,181	MIS	9: $51,200
		Operations	5: $75,400
		Consulting	4: $48,500

LOYOLA COLLEGE IN MARYLAND
SELLINGER SCHOOL OF BUSINESS AND MANAGEMENT

GENERAL INFORMATION

Type of school	private
Affiliation	Roman Catholic-Jesuit
Environment	village
Academic calendar	semester

SURVEY SAYS...

Students love Baltimore, MD
Friendly students
Good peer network
Happy students
Smart classrooms

STUDENTS

Enrollment of parent institution	6,156
Enrollment of MBA program	798
% part-time	100
Average age at entry	28

ACADEMICS

Academic Experience Rating	**74**
Student/faculty ratio	13:1
Profs interesting rating	79
Profs accessible rating	78
% female faculty	27
% minority faculty	15

Academics

Students at the Sellinger School of Business and Management at Loyola College in Maryland love the school's "solid reputation in the Baltimore/Washington DC area" as well as the program's "great flexibility for part-time MBAs." Sellinger's self-paced curriculum suits the lifestyles of its busy students, allowing them to schedule classes around their other commitments. Sellinger's two campuses (Timonium, and Columbia) that "offer most of the same courses," further augments students' options.

Loyola's MBA program requires between 33 and 53 credits, depending on one's undergraduate background in business. Those eligible to waive pre-program competencies and foundation courses can complete the program in as little as 12 months. The Sellinger curriculum is organized around five integrated areas of study: leadership and teamwork, social responsibility and ethics, IT, global markets, and learning through reflection. MBAs here appreciate the "strong focus on ethics throughout the curriculum." They also tell us that international business studies here are greatly enhanced by "mini-mester courses that involve traveling to a foreign country. There is a two-week trip to Europe and a one-week trip to Chile. It's a nice bonus, and a great way to pick up credits between semesters." Concentrations are offered in accounting, finance, general business, international business, management, MIS, and marketing. Loyola also has an Executive MBA Program.

Students give the academics here an "A+" and report that Sellinger "uses people who are well-established in business to teach the core courses. This means there is no gap between what is taught in the classroom and what the 'real world' is doing. The business people who teach these classes greatly enjoy teaching, and it shows." Classes are interactive, too. One MBA candidate explains, "We don't just read the text and do the homework from the book. We read the text, relate it to our business and personal lives, and apply models to help us comprehend what we just learned." When things get rough, "there are tutors available, with the ability to focus on individual needs." Advisors, on the other hand, "are very hands-off. If you want to find out about resources such as programs, you might not be aware these things exist unless you dig for them yourself."

Career and Placement

Loyola students tell us that "because this is a part-time program, almost all students have full-time jobs, and the school does not offer a lot of resources in career counseling and placement." One student writes, "I only know about the career counseling program because I went to this school for my undergraduate degree. Most graduates are probably not aware we have one." Those who are aware of the service would like to see it beefed up. "Yes, we have jobs. However, this does not mean students are not looking for a job change upon graduation," points out one student. A "strong local alumni network" is Loyola's greatest asset in this area.

Scott Greatorex, Graduate Admissions Director
4501 North Charles Street, Baltimore, MD 21210 United States
Phone: 410-617-5020 • Fax: 410-617-2002
E-mail: graduate@loyola.edu/mba@loyola.edu • Website: http://sellinger.loyola.edu

Student Life and Environment

The Sellinger MBA program is entirely part-time, which students say "creates an atmosphere similar to a community college. There is really no life at school," which actually suits students just fine. Students explain, "Obtaining an MBA is an extremely hard thing to do when working full-time, and the students are very respectful of each other and the teacher because of that. We are all here to strengthen our educational background and move up in the world. School life in a part-time MBA program centers around academics." Fortunately, "the administration and faculty are sensitive to student work/school balance issues. They work to strike a balance between maintaining a top-quality curriculum and providing some flexibility when needed by students."

Occasional extracurricular events do occur here, and students make the most of them. For example, "the school sponsors an alumni night every semester where current students and alumni can network in a relaxed atmosphere. It also sponsors a student appreciation night every semester with refreshments before class." Students socialize on a more casual basis as well. "During evening classes, students are able to meet for a cup of coffee at Starbucks, relax in the lounge and read a book, or catch a show on one of its many flat-screen televisions," explains one student.

The Sellinger student body "is a vibrant population of many young professionals, many with type-A personalities." There is "an intense, yet friendly and productive, sense of competition at Loyola," with students generally "more concerned with learning and networking than being the best at the expense of other classmates." Some here observe that "due to the recent economic environment, there is a noticeable percentage of students right out of undergrad, who decided to get more education before jumping into the market." Overall, though, there is "definitely a diverse group here. There are younger students and older students; married students and single students; students completing the MBA program to move up at their current job; and students completing the MBA program to move to a different company."

Admissions

A complete application to the Loyola College MBA program includes: a completed application form; a personal statement; a resume; an official GMAT score report; official transcripts for all degree work and for any post-secondary academic work completed within five years of application; as well as international documents, where appropriate. Applicants with a 3.25 undergraduates GPA and five years of work experience may waive the GMAT requirement, as many students with an advanced degree in any other discipline (e.g., a Masters, a PhD, a JD, etc.). Interviews and letters of recommendation are optional.

FINANCIAL FACTS

Annual tuition	$9,000
Fees	$50
Books and supplies	$540
Room & board	$10,440
% of students receiving aid	36
% of students receiving loans	36
% of students receiving grants	4
Average award package	$16,310
Average grant	$5,400
Average student loan debt	$27,980

ADMISSIONS

Admissions Selectivity Rating	75
# of applications received	558
% applicants accepted	81
% acceptees attending	85
Average GMAT	562
Range of GMAT	440-680
Average GPA	3.3
TOEFL Required of International Students?	Yes
Minimum TOEFL (paper/computer)	550/213
Application fee	$50
International application fee	$50
Regular application deadline	Rolling
Regular notification	Rolling
Deferment Available?	Yes
Maximum length of deferment	1 year
Transfer students accepted?	Yes
Transfer application policy: Transfer credits only accepted from AACSB accredited schools.	
Non-fall admissions?	Yes
Need-blind admissions?	Yes

Career Rating	60*	Grads employed by field:	
		Accounting/Finance	36
		Human Resources	7
		Marketing	19
		MIS	14
		Operations	9
		Consulting	2
		General Management	12
		Other	1

LOYOLA MARYMOUNT UNIVERSITY
COLLEGE OF BUSINESS ADMINISTRATION

GENERAL INFORMATION
Type of school	private
Affiliation	Roman Catholic-Jesuit
Environment	village
Academic calendar	semester

SURVEY SAYS...
Students love Los Angeles, CA
Friendly students
Happy students
Smart classrooms
Solid preparation in:
Teamwork

STUDENTS
Enrollment of parent institution	8,715
Enrollment of MBA program	286
% male/female	55/45
% part-time	70
% minorities	38
% international	33
Average age at entry	26
Average years work experience at entry	4

ACADEMICS
Academic Experience Rating	**77**
Student/faculty ratio	22:1
Profs interesting rating	90
Profs accessible rating	87
% female faculty	21
% minority faculty	21
Joint Degrees	
MBA/JD: 4 years	
MBA/SELP: 3 years	

Academics

Loyola Marymount University capably serves its largely part-time student body with an extremely accommodating program that allows students to enter in either the fall or spring semester, take as many classes as they can handle, and choose from "a cafeteria-style of elective courses in which a variety of subjects are offered."

Students love LMU's "unbelievable" entrepreneurship program taught by "renowned professors." They also love the international business program and the unique Comparative Management Systems (CMS) option, "where you research issues in foreign countries and then travel to those countries to do hands-on research and interview. CMS is a great alternative to a traditional thesis." Dual degree options such as the Systems Engineering Leadership Program (MBA and MS in Systems Engineering) and the JD/MBA program also earn praise.

Students love the "teamwork-oriented and friendly" vibe, with "none of that back-stabbing you hear about on other campuses. It's like 'The Apprentice' for the winning team, not the losing team." Classwork involves "going to class and participating, not just sitting there and listening to the professor lecture. There is a lot of group work, so you really get to know your peers through large projects and presentations." MBAs also appreciate the Jesuit influence on the curriculum, which translates to "a lot of emphasis on ethics." Professors, we're told, are the school's "greatest strength. They challenge us and push our ideas and we get our money's worth for our education." They also "do a great job of applying real-world situations to theory [and] are a great networking resource."

Career and Placement

LMU serves two distinct student bodies: a majority of part-timers who already have full-time jobs, and a minority who attend full-time and will be looking for job placement post-MBA. The MBA Career Services Office (CSO) doesn't see much of the former, whose employers frequently foot the bill for their MBAs. The latter benefit from resume and cover-letter seminars; interview and salary-negotiation workshops; and career counseling. An MBA Mentor program pairs students with area execs, while the annual Meet the Firms event brings employers to campus to meet with prospective employees and interns.

The CSO also offers the CareerLeader assessment tool and access to Vault.com and Monstertrak.com. The office maintains an online bulletin board for job postings. Students feel that "the school could improve in its ability to attract top-notch companies to the career fair. This would allow LMU grads to compete on a more level playing field with the likes of USC and UCLA." They also "would like to see LMU's alumni association have the power and prestige of a USC."

Student Life and Environment

All students, full-time and part-time, attend classes together at LMU. Classes begin at 4:25 P.M. and continue through the evening. MBAs appreciate that the "beautiful campus" is "very safe," that "faculty and staff are usually available from 9 A.M. to 7 P.M.," and that "the business building remains open after classes end at 10 P.M., allowing students to work." They warn, however, that parking is extremely difficult.

Maria McGill, MBA Program Coordinator
One LMU Drive, MS 8387, Los Angeles, CA 90045-2659 United States
Phone: 310-338-2848 • Fax: 310-338-2899
E-mail: mbapc@lmu.edu • Website: www.mba.lmu.edu

FINANCIAL FACTS

Annual tuition	$23,220
Fees	$400
Books and supplies	$1,300
Average award package	$7,450
Average grant	$2,500

ADMISSIONS

Admissions Selectivity Rating	**75**
# of applications received	223
% applicants accepted	75
% acceptees attending	58
Average GMAT	556
Average GPA	3.25
TOEFL Required of International Students?	Yes
Minimum TOEFL (paper/computer)	600/250
Application fee	$50
International application fee	$50
Regular application deadline	Rolling
Regular notification	Rolling
Deferment Available?	Yes
Maximum length of deferment	1 year
Transfer students accepted?	Yes
Transfer application policy: Students from other Jesuit MBA Programs may transfer core and electives through the Jesuit Transfer Network. Students who attend an AACSB accredited MBA Program (not Jesuit) with equivalent course work of B or better may only transfer in 6 units of upper division course credit but may be eligible for core course waivers.	
Non-fall admissions?	Yes
Need-blind admissions?	Yes

LMU offers "many organized social and networking activities" to its business students, but many are too busy with work, class assignments, and family obligations to take advantage. Those who do speak highly of the opportunities as one reports, "The school provides weekday and weekend activities that encourage students, faculty, and alumni to mingle. From yacht cruises to a day at the horse-races, LMU has a great social culture." Students add, "We have multiple Food 'n' Schmooze nights each semester, which give us the opportunity to get to know our fellow students before and after class over dinner. We also do First Fridays by meeting at different bars on the first Friday of every month." Even so, this "is an evening program, so I don't think we have the same intensity of community as full-time MBA programs might have," concedes one MBA. Another explains, "Because the program is geared towards working adults, most students are part-time and thus come to class and leave immediately afterwards. It's almost like a commuter school in that sense. I wish the program would offer day courses and not just evening courses."

The typical LMU professional is "an aerospace or entertainment industry professional who is very smart and highly motivated." In recent years, an increasing proportion of the student body has arrived with little or no professional experience. One student explains, "The student body is changing in that many students used to come from local engineering companies, but they have cut tuition subsidies so students are now younger." Another observes, "About 25 percent of students are recent college grads. They don't participate much in class discussions. About 75 percent are over 24. This group is the most vocal in class, participate more, and are engaging."

Admissions

LMU implements a relatively lenient admissions policy. Work experience, for example, is not required; while most students have worked post-baccalaureate an average of four years, a substantial number of students arrive here with little or no professional experience. The school enforces no minimum undergraduate GPA or GMAT score, although the average GPA of 3.21 among admitted students bespeaks an academically accomplished student body. No prerequisite courses are required of enrollees; however, students must show evidence of college-level math proficiency (i.e., business math or intermediate algebra) before enrolling in quantitative courses. Applicants may be admitted for fall or spring semester. Applications are processed on a rolling basis.

LOYOLA UNIVERSITY—CHICAGO
GRADUATE SCHOOL OF BUSINESS

Academics

"Loyola University—Chicago is the ideal MBA program for students who work full-time and take classes part-time," students report; about four-fifths of the school's MBAs fall into the "part-time student, full-time worker" category. The program suits these students in part because "it is very flexible; [students] can take one to four courses each quarter." The system even suits those without jobs, since it "makes it easy to be full-time in one quarter and in another to easily take an opportunity for a good internship at the same time we are studying," says one such student. LUC operates on a quarterly academic calendar, which "allows students to finish quickly if they load up on classes. This flexibility is often not found in many MBA programs."

Full-timers and part-timers agree that "one of Loyola's main strengths is its value. It offers a Northwestern or University of Chicago education at affordable prices. Many of the professors have their degrees from these other two schools." Students rate the faculty highly, telling us that professors "are all very eager to develop students' skills. I believe they consider the success of a student a personal success. It provides for a better learning environment because the professors are not so focused on their research that they can't spend time discussing their findings with students." Another student adds, "The classes are great; professors are usually up-to-date. We discuss current strategic marketing events or global challenges/opportunities in classes, which is useful and fun! We prepare real-life cases with brand managers from top-notch multinational companies and have great guest speakers in classes who proved themselves to be leaders in their business."

LUC offers specializations in 13 areas, including such unique disciplines as business ethics, derivative markets, and healthcare management. One marketing student reports that Loyola "is a great place to learn about integrated marketing communications. Real-life cases and great in class materials and discussions helped me stay in contact with the business atmosphere." Students also praise the school's research in information systems and operations management. They also cite the "great opportunities to study abroad."

LUC's large part-time population is not without its drawbacks. The LUC curriculum "requires a team project in nearly every class, [and] the nature of our student body makes this twice as difficult to schedule because you have to meet with your team outside of class. Most students are simply too busy with work or other commitments." Further complicating the situation is the fact that some students are too busy with work to prepare adequately for every class, thus unfairly increasing the workload of their teammates.

Career and Placement

Loyola's Business Career Center is dedicated exclusively to Graduate School of Business students and alumni; this is usually a strong indicator of a solid career office. Loyola students, however, find much to fault with the BCC. Many complain that "the office is understaffed, so services are limited. Loyola GSB has great alumni, especially in the Chicago area and Midwest, but unfortunately, the BCC does not utilize these connections well." Some detect a recent trend toward improvement; one full-time student writes, "This year has been better than the last year, but still we need more co-op positions that school arranges with companies, like other schools do."

ANN BEZBATCHENKO, GRADUATE PROGRAMS RECRUITER
25 E. PEARSON CHICAGO, IL 60611 UNITED STATES
PHONE: 312-915-6124 • FAX: 312-915-7207
E-MAIL: GSB@LUC.EDU • WEBSITE: WWW.GSB.LUC.EDU

FINANCIAL FACTS

Annual tuition	$24,408
Fees	$150
Books and supplies	$1,200
Room & board (on/off-campus)	$10,000/$12,000
Average grant	$8,016

ADMISSIONS

Admissions Selectivity Rating	71
# of applications received	825
% applicants accepted	78
% acceptees attending	55
Average GMAT	540
Range of GMAT	500-620
Average GPA	3.2
TOEFL Required of International Students?	Yes
Minimum TOEFL (paper/computer)	550/213
Application fee	$40
International application fee	$40
Regular application deadline	8/1
Regular notification	Rolling
Deferment Available?	Yes
Maximum length of deferment	1 year
Transfer students accepted?	Yes
Transfer application policy: Up to 9 hours of B or better coursework can transfer from AACSB-accredited institutions.	
Non-fall admissions?	Yes
Need-blind admissions?	Yes

Employers who recently hired Loyola MBA students for internships and full-time jobs include Abbott Laboratories, Alcoa, Allstate, Bank One, CitiGroup, Classified Ventures, Emmaus Ministries, the Federal Reserve Bank of Chicago, Graco Inc., IIT, Johnson & Johnson, Merck, Northern Trust, PricewaterhouseCoopers, Richland Mortgage, and Walgreens.

Student Life and Environment

LUC's MBA program "is well designed for part-time students. Almost all MBA classes are offered between 6:00 P.M. and 9:00 P.M. downtown at the Water Tower campus." This location "makes it easy for those that work in the city [as well as commuters, as the site] provides easy access for students who travel from the suburbs and other parts of Chicago. There are buses and trains within a few blocks of the school itself."

While many of the part-timers "arrive just in time for class and leave right afterward, [others] get together after classes fairly often. Many [students] go to Flapjaws, the bar across the street, after class. After midterms, a bunch of people got together to go skating to celebrate." LUC offers "plenty of great student-run organizations such as the Loyola Strategic Consulting Group, [and] the school sponsors a number of events, from International Night to Christmas parties. Each of these events allows the students to network to build friendships and potential business contacts."

The "international and cultural diversity [of LUC's student body] brings together an incredibly diverse body of work experience, helping to expand career choices and networks." On the downside, "Loyola has a fairly open admission policy. The school has a lot of good students. However, sometimes a poorer student is admitted. These students fail to contribute as well in classroom discussion and on group projects." Group projects abound, boosting class cohesion. One MBA explains, "The teamwork allows us to get to know each other. We ask about family and share in new babies and weddings and love to head across the street to the pub for beers after class to catch up. We're kind of like an extended family."

Admissions

According to the GSB Admissions Office, "Applicants are evaluated on the basis of academic GPA, GMAT score, professional work experience, personal statements/essays, letters of recommendation, and their written responses to the questions on our application." Two letters of recommendation from "current or past employers, academic references, or professional colleague," are required. Interviews are not required. Although work experience is not required, nearly all Loyola students—98 percent of them, to be precise—have it; about 80 percent work while attending school part-time. Admissions decisions are made on a rolling basis, usually within 10 days of receiving all application materials.

APPLICANTS ALSO LOOK AT

DePaul University, Illinois Institute of Technology, Northern Illinois University, Northwestern University, University of Chicago, University of Illinois at Chicago, University of Illinois at Urbana-Champaign.

Career Rating	70	Grads employed by field	%: avg. salary
Placement rate (%)	65	Accounting	2: $46,500
# of companies recruiting on-campus	76	Finance	18: $54,250
% grads employed immediately	35	Human Resources	7: $51,588
Average starting salary	$57,710	Marketing	8: $50,000
		MIS	3: $58,000
		Operations	3: $39,667
		Strategic Planning	1: $75,000
		General Management	3: $65,667
		Other	9: $68,755

LOYOLA UNIVERSITY—NEW ORLEANS
JOSEPH A. BUTT, S. J., COLLEGE OF BUSINESS ADMINISTRATION

GENERAL INFORMATION
Type of school	private
Affiliation	Roman Catholic-Jesuit
Environment	metropolis
Academic calendar	semester

SURVEY SAYS...
Friendly students
Good social scene
Happy students
Smart classrooms
Solid preparation in:
Teamwork

STUDENTS
Enrollment of parent institution	5,423
Enrollment of MBA program	77
% male/female	64/36
% out-of-state	33
% part-time	50
% minorities	31
% international	33
Average age at entry	26
Average years work experience at entry	3.5

ACADEMICS
Academic Experience Rating	**78**
Student/faculty ratio	14:1
Profs interesting rating	77
Profs accessible rating	88
% female faculty	33
% minority faculty	3
Joint Degrees	
MBA/JD: 4-5 years	

Academics

MBA students who crave small classes and tons of personal attention should consider the MBA program at Loyola University—New Orleans. With a combined full-time/part-time student body of under 100, Loyola can offer "small classes of 10 to 20 students, which allows for many class discussions and sharing [and] professors who are always available to interact with students." And because the MBA program piggybacks on a much larger undergraduate program (about 20 percent of Loyola's undergrads major in business disciplines), it can offer a relatively wide range of options along with all these boutique-style amenities.

Of course, like any program, this one has areas of relative strength and weakness. Students are especially enthusiastic about the "very informative classes in operations management, e-commerce, and management and organization, [and love the] emphasis on international business." On the downside, they feel that offerings in finance and marketing could stand to improve. In all areas, the MBA program remains true to its Jesuit tradition by "focusing on critical reasoning, discernment, business ethics, leadership, entrepreneurship, and international business." Students tell us the program does a solid job of developing general business acumen. One student reports, "As the lead revenue coordinator for my current company, I feel the depth and breadth of the Loyola MBA program has further developed the skill sets needed to compete in the current corporate environment."

"Like any school, you have a mix of good and bad professors," at Loyola, although students add that "a large percentage of them are very knowledgeable and actually fun to learn from. There's only a small number that make you ask, 'Why am I here?'" MBAs appreciate the "open-door policy maintained by most professors who are willing to assist students, even if one calls them at their home during weekends, [and are satisfied that] the administrative staff as well as the professors and students know the name of each person in the business school. It is just amazing to be known by your name from everyone! That's the real network you should expect for the future." MBAs agree, Loyola's library "is outstanding from a resource and technology standpoint, [and the business building] has excellent technology. All classrooms and conference rooms are equipped with the latest multimedia technology ([like] wireless LAN connectivity [and] computer labs), and class material is also available through Blackboard."

Career and Placement

A program as small as Loyola's obviously cannot dedicate a career office exclusively to MBA students. Instead, MBA students receive career guidance from the university's Counseling and Career Center, which, according to the school's website, "offers personal counseling (individual and group) and informational workshops and prevention programs. The center's staff is sensitive to the stresses and concerns of the students. Additionally, staff members provide resume assistance, job fairs, internships, employer research, and job-search support."

Jan Moppert, Coordinator of Graduate and External Programs
6363 St. Charles Avenue, Campus Box 15, New Orleans, LA 70118 United States
Phone: 504-864-7965 • Fax: 504-864-7970
E-mail: jamopper@loyno.edu • Website: cba.loyno.edu/mba

Student Life and Environment

In most programs that convene classes only in the evening, students typically tell us that they spend relatively little time on campus and/or with classmates off campus. Most programs are not in New Orleans, however. Students report that "since it is a night program, students don't just go to class and go home. We usually go out to dinner or to a bar. We really get to know each other on a more personal level." That is, of course, unless you aren't partial to the New Orleans lifestyle. One student observes, "If you like to get drunk, this is the city (and the school) to be in. I don't drink, so the one thing I dislike about it is that all planned off-campus social activities focus on alcohol. I wish there were more activities planned that were family-oriented or just not all about drinking. I have missed out on getting to know some fellow students better because I do not enjoy those environments." The school's location carries another drawback, as one student notes, "Louisiana ranks either last or next-to-last in the U.S. in job growth, opportunities, and most other positive attributes of acceptable living."

MBAs are "a close-knit community and group of friends." One student explains, "Because the MBA program at Loyola is relatively small, I have had the opportunity to interact with most students. As I do my research assistantship at school, I have had the opportunity to interact and develop a closer relationships with some faculty and other students." This "noncompetitive, supportive [population includes] many Latinos who bring the Latin culture into every classroom and open global knowledge." The main student group is the MBA Association, which provides leadership opportunities to interested students; it also coordinates community-service projects and schedules special events such as guest speakers from the New Orleans and Louisiana business communities.

Admissions

Loyola requires the following of applicants to its MBA program: Official transcripts for all past academic work, GMAT scores, two letters of recommendation, a personal statement of purpose, and a resume. International students whose first language is not English must also submit TOEFL scores. The school's website states, "Applicants are in competition with one another initially on the basis of undergraduate grade-point average and professional work experience." Work experience, though not required, is strongly recommended. Interviews are optional.

FINANCIAL FACTS

Annual tuition	$24,800
Fees	$1,056
Books and supplies	$1,500
Room & board	$8,000
Average grant	$5,000

ADMISSIONS

Admissions Selectivity Rating	79
# of applications received	85
% applicants accepted	59
% acceptees attending	62
Average GMAT	545
Average GPA	3.3
TOEFL Required of International Students?	Yes
Minimum TOEFL (paper/computer)	580/237
Application fee	$50
International application fee	$50
Regular application deadline	6/15
Regular notification	Rolling
Deferment Available?	Yes
Maximum length of deferment	1 academic year
Transfer students accepted?	Yes

Transfer application policy: In applicant comes from an AACSB-accredited program, the foundation work may apply to our program. Also, a maximum of 6 credit hours may be applied to the advanced level. Only a grade of B or better are accepted.

Non-fall admissions?	Yes
Need-blind admissions?	Yes

APPLICANTS ALSO LOOK AT

Louisiana State University, Tulane University, University of Lousiana at Lafayette, University of New Orleans.

EMPLOYMENT PROFILE

Career Rating	70
# of companies recruiting on-campus	225
Average starting salary	$52,000

MARIST COLLEGE

Academics

Many business schools offer students some online options these days, but Marist goes the extra mile; its students can complete their entire degree and barely ever set foot on campus. One student reports, "I am one class away from obtaining my MBA, having taken all required classes online at Marist." Nearly everyone we spoke with at Marist praises the school's "excellent online program, which allows students to go to school anytime, anywhere. Marist is definitely technologically advanced." As one student put it, "The combination of online and classroom-based offerings makes for a very good program that can fit around a wide variety of schedules."

Whether you take courses online, on campus, or pursue both options in combination, Marist serves up a "solidly designed degree that provides a broad-based coverage of business to a student body that has a wide range of backgrounds and levels of managerial experience." This "complete academic experience benefits from the support among faculty members to integrate the different courses to one combined excellent education. Classes are taught by well-established professors who are always available for extra help." MBAs warn that scheduling a combination on campus and online classes can be tricky. Classroom courses take 15 weeks to complete (one three-hour session per week) while online courses are only 8 weeks long (students may log on at any time to "access lectures, share course information, work on group projects, submit class work, and take exams."

The Marist faculty earn students' accolades. MBAs tell us, "The majority of the professors are solid instructors with real-world experience to help them take theory and convert it into applied tools. They are all generally open to new ideas and are usually happy to talk and interact with the students." Their ranks include "a good mix of full-time professors and professionals who hold high-level positions in organizations. This helps to diversify the education. [It's] a good mix of academia and current professionals." One students points out, "There are several assisting professors who are recent Marist MBA grads, people I knew in courses I took who now are assisting professors in classes I'm taking now. It makes it more intimate, and it shows that those who work hard in the program are recognized by the faculty as being good students who can add to the flavor of the classes by teaching them too."

Career and Placement

All career services at Marist College are provided by the Center for Career Services. Over 95 percent of Marist's MBAs are full-time professionals; relatively few seek the help of the center. Those who do find that the office maintains resume books; offers resume critiques; holds workshops in interviewing, resume writing, and job seeking; organizes job expos and coordinates joint job-fair ventures with regional and national organizations; and provides access to self-assessment tools such as DISCOVER. Marist has forged a partnership with IBM to "offer students and faculty opportunities to collaborate with these world-renowned leaders in business, history, and ecology."

ANU R. AILAWADHI, DIRECTOR OF GRADUATE ADMISSIONS
3399 NORTH ROAD, POUGHKEEPSIE, NY 12601 UNITED STATES
PHONE: 845-575-3800 • FAX: 845-575-3166
E-MAIL: GRADUATE@MARIST.EDU • WEBSITE: WWW.MARIST.EDU/MANAGEMENT/MBA

Student Life and Environment

Students tell us that Marist "is primarily an undergraduate institution at this point, and don't really see a need for them to build a culture or 'life' for grad students. Almost none of the grad students live on campus." They also point out that Marist's MBA program "is centered around part-time students who are completing their degrees over a period of several years. Given that, there is not a lot of focus on the grad students in terms of building or catering to a student community. In all fairness, most of the MBA students aren't looking for that from the school, so it is hard to say it is a true weakness. It's more of a factor that might limit the long-term growth of the program." For many, "life at Marist as a grad student is on the Internet, so outside of pure academics, there is no 'life.' The academic environment is great, though."

Those who attend classes on campus tell us, "Our graduate programs offer flexibility for demanding schedules, which is a good thing. While the schedules get hectic with the start of semester, we usually get enough time to do some extracurricular activities if we are so inclined." The school is home to numerous clubs and organizations; the Student Governing Council brings lectures, performing arts, comedy, and musical acts to campus on a regular basis. Marist's athletic teams, the Red Foxes, compete in the Metro Atlantic Athletic Conference. In 2004, the women's basketball team earned its first-ever trip to the NCAA Tournament by winning its conference.

Marist is located in the city of Poughkeepsie, New York, about a 90-minute drive from both New York City and Albany. It's a small city of 30,000 that covers just under five square miles, but it packs a lot into a little space, including a dozen parks, a public boat launch, an 18-hole golf course, and numerous other recreational facilities. The city is also home to the Bardavon 1869 Opera House, which frequently hosts touring productions of Broadway shows. Top employers in Poughkeepsie include IBM, Vassar Brothers Hospital, the county government, the Department of Transportation, Central Hudson Gas and Electric, and various local schools.

Admissions

Applicants to Marist's conventional and online programs follow the same procedure. All must provide the college with official copies of undergraduate and graduate transcripts, GMAT scores, a resume, a personal statement, and letters of recommendation. The school welcomes all students, even those without undergraduate experience in business. Students lacking the requisite academic background must complete seven foundation courses prior to commencing work on the MBA. Students may place out of one or more of these courses through testing.

FINANCIAL FACTS

Annual tuition	$10,116
Fees	$60
Books and supplies	$1,248
% of students receiving aid	38
% of first-year students receiving aid	100
% of students receiving loans	33
% of students receiving grants	33
Average award package	$14,981
Average grant	$2,000

ADMISSIONS

Admissions Selectivity Rating	**62**
# of applications received	102
% applicants accepted	96
% acceptees attending	56
Average GMAT	500
Average GPA	3.3
TOEFL Required of International Students?	Yes
Minimum TOEFL (paper/computer)	550/213
Application fee	$30
International application fee	$30
Regular application deadline	8/1
Regular notification	8/15
Deferment Available?	Yes
Maximum length of deferment	2 years
Transfer students accepted?	Yes
Transfer application policy: No more than six credit hours of core courses accepted from AACSB accredited programs.	
Non-fall admissions?	Yes
Need-blind admissions?	Yes

EMPLOYMENT PROFILE

Career Rating	70	**Grads employed by field**	**%: avg. salary**
Average starting salary	$49,250	General Management	92: $49,250

MARQUETTE UNIVERSITY
COLLEGE OF BUSINESS ADMINISTRATION

Academics

A strong reputation like "the best business school in the area," a "superior faculty," and "a strong international focus in the curriculum" all appeal to the MBA students at Marquette University's College of Business Administration, a nationally known Jesuit-run school in Milwaukee. Marquette belongs to the Network of MBA Programs at Jesuit Colleges and Universities. This means all credits here transfer to any other participating Jesuit MBA program, a significant convenience in today's fluid employment environment. Jesuit sponsorship also ensures a strong curricular focus on ethics.

Marquette offers a part-time and full-time MBA, an Executive MBA, and MS degrees in accounting, applied economics, engineering management, and human resources. The MBA is offered in three locations: Downtown, Waukesha, and Kohler. Programs operate on a semester calendar, which makes for a demanding academic load. But part-time students here—who constitute the majority of the student body—report, "Professors understand the challenges that a working professional faces when going back to school. They are friendly and supportive and really help the transition back into school." Similarly, the administration "offers an impressive level of assistance. They know that most of us have busy lives so they make registering for class simple. If there is a problem, you call and it is taken care of. And they know your name, which is remarkable for a school our size."

MBAs at Marquette may specialize in e-business, economics, finance, human resources, international business, management information systems, marketing, or total quality management. Offerings are especially broad in human resources. Across the curriculum, students commend Marquette professors for "keeping up with new technological trends." MBAs also appreciate "Marquette's focus on teaching. You can tell that, for the most part, professors are here because they like to teach. They like students, people, and helping out. They want to challenge you and make sure that you've learned something along the way. It's a nice balance." Instructors also incorporate "a good balance of text, case work, and projects" to give students a wide range of learning experiences.

Career and Placement

The Career Services Center at Marquette provides counseling and placement services to all undergraduates and graduate students at the university. The office organizes workshops, one-on-one counseling sessions, on-site recruiting events, and job databases. In addition, the College of Business offers career management services. Students are happy to report that the MBA program provides "a number of opportunities to interview with the Big Four firms as well as a number of local and regional firms," and also praise the "strong alumni and business connections in Milwaukee/southern Wisconsin."

Student Life and Environment

Most MBA students at Marquette are part-time students with full-time jobs. They generally "go to class and go home. That's it." One MBA explains, "I feel about as connected to Marquette as one does to say, a parking garage at work: You're there all the time and it's very useful, but you wouldn't notice any difference if you had to park somewhere else one day, and you wouldn't miss it." There are also about 90 full-time students here, however, who involve themselves in the life of the university. One reports, "Marquette offers about 80 clubs and organizations—everything from athletics to cultural groups to arts to academic organizations and honor societies. Athletics (especially basketball) is strongly supported. In addition, the College of Business/MBA program hosts events. There is a strong sense of identity and belonging to a great, dynamic group." The pro-

DR. JEANNE SIMMONS, ASSISTANT DEAN
PO BOX 1881, MILWAUKEE, WI 53201-1881 UNITED STATES
PHONE: 414-288-7145 • FAX: 414-288-1660
E-MAIL: MBA@MARQUETTE.EDU • WEBSITE: WWW.MARQUETTE.EDU/BUSINESS

gram "tries to include the family when possible," which students appreciate.

Students at Marquette see Milwaukee as another asset, one that provides "many activities, connections, and opportunities that come from being near a large city." Some worry about safety on the downtown campus, although others report that "the campus is becoming more enclosed," reducing safety issues. Chicago is less than a two-hour drive to the south.

Marquette's student body consists "mostly of career people who are working toward their MBA part-time. They are friendly and enthusiastic, are good in group work situations, [and] provide a collegial attitude to the program." Because "they come from many different large corporations in the Milwaukee area," they offer "good insight into the economic environment of Milwaukee." Some, though, "are not from business backgrounds. They come from engineering, healthcare, public service, or not-for-profits. The problem with this mix is that these students do not have the ability to offer many strategic business insights because they are just learning the concepts." For many at this Jesuit institution, "spiritual life takes a priority, which is a healthy change from state institutions."

Admissions

Applicants to the Marquette MBA program must provide the Admissions Office official transcripts for all previous post-secondary academic work, an official GMAT score report, a personal essay, and a resume. International students are additionally required to submit three letters of recommendation and an official score report for the TOEFL or another acceptable English proficiency exam. Marquette encourages applicants to apply for full admission but also offers a temporary-admission option for non-international applicants, good for one semester only. Students applying to campuses other than the downtown campus must remember to specify their campus of choice on their application.

FINANCIAL FACTS

Annual tuition	$11,880
Books and supplies	$750
Average grant	$2,975

ADMISSIONS

Admissions Selectivity Rating	**75**
# of applications received	252
% applicants accepted	80
% acceptees attending	77
Average GMAT	560
Average GPA	3.2
TOEFL Required of International Students?	Yes
Minimum TOEFL (paper)	550
Application fee	$40
International application fee	$40
Regular application deadline	Rolling
Regular notification	Rolling
Deferment Available?	Yes
Maximum length of deferment	1 year
Transfer students accepted?	Yes
Transfer application policy: We accept transfers from other Jesuit Schools (JEBNET agreement—see www.jebnet.org). We will also accept up to 12 approved credits from AACSB schools.	
Non-fall admissions?	Yes

APPLICANTS ALSO LOOK AT

Loyola University Chicago, University of Wisconsin—Madison, University of Wisconsin—Milwaukee.

MASSACHUSETTS INSTITUTE OF TECHNOLOGY
MIT SLOAN SCHOOL OF MANAGEMENT

Academics

Students tell us that MIT Sloan "is the very best school for innovation in business," pointing to "the absolute best operations research people in the world;" the fact that "today's leaders in finance and economics were all either educated at Sloan or teach here;" and the university's role as one of the nation's leading engineering, tech, and science research centers. They also cite the Sloan Innovation Period, a week wedged in the middle of each semester during which "students learn from faculty about their current research interests."

Sloan's quant-intensive, two-year, full-time program commences with a rigorous core that involves a large measure of "friendly, team-based learning" as well as "a combination of videos, cases, group exercises, etc. The classes are extremely engaging, and I expect to retain a lot more due to the variation in styles of learning," says one student. Requirements can largely be dispensed with during the first semester here, after which "the design of students' MIT Sloan education is mostly in their own hands, provided they acquire appropriate credits in leadership, research, and practice," according to the school's website.

Students speak highly of MIT's Entrepreneurial Program, noting that it benefits greatly from the research taking place throughout the university. One writes, "Sloan students visit various MIT labs, assessing the marketability of technology projects. They also write business plans and help start-up ventures emerging from MIT's labs, and are heavily involved in supporting new businesses—both locally and globally—through the entrepreneurial department." Another adds, "The environment is very entrepreneurial and with the opportunities students have to take initiative to shape the extracurricular and academic life here, Sloan is a fantastic place to develop your leadership skills."

Other special programs singled out for praise include the Leaders for Manufacturing Program: "The best of its kind, it tailors the MBA experience toward people interested in working for a manufacturing company in the future." Another is the MIT Sloan Fellows Program in Innovation and Global Leadership, "clearly the best program for a mid-career executive due to the intensity of the one-year program." The Cambridge address means "students have many opportunities to network with the school and beyond by cross-registering with other MIT schools or Harvard."

Career and Placement

Sloan's Career Development Office provides MBAs with a range of career management resources, including seminars, self-assessment tools, library materials, and online databases. The CDO hosts on-campus recruiting events throughout the school year to much success. The school reports that approximately 60 percent of students seeking a career change achieve their goal through such events, with the remainder finding new jobs through alumni connections, faculty recommendations, job postings, and other similar methods. Students tell us that the CDO is supportive but could stand to improve in some areas; "Career placement services are non-existent for special programs, like the Biomedical Enterprise Program," writes one student. To make up for it, the "supportive nature of the student body" means "people try to use their network to help other students find jobs."

Employers most likely to hire Sloan MBAs include McKinsey and Co., Merrill Lynch, Boston Consulting Group, Citigroup, Bain and Company, IBM Corporation, Lehman Brothers, Unilever, Goldman Sachs, and United Technologies Corporation.

Student Life and Environment

"The tough part of MIT Sloan is balancing your time to take advantage of all that the school and community offer," students tell us. This is especially true during the first semester core, which students describe as "intense." One first-semester MBA writes,

Rod Garcia, Admissions Director
50 Memorial Drive, E52-118, Cambridge, MA 02139 United States
Phone: 617-258-5434 • Fax: 617-253-6405
E-mail: mbaadmissions@sloan.mit.edu • Website: mitsloan.mit.edu

"People work real hard, and at the same time, companies are coming to campus and there are a lot of clubs. This semester is an exercise in prioritization and balancing tasks." One confesses, "There is so much work that you have to make choices as to which review sessions you can attend." Fortunately, "although there is a lot of work, very little of it is useless or busy work." The MBA continues, "When it's all over, I'll be very happy that I was made to do this much at the beginning of my business school experience." Students tell us that "after first semester, the pressure is off and life consists of an even mix of schoolwork, socializing, career exploration, and personal time."

MIT offers "a plethora of social activity options. A large portion of students play in various intramural sports, [and] there are actually routine options for each weeknight: 'Muddy Mondays' at the on-campus pub, 'Thirst Quenchers' moves the happy hour location each Tuesday, each Wednesday Sloan students gather at the BHP (Beacon Hill Pub), and have 'Consumption Functions' each Thursday night." Clubs "are all student-driven, and there are quite a number of them." There are also "lots of trips, both school-sponsored (company networking) and among the students." One student sums up, "I end every night complaining to myself, 'Why does the day have only 24 hours?' The amount of activities, projects, presentations, and friendships are so abundant and high quality that I'd love if the days were much longer."

Sloan MIT students are "very diverse and extremely impressive with respect to what they did before business school. Many were entrepreneurs who had their own companies." One writes, "What really impresses me is how humble they are. Though most have made remarkable and sometimes extraordinary accomplishments, they rarely speak of them." Although "students are, by nature, competitive and put a lot of effort into winning intramural athletic events, [they are] very collaborative and helpful" in the classroom. "Teams work together to learn yet complete work efficiently leaving time for the other opportunities in graduate school," explains one Sloan MBA.

Admissions

Completed applications to the Sloan MBA program include two letters of recommendation, post-secondary transcripts (self-reported prior to interview; if called for an interview, applicants must provide official transcripts), a resume, four personal essays, supplemental information (hobbies, interests, leadership experience), and GMAT scores. The school requires additional materials from applicants to the Leaders for Manufacturing Program and the Biomedical Enterprise Program. Sloan is extremely competitive; the school's website points out that "nearly all the applicants to the MIT Sloan School of Management have noteworthy academic records, competitive GMAT scores, and an average of five-plus years of professional experience." The nature of the program favors candidates with strong quantitative and analytical skills, as well as those with well-demonstrated leadership potential and a clear vision of their career goals.

FINANCIAL FACTS

Annual tuition	$37,050
Fees	$200
Books and supplies	$4,000
Room & board	$13,880
% of students receiving aid	74
% of first-year students receiving aid	75
% of students receiving loans	68
% of students receiving grants	20
Average award package	$48,616
Average grant	$16,492
Average student loan debt	$59,803

ADMISSIONS

Admissions Selectivity Rating	99
# of applications received	3,228
% applicants accepted	17
% acceptees attending	75
Average GMAT	710
Range of GMAT	610-740
Average GPA	3.5
Minimum TOEFL (paper/computer)	600/
Application fee	$210
International application fee	$210
Regular application deadline	10/20
Application Deadline/Notification	
Round 1:	10/29 / 1/12
Round 2:	1/21 / 4/5
Need-blind admissions?	Yes

EMPLOYMENT PROFILE

		Grads employed by field	%: avg. salary
Career Rating	93		
Placement rate (%)	88	Finance	30: $86,170
% grads employed immediately	77	Marketing	11: $85,095
Average starting salary	$88,217	MIS	2: $90,250
		Operations	10: $86,736
		Consulting	25: $91,085
		General Management	14: $91,844
		Other	8: $86,417

MERCER UNIVERSITY–ATLANTA
EUGENE W. STETSON SCHOOL OF BUSINESS & ECONOMICS

GENERAL INFORMATION

Type of school	private
Affiliation	Baptist
Academic calendar	2 8 week/sem.

SURVEY SAYS...

Students love Atlanta, GA
Friendly students
Good peer network
Cutting edge classes
Happy students
Smart classrooms

STUDENTS

Enrollment of parent institution	7,180
Enrollment of MBA program	347
% male/female	56/44
% part-time	48
% minorities	36
% international	9
Average age at entry	33
Average years work experience at entry	3

ACADEMICS

Academic Experience Rating	64
Student/faculty ratio	20:1
Profs interesting rating	81
Profs accessible rating	68
% female faculty	38
% minority faculty	19

Joint Degrees

MBA/PharmD: 4 years;
Joint MBA/MDiv: 3 years

Prominent Alumni

Karen Romaine Thomas, Vice President, CFO, Schwan's Bakery, Inc.; John F. Hough, Dr. P.H., MPH, MBA, Health Scientist Administrator, NIH; William Astary, Sr. VP of Sales, Acuity Brand Lighting; Paul Gianneschi, Mananging Prin. & Founder, Hatch Medical, LLC; Joann Herold, Vice President, Marketing, Honey Baked Ham Company.

Academics

Designed for the convenience of its predominantly professional student body, Mercer University in Atlanta offers a number of accommodations to suit busy MBAs. Classes here meet only once a week, on weekday evenings or on Saturday. Eight-week sessions help students proceed through the program at a steady pace, while five separate admissions entry points mean students can begin the program at virtually any time of the year. As the school's website asserts, "the program is tailored to meet the needs of individuals already employed as managers," as well as those "preparing for advancement into middle-management and administrative levels."

Mercer is a Baptist university with its main campus an hour south of Atlanta, in Macon, Georgia, and a graduate and professional campus in Atlanta. The school draws on its roots to provide a program that "focuses on ethical leadership and problem-solving skills" in order to give students a "competitive edge" in today's business world. This goal is further achieved through "the establishment of a real-world experience base by maintaining continuous interaction with community organizations, profit and non-profit, through seminars and special programs for practicing managers and administrators." The school's location in a major metropolis is a great asset in achieving this goal.

The heart of the Mercer MBA in Atlanta is a core curriculum covering managerial economics, managerial accounting, marketing, management information systems, corporation finance, operations management science, and ethics. A concluding simulation-student seminar and electives are also part of the program. Prior to beginning core coursework, incoming Mercer students may be required to complete a sequence of four non-graduate-level foundation courses covering micro- and macro-economics, accounting and finance, management and marketing, and business law. Equivalent courses previously completed at the undergraduate level may allow students to place out of these requirements.

Mercer MBAs appreciate their "professional" and "personable" professors who are "helpful outside the class, open to feedback, [and] truly care that the students are learning." One respondent exclaims, "They push you!" Students also love "the timeliness of the program" and the "state-of-the-art equipment in the lecture rooms," but wish that "more class options were available throughout the school year."

Career and Placement

The Office of Career Services at Mercer "provides support to students and alumni in the areas of decision-making and networking," according to the school catalog, which also notes that "students and alumni can view and be informed of ongoing full-time, part-time, and internship opportunities by registering on-line with SUCCESSTRAK. Annual career days, an academic majors fair, a senior kick-off event, and presentations on resume design and other job search topics" are all offered here. Students here tell us that "recruiting, advertising, and corporate sponsorships all could use improvement."

KAREN M. GOSS, ASSISTANT VICE PRESIDENT FOR ADMISSIONS
MERCER UNIVERSITY, 3001 MERCER UNIVERSITY DRIVE, ATLANTA, GA 30341-4155 UNITED STATES
PHONE: 678-547-6417 • FAX: 678-547-6367
E-MAIL: ATLBUSADM@MERCER.EDU • WEBSITE: WWW.MERCER.EDU/BUSINESS

Student Life and Environment

Mercer's Atlanta campus is "primarily a commuter campus" where classes "are held in the evenings to accommodate working individuals." Although most students spend as little time on campus as necessary, a few would like to see a stronger MBA community and call for "more graduate associations, especially for minorities and women."

Mercer MBAs are "mostly full-time workers in the professional world" who "generally have substantial real-world experiences to contribute." This mélange of professionals makes for "good networking because there's lots of different people in different fields." Students also appreciate the "diverse mix of cultural ethnicities" drawn to Mercer's Atlanta campus.

Hometown Atlanta is one of the great cities of the Southeast, a corporate and cultural mecca that is home to Coca-Cola, Home Depot, Delta, and a slew of other business giants. The city is awash in restaurants, clubs, live music venues, theaters, culture of every shape and form, and great professional athletics. Top that off with the fact that the weather's fantastic.

Admissions

Applicants to the Stetson MBA program at Mercer must provide the school with a completed application form, two sets of official transcripts from each post-secondary academic institution attended, a resume, and an official GMAT score report showing test results no more than five years old. In addition, international applicants whose first language is not English must demonstrate English proficiency through TOEFL scores and, upon arrival at the school, through a test administered by the English Language Institute of Mercer University. All students who received undergraduate degrees abroad must, at their own expense, provide an independent evaluation (and, where appropriate, a translation) of their undergraduate records. International students must additionally demonstrate the ability to finance their education at Mercer.

FINANCIAL FACTS

Annual tuition	$12,120
Books and supplies	$1,000
Room & board	$9,450
% of students receiving aid	60
% of first-year students receiving aid	60
% of students receiving loans	60
% of students receiving grants	1
Average award package	$12,666
Average grant	$1,140
Average student loan debt	$20,000

ADMISSIONS

Admissions Selectivity Rating	64
# of applications received	235
% applicants accepted	85
% acceptees attending	64
Average GMAT	500
Range of GMAT	450-610
Average GPA	3.0
TOEFL Required of International Students?	Yes
Minimum TOEFL (paper/computer)	550/213
Application fee	$50
International application fee	$100
Regular application deadline	8/1
Regular notification	Rolling
Deferment Available?	Yes
Maximum length of deferment	5 years past GMAT
Transfer students accepted?	Yes
Transfer application policy: Will consider up to two courses (6 sem. hrs.)for transfer within past five years.	
Non-fall admissions?	Yes
Need-blind admissions?	Yes

EMPLOYMENT PROFILE

Career Rating	75	Grads employed by field	%: avg. salary
Placement rate (%)	91	Accounting	10: $53,609
# of companies recruiting on-campus	85	Finance	11: $53,609
% grads employed immediately	82	Human Resources	2: $51,000
Average starting salary	$52,769	Marketing	21: $64,181
		MIS	5: $57,000
		Operations	12: $54,113
		Consulting	2: $50,000
		General Management	10: $59,867
		Other	27: $57,302

MERCER UNIVERSITY—MACON

EUGENE W. STETSON SCHOOL OF BUSINESS & ECONOMICS

GENERAL INFORMATION

Type of school	private
Affiliation	Baptist
Academic calendar	

SURVEY SAYS...

Friendly students
Happy students
Smart classrooms
Solid preparation in:
Finance
Teamwork

STUDENTS

Enrollment of MBA program	50
% male/female	50/50
% minorities	10

ACADEMICS

Academic Experience Rating	**72**
Student/faculty ratio	20:1
Profs interesting rating	71
Profs accessible rating	67
% female faculty	33
% minority faculty	15
Joint Degrees	

MBA/JD degree: 4 years

Academics

Baptist-affiliated Mercer University provides its MBAs a program that "focuses on ethical leadership and problem-solving skills" in order to give students a "competitive edge" in today's business world. Nearly all the students in this program attend part-time while working full-time. According to the school, "The program is tailored to meet the needs of individuals already employed as managers," as well as those "preparing for advancement into middle-management and administrative levels."

Incoming Mercer students should have at least 18 hours of undergraduate work in business with a grade of C or better; those lacking these credentials will need to complete an additional nine hours of graduate electives. All students must demonstrate mastery in statistics, microeconomics, and principles of finance, either through examination or successfully completed undergraduate work. Students lacking these credentials are required to take the appropriate foundation classes before beginning work on their MBA.

The heart of the Mercer MBA is a 12-course core curriculum covering financial reporting, operations management, applied microeconomic analysis, global macroeconomic environment, management and business law, corporate finance, accounting, leadership, and ethics. A seminar in strategic management, an integrative capstone class, and electives (available in accounting, economics, general business, management, MIS, and marketing) are also part of the program.

Students praise the MBA program for providing "lots of individual attention," an outcome of the school's choice to "keep class sizes small." The "solid faculty make themselves available," which is helpful since "some of the coursework is hard for people who work full-time to get done." A surprising number of students here warn that class times are too often inconvenient for full-time workers, and some suggest class time could be used more wisely ("lectures are too long!" says one). They also point out that "it would be nice to have a wider selection of classes," although they recognize that "at so small a school, it would be hard to offer more without increasing costs."

Career and Placement

The Office of Career Services at Mercer "provides support to students and alumni in the areas of decision-making and networking," according to the school catalog, which also notes that "students and alumni can view and be informed of ongoing full-time, part-time, and internship opportunities by registering on-line with SUCCESSTRAK. Annual career days, an academic majors fair, a senior kick-off event, and presentations on resume design and other job search topics" are all offered here. Students in the MBA program would like to see the services improved.

ROBERT HOLLAND, DIRECTOR OF UNDERGRADUATE ADMINISTRATION
STETSON SCHOOL OF BUSINESS AND ECONOMICS, MERCER UNIVERSITY, MACON, GA 31207 U.S.
PHONE: 478-301-2835 • FAX: 478-301-2635
E-MAIL: HOLLAND_R@MERCER.EDU • WEBSITE: WWW.MERCER.EDU

FINANCIAL FACTS

Annual tuition	$16,400
Books and supplies	$2,000

ADMISSIONS

Admissions Selectivity Rating	83
# of applications received	50
% applicants accepted	70
% acceptees attending	100
Average GMAT	575
Average GPA	3.5
TOEFL Required of International Students?	Yes
Minimum TOEFL (paper/computer)	550/213
Application fee	$50
International application fee	$50
Regular application deadline	Rolling
Regular notification	Rolling
Non-fall admissions?	Yes
Need-blind admissions?	Yes

Student Life and Environment

"Most people in the MBA program work," so "there is limited outside contact" among Mercer MBAs, "but everyone is very close in class." The pace of life here is always a little frantic because most students are juggling full-time jobs and school obligations, but "it is especially frantic around finals and midterms, in part due to the number of classes each professor teaches."

Mercer students include "a mix of people from off campus who have full-time jobs and graduate assistants, as well as other Mercer employees." They "contribute a vast array of experience that enriches the program," students tell us. The school's Baptist affiliation tends to help the school attract minorities.

Hometown Macon, a city of about 125,000, is home to three other colleges and universities, making it a serious college town. The city offers all the typical school-town prerequisites, including clubs, bowling alleys, bars, cheap eats, and plenty of shopping. Medicine is big business here, as is education; insurance is another major player, as both GEICO and the Georgia Farm Bureau Federation maintain major operations in Macon.

Admissions

Applicants to the Stetson MBA program at Mercer must provide the school with a completed application form, two sets of official transcripts from each post-secondary academic institution attended, a resume, and an official GMAT score report showing test results no more than five years old. In addition, international applicants whose first language is not English must demonstrate English proficiency both through TOEFL scores and, upon arrival at the school, a test administered by the English Language Institute of Mercer University. All students who received undergraduate degrees abroad must, at their own expense, provide an independent evaluation (and, where appropriate, a translation) of their undergraduate records. International students must additionally demonstrate the ability to finance their education at Mercer.

MICHIGAN STATE UNIVERSITY
ELI BROAD GRADUATE SCHOOL OF MANAGEMENT

GENERAL INFORMATION
Type of school	public
Environment	town
Academic calendar	semester

SURVEY SAYS...
Friendly students
Good peer network
Solid preparation in:
OperationsTeamwork
Communication/interpersonal skills

STUDENTS
Enrollment of parent institution	42,751
Enrollment of MBA program	203
% male/female	70/30
% out-of-state	63
% minorities	12
% international	32
Average age at entry	28
Average years work experience at entry	5.1

ACADEMICS
Academic Experience Rating	**81**
Profs interesting rating	70
Profs accessible rating	87
% female faculty	23
% minority faculty	7

Joint Degrees
MBA/JD Program (with Michigan State University College of Law): 4 years
MBA/MIM (with Thunderbird, The American School of International Management): 1-2 years

Prominent Alumni
Matthew Barnhill, VP, Corporate Marketing Research, BET; Susan Oaks, VP, A.T. Kearney,Inc.; James Cornelius, Chairman of the Board, Guidant Corp.; Toichi Takenaka, President and CEO, Takenaka Corp.; David Cosper, Chief Financial Officer, Ford Motor Credit Company.

Academics

At Broad School, which rhymes with "road," students can expect a collaborative, well-structured environment and one of the top supply chain management programs in the country. Students praise their fellow MBAs as "friendly and cooperative." Students add, "Our professors work with us outside of class on job searching and with case competitions as advisors."

All first-year students are required to complete the same program of core courses. Students are divided into cohorts-groups of no more than 40—and follow the same class schedule during their first semester. Cohorts switch around and re-form in the second semester to ensure that all students get a chance to work with one another and gain additional perspectives. Students enjoy working with their classmates within this system. Many students agree, "The teamwork dynamic is very good. We even have a class dedicated to it in the first five weeks of our first semester." With this focus in mind, students say that professors do "a great job helping the students realize how important it is to work well together, figure out what to do when things go south, and how to persevere and overcome difficulties working with other people."

In the first year, students build a foundation with core business courses and courses in their selected concentrations (finance, human resource management, marketing, or supply chain management). Students also can take a second concentration in one of the other three primary areas, or select from one of the secondary concentrations. In the second year, students have flexibility as they take only two required courses (strategy and ethics) with the rest consisting of their concentration electives. Students feel that Broad has "a definite presence in supply chain management." One student says, "In this field, I find the material and professors to be top-tier and highly respected. Most [professors] teach from their own textbooks or teaching modules." All students are required to take at least one class with an international perspective along with one noncredit seminar in professional development. Many students also manage to create a customized course of study in topics like business information systems, corporate accounting, international business, and leadership and chain management.

There are two joint-degree options: international business and law and business. The international business degree is acquired through cooperation with Thunderbird—the American Graduate School of International Management in Glendale, Arizona. Students enrolled in this joint-degree program receive the master's of international management from Thunderbird and the master of business administration from Michigan State University. Students say that because international management isn't a strength of their school, "the dual degree relationship with Thunderbird is a plus."

Many students believe that "availability of courses" is a problem, especially outside of the supply-chain management program. They would also like to see more electives added to the curriculum. However, most students feel that overall "the growth potential of the school is great. We already have a great supply-chain program, are building up the finance program, and our HR folks always land great jobs."

Career and Placement

Broad's alumni network is currently about 70,000, and their careers are varied—a helpful factor for any job seeker. Alumni live and work in all 50 states and 88 other countries besides the United States. One student says, "Networking is a large part of school here at MSU. The contacts I have made so far will greatly aid in finding the position I want when I graduate."

ESMERALDA CARDENAL, DIRECTOR OF ADMISSIONS, FULL TIME MBA
215 EPPLEY CENTER, EAST LANSING, MI 48824-1121 UNITED STATES
PHONE: 517-355-7604 • FAX: 517-353-1649
E-MAIL: MBA@MSU.EDU • WEBSITE: WWW.MBA.MSU.EDU

For the most part, the efforts of the career services are appreciated, but some students feel they cater too much to the school's acknowledged strength—supply-chain management. One student complains, "As for the students who are interested in entrepreneurship, forget it! The placement office doesn't even acknowledge that they exist." Another student says that though the office of career services tries, "most of my job hunting has been self-directed."

Student Life and Environment

Charming East Lansing surrounds Michigan State University and offers all of the amenities of a good college town. It is filled with bookstores, coffee houses, cinemas, and hosts annual art and music fairs. A river winds through campus, and the school boasts about a major performing arts center and two museums. Detroit is only a 90-minute drive away, and Chicago and Toronto are both within a five-hour drive. The cost of living is relatively low, and students enjoy the town's laid-back atmosphere.

According to students, the university is not lacking in social opportunities. As one student says, "Whether it's coffee in the MBA lounge, a social hour at a local restaurant/bar, an alumni reception, a tailgate, [or] whatever, there is always something going on." Broad, like most good business schools, understands that the contacts students make in school can be the most important contacts of their careers. Therefore, the school assigns social coordinators for the first year and second year classes. One student explains, "[The coordinators] send out weekly e-mails to all students letting us know what's happening that week. Some typical fall activities are canoe rides, hay rides, and bonfires."

Admissions

The Broad Admissions Committee evaluates students from many different backgrounds using the following criteria: their ability to work in teams, the quality of their work experience, leadership potential, and a very high level of motivation. This results in a very diverse program in regard to professional experiences, gender, national origin, and ethnicity. The average GMAT score of a student in the class of 2004 was 637, and the average undergraduate GPA was 3.4. The average length of work experience is five years. All international students are required to submit a TOEFL score. (If the student has graduated from an English-speaking school, a waiver request is acceptable.) The minimum score required is a 600 on the paper-based test and a score of 250 on the computer-based test.

FINANCIAL FACTS

Annual tuition (in-state/out-of-state)	$16,200/$22,700
Fees (in-state/out-of-state)	$16/$16
Books and supplies	$5,000
Room & board	$7,340
% of students receiving aid	83
% of first-year students receiving aid	84
% of students receiving loans	50
% of students receiving grants	74
Average award package	$23,490
Average grant	$8,362
Average student loan debt	$25,471

ADMISSIONS

Admissions Selectivity Rating	94
# of applications received	648
% applicants accepted	31
% acceptees attending	53
Average GMAT	637
Range of GMAT	570-740
Average GPA	3.4
TOEFL Required of International Students?	Yes
Minimum TOEFL (paper/computer)	600/250
Application fee	$85
International application fee	$85
Regular application deadline	Rolling
Regular notification	Rolling
Application Deadline/Notification	
Round 1:	11/1 / 12/17
Round 2:	1/10 / 3/4
Round 3:	3/7 / 4/29
Round 4:	5/2 / 6/3
Need-blind admissions?	Yes

APPLICANTS ALSO LOOK AT

Emory University, Indiana University, Penn State University MBA, Purdue University, The Ohio State University, University of Illinois at Urbana-Champaign, University of Michigan.

Career Rating	86	Grads employed by field	%: avg. salary
Placement rate (%)	81	Finance	23: $72,089
% grads employed immediately	61	Human Resources	5: $76,530
Average starting salary	$76,313	Marketing	10: $79,688
		Operations	34: $75,348
		Consulting	15: $89,562
		General Management	10: $75,500
		Other	3

MISSISSIPPI STATE UNIVERSITY
COLLEGE OF BUSINESS AND INDUSTRY

GENERAL INFORMATION
Type of school	public
Environment	village
Academic calendar	semester

SURVEY SAYS...
Friendly students
Happy students
Smart classrooms
Solid preparation in:
Teamwork
Communication/interpersonal skills

STUDENTS
Enrollment of parent institution	15,934
Enrollment of MBA program	140
% male/female	81/19
% out-of-state	19
% part time	54
% minorities	13
% international	6
Average age at entry	27

ACADEMICS
Academic Experience Rating	**82**
Student/faculty ratio	3:1
Profs interesting rating	79
Profs accessible rating	83
% female faculty	28
% minority faculty	11

Joint Degrees
MBA in Project Management: 1-2 years

Prominent Alumni
John C. Stennis, Former US Senator; John Grisham, Best-selling novelist; G.V. Montgomery, Former US House Representative; Jerry Thames, Former CEO of GTS, currently at Lehman Bros.; E.B. McCool, Founder, Holiday Inn Motel Chain.

Academics

The MBA program at Mississippi State's College of Business and Industry takes a broad approach to graduate business education, stressing general principles and de-emphasizing details. The idea is to expose students to a broad range of business theories and practices, a methodology students appreciate; as one put it, "The greatest strengths that I have encountered here lie in the fact that the MBA program allows students to experience and learn all aspects of business that will affect them in the future." Another student agrees, "The well-rounded design of the program is very strong. Courses are offered in every aspect of managing a business." Only a few students complain that "more in-depth material could be covered instead of the basics."

MSU's MBA program is small, resulting in "an excellent learning atmosphere in each class [and] lots of personal attention." One MBA notes, "Every professor I have had knows who I am, where I'm from, and what I want to do with my life. It's comforting to know that someone cares whether or not I am in class." Another student adds, "All of the professors are willing to help each student in class and outside of class. Many will take away from their own time and go out of their way to help a student. I know that I have become more competent and more prepared for the business world because of my experience here at Mississippi State."

MSU's program is flexible enough to accommodate both full-timers and part-time students with full-time jobs. In fact, Mississippi State's internet based distance learning program allows students to complete the entire MBA and MBA-Project Management degrees from anywhere. The school offers a wide range of business degrees, including the MBA, an MS in business administration, a master's in professional accountancy, a master's in taxation, an MS in information systems, and several PhDs. The most popular fields of specialization include finance, general management, and operations.

Career and Placement

Placement services for Mississippi State business grads are handled by the university's Career Center. The office provides all the standard career services: career counseling, job fairs, seminars, workshops, interview books, career days, and access to online job databases. But because it serves 15,000 students, it doesn't have much time to tailor services specifically to the school's more than 300 business grad students. One MBA notes, "The biggest improvement this school could make would be to get a better career-placement office. The current office is more geared toward engineering than business." Another student offers, "The school could improve in the areas of possible internships for students within the course of the program." On the plus side, the Career Center can put students in contact with MSU's considerable alumni network.

Companies that most frequently employ MSU MBAs include Amsouth Bank, BellSouth, Cintas, Exxon Mobil, International Paper, JCPenny, Shell Oil, and the U.S. General Accounting Office.

Student Life and Environment

Mississippi State University provides MBAs with a "very intimate setting, since the school makes up the majority of the town." Students love the "small-town setting and college atmosphere," telling us that "the southern charm and friendliness that surround you are the greatest strengths of MSU." Like many other southern schools, MSU has "a great sense of tradition that is upheld very well" by students, faculty, and administrators

Dr. Barbara Spencer, Director of Graduate Studies in Business
PO Drawer 5288, Mississippi State, MS 39762 United States
Phone: 662-325-1891 • Fax: 662-325-8161
E-mail: GSB@COBILAN.MSSTATE.EDU • Website: WWW.CBI.MSSTATE.EDU/GSB

alike; also like its peer institutions, it is crazy for intercollegiate athletics, particularly football. One MBA explains, "For the sports lover, we have plenty of activities like tailgating at football games. There are activities for many sporting events here." Another student adds, "You just can't match the atmosphere of the 'Left-Field Lounge' for college baseball."

Within the College of Business, the MBA Association is the most active force in extracurricular life. It "organizes intramural football, basketball, and softball teams and usually organizes an MBA Social every few weeks. The socials are usually held at local bars and restaurants, and they really give students an opportunity to get to know each other." Students also have access to "more clubs and other organizations than you can count, outdoor sports and recreation, and a very supportive local community." They love the "beautiful campus [and MSU's] state-of-the-art fitness facility that houses a weight room, eight basketball courts, a walking track, climbing wall, pool, and about 10 racquetball courts."

Most of all, though, they love the tight community formed by this small MBA program. One student describes the relationship dynamic, "You form such bonds with your classmates that you spend your outside time with them as well. It is a very tight-knit group. You spend a lot of time at the MBA lab working on projects, but it is well worth it." Another student relates an atmosphere that "is very much like a family. Classmates in general are supportive. I love the people that I am in class with. The school is very laid-back and a fun place to be."

Admissions

Admission to Mississippi State University's graduate business program, the school notes, is "based primarily on results of the Graduate Management Admission Test (GMAT), GPA over the last 60 semester hours of baccalaureate work, and past work experience." The school employs a formula to establish minimum criteria for applicants; that formula is (200 × GPA for final 60 undergraduate credit hours) + GMAT score. All applicants need a score of at least 1110. The school's website states, "Some exceptions to these standards may be granted based on the strength of other materials contained in the student's application." Mitigating factors may include the required letters of recommendation and personal statement. MSU visits a number of minority schools in its efforts to recruit underrepresented minority students.

FINANCIAL FACTS

Annual tuition (in-state/out-of-state)	$4,106/$9,306
Books and supplies	$750
Room & board (on/off-campus)	$5,265/$7,250
% of students receiving aid	66
% of first-year students receiving aid	68
Average award package	$11,603
Average grant	$1,879

ADMISSIONS

Admissions Selectivity Rating	77
# of applications received	85
% applicants accepted	62
% acceptees attending	66
Average GMAT	527
Range of GMAT	420-610
Average GPA	3.5
TOEFL Required of International Students?	Yes
Minimum TOEFL (paper/computer)	575/232
Regular application deadline	7/1
Regular notification	Rolling
Deferment Available?	Yes
Maximum length of deferment	1 year
Transfer students accepted?	Yes
Transfer application policy: 6 hours of transfer credit from accredited institutions.	
Non-fall admissions?	Yes
Need-blind admissions?	Yes

EMPLOYMENT PROFILE

		Grads employed by field:	%
Career Rating	63	Accounting	6
# of companies recruiting on-campus	365	Finance	19
% grads employed immediately	40	Human Resources	3
Average starting salary	$40,124	Marketing	9
		MIS	6
		Operations	14
		General Management	17
		Other	26

MISSOURI STATE UNIVERSITY (FORMERLY SW MISSOURI STATE U.)
COLLEGE OF BUSINESS ADMINISTRATION

GENERAL INFORMATION
Type of school	public
Environment	city

SURVEY SAYS...
Friendly students
Happy students
Smart classrooms
Solid preparation in:
Teamwork
Presentation skills

STUDENTS
Enrollment of parent institution	19,330
Enrollment of MBA program	366
% male/female	63/37
% out-of-state	5
% part-time	46
% minorities	4
% international	29
Average age at entry	29
Average years work experience at entry	2

ACADEMICS
Academic Experience Rating	74
Student/faculty ratio	20:1
Profs interesting rating	78
Profs accessible rating	75
% female faculty	34
% minority faculty	3

Prominent Alumni
David Glass, former CEO of Wal-Mart and CEO of KC Royals; Todd Tiahrt, 4-Term Congressman; Richard McClure, President of Uni Group, Inc.; Jim Smith, President American Banking Association, 2001-02; Terry Thompson, Former President, Jack Henry.

Academics

With a solid reputation in its home state and a growing reputation throughout the country, the College of Business Administration (COBA) at Missouri State University provides a "highly affordable" MBA to a diverse mix of local and international students. Students agree the College is "consistently recognized as a strong business school, especially in technology management." They also love the management and accounting departments at MSU.

Through an arrangement with both the International School of Management Studies in Chennai (Madras), Indian students can complete their "foundation" courses in India, and then complete the remainder of the program (33 credit hours) in Missouri. One of the many Indian students attending MSU writes, "The arrangement allowed me to do my prerequisite courses in India and the regular MBA in the U.S." About one third of the full-time MBA student body is international.

The College offers "true diversity among the faculty. There are conservatives as well as liberals here." Profs earn high marks for "always being willing to take extra time to help a student understand a difficult concept. They expect a lot of preparation and in turn will work their hardest to help you succeed." Most here feel that "this school is definitely headed in the right direction. Class selection is expanding, and the student population is becoming increasingly diverse. The school keeps fairly up-to-date on technology as well."

Career and Placement

MSU hosts "many career fairs, with many companies from the surrounding states recruiting here." Respondents to our survey are satisfied with the school's career center, praising its "commitment to helping students find internship opportunities during school and permanent employment after school." Nearly 400 companies visit the campus looking for full-time hires each year; a little over 100 recruit summer interns on campus. These figures apply to the entire university; the figure for how many of these companies specifically recruit MBAs is unknown.

A little more than half of MSU's MBAs remain in the region after graduation. About a third find work overseas, an unsurprising figure given the large international population. Top employers of MSU MBAs include Wal-Mart, Payless, Hallmark, Samson, FedEx, Anheuser Busch, DataTronics, Edward Jones, State Farm, Caterpillar, Occidental, Petroleum Renaissance Financial, John Hancock, Boeing, State Street, Gateway Financial, the Federal Reserve Bank, Cerner, Target, Toys R Us, Federated Insurance, Enterprise, Archer Daniels Midland, KPMG, Baird Kurtz & Dobson, Deloitte & Touche, Kirkpatrick, Phillips & Miller, CPAs, Sherwin Williams, AG Edwards, and Koch Industries.

Student Life and Environment

MBAs love the "nice and quiet city" of Springfield, with its "unique 'small town' atmosphere with all the amenities of a major city. You get the best of both worlds!" The city boasts "outdoor recreation that is second to none, with several area lakes [and state and national parks], two regional medical centers, a regional shopping mall, and minor league baseball, football, and hockey teams, and even a professional tennis team." Other amenities include "over 300 different churches to attend, plenty of nightlife in the Jordan Valley Park area, [and] several golf and racquet clubs, as well as one of the largest equestrian communities in this region of the country." With "plenty of low cost housing available [and] Branson, one of the entertainment capitals of the world, only 45 minutes away," what's not to love about Springfield?

Tobin Bushman, Graduate College Coordinator
901 South National Avenue, Springfield, MO 65804 United States
Phone: 417-836-5335 • Fax: 417-836-6888
E-mail: GraduateCollege@missouristate.edu • Website: www.coba.missouristate.edu

Best of all, students needn't even leave school grounds to find something to do because "The campus is always brimming with activity." Student organizations "regularly conduct events to keep students involved." Students advise, "Whether you get involved or not is completely up to you. You are accepted if you want to be, and never shunned." Either way you'll feel secure on this "very well-lit and safe campus. A number of safety features are offered throughout [the] campus, including a service where the Safety & Transportation officials will walk you back to your car or residence hall at night." No wonder MBA students agree that "this university is really student-oriented. Everything is done here to create good atmosphere for learning and having fun at the same time."

The rhythm of life in the COBA is such that "life goes on smoothly, and with lots of fun." There is "lots of reading and preparing for classes during the week. Every class has a group project and individual assignments. The midterm times are silent with the libraries full of studies." The weekends, on the other hand, "are crowded with students playing and cheering up." The student body here is drawn "from all different countries, which offers a vast knowledge of other cultures on top of the knowledge of business." Many come from India, where MSU participates in a twinning program to facilitate exchange students. Everyone here enjoys "a very friendly atmosphere where everyone is very helpful towards each other."

Admissions

The admissions office at MSU makes the following minimum requirements of applicants: a GPA of at least 2.75 for the final two years (60 semester hours) of undergraduate work; a minimum GMAT score of 400, with at least a 20-percentile ranking in both verbal and written portions of the test; and a minimum GPA–GMAT score of 1000 based on this formula: (undergraduate GPA in last 60 hours of undergraduate work × 200) + GMAT score. International students who do not initially meet the verbal or written requirements may be admitted conditionally and subsequently required to demonstrate English proficiency through additional testing and/or coursework. For these students, a minimum score of 550 on the paper-based TOEFL is also generally required.

FINANCIAL FACTS

Annual tuition (in-state/out-of-state)	$4,536/$9,072
Fees	$508
Books and supplies	$875
Room & board (on/off-campus)	$4,806/$5,200
% of students receiving aid	54
% of students receiving loans	41
% of students receiving grants	35
Average award package	$7,613
Average grant	$3,112
Average student loan debt	$16,500

ADMISSIONS

Admissions Selectivity Rating	76
# of applications received	173
% applicants accepted	57
% acceptees attending	68
Average GMAT	503
Range of GMAT	440-720
Average GPA	3.4
TOEFL Required of International Students?	Yes
Minimum TOEFL (paper/computer)	550/213
Application fee	$30
International application fee	$30
Regular application deadline	Rolling
Regular notification	Rolling
Deferment Available?	Yes
Maximum length of deferment	1 semester
Transfer students accepted?	Yes
Transfer application policy: Credits may be transferred with advisor's permission.	
Non-fall admissions?	Yes

APPLICANTS ALSO LOOK AT

Arkansas State University, Central Missouri State University, Southeast Missouri State University, University of Arkansas at Little Rock, University of Missouri—Kansas City, University of Missouri—Columbia, University of Missouri—St. Louis.

EMPLOYMENT PROFILE

Career Rating	70	Grads employed by field	%: avg. salary
Placement rate (%)	79	Accounting	25: $47,265
# of companies recruiting on-campus	445	Finance	10: $41,875
% grads employed immediately	62	Human Resources	5: $33,456
Average starting salary	$46,200	Marketing	15: $43,667
		MIS	18: $48,920
		Consulting	5: $39,810
		Entrepreneurship	2
		General Management	10: $40,988
		Other	10: $43,210

MONMOUTH UNIVERSITY
SCHOOL OF BUSINESS ADMINISTRATION

Academics

"The administration and professors at Monmouth University are always looking out for students' best interests," MBAs at this private institution an hour south of New York City tell us. One student observes, "Monmouth keeps up with the changing business world. For example, it added a health care program, and it is constantly updating its courses with new practices and techniques." Monmouth may not be the school for everyone—students warn that "the breadth of the subject matter offered is narrow, as there are only two concentrations, real estate and health care administration,"—but for those looking for a general degree or with interest in those specific areas, Monmouth may well fit the bill. Monmouth also offers an MBA track in accounting. The program is designed to fulfill New Jersey's requirement of 150 credit hours prior to sitting for the CPA exam.

Monmouth's general MBA requires a minimum of 30 credit hours. Note, however, that students with deficiencies in their undergraduate business educations may be required to take core courses that can increase the requirement to up to 48 hours. The accounting track requires a minimum of 33 credit hours, as does the concentration in real estate. The health care concentration requires 36 credit hours. All tracks conclude with an integrative capstone course. Students report that required courses for all MBAs provide "a good foundation in the history and evolution on a business concept." They warn that elective options are scant. One writes, "Of the many non-required courses listed in the catalog, very few are offered each semester. For example, there are only two finance courses offered for the spring 2005 term!" Even more worrisome, is that "required courses fill up quickly, and are packed full with 30 students. Sometimes a new section is added, and sometimes it isn't."

On a positive note, "professors at Monmouth have a vast amount of business experience related to the courses they teach." One student offers, "I feel confident I am learning about how things work in the real business world along the prevalent academic thinking on a given subject." Teachers also "seem to always be available for consultation before class and many other hours as well. It's nice being able to talk to the professors about concepts you may be trying to relate to the current working world, as well as concepts with which you may struggle." Students inform us that "the library is very good, with many valuable resources both print and electronic." One MBA remarks, "The computer labs are good, too. Wi-fi service is a plus; I hope they continue adding more coverage."

Career and Placement

Career services are provided to Monmouth MBAs by the Life and Career Advising Center, which serves the entire university. The office administers aptitude tests and career inventories, and provides a contact point between students and alumni and businesses. One-on-one counseling services are also available.

Student Life and Environment

Monmouth has "an absolutely beautiful campus with lovely historical buildings of import" located "one mile from the beach," a location that provides "a lot of places to go and things to do outside the classroom." Those who stick around campus long enough to socialize report, "Life at Monmouth is very active. While the school is very quiet on weekends, the weekdays are filled with fun, educational activities. There is great school spirit" fostered by "university sporting events, which the majority of students attend." Between classes, students often head for "the Java Coffee Cafe at the student center." These same students get the most out of "a wide range of clubs and a very helpful Career Advising Center staff."

KEVIN ROANE, DIRECTOR, GRADUATE ADMISSION
400 CEDAR AVENUE, WEST LONG BRANCH, NJ 07764-1898 UNITED STATES
PHONE: 732-571-3452 • FAX: 732-263-5123
E-MAIL: GRADADM@MONMOUTH.EDU • WEBSITE: WWW.MONMOUTH.EDU

For the many part-time MBA students here with major commitments outside of school, participation in extracurriculars is a rarity. One such student explains, "In part-time MBA programs, students don't really get to socialize much with their classmates. Most graduate students come to school, put their time in for classes, and then go home to their work and families. We rarely see each other outside of class. It's not the same as a full-time experience." Part-time or full-time, "the majority of graduate students at Monmouth are very friendly and are always looking to share experiences and network with new students."

Campus amenities include "plenty of study areas on campus. Recently the school added two 24-hour computer labs." Monmouth has begun to admit larger MBA classes of late. One student observes, "While the buildings are relatively new, Monmouth has expanded so much that they are already outgrowing their facilities!" Students' wish lists include more classrooms and some on-campus housing for graduate students.

Admissions

Minimum requirements for admission to the Monmouth MBA program include: a GMAT score of at least 450; a formula score of at least 1000 under the formula [(undergraduate GPA ? 200) + GMAT score]; and an overall undergraduate GPA of at least 2.75. Regular admission generally requires a minimum GMAT score of 500. For those whose undergraduate degree is more than eight years old, a GMAT score of 450 is acceptable, provided the applicant has sufficient managerial experience and produces two letters of recommendation and a detailed resume. Students who hold graduate degrees in other areas (PhD, EdD, MD, JD, CPA) may be exempted from the above admissions requirements. International students whose native language is not English must submit official TOEFL score reports in addition to all required documents listed above. Foreign language documents and transcripts must be notarized and translated (Monmouth recommends World Education Service in New York). International students must demonstrate sufficient funds to support at least their first year of study at Monmouth University and sufficient additional resources to fund completion of their degree.

FINANCIAL FACTS

Annual tuition	$10,890
Fees	$596
Books and supplies	$800
% of students receiving aid	83
% of first-year students receiving aid	73
% of students receiving loans	42
% of students receiving grants	60
Average award package	$6,684
Average grant	$1,964

ADMISSIONS

Admissions Selectivity Rating	63
# of applications received	130
% applicants accepted	90
% acceptees attending	58
Average GMAT	502
Range of GMAT	450-540
Average GPA	3.2
TOEFL Required of International Students?	Yes
Minimum TOEFL (paper/computer)	550/213
Application fee	$35
International application fee	$35
Regular application deadline	8/1
Regular notification	Rolling
Deferment Available?	Yes
Maximum length of deferment	1 year
Transfer students accepted?	Yes
Transfer application policy: Students must complete at least 30 credits at Monmouth before credits will be applied towards degree; transfer credits must be within 7 years and with acceptable grade.	
Non-fall admissions?	Yes
Need-blind admissions?	Yes

EMPLOYMENT PROFILE

Career Rating	60*
# of companies recruiting on-campus	188

MONTEREY INSTITUTE OF INTERNATIONAL STUDIES
FISHER GRADUATE SCHOOL OF INTERNATIONAL BUSINESS

Academics

With its "truly international focus," the Fisher Graduate School of International Business at the Monterey Institute of International Studies prepares students for "an exciting future [in] a world of business that is going global." At MIIS, "every course places emphasis on international aspects, from case studies to projects, and everyone speaks at least two languages." MBAs appreciate that "everyone here, from faculty to students, has international experience." Nearly half the student body is international.

The school's Monterey, CA location is a huge advantage, allowing it to "play upon the wealth of business in the San Francisco Bay area. Many top executives and CEOs frequently visit as guest speakers and offer mentorship to students." It also allows the school to "pull professors from Stanford and Berkeley for once-weekly classes and weekend-long seminars." And lastly (it almost goes without saying) Monterey provides an idyllic setting in which students can relax and devote themselves to study.

"The workload is very heavy here," MBAs report, with "lots of simulation, oftentimes in other languages so you don't always understand what is going on—much like in the real world. In these instances we have to rely on each other for translations and try alternative ways of contributing to teamwork." In addition to the curriculum, one student notes the benefits from "a great workshop series [that runs] 15 hours over one weekend exploring a specific topic in-depth with acknowledged leaders. I love the workshops. Plus, the school lets you audit them if your workload doesn't permit you to take the class for a grade." The workshops are frequently led by "visiting professors who are great resources for future career contacts and have a wealth of knowledge in their chosen field of expertise." MIIS's full-time faculty receives similarly high praise. Students say, "We are all on a first-name basis. Not only are the professors very experienced in instruction, but they are also still heavily involved in outside, real-world consulting and/or professions. They are very eager to help, but unwilling to spoon-feed."

Career and Placement

The Career Management Center (CMC) for the Fisher MBA program offers "a customized approach to each individual's goals, skill set, and educational and personal background," according to the school. The office "acts as an 'executive search firm'" to help students "target potential employers and enhance their added value" through online career assessments, one-on-one consultations, and workshops in interviewing skills, salary negotiation, internships, and networking.

Many of the students in our survey tell us however, that they would like to see "more active company involvement in recruiting at the school." They concede that the CMC faces a tough challenge: The school is too small to attract many on-campus recruiters and too new to have much in the way of an alumni network. Most recruiters, we're told, are drawn from within a 30-mile radius, and big international players are unfortunately absent. (The exceptions are NGOs and US government agencies, which do recruit here.) About one-third of Monterey's MBAs move on to jobs in the nonprofit sector. Consulting gobbles up another 20 percent. About half remain on the Pacific coast, while one in five finds work outside the United States.

Student Life and Environment

"The Business School at Monterey is very small," students point out, noting that "the entire institute has only about a thousand students at the most." Full-time MBAs number less than 100, so "students tend to be fairly tight and there is a lot of interaction

JILL STOFFERS, ENROLLMENT MANAGER
460 PIERCE STREET MONTEREY, CA 93940 UNITED STATES
PHONE: 831-647-4123 • FAX: 831-647-6405
E-MAIL: ADMIT@MIIS.EDU • WEBSITE: WWW.MIIS.EDU

between cohorts." MBAs also mix with graduate students in other programs. An MBA reports, "We have institute-wide happy hours every other Friday. There are always opportunities to socialize with fellow students, but no pressure to do things you don't feel comfortable with." Most do feel comfortable, though. As one MBA put it, "It's such a great way to get to know classmates and students in other schools, even the bookworms find a way to make it. It is a good time!"

As you might expect at a school this size, social and extracurricular life isn't exactly buzzing. However, MBAs here point out, "for graduate students wanting to study and focus, that can be a plus." Also in the plus column, "Monterey is a beautiful place to go to school." [Monterey] provides excellent additional resources, as there are two military academic institutions with libraries and research utilities that are accessible to students." Home not only to MIIS but also to the Defense Language Institute, the Navy Postgraduate School, three post-secondary schools, and Language Line Services (a provider of telephone-based interpretation), Monterey has earned its nickname of "the language capital of the world." The benefit is that this combination of schools and businesses "brings an incredible mix of people to the peninsula."

Many of those people can be found on the MIIS campus, where "about half the students are international while the Americans have all spent significant amounts of time abroad and are competent in another language." This makes it "very easy to find a conversation partner to foster an interest in many languages, including Korean, Mandarin Chinese, Arabic, French, Spanish, Italian, Japanese, and many more." Students describe the setting as "a very accurate representation of the future of the global business village. You can be exposed to and appreciate the cultures and behaviors of businesspeople from all over the world—you're interacting with them, not just reading about it in a book." Students "tend to be more collaborative than competitive, more socially responsible than purely financially motivated." The drawback: they're "inexperienced overall in business, [and] lack practical experience."

Admissions

MIIS will consider any applicant with at least a 3.0 undergraduate GPA, provided the applicant speaks English and at least one other language at an advanced (i.e., third-year undergraduate) level. Applicants must also submit GMAT scores, letters of recommendation, and a personal statement. A resume and an interview, while not required, are strongly recommended.

Prominent Alumni

Fumio Matsushima, Vice President Head at Citigroup; J.R. Williams, Vice President at Prudential Securities; Elizabeth Powell, Vice President of Customer Service at Motorola; Naoko Yanaghara, Vice President of AT&T Japan; Venkatesh Baggubati, prominent actor.

FINANCIAL FACTS

Annual tuition	$25,500
Fees	$200
Books and supplies	$900
Room & board	$7,400
% of students receiving aid	58
% of first-year students receiving aid	57
% of students receiving loans	44
% of students receiving grants	33
Average award package	$21,400
Average grant	$4,920
Average student loan debt	$45,000

ADMISSIONS

Admissions Selectivity Rating	64
# of applications received	127
% applicants accepted	90
% acceptees attending	41
Average GMAT	526
Range of GMAT	420-630
Average GPA	3.2
TOEFL Required of International Students?	Yes
Minimum TOEFL (paper/computer)	550/213
Application fee	$50
International application fee	$50
Regular application deadline	3/15
Regular notification	5/1
Transfer students accepted?	Yes
Transfer application policy: Credits must be from an AACSB accredited college or university, with a B or better. Possible to transfer up to 25% of total program. Dean makes final determination.	
Non-fall admissions?	Yes

APPLICANTS ALSO LOOK AT

Babson College, Pepperdine University, Thunderbird, University of California—Berkeley (MFE), University of California—Los Angeles, University of San Francisco, University of South Carolina.

Career Rating	63	**Grads employed by field %: avg. salary**	
% grads employed immediately	80	Accounting	5: $50,000
Average starting salary	$55,700	Finance	10: $50,000
		Marketing	15: $48,000
		Strategic Planning	5: $55,000
		Consulting	20: $67,500
		Communications	5: $50,000
		Entrepreneurship	5: $60,000
		Other	5: $50,000
		Non-profit	30: $56,000

NATIONAL UNIVERSITY OF SINGAPORE
NUS BUSINESS SCHOOL

GENERAL INFORMATION
Type of school	public
Academic calendar	August–May

SURVEY SAYS...
Students love Singapore,
Friendly students
Happy students
Smart classrooms
Solid preparation in:
Quantitative skills

STUDENTS
Enrollment of parent institution	31,346
Enrollment of MBA program	392
% male/female	75/25
% out-of-state	64
% part-time	47
% international	64
Average age at entry	29
Average years work experience at entry	5

ACADEMICS
Academic Experience Rating	**89**
Student/faculty ratio	2:1
Profs interesting rating	83
Profs accessible rating	78
% female faculty	25

Joint Degrees
NUS-Peking University IMBA: 2 years
UCLA-MUS Executive MBA

Prominent Alumni
Ms. Janet Ang, VP, Personel Systems Group, IBM Greater China Grp.; Mr. Wong Ah Long, CEO, Pacific Star Investments Development Pte Ltd.; Mr. Hsieh Fu Hua, CEO, Singapore Exchange Ltd; Mr. Peter Seah, Chairman, Singapore Technologies Engineering Ltd. and SembCorp Industries; Mr. Pratap Nambiar, Regional Partner, KPMG Asia Pacific.

Academics

By delivering a "strong curriculum with an Asian focus," the National University of Singapore Business School has developed a solid reputation in the Asia Pacific. So solid, in fact, that *Asia Inc.* magazine has rated the program among the region's top three MBA programs every year since 1999 and recently ranked the school among the top 15 programs in all of Asia. The magazine cited curriculum, joint programs with such solid institutions as Peking University and UCLA, and the school's reputation among administrators at other MBA programs as the main reasons for its high ranking.

NUS offers both a full-time and part-time MBA. The full-time program is truly international, drawing students from as many as 20 countries around the globe. Both programs consist of 10 core modules and seven elective modules, with electives available in finance and banking, international business, management and organization, management of technology, marketing, strategic management, and decision sciences. Students speak most highly of the finance and marketing courses. Some feel that "the fact that students are required to take 10 core courses leaves them with less time to delve into a specific concentration. Also, courses in communication are conspicuously absent."

In all areas, MBAs agree, the "faculty is the biggest strength. Most of the professors are experienced lecturers from renowned universities in the United States, Canada, and Europe, and they are mostly very knowledgeable in their respective fields." Profs are also "concerned about the student's progress and are always willing to help," which students appreciate. To supplement instruction, "the business school brings in lecturers with working experiences. Such moves allow the lecturers to give insight on how theoretical models could be applied in the actual business world." NUS MBAs warn that "the academic work is a killer, with a heavy workload that lacks time for personal development, generally. Still, it's manageable," in part because of the "easily accessible resources through well-established IT infrastructure, IVLE tools, and wireless Internet connection throughout the campus."

Career and Placement

The MBA Career Services Office at NUS offers the following services: job postings, recruitment talks by employers, career workshops and panel discussions, and on-campus interviews for internships and full-time jobs. The school reports that 60 to 80 employers recruit graduating students each year; 30 to 40 employers recruit summer interns. Students have mixed feelings about the office; some praise both it and the "strong alumni network," while others complain that "career services is nonexistent for most part of the year."

Top employers of NUS MBAs include Barclays, JP Morgan, Ernst & Young, World Bank, Microsoft, KPMG, Pricewaterhouse Coopers, Nestle, Shell, Siemens, Walt Disney TV, Agilent Technology, Avanade, Bax Global, Citigroup Asset Mgt., Courts, DBS Bank, Exxon Mobil, and HP. In the school's most recent employment survey, all students who responded were employed in the region.

Ms. Audrey Yuen, MBA Programs Office
BIZ 2 Building, 1 Business Link, Level 5, Singapore, 117592 Singapore
Phone: 011-065-6874-8871 • Fax: 011-065-6872-4423
E-mail: nusmba@nus.edu.sg • Website: www.bschool.nus.edu.sg

Student Life and Environment

Due to the heavy workload, students tell us that life in the NUS MBA program "revolves around class work, case studies, [and] projects. Time for external community activities is limited." One MBA explains, "Student life has never been a breeze, especially when there are tests and project deadlines. You'll feel like cursing yourself and asking why on earth you're putting yourself through all this in the middle of the night when you're trying to rush out that finance project by 9:00 A.M. the next day. But when it's all over, you'll feel really happy that you've had the chance to go through all that, sweating it out and learning invaluable knowledge while doing the project." When students can break away from their studies, they "try to use it well." Students note that "extracurricular activities in the form of clubs are limited for the school, although there is every opportunity available with a number of activities [and] clubs available for post-graduate students for the university overall."

The NUS student body is "very diverse, with students from different nationalities and different industries. The mixture of part-time students and full-time students enable students to share working experiences and even work on projects from the part-timers' companies." Getting up to speed on life in Singapore is a breeze because "the local students help the foreigners adapt to Singapore life quickly." Women in the program warn that "there are relatively few women, and there is a very slight undercurrent of sexism among the student body." On the positive side, NUS is "a safe environment [where] a lady can jog on campus even at three o'clock in the morning without feeling unsafe."

Admissions

Applicants to NUS School of Business must provide the admissions office with transcripts for all undergraduate and graduate work, GMAT scores, TOEFL scores (for nonnative English speakers), a personal statement, letters of recommendation, and a resume demonstrating at least two years of post-baccalaureate professional experience. The admissions committee also reviews the application for evidence of "the attitude and aptitude of applicant, leadership skills, entrepreneurial quality, and value to alumni." The school's website notes that an "acceptable" GMAT score is one above 600. Scholarships are available.

FINANCIAL FACTS

Annual tuition	$8,455
Books and supplies	$362
Room & board (on/off-campus)	
	$5,024/$2,355
% of students receiving aid	100
% of first-year students receiving aid	100
% of students receiving loans	100
% of students receiving grants	13
Average grant	$2,657

ADMISSIONS

Admissions Selectivity Rating	99
# of applications received	883
% applicants accepted	10
% acceptees attending	91
Average GMAT	672
Range of GMAT	620-700
TOEFL Required of International Students?	Yes
Minimum TOEFL (paper/computer)	620/260
International application fee	$200
Regular application deadline	2/28
Regular notification	5/1
Early decision program?	Rolling
Deferment Available?	Yes
Maximum length of deferment	1 year
Transfer students accepted?	No

EMPLOYMENT PROFILE

		Grads employed by field:	%
Career Rating	61	Finance	9
Placement rate (%)	86	Marketing	16
# of companies recruiting on-campus	120	MIS	3
% grads employed immediately	54	Operations	15
Average starting salary	$28,382	Strategic Planning	12
		Consulting	10
		General Management	27
		Global Management	2
		Quantitative	2
		Other	4

NAVAL POSTGRADUATE SCHOOL
THE GRADUATE SCHOOL OF BUSINESS AND PUBLIC POLICY

GENERAL INFORMATION
Type of school	public
Academic calendar	

SURVEY SAYS...
Students love Monterey, CA

ACADEMICS
Academic Experience Rating	**65**
Student/faculty ratio	10:1
Profs interesting rating	82
Profs accessible rating	88

Academics

At the Graduate School of Business and Public Policy at the Naval Postgraduate School, the MBA that you receive is uniquely defense-focused. Designed to educate officers in the armed forces as well as civilian employees of the Department of Defense (DoD), the school focuses its education exclusively on the current management practices that will be useful in a defense-related position. This does not by any means indicate that the education is below the standards of other schools. As one student puts it, an MBA from the Naval Postgraduate School means a "quality education for no charge from exceptional personnel. The majority of students are navy, but a growing amount of them are from other services and governmental agencies." Still, keep in mind that ordinary civilians—those who are not affiliated with the DoD or armed services—need not apply. This is a shame; as one student says, "the school is great! It's too bad civilians can't attend."

The Naval Postgraduate School is in the unique position to offer, in its own words, an "interdisciplinary approach to problem-solving and policy analysis by applying quantitative, financial, economics, information technology, and other state-of-the-art management techniques and concepts to military management and policy issues." And a graduate of the Naval Postgraduate School's MBA program is guaranteed to "know the latest management theory and practices, embracing leadership, communication, organization design, and planning within large public and private-sector organizations, as well as military sub-units and activities."

To satisfy the unique objectives of the program, an MBA from the Naval Postgraduate School takes 18 months. There's the 33 business core (33 credit hours), the 18 mission-related core (18 credit hours), and the master's application project or thesis. For the most part, students are enthusiastic about their classes. As one puts it, "the professors are experts in their field but respect us as military officers, so the rapport is very good. They are extremely accessible and many will keep in touch even after graduation." Still, many feel overly taxed by the intense concentration of education in such a short period of time. As one says, "the course load is very heavy, and we are made to finish in a very short time period (much less than civilians who choose [what] school they go to). They should either lighten the load or make the length of schooling longer." In addition, "being a military school, joint professional/military education is also a requirement. All said, there is little room left over for anything but school." Still, students are enthusiastic and claim with pride that they attend a "great defense/public policy-oriented program."

Career and Placement

Placement and recruiting are less of an issue at the Naval Postgraduate School, since most of the students are already employed by the United States military and are working toward a degree that will more or less ensure them a job with the Department of Defense. As one student puts it, "this school is geared for people involved in government service of some type. Therefore, it is unnecessary to have employment recruiters or job fairs on campus." And another points out that "the school's contacts with Department of Defense and contractors provide some pretty amazing research possibilities to include sponsoring of students to work on real-world issues."

TRACEY HAMMON,
ONE UNIVERSITY CIRCLUE MONTEREY, CA 93943 UNITED STATES
WEBSITE: WWW.NPS.NAVY.MIL

FINANCIAL FACTS
Annual tuition $0

ADMISSIONS
Admissions Selectivity Rating 60*

Student Life and Environment

Although, like all students, Naval Postgraduate MBAs complain about the workload, the beauty of their natural surroundings (the Monterey Peninsula in Northern California) leaves little room for complaints. As one student puts it, "I can't think of a more gorgeous place to go to school. There is plenty to do outside of school. Whether you're a golfer, kayaker, biker, scuba diver, or you just like to take pleasant oceanfront walks, you'll find something you'll love to do here." Because the school itself was built on the grounds of an aging luxury resort, "the campus preserves the sense of being on a resort. The administration building is located in the old main building of the hotel and is absolutely gorgeous. The gardens are still well tended and it is not uncommon to see peacocks and geese strutting about campus." Another adds, "Monterey is a beautiful location with plenty to do. Beach parties, skiing trips, whale watching, professional sports, and trips to national parks are usually ongoing for student to participate in." The only problem, it seems, is finding the time to enjoy it all. One student complains, "I thought I'd have a lot more time for golf. But I guess it beats being on a boat!"

Despite the grandeur of the physical surroundings, some students feel compelled to point out that "the biggest issue with the Naval Postgraduate School is the cost of living. This is something the school cannot do anything about. It is located in a beautiful luxury vacation area that requires a hefty wallet to support it." Others add, "the housing we live in is substandard—way too small and 50 years old with no improvements been done on them. The navy does not pay enough of a housing allowance to live in the community, so it is prohibitively expensive." In addition, some students who arrive at the school with families find it difficult. According to one, "there is little for children to do," and another complains that "there are no organized functions at the school—those few things that students do together they organize themselves."

Admissions

Requirements for admission to the Graduate School of Business and Public Policy at the Naval Postgraduate School are a little different from most MBA programs. For one thing, civilians—that is those not enlisted in a branch of the military or in government work—are not admitted at all. The school points out, however, that quality is not affected by limiting the applicant pool. To be considered, "a baccalaureate degree with above-average grades is required." In addition, an APC score of 345 is required. The admissions board says that, at the Naval Postgraduate School, "officers from the U.S. services and DoD employees may start the program with widely varied academic backgrounds. Each student's prior academic work and related military and civilian experiences are evaluated for courses previously completed and applicable to the student's concentration area for possible validation examination to satisfy some required core courses."

EMPLOYMENT PROFILE	
Career Rating	60*
% grads employed immediately	100

NEW MEXICO STATE UNIVERSITY
COLLEGE OF BUSINESS ADMINISTRATION AND ECONOMICS

Academics

"Of all strengths" exhibited by the College of Business Administration and Economics at New Mexico State University, "the administration/faculty/staff are the greatest components of the business college," students agree. NMSU, which offers a general MBA with the opportunity to forge an area of specialization in agribusiness, international business, or information systems, has a faculty that is "very helpful and friendly, approachable, encouraging, and respectful of our contributions. Some of them are the greatest teachers." Students have their pet theories about how NMSU attracts its teachers, especially the more experienced ones: "A big reason senior faculty are so prevalent at NMSU is because the wonderful climate," explained one MBA.

The NMSU curriculum consists of thirty hours of required courses, including a capstone course that culminates in a term paper, which must be defended in an oral examination. The school's website states that "while there are no elective courses required in the MBA degree program, students are encouraged to take any additional coursework that fits their interests. Careful scheduling may enable interested students to complete the requirements of a minor or specialization during their courses of study." Students love the curriculum's focus on in-class discussion, telling us that "the class discussion always gives a lot of benefits to students. Because of the super friendly people here, the student always enjoys being in school." However, they wish that the curriculum would reduce the number of lecture courses and incorporate more case studies and hands-on lessons.

The program is among the nation's more affordable, especially for in-state students. One student observes, "Considering the cost of tuition and the value of education at NMSU, there is no other program in the region that can compete. Most would say the business college is a 'diamond in the rough.'" The bargain-basement price occasionally impacts school policy, as when profs have to teach courses outside their fields of expertise; one MBA notes, "The professors are knowledgeable in their fields, but when the university has some [of them] teach other courses outside of their field, that makes it difficult. They struggle with structuring the class instruction to the needs of the students. My overall experience here at NMSU has been great otherwise."

Unlike most state schools, NMSU's MBA program is well run. Students tell us that "NMSU's administration does an admirable job keeping things running smoothly," and that "the business administration is very organized and helpful to students." They also appreciate how the school is "moving into the future by utilizing technology for registering and tuition payments" (among other areas).

Career and Placement

NMSU's Placement and Career Services office provides university students with on-campus employment, internship listings, career listings, workshops, advising, job fairs, and online research tools. The annual Career Expo is the main on-campus recruiting event; because it serves the entire school, only some of the hundreds of companies who visit during the Expo are seeking MBA students. Top employers in the Las Cruces area include Border Foods, the City of Las Cruces, Excell Agent Services, Memorial Medical Center, NASA, New Mexico State University, Wal-Mart, and White Sands Missile Range.

Dr. R. Wayne Headrick, Director, MBA Program
114 Guthrie Hall, MSC 3GSP, Las Cruces, NM 88003-8001 United States
Phone: 505-646-8003 • Fax: 505-646-7977
E-mail: mba@nmsu.edu • Website: http://mba.nmsu.edu

Student Life and Environment

MBAs enjoy a "very mellow and enjoyable life on campus, with a true Southwest climate." The "laid-back atmosphere" is enhanced by "helpful and friendly people, a great education at a low cost, a nice campus, and a climate that is also a great bonus." A confluence of white, Chicano, and Mexican populations (as well as smaller Black and Indian populations) contributes to this "culturally rich area in and around Las Cruces." The student body reflects the region's diversity; MBAs boast that "this is a very multicultural school, no question. The fact that we are a Land Grant institution and highly rated by the Carnegie Foundation helps." Students also love the "pristine location" in this agricultural area bordered on the east by the Organ Mountains.

NMSU works students hard, but not too hard. One MBA explains that "life at school is at a comfortable pace. Professors are willing to push you as far as you are willing. You are not held to any outrageous standards. In fact, you really have an opportunity to discover your own limits and capabilities." Most students work at least part-time, which they can do since classes are held at night. Some students find time for extracurricular activities, such as Delta Sigma Pi, the Professional Business Fraternity; Sigma Iota Epsilon, the Professional Management Fraternity; and numerous professional associations, cultural-heritage groups, and national honor societies.

Admissions

New Mexico State University requires applicants to provide official copies of all transcripts for graduate and undergraduate work, as well as GMAT scores. International applicants must also submit TOEFL scores. NMSU uses the formula GPA x GMAT to eliminate candidates; successful applicants must score at least a 1400 under the formula. All students must demonstrate proficiency in financial accounting, macroeconomics, statistics and calculus, as well as some familiarity with the program's core areas of analysis and markets, domestic and global economic environments of organizations, financial reporting, human behavior in organizations, and the creation and distribution of goods and services.

FINANCIAL FACTS

Annual tuition (in-state/out-of-state)	$3,624/$11,550
Books and supplies	$1,000
Room & board (on/off-campus)	$5,200/$7,000
% of students receiving aid	95
% of first-year students receiving aid	19
% of students receiving grants	23

ADMISSIONS

Admissions Selectivity Rating	75
# of applications received	73
% applicants accepted	60
% acceptees attending	59
Average GMAT	491
Range of GMAT	440-550
Average GPA	3.7
TOEFL Required of International Students?	Yes
Minimum TOEFL (paper/computer)	530/197
Application fee	$30
International application fee	$50
Regular application deadline	7/4
Regular notification	8/4
Deferment Available?	Yes
Maximum length of deferment	1 year
Transfer students accepted?	Yes
Transfer application policy: A maximum of 12 semester credits from AACSB schools.	
Non-fall admissions?	Yes
Need-blind admissions?	Yes

EMPLOYMENT PROFILE			
Career Rating	61	Grads employed by field: %	
# of companies recruiting on-campus	350	Accounting	7
% grads employed immediately	11	Finance	2
Average starting salary	$40,000	Marketing	5
		Operations	2
		Consulting	2
		General Management	7
		Quantitative	2

NEW YORK UNIVERSITY
LEONARD N. STERN SCHOOL OF BUSINESS

GENERAL INFORMATION

Type of school	private
Environment	metropolis
Academic calendar	semester

SURVEY SAYS...

Students love New York, NY
Friendly students
Good social scene
Happy students
Smart classrooms
Solid preparation in:
Finance
Quantitative skills

STUDENTS

Enrollment of parent institution	53,709
Enrollment of MBA program	2,468
% male/female	67/33
% part-time	69
% minorities	12
% international	28
Average age at entry	27
Average years work experience at entry	4.9

ACADEMICS

Academic Experience Rating	**99**
Student/faculty ratio	4:1
Profs interesting rating	90
Profs accessible rating	97

Joint Degrees
MBA/JD: 4 years
MA/MBA (with the Institute of French Studies): 3 years
MA/MBA (with the Department of Politics): 3 years
MPA/MBA (with the School of Public Administration): 3 years

Prominent Alumni
Richard Fuld, Chairman and CEO of Lehman Brothers Holdings, Inc.;
Thomas E. Freston, Co-Pres. and Co-Chief Operating Officer, Viacom;
Abby F. Kohnstamm, Senior Vice President of Marketing, IBM; Robert Greifeld, President and Chief Executive Officer of the Nasdaq;
Kathleen Corbet, President, Standard & Poor's.

Academics

Students at NYU's Leonard N. Stern School of Business are quick to point out that "business schools need to keep pace with the business environment" and even quicker to point out that there may be no better place in the world to do that than New York City. Stern students celebrate the fact that their prime location makes it "well-connected with the large financial institutions [and boast that] there are countless internships offered throughout the school year and opportunities to supplement course work with practical experience." In addition, Stern's location allows it to attract top business people as adjunct faculty. From them, students get practical training and valuable connections. "I've been taught by many 'celebrity'-level professors," says one student. "How many schools have Nobel Prize winners teaching economics?"

Still, celebrity won't mean lack of access, according to most Sternies: "One professor finally had to declare the men's room off-limits to get a little peace. That's the only limit I've ever heard a teacher set on accessibility." And almost everyone agrees that the faculty "teaches concepts in a clear and concise manner and demonstrates how they operate in a real-world context. I could not ask for a more rewarding and challenging academic experience."

With the rapid changes taking place in business today, Stern has made a conscious effort to adapt and change. According to the school, "an international perspective has been formally incorporated into the core program." The core program is covered in the first two semesters with a capstone core course in the second year. There is flexibility to waive by undergraduate degree or proficiency exams certain of the 8 core courses. This allows students to take more elective courses in their program. Summer internships between the first and second years are a critical part of the students' overall MBA experience.

All students graduate with an MBA and can choose as many as three specializations or decide to pursue only a general management degree. And many students believe that, though "some areas such as management lag behind the school's core strength in finance, [Stern is] making a genuine attempt to steer the image from being just a finance school to a general-management school."

Special programs and initiatives abound at Stern. They claim to be able to use New York City as a "learning laboratory," and it shows. In the integrated development program, select first-year students receive a year of in-depth mentoring from alumni and recent graduates working in the students' field of interest. In the Stern Consulting Corps, students work at nonprofits and small businesses all around the city. Student exchange programs send potential MBAs overseas for long- or short-term programs (to Germany, Denmark, and Argentina, most recently). In the Stern Speakers Lunch program, select students wine and dine some of today's best-known business leaders. With all that's going on, it is no wonder most students claim to feel "a strong sense of momentum and energy at the school that is completely revitalizing."

Career and Placement

Being between Wall Street and Midtown definitely has its perks for Stern's Office of Career Development. Recruiters such as American Express, Bank of New York, Bear Stearns & Company Inc., Citigroup, Deloitte Touche Tohmatsu, Goldman Sachs, and JPMorgan Chase all have a strong presence at the school. As one student says, "There is a huge emphasis on career here. It's overwhelming at first, and then you realize how great it is. After all, that is why you are here. Everything is right here—anyone you want to meet with anything you want to do." If there is a downside to this, it is that Stern tends

DINA DOMMETT, ASSISTANT DEAN, MBA ADMISSIONS
44 WEST 4TH STREET, SUITE 6-70, NEW YORK, NY 10012 UNITED STATES
PHONE: 212-998-0600 • FAX: 212-995-4231
E-MAIL: STERNMBA@STERN.NYU.EDU • WEBSITE: WWW.STERN.NYU.EDU

FINANCIAL FACTS

Annual tuition	$34,000
Fees	$1,760
Books and supplies	$1,300
Room & board	$17,320
% of students receiving aid	79
% of first-year students receiving aid	75
% of students receiving loans	68
% of students receiving grants	46
Average award package	$45,873
Average grant	$14,859
Average student loan debt	$65,564

ADMISSIONS

Admissions Selectivity Rating	97
# of applications received	3,403
% applicants accepted	22
% acceptees attending	48
Average GMAT	700
Range of GMAT	650-750
Average GPA	3.4
TOEFL Required of International Students?	Yes
Minimum TOEFL (paper/computer)	600/250
Application fee	$175
International application fee	$175
Regular application deadline	3/15
Regular notification	6/1
Non-fall admissions?	Yes
Need-blind admissions?	Yes

to rely rather heavily on employers within New York City's limits. "Since the school is in New York, having access to many investment banks is not as spectacular an accomplishment on the part of the school as it is a facet of the New York City location. The Office of Career Development needs to focus much more on establishing relationships outside of the core New York City recruiters." According to the school, "while students do accept positions nationally and internationally, by and large students that come to Stern for a 2 year educational experience wind up falling in love with New York and staying. Moreover, its location is a mecca for several key industries and provides Stern students with a broad range of opportunities that meet their career objectives."

Though students report good relations with alumni, particularly those who participate in the Integrated Development Program, others gripe that Stern has only "recently established a formal alumni relations office, and so it is slightly behind other schools in that respect."

Student Life and Environment

For students at Stern, the consensus seems to be that life in the city is fabulous. "We're in the middle of New York City! How could life be any less than fantastic?" one MBA asks. From free music in Washington Square to museums, from fashion shows to ferry rides, Stern's campus boasts all of the advantages of New York City. "Stern is a city school. There's a lot going on outside the campus, and people take advantage. Also, lots of Stern students lived in NYC before school, so they already have social lives that exist outside school. That said, I think there's still a decent amount of social activity around the school." Of course Stern also offers some of the disadvantages of New York City. Some students not native to the city feel that "it is harder to make friends with people in a school in New York City as many people have established their own lives." Overall, though, students seem to enjoy the life. One student relates, "From Thursday night Beer Blasts to a 13-day trip to South Africa where I went cage-diving with white sharks, I've enjoyed every moment of bonding with my classmates and made great friends from the start."

Admissions

Stern admits somewhere between 350 to 400 students each year. The average GMAT score of an admitted full-time MBA student is 700, and the average GPA is 3.4. Almost all the undergraduate degrees of admitted students are in business, math, science and engineering, or economics. Very few were in arts and humanities. Though mastery of English is required for all applicants to Stern, they do not have a minimum TOEFL score requirement.

EMPLOYMENT PROFILE

Career Rating	97	Grads employed by field	%: avg. salary
Placement rate (%)	90	Finance	57: $133,466
% grads employed immediately	80	Marketing	20: $112,627
Average starting salary	$125,443	Operations	2: $96,500
		Consulting	15: $117,748
		General Management	3: $123,571
		Other	3: $142,667

NORTHEASTERN UNIVERSITY
COLLEGE OF BUSINESS ADMINISTRATION

Academics

Northeastern University has long been known as a leader in the field of cooperative education, and full-time MBAs here benefit from the school's expertise through a six-month co-op program that "puts students with brand-name corporations. The program provides a venue for students to apply and prove themselves in the industry they desire." Students love both the idea and the execution of co-op—it is the number-one reason cited by full-time students for choosing Northeastern. They report that "the six month co-op opportunity allows students to graduate with measurable real-world experience, unlike schools that offer six-week internships. NEU has strong relationships with a lot of Boston's biggest companies. Especially if you are looking to gain experience in a new field, this program is great." As an added bonus, a "co-op pays pretty well, too!"

Approximately one-third of MBAs at NEU enroll in the full-time Co-op MBA Program, which can typically be completed in 20 to 24 months. The curriculum consists of foundation courses, interdisciplinary courses that build upon competencies covered in foundation courses, elective work (concentrations are available in accounting, corporate finance, corporate renewal, entrepreneurship, information technology, international business, investments, marketing, and supply chain management), and co-op (optional, but most students opt in). Students report that "the required full-time courses tend to be more challenging than the electives (which are offered in the evenings to accommodate both the full and part-time students)" and praise their professors, telling us that they are "very well-regarded in their field." One student notes, "Several professors have produced highly influential research studies, and many are accomplished professionals in the private/public sectors." Another mentions, "All of my professors have been ivy-league educated, and have taught at many of the leading business schools around the country. The administrators are very accessible as well, and all of my concerns have been addressed promptly."

Northeastern also offers a part-time MBA consisting of 12 core courses and nine electives. Part-time students typically take between two and seven years to finish the degree, taking one or two classes per semester in once-a-week evening and/or Saturday sessions. The school notes that it is possible for students who begin in the part-time program to switch over to the co-op program (and vice versa) "if it is done early enough for the career center to place you in a co-op job." Note, however, that admission to one program does not guarantee the right to transfer to the other, and requests for transfer are handled on a case-by-case basis. Other degree options at Northeastern include a high tech MBA (for tech experts seeking business acumen), an Executive MBA, master's programs in accounting, finance, and taxation, and certificate programs in advanced study of business administration, supply chain management, and taxation.

Career and Placement

Northeastern's co-op program necessitates that the school forge strong connections to Boston-area businesses, and these relationships pay dividends for the efforts of the school's Career Center. "Our Career Center's Co-op placement efforts and relationships with companies for that purpose are outstanding," explains one student. Co-op employers in 2004 included Bayer, Blue Cross Blue Shield, Fidelity Investments, Manulife Financial, Masterfoods, Neutrogena, Sun Microsystems, and Terrapin Capital. NEU students agree the co-op program definitely provides students with a leg up when it comes time for their co-op companies to hire new full-timers.

FINANCIAL FACTS

Annual tuition	$25,700
Fees	$395
Books and supplies	$1,500
Average grant	$20,000

ADMISSIONS

Admissions Selectivity Rating	75
# of applications received	426
% applicants accepted	78
% acceptees attending	59
Average GMAT	581
Average GPA	3.1
TOEFL Required of International Students?	Yes
Minimum TOEFL (paper/computer)	600/250
Regular application deadline	4/15
Regular notification	Rolling
Deferment Available?	Yes
Maximum length of deferment	1 year
Transfer students accepted?	Yes
Transfer application policy: Please visit website for transfer policy.	
Non-fall admissions?	Yes
Need-blind admissions?	Yes

All told, more than 50 companies typically recruit MBAs on campus each year; another 80 come looking for summer interns and co-op employees. Employers most likely to hire Northeastern MBAs after graduation include TJX Corporation, Raytheon Company, Masterfoods, Maersk Logistics, WR Grace, Texas Instruments, Mellon Financial Corporation, and the State Street Corporation.

Student Life and Environment

Full-time students in Northeastern's MBA program describe a "very close-knit group" of students who "go out with each other every week and often have get-togethers outside of school. The business school also sets up weekly events that we all go to." The program helps, as "classes stress group work, and students have a chance to bond and form lifetime friendships" through group work. So too does life in Boston, a city that "is good fun. You can live, shop, and go to school in the best parts of Boston. Newbury, Commonwealth, and Marlborough Streets are all only a couple of blocks away." Part-time students, on the other hand, are generally too busy with work and family commitments to participate regularly in extracurricular life.

The Northeastern student body "is very diverse with students from all areas. Aside from US students, there are international students from Asia, Africa, Europe, Central/South America, and the Caribbean represented. This gives students a global business perspective and a chance to share different ideas." MBAs observe that "the student body is a happy medium of older students who are more career-focused and younger students who want to enjoy the grad-school lifestyle."

Admissions

All applicants to the Northeastern MBA program must provide the Admissions Office with the following: a completed application in the form of either a hard-copy (preferably typed) or online; sealed copies of official transcripts for all post-secondary schools attended; a current resume; three essays; two professional letters of recommendation; and an official GMAT score report. In addition, international students whose first language is not English must submit TOEFL results. All international students must submit transcripts that have been translated with U.S. grade equivalents assigned for work completed, as well as a certified Declaration and Certification of Finances Statement. Neither an undergraduate degree in business nor previous work experience is required for admission to the program, although those lacking both are unlikely candidates for admission. The school advises such students to take college-level introductory business courses prior to or while applying to the school.

Career Rating	80	Grads employed by field: %	
Placement rate (%)	86	Finance	40
# of companies recruiting on-campus	53	Human Resources	4
% grads employed immediately	51	Marketing	22
Average starting salary	$63,000	MIS	3
		Operations	5
		Consulting	19
		General Management	3
		Other	6

NORTHERN ARIZONA UNIVERSITY
COLLEGE OF BUSINESS ADMINISTRATION

Academics

Students who are in a hurry to get their MBAs might want to consider the program at Northern Arizona University, whose "big strength is the fact that the program is compressed into 10 months. While it is hell completing those 10 months, we all know we won't have to spend another year in school, and we'll be able to start our careers earlier than if we had chosen a different MBA program." Those who love beautiful surroundings are in for an added bonus; NAU's Flagstaff campus is surrounded by the world's largest ponderosa pine forest, which in turn is bordered by the San Francisco Peaks. The campus setting is simply gorgeous.

Because of the intensive curriculum, however, students rarely have time to take in the stunning scenery. Course work begins with a five-week summer session that starts in early July; the summer session covers PC and communication skills for professionals, system orientation, and a survey of human-asset issues. Three core courses and two electives make up the fall semester, which "focuses on organizational processes that provide customer value." The spring semester, which consists of two core courses and two electives, centers on analytical approaches to managerial decision-making. Students may use their electives to forge a concentration in one of three areas of new emphasis: accounting, finance, or general management. In the summer of 2006, three new career tracks will be introduced: Marketing Analysis & Distribution Management, Environmental Management, and Geographic Information Systems. The last two will be in partnership with the renowned programs in GIS and Environmental Sciences at Northern Arizona University.

Students tell us that the entire curriculum stresses "a teamwork environment, integrated studies, topical issues, and plenty of case studies." They appreciate this approach, explaining, "the collaborative environment and emphasis on team projects help [them] learn to work well with others and show [them] that the output is better and [they] learn more." The school website reinforces this point, stating that "the goal of the core curriculum is to develop an integrated systems perspective that facilitates management of functional areas as a related unit. This integrative approach to curriculum is essential to quality systems approaches that increasingly focus on continuous improvement to enhance customer value." NAU MBAs give the faculty a thumbs-up, noting that "we have some excellent professors who are well known in the academic world."

Career and Placement

NAU MBAs receive personalized career development advising from the MBA Director. In addition, students take a 1 credit hour course in Career Management during both the Fall and Spring semesters. Throughout the year, employers participate in workshops, mock interviews, and company presentations. Students feel that "the placement office could do a better job of bringing recruiters up to meet [them]," but concede that "it's difficult for a small public school high up in the mountains" to attract such traffic. Between 40 and 50 companies pay recruiting visits to the campus each year.

Top employers of NAU MBAs include Intel, Pulte Homes, and General Dynamics. About one in five graduates finds a first job outside the United States.

TED BOURAS, DIRECTOR, MBA PROGRAM
PO BOX 15066, FLAGSTAFF, AZ 86011-5066 UNITED STATES
PHONE: 928-523-7342 • FAX: 928-523-7996
E-MAIL: MBA@NAU.EDU • WEBSITE: WWW.CBA.NAU.EDU/MBA

Student Life and Environment

Full-timers at NAU finish their MBAs in less than a year's time, which makes for an extremely accelerated academic pace. One explains, "since the NAU MBA is less than one year in length, it is very intense. There is little time to spend on anything other than school. Although school is demanding, the workload is manageable." Another adds, "when not studying (which is rare), time is usually spent downtown at the bars or at small parties held by other MBA students." Flagstaff's bars "are numerous," we're told, and students in the program "enjoy getting together, especially on Thursday nights. We hit the bars to decompress."

While Flagstaff is hardly a booming economic center, it does have its benefits, especially for students in an intensive program like NAU's. One student explains, "the pace of life in Flagstaff is slower and less stressful than other places. It's laid back, and there really is time to smell the roses (or pine trees) when we're not in class, which isn't often." The region offers plenty of opportunities to blow off steam in a healthy way; many "enjoy the outdoors (rock climbing [or] mountain biking) and they love the environment to do those activities. It's beautiful here, and doing outdoor activities is a must when living in Flagstaff." The mountain location means that things never get too hot in the summer (the average high temperature is 81 degrees F) and that skiing is readily available in the winter. The campus is not too far from Sedona and the Grand Canyon.

Students currently enjoy "modern resources such as multimedia presentation facilities, three computer-equipped classrooms, two state-of-the-art student computer laboratories, and classrooms, offices, and labs that all have access to the Internet." Future MBAs will enjoy a whole lot more; construction began on a new College of Business Administration facility in May 2004. The 110,000-square-foot facility, complete with 8 breakout rooms, 20 team-meeting rooms, and a number of network-ready public space, will be ready for occupancy in January 2006.

Admissions

The admissions committee at NAU requires applicants to submit official copies of all undergraduate and graduate transcripts, GMAT scores, two required essays, two letters of recommendation, and a resume. MBA students are required to possess a common body of knowledge (CBK), covered at NAU in its CBK classes. All CBK course work must be completed successfully before a student can register for a 600-level class (these are core courses that are offered during summer session II).

FINANCIAL FACTS

Annual tuition (in-state/out-of-state)	$5,867/$14,515
Fees	$3,500
Books and supplies	$1,295
Room & board (on-campus)	$7,520
% of students receiving aid	80

ADMISSIONS

Admissions Selectivity Rating	78
# of applications received	53
% applicants accepted	58
% acceptees attending	65
Average GMAT	529
Range of GMAT	470-570
Average GPA	3.48
TOEFL Required of International Students?	Yes
Minimum TOEFL (paper/computer)	600/250
Application fee	$50
International application fee	$50
Regular application deadline	5/1
Regular notification	6/1
Early decision program?	Yes
ED Deadline/Notification	11/1 / 12/1
Deferment Available?	Yes
Maximum length of deferment	1 year
Transfer students accepted?	Yes
Transfer application policy: 9 hours are transferable towards elective credits only.	
Non-fall admissions?	Yes
Need-blind admissions?	Yes

EMPLOYMENT PROFILE

Career Rating	60*
# of companies recruiting on-campus	43

NORTHWESTERN UNIVERSITY
KELLOGG SCHOOL OF MANAGEMENT

Academics

At The Kellogg School of Management at Northwestern University, you can almost feel the cooperation in the air. Students are besieged with constant surveys and reviews, their input is always sought, and their voices and desires have a huge impact on the course the school takes both academically and socially. According to one student, "Kellogg almost doesn't have a formal administration. Students run everything." Other students agree that "it's not always the most efficient approach, but it is the best way to train tomorrow's business leaders." It also lends the school "a certain energy around the campus that brings excitement to each and every day." In the past nine years, over 50 new courses have been added to the school's curriculum, often as a result of student initiative. The continual curricular development, along with the constant initiation of new clubs and ventures, ensure that classes keep up with the cutting edge of business management. One facet of the cooperative spirit is that both professors and students receive regular evaluations. Students review the performance of the professors both at mid- and end-of-quarter, and "student feedback is even made part of the tenure selection process." According to some students, another incentive for professors to stay at the top of their game is that "[their] year-end bonuses are based on their ratings from students." Students aren't exempt from the scrutiny of their peers, either. Through a Web-based program called TeamNet, Kellogg students are able to receive "confidential, detailed, and honest feedback on how they work in teams" from fellow students, faculty, and staff. According to the school, this produces an unparalleled ability to "respond to and give confidential peer feedback, something excellent managers do well."

Kellogg also features a unique four-quarter program, in which students attend classes during the fall, winter, and spring programs. Students in the full-time, two-year program are required to complete an internship in the summer after their first year. The core-curriculum classes consist of nine courses in the "fundamental areas of accounting, management and organizations, marketing, finance, decision sciences, and management and strategy."

The four-quarter program also allows students to earn their MBAs in just one year. "Kellogg's one-year program is one-of-a-kind," one enthusiastic MBA says. "It's the best return on investment and offers great flexibility combined with small classes and highest-quality students." The school's other unique program is the Master's of Management and Manufacturing (MMM), which is designed to aid students who wish to pursue "management roles in product-driven companies." This program is shared with Northwestern's McCormick School of Engineering.

Kellogg offers a lengthy list of majors in which students can specialize, from biotechnology to technology industry management. However, students often feel that "application of technology is a little slow compared to other schools." Most students who have had contact with the finance department say it's "outstanding." However, even though they have been "as well trained or better trained than peers at other top finance-business schools," Kellogg has not really developed a reputation as a premier finance school; yet, students feel that "Kellogg deserves it." One student says, "For some reason, people think Kellogg grads are not quant heavy, but [one-]third of my class are finance majors."

Career and Placement

Major recruiters with a presence at Kellogg include McKinsey and Company, Merrill Lynch, and Bain and Company, Inc.; most students are confident that their school has a "sterling reputation among corporate recruiters." One student says, "Kellogg is not a tech school; nor is it particularly well-connected on Wall Street. I personally don't care, but some people might." Many students would also like to see "more recruiting in fields other than marketing, finance, and consulting." While students agree that the team-focused

BETH FLYE, DIRECTOR OF ADMISSIONS AND FINANCIAL AID
2001 SHERIDAN ROAD, 2ND FLOOR, EVANSTON, IL 60208 UNITED STATES
PHONE: 847-491-3308 • FAX: 847-491-4960
E-MAIL: MBAADMISSIONS@KELLOGG.NORTHWESTERN.EDU
WEBSITE: WWW.KELLOGG.NORTHWESTERN.EDU

FINANCIAL FACTS

Annual tuition	$36,372
Books and supplies	$1,647
Room & board	$13,515
% of students receiving aid	75
Average award package	$18,500
Average grant	$7,000
Average student loan debt	$50,000

ADMISSIONS

Admissions Selectivity Rating	98
# of applications received	4299
% applicants accepted	22
% acceptees attending	56
Average GMAT	700
Average GPA	3.4
TOEFL Required of International Students?	Yes
Application fee	$210
International application fee	$210
Regular application deadline	1/7
Regular notification	3/31
Application Deadline/Notification	
Round 1:	10/22 / 1/7
Round 2:	1/7 / 3/31
Round 3:	3/11 / 5/2
Deferment Available?	Yes
Maximum length of deferment	case by case
Non-fall admissions?	Yes
Need-blind admissions?	Yes

environment ensures that "networking at Kellogg is tremendous," many would like to see the career center focus more on locating smaller job opportunities. Some students worry that the center "is not focused enough on helping out international students get jobs—either in the U.S. or internationally."

Student Life and Environment

Kellogg is situated in Evanston, Illinois along the shores of Lake Michigan. It is just a short commute on the El (elevated train) into downtown Chicago. According to some students, because there aren't "a lot of activities in the city of Evanston," most students appreciate the proximity to all that Chicago has to offer. However, for those who choose not to make the 30-minute commute, "there is a lot going on [at] school." There are regular social hours on Tuesdays, and Fridays, and there are no classes on Wednesdays. Students say that because "a large group of students go out together regularly, you can feel confident about going out alone and meeting at least a few friends at whatever bar you choose." As one student says, "When it's time to study, we study, and [we] study hard. When it's time to play, we play well."

Many students feel that for a school whose classes hover somewhere around 700 students, "Kellogg could stand to work on its diversity—both ethnically and in terms of people from industries other than consulting."

Though the school has done multiple renovations to its facilities, which now features "15 new classrooms wired for network access, 20 group study rooms, a quiet study room, a 20-terminal computer training facility, an expanded computer lab, free-standing computer terminals for checking e-mail and accessing the Web, a student lounge, lockers, and a sky-lit atrium," many students would like to see more care taken with their physical environment. According to some students, "[The] buildings are getting long in the tooth."

Admissions

Admissions officers at Kellogg have the unenviable job of having to reduce a pile of approximately 6,000 applications down to an admitted class of about 700. During this process, they look for work experience, academic excellence, and personality. The school's admissions board conducts thousands of interviews each fall. The average GMAT score is 703. Of the applicants who scored above 700 (about 3,000 in all), 21 percent were offered admission. Over 15 percent of applicants who scored within the 650 to 690 range were also accepted for admission. All Kellogg's incoming students had some full-time work experience, and the average amount of employment time was about five years. Almost 33 percent of Kellogg students hail from outside of the United States, and for those applicants, TOEFL scores are required. The average TOEFL score for enrolled students is 650.

Career Rating	94	Grads employed by field	%: avg. salary
Placement rate (%)	90	Finance	24: $89,700
% grads employed immediately	85	Marketing	30: $86,500
Average starting salary	$91,390	Consulting	32: $99,200
		General Management	13: $91,600
		Other	1: $98,500

THE OHIO STATE UNIVERSITY
FISHER COLLEGE OF BUSINESS

GENERAL INFORMATION

Type of school	public
Environment	metropolis
Academic calendar	quarter

SURVEY SAYS...

Friendly students, Good peer network, Happy students, Smart classrooms
Solid preparation in:
Teamwork

STUDENTS

Enrollment of parent institution	58,365
Enrollment of MBA program	541
% male/female	77/23
% out-of-state	15
% part-time	51
% minorities	19
% international	32
Average age at entry	27
Average years work experience at entry	4.6

ACADEMICS

Academic Experience Rating	94
Student/faculty ratio	5:1
Profs interesting rating	91
Profs accessible rating	88
% female faculty	24
% minority faculty	18

Joint Degrees

MBA/JD: 4 years
MBA/MHA: 3 years
MBA/MD: 5 years
MBA/PharmD: 5 years
MBA/MBLE: 15 months

Prominent Alumni

Mr. Leslie Wexner, Chairman & CEO The Limited, Inc.; Mr. Alan J. Patricof, Chairman Patricof & Company Ventures, Inc.; Mr. Lionel Nowell, Executive Vice President and CFO Pepsi Bottling Gr; Mr. Ray Groves, Chairman Legg Mason Merchant Banking; Mr. Max Fisher, Industrialist and Philanthopist; James O'Brien, Chairman and CEO, Ashland, Inc., Mark Johnson, Vice Chairman, Checkfree Corp., Clayton Daley, CFO, Procter & Gamble.

Academics

"If you want a challenge and you don't want a school where you can hide in the back row or behind a laptop, consider the Fisher College of Business at Ohio State University," where "there's ample opportunity to access incredible minds and develop your own personal style to problem solving." As "a small school with intimate classes complemented by the resources of a large university," Fisher is small enough to hear students' suggestions and big enough to find quick solutions to problems. As one student explains, "The administration is very responsive to students' requests for changes to the program. The orientation for first-year students, for example, was far better this year after comments from my class."A fast-moving program (Fisher is on a quarterly academic calendar), the Fisher College MBA stresses teamwork to manage the heavy workload. One student explains, "one of the primary strengths of the program is the team concept created in the first year. You are provided with a group of four to five fellow classmates who become your team (or cohort) for the year. This concept allows students the opportunity to develop immediate connections with fellow students and teaches you the importance of team values. It also helps to ease some of the competitive pressures associated with business schools."

Fisher MBAs tout courses in supply chain, finance, operations, and "various technical specialties of business." The marketing program "needs more options," and some wish the school "would dedicate more resources for those going into nonbusiness fields after graduation (i.e., government and public service)." Fisher has "excellent international programs" whose offerings are enhanced by the university's Center for International Business and Research (CIBAR). One MBA reports, "I did a course involving emerging-market field studies in Hungary and the Czech Republic in my first year and am studying abroad in Australia in my second year. Great stuff." Fisher profs are "all extremely knowledgeable about the latest trends in their fields and publish heavily in very reputed journals," but one students says, "their quality as teachers vary. I have a professor who murmurs in class and nobody can hear her clearly. Another professor is a research leader in his field but does a horrible job teaching." Students happily take the bad with the good, noting that "while their teaching styles vary, they know their material (and expect us to know it too!)" and that "they are more than willing to help anyone who requests it of them and encourage informal conversation." Some students complain that "there are too many night classes. This is one of the disadvantages of being small. We need the part-timers to create sufficient interest in some classes; hence, the evening classes."

Career and Placement

Most Fisher MBAs agree that "the Career Services office is good, but tends to be limited to local companies. The school's reputation is very strong in Ohio and the Midwest, but needs to continue marketing the Fisher brand so that graduates have more opportunity on the coasts and abroad." For those students who do secure employment outside of the Midwest (40%), a travel fund has been established to help offset the student costs associated with school-sponsored trips to a variety of job fairs and alumni events in numerous cities. Many students feel that "there is tremendous potential to leverage the alumni better, both of Fisher and OSU in general," in the past. In response, an Internet-based alumni database was established at Fisher in 2004 that contains contact information for alumni who have volunteered to assist current MBA students with their job search and internship searches. International students feel that "the school should improve its international program, especially career service. It is hard to imagine that with so many international students, there is no one who specifically focuses on international students in Career Services." These students will be happy to hear that in August 2004, a full-time career consultant was hired to work exclusively with international students in securing employment opportunities. Gripes aside, most con-

ASSOCIATE DIRECTOR, GRADUATE PROGRAMS OFFICE
100 GERLACH HALL, 2108 NEIL AVENUE, COLUMBUS, OH 43210 UNITED STATES
PHONE: 614-292-8511 • FAX: 614-292-9006
E-MAIL: COBGRD@OSU.EDU • WEBSITE: WWW.FISHER.OSU.EDU

cede that the office does good work; as one student observes, "despite the downturn, only 15 students from last year's class [were] still hunting for jobs" at the start of the fall quarter. Major employers of OSU MBAs include Accenture; American Electric Power; AT Kearney; Deloitte; Eaton; Ford Motor Company; General Electric; Kimberly-Clark; IBM; Lexmark; Limited Brands; Nationwide; National City; Nestle; PwC; Ross/Abbott Labs; Procter & Gamble and The Scotts Company. Over 200 companies make recruiting trips to the OSU campus each year. One in five students finds work outside the U.S. following graduation.

Student Life and Environment

Extracurricular life at Fisher is driven by the program's many student-run organizations. The MBA Association, for one, "organizes several activities every week. Thursdays we have Event of the Week, which is often cosponsored by another MBA organization. They also organize tailgates for the football games and publicize events/concerts where our classmates are performing." Each of the many function- and interest-specific MBA organizations sponsor events as well, "including festival hops, industry-related networking trips, golf tournaments—the list seems endless!" There's even a group dedicated to community service. Students join as many organizations as they can handle; one MBA writes, "I am involved with three clubs and will probably be involved with more as the year goes on."

Ohio State football is practically a religion among MBAs; they report that "the football tailgating is incredible. You not only create a solid network of associates for the future, but you also create a solid network of friends, which will last a lifetime." Hometown Columbus "is a fun and growing city. There's lots to do here for all interests," including Columbus Clippers baseball (AAA level), ski trips, whitewater rafting, and lots of great local restaurants. Students warn that it is "not a city for people with seasonal mood disorder. Columbus can be miserable in winter. Take it as a hint: There are tunnels underneath the business-school complex to walk to class." Fisher is housed in a six-building complex. Students love it, describing it as "phenomenal. The classrooms are great and are well-equipped with all of the technology we need." One architect pursuing his MBA writes, "The facilities are the best of any school I have visited or seen. They are designed for the student and not for show like many other schools."

Admissions

The admissions office at Fisher requires applicants to provide two official copies of transcripts for all undergraduate and graduate institutions attended, GMAT scores, TOEFL scores (for students whose first language is not English), three letters of recommendation, essays, and a resume of work experience (three or more years preferred), extracurricular activities, and community service. The admissions office carefully considers "the caliber of undergraduate institution and major, the quality of work experience, evidence of leadership and teamwork, and communication skills." Minority outreach programs include Graduate and Professional Schools Visitation Day, the Graduate Enrichment Fellowship Program, the Targeted Minority Recruitment Initiative, and Minority Student Visitation Weekend.

FINANCIAL FACTS

Annual tuition (in-state/out-of-state)	$14,970/$26,853
Fees (in-state/out-of-state)	$585/$585
Books and supplies	$600
Room & board (on/off-campus)	$6,201/$6,372
% of students receiving aid	52
% of first-year students receiving aid	57
% of students receiving grants	45
Average award package	$13,200
Average grant	$11,500

ADMISSIONS

Admissions Selectivity Rating	88
# of applications received	609
% applicants accepted	56
% acceptees attending	40
Average GMAT	664
Range of GMAT	500-770
Average GPA	3.4
TOEFL Required of International Students?	Yes
Minimum TOEFL (paper/computer)	600/250
Application fee	$40
International application fee	$50
Regular application deadline	4/30
Regular notification	5/30
Application Deadline/Notification	
Round 1:	11/15 / Rolling
Round 2:	12/30 / Rolling
Round 3:	3/15 / Rolling
Round 4:	4/30 / 5/31
Early decision program?	Yes
ED Deadline/Notification	12/30 / 2/28
Deferment Available?	Yes
Maximum length of deferment	1 year
Need-blind admissions?	Yes

APPLICANTS ALSO LOOK AT

Case Western Reserve University, Indiana State University, Michigan State University, Northwestern University, Purdue University, University of Michigan, University of Wisconsin-Madison.

Career Rating	90	Grads employed by field	%: avg. salary
Placement rate (%)	92	Accounting	1: $60,000
# of companies recruiting on-campus	175	Finance	26: $76,938
% grads employed immediately	80	Marketing	20: $73,905
Average starting salary	$75,895	MIS	6: $71,000
		Operations	14: $74,250
		Consulting	15: $77,290
		General Management	18: $74,000

OLD DOMINION UNIVERSITY
COLLEGE OF BUSINESS AND PUBLIC ADMINISTRATION

GENERAL INFORMATION
Type of school   public
Environment   city

SURVEY SAYS...
Happy students
Smart classrooms
Solid preparation in:
General management
Teamwork

STUDENTS
Enrollment of parent
  institution   21,000
Enrollment of MBA program   382
% male/female   57/43
% part-time   72
% minorities   13
% international   40
Average age at entry   28
Average years work experience
  at entry   6.5

ACADEMICS
Academic Experience Rating   64
Student/faculty ratio   14:1
Profs interesting rating   63
Profs accessible rating   61
Prominent Alumni
Elizabeth Duke, Chairman & EVP;
Linda Middleton, Senior VP; John
Sanderson, President; Larry
Kittelberger, Senior VP & CIO; Lloyd
"Skip" Sorenson, CFO.

Academics

Asked to list the strengths of the MBA program at Old Dominion University's College of Business and Public Administration, one student responded thus: "(1) affordability; (2) value for the price; (3) facilities; (4) laid-back atmosphere." And most other students agree. One student says, "I truly enjoy the atmosphere and the way all of my classes have been taught," while another student exclaims, "I have been surprisingly pleased with the school, what I am learning, and the value I am receiving for my dollar." A third student adds, "I am thrilled with the course curriculum and how well the business school is operated. My professors are wonderful, and I have learned more in my first year of business school at ODU than my entire undergraduate career, where I majored in business."

The MBA program at Old Dominion University (ODU) is, according to the school, designed to "present broad but thorough insights into issues relevant to all effective managers. Our focus is on quality." Students agree; as one puts it, "my professors were knowledgeable in their fields. They include an operational expert and MSCE for e-commerce, a former Wall Street Investment banker for finance, a senior VP of Carlson Company for accounting, a former university dean for marketing, and other elite academicians as instructors who are stewards of business and operational knowledge."

But perhaps "excellence with flexibility" would be a better motto. With programs around the state, and ample opportunity for distance learning, prospective MBAs are faced with a wide array of choices. Students can choose to specialize in any of the following areas: decision science, assurance services, information technology, international business management, management accounting, business and economics forecasting, finance, maritime and port management, marketing, public administration, or they can choose a general MBA. Students are extremely excited about "the Maritime Institute. This is the only school in the country that offers an MBA with a concentration in maritime management/port management." Many students, however, say that they're "disappointed with the school's marketing emphasis but all other areas are good" and one complains that "A structured entrepreneurial class would be beneficial."

ODU offers several other masters-level programs in addition to the MBA, including a master of science in accounting, master of arts in economics, master of science in computer science, master of urban studies, and master of public administration degree. Although most students seem to truly enjoy their work, some lament the dearth of big-name professors in the school's program. As one student says, "We need more outstanding professors in business courses." Another adds that although students would "like to have more teachers that are recognized leaders in their field," most "teachers overall are committed to the material and care about the student's learning experience." And others point out that although "the curriculum is demanding, it's not to the point of all-nighters."

Career and Placement

Although the school proudly claims "active support for faculty and students from its alumni, more than half of whom reside within a 100-mile radius of the campus," most students wish that ODU would exert more energy in utilizing its alumni network—and in placing students in jobs. Students complain that they definitely need to "have more opportunities to meet with people in the business community." And while some point out that "there is an MBA association that offers a social outlet and some job search assistance," most regret that the "on-campus recruiting is far from helpful."

Mrs. Rhyanne Henley, MBA Program Manager
Constant Hall 1026 Norfolk, VA 23529 United States
Phone: 757-683-3585 • Fax: 757-683-5750
E-mail: mbainfo@odu.edu • Website: www.odu-mba.org

Student Life and Environment

Located in historic Norfolk, Virginia, Old Dominion University is blessed with lovely weather, happy students, proximity to major business centers, and a brand-new Business School building—Constant Hall—which boasts state-of-the-art facilities. As one student puts it, "the actual building in Norfolk is brand new and equipped with all technology aides for training." Because the building opened so recently, students are still excited about the "media-equipped classrooms," although other aspects of the school's facilities could be improved, according to most. As one student says, "it is a nightmare to park, even in the evening," and others claim that something needs to be done to prevent the undergrads from driving like crazy people.

Still, "there are many activities organized by the school's associations and organizations. However, it doesn't seem to be heavily advertised. Many services are offered to students ([such as] health, off-campus housing, [and] banks), which makes life on campus easier." Despite all these activities, many students would like to see a greater effort on ODU's part to "build a substantial school culture." As one student says, "until 2004, the social scene at Old Dominion was virtually nonexistent outside of the classroom. Hopefully this year will be different with the formation of a strong MBA association and a social club called The Loop. Only time will tell."

Admissions

Anyone applying to be one of the 120-odd full-time MBA students at ODU should have a GMAT score around the average (530) and a competitive GPA. Those students applying from countries in which English is not the native language should be prepared to take the TOEFL exam. The minimum required score is 550 paper-based and 213 computer-based. The program currently hosts about 300 part-time students on-campus and around 50 part-timers working through the distance program. There are 20-odd PhD candidates, and about 1,500 undergraduates in the business school. Graduate assistantship positions are highly coveted and competitive; approximately 60 percent of students applying for a teaching or research assistantship are awarded one.

FINANCIAL FACTS

Annual tuition (in-state/out-of-state)	$5,904/$15,144
Fees	$168
Books and supplies	$1,000
Room & board (on-campus)	$5,232
Average grant	$14,000

ADMISSIONS

Admissions Selectivity Rating	76
# of applications received	210
% applicants accepted	65
% acceptees attending	86
Average GMAT	530
Average GPA	3.2
TOEFL Required of International Students?	Yes
Minimum TOEFL (paper/computer)	550/213
Application fee	$40
International application fee	$40
Regular application deadline	6/1
Regular notification	Rolling
Application Deadline/Notification	
Round 1:	11/1 / 12/1
Round 2:	3/1 / 4/1
Round 3:	6/1 / 7/1
Deferment Available?	Yes
Maximum length of deferment	1 year
Transfer students accepted?	Yes
Transfer application policy: Credits accepted from AACSB accredited schools only.	
Non-fall admissions?	Yes
Need-blind admissions?	Yes

PENNSYLVANIA STATE UNIVERSITY
SMEAL COLLEGE OF BUSINESS

GENERAL INFORMATION
Type of school   public
Environment   village
Academic calendar   7-1-7 modules

SURVEY SAYS...
Friendly students
Smart classrooms
Solid preparation in:
Communication/interpersonal skills
Presentation skills

STUDENTS
Enrollment of parent
  institution   41,289
Enrollment of MBA program   173
% male/female   74/26
% out-of-state   79
% minorities   17
% International   34
Average age at entry   27
Average years work experience
  at entry   4.5

ACADEMICS
Academic Experience Rating   93
Student/faculty ratio   2:1
Profs interesting rating   88
Profs accessible rating   83
% female faculty   15
% minority faculty   21
Joint Degrees
Science BS/MBA: 5 years
MHA/MBA: 3 years
MBA/JD: 5 years
Prominent Alumni
John Arnold, MBA '87, Chairman
and CEO, Petroleum Products
Corporation; J. David Rogers, MBA
'80, Chairman and CEO, JD Capital
Management; James R. Stengel
MBA '83, CMO, Proctor and Gamble
Corporation.

Academics

Even at a large institution like Pennsylvania State University, Smeal maintains a strong feeling of intimacy and comfort. With only about 100 students in each entering class, "the size of the class gives it a personal touch." The faculty members are always available to students. Students say, "The dean is accessible and so is the program director. In fact, we've all been to their homes!" The program is filled with "collaborative, not competitive students, [and] second-years invest so much time in helping first-years." Even alumni are willing to do anything they can to help current students. Students are "energetic and eager to get involved" and are heartened by the fact that, even with a small program, huge investments are made. One student comments, "The school is putting great effort and money into becoming one of the top programs in the United States, and that shows in the quality of faculty, career services, and the new business building being constructed."

Smeal's academic calendar is divided into an unusual module program referred to as the "7-1-7" system. Each semester of the first year is divided into two learning modules, separated by an immersion program. In the first seven-week module, for example, students study communications, introduction to managerial accounting, management, and teams, and then break midway through for a one-week immersion program in negotiations. After the immersion program, they go on to their second seven-week module, which teaches analysis for managerial decision-making, communication, economics for managers, financial accounting, and a second immersion experience where every student experiences an international culture. It isn't until the fourth module (in the second half of the spring semester) that students start taking electives for their chosen portfolios.

Despite the rigor of this system, students feel comfortable and capable. Students say, "We spent an entire year becoming completely comfortable in public-speaking situations, based on a rigorous methodology that incorporates oral, written, and graphic communication. It will undoubtedly differentiate us from [our] peers at other schools." Other students add, "this is tops in the b-school community."

There are six academic departments from which Smeal students can choose to specialize: corporate, finance, investment banking, strategic consulting, entrepreneurship, marketing, and supply chain and information systems. Students say that "finance, accounting, entrepreneurship, and communications [programs] are top-notch." The school also offers three joint degrees: an MBA/JD, a MBA/MHA, and a MBA/QMM.

Diversity remains something of a problem for some students. Many students agree that they would like to see Smeal "create activities or clubs to cater to nontraditional students and also admit more of these nontraditional students instead of so many engineers."

Career and Placement

A strong alumni network is one of Smeal's biggest strengths. One student says, "There are so many successful alumni that stay very actively involved—it is overwhelming. I have several VP- and officer-level contacts already that I can contact personally if I wish, and I've only been here three months!"

In terms of career services—which are "being revamped"—many students believe that "the finance area for jobs needs improvement." Students agree that "not many firms travel [to the university] from New York City," but yet more students end up in finance/accounting than in any other field. By the September following the completion of their degree, 74 percent of the 2003 class had one or more job offers. A few years ago, IBM was the top recruiter, but now Andersen, Bear Stearns, Merrill Lynch, Sony Electronics, and Wyeth Pharmaceuticals (among many others) all maintain a presence on campus. Still, students would like to see a little more action from the office itself. According to some students, "Smeal is a place where you have to be somewhat creative and show a great deal of personal commitment to get a great job." One student adds, "But that's a good thing in my opinion."

Student Life and Environment

"Although we're in a small town, there's plenty to do," one student says. "Dinners hosted by the International Students Association are big hits, and intramural sports are a popular way to blow off some steam." Students add, "We have our nightly happy-hour spots. A great number of students live in one building downtown, so there are 'apartment crawls' and lots of opportunities to study in groups." The school, situated right in the middle of Pennsylvania, is equidistant from "major nerve centers of the Northeast, Mid-Atlantic, and Midwest," which means Baltimore; Cleveland; Detroit; New York City; Philadelphia; Pittsburgh; Washington, DC; and many other places are accessible by trains, planes, and automobiles. The area's unofficial name is "Happy Valley." *Psychology Today* ranked State College (yes, that's the name of the town) as one of the least stressful places to live in the nation. Students say the town has an "active downtown area, but little beyond restaurants and bars." For them, life is more about "tailgates, tailgates, tailgates." Another student says, "Football games are a big part of the weekend relief at Smeal. It is an opportunity to network with alumni, and all the festivities are coordinated by our MBA Association, a student-run group."

As for actual campus life, one student says, "The Smeal MBA Program is a very small program in a very large school. So it allows students to feel a part of community within the program." Being a part of a huge university, "there are amazing resources for literally anything you could want: sports facilities, international student clubs, investment and finance clubs, great intercollegiate sports teams, [and] good classrooms." In an effort to make the campus still more attractive to students, Smeal has broken ground on a new 210,000-square-foot building. When the building is completed in the summer of 2005, it will be the largest academic facility at Penn State.

Admissions

With only about 100 students admitted each year, Smeal's goal is to "recruit, admit, and enroll candidates who will be successful in the MBA program and as Smeal alumni." In order to be considered for admission, students must be computer literate, demonstrate competency in mathematics (including linear algebra), knowledge of statistics, and some knowledge of micro and macroeconomics. International students who are not fluent in English are required to submit TOEFL scores. Students admitted in the program have an average of five years work experience; 29 percent of them are female, and 18 percent are part of a minority group. The mid-80 percent range for their GMAT scores was 580 to 720, and the mid-80 percent range for undergraduate GPA was 2.7 to 3.8.

FINANCIAL FACTS

Annual tuition (in-state/out-of-state)	$14,500/$24,796
Fees	$2,248
Books and supplies	$1,500
Room & board (on/off-campus)	$8,800/$16,000
% of students receiving aid	86
% of first-year students receiving aid	84
% of students receiving loans	38
% of students receiving grants	75
Average award package	$15,615
Average grant	$9,888
Average student loan debt	$24,048

ADMISSIONS

Admissions Selectivity Rating	90
# of applications received	439
% applicants accepted	39
% acceptees attending	42
Average GMAT	643
Range of GMAT	590-690
Average GPA	3.2
TOEFL Required of International Students?	Yes
Minimum TOEFL (paper/computer)	600/250
Application fee	$60
International application fee	$60
Regular application deadline	4/15
Regular notification	6/1
Early decision program?	Yes
ED Deadline/Notification	12/1 / 2/1
Deferment Available?	Yes
Maximum length of deferment	1 year
Need-blind admissions?	Yes

APPLICANTS ALSO LOOK AT

Indiana University, Michigan State University, Purdue University, The Ohio State University, University of Illinois at Urbana-Champaign, University of Maryland—College Park.

EMPLOYMENT PROFILE

Career Rating	90	Grads employed by field	%: avg. salary
Placement rate (%)	92	Finance	37: $79,200
% grads employed immediately	59	Marketing	14: $75,250
Average starting salary	$76,096	MIS	1
		Operations	26: $77,244
		Consulting	9: $74,640
		General Management	7: $71,250
		Other	6

PENNSYLVANIA STATE UNIVERSITY ERIE—THE BEHREND COLLEGE
SAM AND IRENE BLACK SCHOOL OF BUSINESS

Academics

At the Sam and Irene Black School of Business at Penn State Erie—The Behrend College, the MBA program primarily serves students who are already fully employed. The MBA degree stresses integration of business knowledge across disciplines, and emphasizes the development of "planning and problem-solving skills crucial in middle and upper management." Because so many of the prospective MBAs are "mature students with significant work experience," many students "juggle their work, family, and school responsibilities and have little free time." However, students point out that "the average age of the typical MBA student is decreasing due to an influx of recent business under-graduates who are staying in school for their MBA because of a poor job market." Still, quality of instruction remains the same. As one student says, "Professors are good at relating today's business trends into classroom activities and discussions;" another adds, "I feel very lucky to have found a great school."

Although the amount of time it takes to complete an MBA at the Sam and Irene Black School of Business varies depending on students' needs, all students are required to complete between 30 and 48 credits (depending on their undergraduate degree). The curriculum consists of 18 credits of foundation-core course work, 15 credits of advanced-required course work, and 15 credits of electives designed to allow students to pursue their areas of special interest. To accommodate the differing schedules of its students, courses are taught in the late afternoons, evenings, and weekends. Students say that "professors are good people and their command of the material is good." Others complain that "the MBA program is geared more toward production and the manufacturing segments of the economy. I would like to see more classes aimed at service-related issues." Some worry that "information technology professors are not providing current applications of software/hardware."

Career and Placement

Each fall, the career-development center sponsors a business fair, which is well attended by both MBA students and recruiters. According to the school's website, "a growing number of local, regional, national, and international companies participate in the fair each year, and many return to campus in the spring to recruit our graduates for jobs."

Still, because many of the students at the Black School are already employed and are being educated on their company's dime, post-graduation employment is less of an issue in Behrend's MBA program as it is at others.

Student Life and Environment

Erie is, according to most students at Behrend's b-school, an overlooked gem. Students cite the "beautiful location" of their school as one very good reason to attend. The Black School's facilities themselves are located in the campus' historic center, and Turnbull Hall, the center, is graced with a special management information science computer lab with more than forty PCs, which provides constant access to "the latest in business-application software." A new location is in the works as well, and the school's administrators feel confident that "students and faculty will benefit greatly when the School of Business relocates into the $30 million Research and Economic Development Center." As one student says, "most of its campus facilities are relatively new, and the campus itself is visually appealing."

Ann M. Burbules, Graduate Admissions Counselor
5091 Station Road, Erie, PA 16563 United States
Phone: 814-898-7255 • Fax: 814-898-6044
E-mail: PSBehrendMBA@psu.edu • Website: www.pserie.psu.edu

FINANCIAL FACTS

Annual tuition (in-state/out-of-state)	
	$9,882/$15,624
Books and supplies	$996
Room & board	$7,650
% of students receiving aid	40
% of first-year students	
receiving aid	50
% of students receiving loans	33
% of students receiving grants	4
Average award package	$14,250
Average grant	$1,600

ADMISSIONS

Admissions Selectivity Rating	**70**
# of applications received	56
% applicants accepted	86
% acceptees attending	90
Average GMAT	522
Average GPA	3.3
TOEFL Required of	
International Students?	Yes
Minimum TOEFL	
(paper/computer)	550/213
Application fee	$45
International application fee	$45
Regular application deadline	7/4
Regular notification	Rolling
Deferment Available?	Yes
Maximum length of	
deferment	2 years
Transfer students accepted?	Yes
Transfer application policy: Up to 10 credits from an accredited institution may be transferred; grade must be a B or higher, and less than 5 years old.	
Non-fall admissions?	Yes

The social life for MBAs at Behrend leaves a little something to be desired, according to many. Although student activities programming is open to all students, one student observes that "approximately 80 percent of MBA students are working professionals, attending school during the evening on a part-time basis. Activities are very strongly skewed toward the undergraduate student enrollment. Undergrads have lots of things to keep them busy." Another explains the dearth of social activity saying, "Students in the MBA program have little time to spend socializing with other students as most work full-time jobs." And because "most are married with children," students often feel they lack a cohesive community. "Everyone tends to come to class and that's the only time you interact with them."

But in fact, the community is not that homogenous. According to one student, "A lot of students are from GE or Erie Insurance where the company pays for their education. They are friendly and everyone is diverse in background." Because of the economy, many students who recently completed undergraduate degrees "enrolled in the MBA program to finish in one year," which means that all ages and experience levels are welcomed.

Admissions

The admissions process at the Sam and Irene Black School of Business is in some ways more forgiving than at other schools. Although they, like almost everyone, require GMAT scores, the minimum GMAT total score is 400. All applicants must score a 4.0 or better on the Analytical Writing Assessment section of the GMAT exam, in addition to that. A GPA of no lower than 3.0 is preferred, but the school will allow students with a GPA lower than that to apply, as long as their GMAT score is higher in proportion. In other words, they use the following formula to determine admissibility: Grade Point Average x 200 - 1000 = GMAT score required to be admissible to the MBA program. Students for whom English is not the first language are also required to take the TOEFL exam and are expected to score no lower than 550 (paper-based exam) or 213 (computer-based exam).

EMPLOYMENT PROFILE

Career Rating	**72**	**Grads employed by field %: avg. salary**	
Placement rate (%)	90	Finance	11
# of companies recruiting on-campus	8	MIS	11
Average starting salary	$52,222	Operations	11
		Consulting	11
		General Management	11
		Other	44: $49,375

PEPPERDINE UNIVERSITY
THE GRAZIADIO SCHOOL OF BUSINESS AND MANAGEMENT

GENERAL INFORMATION

Type of school	private
Environment	village
Academic calendar	trimester

SURVEY SAYS...
Students love Los Angeles, CA
Friendly students
Smart classrooms
Solid preparation in:
Teamwork
Communication/interpersonal skills
Presentation skills

STUDENTS

Enrollment of parent institution	8,324
Enrollment of MBA program	2,338
% male/female	66/34
% part-time	09
% minorities	8
% international	22
Average age at entry	27
Average years work experience at entry	3

ACADEMICS

Academic Experience Rating	74
Student/faculty ratio	20:1
Profs interesting rating	76
Profs accessible rating	77
% female faculty	22

Joint Degrees
MBA/JD: 4 years
MBA/MPP (Master of Public Policy): 3 years

Prominent Alumni
Victor Tsao, Founder, Linksys, 2004 Inc. Magazine Entrepreneur; Shirley Choi, Executive Director and CEO, Seapower Group; David T. Mount, Former Chairman and CEO, Warner Elektra Atlantic; Laura Skandera Trombley, President, Pitzer College.

Academics

Los Angeles now boasts the eleventh largest economy in the world, and the Graziadio School, located just 30 minutes away in Malibu, is poised to take advantage of that. In the past few years, the school has built an entirely new graduate campus along the Pacific Coast, increased the size of their student body by several hundred students, and revamped their administration. With "a brand-new campus and a new administration with full support from full-time faculty, [most students] imagine that the school can only move forward from here." Not to say the transition has happened without any troubles—many students have had considerable difficulty adjusting—most agree however, that the administration "seems to be on the right track now."

Students have already seen improvements in the campus and say that the administration has attempted to be responsive to their input. For the most part, students are positive about their interactions with professors. One MBA observes, "The teachers are usually current consultants or former top executives with PhDs, and they bring real-life cases in their classes, a source of knowledge very precious for managers who want practical solutions to current business issues they are likely to face once out of school." For the most part, students applaud the practical application of knowledge that their professors are able to demonstrate, although some students feel that "some departments seem to be stuck in the world of academia rather than the business world."

Pepperdine's tradition as a religious school has an effect on the business school, though students say that "the label 'Church of Christ' is much less influential in the graduate campus than it is in the undergrad campus." But students do attribute one of the Graziadio program's greatest strengths to a religious background. "Ethics, ethics, ethics. It is a moral place to learn where gray areas are explored and analyzed and the current environment of business is studied and reviewed." According to students, most of the classes focus on ethical choices and practices, and "this focus challenges the students to give thought to their personal ethics so that we will be more likely to make the right choices when faced with ethical dilemmas."

Core requirements make up 30 to 40 units of study out of 54 to 60 total, and the first year is almost all core classes. Students have freedom in their second year to take electives, though they'd like to see more options. In accounting and finance, students rate their courses as "outstanding." One student adds, "However, some classes, such as organization behavior or information technology need to be more practical. As I was a manager, I don't think I learned efficient tools to turn into practice. I need less theory and more practical tools."

Career and Placement

Like many students at business schools in today's economy, students would like to see their Career Services Office working harder. Students say, "Relations with the business community in Southern California could be stronger. People don't have negative perceptions about the school. The problem is they don't have any perceptions of the school, as everything in LA is focused on the two big schools." In an attempt to better leverage its relationship with the business community, Graziadio recently merged its Career Services and Alumni Offices.

Many major companies have found their employees at Graziadio, including American Express Financial Advisors, Arthur Andersen LLP, the City of Los Angeles, Deloitte Touche Tohmatsu, The Disney Channel, Gap, Herbalife International, Kaiser Permanente, Morgan Stanley Dean Witter, Salomon Smith Barney, and Wells Fargo. Still, some students feel "on-campus recruiting is weak."

DARRELL ERIKSEN, DIRECTOR OF ADMISSIONS
6100 CENTER DRIVE, LOS ANGELES, CA 90045 UNITED STATES
PHONE: 310-568-5535 • FAX: 310-568-5779
E-MAIL: GSBM@PEPPERDINE.EDU • WEBSITE: WWW.BSCHOOL.PEPPERDINE.EDU

Student Life and Environment

In terms of natural beauty, there are few campuses that can rival Graziadio's. Students call it the "most beautiful campus in the country." Nestled in the Santa Monica mountains and facing the winding coast of the Pacific Ocean, "the weather and campus beauty are great forms of therapy. Stepping outside for five minutes for a break from an intensive econometrics class or a tense group meeting is amazing." "B-school in Malibu—there's not much more to say. Classes are great, and the views are gorgeous. You haven't lived until you hit the bar after classes end on Thursday and chatted with colleagues while the surf crashes against the beach."

With a school so close to a major metropolitan area, students are "out of LA enough to have a more relaxed feel but close enough to tap into the job resources." Being in Southern California, "the overall atmosphere is laid-back and friendly, but it is obvious that everyone is hard-working and ambitious."

Students do lament one thing about the social scene. "We are a dry campus," reports one student. "The campus social scene is somewhat limited by the complete prohibition of alcohol." Still, students take advantage of "big house parties once a month or so and occasional trips to the beach after class." Because Malibu is an extremely expensive area and many students opt not to live on campus, "study groups and other networking takes place almost exclusively on campus since everyone is spread out so far."

Admissions

Each admitted class is only about 130 students, and Graziadio's board of admissions looks carefully at the applications, searching for "highly motivated self-starters who thrive on challenge. We carefully select each new class to represent diverse academic, cultural, and professional backgrounds." For the class of 2004, the average GMAT score for admitted full-time MBA students was 635. Many incoming students had about four years of full-time post-graduate work experience before they applied for the MBA. TOEFL scores are required of those students for whom English is not the first language, and the minimum score required for admission is a 600. The school awards merit-based scholarships.

FINANCIAL FACTS

Annual tuition	$27,432
Fees	$262
Books and supplies	$1,000
Room & board (on/off-campus)	
	$8,640/$11,000
% of students receiving aid	66
% of students receiving loans	48
% of students receiving grants	38
Average award package	$29,146
Average grant	$16,387
Average student loan debt	$62,500

ADMISSIONS

Admissions Selectivity Rating	82
# of applications received	433
% applicants accepted	66
% acceptees attending	36
Average GMAT	633
Range of GMAT	580-700
Average GPA	3.2
TOEFL Required of International Students?	Yes
Minimum TOEFL (paper/computer)	600/250
Application fee	$50
International application fee	$50
Regular application deadline	5/1
Regular notification	Rolling
Early decision program?	Yes
ED Deadline/Notification	12/15 / 1/15
Deferment Available?	Yes
Maximum length of deferment	1 year
Transfer students accepted?	Yes
Transfer application policy: No more than 2 courses may be transferred, contingent upon approval of policy committee.	
Need-blind admissions?	Yes

EMPLOYMENT PROFILE

Career Rating	79	Grads employed by field	%: avg. salary
Placement rate (%)	74	Finance	26: $66,333
% grads employed immediately	41	Marketing	48: $56,818
Average starting salary	$66,130	MIS	4: $75,000
		Operations	9: $65,000
		Consulting	9: $74,000
		General Management	4: $145,000

PITTSBURG STATE UNIVERSITY
GLADYS A. KELCE COLLEGE OF BUSINESS

GENERAL INFORMATION
Type of school	public
Environment	village
Academic calendar	semester

SURVEY SAYS...
Friendly students
Happy students
Smart classrooms
Solid preparation in:
Presentation skills

STUDENTS
Enrollment of parent institution	6,500
Enrollment of MBA program	136
% male/female	55/45
% out-of-state	53
% part-time	27
% international	43
Average age at entry	25
Average years work experience at entry	1

ACADEMICS
Academic Experience Rating	72
Student/faculty ratio	25:1
Profs interesting rating	80
Profs accessible rating	84
% female faculty	15
% minority faculty	10

Prominent Alumni
Lee Scott, President & CEO Walmart; John Lampe, President & CEO Firestone/Bridgestone; John Lowe, Executive VP ConocoPhillips; Orvil Bicknell, CEO NPC International; Richard Colliver, Executive VP American Honda.

Academics

Students choose the MBA program at Pittsburg State University because "it's reasonably priced, convenient to home, [and perhaps most importantly,] because it is one of the best in the state of Kansas." In fact, the school's reputation is such that—despite its relatively remote location—PSU's MBA program attracts a substantial international student population on a consistent basis. This "strong international student community" contributes significantly to classroom instruction here.

Students may attend PSU on either a full-time or part-time basis; part-time classes are offered in Kansas City as well as on the Pittsburg campus. Either program requires a minimum of 34 course hours beyond foundation courses; some or all of the 30 hours of foundation courses may be waived for students with undergraduate degrees in business. A waiver of all 30 hours of foundation classes makes it possible to receive an MBA in 12 months. The part-time program requires a minimum of two and a half years to complete.

PSU's professors are "accessible and approachable [and] dedicated to making you work hard and learn, but doing it in a caring and fun way." One student writes, "A high ratio of PhDs teach the core courses." Like the students, "Professors come from a variety of different countries." Classes at PSU "are relatively small, allowing for good interaction between instructors and the class," which students appreciate. They also appreciate how "the administration is very supportive of the MBA program and interested in the views of the students."

PSU MBAs may earn concentrations in accounting and general administration. Although no concentration is offered in marketing, students single the discipline out for praise, telling us the school is "famous for its marketing section."

Career and Placement

According to PSU's website, the university's relationship with area businesses and its reputation for applying high admissions standards result in "an excellent record of placement of [the school's] MBA candidates." Students confirm this assertion; one writes, "I chose PSU because of its reputation for being a great business school and because of the many job opportunities that are available through PSU's career service after you graduate."

Career services are provided through the university's Career Services Office. Employers who most frequently hire PSU MBAs include Deloitte, PriceWaterhouseCoopers, Payless ShoeSource, Core-Mark, Sprint, Hallmark, Cessna, Koch Industries, Inc., Wal-Mart, and Allstate.

Student Life and Environment

"Located in a peaceful small town," Pittsburg State offers students a lifestyle that "is pretty laid back." The university at large "not only offers excellent academic programs but also excellent entertainment programs, such as outdoor movies [and] comedians." Besides "various clubs and organizations to join for nearly any student's taste or major" and a recently remodeled student center, the school offers events such as "recitals at the music school building. There are also plays at the theatre department to attend, and there are about five art exhibits, both student and traveling, per school year."

MARVENE DARRAUGH, ADMINISTRATIVE OFFICER—GRADUATE STUDIES
1701 SOUTH BROADWAY, PITTSBURG, KS 66762-7540 UNITED STATES
PHONE: 620-235-4222 • FAX: 620-235-4219
E-MAIL: GRAD@PITTSTATE.EDU • WEBSITE: WWW.PITTSTATE.EDU/KELCE/

The majority of Pittsburg MBAs attend full-time, although there is also a sizeable part-time population here. One student notes a distinction between the two groups: "The majority of the full-time students at my school are international students, and they tend to stick together in their own groups. Most of the American students work during the day and go to class at night." Students are typically "hardworking, goal-oriented, [and] very friendly." With just over 100 MBAs in the entire program, "students know virtually everyone in the MBA program, which is nice." An MBA Association promotes the goals of MBA students and helps organize recruiting events.

Pittsburg is a town of just under 20,000. It is situated in the southeast corner of Kansas, 120 miles to the south of Kansas City. The region's rolling prairies attract outdoor enthusiasts; hunters, fishers, and hikers are all welcome. The university occupies a central role in the life of the community, providing entertainment as well as employment to the town's citizens. PSU's athletic teams, the Gorillas, receive enthusiastic support from sports fans throughout the area.

Admissions

Applicants to Pittsburg's MBA program must provide the admissions department with official copies of transcripts for all post-secondary academic work, official GMAT score reports, and a completed application to the Graduate School of PSU. International students whose first language is not English must also submit TOEFL scores. All applicants must achieve a minimum GMAT score of 400 and must receive a formula score of at least 1050 under the formula [(undergraduate GPA × 200) + GMAT score]. Students with undergraduate degrees in non-business areas are typically required to complete foundation courses in statistics; organizational theory; marketing; business law; production management; financial and managerial accounting; MIS; business finance; and micro and macro economics prior to beginning the MBA program. Such applicants may be admitted to the program conditionally, pending successful completion of these courses.

FINANCIAL FACTS

Annual tuition (in-state/out-of-state)	$3,728/$9,652
Books and supplies	$1,200
Room & board (on/off-campus)	$4,570/$6,000
% of students receiving aid	50
% of first-year students receiving aid	25
% of students receiving loans	25
% of students receiving grants	15
Average award package	$8,500
Average grant	$3,500

ADMISSIONS

Admissions Selectivity Rating	71
# of applications received	270
% applicants accepted	76
% acceptees attending	67
Average GMAT	510
Range of GMAT	400-710
Average GPA	3.5
TOEFL Required of International Students?	Yes
Minimum TOEFL (paper/computer)	550/213
Application fee	$30
Regular application deadline	7/15
Regular notification	8/1
Deferment Available?	Yes
Maximum length of deferment	1 year
Transfer students accepted?	Yes
Transfer application policy: Up to 9 semester hours may be transferred from another accredited program.	
Non-fall admissions?	Yes
Need-blind admissions?	Yes

EMPLOYMENT PROFILE

		Grads employed by field	%: avg. salary
Career Rating	72		
Placement rate (%)	90	Accounting	30: $48,000
# of companies recruiting on-campus	66	Marketing	17: $44,000
% grads employed immediately	80	MIS	15: $45,000
Average starting salary	$46,000	General Management	38: $45,000

PORTLAND STATE UNIVERSITY
SCHOOL OF BUSINESS ADMINISTRATION

GENERAL INFORMATION

Type of school	public
Environment	city
Academic calendar	2005–2006

SURVEY SAYS...

Students love Portland, OR
Friendly students
Happy students
Solid preparation in:
Teamwork
Presentation skills

STUDENTS

Enrollment of parent institution	23,486
Enrollment of MBA program	344
% male/female	65/35
% out-of-state	9
% part-time	81
% minorities	10
% international	11
Average age at entry	30
Average years work experience at entry	6

ACADEMICS

Academic Experience Rating	82
Student/faculty ratio	35:1
Profs interesting rating	80
Profs accessible rating	85
% female faculty	29
% minority faculty	8

Prominent Alumni

Gary Ames, former President/CEO, U.S. West; Gerry Cameron, retired Chairman of the Board, U.S. Bancorp; Scott Davis, Chief Financial Office, UPS; Ray Guenther, Northwest Operations Director, Intel; Darrell Webb, President, Fred Meyer/ Kroger.

Academics

The Portland State University School of Business Administration's "strong ties to the business community" are what appeal most to the school's MBA students. "Thanks to the efforts of the deans and faculty, Portland State is extremely well-connected with the Portland Business community," one student writes, adding that "this program has provided exceptional opportunities to meet and learn from top business leaders." The school notes that "[they] consider ourselves partners with area businesses and continually seek joint opportunities to further enrich the livability and economic well-being of the region. Resources available to business are many, ranging from faculty research expertise and professional development courses to small business consulting and the MBA Business Project."

Although small, PSU offers some unique, off-the-beaten-path areas for students to investigate. "The Food Industry Leadership Center deserves special recognition for its exceptional work on behalf of students," MBAs brag; also noteworthy is the school's Interdisciplinary Center for Law and Entrepreneurship. Among more conventional fare, students tell us that "stand-out courses include financial accounting, financial management and theory, and business strategy and policy. These courses have really delivered." Some feel the school "should incorporate more quantitative material both in existing classes and [by] adding more quantitative classes," and that "a greater emphasis on small, entrepreneurial business issues would be welcome, as would an opportunity to focus on sustainable, socially-responsible operations."

Throughout the curriculum, "the PSU MBA program puts strong emphasis on teamwork and interpersonal communication and conflict-management skills. Many of the PSU instructors are able to successfully incorporate their career experiences into meaningful class discussion." The faculty offers "a good balance between tenured professors to teach the more academic subjects and adjunct professors for topics where business experience is critical to teaching the subject." The majority, students agree, "are very enthusiastic, animated, and passionate about their areas of expertise. Class discussions are generally very lively and quite often humorous." On the downside, the school "needs more funding to have better facilities and technology. The classrooms are dumpy, and we are starved for resources."

Career and Placement

The School of Business Administration Career Services office serves both undergraduate and graduate b-students at PSU. The office provides a number of counseling services, workshops, and online job-search tools to students ("the school has great networking events and always keeps the students informed of what job opportunities open up with the GradListServe," MBAs tell us). On-campus recruiting is minimal; "due to the school's small size, big companies are not interested in recruiting here," one student explains. Part-timers gripe that they get "zero placement help. The career coach says 'Well, part-timers never come to my seminars.' But that's because we're at work! The school needs to integrate all of the career-management components directly into the curriculum for part-timers."

Companies that most frequently hire PSU MBAs include Adidas, AT&T, Coca Cola, Freightliner, IBM, Intel, KPMG, Lufthansa, Nike, OHSU, Planar, Tektronix, The Standard, U.S. Bancorp, U.S. Bank, Wells Fargo Bank, and Xerox. Approximately one in five PSU MBAs finds work outside the United States; most of the rest remain in the Portland area.

PAM MITCHELL, GRADUATE PROGRAMS ADVISOR
631 SOUTHWEST HARRISON STREET, PORTLAND, OR 97201 UNITED STATES
PHONE: 503-725-8001 • FAX: 503-725-5740
E-MAIL: MBAINFO@PDX.EDU • WEBSITE: WWW.MBA.PDX.EDU

Student Life and Environment

The majority of PSU's MBAs are part-time students, meaning they typically have jobs, families, and lots of other responsibilities to go along with their schoolwork. That cuts back on campus life. Even so, students see their demographic as a plus, telling us that "the part-time program brings together a more mature and experienced group. You learn a lot more from other students when they actually have some real-world experience to share." Part-timers generally "grind it out every Tuesday and Thursday nights from 5:40 to 9:20 pm, and then usually have group team meetings on most weekends."

The school is also home to about 90 full-time MBAs, for whom a typical day consists of "meeting with study groups and go[ing] to your classes. In between you relax in the student lounge, [and] meet lots of international students. Discussions range from current presidents to recipes for Swedish food. You end your day with a pint from one of the numerous microbreweries." Students become especially close with those in their cohort; they tell us that "the school pools together a great team of students for each cohorts. I think that the types of people that you are taking intense classes with can make or break a program, and PSU brings together excellent people for a great school experience." The program offers MBAs access to "organizations for any interest or hobby. Meetings can be a problem, however, with people living in various parts of the city."

Hometown Portland "is a great place, and nearly all of the students want to stay here" when they graduate. Students love that "PSU is an urban campus, adjacent to downtown Portland, on the trolley line. Most students live off campus but are active socially. Portland is a friendly community, and the campus reflects the city. Portland has an active, urban, lifestyle with a [lot of] respect for diverse interests."

Admissions

Admission to the MBA program is competitive based on GMAT scores, undergraduate GPA, and letters of reference. Applicants must achieve at least a 470 on the GMAT, with both verbal and quantitative scores exceeding the 35th percentile. Their undergraduate GPA must be above 2.75; those with lower GPAs may be asked to complete at least 12 hours of graduate work with a minimum GPA of 3.0 before gaining admission to the MBA program. Applicants must also provide two letters of recommendation and a one-page personal statement. Some international students are required to take the TOEFL. Students need a working knowledge of introductory calculus and basic computer functions. The school prefers applicants with a minimum of two years of business work experience.

FINANCIAL FACTS

Annual tuition (in-state/out-of-state)	$9,417/$17,427
Fees (in-state/out-of-state)	$1,050/$1,050
Books and supplies	$1,300
Room & board	$15,324
% of students receiving aid	70
% of students receiving grants	53
Average grant	$7,500

ADMISSIONS

Admissions Selectivity Rating	89
# of applications received	298
% applicants accepted	54
% acceptees attending	45
Average GMAT	620
Range of GMAT	520-730
Average GPA	3.3
TOEFL Required of International Students?	Yes
Minimum TOEFL (paper/computer)	550/213
Application fee	$50
International application fee	$50
Regular application deadline	4/1
Regular notification	6/30
Early decision program?	Yes
ED Deadline/Notification	1/1 / 4/1
Transfer students accepted?	Yes
Transfer application policy: Maximum of one third of the total number of PSU credits may be transferred from a US accredited university.	

APPLICANTS ALSO LOOK AT

Oregon State University, University of Oregon, University of Portland.

EMPLOYMENT PROFILE

Career Rating	77	Grads employed by field %: avg. salary	
# of companies recruiting on-campus	9	Finance	3: $57,600
% grads employed immediately	48	Marketing	2: $70,000
Average starting salary	$64,600	Consulting	1: $75,000

PURDUE UNIVERSITY
KRANNERT SCHOOL OF MANAGEMENT

GENERAL INFORMATION

Type of school	public
Environment	village
Academic calendar	semester

SURVEY SAYS...
Smart classrooms
Solid preparation in:
Teamwork
Quantitative skills

STUDENTS

Enrollment of parent institution	38,653
Enrollment of MBA program	281
% male/female	80/20
% out-of-state	86
% minorities	6
% international	38
Average age at entry	28
Average years work experience at entry	4

ACADEMICS

Academic Experience Rating	92
Student/faculty ratio	3:1
Profs interesting rating	86
Profs accessible rating	89
% female faculty	14
% minority faculty	10

Joint Degrees
BS Management/MBA 3+2 Program: 5 years; PhG/MSIA: 6 years; BS Industrial Engineering/MBA: 5 years; BS Mechanical Engineering/MBA: 5 years

Prominent Alumni
Joseph Forehand, Chairman, CEO, Accenture; Marshall Larsen, President, COO, Goodrich; Marjorie Magner, Chairman, CEO, Global Consumer Group, Citigroup; Albert Nahmad, Chairman, CEO, Watsco, Inc.; Jerry Rawls, CEO, Finisar.

Academics

Students who enroll in Krannert's School of Management at Purdue University can expect to receive a "no-nonsense MBA." According to most students, "the workload is extremely high, but the results include the ability to tackle any type of business problem." This is in part due to the faculty. Students say, "Professors range from very good to outstanding." Aside from being experts in their fields, they're "extremely accessible and are very open to students, even when the students are no longer in the professor's classes, [and know how to] seamlessly blend detailed academic understanding into real-world applications that create an enjoyable learning experience." And it's not just the faculty that is committed to the success of Krannert students. "The general administration faculty are outstanding. They go out of their way to make you feel at home and let you know they are always there if you need them." The student body, which is (internationally speaking, at least) very diverse, is also counted among Krannert's greatest strengths. "I believe we have the largest international population of any business school. This diverse group of people help enrich the learning experience here."

Krannert offers three full-time master's programs: a master's of business administration (MBA), a master's of science in human resource management (MSHRM), and a master's of science in industrial administration (MSIA). The MBA program is a two-year, 60-credit course of study, with 35 credits of required core courses. Students may choose to specialize in any of the following areas: accounting, finance, marketing, strategic management, operations management, information systems, e-business, and human-resource management. They may also select from three interdisciplinary options: general management, international management, and manufacturing management.

The MSHRM, also two years, requires 61 credits, divided into 24 credits for human-resource management and organizational behavior, twenty-five for general management with an analytical core, and 12 for a wide range of electives. The MSIA, however, is a one-year program and is considered the equivalent of an accelerated MBA. MSIAs aren't required to select a formal concentration but have the option of specializing during their spring and summer courses. According to Krannert's website, the MSIA program is "intended for highly ambitious students who are prepared for complete immersion into a very demanding and rewarding professional business-management curriculum."

For the most part, students appreciate the quant-oriented appeal of the program, especially because professors are skilled at teaching through case study. According to one student, "Only Harvard uses more cases to teach than Krannert. Case analysis takes a long time to complete, but I am refreshed to see that there is an emphasis placed on actual business-related scenarios instead of made-up examples." Students say courses in strategy, operations, quantitative skills, and finance are "top-notch," but many of them would like to see "more soft skills like negotiations and communication," and others think the school would benefit from more marketing electives.

Overall, most students say Krannert "boasts a warm, friendly environment, a solid curriculum, excellent placement assistance, and talented students. The burden truly is upon the student to take advantage of the wonderful resources available." Another student says, "Purdue's strength is its commitment to excellence and its challenging atmosphere. Even the best student would learn a lot."

Career and Placement

From the moment students arrive on campus, they're prepped for their eventual job search. According to one student, "Placement is a big focus here. They provide all the

JAMIE HOBBA, DIRECTOR OF ADMISSIONS
RAWLS HALL, ROOM 2020, 100 SOUTH GRANT STREET, WEST LAFAYETTE, IN 47907 UNITED STATES
PHONE: 765-494-0773 • FAX: 765-494-9841 • E-MAIL: MASTERS@KRANNERT.PURDUE.EDU
WEBSITE: WWW.KRANNERT.PURDUE.EDU/PROGRAMS/MASTERS/

resources we need to find the perfect placement for our desires and needs." Students complain, however, that "the companies recruiting here are often small divisions or groups with a few Purdue MBA alumni. We are not on many of the corporations' official recruiting stops. If companies don't come, you need to search through databases, write cover letters, and practically jump through hoops in order to try and get an interview!" Others wish that career services would "increase its efforts in attracting companies interested in recruiting international students to campus." Indeed, Purdue has recognized these issues and is continuing to work on attracting and retaining employers to recruit students; 2004–2005 recruiting was up 21 percent from the previous year.

Despite their gripes, numbers show that most students manage to find employment pretty quickly. By the August after they'd completed their degree, 80 percent of the class of 2003 had at least one offer of employment, and 75 percent had accepted an offer. Almost 75 percent of students ended up in the industry of manufacturing, but marketing/sales was the job function more popular than any other.

Student Life and Environment

Krannert is only home to about 375 students at any one time, so it makes sense that people talk about the school's "family atmosphere." Located in West Lafayette, Indiana, students say that while "most of the cultural life is found in Chicago, two hours away, or Indianapolis, a one-hour drive away," Krannert life is quite simple. "Of course," says one MBA, "West Lafayette does not provide any distractions that would make life complicated." Still, students say that on-campus activities comprise "almost anything anyone would want with nightlife, plays, entertainment, varsity sports, Greek life, and other activities." Students congregate at Harry's Chocolate Shop—a converted speakeasy—every Thursday night for drinks and networking, and there are "many, many clubs, both academic (i.e., finance club) and social (i.e., sushi club) for everyone to participate in."

West Lafayette's low cost of living is also a large draw, and the family feel ensures that "people say 'hi' to each other in the halls, and faculty have more time to give to individual students." In addition, an "incredible" new state-of-the-art building was recently completed, and the school continues to work on the building that houses the Morgan Center for Entrepreneurship.

Admissions

Of the thousands of applications Krannert receives each year, the ones that often stand out to admissions officers are those that "have substantial industry or military work experience." The mean GMAT score is 667, while the median is 670. The mean undergraduate GPA is 3.3, and 88 percent of the students had some full-time post-graduate work experience; 40 percent were international students, 17 percent were minority students, and 23 percent were female students in 2003.

FINANCIAL FACTS

Annual tuition (in-state/out-of-state)	$13,372/$26,488
Fees	$500
Books and supplies	$1,900
Room & board	$7,500
% of students receiving aid	73
% of first-year students receiving aid	66
% of students receiving grants	26
Average award package	$17,931
Average grant	$5,288
Average student loan debt	$32,530

ADMISSIONS

Admissions Selectivity Rating	91
# of applications received	828
% applicants accepted	44
% acceptees attending	33
Average GMAT	667
Range of GMAT	640-710
Average GPA	3.3
TOEFL Required of International Students?	Yes
Minimum TOEFL (paper/computer)	575/230
Application fee	$55
International application fee	$55
Regular application deadline	3/1
Regular notification	4/15
Application Deadline/Notification	
Round 1:	11/1 / 12/15
Round 2:	1/1 / 3/1
Round 3:	3/1 / 4/15
Round 4:	5/1 / 6/15
Early decision program?	Yes
ED Deadline/Notification	11/1 / 12/15
Deferment Available?	Yes
Maximum length of deferment	2 years
Need-blind admissions?	Yes

APPLICANTS ALSO LOOK AT

Indiana University, The Ohio State University, The University of Texas at Austin, University of Chicago, University of Michigan, University of North Carolina at Chapel Hill, University of Southern California.

Career Rating	86	Grads employed by field	%: avg. salary
Placement rate (%)	87	Finance	18: $77,284
% grads employed immediately	69	Human Resources	3: $67,647
Average starting salary	$74,915	Marketing	25: $69,426
		MIS	7: $71,604
		Operations	22: $77,175
		Consulting	5: $73,475
		General Management	16: $81,573
		Other	4: NR

QUINNIPIAC UNIVERSITY
SCHOOL OF BUSINESS

GENERAL INFORMATION
Type of school	private
Environment	town
Academic calendar	2005–2006

SURVEY SAYS...
Friendly students
Happy students
Smart classrooms
Solid preparation in:
Teamwork
Presentation skills

STUDENTS
Enrollment of parent institution	7,253
Enrollment of MBA program	222
% male/female	85/15
% part-time	68
% minorities	8
% international	9
Average age at entry	27
Average years work experience at entry	3

ACADEMICS
Academic Experience Rating	**61**
Student/faculty ratio	12:1
Profs interesting rating	67
Profs accessible rating	74
% female faculty	22
% minority faculty	30

Joint Degrees
MBA/JD: 4 years

Academics

The School of Business at Quinnipiac University capably serves both a part-time and a full-time MBA population. Part-time students make up about two-thirds of the MBA program and are primarily full-time working professionals, while one-third of the program is comprised of full-time students. The School of Business offers "extraordinary resources [and] small classes with ample instructor attention" to its MBAs.

Full-time students can complete the Quinnipiac MBA—which can be taken with either a thesis or non-thesis option—in as little as 15 months. Students who opt for the thesis research project must complete a thesis paper over the course of two semesters, under the supervision of a faculty member. Thesis topics must be approved by the department head and the director of the MBA program; theses are reviewed by the student's thesis advisor and a second faculty member. Students choosing the non-thesis option complete three electives in lieu of a thesis.

Quinnipiac offers concentrations in accounting/taxation, computer information systems, economics, finance, health administration, international business, management and marketing. While some here complain that "classes should focus more on how topics are applied in the real world, rather than their theoretical applications," most are "more than pleased with the learning environment and the pro-student attitude from the faculty and administrative personnel." Students tell us that the faculty across departments is "very well rounded. Every teacher at the MBA level has a PhD from a top business school and business experience in the given course." They are "generally accessible and great teachers," leading to "a good all-around experience."

Career and Placement

Quinnipiac maintains a central Office of Career Services, which serves both undergraduates and graduate students at the university. Many of Quinnipiac's part-time students are concurrently employed by such prominent area concerns as SBC-SNET, Anthem Blue Cross/Blue Shield, Yale New Haven Hospital, the Hospital of St. Raphael, Bayer, and United Technologies.

Student Life and Environment

Quinnipiac's MBA program makes its home in the Lender School of Business Center, whose assortment of classroom styles (tiered, semicircular, and conventional) accommodates a wide range of teaching and presentation styles. The facility also includes six breakout rooms for small meetings, two LAN rooms equipped with 24 workstations, wireless Internet access, and television monitors continually broadcasting CNBC and CNN. The school's network makes business databases available to students both on campus and at home, via the Internet. Quinnipiac's 47,000-square-foot Arnold Bernhard Library boasts a high-tech infrastructure that allows for access to numerous digital archives and online business resources. The newest resource to grace the campus is The Terry W. Goodwin 1967 Financial Technology Center. Dedicated in February 2005, it is a 1500 square foot simulated financial trading room with 31 dual-monitor computer workstations. This state-of-the-art facility allows students to access real-time financial data, practice analytical finance methods, conduct trading simulations, analyze economic databases and develop financial models.

LOUISE HOWE, ASSOCIATE DIRECTOR OF GRADUATE ADMISSIONS
275 MOUNT CARMEL AVE, AB-GRD, HAMDEN, CT 06518-1940 UNITED STATES
PHONE: 203-582-8672 • FAX: 203-582-3443
E-MAIL: GRADUATE@QUINNIPIAC.EDU • WEBSITE: WWW.QUINNIPIAC.EDU

Those students on the five-year plan constitute the bulk of the full-time MBA population; working students make up most of the part-time program. One student writes, "Each group has a different approach to coursework. Those students on the five-year plan who I have been involved with on group projects rely heavily on the more experienced students, in part because their course load is too heavy (six or seven classes a semester)." They also rely on more experienced students because "they are young and inexperienced, and they are in graduate-level courses which require business experience to participate. They are unprepared." Fortunately, "everyone seems to support each other within the framework of a healthy competitive environment. There is diversity, respect, and always something enriching to the learning experience." Part-timers note that "there is very little social activity offered for graduate students, especially those of us who attend part-time. The school life is really focused on the undergraduate campus community." Hopefully, the March '05 social event hosted by the newly formed Graduate Student Council is a sign for better things to come.

The Quinnipiac campus, set amid 400 wooded acres on the periphery of Sleeping Giant State Park, "is very beautiful. The setting of the state park sells itself; it creates a beautiful atmosphere." The bucolic location is very convenient to New Haven, which is eight miles away. New York City is 1.5 hours away by train or (theoretically within that timeframe) by automobile. Boston is about two hours to the Northeast.

Admissions

Quinnipiac processes MBA applications on a rolling basis. A complete application includes official transcripts for all post-secondary academic work, a recent resume, an official GMAT score report, two letters of recommendation, and a completed application form. The admissions office screens applicants using the formula [(undergraduate GPA × 200) + GMAT score], with a minimum acceptable score of 1000, a minimum undergraduate GPA of 2.7, and a minimum GMAT score of 500 generally required. Not all applicants who meet these criteria are admitted to the program. The school notes that "work experience and recommendations also are strongly considered in the process." Many Quinnipiac MBAs enter through the BS/MBA program, which is open to Quinnipiac undergraduates only; the school expects such students to have a minimum undergraduate GPA of 3.0 with at least a 3.25 GPA in their major. BS/MBA applicants are required to submit GMAT scores. International applicants must provide an official statement of sufficient financial support and, if their native language is not English, TOEFL scores.

FINANCIAL FACTS

Annual tuition	$9,540
Fees	$540
Books and supplies	$1,000
Room & board	$9,408
% of students receiving aid	55
% of first-year students receiving aid	65
% of students receiving loans	41
Average award package	$13,789
Average student loan debt	$13,074

ADMISSIONS

Admissions Selectivity Rating	66
# of applications received	123
% applicants accepted	77
% acceptees attending	68
Average GMAT	502
Range of GMAT	420-570
Average GPA	3.2
TOEFL Required of International Students?	Yes
Minimum TOEFL (paper/computer)	575/233
Application fee	$45
International application fee	$45
Regular application deadline	Rolling
Regular notification	Rolling
Deferment Available?	Yes
Maximum length of deferment	1 year
Transfer students accepted?	Yes
Transfer application policy: 9 transfer credits allowed with equivalent courses.	
Non-fall admissions?	Yes
Need-blind admissions?	Yes

APPLICANTS ALSO LOOK AT

Fairfield University, University of Connecticut, University of Hartford.

EMPLOYMENT PROFILE

Career Rating	60*
# of companies recruiting on-campus	150

RADFORD UNIVERSITY
COLLEGE OF BUSINESS AND ECONOMICS

GENERAL INFORMATION

Type of school	public
Environment	village
Academic calendar	

SURVEY SAYS...
Happy students
Smart classrooms
Solid preparation in:
Teamwork
Communication/interpersonal skills

STUDENTS

Enrollment of parent institution	8,368
Enrollment of MBA program	83
% male/female	55/45
% part-time	80
% minorities	5
% International	12
Average age at entry	29

ACADEMICS

Academic Experience Rating	80
Student/faculty ratio	3:1
Profs interesting rating	86
Profs accessible rating	76
% female faculty	25
% minority faculty	10

Academics

The College of Business and Economics at Radford University is home to a large undergraduate population; nearly one in four RU undergrads majors in a business-related area. The much smaller MBA program capitalizes on the resources and strengths of the school's undergraduate program to provide a solid generalist graduate degree. As one student assessed the program says, "the school is affordable, and it is good for someone who does not plan on conquering the world, but rather [someone who] wants to stay in their community and better themselves."

Because of the size of the program, MBAs at Radford enjoy "small classes with plenty of personal attention." One student notes, "after only one semester, I am already convinced going to this school was the right decision for future endeavors. Professors are easily accessible and responsive to students' needs, and the administration is very attentive." Radford's curriculum focuses on "the presentation experience" and a large dose of writing; "there are lots of challenging papers assigned," students warn. Because of the predominantly part-time nature of the program (classes are held almost exclusively in the evening), the program tends to be a little more lecture-based and academic than others. Some feel that "they need more opportunities to work with outside companies and more real-life examples of local companies and speakers" in order to gain more practical experience within the program.

What Radford isn't is a place to forge a high degree of expertise in one area. That's because "it is a basic MBA program that does not allow for specialization." Some students see this as a drawback; one writes, "I would like more marketing courses because I would like to go into the marketing field upon graduation. This program only offers one marketing course." Others feel they are best served by the program's broad approach; one student explains, "My analytical business-diagnosing skills and presentation skills have been greatly enhanced by this MBA program." Radford's curriculum consists of eight required courses and two electives; the greatest number of electives are available in economics, finance, and management. Aggressive students can complete the degree in as little as 12 months, although most students work full-time and accordingly attend the program on a part-time basis. MBA courses are offered in two locations: the main campus in Radford, Virginia, and the Roanoke Higher Education Center in Roanoke, Virginia.

Radford's "tough but fair" professors "are excellent and even inspiring. Students find that they want to do their best work for all of them." They also "have a good sense of humor," which comes in handy during those long three-hour classes following a full work day.

Career and Placement

The Center for Experiential Learning and Career Development at Radford University offers a variety of resources to undergraduates, graduates, and alumni. These include a virtual resume, internship, and job database "where students and employers come together to post and view resumes and position openings," as well as workshops in resume and portfolio development, career fairs, and career-assessment tools. In the spring of 2004, on-campus recruiters included DMG Securities, Ferguson Enterprises, Northwestern Mutual, State Farm, Wachovia Securities, and the federal government.

DR. DUNCAN HERRINGTON, DIRECTOR, MBA PROGRAM
MBA OFFICE, BOX 6956, RADFORD, VA 24142 UNITED STATES
PHONE: 540-831-5258 • FAX: 540-831-6655
E-MAIL: RUMBA@RADFORD.EDU. • WEBSITE: WWW.RADFORD.EDU/~COBE-WEB/

Student Life and Environment

Radford's MBA program serves two identifiable populations. The larger of the two consists of full-time workers who live in the area or in nearby Roanoke. The second, which is also substantial, is made up of "students fresh from Radford undergraduate programs. Many of these are relatively immature in behavior and in life knowledge." Wrote one of the professional students of his younger peers, "some of their writing skills have not been up to graduate-level quality, which can be a real problem in team situations. All of these issues should be taken care through the admissions process."

The Radford campus "has many formally organized activities," but most students are too busy to participate. The campus is small and pretty, attributes appreciated by the school's MBAs. Those who attend classes at the Roanoke Higher Education Center tell us that "the RHEC is a newly remodeled, high tech, and comfortable facility more suited to providing an appropriate atmosphere for educating older MBA students." Students at both campuses praise the school's "excellent website, telecommunications equipment, [and] library."

Hometown Radford is a small town in the Blue Ridge Mountains; Roanoke is about a half-hour away. The area is most amenable to outdoor enthusiasts, as it provides easy access to the Appalachian Trail, the New River, and Clayton Lake. Shopping, restaurants, nightlife, and such are not in great supply, students warn, although the proximity of Roanoke helps to make up for this deficiency. Charleston, Virginia, and Greensboro, North Carolina, are also within a reasonable driving distance.

Admissions

Admission to Radford's MBA program requires successful completion of an undergraduate degree with a minimum GPA of 2.75. Applicants must also submit an official report of GMAT scores, TOEFL scores (international students), two letters of recommendation, a resume of work experience, a personal statement of purpose, and "evidence of creativity and leadership." Also, "applicants must also have taken accredited collegiate preparation in the following foundation areas (or equivalents): fundamentals of financial accounting, fundamentals of managerial accounting, principles of economics I and II, organizational behavior, essentials of marketing, introduction to business finance, business statistics, and business calculus." Students can earn credit for some of these prerequisites through CLEP testing. Competency with computers is also a prerequisite.

FINANCIAL FACTS

Annual tuition (in-state/out-of-state)	$5,710/$10,524
Fees	$450
Books and supplies	$800
Room & board	$6,040

ADMISSIONS

Admissions Selectivity Rating	74
# of applications received	75
% applicants accepted	60
% acceptees attending	51
Average GMAT	480
Average GPA	3.1
TOEFL Required of International Students?	Yes
Minimum TOEFL (paper/computer)	550/215
Application fee	$40
Regular application deadline	Rolling
Regular notification	Rolling
Deferment Available?	Yes
Maximum length of deferment	1 year
Transfer students accepted?	Yes
Transfer application policy: Maximum of six credit hours may be transferred.	
Non-fall admissions?	Yes
Need-blind admissions?	Yes

APPLICANTS ALSO LOOK AT

Virginia Polytechnic Institute and State University.

EMPLOYMENT PROFILE

Career Rating	60*
# of companies recruiting on-campus	210

RENSSELEAR POLYTECHNIC INSTITUTE
LALLY SCHOOL OF MANAGEMENT AND TECHNOLOGY RESEARCH

Academics

The Lally School is located in Troy, New York, a historic town along the Hudson river that's over 200 years old. Once a major center of the Industrial Revolution (during the 1800s), Troy now finds itself at the center of a technological revolution. Rensselear's sterling reputation as a technical school has influenced Lally's direction. They have created an MBA program that combines technological innovation and a focus on entrepreneurship in a faculty team-taught curriculum that cuts across all business functions.

Lally's students, only about 70, find themselves in a place feverishly dedicated to the creation of entrepreneurial energy. Rensselear has state-of-the-art technical facilities, including a Center for Entrepreneurship, Business Incubator Program and the RPI tech-park, so it's no surprise that the Lally School's strength is in technological entrepreneurship. As the school says, "Technology creation and commercialization do not occur in an ivory tower; they happen in a competitive, increasingly global marketplace. Our students and faculty have a passion for taking ideas and turning them into real-world products." The students concur that "everybody at Rensselaer thinks about initiating a company." One student adds, "This makes it one of the best schools in providing a technology-driven MBA."

This year, Lally introduced a dynamic new MBA curriculum that identifies five critical areas for advancing business through innovation and mimics real-world decision-making. The curriculum is based on "streams of knowledge" modeled after their signature course, "Developing Innovative Products and Services", in which student teams develop a new product or service, write a business and marketing plan, and learn how to market and sell it. Students love this program, arguing that it "prepares future business leaders and strategic thinkers. Most courses incorporate projects that are applied to real businesses in the community." Some of the groups have even taken their products to compete in the "Tech Valley Collegiate Business Plan Competition" sponsored by the school's own Severino Center for Technological Entrepreneurship. There, teams compete for the money to make their theoretical venture a reality. Some groups from these classes have "actually now established themselves as startups!" Some students point out that "even if you don't have a desire to start your own company, the experiences you gain can be used in established tech companies."

However, none of this means that traditional b-school material is lacking. The school has a strict core curriculum, which takes up the entire first year of the MBA program and a summer internship is encouraged. In the second year, there are only three required classes; that year is primarily dedicated to specialization. A summer internship between the two years is strongly recommended, but is not a degree requirement. Throughout the academic program, students say that "professors are exceptional and expect high technical standards from students." Still, students would like to be allowed "more freedom to take electives" and would like to see "more seminars and more of a focus on financial-market topics."

Another specialized aspect of the Lally School is the strong connection it has with international businesses—particularly business education in Asia. An international management exchange program is offered, in which students can elect to spend a semester abroad at one of several universities in Europe and Asia. This creates a "diverse composition of student body" that students appreciate. In short, at a school described as "very techie and wired," there are plenty of opportunities to learn from the "cutting-edge research going on across campus."

FRANK J. MENDELSON, DIRECTOR OF GRADUATE ADMISSIONS, MBA/MS PROGRAMS
110 EIGHTH STREET, PITTSBURGH BUILDING, TROY, NY 12180-3590 UNITED STATES
PHONE: 518-276-6565 • FAX: 518-276-2665
E-MAIL: MENDEF@RPI.EDU • WEBSITE: WWW.LALLYSCHOOL.RPI.EDU

Career and Placement

Though the emphasis at Lally is so much about creating jobs rather than looking for them, career services reports that they've managed to place plenty of their students. The average salary for their MBA graduates in 2002 was around $75,000; 70 percent of those who completed the MBA were employed in the Northeast region of the United States, but 17 percent (the next-largest group) were employed internationally. Companies like GE Power Systems, Kaiser Permanente, and PricewaterhouseCoopers all recruit on campus, and about 30 percent of Lally graduates in 2002 ended up in project management. According to some students, the weakest link in the employment chain is Lally's "circle of alumni," who are not as involved as most current students would like to see.

Student Life and Environment

Troy is home to just about 55,000 people and once boasted such illustrious citizens as Samuel Wilson—that's Uncle Sam to you. Though it's a relatively small city, Troy—and students who make Troy their home—benefit from its proximity to Albany, which, despite what New York City likes to believe, is still the capital of the state. And students who manage to make time in their hectic academic schedule point out that there are "tons of cultural opportunities like readings, speakers, and music on campus and in town. We have a brewpub in town making great beer. There is a good live music scene." The school, along with student-run groups, tries to facilitate student interaction as well. "We have regular social functions that get both classes together and try to involve faculty as well. Since it's a smaller program, it's pretty close-knit and a lot of students organize social activities and invite the entire class."

Despite the assurances of most students that all the whole Rensselear campus boasts top-of-the-line technology, some students would like to see Lally "upgrade some of its classrooms." Another common complaint is that recent changes in administration have led to breakdowns in communication. Though the administration overall scores a high rating, most students wish the school could better communicate its goals to its students.

Admissions

Though the majority of Lally's admitted students come from some sort of technical background, 29 percent have some background in liberal arts or business. The average age for an admitted student at Lally is 29, but ages range from 21 to 39. The average work experience is about five years, the average GMAT is 643, and the average undergraduate GPA is 3.28.

FINANCIAL FACTS

Annual tuition	$31,000
Fees	$1,469
Books and supplies	$1,631
Room & board	$9,000
Average grant	$40,967

ADMISSIONS

Admissions Selectivity Rating	82
# of applications received	251
% applicants accepted	67
% acceptees attending	60
Average GMAT	618
Average GPA	3.1
TOEFL Required of International Students?	Yes
Minimum TOEFL (paper/computer)	600/250
Application fee	$60
International application fee	$60
Regular application deadline	Rolling
Regular notification	Rolling
Early decision program?	Yes
ED Deadline/Notification Fall semester,	1/15 / 2/15
Deferment Available?	Yes
Maximum length of deferment	1 year
Need-blind admissions?	Yes

APPLICANTS ALSO LOOK AT

Babson College, Boston University, Carnegie Mellon, Case Western Reserve University, Cornell University, Georgia Institute of Technology, Massachusetts Institute of Technology.

EMPLOYMENT PROFILE			
Career Rating	87	**Grads employed by field**	**%: avg. salary**
Placement rate (%)	100	Finance	33: $67,125
# of companies recruiting on-campus	35	Marketing	17: $68,750
% grads employed immediately	56	MIS	17: $61,700
Average starting salary	$65,033	Operations	11: $75,000
		Consulting	11: $56,000
		General Management	11: $60,000

RICE UNIVERSITY
JESSE H. JONES GRADUATE SCHOOL OF MANAGEMENT

GENERAL INFORMATION

Type of school	private
Environment	metropolis
Academic calendar	semester

SURVEY SAYS...
Smart classrooms
Solid preparation in:
Finance
Teamwork
Communication/interpersonal skills
Presentation skills

STUDENTS

Enrollment of parent institution	4,805
Enrollment of MBA program	325
% male/female	70/30
% out-of-state	22
% minorities	13
% international	21
Average age at entry	28
Average years work experience at entry	5

ACADEMICS

Academic Experience Rating	**87**
Student/faculty ratio	6:1
Profs interesting rating	86
Profs accessible rating	92
% female faculty	23
% minority faculty	23

Joint Degrees
MBA /Master of Electrical Engineering: 2 years; MBA/Master of Computer Science; MBA/Master of Chemical Engineering; MBA/Master of Civil Engineering; MBA/Master of Environmental Engineering; MBA/Master of Science in Mechanical Engineering; MBA/Master of Engineering; MBA/MD (with Baylor College of Medicine): 5 years

Academics

Because business schools contribute so heavily to the workforce of their local communities, the synergy between school and location can be an especially important factor in an MBA program. Rice—which would be a world-class university even if it were located in the middle of the tundra—benefits greatly from its location in Houston, a city second only to New York in the number of *Fortune* 500 companies hosted. A demanding curriculum with a number of standout features contributes equally to the high regard given Rice's Jones Graduate School of Management.

Rice piles on the work in the first-year core, doled out in 5- and 10-week modules to "allow for more flexibility and the opportunity to be exposed to a wider array of topics." The core includes courses in Rice's three strongest areas: finance, communications, and entrepreneurship. The highlight of first year is the action learning project, a 10-week undertaking that has students "working in teams on real-world problems on behalf of a wide variety of significant companies, such as Continental Airlines, ConocoPhillips, ExxonMobil, and Deloitte Touche Tohmatsu, as well as smaller start-ups and nonprofits." At least one student feels, "The Action Learning Project offered at Rice has helped me become an attractive candidate to employers," an added benefit of the project. Overall, students feel that "the course load is a bit too heavy for first years," noting that "the school offers fabulous enrichment experiences (such as guest speakers, seminars, and training programs), but we are too busy with schoolwork to enjoy all of them." Even so, they also praise the curriculum as "well-structured to impart the basics of the business experience while simultaneously enhancing writing, presentation, and communication skills so as to be prepared for internships and other outside business-related projects hosted by the school."

Second-year course work includes five more five-week core courses (including unique offerings in business-government relations, business ethics, and globalization); the rest of the year is given over to the electives (two of which must come from a pre-selected list of entrepreneurship classes). Older MBAs observe that "the full-time program is very much geared towards very young, relatively inexperienced people. This includes the career-placement center. Students with more than eight years of experience should definitely enroll in the EMBA program or go to another school."

Career and Placement

Most MBAs agree that "Rice has a very good career center, which brings top recruiters to the school and helps immensely with finding employment/internship positions for MBA students." They also praise the "close-knit alumni network;" one student notes, "Every Rice alumni I have contacted has offered to help with job opportunities, which I found really impressive." Asked where the service could improve, students suggested that "the office should pay greater attention to recruiting a wider variety of companies, such as marketing and real estate companies. There is perhaps too much focus on finance, oil, and gas, to the detriment of other areas."

Top employers of Rice MBAs include BP, CapRock, Deloitte Touche Tohmatsu, Deutsche Bank, ExxonMobil, FMC Technologies, Goldman Sachs, Hewlett-Packard, JPMorgan Chase & Co., Lehman Brothers, the Methodist Hospital, Noble Drilling, Sabre, Stewart & Stevenson, and UBS Warburg. About three-quarters of all Rice MBAs remain in the Texas region, with many of them remaining in Houston.

LISA W. ANDERSON, DIRECTOR OF ADMISSIONS
6100 MAIN STREET , MS 531, JONES SCHOOL STE. 109, PO BOX 2932, HOUSTON, TX 77005-1892 U.S.
PHONE: 888-844-4773 • FAX: 713-348-6147
E-MAIL: RICEMBA@RICE.EDU • WEBSITE: WWW.JONESGSM.RICE.EDU

Student Life and Environment

Life at Rice "is balanced between personal studies and numerous team projects," an equation most students find agreeable. The academic week ends on Thursday, students report, "and is typically capped with a first-year and second-year joint party on the patio—or as we say, 'partio'—at which time pizza is sponsored either by the student association or an outside firm that may want to mingle and informally meet with students." Other program-wide events include "alumni receptions and golf tourneys twice a year to network with alumni." In addition, there are "twice-a-week coffee colloquiums for students and faculty to mingle, and weekends frequently consist of groups of students planning social outings at area night establishments."

The Jones MBA program is housed in an "incredible state-of-the-art building" with "lots of team rooms, cutting-edge technology in all classrooms (incredible audiovisual tools)," and "comfortable classrooms with seats that can be changed to fit your comfort." Wireless connectivity "is everywhere." In sum, students agree that "the building and facilities are second to none. They really facilitate a learning environment where your options are almost unlimited."

They're just as enthusiastic about the Rice campus and hometown Houston. A typical MBA writes, "The campus is absolutely beautiful; the weather is great most of the time. Rice is located inside of Houston, so it gives you both the cozy campus life and the opportunity to venture into the city for more diverse entertainment. In Houston, there are more restaurants per capita than in any other city in the United States. Houston is a very international city with a great deal of diversity in terms of its people, its restaurants, and its entertainment."

Admissions

Applicants to Jones must provide the admissions committee with official copies of all undergraduate and graduate transcripts, GMAT scores, two letters of recommendation, three personal essays, and a resume. An interview is also required. "Meaningful post-undergraduate leadership and professional experience" is "strongly encouraged" but not required. The admissions committee considers an applicant's "leadership experience and team-based experiences, as well as the unique qualities that the candidate will contribute to the program." The school reports that "an independent organization, RICE-TMS, offers merit-based scholarships for underrepresented minority students completing an MBA at Rice."

Prominent Alumni

James S. Turley, Chairman, Ernst & Young LLP, Worldwide; Abby Rodgers, Vice President of Innovation, Coca-Cola; Keith Anderson, Founding Partner, BlackRock, Inc.; Doug Foshee, President & CEO, El Paso Energy Company; Caroline Caskey, Founder and CEO, Identigene.

FINANCIAL FACTS

Annual tuition	$30,000
Fees	$1,860
Books and supplies	$1,125
Room & board (on/off-campus)	$7,500/$10,500
% of students receiving aid	75
% of students receiving loans	62
% of students receiving grants	61
Average award package	$38,500
Average grant	$7,000
Average student loan debt	$63,690

ADMISSIONS

Admissions Selectivity Rating	86
# of applications received	684
% applicants accepted	53
% acceptees attending	44
Average GMAT	625
Range of GMAT	570-680
Average GPA	3.2
TOEFL Required of International Students?	Yes
Minimum TOEFL (paper/computer)	600/250
Application fee	$100
International application fee	$100
Regular application deadline	4/5
Regular notification	5/5
Application Deadline/Notification	
Round 1:	10/11 / 11/19
Round 2:	12/6 / 1/28
Round 3:	2/7 / 4/1
Round 4:	4/18 / 5/2
Early decision program?	Yes
ED Deadline/Notification	10/11 / 11/19
Deferment Available?	Yes
Maximum length of deferment	2 years
Need-blind admissions?	Yes

APPLICANTS ALSO LOOK AT

Emory U., Georgetown U., Indiana U., Purdue U., Southern Methodist U., U. of Texas at Austin, Vanderbilt U.

EMPLOYMENT PROFILE

Career Rating	88	Grads employed by field	%: avg. salary
Placement rate (%)	85	Finance	54: $74,881
# of companies recruiting on-campus	194	Marketing	13: $68,107
% grads employed immediately	57	Operations	2: $74,250
Average starting salary	$75,110	Consulting	17: $83,778
		General Management	9: $73,000
		Other	5: $73,750

ROLLINS COLLEGE
CRUMMER GRADUATE SCHOOL OF BUSINESS

GENERAL INFORMATION

Type of school	private
Environment	town
Academic calendar	semester

SURVEY SAYS...
Smart classrooms
Solid preparation in:
Teamwork
Computer skills

STUDENTS

Enrollment of parent institution	3,726
Enrollment of MBA program	422
% male/female	65/35
% out-of-state	26
% part-time	60
% minorities	18
% international	23
Average age at entry	26
Average years work experience at entry	3

ACADEMICS

Academic Experience Rating	**85**
Student/faculty ratio	20:1
Profs interesting rating	91
Profs accessible rating	95
% female faculty	18
% minority faculty	14

Prominent Alumni
Al Weiss, President; Thomas Jones, Senior Vice President Operations; Steve Grune, Punlisher; Charles Rice, President; F. Duane Ackerman, President & CEO.

Academics

Rollins College's Crummer Graduate School of Business offers students an MBA program "geared for general managers, not specialists" that "truly prepares students for general management and big-picture issues." For convenience's sake, Crummer, which has "a great regional reputation," serves the program up in five different varieties: full-time students can choose either a one-year or two-year program, while part-timers have the option of attending either the professional MBA program (part-time evening program) the Saturday MBA Program (classes are held on Saturdays), or the executive MBA program (alternating Fridays/Saturdays for students with extensive professional experience). All five programs include core courses, electives, and integrative capstone course work; the full-time programs also include an international study trip. Crummer tells us that its "experienced faculty has developed an international reputation for teaching through a hands-on method of applying business concepts." Students approve, telling us that "the faculty and administration at Crummer are completely committed to making the student experience as successful as possible. I believe that the professors take pride in the art of teaching." Noted one MBA, "I was really surprised by the teachers I got for my classes. Not only are they leaders in their field of work, but also they convey their knowledge in an understandable manner. Excellent teacher selection!" Administrators, we're told, "are constantly initiating innovative programming to enhance the student experience." Students also appreciate the curriculum's "strong focus on working in teams, giving presentations, class participation, and use of technology" and the "small class size, which helps us greatly." The program "has less of a focus on quantitative than expected, yet with very intensive use of Excel spreadsheets."

Top concentrations at Crummer include management, finance, e-commerce, and international business. MBAs observe that "[twenty percent] of our students are international, and a focus on international business issues are woven into most classes." Crummer "has an excellent mentor program and is very active in the community;" all students must fulfill a ten-hour service requirement to a not-for-profit organization.

Career and Placement

The Crummer Career Management Center offers skill-development workshops, online self-assessment tools, job listings, and online job databases and resume books. Crummer depends on participation in consortia for recruiting to offset the trend that fewer companies are scheduling on-campus interviewing sessions. Students feel that "a much greater emphasis needs to be put on bringing more companies to campus for recruiting. The office also needs to put more pressure on the MBA Consortium it is a member of to include only MBA-caliber jobs at its career events." Many feel that "the office is understaffed to properly serve the needs of all five MBA programs, although the center just increased the staff this year."

Major employers of Rollins MBAs include Anderson Consulting, AT&T, CIA, Citigroup, CNL, Darden Restaurant Group, Dyntech, FedEx, General Mills, Harris Corporation, Bank of America, The Marriott Corporation, Dell, Seimens Westinghouse, SunTrust Bank, Tupperware, Universal Studios, and Walt Disney. About 1 in 10 Rollins MBAs finds a first post-degree job outside the United States.

Student Life and Environment

Crummer MBAs agree that Rollins and hometown Winter Park offer an extraordinary quality of life. As one student put it, "Central Florida is paradise, so what more needs be said? When we're not involved in schoolwork, the area offers anything you could ever want to do, from beaches to amusement parks to lively entertainment districts. The warm climate allows me to participate year-round in outdoor activities such as biking, golf, and soccer." Another writes, "Winter Park is very upscale, so there is a wide variety

STEPHEN GAUTHIER, ASSOCIATE DEAN
1000 HOLT AVEENUE, 2722, WINTER PARK, FL 32789-4499 UNITED STATES
PHONE: 407-646-2405 • FAX: 407-646-1550
E-MAIL: CRUMMER@ROLLINS.EDU • WEBSITE: WWW.CRUMMER.ROLLINS.EDU

of top restaurants and bars in town and some more reasonably priced sports bars. Orlando is close by, so there are clubs and bars." Students in the full-time Early Advantage MBA programs are a tight-knit group of "mostly young people (with little business experience and with strong academic backgrounds), so there are regular bar outings for those who party." One full-timer writes, "Whether it be happy hour at the local Irish pub, dinner at one of the bistros on Park Avenue, paintball, a bowling competition, or a casino cruise, this school knows how to offer students a good break from the grueling world of case studies and marketing plans." The pace of life has quickened of late; students report that the "2003 to 2004 has been the year of student activities. Existing clubs were reinvigorated and new clubs have been created, such as the Entrepreneurship Club." One student gleefully claims that "students here are more alive than ever."

Crummer has a large international population, with "students from the U.K., India, Belgium, China, Romania, and many more. There's a real international focus; last summer the entire class went on a trip to London and Dublin. (This is included in tuition.) This trip focused on visiting businesses and academic institutions. It was also a great chance to party together and see some sights."

The Rollins campus "is beautiful in both appearance and people," and because "there are only four main classrooms, students tend to see a lot of each other. The student lounge just got a face lift and looks better, but it still needs some work." Also in need of an upgrade are nuts-and-bolts tech facilities; one MBA explains, "There is high-speed Internet, but some of the connections work while others do not. True, there is state-of-the-art technology, videoconferencing, and speaker phones for group interviews. Nevertheless, it is the little things that count, and in this arena, the school really needs to make sure all the Ethernet ports work, without question." Agreed another student, "The b-school study area could use an upgrade in technology. Our copier, printing capabilities, and wireless system always seem to be having problems, forcing us to run across to the Kinko's or the UPS store." However, the school has reacted by replacing some of the older printers and is in the process of upgrading the campus-wide Internet system.

Admissions

"Previous academic records, score on the Graduate Management Admission Test (GMAT), prior work experience, and evidence of maturity and motivation" all factor into the Rollins admissions decision. Admission to the school's five MBA programs is competitive. Applicants are required to submit official transcripts for all undergraduate and graduate work, GMAT scores, personal essays, two letters of recommendation, and a resume. A personal interview is required phone or teleconference interviews can be arranged for candidates who cannot visit the campus. Rollins offers scholarships and graduate assistantships to attract minority students and students from disadvantaged backgrounds.

FINANCIAL FACTS

Annual tuition	$24,800
Fees	$60
Books and supplies	$1,500
Room & board	$14,520
% of students receiving aid	50
% of first-year students receiving aid	50
% of students receiving grants	50
Average award package	$12,000
Average grant	$13,447
Average student loan debt	$28,900

ADMISSIONS

Admissions Selectivity Rating	80
# of applications received	237
% applicants accepted	68
% acceptees attending	68
Average GMAT	585
Range of GMAT	530-640
Average GPA	3.2
TOEFL Required of International Students?	Yes
Application fee	$50
International application fee	$50
Regular application deadline	Rolling
Regular notification	Rolling
Deferment Available?	Yes
Maximum length of deferment	1 year
Transfer students accepted?	Yes

Transfer application policy: The school accepts up to 6 credits transferred from an MBA program that is accredited by the AACSB.

Non-fall admissions?	Yes
Need-blind admissions?	Yes

APPLICANTS ALSO LOOK AT

Florida State University, Stetson University, University of Central Florida, University of Florida, University of Miami, Vanderbilt University, Wake Forest University.

Career Rating	76	Grads employed by field	%: avg. salary
Placement rate (%)	82	Finance	34: $47,340
# of companies recruiting on-campus	12	Human Resources	4: $52,700
% grads employed immediately	55	Marketing	25: $50,000
Average starting salary	$51,600	MIS	3: $70,000
		Operations	8: $66,200
		Consulting	7: $62,500
		General Management	4: $55,800
		Other	15: $50,750

ROWAN UNIVERSITY
COLLEGE OF BUSINESS

Academics

Rowan University's MBA program, the school tells us, "is especially suited for full-time employees working in the tristate area" encompassing Pennsylvania, New Jersey, and Delaware. "As working adults, we have been treated like valued customers," one student notes, pointing out that the once-a-week, three-hour classes (mostly weeknight evenings, with some classes held on Saturday mornings) best fits her busy work schedule. Because most students attend part-time, a Rowan degree usually takes between three and six years to complete; the school's few full-time students can conceivably complete the program in a single year.

The Rowan MBA curriculum commences with 27 hours of required core courses covering fundamental general-management skills and concludes with an integrative capstone seminar. The curriculum also leaves room for nine hours of electives; students may choose to take a variety of courses that match their career needs or may use these courses to specialize in finance, accounting, or management. MBAs tell us that "every class involves group work, which teaches students to work well with each other and share work. This skill set has helped in the workforce as well." They also wish the school would expand its selection of electives; one student observes, "Rowan could offer specializations in some different tracks, such as human resources and marketing. This would help the program grow."

The program has been growing in recent years, a fact that students acknowledge and appreciate. The school recently earned AACSB accreditation, placing it among the nation's top programs. Students tell us that "there has been an increase in the quality of the program, and [they] were delighted when the Rowan program was accredited last year. Enrollment has increased, and [they] see a great future for Rowan's MBA program." One graduating BA/MBA student told us that "although the program started at a low level, it is now getting tougher and tougher to get into." The increased standards, we're told, have paid dividends in more challenging classes and more illuminating in-class discussions.

Rowan MBAs love that "we are able to access the library's databases from our home computers. It's great to be able to look up material 24/7. Also, online and tele-registrations have reduced the hassle of registering to zero." Technology remains in the spotlight in the classroom; "Rowan teaches computer skills that have proven invaluable in the workforce," students tell us, although they also complain that "the audiovisual capabilities are terrible in all but one classroom. It is a very limiting feature when trying to receive information or do presentations." Overall, students feel that Rowan "is a great regional school whose current programs and commitment to expansion of the program will continue to take great strides in drawing students from outside this region."

Career and Placement

Rowan maintains a Career and Academic Planning Center "to provide developmental advising" to all students in their pursuit of academic and professional goals. The CAPC serves the entire school; there is no office dedicated specifically to MBAs or to business students on the undergraduate and graduate levels. CAPC Services include one-on-one counseling, workshops, online self-assessment and job databases (jobdirect.com, Career Key), career publications, and employer directories. Services are available to alumni as well as to current students. It should be noted that most current students are full-time workers looking to advance within their current places of work; relatively few students seeking MBAs are actively searching for new jobs.

THE GRADUATE SCHOOL, DIRECTOR OF GRADUATE ADMISSIONS
MEMORIAL HALL, 201 MULLICA HILL ROAD, GLASSBORO, NJ 08028 UNITED STATES
PHONE: 856-256-4050 • FAX: 856-256-4436
E-MAIL: GILCHRIST@ROWAN.EDU • WEBSITE: WWW.ROWAN.EDU

Student Life and Environment

Because Rowan serves part-time students almost exclusively, its student body is more "a collection of people that get together in the evening for three hours" than a coherent and cohesive community. That's not to say the opportunities to socialize and network aren't there; as one BA/MBA student explains, "As an undergraduate, I found many activities that were available to students who lived on and off campus. I enjoyed my four years living on campus. Rowan had activities for everyone, including day and evening events, student government, community-service efforts, fraternities, and campus-wide events. As a graduate student, however, I am a working professional, so I do not have any time to participate in the activities available."

Rowan's suburban New Jersey home town of Glassboro is a mere half-hour's drive from Philadelphia; the Jersey shore is less than an hour to the east, and Atlantic City is only 50 miles away. New York; Washington, DC; and the Chesapeake are all within easy travel distances. The Rowan campus is in the middle of an ambitious expansion program, with makeovers planned for most facilities and several new buildings going up. Students praise the new athletic center and enjoy watching Rowan's Division III excellent men's and women's basketball teams.

Admissions

Rowan's graduate b-students are required to complete seven foundation courses, or their undergraduate equivalents, prior to enrolling in the MBA program; those courses are foundations of accounting, statistics I, principles of finance, principles of marketing, calculus, operations management, and global perspective on economics. Those lacking the required course work must enroll in the pre-MBA program; admission to the pre-MBA program does not ensure admission to the MBA program. Applicants to the MBA program must submit official transcripts for all undergraduate work (with a minimum GPA of 2.5. overall or 2.8 for final 60 semester hours), GMAT scores, two letters of recommendation, a personal statement of career objectives, evidence of computer proficiency, and a resume. International students whose first language is not English must also provide TOEFL scores.

FINANCIAL FACTS

Annual tuition (in-state/out-of-state)	$4,577/$7,331
Fees	$859
Books and supplies	$700
Room & board (on-campus)	$5,600

ADMISSIONS

Admissions Selectivity Rating	64
# of applications received	45
% applicants accepted	98
% acceptees attending	89
Average GMAT	505
Range of GMAT	460-550
Average GPA	3.2
TOEFL Required of International Students?	Yes
Minimum TOEFL (paper/computer)	550/213
Application fee	$50
International application fee	$50
Regular application deadline	Rolling
Regular notification	Rolling
Deferment Available?	Yes
Maximum length of deferment	1 year
Transfer students accepted?	Yes
Transfer application policy: Student may transfer up to 9 credit hours.	
Non-fall admissions?	Yes
Need-blind admissions?	Yes

APPLICANTS ALSO LOOK AT

Rutgers—The State University of New Jersey—Camden.

RSM ERASMUS UNIVERSITY

Academics

An international curriculum well-suited to an international student body—that's the formula at RSM Erasmus University, and it's one students endorse. In a typical year, aspiring MBAs representing more than 50 countries attend the school; the faculty has a similarly international aspect. Course materials, case studies, and class discussion all focus steadily on global business issues. With nearly 30 exchange partner schools available to students, MBAs can even take their business studies abroad to any continent (well, except Antarctica).

RSM Erasmus University's full-time MBA is a 15-month intensive program divided into four terms. The first term covers core competencies and career- and professional-development skills; the second investigates business disciplines and continues career-development work; the third consists of core career concentration courses, followed by an internship and a research project on the company sponsoring the internship; and the fourth term allows students to pursue electives. Students praise the curriculum's "recognition of environmental and sustainability issues in business" and rate the accounting and marketing faculty very highly. They are less enthusiastic about economics and statistics professors. "Overall, this is a great program for general management studies," sums up one MBA, adding that "the visiting professors are generally better than the resident professors."

Throughout the RSM Erasmus University curriculum, "an important part of the learning process is working on assignments in groups. Group members not only come from different cultures but also from different backgrounds. This diversity results in sharing both knowledge and experiences and, of course, learning how to cope with such cultural diversity. Not easy during tough times!" Students also appreciate how "the small class size ensures that everybody gets individual attention. The sessions are highly interactive, making our classes very interesting."

Career and Placement

The Career Management Centre at RSM Erasmus University, according to the school, "is dedicated to helping students make sound career choices. They provide guidance, training, and support to help you. The CMC also supports, coordinates, and facilitates company presentations and other recruitment events for many top international firms to provide you with the opportunity to meet as many companies as possible on campus." Students tell us that the office does a good job of attracting recruiters from consultancies and banks but is less adept with other sectors.

Major employers of MBAs include ABN Amro, AT Kearney, Bain and Company, Barclays Capital, Benson, Bertelsmann, Boston Consulting Group, Citibank, Citigroup, Eli Lilly, Ford Motor Company, General Electric, Hilti, Johnson & Johnson, Lehman Brothers, McKinsey, Novartis, Roland Berger Strategy Consultants, and Royal Dutch Shell. About one in four graduates finds work in the Netherlands; another 40 percent take jobs in Western Europe, and 14 percent of all graduates find jobs in the Americas.

Student Life and Environment

The 15-month curriculum condenses a lot of information into a relatively short period, placing a substantial academic burden on students. MBAs observe, "It is crucial to find a balance between hard work and social life. As a first-class European MBA program, the school puts significant pressure with lots of readings and work, either in groups or class preparation. On the other hand, it does give you time to enjoy other activities (i.e., social events like the Chinese celebration of New Year, where many students had a beautiful

LUISA MAGALHAES/KIRSTY JOHNSTON, MARKETING & ADMISSIONS MANAGER
BURGEMEESTER OUDLAAN 50—J BUILDING, 3062 PA ROTTERDAM, NETHERLANDS
PHONE: 011-31-10-4082222 • FAX: 011-31-10-4082222
E-MAIL: MBA.INFO@RSM.NL • WEBSITE: WWW.RSM.NL

dinner together) and help you understand what your career should really look like."

A collegial student body helps MBAs manage the workload, which "is so intense that you are constantly running to and from lectures or group meetings. Fortunately, people are very helpful and friendly, and everyone looks out for each other regardless of nationality." Students are "an extremely diverse and international group. It is amazing to talk with people from different backgrounds." Many convene in program-related clubs serving many different professional and extracurricular interests.

Rotterdam, a large port city of 600,000, is located just 45 miles from Amsterdam. It lacks the many tourist attractions common to large European cities, primarily because the city was nearly destroyed during World War II. The city harbor, considered by many the world's largest, brings in trade from around the world and makes Rotterdam a truly international city. Shopping areas and restaurants are plentiful, although students warn that "prices in the Netherlands are high."

Admissions

Admission to the RSM Erasmus University MBA program is contingent on all the following factors: professional achievements and goals, as reflected in one's resume/curriculum vitae; academic achievement, as reflected in one's academic transcripts and GMAT scores; leadership qualities; English-language proficiency; personality; and ability to contribute to an international atmosphere. Two letters of recommendation and a personal interview are required. The school estimates that the entire review process takes about 6 weeks from the time the admissions office receives all application materials.

FINANCIAL FACTS

Annual tuition	$43,800
Books and supplies	$23,800

ADMISSIONS

Admissions Selectivity Rating	89
# of applications received	486
% applicants accepted	49
% acceptees attending	48
Average GMAT	630
Range of GMAT	550-700
Average GPA	3.5
Minimum TOEFL (paper/computer)	600/250
Application fee	$100
International application fee	$100
Regular application deadline	7/15
Regular notification	Rolling
Need-blind admissions?	Yes

EMPLOYMENT PROFILE

Career Rating	83	Grads employed by field:	
Placement rate (%)	95	Finance	26
# of companies recruiting on-campus	100	Human Resources	1
% grads employed immediately	56	Marketing	18
Average starting salary	$72,500	MIS	2
		Operations	5
		Consulting	34
		General Management	9

RUTGERS, THE STATE UNIVERSITY OF NJ—CAMDEN
SCHOOL OF BUSINESS MBA PROGRAM

GENERAL INFORMATION
Type of school	public
Academic calendar	semester

SURVEY SAYS...
Friendly students
Happy students
Smart classrooms
Solid preparation in:
Marketing
Teamwork
Communication/interpersonal skills
Presentation skills

STUDENTS
Enrollment of parent institution	5,052
Enrollment of MBA program	305
% male/female	60/40
% part-time	85
% minorities	9
% international	15
Average age at entry	28

ACADEMICS
Academic Experience Rating	**78**
Profs interesting rating	88
Profs accessible rating	85
Joint Degrees	
MBA/JD: 3-5 years	
MBA/MD: 5-6 years	

Academics

Located just across the Benjamin Franklin Bridge from Philadelphia, the School of Business MBA Program at Rutgers—Camden offers a convenient and affordable graduate degree option for both Garden State and City of Brotherly Love residents. This small program consists almost entirely of part-time students pursuing degrees while simultaneously engaging in careers and, quite often, starting families.

Fortunately for these busy students, "professors and administrators bend over backwards for the students to ensure they are achieving their educational goals" by "making themselves very accessible. Their main priority is ensuring that we understand everything gone over in class and can apply it to the real world." Students here also appreciate that "classes are well organized and there are many opportunities to enroll in unique courses that include exposure to industry professionals." On the downside, some here feel that "expectations for student performance are too low in general and the amount of material covered is not enough to feel really comfortable in a number of areas."

The Rutgers MBA consists of 60 credits, 36 devoted to the core curriculum and 24 to electives. The school website notes, "Some course requirements may be waived based upon prior knowledge gained at the undergraduate level." Students may combine four electives to create a concentration in one of the following disciplines: accounting, e-commerce technology, finance, international business, health-care management, management, or marketing. Concentrations in international business and health-care management piggyback on other divisions of the university, allowing students to gain exposure to the School of Law and the Department of Public Policy and Administration. Students are not required to concentrate in an area; they may opt instead for a general MBA. Thanks to "institutional relationships with universities and companies in Namibia and South Africa," Rutgers MBAs have the opportunity to study abroad and "experience firsthand the issues facing emerging global markets." Study in Europe is also an option. The business school also offers classes in Voorhees and Atlantic City.

Career and Placement

The Career Center at Rutgers University/Camden handles counseling and placement services for all undergraduate and graduate students. The office provides all the following services: assessment inventories; career counseling; a career library; job fairs; on-campus recruiting events; resume critique; skills seminars; and Web-based resume posting. More than one hundred recruiters visit the Camden campus each year. Top recruiters include: Bally's Park Place Casino and Resort, Bristol-Myers Squibb, Campbell Soup Company, PHH Mortgage, Commerce Bank, Galaxy Scientific, J&J Snack Foods, Lockheed Martin, Merck, Mobil, Okidata, PaineWebber, PSE&G, Rohm and Haas, and the U.S. Air Force.

Dr. Barbara Bickart, MBA Program Director
MBA Program, Camden, NJ 08102-1401 United States
Phone: 856-225-6452 • Fax: 856-225-6231
E-mail: mba@camden-sba.rutgers.edu • Website: www.camden-sbc.rutgers.edu

FINANCIAL FACTS
Annual tuition (in-state/out-of-state)
$13,310/$20,170

ADMISSIONS
Admissions Selectivity Rating	**79**
# of applications received	160
% applicants accepted	63
% acceptees attending	63
TOEFL Required of	
International Students?	Yes
Minimum TOEFL (computer)	230
Application fee	$50
Regular application deadline	
	8/1 (Fall)
	11/1 (Spring)
Regular notification	Rolling

Student Life and Environment

Most Rutgers-Camden MBAs "are married with children and work full-time. In spite of this, they show up to class regularly, have their work done on time, and participate a lot in class. We do a lot of group work, and most people are easy to work with." One student observes, "Everyone is really nice and willing to help you out with knowledge from other classes they may have taken already. Throughout the semester you get real close with your classmates. The business school is really like a family here." Rutgers' on-the-go grads appreciate how "the campus is specifically geared toward the busy professional who wants to jump start his or her career. The library is open late during the regular semesters, although it closes early in the summer and winter intermission sessions."

Those who seek opportunities on this campus usually find them. One MBA explains, "The business school has connected me with a lot of great employers and I have been doing a lot of interviews. The campus offers a lot of activities and events that are open to all students regardless of what school they are in." Students love the convenience of Camden, which can be easily accessed via public transportation (the PATCO Hi-Speed train line) or automobile. They warn that "there's not a lot to do in Camden," but with Philadelphia so close by (and Atlantic City an easy drive or bus ride away), there's always plenty to do within a reasonable travel distance.

Admissions

Applicants to the School of Business MBA Program at Rutgers-Camden must submit the following materials: an online application form; an official score report for the GMAT the average score is approximately 560; two official copies of transcripts for all post-secondary academic work (minimum undergraduate GPA of 2.5 required); three letters of recommendation; a personal statement; and a resume. International students must also submit appropriate financial documentation; those whose first language is not English must submit official score reports for the TOEFL (minimum acceptable score of 550 paper-based test or 230 computer-based test) or IELTS (minimum acceptable score of Band 7).

Career Rating	**84**
Placement rate (%)	97
# of companies recruiting on-campus	150
% grads employed immediately	92
% grads employed within three months	98
Average starting salary	$76,000

SAGINAW VALLEY STATE UNIVERSITY
COLLEGE OF BUSINESS AND MANAGEMENT

GENERAL INFORMATION

Type of school	public
Academic calendar	year round

SURVEY SAYS...
Friendly students
Smart classrooms

STUDENTS

Enrollment of parent institution	9,448
Enrollment of MBA program	60
% male/female	40/60
% part-time	67
% minorities	15
% international	35
Average age at entry	30
Average years work experience at entry	7

ACADEMICS

Academic Experience Rating	**67**
Student/faculty ratio	5:1
Profs interesting rating	71
Profs accessible rating	62
% female faculty	8
% minority faculty	8

Academics

Students cite convenience, affordability, and AACSB accreditation as their main reasons for choosing the MBA program at Saginaw Valley State. Most students attend the school part-time while holding down full-time jobs. That's why they appreciate the flexibility of the program, which allows them to complete their degree at their own pace. Full-timers here are typically international students or accounting undergraduates participating in the 3/2 BBA/MBA degree program.

The MBA program at SVSU begins with a nine-course business and management foundation sequence covering the basic principles of accounting, economics, statistics, finance, business law, organization, operations, MIS, and marketing. Students with related undergraduate course work are generally allowed to waive these courses and proceed directly to the business core, a nine-course curriculum of required courses. The business core courses focus on global business, business ethics, managerial accounting, macroeconomics, managerial finance, organizational behavior and leadership, business process design, integrated marketing management, and management of global corporations. Students must also complete three elective courses. The school offers an international business concentration.

Students at SVSU say, "Most of the professors have taught us through real-life experiences of their own, which is a definite plus." (Though some students remark that several professors could "use even more real life experience to teach from.") Another plus is that "professors make themselves available more than I would have imagined. Sometimes e-mail is most convenient, and they seem to be quick at getting back with me," notes one student. Students also praise the school's "relatively new equipment and facilities," the "small class size," and "the option to take a class as an independent study for some classes." Their complaints generally derive from the size of the program, which limits options. One student writes, "There are limited electives every term and it's hard to wait until one is offered that looks interesting, so sometimes you have to take one just because it is the only class available for you during the term." Another warns, "Classes get dropped frequently. Many classes are rarely offered, yet are required to graduate."

Career and Placement

Though Saginaw Valley State's Career Planning and Placement Office primarily serves undergraduates, MBA students also receive assistance and counseling in the areas of online databases, counseling, mock interviews, and coordination between students and alumni. For MBAs, professors are generally more helpful; many are, or recently were, active in the area business community and can provide contacts and recommendations to students. A recent SVSU internal survey showed that 93 percent of its MBA holders were employed full-time; 83 percent were employed in fields related to their major. Of the many students who attended SVSU while working full-time, 61 percent received a promotion from their employer after completing the degree.

JILL WETMORE, ASSISTANT DEAN, COLLEGE OF BUSINESS AND MANAGEMENT
7400 BAY ROAD., 320 CURTISS HALL, UNIVERSITY CENTER, MI 48710 UNITED STATES
PHONE: 989-964-4064 • FAX: 989-964-7497
E-MAIL: CBMDEAN@SVSU.EDU • WEBSITE: WWW.SVSU.EDU/CBM

Student Life and Environment

SVSU's 782-acre campus is located in east central Michigan's tri-city area and serves the communities of Bay City, Midland, and Saginaw. The MBA program makes its home in Curtis Hall, a facility that also houses the University Conference and Events Center. As a result, students needn't leave the building to attend plays, conferences, and lectures.

Most SVSU MBA students have full-time commitments beyond school—work, family, community, often all three—and thus have time to visit campus only for classes, study, group meetings, and meetings with professors. Students are relieved to find that "the environment has worked out well" to meet their busy schedules, noting that "professors are very accommodating." One student writes, "Most of the group projects have team members who are willing to meet to get the project done and they are flexible in meeting times."

Although they don't spend as much time with each other as do their peers in predominantly full-time programs, SVSU MBAs manage to bond through classes and projects. One explains, "Classes encourage interaction and we get to know most of our fellow students because the average class size is relatively small." They tell us that their classmates "tend to be here because of a desire to be more competitive in the professional world, but do not tend to be overly competitive with each other." SVSU "seems to attract a large percentage of its students from the professional world, and a fair number of students internationally. The number of international students is surprising because SVSU is a smaller school in a smaller community."

Admissions

The admissions department applies a formula to establish a floor for all applicants. To be considered for admission, students must score above 1050 under the formula [(undergraduate GPA for final two years of four-year undergraduate program × 200) + GMAT score], and must have a GMAT score of at least 450. Applicants must also submit a current resume, a one-page personal essay (statement of goals), two letters of reference, and official copies of all undergraduate and graduate transcripts. International students also need to demonstrate sufficient finances to support themselves while studying in the United States; additional documents are also required of them. Applicants whose first language is not English must submit official TOEFL scores. Undergraduates in the SVSU Accounting Program may opt for a 3/2 option at the end of their junior year—successful completion of which results in a BBA and MBA at the end of five years' study.

FINANCIAL FACTS

Annual tuition (in-state/out-of-state)	$4,271/$10,377
Fees	$642
Books and supplies	$800
Room & board	$5,850
% of students receiving aid	55
% of first-year students receiving aid	56
% of students receiving loans	46.5
% of students receiving grants	19.5
Average award package	$6,140
Average grant	$3,236
Average student loan debt	$3,395

ADMISSIONS

Admissions Selectivity Rating	69
# of applications received	26
% applicants accepted	92
% acceptees attending	92
Average GMAT	530
Range of GMAT	480-580
Average GPA	3.3
TOEFL Required of International Students?	Yes
Minimum TOEFL (paper/computer)	525/197
Application fee	$25
International application fee	$25
Regular application deadline	Rolling
Regular notification	Rolling
Deferment Available?	Yes
Maximum length of deferment	7 semesters
Transfer students accepted?	Yes
Transfer application policy: May transfer 6 credits.	
Non-fall admissions?	Yes
Need-blind admissions?	Yes

APPLICANTS ALSO LOOK AT

Central Michigan University, Michigan State University, Northwood University, University of Michigan—Flint.

EMPLOYMENT PROFILE	
Career Rating	70
# of companies recruiting on-campus	40

SAINT JOSEPH'S UNIVERSITY
ERIVAN K. HAUB SCHOOL OF BUSINESS

GENERAL INFORMATION
Type of school	private
Affiliation	Jesuit
Environment	metropolis
Academic calendar	semesters

SURVEY SAYS...
Students love Philadelphia, PA
Smart classrooms
Solid preparation in:
Teamwork
Communication/interpersonal skills
Presentation skills

STUDENTS
Enrollment of parent institution	7,230
Enrollment of MBA program	561
% male/female	56/44
% part-time	90
% minorities	10
% international	51
Average age at entry	28
Average years work experience at entry	4

ACADEMICS
Academic Experience Rating	**75**
Student/faculty ratio	20:1
Profs interesting rating	80
Profs accessible rating	78
% female faculty	20
% minority faculty	10

Joint Degrees
DO/MBA Program with Philadelphia College of Osteopathic Medicine (2 years for MBA component)

Academics

The Erivan K. Haub School of Business at Saint Joseph's University has about 60 full-time students, but the vast majority of MBAs here attend part-time, and the program is designed for their convenience. One part-timer explains, "The academic experience appeals to those who work full-time, offering night classes for the MBA program, which opens the doors to many other people in professional careers." Saint Joseph's recognizes that not all its potential students can finish work and make it into Philadelphia by class time; therefore, they offer classes at Ursinus College in Collegeville (about 30 miles northwest of downtown Philly) as well as on its main campus.

The Haub MBA program is distinguished in part by "a constant focus on ethics. Given the number of scandals in the news today, ethics has become increasingly important. This continues to be a core competency for Saint Joseph's, as it has been since 1978." That's not to suggest that the Haub curriculum is written in stone; on the contrary, the administration here is not afraid to adapt the program to meet the ever-changing needs of the business world. Students admire how "the administration is constantly looking for ways to improve the MBA program, whether it is by offering courses relevant to hot topics in industry or hosting lectures from industry leaders." They also appreciate the "great use of technology and state-of-the-art equipment in the classrooms."

The Haub faculty "offers a nice combination of full-time professors, who bring academic knowledge to the classroom, and adjunct professors, who bring real-world experience, which actually enhances the learning experience in a business school. The caliber of students here is also high," MBAs report. One student writes, "There are some awesome professors here, and the intellectual abilities of my classmates make classes even more challenging and intriguing." Students also tell us that "if one gets to know faculty members, they can be a great asset when it comes to finding a job. Almost all of the best employment opportunities presented to me came from faculty members and people they knew."

Haub offers a wide selection of areas of concentration, but students wish the school would "give more choices of elective courses within each concentration." The curriculum allows students only six credits worth of electives—that's only two courses—which helps explain the relative lack of selection.

Career and Placement

The Career Services Office at Saint Joseph's University "is currently working to help MBA students find new jobs through a resume network and online support," according to the school's website. The university encourages MBAs to take advantage of MBAFutureStep, a free online service introduced by the Graduate Management Admissions Council (the same folks who bring you the GMAT). Some of the students feel that the CSO focuses too little on graduate students. One student explains, "Almost everything encountered in the Career Services office is tailored toward undergraduate placement." Another student adds, "They need to improve the career services. The same types of companies recruit here all the time and most are for just marketers and accountants. If you are in finance and do not want to do financial services, you are basically out on your own. Also, forget about [companies] out of the Philly area."

In 2003 the average graduating Haub MBA earned a salary of $71,600 with an average signing bonus of $9,000. Companies and organizations that recruit graduate students on Saint Joseph's campus include Bryn Mawr Trust, Citigroup, SEI Investments, Wachovia Securities, and Wilmington Trust.

SUSAN KASSAB, DIRECTOR
5600 CITY AVENUE, PHILADELPHIA, PA 19131 UNITED STATES
PHONE: 610-660-1101 • FAX: 610-660-1224
E-MAIL: GRADSTAFF@SJU.EDU • WEBSITE: WWW.SJU.EDU

Student Life and Environment

Haub's full-time student body is small but active. Even so, they concede that their extracurricular life "is not as rich as it could be;" since most students attend class after work, out-of-class networking opportunities get short shrift. One student says, "If Saint Joe's can improve and develop the social aspect of the program, there is no reason why our school cannot be competitive with top-tier schools given its proven and strong academic curriculum."

Saint Joseph's University is home to "a great basketball team" and "really makes [students] feel at home on the campus," as well as being "a good place to hang out, with good weekend entertainment." The campus is located 20 minutes outside the downtown area in the pleasant, quiet northwest corner of the city. Philadelphia's extensive SEPTA system of buses and trains connects the campus to the heart of America's fifth-largest city. The campus is only a half-mile walk from the closest commuter train station.

Admissions

Haub admits MBA candidates for all three academic semesters (fall, spring, and summer). A completed application to the program includes copies of official transcripts for all undergraduate and graduate academic work, an official GMAT score report (results no more than seven years old), two letters of recommendation, a personal statement, and a resume reflecting professional experiences. The TOEFL is required of international students, as is a WES (World Education Services) evaluation of transcripts and proof of financial support. The Haub curriculum includes seven foundation courses. Completion of equivalent undergraduate courses (equivalency determined by the admissions committee) can also earn students a waiver on up to 18 credits or foundations.

FINANCIAL FACTS

Annual tuition	$12,996
Books and supplies	$800
% of students receiving aid	14
% of students receiving loans	12
Average award package	$14,900
Average student loan debt	$14,500

ADMISSIONS

Admissions Selectivity Rating	**74**
# of applications received	248
% applicants accepted	65
% acceptees attending	61
Average GMAT	520
Average GPA	3.2
TOEFL Required of International Students?	Yes
Minimum TOEFL (paper/computer)	550/213
Application fee	$35
International application fee	$35
Regular application deadline	Rolling
Regular notification	Rolling
Transfer students accepted?	Yes
Transfer application policy: Transfer students must provide a completed application including original test scores.	
Non-fall admissions?	Yes
Need-blind admissions?	Yes

APPLICANTS ALSO LOOK AT

La Salle University, Penn State University—Great Valley Campus, Temple University, Villanova University.

EMPLOYMENT PROFILE	
Career Rating	75

SAINT LOUIS UNIVERSITY
JOHN COOK SCHOOL OF BUSINESS

GENERAL INFORMATION

Type of school	private
Affiliation	Roman Catholic
Environment	metropolis
Academic calendar	semester

SURVEY SAYS...
Students love St. Louis, MO
Friendly students
Happy students
Smart classrooms
Solid preparation in:
General management
Teamwork
Presentation skills

STUDENTS

Enrollment of parent institution	11,422
Enrollment of MBA program	324
% male/female	70/30
% out-of-state	69
% part-time	83
% minorities	9
% international	15
Average age at entry	26
Average years work experience at entry	3.3

ACADEMICS

Academic Experience Rating	**77**
Student/faculty ratio	15:1
Profs interesting rating	73
Profs accessible rating	79
% female faculty	15
% minority faculty	2

Joint Degrees
MBA/JD: 3-4 years
MBA/MHA: 3 years
MBA/MD: 5 Years

Academics

The John Cook School of Business at Saint Louis University offers both a full-time and a part-time Professional MBA (PMBA) program. A substantial majority of the students here attend the part-time program, usually while working full-time jobs in the Saint Louis area.

The "enhanced, flexible" curriculum of the PMBA program, which was first introduced in the fall of 2004, is designed to allow working professionals to take as many or as few courses as they want, when they want. The sequence of 11 to 15 courses (four foundation courses may be waived, depending on the student's undergraduate and professional qualifications) can be completed in as little as two years. All classes are offered in the evenings, typically once a week from 6 P.M. to 9 P.M. Besides the foundation courses, the PMBA curriculum includes five breadth courses; a capstone course; three mini-courses (together constituting one full course) covering business law, business ethics, and career management; and four electives.

The SLU full-time MBA is also a relatively recent arrival, with its first classes convening in 1999. The two-year program covers the same fundamental business functions covered in the PMBA program, but also "emphasizes oral and written communications, teamwork skills, and other leadership competencies, linked with a practical, working knowledge of business ethics and a global perspective," according to the school's website. The 45-credit curriculum, offered primarily during the day, includes five electives, allowing students to specialize in accounting, economics, entrepreneurship, finance, international business, management, marketing, MIS, or operations and supply chain management.

"Because of the relatively small class size" in both MBA programs, "professors are able to interact with students easily and frequently" at SLU. One student explains, "The school is like a tight-knit community where faculty, staff, and administration make students the first priority. This is obvious in every aspect of campus interaction." Students praise offerings in finance and international business, telling us that the latter benefits from "excellent study-abroad opportunities." A few here complain that "some professors lack the necessary real-world experience to teach graduate students" and feel that "the school could upgrade the technology in the classroom. Lectures should be taped and made available online."

Career and Placement

The Career Resources Center at the John Cook School of Business provides career services and counseling for all MBAs. The center offers self-assessments, personal advising, resume assistance, mock interviews, and access to multiple online and hard-copy databases and reference sources. Students tell us that the school's regional reputation and alumni network are its most effective career-enhancing assets. One writes, "I chose the school for its regional name recognition and the quality associated with the education given here. In the St. Louis area, this school opens many doors in the business field. The school is also well-networked in the community." Another adds, "The variety and reputations of the companies at which SLU alums and faculty currently work or have worked at in the past are impressive. I know that when I am close to graduating, I will have no trouble finding a great job."

Janell Kiel Nelson, Associate Director
3674 Lindell Boulevard, Suite 132, St. Louis, MO 63108 United States
Phone: 314-977-6221 • Fax: 314-977-1416
E-mail: mba@slu.edu • Website: www.mba.slu.edu

Student Life and Environment

SLU's "beautiful campus" is a park-like setting peppered with sculptures, fountains, archways, and verdant open spaces. Because the Jesuit tradition seeks to educate the whole person, SLU brings numerous cultural events to campus. Through the campus ministry, opportunities for service and spiritual growth are readily available. SLU competes in 16 NCAA Division I sports; the men's basketball and soccer teams both draw hefty crowds. The school's midtown location provides students easy access to the Fox Theatre, the Sheldon Concert Hall, the Grandel Square Theatre, and the Powell Symphony Hall.

"On-campus activities are readily available and student-driven," MBAs report, although many part-timers have difficulty making time to take advantage of them. One first semester, part-timer writes, "I plan to join various business clubs eventually, such as the Marketing Club and/or MIS Club, after I have chosen a concentration in the program." The student body here includes "new college graduates and seasoned professionals. Some are single while others have kids and are married. Some have business backgrounds while others have engineering and other backgrounds. It is a fairly diverse cross-section of people." Students are "competitive, friendly, smart, anxious to learn," yet "always willing to help each other out."

Admissions

St. Louis University accepts both online and paper-and-pencil applications; an Adobe Acrobat file of the application can be downloaded at the school's website. All applications must include a completed application form, personal essays, two letters of recommendation (at least one professional), official transcripts for all post-secondary academic work, and an official GMAT score report. International applicants must provide all of the above plus certification of financial support and, for non-native English speakers, an official TOEFL score report. According to the school, "Work experience plays a large role [in the admissions decision]. For applicants with limited or no work experience, the GMAT and GPA become very important. Interviews are recommended for all applicants, but are required for applicants with no work experience."

FINANCIAL FACTS

Annual tuition	$28,960
Fees	$100
Books and supplies	$1,250
Room & board	$11,000
% of students receiving aid	75
% of first-year students receiving aid	85
% of students receiving grants	84
Average grant	$9,000

ADMISSIONS

Admissions Selectivity Rating	80
# of applications received	70
% applicants accepted	60
% acceptees attending	57
Average GMAT	580
Range of GMAT	530-600
Average GPA	3.1
TOEFL Required of International Students?	Yes
Minimum TOEFL (paper/computer)	600/250
Application fee	$90
International application fee	$90
Regular application deadline	4/15
Regular notification	5/7
Application Deadline/Notification	
Round 1:	1/15 / 2/14
Round 2:	3/1 / 3/21
Round 3:	4/15 / 5/7
Deferment Available?	Yes
Maximum length of deferment	1 year
Transfer students accepted?	Yes
Transfer application policy: 6 credit hours only from another AACSB accredited school.	
Need-blind admissions?	Yes

APPLICANTS ALSO LOOK AT
Washington University in St. Louis.

EMPLOYMENT PROFILE	
Career Rating	83
Placement rate (%)	90
% grads employed immediately	50

SAN FRANCISCO STATE UNIVERSITY
COLLEGE OF BUSINESS

GENERAL INFORMATION

Type of school	public
Environment	metropolis
Academic calendar	2005-2006

SURVEY SAYS...
Students love San Francisco, CA
Friendly students
Happy students

STUDENTS

Enrollment of parent institution	26,500
Enrollment of MBA program	741
% male/female	49/51
% part-time	65
% minorities	25
% international	40
Average age at entry	29
Average years work experience at entry	3

ACADEMICS

Academic Experience Rating	70
Student/faculty ratio	10:1
Profs interesting rating	69
Profs accessible rating	61
% female faculty	36
% minority faculty	40

Academics

The College of Business at San Francisco State University offers a range of MBA options to satisfy the needs of every student. A conventional MBA, the most popular of the school's choices, is offered on both a full-time and part-time basis and includes a thorough complement of foundation courses for those with little undergraduate or practical business experience (such courses may be waived for students with a deeper academic background in business). Two part-time MBA programs are available off campus: the Accelerated MBA, a fixed-curriculum cohort program that ensures a degree in 23 months (students attend class for seven hours a week), and the Alliance MBA, a flexible, intensive program delivered via audio-video teleconferencing technology (and occasional on-site visits by professors) to students' workplaces. SFSU also offers a master's in business, the MSBA, for students seeking a personalized curriculum that allows for in-depth specialization in one or more areas, such as accounting, finance and information systems.

Students at SFSU appreciate "the flexibility of the program" and praise its "strong accounting department, [the] great faculty in the Decision Sciences department, [and the] access to great professors, contacts, and networking in the field of marketing." San Francisco itself is seen as a tremendous asset. One student explains, "Many top-quality professors want to live in the San Francisco Bay area, but there are only so many jobs at Stanford and Berkeley, so SFSU benefits from the overflow of top-quality professors. Overall, I feel that I'm getting Stanford-level instruction at community college-level prices. The professors and the program structure are excellent. It's like getting a Porsche at Hyundai prices." Another student agrees, "This could be the best value MBA program in the country, and it's in a great city with a great professional environment, including Silicon Valley and the San Francisco financial district nearby."

Like many state-run schools, SFSU is sometimes a little deficient in administrative functions. Students tell us that the program "needs to provide more advising time, especially for new students, at the beginning of the semester. We also need clearer guidelines in terms of classes that the students need to take." The administration itself, reports one student, "has been in almost constant turnover since I began the program. The staff is very knowledgeable, yet they can provide different answers to the same questions, which causes confusion among the students."

Career and Placement

SFSU maintains a Business Relationship Center dedicated exclusively to its College of Business. This office provides career counseling services, organizes job fairs, conducts career skills seminars, and assists students in their search for internships. Online services include job databases and an alumni networking site. Students are unimpressed, "career placement is non-existent here. Students are on their own when it comes to the job/internship search. Although students ask for job-placement assistance, the school provides no valuable help at all," writes one student. Another MBA observes, "In exchange for the low tuition, one cedes the network that would have come from attending a UC or private school."

Student Life and Environment

The MBA program at SFSU is in the process of relocating from the school's main campus to a new downtown campus. Many part-timers applaud the move, telling us that "the development of the downtown campus will make the program extremely convenient for those of us who work in the financial district." A few opponents ask, "What about the people who don't work downtown? There is no parking and I don't want to take public

VICTOR V. CORDELL, PhD, DIRECTOR
1600 HOLLOWAY AVENUE, SAN FRANCISCO, CA 94132 UNITED STATES
PHONE: 415-338-1279 • FAX: 415-405-0495
E-MAIL: MBA@SFSU.EDU • WEBSITE: HTTP://COB.SFSU.EDU/MBA

FINANCIAL FACTS

Annual tuition (in-state/out-of-state)	$3,366/$11,502
Books and supplies	$2,000
Room & board	$10,000

ADMISSIONS

Admissions Selectivity Rating	**80**
# of applications received	625
% applicants accepted	47
% acceptees attending	48
Average GMAT	550
Range of GMAT	500-600
Average GPA	3.15
TOEFL Required of International Students?	Yes
Minimum TOEFL (paper/computer)	570/230
Application fee	$55
International application fee	$55
Regular application deadline	5/1
Regular notification	5/15
Transfer students accepted?	Yes
Transfer application policy: Applicants need to apply to the program and waive out our foundation requirements.	
Non-fall admissions?	Yes

transportation home after a night class. The current location is excellent. People working downtown can easily hop on the M streetcar to arrive at the front door of the school in 20 minutes." Regardless of how they feel about the move, nearly everyone here agrees that "the school's greatest strength is that it's located in San Francisco, where there are lots of opportunities around."

Because SFSU "is a commuter school," MBAs "come on campus only to go to their classes or meet with other students to work on group projects." Students feel that "more social functions to connect fellow MBA students with each other would be a plus." One student writes, "There is not a lot of time for social interaction. The group work assignments help compensate for this deficiency and is something I have, eventually, learned to appreciate, despite the added onus of making time." Students also love such high-tech campus amenities as "wi-fi throughout the building and great online research possibilities through the library."

SFSU draws a large international population, "especially from Asia and Europe, although I also know people from Georgia (former USSR), Turkey, Egypt, Venezuela, Chile, [and] Brazil," observes one student. Another notes, "Having received my undergraduate degree from a small private college that touted its 'diversity,' I was unsure what to expect from a larger state school. But the diversity of the students in my classes is amazing. This is what my private undergrad college was trying to accomplish. We have all types, colors, background—married, unmarried, old, young, you name it. It makes for a very interesting and stimulating learning environment." Many students here "have worked for high-tech companies in Silicon Valley," although the general impression is that most international students arrive with little work experience.

Admissions

The admissions office at SFSU requires all of the following materials of applicants: a completed application (pencil-and paper or computer-based); two sealed copies of official transcripts from all post-secondary programs attended; a sealed official GMAT score report; and a letter of intent (i.e., personal statement of purpose). Letters of recommendation are optional. International students whose first language is not English must submit sealed official TOEFL score reports. All international students must submit a financial statement demonstrating that the student has at least $20,000 to cover the cost of the program, and a signed form indicating agreement to purchase medical health insurance. The minimum GMAT score for all applicants is 500; a minimum rank of 25th percentile on the verbal, math, and writing sections is also required.

EMPLOYMENT PROFILE	
Career Rating	71

SAN JOSE STATE UNIVERSITY
COLLEGE OF BUSINESS

Academics

San Jose State University serves the MBA needs of the Silicon Valley with a variety of convenient options. SJSU's intensive MBA-One program gets students in and out of the program in one year. For those working full-time, the school offers several part-time options, including an off-campus program located conveniently in the Rose Orchard Technology Center (near the Cisco campus). The College of Business also offers an MS in transportation management, an MS in taxation, an MS in accountancy, a dual degree program, an MBA/Masters in Engineering Management, and an off-campus MBA/MSE.

SJSU's MBA-One is "for nonworking individuals who prefer an intensive, cohort style of learning." The 16-course curriculum is entirely lock-step (no electives), taught in six terms of varying duration. The final term of the curriculum includes a comprehensive project. Students tell us that the MBA-One is "very well coordinated" but caution that it is "intense and rigorous. Basically, you can kiss your social life good-bye for one year. On the plus side, you cover a complete two-year curriculum in a single year." Students love the cohort system, as it allows them to share work and to get to know one another well.

Two part-time options are available at SJSU. The on-campus MBA offers students a wider variety of courses than the off-campus option but is, of course, less convenient to the many students who work on the north end of the city. The on-campus calendar consists of two 16-week semesters and a 6-week summer session. Off-campus classes run year-round in three 16-week trimesters, broken down into two eight-week sessions offered each term. Students in the off-campus program generally complete their MBAs in less time than those on campus. Students in both part-time programs praise their convenience and affordability. They also speak highly of their professors, who "know how to relate course material to real-life situations and how to help us understand complicated material." Students warn, however, that their classmates' busy work and home schedules sometimes negatively impact classroom instruction.

Although both part-time programs include elective courses, areas of concentration are not part of the SJSU program. Students tell us that elective choices include "great entrepreneurship classes" but that "marketing and general-management instruction should be improved."

Career and Placement

The school tells us that its career center "offers a range of resources to help students and recent graduates meet with success in the search for employment. Services include career advising and assistance with resume preparation and interview skills. The center maintains a resource library, a career lab with workstations and career-guidance software, and a job bank. On-campus recruiting and job fairs are organized by the center, putting students and recent graduates in touch with potential employers," but many full-time students are unimpressed, reporting that "career help seems limited to meager listings on job websites."

With a population of nearly one million, San Jose is one of California's major cities. Even after the dot-com bust, it has remained a major hub of U.S. tech industry. Major employers include Adobe Systems, BEA Systems, Cisco, eBay, Hewlett-Packard, IBM, Lockheed Martin, and MicroSystems.

ADMISSIONS COORDINATOR, ADMISSIONS COORDINATOR
ONE WASHINGTON SQUARE, SAN JOSE, CA 95192-0162 UNITED STATES
PHONE: 408-924-3420 • FAX: 408-924-3426
E-MAIL: MBA@COB.SJSU.EDU • WEBSITE: WWW.COB.SJSU.EDU/GRADUATE

Student Life and Environment

SJSU attracts "awesome and open students" with "good industry experience." The student population is "very diverse in terms of international students. We lack African American and Hispanic students, though." Part-timers are generally "too busy to be sociable" and "not very network-oriented outside of class." Students in the MBA-One program "spend a lot of time together and are a very tight-knit group, even though [they] are mainly a commuter community." They count on one other's help to complete the curriculum, since "the MBA-One program is quite demanding and [they] are quite involved in schoolwork. On weekends, [they] still need to study."

The main SJSU campus is located in downtown San Jose. Business classes meet in the recently renovated Boccardo Business Education Center. All classrooms are wired for Internet access, and many are equipped for multimedia instruction. Off-campus classes are held at the Rose Orchard Technology Center "in the heart of the Silicon Valley high tech corridor, making it convenient to many working adults."

Admissions

The following are the minimum admission requirements to graduate business programs at SJSU: a four-year undergraduate degree with a GPA of at least 3.0 for the final 60 semester hours of course work; a GMAT score of at least 500, with a minimum 50th-percentile ranking in both Verbal and Math scores; and, for any student whose main language is not English, a TOEFL score of at least 550 (paper-based) or 213 (computer-based). A personal statement of purpose is also required with the application.

FINANCIAL FACTS

Annual tuition	$22,560
Books and supplies	$3,000

ADMISSIONS

Admissions Selectivity Rating	89
Average GMAT	564
Average GPA	3.3
TOEFL Required of International Students?	Yes
Minimum TOEFL (paper/computer)	550/213
Application fee	$55
International application fee	$55
Regular application deadline	4/1
Regular notification	7/1
Transfer students accepted?	Yes
Transfer application policy: Applicant must meet admission requirements. Up to 6 units transferred from AACSB accredited institution.	
Non-fall admissions?	Yes

APPLICANTS ALSO LOOK AT

Santa Clara University, University of California—Berkeley (MFE), University of California—Davis.

EMPLOYMENT PROFILE	
Career Rating	61
Average starting salary	$57,000

SANTA CLARA UNIVERSITY
LEAVEY SCHOOL OF BUSINESS

GENERAL INFORMATION

Type of school	private
Affiliation	Roman Catholic-Jesuit
Environment	city
Academic calendar	quarters

SURVEY SAYS...

Students love Santa Clara, CA
Friendly students
Good peer network
Happy students
Solid preparation in:
General management
Teamwork

STUDENTS

Enrollment of parent institution	8,213
Enrollment of MBA program	1,064
% male/female	66/34
% part-time	82
% minorities	15
% international	22
Average age at entry	29
Average years work experience at entry	7

ACADEMICS

Academic Experience Rating	**76**
Student/faculty ratio	34:1
Profs interesting rating	84
Profs accessible rating	77
% female faculty	16
% minority faculty	13
Joint Degrees	
MBA/JD: 4 years	

Academics

The Leavey School of Business at Santa Clara University combines "Jesuit values, primarily in the quality of education and the emphasis on high integrity," with a Silicon Valley location that draws "the cream of the crop to the faculty, such as the former 3Com CEO." The result is a unique MBA program that "caters to part-time students" but also has plenty to offer full-timers.

Customer service is the name of the game at Leavey, where "the dean runs the school as if it was a company in itself. He provides quarterly reports of the progress of school and reviews student evaluations as a measure of the progress." Administrators "do everything they can to keep up with the changing trends in business and business schools. For example, this year, they introduced international exposure for the student. Every summer, one or two student groups visit another country to meet with business leaders and financial institutions to understand how business is done in that country. This year, the group went to China. Next year, one group will go to China and another, to Germany." Professors take a similar student-first approach; they are "eager to help students in the classroom and to introduce them to colleagues for future employment opportunities. They are always available for personal/professional consultation."

Leavey's curriculum employs "a great case-study approach" that "is structured to maximize teamwork abilities." Students find this pedagogical approach immediately applicable to their professional lives. MBAs also "love the 'experimental' classes that students can choose as electives, such as Spirituality and Leadership, which really gets you to focus on your inner self and become a better, less stressed person." Students tell us the school excels in accounting, general management, and marketing. Asked where the school should improve, one student comments, "For some reason, the school is not so well recognized as other schools in the area, namely Stanford and Berkeley. But I have been quite impressed with SCU so far. The campus is good and the academic standards are excellent. I think the school will stand to gain if marketed better."

Career and Placement

Students appreciate the "great Bay Area network" connected to SCU; MBAs here benefit from "a terrific level of interaction with leaders and innovators in Silicon Valley." The Graduate Business Career Services Office capitalizes on these connections to help students procure internships ("The quarter system allows for some interesting internship opportunities in the area because local employers know some students can be available part-time or full-time for a quarter or two," explains one student) and post-graduation jobs. Even so, students feel the service isn't all it could be. As one observes, "Since most students are working, there are limited resources devoted to the internship/career placement program. Also, SCU also does not do enough promotion of the program out in the business community. Its reputation is only good regionally, despite its high ranking as a part-time business program."

The top ten employers of graduates of the class of 2004 were Applied Materials, Inc.; Cisco Systems, Inc.; eBay; Hewlett-Packard; KLA-Tencor Corporation; Silicon Valley Bank; Sun Microsystems; VERITAS Software; Wells Fargo Bank; and Xilinx.

JULIE KRUGMAN, DIRECTOR, GRADUATE BUSINESS ADMISSIONS
223 KENNA HALL, 500 EL CAMINO REAL, SANTA CLARA, CA 95053-0001 UNITED STATES
PHONE: 408-554-4539 • FAX: 408-544-4571
E-MAIL: MBAADMISSIONS@SCU.EDU • WEBSITE: WWW.SCU.EDU/BUSINESS

FINANCIAL FACTS

Annual tuition	$17,496
Fees	$120
Books and supplies	$700
Room & board	$13,000

Student Life and Environment

MBAs report that SCU "provides a safe, clean, study environment coupled with a very caring and personal staff. The school really treats students as 'customers' and caters to their needs, offering extended library hours during exams. The staff wants the students to succeed." Part-timers also appreciate that "the schedule is really terrific [and] works for working folks as well as commuters." A new facility is in the works, we're told, which is a good thing; students agree that "the current facility is old and cramped."

SCU's "gorgeous and safe campus" offers a number of top amenities, including "a state-of-the-art gym and pool, great recreation areas, and a late-night venue called The Bronco with a pool table and a large television and several couches," as well as "campus-wide wireless access, [and] a peaceful rose garden and a church for when you need serenity." Although most students are part-timers with numerous other commitments outside school, MBAs here do occasionally socialize. One writes, "There are quarter-end bar nights which are great for relaxing after your last final with current classmates, catching up with past classmates, and meeting new people." Another student points out that "life at school can be great for those who do the work to get involved. It can be a commuter school if that is all a student wants to get out of it. [But] there is always something social to do on the weekends, either sponsored by the school or just going out with other MBA students."

"Many students here have jobs," which "provides the best opportunity for networking and recruiting after graduation, as you have gained so many resources at numerous organizations," students here tell us. MBAs range from the mid 20s to the mid 40s. Their "backgrounds are extremely diverse; they come from such areas as financial services, banking, semiconductors, software, technology management, finance, and human resources, to name a few." Engineers from the Silicon Valley are the single most visible contingent.

Admissions

Applicants to Leavey MBA programs at SCU must provide the Admissions Office with all of the following: official transcripts for all post-secondary academic work; official GMAT score reports reflecting scores no more than five years old; a completed application and a copy of same; two letters of recommendation; and personal essays. A third essay is optional. Candidates whose first language is not English must also submit official score reports for the TOEFL (minimum required score: 600 paper-based test, 250 computer-based test). Work experience is not a prerequisite to admission, although a minimum of two years of experience is recommended; on average, admitted students have between five and seven years of post-undergraduate professional experience. All applicants must demonstrate competency in four areas: college algebra, calculus, and oral communications. SCU uses targeted advertising and recruiting events to enhance its minority and disadvantaged populations.

ADMISSIONS

Admissions Selectivity Rating	78
# of applications received	377
% applicants accepted	86
% acceptees attending	73
Average GMAT	619
Range of GMAT	530-710
Average GPA	3.2
TOEFL Required of International Students?	Yes
Minimum TOEFL (paper/computer)	600/250
Application fee	$75
International application fee	$100
Regular application deadline	6/1
Regular notification	Rolling
Early decision program?	Yes
ED Deadline/Notification	3/1 / 4/15
Deferment Available?	Yes
Maximum length of deferment	2 quarters
Transfer students accepted?	Yes
Transfer application policy: Apply as all others.	
Non-fall admissions?	Yes
Need-blind admissions?	Yes

APPLICANTS ALSO LOOK AT

San Jose State University,
University of California—Berkeley,
University of California—Davis,
University of San Francisco.

EMPLOYMENT PROFILE	
Career Rating	89
% grads employed immediately	95
Average starting salary	$83,909

SEATTLE PACIFIC UNIVERSITY
SCHOOL OF BUSINESS AND ECONOMICS

GENERAL INFORMATION
Type of school	private
Affiliation	Free Methodist
Environment	metropolis
Academic calendar	quarters

SURVEY SAYS...
Students love Seattle, WA
Friendly students
Helfpul alumni
Happy students
Smart classrooms
Solid preparation in:
Teamwork

STUDENTS
Enrollment of parent institution	3,779
Enrollment of MBA program	118
% male/female	54/46
% part-time	92
% minorities	12
% international	6
Average age at entry	31
Average years work experience at entry	7

ACADEMICS
Academic Experience Rating	**72**
Student/faculty ratio	17:1
Profs interesting rating	88
Profs accessible rating	85
% female faculty	25
% minority faculty	5

Academics

The School of Business and Economics at Seattle Pacific University is distinguished by its dedication to mission and vision. Students say, "The school does a good job of staying close to its Christian vision and integrating it into their studies." Both the MBA and the MS-ISM (master's of science in information systems management) programs "maintain a commitment to competence, character, and ethical decision-making from a Christian perspective." According to the school, "[The programs] teach students to provide values-based leadership in organizations from a general-management perspective."

Students are drawn by the school's ethical focus, as well as by its caring atmosphere and adaptability to the needs of its part-time student body. Professors and administrators "care a lot about the students, and they are understanding about other influences (like work and family) and try to be as accommodating as possible." Classes are generally offered once a week, for 11 weeks, in three-hour evening or weekend sessions; this arrangement allows most part-timers to complete an MBA in three years or an MS-ISM in two years.

The SPU MBA program commences with nine core courses; these courses cover basic principles of business and can be waived for those who have completed equivalent undergraduate courses within the previous seven years. Ten advanced courses and five electives round out the curriculum. Students can use their electives to develop a specialization in any of the following areas: e-business, human-resource management, information-systems management, finance, and management of business processes. The MS-ISM is a shorter program consisting of 2 core courses, 12 required courses, and 3 electives. Both curricula "approach instruction with an eye to the practical" and a "stress on applied learning." Students note that the program also places "a continuing emphasis on teamwork and team achievement."

Most of all, students love the atmosphere at SPU, which emanates from "warm professors and staff who make the experience very enjoyable." They also appreciate the school's desire to improve and to act on student feedback. Students who say "some professors are outstanding while others are only okay," also point out that students are able to evaluate professors at the end of each quarter. Students note, "The dean of the school meets with professors who receive less-than-satisfactory feedback, and improvements in instruction occur because of this feedback." As an added bonus, SPU's location allows the school to offer "great business-world networking with companies like Boeing, Microsoft, and Starbucks."

Career and Placement

The Career Development Center at SPU handles career services for all students at the school. These services include on-site job listings, workshops, a career library, one-on-one career counseling, and access to online job databases. In addition, the School of Business and Economics maintains the Center for Applied Learning, which helps students develop "mentorship contacts, internship training, entrepreneurial ingenuity, and service appreciation" through projects in the business and nonprofit communities. The school also notes, "SPU's strong ties to the business community offer further networking and learning opportunities. Business leaders are welcomed into the classroom as guest speakers, sources for team projects, and informal advisors. The MBA and MS-ISM programs, along with the Center for Integrity in Business, also sponsor quarterly events such as the Faith and the Marketplace Speaker Series, where executives share their career experiences and commitment to Christian faith."

DEBBIE WYSOMIERSKI, ASSOCIATE GRADUATE DIRECTOR
3307 THIRD AVENUE WEST, SUITE 201, SEATTLE, WA 98119-1950 UNITED STATES
PHONE: 206-281-2753 • FAX: 206-281-2733
E-MAIL: MBA@SPU.EDU • WEBSITE: WWW.SPU.EDU/SBE

FINANCIAL FACTS

Annual tuition	$15,282
Books and supplies	$1,200
Room & board	$10,505

ADMISSIONS

Admissions Selectivity Rating	67
# of applications received	36
% applicants accepted	86
% acceptees attending	81
Average GMAT	501
Range of GMAT	430-550
Average GPA	3.3
TOEFL Required of International Students?	Yes
Minimum TOEFL (paper/computer)	565/225
Application fee	$50
International application fee	$50
Regular application deadline	8/1
Regular notification	8/31
Deferment Available?	Yes
Maximum length of deferment	1 year
Transfer students accepted?	Yes
Transfer application policy: Regular admission process.	
Non-fall admissions?	Yes
Need-blind admissions?	Yes

Companies most frequently employing SPU MBAs include Boeing, Microsoft, Safeco, and Starbucks. Approximately 1 in 12 MBAs finds their first post-degree job outside the United States.

Student Life and Environment

The average SPU business graduate student is 31 years old and has been in the professional workforce for seven years. Most attend part-time while working full-time at such companies as Adobe Systems, AT&T Wireless, Boeing, Eldec, Microsoft, Safeco, Starbucks, Virginia Mason Medical Center, and Washington Mutual. Despite the fact that most students come in at night, take a class, and then leave, MBAs tell us that "SPU has a true sense of community that they enjoy." One student writes, "Everyone is friendly, and the values and mission of the school serve it and its students and faculty well. There is always something going on and interesting things to do and see." Extracurricular events include lectures at the school's Center for Integrity in Business.

The university is located on the north slope of Queen Anne Hill, less than 10 minutes from downtown Seattle. Students agree that "[it's] a pretty campus with an intimate feel" that's "easily accessible." McKenna Hall, home to the School of Business and Economics, is also "well-wired with technology." Students love the setting, but they complain that "many facilities are closed when [they] take classes in the evening."

Hometown Seattle offers aspiring business mavens many benefits. The city is a gateway to international trade, home to a number of major corporations and organizations, and offers plenty of great dining, entertainment, arts, sports, and shopping. The cherry on the sundae is the area surrounding Seattle: the Pacific Northwest is an outdoor lover's paradise, offering (besides plenty of rain) opportunities ranging from skiing and hiking to fishing, kayaking, and scuba diving.

Admissions

Applicants to SPU must submit an official undergraduate transcript demonstrating a 3.0 grade point average (overall or final three semesters, whichever is higher), GMAT scores (MBA program) or GRE scores (MS-ISM program), two letters of recommendation, TOEFL scores (international students), a three- to four-page personal statement, and a resume demonstrating at least one year of full-time, substantive professional experience. Additional work experience is preferred; work experience is a significant factor in the admissions decision process.

APPLICANTS ALSO LOOK AT

Seattle University, University of Washington.

EMPLOYMENT PROFILE

Career Rating	60*
% grads employed immediately	90

SEATTLE UNIVERSITY
ALBERS SCHOOL OF BUSINESS AND ECONOMICS

Academics

Students praise the convenient flexibility of the Albers MBA program at Seattle University, telling us that "both in scheduling classes for each term and in the order that you take your classes, the curriculum is very open. Thus, people who are going to school in addition to a job and family can manage their time effectively." Students say, "There are both full-time and part-time options with most classes being offered during the evenings on Monday to Thursday, which gives us the time to work for a living during the day and be with our families on the weekends." This is, in short, "a good-quality program for those who can't quit working for two years to go to school."

Ethics are featured prominently in the Albers curriculum because "Seattle University is a private Jesuit organization that reflects Christian principles." Students agree that "it has a very friendly atmosphere." The school also places a premium on the teaching ability of its faculty; as one MBA explains, "The professors at Seattle University are rated by the school on three areas: research and publications, service to the university community, and on the quality of teaching (as rated by student evaluations)—with teaching quality being the most heavily emphasized metric. Because of this, Seattle University is a place where professors come to teach and enjoy the quality of life in the Pacific Northwest." MBAs praise the "willingness of professors to engage with students in class and outside of class." One student writes, "The professors here are great. It is wonderful to be at a school where the professors care about the students and want to see them succeed."

Professorial instruction here is supplemented by "CEOs from Wells Fargo to Boeing to Starbucks to Safeco coming to [speak in] class," a windfall of the school's location in a major corporate city. Students tell us that the program is "really strong in finance, accounting, entrepreneurship, and ethics. It's also a very good program for building teamwork and leadership skills." In addition, one student says, "The administration is outstanding, giving quick and professional responses and help every time I need to contact someone, and [they provide] constant updates on ongoing events." Several students note, "No wonder students love this program, [but] they would love it even more if the tuition weren't so high." One MBA sums up, "The academics here are comparable to traditional programs in the region, but the program is as flexible as those of nontraditional programs. [This] flexibility helps students complete their degree while still working. That is a huge strength!"

Career and Placement

The Albers Placement Center serves both undergraduates and graduate students in business at Seattle University. The office sponsors a mentoring program that pairs MBAs with area senior executives and provides a standard roster of career-related services including counseling and job posting. The office organizes a career fair: employers attending the 2005 fair included Boeing, Costco, Russell Investment, Washington Mutual, Smith Barney, and Wells Fargo Financial. Approximately 30 employers visit campus each year for the purpose of recruiting MBAs.

Employers most likely to hire Albers MBAs include Boeing, Paccar, Deloitte Touche Tohmatsu, Alaska Airlines, Amazon, PricewaterhouseCoopers, Washington Mutual Bank, and Weyerhaeuser. At least 10 percent of Albers MBAs find a post-degree job outside the United States.

JANET SHANDLEY, DIRECTOR, GRADUATE ADMISSIONS
901 12TH AVENUE, PO BOX 222000, SEATTLE, WA 98122-1090 UNITED STATES
PHONE: 206-296-2000 • FAX: 206-296-5656
E-MAIL: GRAD-ADMISSIONS@SEATTLEU.EDU • WEBSITE: WWW.SEATTLEU.EDU/ASBE

Student Life and Environment

Albers does "a really good job of making life easy for its many part-time students." It has extended bookstore hours during the beginning of quarters and an espresso stand is open throughout evening class hours in the b-school building. There are also two campuses with duplicate sections for almost all of the initial courses, allowing students to choose the one that is more convenient for their schedule and location in the area. Some students comment that the only problem with the East Side campus in Bellevue is that it "has no sense of community; it's simply a drab office park in which students spend as little time as possible." The downtown campus, located near Capitol Hill is "very beautiful, and the buildings are new. There is wireless Internet all over the campus for student use."

Students say that "because our [program] is an evening program, it's very difficult to participate in school activities. But the school recognizes this factor and provides events specifically targeting the evening programs such as the pizza get-togethers after class to meet and [talk] with professors and students." Students also bond during the required leadership and teambuilding course. Students say, "[The course] is an excellent networking class that allows roundtable discussions about solutions to the real pitfalls in the business world."

The student body at Albers has "a lot of age diversity." MBAs say, "We have students in their early 20s fresh in the work force, and we have students with 10, 20, and even more years of experience. Many students run their own companies or manage departments for local corporations. The breadth of experience within the student body surpasses every other MBA program in the region." There's also "a nice mix of international students, and a very good travel-abroad program where course credit can be obtained while studying aspects of business in another country (like France, Italy, or China)."

Admissions

Applicants to Seattle University must provide the admissions committee with official transcripts from all schools attended, GMAT scores, TOEFL scores (for applicants whose native language is other than English), and a resume. The school's website notes that "most successful applicants have a 3.0 undergraduate GPA, score a minimum of 500 on the GMAT, and have at least one year full-time of work experience." Applicants must meet the math and computer proficiency requirement; the former requires an understanding of calculus, while the latter requires the ability to use e-mail, web browsing, word processing, and spreadsheet applications.

FINANCIAL FACTS

Annual tuition	$15,741
Books and supplies	$1,107
Room & board	$6,738
% of students receiving aid	43
% of first-year students receiving aid	35
% of students receiving loans	42
% of students receiving grants	3
Average award package	$16,994
Average grant	$7,077

ADMISSIONS

Admissions Selectivity Rating	79
# of applications received	171
% applicants accepted	68
% acceptees attending	68
Average GMAT	572
Range of GMAT	500-610
Average GPA	3.3
TOEFL Required of International Students?	Yes
Minimum TOEFL (paper/computer)	580/237
Application fee	$55
International application fee	$55
Regular application deadline	8/20
Regular notification	9/10
Deferment Available?	Yes
Maximum length of deferment	1 year
Transfer students accepted?	Yes
Transfer application policy: Applicants must meet standard admission requirements. University will accept 9 quarter credits from AACSB accredited schools. Students transferring from an accredited Jesuit MB program (JEBNET) may transfer up to 50% of credits.	
Non-fall admissions?	Yes
Need-blind admissions?	Yes

APPLICANTS ALSO LOOK AT

Pacific Lutheran University, San Francisco State University, Seattle Pacific University, University of Washington, Washington State University, Western Washington University.

EMPLOYMENT PROFILE	
Career Rating	75
# of companies recruiting on-campus	30
% grads employed immediately	80
Average starting salary	$61,067

SOUTHEAST MISSOURI STATE UNIVERSITY
DONALD L. HARRISON COLLEGE OF BUSINESS

Academics

The Donald L. Harrison College of Business at Southeast Missouri State University (SEMO) offers students plenty of "bang for their buck." In 2003, *U.S. News & World Report* reported that the school produces some of the "least indebted students" in the nation. As one MBA student says, "It's not Kellogg, but it's as good as you'll find for the money. I was an MBA at another university for a semester and transferred because the education there was not up to par with the tuition charged. SEMO, which charges much less, has provided a much better value." Harrison MBAs can choose from seven different degree options: accounting, environmental management, finance, general management, industrial management, international business, and a recently added concentration in health administration. MBAs praise "the variety of available disciplines of study, given the size of the institution," although they also warn that "there should be a wider variety of courses offered each semester." One student adds, "Sometimes you may be very limited to what [courses] you will be able to take. For instance, I can't take any summer courses because the courses that will be offered are ones that I have already taken." Internships play an integral role in the Harrison MBA—at least for its younger full-timers. The school notes, "Students have the opportunity to participate in internship assignments (and receive full credit as an elective course) that bring our graduate students into contact with the managerial practice of business. Our students have benefited from internships with American Express Financial, Coca-Cola, KPMG Peat Marwick, Merrill Lynch, [and] Northwestern Mutual Life, to name just a few." Many Harrison MBAs have jobs (they attend evening classes), and so, do not participate in the internship program. Students love Harrison's small classes and the focus on in-class discussion. One older MBA student writes, "As a nontraditional student with over 30 years [of] business experience, my reflections and experiences were sometimes sought [after] and discussed as another means to broaden the overall picture of the real work place. I felt valued as a contributor by most professors and younger students. Diversity and variety seemed to be positive influences in most of my classes. Students were supportive of each others' efforts." However, some other students feel that "some professors do not demand enough from students, especially in the area of presentation and revision of work. Overall, this school's MBA program should be more challenging."

Career and Placement

Harrison placement services are provided by SEMO's Career Services Office, which serves all undergraduates and graduate students at the university. In conjunction with the Alumni Affairs office, Career Services has established the Southeast Career Alumni Network to facilitate job searches. The office also offers the standard array of services including counseling, workshops, and online support. Students are unimpressed; they feel that "the biggest area the MBA administration must improve on is the career center. The business school doesn't have a career center. We must use the undergraduate career center that focuses on attracting jobs for undergraduates. Obtaining a job through the career center at Southeast is nearly impossible. All work must be self-initiated and completed." Harrison MBAs who seek new jobs after graduation most often find themselves working for Accenture, Bausch and Lomb, Dow Jones, PricewaterhouseCoopers, TG Missouri, and Texas Instruments. About one in ten students finds a job outside the United States.

Student Life and Environment

"Life at school is good!" one Harrison MBAs reports. The student body is tight and the surrounding town of Cape Girardeau is pleasant and quiet. Another student explains, "Cape Girardeau is a fairly small town, so there are some limitations on recreational activity. In warm months, there are many lakes, parks, and trails nearby to enjoy. The people in the community are friendly overall." One MBA student says, "Even though Cape Girardeau is a relatively small town, there is actually quite a lot to do, and it is close to Memphis and St. Louis for people who want to get to a city every once in a while." Campus life centers on the MBA Association, which "has holiday parties, happy-hour gatherings, intramural sports teams, [and] sponsors speakers." One student says, "I must give credit to the MBA Association because they work hard to create a positive social atmosphere for students." However, other MBAs believe that is pretty much the only school-related extracurricular. One student writes, "It seems the only student organization that MBA students are a part of is the MBA Association. This may be because MBA students have busy schedules." Other students feel that "the administration needs to work at creating more community. Although the student-run MBA Association does well, the administration does little to make new students feel welcomed." Students agree that "[SEMO's campus] is nice and fairly attractive [with] good facilities on-campus for student recreation, exercise, leisure, activities, and so on. The library resources are adequate and [continue to] improve—considering the budget crisis of the past couple years. The surrounding community is fairly supportive of the university and recognizes the impact it plays on its economy." Although one student comments, "For those who work during the day and study at night, some of the facilities are not open (for example, the bookstore). Sometimes the working student just simply cannot get to campus before it closes and has to take time off work to get necessary books for class." Students agree, "[The Harrison student body] comes from a wide array of backgrounds: rural, urban, suburban, international, and so on. The mix of such a diversity of students offers a relatively interesting interesting student population." The school notes, "Approximately 36 percent of our MBA students and half of our alumni are international students. Since Southeast Missouri State University launched its MBA program in fall 1996, students from more than 25 countries have studied in the program. Currently, students from more than 15 countries represent their nations and bring the world to the classroom."

Admissions

Harrison admissions officers use a formula to establish a floor for all MBA applicants: (200 × GPA [on a four-point scale] + GMAT score). Applicants must score at least 1000 to be considered for admission. In addition, applicants must score at least 400 on the GMAT and must have earned at least a C in all required foundation courses for the GMAT program. These foundation courses are applied calculus, financial management, introductory statistics, management and organizational behavior, management information systems, principles of financial accounting, principles of macroeconomics, principles of managerial accounting, principles of marketing, and principles of microeconomics. Students without the requisite undergraduate work may place out of foundation courses through local and/or CLEP exams.

FINANCIAL FACTS

Annual tuition (in-state/out-of-state)	$4,320/$7,752
Books and supplies	$500
Room & board	$4,500
% of students receiving aid	38
Average grant	$6,200

ADMISSIONS

Admissions Selectivity Rating	71
# of applications received	53
% applicants accepted	79
% acceptees attending	93
Average GMAT	510
Range of GMAT	460-560
Average GPA	3.2
TOEFL Required of International Students?	Yes
Minimum TOEFL (paper/computer)	550/213
Application fee	$20
International application fee	$100
Regular application deadline	Rolling
Regular notification	Rolling
Deferment Available?	Yes
Maximum length of deferment	1 year
Transfer students accepted?	Yes
Transfer application policy: May transfer 9 hours authorized by Director of MBA program.	
Non-fall admissions?	Yes
Need-blind admissions?	Yes

APPLICANTS ALSO LOOK AT

Saint Louis University, Southern Illinois University—Carbondale, Southwest Missouri State University, University of Missouri—Columbia,

EMPLOYMENT PROFILE

Career Rating	73	Grads employed by field	%: avg. salary
Placement rate (%)	85	Accounting	15: $45,000
# of companies recruiting on-campus	45	Finance	20: $45,000
% grads employed immediately	60	MIS	15: $55,000
Average starting salary	$50,000	Consulting	10: $55,000
		General Management	40: $40,000

SOUTHERN METHODIST UNIVERSITY
COX SCHOOL OF BUSINESS

GENERAL INFORMATION

Type of school	private
Affiliation	
Environment	town
Academic calendar	semester

SURVEY SAYS...

Students love Dallas, TX
Friendly students
Smart classrooms
Solid preparation in:
Communication/interpersonal skills
Presentation skills

STUDENTS

Enrollment of parent	
institution	10,000
Enrollment of MBA program	1,008
% male/female	75/25
% out-of-state	51
% part-time	82
% minorities	13
% international	22
Average age at entry	28
Average years work experience	
at entry	5

ACADEMICS

Academic Experience Rating	**94**
Student/faculty ratio	4:1
Profs interesting rating	95
Profs accessible rating	97
% female faculty	11

Joint Degrees
JD/MBA, 4 years

Prominent Alumni
Thomas W. Horton, Senior VP/CFO, American Airlines; David B. Miller, Managing Director, El Paso Energy; Ruth Ann Marshall, President, MasterCard; James MacNaughton, Managing Director, Rothschild, Inc.; C. Fred Ball, CEO, Bank of Texas.

Academics

For students looking for a prime business-school education combined with more than a dash of southern hospitality, there may be no better place than the Edwin L. Cox School of Business at Southern Methodist University. Located in the Dallas/Fort Worth area, the school certainly benefits from Dallas's reputation as one of the "Best Cities for Business" (according to *Fortune* magazine). Though it's a businessperson's paradise, students say Cox is not as straight-laced as you might expect. Students describe their school as "friendly, laid-back, and enjoyable." And, they add, "environment is emphasized more than the academics, so its students don't have sharp elbows like at other large schools." The administration is "outstanding. Everyone in the admissions department is very accessible. They basically carry you through the entire process. The dean has an open-door policy as well."

Each term of the two years is divided into two modules (called A and B). Each of these consists of an eight-week-long, two-hour-credit course. Students appreciate the module system for the amount of information that's crammed in and the "greater flexibility to customize an MBA experience." However, students confess to sometimes being a bit "overwhelmed." As in most b-schools, the first year is comprised almost entirely of general knowledge style classes like accounting, economics, statistics, finance, marketing, organization behavior, operations, and team-interaction skills. The second year, however, is designed to allow students to really focus on their own professional goals. To that end, a wide range of electives is offered. But it's neither the core courses nor the range of electives that sets Cox apart. Though students say that "Cox made its name with finance, but the marketing faculty is rock-solid in everything from research and analytics to marketing communications," it's the international focus of the program that garners the most attention. In partnership with American Airlines, Cox developed a Global Leadership Program in 2000 in which all students participate. In this program, students begin their first semester with a "comprehensive study of the culture, politics, and business of [their] region of choice." Cox is also notable for its mentoring program, in which every student is paired with a mentor—"business leaders representing every major industry and many of the most prominent companies in the Dallas/Fort Worth metroplex"—each of whom provides students with "the business contacts, career advice, and industry insight that only experienced professionals can offer." For a school located so close to the "telecom corridor," however, Cox seems to be somewhat lacking in technology. Students "wish the school had more emphasis on high tech." Others point out that "if Cox concentrated a little more on building better [high tech] connections, starting salaries would improve significantly."

Career and Placement

As is the case with so many b-school programs, recruiting and placement can often be focused on the region in which the school resides. Cox is no exception. Luckily for students at SMU, Dallas's economy is strong, and top businesses abound. Students say the "alumni network is the greatest advantage—especially if you want to work in Dallas. The school does a tremendous job of putting us in front of alumni." In addition, "prestigious business leaders serve on the Cox board and are very willing to help students." For most students, this is a plus. Some, however, would like to see the "geographic diversity of the companies that recruit on-campus" increase. Others point out that for those with interests in nontraditional business fields, career placement can be difficult. One student seeking a change comments, "Our career center is mostly devoted to the traditional Dallas economy drivers (oil, banks, real estate, Frito-Lay). I would like to see some companies that stray outside these fields onto more unconventional ground."

ARRION RATHSACK, DIRECTOR, MBA ADMISSIONS
P.O. BOX 750333 DALLAS, TX 75275 UNITED STATES
PHONE: 214-768-1214 • FAX: 214-768-3956
E-MAIL: MBAINFO@MAIL.COX.SMU.EDU • WEBSITE: HTTP://WWW.MBA.COX.SMU.EDU

Students say that although "career management is still building itself up from two very slow years, the new office of corporate relations has done an amazing job of pulling in new companies this year to recruit." Among the many companies that recruit on the Cox campus are AT&T, Citigroup/CitiFinancial, Coca-Cola, the ExxonMobil Corporation, Morgan Stanley, Philip Morris, and Red Bull.

Student Life and Environment

With such an emphasis on international business, it's no surprise that on any given day, students at Cox might encounter students who speak Bengali, Japanese, Italian, Spanish, Hebrew, Punjabi, Bulgarian, Russian, French, Tagalog, or Urdu, just to name a few. Add this international feel to the fact that Cox School of Business is located in "a residential area" between Dallas's downtown and the North Texas telecom corridor, and it is obvious that cultural opportunities abound. With dozens of museums, theaters, shopping centers, and sports venues at their fingertips, Cox students are rarely bored (not that they'd have time to be). One student says, "The school is a very vibrant place to be. There are more opportunities than time available to take advantage of them. Some event is always taking place on the arts and culture front." And like most schools, students have the opportunity to socialize and network at weekly happy hours. "We're a little crazy with the intramural sports, too. Rugby, soccer, volleyball—there's always a turn-out. And the SMU football games are marked with campus-wide festivities that crowd the grass areas. (Our dean provides free beer, which has made him very popular.)"

Facilities are somewhat lacking, as the MBAs still find themselves cheek-by-jowl with undergraduates, but, for the most part, students can expect a "very social atmosphere, [in an exciting area, and a] close-knit community of full-time students."

Admissions

Cox admissions officers seek to create a qualified and diverse student body. In doing this, they put together a class that is 22 percent international students, 25 percent female, and 20 percent minority students. The average GMAT is 661, and the average GPA is 3.26. Average work experience was around five years, and the undergraduate degrees were mostly in business and engineering, but also included a surprisingly large number of social sciences. Cox is committed to making private education affordable, and for that reason, 80 percent of the most recent group of MBAs received some form of a scholarship. Scholarships range from as little as 10 percent of tuition to as much as 100 percent, but it's best to apply early to snatch these opportunities up.

FINANCIAL FACTS

Annual tuition	$30,255
Fees	$3,034
Books and supplies	$2,000
Room and board	$10,000
% of students receiving grants	77
Average grant	$17,500

ADMISSIONS

Admissions Selectivity Rating	90
# of applications received	336
% applicants accepted	46
% acceptees attending	45
Average GMAT	661
Range of GMAT	580-720
Average GPA	3.3
TOEFL Required of International Students?	Yes
Minimum TOEFL (paper/computer)	600/250
Application fee	$75
International application fee	$75
Regular application deadline	4/30
Regular notification	6/15
Application Deadline/Notification	
Round 1:	11/30
Round 2:	1/31
Round 3:	3/15
Round 4:	4/30
Early decision program?	Yes
ED Deadline/Notification	11/30
Deferment Available?	Yes
Maximum length of deferment	1 year
Need-blind admissions?	Yes

APPLICANTS ALSO LOOK AT

Duke University, Emory University, Georgetown University, Rice University, The University of Texas at Austin, Vanderbilt University, Washington University in St. Louis,

Career Rating	87	Grads employed by field %: avg. salary	
% grads employed immediately	45	Finance	45 $68,180
Average starting salary	$69,359	Human Resources	3 $59,000
		Marketing	16 $70,695
		MIS	3 $80,000
		Operations	7 $63,333
		Consulting	10 $79,625
		General Management	11 $68,944
		Other	5 $69,625

ST. JOHN'S UNIVERSITY
PETER J. TOBIN COLLEGE OF BUSINESS

Academics

"New York City is the financial capital of the world," one MBA student at St. John's Tobin College of Business correctly observes, "and SJU's proximity to the city is one of its greatest strengths." Indeed, Tobin offers three location options to students seeking an MBA at a New York address: the university's main campus in Jamaica, Queens; a small campus in the financial district of Manhattan (the focus here is primarily on risk management, insurance, and financial services); and another small campus on Staten Island (most courses here are in accounting-related fields). A fourth campus gives students yet another fabulously urban option: Rome, Italy, where international business and finance are in the spotlight.

Access to New York means access to great faculty, and MBAs at Tobin tell us that St. John's has recruited a solid core of teachers. "Most of my accounting/tax professors have graduated from prestigious law schools and have had successful careers. Learning from them has been a huge benefit," writes one accounting student. Students also praise the faculty in insurance and marketing. MBAs here appreciate the fact that "New York City is known throughout the world as a financial hub. This can provide many opportunities for employment, or even education experiences for students."

Students love how Tobin "is currently updating curriculum, constantly improving teaching methods, implementing new technology, and hiring new professors educated in the academic and professional fields. The result is a positive and worthwhile experience." The program "places a lot of emphasis on team-building and presentation skills," which students find useful. One writes, "Most classes are presented, in full or in part, as seminars, requiring students to work in groups and presenting to the class. These activities are helpful in developing needed skills." Students also approve of "the strong emphasis the school places on ethics in business practice." The administration scores high marks in the helpfulness department. Asked where SJU needs an upgrade, students suggest that Tobin "could further improve by continuing the technology program currently being undertaken to encompass the entire campus, with emphasis on including wireless capabilities in lecture halls and on laptop computers in standard course procedures for the MBA program." Some even feel that "the emphasis on technology within the program will allow SJU to propel the MBA program years ahead of other comparable universities."

Career and Placement

The Career Center at St. John's University provides placement and counseling services for Tobin MBAs as well as for all other students of the university. Students remind us that St. John's location is a great boon to their career searches. Being in New York provides "great networking opportunities with companies long before you start working through clubs and departmental events."

Employers most likely to hire Tobin MBAs include Accenture, American Express, Citi Group, City of New York, JP Morgan Chase, Merrill Lynch, and Revlon.

SHEILA RUSSELL, ASSISTANT DIRECTOR OF MBA ADMISSIONS
8000 UTOPIA PARKWAY, 111 BENT HALL, QUEENS, NY 11439 UNITED STATES
PHONE: 718-990-1345 • FAX: 718-990-5242
E-MAIL: MBAADMISSIONS@STJOHNS.EDU • WEBSITE: WWW.STJOHNS.EDU/TOBINCOLLEGE

Student Life and Environment

The Tobin MBA program "is mostly designed for those who work during the day, so classes are only offered at night." One full-time student writes, "The schedule took some getting used to, but once I got used to it, I began to appreciate it, as I can spend my days studying and doing research for my graduate assistant program." Full-timers are otherwise "very active and very proactive on campus. Within the past year, many students have combined their efforts to implement clubs and activities that provide networking opportunities, academic opportunities, and social gatherings." Even the campus itself "is an active one. Due to the NYC area and the fast-paced environment, the campus is always fluttering with excitement, from sports events to guest lectures by individuals such as Spike Lee and Cornell West." The majority of MBA students, however, experience little of this excitement; they're here as part-timers who come to campus for class, then leave. One MBA Explains, "Unfortunately, my work and school schedule do not provide me with many opportunities to participate in campus activities. I attend St. John's on a part-time basis while working full-time."

One look at the student body here tells you that Tobin is "a real New Yorker school" with "type-A MBA students in abundance,"—and they wouldn't have it any other way. "Their aims are clear, their motivations are apparent, their goals are attainable, and their willingness to increase the level of competition in the program produces professionals uniquely qualified and highly valued in their particular professional fields," explains one student. With its main campus in Queens, Tobin needn't look far to attract an international student body; one of the world's most international populations lives within a 10-mile radius of the school. Students "come from different countries and bring their business experience to the table." One student comments, "It has also been a pleasure meeting such a diverse group of students and having the opportunity to study and prepare group projects with them while surrounded by the energetic city of New York."

Admissions

Tobin requires all applicants to provide the admissions with: official transcripts for all undergraduate, graduate, and professional school academic work attempted; an official GMAT score report for an exam taken within the last five years; letters of recommendation; a personal statement; and a resume. Students whose native language is not English must also submit an official TOEFL score report. Work experience is not required for admission to the program, although it is preferred. Informal on-campus interviews are available for prospective students but are not required, except in special cases.

FINANCIAL FACTS

Annual tuition	$20,750
Fees	$250
Books and supplies	$3,000
Room & board (on/off-campus)	$12,000/$15,000
% of students receiving aid	25
% of first-year students receiving aid	25
Average award package	$14,914
Average grant	$1,812

ADMISSIONS

Admissions Selectivity Rating	74
# of applications received	565
% applicants accepted	62
% acceptees attending	43
Average GMAT	530
Range of GMAT	440-630
Average GPA	3.2
TOEFL Required of International Students?	Yes
Minimum TOEFL (paper)	580
Application fee	$40
International application fee	$40
Regular application deadline	6/1
Regular notification	Rolling
Deferment Available?	Yes
Maximum length of deferment	1 year
Transfer students accepted?	Yes
Transfer application policy: Must use regular application. Individual review of transfer credits.	
Non-fall admissions?	Yes
Need-blind admissions?	Yes

APPLICANTS ALSO LOOK AT

Fordham University, Hofstra University, New York University.

EMPLOYMENT PROFILE	
Career Rating	89
Placement rate (%)	96
# of companies recruiting on-campus	90
% grads employed immediately	85
Average starting salary	$68,000

STANFORD UNIVERSITY
STANFORD GRADUATE SCHOOL OF BUSINESS

GENERAL INFORMATION
Type of school   private
Environment   city
Academic calendar   quarter

SURVEY SAYS...
Good social scene
Good peer network
Happy students
Solid preparation in:
General management

STUDENTS
Enrollment of parent
  institution   14,454
Enrollment of MBA program   753
% male/female   65/35
% minorities   24
Average years work experience
  at entry   4

ACADEMICS
Academic Experience Rating   98
Student/faculty ratio   6:1
Profs interesting rating   85
Profs accessible rating   93
% female faculty   16
% minority faculty   13
Joint Degrees
It is possible to earn dual degrees
with other departments. Common
area is MBA/JD and MBA/MA in
Education.
Prominent Alumni
Phil Knight, Former Chairman, Nike
Inc.; Charles Schwab,
Chairman/CEO, Charles Schwab &
Co.; Henry McKinnell,
Chairman/CEO, Pfizer Co.; Mads
Ovlisen, Chairman, Novo Nordisk
A/S Denmark; Jeff Bewkes,
Chairman, Ent. & Networks Group,
Time Warner; Miles White,
Chairman/CEO, Abbott Labaratories;
Jean-Pierre Garnier, CEO,
GlaxoSmithKline.

Academics

It's the company you'll keep at Stanford Graduate School of Business (GSB) that ultimately distinguishes a Stanford MBA from all but a few other elite programs. First there's the faculty, who "are brilliant. Most are world leaders in their fields." One student notes, "I am amazed at how accomplished my professors are in the nonacademic world. For example, my entrepreneurship professor this quarter founded a large cable company and now owns the Boston Celtics! Other professors hold similar experiences; better still, all hold a true zest for teaching." Then there are the visiting lecturers, who include "frequent luminaries such as top CEOs. Three winners of the Nobel Prize for economics gave separate guest lectures in the same week not too long ago." Finally, there are your classmates, whom students describe as "amazingly accomplished." One MBA observes, "The admissions office takes great care to bring in the right students, not just the students with the highest test scores and grades—the director said he didn't accept one 800 GMAT for the Class of 2005."

Students tell us that Stanford excels in large part because of its location. One student explains, "While the school itself is phenomenal, I don't think it would be possible if it were in any other place. The location in the Silicon Valley gives us instant access to an amazing group of entrepreneurs, so our school is consequently very entrepreneurial. There are always some great ideas floating around here." Among top programs, Stanford is relatively small, which students describe as "both a strength and a weakness." One student writes, "I'm sure that Harvard Business School or Wharton are better-run academic machines, but Stanford does have a small-school feel that is quite nice. You do get the sense that if everyone wasn't pulling an oar, the school would break down." Another student adds, "The class offering is not as deep as some other schools (I was a Wharton undergrad, so I have some basis for comparison), but the classes that are taught are excellent."

That's because a "relentless pursuit of best teaching methods and material" and a "level of subject matter that is both intellectually challenging and strong enough for practical application when we leave" ensure that students are constantly testing their limits. One MBA reports, "The emphasis here is on learning, not grades. We are encouraged to take risks, even at the risk of failure—because this is when the deepest learning occurs." In order to encourage risk-taking, Stanford neither posts grades publicly nor includes class rank in students' transcripts. Students add, "Our collaborative culture frees you from focusing on grades and enables you to take academic risks and broaden your general management skills."

Career and Placement

The Career Management Center at Stanford doesn't have to do a whole lot; companies come looking for Stanford MBAs without much prompting. According to students, the office does a fine job of providing the standard complement of career services including personal counseling, self-assessment exercises, workshops, seminars, networking events, lectures and presentation, online job posting, and alumni events. Students agree that Stanford has "a strong alumni network where you can get help when needed."

Major employers of Stanford MBAs include Bain and Company; McKinsey & Co.; The Boston Consulting Group; Lehman Brothers; Yahoo!; Gap Inc.; Morgan Stanley; GerenTech; Amazon; Deutche Bank; General Mills; Goldman Sachs; and Devry Capital. Last year, Stanford MBAs dispersed across the globe to take their first post-degree jobs; half remained on the Pacific coast, one in five headed to the Northeast, and one in eight found work outside the United States.

Student Life and Environment

"There is an amazing balance of hard work and enjoyment" at Stanford, whose idyllic setting is praised by one and all. With "an amazingly beautiful campus, one of the best golf courses in the country, [and] a sunny climate that definitely makes people happier than gray skies, [Stanford] in many ways feels like a country club, but without the negative connotation. People play hard here, but they also work hard." Stanford is also a "great environment for families with children. You can rollerblade with your family every Sunday morning, bike to school everyday, have lunch at the Stanford museum. It's simply amazing!"

The Stanford campus is constantly abuzz with activity; students report that "there's tons of stuff going on all the time. We are often hard-pressed to choose between talks, visits, trips, and other academic and social events. It is not uncommon for me to have to choose between three different brown-bag lunch events every day or every other day." One MBA explains, "The GSB is more than simply a business school; it is an experience. There are no boundaries between classroom and everyday, real-life learning. The most difficult thing I find here is choosing amongst so many extraordinary opportunities and focusing on only a few. It is easy to overextend yourself, when learning to achieve life balance and prioritize one's time is a critical centerpiece of living a high-impact, successful life."

Hometown Palo Alto "can be somewhat boring, [but] the small-town atmosphere makes people bond more, especially since it is such a small class." Students note, "We're just 30 minutes from San Francisco and 20 minutes from San Jose, so we get the best of both areas. The Bay Area has so much to offer that you will never be bored."

Admissions

Admissions are highly competitive at Stanford GSB. The admissions office sets no minimum standards for work experience, GMAT score, or GPA, but don't let that fool you; only exceptional candidates receive the precious invite to attend. The school reports that it is most interested in "a unique combination of high leadership potential, academic excellence, and individual background and interests." The school also seeks students who "contribute to a diverse community, because we believe that all students learn invaluable lessons from sharing experiences and perspectives with classmates from many different backgrounds." Applicants must provide the school with GMAT scores, TOEFL scores (if applicable), undergraduate and graduate transcripts, letters of reference, two essays, and a resume.

FINANCIAL FACTS

Annual tuition	$37,998
Books and supplies	$3,540
Room & board (on/off-campus)	$16,180/$15,877
% of students receiving aid	72
% of students receiving loans	70
% of students receiving grants	56
Average student loan debt	$66,457

ADMISSIONS

Admissions Selectivity Rating	99
# of applications received	4,697
% applicants accepted	10
% acceptees attending	79
Average GMAT	711
Average GPA	3.5
TOEFL Required of International Students?	Yes
Minimum TOEFL (paper/computer)	600/250
Application fee	$225
International application fee	$225
Application Deadline/Notification	
Round 1:	10/19 / 1/18
Round 2:	1/4 / 3/31
Round 3:	3/15 / 5/12
Deferment Available?	Yes
Maximum length of deferment	Very limited
Need-blind admissions?	Yes

APPLICANTS ALSO LOOK AT
Harvard University.

EMPLOYMENT PROFILE

Career Rating	99	Grads employed by field	%: avg. salary
% grads employed immediately	74	Finance	28: $102,237
% grads employed at 3 months	91	Marketing	14: $92,268
Average starting salary	$100,400	Operations	2: $113,833
		Strategic Planning	9: $93,400
		Consulting	18: $102,031
		General Management	7: $98,143
		Venture Capital	5: $126,650
		Other	10: $92,001
		Internet/New Media	5: $98,949
		Non-profit	4: $77,318

STATE UNIVERSITY OF NEW YORK AT OSWEGO
SCHOOL OF BUSINESS

GENERAL INFORMATION
Type of school	public
Academic calendar	semester

SURVEY SAYS...
Smart classrooms
Solid preparation in:
Teamwork
Presentation skills

STUDENTS
Enrollment of MBA program	70
% male/female	62/38
% minorities	12.5
% international	20
Average age at entry	26
Average years work experience at entry	5

ACADEMICS
Academic Experience Rating	**74**
Student/faculty ratio	6:1
Profs interesting rating	80
Profs accessible rating	73
% female faculty	32

Academics

Students who enroll in the School of Business at SUNY Oswego can expect several things: excellent value for their money, intimate classes, knowledgeable professors, state-of-the-art facilities, and an excellent hockey team. As one student puts it, "in most areas, the school of business is at the top of its class. The classes are challenging and worthwhile. Most professors are really good at their areas. They are also widely available to help students both inside and out of class." According to most of the students, the "very small classes promote learning and student-professor interaction."

Designed as a degree in general management, an MBA from SUNY Oswego provides a solid grounding in the basics of modern business organization. The school says that "this program is intended to be equally applicable to private, public, and governmental sectors of management." The core subjects required of students include management, accounting, marketing, organization, law, and finance. In addition, students can choose to specialize in a specific field such as international management, manufacturing management, organizational leadership, or financial services. Core requirements include management information systems, managerial finance, marketing management, management science I, international business, global perspectives on organizational management, and management policy. A wide range of electives is also available to students at SUNY Oswego, including management economics, database development, collective bargaining, industrial and organizational psychology, industrial sociology, principles of forecasting, business research, futures and options markets, database development, project management, public-sector accounting, and advanced auditing.

Students find their course work both rigorous and exciting. As one puts it, "the professors are excellent and the classes are fun and challenging." Another says, "the course load is challenging, requiring solid communication and organization skills. Many professors are conducting research on global trade, accounting, and management science. My academic experience has been very positive. I would suggest Oswego to all prospective business students (undergraduate or graduate)."

Career and Placement

Although Oswego has a lot to offer—lovely campus, low cost, quality education, intimate program—most students wish it would go further in strengthening its career-services department. There is little aid specifically for prospective MBAs, and the job search is often directed almost entirely by the student. As one puts it, "Connecting with employers is a difficult task. Linking up with quality employers looking for graduates with post-graduate degrees needs to be addressed."

GRADUATE OFFICE, DAVID W. KING, INTERIM DEAN GRADUATE STUDIES
602 CULKIN HALL, SUNY OSWEGO OSWEGO, NY 13126 UNITED STATES
PHONE: 315-312-3692 • FAX: 315-312-3577
E-MAIL: MBA@OSWEGO.EDU • WEBSITE: WWW.OSWEGO.EDU/BUSINESS/MBA

Student Life and Environment

Students at SUNY Oswego rave about their "beautiful campus," which, they proudly point out, is also extremely "technologically advanced and mostly wireless." The typical MBA's social life is strong, and there are "plenty of bars around for an active nightlife." As one student says, "At Oswego, I had the opportunity to make new friends from all over the world. The social life is active and I consider myself lucky." For the most part, students claim to be "very active on campus. There is a multitude of clubs and organizations to choose from." Students enjoy their "great gyms to work out in or play a game of racquetball." Plus—as is typical in upstate New York—the school's athletic life centers on their "excellent hockey team, instead of football." As one student puts it, "what's excellent about living on campus here is that there is every resource that you could possibly need available on-campus. There are new buildings and renovations, from a new student center to the newly renovated freshman residence hall and new business center with technology classrooms."

Admissions

To be considered for admission to the small MBA program at the School of Business at SUNY Oswego, a candidate must have a minimum GPA of 2.6 out of 4.0. The minimum required score for the GMAT is 450, unless the applicant's native language is not English, in which case the minimum score is 400. Taking the TOEFL test is also required for students whose native language is not English.

FINANCIAL FACTS

Annual tuition (in-state/out-of-state)	$7,100/$11,340
Fees	$606
Books and supplies	$800
Room & board (on-campus)	$3,348
% of students receiving aid	28
% of first-year students receiving aid	16
% of students receiving grants	3
Average grant	$12,000

ADMISSIONS

Admissions Selectivity Rating	69
# of applications received	40
% applicants accepted	80
% acceptees attending	75
Average GMAT	500
Range of GMAT	350-650
Average GPA	3.22
TOEFL Required of International Students?	Yes
Minimum TOEFL (paper/computer)	550/213
Application fee	$50
Regular application deadline	4/1
Regular notification	6/1
Deferment Available?	Yes
Maximum length of deferment	1 year
Transfer students accepted?	Yes
Transfer application policy: Two classes (6 credits) may be transferred into the program.	
Non-fall admissions?	Yes
Need-blind admissions?	Yes

APPLICANTS ALSO LOOK AT

Albany Law School, SUNY—Brockport, SUNY—University at Buffalo.

EMPLOYMENT PROFILE

Career Rating	67	Grads employed by field	%: avg. salary
Placement rate (%)	65	Accounting	50: $39,000
# of companies recruiting on-campus	65	Finance	10: $38,000
% grads employed immediately	65	Human Resources	5: NR
Average starting salary	$38,000	MIS	5: NR
		Operations	10: NR
		General Management	5: NR
		Quantitative	5: NR
		Non-profit	10: NR

Stetson University
School of Business Administration

Academics

One of the advantages of small programs like the Stetson University School of Business Administration—which sometimes hosts fewer than 20 students—is that you really get a chance to get to know everyone. As one student says, "The faculty and administration at Stetson are easily accessible and extremely supportive. Everyone is on a first-name basis, and the individual attention makes me feel as if my money was well-spent." Other students are enthusiastic about the "low ratio of students to faculty," and many claim that the "nicest thing is that the school is small and class sizes are small." One student says, "Each and every professor I have taken a class with at Stetson has been excellent! I would recommend this school to any and everyone!"

The school, which is located on campuses throughout central Florida, "offers classes in three locations to serve the needs of not just the full-time student but also the working student. The locations are geographically located throughout central Florida, including Orlando and Tampa, two of the largest metropolitan areas in Florida and two major job markets," one student says. Other students also point out that "the proximity of the school to major job markets like Orlando, Tampa, and Jacksonville is a major strength of the program and helps to draw a diverse mixture of students including international, female, and minority students."

Stetson's MBA offers a general business-management degree, though students can choose to specialize in a number of different areas. According to the school, "[The] programs are designed not to make you a technical specialist, but rather to provide you with a range of knowledge needed by the professional manager." The MBA program is divided into two parts: the business foundation and the advanced level courses. Foundation-level courses include business statistics, information system, law or legal environment and ethics, macro and microeconomics, principles of management, and principles of marketing. Advanced-level courses include an advanced accounting seminar, electronic commerce, international business and finance, and a variety of business electives. Students appreciate the focus of the program and say that "professors are very concerned with students learning and integrate their professional experience into the curriculum." Others have been extremely impressed by "the professional experience that the faculty brings from there diverse backgrounds" and the "camaraderie among the students and faculty at [the] school."

Stetson also offers several special programs for its business students including the Family Business Center, the Joseph C. Prince Entrepreneurial Program, and the Roland George Investments Program. Stetson also has a summer school abroad program in Innsbruck, Austria, that is open to students in all majors and concentrations. Still, many students would like to see a stronger focus on "an entrepreneurship program for students interested in that field." Another complaint is the uneven distribution of classes among the campuses. Though DeLand houses the main campus, many students complain that "the course offerings at the Celebration campus in Orlando and the Law School campus in Gulfport are not as plentiful as in DeLand."

Career and Placement

Stetson's Career Management Office offers a variety of services to its MBA students including "individual career counseling, career planning and development in the classroom, resume referrals, internship development, full-time placement, on-campus recruiting, mock interviews, and the Business and Industry Speaker Series presentations." Their

DRIVE FRANK A. DeZOORT, DIRECTOR, GRADUATE BUSINESS PROGRAMS
421 NORTH WOODLAND BOULEVARD, UNIT 8398, DELAND, FL 32723 UNITED STATES
PHONE: 386-822-7410 • FAX: 386-822-7413
E-MAIL: JBOSCO@STETSON.EDU • WEBSITE: WWW.BUSINESS.STETSON.EDU

new, more aggressive approach to marketing their students also seems to be paying off. Industry and employer presence was up 75 percent from four years ago, and on-campus recruiting had increased 85 percent. In 2002 and 2003, every student seeking an internship was able to get one, and, though jobs in the private sector have been rare, the center proudly points out that even in a depressed economy there has "been more activity in government jobs, health care, sales positions, and education."

Student Life and Environment

With campuses in DeLand (20 minutes north of Orlando), Celebration (located in Orlando, right near Disney World), and Gulfport, Stetson University has the advantages of pleasant weather, active campus life, vital student athletics, and an extremely friendly student body. As a "values-centered, comprehensive, private liberal-arts university," Stetson promises on its website that all of its students will be "challenged by [the] academic programs in more than 40 disciplines. Just as importantly, [students] will learn about life and all the opportunities it holds." As one student says, "Overall, the life at Stetson has been incredible. The school is continuously improving and staying on top of technology. Our campus is outstanding as well as our library, computer labs, and tutorial sessions." Another student adds, "It is not uncommon for large groups of students to go out to dinner after class or meet on the weekends for extracurricular activities. There are many activities and clubs to choose from, and all serve to enrich the Stetson experience."

Besides the fact that "the student body feels like a small community where most people know each other," students are impressed that they've "met so many wonderful people while going to Stetson." Because it's a b-school, students need time to decompress as well as study and bond with their peers, which is why having campuses so close to beaches, and Disney World is a major plus for the prospective MBAs. As one student says, "It is also conveniently located less than 30 minutes from Daytona, which offers students wonderful, inexpensive nightlife and vacation spots."

Admissions

In order to be eligible for admission to Stetson's MBA program, all applicants must have received a BA from an accredited college or university. Stetson is quick to point out that "the undergraduate degree need not be in business administration. The course of study is specifically designed to accommodate the nonbusiness as well as the business degree holder. Combining the MBA with a nonbusiness undergraduate degree is considered outstanding career preparation in many fields." Applicants must submit an acceptable GMAT score, recommendation forms, and a recent photograph of themselves in order to be considered.

FINANCIAL FACTS

Annual tuition	$11,400
Books and supplies	$1,300
Average grant	$3,970

ADMISSIONS

Admissions Selectivity Rating	**74**
# of applications received	221
% applicants accepted	178
% acceptees attending	173
Average GMAT	531
Range of GMAT	425-690
Average GPA	3.5
TOEFL Required of International Students?	Yes
Minimum TOEFL (paper/computer)	550/213
Application fee	$25
Regular application deadline	1/1
Regular notification	1/11
Application Deadline/Notification	
Round 1:	1/1 / 1/11
Round 2:	3/1 / 3/15
Round 3:	5/1 / 5/15
Round 4:	8/1 / 8/12
Early decision program?	Yes
ED Deadline/Notification	Fall 8/1,
Spring 10/15, Summer 4/15 / 06/15	
Deferment Available?	Yes
Maximum length of deferment	1 year
Transfer students accepted?	Yes
Transfer application policy: Maximum 6 credit hours from AACSB accredited school.	
Non-fall admissions?	Yes
Need-blind admissions?	Yes

EMPLOYMENT PROFILE	
Career Rating	**80**
Placement rate (%)	98
# of companies recruiting on-campus	90
Average starting salary	$43,925

SUFFOLK UNIVERSITY
SAWYER SCHOOL OF MANAGEMENT

Academics

With five MBA options and four campuses in Massachusetts, the Sawyer School of Management at Suffolk University is the model of flexibility. Add to that "the diversity of students from different careers and from different countries," and professors "representing all corners of the Earth," and the options at Sawyer seem almost too broad. Luckily, students are saved by the administration from drowning in choices. "[The administration] works very closely with the students and is incredibly approachable." Overall, most students agree that "the academic experience seems to be the conventional combination of sweat and idealism, but the interactivity of this program is what puts it over the top." Another adds, "the school's administration provides events that bring distinguished Boston business leaders in (many of whom are Suffolk alumni), which have been very resourceful. I have yet to be unimpressed. My overall academic experience has been more than I could have ever imagined."

The five MBA options include the full-time MBA, the part-time MBA, the global MBA, executive MBA, and the online MBA. The program that garners the most enthusiasm from our survey respondents is the global MBA. One student reports "The focus is very international and very cutting edge." Another warns that the program is "condensed and very intense. Nine classes per semester doesn't leave for much outside school." Of all departments, professors in accounting receive particular praise.

In the full-time and part-time MBA, eight elective courses allow students to specialize their education in accounting, finance, organizational behavior, business law, health administration, marketing, entrepreneurship, taxation, nonprofit, international business, or corporate financial executive skills.

The school also offers a number of overseas seminars and study options. According to the school's website, students who take one of these routes "make corporate site visits, meet government officials to discuss business policies, and attend lectures in English at a leading international university. Suffolk MBAs have recently studied in Belgium, China, France, Ireland, Italy, and Turkey." This outright focus on the global isn't lost on students, either; an international student echoes the sentiments of many of his classmates and says, "Cultural diversity is the main strength of Suffolk. It is easy to have a truly multinational network [at this school]."

Career and Placement

Although students recognize the strengths of their program, many wish there were a better way to make more companies recognize them, too. One student says that the school could be better "in creating on-campus meetings with top recruiters more frequently to show them the great quality of our education, which they can use to add value to their companies." Still other students complain that there simply isn't enough "help for the students who are looking for jobs."

Despite these complaints, students from the Sawyer School have been recruited at companies as various as the Associated Press, *The Boston Globe*, Fidelity Investments, Fleet Financial, the Peace Corps, and PricewaterhouseCoopers.

Judith L. Reynolds, Director of Graduate Admissions
8 Ashburton Place, Boston, MA 02108 United States
Phone: 617-573-8302 • Fax: 617-305-1733
E-mail: grad.admission@suffolk.edu • Website: www.suffolk.edu/business

Student Life and Environment

Although many students take advantage of the online and off-site options that the school offers, those who opt to attend regular classes at the main Boston campus have little to complain about. Students rave about "downtown Boston and Boston's life" and say it is "very usual to go for a drink after class. People are outgoing and very active around the city. I see classmates in all sorts of happenings." According to one student, "From my point of view Boston is one of the most beautiful cities...with a lot of cultural activities and entertainment." The school itself ranks community building high on its list of priorities, and students say Suffolk offers "several cultural activities, like ski trips, Latin events, [and] food festivals." Besides this, one students raves that "the small feel of the school is great. Everyone knows who I am, and they know my story. You really feel connected to the administration, and we are treated as clients whom they want to succeed."

Despite the wealth of activities available and the cultural variety of Boston, some students complain that they barely get a chance to enjoy them. "Life at our school is basically the classroom and tons of meetings on a daily basis. Socializing, clubs, or activities are definitely not one of the strengths of our school," one typical student offers.

Admissions

To be considered for admission to the Sawyer School, students' undergraduate GPAs should be a solid B, which is the average for most of Sawyer's programs. The average GMAT is 510. Applicants who are not native speakers of English must take the TOEFL and score a minimum of 550 (paper-based) and 213 (computer-based) on the exam.

FINANCIAL FACTS

Annual tuition	$25,800
Fees	$140
Books and supplies	$1,000
Room & board	$10,651
% of students receiving aid	30
% of first-year students receiving aid	37
% of students receiving loans	18
% of students receiving grants	10
Average award package	$20,171
Average grant	$2,000

ADMISSIONS

Admissions Selectivity Rating	69
# of applications received	356
% applicants accepted	76
% acceptees attending	51
Average GMAT	510
Range of GMAT	430-580
Average GPA	3.2
TOEFL Required of International Students?	Yes
Minimum TOEFL (paper/computer)	550/213
Application fee	$50
International application fee	$50
Regular application deadline	6/15
Regular notification	Rolling
Deferment Available?	Yes
Maximum length of deferment	1 year
Transfer students accepted?	Yes
Transfer application policy: Same as regular applicants.	
Non-fall admissions?	Yes
Need-blind admissions?	Yes

APPLICANTS ALSO LOOK AT

Babson College, Bentley College, Boston College, Boston University, Northeastern University.

EMPLOYMENT PROFILE

Career Rating	87	Grads employed by field	%: avg. salary
Placement rate (%)	95	Accounting	15: $47,500
# of companies recruiting on-campus	30	Finance	17: $67,300
% grads employed immediately	65	Marketing	17: $68,400
Average starting salary	$67,800	MIS	6: $77,300
		Operations	2: $62,000
		Consulting	6: $95,000
		Entrepreneurship	2: $85,000
		General Management	17: $63,500
		Global Management	2: $40,000
		Other	9: $64,800
		Internet/New Media	4: $58,000
		Non-profit	2: $70,000

SYRACUSE UNIVERSITY
MARTIN J. WHITMAN SCHOOL OF MANAGEMENT

GENERAL INFORMATION

Type of school	private
Environment	city
Academic calendar	semester

SURVEY SAYS...
Friendly students
Cutting edge classes
Happy students
Smart classrooms
Solid preparation in:
Teamwork

STUDENTS

Enrollment of parent institution	18,000
Enrollment of MBA program	194
% male/female	68/32
% part-time	34
% minorities	9
% international	58
Average age at entry	26
Average years work experience at entry	4

ACADEMICS

Academic Experience Rating	**70**
Student/faculty ratio	7:1
Profs interesting rating	64
Profs accessible rating	80
% female faculty	14
Joint Degrees	

MBA/JD: 4 years
MBA/Master of Public
Administration: 3 years

Academics

The Martin J. Whitman School of Management at Syracuse University is among the oldest business schools in the nation, but this is not a program content to rest on its considerable laurels. On the contrary, Whitman's administration continually retools its MBA to meet the ever-changing needs of the modern business world. In its search to offer areas of study that are both unique and valuable, Whitman has developed concentrations and specialty tracks in such areas as innovation management; entrepreneurship, innovation, and global leadership; management of technology; and supply-chain management. These complement more traditional offerings in accounting, finance, general management, and marketing management.

A Whitman MBA consists of 18 courses, 10 of which are required core courses; the remaining courses are electives. Full-time, two-year MBAs complete an internship during the summer between their first and second years; a number of international internships are available, as are some six-month internships. (Students who choose this option increase their second-year spring course load in order to graduate on time.) An accelerated MBA is available to students who enter with highly developed business skills and knowledge. Students may also choose to pursue an iMBA that relies heavily on Internet-based distance learning. MBAs tell us, "The academics are tough but not impossible. You just need to have time-management skills. Professors are aware of other courses and their assignments, and [they] work with each other to make sure [the] workload is equally balanced."

Students at Whitman say, "[We appreciate the] vast number of resources available at our disposal at this school including computer clusters, libraries, tutors, [and] the resources of top schools in other areas, such as the Maxwell School for Public Administration and Newhouse School for Communication." Students agree that "[the faculty members] are very approachable outside of the classroom and give valuable insight," although "their effectiveness as teachers ranges widely. More emphasis needs to be placed on professors that have consistently shown poor performance in communicating effectively." Students comment that when professors are "on their game, the overall experience is very good. The discussion (rather than lecture) format is popular and seems to be more beneficial for overall understanding of topics. Also, casework is a popular technique and has been very effective."

Career and Placement

Whitman's Career Center provides a full range of services to all business undergraduates and graduate students including access to Internet job databases, in-office job postings, and an alumni database. The office maintains an online and traditional library of career resources, conducts workshops, seminars, mock interviews, and they also organize on-campus recruiting sessions. Students feel the office needs to do more, and they agree that "there are not enough valuable events for networking and career service." Students add, "We need to improve alumni connections. Those that are available are very helpful, but not many alumni are available, and [the] system for keeping track of them is poor."

In the spring of 2004, employers seeking Whitman MBAs included CallStreet LLC, Forest Laboratories, Johns Hopkins Health System, the Noel Group, and Xerox. One in five MBAs found work outside of the United States; nearly as many took jobs on the Pacific coast.

CAROL J. SWANBERG, DIRECTOR OF ADMISSIONS AND FINANCIAL AID
900 SOUTH CROUSE AVENUE, SUITE 100, SYRACUSE, NY 13244-2130 UNITED STATES
PHONE: 315-443-9214 • FAX: 315-443-9517
E-MAIL: MBAINFO@SOM.SYR.EDU • WEBSITE: WWW.WHITMAN.SYR.EDU

Student Life and Environment

Like many small MBA programs on big campuses, Whitman fosters a community unto itself, one in which, "students are all pretty close. The MBA Student Association organizes functions like happy hours, parties, and trips to the movies." One student elaborates, "Despite the normal gripes of student life, there is a familial atmosphere here at Syracuse that's hard to explain. For example, we recently appointed a new chancellor, and everyone—grad students, undergrad students, and faculty—seemed to view this as a very personal act. [It was] as if we were inducting a new patriarch (actually, a matriarch in our case) of sorts. I think it's a sign of the personal level of involvement that accompanies enrollment in the School of Management."

Students also enjoy the assets of the university at large, especially the intercollegiate athletics. One MBA explains, "Sports are big here. Many students go to the football and basketball games." Students also brag that "the campus itself is beautiful and is well maintained." As a major research university, Syracuse attracts a number of prominent speakers every semester.

The city of Syracuse has "a good local bar scene" that includes the famous Dinosaur, a blues club that serves some of the best and most authentic barbecue north of the Carolinas. Unfortunately, according to students, that's about all it has. Students say, "The city of Syracuse is not a very nice city. It is generally very filthy and in very poor economic condition. Crime is a problem." Also, winter arrives early here and really digs in its heels. Other students see a positive side of the situation; one student explains "The weather's so bad, you have no choice but to put in extra time studying."

Admissions

Applicants to the Whitman MBA program must submit official copies of all undergraduate and graduate transcripts, GMAT scores, TOEFL scores (international students), three short essays, two letters of recommendation, and a personal history detailing work and academic achievement. The school tells us that the admissions committee looks at "the quality of full-time work experience, the student's appropriateness for Syracuse's program, and evidence of leadership potential, motivation, teamwork ability, and perseverance." An admissions interview is strongly encouraged but not required.

FINANCIAL FACTS

Annual tuition	$24,180
Fees	$850
Books and supplies	$1,325
Room & board (on/off-campus)	$12,000/$12,000
% of students receiving aid	60
% of first-year students receiving aid	70
% of students receiving grants	49
Average award package	$13,000
Average grant	$10,000
Average student loan debt	$16,000

ADMISSIONS

Admissions Selectivity Rating	76
# of applications received	291
% applicants accepted	65
% acceptees attending	37
Average GMAT	568
Range of GMAT	530-620
Average GPA	3.2
TOEFL Required of International Students?	Yes
Minimum TOEFL (paper/computer)	600/250
Application fee	$65
International application fee	$65
Regular application deadline	3/1
Regular notification	4/1
Application Deadline/Notification	
Round 1:	1/15 / 2/15
Round 2:	3/1 / 4/1
Round 3:	5/1 / 6/1
Deferment Available?	Yes
Maximum length of deferment	1 year
Need-blind admissions?	Yes

APPLICANTS ALSO LOOK AT

Boston University, Cornell University, New York University, Penn State University-Great Valley Campus, University of Illinois at Urbana-Champaign, University of Rochester, University of Wisconsin—Madison.

EMPLOYMENT PROFILE			
Career Rating	73	**Grads employed by field %: avg. salary**	
Placement rate (%)	82	Accounting	20: $55,375
# of companies recruiting on-campus	22	Finance	26: $64,000
% grads employed immediately	63	Marketing	25: $53,125
Average starting salary	$60,500	Operations	17: $68,500
		Consulting	12

TEMPLE UNIVERSITY
THE FOX SCHOOL OF BUSINESS AND MANAGEMENT

GENERAL INFORMATION
Type of school   public
Environment   metropolis
Academic calendar

SURVEY SAYS...
Friendly students
Happy students
Smart classrooms

STUDENTS
Enrollment of parent
  institution   34,578
Enrollment of MBA program   650
% male/female   64/36
% out-of-state   54
% part-time   72
% minorities   7
% international   36
Average age at entry   28
Average years work experience
  at entry   5

ACADEMICS
Academic Experience Rating   82
Student/faculty ratio   8:1
Profs interesting rating   67
Profs accessible rating   65
% female faculty   18
% minority faculty   20
Joint Degrees
MBA/JD
MD-MBA
DMD/MBA
MBA/MS in Healthcare
Management/Healthcare Financial
Management: 2 years

Academics

Flexibility is a key selling point of Temple's Fox School of Management, which offers 11 areas of concentration to a good mix of both full-time and part-time students. With programs in accounting, business administration, e-business, economics, finance, general and strategic management, health-care management, human resource administration, international business administration, international business (tri-continent), management-information systems, and risk management and insurance, Temple gives graduate students an unusually wide array of choices, especially given the relatively intimate size of their program. The school also offers a variety of master's of science degrees, a master's of arts in economics, and a solid assortment of joint degrees.

"The health care and IMBA groups are the strongest of all the majors [at Fox]," according to students. The former, the first accredited program of its kind in the United States, benefits from its relatively long history as well as the presence of 5 medical schools and 30 teaching hospitals in the Philadelphia area. The latter is a natural outgrowth of Temple's "huge international student body," which has helped drive the focus of the curriculum toward globalization. Students also praise Temple's "great strategic management and MIS professors" as well as its "excellent consulting practicum" and "first-rate faculty in finance."

Temple recently revamped the MBA curriculum; it currently consists of six foundation courses, a seven-course sequence in advanced managerial perspectives, electives (leading to an area of concentration), and a capstone course. Students appreciate the administration's "willingness to take student assessment into consideration and re-evaluate current offerings (for the next class of students)." In general, students are happy with the program, but they would like to see more in-class practical application of the material. As one student says, "Theory is great and all, but practical experience in consulting, systems analysis, financial analysis, [or] project management is what matters. [The] extensive client-based project work with professors as mentors is by far the best teaching method applied here. Those that teach solely out of a textbook seem to be missing the big picture. The school is moving toward this type of learning, but it hasn't completely embraced it yet."

Career and Placement

Fox MBAs receive career services from the Fox School of Business Graduate Career Management Center (GCMC). "[It] provides [students with] assistance in focusing and preparing for both summer internships and post-MBA careers and provides opportunities for networking, meeting, and interviewing with top employers." Services include seminars, networking events, online job databases, and recruiting events. Students say, "A whole lot more needs to be done as far as MBA recruitment is concerned—especially for international students, as they constitute about 40 percent of the student population." Job searches benefit from "a strong alumni network and heavy presence in the Philadelphia/New Jersey/New York region, as well as strong connections with regional executives and industry experts."

Among the companies that most frequently hire Fox MBAs are Cigna, Eli Lilly, First Union, GlaxoSmithKline, IBM, Independence Blue Cross, JPMorgan, Mass Mutual, McNeil, Merck, Subaru of America, Unisys, Vanguard, William M. Mercer, and Wyeth.

Student Life and Environment

Temple principally operates its MBA program out of two campuses: the university's main campus, located a mile north of Center City, and a smaller downtown campus in

DAN CHATHAM, ASSOCIATE DIRECTOR, RECRUITING AND ADMISSIONS
1810 NORTH 13TH STREET, SPEAKMAN HALL, ROOM 5, PHILADELPHIA, PA 19122 UNITED STATES
PHONE: 215-204-5890 • FAX: 215-204-1632
E-MAIL: FOXINFO@TEMPLE.EDU • WEBSITE: WWW.FOX.TEMPLE.EDU/MBAMS

Center City. Students explain, "The downtown campus is in a convenient location, [while] the main campus is in the middle of 'the hood'; however, it is pleasant within the surrounding school streets." Students are quick to add that "both campuses are very safe." However, one student notes, "I would not walk too far away from the main campus because safety then becomes an issue." The main campus "is a lively place with lot of activities, [while] the center city campus only holds classes, primarily in the afternoons and evenings." MBAs appreciate that "shuttle buses provide handy service" between the two campuses. Temple also operates some satellite campuses in and around the city, some of which also offer MBA courses. One student writes, "I love the classes at Fort Washington, where the MBA crowd has much more job experience, and the place itself is so scenic during the spring season."

Full-time MBAs at Temple enjoy "active student organizations that organize networking events. There's also very active involvement in seminars by internationally recognized social, economic, and political leaders." Students add that fortunately "before we become exhausted from all the schoolwork and such, the MBA Association provides happy hours, networking events, club parties, and a lot of [enjoyable] things." Students also blow off steam by attending the games of the school's popular men's basketball team. Part-timers are less connected; one student explains, "Everyone at my school is very busy attempting to balance schoolwork, family, and a social life. It becomes very stressful. But everyone seems to work together to achieve a common goal: graduating."

Students love hometown Philadelphia, the second-largest metropolitan area in the eastern United States. The city not only provides innumerable business opportunities, but also lays out an impressive spread of restaurants, clubs, museums, parks, galleries, tourist attractions, professional sporting events, and shopping venues. One student notes that public transportation makes "traversing Philly a snap."

Admissions

Fox admissions officers review all undergraduate and graduate transcripts, GMAT scores, TOEFL scores (international students), and letters of recommendation for all candidates. In addition, the committee seriously considers "work experience and the applicant's statement of goals. Prospective students should have a statement of goals that expresses the direction [in which] they wish to move their career and how an MBA will serve that goal." Interviews are granted only on request of the applicant. To enhance recruitment of under-represented minority students and students with disadvantaged backgrounds, Temple "participates in annual state-wide and national conferences for minority candidates looking to further their education and participates with KPMG in their diversity recruiting."

FINANCIAL FACTS
Annual tuition (in-state/out-of-state)	$8,514/$12,636
Fees	$810
Books and supplies	$1,100
Room & board (on/off-campus)	$11,000/$11,000
% of students receiving grants	10
Average grant	$5,000
Average student loan debt	$36,000

ADMISSIONS
Admissions Selectivity Rating	91
# of applications received	502
% applicants accepted	50
% acceptees attending	64
Average GMAT	655
Range of GMAT	600-720
Average GPA	3.3
TOEFL Required of International Students?	Yes
Minimum TOEFL (paper/computer)	575/230
Application fee	$40
International application fee	$40
Regular application deadline	3/15
Regular notification	Rolling
Deferment Available?	Yes
Maximum length of deferment	1 year
Transfer students accepted?	Yes
Transfer application policy: May transfer up to six upper level credits if applicable to the program.	
Non-fall admissions?	Yes
Need-blind admissions?	Yes

APPLICANTS ALSO LOOK AT
Drexel University, Penn State University MBA, Rutgers, The State University of New Jersey—Thunderbird, University of Pittsburgh, University of South Carolina, Villanova University.

EMPLOYMENT PROFILE
Career Rating	79	Grads employed by field	%: avg. salary
Placement rate (%)	82	Finance	8: $51,350
# of companies recruiting on-campus	20	Marketing	14: $84,500
% grads employed immediately	45	MIS	1: $73,000
Average starting salary	$75,346	Operations	1: $60,667
		Consulting	20: $93,190
		General Management	4: $58,333

TENNESSEE TECHNOLOGICAL UNIVERSITY
TENNESSEE TECH MBA PROGRAM

GENERAL INFORMATION
Type of school	public
Environment	rural
Academic calendar	semester

SURVEY SAYS...
Friendly students
Happy students
Solid preparation in:
General management
Teamwork
Communication/interpersonal skills

STUDENTS
Enrollment of parent institution	9,107
Enrollment of MBA program	145
% male/female	68/32
% part-time	59
% minorities	15
% international	15
Average age at entry	29
Average years work experience at entry	5

ACADEMICS
Academic Experience Rating	65
Student/faculty ratio	22:1
Profs interesting rating	84
Profs accessible rating	66
% female faculty	18
% minority faculty	3

Prominent Alumni
Harry Stonecipher, President/COO of Boeing; Lark Mason, VP of Sotheby's Inc.-World's largest auction house; Jimmy Bedford, Master Distiller at Jack Daniel's (top position); Roger Crouch, Astronaut; C. Stephen Lynn, Former CEO of Shoney's Inc.

Academics

Accessibility and convenience are the most frequently cited attributes of the MBA program at Tennessee Tech, a midsize state university located halfway between Nashville and Knoxville. Students here may take classes on campus or at home through the school's distance-learning option. The program actually allows students to exercise both options simultaneously, so it's not either/or. In fact, MBAs are encouraged to find the ideal combination of on- and off-campus classes to suit their personal schedules. Students may attend part-time or full-time (more than half are part-timers), and may enter the program in the fall, spring, or summer. The program is also accessible to most students' budgets, especially those who reside in the state of Tennessee.

Enrollees love the distance program. One MBA writes, "The DMBA (Distance MBA) is a big strength of TTU. It allows students to get their MBA without ever stepping foot on campus. This is very valuable to out-of-state students and to those of us who work full-time." Despite the novelty of the program, most report that it runs smoothly. One student writes, "My graduating class is the first class of the Distance MBA program, and we have had an excellent experience. Our professors are very flexible and the staff is top-notch. The coursework is the same for the on-campus program, so we are fully prepared to succeed in today's business environment." Lectures are delivered on a set of CD ROMs, providing students with a rare and valuable permanent record. Class interaction is facilitated through WebCT; students log on to a site that provides access to e-mail, a course calendar, bulletin boards, quizzes and exams, and chat rooms, as well as downloadable PowerPoint presentations.

Even the campus-based courses incorporate "some online components," which students appreciate, noting the school's "total commitment to staying current with technological trends, which ensures Tech students have the latest tools for use in their jobs." Professors here represent "a good mix. Some are more traditional, others very technological. Some are really laid back and may have a class meeting at a downtown restaurant during happy hour. Some bring things to life by presenting research in an understandable form. For example, did you know that just the smell of fresh-baked cookies can increase productivity? There's a little bit of everything to keep it interesting." Administrators are "very approachable. They are always willing to go the extra mile to help the students. They truly care about giving us a quality education, and they do it with a smile."

TTU offers concentrations in accounting and MIS. The MBA program, which consists of seven, three-hour core courses and nine hours of electives, can be completed in one year by a full-time student.

Career and Placement

Career services at Tennessee Tech are of interest primarily to the school's full-time MBAs, since most of the part-timers and distance-learning enrollees are currently employed. Placement services are handled through the university's Career Services Office; there is no career office dedicated solely to the MBA program or to the College of Business. The MBA office does provide some supplemental career counseling and placement assistance. The school's website states that "the key to placement is flexibility. We generally place all MBAs who are seriously looking for a position."

Nearly all graduates remain in the Tennessee region following graduation. A few find work in the southern Atlantic states, while a few others relocate to the Southwest. On average, 85 employers recruit each year on the Tennessee Tech campus.

Drive Bob Wood, Director of MBA Studies
Box 5023 TTU, 1108 North Peachtree, Cookeville, TN 38505 United States
Phone: 931-372-3600 • Fax: 931-372-6544
E-mail: mbastudies@tntech.edu • Website: www.tntech.edu/mba/

Student Life and Environment

The MBA Program at Tennessee Tech provides a "small school environment within a larger university" for the cadre of students who attend classes on campus. Full-timers tell us that "life at Tech is thoroughly enjoyable. There is enough diversity to offer something for everyone as well as being small enough that you don't get lost in the crowd." Students "can join the MBA society and get involved in the panel discussions" to fill out their extracurricular schedules. Part-timers, on the other hand, "do not get very involved with the student activities that are offered" but they can still "enjoy going to Tech because," as one says, "I can go to on-campus courses as opposed to taking them online."

Many Tech MBAs do take the courses online, however, and for them "there is not any face-to-face contact with classmates." Even so, one distance learner reports that "the WebCT experience has been more enriching for me than my on campus classes. I do miss the amenities found on campus, such as the library, help desk, and fitness center, though." In the plus column, distance learners needn't cope with a parking situation that "will give you a headache."

Hometown "Cookeville and the surrounding area provide many outdoor activities. With major cities like Nashville and Knoxville within 100 miles, many students leave for the weekend." The student body is a mix of people who "just graduated from Tech as undergrads and are somewhat insular" and professionals "with strengths in various fields: some financial, some technology, some creative." One student writes, "I can't count the times I've leaned on my fellow classmates for support and vice versa. The morale here is wonderful." Full-timers form a tight group, saying they "study together, get our work done, and then go out and have a couple of drinks. Even though we're in the heart of the 'Bible Belt,' we know how to have a good time."

Admissions

Successful applicants to the Tennessee Tech MBA Program must have a minimum undergraduate GPA of 2.5, a minimum GMAT score of 450, and a minimum formula score of 1000 using the formula [(undergraduate GPA × 200) + GMAT score] or 1050 using the formula [(undergraduate GPA for final 60 semester hours ? 200) + GMAT score]. Applicants must also provide a statement of computer proficiency attesting to aptitude in word processing, spreadsheet, and presentation software. Students whose native language is not English must provide TOEFL scores (minimum 550 paper-and-pencil, 213 computer-based). Entering students who have not completed an undergraduate business core are required to complete pre-MBA foundation modules in accounting, business law, economics, finance, management, marketing, and business statistics/quantitative methods. Special minority fellowships and graduate assistantships are offered to attract students from underrepresented populations.

FINANCIAL FACTS

Annual tuition (in-state/out-of-state)	$0/$9,996
Fees	$6,550
Books and supplies	$1,500
Room & board (on/off-campus)	$4,380/$5,500
% of students receiving aid	50
% of first-year students receiving aid	16
% of students receiving grants	24
Average award package	$8,426
Average grant	$1,336
Average student loan debt	$5,000

ADMISSIONS

Admissions Selectivity Rating	67
# of applications received	94
% applicants accepted	93
% acceptees attending	63
Average GMAT	538
Range of GMAT	450-760
Average GPA	3.2
TOEFL Required of International Students?	Yes
Minimum TOEFL (paper/computer)	550/213
Application fee	$25
International application fee	$30
Regular application deadline	Rolling
Regular notification	Rolling
Deferment Available?	Yes
Maximum length of deferment	1 year
Transfer students accepted?	Yes
Transfer application policy: TTU will transfer 9 hours or less from an AACSB accredited school.	
Non-fall admissions?	Yes
Need-blind admissions?	Yes

EMPLOYMENT PROFILE

Career Rating	73	Grads employed by field:	
Placement rate (%)	95	Accounting	17
# of companies recruiting on-campus	85	Finance	8
% grads employed immediately	45	Marketing	3
Average starting salary	$41,800	MIS	8
		Strategic Planning	3
		Consulting	8
		Entrepreneurship	3
		General Management	14
		Other	33
		Internet/New Media	3

TEXAS A&M INTERNATIONAL UNIVERSITY
COLLEGE OF BUSINESS ADMINISTRATION

GENERAL INFORMATION
Type of school   public
Academic calendar

SURVEY SAYS...
Friendly students
Happy students
Smart classrooms
Solid preparation in:
Finance
General management
Teamwork

ACADEMICS
Academic Experience Rating   64
Profs interesting rating   74
Profs accessible rating   64

Academics

The College of Business Administration at Texas A&M International University "is dedicated to the delivery of a high quality professional and internationalized education to a graduate student population that is drawn from a wide variety of countries and cultures," according to the College's website, which also points out that "these programs [are intended to] contribute to the students' success in leadership positions in both domestic and international settings." This AACSB-accredited school offers a general MBA, an MBA in international banking (MBA-IBK), an MBA in international trade (MBA-IT), and a PhD in International Business Administration.

All MBA programs at TAMIU require mastery of eight foundation areas: accounting, information systems, quantitative methods, economics, finance, management, marketing, and operations. Students may fulfill these requirements by completing corresponding undergraduate courses at TAMIU, by showing evidence of equivalent coursework at another undergraduate institution, or by having earned an undergraduate business degree from an AACSB-accredited program. Waivers are only granted for coursework completed within the previous seven years.

TAMIU's general MBA is taught in both English and Spanish. The 30-hour program allows students to concentrate in one of the following areas: accounting, information systems, international business, international finance, international trade economics, logistics, and management marketing. The strong international focus of the program "gives students the opportunity to immerse themselves in an international environment in which we can analyze situations of different countries. The diversity of the student body helps." Students also praise the "extremely optimistic" professors who "honestly care about their students and are always willing to offer a helping hand." One student writes, "Teachers are very good and highly cooperative, with great academic ability. They have the knowledge to impart, help the students and, offer their valuable suggestions to guide their further course of action."

Students also point out that "the small size of the program is a great strength. The student population is not big, so there is enough opportunity to interact with your professors and get to know everyone in your college." MBAs here appreciate how "professors acknowledge that the majority of the class works full-time and also goes to school, so they make the assignments challenging, but not impossible." In addition to the above-mentioned degrees, TAMIU also offers a master of professional accountancy (MPAcc), a master of science in international logistics (MS-IL), a master of science in information systems (MS-IS), and a doctorate in international business administration (PhD-IB).

Career and Placement

The Texas A&M International Career Services Office provides counseling and placement services to the entire undergraduate and graduate student body. The office organizes on-campus recruiting events, career expos, and job fairs. It also offers one-on-one counseling, workshops, library services, and resume review.

FINANCIAL FACTS
Annual tuition (in-state/out-of-state)
$1,222/$3,544
Room & board (on/off-campus)
$3,083/$2,682

ADMISSIONS
Admissions Selectivity Rating   71

Student Life and Environment

Nearly three-quarters of TAMIU's MBA students attend full-time, providing a sizeable base for clubs, organizations, and extracurricular activity. Students tell us that "campus life offers a diverse field of organizations. New clubs and sports are always developing." They also report that "seminars provided by the school are good. Many important speakers visit the campus to deliver inspirational speeches on important current topics, including politics, finance, economics, and health." Part-timers generally "don't get to spend much time on campus, but rather just get here for class at night and leave once classes are done." They "visit the computer labs and library to do research and work," but otherwise spend little extra time socializing.

Hometown Laredo "is poised at the gateway to Mexico," placing it "at an enviable crossroads of international business and life." 156 miles south of San Antonio and 153 miles north of Monterrey, Mexico, this city of over 150,000 is the fastest growing in the state of Texas. The area's growth has been spurred by Laredo's increasing role as a center for international manufacturing and trade. Top employers in the area, outside of education and government, include the Laredo Medical Center, the H-E-B Grocery Company, Doctor's Hospital, Laredo Candle, and area banks.

TAMIU's "friendly, frank, cheerful and helpful" students "enjoy the challenge of studying in a foreign country and expect the experience to give them a better professional future." Nearly half the MBAs here are international students; not quite half of these are Mexican and Latin American. Thirty percent of the international student body comes from Asia.

Admissions

Applying to the TAMIU MBA program is a two-step process, as applicants must be admitted to both the university at large and the College of Business in order to enroll in the MBA program. Applicants must submit the following materials to the Office of Graduate Admission: a completed application; an official copy of transcripts for all post-secondary academic work undertaken; and an official score report for the GMAT. Applicants must also provide a statement of purpose, a resume, and two letters of recommendation. The TOEFL is required of all students who completed undergraduate study in a country where English is not the language of instruction; a minimum score of 550 paper-based or 213 computer-based is required. International students must also submit documentation demonstrating the ability to support themselves financially while studying at TAMIU.

EMPLOYMENT PROFILE	
Career Rating	62

Texas A&M University—College Station

Mays Business School

Academics

The top-ranked Mays Business School at Texas A&M University—College Station combines a one-size-fits-all approach with specialization options to provide its small student body a cost-effective and streamlined, yet flexible, MBA degree. This inexpensive public school offers one of the 10 quickest returns on investment, according to *Business Week*. *Financial Times* ranked it the fourth best value in US graduate business education. One MBA agrees, "The education you receive is top notch for the cost."

All Mays students complete a 48-credit core sequence over a 16-month period. This core covers accounting, business communication, finance, global management, information and operations management, marketing, negotiations, and management, all with "an emphasis on character and ethics, a very appealing aspect of the program." This mandatory curriculum that combines "business competencies, communications, international issues, teamwork, and ethics" means all Mays MBAs "are prepared to be strategic thinkers, effective communicators, and accountable team members and leaders in today's global marketplace," according to the school.

Those seeking specialization are welcome to remain at Mays for an additional semester, participate in study abroad, or undertake other enrichment opportunities. The school offers specialization in 11 predefined areas (students speak most highly of accounting, marketing, management, and real estate). MBAs may also design specializations of their own. Other unique aspects of the program include the Technology Transfer Challenge, in which MBAs compete to develop commercial applications for promising new technologies. The school writes, "The Challenge's design is based on state-of-the-art knowledge management theory, demonstrating how knowledge management principles can be used to help evaluate the potential of patents and other raw technologies. It demands a level of creativity not possible with traditional case competitions."

Students here love the "low cost and excellent financial aid," as well as the school's vision. One MBA exclaims, "The school continues to replace weak faculty in an effort to improve. And the program is definitely improving, with great faculty leading the way." They also appreciate that it's a "conservative, strong program with high starting salaries and great recruiting companies." Naturally, though, a few see its small size as a drawback. One such student opines, "The Mays MBA Class of 2006 is only 70 students strong. If the school is ever to be mentioned amongst Harvard, Texas, and Michigan, then it will have to expand to upwards of 500 students."

Career and Placement

A&M's legendary alumni network works its magic for MBAs. Students exploit this valuable asset through publications, a website, newsletters, and on- and off-campus events. The Mays Graduate Business Career Services (GBCS) Office also provides one-on-one counseling, online assessment tools, and frequent workshops on crafting resumes and cover letters, networking, interviewing, and negotiating your salary.

Hundreds of companies recruit on the College Station campus each year—just how many come for the purpose of interviewing MBAs is less clear. What counts is that the results are pretty impressive. Employers of Mays MBAs include BP, CattleSoft, ChevronPhillips, China National Petroleum Corp, CIA, Citibank, Citigroup, DuPont, Eagle Pass Winery, the Federal Reserve Bank, First Houston Mortgage, Ford, Hewlett Packard, Johnson-Lancaster & Associates, Proctor & Gamble, Smith Barney, Solutions Inc., Sovico Trading Ltd, USAA, Wal-Mart, and World Savings. In 2004, the mean starting salary of a Mays MBA was $77,153. One student sums up, "One of the greatest facets

WENDY FLYNN, ASSOCIATE DIRECTOR, MAYS MBA
4117 TAMU COLLEGE STATION, TX 77843-4117 UNITED STATES
PHONE: 979-845-4714 • FAX: 979-862-2393
E-MAIL: MAYSMBA@TAMU.EDU • WEBSITE: MBA.TAMU.EDU

of a Texas A&M education is the high salary upon graduation with relatively low tuition costs."

Student Life and Environment

Although "school requires much of a student's time" at A&M, "the lifestyle in College Station is still very enjoyable." Furthermore, "those who wish to participate in social activities will not be disappointed," MBAs write, since "there are weekly events organized, as well as plenty of hot spots to frequent." It will come as no surprise to anyone who knows anything at all about the school that "football is the major activity" and that A&M is "big into traditions, and it really enhances the life here." Lesser-known but popular diversions also include "rollerblading, volleyball, tennis, and other sports." Overall, MBAs here agree that "Texas A&M is very conservative and an excellent environment to learn quality business practices."

With a substantial international population, Mays' student body is "very diverse in ethnicity, education, and experience," although not so much in gender. MBAs tend to be "boisterous in class, friendly and intelligent, [and] proactive in regards to career advancement and networking." All "have some special skills which make them unique. If one is good in math, another is very good in communications." One MBA observes, "Fellow students are like good coworkers at the office: During class and study time they work hard, but after class, they know how to have fun."

Admissions

With a limited number of slots available, the Mays MBA program can keep admissions very competitive. Successful applicants typically have at least two years of post-college, full-time work experience, good GMAT scores ("quant and verbal sections must have scores at least at the 50th percentile for consideration," notes the Admissions Office), and evidence of leadership and professional skill. All applicants must submit a current resume, three letters of recommendation from professional sources, and application essays. International students must provide TOEFL scores (minimum 600 on the paper-and-pencil test, 250 on the computerized test for admission). A&M "aggressively seeks to enhance diversity on all levels in the program, and has programs in place to recruit all students who will bring diversity to our program."

FINANCIAL FACTS

Annual tuition (in-state/out-of-state)	$3,456/$16,056
Fees	$8,289
Books and supplies	$1,428
Room & board	$9,306
% of students receiving aid	75
% of first-year students receiving aid	75
% of students receiving loans	65
% of students receiving grants	75
Average grant	$10,237
Average student loan debt	$7,500

ADMISSIONS

Admissions Selectivity Rating	93
# of applications received	348
% applicants accepted	35
% acceptees attending	57
Average GMAT	637
Average GPA	3.3
TOEFL Required of International Students?	Yes
Minimum TOEFL (paper/computer)	600/250
Application fee	$50
International application fee	$75
Regular application deadline	5/31
Regular notification	6/15
Deferment Available?	Yes
Maximum length of deferment	1 year
Need-blind admissions?	Yes

APPLICANTS ALSO LOOK AT

Arizona State University, Brigham Young University, Rice University, The University of Texas at Austin, University of Maryland—College Park, University of Notre Dame, Vanderbilt University.

EMPLOYMENT PROFILE

Career Rating	85	Grads employed by field	%: avg. salary
% grads employed immediately	90	Finance	37: $77,335
Average starting salary	$77,153	Human Resources	6: $77,000
		Marketing	21: $76,120
		MIS	7: $74,233
		Operations	11: $74,126
		Consulting	7: $75,000
		General Management	11: $82,778

TEXAS A&M UNIVERSITY—COMMERCE
COLLEGE OF BUSINESS AND TECHNOLOGY

GENERAL INFORMATION
Type of school	public
Academic calendar	semester

SURVEY SAYS...
Friendly students
Happy students
Smart classrooms
Solid preparation in:
Finance
General management

STUDENTS
Enrollment of parent institution	4,170
Enrollment of MBA program	195
% male/female	49/51
% out-of-state	25
% part-time	57
% minorities	25
% international	23
Average age at entry	29

ACADEMICS
Academic Experience Rating	61
Student/faculty ratio	27:1
Profs interesting rating	62
Profs accessible rating	61
% female faculty	33
% minority faculty	28

Joint Degrees
BPA/MBA in Accounting: 4-5 years

Academics

With classes offered in five locations, the College of Business and Technology at Texas A&M Commerce has made convenience one of its chief selling points. The approach seems to be working; the program is now one of the biggest MBA programs in the Dallas/Fort Worth region, according to the *Dallas Business Journal*. The school uses only its regular, full-time graduate faculty to teach MBA classes in Commerce, Mesquite, McKinney, Dallas, and Waco. (The Waco program, which began in the spring of 2004, is cohort-based.) According to a survey, easy-to-reach locations, affordability, and connections to area industry are the reasons most students choose to pursue a Commerce MBA.

Students can choose not only from a wide range of sites, but also from a variety of program options. The Fast Track MBA offers a general management degree consisting of 10 courses. This program, which can be finished in one year, is favored by the school's five-year BA/MBA students. The Comprehensive MBA can also be completed in a year, although most students take longer due to required foundation courses (which can be waived for students with mastery in foundation areas). The school also offers MBAs a minor that is available in accounting, economics, finance, human-resources management, international business, management-information systems, marketing, and management of technology. In addition, students at Commerce can pursue a British study option, study in China through the China University of Geosciences Partnership, and MS degrees in e-commerce, economics, finance, management, and marketing. The MS in management can be completed entirely online; there are select MBA classes also available over the Internet.

Big things are ahead for Texas A&M Commerce. The school introduced an online MBA program in the fall of 2004 and will soon offer an A&M MBA in Beijing, China. "If they cannot come here to Commerce, we will take the MBA program to them," explains university President Keith McFarland, alluding to the difficulty foreign students have receiving United States visas in the post-9/11 world. "They will receive the same high quality education we are known for." That means Chinese students will soon benefit from "very experienced faculty [and] a low student-teacher ratio that shows the school really cares about the students and tries to get to know them."

Career and Placement

The university maintains a career-services office on its main campus in Commerce. The office includes a library of job-related materials and a bulletin board of job postings; its staff offers one-on-one counseling to students searching for jobs. The school is one of 44 members of the Metroplex Area Consortium of Career Centers (MAC3), "organized for the purpose of 'uniting students, employers, educators, and the community to form a better workplace.'" MAC3 maintains an online job database and holds regular career fairs.

Tammi Thompson, Admissions Advisor
PO Box 3011, Commerce, TX 75429 United States
Phone: 903-886-5167 • Fax: 903-886-5165
E-mail: graduate_school@tamu-commerce.edu
Website: www.tamu-commerce.edu/graduateprograms

Student Life and Environment

The cooperative students in Commerce's various programs constitute "a melting pot of many ethnic backgrounds; [there are] both male and female students [with] fairly large variances in age and work experience." The population includes "a large proportion of international students from East Asia and India." MBAs say, "Students are either really involved in extracurricular life or not at all," and that their ranks contain "many commuters who don't participate in on-campus activities."

The Commerce campus includes "a brand-new, multimillion-dollar recreation center. The students love it." MBAs comment that "even though it is a small campus, there is plenty to do." Nationally touring performers, lecturers, festivals, and parties fill the extracurricular calendar here. The school's athletic programs are hit-and-miss; the women's soccer team is quite competitive, while the men's football and basketball teams are dolorous endeavors.

Commerce, Texas is a quaint town sixty miles east of Dallas. Its population totals around 7,500 permanent residents; when school is in session, the population doubles. Major employers in the area include Bank One, Ben E. Keith Foods, Tyco, and the university. MBAs warn that "the town is a very low-income town, which results in a low-income lifestyle at the school."

Admissions

Applicants to the MBA program at the College of Business must send the Admissions Office copies of all undergraduate and graduate transcripts, GMAT or GRE scores, three letters of recommendation (from present or past employers and/or from professors), a personal statement describing one's goals in pursuing a graduate degree, and a current resume. A minimum undergraduate GPA of 2.75 and a GMAT score of at least 400 are both required to qualify for full admission; students not meeting these requirements may still enter under probationary status, or they may enter with nondegree status. Applicants to MS programs may take the GRE or GMAT. To gain entrance into the 33-hour program, students must have successfully completed introductory undergraduate classes in accounting, finance, macroeconomics, management, marketing, microeconomics, operations, and statistics.

FINANCIAL FACTS

Annual tuition (in-state/out-of-state)	$3,600/$8,832
Books and supplies	$800
Room & board	$4,100
% of students receiving aid	8
Average grant	$4,798

ADMISSIONS

Admissions Selectivity Rating	62
# of applications received	600
% applicants accepted	31.5
% acceptees attending	205
Average GMAT	460
Range of GMAT	380-620
Average GPA	3
TOEFL Required of International Students?	Yes
Minimum TOEFL (paper/computer)	500/173
Application fee	$35
International application fee	$50
Regular application deadline	6/1
Regular notification	Rolling
Deferment Available?	Yes
Maximum length of deferment	2 semesters
Transfer students accepted?	Yes
Transfer application policy: Students can transfer up to 12 credits in the 36-48 credit program and 9 credits for the 30-33 credit program.	
Non-fall admissions?	Yes

APPLICANTS ALSO LOOK AT

Southern Methodist University, Texas Christian University (TCU), The University of Texas at Arlington, University of Dallas, University of North Texas, University of Phoenix.

EMPLOYMENT PROFILE	
Career Rating	70
Placement rate (%)	93
Average starting salary	$62,000

TEXAS CHRISTIAN UNIVERSITY
THE M. J. NEELEY SCHOOL OF BUSINESS

GENERAL INFORMATION

Type of school	private
Academic calendar	semester

SURVEY SAYS...

Friendly students
Happy students
Smart classrooms
Solid preparation in:
Teamwork
Presentation skills

STUDENTS

Enrollment of parent institution	8,632
Enrollment of MBA program	298
% male/female	71/29
% part-time	66
% minorities	7
% international	22
Average age at entry	27
Average years work experience at entry	4

ACADEMICS

Academic Experience Rating	**85**
Student/faculty ratio	5:1
Profs interesting rating	85
Profs accessible rating	83
% female faculty	15
% minority faculty	3

Joint Degrees
MBA/EdD in educational leadership: 3 years
MBA/PhD in Physics: 6 years
MBA/MIM: 2 years

Prominent Alumni
John Roach, Roach Investments/Field Electronics; Luther King, Luther King Capital Management; Gordon England, Secretary of the Navy; John Davis III, CEO and Chairman, Pegasus Systems; Vivian Noble Dubose, President, Noble Properties.

Academics

The greatest strengths of the M. J. Neeley School of Business, the boutique-size MBA program at Texas Christian University, "all have to do with its size," students say. "Because it is small, students' needs are recognized and addressed quickly, professors give students a lot of attention, and the students are all very close. It all makes for good learning environment and good networking." Neeley excels in a variety of areas; finance and investments, supply-chain management, and the entrepreneurs program all received plaudits from our survey respondents, who happily added that the school is not content to rest on its laurels. "They want to break into the top-50 business schools and stay there, and they push us accordingly," MBAs tell us. "The recent additions of several prominent and recognizable faculty" represent just one stage of TCU's efforts in this area.

Not that the faculty has never been a group of slouches. According to one second-year student, "The professors are great teachers and are available at all times. Some outstanding teachers were Vassil Mihov, Steve Lim, Bill Cron, Chuck Williams, Rob Rhodes, Larry Lockwood, and In-mu Haw. All of these men have great minds and are great teachers." They also "go the extra mile to ensure that we learn and feel prepared for exams or for our future careers." Instruction is often integrated; "course material overlaps, and we are looking at similar issues from different perspectives in different classes." While "professors do lecture, students must be prepared to discuss the reading materials in class." The workload can be heavy, but rarely is it overly quant-heavy. One student explains, "The professors design classes to help bring nonbusiness majors quickly up to speed. This is a good school to attend if you have a liberal-arts background."

TCU offers students a number of user-friendly options, including "the ability to take classes with other graduate-program students," which as one student notes is "very helpful." The school's location, near the Dallas/Forth Worth area, offers "networking opportunities and close ties to companies in the area." An Executive MBA program is "open to qualified candidates with eight or more years of work experience, five of which must be managerial in nature."

Career and Placement

Neeley offers its MBAs free access to a number of premium online career services, including CareerTools, CareerSearch, and WetFeet. The school also offers a series of workshops throughout students' tenure to teach them everything from how to prepare a great resume to which fork to use during the salad course. In 2003, 98 percent of the class of 2004 sought summer internship; 93 percent received offers, and 91 percent accepted those offers. Students report approvingly, "Since we are a relatively small program, there is not as much competition for jobs or interviews, and we get a lot of personal attention from the faculty and staff."

Employers who most frequently hire Neeley graduates include Alcon Labs, American Airlines, Bell Helicopter Textron, Burlington Northern Santa Fe, Champion Communications, Crescent Real Estate, Energy Reliability Council of Texas, First Command Financial Planning, Fort Worth Business Press, Handango, IBM China, Intuit, PepsiCo, Sabre Holdings, SBC, 7-Eleven, Southwest Securities, and Timera. More than 80 percent of Neeley graduates are able to secure positions in Texas or the states immediately surrounding it; 8 percent find employment overseas.

Student Life and Environment

Neeley recently relocated to a "great new building with a number of team rooms." Students tell us, "Having so many available rooms keeps many students on campus the

OLIVIA WILLIAMS, ASSISTANT DIRECTOR OF MBA ADMISSIONS
PO BOX 298540, FORT WORTH, TX 76129 UNITED STATES
PHONE: 817-257-7531 • FAX: 817-257-6431
E-MAIL: MBAINFO@TCU.EDU • WEBSITE: WWW.MBA.TCU.EDU

FINANCIAL FACTS

Annual tuition	$19,200
Fees	$2,040
Books and supplies	$1,600
Room & board	$10,000
% of students receiving aid	90
% of students receiving loans	52
% of students receiving grants	88
Average award package	$23,145
Average grant	$17,000
Average student loan debt	$34,463

entire day and evening. The rooms are very conducive to getting to know each other. Not only do we all study together and help each other, we also get to know each other well. We have everything we need in the new building [like] study rooms, a sandwich shop, [and a] lounge." MBAs describe an unusually congenial atmosphere at their school; it's the kind of place where students stay in touch year-round. One student reports, "During the summer, most of us had internships here in the area, so we would meet for happy hour on Friday to discuss our work for the week and just keep in touch."

A typical day at Neeley is "busy, but good. The workload is manageable but challenging. There is always some project to be working on, a case to read, or a problem set to complete." When school is done, "there's always something going on, whether it's an employer-appreciation reception, industry speaker or presentation, mentor dinner, community-service project, or tailgate party." Tailgates are central to the TCU experience; "the MBA student association has sponsored a tailgate at each home football game." Students also "often go out together on Thursday nights, first-years and second-years. Happy hours are also very common on Fridays. The MBA Association is making more of an effort to include the professional MBA students in the activities."

Students praise TCU's efforts to diversify its student body but report that it still has some ground to cover. One student writes about the diversity, "While women, Hispanic students, and international students are well represented, there [are only a few] African American students found in either of the full-time classes," although efforts are underway to attract a more diverse group of students. Students love TCU's location "in the Dallas/Fort Worth area because it gives the school several connections within the metroplex, which makes us very accessible to local employers." TCU, we're told, enjoys "a great relationship with both the city and the businesses [in Dallas/Fort Worth]."

ADMISSIONS

Admissions Selectivity Rating	79
# of applications received	112
% applicants accepted	72
% acceptees attending	56
Average GMAT	602
Range of GMAT	570-650
Average GPA	3.3
TOEFL Required of International Students?	Yes
Minimum TOEFL (paper/computer)	550/213
Application fee	$50
International application fee	$50
Regular application deadline	4/30
Regular notification	Rolling
Deferment Available?	Yes
Maximum length of deferment	1 year
Transfer students accepted?	Yes
Transfer application policy: Maximum transferable credits are six semester hours from an AACSB accredited institution.	
Non-fall admissions?	Yes
Need-blind admissions?	Yes

Admissions

Applicants to the Neeley MBA program must submit undergraduate transcripts, GMAT scores, letters of recommendation, a personal statement, and a resume. An interview, while not required, is "strongly encouraged"; interviews can be conducted via telephone for applicants unable to visit the campus. At least two years of work experience is recommended. The school reports that "a holistic admissions approach is used to assess the applicant's fit with the program. In addition to academic ability, applicants must demonstrate the desire and ability to perform in a highly interactive, team-based environment." To attract minority students, the school awards "scholarships to recognize the achievements of Henry B. Gonzalez and Martin Luther King, Jr., made available to TCU MBA students by the PepsiCo Foundation." The school also offers National Hispanic MBA and National Black MBA scholarships.

APPLICANTS ALSO LOOK AT

Baylor University, Rice University, Southern Methodist University, The University of Texas at Austin, Tulane University.

EMPLOYMENT PROFILE

		Grads employed by field %: avg. salary	
Career Rating	83		
Placement rate (%)	88	Finance	27: $61,944
% grads employed immediately	48	Marketing	38: $58,750
Average starting salary	$59,075	Operations	11: $61,407
		Consulting	18: $51,667
		Other	6: $66,000

TEXAS TECH UNIVERSITY

JERRY S. RAWLS COLLEGE OF BUSINESS ADMINISTRATION

GENERAL INFORMATION

Type of school	public
Environment	city
Academic calendar	Rolling

SURVEY SAYS...
Friendly students
Smart classrooms
Solid preparation in:
Teamwork
Communication/interpersonal skills
Presentation skills

STUDENTS

Enrollment of parent institution	28,412
Enrollment of MBA program	393
% male/female	74/26
% out-of-state	13
% part-time	82
% minorities	7
% international	11
Average age at entry	24
Average years work experience at entry	2.9

ACADEMICS

Academic Experience Rating	70
Student/faculty ratio	8:1
Profs interesting rating	74
Profs accessible rating	84
% female faculty	12
% minority faculty	1

Joint Degrees
MD/MBA: 4 years
MBA/JD: 3 years
MBA/MA in foreign language: 2 years
MBA/MArch: 2.5 years
Dual MBA programs with:
Universidad Anahuac/Mexico 2 years; Sup de Co Montpellier 2 years

Prominent Alumni
Jerry V. Smith, President/Jerry V. Smith Professional Corporation; Robert C. Brown, Director, Wayne & Gladys Valley Foundation; Michael Lynn Marshall, President, American State Bank, Odessa.

Academics

"Excellent cost-benefit" is the fare of the day at Texas Tech University's Rawls College of Business Administration, where "[students] can get an inexpensive MBA in a year-and-a-half program." Students love the price tag, but they also appreciate Texas Tech's regional reputation; according to students, "It's a big school known for its research activities and is considered among the best schools in Texas." The program also accommodates part-time students by offering all required MBA courses in the evening each academic year.

The Rawls MBA curriculum consists of 27 hours of required general business courses, 6 hours of credited out-of-class experience (internship, international study, directed experience), a 3-hour capstone course, and 12 hours of electives. Students can earn a concentration by dedicating all 12 elective hours to a single subject; Rawls offers concentrations in agribusiness, energy commerce, entrepreneurship, finance, health-organization management, international business, management-information systems, and marketing. Rawls also offers a more specialized MS in business administration, an IMBA (international MBA), and an MSA (master of science in accounting).

MBAs note that "[the professors] are world leaders in research and consulting and yet remain easily accessible to all of their students." Students add, "[We] really like the professors' attitudes here—they teach as well and as much as they can. [They] want their students to know everything they do, instead of concealing some things to retain their status and power." One student comments, "Our professors are constantly trying to incorporate the demands of the working world into our courses, which I think makes us very prepared. Our courses are constantly being updated and changed to fit the current climate of the business world." They are also good contacts and mentors. One MBA reports, "Several [professors] have offered to help me as I begin my job search, and most know me by my first name."

The wish lists of many students include the addition of "leveling courses for nonbusiness majors." (Texas Tech welcomes students with little previous business education or experience.) One student notes, "I'm completely lost in half of my classes because we just jumped right in, and starting intermediate accounting after majoring in journalism was a bit of a shock." Some students would also "like to see Texas Tech get involved with the city of Lubbock [and] get companies to set up shop in the city. A commonality of top MBA programs seems to be their proximity to large cities, and the opportunities that are created with companies located there. It would be in the interest of Tech to have companies as liaisons." One student says, "I believe the school should be more active in participating with Lubbock in creating beneficial opportunities."

Career and Placement

According to students, "Rawl's Business School [built] its own career center about a year ago." Students add, "It's doing very well for only being there almost a year. However, the opportunities that it brings in for MBA students is very much lacking. Most of the opportunities are for undergrad degrees." Students also feel that the center needs to "improve counseling for career opportunities for students, especially international students" and "provide one-to-one counseling to help students decide their courses, internships, jobs, and finally to choose career paths." They also see great potential in the new office, though, and have high hopes for its future.

CINDY BARNES, DIRECTOR, GRADUATE SERVICES CENTER
RAWLS COLLEGE OF BUSINESS, GRADUATE SERVICES CENTER LUBBOCK, TX 79409-2101 U.S.
PHONE: 806-742-3184 • FAX: 806-742-3958
E-MAIL: MBA@BA.TTU.EDU • WEBSITE: WWW.GRAD.BA.TTU.EDU

Companies that most frequently employ Rawls MBAs include Accenture; Andersen; Cap Gemini; CINTAS; Comerica; Covenant Health Systems; Dell; Deloitte Touche Tohmatsu; DePuy Orthopaedics, Inc.; First Investors Corporation; Kellogg's; KPMG; National Instruments; NHK International; PNB Financial; PricewaterhouseCoopers; Ryan and Company; SBC; Walgreens; Wells Fargo Financial; and Yvew Socher. About 10 percent of Rawls graduates find their first post-graduation jobs outside of the United States.

Student Life and Environment

Texas Tech MBAs praise their hometown of Lubbock, where "good old West Texas friendliness" is always the rule. Students say, "Life in Lubbock is relaxed. There is plenty of shopping, a good selection of housing, and diversified activities available." Located in the midst of a rich agricultural area, this city of approximately 200,000 has developed into a regional commercial, financial, cultural, educational, and medical center (the school even offers a concentration in health-facility management). The cost of living is reasonable, and the city is hospitable to entrepreneurial enterprise. The area also has a rapidly growing—and surprisingly well-regarded—wine industry.

Texas Tech is home to a huge undergraduate population (approximately 22,000), and according to students, "Texas Tech has a good nightlife. Lots of students go Greek and there are tons of clubs for undergrad and grads alike." MBAs note, "If you're doing your schoolwork right, you stay busy, but there is still time to enjoy yourself." Nearly all students enjoy Texas Tech's "excellent football team" and the tailgating parties preceding home games; the school also has a well-loved women's basketball team. Texas Tech's campus has "an excellent recreation center with lots of other opportunities for physical activities, a theater that shows movies, a sprawling campus with greenery, a great bookstore, and a coffee place in the university center. There is always something happening on campus," according to students.

Admissions

In considering candidates for its MBA program, the admissions department at Texas Tech reviews "work experience, awards, leadership positions held in college and/or industry, likelihood of bringing a unique perspective to the program, civic and volunteer activities, motivation, past success, and letters of recommendation." The school requires students to submit official transcripts of all undergraduate and graduate work and GMAT scores; international students whose first language is not English must also provide TOEFL scores. To increase minority interest in the school, Texas Tech advertises in minority magazines, recruits in minority colleges in New Mexico and Texas, and attends and recruits at minority forums and conferences, such as the National Black Graduate Student Conference.

FINANCIAL FACTS

Annual tuition (in-state/out-of-state)	$4,128/$10,320
Fees	$2,440
Books and supplies	$1,500
Room & board	$6,000
% of students receiving grants	18
Average grant	$1,000
Average student loan debt	$10,777

ADMISSIONS

Admissions Selectivity Rating	71
# of applications received	342
% applicants accepted	87
% acceptees attending	79
Average GMAT	539
Range of GMAT	490-590
Average GPA	3.4
TOEFL Required of International Students?	Yes
Minimum TOEFL (paper/computer)	550/213
Application fee	$50
International application fee	$60
Regular application deadline	Rolling
Regular notification	Rolling
Deferment Available?	Yes
Maximum length of deferment	1 year
Transfer students accepted?	Yes
Transfer application policy: Up to six hours may transfer.	
Non-fall admissions?	Yes

APPLICANTS ALSO LOOK AT

Texas A&M University, The University of Texas at Austin.

Career Rating	62	Grads employed by field	%: avg. salary
Placement rate (%)	61	Accounting	2: $50,750
# of companies recruiting on-campus	300	Finance	25: $43,333
% grads employed immediately	38	Human Resources	2: $49,000
Average starting salary	$44,736	Marketing	12: $42,363
		MIS	12: $43,476
		Operations	6: $47,880
		Consulting	6: $54,700
		General Management	15: $42,933
		Other	20: $44,882

THUNDERBIRD
THE GARVIN SCHOOL OF INTERNATIONAL MANAGEMENT

Academics

"Thunderbird has an international focus and curriculum that others try to emulate," students say, explaining why their school often turns up atop lists of the best international-business programs in the United States. MBAs here love that certain tracks have a "very flexible program that allows students to complete their MBA in one year or two years;" it's a "tripartite curriculum focusing in global business, international studies, and modern languages." However, students warn that "the overall academic rigor is unbelievably challenging. It gets more and more difficult each module (we have two modules per trimester). The program is condensed and very fast-paced, so it is very demanding." Number-crunching is a must; according to "[one] nonquant person, the learning curve through the first two-thirds of the program was vertical. I have worked harder in this program, for a longer period of time, than I have ever worked at anything in my life (including 10 years of business experience and past participation in a Big Ten major sports program); and, despite the painful moments, I've probably enjoyed it more than any prior experience as well." Casework is also critical; one MBA explains, "Thunderbird does a good job of using casework to reinforce the concepts learned in class. It also does a good job promoting team and project work."

Students say that there are "down-to-earth [professors]" who "are all high achievers in their field, erudite (knowledgeable outside of their field), interesting, fun, and from diverse backgrounds." This includes a number of professors who "are truly top-shelf. They are not afraid to challenge you, and many demand (and usually get) more from you than you may think you have." Students also appreciate such technical perks as wireless Internet and "a powerful Intranet community; we communicate by 'My Thunderbird' (MTB). It is a way of life bringing information to our fingertips and maximizing interaction. At Thunderbird, class is always in session." Students also praise the library, Thunderbird International Business Information Center (TBIC) describing it as "second to none."

Career and Placement

Thunderbird's website lists over 200 companies that "have visited the Thunderbird campus to interview students and/or have hired recent graduates in the past year." The school's biggest on-site recruiting activity is the fall Career Fair, which drew at least 56 companies last year. Off-campus events in which Thunderbird participates include the International MBA Conference, the National MBA Consortium, the National Black MBA Association, the National Society of Hispanic MBAs, and Winterim programs in Washington, DC; Wall Street; Cuba; South Africa; Chile; Peru; Argentina; Prague; Singapore; India; and Switzerland. The Career Fair, designed to procure summer work for first-year students, drew 49 companies this year. Students generally agree that "the Career Management Center is very good, but not excellent." One MBA student opines, "The school needs to market itself more to the United States. Thunderbird is recognized around the world and in the United States as the best MBA international-business program around. However, its brand management needs to improve with all companies and with undergraduate schools so that it can recruit the best companies and students to its campus." The school has addressed this by intensifying its marketing efforts in the U.S. and abroad with a new web marketing/lead generation program, a worldwide branding campaign and is currently in the process of upgrading its corporate website to reflect the new "Truly Global" brand and provide increased accessibility for prospective students.

Companies looking at Thunderbird graduates include Abbott Japan, AIG, American Express, Citigroup, Daimler Chrysler, Dell Computer Corporation, Deloitte & Touche Deutsche, Echo Star, GE, Honeywell, IBM, Intel, Johnson & Johnson, LG Electronics,

JUDY JOHNSON, DEAN OF ADMISSIONS
15249 NORTH 59TH AVENUE, GLENDALE, AZ 85306-6000 UNITED STATES
PHONE: 602-978-7100 • FAX: 602-439-5432
E-MAIL: ADMISSIONS@THUNDERBIRD.EDU • WEBSITE: WWW.THUNDERBIRD.EDU

L'Oréal, Lufthansa, Microsoft, Novartis, Post World Net, Samsung Electronics, and UBS Warburg. Average starting salary for 2004 graduates was $66,675. Average signing bonus was $8,651.

Student Life and Environment

Students at Thunderbird agree that there is a "good mix of social life and school life." Sometimes both come rolled up in the same activity; one MBA notes, "There are a million clubs for all ethnicities, for business interests, and for personal/social interests. We attract a lot of ambassadors and former princes or presidents to speak, and the quality of speakers is excellent. The clubs on campus are also very active in putting together topical panels and networking events." Another adds, "We have fantastic cultural nights that allow a group of international students to present their customs and cuisine. There are always great events and good excuses to sample a seemingly endless variety of regional alcoholic delights." MBAs also appreciate the presence of "a very nice pub on campus. It's a great place to network on the weekends. It's like a small family reunion every weekend." These get-togethers are unusually festive because Thunderbird students genuinely appear to like each other a lot; they regard each other as "the school's greatest strength. I can (and do) sit down at lunch every day with students from any number of countries. The cultural mix here is fantastic. I can have conversations every day with people from Finland to Fiji; everyone speaks two, three, even four or more languages. There are also many more 'nonstandard' business types here than you might find at traditional b-schools; that is, people bring perspectives from all walks of personal and professional experience. I know I could pick out almost anyone on campus for a dinner out and have a great conversation about something besides net present value or statistical anomalies," according to one student. Students agree that the benefits of the school's social life extend beyond graduation, as MBAs "all know that the Thunderbird Network is one of the most valuable aspects of this school. Wherever we are in the world after we graduate, either for business or leisure, a Thunderbird graduate is not far away." What more could you ask for in a student body? How about "the best rugby team of all the United States b-schools?" You got it.

Admissions

Thunderbird considers all of the following in evaluating its MBA program applicants: GMAT scores, personal essays, TOEFL scores (if required), letters of reference (preferably from a supervisor or professional peer), college transcripts, and a resume. Applicants must demonstrate at least two years of work experience; international or cross-cultural experience is recommended. Applications are considered on a rolling basis; offers of admission are term-specific and are valid only until all spaces in a particular term's class have been filled. Applications may be submitted online at www.PrincetonReview.com.

FINANCIAL FACTS

Annual tuition	$29,300
Fees	$125
Books and supplies	$1,500
Room & board (on/off-campus)	$6,200/$7,500
% of students receiving aid	55
% of first-year students receiving aid	66
% of students receiving loans	46
% of students receiving grants	25
Average award package	$24,335
Average grant	$21,942
Average student loan debt	$27,475

ADMISSIONS

Admissions Selectivity Rating	76
# of applications received	724
% applicants accepted	81
% acceptees attending	47
Average GMAT	600
Range of GMAT	570-640
Average GPA	3.3
TOEFL Required of International Students?	Yes
Minimum TOEFL (paper/computer)	600/250
Application fee	$125
International application fee	$125
Regular application deadline	8/15
Regular notification	Rolling
Deferment Available?	Yes
Maximum length of deferment	1 trimester
Non-fall admissions?	Yes
Need-blind admissions?	Yes

APPLICANTS ALSO LOOK AT

Babson College, Southern Methodist University, University of Notre Dame, University of South Carolina, University of Southern California.

EMPLOYMENT PROFILE

Career Rating	79	Grads employed by field	%: avg. salary
% grads employed immediately	18	Finance	23: $65,000
Average starting salary	$65,500	Human Resources	1: $61,000
		Marketing	42: $65,000
		Operations	7: $64,000
		Consulting	10: $64,000
		General Management	11: $72,000
		Other	6: $66,000

TULANE UNIVERSITY
FREEMAN SCHOOL OF BUSINESS

Academics

"Class size is one of the strong points at the Freeman School of Business, [the MBA program at Tulane University, where] MBA classes are limited to around 100, which places a personal touch on classroom lectures." All small schools must perform a balancing act; of course, it is difficult to cover all areas unless your customer base is large enough to support them all, but Tulane manages well. "Course offerings are numerous for a small student body. The academic experience can be tailored many different ways," students tell us. Of course, all business schools have standout departments; at Freeman, it's finance. One MBA tells us, "Tulane is very heavy on the finance area, with the majority of my classmates undertaking at least a supporting concentration in finance." While other areas receive sufficient coverage, we're told, they do not receive the five-star handling that Tulane lavishes on its finance department.

Freeman's size is designed to maximize contact between students and professors, and in that area the school also succeeds. MBAs tell us that the "knowledgeable, outgoing, and sometimes brilliantly innovative [professors] are always approachable either face-to-face or via e-mail." Students especially appreciate that "some top-notch professors teach core courses. The recent additions to the faculty are first-rate, reflecting the school's commitment to improving quality." Students can "get very involved, with professors acting as their teachers' assistants or research assistants due to small class size." That is, if they can find the time. Freeman's intensive seven-week academic terms mean that heavy course work starts on day one and doesn't let up until exam day. "I haven't been able to spend as much time on Bourbon Street as I had planned," is how one student put it.

How long Tulane intends to maintain its little-school charm is open to question. Enrollment has grown 57 percent in the past six years in anticipation of the school's new home, Goldring/Woldenberg Hall II; the new business-school facility opened in November of 2003. Students feel that "with the new building opening and bigger MBA class enrollment, it will be very possible in the next couple of years for the administration to improve practices and invite more leading professors." One thing that probably will not change is Freeman's overriding philosophy, which "is very concerned with providing the skills that will be directly applicable to your career. I think they've got the recipe for professional success right," notes one student.

Career and Placement

Career prep begins as soon as students arrive at the Freeman School; orientation includes training in the use of e-recruiting, Tulane's online student information-management system. Subsequent training in interviewing, resume building, internship hunting, and salary negotiation follows and is offered throughout the program. Tulane also maintains a database (called the Career Consultants Network) of Freeman alumni willing to counsel current students. Job fairs and other recruiting events pepper Freeman's academic calendar.

The school's best efforts notwithstanding, students are less than 100 percent satisfied with their career office. One MBA complains, "We only had less than 10 *Fortune* 500 companies visiting last year. You do the math." Most students concede that "perhaps the biggest disadvantage with the school is the limited employment opportunities around New Orleans; [the] tough economy" hasn't helped either. Things are looking up, however, as "the Career Development Center just hired a new director from one of the leading business schools who is making a lot of great changes."

BILL D. SANDEFER, DIRECTOR OF GRADUATE ADMISSIONS AND FINANCIAL AID
7 MCALISTER DRIVE, SUITE 401, NEW ORLEANS, LA 70118 UNITED STATES
PHONE: 504-865-5410 • FAX: 504-865-6770
E-MAIL: FREEMAN.ADMISSIONS@TULANE.EDU • WEBSITE: WWW.FREEMAN.TULANE.EDU

Companies most likely to hire Freeman MBAs include Bank of America, Citibank, Credit Suisse First Boston, D&T Management Solutions, Dynegy, El Paso Energy, Entergy, FedEx, First Union Securities, Jackson & Rhodes, JP Morgan Chase, Mirant, PA Consulting, Reliant Energy, Towers Perrin, and TXU. One-fifth of Freeman graduates find their first jobs outside the U.S.; about 60 percent wind up working somewhere in the South.

Student Life and Environment

With the November 2003 completion of the Goldring/Woldenberg Hall II, the A.B. Freeman Business school has "finished its expansion and now it can host more students and faculties." The facility earns top marks from all students, who tell us that the "attractive and technologically advanced [business-school home is] amazing. It boasts the latest and greatest technology, including a trading floor, digital media theater, 60-inch plasma TVs, all the latest technology, [and] a number of breakout rooms for students to use for group work."

The new facility also has plenty of room to host speakers, club meetings, and social functions. "We have several school-sponsored events that are usually well-organized, though in New Orleans style," MBAs report. They add, "Social functions are extremely fun and occur quite often. We usually have a great turnout for each and every one, which makes for great friendships and networking opportunities within the MBA program." Students enjoy a "very broad choice of clubs to join depending on interests." One student approvingly notes, "Student organizations also invite speakers, do community consulting and other helpful jobs for the communities in New Orleans."

New Orleans, as you probably already know, "is a great place to live; [its legendary party scenes makes it] ideal for honing or exploiting social skills." One MBA explains, "Life in New Orleans is pretty terrific for all ages. There is always something fun to do for everyone; the weather is great almost year-round; the city is beautiful; and the people are friendly." Tulane's student body has a global flavor, as "more than 40 percent of the students are international." Those seeking employment in the East, take note: "Tulane also has over 1,000 alumni in Asia."

Admissions

Freeman reviews applications to its graduate programs in three separate rounds; the school encourages students to apply as early as possible to maximize their chances of gaining admission. All of the following are required components of the application: undergraduate transcript, GMAT scores, TOEFL scores, letters of recommendation, work resume, personal statement, and interview. Minority recruitment efforts include Destination MBA, the National Black MBA Association Career Fair, targeted GMASS searches, and minority fellowships.

FINANCIAL FACTS

Annual tuition	$30,450
Fees	$1,590
Books and supplies	$1,600
Room & board	$9,090
% of students receiving aid	68
% of first-year students receiving aid	71
% of students receiving loans	42
% of students receiving grants	52
Average award package	$39,055
Average grant	$8,172
Average student loan debt	$82,730

ADMISSIONS

Admissions Selectivity Rating	87
# of applications received	338
% applicants accepted	60
% acceptees attending	41
Average GMAT	655
Range of GMAT	570-680
Average GPA	3.35
TOEFL Required of International Students?	Yes
Minimum TOEFL (paper/computer)	600/250
Application fee	$40
International application fee	$50
Regular application deadline	5/1
Regular notification	6/1
Application Deadline/Notification	
Round 1:	11/15 / 12/15
Round 2:	1/15 / 2/15
Round 3:	3/15 / 4/15
Round 4:	5/1 / 6/1
Need-blind admissions?	Yes

APPLICANTS ALSO LOOK AT

Emory University, Rice University, Southern Methodist University, The University of Texas at Austin, University of North Carolina at Chapel Hill, Vanderbilt University, Washington University in St. Louis.

EMPLOYMENT PROFILE

Career Rating	81	Grads employed by field	%: avg. salary
Placement rate (%)	88	Finance	64: $76,273
# of companies recruiting on-campus	46	Marketing	15: $67,417
% grads employed immediately	63	Consulting	8: $71,000
Average starting salary	$72,961	General Management	13: $66,333

THE UNIVERSITY OF AKRON
COLLEGE OF BUSINESS ADMINISTRATION

GENERAL INFORMATION
Type of school   public
Environment   city

SURVEY SAYS...
Friendly students
Happy students
Smart classrooms
Solid preparation in:
Communication/interpersonal skills
Presentation skills
Computer skills
Doing business in a global economy

STUDENTS
Enrollment of parent
  institution   24,129
Enrollment of MBA program   252
% male/female   45/55
% out-of-state   2
% part-time   56
% minorities   6
% international   38
Average age at entry   30
Average years work experience
  at entry   4

ACADEMICS
Academic Experience Rating   66
Student/faculty ratio   21:1
Profs interesting rating   73
Profs accessible rating   77
% female faculty   19
% minority faculty   17
Joint Degrees
MBA/JD
MBA in Tax/JD
MSM-HR/JD
Prominent Alumni
Ernest Pouttu, VP of Finance & CFO,
Harwick Standard Distribution;
James McCready, Chairman of
Cypress Companies; John Piecuch,
Retired Pres. & CEO of LaFarge
Coppee; Joanne Rohrer,
Secretary/Treasurer, Rohrer
Corporation.

Academics

Full-time students in the University of Akron's MBA program have a number of options available to them. They can choose to pursue the conventional two-year program, or—if they have the requisite undergraduate course work to place out of all foundation courses—they can complete the degree more quickly via the accelerated 12-month program. The College of Business Administration (CBA) also offers a part-time MBA, an International Executive MBA, a masters of science (MS) in accountancy, an MS in management, and a master of taxation degree.

Akron's MBA program is large enough to offer a wide range of concentrations. Students here may specialize in accounting, e-business, finance, global sales management, health-care management, international business, international finance, management, management of technology and innovation, marketing, and supply-chain management. Students appreciate the way the curriculum "emphasizes real cases to study" and "always tries to bring the latest technology to students." Most agree that "the greatest strength of the College of Business at the University of Akron is the professors. They take the initiative to make sure the students are exposed to the topics by giving real-world problems to the students." One part-time student notes, "I have found with my own background in operation, the examples used in class are very similar to what really happens on the job." Students also report that "the professors are friendly and approachable and are very willing to help by any means they can."

Specialized education is enhanced by the many institutes and research centers at the university; these include the Fisher Institute for Professional Selling (a sales-simulation and skills-practice facility), the Institute for Global Business (which provides "plenty of opportunities to study abroad"), the Center for Information Technology and e-Business, the Center for Organizational Development, and the Fitzgerald Institute for Entrepreneurial Studies. *Entrepreneur* magazine recognized the last of these in 2003 when it ranked the University of Akron among the top-25 schools offering a program in entrepreneurial studies. Students are proud that "the school is very focused on the latest trends in business; it is one of the few business schools with an e-business concentration for the MBA program. Also, the facilities are very modern have the latest technology."

Career and Placement

The University of Akron's Center for Career Management provides career services for all undergraduates, graduate students, and alumni; the school does not maintain a separate career office for graduate students or business students. The office provides assistance in career planning, procuring a summer internship, developing job-search, interviewing, and resume-writing skills, and locating potential employers. Opinions about the office are widely mixed; some praise its work, while others feel that services for graduate students are minimal.

A paucity of on-campus recruiters led one student to state that "the career fairs are a waste of time. It is the same employers year after year. I stopped going because of this." Some of the employers who frequently hire Akron MBAs include Sogistics Corporation, Rhein Chemie Corporation, Lockheed Martin, Computer Sciences Corporation, and the Greater Cleveland Regional Transit Authority.

MYRA WEAKLAND, ASSISTANT DIRECTOR
THE UNIVERSITY OF AKRON, 259 SOUTH BROADWAY, ROOM 412, AKRON, OH 44325-4805 U.S.
PHONE: 330-972-7043 • FAX: 330-972-6588
E-MAIL: GRADCBA@UAKRON.EDU • WEBSITE: WWW.UAKRON.EDU/CBA/GRAD

Student Life and Environment

CBA students are a varied group, with "friendly and intelligent international students" and a mix of people who "either have full-time jobs or have recently graduated from undergrad. There is a good diversity of age, experience, gender, and race here." One student happily notes, "I have met lots of really nice people and have study groups for almost all of my classes, which in my opinion is essential to being successful in grad school." Students convene in clubs—"there is one for every concentration"—and "parties hosted by students outside of school." Most agree, however, that this is not an especially social program; students generally spend their free time away from the program, not with classmates.

The University of Akron is a large school, with more than 24,000 undergraduates and graduate students. It is widely heralded for its science and engineering programs; these programs are outgrowths of the city of Akron's historical role as "the Rubber Capital of the World," which has spurred polymer research and development for well over a century. Students appreciate that "the business school is very accessible off the interstate. Most business classes are in one of two buildings that are connected by a parking deck."

Akron itself "is very small and there is not much to do except go to the movies or go see a play sometimes," students tell us. The historic downtown region is currently undergoing a revitalization program; it's too early into the process to judge the results. Cleveland is only an hour to the north, and it offers many of the cosmopolitan amenities currently absent from Akron.

Admissions

The admissions committee at the University of Akron considers all of the following components of a business graduate student's application: undergraduate GPA, GMAT scores, TOEFL scores (international applicants), two letters of recommendation, a letter of purpose, resume, previous graduate and post-baccalaureate performance, and professional-association and student-organization memberships. The Graduate School of the University of Akron sponsors a diversity program to enhance minority recruitment within the MBA program.

FINANCIAL FACTS

Annual tuition (in-state/out-of-state)	$12,932/$20,784
Fees	$780
Books and supplies	$1,200
Room & board	$10,000
% of students receiving aid	20
% of first-year students receiving aid	12
% of students receiving grants	4
Average award package	$16,978
Average scholarship	$2,500

ADMISSIONS

Admissions Selectivity Rating	71
# of applications received	114
% applicants accepted	83
% acceptees attending	56
Average GMAT	554
Range of GMAT	510-600
Average GPA	3.3
TOEFL Required of International Students?	Yes
Minimum TOEFL (paper/computer)	550/213
Application fee	$30
International application fee	$40
Regular application deadline	8/1
Regular notification	8/15
Deferment Available?	Yes
Maximum length of deferment	2 years
Transfer students accepted?	Yes
Transfer application policy: Up to 24 credits of foundation courses may be waived. Nine credits of the core may transfer from AACSB accredited schools if approved by the director.	
Non-fall admissions?	Yes
Need-blind admissions?	Yes

APPLICANTS ALSO LOOK AT

Case Western Reserve University, Cleveland State University, John Carroll University, Kent State University, The Ohio State University, University of Cincinnati, Youngstown State University.

EMPLOYMENT PROFILE

		Grads employed by field	%: avg. salary
Career Rating	66		
Placement rate (%)	58	Finance	21: $68,500
% grads employed immediately	58	Marketing	21: $47,333
Average starting salary	$57,536	Operations	21: $58,333
		Strategic Planning	21: $65,000
		Non-profit	14: $44,000

UNIVERSITY OF ALABAMA—BIRMINGHAM
SCHOOL OF BUSINESS

GENERAL INFORMATION
Type of school	public
Environment	metropolis
Academic calendar	semester

SURVEY SAYS...
Friendly students
Happy students
Smart classrooms
Solid preparation in:
Teamwork

STUDENTS
Enrollment of parent institution	16,000
Enrollment of MBA program	334
% male/female	62/38
% out-of-state	17
% part-time	95
% minorities	11
% international	10
Average age at entry	27
Average years work experience at entry	5

ACADEMICS
Academic Experience Rating	76
Student/faculty ratio	15:1
Profs interesting rating	80
Profs accessible rating	76

Joint Degrees
MBA/MPH: 2-3 years
MBA/MS: 2-3 years

Academics

The School of Business MBA program at the University of Alabama—Birmingham is a part-time, evening program designed for students who are working full-time. Cost and convenience are the main reasons they choose this affordable program. Once MBAs arrive at UAB, they discover one of the university's lesser-known assets: a faculty of "inspiring, truly top-notch lecturers and researchers." Students say, "[The faculty] are always willing to offer real-world advice and assist us in reaching our goals once we are finished with the program." One student adds, "The faculty are very knowledgeable, and they all have great life experiences to use as valuable teaching tools. I have learned more about the real world through their experiences than I would have any other way. I feel that I am well prepared for life in the business world."

UAB has other assets as well. The administration here "has been working hard to increase the value of the program through class changes and student contact. The overall experience has been smooth and extremely educational." Students also love the classroom experience, which is "very informative and open to discussion." Students say, "Most of the faculty know us on a first-name basis. The classes are not excessively large, and the overall environment is conducive toward the learning process." Courses are offered at convenient times; students explain that "the class scheduling works well around the working students, which [includes] the majority of graduate students at UAB."

As at most state schools, UAB has problems stemming from a lack of funding. Some students grumble about "limited class offerings in the summer" and would like to see "more class offerings and concentrations during the year." In addition, while all classrooms have computer based multi-media systems and Internet access, at present the MBA program offers "no online or video conferencing classes." But, despite these drawbacks, most students are extremely happy with the MBA at UAB. When students take the entire package into view, they conclude that "the MBA program here at UAB is outstanding, and it could benefit all students even more if the business school were given more funds to work with."

Career and Placement

UAB maintains a branch office of its Career Services in the business wing of the Business-Engineering Complex to serve business undergraduates, graduates, and alumni. While a considerable 44 percent of current MBA students plan to stay with their current employer after graduation, the center works with the remaining students looking for assistance with job searches. The staff there "offers career counseling, coaching, and consultation, provide up-to-date information about the job market, career options, salary, and graduate school." Several students, however, feel that the school needs to create "more networking opportunities with large and prominent employers in Birmingham and surrounding areas."

Many students love Birmingham and feel that the city location "benefits the school because of the large business community it surrounds. It also allows the school to recruit professors with exceptional work experience." The manufacturing and service sectors supply most of the jobs; the city has steadily moved away from its past reliance on iron and steel.

Top employers in Birmingham include the university; the state and city governments; Alabama Power; AmSouth Bank; Baptist Health System; BellSouth; Blue Cross-Blue Shield; Bruno's, Inc.; and Wal-Mart.

GLENN KINSTLER, MBA PROGRAM COORDINATOR
1530 3RD AVENUE SOUTH, BEC 219, BIRMINGHAM, AL 35294-4460 UNITED STATES
PHONE: 205-934-8815 • FAX: 205-934-9200
E-MAIL: GKINSTLER@BUSINESS.UAB.EDU • WEBSITE: WWW.BUSINESS.UAB.EDU

Student Life and Environment

Some students say that because "UAB is a commuter college," the school has "no campus identity; therefore, no real affiliation or bond is ever solidified between students and the school." Other MBAs with busy schedules ask, "Who has time to be involved in student life? It is extremely tough to balance full-time work while being a full-time student." Even so, some would like to feel more like part of a community and would welcome more "opportunities for students to become involved."

With a metropolitan-area population of nearly one million, Birmingham is the biggest city in Alabama and one of the bigger cities in the South. Sports fans will appreciate that the area is home to competitive college football teams, arena football, an AA baseball team, and tons of excellent golf courses. Outdoor lovers will enjoy the easy access to fishing, hunting, boating, and hiking areas.

Admissions

Admission to UAB's MBA program is based on evaluation of official transcripts, GMAT scores, and TOEFL scores (and work experience). A minimum score of 480 on the GMAT is required, as is a minimum score of 1050 when the formula (200 × undergraduate GPA) + GMAT score) is applied. A minimum TOEFL score of 550 (paper-based; 213 computer based) is also required of international students. UAB has a calculus prerequisite that students can waive by passing a proficiency exam or short review offered by the school.

FINANCIAL FACTS
Annual tuition (in-state/out-of-state)
$162/$405 (per credit hour)

ADMISSIONS
Admissions Selectivity Rating	77
# of applications received	275
% applicants accepted	68
% acceptees attending	78
Average GMAT	553
Range of GMAT	510-600
Average GPA	3.2
TOEFL Required of International Students?	Yes
Minimum TOEFL (paper/computer)	550/213
Application fee	$50
International application fee	$75
Regular application deadline	7/1
Regular notification	8/1
Application Deadline	
Round 1:	7/1
Round 2:	11/1
Round 3:	4/1
Deferment Available?	Yes
Maximum length of deferment	1 year
Transfer students accepted?	Yes
Transfer application policy: Must meet UAB MBA admission requirements, transfer courses must be from AACSB accredited program and equivalent to our required courses.	
Non-fall admissions?	Yes
Need-blind admissions?	Yes

APPLICANTS ALSO LOOK AT
Samford University.

EMPLOYMENT PROFILE	
Career Rating	77
Placement rate (%)	92
# of companies recruiting on-campus	231
% grads employed immediately	75
Average starting salary	$59,400

UNIVERSITY OF ALABAMA—TUSCALOOSA
MANDERSON GRADUATE SCHOOL OF BUSINESS

GENERAL INFORMATION
Type of school	public
Environment	city
Academic calendar	semester

SURVEY SAYS...
Friendly students
Happy students
Smart classrooms
Solid preparation in:
Teamwork
Communication/interpersonal skills

STUDENTS
Enrollment of parent institution	22,000
Enrollment of MBA program	105
% male/female	72/28
% out-of-state	37
% minorities	14
% international	10
Average age at entry	25
Average years work experience at entry	2.1

ACADEMICS
Academic Experience Rating	**96**
Student/faculty ratio	12:1
Profs interesting rating	96
Profs accessible rating	99
% female faculty	13
% minority faculty	10

Joint Degrees
MBA/JD: 4 years
MBA/MA in Modern Languages: 3 years
MBA/MSN in Nursing: 3 years
MBA/MS Engineering

Prominent Alumni
Thomas Cross, Managing partner, PricewaterhouseCoopers; Samuel D. DiPiazza, Vice Chairman, PricewaterhouseCoopers; Marvin Mann, Founding CEO, Lexmark.

Academics

With fewer than 55 full-time students per class, University of Alabama's Manderson Graduate School of Business truly offers its MBAs "the ability to develop personal relationships with all of [the] professors." It does so at a "very affordable" tuition rate, thanks to both the state sponsorship and to the assistantships that most students receive; many students at U of A feel that the university offers one of the best returns on investment available anywhere.

Students love U of A's "cutting-edge technology, which is a huge strength of [the] program. There are multimedia podiums in every classroom, and students have access to numerous computer labs. The business school has invested in wireless routers to allow students to access the Internet from laptops and PDAs. The classrooms and library have all the relevant technology," according to students. They also appreciate the "great atmosphere and the sense of tradition and pride at the University of Alabama." One MBA reports, "The campus is beautiful, and the architecture is superb. There are a few buildings that date back to before the Civil War. The grounds and facilities are well-maintained."

Manderson brags about the flexibility of its program, which allows students to create their own "niche of interest." MBAs concur and explain that "the flexibility of the program allows students to take on more than just a general degree but allows study abroad and dual concentrations." This flexibility arrives in the second year of the program, as the first year is given over to "a prescribed program of courses and cross-discipline work that blends an introduction to the analytical tools of management and the functional areas of business into a general management perspective." Throughout the curriculum, "teamwork is a focus of the program and students get a lot of practice in it," and "lectures, case studies, and current-event publications create an interactive learning experience." Students also add that "the class atmosphere encourages participation, and the instructors do an excellent job of letting class discussion lead the direction of the course, while still providing all the necessary tools to be a contributor in the business world."

Students explain that the professors at Manderson "are all recognized leaders in their perspective fields, and they are very compassionate. Our professors truly care about us and work with us." Students are particularly enthusiastic about the MIS faculty. Other students add that "more widespread project-management hands-on training would help the school."

Career and Placement

Career services are provided to Manderson MBAs through the university's Career Center and the College of Commerce and Business Administration Satellite Center. The office provides counseling services, workshops, online job databases, and biannual job fairs, which students say "assist [them] in the job hunt. Excellent companies are brought in for recruitment specifically from the MBA program." However, many feel that "the school could improve its recruitment of companies outside of the Southeast to come to campus for recruiting."

Top recruiters at the University of Alabama include Accenture, AmSouth Bank, Cap Gemini, Ernst & Young, Compass Bank, Eli Lilly, FedEx, Lithonia Lighting, Procter & Gamble, Southern Company, and Tait Advisory Services.

Student Life and Environment

Despite the school's laid-back southern setting, "life at the University of Alabama is fast-paced." Students describe a typical day: "Generally, each MBA class meets twice a week for an hour and 15 minutes. Each class has a heavy amount of team-based cases. Our entire class is divided into four- or five-member teams, which typically meet twice a week for an hour to discuss projects and divide responsibilities. In addition to the academic course load, the majority of our students are employed through student assistantships on campus or extended internships in the Tuscaloosa business community. Students' work schedules vary; however, the hour requirements range from 10 to 20 hours per week."

On top of their school and work responsibilities, "the majority of MBA students are active in the recruitment process. First-year students serve as MBA Hosts by giving tours to prospective students and corporate recruiters. Second-year students volunteer as Interview Fellows and actually interview all prospective students." These commitments leave some MBAs too busy to enjoy all the Tuscaloosa area has to offer. One student writes, "I wish I had more time for fishing in one of the area's many beautiful lakes, rivers, or nearby Gulf coast. There is some world-class golf nearby as well. Instead, I pretty much wake up, go to class, work as a grad assistant, study, and go to sleep."

Most students, however, manage to find time for social life. One student explains, "Everyone is voluntarily involved in the MBA Association. This provides many social activities and philanthropic opportunities for students. We also have events that bring us together as a class and help with networking opportunities, including hosting a golf tournament each year. My classmates also often hold impromptu parties to watch the latest sporting event or have a 'themed' dinner party, from Thai to a traditional Christmas dinner." Active organizations include: "Toastmaster's International, Women in Business, Finance Association, and the Dinner Club. Leadership positions are available for both first- and second-year students." Students also report that "weekends are filled with relaxation, social time, and great bands. During football season, two words: 'Roll Tide!'"

Admissions

Applicants to Manderson must provide the admissions department with official copies of all undergraduate and graduate transcripts, GMAT scores, TOEFL scores (for applicants whose native language is not English), professional recommendations, and a resume. An interview is typically required of candidates. According to the school's catalog, "applicants must show evidence of career interest in management, and relevant employment experience is considered in the admissions decision." An understanding of introductory calculus and facility with basic computer functions (word processing, spreadsheets, databases) is expected.

FINANCIAL FACTS

Annual tuition (in-state/out-of-state)	$4,630/$12,664
Fees	$1,600
Books and supplies	$800
Room & board	$8,800
% of students receiving aid	70
% of first-year students receiving aid	100
% of students receiving loans	25
% of students receiving grants	65
Average award package	$14,522
Average grant	$7,956
Average student loan debt	$13,424

ADMISSIONS

Admissions Selectivity Rating	95
# of applications received	248
% applicants accepted	32
% acceptees attending	62
Average GMAT	641
Range of GMAT	600-690
Average GPA	3.4
TOEFL Required of International Students?	Yes
Minimum TOEFL (paper/computer)	550/213
Application fee	$25
International application fee	$25
Regular application deadline	4/15
Regular notification	Rolling
Application Deadline/Notification	
Round 1:	1/5 / 1/20
Round 2:	2/15 / 3/1
Round 3:	4/15 / 5/1
Round 4:	7/1 / 7/15
Early decision program?	Yes
ED Deadline/Notification	Rolling
Deferment Available?	Yes
Maximum length of deferment	1 year
Transfer students accepted?	Yes
Transfer application policy: Up to 12 credit hours accepted for transfer from AACSB accredited programs subject to committee approval.	
Need-blind admissions?	Yes

APPLICANTS ALSO LOOK AT

Auburn University, University of Florida, University of Georgia, University of Mississippi, University of South Carolina, University of Tennessee, Wake Forest University.

EMPLOYMENT PROFILE

Career Rating	84	Grads employed by field	%: avg. salary
Placement rate (%)	91	Finance	17: $51,500
# of companies recruiting on-campus	125	Marketing	17: $51,000
% grads employed immediately	59	MIS	21: $53,625
Average starting salary	$58,404	Operations	8: $67,500
		Consulting	12: $51,667
		General Management	8: $71,000
		Other	17: $73,500

UNIVERSITY OF ALBERTA
SCHOOL OF BUSINESS

GENERAL INFORMATION
Type of school   public
Environment   city

SURVEY SAYS...
Students love Edmonton, AB
Friendly students
Happy students
Smart classrooms

STUDENTS
Enrollment of parent
 institution   34,367
Enrollment of MBA program   302
% male/female   64/36
% part-time   53
% international   18
Average age at entry   30
Average years work experience
 at entry   7

ACADEMICS
Academic Experience Rating   90
Student/faculty ratio   4:1
Profs interesting rating   89
Profs accessible rating   89
% female faculty   18
Joint Degrees
MBA/LLB:4 years
MBA/MEng: 2 years
MBA/MAg: 2 years
MBA/MF: 2 years
Prominent Alumni
Guy Kerr, Pres. & CEO; Gay
Mitchell, Executive Vice-Pres.-
Ontario; Guy Turcotte, Chairman &
CEO; Eric Morgan, Pres.; Michael
Lang, Chairman.

Academics

Why trek up to the northland of Edmonton for an MBA, you may ask yourself? Well, you may be the type who wants a program with "a great reputation and excellent research in a broad array of fields." Or you may be the cost-conscious type who values "a reasonably affordable education that returns excellent education value per dollar." Maybe you want to pursue an unusual specialization, such as natural resources and energy, technology commercialization, or leisure and sport management. All are good reasons to choose the Alberta School of Business, but the best of all might well be the quality of the faculty. As students here justifiably brag, "The professors at the U of A School of Business have won more 3M Teaching Fellowships (which recognize excellence in teaching and educational leadership) than any other school in Canada, and it shows in the lectures. The lectures are as real-world as possible."

Only a chosen few can enjoy this embarrassment of riches, unfortunately, as "only 50 full-time MBAs are accepted each fall." Students love how "this keeps classes small. You take almost all of your courses together and this becomes a very tight-knit group. The small class size means that professors know your name and recognize you in the hallways." They also love the curriculum; another student says that "[the courses] provide core business fundamentals without the hype of other schools. Also, U of A has just the right mix of lecture and case learning. In recent years, schools have shifted to mainly case learning, which in my opinion does a poor job in communicating fundamentals. [U of A's] method of learning is the right one for me."

Those interested in research are well-served by 12 separate research centers in diverse areas such as social entrepreneurship, cultural industries, and professional service firm management. Those with an eye toward international markets will happily observe that "the program is very sensitive to ethnic and cultural differences, and it shows in the lectures. All professors are very aware of cultural differences and will take the time to explain examples, which may be lost on international students because of cultural differences." And those just looking for a solid MBA will be pleased to hear that "overall, academically, the program is challenging, but with good reason. The students here want to be as prepared as possible for their chosen career paths, and the faculty here assists with that by presenting us with a very high level of learning paired with incredible extracurricular activities. It's a program and culture well worth engaging in," according to students.

Career and Placement

U of A's MBA Career Management Services does a solid job of serving students and alumni of the School of Business. Students explain that "one of the greatest strengths of the university is the connection to the local job market and the MBA program's adaptation using the specialization programs to better serve that market." MBAs also note that "there is less representation from other job markets than maybe there could be."

Employers most likely to hire Alberta MBAs include Alberta Energy; Alberta Environment; Alberta Sustainable Resources; ATB Financial; Lilydale Foods; Maple Leaf Foods; PepsiCo; Petro-Geotech RBC Financial; Sask Power; SCIMED; Stantec, Inc.; Vogel Publishing; and the University of Alberta.

Student Life and Environment

"The culture is unique at the U of A; it is incredibly social, friendly, and collaborative." Students say, "There are always several different activities going on consecutively or at once, ranging from TGIFs to international potluck dinners, to guest-speaker lectures and

JOAN WHITE, EXECUTIVE DIRECTOR, MBA PROGRAMS
2-30 BUSINESS BUILDING, EDMONTON, AB T6G 2R6 CANADA
PHONE: 780-492-3946 • FAX: 780-492-7825
E-MAIL: MBA.PROGRAMS@UALBERTA.CA • WEBSITE: MBA.BUS.UALBERTA.CA

Annual tuition (in-state/out-of-state)	$8,300/$16,600
Fees	$590
Books and supplies	$1,000
Room & board (on/off-campus)	$3,800/$6,000
% of students receiving aid	35
% of first-year students receiving aid	45
% of students receiving grants	25
Average grant	$3,100

ADMISSIONS

Admissions Selectivity Rating	89
# of applications received	343
% applicants accepted	37
% acceptees attending	45
Average GMAT	600
Range of GMAT	550-640
Average GPA	3.3
TOEFL Required of International Students?	Yes
Minimum TOEFL (paper/computer)	600/250
Application fee	$75
International application fee	$75
Regular application deadline	4/30
Regular notification	Rolling
Deferment Available?	Yes
Maximum length of deferment	1 year
Need-blind admissions?	Yes

recruiting events. Everyone is invited and welcome to participate, and almost everybody does." The result of all this activity is "a tight-knit group that studies and plays hard together." As one student notes, "We placed third at the annual MBA games this year, which was pretty good. However, the real bonus for me was all the relationships and teamwork that was developed to make it there."

Because admission is so competitive, the student body is an exceptional lot. "A high percentage of international students from both Europe and Asia are both competent in the English language and willing to integrate and socialize with the other students." This enhances classroom and social interaction, while the "true team spirit" of the student body contributes to the "very cooperative, rather than overly competitive atmosphere. If someone has an undergrad in, say, economics, that person will lead study groups to bring those without an economic background up to speed before exams. Quants are happy to help out nonquants on their stats, [and] nonquants [assist in] proofreading quant papers," according to students.

Alberta MBAs enjoy "state-of-the-art facilities in classrooms, which have considerably enhanced the learning environment." One student comments, "We have access to our own computer lab, and many locations on campus have wireless connections (including our MBA classrooms). Our professors have excellent websites where we can access lecture notes in advance." Students concede that their Edmonton address "allows some of the great aspects of the school to come through, but also causes some difficulties. Given the living costs of the location, students can get a much higher standard of living for a lower cost than larger cities. However, this can be a negative for placement opportunities." Other assets of the locale include a campus boasting "many beautiful historic and modern buildings. It's situated adjacent to the beautiful River Valley and several large parks. U of A is certainly a beautiful campus."

Admissions

Applicants to the Alberta MBA program must provide the school with all academic transcripts; GMAT scores; TOEFL, IELTS, or MELAB scores (non-native English speakers); three letters of reference; a personal statement of educational and professional goals; and a resume. Applicants should have a GPA of at least 3.0, a GMAT score of at least 550, and at least two years of post-baccalaureate employment experience in the business world. At the U of A website, the school notes that "admission into the MBA program is competitive and only a small number of applicants are admitted. We receive more applications from qualified individuals than we can admit."

Career Rating	82	Grads employed by field:	
Placement rate (%)	93	Finance	5
# of companies recruiting on-campus	25	Operations	5
% grads employed immediately	85	Strategic Planning	7
Average starting salary	$55,000	Consulting	5
		Communications	7
		General Management	33
		Other	35
		Non-profit	3

UNIVERSITY OF ARIZONA
ELLER COLLEGE OF MANAGEMENT

GENERAL INFORMATION
Type of school   public
Academic calendar   semester

SURVEY SAYS...
Students love Tucson, AZ
Friendly students
Smart classrooms
Solid preparation in:
Entrepreneurial studies

STUDENTS
Enrollment of parent
  institution   35,000
Enrollment of MBA program   240
% male/female   68/32
% out-of-state   78
% part-time   46
% minorities   9
% international   40
Average age at entry   26.5
Average years work experience
  at entry   3.5

ACADEMICS
Academic Experience Rating   64
Student/faculty ratio   38:1
Profs interesting rating   61
Profs accessible rating   61
% female faculty   21
% minority faculty   15
Joint Degrees
MBA/JD: 4 years
MBA/MIM: 2-4 years
MIS/MBA: 3 years
MBA/PharmD: 5 years
MBA/MMF: 2-3 years
MBA/MS in engineering and optical
science: 2 years
Prominent Alumni
Mark Hoffman, CEO, Commerce
One; Thomas Kalinske,, Pres.,
Knowledge Universe; Chairman,
LeapFrog; Jim Whims, Managing
Partner, Tech Fund; Stephen Forte,
Sr. VP, Flight Operations, United
Airlines; Cephas Bowles, General
Manager, WBGO-FM Jazz Radio.

Academics

"The Eller MBA is highly quantitative, reasonably priced, and close-knit," one student writes about the University of Arizona's MBA program, neatly summarizing many of it's greatest strengths. Eller students especially appreciate the intimate size of the program. One student explains, "Because of its small size, it's more responsive when changes are effected, and the administration has the ability to work with a student to create a custom solution for the student." Another student notes, "The program has a lot of potential, and administrators spend time with students to empower them to improve the program."

Eller's heavy focus on quantitative skills feeds its strongest disciplines, MIS and finance. It also means a deluge of challenging work in the first semester of the program, especially for students with little quant or business experience. "Students with little or no business background struggle mightily with the course load," one student writes.

According to the school, Eller's core courses for the year-one schedule "build the analytic skills in economics, statistics, accounting, finance, and communication that form the basis of managerial decision-making. [These courses also] develop the viewpoint of the general manager, introducing MBAs to the functional areas of the firm and the tools for integrating technological and human resources to achieve organizational goals." Year two consists primarily of electives, though students may choose to develop a concentration or "construct a plan of study suited to [their] unique career goals." The curriculum culminates in a required capstone course called dynamics of strategy.

Along with MIS and finance, entrepreneurship is one of Eller's major focal points. Its McGuire Entrepreneurship Program was named a NASDAQ Center for Entrepreneurial Excellence in 2002. The program's success has resulted in the integration of entrepreneurship into the core and has created opportunities for students to participate in business-plan competitions across the country. The program also helps students find internships with area startup companies during the summer between the first and second year.

Career and Placement

The Eller Office of Career Development provides career services including self-assessment tools, job-skills seminars, online research resources, executive mentoring, counseling, career fairs, and on-campus interviews. Students explain that the office labors under the handicap of "our small program. The size causes many recruiters to stay away from our school." Students also complain that "international students are not hired by 80 percent of the companies coming to campus for recruiting. The school should cut down on international admissions if it's not going to offer them any career assistance."

Eller MBAs most frequently find jobs with the following employers: America West Airlines, Avery Dennison, Deloitte Consulting, First Magnus Financial Corporation, Ford Motor Company, E & J Gallo Winery, Honeywell, IBM, Intel Corporation, Raytheon Company, and Target Corporation-Mervyn's Division. Slightly more than half of graduates find work in the Southwest or on the Pacific coast; one in five finds a job outside the United States, a statistic that reflects Eller's large international population.

SIMONE L. POLLARD, ASSOCIATE DIRECTOR OF MBA PROGRAMS
McCLELLAND HALL 210, BUILDING 108, 1130 E HELEN STREET, PO BOX 210108 TUCSON, AZ
85721-0108 UNITED STATES
PHONE: 520-621-4008 • FAX: 520-621-2606
E-MAIL: MBA_ADMISSIONS@ELLER.ARIZONA.EDU • WEBSITE: WWW.ELLERMBA.ARIZONA.EDU/

Student Life and Environment

The University of Arizona offers a comfortable, casual setting that allows students to pursue an MBA. The school states that "MBA spaces at Eller blur the distinctions between in and out, work and play. Classrooms, meeting spaces, study centers, and technical labs all reflect the casual comfort and relaxed living of Southwest style." There's nothing casual or laid-back about the program itself; however, MBAs caution that "most students spend a significant amount of time studying. It's a lot of work."

Fortunately, students have plenty of opportunities to unwind. One student reports, "Happy hour on Thursdays (which is the last day of the school week for us) and tailgates, when applicable on Saturday, are just a couple of the regular social activities on campus. The mix of social and academic life is pretty good and has helped the student body become more integrated." Students note that "much of the work is group work," with "social breaks occurring with study buddies frequently before, after, or during study sessions." The schoolwork itself brings students closer together, as they "all work together to help each other achieve a higher level [of learning]. There is certainly competition, but it's not cutthroat."

Hometown Tucson is a growing city with a population of about 870,000. The city's architecture retains elements of the city's past with a mixture of frontier, Hispanic, and Native American styles. Winter barely glances the city (from November to March, the average daily temperature range is from 38 to 65 degrees Fahrenheit), and the desert setting means that humidity is rarely a concern; this is a dry place that heats up considerably in the summer. The university and defense-related industries are among the city's top employers. The Grand Canyon, Mexico, and Phoenix, are all within reasonable driving distance.

Admissions

Major factors in the decision process of Eller's admissions committee include undergraduate GPA (at least 3.0 preferred); evidence of a rigorous undergraduate curriculum (the committee has no preference for particular majors; nonbusiness majors are welcome); GMAT score; and a minimum of two years work experience postdating undergraduate schooling (this requirement cannot be waived, according to the school). The school warns that the program is "highly quantitative," and accordingly the admissions committee looks for "evidence of your capacity to successfully handle the analytic parts of the program in undergraduate coursework, the quantitative portions of GMAT scores, and work experience." Applications must include an essay, letters of recommendation, and a resume. An interview is "strongly recommended."

FINANCIAL FACTS

Annual tuition (in-state/out-of-state)	$14,451/$23,431
Fees	$99
Books and supplies	$2,000
Room & board (on/off-campus)	$12,000/$14,000
% of students receiving grants	80
Average grant	$13,337

ADMISSIONS

Admissions Selectivity Rating	86
# of applications received	216
% applicants accepted	62
% acceptees attending	52
Average GMAT	638
Range of GMAT	580-710
Average GPA	3.5
TOEFL Required of International Students?	Yes
Minimum TOEFL (paper/computer)	600/250
Application fee	$50
International application fee	$50
Regular application deadline	Rolling
Regular notification	Rolling
Application Deadline/Notification	
Round 1:	11/15 / 12/15
Round 2:	2/15 / 3/15
Round 3:	4/15 / 5/15
Early decision program?	Yes
ED Deadline/Notification	11/15 / 12/15
Deferment Available?	Yes
Maximum length of deferment	1 year
Need-blind admissions?	Yes

APPLICANTS ALSO LOOK AT

Arizona State University, Babson College, California State University—Los Angeles, The University of Texas at Austin, Thunderbird, University of California—Irvine, Wake Forest University—Full-time MBA Program, University of Washington.

Career Rating	68	Grads employed by field	%: avg. salary
Placement rate (%)	87	Finance	38: $58,847
% grads employed immediately	53	Human Resources	7: $58,000
Average starting salary	$64,609	Marketing	16: $69,483
		MIS	16: $71,143
		Operations	4: NR
		Consulting	2: NR
		General Management	4: NR
		Other	13: $73,750

UNIVERSITY OF ARKANSAS—FAYETTEVILLE
SAM M. WALTON COLLEGE OF BUSINESS

GENERAL INFORMATION
Type of school   public
Environment   town
Academic calendar   July–June

SURVEY SAYS...
Students love Fayetteville, AR
Friendly students
Smart classrooms
Solid preparation in:
Presentation skills

STUDENTS
Enrollment of parent
  institution   16,449
Enrollment of MBA program   147
% male/female   71/29
% out-of-state   13
% part-time   63
% minorities   10
% international   24
Average age at entry   27
Average years work experience
  at entry   3.5

ACADEMICS
Academic Experience Rating   80
Student/faculty ratio   20:1
Profs interesting rating   70
Profs accessible rating   86
Joint Degrees
MBA/JD: 4 years
Prominent Alumni
S. Robson Walton, Chairman, Wal-
Mart Stores Inc.; William Dillards
Sr., Chairman, Dillards Inc.; Frank
Fletcher, Entrepreneur; Jack
Stephens, Stephens Inc.; Thomas F.
McLarty, Former U.S. Pres.al
Advisor.

Academics

From the name above the door to the endowment that funds its high tech facilities to the employer who hires many of its MBAs, it's difficult to avoid the influence of Wal-Mart at University of Arkansas' Sam M. Walton College of Business. Students can't resist drawing comparisons to their megacorporate neighbor and benefactor; one student writes, "The school offers good quality at low cost. It's the Wal-Mart of schools." And Wal-Mart money, students brag, has made Walton College "the most technologically advanced of any school in the U of A system. The classrooms and facilities are second to none."

In order to maximize return on students' investment, Walton offers a one-year accelerated MBA program. It begins with a set of optional one-week "short courses" in basic management and number-crunching skills. Mandatory foundations courses, which cover intermediate skills and concepts, run from late June through early August. The core is covered in two 8-week integrated modules in the fall; the spring starts with a five-week strategic management course followed by an 11-week consulting project, during which, students apply classroom lessons to the real-world problems of local companies (many of which are *Fortune* 500 companies drawn to the area by Wal-Mart; students describe this phenomenon as "the Wal-Mart effect"). Students take electives concurrently with the consulting project and then wind up the program with two more electives in a summer session.

MBAs report that "this program is intense and requires you to manage your time." They love the school's "local reputation and contacts, especially if you want to get involved in the retail/Wal-Mart vendor industry." However, most students agree that "the faculty is what makes this program great. Most of the classes are very interactive, and a top-notch faculty applies and teaches the most current tools to solve today's business problems. They really do challenge us to think outside the box." Students also appreciate how "the administration tries their hardest to accommodate [them] despite all the red tape and bureaucracy that come with a large university." They also have high hopes for the program's future; as one student comments, "I know the school is looking to the future. With a $50 million gift to the business school and a $300 million gift to the entire university, I am aware of many new things the school is planning, including a new graduate building and a quad devoted just to business students."

Career and Placement

The Career Development Center at Walton offers students a number of job fairs each year, some aimed specifically at a particular function (supply-chain management, engineering, IT), and others that are open to the entire campus. The office promises "personalized career planning and placement" with lots of "one-to-one attention; it employs four full-time staffers to serve the university's business students. Over 200 employers use the school's interview rooms each year; roughly a quarter of those employers are looking specifically for MBAs."

Top employers of Walton MBAs include J.B. Hunt, Masterfoods, Tyson Foods, Unilever, and, of course, Wal-Mart Stores, Inc. About three in five graduates remain in the area; approximately 10 percent find jobs outside of the United States.

MICHELE HALSELL, MANAGING DIRECTOR, GRADUATE SCHOOL OF BUSINESS
475 BUSINESS BUILDING, FAYETTEVILLE, AR 72701 UNITED STATES
PHONE: 479-575-2851 • FAX: 479-575-8721
E-MAIL: GSB@WALTON.UARK.EDU • WEBSITE: WWW.GSB.UARK.EDU

Student Life and Environment

The old real-estate cliché holds true; it's all about "location, location, location." In Fayetteville, students enjoy "close proximity to Wal-Mart headquarters and 'Vendorville' (all Wal-Mart suppliers, including Newell-Rubbermaid, Procter & Gamble, and Unilever, have offices here) in the fastest-growing region in the country (according to the Milken Institute). It creates great opportunities for newly minted MBAs." In addition, students agree, "Fayetteville is a great town to be in. There is plenty to do socially after hours. Dixon Street, Fayetteville's version of Bourbon Street in New Orleans, is a common place for our networking activities." Although a city of just under 60,000, Fayetteville is home to a symphony orchestra, an arts center, and a film society. It is an understatement to say that college athletics are huge here.

According to students, MBAs form a tight-knit community at the university. The rigors of the accelerated academic program also help forge an esprit de corps, but there's more to it than that. One student explains, "The students in the Walton College of Business have formed a collegial and cohesive group. The small size of the program and efforts of the MBA program administration have fostered a supportive and team-oriented approach to our business education." Another students adds, "I went to undergrad at a small liberal arts college, so the large university is somewhat overwhelming and not really my cup of tea. However, the MBA program is small and caters to us, so it still has that small-school feel."

Admissions

The Walton admissions committee reports that successful applicants typically have high undergraduate GPAs (at least 3.4), score at least 580 on the GMAT, have at least two years of work experience (or substantial extracurricular involvement in their undergraduate programs), produce three strong letters of recommendation, and write a compelling personal statement. Although work experience is not required, applicants with at least two years of experience are given preference for admission. The school tells us that "underrepresented minorities are encouraged to apply, and special financial assistance is available to minority students."

FINANCIAL FACTS

Annual tuition (in-state/out-of-state)	$12,312/$24,871
Fees	$1,542
Books and supplies	$1,000
Room & board	$11,746
% of students receiving aid	93
% of first-year students receiving aid	93
% of students receiving loans	33
% of students receiving grants	11
Average award package	$24,576
Average grant	$4,754
Average student loan debt	$14,950

ADMISSIONS

Admissions Selectivity Rating	82
# of applications received	222
% applicants accepted	65
% acceptees attending	69
Average GMAT	594
Range of GMAT	530-660
Average GPA	3.3
TOEFL Required of International Students?	Yes
Minimum TOEFL (paper/computer)	550/213
Application fee	$40
International application fee	$50
Regular application deadline	2/15
Regular notification	3/15
Deferment Available?	Yes
Maximum length of deferment	1 year
Transfer students accepted?	Yes
Transfer application policy: Max 6 hours,electives from an AACSB accredited school, A or B grades.	
Non-fall admissions?	Yes
Need-blind admissions?	Yes

APPLICANTS ALSO LOOK AT

Oklahoma State University, South Texas College of Law, The University of Texas at Austin, University of Georgia, University of Mississippi, University of Oklahoma, University of Tennessee.

EMPLOYMENT PROFILE

Career Rating	79	Grads employed by field:	
Placement rate (%)	95	Accounting	10
% grads employed immediately	56	Finance	16
Average starting salary	$55,000	Marketing	7
		MIS	2
		Operations	21
		Strategic Planning	2
		Consulting	10
		Entrepreneurship	5
		Other	25
		Non-profit	2

UNIVERSITY OF BRITISH COLUMBIA
SAUDER SCHOOL OF BUSINESS

GENERAL INFORMATION
Type of school   public

SURVEY SAYS...
Students love Vancouver, BC
Happy students
Smart classrooms
Solid preparation in:
Teamwork

STUDENTS
Enrollment of parent
  institution   40,000
Enrollment of MBA program   245
% male/female   63/37
% part-time   18
% minorities   60
% international   65
Average age at entry   30
Average years work experience
  at entry   6

ACADEMICS
Academic Experience Rating   **85**
Student/faculty ratio   20:1
Profs interesting rating   90
Profs accessible rating   96
% female faculty   18

Academics

Students in this prestigious 15-month, full-time-only MBA program at Vancouver's University of British Columbia report that "Sauder professors look for an integrated approach that develops every student's overall understanding of each facet of business, using relevant materials and current events. This results in ensuring that Sauder students are ready for the challenges of today's business world without burdening them with outdated business concepts." Through "a mix of theory and concepts, case studies, real-project analysis, and internships," students agree, "this program provides [them] with very good opportunities [to develop] practical, useful management practices."

"The most valuable part of the Sauder MBA program is the integrative core," students report. The core, an intensive 13-week sequence, is taught as a single course rather than as a set of discrete disciplines, an approach befitting Sauder's focus. Because of both the sheer quantity of work and the level of complex thinking required, the core is extremely challenging. One student explains, "I feel I'm going through the business equivalent of Navy Seal training. Surviving the core is the toughest thing I've ever done...but I can honestly say I've never laughed this hard nor had so much fun." Students happily note that "after solving so many cases, analyzing so many businesses, and critically tearing apart complex business theories, you come out of the core thinking you can do almost anything. It really is inspiring." Another benefit of the workload is that "it prepares students to cope with demanding deadlines and timelines in their chosen careers." But such preparation results from rigorous training, including "24 hours a week of class lectures, case studies and presentations, assignment submissions, course readings to catch up on, and multiple submissions due on some days."

The remainder of the program post-core is devoted primarily to specialization and professional development. Students tell us that finance is "by far" the school's strongest area, although supply chain management, entrepreneurship, and international business also earn praise. Administrators here "do their job and more. They are service-oriented and very focused in addressing students' needs." When students find spare time to put down the business books, they "can learn about the interesting research happening in other faculties, because the school has so much interesting research-oriented stuff happening all the time."

Career and Placement

UBC's Business Career Centre offers both personal consultation as well as a structured program to help students identify goals and then develop strategies to meet those goals. Its services include self-assessment assistance, coaching sessions, skills training programs (in resume writing, interviewing, and networking), recruiting events (which bring "corporate recruiters from prominent companies" to interview job candidates), and job postings. Students wish the office could do more to attract companies from the east coast, and many emphasize that "UBC needs to continue to build its alumni network, and its Business Career Centre needs more resources to attract recruiters and companies to come to UBC to find qualified MBA grads in all areas, not just finance," the school's strongest discipline.

Employers likely to hire UBC MBAs include Accenture, Bank of Montreal, Bombardier, Citibank, General Motors of Canada, Genome BC, Ledcor Industries, MacDonald Dettwiler & Associates, the Ministry of Energy & Mines, the Pepsi Bottling Group, Procter & Gamble, Westport Innovations, and Xantrex Technology.

FINANCIAL FACTS

Annual tuition	$21,500
Books and supplies	$1,200
Average grant	$5,000

ADMISSIONS

Admissions Selectivity Rating	**81**
# of applications received	358
% applicants accepted	21
% acceptees attending	100
Average GMAT	621
Range of GMAT	590-680
Average GPA	3.3
TOEFL Required of International Students?	Yes
Minimum TOEFL (paper/computer)	600/250
Application fee	$125
International application fee	$125
Regular application deadline	4/30
Regular notification	Rolling
Need-blind admissions?	Yes

Student Life and Environment

It's impossible to separate the quality of life at UBC from its hometown of Vancouver, which students unanimously proclaim "one of the best places on earth." This "vibrant city [is] a great place to live. It's very safe, and there's always so much to do. Whistler Mountain is on your doorstep, so lots of ski trips are planned, with hiking in the Rockies during the summer. The wineries aren't too far away, either!" Vancouver's "strategic location—facing directly into the Asian market"—provides excellent internship and career opportunities for UBC MBAs. Non-Canadian students happily report that "our spouses can work here legally for the duration of our courses! In the U.S., my wife would have had to do nothing for two years." About the only downside is that "because Vancouver is a great place to live, people are willing to take lower wages. There are a lot of excellent-quality people looking for jobs in Vancouver too, so the competition is tough. It is difficult to get a really high-paid job in Vancouver, but your quality of life makes [taking a lower-paying job] worth it!"

UBC's "park-like campus" is located "on a peninsula with vistas of mountains and oceans." The facilities are "excellent. The commerce building is wireless-enabled, the MBA lounge is a great place to hang out, and there are adequate restaurants for all tastes." Furthermore, "the facilities include pools and gyms, and a movie theater located in the university. There's also a graduate bar on campus that provides a beautiful view of Vancouver, and the school has a great 18-hole golf course." Students can participate in "tons of different clubs" that help them network while developing business-related or recreational skills. "There is a good balance between the workload and time for yourself," with "plenty and diverse social and development events."

Admissions

Admission to the Sauder MBA program is extremely competitive. All applicants must submit official transcripts for undergraduate work (students who attended schools where English was not the primary language must arrange for a literal translation of their transcripts to be delivered to UBC), official GMAT score reports, evidence of English proficiency (TOEFL scores for students whose first language is not English), a resume, and three letters of reference. Interviews are by invitation only; the school interviews roughly half of its applicant pool. The school's viewbook notes that "only under exceptional circumstances will applicants with less than two years of full-time work experience be admitted to this program." On average, students enter the program with between six and eight years' full-time professional experience. Applications are processed on a rolling basis; admitted students may not defer admission.

EMPLOYMENT PROFILE			
Career Rating	**88**	**Grads employed by field**	**%: avg. salary**
Placement rate (%)	92	Finance	13: $88,000
# of companies recruiting on-campus	50	Marketing	15: $76,000
% grads employed immediately	92	Operations	6: $59,000
Average starting salary	$79,000	Strategic Planning	25: $67,000
		Consulting	8: NR
		General Management	19: $77,000
		Other	14: NR

UNIVERSITY AT BUFFALO—STATE UNIVERSITY OF NEW YORK
SCHOOL OF MANAGEMENT

GENERAL INFORMATION

Type of school	public
Environment	metropolis
Academic calendar	semester

SURVEY SAYS...
Friendly students
Smart classrooms
Solid preparation in:
Teamwork
Communication/interpersonal skills

STUDENTS

Enrollment of parent institution	26,000
Enrollment of MBA program	720
% male/female	61/39
% out-of-state	50
% part-time	26
% minorities	5
% international	47
Average age at entry	26
Average years work experience at entry	3

ACADEMICS

Academic Experience Rating	**75**
Student/faculty ratio	9:1
Profs interesting rating	64
Profs accessible rating	71
% female faculty	20
% minority faculty	30

Joint Degrees
MBA/JD
MBA/MD
MBA/March
MBA/PhG
MBA/MS in Geography
BS/MBA Business or Engineering
MBA/MSW
MBA/AuG
MBA/MPH

Prominent Alumni
Harold Kutner, VP of Worldwide Purchasing, GM; Jeremy Jacobs Sr., CEO, Delaware North Cos.; Robert Rich Sr., Chairman & Founder, Rich Products; David Gasiewicz, General Manager, Microsoft.

Academics

Students look at the bottom line and like what they see at University of Buffalo School of Management. As one student explains, "The sheer cost of an MBA today can be overwhelming, but UB combines affordability and a great academic reputation to make it one of the best returns on an investment in graduate education that anyone can get." ROI is boosted by the school's excellent reputation with recruiters; according to *The Wall Street Journal*, the full-time MBA program has ranked among the world's top programs for the past four years.

UB offers a full-time MBA, a professional MBA (part-time), an executive MBA, and an international MBA with programs in Beijing and Singapore. (UB's focus on international business affords students study-abroad opportunities in 20 countries around the world as well as numerous international internships. Even when they're in Buffalo, students are exposed to international perspectives; more than one third of the student body is international.) The school also offers MS degrees in accounting, management/information systems, and supply/chains and operations management. UB offers formal concentrations in accounting, biotechnology management, finance, information systems and e-business, international management, management consulting, marketing management, and supply chain and operations management. Students often pursue dual concentrations.

In all programs, students praise the "small, well-connected atmosphere where all classmates help each other out and network well together." The use of "study teams" in many courses helps students develop "team skills, including things such as oral and written communication, managing diversity and conflict, making meetings work, and leadership. In addition, students can work together to minimize weaknesses and maximize strengths." Students tell us that their professors cover "a wide range [of material] in quality, with some of the best teachers and also some of the worst. On average, they are very good." Overall, students describe study at UB as "an excellent experience. Most professors are very available, and the administration has done everything possible to make our experience meaningful."

Career and Placement

The School of Management Career Resource Center offers a wide range of services to MBAs including participation in a major MBA consortium, the alumni Telementor Program (through which students receive guidance from alumni and other mentors via e-mail and telephone contact), recruiting events, workshops and seminars, online job databases, and on-campus recruiting sessions. State-of-the-art facilities allow for videoconference interviews and the maintenance of a student information system database that is "used to complement traditional methods of on-campus and off-campus recruiting."

Employers most likely to hire Buffalo MBAs include Advantage Energy, Aldi Foods, Citigroup, Deloitte Touche Tohmatsu, Delphi Harrison, Dopkins and Co. CPA, Eli Lilly, Ernst and Young, Fisher Price, General Dynamics, International Monetary Fund, Itochu/USA, J&J Medical, Kalieda Health, Lockheed Martin, M&T Bank, Mentholatum, Morgan Stanley, National Fuel, Praxair, PricewaterhouseCoopers, Rich Products, Samsung Capital, Turner Construction, Washington Mutual, Bearing Point, Eastman Kodak, HSBC Bank, IBM, and Unifrax Corp.

ADMISSIONS CONTACT: JAIMIE TAYLOR, ASSOCIATE DIRECTOR OF MBA RECRUITING & ADMISSIONS
ADDRESS: 203 ALFIERO CENTER, BUFFALO, NY 14260 UNITED STATES
PHONE: 716-645-3204 • FAX: 716-645-2341
E-MAIL: SOM-MBA@BUFFALO.EDU • WEBSITE: WWW.MGT.BUFFALO.EDU

Student Life and Environment

UB's international business program translates into a student body that is "extremely diversified, with fellow students hailing from Japan, China, India, Bulgaria, Sweden, Brazil, Taiwan, Egypt, and the United States, to name a few. This mix provides a culturally rich environment and an excellent opportunity to learn about other cultures." Students overcome cultural and, in some cases, language barriers to work and play together. One MBA student reports, "The culture is upbeat around the school. Most of the students seem to have developed a bond in and out of class. There is great opportunity to learn about different cultures from international students."

Extracurriculars are largely the function of the Graduate Management Association, which "organizes happy hours, sometimes with other schools such as the law school, at least once a month." One student says, "The GMA also provides School of Management grad students with an opportunity to assume leadership roles as well as contribute to graduate life in terms of organizing social and community functions by way of participating on committees. In addition, there are clubs that cater to just about every interest imaginable, and if there isn't one that covers your particular interest, I understand clubs are fairly easy to form." The recently-added Alfiero Center provides offices and rooms for these student clubs, as well as lecture halls, and academic advisement offices.

The university community and the city of Buffalo both contribute to "a fun social atmosphere" within the MBA program. As the state's "largest and most comprehensive public university," UB can support thriving social, artistic, and athletic scenes that literally offer something to just about everyone (the exception: people who hate cold weather). The city of Buffalo, known as "the City of Good Neighbors," offers students plenty of entertainment outlets as well as "a wide range of living situations to accommodate any income level. In addition, a comprehensive public transportation system precludes the need for private transportation."

Admissions

According to the school's website, admissions decisions at the School of Management "are based on quantitative and qualitative factors within the scope of the enrollment and academic goals of the program. GMAT, GPA, TOEFL (for international applicants), undergraduate degree field, undergraduate institution, work experience, recommendations, and essays all factor into a decision." The school reports that it "offers competitive fellowships and assistantships to highly qualified minority applicants." Post-baccalaureate professional experience is recommended but not required. Entering students are required to have a functional understanding of calculus.

FINANCIAL FACTS

Annual tuition (in-state/out-of-state)	$7,390/$11,340
Fees	$1,131
Books and supplies	$1,150
Room & board	$7,543
% of students receiving aid	15
% of first-year students receiving aid	12
% of students receiving grants	15
Average award package	$11,610
Average grant	$11,610
Average student loan debt	$14,779

ADMISSIONS

Admissions Selectivity Rating	83
# of applications received	567
% applicants accepted	56
% acceptees attending	47
Average GMAT	595
Range of GMAT	560-640
Average GPA	3.2
TOEFL Required of International Students?	Yes
Minimum TOEFL (paper/computer)	573/230
Application fee	$50
International application fee	$50
Regular application deadline	6/1
Regular notification	Rolling
Need-blind admissions?	Yes

APPLICANTS ALSO LOOK AT

Albany Law School, Baruch College—City University of New York, Binghamton University, State University of New York, Syracuse University, University of Illinois at Chicago, University of Illinois at Urbana-Champaign.

EMPLOYMENT PROFILE

Career Rating	75	Grads employed by field	%: avg. salary
Placement rate (%)	66	Accounting	11: $51,000
% grads employed immediately	56	Finance	23: $52,667
Average starting salary	$51,997	Marketing	15: $51,000
		MIS	10: $49,480
		Operations	20: $51,606
		Consulting	7: $52,000
		General Management	10: $45,300
		Other	4: $52,000

University of Calgary
Haskayne School of Business

GENERAL INFORMATION
Type of school	public
Affiliation	
Environment	
Academic calendar	semester

SURVEY SAYS...
Students love Calgary, AB
Friendly students
Happy students
Smart classrooms
Solid preparation in:
Teamwork

STUDENTS
Enrollment of parent institution	27,928
Enrollment of MBA program	375
% male/female	62/38
% part-time	56
% international	42
Average age at entry	30
Average years work experience at entry	6

ACADEMICS
Academic Experience Rating	**80**
Student/faculty ratio	3:1
Profs interesting rating	62
Profs accessible rating	72
% female faculty	29

Joint Degrees
MBA/LLB: 4 years
MBA/MSW: 2 years
MBA/MD: 5 years
MBA/MBT: 2 years

Prominent Alumni
Al Duerr, CEO Emergo Projects International; Charlie Fisher, Pres. and CEO, Nexen; Hal Kvisle, Pres. & CEO, TransCanada; Brett Wilson, Managing Director, First Energy Capital; Byron Osing, Chairman, Launchworks Inc.

Academics

Because Calgary is "the center of Canada's energy markets, [it] is the perfect location for a program like the one offered by the Haskayne School of Business" at the University of Calgary. One MBA explains, "I think Haskayne's strength lies in the potential of alliances and joint ventures with the large business sector for such a small community. With so many head offices located in our community, I think Haskayne has the ability to capitalize on this available resource." Indeed, it already does, by offering "such unique features as its global energy and sustainable development program."

Haskayne MBAs may pursue their degrees during the day as a full-time student or part-time in the evening. This course-based track requires up to 20 courses; 12 required and 8 electives. (Some foundation courses can be waived for students with demonstrable knowledge in the subject matter covered.) Specializations—completed by taking four electives in a single area—are available in entrepreneurship and innovation, finance, global energy and sustainable development, and marketing. A select few students (all with relatively deep academic and professional backgrounds in business) are admitted to a thesis-based MBA program, which consists of eight half-courses and a research paper that is completed under the supervision of a faculty sponsor.

Students give the Haskayne faculty mixed reviews and explain that "there are some professors who are nice and intelligent individuals, but [they] seriously lack the ability to teach." One MBA elaborates, "There's a vast difference between having a PhD professor, who may have submitted umpteen research papers for publication, but can't teach [and someone with a master's degree who can. If there was a master's lecturer who can get the information across in a more meaningful manner, without the same knowledge base as the PhD, I would take the lecturer any day." MBAs are firmly behind the administration and say that "[the university] has been excellent in planning. Contingency situations are handled with ease." One student notes, "Administrators are very helpful when questions need to be answered, timely at getting new information out to us, and generally courteous."

Haskayne draws on its geographical advantage to offer students mentorship opportunities. According to the school, "Senior business leaders from a diverse range of industries with an economic and operational impact locally, regionally, and internationally provide professional development opportunities for full-time MBA students." Overall, students feel that "the program provides students with the basic skills necessary to begin a career in management." One student says, "I believe that the learning environment is very positive and allows students to develop their communication and social skills."

Career and Placement

Students either seem to have mixed feelings about the Haskayne Career Center. Its champions tell us that "the Career Center is second to none with respect to the services offered. The center tries to promote networking opportunities." One international student notes, "The Career Center in this school provides us with amazing experience. For example, they provide business etiquette courses which encourage international students to attend local business events and behave correctly." The bottom line, however, is how effective the office is in facilitating the job search. At least one student feels it comes up short in this area; the disgruntled MBA writes, "There are no quality jobs for MBA students. We all struggle to find work."

PENNY O'HEARN, ADMISSIONS OFFICER
2500 UNIVERSITY DRIVE, NW, CALGARY, AB T2N 1N4 CANADA
PHONE: 403-220-3808 • FAX: 403-282-0095 • E-MAIL: MBAREQUEST@MGMT.UCALGARY.CA
WEBSITE: WWW.HASKAYNE.UCALGARY.CA/MBA

Employers of Haskayne MBAs include Calgary Catholic School Board; Canadian Natural Resources Limited; Cap Gemini Ernst & Young; CIBC; Coral Energy; Deloitte Touche Tohmatsu; Dustsoft Technologies, Inc.; Encryption Systems, Inc.; ENMAX; Gibson Petroleum; Merak; Opportunity Capital Corporation; PanCanadian Petroleum Limited; Rainbow Contractors; RLG International Ltd.; SagaTech Electronic, Inc.; SAP Canada; and TELUS Communications, Inc.

Student Life and Environment

Life within the Haskayne program "is comfortable and safe. Students can study right into midnight without worrying about personal or property security. There are security officers wandering on the building regularly, and school security office offers 24-hour accompany services to all students who stay late or need accompaniment to the parking lot." Students say, "The school puts real efforts to make our study experience convenient, secure, and enjoyable." Haskayne's facility boasts "state-of-the-art technology utilization for studies (like online access to teaching staff and on-campus wireless access)."

The MBA program also offers "excellent opportunities for participation in extracurricular activities. Students can practice skills through involvement in MBA Society activities like hosting business conferences or participating in MBA games. There are excellent opportunities for networking, career counseling, and the MBA student business case competition." While "people are very involved in their studies and work together, any outside social activities are segmented into cliques." In part because many students attend part-time, Haskayne is not an especially social program.

Hometown Calgary is "a good business city" with a population approaching one million. Proximity to the Rocky Mountains means that "students can go skiing and camping in marvelous surroundings." Calgary is an international city, and this is reflected in the student population. Students explain that "the focus on a diverse mix of students in the MBA class provides a global perspective to [the] learning process."

Admissions

Minimum admission requirements to the Haskayne MBA program include a four-year undergraduate degree completed with at least a 3.0 GPA over the final two years of study, a GMAT score of 550, a personal statement of career and academic goals; three letters of reference, and a resume. Non-English speaking applicants must submit TOEFL scores (minimum 600). A minimum of three years of appropriate employment are required. Applicants to the thesis-based program must have a minimum GPA of 3.3 and a minimum GMAT score of 600.

FINANCIAL FACTS

Annual tuition (in-state/out-of-state)	$11,250/$22,500
Fees (in-state/out-of-state)	$715/$1,430
Books and supplies	$2,000
Room & board (on/off-campus)	$5,000/$15,000
Average grant	$5,000

ADMISSIONS

Admissions Selectivity Rating	87
# of applications received	291
% applicants accepted	54
% acceptees attending	58
Average GMAT	621
Range of GMAT	540-690
Average GPA	3.3
TOEFL Required of International Students?	Yes
Minimum TOEFL (paper/computer)	600/250
Application fee	$60
International application fee	$60
Regular application deadline	5/1
Regular notification	Rolling
Application Deadline/Notification	
Round 1:	11/15 / 1/15
Round 2:	1/15 / 3/1
Round 3:	3/1 / 5/1
Round 4:	5/1 / 6/15
Deferment Available?	Yes
Maximum length of deferment	1 year
Transfer students accepted?	Yes
Transfer application policy: May transfer up to nine courses.	

EMPLOYMENT PROFILE

Career Rating	85	Grads employed by field: %	
% grads employed within three months	89	Finance	23
Average starting salary	$79,705	Human Resources	3
		Marketing	7
		MIS	2
		Operations	19
		Consulting	14
		General Management	13
		Other	15

UNIVERSITY OF CALIFORNIA—BERKELEY
HAAS SCHOOL OF BUSINESS

Academics

The Haas School of Business at the University of California—Berkeley offers students "a truly interactive environment," one in which "professors learn from the students as well as the other way around" thanks to students' substantial input into the program. The full-time program in particular is designed to provide students with an unusual degree of autonomy; explains one student, "Student initiative comes into play in every aspect of the program, from scheduling speakers to career search." Students here also design and run, with faculty oversight, a number of electives every semester. The result of all this freedom is that "students are forced to become entrepreneurs as part of their education." The small size of the program (only 250 full-time students and about as many part-timers) contributes to the experience by "forcing a collaborative environment where competition is put aside in order to help one another."

Haas backs up its unique approach to graduate business education with a strong curriculum and a solid faculty. The school excels in Social Entrepreneurship, Corporate Social Responsibility, General Management, and Technology; this last area capitalizes on Berkeley's location "across the bay from San Francisco and just one hour from Silicon Valley." The faculty includes a number of stars; boasts one MBA, "Our finance professor is serving as the president of the San Francisco Federal Reserve. Our dean is on leave as [Governor] Arnold Schwarzenegger's Finance Director. They don't get better than this." Better still, "not only are the professors outstanding in their fields, but they are also highly approachable and willing to make changes to the class to meet the students' needs." Semesters move along quickly here; "The academic pace is very fast," students observe, "but the workload is not overwhelming." While the core "is solid," most here prefer the "awesome electives that give you some great opportunities outside the classroom."

Career and Placement

When it comes time to find a career, Haas MBAs benefit from their program's high profile and sound reputation. As is often the case at such schools, the Haas Career Center provides a broad range of excellent services. Students here benefit from one-on-one advisement, access to numerous online job databases, industry clubs, workshops, seminars, and a mentoring program in which second-year students counsel first years in their search for internships.

Employers most likely to hire Haas MBAs include Bank of America; the Clorox Company; Deloitte; Gap, Inc.; Johnson & Johnson; LeapFrog Enterprises, Inc.; McKinsey & Company; Microsoft Corporation; Samsung Group; and Wells Fargo Bank.

Student Life and Environment

For full-time students, "student clubs are at the heart of the school" because they help organize student input to the program. Explains one MBA, "Nothing happens at Haas without student involvement. Just about every full-time student is heavily involved in all aspects of the school. From student government to admissions to industry clubs to sports and wine clubs, everyone is able to express their interests and tap their fellow students for more information or just someone to share a good meal." The administration "fully supports club activities and has our needs on their minds continuously. It is only with their aid that we have been able to accomplish so much in our short time here."

Between classes, clubs, and other extracurricular options, "live is very busy" for full-time students at Haas. There are "groups constantly getting together to go to arts festivals, AIDS walks, golfing, cycling, surfing, skiing, attending seminars, hearing guest lecturers, and hiking, to name just a few activities. The opportunities are endless and everyone loves being here." Thursday nights "are a tradition at Haas. We have BoW (Bar of the Week) in Berkeley and San Francisco, so there are always fun places to check out as you get to know the area." Students also appreciate their "access to the Bay Area's business, culture, natural beauty, and geographic diversity. Networking opportunities abound because so many business and thought leaders either live in the area or pass through here."

The "great, resourceful, creative, and mellow" students of Haas are "warm, but with a competitive edge—in the best sense of the word." Students speculate that "Haas' long-standing 'no grade-disclosure' policy" results in "students who are extremely helpful to each other, making certain that learning is truly a collaborative process." Indeed, our survey respondents all agree that "students at Haas are extremely team-oriented. They very much work together to get things done. The Berkeley MBA attracts top-notch students from all over the world and we mutually benefit from one another's experiences." Adds one student, "Given how diverse the work experiences are here, I find myself learning from those around me every day. These are truly the type of people I want to work with and for after graduation."

Admissions

Applicants to Haas graduate programs must submit all the following materials to the admissions department: official copies of transcripts for all post-secondary academic work, an official GMAT score report, letters of recommendation, a personal statement, and a resume. Interviews are optional. In addition to the above materials, international applicants whose first language is not English must also submit official score reports for the TOEFL (minimum score of 570 for the paper-based test, 230 for the computer-based test). The school considers all of the following in determining admissions status: "demonstration of quantitative ability; quality of work experience, including depth and breadth of responsibilities; opportunities to demonstrate leadership, etc.; strength of letters of recommendation; depth and breadth of extracurricular and community involvement; and strength of short answer and essays, including articulation of clear focus and goals."

FINANCIAL FACTS

Annual tuition (in-state/out-of-state)	$21,512/$33,758
Books and supplies	$2,500
Room & board	$13,330
% of students receiving aid	67
% of first-year students receiving aid	64
% of students receiving loans	55
% of students receiving grants	21
Average award package	$27,916
Average grant	$18,921
Average student loan debt	$42,856

ADMISSIONS

Admissions Selectivity Rating	98
# of applications received	2858
% applicants accepted	17
% acceptees attending	47
Average GMAT	701
Range of GMAT	670-730
Average GPA	3.5
TOEFL Required of International Students?	Yes
Minimum TOEFL (paper/computer)	570/230
Application fee	$175
International application fee	$175
Regular application deadline	3/4
Regular notification	5/31
Application Deadline/Notification	
Round 1:	10/29 / 1/31
Round 2:	12/10 / 3/18
Round 3:	1/21 / 5/2
Round 4:	3/4 / 5/31
Need-blind admissions?	Yes

APPLICANTS ALSO LOOK AT

Columbia University, Harvard University, New York University, Northwestern University, Stanford University, University of California—Los Angeles, University of Pennsylvania.

EMPLOYMENT PROFILE

Career Rating	98	Grads employed by field	%: avg. salary
Placement rate (%)	92	Finance	29: $84,636
% grads employed immediately	78	Marketing	24: $88,308
Average starting salary	$88,234	Operations	3: $84,174
		Consulting	17: $93,879
		General Management	17: $92,063

UNIVERSITY OF CALIFORNIA—DAVIS
GRADUATE SCHOOL OF MANAGEMENT

GENERAL INFORMATION
Type of school	public
Environment	town
Academic calendar	quarters

SURVEY SAYS...
Students love Davis, CA
Friendly students
Good peer network
Happy students
Solid preparation in:
Teamwork

STUDENTS
Enrollment of parent institution	30,065
Enrollment of MBA program	123
% male/female	70/30
% minorities	8
% international	10
Average age at entry	30
Average years work experience at entry	5

ACADEMICS
Academic Experience Rating	93
Student/faculty ratio	8:1
Profs interesting rating	82
Profs accessible rating	96
% female faculty	15
% minority faculty	21

Joint Degrees
MBA/JD: 4 years
MD/MBA: 6 years
MBA/MEng: 2 years
MBA/Ag Econ: 2 years

Prominent Alumni
David H. Russ, UC Treasurer & VP of Investments; Christine Smith, UltraDots, Inc., Founder; Gordon C. Hunt, Jr., MD, Sutter Health, Senior VP and Chief Medical Officer; Eric Robison, IdeaTrek, Inc., Owner & Pres.; Steve Spadarotto, Diageo Chateau & Estate Wines, VP.

Academics

UC Davis' Graduate School of Management still has the glow of youth about it. Its proud students state confidently, "We're only 20 years old, and we're doing great!" That youthful energy carries into most aspects of the program and influences the teaching styles of the professors, the attitudes of the administrators, and the caliber of the students. One student says, "The GSM provides student reviews to all faculty at midterm. Every one of my teachers (even tenured ones) has embraced this feedback and tried to improve their classes." Others say, "Because the school is young, we do have some green professors. The positive aspect of these new professors is that they are totally committed to learning how to best teach us, and they bring fresh ideas into the classroom."

Another part of being a young program is flexibility. There are only six core courses, all of which must be taken in the first year. Core courses are "designed to provide students with a foundation in the functional areas of business—accounting, economics, finance, marketing, organizational behavior, and statistics." Most disciplines are taught through the use of case studies, lectures, and the study of real companies and the problems they face. Along with the core classes in the first year, students have to select three "breadth" classes, which "prepare them for in-depth study in their concentration." Breadth classes "are designed to bring into focus the initial required topics of study and apply them to each student's chosen concentration." This gives GSM students much earlier access to electives than they would have at many schools.

Students are encouraged to design their own concentrations. As one student says, "If we want something done, the administration will find a way to do it." The school also has four joint-degree program options. Students can choose between an MBA/JD, an MBA/master's of engineering, an MBA/master's of agricultural economics, and an MBA/MD. In addition, there is one interdisciplinary degree program, a master's of agriculture and management.

While students would still like to see better technology on campus and more classes that cater to the nonprofit concentration, for the most part, they agree that their experience has "more than exceeded expectations." Davis also seems to have applied the management skills they teach to the work they do. "The staff and administration are incredible. The amount of resources at the student's disposal is almost overwhelming. The dean invites us to 'just drop in,'" one student says. In the end, it seems, administration and faculty "consider the students the product of the school and make every effort to turn out a top-notch product."

Career and Placement

UC Davis students are in the relatively rare position of being able to praise their Career Services Center, which is "really the cream of the crop." Students say, "The career counselors are absolutely stellar in helping students identify their career goals as well as helping them find an internship or job." Students admire the center's "efforts to get the school name more recognition among the recruiting landscape. We can continue to do better in this regard." Some students, however, would like to see a "stronger conduit between UC Davis and the Bay Area for additional career-placement opportunities." Companies that recruit on campus include Genentech, Inc.; Accenture; Hewlett-Packard Company; IBM; Calama Wines; Packard Bell; Deloitte Touche Tohmatsu; E & J Gallo Winery; UBS PaineWebber; and many more.

Students point out that Davis's "small size is a great advantage in some respects, but a bit of a disadvantage when it comes to recruiters and the size of the alumni database. Luckily,

James Stevens, Assistant Dean, Student Affairs
One Shields Avenue, Davis, CA 95616 United States
Phone: 530-752-7658 • Fax: 530-754-9355
E-mail: admissions@gsm.ucdavis.edu • Website: www.gsm.ucdavis.edu

this is made up for by a very helpful and friendly alumni group." The size certainly has not stopped the students from finding employment—97 percent of the class of 2000 had been placed in a position just three months after graduation. As for where they end up, "the majority of Graduate School of Management students find positions in the high tech industries, in corporate finance, or in consulting," according to the school's website.

Student Life and Environment

Half of Davis's population of 50,000 is made up of students at the university, which makes it, according to students, "the perfect small college town." As one says, "It allows you to immerse yourself in your schoolwork, but still have enough distractions to keep you busy during those much needed 'study breaks.'" Since the GSM student population is so small, the feeling is pretty intimate, and "students get to know each other well and become almost a surrogate family." Most are confident that their "relationships will continue long after school ends, especially since so many classmates will likely stay in beautiful Northern California!" Despite being a small town, Davis is "near beaches, mountains, rivers, lakes, cities, and just about everything else that California has to offer." For most students, "weekends are filled with trips to San Francisco, Lake Tahoe, Yosemite, and Las Vegas. There's never a dull moment, especially when you organize a group skydiving trip to Lodi." UC Davis prides itself on its environmental and ecological awareness, and the graceful campus shows that care. Davis boasts multiple greenbelts and 18 landscaped parks. Miles of bike paths and jogging paths link the campus to the town. Students appreciate the emphasis on the natural and say "a school that doesn't allow private vehicles on campus is really cool. It isn't often that you can own the street with an old clunker bike." Students say the current facilities leave much to be desired, but the school is diligently at work on a new, state-of-the-art building, which should be completed in late 2005/early 2006. Students often find housing in Davis prohibitively expensive and advise prospective students to "get housing early! It's expensive and difficult to come by."

Admissions

Only one out of three applicants is admitted to Davis' GSM. Admissions looks for "applicants whose academic background, intellectual capability, work experience, demonstrated leadership, and communication skills meet the demands of the MBA program and a managerial career." Davis' GSM doesn't have a minimum GMAT or GPA, but the average GMAT was 678, and scores ranged between 580 and 760. The average GPA was 3.4, with a range of 2.5 to 4.0. Unless they've earned a degree at a college or university within the United States or their undergraduate education was conducted in English, all international students must take the TOEFL exam. The minimum score requirements are 600 (paper-based) and 250 (computer-based). More than 70 percent of the GSM students who apply for financial assistance receive some type of support, either from the GSM program or from the university itself.

FINANCIAL FACTS

Annual tuition (in-state/out-of-state)	$21,462/$33,707
Books and supplies	$1,650
Room & board	$12,200
% of students receiving aid	74
% of first-year students receiving aid	80
% of students receiving loans	52
% of students receiving grants	66
Average award package	$23,326
Average grant	$13,158
Average student loan debt	$33,455

ADMISSIONS

Admissions Selectivity Rating	96
# of applications received	329
% applicants accepted	28
% acceptees attending	65
Average GMAT	678
Range of GMAT	650-710
Average GPA	3.3
TOEFL Required of International Students?	Yes
Minimum TOEFL (paper/computer)	600/250
Application fee	$150
International application fee	$150
Regular application deadline	1/6
Regular notification	3/31
Application Deadline/Notification	
Round 1:	11/1 / 1/31
Round 2:	1/6 / 3/31
Round 3:	3/15 / 5/31
Round 4:	5/16 / 6/30
Early decision program?	Yes
ED Deadline/Notification	11/1 / 1/31
Deferment Available?	Yes
Maximum length of deferment	1 year
Need-blind admissions?	Yes

APPLICANTS ALSO LOOK AT

Stanford University, The University of Texas at Austin, University of California—Berkeley, University of California—Irvine, University of California—Los Angeles, University of Southern California, University of Washington.

EMPLOYMENT PROFILE

Career Rating	90	Grads employed by field	%: avg. salary
Placement rate (%)	98	Accounting	10: $71,364
% grads employed immediately	66	Finance	20: $71,364
Average starting salary	$74,000	Marketing	34: $79,893
		Consulting	11: $79,560
		General Management	11: $63,196

UNIVERSITY OF CALIFORNIA—IRVINE
PAUL MERAGE SCHOOL OF BUSINESS

GENERAL INFORMATION
Type of school	public
Environment	city
Academic calendar	Sept–June

SURVEY SAYS...
Students love Irvine, CA
Friendly students
Happy students
Smart classrooms
Solid preparation in:
Teamwork

STUDENTS
Enrollment of parent institution	21,550
Enrollment of MBA program	820
% male/female	68/32
% out-of-state	6
% part-time	74
% minorities	5
% international	28
Average age at entry	28
Average years work experience at entry	4.75

ACADEMICS
Academic Experience Rating	**86**
Student/faculty ratio	7:1
Profs interesting rating	69
Profs accessible rating	73
% female faculty	32
% minority faculty	13

Joint Degrees
MBA/MD: 5-6 years

Prominent Alumni
Lisa Locklear, VP, Ingram Micro; Darcy Kopcho, Executive VP, Capital Group Companies; George Kessinger, Pres.. and CEO, Goodwill Industries International; Norman Witt, VP Community Development, The Irvine Co.

Academics

Students praise the "great IT focus" at UC—Irvine's Paul Merage School of Business; as one student points out, "IT management, which is the major focus of the school, is something every manager must understand and be able to do successfully in the current economy. The UC Irvine MBA stresses the appropriate use of technology to improve business processes." Research plays a major role in this aspect of the program; the school explains, "[It is] our distinguished faculty conduct [and] leading-edge research that brings the very latest thinking on management practices to classrooms and corporations. Their work has an international impact on management knowledge, deepening our understanding of how technological innovations are transforming the way business is done. As a full-time MBA, you can gain hands-on experience in our ITM labs with the tools you will need to lead change, whether you are reinventing an established firm or launching a new one. In ITM labs or electives across all the business disciplines, you will learn how technology and information transform business functions and business models." Students concur; one MBA explains, "This school is a global leader in IT." Study at Irvine commences with management of complex organizations, a residential course (held off campus at a nearby hotel) that doubles as a 'get to know your classmates' orientation event. What follows is "a solid core curriculum focused on the fundamental disciplines of management" and electives. The program does not have formal areas of concentration; instead, students are encouraged to "develop depth in a discipline or interdisciplinary area, to gain expertise with a particular set of analytical or technical tools, or to choose electives across disciplines to match [their] individual goals."

While acknowledging the cutting-edge research, world-class facilities, and fine curriculum, students say that "the greatest strength of Irvine is the people at the school—not [only] the students (who are fantastic), but also the administration and faculty." One student says, "There is a culture of teamwork and friendship that has been fostered here, which I don't think a big school can attain. [Professors] are very willing to talk and accommodate any of our needs, for the most part. They are not only researchers, but they also really care about the quality of your learning. I've even had a great time getting to know some of them outside of class." MBAs also appreciate that "Irvine offers excellent opportunities for the students to become a part of the direction for the school. Professors will change curriculum mid-course based on feedback from students."

Career and Placement

The Irvine MBA program maintains a staff of five who are "dedicated to providing students with career guidance." Available resources include career workshops, interactive Web tools, on-campus recruiting sessions, and career-assessment tools. The office maintains corporate contacts across the country, but they note that "our best company contacts are centered around our geographic location." The school hosts 120 on-campus recruiters each year; 85 employers visit the campus to recruit summer interns.

Employers who most frequently hire UC—Irvine MBAs include Accenture, Beckman Coulter, Bristol Myers Squibb, Conexant, Deloitte Touche Tohmatsu, Experian, Gateway, Hewlett-Packard, Honda Motor Co., IBM, Intel, KPMG, Microsoft, Nissan, PacifiCare, PricewaterhouseCoopers, Roth Capital Partners, Taco Bell, and Wells Fargo. Approximately one in five students finds post-degree work in the Southwestern United States; 1 in 20 finds work outside the country.

Student Life and Environment

According to students, "UC—Irvine's business school is located in a great area," a spot where "the weather is second to none, and there are many prosperous businesses nearby."

BRYAN MCSWEENEY, ASSOCIATE DIRECTOR, MBA ADMISSIONS
GSM 220, IRVINE, CA 92697-3125 UNITED STATES
PHONE: 949-824-4622 • FAX: 949-824-2235
E-MAIL: MBA@UCI.EDU • WEBSITE: WWW.GSM.UCI.EDU

We have a balanced life. Academics, charity, sports, networking, and family life" can all fit into the mix. Students appreciate that "the campus is very safe, and the location is ideal for studying. Irvine is a quite, beautiful area, with a very well-organized city master plan." The program constitutes "a small community with strong bonds," a place where students "are top-notch, and they are more focused on helping one another than being cutthroat." Remarkably, students feel that this sense of community exists even though "many students are commuters, and a lot of them have lives outside the school, so we barely get together to do things."

The program is also home to a substantial group who participate in campus and social activities within the program. For those seeking extracurricular opportunities, "there is a wide array of opportunities for school involvement and networking. From clubs to community service, executive speakers, or networking events, there are many activities outside of the classroom." One student reports, "I am very involved in club leadership and school life. It's a great experience because I have had opportunities to join into many leadership positions. I also have made a ton of great friends at the school, whom I socialize with during and after school. There is always a happy hour on Thursday nights and get-togethers during the weekends." Socializing isn't limited strictly to students; some students add that "faculty and administration are also a core part of the community. It's not unheard of to meet a professor for coffee or have a beer with the administration staff at the weekly Thursday happy hour."

The student body is relatively diverse, with "a population of about 25 percent internationals, which brings an extra splash of diversity to the school." A student with a family tells us that "[there] are very few students with children my son's age in the program; the area has its own great resources for children, including Boys and Girls Clubs, Boy Scouts, and excellent schools. My family and I have had excellent opportunities to get involved on campus."

Admissions

The Irvine Graduate School of Management requires incoming students to be proficient in introductory calculus and introductory statistics with probability; students lacking these qualifications can earn a provisional admission but must complete both courses successfully before gaining full admission. The school strongly recommends, but does not require, an introductory accounting course for students with no accounting background. All applicants must submit one copy of official transcripts for all previous academic work, GMAT scores, TOEFL scores (for international students), several "self-evaluation essays," two letters of recommendation, and a resume. The admissions committee looks for evidence of "career progression, well-articulated educational and professional goals, a clear understanding of MBA programs, presentation skills, and leadership potential." The UC Irvine MBA is an Equal Opportunity program.

FINANCIAL FACTS

Annual tuition (in-state/out-of-state)	$21,635/$33,880
Books and supplies	$2,500
Room & board (on/off-campus)	$11,089/$12,443
% of students receiving aid	85
% of first-year students receiving aid	70
% of students receiving loans	80
% of students receiving grants	48
Average award package	$20,500
Average grant	$9,950
Average student loan debt	$31,500

ADMISSIONS

Admissions Selectivity Rating	92
# of applications received	530
% applicants accepted	43
% acceptees attending	46
Average GMAT	660
Range of GMAT	600-710
Average GPA	3.4
TOEFL Required of International Students?	Yes
Minimum TOEFL (paper/computer)	600/250
Application fee	$110
International application fee	$110
Regular application deadline	11/15
Regular notification	1/15
Application Deadline/Notification	
Round 1:	11/15 / 1/15
Round 2:	1/15 / 3/1
Round 3:	2/15 / 4/1
Round 4:	4/1 / 5/15
Deferment Available?	Yes
Maximum length of deferment	1 year
Non-fall admissions?	Yes
Need-blind admissions?	Yes

APPLICANTS ALSO LOOK AT

University of California—Berkeley, University of California—Davis, University of California—Los Angeles, University of Southern California, University of Washington.

EMPLOYMENT PROFILE

Career Rating	84	Grads employed by field	%: avg. salary
Placement rate (%)	98	Accounting	15: $65,000
# of companies recruiting on-campus	120	Finance	18: $65,000
% grads employed immediately	53	Marketing	27: $64,000
Average starting salary	$70,000	MIS	4: $72,000
		Operations	3: $67,000
		Consulting	20: $82,000
		Entrepreneurship	3: NR
		General Management	6: $68,000
		Other	4: NR

UNIVERSITY OF CALIFORNIA—LOS ANGELES
UCLA ANDERSON SCHOOL OF MANAGEMENT

Academics

Students suggest that a good slogan for the UCLA Anderson School of Management might be "excellence without attitude." One student continues the compliment saying, "This school is gold! Students are motivated but not overly competitive. No one's going to rip pages out of books in the library." Anderson's students are crazy about their professors, describing them as "understanding, tremendous, top-notch, [and] distinguished." Most everyone at Anderson, even the occasional administrator, exhibits a "free thinking, entrepreneurial spirit," and students assure that "backstabbers need not apply."

Academics, as one might expect, are "rigorous but fully engaging." And because Anderson is "run by the students, attendees are afforded opportunities to put their skills to work." Many say that, due to its Los Angeles location, MBAs who are "interested in entertainment or entrepreneurship in particular, I can't think of a better place to be."

The academic schedule consists of the five-day "Leadership Foundation" course which initiates the program, the management core (10 classes), and electives, which make up over half of the MBA curriculum. The management core, in which students are divided into cohorts of 65 students, "grounds students in business fundamentals and prepares them for advanced study in areas of their own choosing." Students say the "core teachers are all extremely interesting and cover a lot of material quickly." The broad array of electives, on the other hand, affords students enormous flexibility in designing their own curriculum.

Special aspects of the school include the eight-unit "Management Field Study." In the second year, small field teams of students conduct a six-month investigation on a major strategic consulting project. Field study programs are designed to expand "students' capacity to solve complex business problems in real-world settings." Students say, "The field study program gives students real-life consulting experience working with world-class companies." Another such program is the Advanced International Management program (AIM), in which students tailor their own programs by selecting courses from among many international opportunities at UCLA and UCLA Anderson. Students who opt to participate in AIM work on research with UCLA Anderson's international faculty and interact with business and governmental leaders from around the world.

Students at UCLA Anderson also face an unusually broad selection of joint-degree options (nine in all): MBA/JD, MBA/MD, MBA/master of computer science, MBA/master of Latin American studies, MBA/master of library and information science, MBA/master of nursing, MBA/master of public health, MBA/master of public policy and an MBA/master of urban planning. Because of the broad range of options and the flexibility inherent in the program, students feel confident in the school's "ability to create leaders through teaching and experiential learning."

Students report relatively few complaints, though some wish for "a greater emphasis on life sciences, both in terms of course offerings and career-planning opportunities." And others worry that the entrepreneurial spirit affects the relations with recruiters. "Anderson gets dinged for poor relations because a lot of students start their own businesses."

Career and Placement

UCLA Anderson students are in the fortunate position of being able to draw upon an alumni network that includes more than 33,000 "corporate executives, entrepreneurs, consultants, film producers, high tech innovators, financiers, and other professionals" in

LINDA BALDWIN, DIRECTOR OF ADMISSIONS
110 WESTWOOD PLAZA, GOLD HALL, SUITE B201, LOS ANGELES, CA 90095-1481 U.S.
PHONE: 310-825-6944 • FAX: 310-825-8582
E-MAIL: MBA.ADMISSIONS@ANDERSON.UCLA.EDU • WEBSITE: WWW.ANDERSON.UCLA.EDU

50 states and 80 countries. Students say, "The school makes good use of its alumni network and the diverse industries in the Los Angeles area." They also really appreciate "the support from everyone, especially the Career Center. They are really making a grand effort to help us find direction and jobs, of course!"

Top recruiters at UCLA Anderson over the past two years include A.T. Kearney, Inc.; Bear, Deutsche Bank; Goldman Sachs; Lehman Brothers; Morgan Stanley; Stearns and Co., Inc.; and Twentieth Century Fox, among many others.

Student Life and Environment

When imagining life at UCLA Anderson, one student asks you to picture this: "The sun is shining. You stop by In-N-Out for a burger, animal-style, and you're on your way to mingle with the entertainment industry's top executives. Life is good." At UCLA Anderson, you can expect a "healthy mix of Hollywood glamour, fashion, and parties." Students boast of a rigorous social schedule including "Lit Club (a bar event featuring tongue-in-cheek 'readings' by students) on Wednesday nights, beer busts on Thursday afternoons, and surfing, barbecues, golf, and tailgating at football games on the weekends."

Students occasionally complain that their fellow MBAs are "very friendly but way too focused on alcohol. There are very few other social types of events." Still, even for those to whom this lifestyle does not appeal, there's always the "perfect weather, [the] beautiful campus and city, [and of course] top-notch academics" to keep you occupied. The size of the program leaves some people wishing they had more contact with school administrators and "closer relationships between faculty and students." And almost all point out that living in LA is expensive—both in terms of housing and basic amenities. But "that's out of the hands of the school," say the students, who also repeatedly point out that "Los Angeles has something for everyone."

Admissions

UCLA Anderson receives approximately 3,500 applications every year. Of these, only about 330 students actually enter the school. There is no minimum GMAT or GPA, but they do tend to be high. The mean GMAT was 705, and the 80 percent range was 650 to 730. The mean GPA was 3.6, and the middle 80 percent range was 3.2 to 3.9. Nor does Anderson have a minimum TOEFL score, but they say "few applicants have been admitted with a score below 260." The average number of years of work experience for the entering class of 2005 was a little over four years. Fellowship support is offered to "exceptional admitted students," and about 20 percent of the incoming class received some sort of fellowship.

FINANCIAL FACTS

Annual tuition (in-state/out-of-state)	$23,516/$33,829
Books and supplies	$5,900
Room & board	$12,084
% of students receiving aid	80
% of first-year students receiving aid	60
% of students receiving loans	75
% of students receiving grants	35
Average award package	$34,400
Average grant	$5,000
Average student loan debt	$62,000

ADMISSIONS

Admissions Selectivity Rating	97
# of applications received	2941
% applicants accepted	100
% acceptees attending	11
Average GMAT	710
Range of GMAT	650-750
Average GPA	3.6
TOEFL Required of International Students?	Yes
Minimum TOEFL (paper/computer)	600/260
Application fee	$175
International application fee	$175
Regular application deadline	4/18
Regular notification	6/23
Application Deadline/Notification	
Round 1:	11/3 / 1/19
Round 2:	1/5 / 3/25
Round 3:	2/2 / 5/20
Round 4:	4/18 / 6/23
Early decision program?	Yes
ED Deadline/Notification	11/5 / 1/21
Deferment Available?	Yes
Maximum length of deferment	case by case basis
Need-blind admissions?	Yes

APPLICANTS ALSO LOOK AT

Duke University, Harvard University, Northwestern University, Stanford University, University of California—Berkeley, University of Pennsylvania.

Career Rating	96	Grads employed by field	%: avg. salary
Placement rate (%)	91	Finance	43: $85,000
# of companies recruiting on-campus	200	Marketing	20: $82,500
% grads employed immediately	88	Operations	3: $75,000
Average starting salary	$87,022	Strategic Planning	4: $85,000
		Consulting	15: $100,000
		Entrepreneurship	2: $100,000
		General Management	5: $85,000
		Other	8: $84,000

UNIVERSITY OF CALIFORNIA—RIVERSIDE
A. GARY ANDERSON GRADUATE SCHOOL OF MANAGEMENT

GENERAL INFORMATION
Type of school	public
Environment	city
Academic calendar	quarter

SURVEY SAYS...
Friendly students
Happy students
Smart classrooms
Solid preparation in:
Accounting
General management
Teamwork
Presentation skills

STUDENTS
Enrollment of parent institution	17,000
Enrollment of MBA program	101
% male/female	34/66
% out-of-state	5
% part-time	10
% minorities	26
% international	55
Average age at entry	26
Average years work experience at entry	2.5

ACADEMICS
Academic Experience Rating	**71**
Student/faculty ratio	15:1
Profs interesting rating	70
Profs accessible rating	70
% female faculty	23
% minority faculty	43

Academics

It may be in part due to the sunny California weather, but students at the A. Gary Anderson Graduate School of Management at UC Riverside are almost nauseatingly enthusiastic about their program. As one student raves, "I am at a fantastic school, and I am having the time of my life. I feel very privileged to be here. As a returning student, having been out in the workforce for some time, this experience is doubly beneficial to me. The rigorous curriculum, the superb professors—what a gift they are!" Students appreciate the fact that "professors are all very accessible, both inside and outside of the classroom." One student says, "[The professors] make an effort to get to know everyone's name, so that you're not just a face in the crowd." And several shy students are enthusiastic about the way the program has "improved [their] professional skills, especially in interpersonal communication, teamwork, and presentational skills."

The six components of an MBA from AGSM are the core courses, an internship, the communication workshop, the electives, "capstone course," and a case project or thesis. Though the core courses take up more time than any other single component, students are most enthusiastic about the wide variety of electives, which are all seminar size and designed to "encourage participative learning." As one student says, the program offers a very "wide diversity of elective courses, and it's very easy to get into any course." There are 11 areas of electives, and students are allowed to take up to 9 electives from any area. These areas are accounting, corporate environmental management, entrepreneurial management, finance, general management, human-resources management/organizational behavior, international management, management information systems, management science, marketing, and production and operations management.

In regard to the teaching style, most students agree that "discussion is greatly encouraged. A lot of courses require presentation with business formal attire; some courses even require group debate." One student notes, "It gives you some pressure, but it's fun." However, others are sorry to point out that "it is a research-oriented university and feel [that they] are not getting attention from some professors. There are one or two professors who [have tenure] and are good at research. Their teaching is very bad, and they don't care about students learning; the university doesn't do anything about them." Other students complain that because "the tuition is very high and is still increasing. Students need to have professors who teach well and care about students, not just good researchers and paper-publishers."

Career and Placement

Aside from recent budget cuts, the thing that has most students at AGSM up in arms about is the career-resources center. As one student says, "The school desperately needs a stronger career-counseling center designed just for the MBA students." And students consider career services, "job placement for MBA graduates, and internships" among the school's greatest failings, although the recent addition of a full-time career services coordinator should help to alleviate these problems. They'd also like to see AGSM work on "improving on-campus recruiting and relationship with alumni," and "community relations and professional networking."

Lori Muramoto, Director of MBA Recruiting & Alumni Relations
Anderson Hall 133, University of California—Riverside, Riverside, CA 92521-0203 U.S.
Phone: 951-827-7060 • Fax: 951-827-3970
E-mail: lorim@ucr.edu • Website: www.agsm.ucr.edu

Student Life and Environment

Lovely Riverside, California, is home to not only UC—Riverside, but also three other colleges or universities. Students at AGSM will never have to look far to find like-minded compatriots. And between exams and case studies, there is always something to do. A guide compiled by a group of students from the different schools says, "Riverside has plenty of unique hangouts, interesting shopping, and a wide variety of eats to fit anyone's desires (and budget)." Whatever you're looking for, from "a night out on the town or just a good place to go hiking," Riverside has it. As one student says, "Although I am busy with school, I always have time to mingle with my classmates and outside friends." Another student adds, "Most students go to a local lounge on Thursday nights to listen to a fellow MBA student play bass in a band. We have a great social circle!"

The school itself is housed in a 30,000-square-foot building that features "state-of-the-art research and teaching facilities." MBA students agree that their "computer lab is very nice," but complain that "the undergraduate business majors have the better systems." Other students gripe that they're stuck in "a small building that consists of one lecture room and one classroom. Our school has suffered greatly from the previous budget cuts." Still, the building must have something going for it because "MBA students rarely venture onto the main campus at [UC—Riverside], unless it's to go to the library or bookstore."

Students agree that it is worth venturing out to UC—Riverside library. It is home to "more than two million bound volumes; 13,000 serials; and 1.6 million microforms, including extensive literature in the management field." This superb research library "provides substantial support for student and faculty research."

Admissions

At AGSM, students from all undergraduate majors and levels of business experience are eligible for admission. In fact, more than 30 percent of all incoming students come from a background other than business, including social sciences, math, engineering, physical and natural sciences, humanities, and languages. According to the school, "There is no minimum GPA or GMAT requirement for MBA admission consideration. However, please consider that the average GPA for new students admitted for the fall 2004 quarter was 3.41, and the average GMAT score was 583." AGSM does not require prior work experience for its MBA students (though it is, of course, encouraged) and feels that a diverse student body can only add to the learning experience. However, because they don't require prior work experience, they do require that all prospective MBAs complete an internship "to ensure your success upon graduation."

FINANCIAL FACTS

Annual tuition (in-state/out-of-state)	$0/$12,246
Fees	$21,203
Books and supplies	$1,350
Room & board	$10,105
Average grant	$13,860

ADMISSIONS

Admissions Selectivity Rating	83
# of applications received	229
% applicants accepted	48
% acceptees attending	31
Average GMAT	583
Range of GMAT	540-640
Average GPA	3.4
TOEFL Required of International Students?	Yes
Minimum TOEFL (paper/computer)	550/213
Application fee	$60
International application fee	$60
Regular application deadline	7/1
Regular notification	8/1
Transfer students accepted?	Yes
Transfer application policy: A maximum of 2 graduate courses taken in residence may be transferred.	
Non-fall admissions?	Yes
Need-blind admissions?	Yes

APPLICANTS ALSO LOOK AT

California State Polytechnic University Pomona, Pepperdine University, University of California—Irvine, University of California—San Diego, University of California—Los Angeles.

UNIVERSITY OF CENTRAL ARKANSAS
COLLEGE OF BUSINESS ADMINISTRATION

GENERAL INFORMATION

Type of school	public
Environment	rural
Academic calendar	semester

SURVEY SAYS...

Friendly students
Happy students
Smart classrooms
Solid preparation in:
Finance
Teamwork
Presentation skills

STUDENTS

Enrollment of parent	
institution	10,000
Enrollment of MBA program	196
% male/female	50/50
% part-time	66
% minorities	6
% international	12
Average age at entry	23

ACADEMICS

Academic Experience Rating	**63**
Student/faculty ratio	20:1
Profs interesting rating	66
Profs accessible rating	61
% female faculty	25
% minority faculty	12.5

Joint Degrees

MBA/IMBA

Academics

Affordability, location, the flexibility of the program, and the opportunity to complete a degree in one year are the primary reasons students choose one of the MBA programs at the University of Central Arkansas. UCA offers both a standard MBA and an International MBA. A Pre-MBA Program Certificate Program is also available for students who lack the necessary related undergraduate coursework.

UCA's conventional MBA requires 30 credit hours, making it possible for full-time students to complete the program in one year. The program is comprised of 10 three-credit classes offered in the afternoons and evenings. Courses cover information systems, accounting, managerial economics, communication, financial decision making, business law, entrepreneurship, marketing, and strategic management. The program concludes with an integrative class. Elective and specialization options are not available.

The International MBA program requires 36 credit hours, meaning that it, too, can be completed in one year by full-time students. The program is comprised of 12 three-credit classes offered in the afternoons and evenings. Courses cover information systems, accounting, managerial economics, financial decision making, business law, global entrepreneurship, marketing, international strategic management, and multicultural communications. In addition, students must take an integrative capstone class and two graduate-level electives in business, international culture, or foreign language. Students may complete an internship with a global company in lieu of the two electives.

Students wishing to receive an MBA but who lack the necessary undergraduate coursework in business may complete that coursework through the Pre-MBA Program Certificate Program. Applicants to the program must meet the same requirements as applicants to the MBA program; completion of the Pre-MBA Program does not guarantee admission to the MBA program. The program consists of six courses covering basic concepts in accounting, economics, finance, management, marketing, and quantitative analysis.

Professors get mixed reviews here. More than one respondent points out, "We have some very good professors, but some are unorganized and have a hard time communicating their subjects to students."

Career and Placement

Because UCA's MBA program is so small and many of the students are part-timers who already have jobs, the school offers few career and placement services directed exclusively to MBAs. Still, several students express a desire for better relations with local companies and overall "better job placement." Students may use the Career Services Office, which serves the entire university; the office provides counseling, training, mock interviews, workshops, access to online job databases, and school-wide career fairs and other recruiting events. Only a handful of employers visit campus each year for the express purpose of recruiting MBAs. Employers most likely to hire UCA MBAs include Acxiom, ALLTEL, Entergy, First Security Bank, and Kimberly-Clark.

REBECCA GATLIN-WATTS, MBA DIRECTOR
BURDICK BUSINESS BUILDING, ROOM 224, CONWAY, AR 72035 UNITED STATES
PHONE: 501-450-5316 • FAX: 501-450-5302
E-MAIL: MBA@UCA.EDU • WEBSITE: WWW.BUSINESS.UCA.EDU

Student Life and Environment

The University of Central Arkansas is located in Conway, one of the state's fastest growing cities. The city is home to a number of industries, including Kimberly Clark, AmTran, Virco, and Baldwin Piano. Database magnate Acxiom makes its headquarters in Conway. A number of government headquarters are located in Conway as well. Besides UCA, the city is also home to Hendrix College and Central Baptist College.

The UCA campus is "a unique mix of Georgian-style architecture and up-to-date technology," according to the school's view book. The school has a long and proud tradition in intercollegiate athletics—Scotty Pippin played his college ball here—and the school's 10,000+ students regularly turn out to cheer on their Bears and Sugar Bears. The MBA program is located in the Burdick Business Administration Building, which was built in 1973.

Because of the International MBA program, the student body here includes "fairly diverse nationalities, which is good." Not so good is the fact that "many American students seem to have come directly from undergraduate programs" and thus lack the practical business experience necessary to contribute meaningfully to classroom discussion.

Admissions

All applicants to the MBA program at UCA must have earned an undergraduate degree from an accredited US institution or its overseas equivalent, with a minimum GPA of 2.7, or a minimum GPA of 3.0 for the final 60 hours of undergraduate study. Applicants must also submit official GMAT scores; the admissions committee requires a minimum GMAT score of 450 from all applicants. UCA uses formulas to create minimum cut-offs for applicants. Applicants must have a minimum formula index of 1000 under the formula [(undergraduate GPA × 200) + GMAT score], or a minimum formula index of 1050 under the formula [(undergraduate GPA for the final 60 hours of study × 200) + GMAT score]. International applicants whose first language is not English must also submit TOEFL scores.

FINANCIAL FACTS

Annual tuition (in-state/out-of-state)	$3,778/$7,054
Books and supplies	$1,500
Room & board	$6,000

ADMISSIONS

Admissions Selectivity Rating	77
# of applications received	45
% applicants accepted	76
% acceptees attending	96
Average GMAT	494
Average GPA	3.4
TOEFL Required of International Students?	Yes
Minimum TOEFL (paper/computer)	550/213
Application fee	$25
International application fee	$40
Regular application deadline	Rolling
Regular notification	Rolling
Deferment Available?	Yes
Maximum length of deferment	text marker
Transfer students accepted?	Yes
Transfer application policy: A maximum of 6 graduate hours is transferrable from a AACSB institution.	
Non-fall admissions?	Yes

EMPLOYMENT PROFILE

Career Rating	60*
Placement rate (%)	85
# of companies recruiting on-campus	71
% grads employed immediately	70
Average starting salary	$35,000

UNIVERSITY OF CENTRAL FLORIDA
COLLEGE OF BUSINESS ADMINISTRATION

GENERAL INFORMATION
Type of school   public
Environment   city
Academic calendar   semester

SURVEY SAYS...
Students love Orlando, FL
Friendly students
Smart classrooms
Solid preparation in:
Teamwork

STUDENTS
Enrollment of parent
  institution   42,837
Enrollment of MBA program   490
% male/female   58/42
% out-of-state   13
% part-time   69
% minorities   4
% international   19
Average age at entry   28
Average years work experience
  at entry   8

ACADEMICS
Academic Experience Rating   70
Student/faculty ratio   35:1
Profs interesting rating   62
Profs accessible rating   63
% female faculty   9
% minority faculty   3
Joint Degrees
MBA/Sport Business Management
(21 months)

Academics

Students pursing an MBA at the University of Central Florida have three options: the traditional MBA, a part-time evening program designed for working professionals; the full-time one-year MBA, a daytime program for freshly minted BAs as well as mid-career professionals looking to jumpstart their careers; and an Executive MBA, designed for current executives and managers. The school also offers an MA in applied economics and MS degrees in accounting, taxation, human resources, change management, information systems, and sports business management.

UCF offers concentrations in accounting, economics, finance, entrepreneurship, environmental management and policy, human resources and change management, international business, and management information systems. Both the full-time and part-time MBA programs require between 39 and 51 course hours, depending on one's undergraduate background in business. The school reports that its greatest strengths lie in applied economics, environmental economics, MIS, hi-tech marketing, and entrepreneurship. In addition, students appreciate "the school's focus on technology, which gives it a leg up over more traditional institutions," as well as the program's "strong emphasis on leadership, integrity, academia, and community involvement."

Students interested in the popular Sports Business Management Track must apply for separate admission to the Master in Sports Business Management Program. The program, which awards an MBA as well as the master's degree, requires a 10-week internship.

While students love both the cost and convenience of UCF's graduate business programs, they tell us that the programs are not without their faults. Some complain that "electives aren't clearly laid out, and many of the classes aren't focused enough, making them a repeat of undergraduate business courses." Just as many believe that "the school has more research-oriented teachers than teachers who can actually teach," and that too many profs "lack real-world experience. They are so focused on theory that they do not focus enough on practice." On the other hand, others point out that "professors are generally very experienced in their fields and have a great deal of related knowledge to share."

Career and Placement

UCF's Career Resource Center operates a satellite office at the College of Business Administration to serve business graduates and undergraduates. The office includes a Career Information Library stocked with job binders, salary surveys, employer databases, and other reading materials. Workshops are offered in resume writing, job search strategies, interviewing techniques, and federal employment opportunities. Students have free access to MonsterTrak during their tenure at the school and for one semester following graduation.

Employers who most frequently hire UCF MBAs include AmSouth Bank, Darden, SunTrust, CitiBank, Coca Cola Bottling Company, Disney, Aventis, Cendant, Dynetech, IRS, Intersil, and Marriott Vacation Clubs.

JUDY RYDER, DIRECTOR OF GRADUATE ADMISSIONS
PO BOX 161400, BA I, ROOM 240, ORLANDO, FL 32816 UNITED STATES
PHONE: 407-823-2412 • FAX: 407-823-0219
E-MAIL: CBAGRAD@BUS.UCF.EDU • WEBSITE: WWW.BUS.UCF.EDU

Student Life and Environment

Students in UCF's traditional MBA program attend classes in the evenings, as most are working during the day. These students typically "go to classes and then leave" without participating in the university's extracurricular life. Students in the one-year full-time program, on the other hand, do immerse themselves in the UCF environment. One writes, "You could actually live your whole life on campus—it is almost its own town! We have absolutely everything so you don't even need a car! The gym is spectacular, the food selection is extensive, and there are hundreds of clubs doing great things in the community as well as encouraging students to network." Facilities are equally edifying; one MBA observes, "There are computers everywhere. The dorms are very nice and clean, most even have individual bedrooms and common rooms with kitchens." Everyone here appreciates that "the environment is relatively safe. The campus is well-lit at night and there is a free escort service anywhere on campus if you don't want to walk alone."

Students love Orlando, "a city known throughout the world and one that everyone would like to visit at some point in their lives." The city is an excellent resource for students seeking internships and post-degree jobs. The campus is located "on the outskirts of the city," which some feel is a "great location." Others complain that "it is difficult to access the campus from downtown Orlando. Drive time is between 40 minutes and one hour."

The UCF College of Business Administration attracts "mostly younger professionals or those who are recent graduates and are looking to get a start in a career field," along with "some older students with families and long-time careers. Many students are married." They tend to be "warm and cordial, competitive, yet also good team players who are willing to help others in need." Some feel that "many of the non-business students in the MBA program seem to lag behind, dragging classes to a lower level. More stringent requirements should be implemented for acceptance into the MBA program, possibly including prior business experience."

Admissions

Applicants to the UCF College of Business MBA program must complete an online application to the UCF School of Graduate Studies. Additionally, applicants must submit official transcripts for each university or college attended, an official GMAT score, a personal essay, a resume, and three letters of recommendation. International students whose first language is not English must also submit TOEFL scores. All international students need to provide translations of non-English documents and an accredited course-by-course evaluation of transcripts from institutions that do not employ the American system. UCF requires a minimum GMAT score of 540 (550 for the one-year full-time program) for its MBA programs; requirements for other master's programs are less restrictive. An undergraduate GPA of at least 3.0 is also required.

FINANCIAL FACTS

Annual tuition (in-state/out-of-state)	$5,520/$20,880
Fees (in-state/out-of-state)	$250/$350
Books and supplies	$1,800
Room & board	$10,000
% of students receiving grants	10
Average grant	$10,000

ADMISSIONS

Admissions Selectivity Rating	77
# of applications received	258
% applicants accepted	71
% acceptees attending	77
Average GMAT	558
Range of GMAT	510-660
Average GPA	3.3
TOEFL Required of International Students?	Yes
Minimum TOEFL (paper/computer)	575/233
Application fee	$30
International application fee	$30
Regular application deadline	6/15
Regular notification	Rolling
Early decision program?	Yes
ED Deadline/Notification	Fall Only: 4/15 / 6/15
Transfer students accepted?	Yes
Transfer application policy: Transfer applicants must be from a regionally or nationally accredited university.	
Non-fall admissions?	Yes
Need-blind admissions?	Yes

APPLICANTS ALSO LOOK AT

Florida State University, Rollins College, University of Florida, University of South Florida.

EMPLOYMENT PROFILE

Career Rating	81	**Grads employed by field %: avg. salary**	
Placement rate (%)	98	General Management	98: $61,556
% grads employed immediately	98		
Average starting salary	$61,556		

UNIVERSITY OF CHICAGO
GRADUATE SCHOOL OF BUSINESS

Academics

Established in 1898, the University of Chicago's GSB is the second-oldest program in the country. This means, as the students will tell you, that the school has had over a hundred years to perfect its craft. Students tout the impressive qualifications of their teachers: "Professors are Jedi-smart and are passionate about their work. Each [professor] is here because they know that working here exposes them to: the best and the brightest." The word "Nobel" comes up a lot, too—as in, "my faculty advisor is a Nobel laureate." Other students admit that, while "it is daunting to study finance theory at the school where a lot of the theory originated," the "challenge is quite stimulating." However, a few specific departments shine more than others; GSB students say without qualms that their "finance, accounting, entrepreneurship, and marketing are at or near the top across business schools." The one drawback to having the very best in academia at your doorstep is that "most faculty have very limited business experience, so they can teach only the theory and not the practice of business." One student explains, "By far the best courses I have taken are entrepreneurship classes, which are taught by practitioners."

Though the academic program is "intense," students say it's not because of pressures in the program. They explain that it's "because the students are inherently competitive. Grade nondisclosure works very well in increasing the friendliness among students."

Compared to most full-time MBA programs, Chicago's list of requirements is amazingly flexible, and the choice of electives they offer is enormous. Among the few required courses is LEAD (Leadership Effectiveness and Development), which first-year students take as part of a cohort to develop professional personal skills. LEAD is popular and acknowledged as a valuable resource, but some students say that it "could use some revisions. It is a great idea to teach management, negotiation, ethics, and public speaking in the LEAD program, but the modules are not as effective as it could be. The examples used in class are sometimes not relevant, and students don't get as much out of the exercises as they should."

Of the 11 electives, students have the option to take 6 with other departments. This means that, according to the school, GSB students are able to "study with some of the world's most renowned scholars in economics, law, languages, philosophy, or literature." Students appreciate that the curriculum is "flexible enough that students can tailor it to their every need." Students also report that "the flexible curriculum offered at the GSB is one of the [university's] greatest strengths. Recruiters tell us how much more prepared we are for finance internships because we can choose [the] courses we want to take during the first year."

Full-time MBAs can also choose to pursue the international MBA degree. To do this, students must master a foreign language, complete a rigorous course of studies in international business, and study abroad. An internship abroad doesn't hurt either. Joint degrees with other schools within the University of Chicago include an MBA/JD, and MBA/MD, and MBA/master's of public policy studies (MPP), and an MBA/master's of social services administration (AM).

While most students readily applaud the rigor of the academic program, they often wish for diversity, both in the student body and in job opportunities. They would like the GSB to "offer a better mix of different types of marketing, so marketing grads could walk out [of the program] equal to peers at other schools." Other students add that they wish the school "would make more of an effort to develop East Coast career opportunities."

ROSEMARIA MARTINELLI, ASSOCIATE DEAN FOR STUDENT RECRUITMENT & ADMISSION
5807 SOUTH WOODLAWN AVENUE CHICAGO, IL 60637 UNITED STATES
PHONE: 773-702-7369 • FAX: 773-702-9085
E-MAIL: ADMISSIONS@CHICAGOGSB.EDU • WEBSITE: WWW.CHICAGOGSB.EDU

Career and Placement

Students have nothing but good things to say about the university's 37,000 alumni. "They're great—perhaps not as proactive as those that cheerlead at other schools, but they are very excited to help and build presence at their firms." Another student points out that Chicago is "one of only a few schools to have been at the top for nearly 100 years, so there is an amazing, deep alumni network of professionals at all levels, especially in finance and general management."

Even without the help of alumni, graduates find jobs and are well-placed in their field. The career services center reports that school-facilitated sources accounted for about 80 percent of all hires for their classes. And three months after graduation, 87 percent of graduates in 2003 had job offers, compared with 82 percent for the class of 2002. The economy was less harsh for the intern class; 99 percent of students who sought an internship in the class of 2004 accepted an offer. Companies that recruit on-campus include Bear Stearns, Goldman Sachs, Merrill Lynch, and McKinsey & Company. Because the career office is so helpful, some students have gone so far as to say that "the office of career services is almost too much of a resource." One student comments, "I think the wealth of materials available to us could be presented in more concise ways in order to free up our schedules a little."

Student Life and Environment

With a brand new $125 million Hyde Park Center, just a few minutes by train from downtown Chicago, and a handful of blocks from Lake Michigan, "life on campus is relaxed. It is like living in a small village 10 miles from downtown. You can choose when [to] go little and when [to] go big," according to students. Many students live in other Chicago neighborhoods and commute to school; other students complain that "many members of the class have lived in Chicago and [already] have friends in the city, so integrating into the GSB community is not as important to [them]."

Though the neighborhood around Hyde Park is sometimes considered dangerous, students say that "the University of Chicago is striving mightily to improve the surrounding neighborhood. There are areas adjacent to campus that are beautiful and expensive to live in and unfortunately there are areas nearby that are traditionally tough neighborhoods."

Admissions

Of approximately 3,400 applicants who apply to Chicago GSB every year, only about 800 are admitted and 520 enroll. Approximately 26 percent are international, and about 70 percent are male. All of those admitted have at least some full-time work experience, and their average age is 28. The average GMAT score is 689 (though the median is 700), and the average undergraduate GPA is 3.4. Many students appreciate that, unlike some other universities, the University of Chicago is "one of the few top schools that gives scholarships. About 25 percent of [those admitted] received some form of scholarship."

FINANCIAL FACTS

Annual tuition	$36,520
Fees	$555
Books and supplies	$1,650
Room & board	$17,100
% of students receiving aid	75
% of first-year students receiving aid	75
% of students receiving loans	70
% of students receiving grants	16
Average award package	$55,000
Average grant	$21,000
Average student loan debt	$85,000

ADMISSIONS

Admissions Selectivity Rating 60*

Average GMAT	695
Range of GMAT	640-750
Average GPA	3.4
TOEFL Required of International Students?	Yes
Minimum TOEFL (paper/computer)	600/250
Application fee	$200
International application fee	$200
Deferment Available?	Yes
Maximum length of deferment	1 year
Need-blind admissions?	Yes

EMPLOYMENT PROFILE			
Career Rating	96	**Grads employed by field**	**%: avg. salary**
Placement rate (%)	88	Finance	59: $87,975
% grads employed immediately	78	Marketing	10: $84,717
Average starting salary	$90,121	Consulting	22: $99,213
		General Management	3: $90,572
		Other	5: $84,010

UNIVERSITY OF CINCINNATI
COLLEGE OF BUSINESS

Academics

Future MBAs may choose from multiple options at the University of Cincinnati's College of Business. For full-timers in a hurry, UC offers a full-time 12-month MBA; a 15-month degree that packs the coursework just as tightly but adds a three-month internship; and a 21-month degree that, along with a three-month internship, combines an MBA and MS for those "seeking a high degree of rigorous specialization in addition to an applied general management education." UC's full-time programs take advantage of their ability to sequence classes, allowing advanced classes to build on concepts taught in previous classes.

UC also offers part-time options at a variety of sites, including the Clifton Campus, the Blue Ash Professional Development Center (both evening programs) and Wright Patterson Air Force Base (a mid-afternoon program). The part-time program is by necessity more flexible than its full-time counterpart, but is otherwise similar, employing the same professors and providing the same support services. In both the full-time and part-time programs, concentrations are available in construction management, finance, information systems, international business, management, marketing, operations management, quantitative analysis, and commercial real estate.

The UC MBA program stresses teamwork, which students appreciate. One writes, "The team structure that is fostered from day one is instrumental in making our program unique and successful. The teams are organized in such a way that no one gets left behind. There is almost an imperative that everyone graduates; an instilled sense of community and support, which has been so refreshing. Coming from Procter & Gamble, I recognize the necessity of teaching a team-based structure. It's remarkable." The small size of the program "means students get a lot of attention, something you can never have too much of." However, for many, "the greatest strength of UC is its focus on global business. The College of Business stresses to every student the need to look at business from a global perspective. There are study-abroad opportunities. There are also many foreign students in class with us to give us a different viewpoint of a situation." Offerings in quantitative analysis and commercial real estate also receive high marks.

Career and Placement

Students tell us that "the MBA Career Office puts extensive effort into assuring us that we have the tools to find a job and brings in various employers for recruiting activities." The office's efforts include one-on-one counseling meetings; career development workshops; career days; online recruiting and contact databases; videotaped mock interviews; and on-campus recruiting events.

Employers most likely to hire UC MBAs include Fifth Third Bank, Deloitte, P & G (Procter & Gamble), The ARS Group, Toyota Motor Manufacturing, L'Oreal, Cincinnati Bell, Sara Lee, Cintas, Eli Lilly and Company, Burke, Inc., Steak 'n Shake, and Charter Consulting.

VALERIE O. ROBINSON, ASSOCIATE DIRECTOR, MBA ADMISSIONS
CARL H. LINDNER HALL, SUITE 103, PO BOX 210020, CINCINNATI, OH 45221-0020 U.S.
PHONE: 513-556-7020 • FAX: 513-558-7006
E-MAIL: GRADUATE@UC.EDU • WEBSITE: WWW.BUSINESS.UC.EDU/MBA

Student Life and Environment

The "driven and intelligent" MBAs at UC enjoy a "diverse mix" that includes a one-quarter international population, a range of experience levels ("we have students right out of undergraduate schools, as well as students well into their careers"), and backgrounds ("a lot of the students are engineering undergrads looking to utilize an MBA for the opportunity of advancement in the engineering field; most others are business undergrads looking for career advancement"). The program has an unusually even gender split as well. One student sums up, "UC doesn't recruit a specific mold of what is perceived as 'the MBA Student.' They recruit a diverse mix that makes the experience surprisingly worldly in decidedly Midwestern Cincinnati." The mix "adds a lot of value to the classes."

"The majority of students are commuters" in the UC MBA program, "and it is challenging to have graduate students involved in on-campus activities. We do enjoy the academic strength and fellow classmates, but not all of us feel fully integrated into the campus." The opportunities are there, though, and full-time students generally take advantage of them, reporting that "the administration is focused on activities and connecting students to the university and community. We have weekly networking dinners or happy hours with people from General Electric, Procter & Gamble, and Cincinnati Bell. The MBA Association has been active in organizing social activities for students as well." In addition, "we have a lot of free lunches associated with training sessions and academic and career development sessions. They are wonderful. And we have all kinds of recreational facilities and free movies to broaden our view of the world." UC's men's basketball team is "amazing, and everyone rallies around it. As one student puts it, "For being a mostly commuter campus, there are plenty of opportunities to get involved on campus."

Admissions

Applicants to the UC MBA program must submit an official GMAT score report, official copies of all post-secondary academic transcripts, two essays, two letters of recommendation, a resume, and a completed application form. Applicants need not have earned undergraduate degrees in business; in fact, only half the students here have. The rest are primarily split among engineering and liberal arts majors, with a few science majors thrown in to the mix. Completion of a college-level calculus course is required of all applicants. International applicants must also submit results for the TOEFL exam and certification of finances. In an effort to increase the population of underrepresented students, "UC offers the Albert C. Yates Scholarships and Fellowships to candidates from underrepresented groups. The scholarships cover full tuition and fees and the fellowship additionally provides a stipend each quarter."

FINANCIAL FACTS

Annual tuition (in-state/out-of-state)	$19,184/$24,188
Fees	$1,900
Books and supplies	$3,300
Room & board (on/off-campus)	$13,000/$14,500
% of students receiving aid	86
% of first-year students receiving aid	86
% of students receiving loans	40
% of students receiving grants	69
Average award package	$21,347
Average grant	$17,957

ADMISSIONS

Admissions Selectivity Rating	78
# of applications received	205
% applicants accepted	73
% acceptees attending	60
Average GMAT	586
Range of GMAT	540-640
Average GPA	3.3
TOEFL Required of International Students?	Yes
Minimum TOEFL (paper/computer)	600/250
Application fee	$40
International application fee	$40
Regular application deadline	4/30
Regular notification	Rolling
Early decision program?	Yes
ED Deadline/Notification	Fall, 2/15 / 3/30
Deferment Available?	Yes
Maximum length of deferment	1 year
Transfer students accepted?	Yes
Transfer application policy: Transferring from an AACSB accredited institution, no more than 3 classes	
Non-fall admissions?	Yes
Need-blind admissions?	Yes

APPLICANTS ALSO LOOK AT

Indiana University, Miami University, Northern Kentucky University, The Ohio State University, University of Dayton, Wright State University, Xavier University.

EMPLOYMENT PROFILE

Career Rating	78	Grads employed by field	%: avg. salary
Placement rate (%)	74	Finance	17: $47,700
# of companies recruiting on-campus	10	Marketing	29: $43,071
% grads employed immediately	74	MIS	4: $72,000
Average starting salary	$48,500	Operations	4: $50,000
		Consulting	10: $65,500
		General Management	29: $52,400
		Other	7: $46,000

UNIVERSITY COLLEGE DUBLIN
THE MICHAEL SMURFIT GRADUATE SCHOOL OF BUSINESS

GENERAL INFORMATION
Type of school   public

SURVEY SAYS...
Students love Co. Dublin,
Good social scene
Happy students
Smart classrooms
Solid preparation in:
Finance

STUDENTS
Enrollment of MBA program   330
% male/female   72/37
% part-time   64
% international   45
Average age at entry   30
Average years work experience
  at entry   7

ACADEMICS
Academic Experience Rating   86
Student/faculty ratio   3:1
Profs interesting rating   71
Profs accessible rating   79
Joint Degrees
CEMS Masters (Community of
European Management School): 1
year
Prominent Alumni
Patrick Haren, MBA 1986, Group
Chief Executive, Viridian; Cathal
McGloin, MBA 1992, CEO and
Founder, Perform; JP Donnelly,
MBA 1993, Managing Director,
Ogilvy.

Academics

There are worse ways to spend a year than by getting an MBA in a beautiful, historic city like Dublin, especially when the conferring institution is the well-respected University College Dublin. As Dubliners are well aware, theirs is a city that boasts an appealing blend of commerce, art, and nightlife. Visitors—international business students, for example—may find themselves enthralled by its quaint streets and raucous pubs. On the other hand, they may never find the opportunity to leave the b-school and explore their surroundings. This is one demanding MBA program.

The Smurfit MBA begins with an orientation week, followed by a sequence of nine quant-heavy foundation courses. Corporate and integrative courses, electives, and an applied research project all follow. The program concludes with final examinations. Students warn that "the one-year program is a great test of inner desire to achieve and thrive in a pressure-filled environment." First semester is by far the worst; as one student says, "Semester one in this school is grueling, with very heavy workload and high pressure. It's not as bad, though, for those with a finance background. In semester two, there's more time to actually allow the knowledge to be absorbed." Another MBA agrees, "Second semester is more balanced and sociable than [the] first semester, with the exception that electives run at night and on the weekend, making it less like a full-time course and more like a part-time one!"

MBAs explain that "overall, the greatest strengths of the school [are] the well-developed finance faculty, human-resource faculty, and the team culture that students develop while [at the Smurfit School]. The international business faculty is also great." Smurfit professors are "generally approachable and extremely willing to help out with advice on any quirky idea that emerges," and they "bring together lots of experience and knowledge and, more importantly, a huge amount of enthusiasm that is infectious." Another plus: "Communication facilities, e-mail, Internet, and multimedia facilities are excellent."

Career and Placement

The Career Management Center at the Smurfit School is, according to the school's website, "a full career-guidance service with a comprehensive array of research and online facilities. These include a large bank of data and publications relating to potential employers around the world, as well as reference materials such as guides to psychometric testing, job hunting, or CV preparation." The service also arranges corporate workshops, one-on-one counseling, and seminars covering interviewing, job search, and resume writing. An MBA-dedicated office is located on the Blackrock campus, home to the Smurfit MBA program.

Employers most likely to hire Smurfit MBAs include A&L Goodbody, Citibank, Elan, Eli Lilly, GE, KPMG, and Riverdeed.

FINANCIAL FACTS	
Annual tuition	$33,700

ADMISSIONS	
Admissions Selectivity Rating	88
# of applications received	221
% applicants accepted	48
% acceptees attending	56
Average GMAT	598
Range of GMAT	530-740
Average GPA	3.5
TOEFL Required of International Students?	Yes
Application fee	$55
International application fee	$55
Regular application deadline	3/31
Regular notification	Rolling
Deferment Available?	Yes
Maximum length of deferment	1 year
Non-fall admissions?	Yes
Need-blind admissions?	Yes

Student Life and Environment

"Smurfit totally lives up to the phrase 'work hard, play hard,'" according to MBAs. One student writes, "I have never worked so intensely or socialized as much. There are many different committees [that] all students are encouraged to participate in: Smurfit rugby, networking club, or social committee, just to name a few. It has been a life-altering experience [that] I have thoroughly enjoyed." Another student adds, "I never expected an MBA to be so much fun. Sure, if you want to spend every hour studying, you can find the work, but you will miss out on a vital part of the MBA experience."

Dublin offers plenty of options for students when they need to blow off steam. Students say that its sometimes necessary for the health of the program; one student explains, "One moment you are in a team meeting, fighting over a strategic posture your team needs to take in case review, and you could be sometimes furious at your inability to get your team members to your point of view. But if you seem really furious at the outcome of this meeting, just hold it; it will be time to meet at the pub soon and all that disagreement will be history. The pub seems to be a place to bury most disagreements." The school also offers "a number of balls and networking events during the course of the year. Other formal events occur from time to time, in which guest speakers, normally CEOs of companies like IBM operating in Ireland, come to give lectures and presentations about their company. Their staff [also comes] in order to get some networks running. These are all a good respite from the tough MBA curricula."

Smurfit students evince "diversity in every dimension you can think of: language, nationality, gender, work experience, age, even hair color." MBAs here enjoy an "open, friendly atmosphere" with a collegial vibe; as one student explains, "The program is set up under one roof, which imparts a strong sense of togetherness and focus."

Admissions

The Smurfit admissions office requires applicants to provide all of the following: a completed application form and a photocopy of the completed form; two photographs, passport size; one set of official transcripts for all previous undergraduate work, plus a photocopy of all transcripts; two letters of recommendation; three essays; and a resume/curriculum vitae. Non-native English speakers must take the TOEFL to demonstrate English proficiency.

EMPLOYMENT PROFILE			
Career Rating	85	Grads employed by field %: avg. salary	
% grads employed immediately	99	Accounting	24
Average starting salary	$105,000	Human Resources	2
		Marketing	7
		Operations	17
		Consulting	15
		Entrepreneurship	4
		General Management	17
		Other	5
		Internet/New Media	9

UNIVERSITY OF COLORADO—BOULDER
LEEDS SCHOOL OF BUSINESS

GENERAL INFORMATION
Type of school	public
Environment	city
Academic calendar	semester

SURVEY SAYS...
Students love Boulder, CO
Friendly students
Good social scene
Solid preparation in:
Teamwork
Entrepreneurial studies

STUDENTS
Enrollment of parent institution	29,151
Enrollment of MBA program	179
% male/female	76/24
% out-of-state	48
% part-time	35
% minorities	9
% international	19
Average age at entry	28
Average years work experience at entry	5.22

ACADEMICS
Academic Experience Rating	86
Student/faculty ratio	4:1
Profs interesting rating	881
Profs accessible rating	82
% female faculty	12
% minority faculty	20

Joint Degrees
MBA/JD: 4 yrs.
MBA/MS in Telecommunications and/or Computer Science: 3-3.5 yrs.
MBA/MA in Fine Arts: 3 yrs.
MBA/MA Germanic Languages: 3 yrs.
MBA/MS Environmental Studies: 3 yrs.
MBA/MA in Anthropology: 3 yrs.

Prominent Alumni
Kevin Burns, Managing Principle/Lazard Technology Partners; John Puerner, Pres. & CEO/Los Angeles Times; Patrick Tierney, CEO/Reed Elsevier; Dick Fuld, CEO/ Lehman Brothers; Michael Leeds, Pres. & CEO/Flightstar.

Academics

In 2001, the business school at the University of Colorado—Boulder received a $35 million donation—the country's sixth largest such donation in history—from the Leeds family of Long Island, New York (two of the sons attended the school). The school, originally founded in 1923, was renamed the Leeds School of Business as a result, and students feel confident that the huge influx of money "is working to bring top-tier professors to the university, so quality will continue to improve."

The program is small, with only about 50 students per class, and each class is divided into two cohorts of about 30 students. As a small school, "Leeds has both the advantages (small class size, easy course access, access to professors, access to entrepreneurship and real-estate center staff) and disadvantages (limited course offerings, reduced access to large corporate recruiters) that are part and parcel of the small school experience." But most agree that the small size lends an intimacy and familiarity that will ensure their future success. "The high caliber of students and faculty is rare for a program of this size," says one student. "Definitely a great group of people that don't take themselves too seriously. If you are looking for a group of people who understand [that] life should be balanced (after first semester), you will love it here."

Leeds has only nine required courses and nine electives, and students can choose to take two electives in the spring of the first year. The second year is mainly electives—only two required classes, but the program is very quant-heavy, and students who don't come into the program with a strong background in statistics, college-level algebra, and principles of microeconomics are advised to take college-level courses in these subjects before they enroll. Students say that both the "entrepreneurial course work and real-estate course work are excellent."

Leeds offers more than 25 "career tracks" or sets of electives designed to lead students down specific career paths. Some career paths include "corporate finance, financial consulting, social and ethical venturing, entrepreneurship, real-estate capital markets, marketing management, operations management, and corporate entrepreneurship." When following one of these career paths, students are allowed to enroll in graduate classes in other schools on the university's campus. Dual-degree programs such as an MBA/JD, an MBA/MS in telecommunications or computer science, and an MBA/MA (in anthropology, fine arts, or Germanic languages) are available. And exchange programs are offered at any of the following locations: the ITESM (Monterrey Tec) located in Monterrey, Mexico; and the Instituto de Empresa, located in Madrid, Spain.

Leeds also hosts specialized centers devoted to entrepreneurship, real estate, and financial markets. Students warn, however, that course selection is important: "The professors are a mixed bag. Sometimes you get duds; other times, rock stars." And others amend this by saying, "The majority of professors are very good, but the administration has been unresponsive to students' complaints about the occasional inadequate instructor." Some say that they'd like to see the teaching style change a bit. "The largest flaw in the academics is not the workload, the professors, or the administration, but the classroom style. Even in case studies, there is limited class debate—this is certainly something that must be directly addressed and changed."

Career and Placement

The school only recently appointed someone to the position of Director of Alumni Relations, and so students occasionally complain about the "lack of alumni network." How bad can it be, though, if alumni are donating $35 million to the school? Though students might gripe about the efforts of Career Services, 85 percent of the graduating class of 2002 had found employment within three months of graduation, and the average salary as about $69,000. About 28 percent of students who were hired received a signing bonus, and the average bonus was almost $15,000; 19 percent of the graduates started their own companies, and about 33 percent ended up working for very small companies (between 2 and 50 employees).

Student Life and Environment

Pretty much all Leeds students agree that living in Boulder can't be topped. Ranked "Best Place to Live" by *Money* magazine, Boulder hosts just over 96,000 residents, and yet is home to multiple high-technology businesses, natural beauty, and multiple cultural institutions. Students say "There is no nicer place to be a student than Boulder, Colorado. The campus is beautiful, architecturally significant, and safe. The school is situated in the foothills of the Rocky Mountains, and world-class ski resorts are but an hour away. The social scene and nightlife are fantastic, and Boulder has an eclectic mix of cafes and restaurants." School or student-organized events include "TNO [Thursday Night Out] at a different bar every week, free tailgates before every football game, a night hike/snowshoe/cross-country ski trip every full moon, and an annual retreat that is a traditional highlight of the year. It's never long before the next event, and with our location, the opportunities are virtually endless."

The only problem with life at Leeds, it seems, is the building in which the school is housed, which students say is "horribly ugly and has a bad feel to it." State funds were allocated to the school, but "held back during the recent budget crunch." Students have high hopes, though, that with money from the Leeds family, a new building will soon be in the works.

Admissions

When selecting their incoming class of 60 students, admissions officers at Leeds seek out applicants "with a wide variety of backgrounds—both educational and professional. We are not looking for specific work experience in a certain field or for a particular undergraduate degree. Rather, we look for applicants who have compelling reasons to earn an MBA and who will add perspective and experience to their classmates' experiences." The average GPA of this diverse group is a 3.31, and the average GMAT is 648. The student body is 27 percent female, 73 percent male, and 19 percent international. The TOEFL exam is required for international students, and the minimum score is 250 (computer-based) and 600 (paper-based).

FINANCIAL FACTS

Annual tuition (in-state/out-of-state)	$6,732/$23,130
Fees (in-state/out-of-state)	$869
Books and supplies	$3,000
Room & board (on/off-campus)	$13,000/$13,000
% of first-year students receiving aid	74
Average award package	$23,103
Average grant	$4,132
Average student loan debt	$29,956

ADMISSIONS

Admissions Selectivity Rating	88
# of applications received	249
% applicants accepted	53
% acceptees attending	42
Average GMAT	648
Range of GMAT	610–690
Average GPA	3.31
TOEFL Required of International Students?	Yes
Minimum TOEFL (paper/computer)	600/250
Application fee	$70
International application fee	$70
Regular application deadline	4/1
Regular notification	6/15
Application Deadline/Notification	
Round 1:	12/1 / 2/15
Round 2:	2/1 / 4/15
Round 3:	4/1 / 6/15
Early decision program?	Yes
ED Deadline/Notification	12/1/ 2/15
Transfer students accepted?	Yes
Transfer application policy: No transfers are allowed in the full-time MBA program. Evening MBA students may transfer up to 6 credits on a case-by-case basis with approval from the MBA Programs office.	
Need-blind admissions?	Yes

APPLICANTS ALSO LOOK AT

Arizona State University, Colorado State University, The University of Texas at Austin, University of California—Berkeley, University of Colorado at Denver, University of Denver, University of Washington.

EMPLOYMENT PROFILE			
Career Rating	76	**Grads employed by field %: avg. salary**	
Placement rate (%)	87	Finance	19: $64,455
# of companies recruiting on-campus	40	Marketing	16: $69,000
% grads employed immediately	46	Operations	5: $64,000
% grads employed within three months	86	Consulting	11: $69,000
Average starting salary	$65,300	General Management	14: $64,570

UNIVERSITY OF CONNECTICUT
SCHOOL OF BUSINESS

GENERAL INFORMATION
Type of school	public
Environment	town
Academic calendar	semester

SURVEY SAYS...
Friendly students
Smart classrooms
Solid preparation in:
Teamwork

STUDENTS
Enrollment of parent institution	27,579
Enrollment of MBA program	1,047
% male/female	66/34
% out-of-state	22
% part-time	89
% minorities	14
% international	38
Average age at entry	28
Average years work experience at entry	5.70

ACADEMICS
Academic Experience Rating	84
Student/faculty ratio	13:1
Profs interesting rating	74
Profs accessible rating	86
% female faculty	18
% minority faculty	27

Joint Degrees
MBA/JD
MBA/MD
MBA/MSW
MBA/MIS
MBA/MIM
MBA/MSN in Nursing, 3 years

Prominent Alumni
Mr. Robert W. Crispin, CEO, ING Investment Management, Inc.; Mr. Robert E. Diamond, CEO, Barclays Capital; Ms. Penelope A. Dobkin, Portfolio Manager, Fidelity Investments; Mr. John Y. Kim, Pres., Prudential Retirement; Mr. Denis Nayden, Managing Partner, Oakhill Capital.

Academics

The University of Connecticut's School of Business stands out as one of the highest-ranked low-cost public schools in the country; students get a bargain and rarely feel that they compromise quality. Students say, "The professors at UConn MBA are first-class. Not only are they your professors, but they are also your friends by the end of the program." Students also point out that "the administration is very much 'for the students.' They listen to concerns and suggestions." In addition, there was a recent multi-million dollar investment in the School of Business. These things combined give students a great deal of confidence in the program. One student says, "The state-of-the-art building is creating a fantastic environment for learning and interaction. The University of Connecticut's School of Business is preparing itself for a bright and prestigious future."

Since there are only about 100 full-time MBA students, classes in the school are small, and "every student has the opportunity to speak their opinions." Academic departments include accounting, finance, health care, information management, management, marketing, operations, and real estate. Students say, "The school really excels in finance, marketing, and application of technology." According to most students, "the technology component of the program, and the diversity of the student body, gives [students] a wide range of experiences in the learning process."

In the first year, students mostly attend core classes and participate in consulting partnerships with real companies. Recent corporate partners in this program include General Electric, United Technologies Corporation, Xerox Engineering Systems, and Aetna. This allows students to apply their knowledge to practical situations almost immediately, under the tutelage of some of the best minds in business. Students will also be better prepared for a summer internship, as they would have already had the experience most students have to wait for. As the school says, "This unique program also mirrors the corporate world by allowing students to integrate all of their course work into one project, thereby realizing the synergistic effect classes in finance, marketing, accounting, management, and operations information management provide." Students say, "The Integration Project was a great way to give students real-world experience, while teaching them important academic skills." Students also have the opportunity to "bridge the gap between theory and practice" with the Student-Managed Fund, Edgelab, and the SS&C Technologies Financial Accelerator.

During the second year, there are only two required core courses, and students engage in any two of the five areas of concentration offered by the school. These concentrations are finance, health-care management, operations and information management, management consulting, and marketing intelligence. There are also opportunities to design an individualized secondary concentration.

UConn MBA students also have an unusually broad array of dual degree programs from which to choose. These programs include MBA/JD, MBA/master of international management (MIM), MBA/MA international studies, MBA/MS nursing, MBA/MSW, and MBA/MD.

Students gripe that they would like to see more opportunities to pursue studies in entrepreneurship. One student comments, "A part of a business education should prepare [you] to become a business owner."

RICHARD N. DINO, ASSOCIATE DEAN
2100 HILLSIDE ROAD UNIT 1041, STORRS, CT 06269-1041 UNITED STATES
PHONE: 860-486-2872 • FAX: 860-486-5222
E-MAIL: UCONNMBA@BUSINESS.UCONN.EDU • WEBSITE: WWW.BUSINESS.UCONN.EDU

Career and Placement

Although students typically complain about UConn's business placement and career center (BPCC), the center has actually done pretty well. For more than 10 years, between 95 and 98 percent of the class have been placed in a position within six months of graduation. The mean salary for the graduating class of 2003 was $78,500, and the median was $82,000; 60 percent of the graduates received some sort of sign-on bonus, and the range for that was between $5,000 and $20,000. UConn's top employers are CIGNA, CitiCorp, Aetna, GE, Hartford Financial Services, Hartford Life, Purdue Pharma, Travelers, General Dynamics, UBS Warburg, and United Technologies Corporation Other companies include ABC; ESPN, Inc.; IBM; and United Health Care. Still, students agree that "career placement of international students is a definite sore point, both in terms of internships and permanent jobs after graduation."

Located in Storrs, Connecticut, UConn's School of Business finds itself placed right in the "*Fortune* 500 Heartland" between Boston and New York, and students take advantage of the abundance of opportunities. A recent influx of money has helped the school a great deal. Students say, "UConn is a big school with a new face-lift. Almost all of the academic buildings have been recently renovated and equipped with top-of-the-line technology. Life on campus is fun and safe, and there's an overall lively spirit that exists."

Still, there's no getting around the fact that the school is in a small town, though most consider that an advantage. One student says, "Because we're in a small town, we have to get creative about doing things together socially. Because of this, I think we have a better time than do students in big cities!" Other students concur, "It's a college town [and] there's not much to do outside of school. But within the school, there is ample opportunity to discover new things all the time, given the huge number of top-rated programs on campus."

Admissions

When selecting a new class for admission, the UConn MBA program looks for "bright, innovative leaders, who are motivated by change and challenge, and each year [they] strive to create a class with a diversity of professional experience, educational achievement, and cultural background." Approximately 40 to 50 percent of students in each class are international students, and 34 percent are female. The average GMAT for last year's class was 625, and the average undergraduate GPA was 3.52. Most students had at least one year of full-time work experience after college, and the average amount of time spent in the work place was 5.7 years. The average age for those who attended was 28. UConn offers an unusually high amount of financial aid, and graduate assistantship positions are also available.

FINANCIAL FACTS

Annual tuition (in-state/out-of-state)	$7,524/$19,584
Fees	$1,446
Books and supplies	$3,000
Room & board (on/off-campus)	$8,412/$9,000
% of students receiving aid	51
% of first-year students receiving aid	39
% of students receiving loans	29
% of students receiving grants	9
Average award package	$26,500
Average grant	$3,000

ADMISSIONS

Admissions Selectivity Rating	88
# of applications received	241
% applicants accepted	52
% acceptees attending	47
Average GMAT	630
Range of GMAT	590-630
Average GPA	3.48
TOEFL Required of International Students?	Yes
Minimum TOEFL (paper/computer)	575/233
Application fee	$65
International application fee	$65
Regular application deadline	4/15
Regular notification	Rolling
Deferment Available?	Yes
Maximum length of deferment	1 year
Transfer students accepted?	Yes
Transfer application policy: All students requesting to transfer are required to meet with the director of the MBA Program. A maximum of 15 credits are accepted.	
Need-blind admissions?	Yes

APPLICANTS ALSO LOOK AT

Boston College, Michigan State University, Penn State University MBA, The Ohio State University, University of Illinois at Urbana-Champaign, University of Wisconsin—Madison.

Career Rating	83	Grads employed by field %: avg. salary	
Placement rate (%)	87	Finance	41: $70,000
# of companies recruiting on-campus	25	Human Resources	4: $60,000
% grads employed immediately	65	Marketing	12: $70,000
Average starting salary	$72,000	MIS	12: $65,000
		Operations	10: $62,500
		Consulting	15: $65,000
		Entrepreneurship	3: $85,000
		General Management	3: $92,500

UNIVERSITY OF DENVER
DANIELS COLLEGE OF BUSINESS

GENERAL INFORMATION
Type of school	private
Environment	metropolis
Academic calendar	quarter

SURVEY SAYS...
Students love Denver, CO
Cutting edge classes
Smart classrooms
Solid preparation in:
Teamwork
Communication/interpersonal skills
Presentation skills

STUDENTS
Enrollment of parent institution	9,521
Enrollment of MBA program	507
% male/female	64/36
% out-of-state	20
% part-time	44
% minorities	8
% international	25
Average age at entry	27
Average years work experience at entry	5

ACADEMICS
Academic Experience Rating	**73**
Student/faculty ratio	30:1
Profs interesting rating	85
Profs accessible rating	80
% female faculty	15
% minority faculty	10

Joint Degrees
MBA/JD: 3-4 years
JD/IMBA: 3-4 years
JD/MSRECM: 3-4 years
IMBA/MA in Global Finance, Trade, and Economic Integration: 2-3 years

Prominent Alumni
Peter Coors, Chaiman, Coors Brewing Company; Andrew Daly, Former Pres., Vail Resorts; Condoleezza Rice, U.S. Secretary of State; Gale Norton, U.S. Secretary of Interior; Carol Tome, Executive VP and CFO, The Home Depot.

Academics

Students at Daniels College of Business at the University of Denver are faced with an almost dizzying array of options. Their classmates are ethnically and nationally diverse and come from a variety of business backgrounds. The city of Denver offers a multitude of cultural, natural, and sporting respites for those looking to take a break from studying. And apart from an 18-month MBA program, the school offers an enormous selection of joint degrees and special concentrations, as well as a part-time evening course of study. For some students, the only problem is narrowing down the field.

Most of the school's curriculum is taken up by the 56 (out of 72) credit hours of core classes, including Daniels' own core, which consists of three classes: values-based leadership, twenty-first-century professional, and global information economy. For the remaining 16 credits, students choose their own electives and are allowed to select any graduate-level courses they like to fulfill these requirements. Travel courses during interim periods are also an option. Of the departments in their school, students say that the "finance department in particular is filled with well-respected, smart teachers." But students add that professors from all departments are good, and "many of the higher-level professors serve as consultants to big players such as First Data, HP/Compaq, and Qwest." The school "has a strong ethics and values program," and students say that these classes "are very thought-provoking. Ethics has been a tradition at Daniels College of Business for many years." Students do gripe, however that there ought to be "better availability and times of core and elective classes."

Another complaint is the relative lack of real-world work experience some students find in their peers. One older student tells us that "some students are getting both an undergraduate degree as well as an MBA, and these students don't seem prepared." Some students feel, "The school should work harder to cater to the needs of the experienced student."

Daniels offers a dual-degree program in which students can earn any two approved graduate level degrees, including the following at once: MBA/international, MBA/master's of accountancy, master's of science in finance, master's of science in information technology, master's of science in management, master's of science in marketing, master's of science in real estate and construction management, master of taxation, and master of data mining.

The school's customized MBA programs include concentrations in applied communication and leadership, art museum administration, environmental policy and management, geographic information systems, human-resource management and development, not-for-profit management, organizational training and development, sport management, strategic management, technology management, and telecommunications. Students are understandably wowed by this smorgasbord of options. One student excitedly notes, "The number of program combinations offered are amazing! If I had the time and money, I would stay on for another year and get another degree."

SCOTT CAMPBELL, DIRECTOR OF ADMISSIONS AND FINANCIAL AID
2101 SOUTH UNIVERSITY BOULEVARD #255, RIFKIN CENTER FOR STUDENT SERVICES,
DENVER, CO 80208 U.S.
PHONE: 303-871-3416 • FAX: 303-871-4466
E-MAIL: DANIELS@DU.EDU • WEBSITE: WWW.DANIELS.DU.EDU

Career and Placement

Like so many other schools, Daniels must deal with complaints about its career-resource center. Some students say, "It would help to have a more aggressive job placement service." But others find career resources to be a "helpful advice center for both curriculum and career," and indeed, the school boasts a placement rate of 89 percent. They cite the fact that a student's average salary pre-Daniels was $43,364 while post-Daniels, it was $59,900 as an indicator that they're doing well in spite of the poor economy.

Some of the major companies that recruit on-campus include Accenture, Johnson Controls, Keane Consulting Group, Boston Market, Citibank/Citicorp, Peace Corps, Republic Financial, Enterprise Rent-a-Car, Cap Gemini, Ernst & Young, First Data Corporation, Forest Oil, MicroSystems, and Time Warner Telecom.

Student Life and Environment

Students at Daniels are surrounded by what they call a "very rich environment." The city of Denver enjoys a relatively mild climate year-round. Outdoor recreation abounds, and students take advantage of hiking, skiing, camping, and myriad sporting events, professional and otherwise. The city hosts numerous music festivals and museums as well as several centers for the performing arts. The school itself boasts the current two-time NCAA Division I national championship hockey team, and, according to the students, among the best aspects of the school's cultural life are that there's "no football team (yay!), a brand-new performing-arts center, and top speakers (like Michael Moore and former presidential cabinet members)." One student enthusiastically adds, "Denver is a great city." As for the student body, MBAs say it is "diverse and has an entrepreneurial edge, though some students just want to get their diploma and a higher salary (how boring!)." People are "warm and friendly, and the atmosphere is light as the building is also used by undergrads." That building, they add, is "world-class [and] provides a good basis for orientation to business technology."

Some students complain that, due to the variety of different programs, and the preponderance of part-time students, the atmosphere can sometimes feel a little "transient. Most students are in and out."

Admissions

In fall of 2003, the average undergraduate GPA at Daniels was 3.24, and the mean GMAT was 565. Out of 549 students total, 355 were male and 194 were female. The average age was 30, and students hailed from countries as diverse as Serbia, South Africa, Kuwait, Germany, and Canada. A minimum TOEFL score of 550 (paper-based) or 213 (computer-based) is required.

FINANCIAL FACTS	
Annual tuition	$25,956
Fees	$324
Books and supplies	$1,200
Room & board	$9,600
% of students receiving aid	58
% of first-year students receiving aid	42
% of students receiving loans	60
% of students receiving grants	66
Average award package	$22,914
Average grant	$6,746

ADMISSIONS	
Admissions Selectivity Rating	72
# of applications received	399
% applicants accepted	86
% acceptees attending	56
Average GMAT	572
Range of GMAT	510-600
Average GPA	3.2
TOEFL Required of International Students?	Yes
Minimum TOEFL (paper/computer)	550/213
Application fee	$50
International application fee	$50
Regular application deadline	3/15
Regular notification	5/1
Application Deadline/Notification	
Round 1:	1/15 / 3/1
Round 2:	3/15 / 5/1
Round 3:	5/15 / 7/1
Deferment Available?	Yes
Maximum length of deferment	1 year
Transfer students accepted?	Yes
Transfer application policy: 12 quarter hours (9 semester hours) toward electives.	
Non-fall admissions?	Yes
Need-blind admissions?	Yes

APPLICANTS ALSO LOOK AT

American University, Arizona State University, Boston University, Brigham Young University, University of Arizona, University of Colorado at Denver, University of Colorado.

EMPLOYMENT PROFILE

Career Rating	82	Grads employed by field	%: avg. salary
Placement rate (%)	89	Accounting	8: $46,125
# of companies recruiting on-campus	65	Finance	22: $61,335
% grads employed immediately	57	Human Resources	2: $49,500
Average starting salary	$55,756	Marketing	12: $50,051
		MIS	6: $61,867
		Operations	6: $59,500
		Strategic Planning	1: $80,000
		Consulting	13: $63,571
		General Management	20: $55,614
		Other	4: $24,000
		Non-profit	6: $39,857

UNIVERSITY OF FLORIDA
WARRINGTON COLLEGE OF BUSINESS

GENERAL INFORMATION

Type of school	public
Environment	city
Academic calendar	semester

SURVEY SAYS...
Friendly students
Happy students
Smart classrooms
Solid preparation in:
Finance
Teamwork
Communication/interpersonal skills

STUDENTS

Enrollment of parent institution	49,000
Enrollment of MBA program	763
% male/female	80/20
% part-time	83
% minorities	15
% international	28
Average age at entry	28
Average years work experience at entry	5

ACADEMICS

Academic Experience Rating	**97**
Student/faculty ratio	13:1
Profs interesting rating	90
Profs accessible rating	89
% female faculty	14
% minority faculty	23

Joint Degrees
MBA/JD (4 years); MBA/MS in Medical Sciences, Biotechnology; MBA/Ph.D in Medical Sciences, Biotechnology; MBA/B.S. in Industrial and Systems Engineering; MBA/Doctor of Pharmacy; MBA/PhD in Medical Sciences; MBA/MD; MBA/Master of Exercise and Sport Science (3 years)

Academics

Finance "is the greatest strength of the program" at University of Florida's Warrington College of Business, where "entrepreneurship is also a rising star." The school offers students lots of options, everything from course schedules that accommodate UF's many part-timers, to an intensive one-year MBA for those who just want to grind out a degree and get on with their careers.

To maximize opportunities for electives without skimping on core requirements, the school splits each semester into two eight-week modules. Warrington MBAs may choose from 16 areas of concentration including joint ventures with other university branches (for example, arts administration, Latin American business, and sports administration) and six certificate programs (for example, e-commerce and supply-chain management). First, of course, students must master the core curriculum, which includes twelve classes spread over the first four modules. One marketing student writes, "I was challenged by the core classes (especially in unfamiliar topics) as well as my electives. I feel that I was given a great opportunity to learn core business skills while digging deeper and enriching my marketing knowledge."

Despite the enormity of the University of Florida, students report a high degree of personal attention at Warrington. The administration "runs the MBA programs like a business. They do not lose focus of the fact that their primary customer is the student. The MBA programs reflect a milieu that is both student-oriented and student-friendly." According to students, the program does not rest on its considerable laurels; MBAs say, "The school is totally dedicated to improvement. They are always evaluating, changing, modifying, and asking about every part of the program. They are always asking how they can make things better. The best part is that they actually act on what we tell them." MBAs also appreciate their access to "excellent university resources."

Warrington's faculty is yet another feather in the school's cap. As one student notes, "I didn't expect the quality of the professors to be so high. I have been learning from people who [are] educated and worked at the best places in the country. They all say how great it is to teach in Florida. It is awesome to know that your professors could be successful anywhere, and they want to be at your school." Students add that "[faculty accessibility] is amazing. Whether we just stop by the office or send an e-mail at midnight, the administration and professors are always willing to help."

Career and Placement

The Graduate Business Career Services Office (CSO) earns mixed reviews from Warrington students. The majority of them feel that "the CSO leaves something to be desired. It is moving in the right direction, but most students will need to do their own job search." Some students believe that "the problems may just be a reflection of the economy/environment and not the quality of the department."

Warrington MBAs are most likely to go to work for American Express, Bank America, Citibank, CSX, Darden Restaurants, Disney, Ernst & Young, ExxonMobil, Ford, General Electric, IBM, Johnson & Johnson, Pratt & Whitney, Procter & Gamble, Ryder Systems, and SunTrust. About one-quarter of graduates find their first jobs outside of the United States.

Student Life and Environment

Florida MBAs can't think of enough good things to say about hometown Gainesville, "a wonderful college town." Students say, "There's plenty of stuff to do, whether it be biking, catching a play, fishing, or hitting downtown for a night out with the gang. Plus,

ROBERT BREWER, ASSOCIATE DIRECTOR OF ADMISSIONS
134 BRYAN HALL, PO BOX 117152 GAINESVILLE, FL 32611-7152 UNITED STATES
PHONE: 877-435-2622 • FAX: 352-392-8791
E-MAIL: FLORIDAMBA@CBA.UFL.EDU • WEBSITE: WWW.FLORIDAMBA.UFL.EDU

UF has an excellent tradition of strong sports teams!" Another student adds that "the beach is close," and "the weather allows for year-round outdoor activities." One student notes, "Gainesville is a great place to live. It was named 'Best Place to Live' by *Money* magazine in the late [1990s]. All of my other b-school opportunities were in the Midwest. My wife and I laugh as we watch the Weather Channel." As an added bonus, "it is also nice being a little over an hour away from Orlando."

The University of Florida campus earns similar plaudits. Students describe it as "awesome" and explain that "[the] university resources like athletics, both personal and varsity (like football and basketball), the libraries, and the caliber of people accentuate a great learning environment." One student says, "It's a huge university, and with so many students (including 10,000 graduate students), I know I can go somewhere any night of the week and see people I know. Meeting people couldn't be any easier [because] people here are friendly, warm, and easy to talk to. I had a group of friends within a week or so. The social life at Florida is wonderful!" MBAs agree that "the combination of student-run activities, competitive athletics, abundant nightlife, and fantastic weather make this a great place to live."

Of course, not everyone has time to enjoy the great town and the great campus. Students in the one-year program have "an incredibly heavy workload, so as a group, we tend to stay close and work together most of the time. We work hard, and we play hard. We may be in the MBA lounge studying at one o'clock on a Saturday night, but we were probably up all night Friday drinking beers and talking. It is easier to deal with so much schoolwork when you like the people you are teamed with," according to students. Everyone else here clears their schedules occasionally to enjoy "school clubs and students who accept everyone, making life here a blast. There is the right balance of studying and fun to make life enjoyable." Warrington's student body includes a large international presence; one student observes, "The ethnic diversity has opened my eyes to a wide range of cultures and opportunities that I have not seen before."

Admissions

Applicants of the Warrington MBA program are required to have a minimum of two years of full-time, post-undergraduate professional experience; prospective executive MBAs must have at least eight years of experience. Applicants must submit official copies of all undergraduate and graduate transcripts, GMAT scores, TOEFL scores (when applicable), two letters of recommendation (preferably from supervisors at work), personal essays, and a resume. The school "strongly encourages preparation in financial accounting and quantitative skills (like calculus and statistics) prior to enrollment."

Prominent Alumni

John Dasburg, MBA '70, Chairman & CEO ASTAR Air Cargo; Don McKinney, MBA '72, Venture Capitalist; partner in Watershed Capital; William R. Hough, MBA '48, Pres. of William R. Hough & Co. & WRH Mortgage; Laurie Burns, MBA, Pres. Bahama Breeze; Hal Steinbrenner, MBA, General Parnter, New York Yankees.

FINANCIAL FACTS

Annual tuition (in-state/out-of-state)	$5,484/$21,359
Fees	$500
Books and supplies	$3,685
Room & board (on/off-campus)	$6,870/$7,130
% of students receiving aid	65
% of first-year students receiving aid	76
% of students receiving loans	50
% of students receiving grants	27
Average award package	$19,531
Average grant	$9,671
Average student loan debt	$14,196

ADMISSIONS

Admissions Selectivity Rating	93
# of applications received	406
% applicants accepted	41
% acceptees attending	50
Average GMAT	666
Range of GMAT	640-700
Average GPA	3.3
TOEFL Required of International Students?	Yes
Minimum TOEFL (paper/computer)	600/250
Application fee	$30
International application fee	$30
Regular application deadline	4/15
Regular notification	Rolling
Non-fall admissions?	Yes
Need-blind admissions?	Yes

APPLICANTS ALSO LOOK AT

Emory University, Georgetown University, The University of Texas at Austin, University of Georgia, University of North Carolina at Chapel Hill, University of Notre Dame, University of Southern California.

Career Rating

EMPLOYMENT PROFILE			
80		**Grads employed by field**	**%: avg. salary**
Placement rate (%)	91	Finance	55: $60,300
% grads employed immediately	65	Marketing	8: $53,000
Average starting salary	$61,380	Consulting	11: $63,000
		General Management	13: $64,000
		Other	13: $71,500

UNIVERSITY OF GEORGIA
TERRY COLLEGE OF BUSINESS

Academics

The Terry MBA program at the University of Georgia offers "a good mix of the 'hard' technical skills and 'soft' skills, which are equally required in today's business community." This translates into "a great return on investment," especially for Georgia residents. For a small program—the full-timers number fewer than 200—Terry provides a surprising number of strong concentrations; students praise its programs in entrepreneurship, MIS, real estate, and finance. Students love Terry's "flexibility to create rigorous academic programs suited to the needs of the individual student," and they appreciate how the program draws on the resources of the University of Georgia. One MBA explains, "This a large school with many different opportunities, including taking classes in areas outside of the business school." Students with undergraduate business degrees can earn MBAs in under a year, thanks to the school's eleven-month program, which substitutes a summer of intensive review for the first-year core requirements of the more traditional two-year program. Students in both the eleven-month and two-year programs warn that "the workload is high, especially given that so many of the students have assistantships, which require ten to fifteen hours of work per week." The small size of the program is seen as both an asset and a drawback. In the credit column, the program's size "gives every student complete access to all facilities including lecturers and administrative staff" and "helps build closer relationships between students, create more engaging classes, and make students feel more a part of the school." In the debit column, "the smaller size keeps some recruiters off campus."

Instructors at the University of Georgia include "some very knowledgeable and respected professors," according to one student. "My accounting professor was president of the FASB for 10 years, and my statistics professor was CFO for Kodak." By and large, they are "very good at teaching, not just lecturing about their research," and they deftly communicate "a wealth of real-life experience, which is something that books can't translate." They are also "always very helpful outside of class, whether it's with subject matter or introducing you to people in a particular industry."

Career and Placement

Because its MBA program is too small to attract some larger recruiters to campus and contrasts with Stanton Chase International, the University of Georgia participates in two consortia (one regional, one national) and contracts with Stanton Chase International. The Career Services office provides all the standard services—workshops, panel presentations, breakfast speakers, career fairs, and one-on-one counseling. The school also offers students access to Career Leader, an online assessment tool developed by career specialists and psychologists. Students explain that the career office "works very hard" but is hampered by the size of the program. One student says, "Terry needs to grow in order to be considered a top-20 business school. The large schools attract more employers, and employers attract better and better students." Top recruiters of Terry MBAs include Bank of America, BB&T, Capital One, Cintas, Cushman & Wakefield, FedEx, First Union, Hewitt Associates, Home Depot, Liberty Mutual, Prudential, Sun Trust, UPS, and Wachovia. About three-quarters of Terry MBAs take their first jobs in the Southeast.

Student Life and Environment

The Terry curriculum is demanding, but MBAs here still manage to find some time for "R&R." Students explain that "while we spend a large portion of our time studying, the first-year, 11-month, and second-year students make an effort to continue a normal lifestyle away from campus by organizing social get-togethers, community volunteer opportunities, and athletic activities." Integration into the mainstream is toughest for the

ANNE C. COOPER, DIRECTOR, MBA ADMISSIONS
362 BROOKS HALL, ATHENS, GA 30602-6264 UNITED STATES
PHONE: 706-542-5671 • FAX: 706-542-5351
E-MAIL: TERRYMBA@TERRY.UGA.EDU • WEBSITE: WWW.TERRY.UGA.EDU/MBA

11-month students, "who are rolled in with the returning two-year students for the fall semester, with no formal get-to-know-each-others." One student says, "While this hasn't been terribly difficult for me to handle, I know other 11-month students who don't know the names of most of the second-year students they are in class with. I think this is unfortunate."

Students tell us that the school "strongly encourages extracurricular activities as much as it drives academic excellence." Terry "offers a wide array of activities [like] guest lectures, seminars, workshops, clubs/organizations, socials, and community service. Strong ties with the external business community means that we get eminent speakers (such as, Vernon Smith, the current Nobel winner for economics) to come to the campus to address us on relevant business topics affecting our world." The university at large offers even more options including Bulldog football and the inevitable tailgating that precedes each home game. The university is also home to the Ramsey Student Center, "the best university sports complex in the United States!"

An up-to-date facility houses the Terry program; students report approvingly that "the main building used for classrooms is fairly new and contains complete multimedia in most classrooms (such as, projection, whiteboards, television, video, PowerPoint, and computer demonstration), is wireless (as is most of north campus), and has many areas where students can work in groups. The main administrative building is an older, grand structure that is easily accessible and beautiful to look at." The program makes its home "on UGA's gorgeous north campus, about 200 yards away from downtown Athens." Students call their hometown "an eclectic Mecca, known mainly because of its contributions to the music scene (like REM, B-52's, and Widespread Panic), [that] is comparable, and often ranked above Austin, Texas, as the best college town. It contains many great eateries and more than [an] adequate nightlife, which is hard to resist." Students also appreciate the "access and proximity to Atlanta."

Admissions

Applicants to the Terry MBA program must submit two sealed copies of all undergraduate and graduate transcripts, two letters of recommendation, GMAT scores, TOEFL scores (for international students), essays, and a resume. The school regards favorably any evidence of "unique life experiences and growth opportunities." Interviews are encouraged but not required. Candidates are expected to demonstrate computer proficiency and strong math skills; a minimum of two years of work experience is strongly recommended. The admissions office admits students on a rolling basis, beginning in December; the school encourages applicants to apply early.

FINANCIAL FACTS

Annual tuition (in-state/out-of-state)	$5,392/$19,778
Fees	$904
Books and supplies	$1,000
Room & board (on/off-campus)	$12,400/$16,500
% of students receiving aid	74
% of first-year students receiving aid	58
% of students receiving grants	74
Average award package	$20,500
Average grant	$20,500

ADMISSIONS

Admissions Selectivity Rating	92
# of applications received	333
% applicants accepted	46
% acceptees attending	64
Average GMAT	663
Range of GMAT	590-730
Average GPA	3.3
TOEFL Required of International Students?	Yes
Minimum TOEFL (paper/computer)	577/233
Application fee	$62
International application fee	$62
Regular application deadline	5/1
Regular notification	Rolling
Application Deadline/Notification	
Round 1:	12/1 / 1/17
Round 2:	2/1/ 3/1
Round 3:	3/1 / 4/1
Round 4:	5/1 / 6/1
Deferment Available?	Yes
Maximum length of deferment	1 year
Non-fall admissions?	Yes
Need-blind admissions?	Yes

APPLICANTS ALSO LOOK AT

Emory University, University of North Carolina at Chapel Hill, Vanderbilt University.

EMPLOYMENT PROFILE			
Career Rating	86	Grads employed by field	%: avg. salary
Placement rate (%)	84	Finance	35: $62,592
# of companies recruiting on-campus	56	Marketing	18: $64,444
% grads employed immediately	50	Consulting	12: $72,363
Average starting salary	$65,438	Other	25: $66,969

UNIVERSITY OF HARTFORD
BARNEY SCHOOL OF BUSINESS

GENERAL INFORMATION
Type of school	private
Environment	village
Academic calendar	

SURVEY SAYS...
Friendly students
Happy students
Smart classrooms
Solid preparation in:
Teamwork
Communication/interpersonal skills
Presentation skills

STUDENTS
Enrollment of parent institution	7,246
Enrollment of MBA program	394
% male/female	57/43
% out-of-state	10
% part-time	76
% minorities	11
% international	46
Average age at entry	32

ACADEMICS
Academic Experience Rating	76
Student/faculty ratio	8:1
Profs interesting rating	75
Profs accessible rating	80
% female faculty	28
% minority faculty	16

Academics

Convenience and a marketable degree are the chief drawing cards for most graduate students at the University of Hartford's Barney School of Business. This predominantly part-time population comes here because the school is local to their homes and employment, flexible to their scheduling needs, and able to deliver a prestigious degree recognized throughout the Northeastern business community.

The Hartford MBA has achieved the gold standard of excellence—AACSB accreditation. The program owes a large measure of its success to an excellent faculty who "are a wealth of knowledge in their areas and are usually very willing to ensure that students get the knowledge they desire." One student says that instructors "come from very diverse backgrounds with a wide array of previous work experience, which I feel helps creates an extremely interesting learning environment." Plus, they know how to teach; according to students, "The professors' methods of class delivery is outstanding. Maintaining interest after [a] full day of work can be difficult. operations management—amazing. accounting, which can be so boring—quite the eye-opener. Even the dry statistics were enjoyable."

None of this would do students any good, of course, if it weren't offered in a form adaptable to their busy work schedules. Hartford accommodates its students by scheduling classes once a week on evenings and weekends. Professors here are "very accessible and also understand the demands of the work-school balance," offering "great flexibility to help those who have constraints in both time and money." The administration has pitched in by formulating its "no-hassle" approach which makes books and other curricular materials, identification cards, and parking permits (included in the cost of tuition) available at the same site in which MBA classes are held.

The Hartford MBA consists of 17 three-credit courses. Six core courses cover material mastered by undergraduates with business majors and may be waived on that basis. All other courses—five breadth courses (leadership, managing technology, managing customer interfaces, business law, and performance analysis), five electives, and a capstone course that "integrates functional approaches and environment issues by having students make strategic business decisions" are mandatory. MBAs praise the curriculum's "emphasis on group-based assignments and its emphasis on practical cases and examples in classes."

Career and Placement

Placement and career-counseling services are provided to Barney MBAs by the Career Services Office, which serves the entire undergraduate and graduate student body of the university. Services include resume and cover-letter writing workshops, seminars on networking and interviewing strategies, job banks, on-campus interviewing, and job fairs.

CLAIRE SILVERSTEIN, DIRECTOR OF GRADUATE PROGRAMS
200 BLOOMFIELD AVENUE, CENTER FOR GRADUATE & ADULT SERVICES, CC231
WEST, HARTFORD, CT 06117 UNITED STATES
PHONE: 860-768-4444 • FAX: 860-768-4821
E-MAIL: BARNEY@HARTFORD.EDU • WEBSITE: HTTP://BARNEY.HARTFORD.EDU

FINANCIAL FACTS

Annual tuition	$9,270
% of students receiving aid	14
% of first-year students receiving aid	45
% of students receiving loans	13
% of students receiving grants	4
Average award package	$13,207
Average grant	$3,885

ADMISSIONS

Admissions Selectivity Rating	78
# of applications received	146
% applicants accepted	58
% acceptees attending	91
Average GMAT	530
Range of GMAT	480-570
Average GPA	3.0
TOEFL Required of International Students?	Yes
Minimum TOEFL (paper/computer)	550/213
Application fee	$40
International application fee	$55
Regular application deadline	Rolling
Regular notification	Rolling
Deferment Available?	Yes
Maximum length of deferment	1 year
Transfer students accepted?	Yes
Transfer application policy: Transfer credits accepted on case by case basis.	
Non-fall admissions?	Yes

Student Life and Environment

Nearly all part-timers at the Barney MBA program arrive on campus as classes begin and leave as soon as they end; if they spend any more time there, it's to study, meet with a professor, or participate in a study group. MBA Association, major-related clubs, and pub nights simply aren't part of the equation here. As a typical student explains, "I am a commuter with children at home; therefore, hanging out at the school is not in my schedule. Barbeques and networking get-togethers I do attend, and they are very good." Full-time students benefit from such campus programs as the Lunch and Learn Series, which brings in executives to address students, and non-credit enrichment workshops.

The business school makes its home in Beatrice Fox Auerbach Hall, which recently received a partial makeover to renovate its entry hall. The facility houses a "newly refurbished reading room with daily newspapers and periodicals" and two information technology centers on the wireless campus are loaded with computers complete with flat screens. Students appreciate the effort, but many agree that the school needs a more dramatic technological upgrade.

Hartford benefits from its location in one of the nation's insurance centers. The school attracts students from "a wide variety of business and even engineering specialists" whose experiences add to instruction. The school's proximity to "the biggest financial industry in the world—New York City" is also an asset, allowing for guest speakers, internship opportunities, and day trips for interviews and recruiting.

Hartford MBAs "range in age from recent college graduates up to their 50s and higher. It is good, particularly during group projects, to have such diversely experienced co-group members." With about "half the class made up of international students native to foreign countries, the MBA student body is quite diverse, and not just ethnically. Our working backgrounds are so different: engineers, stockbrokers, chemists, a physicist, insurance, business administrators, accountants—oh, boy. You get all of us in a working group [and] it is quite the experience, especially for a class project," notes one MBA.

Admissions

The Barney admissions office requires all MBA applicants to submit official transcripts from all previously attended post-secondary schools, two letters of recommendation, official GMAT results, a resume, a letter of intent describing the applicant's academic and career goals, and a completed application. Applicants with at least three years of continuous work experience may apply for a GMAT waiver. International students must submit TOEFL scores and a Guarantor's Statement of Financial Support in addition to the above.

UNIVERSITY OF HAWAII
COLLEGE OF BUSINESS ADMINISTRATION

Academics

For most students at the University of Hawaii College of Business, the most exciting thing about their program is "its proximity to Asia and the large number of Chinese and Japanese students." Because so many students plan to go on to work in the rapidly growing markets of Asia, the program is not only helpful to their education, but also to their manners. Through a variety of exchange programs, as well as friendships with students from so many different cultures, students learn how to interact with cultures not their own, and, in many cases, learn how to avoid embarrassing social gaffes that could spoil a deal. As one student says, "[The school's] greatest strengths are the international business ties the school has with countries around the Pacific Rim. The MBA program offers exchange opportunities like the PACIBER program, which requires fluency in a language spoken in the Pacific region other than English, one semester of study abroad, and an internship with a focus on international business." UHM's MBA program is a general one, and its classes are all taught at night to accommodate the needs of its many working students. Students can choose part-time or full-time courses of study and can pick from the following departments: financial economics and institutions, information-technology management, management and industrial relations, marketing, and the school of accountancy. In addition, the school offers a variety of dual degree programs (MBA/MA, or MBA/MS, and JD/MBA) and a Japan- or China-focused MBA: a full-time, 15-month specialized program. As far as students are concerned, however, all of the departments have one strength in common: "The professors! They are the ones who point you in the right direction and help with the networking process." Another student concurs, adding that the school is home to "great and knowledgeable faculty. My classmates are also excellent." And because of the nontraditional curriculum and the small program, "in general, the environment is noncompetitive."

Although there are few complaints about the curriculum, some students feel that "the offerings of noncore classes could be increased, especially in the areas of finance and marketing." Others make the case that "academically, the school could make the course work more vigorous, but with more than 50 percent of the students working full-time, those students may not be able to accommodate more rigorous work." Another student agrees and adds that "though the classes require a lot of work, I think that in general they should be more challenging." In keeping with the multinational tone of the school, one of the more popular aspects of the College of Business Administration is their study-abroad program. The school has multiple exchange programs with universities in Asia and Europe and a summer Asian field-study elective, which "enables students to earn six credits while visiting factories and other businesses in four Asian countries." As one student says, " I went on a three-week long field study, where we visited Korea, Japan, and Thailand. As a group of 15 students with a well-known advisor, we were able to visit with executive managers at companies such as Nissan, POSCO, and K. Cotton." UHM also offers a number of different international activity groups, such as the Academy of International Business; the Asia Pacific Economic Cooperation (APEC) Study Center, the Asia-Pacific Financial Markets Research Center, the Family Business Center of Hawaii, the Pacific-Asian Center for Entrepreneurship and E-Business, and the Native Hawaiian Leadership Project.

Career and Placement

Many students who graduate from UHM remain in Hawaii to work, though some return to the United States mainland or to Asia, and students are wild about the "networking opportunities for international and local students across Asia and the Pacific Rim." Employers of recent MBAs include AIG Insurance, Bank of Hawaii, Booz Allen Hamilton, PricewaterhouseCoopers, First Hawaiian Bank, Foodland, Frito Lay, Nabisco,

MARY DUMAS, ACTING ASSISTANT DEAN
2404 MAILE WAY C-202, HONOLULU, HI 96822 UNITED STATES
PHONE: 808-956-8266 • FAX: 808-956-2657
E-MAIL: MBA@HAWAII.EDU • WEBSITE: WWW.CBA.HAWAII.EDU

Hewlett-Packard, Hilton Hotels, the Internal Revenue Service, and many others. Many MBAs have also been inspired to start their own businesses after their time at UHM.

Still, some students feel that the alumni network could be improved. One student says, "It would be great if the alumni could get more involved with the program. I am lucky to have a good alumnus who takes participation in my attendance, but I wonder if my other classmates are just as lucky."

Student Life and Environment

One look at the school's website should tell you all you need to know about campus life at the University of Hawaii, Manoa. Palm trees, mountains, airy beaches, and wide expanses of deep blue sea abound. As one student says on the school's site: "Life in Hawaii... well, what can I say? It's Hawaii!" Another student adds, "Located in beautiful Hawaii, UHM is an ideal location for students who are looking for a change of scenery. The students are extremely diverse, and the program is very flexible to accommodate various needs." And another student points out that the great thing about UHM is that "the location and the diverse student body make it exciting to learn. There are people who are here for different reasons, so it is exciting to meet engineers, psychologists, astronomers, chemists, and economists. The city and community is beautiful and safe." Still, many students feel that "the facilities at this school could stand a lot of improvement, and the negative attitude of most of the faculty toward technology is unacceptable." Many students strongly feel that "the friendships made from the intensive group work make up for all this. In my first semester alone, I have made several friends I am proud to call my friends for life." But others point out that because it's a commuting campus, "extracurriculars are limited, especially with students working full-time. But the Graduate Business Students Association does put on monthly 'relaxers' after classes to get the students to mingle with each other and with professors." Relaxers provide drinks, snacks, and a place to socialize, and students consider them "a good but rare offering." Also, many students feel that "it would be great if the school could involve the spouses and families a bit more. More opportunities to meet socially, instead of just academically (for group work) would be great."

Admissions

In order to join UHM's diverse community of students, applicants must have a minimum GPA of 3.0 and a minimum GMAT score of 500. The school requires that its applicants have at least two years of post-graduate, full-time work experience. Because international students representing more than 80 countries account for about 25 percent of UHM graduate student population, the TOEFL is required. Students whose native language is not English must score at least a 600 (paper-based) test 250 (computer-based). Students who score 550/213 are considered, but will be tested again by the university's English Language Institute.

FINANCIAL FACTS

Annual tuition (in-state/out-of-state)	$8,928/$14,544
Fees	$172
Books and supplies	$900
Room & board (on/off-campus)	$12,000/$14,000
% of students receiving aid	25
% of first-year students receiving aid	5
% of students receiving loans	22
% of students receiving grants	10
Average award package	$12,281
Average grant	$25,000
Average student loan debt	$7,644

ADMISSIONS

Admissions Selectivity Rating	88
# of applications received	313
% applicants accepted	39
% acceptees attending	55
Average GMAT	575
Range of GMAT	500-710
Average GPA	3.3
TOEFL Required of International Students?	Yes
Minimum TOEFL (paper/computer)	550/213
Application fee	$50
International application fee	$50
Regular application deadline	5/1
Regular notification	Rolling
Transfer students accepted?	Yes
Transfer application policy: Credits may be transferred into the MBA program from other AACSB-accredited business schools, from other University of Hawaii graduate programs, or by petition.	
Non-fall admissions?	Yes
Need-blind admissions?	Yes

Career Rating	74	Grads employed by field	%: avg. salary
Placement rate (%)	92	Accounting	5: $45,000
# of companies recruiting on-campus	45	Finance	15: $45,000
% grads employed immediately	67	Human Resources	5: $40,000
% grads employed within three months	85	Marketing	25: $50,000
Average starting salary	$50,000	MIS	10: $55,000
		Consulting	5: $40,000
		General Management	10: $55,000
		Global Management	25: $55,000

UNIVERSITY OF HOUSTON
C.T. BAUER COLLEGE OF BUSINESS

GENERAL INFORMATION

Type of school	public
Environment	metropolis
Academic calendar	semester

SURVEY SAYS...
Friendly students
Cutting edge classes
Happy students
Smart classrooms
Solid preparation in:
Accounting

STUDENTS

Enrollment of parent institution	35,180
Enrollment of MBA program	622
% male/female	59/41
% out-of-state	28
% part-time	67
% minorities	7
% international	31
Average age at entry	27
Average years work experience at entry	4

ACADEMICS

Academic Experience Rating	**74**
Student/faculty ratio	4:1
Profs interesting rating	68
Profs accessible rating	61
% female faculty	25
% minority faculty	20

Joint Degrees

MBA/JD: 4 to 6 years
MBA/MIE in Industrial Engineering: 2 to 5 years
MBA/MA in Spanish: 2 to 5 years
MBA/Master's in Hospitality Management: 2 to 5 years
MBA/MSW: 3 to 5 years
MBA/MIM: 3 to 5 years

Prominent Alumni

Fran Keeth, Pres. and CEO, Shell Chemical, LP; Karen Katz, Pres. and CEO, Neiman Marcus Stores; David McClanahan, Pres. and CEO, CenterPoint Energy; Harry Lambroussis, Pres., International Paper-Latin America; John Beard, Pres., Lyondell Europe Inc.

Academics

The University of Houston is riding high from a $40 million donation from Charles T. Bauer—so high, in fact, that they renamed the business school in his honor. Bauer's gift, the largest in university history, has spurred the school to greater heights, allowing it to attract top-line faculty, upgrade facilities, and fuel cutting-edge research at its many centers and institutes. Yet, to the delight of students, the school remains "reasonably priced."

Despite the emphasis on big names and research, students at Bauer tell us that "the MBA from UH is definitely a real-life, practical MBA that will be useful in the real world" and that "the best professors are not always the academics, but rather the practitioners of business who bring to the table a lot of relevant real-life experience." Students point out that "some of these teachers are not regular faculty but are rather designated 'Executive Professors' who teach only one or two classes per semester." These teachers "are often drawn from such big-name businesses as ExxonMobil, Royal Dutch Shell, Price Waterhouse, etc."

Bauer's students, two-thirds of whom attend part time, extol the program's "focus on meeting the needs of part-time students who are working full-time." The school offers "cohort scheduling with night classes [and] low tuition costs compared to other schools in the area,"—both high priorities for the school's aspiring MBAs. In addition, the Bauer College has introduced a new full-time day program for Fall 2005 that allows students to complete almost all their required core classes in their first year of study. Bauer's 'mini-lockstep' 30-hour core curriculum helps create cohesion even among the part-time student body. It also allows the school to organize material in thematically related modules, each culminating in an integrative capstone course. This ensures that students learn and apply multiple skills to solve problems and improve their understanding of the business world. MBAs praise the "extensive use of case histories and research papers" in their classes and appreciate the "good selection of advanced electives." The curriculum allows for six electives over the course of the program. Concentrations are offered in accounting, finance, decision and information sciences, management, and marketing. Bauer students' main desire is for the "administration to be more open to change."

The Bauer College also offers an Executive MBA Program as well as graduate certificate programs. Students enrolled in the Executive MBA Program have the option of pursuing the traditional Leadership track, or the brand new track in Global Energy Management. Graduate certificate program offerings include energy accounting, energy risk management, and financial services management.

Career and Placement

Bauer students may employ the services of the Elizabeth D. Rockwell Career Services Center. The center offers a number of career-readiness workshops in such areas as resume writing, interviewing strategies, networking, and developing a professional image. The office also assists students in finding jobs and internships, and organizes career fairs. Career counseling services are provided at the Rockwell Center, and students may use the office to access proprietary online job databases. Bauer students may also use a variety of online services free of charge; other career assessment tools are also available through the Rockwell Center.

Employers most likely to take on Bauer MBAs include AIM Management Group, Inc., Duke Energy, Hewlett-Packard, ExxonMobil, and Shell Services International.

DAVID SHIELDS, ASSOCIATE DEAN FOR GRADUATE AND PROFESSIONAL PROGRAMS
334 MELCHER HALL, SUITE 275, HOUSTON, TX 77204-6021 UNITED STATES
PHONE: 713-743-5936 • FAX: 713-743-4368
E-MAIL: HOUSTONMBA@UH.EDU • WEBSITE: WWW.BAUER.UH.EDU/MBA

Student Life and Environment

The Bauer College of Business is housed in Melcher Hall on the east end of the University of Houston campus. The facility includes the AIM Center for Investment Management, a $5-million learning laboratory that students use to manage a mutual fund called The Cougar Fund. The facility is also home to several of Bauer's research institutes, including the Global Energy Management Institute and the Center for Entrepreneurship & Innovation, and programs that serve the Houston business community (e.g. the Center for Executive Development, the Program for Excellence in Selling).

Students note that Bauer "is a commuter school" that "is not really comparable with a conventional MBA program. This one is geared towards working professionals who already live and are working in Houston. We barely have time to handle school and work, much less social activities. Those activities that are scheduled here are geared more towards the international students, many of whom attend full-time." When school is done, "there is no 'Let's hit the bars' attitude. Students generally are tired—they want to go home to their families after class. If we meet on the weekends, it is to do work on group projects, not for fun." MBAs report that "fellow students bring to the table a diversity of experience and background. This makes for really rich discussions."

Admissions

Applicants to the Bauer MBA program must submit all of the following materials: a completed application; official transcripts for all undergraduate work; an official GMAT score report; a resume; two letters of reference; and a short, personal essay explaining the student's choice of the Bauer MBA Program. International students whose first language is not English must also submit official score reports for the TOEFL or IELTS, unless they have already earned a degree in the U.S. Those with transcripts from overseas must provide translations but need not provide evaluations, as Bauer prefers to make its own assessment of the transcripts. The school admits students for the fall semester only. Proficiency in college-level calculus is required of all non-executive MBA students prior to enrolling in the program.

FINANCIAL FACTS

Annual tuition (in-state/out-of-state)	$4,194/$8,838
Fees	$3,140
Books and supplies	$1,400
Room & board (on-campus)	$7,900
% of students receiving aid	45
% of first-year students receiving aid	49
% of students receiving loans	31
% of students receiving grants	23
Average award package	$11,300
Average grant	$1,800
Average student loan debt	$14,300

ADMISSIONS

Admissions Selectivity Rating	85
# of applications received	303
% applicants accepted	61
% acceptees attending	67
Average GMAT	605
Range of GMAT	570-640
Average GPA	3.3
TOEFL Required of International Students?	Yes
Minimum TOEFL (paper/computer)	620/260
Application fee	$75
International application fee	$150
Regular application deadline	5/1
Regular notification	6/1
Deferment Available?	Yes
Maximum length of deferment	1 year
Non-fall admissions?	No
Need-blind admissions?	Yes

APPLICANTS ALSO LOOK AT

Rice University, Texas A&M, The University of Texas at Austin, University of Houston-Clear Lake.

EMPLOYMENT PROFILE

Career Rating	75	Grads employed by field	%: avg. salary
# of companies recruiting on-campus	103	Accounting	10: $52,000
% grads employed immediately	81	Finance	17: $67,500
Average starting salary	$68,500	Marketing	10: $59,300
		MIS	10: $80,300
		Operations	17: $73,800
		Strategic Planning	2: NR
		Consulting	2: $80,000
		Entrepreneurship	3: NR
		General Management	12: $67,000
		Other	17: $70,660

UNIVERSITY OF ILLINOIS—CHICAGO
LIAUTAUD GRADUATE SCHOOL OF BUSINESS

Academics

When it comes to resources, the Liautaud Graduate School of Business has two power-houses at its disposal: the University of Illinois—Chicago and the city of Chicago itself. The benefits of location are obvious and bountiful, students tell us; one student writes, "UIC is located in the heart of Chicago. The culturally and economically diverse environment truly makes studying international business not just an in-the-classroom experience. UIC takes advantage of its location by promoting trips to the Federal Reserve and inviting top business leaders in the city to teach professional topics courses. I learn every day about how to function in an international business environment, whether I'm in the classroom or not." Another MBA adds, "We are right in the heart of downtown Chicago, so the city really becomes our campus in a sense. You can access anything you want, and most importantly, you have the resources of Chicago at your disposal."

UIC offers both full-time and part-time programs; each is flexible enough that students can begin in the fall, spring, or summer semester. The program also allows students to switch back and forth from the full-time to part-time programs, a real plus in today's unpredictable job market. Those in a hurry to earn their degrees can assay the intensive core, which covers all core disciplines in a single semester. With many classes offered in the evening, "class scheduling makes this a great school for the middle levels to upgrade themselves on the job." The substantial presence of part-timers benefits classroom discussions, which "have more depth due to the high percentage of currently working professionals that attend classes at Liautaud."

UIC MBAs explain that their curriculum "is very intellectually stimulating. The emphasis is not only on the practical/business knowledge, but also on the social-science nature of business (for example, interactions between individuals). Professors challenge students to apply concepts from all aspects of life." Course work places "much emphasis on group effort. If you have difficulty communicating or working with others, this will be a difficult program. If you like group projects, you will do fine." Students are especially keen on the school's programs in entrepreneurship and finance. They also love the low tuition, which gives a UIC MBA a great return on investment. One student sums up, "Arguably, with the exception of Kellogg and Chicago, this is the best MBA program in Chicago, and it is certainly the best public MBA program in the area."

Career and Placement

UIC students agree that their Business Career Center "is the area of the school in greatest need of improvement." MBAs complain that "the office really does a bad job of distinguishing between the needs of an MBA student and the needs of an undergraduate. They kind of clump us together when it comes to most of their services. They seriously need to develop some MBA career placement initiatives." Another student adds, "Other than looking over your resume and doing a mock interview, you're pretty much on your own. The career center doesn't act as though it has a vested interest in showing high placement rates at all."

Employers who have hired UIC MBAs in recent years include Accenture; Aegon Insurance; Alphants Trading; Caterpillar; Citibank; Discover Financial Services; Fujisan.com; KPMG; LG Chemical; MacArthur Foundation; Maytag; Nestle; Netsource; R.R. Donnelley; SAP America; S. C. Johnson & Son, Inc.; Siemens; Takeda Pharmaceuticals; Unilever; and Wirthlin Worldwide.

RITA BIELIAUSKAS, ASSISTANT DIRECTOR
815 WEST VAN BUREN, SUITE 220, CHICAGO, IL 60607 UNITED STATES
PHONE: 312-996-4573 • FAX: 312-413-0338
E-MAIL: MBA@UIC.EDU • WEBSITE: WWW.MBA.UIC.EDU

Student Life and Environment

Students say, "Going to school in Chicago is amazing." One student reports that "the city is unbelievable, and, as a business student, it is very important to me that UIC is located in the heart of the Chicago business scene." MBAs explain that "many parts of the city of Chicago have been rejuvenated, and the UIC campus area is one of them. There are plenty of great restaurants and pubs in the area. The United Center where the Bulls and Blackhawks play is within walking distance of campus, and the subway cuts right through the UIC for easy access to everything." However, some students warn that "the safety around the campus isn't the best, but the school has really tried to help with that by putting emergency light posts all over the campus." UIC also offers an MBA program at its Oak Brook campus in Chicago's western suburbs.

The UIC MBA student population includes "a wide variety of students from diverse ethnic and social backgrounds. This helps to make all students more aware of the world and keeps them in touch with the global business environment." Because "it's very much a commuter campus" and "students live all over the city, it's not easy to organize social activities that all may attend." Regular get-togethers include MBA Bar Night, as well as "other great events organized by the MBA Association, so that we can socialize outside of school," according to students.

The MBA program currently shares its facility with business undergraduates, a situation that many here find irksome. "The MBA program wants to build their own building to house classes and offices. This will be the best thing to bring students and the program more cohesion," one student notes.

Admissions

The admissions committee at UIC considers all the following components of an application: undergraduate and graduate transcripts, GMAT scores, TOEFL scores (international students), employment history (the school "strongly recommends" a minimum of two to three years full-time work experience following undergraduate work), two letters of reference, a personal statement of purpose, and record of organizational involvement. Students are expected to enter with a working knowledge of business statistics. Interviews are given by invitation of the admissions committee only.

FINANCIAL FACTS

Annual tuition (in-state/out-of-state)	$14,308/$25,522
Fees	$1,900
Books and supplies	$1,695
Room & board	$10,305

ADMISSIONS

Admissions Selectivity Rating	82
# of applications received	397
% applicants accepted	50
% acceptees attending	51
Average GMAT	570
Average GPA	3.1
TOEFL Required of International Students?	Yes
Minimum TOEFL (paper/computer)	570/230
Application fee	$55
International application fee	$65
Regular application deadline	5/15
Regular notification	Rolling
Deferment Available?	Yes
Maximum length of deferment	1 semester
Transfer students accepted?	Yes
Transfer application policy: Need to apply and be accepted to the UIC MBA Program. Can submit transcripts from previous coursework with a grade of B or better and a course description. Must be from an AACSB accredited institution. Maximum of 24 semester hours may transfer.	
Non-fall admissions?	Yes
Need-blind admissions?	Yes

APPLICANTS ALSO LOOK AT

DePaul University, Loyola University—Chicago, Northwestern University, The University of Chicago.

EMPLOYMENT PROFILE

		Grads employed by field	%: avg. salary
Career Rating	70		
Placement rate (%)	71	Finance	30: $58,000
# of companies recruiting on-campus	60	Marketing	35: $44,000
% grads employed immediately	20	General Management	25: $61,000
Average starting salary	$57,204		

UNIVERSITY OF ILLINOIS—URBANA-CHAMPAIGN

GENERAL INFORMATION

Type of school   public
Environment   city
Academic calendar   semester

SURVEY SAYS...
Friendly students
Happy students
Smart classrooms
Solid preparation in:
Teamwork
Communication/interpersonal skills
Presentation skills

STUDENTS
Enrollment of parent
  institution   38,904
Enrollment of MBA program   267
% male/female   73/27
% minorities   3
Average age at entry   27
Average years work experience
  at entry   4

ACADEMICS
Academic Experience Rating   93
Student/faculty ratio   3:1
Profs interesting rating   95
Profs accessible rating   84
% female faculty   18
% minority faculty   14

Joint Degrees
MBA/MArch: 2.5 years
MBA/MS Computer Science: 2.5
years
MBA/MS Civil and Environmental
Engineering: 2.5 years
MBA/MS Electrical Engineering: 2.5
years
MBA/MS Industrial Engineering: 2.5
years
MBA/MS Mechanical Engineering:
2.5 years
MBA/MD: 5 years
MBA/MS Journalism: 2.5 years
MBA/JD: 4 years
MBA/MS Human Resource
Education: 2.5 years

Academics

"Our greatest strength lies in research," one satisfied MBA at the University of Illinois—Urbana-Champaign writes. "[The] professors are often on the cutting edge of research, so we are often taught things that won't show up in textbooks for several years." Some of that cutting-edge research goes on outside of the b-school—Urbana-Champaign boasted two Nobel Prize winners in 2003, one in medicine, one in physics—but MBAs can access it all the same through the school's well-regarded joint-degree programs. One student explains pursuing simultaneous degrees in business and engineering: "The MBA program here is excellently paired with the engineering department in the form of a joint degree. It only takes four or five semesters to get both master's degrees."

Throughout the curriculum, "teachers work together to prevent overlapping cases and subjects and to complement one class with another one." This "effective integration of instruction" earns the praise of the students; one MBA writes, "The classes and activities for the first year are well-organized and fully integrated. The program is designed for students to occupy nearly all of their time doing something—homework, study teams, intramurals, clubs, events—related to the school." Things open up in the second year, as the curriculum "offers more flexibility. In fact, there are far too many offerings in the second year for you to do them all."

Illinois MBAs are bullish on their school's future, and they report that "our new administration comprises many folks formerly from Stern Business School of New York University, and it's doing wonders with the MBA program." As one student explains, "Academically, Illinois MBA can take any other business school by its horns and give it a good run for its money. In coming years, I expect the program to catch up with the leading business school in administration domain and then smoothly slip into the tier-one business school rankings." Students comment that finance is the strongest core area.

Career and Placement

University of Illinois maintains a fully automated resume-posting and job-listing board for its students; the site is called Compass and even e-mails students automatically when positions suiting their qualifications are posted. The school hosts "over 20" career fairs over the course of the school year. Some are exclusively for MBAs, others are open to a wider range of students; in all, there are more than 2,000 employers make recruiting visits to the campus each year. An executive skills program for students sharpens their job-seeking skills; a new externship program gives them a little extra to put on their resumes. While some students complain that "career services needs to get their act together and get more alumni support for current students, and more effort needs to be made to support international students in finding careers;" other students feel that "the administration [is working] very hard." Students say, "We can feel the positive effects of its effort in career services and organizing business events." Most MBAs understand the handicap under which administrators labor; one MBA writes, "Because the location of our schools is far from the big cities, it's hard to attract as many employers as possible to come here to recruit us."

Companies that most frequently hire Illinois graduates include AC Nielsen, Accenture, Agilent Technologies, Aquila, AT&T, Deloitte Touche Tohmatsu, Dynegy, Ford Motor Company, Gallup Organization, Kraft Foods, Procter & Gamble, and Samsung. The school's alumni network is more than 10,000 strong. Average starting salaries range from $52,000 (production/operations) to over $80,000 (human resources, other). Over one-third of Illinois graduates wind up in finance and accounting (average starting salary in 2003: $71,000).

SARAH ZEHR, ASSOCIATE DIRECTOR OF ADMISSIONS
405 DAVID KINLEY HALL, 1407 WEST GREGORY DRIVE, URBANA, IL 61801 UNITED STATES
PHONE: 217-244-7602 • FAX: 217-333-1156
E-MAIL: MBA@UIUC.EDU • WEBSITE: WWW.MBA.UIUC.EDU

Student Life and Environment

Urbana-Champaign students report, "[The school] has the best of both worlds: lots of cultural things, but with small-town charm, little traffic, and lots of nature and hiking nearby." While "being located in Champaign does have its drawbacks"—primarily, isolation from the big city and big-city jobs and internships—"there are plenty of opportunities to be involved if you take the initiative." In addition, "it's only a short trip to Chicago or Indianapolis if you crave bigger cities."

Not that there's any need to leave campus because "each day is full, whether it's classes and teamwork, or company presentations and extracurriculars, or simply having fun and relaxing with classmates." The school hosts "many clubs formed by MBA students, MBA softball team, MBA soccer team, [and] MBA volleyball team. Everybody can become friends through various club activities." MBAs say, "Student participation in clubs outside of class is heavy." Students explain that they are particularly proud of the Office of Strategic Business Initiatives (OSBI) Consulting, "a student-run consulting organization" that "provides a meaningful interface among MBA students, the faculty, and business leaders." MBAs add that "over two-thirds of students join, even though involvement is not mandatory, and classwork is really demanding." Students also praise the "first year-second year mentoring program, which is designed to help everyone acclimate to the IMBA program; also, second-year mentors help first years in the job search. It's totally their own thing on their own time, which is great."

Social life at the University of Illinois piggybacks on university-at-large events, especially Big Ten football and basketball games, which "can't be beat, especially when attending and tailgating with fellow students." Overall, students work hard, but not without a sense of proportion; they also "seem to be very concerned about having fun. [The University of Illinois] is seen as a party school, and the MBA students do their fair share of partying." Students also report approvingly that "off-campus housing is widely available" and that "public transportation is good; though the campus is large, the transportation provided makes varied destinations accessible."

Admissions

The University of Illinois admissions department considers GPA, GMAT scores, letters of recommendation, personal essay, interview, and, where appropriate, TOEFL scores; all of these are required. Optional, but also important, are extracurriculars and work experience. The school stresses that "work experience is weighted heavily in admissions decisions. At least two years of full-time, post-undergraduate experience is strongly recommended, although exceptions have been made in the cases of joint degree applicants and applicants with compelling part-time experience." Prior internships and military experience can also work in the favor of applicants.

Prominent Alumni

Mike Tokarz, Chairman, The Tokarz Group; Tom Siebel, Founder, Chairman & CEO, Siebel Systems, Inc.; Jan Klug Valentic, Executive VP, Young and Rubican; Alan Feldman, Pres. & CEO, Midas, Inc.; Bruce Holecek, CEO, Hobbico.

FINANCIAL FACTS

Annual tuition (in-state/out-of-state)	$16,400/$23,500
Fees	$1,640
Books and supplies	$1,000
Room & board	$15,168

ADMISSIONS

Admissions Selectivity Rating	92
# of applications received	643
% applicants accepted	38
% acceptees attending	38
Average GMAT	649
Range of GMAT	620-680
Average GPA	3.4
TOEFL Required of International Students?	Yes
Application fee	$40
International application fee	$50
Regular application deadline	3/15
Regular notification	Rolling
Early decision program?	Yes
ED Deadline/Notification	12/15 / 2/15
Need-blind admissions?	Yes

APPLICANTS ALSO LOOK AT

Indiana University, Northwestern University, Purdue University, University of Chicago, University of Michigan, University of Wisconsin-Madison, Washington University in St. Louis.

EMPLOYMENT PROFILE			
Career Rating	88	**Grads employed by field %: avg. salary**	
Placement rate (%)	96	Finance	18 $64,300
Average starting salary	$68,997	Human Resources	6 $60,000
		Marketing	18 $71,500
		MIS	3 $60,000
		Operations	6 $82,500
		Consulting	29: $68,500
		General Management	15: $72,800
		Other	5

UNIVERSITY OF IOWA
HENRY B. TIPPIE SCHOOL OF MANAGEMENT

GENERAL INFORMATION

Type of school	public
Environment	village
Academic calendar	semester

SURVEY SAYS...
Students love Iowa City, IA, Friendly students, Happy students, Smart classrooms
Solid preparation in:
Finance, Teamwork

STUDENTS

Enrollment of parent institution	29,745
Enrollment of MBA program	896
% male/female	71/29
% out-of-state	65
% part-time	83
% minorities	3
% international	41
Average age at entry	28
Average years work experience at entry	3.95

ACADEMICS

Academic Experience Rating	87
Student/faculty ratio	6:1
Profs interesting rating	73
Profs accessible rating	87
% female faculty	24
% minority faculty	14

Joint Degrees
MBA/JD: 4 years
MBA/Hospital and Health Administration: 2.5 years
MBA/MLS: 3 years
MBA/MS in nursing, 3 years
MBA/MD: 5 years

Prominent Alumni
Steven L. Caves, President, Firstar Bank Iowa (Banking); Kathleen A. Dore, President, TV & Radio CanWest Mediaworks; Kerry Killinger, Chairman, Pres. & CEO, Washington Mutual Sav. Bank; Michael Maves, M.D., Executive VP & CEO, American Medical Assn.; Ted E. Ziemann, President, Cargill Health & Food.

Academics

With standout concentrations in finance and marketing, and a dedication to bestowing a "personal touch" on all its students, the Henry B. Tippie School of Management at the University of Iowa provides one of the best publicly funded MBAs in the United States. And thanks to its state-level tuitions, Tippie offers a fabulous return on investment; *Business Week* recently ranked it the MBA with the eighth-fastest payback. Small class sizes and a dedicated administration allow for the personal touches Tippie justly brags about. Students explain that "everyone is very committed to making Tippie as strong a program as possible, and it shows. Just as the primary responsibility of the board is to maximize shareholder value, the faculty [does] a great job of maximizing student value in the MBA program." One student notes, "I've been very impressed. The dean of the school has an open-door policy and is incredibly accessible. He and many professors have made student support a priority. Faculty and staff attend the majority of student social functions and are completely accessible." The University of Iowa's integrated core means "the classes inform each other to a great extent. For example, shortly after we learned regression in statistics, we used regression modeling in marketing to analyze the relationship between the price and market share of several ketchup brands," according to students. The core is flexible enough "to give students the opportunity during the second semester to begin course work in their area of concentration," an option that students appreciate. The core is strongest in Tippie's top disciplines; one student explains, "The finance and marketing faculty are terrific. I'm still in my first semester, and they have already walked us through basic concepts and decision-making tools so well that I scored better on midterms than some students who were already practitioners in those fields."

Overall, Tippie professors "are demanding, but take interest in each student's development. They not only are available for help with a particular subject, but also assist students in exploring career goals." While "the academics are very demanding, especially in relation to quantitative skills," the "small size of the program and the social life allows you to create strong friendships immediately, which in turn helps any academic weakness you might have," according to the students. MBAs love the school's resources, and they explain that "every classroom is perfectly equipped with useful technology. The building itself is modern yet comfortable." However, some students warn that "A lot of the course documents are posted online, and the [support program] goes down a lot. It's a huge time-waster." The university-at-large offers "many fabulous resources," and students say that "there are tons of opportunities to do directed studies with professors or consulting engagements with outside companies. Additionally, we get pushed hard in the classroom which prepares us well for internships and jobs."

Career and Placement

The MBA Career Services Office at Tippie earns praise for its personalized service. This "dedicated placement center that knows each student individually learns what each of us wants to do, so they can proactively 'sell' us to employers," students say. Career services are enhanced by "alumni who [help] in networking and opening up internship opportunities. Also, outside speakers are brought in regularly to give another perspective and networking opportunity." Students point out that "perhaps due to its location, Iowa fails to attract a wide range of companies to campus—no high-tech companies or investment banks."

Top employers of Tippie MBAs include AEGON, N.V.; Allstate Corporation; Allsteel, Inc.; Best Buy Co.; CitiGroup; General Electric; HNI Co.; John Deere Credit Co.; Kimberly-Clark Corporation; Lil' Drug Store Products, Inc.; Northwest Airlines Corporation; Pearson; Principal Financial Group, Inc.; Procter & Gamble; and Rockwell Collins, Inc.

MARY SPREEN, DIRECTOR OF MBA ADMISSIONS AND FINANCIAL AID
108 JOHN PAPPAJOHN BUSINESS BUILDING, C140, HEY B. TIPPIE SCHOOL OF MANAGEMENT, THE
UNIVERSITY OF IOWA, IOWA CITY, IA 52242-1000 UNITED STATES
PHONE: 319-335-1039 • FAX: 319-335-3604
E-MAIL: TIPPIEMBA@UIOWA.EDU • WEBSITE: WWW.BIZ.UIOWA.EDU/MBA

Student Life and Environment

Tippie MBAs have nothing but praise for their classmates and explain that "because Iowa is fairly tough to get into, the students here tend to be highly intelligent and very serious about classes. Some of my classmates include a writer, a musician, a scientist, and, of course, people with business and engineering backgrounds. Iowa accepts people from all disciplines, and I consider this to be a strength." This mutual admiration society loves to hang together; as one student explains, "There is a great deal of camaraderie among the students, which makes for a pleasant class scene. Although it's not as party-intense as college, it's nice to know that grad students can still have fun!"

The high point of the Tippie social calendar arrives on Thursday evening with TGIT (short for "Thank God It's Thursday"). The event "is held each week, and almost all the MBA students of two years attend this fascinating activity." It usually takes place "at one of the many local bars. It's a great atmosphere, and there are always drink specials. It's great because there are no classes on Friday." Besides TGIT, students also convene for "team sports, especially football—the MBA Association sponsors tailgates before each game," and "international lunches where international students prepare food and educate us about their countries and cultures." The many MBA student organizations "provide a wide array of activities to get involved in, either by participating or by assuming a leadership role."

Although not located in a major business center, Tippie's Iowa City location has a lot to recommend it. For one, the cost of living in this "great and very friendly community of students" is "so affordable that a number of students have bought their own houses. Three of my classmates live in my neighborhood, and we do what most late-20s and early-30s couples do, when we have time." Further easing the financial burden of school is the fact that "almost anyone who wants an assistantship (TA or GA) can have one. For out-of-state students, this earns them in-state tuition. For all students, these pay roughly $8,000 for the nine months of school."

Admissions

Tippie applicants must submit official copies of all undergraduate and graduate transcripts, GMAT scores, TOEFL scores (for the school's considerable pool of international applicants whose first language isn't English), letters of recommendation, a personal statement, and a resume; two years of full-time, post-baccalaureate professional experience is required. Applications are evaluated for evidence of leadership qualities. Tippie is the recipient of a FISPE grant to the Iowa Electronic Markets' initiative, whose goal is to promote knowledge of markets among minority students.

FINANCIAL FACTS

Annual tuition (in-state/out-of-state)	$10,500/$19,262
Fees	$694
Books and supplies	$2,000
Room & board (on/off-campus)	$7,358/$7,875
% of students receiving aid	62
% of first-year students receiving aid	56
% of students receiving grants	43
Average award package	$15,023
Average grant	$2,443
Average student loan debt	$21,059

ADMISSIONS

Admissions Selectivity Rating	90
# of applications received	273
% applicants accepted	47
% acceptees attending	49
Average GMAT	645
Range of GMAT	610-670
Average GPA	3.36
TOEFL Required of International Students?	Yes
Minimum TOEFL (paper/computer)	600/250
Application fee	$60
International application fee	$85
Regular application deadline	7/15
Regular notification	Rolling
Deferment Available?	Yes
Maximum length of deferment	1 year
Transfer students accepted?	Yes
Transfer application policy: Maximum of nine credits are transferable (from AACSB-accredited programs only).	
Non-fall admissions?	Yes
Need-blind admissions?	Yes

APPLICANTS ALSO LOOK AT

Indiana University, Michigan State University, Ohio State University, Purdue University, University of Illinois at Urbana-Champaign, University of Minnesota, University of Wisconsin—Madison.

EMPLOYMENT PROFILE			
Career Rating	87	**Grads employed by field %: avg. salary**	
Placement rate (%)	91	Finance	26: $67,960
% grads employed immediately	73	Marketing	37: $70,889
Average starting salary	$72,020	Operations	11: NR
		Consulting	5: NR
		General Management	11: NR
		Other	10: NR

UNIVERSITY OF KANSAS
SCHOOL OF BUSINESS

GENERAL INFORMATION
Type of school	public
Environment	city
Academic calendar	semester

SURVEY SAYS...
Students love Lawrence, KS
Friendly students
Good peer network
Cutting edge classes
Happy students
Smart classrooms

STUDENTS
Enrollment of parent institution	26,894
Enrollment of MBA program	380
% male/female	70/30
% out-of-state	33
% part-time	83
% minorities	4
% international	24
Average age at entry	28
Average years work experience at entry	7

ACADEMICS
Academic Experience Rating	84
Student/faculty ratio	8:1
Profs interesting rating	75
Profs accessible rating	76
% female faculty	30
% minority faculty	2
Joint Degrees	
MBA/JD: 4 years	

Academics

Brand-name recognition is one of the chief drawing cards of the University of Kansas School of Business; students note that the b-school's parent university is "the best school in Kansas and is among the best schools in the Midwest. It has a long tradition as a top university in the nation." Students expect to parlay that reputation into solid job offerings following graduation from this MBA program, whose greatest strengths lie in finance and international business.

KU's core curriculum divides first-year semesters into eight-week half-semester modules "so students can move quickly into electives and areas of concentration." Students approve of the concept but say there are a few kinks in its execution. One MBA notes, "Last October, I had new classes begin before I was done with finals from the last module. It was just dumb luck that they weren't scheduled at the same time. They need to work on coordinating classes better."

"International business is probably the best part of the KU program," many students feel, citing the school's unique one year MBA in Italy program as well as the presence of the Center for International Business Education and Research on the Lawrence campus. Student say, "There are many excellent opportunities to study abroad." KU MBAs may concentrate in international business; other options include finance, marketing, e-business, information systems, information technology, and human-resource management.

The KU faculty is "very distinguished, very accessible, very open to sharing real-world experiences, and very sensitive to students' needs. They pick up a lot of slack and make the program worthwhile." The administration for the university at large is "a nightmare," but the b-school's administration is much better; students explain that it "has demonstrated knowledge, accuracy, and follow-through." Students also add that "the school needs to develop much more if it wants to go places. But there is a lot of potential, as the administration is very student friendly and will listen to our suggestions and ideas."

Career and Placement

The Business Career Services Center at KU serves the school's undergraduates and graduates in business disciplines with a variety of workshops, counseling sessions, and career fairs. The school belongs to the 11-school Southwest MBA Alliance, which allows members to "combine efforts each year in order to foster connections between progressive businesses and our outstanding MBA students." The office also maintains a Listserv to notify students when its job listings are updated. Students explain that "career development and placement has been a very low priority in the past. The b-school is planning to raise tuition for improvements that include this area."

Top employers of KU MBAs include Accenture, Anderson Consulting, Aquila, Cap Gemini, Cerner Corporation, Deloitte Consulting, Ernst & Young, KPMG, McGladrey & Pullen, Payless ShoeSource, and Sprint. Approximately one in five KU graduates find their first post-MBA job outside the United States.

Dee Steinle, Associate Director of Master's Programs
206 Summerfield Hall, 1300 Sunnyside Avenue, Lawrence, KS 66045 United States
Phone: 785-864-3844 • Fax: 785-864-5376
E-mail: bschoolgrad@ku.edu • Website: www.business.ku.edu

Student Life and Environment

KU's full-time MBA program is headquartered at the main campus in Lawrence. The campus is "attractive and well-maintained. The classrooms are comfortable and conducive to learning. The library and computer labs are state-of-the-art and very comfortable for studying." Full-time students also take some courses at the Edwards Campus in Overland Park. The drive from Lawrence is approximately 40 minutes; this campus is home to KU's part-time MBA program, and it offers classes in the evening only. This satellite campus "needs to improve its facilities," but "renovations are under way," so those improvements should come soon. Students wish that the bookstore, library services, and similar amenities would keep evening hours. One student complains, "Right now many of these places close at 7:00 P.M., which does us no good at all."

Part-time students also report that there's little more to their program than "getting to class lectures and back. Group and teamwork is carried out, but I think it's looked upon as quite a burden by the students." Extracurricular activity is at a minimum. One student explains, "This is a professional MBA program. Most people work full-time and attend classes at night." Students add that "there is no interaction between full-timers and the part-time business school students other than a 10 to 15 minute break in a 3.5 hour period."

Full-time students tend to be younger than the part-timers, and they enjoy a life that more closely resembles a typical undergraduate social scene. Students explain that "life at KU is very nice, with tons of things to do. Lawrence is a beautiful college town, and basketball is a religion at KU," and "there are plenty of social opportunities. MBA students often go out on the town together." Lawrence, a city of about 100,000, has a vital arts community, great golf courses, and an environment conducive to business; Inc.com named the Lawrence area one of the nation's 20 best in which to start and grow a company. KU's MBA student body is "a pretty good crowd of mid-20-year-olds" with a "substantial international community" figuring into the mix.

Admissions

Students applying to the University of Kansas School of Business must submit GMAT scores, TOEFL scores (if applicable), two copies of official transcripts from each postsecondary school attended, two letters of recommendation from employers and/or professors, responses to three essay questions, and a resume. Two years of postbaccalaureate full-time professional experience are recommended, and "those without this experience will be at a competitive disadvantage in admissions. However, demonstrating exceptional personal attributes may, to an extent, offset this disadvantage." Limited scholarship funding is available to all students in the full-time program based on academic excellence and/or need.

FINANCIAL FACTS

Annual tuition (in-state/out-of-state)	
	$3,777/$12,333
Fees	$470
Books and supplies	$800
Room & board (on/off-campus)	
	$5,600/$6,686
% of students receiving aid	50
% of first-year students	
receiving aid	50
% of students receiving grants	25
Average grant	$1,500

ADMISSIONS

Admissions Selectivity Rating	87
# of applications received	182
% applicants accepted	58
% acceptees attending	90
Average GMAT	607
Range of GMAT	540-690
Average GPA	3.3
TOEFL Required of	
International Students?	Yes
Minimum TOEFL	
(paper/computer)	600/250
Application fee	$60
International application fee	$60
Regular application deadline	6/1
Regular notification	Rolling
Deferment Available?	Yes
Maximum length of	
deferment	1 year
Transfer students accepted?	Yes
Transfer application policy:	
Maximum number of transferable	
credit hours is six.	
Non-fall admissions?	Yes
Need-blind admissions?	Yes

APPLICANTS ALSO LOOK AT

Iowa State University, University of Iowa, University of Missouri—Columbia, University of Nebraska—Lincoln, University of Oklahoma.

EMPLOYMENT PROFILE

Career Rating	71	Grads employed by field %: avg. salary	
Placement rate (%)	76	Finance	35: $61,000
% grads employed immediately	60	Marketing	10: $41,200
Average starting salary	$52,999	MIS	5: $41,000
		Operations	8: NR
		Consulting	5: $65,660
		General Management	5: $56,650
		Other	32: $56,650

UNIVERSITY OF KENTUCKY
THE GATTON COLLEGE OF BUSINESS AND ECONOMICS

GENERAL INFORMATION

Type of school	public
Environment	city
Academic calendar	semester

SURVEY SAYS...
Friendly students
Smart classrooms
Solid preparation in:
Teamwork
Presentation skills

STUDENTS

Enrollment of parent institution	26,260
Enrollment of MBA program	245
% male/female	67/33
% out-of-state	20
% part-time	39
% minorities	7
% international	12
Average age at entry	26
Average years work experience at entry	2.4

ACADEMICS

Academic Experience Rating	**82**
Student/faculty ratio	4:1
Profs interesting rating	62
Profs accessible rating	63
% female faculty	15
% minority faculty	5

Joint Degrees
MBA/JD: 4 years
MBA/BS in Engineering: 5 years
MBA/MD: 5 years
MBA/PhG: 4 years
MBA/MA in International Relations: 3 years

Prominent Alumni
Chris Sullivan, Chairman of the Board, Outback Steakhouse; Paul Rooke, Executive VP, Lexmark International, Inc.; Gretchen Price, VP, Finance & Accounting, Global Operations, P&G; Greg Burns, Chairman and CEO, O'Charley's, Inc.; James E. Rogers, Jr., Chairman, Pres. and CEO, Cinergy Corp.

Academics

Everyone from the most experienced businessperson to the liberal-arts undergraduate, who has never before used a calculator, is welcome at the Gatton College of Business and Economics at the University of Kentucky. In fact, the program is set up to accommodate all levels of experience; it features two MBA tracks, one for those with undergraduate business degrees (business track) and those without (nonbusiness track).

Gatton's business track, geared toward students who "seek a course of study designed to develop more advanced skills across a wide range of business functions or focused within a particular functional area of business," affords ample opportunities to sample electives in accounting, finance, management, marketing, MIS, and international business. (Students explain that the program has "comparative advantages in finance and accounting, especially in the regional job market.") The nonbusiness track imposes many more required courses; in addition, many entering this track are required to complete pre-MBA foundation course work before commencing MBA work (see Admissions). Both tracks consist of 36 class hours, requiring three semesters of full-time study to complete. Students give the curriculum high marks; although, some students feel that "we could use less theory and more case study/practical application," and that "maybe [the curriculum] could add a little more emphasis on some quantitative areas."

Students love the friendly vibe of the Gatton program, and they explain that "the non-condescending attitude is the greatest strength at UK. We are a strong academic school, but we are all accepting of others. It makes for a positive working environment. The faculty is available and knowledgeable, making it easy to get one-on-one help." Gatton's administration "is visible, involved, and constantly asking our advice on what improvements should be made to increase the value of our MBA," according to students. Unfortunately, the bureaucracy of the university at large makes it difficult for MBAs to take advantage of UK's many other fine programs. One student complains, "The administration of other programs does not seem to communicate well with the business school to facilitate taking courses in areas outside of the business school."

Career and Placement

MBAs at Gatton College are served by the James W. Stuckert Career Center. Students explain that one officer handles placement services for both business undergrads and MBAs, but they feel that "[they] need career services focused on MBAs alone, not a joint person for undergrad and grad." The office provides opportunities through networking, job fairs, on-campus recruitment (about 180 companies make recruiting trips to the campus each year), job banks, and professional organizations. The career center also provides counseling services.

Top recruiters at Gatton include Bank One, Citigroup, Ernst and Young, Johnson & Johnson, Lexmark International, Procter & Gamble, Sunoco, University of Kentucky, and Yum! Brands. About 1 in 20 UK MBAs moves on to a job outside the United States.

Student Life and Environment

Gatton MBAs enjoy the benefits of a small-program environment within a university community; one student explains, "UK is a large university, but the MBA program has a distinct family feel that is very helpful at times." The advantages conferred by the university include first-class research and fitness facilities, a population large enough to attract prominent guest speakers and famous entertainers, and, of course, competitive and fanatically followed athletic teams. "Be prepared to become a big-time UK fan if you are not already. It's all about football and basketball here," one student observes.

BEVERLY KEMPER, MBA ACADEMIC COORDINATOR
145 GATTON COLLEGE OF BUSINESS AND ECONOMICS LEXINGTON, KY 40506-0034 UNITED STATES
PHONE: 859-257-7722 • FAX: 859-323-9971
E-MAIL: KEMPER@UKY.EDU • WEBSITE: GATTON.UKY.EDU

The Gatton program provides students with more cozy environs, including "an MBA center with a big lounge, a big-screen TV, and snacks available. At any given time, there are 5 to 10 students conversing together, laughing [and] hanging out. We eat lunch together at the popular pizza pubs, go to basketball and football games, and we even hang out at Makers' Mark. We are more than classmates: we're friends," students say. The community gels around the MBA Association, which "has been very successful in social activities and bringing the students closer together outside the classroom." All in all, "MBAs spend a lot of time together, in group projects, with homework, and in outside activities. We have all become very close and are all currently trying to help each other find jobs, so we have a unique type of competition." One student says, "I will really miss this program and especially my classmates." Students at UK "have a unique identity. We have a wide range of backgrounds and demographics so that we all learn from each other in one way or another."

Hometown Lexington is yet another one of Gatton's advantages. One student explains, "Location is the greatest asset for the school. It's a relatively small town close to a metropolitan area (Louisville)." There are plenty of businesses headquartered in the area, including Ashland, Inc.; Bank One; General Electric; Lexmark; Square D; and Toyota. As a result, Lexington provides "many opportunities for outside independent-study projects with companies." The city is home to an active arts scene; fans of the ponies will find plenty to cheer about at the area's two racetracks, Keeneland (thoroughbreds) and Red Mile (harness racing).

Admissions

A complete application to the Gatton MBA program includes official copies of all undergraduate and graduate transcripts, GMAT scores, TOEFL scores (international students), a personal statement, letters of recommendation, and a resume. The school reports that "the admissions decision is also influenced by communication skills, international experience, and work experience." Proficiency in the basics of financial and managerial accounting, micro- and macro-economics, calculus, and statistics is a prerequisite to entering the MBA program. Those lacking proficiency may be admitted provisionally but cannot commence MBA work until they complete pre-MBA foundation course work. The school lists the following programs aimed at recruitment of minority/disadvantaged students: the Academic Excellence Scholarship, Commonwealth Minority Scholarship Program, the Kentucky Scholars program, and Lyman T. Johnson fellowships.

FINANCIAL FACTS

Annual tuition (in-state/out-of-state)	$5,978/$15,122
Fees	$1,163
Books and supplies	$1,200
Room & board (on/off-campus)	$8,250/$9,100
% of students receiving aid	29
% of first-year students receiving aid	32
% of students receiving grants	27
Average award package	$7,060
Average grant	$3,921

ADMISSIONS

Admissions Selectivity Rating	87
# of applications received	214
% applicants accepted	56
% acceptees attending	78
Average GMAT	607
Range of GMAT	570-640
Average GPA	3.3
TOEFL Required of International Students?	Yes
Minimum TOEFL (paper/computer)	550/213
Application fee	$40
International application fee	$55
Regular application deadline	4/1
Regular notification	Rolling
Transfer students accepted?	Yes
Transfer application policy: File must be completed and applicant is considered as a regular applicant.	
Need-blind admissions?	Yes

APPLICANTS ALSO LOOK AT

Eastern Kentucky University, Indiana University, The Ohio State University, University of Cincinnati, University of Louisville, University of Tennessee, Xavier University.

EMPLOYMENT PROFILE

		Grads employed by field	%: avg. salary
Career Rating	70		
Placement rate (%)	79	Accounting	8: $42,000
# of companies recruiting on-campus	153	Marketing	23: $46,333
% grads employed immediately	68	MIS	15: $62,639
% grads employed within three months	75	Operations	31: $50,000
Average starting salary	$57,772	Strategic Planning	8: $80,000
		General Management	15: $40,000

UNIVERSITY OF LONDON
LONDON BUSINESS SCHOOL

Academics

"The international slant of the London Business School is its greatest strength," students agree, pointing to both the international focus of the curriculum and the school's location in "the most important financial and business centre of Europe." One MBA explains, "Everything that is done by the school—from creating the study-group teams to the content of the case studies in class—is centered around promoting internationalism. It is very impressive." The school's rare language requirement—students must be proficient in English and a second language (French, Spanish, German, Japanese, or Mandarin) demonstrates the prominence of international business.

LBS's 14-course first-year core is divided into three terms, throughout which "the integration of the different topics is very strong, helping one grasp the big picture quickly and efficiently prepare for the electives." Students caution that "the first-term workload is extremely heavy, but the second term is lighter, which lets time for the milk round." (Note: "Milk round" is a British term for "making the rounds," and usually refers to company-recruiting visits to university campuses.) Students especially appreciate how "the entire stream sits down to give feedback on each of the core classes at the end of the first year, and our comments are immediately fed back to the professors for improvement and/or encouragement. Unpopular electives are either drastically altered or discontinued."

Second year at LBS is a "year of choice," offering seven possible areas of concentration. Students identify strategy, entrepreneurship, and finance as the strongest areas; "London has a great position in the finance centre of Europe. There is no doubt it has deep and strong links with the finance industry with practically every investment bank I have ever heard of presenting at campus," noted one student. Electives in marketing, technology, and decision sciences also earn students' praise. Overall, students describe the LBS curriculum as "balanced, with lots of practical courses and interactions with the outside/real world." They praise the program's shadowing project (in which student's trail a manager for up to five days, then report on the experience) and the capstone second-year consulting project.

LBS faculty "deal daily with today's business issues either through their research or their consulting assignments. It is absolutely fantastic to see them bring that experience to class every week. Moreover, professors recognize they have a class full of bright and intelligent people in front of them and therefore engage them in the discussion and exploration of the latest business thinking. You do not have the feeling that you are back at high school where the teacher reads out what you should know." MBAs point out that profs "have to be good teachers to stay at London Business School. They're rigorously critiqued by students and administration."

Career and Placement

Students give Career Services at London Business School mixed reviews, noting that "in the past, the emphasis of Career Services has been strongly slanted toward finance and consulting, with industry being basically ignored. This focus is starting to shift and hopefully will continue to expand." Several MBAs observed that "the school has recruited new director for the career services and things seem to be improving." Until things get entirely up to speed, students can turn to their peers for added job-search assistance, as "the student clubs are especially effective at networking and helping with career strategies and contacts." They can also seek help from the school's 16,000 alumni working in over 100 countries across the globe.

Julie Ahrens, MBA Marketing & Admissions Manager
Regent's Park, NW1 4SA, London, England
Phone: 011-44-20-7262-5050 • Fax: 011-44-20-7724-7875
E-mail: mbainfo@london.edu • Website: www.london.edu

Top employers of LBS MBAs include A. T. Kearney, Accenture, American Express, Bain, Bank of America, Barclays Capital, Capital One, Booz Allen Hamilton, Citigroup, Deloitte Touche Tohmatsu, Deutsche Bank, Johnson & Johnson, JPMorgan, KPMG, Lehman Brothers, McKinsey, Merrill Lynch, Morgan Stanley, and UBS Warburg.

Student Life and Environment

LSB attracts a "truly international student and faculty body. More than 80 percent of students comes from outside U.K., giving an indescribable wealth of experience and network." Explains one MBA, "You will never be 'one of the foreign students' at LBS, since there is no dominating nationality. The students are amazingly diverse." Students learn about each others' cultures through the regional clubs, "such as the Indian and Asian clubs, which are very active and host a variety of activities and parties that introduce their country's culture to the student body. In fact, there are so many themed parties that it is sometimes hard to tear yourself away from school and remember that there is an amazing city to explore outside of the school neighborhood." Other clubs "run lectures or other events in the evening, which are good both for learning and networking." Students also have "a plethora of sports options, with men and women's rugby and football being the most popular. Everyone is involved in a club or sport."

Going to school in central London "provides the school access to business leaders from around the globe and direct access to companies," students tell us. One student observed that "London Business School's location limits the school's expanding capabilities—there's really nowhere to expand to in London—but overall the campus is great. It is much smaller than American b-schools, but I'd rather be in a smaller campus in London than in larger one outside the city." "The nightlife and culture are also great" in London; as one student told us, "It is hard to imagine a better social scene at your fingertips at any other school in the world. The only issue is that there may be too many distractions." The chief drawback: "Life in central London can be quite expensive (probably more expensive than Manhattan, even)."

Admissions

Admission to University of London requires "two to three years of work experience." The school notes that "candidates do not have to have international experience, but they must have international aspirations." Applicants must supply the school with official copies of all undergraduate and graduate transcripts, GMAT scores, two letters of reference, scores on an English proficiency test (where applicable), three essays, and a one-page curriculum vitae. The school reviews applications for evidence of management potential, personal motivation, interpersonal skills, language proficiency, and international orientation.

FINANCIAL FACTS

Annual tuition	$34,850
Books and supplies	$500
Room & board	$25,500
% of students receiving loans	56
Average grant	$5,000

ADMISSIONS

Admissions Selectivity Rating	60*
# of applications received	1,950
Average GMAT	685
Range of GMAT	650-710
Average GPA	3.5
TOEFL Required of International Students?	Yes
Application fee	$180
International application fee	$180
Regular application deadline	4/30
Regular notification	5/28
Application Deadline/Notification	
Round 1:	10/24 / 11/28
Round 2:	1/9 / 2/13
Round 3:	2/27 / 4/9
Round 4:	4/30 / 5/28
Deferment Available?	Yes
Maximum length of deferment	1 year

EMPLOYMENT PROFILE

Career Rating	60*	Grads employed by field:	
		Finance	30
		Consulting	22
		General Management	48

UNIVERSITY OF LOUISIANA—LAFAYETTE
B. I. MOODY III COLLEGE OF BUSINESS

GENERAL INFORMATION
Type of school   public
Environment   city
Academic calendar   semester

SURVEY SAYS...
Students love Lafayette, LA
Friendly students
Good social scene
Solid preparation in:
Teamwork

STUDENTS
Enrollment of parent
  institution   16,500
Enrollment of MBA program   187
% male/female   55/45
% out-of-state   9
% part-time   80
% minorities   8
% international   4
Average age at entry   30
Average years work experience
  at entry   7

ACADEMICS
Academic Experience Rating   74
Student/faculty ratio   18:1
Profs interesting rating   68
Profs accessible rating   81
% female faculty   40
% minority faculty   12
Prominent Alumni
Conrad Comeaux, Lafayette Parish
Tax Assessor; Mike DeHart, Stuller
Management Services, Inc.; Stefni
Lotief, UL Women's SoftBall Coach;
Greg Roberts, Dir. of Avaiation,
Lafayette Airport; Dr. Ross Judice,
Acadian Ambulance and Air Med,
EVP and CMO.

Academics

Students at the University of Louisiana—Lafayette's B.I. Moody College of Business appreciate that theirs is an MBA program constantly in search of improvements. Students explain that "UL has spent a lot of time and effort bringing the university up-to-date with the growing economy, and it has high standards which make getting a degree hard work and valuable." One student notes, "The school continually strives to increase enrollment and improve facilities." MBAs also report that Moody, a new b-school facility. The new structure, opened in January 2005, includes wi-fi capabilities, multimedia communications facilities, and new, state-of-the-art classrooms capable of accommodating a larger student body.

According to some students, the new building is the crowning piece of a long, concerted effort to "guide the university from a small, regional university to become the national-ly recognized university that it is today." Part of the effort involves "actively [pursuing] the best professors in the field," students report. Best of all, "administrators have grown this university while still providing the small university atmosphere where professors care about their students. This is evident from the first day on campus at orientation when our vice president of student affairs gives every new student a card with his home phone number. He urges all students to call him if they are ever in trouble [and explains] that we are his 'kids' now."

Moody MBAs also speak highly of their instructors. Students say that "many [professors] have or had prestigious careers in the fields they teach. This seems to help in giving students real-world examples of the ideas [they] are teaching." Students only complaint is with the scheduling of classes, which many report is inconvenient for those with full-time jobs. One student warns, "For anyone looking to pursue an MBA while still working, I would advise a different school. The MBA program here is offering fewer and fewer courses at night each semester." Another student adds, "[Making matters worse is that] many of the classes offered each semester conflict with each other, which makes it difficult to take all of the courses required in a timely manner."

Career and Placement

Career guidance is provided to Lafayette MBAs by the university's Career Services Center. According to the school's website, "the center serves as a major link between the students and potential employers and confirms its commitment to support and advance university/employer relationship." The office offers students workshops, seminars, one-on-one counseling, and access to various job-listing sources. Students explain that "alumni are supportive" and serve as a major resource in their job searches. Companies recruiting on campus in the spring of 2004 included BJ Services, Cameron Corporation, Drill-Quip, Halliburton, Magnolia Marketing, New York Life, and Union National.

Student Life and Environment

"UL is located in a part of Louisiana that is known for its hospitality and down-home feel," students say, and they add that "no matter where you are from, you are welcomed to this area with open arms." Lafayette is part of Louisiana's Acadiana region, historical home to French settlers and Creoles, among others. Its location near the Gulf of Mexico feeds the area's many oil- and gas-industry employers; the region has attempted to diversify its economy in recent years and has had some luck attracting manufacturers and companies in the transportation sector.

Dr. C. Eddie Palmer, Dean of the Graduate School
Martin Hall, Room #243, PO Box 40200, Lafayette, LA 70504-0200 United States
Phone: 337-482-6491 • Fax: 337-482-6195 • E-mail: MBA@louisiana.edu
Website: www.moody.louisiana.edu

Students say that campus life "offers the perfect blend of educational opportunities and extracurricular activities." UL "has many different clubs to be involved in, allowing students to feel like a part of the university. The faculty encourages involvement on campus and in the community." Recreational opportunities abound; one student reports, "My undergraduate and graduate life at UL Lafayette has been an even mix of studying and partying. While studies consume most of the week, the city of Lafayette always provides party opportunities such as Mardi Gras, Festival Acadiens, Downtown Alive, and many other cultural gatherings."

While hardly a small school, UL "is not a huge place where you get lost in the crowd, and that is what draws me to it the most," one student says. The MBA program is small enough that "everyone knows each other in the business school, and that creates a family atmosphere for everyone." Minority enrollment in the MBA program is small; non-white Americans make up only 8 percent of the student body. International students, who make up 10 percent of the program, arrive from the Caribbean, Europe, France, Greece, India, and Southeast Asia. About 30 percent of all MBA students majored in business and commerce as undergrads, another 50 percent majored in math or science, 10 percent studied engineering, and 10 percent were in humanities and social-science programs.

Admissions

Applicants to the Moody College of Business at UL must provide the school with an undergraduate transcript demonstrating a GPA of at least 2.75; GMAT scores (450 minimum); three letters of recommendation; and a resume "including (at a minimum) the dates and awarding institutions of academic degree(s); employment and salary history; a list of honors, awards, and professional certificates; a summary of basic computer skills; and a list of overseas travels and multilingual abilities. Prospective students are also encouraged to include a resume 'supplement' listing and briefly describing all relevant extracurricular and/or community involvement(s)." Undergraduate grades and GMAT score are "major selection criteria;" recommendations and resume are "significant (of moderate importance)" criteria. Students must also send the school "a written statement of purpose of 750 words or less describing the reasons why the prospective student wishes to pursue an MBA degree."

FINANCIAL FACTS

Annual tuition (in-state/out-of-state)	$3,104/$9,284
Books and supplies	$1,000
Room & board (on/off-campus)	$3,750/$6,750
% of students receiving aid	60
% of first-year students receiving aid	50
% of students receiving loans	40
% of students receiving grants	25
Average grant	$8,605
Average student loan debt	$5,000

ADMISSIONS

Admissions Selectivity Rating	78
# of applications received	116
% applicants accepted	52
% acceptees attending	62
Average GMAT	533
Range of GMAT	470-610
Average GPA	3.1
TOEFL Required of International Students?	Yes
Minimum TOEFL (paper/computer)	550/213
Application fee	$20
International application fee	$30
Regular application deadline	6/30
Regular notification	8/1
Early decision program?	Yes
ED Deadline/Notification	Rolling 6/1
Deferment Available?	Yes
Maximum length of deferment	1 year
Transfer students accepted?	Yes
Transfer application policy: Can transfer in a maximum of 9 credit hours. Must apply through regular process.	
Non-fall admissions?	Yes
Need-blind admissions?	Yes

APPLICANTS ALSO LOOK AT

Louisiana State University, Louisiana Tech University, Loyola University New Orleans, McNeese State University, Nicholls State University, Tulane University, University of New Orleans.

EMPLOYMENT PROFILE

Career Rating	77
Placement rate (%)	90
# of companies recruiting on-campus	63
% grads employed immediately	92
Average starting salary	$55,000

UNIVERSITY OF MARYLAND—COLLEGE PARK

ROBERT H. SMITH SCHOOL OF BUSINESS

GENERAL INFORMATION

Type of school	public
Environment	metropolis
Academic calendar	semester

SURVEY SAYS...

Friendly students
Cutting edge classes
Happy students
Smart classrooms
Solid preparation in:
Teamwork
Quantitative skills

STUDENTS

Enrollment of parent institution	34,933
Enrollment of MBA program	1,336
% male/female	67/33
% out-of-state	36
% part-time	76
% minorities	12
% international	35
Average age at entry	29
Average years work experience at entry	5.65

ACADEMICS

Academic Experience Rating	**91**
Student/faculty ratio	8:1
Profs interesting rating	97
Profs accessible rating	84
% female faculty	24
% minority faculty	20

Joint Degrees

MBA/MS: 2-5 years
MBA/JD: 3-5 years
MBA/MPM: 2-5 years
MBA/MSW: 2-3 years

Prominent Alumni

Carly Fiorina, Former Chairman & CEO, Hewlett Packard; James F. O'Brien, Head Coach, Philadelphia 76ers; Harold Kahn, CEO, Macy's East; Paul Norris, Chairman, Pres. & CEO, W.R. Grace & Company; Kevin Plank, Founder & Pres., Under Armour.

Academics

The Robert H. Smith School of Business at the University of Maryland—College Park places "an extraordinary emphasis on technology in business," refocusing traditional disciplines such as finance, management, and marketing on the emerging world of e-business. Thanks to the largesse of the school's namesake—an area real estate developer who recently donated $30 million to the university—the Smith School has the resources necessary to maintain and develop the state-of-the-art facilities its curriculum requires.

Smith MBAs commence their work with a core curriculum that "is very comprehensive and prepares students well with a solid foundation." Students report that "it is fast-paced and challenging, but the professors make sure the students keep pace." To ensure that students can tailor their MBAs to the areas that interest them most, Smith sets aside "a huge portion of degree requirements for elective courses." Electives can be used to fashion an area of specialization in one of 18 disciplines; students are especially enthusiastic about Smith's offerings in entrepreneurship and information technology. A general management degree without specialization is also an option here. In addition to the traditional curriculum, MBAs may also pursue Experiential Learning Modules (ELMs), such as case competitions, which "provide a great opportunity to continue learning and applying it outside of the classroom."

Smith professors, students agree, "are great. They are genuinely interested in our progress. Very approachable and down-to-earth, too." Observes one student, "Subjects I hated in my undergraduate university—economics and statistics, for example—I enjoy taking at Smith just because of the professors who teach them."

Career and Placement

Smith's Office of Career Management (OCM) offers MBA students the full complement of career-related services, including a number of high-tech interviewing and job-search facilities. Students report that "the office has made improvements in recent years but has a lot more room for growth." They also tell us that OCM "brings a good number of companies to campus, although more would certainly be better," but they also concede that "the size of the program—each full-time class is about 150 students—makes it more difficult to organize events and attract large companies." International students would love to see "at least one officer devoted exclusively to helping [us] find jobs." These students will be happy to hear that in April 2005 the school retained a leading immigration law firm, Reed Smith LLP, to help recruiters hire international students.

Employers most likely to hire Smith MBAs include: Avaya; Citigroup; Constellation Power Source; Deloitte; Delta; General Electric; Fannie Mae; IBM; Intel; Johnson & Johnson; Navigant; PepsiCo; PriceWaterhouseCoopers; UBS; Wachovia; and World Bank.

Student Life and Environment

Life at Smith is hectic, as "the pressure of the MBA is always looming overhead, with generally two case studies, one to two tests per week, and exams around the corner." Even so, "people still find time to enjoy themselves and hang around with friends." There's "Happy Hour every Thursday, sports clubs for those who like to play intramurals, and cultural clubs (Black, Hispanic, Indian, Asian, Chinese, International, and Jewish) that are very active within the school organizing dinners and fundraising." Students also like to "hit the DC club and bar scene on weekends, and any night of the week you can usually find someone who's willing to join you for a few beers at a local watering hole." One student observes, "There are enough activities inside and outside of

SABRINA WHITE, DIRECTOR, MBA & MS ADMISSIONS
2308 VAN MUNCHING HALL, UNIVERSITY OF MARYLAND, COLLEGE PARK, MD 20742-1871 U.S.
PHONE: 301-405-2278 • FAX: 301-314-9862
E-MAIL: MBA_INFO@RHSMITH.UMD.EDU • WEBSITE: WWW.RHSMITH.UMD.EDU

the classroom to keep anyone occupied. Formals, tailgates, sporting events, speakers, forums, career development—you name it, we have it." Maryland's part-time students are, of course, much less intimately integrated into extracurricular life. These students, who attend on evenings and weekends, generally spend the minimum amount of time necessary on campus.

Smith MBAs include "a large number of international students" and "a diverse blend of backgrounds, nationalities, ethnicities, and experience. Despite these differences, there is an amazingly strong team-oriented feeling here at Smith School." This "sense of community" is all the more amazing when you realize that "the student body is naturally fragmented by the fact that we live everywhere from Baltimore to Northern Virginia, not just in suburban Maryland and DC."

Admissions

All applicants to Smith MBA programs at College Park must submit the following to the School: two official copies of transcripts for all post-secondary academic work; an official GMAT score report; personal essays; two letters of recommendation; and a completed application form. Interviews are optional but recommended. International students must also provide an official TOEFL score report (minimum required score: 600 paper-based test, 250 computer-based test) and a financial certification form, with supporting documents. The school lists the following outreach programs for minority and disadvantaged students: Kaleidoscope: Advancing Diversity at Smith, a fall semester recruitment event for underrepresented minority students; Women and the MBA, a symposium oriented to educating women about the advantages of the MBA; Management Leadership for Tomorrow: a partnership that focuses on guiding minority students through the MBA application preparation process; online chats for prospective MBA students from underrepresented groups (Africa, South America, Women, African American,— and Hispanics); and participation at conferences of minority professional organizations, including the Society for Hispanic Professional Engineers, the Women's Information Network, Graduate Women in Business, the National Society for Black Engineers, and the Black MBA Association."

FINANCIAL FACTS

Annual tuition (in-state/out-of-state)	$14,454/$23,814
Fees	$6,777
Books and supplies	$1,600
Room & board	$10,500
% of students receiving aid	50
% of first-year students receiving aid	52
% of students receiving grants	11
Average grant	$15,086

ADMISSIONS

Admissions Selectivity Rating	89
# of applications received	1306
% applicants accepted	54
% acceptees attending	68
Average GMAT	629
Range of GMAT	570-670
Average GPA	3.3
TOEFL Required of International Students?	Yes
Minimum TOEFL (paper/computer)	600/250
Application fee	$50
International application fee	$50
Regular application deadline	Rolling
Regular notification	Rolling
Application Deadline/Notification	
Round 1:	11/15 / 1/15
Round 2:	1/15 / 3/15
Round 3:	2/15 / 4/1
Round 4:	3/15 / 5/1
Early decision program?	Yes
ED Deadline/Notification	11/15 / 2/2
Deferment Available?	Yes
Maximum length of deferment	1 year
Need-blind admissions?	Yes

APPLICANTS ALSO LOOK AT

Georgetown University, Rochester Institute of Technology, The George Washington University, The University of Texas at Austin, University of North Carolina at Chapel Hill.

EMPLOYMENT PROFILE

Career Rating	89	Grads employed by field	%: avg. salary
Placement rate (%)	89	Finance	44: $75,632
# of companies recruiting on-campus	40	Human Resources	1: $100,000
% grads employed immediately	61	Marketing	19: $68,817
% grads employed within three months	89	MIS	7: $78,000
Average starting salary	$75,090	Operations	2: $74,500
		Consulting	16: $83,200
		General Management	10: $68,583
		Other	1: $64,000

University of Massachusetts—Amherst
Isenberg School of Management

GENERAL INFORMATION
Type of school	public
Environment	village
Academic calendar	semester

SURVEY SAYS...
Friendly students
Good peer network
Happy students
Smart classrooms
Solid preparation in:
Teamwork
Communication/interpersonal skills

STUDENTS
Enrollment of parent institution	22,393
Enrollment of MBA program	479
% male/female	61/39
% out-of-state	45
% part-time	85
% minorities	11
% international	21
Average age at entry	27
Average years work experience at entry	4.5

ACADEMICS
Academic Experience Rating	**98**
Student/faculty ratio	8:1
Profs interesting rating	98
Profs accessible rating	98
% female faculty	22
% minority faculty	8

Joint Degrees
MBA/MS in Sport Management: 2 years

Prominent Alumni
John P. Flavin, Chairman of the Board, Flavin, Blake & Co. Inc.; Eugene M. Isenberg, Chairman and CEO, Nabors Industries, Inc.; Jayne A. McMellen, VP Fund Admin., State Street Bank & Trust Co. Inc.; John F. Smith, Jr., Retired Chairman, General Motors Corporation.

Academics

Students praise the affordability and the "small size of the program, which makes it extremely possible for students to have one-to-one contact with great faculty" at the Isenberg School of Management at the University of Massachusetts at Amherst. The school's already low public-school tuition is made even more affordable by financial aid and fellowships; in fact, many students receive assistantships that carry a full-tuition waiver plus a stipend. "The university works hard to make sure that students get enough financial aid," MBAs say.

Isenberg offers both full-time and part-time programs; the part-time program is taught at three satellite campuses (Shrewsbury, Pittsfield, and Springfield) and is also available online in order to maximize convenience for working students. The full-time program dispenses with all core courses during the first year, which "makes it a very fast-paced environment and hard to digest everything. But it is a good program overall." Students build their fields of specialization (accounting, finance and operations management, management, and marketing) through electives offered by the School of Management or by other schools at the University. Full-time students say, "There is a real sense of community. The administration [and the teachers] are always available. I am having an amazing experience!" They also appreciate how "the atmosphere strongly encourages teamwork over cutthroat competition." However these students warn that "the small size of program severely limits the number of electives available. The majority of electives are in finance and operations."

The part-time program, available only to working adults, consists of 12 courses taken at the student's pace. Students typically complete the program in 2 years, although the program can be completed in as little as 18 months. The online program can be completed entirely in the online format, without visiting the university's campus.

Students brag that Isenberg has "a very impressive faculty. They have the best mix of outstanding intellect and pure teaching skills that I have ever seen. It is one thing to know an incredible amount about a particular subject, [but] it is another thing to actually be able to teach it. UMass has hired individuals capable of accomplishing both." According to the school, faculty specialties include investments, alternative risk management, technology management, organizational change, information technology, corporate creativity, supply-chain management, strategic marketing, and social marketing.

Career and Placement

Isenberg has a career management office dedicated exclusively to MBAs, which is unusual for a small program. The office schedules networking events and interview sessions, conducts workshops and seminars, and provides students with access to job databases. MBAs say that, unfortunately, it's not enough; in fact, they say that "students are pretty much on their own finding jobs and internships. If you are not prepared to do your own career research and networking, you will easily be unemployed at graduation. Only a handful of companies recruit on campus." Some students suggest that "off-campus social tours should be organized, and, most importantly, career opportunities and assistance should be improved via more structured courses like the professional seminars."

Employers who most frequently hire Isenberg MBAs include Deloitte Touche Tohmatsu, EMC, Frito-Lay, General Electric, Hamilton Sundstrand, IBM, Liberty Mutual, MassMutual Financial Group, Morgan Stanley, PricewaterhouseCoopers, RSA Security Teradyne, and United Technologies Corporation.

MARYBETH HARRIS, DIRECTOR OF STUDENT SUPPORT SERVICES
305 ISENBERG SCHOOL OF MANAGEMENT, UNIVERSITY OF MASS.—AMHERST, MA 01003 U.S.
PHONE: 413-545-5608 • FAX: 413-577-2234
E-MAIL: GRADPROG@SOM.UMASS.EDU • WEBSITE: WWW.UMASS.EDU/MBA

Student Life and Environment

Isenberg is housed in "a brand-new building with state-of-the-art computers and multimedia resources, which makes the students more productive and classes easier to comprehend." The completely wireless Alfond Management Center, which opened in 2002, features audio- and videoconferencing facilities as well as a real-time trading center. A number of breakout rooms are available for meetings and recruiting.

Full-timers describe a very socially active program with regular events including a Thursday night pub crawl, "a weekly festivity in which MBA students meet up at a local bar. It provides an opportunity for first- and second-year students to intermingle outside [of] class." Students also have house parties during the weekends. "[The] Graduate Business Association helps with many out-of-school social activities" that are MBA-specific. Students also report that "because we are located in large university campus of 25,000 students, opportunities abound throughout the campus. There are plenty of activities, from watching theater productions at the university's theater to catching a comedy show at the Student Union. UMass has great athletic programs, especially its football program. Students go down and tailgate before Minuteman games at the stadium."

Isenberg students are a group of "handpicked intelligent people. The admission [office] is very selective about who they accept into the program." MBAs explain, "It's delightful to have a high percentage of international students in [a] program located in a relatively rural area." MBAs only wish that there were more students in the program. One student comments, "The school could try to increase the number of students in the full-time program from a current total of 70 (first and second) to 100 or more. This would allow for more critical mass when it comes to recruitment."

Amherst is a quintessential New England college town, home not only to UMass, but also to Amherst College and Hampshire College. The town offers "plenty of things to do. There is no better place to be than New England on a crisp autumn day, and Amherst might be the best place in New England."

Admissions

According to the Isenberg Admissions office, "no one academic background is favored in the selection of candidates. Academic history, GMAT performance, motivation, aptitude for graduate-level work, and managerial experience are all taken into consideration." The school seeks candidates with two to four years of professional work experience. Applicants must submit two official copies of all undergraduate and graduate transcripts, GMAT scores, TOEFL scores (international students), two letters of recommendation, essays, and a resume. Students applying for fellowships must apply by February 1. Isenberg maintains a Diversity Recruitment Committee that "meets regularly to design and implement effective strategies to continue development of diversity in the program."

FINANCIAL FACTS

Annual tuition (in-state/out-of-state)	$2,640/$9,937
Fees (in-state/out-of-state)	$6,639/$7,544
Books and supplies	$2,000
Room & board (on/off-campus)	$6,189/$8,500
% of students receiving aid	93
% of first-year students receiving aid	88
% of students receiving loans	36
% of students receiving grants	5
Average award package	$15,334
Average grant	$17,768
Average student loan debt	$16,663

ADMISSIONS

Admissions Selectivity Rating	95
# of applications received	234
% applicants accepted	28
% acceptees attending	66
Average GMAT	629
Range of GMAT	590-720
Average GPA	3.4
TOEFL Required of International Students?	Yes
Minimum TOEFL (paper/computer)	600/250
Application fee	$40
International application fee	$65
Regular application deadline	2/1
Regular notification	3/15
Deferment Available?	Yes
Maximum length of deferment	1 year
Need-blind admissions?	Yes

APPLICANTS ALSO LOOK AT

Babson College, Boston College, Boston University, University of Connecticut, Yale University.

EMPLOYMENT PROFILE

Career Rating	80	Grads employed by field	%: avg. salary
Placement rate (%)	82	Accounting	4: NR
% grads employed immediately	61	Finance	30: $69,000
Average starting salary	$63,071	Marketing	30: $62,000
		Operations	13: $62,500
		General Management	18: $65,500
		Other	5: NR

UNIVERSITY OF MEMPHIS
FOGELMAN COLLEGE OF BUSINESS AND ECONOMICS

GENERAL INFORMATION

Type of school	public
Environment	city
Academic calendar	semester

SURVEY SAYS...
Friendly students
Smart classrooms
Solid preparation in:
Teamwork
Presentation skills

STUDENTS

Enrollment of parent institution	20,668
Enrollment of MBA program	266
% male/female	98/2
% part-time	47
% minorities	43
% international	77
Average age at entry	31

ACADEMICS

Academic Experience Rating	**63**
Student/faculty ratio	20:1
Profs interesting rating	68
Profs accessible rating	61
% female faculty	22
% minority faculty	24

Joint Degrees
MBA/JD: 4 years

Academics

The Fogelman College of Business and Economics at the University of Memphis is a program on the rebound. Students report that "the school had lost its focus during the mid-to-late '90s but has really pulled things together lately." One MBA student writes, "I have been here off and on since 1987, and it is now regaining its previous level." Central to the school's rehabilitation is a recent curriculum overhaul, from which the school identifies four resulting improvements: the creation of a more structured, more focused program stressing integration and thematic links among different courses and areas of study; an upgrade to program prerequisites that relegates remedial work to pre-MBA study; a "beefing up" of the MIS program; and the elimination of concentrations (in order to allow students to complete the program in a reasonable amount of time).

To better serve the majority of students, who attend part-time while working full-time, Fogelman offers most classes in the evenings. Students appreciate the convenience but warn that scheduling can be difficult. One MBA complains, "Every decent class is offered from 5:30 to 7:00 [P.M.] only on Tuesdays and Thursdays." Another student notes, "The scheduling of various courses is determined by each department with no input from the students. Class conflicts between departments offering core courses are unfortunately not taken into consideration." Most classes at Fogelman are required, which complicates matters further; only 3 of the 11 classes required for graduation are electives, and one elective must cover international business.

Fogelman faculty members earn good marks from students, who explain that "the majority of the professors are well-known in their academic fields and are very nice individuals. [They] have gone out of their way to be helpful with questions asked." "[Many professors] have life experiences that relate [to] the material," which "enhances their ability to teach. Once you've studied with these professors, you can understand why they have such well-deserved reputations." Students also appreciate the school's "partnerships with local corporations," which facilitate internships, and also that "tuition is very reasonable."

Career and Placement

There is no dedicated career office for the Fogelman MBA program; all students at the university utilize the school's Career and Employment Services (C&ES) Office, which "provides leadership and administers university-wide part-time and full-time placement programs; works with local and regional employers to identify part-time jobs and full-time career opportunities for University of Memphis students and alumni, prepares students with proficient job-search skills that will enable them to effectively present themselves to prospective employers, provides an opportunity for prospective employers and University of Memphis students/alumni to meet, and enhances faculty support of and interest in the professional employment process."

Carol Danehower, Director of Master's Programs

Graduate School, Administration Building, Room 216, Memphis, TN 38152-3370 U.S.

Phone: 901-678-2911 • Fax: 901-678-5023

E-mail: gradsch@memphis.edu • Website: www.fcbe.memphis.edu

Student Life and Environment

Fogelman welcomes full-time MBA students, but "the college is designed for part-time students with all classes offered in the evening" because part-timers make up the bulk of the population. Accordingly, "it's a commuter school" where "[the] only real campus experience [for most students] is taking classes" and studying. Students grouse that facilities are "in poor shape" and that "more computers are needed in the classrooms." One student writes, "I'm taking a programming class in a room with no computers [and] where the instructor has to bring in his own laptop to teach us." In the asset column, the campus is surprisingly cozy for such a large-scale university. One student explains, "I came from a small, private university in my undergrad and was afraid of the large university feel, but the proximity of all the buildings and all my classes makes the feel less overbearing."

Hometown Memphis is the headquarters of FedEx shipping; it is also a major manufacturing center. The city is home to an NBA franchise, a AAA baseball team, and more great barbecue joints and live music venues than you can count. Tourist attractions include Graceland, Elvis Presley's home and burial place; Beale Street, where blues legend B.B. King (among others) built his reputation as a blues master; and the National Civil Rights Museum, located on the site where Martin Luther King, Jr. was assassinated. Memphis is home to seven colleges and universities.

Admissions

Applicants to the Fogelman College of Business and Economics must submit official copies of all undergraduate transcripts, official GMAT scores, TOEFL scores (international students), a current resume reflecting at least one year of professional work experience, a personal statement of purpose for pursuing a Fogelman MBA, and a written response to an essay question provided by the school. The school does not require letters of recommendation or an interview; however, letters of recommendation are "suggested." Fogelman recently raised admissions standards; a work requirement was added, the minimum GPA score was increased, and standardized test scores are now required for consideration of admission.

FINANCIAL FACTS

Annual tuition (in-state/out-of-state)	$5,930/$14,654
Fees	$568
Books and supplies	$10,000
Room & board (on/off-campus)	$3,000/$8,000

ADMISSIONS

Admissions Selectivity Rating	73
# of applications received	152
% applicants accepted	73
% acceptees attending	78
Average GMAT	530
Range of GMAT	530-700
Average GPA	3.1
TOEFL Required of International Students?	Yes
Minimum TOEFL (paper/computer)	550/213
Application fee	$35
Regular application deadline	8/1
Regular notification	Rolling
Deferment Available?	Yes
Non-fall admissions?	Yes

EMPLOYMENT PROFILE

Career Rating	71
Placement rate (%)	90
# of companies recruiting on-campus	100
% grads employed immediately	49
Average starting salary	$63,800

UNIVERSITY OF MICHIGAN—ANN ARBOR
STEPHEN M. ROSS SCHOOL OF BUSINESS

Academics

The University of Michigan Business School made history in 2004 when it accepted the largest gift to any U.S. business school—$100 million—from New York real estate developer and alumnus Stephen M. Ross. In honor of the unprecedented gift, the school was renamed the Stephen M. Ross School of Business. Early in 2005, the Ross School announced plans to build a new $145 million facility to support its action-based curriculum. This announcement came on the heels of the school rolling out for the Class of 2006 a revised MBA curriculum. Benefits include carefully sequenced core courses, more electives and the opportunity to focus on specific areas of interest prior to internship interviews.

Most students agree that the program was and remains "extremely strong in corporate strategy, entrepreneurial studies, management accounting, marketing, organizational behavior, nonprofit organizations, social venturing, and venture-capital/private-equity/entrepreneurial finance." Because of the size of the program, Michigan is able to offer a wide variety of choices—more than 100 electives in nine disciplines by the school's reckoning, plus entreprenurial studies and plenty of dual-degree options. In addition, because the Business School does not require students to specialize, MBAs "have a lot of flexibility in the second-year schedule to focus on the classes [they] want." Students must first complete a rigorous core [curriculum], however, before moving on to electives. For full-time students, the core takes up their entire first year with 10 courses "in elemental business functions" as well as a seven-week Multidisciplinary Action Project (MAP). Students say, "[The program] essentially allows us to get real-world experience and learn a heck [of a] lot while we're doing it." MBAs add that the workload is fairly heavy. One student reports, "We take five classes per semester, and each class usually meets twice a week for one and [one] half hours at a time. For every one and [one] half hour class, there's probably about that much preparation time that is put in outside of class." The evening MBA core is no less demanding, although it does not include a MAP Team-Project experience. As a major research institution, U of M gives its MBAs access to world-class research facilities including institutes in emerging and transitional economies worldwide, entrepreneurial studies, environmental management, and manufacturing. Students especially praise the environmental management and transitional economies worldwide institutes. MBAs say, "[The] U of M's self-positioning [is] on the cutting edge of corporate-responsibility issues."

Career and Placement

"[The university] literally [has] the largest alumni network of any business school in the world." U of M's Student Career Services Office at the Ross School of Business, which serves both undergraduates and graduate students. Among 2003 graduates, approximately three-fifths reported that they found positions through school-affiliated channels (on-campus recruiting, 35 percent; on-campus job posting, 17 percent; return to place of first-year summer internship, 10 percent).

Top employers of Michigan MBAs include Citigroup, Booz Allen Hamilton Inc., Dell, Inc., McKinsey & Company, Deloitte Consulting, Johnson & Johnson, A Family of Companies, American Express Company, JPMorgan Chase & Co., A.T. Kearney, Inc., Eli Lilly & Company, Bain & Company, Inc., Ford Motor Company, Medtronic, Inc., 3M Company, Cummins Inc., DiamondCluster International, Inc., General Mills, Inc., Guidant Corporation, Intel Corporation, Kraft Foods Inc., Lehman Brothers, Microsoft Corporation, National City Corporation and S.C. Johnson & Son, Inc. The desirability of U of M MBAs can be seen in the geographic diversity of their first-job locations. While

James P. Hayes, Director of Admissions
701 Tappan Street, D2260, Ann Arbor, MI 48109-1234 United States
Phone: 734-763-5796 • Fax: 734-763-7804
E-mail: ROSSMBA@UMICH.EDU • Website: WWW.BUS.UMICH.EDU

one in three remains in the Midwest, others head everywhere from the mid-Atlantic (9 percent) to the Pacific Coast (13 percent) to companies outside the United States (12 percent).

Student Life and Environment

"If you like college towns, you will love Ann Arbor," students at U of M agree. MBAs add that "there's happy hour every Thursday, tailgates every Football Saturday, and numerous club parties in between." The hub of campus life is the school's athletic program; one student explains, "You can't beat Michigan football, hockey, and basketball. Tailgates make a great way to bond in the spirit of the university." The city also "offers a lot of entertainment options like jazz, dance clubs, and restaurants." About the only drawback to Ann Arbor life is that "the weather is cold in the winter, and students do spend too much time studying because there's not much else to do when it's 15 degrees out." The MBA program offers "abundant opportunities to get involved, from professional to social clubs, newspaper, admissions, and career counseling. There's even a wine-tasting club." The program also "provides lots of opportunities for spouses to get together. It also has joint programs with other schools in the university, which provide meaningful activities." All in all, students agree that the program provides a "good work-life balance. We work quite hard, but on Thursday evenings, practically all MBAs flock to the b-school happy-hour bar, Mitch's. No weekend goes by without lots of prep for class, several group meetings, and at least one party or social/fun activity. We live the two years at b-school [like they] are the last of our lives. We've gotta do everything while having fun!"

Admissions

Applications to the University of Michigan MBA program must include undergraduate transcripts, GMAT test scores, TOEFL test scores (international students—see website for exceptions), letters of recommendation, a personal statement, and a resume. The school also looks at an applicant's track record of success, clarity of goals, and management and leadership potential. The program does require previous work experience. Interviews are "highly recommended" but not required. Minority recruitment efforts include membership in the Consortium for Graduate Study in Management; the UpClose Program a weekend for prospective minority students; Robert F. Toigo Fellowships in Finance, Management Leadership for Tomorrow (MLT)-mentorship opportunities, National Society of Hispanic MBA Conference, National Black MBA Conference, faculty and alumni outreach and a student phonathon.

FINANCIAL FACTS

Annual tuition (in-state/out-of-state)	$31,500/$36,500
Fees	$188
Books and supplies	$7,632
Room & board	$9,296
% of students receiving aid	75
% of first-year students receiving aid	75
% of students receiving loans	47
% of students receiving grants	48
Average award package	$53,799
Average grant	$10,904
Average student loan debt	$58,667

ADMISSIONS

Admissions Selectivity Rating	96
# of applications received	2041
% applicants accepted	36
% acceptees attending	60
Average GMAT	690
Range of GMAT	640-740
Average GPA	3.3
TOEFL Required of International Students?	Yes
Minimum TOEFL (paper/computer)	600/250
Application fee	$180
International application fee	$180
Regular application deadline	11/3
Regular notification	1/4
Application Deadline/Notification	
Round 1:	11/1 / 1/15
Round 2:	1/7 / 3/15
Round 3:	3/1 / 5/15
Deferment Available?	Yes
Maximum length of deferment	1 year
Transfer students accepted?	Yes
Transfer application policy: Transfer applicants are welcome to apply, but no credits will transfer into our program.	
Need-blind admissions?	Yes

APPLICANTS ALSO LOOK AT

Duke University, Northwestern University, University of Chicago, University of Pennsylvania.

Career Rating	95	Grads employed by field	%: avg. salary
Placement rate (%)	87	Finance	31: $83,649
% grads employed immediately	76	Human Resources	1: $95,750
Average starting salary	$85,734	Marketing	30: $82,549
		Operations	4: $80,375
		Strategic Planning	5: $80,651
		Consulting	21: $94,456
		General Management	4: $81,214
		Other	4: $91,964

UNIVERSITY OF MICHIGAN—FLINT
SCHOOL OF MANAGEMENT

GENERAL INFORMATION
Type of school	public
Environment	city
Academic calendar	semester

SURVEY SAYS...
Smart classrooms
Solid preparation in:
Teamwork
Communication/interpersonal skills
Presentation skills

STUDENTS
Enrollment of MBA program	169
Average age at entry	31
Average years work experience at entry	3

ACADEMICS
Academic Experience Rating	**61**
Student/faculty ratio	30:1
Profs interesting rating	73
Profs accessible rating	69
Joint Degrees	
BA/MBA: 5 years	

Academics

The School of Management at University of Michigan—Flint offers its entirely part-time student body two MBA options: a traditional MBA conducted on the Flint campus, and the NetPlus! MBA, a "mixed-mode" program that combines online instruction with classroom interaction. The NetPlus! calendar includes a mandatory campus session one weekend every six weeks.

U of M Flint's traditional MBA program is unusual among part-time programs, in that, it is cohort-based, which "enables students to develop a strong support network for personal and professional development beyond the time they are in the MBA program." This 18-course program does not allow students to develop an area of specialization—in fact, it allows for only two electives, chosen from a limited list of options—preferring instead to emphasize generalization. This program "provides [students] with a solid foundation for making decisions, which has an impact beyond one functional area." Students in the program explain that it is "outstanding in every way; however, the work involved to get through the program is incredible!" One student says, "I still question whether I'll make it through, with all the other work, home, and parenting responsibilities of life competing for [my] time."

Students seeking more flexibility and convenience should consider the NetPlus! MBA because it allows students to view online lectures "anytime [and] anywhere." In this program, each 12-week term commences with a one-day on-campus orientation; subsequent campus visits are required three and nine weeks into each term. On-campus sessions mean that students reap the benefits of cohort-based instruction. One participant explains, "The mixed-mode concept provides networking opportunities, classroom interaction, and flexible scheduling for studies, assignments, and exams." However, "all students and professors new to the program experience behavioral challenges switching from a traditional classroom environment to an online classroom dependent on evolving technology;" some professors are reportedly better at handling the technical demands of the program than are others. Students point out that "this is a new program. There have been some kinks, but overall, I am impressed with the attention to detail in administering this program."

In both programs, U of M—Flint features "committed, interested professors who are willing to assist and provide up-to-date information and discussion on today's business trends and events; extremely up-to-date textbooks with recent business case studies and trends incorporated into the syllabus;" and perhaps best of all, "an affordable tuition." The cherry on the sundae: "The name 'University of Michigan' on a resume is valuable to employers."

Career and Placement

The U of M—Flint Career Development Center serves all undergraduate and graduate students at the university. Because MBA students are already employed full-time, relatively few use the office's services.

D. Nicol Taylor, MBA, MBA Program Coordinator
School of Management, UM-Flint, 3139 William South White Building, 303 East
Kearsley Street, Flint, MI 48502-1950 United States
Phone: 810-762-3163 • Fax: 810-237-6685
E-mail: UMFlintMBA1@umich.edu • Website: www.mba.umflint.edu

FINANCIAL FACTS

Annual tuition	$4,347
Average grant	$1,000

ADMISSIONS

Admissions Selectivity Rating	64
# of applications received	48
% applicants accepted	98
% acceptees attending	81
Average GMAT	519
Range of GMAT	453-585
Average GPA	3.2
TOEFL Required of International Students?	Yes
Minimum TOEFL (paper/computer)	550/213
Application fee	$55
Regular application deadline	Rolling
Regular notification	Rolling
Deferment Available?	Yes
Maximum length of deferment	1 year
Transfer students accepted?	Yes
Transfer application policy: AACSB accredited, B or better, grad level, 9 credit hours; credits cannot be part of another degree.	
Non-fall admissions?	Yes
Need-blind admissions?	Yes

Student Life and Environment

U of M—Flint is "a commuter college with very little life at the school," students say. That's especially true for students in the NetPlus! program, who only see each other a few times a year. One participant in the program explains, "The online concept minimizes school-activity involvement unless you are local to the area. Most students commute to the town for weekend residencies and spend the majority of the time in the classroom or dining in the evening with classmates." Those who travel note with approval that "there are excellent discounts provided with area hotels through the school program. Breakfast and lunch are catered-in to increase class networking time, and many professors in the school of business join us for the meals providing additional networking opportunities."

Those amenities minimize the time that students spend venturing about Flint, which most see as a very good thing. "The city is not the best," say students of this "mostly unsafe" town, "but the campus and especially the business building is well-equipped and very nice." The program's facility "has state-of-the-art technology for presentations and Internet access. It makes it easy to prepare professional projects for class." One student observes, "The facilities are excellent. They are clean and consistent with what you see in top corporations. You feel like you are in a business meeting and not just a classroom."

Admissions

All applicants to the School of Management at U of M—Flint must provide the school with official copies of all undergraduate and graduate transcripts, GMAT scores, TOEFL scores (international students), three letters of recommendation (preferably from employers and/or professors), a statement of purpose, and a resume. One year of finite mathematics or college algebra is a prerequisite. A background in statistics, economics, or accounting is not required, but it is helpful in getting the entire class quickly up to speed. Work experience is preferred; the average student arrives with three years of professional experience.

UNIVERSITY OF MINNESOTA
CARLSON SCHOOL OF MANAGEMENT

GENERAL INFORMATION
Type of school	public
Environment	city
Academic calendar	semester

SURVEY SAYS...
Students love Minneapolis, MN
Friendly students
Happy students
Smart classrooms
Solid preparation in:
Teamwork
Communication/interpersonal skills

STUDENTS
Enrollment of parent institution	45,413
Enrollment of MBA program	1,787
% male/female	78/22
% out-of-state	33
% part-time	88
% minorities	8
% international	28
Average age at entry	29
Average years work experience at entry	5.8

ACADEMICS
Academic Experience Rating	**90**
Student/faculty ratio	13:1
Profs interesting rating	84
Profs accessible rating	84
% female faculty	23
% minority faculty	9

Joint Degrees
MBA/JD: 4 years
MBA/MHA: 3 years

Prominent Alumni
Charles W. Mooty, CEO, International Dairy Queen; William G. Van Dyke, Chairman, Pres. & CEO, Donaldson Company, Inc.; Curtis C. Nelson, Pres. & COO, Carlson Companies; Robert A. Kierlin, Chairman, Fastenal Company; Barbara J. Mowry, Pres. & CEO, TMC Consulting.

Academics

The Carlson School of Management MBA program "combines research and reality" in a curriculum that capitalizes on university resources and the school's urban location. The business school's 11 research centers have elevated it to the nation's 13th-ranked institution in business-research productivity, according to the school. MBAs benefit from Carlson cutting-edge work, but their greatest enthusiasm is for the "reality" portion of the equation. They love the program's emphasis on experiential learning, especially through its four enterprise programs: Carlson Funds Enterprise, Carlson Consulting Enterprise, Carlson Ventures Enterprise, and Carlson Brand Management Enterprise. These programs "allow students to get real-world experience before entering the job market, while working with local and national companies" through their "student-run businesses within the school."

The Carlson School's "unbelievably integrated curriculum is one of the school's major strengths. Carlson breeds outstanding generalists who are capable of working well in teams." Course work commences with an intensive—some say too intensive—core. One student warns, "The workload during the first semester is too much. It's seven classes (19 credits), two required workshops, Leadership Edge (a cocurricular program designed to help students cultivate their leadership skills), Career Exploration (a career conference), and the hunt for a summer internship." Students generally survive the grind, and the pressure lessens somewhat thereafter. Throughout the first year, "there is a huge focus on group projects. Teams are hand-picked before classes begin to ensure a good mix of first-year students. These teams work on over a dozen projects together during the first semester; plus, they often form strong friendships while socializing after helping each other with homework. The school places significant emphasis on networking with fellow students, faculty, and alumni," according to students.

Students also love that the focus of the university "is on creating leaders. There's a real emphasis on so-called 'soft skills' such as, negotiations, group dynamics, and new technology sales." One student says, "Coming into the program I expected that most, if not all of my classes would be focused on finance, statistics, or operations. But having been encouraged and having taken the opportunity to take these soft-skill classes, I believe I am much better qualified to work as a manager." The program has "a very strong brand-management faculty" and "is a prominent leader in strategic and marketing research." The Carlson School "also has a very strong finance and accounting department."

Career and Placement

Carlson MBAs appreciate their program—dedicated career services office—the Graduate Business Career Center (GBCC)—and explain that "the initiatives introduced by the GBCC to build skills such as networking, interviewing, and leadership are one of the great strengths of the program." The office "counsels each and every student one-on-one on a constant basis, giving feedback on strengths and weaknesses." Students report that "alumni connections and career opportunities within the Twin Cities area [of Minneapolis/St. Paul] specifically are strong." However, some students feel that "the GBCC needs to work with more companies outside the Twin Cities as well as working with companies that are smaller, providing more diverse on-campus opportunities." Employers of Carlson School MBAs include 3M, Boston Scientific Scimed, Ernst & Young LLP, Cargill, Carlson Companies, Deloitte Consulting, Ecolab, General Electric, General Mills, Guidant, Honeywell, Johnson & Johnson, Kimberly-Clark, Kurt Salmon Associates, McKinsey, Medtronic, Multifoods, Northwest Airlines, Philip Morris, RBC Capital Markets, RBC Dain Rauscher, Samsung Electronics, Taylor Corporation, Target, US Bancorp, and US Bancorp Piper Jaffray.

DUSTIN CORNWELL, DIRECTOR OF ADMISSIONS & RECRUITING
321 NINETEENTH AVENUE SOUTH, SUITE 2-210, MINNEAPOLIS, MN 55455 UNITED STATES
PHONE: 612-625-5555 • FAX: 612-626-7785
E-MAIL: FULL-TIMEMBAINFO@CARLSONSCHOOL.UMN.EDU
WEBSITE: WWW.CARLSONSCHOOL.UMN.EDU

Student Life and Environment

The Carlson School has substantial populations of both full-time and part-time MBAs. The full-timers take a mix of daytime and evening courses; part-time students attend courses in the evenings and Saturdays. The part-timers have less available time to participate in nonacademic activities, but all students enjoy the "excellent camaraderie between students and between students and faculty." Students say, "We have lounge parties every Thursday, monthly interaction with the alumni base, the MBA Follies (a talent show), and almost-daily speakers or company information sessions." One student reports, "I have made many friends at the school, and we spend quite a bit of time together, whether it is by going out on the town, dinners at [our] homes with our significant others, competing in intramural sports, or by getting a block of tickets to cheer on the university's football, basketball, or hockey teams."

The full-timers, though, are hard-pressed to enjoy extracurriculars during their first semester because the core is extremely demanding. One student writes, "During the first semester (for example, the 'core'), life is totally focused on studies. It was all day on the weekdays, and then I usually studied every evening from 6:00 P.M. until 12:00 or 1:00 A.M. I also studied both weekend days, trying to take one weekend night off to do something with my fiancée or friends outside of the program. Total time spent studying or preparing [for courses] (outside of class) was about 65 to 75 hours a week." The second year is a little better because "during the second year, less time is spent on studying, but students are still very busy focusing on internships, job searching, [and] working in Carlson Enterprise programs."

The Carlson School's recently constructed facilities "offer a great environment for learning with wireless and other new technology enhancing the educational experience." Students comment that "the campus is large but nice. It sits on both sides of the Mississippi River and is very attractive." Students with families complain that "the school is not really set-up to be kid- or spouse-friendly. Few people bring their spouse or kids to extracurricular activities."

Admissions

The University of Minnesota admissions office considers applicants' undergraduate records, GMAT scores, TOEFL or IELTS scores (international students), letters of recommendation from employers and/or professors, a personal statement, and a resume. An interview is "required," and "a minimum of two years' work experience is strongly recommended." The school reports that "Minnesota Boulevard is a group of locally based companies working jointly with the Carlson School to bring minority MBA candidates to Twin Cities for jobs, mentoring, and the MBA. The school maintains close ties with the National Black MBA Association (NBMBAA) and NSHMBA, who help and call students for recruiting, scholarships, and retention."

FINANCIAL FACTS

Annual tuition (in-state/out-of-state)	$19,820/$28,200
Fees	$2,000
Books and supplies	$4,000
Room & board (on/off-campus)	$7,500/$10,500
% of students receiving aid	75
% of students receiving loans	50
% of students receiving grants	60
Average grant	$16,273
Average student loan debt	$36,020

ADMISSIONS

Admissions Selectivity Rating	91
# of applications received	509
% applicants accepted	44
% acceptees attending	49
Average GMAT	655
Range of GMAT	620-700
Average GPA	3.25
TOEFL Required of International Students?	Yes
Minimum TOEFL (paper/computer)	580/240
Application fee	$60
International application fee	$90
International application deadline	2/15
International notification	4/15
Regular application deadline	4/15
Regular notification	5/15
Application Deadline/Notification	
Round 1:	12/15 / 2/15
Round 2:	2/15 / 4/15
Round 3:	4/15 / 5/15
Early decision program?	Yes
ED Deadline/Notification	12/15 / 2/15
Deferment Available?	Yes
Maximum length of deferment	1 year
Need-blind admissions?	Yes

EMPLOYMENT PROFILE

Career Rating	90	Grads employed by field	%: avg. salary
Placement rate (%)	93	Finance	28: $77,205
% grads employed immediately	68	Marketing	32: $75,976
Average starting salary	$77,821	MIS	6: $82,125
		Operations	12: $74,875
		Consulting	17: $77,118
		General Management	5: $99,333

University of Missouri—St. Louis
College of Business Administration

GENERAL INFORMATION
Type of school	public
Environment	metropolis
Academic calendar	semester

SURVEY SAYS...
Happy students
Smart classrooms
Solid preparation in:
Teamwork
Communication/interpersonal skills
Presentation skills

STUDENTS
Enrollment of parent institution	12,100
Enrollment of MBA program	347
% male/female	62/38
% out-of-state	18
% part-time	72
% minorities	1
% international	15
Average age at entry	29
Average years work experience at entry	5

ACADEMICS
Academic Experience Rating	**78**
Student/faculty ratio	12:1
Profs interesting rating	78
Profs accessible rating	82
% female faculty	22
% minority faculty	4

Academics

The College of Business Administration at the University of Missouri—St. Louis offers two options to the busy professional who is in search of the MBA. Its traditional MBA is a 39 to 54-hour program (depending on the number of general requirements courses a student can place out of) that convenes on weeknight evenings. The school's professional MBA online is a 48-hour program that requires students to visit campus only one weekend per month; most other work is completed via the Internet. Students in this program "love its flexibility" and note that "although we are only at school for two full days per month, the class schedules and assignments require us to meet in groups almost weekly and sometimes more. Each class requiring at least one presentation allows us to polish our communication skills for the real world quite often."

The degree of convenience is not the only difference between UM—St. Louis's two MBA options. The professional MBA online curriculum is entirely prescribed, while the traditional MBA afford the opportunity to take electives and develop an area of specialization (accounting, finance, logistics and supply-chain management, management, marketing, operations management) or earn a graduate certificate (e-commerce, human-resources management, information-resource management, information-systems development, logistics and supply-chain management, marketing management, telecommunications management). Students in our survey were especially enthusiastic about accounting, logistics, marketing, and operations management.

UM—St. Louis professors "are top rate. They have almost all authored books or teach at other well-known and more expensive schools." Students also report that instructors "are all very willing to help with any problems you may have and especially seem to enjoy working with professionals who are working within industry. I have approached several professors who have helped me develop processes that assist me at work. Additionally, the professors are easy to access and seem to be available whenever you need help or will make time to meet your schedule." That's important since this program is no walk in the park; warns one student, "The course load is very intensive, considering that the entire class is full of professionals who work forty hours a week, have families, and are trying to get their MBAs." Students predict a bright future for the program; as one told us, "It is overall a progressive school that changes to current needs of students. Because of this and their continuous surveys, UM—St. Louis is always improving their education experience."

Career and Placement

The Career Services Office at UM—St. Louis serves the entire university's undergraduate and graduate student bodies. Available services include a research library, counseling, workshops, seminars, e-recruiting resources, Web-based support, job fairs, and alumni events. Each degree program maintains its own Listserv through which subscribers can learn immediately about new job openings in their area. Top employers of UM—St. Louis MBAs include Boeing Company, CitiMortgage, Edward Jones, and May Company.

Thomas H. Eyssell, Director, Grad. Programs in Business
One University Boulevard, 250 University Center, St. Louis, MO 63121-4499 United States
Phone: 314-516-5885 • Fax: 314-516-7202
E-mail: mba@umsl.edu • Website: www.mba.umsl.edu

Student Life and Environment

The MBA program at UM—St. Louis "is split between students who work full-time and try to spend the least amount of time on campus and those that are involved on campus with every aspect of their lives." Those most involved tell us that "we have an active Student Union and a good student newspaper. Student life is enriched by the diversity of student backgrounds and culture. For example, African students put up an annual dinner at which they share their different cultures with U.S. students and others. My school is a rich mix of social life." Nearly all international students attend the full-time program; the majority of local students are enrolled part-time. The full-time/part-time mix prevents cohort-based instruction, which in turn reduces communal spirit. One part-timer writes, "It would be nice to have more of a sense of community with others in my year. I am in class with people in their first and last semesters, and I don't know who is who."

The program's facility receives mixed reviews. Students report approvingly that "most classrooms have a computer and overhead screen that instructors and students have access to" but complain that "there is really nowhere in the business building to study except one small room." They also complain that "the campus grounds at UM—St. Louis are not what I'd hoped they'd be; they're not kept very well." On a positive note, the campus is easy to reach by public transportation.

St. Louis is a sizeable city, home to major league sports teams, one of the nation's best zoos, and numerous cultural sites and ethnic neighborhoods. Its most famous attraction, of course, is the Gateway Arch, and its most famous business is probably Anheuser-Busch. Other major employers in the city include Monsanto, Ralston Purina, Boeing, and many of the major automobile manufacturers. St. Louis was once a major center of shoe manufacturing; while that is no longer the case, many shoe companies continue to run their corporate operations from the city. The city is well-known for great music and great barbecue, two commodities that are still available in abundance.

Admissions

Applicants to the UM—St. Louis MBA program must submit official copies of all undergraduate and graduate transcripts, official GMAT score reports, TOEFL scores (international students), a brief personal statement, two letters of recommendation, and a resume. The admissions committee looks for "professional experience since graduation, motivation, and other indicators of ability" in assessing applicants' fitness for the program. A minimum GMAT score of 500 (with both Math and Verbal scores above the 30th percentile) and a minimum undergraduate GPA of 3.0 are both required for unrestricted admission. Interviews are not required, but they are available to those who are interested.

FINANCIAL FACTS

Annual tuition (in-state/out-of-state)	$7,098/$19,170
Fees	$1,287
Books and supplies	$3,000
Room & board (on/off-campus)	$5,600/$6,180
% of students receiving aid	53
% of first-year students receiving aid	48
% of students receiving loans	32
% of students receiving grants	24
Average award package	$10,139
Average grant	$6,159
Average student loan debt	$5,933

ADMISSIONS

Admissions Selectivity Rating	72
# of applications received	106
% applicants accepted	80
% acceptees attending	71
Average GMAT	540
Range of GMAT	470-590
Average GPA	3.2
TOEFL Required of International Students?	Yes
Minimum TOEFL (paper/computer)	550/213
Application fee	$35
International application fee	$40
Regular application deadline	7/1
Regular notification	Rolling
Deferment Available?	Yes
Maximum length of deferment	1 year
Transfer students accepted?	Yes
Transfer application policy: Transcripts are evaluated for relevant course work. Maximum of nine hours of acceptable graduate credit allowed to transfer in.	
Non-fall admissions?	Yes
Need-blind admissions?	Yes

EMPLOYMENT PROFILE

Career Rating	76	Grads employed by field	%: avg. salary
Placement rate (%)	80	Finance	50: $51,600
# of companies recruiting on-campus	13	Consulting	17: $42,500
% grads employed immediately	40	Communications	16: $43,000
Average starting salary	$48,067	Other	17: $48,000

UNIVERSITY OF NEBRASKA AT OMAHA
COLLEGE OF BUSINESS ADMINISTRATION

GENERAL INFORMATION

Type of school	public
Environment	metropolis
Academic calendar	semester

SURVEY SAYS...
Students love Omaha, NE
Friendly students
Happy students
Solid preparation in:
General management
Teamwork
Communication/interpersonal skills

STUDENTS

Enrollment of parent	
institution	14,667
Enrollment of MBA program	293
Average age at entry	28
Average years work experience	
at entry	5

ACADEMICS

Academic Experience Rating	**73**
Student/faculty ratio	15:1
Profs interesting rating	68
Profs accessible rating	80
% female faculty	40
% minority faculty	5

Prominent Alumni

James R. Young, Pres. and COO, Union Pacific Railroad; R. Craig Hoenshell, Former CEO, Avis and American Express International; Ronald J. Burns, Former Pres. and CEO, Union Pacific; Bernard R. Reznicek, Former Chairman, Pres. and CEO, Boston Edison Company; Samuel G. Leftwich, Former Pres., K-Mart Corporation; Howard Hawks, Former Chairman and CEO, Tenaska, Inc.; Charles J. Marr, Former CEO, Alegent Health; Fred M. Petersen, Former CEO, Omaha Public Power District.

Academics

"The MBA program at UNO's College of Business Administration concentrates on the working professional, and most, if not all, classes are offered at night. This is a big plus for me," one typical student in this solid local program writes. Students are pragmatic about what the CBA can and cannot offer, and they are confident that it is by far the best option for Omaha-area students. One student writes, "It's a great school if you're working full-time. There's good, cheap parking; a safe campus, business-focused classes; and professors with real-world experience." Another student agrees, "I'm glad that I chose UNO because, I think proportionally, there are just as many students and teachers that aren't the highest caliber at other graduate schools. I would be highly upset if I had to drive twice the distance and pay three times as much for teachers and students who weren't all smarter than the best at UNO. It's not realistic to expect that much from any local school."

Students entering the CBA must demonstrate proficiency in accounting and finance fundamentals, basic business statistics, and foundations of economics; those lacking these skills must take the corresponding foundation courses at the outset of the program. The MBA curriculum includes nine core courses (27 hours) and nine hours of electives; students may elect to devote six curriculum hours to writing and subsequently defending orally a thesis paper. Students must also participate in at least three business leadership seminars during their tenure; complete a business case study as part of the capstone course policy, planning, and strategy; and pass a comprehensive exam that requires them to synthesize core skills and concepts.

While some students wish that the program were even broader and more demanding one student, for example, complains that "the conventional MBA program does not even offer a specialization in finance," most are satisfied with what UNO offers. Professors are generally good; they "make the material very interesting, and most [professors] teach the material as it applies to both academic and real-world settings." In addition, they are "very supportive, very prepared, and always available for questions." On the downside, "some are a bit long in the tooth and do not relate well to current technology for the students. That's frustrating and a waste of time in class." MBAs also complain that "state budget cuts have led to fewer times available for some classes."

Career and Placement

UNO's Career Center "assists undergraduates, graduate candidates, and alumni from all colleges of the university in their search for career employment." According to the school's catalog, the center provides counseling services, a library of information on local and national employers, and recruiting and referral programs. The school also offers university-wide career fairs. Students explain that "the local reputation is key" in parlaying their degrees into successful careers; in addition, "good corporations in town and working adult students bring in current information" that assists in their job searches. Companies recruiting on campus during the spring of 2004 included Deloitte Touche Tohmatsu, EFG Companies, First National Bank of Omaha, Mutual of Omaha, the state of Nebraska, Northwestern Mutual, State Farm, and Union Pacific.

LEX KACZMAREK, DIRECTOR, MBA PROGRAM
6001 DODGE STREET, OMAHA, NE 68182-0048 UNITED STATES
PHONE: 402-554-2303 • FAX: 402-554-3747
E-MAIL: MBA@UNOMAHA.EDU • WEBSITE: WWW.CBA.UNOMAHA.EDU/MBA

Student Life and Environment

According to students, UNO MBAs form a "close-knit group, even though [they] have few out-of-class activities because most of the students have responsibilities outside of school." As one student says, "Other than networking through the various clubs and associations, the extracurriculars are limited to the undergraduate population." MBAs are friendly enough to watch out for each other, students say. One student adds, "We become friends, and we all use the friendships developed at school to network and that eventually leads to new jobs. Also, because all the students know each other, they get guidance from each other on what classes are better and the teaching styles of the professors."

UNO is the state's only metropolitan-area university, and this allows it to offer some of the best student-business connections available in Nebraska. Major employers in the city include Alegent Health, ConAgra, First Data Corporation, Methodist Health, Mutual of Omaha, Odyssey Staffing, Staff Mid-America, Union Pacific, and West Corporation. Omaha's metropolitan population of over 600,000 supports a variety of museums, the world's best-endowed community theater, and a zoo.

Admissions

Students applying to the University of Nebraska—Omaha must provide the admissions department an official transcript for each undergraduate and graduate program attended, official GMAT test results, and a current resume detailing work experience. Letters of recommendation, an essay or personal statement, and an interview are all optional for domestic applicants. International applicants "must provide letters of recommendation, statements of financial independence, and evidence of ability to speak and write the English language." The CBA accepts applications for admission three times a year; students may enter in the fall, spring, or summer.

FINANCIAL FACTS

Room & board (on/off-campus)	$6,500/$9,500
Average award package	$8,414
Average grant	$2,981
Average student loan debt	$7,625

ADMISSIONS

Admissions Selectivity Rating	77
# of applications received	86
% applicants accepted	79
% acceptees attending	78
Average GMAT	568
Range of GMAT	500-610
Average GPA	3.45
TOEFL Required of International Students?	Yes
Minimum TOEFL (paper/computer)	550/213
Application fee	$45
International application fee	$45
Regular application deadline	7/1
Regular notification	Rolling
Deferment Available?	Yes
Maximum length of deferment	1 year
Transfer students accepted?	Yes
Transfer application policy: A maximum of nine hours of transfer credit may be accepted from another. accredited (AACSB) institution. Requires submission of course syllabi and relevant catalog information.	
Non-fall admissions?	Yes
Need-blind admissions?	Yes

APPLICANTS ALSO LOOK AT

Creighton University, University of Nebraska—Lincoln.

EMPLOYMENT PROFILE	
Career Rating	60*
# of companies recruiting on-campus	118
% grads employed immediately	72

UNIVERSITY OF NEVADA—LAS VEGAS
COLLEGE OF BUSINESS

Academics

The College of Business at the University of Nevada, Las Vegas offers both a full-time and part-time evening MBA as well as a cohort-based weekend Executive MBA program for more experienced professionals. Roughly half the students in these programs attend the College full time.

UNLV's evening MBA consists of 48 credit hours, 33 of which are devoted to core courses. Students must devote five electives to a single area in order to achieve a concentration; the College offers concentrations in finance, management information systems, service marketing, and venture management. An accelerated program is open to students who score at least a 600 on the GMAT (with a score exceeding the 50th percentile in both verbal and quantitative skills) and an undergraduate business degree from an AACSB-accredited university. Students who meet these conditions may be allowed to waive up to six of the ten required core courses.

The 18-month Executive MBA program offers a general management degree; in order to preserve the program's cohort-based approach to learning, all students follow the same curriculum. The program begins with a week of intensive work; afterwards, students meet every Friday and Saturday from 8:30 A.M. to 5:30 P.M. Applicants to the program must have at least seven years of professional experience, at least three of which have been spent in "a key decision-making role."

UNLV also offers combined-degree programs in Hotel Administration, Dental Medicine, and a JD/MBA. Students point out that the "hotel concentration feeds off the Las Vegas resort market."

Career and Placement

The UNLV College of Business Career Services Center serves only graduate students in business. According to the College's website, the office seeks to help students define career goals, develop a career plan, market themselves, develop job-search skills, sharpen interviewing skills, and contact alumni. The office serves as a liaison to the local business community, maintains a number of hard-copy and online job databases, and organizes lectures and on-campus recruiting events.

Employers most likely to hire UNLV MBAs include Bechtel Nevada, Bechtel SAIC, Citibank, Harrah's Entertainment, Pulte Homes, U.S. Bank, and Wells Fargo. A plurality of the class of 2004 wound up in the finance sector, and almost everyone had found employment by graduation.

ROBERT CHATFIELD, MBA PROGRAMS DIRECTOR
4505 MARYLAND PARKWAY BOX 456031, LAS VEGAS, NV 89154-6031 UNITED STATES
PHONE: 702-895-3655 • FAX: 702-895-4090
E-MAIL: COBMBA@CCMAIL.NEVADA.EDU • WEBSITE: WWW.BUSINESS.UNLV.EDU

Student Life and Environment

Las Vegas is one of America's top tourist destinations, primarily because "it's fun every single night." Those who live here know that Vegas has a lot more to offer than just gambling, over-the-top floor shows, and cheap buffets. The Las Vegas metropolitan region is home to 1.5 million residents, many of whom never set foot inside a casino. The city boasts all the amenities of a midsize metropolis and adds to the mix a perennially sunny climate and proximity to plenty of outdoor fun; Lake Mead, the Colorado River, and the Hoover Dam are all within a half-hour's drive of the city. Some fabulous skiing and hiking awaits residents on Mount Charleston, less than an hour northwest of Sin City.

UNLV does its part to keep things interesting, providing "new cultural and entertainment attractions to the community every day," according to the College's website. Prominent lecturers and touring performing artists regularly stop by this desert campus.

Admissions

Applicants to the MBA program at UNLV must submit the following to the Admissions Committee: official transcripts for all post-secondary academic work undertaken; an official score report for the GMAT; two letters of recommendation; a personal essay; and a resume. An interview is required for admission to the Executive MBA program, but not for other graduate programs. The TOEFL is not required of students who completed degree programs conducted in English in the U.S., U.K., Australia, Canada, or New Zealand. All international applicants must provide financial certification documents.

FINANCIAL FACTS

Annual tuition	$8,674
Fees	$456
Books and supplies	$800
Room & board (on/off-campus)	$5,000/$7,000
% of students receiving aid	24
% of first-year students receiving aid	34
% of students receiving loans	23
% of students receiving grants	3
Average award package	$16,000
Average grant	$2,500
Average student loan debt	$30,957

ADMISSIONS

Admissions Selectivity Rating	84
# of applications received	224
% applicants accepted	58
% acceptees attending	75
Average GMAT	590
Range of GMAT	520-760
Average GPA	3.25
TOEFL Required of International Students?	Yes
Minimum TOEFL (paper/computer)	550/213
Application fee	$60
International application fee	$75
Regular application deadline	6/1
Regular notification	7/1
Deferment Available?	Yes
Maximum length of deferment	1 semester
Transfer students accepted?	Yes
Transfer application policy: Total of 6 credits from an AACSB accredited school.	
Non-fall admissions?	Yes
Need-blind admissions?	Yes

EMPLOYMENT PROFILE

Career Rating	72	Grads employed by field	%: avg. salary
Placement rate (%)	90	Accounting	10: $50,000
# of companies recruiting on-campus	3	Finance	40: $52,000
% grads employed immediately	95	Human Resources	2: $50,000
Average starting salary	$57,000	Marketing	20: $45,000
		MIS	3: $50,000
		Operations	2: $65,000
		Consulting	3: $60,000
		General Management	10: $70,000
		Other	10: $35,000

UNIVERSITY OF NEW MEXICO
ROBERT O. ANDERSON GRADUATE SCHOOL OF MANAGEMENT

Academics

Students turn to the Robert O. Anderson Graduate School of Management at the University of New Mexico for "an excellent education at a reasonable cost," and most students are extremely satisfied with the results. MBAs can choose from nine areas of concentration including organizational behavior/human resources, management of technology ("the most reputable program at the business school," one MBA notes), and policy and planning (the last abroad, cross-functional approach to problem-solving analysis). One student says, "[The policy and planning concentration] really sets the school apart from any of the others I considered." The Anderson School also offers a master's of accounting, and dual degrees that incorporate law, engineering, or Latin American studies.

Although many of its students register for full-time instruction, Anderson provides "plenty of flexibility for working professionals," with "classes usually held in the evenings." The core curriculum consists of ten classes; students with undergraduate business degrees may be able to receive a waiver for some of these; six management electives round out the requirements. Students pursuing a specialization may arrange the six electives to satisfy concentration requirements. The curriculum concludes with a capstone course in strategic management.

Students praise the Anderson faculty "in both core and concentration areas." One MBA writes, "The professors are wonderful, supportive, and challenging. I have had the opportunity to make friends with them and will be in touch with them after graduation." Another student adds, "The professors are incredibly helpful and have open minds about teaching. More than book work, the professors often engage the class in case studies, group work, interactive discussions, and role-play negotiations. Nearly every course is unique in the way the teacher presents the material." One student neatly sums up, "Who could make accounting interesting? Our faculty does!"

While some students feel that standards should be raised in order to increase the program's ranking and national profile, most of them believe that Anderson serves a valuable function for its mostly local student body. As one student concludes, "The academic experience has been rewarding for me, and I have grown as an individual and a professional. My analytical and problem-solving skills have been sharpened, and I have had the opportunity to explore where I would like for my career path to head."

Career and Placement

The school's Career Planning and Placement Office manages career services for all Anderson undergraduate and graduate students. The office provides information sessions, schedules on-campus interviews, organizes job fairs, manages access to online job databases, and provides job search skills coaching. The school reports that 60 employers recruit full-time employees on campus each year; 25 recruit first-year students for summer internships.

Employers who most frequently hire Anderson MBAs include Cardinal Health, Eli Lilly & Company, the EPA—Office of Inspector General, Goldman Sacks & Co., IBM, Intel, Lawrence Livermore National Laboratory, Los Alamos National Laboratory, Pulte Homes, Sandia National Laboratories, the state of New Mexico, University of New Mexico, and the U.S. General Accounting Office.

LOYOLA CHASTAIN, GRADUATE PROGRAMS MANAGER
THE UNIVERSITY OF NEW MEXICO, 1924 LAS LOMAS BOULEVARD, ALBUQUERQUE, NM 87131 U.S.
PHONE: 505-277-3147 • FAX: 505-277-9356
E-MAIL: CHASTAIN@MGT.UNM.EDU • WEBSITE: WWW.MGT.UNM.EDU

Student Life and Environment

The Anderson Graduate School of Management is "a total commuter school" that "tends to be for working professionals." Those who don't work will find that "there are several internships that are available to graduate students as well as TA and GA positions," which will give them something to do during the daytime hours (classes are largely conducted in the evening). One student observes, "It is not a lively campus. There is little connection between MBA students because [the University of New Mexico] is a commuter campus. Everyone comes to class [and] then leaves."

Hometown Albuquerque "is okay, but nightlife is substandard in comparison to other towns. There isn't any specific hang out that students frequent, so between classes, students hang out and talk or usually go to the computer lab." They also head outside because "the warm weather allows lots of interaction outdoors between classes." Students also appreciate the opportunities afforded by Albuquerque's setting, which is "in the midst of a growing Southwestern community with tons of local opportunities for entrepreneurship."

Although UNM is a sizeable university, "the business school has a small-school feel with students, instructors, [and] professors getting to know each other well." Students explain that "the diversity of the student population is one of the greatest strengths of the school. It is cultural, geographic, and gender-based." Hispanic Americans constitute the largest minority population here (approximately 20 percent of the student body).

Admissions

A completed application to the Anderson MBA program includes all of the following: two official transcripts from each undergraduate and graduate school attended, GMAT scores, TOEFL scores (international students), a brief statement of purpose, three letters of recommendation ("the most meaningful evaluations come from people who been responsible for evaluating your academic or managerial performance"), two application forms, and a resume. Students may apply for admission for the fall, spring, or summer term.

FINANCIAL FACTS

Annual tuition (in-state/out-of-state)	$4,110/$12,811
Fees	$280
Books and supplies	$2,000
Room & board (on/off-campus)	$10,270/$8,520
% of students receiving aid	55
% of first-year students receiving aid	52
% of students receiving loans	36
% of students receiving grants	30
Average award package	$5,424
Average grant	$2,849
Average student loan debt	$25,134

ADMISSIONS

Admissions Selectivity Rating	87
# of applications received	168
% applicants accepted	51
% acceptees attending	100
Average GMAT	561
Range of GMAT	420-760
Average GPA	3.54
TOEFL Required of International Students?	Yes
Minimum TOEFL (paper/computer)	550/213
Application fee	$40
International application fee	$40
Regular application deadline	6/1
Regular notification	Rolling
Deferment Available?	Yes
Maximum length of deferment	1 year
Transfer students accepted?	Yes
Transfer application policy: Up to 6 credit hours may transfer	
Non-fall admissions?	Yes

EMPLOYMENT PROFILE

Career Rating	74	Grads employed by field	%: avg. salary
Placement rate (%)	85	Accounting	18: $47,800
# of companies recruiting on-campus	41	Finance	18: $54,500
Average starting salary	$53,025	Marketing	9: $34,000
		MIS	9: $61,100
		Operations	9: $54,600
		General Management	22: $44,200
		Other	15: $50,045

UNIVERSITY OF NORTH CAROLINA AT CHAPEL HILL
KENAN-FLAGLER BUSINESS SCHOOL

Academics

Students have a lot of reasons to be happy at Kenan-Flagler Business School at UNC—Chapel Hill. Students explain that "there is an intense focus on student satisfaction, and the administration is really focused on the MBA program as key to UNC's success." UNC Kenan-Flagler MBAs get to voice their opinions at "monthly town-hall meetings; [students] are also highly encouraged to give feedback to the dean of the MBA program and the business school dean." Students report that their feedback is quickly acted upon. Some students note, "There was weakness in the core finance curriculum for the class of 2004. We told the dean about it, and it was dramatically improved for the 2005 class."

This student-friendly attitude is emblematic of UNC Kenan-Flagler, where collegiality and learning constantly trump competitiveness and grade-grubbing. "Any student will drop what they are doing and help you with your work," according to students. This is because the grading system (high pass, pass, low pass, and fail, rather than the traditional A-through-F grades) "is such that one needs to be almost flawless on exams to earn a high pass. This leaves the vast majority of students with no incentive to restrict the aid they give to other students." Another student adds, "Not having grades creates an atmosphere that encourages learning, but more importantly, challenges students to take courses outside of their comfort zone. This is critical for those that want to be well-rounded leaders."

Even without its approach to customer service, UNC Kenan-Flagler would still be among the nation's top MBA programs, one with "excellent entrepreneurship and real estate efforts, great strength in marketing and finance, [a] sustainable enterprise program that's the best in the country," and a "strong general-management focus." Students love how "international opportunities abound: you can take a language class [or] a business-outside-the-United States course that culminates in a trip overseas (there are about eight of these per year [in] various countries), get an internship overseas (we have strong connections in Southeast Asia), or spend half a semester to [one] year abroad studying at another school."

The quality of the program justifies the effort needed to complete it, which is considerable. The grueling core curriculum "is like a pain you know you must live with for a little while, but in the end you will be stronger for it." Students also point out that "while the first-year course load is heavy, most concepts are covered again in the second year, which allows you to thoroughly understand the topics in a way that is relevant to your career interest." Comprehension is also enhanced by "outstanding coordination among the faculty, which allows for the 'a-ha' effect to be much more profound." The faculty, "a split of all-stars and good younger professors, who are trying to make it," are "amazingly capable, challenging, and engaging."

Career and Placement

UNC b-students praise the Office of Career Services; they explain that the office makes MBAs feel as though it "has a personal stake in [their] careers and wants [them] to succeed." Students also note that the office "does an outstanding job of preparing students for the interview process and helping them find full-time and intern positions. In addition, they put a great deal of energy into maintaining current corporate relationships as well as building and improving new corporate relationships. The companies that recruit at Carolina come here because of the quality of the people. Once they recruit from UNC, they rarely leave!" As at most career offices, the services are strongest within the immediate region of the school; "OCS is not incredibly helpful if you're looking for positions outside of the East Coast," students observe.

SHERRY WALLACE, DIRECTOR, MBA ADMISSIONS
CB #3490, McCOLL BUILDING, CHAPEL HILL, NC 27599-3490 UNITED STATES
PHONE: 919-962-3236 • FAX: 919-962-0898
E-MAIL: MBA_INFO@UNC.EDU • WEBSITE: WWW.KENAN-FLAGLER.UNC.EDU

Companies that most frequently hire Kenan-Flagler MBAs include Bank of America, Bayer Corporation, BellSouth Corporation, Blue Cross Blue Shield of North Carolina, Deloitte Consulting, Hewlett-Packard Company, IBM, Johnson & Johnson, Kraft Foods, Lehman Brothers, Microsoft, Pulte Homes, Scott Madden & Associates, Wachovia, and Wood Partners.

Student Life and Environment

"Life at Kenan-Flagler is always challenging and usually a lot of fun," students note. One student adds, "The school operates on a modular system, so your class schedule changes regularly. I like the mod system because it makes the most of your time here. If the school feels like they only need 8 weeks to teach intro statistics, then the class is only 8 weeks long. They don't make it 12 weeks just because finance needs to be 12 weeks." Outside of class, "social and cultural activities can't be beat. [Some activities include] semi-annual bar golf, golf tournaments every week, free golf lessons for women, small group potluck dinners every quarter (with a new mix of people each time), Asia night, Latin parties, speaker series, bonfires, 'Prom,' and a slew of athletic activities." In addition, students say, "Club activities abound. We have a very active student-run career network for every conceivable track," as well as "a very active partners' club for spouses."

Hometown Chapel Hill—part of Raleigh's Triangle region (Raleigh and Durham round out the triumvirate)—is highly regarded by all. One student observes, "The community is diverse in cultural background, is beautifully kept, and is safe; the bus system is free; the public library is top-notch; the elementary school system is in the top 10 in the country, which is great for my family. You really couldn't ask for more." The town serves up "a great nightlife, especially if you like music." The university at large contributes "great sporting events, super social interactions, stimulating reading clubs, and lecture series," as well as "a beautiful campus."

Admissions

Applicants to UNC Kenan-Flagler must submit the following to the school: official copies of all undergraduate and graduate transcripts, GMAT scores, TOEFL scores (international students), two letters of recommendation, three essays, and a resume. An interview is also required. Applicants must have at least two years of post-baccalaureate professional experience; the school notes that "most successful candidates have closer to five years of work experience." The school also reports that "at UNC Kenan-Flagler, current minority students play an active role in recruiting other high-achieving students of color." The school hosts on-campus recruiting events for minority and underprivileged students, participates in the National Black MBA Association annual conference and the National Society of Hispanic MBAs annual conference, and recruits talented minorities to compete for merit-based fellowships.

FINANCIAL FACTS

Annual tuition (in-state/out-of-state)	$16,375/$32,749
Fees	$2,551
Books and supplies	$4,538
Room & board	$15,032
% of students receiving aid	76
% of first-year students receiving aid	76
% of students receiving loans	71
% of students receiving grants	39
Average award package	$35,727
Average grant	$8,395

ADMISSIONS

Admissions Selectivity Rating	89
# of applications received	1500
% applicants accepted	47
% acceptees attending	40
Average GMAT	652
Range of GMAT	620-700
Average GPA	3.3
TOEFL Required of International Students?	Yes
Minimum TOEFL (paper/computer)	600/250
Application fee	$110
International application fee	$110
Regular application deadline	3/5
Regular notification	5/16
Application Deadline/Notification	
Round 1:	10/28 / 12/13
Round 2:	12/2 / 2/7
Round 3:	1/13 / 3/23
Round 4:	3/5 / 5/16
Early decision program?	Yes
ED Deadline/Notification	
Early Action deadline is	10/28 / 12/13
Deferment Available?	Yes
Maximum length of deferment	1 year
Need-blind admissions?	Yes

APPLICANTS ALSO LOOK AT

Duke University, Northwestern University, University of Michigan, University of Virginia.

EMPLOYMENT PROFILE

Career Rating	89	Grads employed by field	%: avg. salary
Placement rate (%)	81	Finance	44: $77,839
% grads employed immediately	59	Human Resources	2: $58,666
Average starting salary	$78,751	Marketing	21: $78,546
		Operations	3: $77,833
		Consulting	10: $85,444
		General Management	7: $79,666
		Other	12: $79,328

UNIVERSITY OF NORTH CAROLINA AT CHARLOTTE
BELK COLLEGE OF BUSINESS ADMINISTRATION

GENERAL INFORMATION
Type of school	public
Environment	metropolis
Academic calendar	semester

SURVEY SAYS...
Students love Charlotte, NC
Cutting edge classes
Happy students
Smart classrooms
Solid preparation in:
Teamwork
Quantitative skills

STUDENTS
Enrollment of parent institution	19,846
Enrollment of MBA program	310
% male/female	69/31
% out-of-state	6
% part-time	80
% minorities	8
% international	28
Average age at entry	30
Average years work experience at entry	8.7

ACADEMICS
Academic Experience Rating	**84**
Student/faculty ratio	5:1
Profs interesting rating	82
Profs accessible rating	75
% female faculty	23
% minority faculty	14

Prominent Alumni
Verl Purdy, Executive VP and Pres., AGDATA; Manuel Zapata, Pres., Zapata Engineering; David Hauser, CFO, Duke Energy; Dr. Robert Rucho, DDS, Senator, North Carolina General Assembly; Kathy B. Harris, VP, Software Sector Chief of Research, Gartner,Inc.

Academics

A large part-time program "allows working professionals to earn their degree in the evening without interrupting their careers" at the University of North Carolina at Charlotte, a state school located in one of the nation's major banking centers. MBAs in this "incredibly flexible program" can take one to four courses per term at two convenient locations, and as long as they're North Carolina residents, they can do it for a remarkably low price. "I think it's probably one of the top five business schools in terms of return on investment," one Tar Heel tells us.

Belk offers a whopping 9 areas of concentration (business finance, information & technology management, international business, management, marketing, economics, real estate finance and development, supply chain management, and financial institutions/commercial banking), as well as the option to design one of your own. Banking and finance-related disciplines are strong, benefiting from the school's location. Other disciplines also benefit from Charlotte's status as a business center. One MBA explains, "Many of the professors are very active within their fields as well as in the community, and often run their own businesses. They bring valuable knowledge and experience into the classroom, and keep current events in the forefront of class discussion." The program has recently intensified its focus on international business, employing technology to run joint learning ventures with students in Mexico, Europe, Asia, and Latin America.

Students here warn that "Most of the time, the course load is very heavy, but that's the only way you learn a lot from a master's program." Fortunately, when work becomes overwhelming, the professors "are very helpful and knowledgeable" and administrators "are willing to meet one-on-one and they respond to your e-mails almost immediately, even during registration week." Best of all, the school's leaders are "very committed to implement students' input and develop a stronger program." No wonder MBAs express a high degree of satisfaction with Belk, telling us that "it offers a well-diversified and challenging program that's most likely as good as any."

Career and Placement

Belk students receive career and placement assistance from both the administration of their program and the university's Career Center. The Career Center maintains a list of job postings and recruiting schedules; conducts workshops and counseling sessions in resume writing, interviewing, and networking; and provides assistance in employment searches. A total of 37 companies visit the UNC—Charlotte campus each year to recruit MBAs for full-time employment; another 7 recruit summer interns here. Many students attend part-time on their employer's dime and do not use the school's career services—some because they deem the services "weak."

Top employers of Belk MBAs include AG Edwards, Bank of America, BB&T, Belk Stores Services, Carolina Health Care System, Cisco Systems, Compass Group, Duke Energy, IBM, Ingersoll-Rand, Northwestern Mutual, TIAA-CREF, and Wachovia.

Student Life and Environment

Belk MBAs "are very career-focused . . . working adults" who "spend very little time on campus," and accordingly "many do not have time for much outside of class." When attending classes, students appreciate the "clean, safe, new buildings, and well-kept grounds," but they rarely stick around once classes end. Full-timers note that "there are a lot of activities which are cocurricular [and] a lot of extracurricular activities, like plays, dramas, and movies to watch together on weekends here on campus. There are

Ron Veith, Director of the MBA Program
9201 University City Boulevard, Charlotte, NC 28223-0001 United States
Phone: 704-687-2569 • Fax: 704-687-2809
E-mail: mba@email.uncc.edu • Website: www.mba.uncc.edu

also a few international festivals organized by UNC—Charlotte each year." Even so, most feel that "the MBA program needs to be more involved in the community and more active in sponsoring seminars, etc. The school in general should do more to make it a 'non-commuter' school." They report optimistically, "The association representing business school students is trying to bring about these changes."

Students see great benefit in attending school in Charlotte, a "growing city" with "diverse companies that allow UNC—Charlotte to attract students who could go to better schools." Charlotte is a major global banking center and is the U.S. headquarters to over 400 global corporations (among which are nine Fortune 500 companies). Health care and technology are also major players in the employment market here. The program's thousand-acre main campus is both beautiful and easily accessible. Students may also attend classes at the uptown campus in the Mint Museum of Craft & Design.

The Belk student body consists primarily of "two general types of students. One type is the recent undergraduate who has either not found employment or is not ready to commit to a full-time job yet. The other type is the achieving professional, typically with four or more years of experience and family commitments that prevent him or her from attending a 'name school' full-time. Thankfully, UNC—Charlotte is devoting its resources to attracting the second type of student." Of the latter, MBAs agree that "Full-time employment gives students excellent working experience to bring to class, probably more so than in a full-time program." Wachovia, Bank of America, Duke Energy, IBM, and Bell South are all major feeders into the program, but over 210 companies are represented here, including nonprofits, real estate developers, and sole proprietorships.

Admissions

Belk prefers students with at least three years of professional experience. Eighty percent of its students are part-timers who also work full-time. Applicants must provide the school with two official copies of all transcripts for post-secondary-school work, GMAT scores, a personal essay "describing the applicant's experience and objectives in undertaking graduate study," a resume, and three evaluations from "persons familiar with the applicant's personal and professional qualifications." International applicants must provide TOEFL scores (minimum 557 paper-and-pencil, 220 computer-based), IELTS scores (minimum overall band score 6.5), or MELAB scores (minimum 78), as well as a statement of sufficient financial resources to cover the cost of education and living in Charlotte.

FINANCIAL FACTS

Annual tuition (in-state/out-of-state)	$4,704/$14,911
Fees	$1,348
Books and supplies	$1,000
Room & board (on/off-campus)	$7,000/$8,500
% of students receiving aid	22
% of first-year students receiving aid	10
% of students receiving loans	16
% of students receiving grants	2
Average award package	$10,846
Average grant	$7,250
Average student loan debt	$28,812

ADMISSIONS

Admissions Selectivity Rating	81
# of applications received	170
% applicants accepted	62
% acceptees attending	68
Average GMAT	575
Range of GMAT	530-630
Average GPA	3.25
TOEFL Required of International Students?	Yes
Minimum TOEFL (paper/computer)	557/220
Application fee	$55
International application fee	$55
Regular application deadline	5/1
Regular notification	Rolling
Deferment Available?	Yes
Maximum length of deferment	1 year
Transfer students accepted?	Yes
Transfer application policy: All students have to complete the graduate application materials and submit official test scores. With permission, it may be possible to transfer graduate level work from an AACSB-accredited university.	
Non-fall admissions?	Yes
Need-blind admissions?	Yes

EMPLOYMENT PROFILE

Career Rating	78	Grads employed by field:	
% grads employed immediately	84	Accounting	2
Average starting salary	$68,251	Finance	35
		Human Resources	2
		Marketing	7
		MIS	5
		Operations	14
		Consulting	12
		General Management	5
		Other	18

University of North Carolina at Greensboro

Joseph M. Bryan School of Business & Economics

Academics

Most of the students in the Bryan MBA program at University of North Carolina Greensboro are part-timers, and the school accordingly tailors its evening program to their needs. MBAs tell us that their school gets the job done, praising the flexible scheduling system that allows them to shoehorn schoolwork into their busy lives. They also appreciate a "very affordable price" that doesn't impinge on the "outstanding quality of the program" and technological assets that are "a huge plus for UNCG," including a wireless network that supports "a variety of computing environments and provides access to a wide range of software to support instructional and research activities," numerous computer labs, and modern computing and projection equipment in classrooms.

Classes for experienced students at Bryan are offered in the evening, a system that "allows maximum flexibility for working students, and allows daytime internship opportunities for full-time students." In addition to prerequisite courses (which can be waived for students with appropriate academic or professional backgrounds) and foundation courses, Bryan offers electives in advanced accounting, finance, management information systems, marketing, international business, and economics. Students may also take electives through the masters of textile design and marketing program, a program that capitalizes on Greensboro's historic role as a textile manufacturer. All classes "are taught in eight-week increments, so the pace of the courses is fast. Having this type of class enables you to learn quickly and then apply that knowledge to the next layer of classes you take."

Bryan "does well in pulling experts from the field to teach one or two courses, including CEOs from top firms. Some still practice in their field but most are on a 'second' career as a teacher." The professors "demand that students set high standards ethically, professionally, and academically," but are also "understanding of the multitude of priorities in life in addition to coursework. It takes self-motivation to excel in this program," in which "class interaction is encouraged and stressed." The MBA program recently introduced a full-time day MBA option in August 2004 to attract recent graduates with little or no work experience. The course structure is similar to the evening option but more emphasis is placed on practical learning experiences through summer internships, study abroad and a capstone consulting course. The students in the daytime option go through "Boot camp"—a four day skill and team building program before they begin graduate level coursework.

Career and Placement

The office providing career services to Bryan MBAs is new and dedicated to providing service to MBA and MSITM students. It will assist current students and alumni, at no charge, in career and internship placement services.

Top employers of Bryan MBAs include Wachovia, VF Corporation, Sara Lee, Volvo Finance, American Express, Gilbarco, Inc., Syngenta, Konica, the Moses Cone Health Care System, the Center for Creative Leadership, Eveready, Kayser-Roth, Stockhausen Inc., Dow Corning, Labcorps, Banner Pharmacaps, North Carolina Baptist Hospital, Cone Mills Corporation, Deloitte & Touche, Proctor & Gamble, Dixon Odom & Company, and RJR Nabisco.

Student Life and Environment

Because the Bryan MBA is largely a part-time evening program, "Most of the students work a full week and attend classes at night. Add to that the pressures of family and basic household responsibilities, and there's not much time for social clubs and organizations." Even so, the program makes "some attempts at activities, but it's hard because

Dr. Catherine Holderness, Associate Director, MBA Program
PO Box 26165, Greensboro, NC 27402-6165 United States
Phone: 336-334-5390 • Fax: 336-334-4209
E-mail: mybryanmba@uncg.edu • Website: www.mybryanmba.com

most of us work and go to school." On a positive note, "a lot of the MBA social events try to include alumni, which is important and helps with networking for jobs when you get out." The university at large is busy, with plenty of athletic events, theatrical productions, and lectures. As one MBA puts it, "Many of us in the MBA program are too tired to take advantage of all that's offered by the university."

Bryan students enjoy a genial classroom atmosphere in which "the environment is competitive, but students look out for one another and try to help one another out." Full-timers "tend to stick together. Almost any time of day you can find a group of them in the business school studying, conversing, eating, etc." Full-timers also note that "the recreational facilities are outstanding [and] the campus is well-lit and safe." All students complain that "parking is an issue, due to the increased enrollment in the MBA program."

Students tell us that hometown Greensboro, a midsize city with a small-town feel, "is full of entertainment options." The city is part of North Carolina's Triad metropolitan region (which also includes High Point and Winston-Salem), home to 11 colleges and universities as well as a 24,000-seat arena (home of the ACC basketball tournaments), minor-league baseball, and numerous theaters, galleries, and restaurants. The location provides easy access to mountain getaways, Sandhills golf, and North Carolina's two largest cities, Charlotte (a major banking center) and Raleigh (the state capital).

"There is a large group of international students" in the Bryan MBA program, "which enables U.S. students to understand the global business world more clearly." Students come from Germany, France, Italy, China, India, Japan, Thailand, and Holland, we're told. Local students "are a good mix of younger students who recently graduated from undergrad school and students in their 30s or 40s (or higher) who have been in the work force for some time." Many "are technically oriented by degree and experience."

Admissions

Applicants to the Bryan MBA program must provide the admissions office with a completed application, two sets of official undergraduate transcripts, GMAT scores, a personal essay, and three letters of recommendation from coworkers and/or current/former instructors. International students must also submit TOEFL scores and an affidavit of financial support. The school reports that the average successful applicant has a GMAT score of 570 and an undergraduate GPA of 3.2. Note, however, that half of all successful applicants fail to meet at least one of those benchmarks. Previous work experience is preferred but not required. Bryan fellowships, scholarships and graduate assistantships are available to outstanding and well deserving students.

FINANCIAL FACTS

Annual tuition (in-state/out-of-state)	$2,832/$13,882
Fees	$1,407
Books and supplies	$1,200
Room & board	$7,000
% of students receiving aid	10
% of first-year students receiving aid	17
% of students receiving grants	1
Average award package	$6,667
Average grant	$14,000

ADMISSIONS

Admissions Selectivity Rating	81
# of applications received	180
% applicants accepted	60
% acceptees attending	77
Average GMAT	562
Range of GMAT	520-600
Average GPA	3.4
TOEFL Required of International Students?	Yes
Minimum TOEFL (paper/computer)	550/213
Application fee	$45
International application fee	$45
Regular application deadline	7/1
Regular notification	Rolling
Deferment Available?	Yes
Maximum length of deferment	1 year
Transfer students accepted?	Yes
Transfer application policy: Students must be in good standing at a fellow AACSB Accredited MBA Program and may transfer no more than 12 semester credit hours of approved coursework.	
Non-fall admissions?	Yes
Need-blind admissions?	Yes

APPLICANTS ALSO LOOK AT

North Carolina State University, University of North Carolina at Chapel Hill, Wake Forest University.

EMPLOYMENT PROFILE	
Career Rating	83
Placement rate (%)	95
# of companies recruiting on-campus	55
% grads employed immediately	80
Average starting salary	$70,605

UNIVERSITY OF NORTH DAKOTA
COLLEGE OF BUSINESS AND PUBLIC ADMINISTRATION

GENERAL INFORMATION
Type of school	public
Environment	town

SURVEY SAYS...
Solid preparation in:
Operations
Communication/interpersonal skills
Presentation skills
Quantitative skills

STUDENTS
Enrollment of parent institution	11,300
Enrollment of MBA program	121
% male/female	60/40
% out-of-state	30
% part-time	30
% minorities	15
% international	10
Average age at entry	27
Average years work experience at entry	5

ACADEMICS
Academic Experience Rating	62
Student/faculty ratio	15:1
Profs interesting rating	76
Profs accessible rating	69
% female faculty	40
% minority faculty	20

Prominent Alumni
Jason Coffel, Finance Manager;
Dave Goodin, Vice Pres of
Operations; Odella M. Fuqua,
Assistant Dean of Finance &
Information Technology; Rick Pauls,
Managing Director.

Academics

Affordability, convenience, a "solid reputation in the area," and a popular 3/2 combined bachelor's-MBA program draw students to the College of Business and Public Administration at the University of North Dakota, one of only two AACSB-accredited programs in the state. More than half the students here attend full-time, many under the Combined Model that yields a baccalaureate in business and an MBA in five years' time. The part-time population include a number of distance learners; UND has offered long-distance learning for more than 10 years through IVN, the state-run interactive video network.

The UND MBA consists of 32 hours of coursework (35 hours for students pursuing a concentration). Twenty-four hours are committed to core classes, two hours are set aside for independent study, and the remaining hours are allotted to electives. Because this is a small program, concentrations are available in two areas only: accounting, and international business. The former program can be used to help fulfill the 150-hour requirement for taking the CPA exam; the latter program requires students to complete nine hours of coursework at the Business Institute University of Norway. Students here praise the "outstanding accounting concentration" and also love the college's courses in entrepreneurship. In all areas, classes at UND are "small and discussion based," leading to "a more intimate student-teacher relationship." Sums up one student, "This is the best school in the state of North Dakota. It's also great having a Division I hockey team. It helps with recruiting, believe it or not."

Career and Placement

The UND Career Services Office provides counseling and placement services for all enrolled students of the university. The office organizes career fairs and on-campus recruiting events. On average, about 25 companies visit the campus to recruit MBAs each year; another three visit to recruit summer interns. Employers most likely to hire UND MBAs include Cargill, Deloitte & Touche, PricewaterhouseCoopers, Honeywell, Microsoft Great Plains, Eide Bailley, and McGladdrey Pullen.

SUSAN NELSON, MBA DIRECTOR
GAMBLE HALL, PO BOX 8098, GRAND FORKS, ND 58202 UNITED STATES
PHONE: 701-777-2975 • FAX: 701-777-2019
E-MAIL: MBA@UND.NODAK.EDU • WEBSITE: WWW.BPA.UND.NODAK.EDU/MBA/

Student Life and Environment

The College of Business and Public Administration building at UND boasts a number of high-tech facilities, including the A. Kirk Lanterman Investment Center, which "provides students access to real-time financial market data and research information, which augments student education at the graduate and undergraduate levels," according to the college's website. The Page Family Marketing Center provides marketing students with a research lab, breakout rooms, a conference room, and a focus group area equipped with video cameras for taping focus-group sessions. Students appreciate these assets, but are most pleased that "all the classes are in the same building, which means we don't have to go outside in the winter!"

Students can make their extracurricular lives at UND as busy as they want. The program hosts a solid complement of professional groups and student organizations. There are plenty of opportunities for physical activity, both indoor and out: students have access to an Arnold Palmer-designed golf course, parks, swimming pools, and a gym. The university's hockey team draws large crowds of winter sports enthusiasts. The area is also ideal for skaters, sledders, snowmobilers, and cross-country skiers. Students report that "the various seasons provide a diverse climate" in Grand Forks, but warn that "the winter session is very harsh because of the weather."

"Many students come straight out of undergraduate school and into the program" at UND, but the student body as a whole is drawn "from all different backgrounds and all different locations." Nearly one-third of the student body originates from outside North Dakota. Students form a "friendly community" of "smart and self-sufficient" future MBAs.

Admissions

Admissions requirements to the MBA program at UND include: an undergraduate degree from an accredited institution, with a GPA of at least 2.75 for the full four years or 3.00 for the final two years of undergraduate work (a 3.00 GPA is required for admission under the Combined Model, which allows students to begin their MBA work after three years of undergraduate work); a GMAT score of at least 450 (500 under the Combined Model); and demonstrated proficiency in basic accounting, administrative process, economics, functional areas of business, mathematics, and quantitative methods. Applicants who do not meet this final requirement may be admitted conditionally, pending completion of coursework in the prescribed areas. International students whose first language is not English must additionally demonstrate language mastery through the TOEFL.

FINANCIAL FACTS

Annual tuition (in-state/out-of-state)	$1,943/$4,598
Books and supplies	$3,300
Room & board (on-campus)	$3,932
Average grant	$7,000

ADMISSIONS

Admissions Selectivity Rating	**66**
# of applications received	90
% applicants accepted	93
% acceptees attending	83
Average GMAT	520
Range of GMAT	440-680
Average GPA	3.2
TOEFL Required of International Students?	Yes
Minimum TOEFL (paper/computer)	550/213
Application fee	$35
International application fee	$35
Regular application deadline	Rolling
Regular notification	Rolling
Deferment Available?	Yes
Maximum length of deferment	1 year
Transfer students accepted?	Yes
Transfer application policy: Up to nine credits of approved coursework can be transferred.	
Non-fall admissions?	Yes
Need-blind admissions?	Yes

APPLICANTS ALSO LOOK AT

University of Minnesota.

EMPLOYMENT PROFILE

		Grads employed by field	%: avg. salary
Career Rating	73		
Placement rate (%)	98	Accounting	25: $50,000
# of companies recruiting on-campus	25	Finance	20: $45,000
% grads employed immediately	45	Human Resources	15: $38,000
Average starting salary	$39,000	Marketing	20: $45,000
		MIS	5: $40,000
		Consulting	5: $42,000
		Communications	5: $37,000
		General Management	5: $40,000

UNIVERSITY OF NORTH FLORIDA
COGGIN COLLEGE OF BUSINESS

GENERAL INFORMATION
Type of school	public
Environment	metropolis

SURVEY SAYS...
Students love Jacksonville, Fl
Friendly students
Happy students
Smart classrooms
Solid preparation in:
Teamwork

STUDENTS
Enrollment of parent institution	14,641
Enrollment of MBA program	459
% male/female	50/50
% out-of-state	5
% part-time	68
% minorities	24
% international	10
Average age at entry	29

ACADEMICS
Academic Experience Rating	**80**
Student/faculty ratio	17:1
Profs interesting rating	85
Profs accessible rating	82

Academics

When you consider the cost-benefit ratio, The University of North Florida Coggin College of Business is an excellent choice for the sensible business student, as it offers "quality instructors and overall programs at an affordable price." Intended for students with a bachelor's degree in any field, Coggin offers general graduate level coursework in a wide range of business topics, including accounting, finance, international business and e-commerce. As a vast majority of the school's 450 graduate students are working professionals, the school offers a flexible evening schedule, and classes are also offered on the weekends.

Coggin has a strong "focus on application-based learning." All UNF professors join the faculty with real world experience, and students are expected to take a hands-on, practical approach to their education. A student reports, "I have been very pleased with my professors at UNF. A majority of them have published several books, journal articles, and have also been part of corporate America, such as Dun & Bradstreet and Fortune 500 companies. They have brought valuable corporate experience into the classroom." Another student adds, "I have seen a direct correlation between my performance at work and the additional knowledge gained through my MBA courses. Most professors have done an excellent job relating the course material to real-world business examples."

A distinguishing characteristic of the Coggin MBA program is its strong focus on international business. In particular, Coggin offers the unique GlobalMBA program, a business school exchange operated in conjunction with three partner universities in France, Germany, and Poland. The GlobalMBA brings "a ton of international students" to the UNF campus each year, a benefit to the entire student community. "The GlobalMBA attracts students from across the world," writes one student. "My current cohort has nationalities of Greece, Iran, Bulgaria, Germany, France, Poland, and the U.S.A. This makes for a great intercultural experience, as well as a wonderful interactive learning environment." For students in the regular MBA program, "There are several opportunities for UNF students to study abroad all over the world."

Coggin offers a number of concentrations for those who wish to focus their education on a specific business field. Currently, the faculty has approved concentrations in the following fields of study: accounting, construction management, e-commerce, economics, finance, human resource management, international business, logistics, or management application. Students also point out that UNF offers the unique "opportunity to be selected in the Osprey Financial Group, the student run investment portfolio" that manages a $600,000 portfolio of equity and fixed income securities. Still, many students believe Coggin could offer "more options for electives." Many tell us that the research facilities need to be updated; "Really, the biggest improvement [is] the library. It is dated and the material is lacking. You have to go to your local library or order the book you need from another university," writes a second-year student. Luckily, a library extension is underway.

Career & Placement

Coggin students "mostly consist of local Jacksonville residents who intend to continue their careers in the area." As such, the school is an excellent choice for those interested in finding quality employment in the burgeoning Jacksonville region, as it is "well regarded in the community." This is mainly due to that fact that faculty and administrators work "diligently at keeping their business school on the cutting edge and involving the local business community."

PEGGY TATTERSALL, GRADUATE STUDIES COORDINATOR
4567 ST JOHN'S BLUFF ROAD SOUTH, BUILDING 2, JACKSONVILLE, FL 32224 UNITED STATES
PHONE: 904-620-1361 • FAX: 904-620-1362
E-MAIL: PTATTERS@UNF.EDU • WEBSITE: WWW.UNF.EDU/CCB/

Student Life & Environment

With its international focus and active part-time program, Coggin attracts "a very diverse group of students. Some with families, some...straight out of undergrad." Satisfied part-time students praise the fact that "for the working student, UNF is a great university that allows you to balance your educational objectives." While the campus vibe is low-key and friendly, most business students "have busy lives and would really like to minimize the time spent on campus." Therefore, most are uninterested in participating in campus clubs or social activities. In fact, "many of us only attend functions that are mandatory on campus or for our group work."

Nonetheless, UNF still also manages to appeal to full time students. For those who want a more traditional college experience, "the campus housing is pretty good," and "UNF has tons of clubs, sororities, and sports" in which MBA students are free to participate. Students also note that "the weather, the people, the campus are all wonderful." In fact, "the city itself is full of activities from the beach to NFL football games, to clubs to hockey games. You can't get bored!"

Admissions

To apply to the Coggin School of Business, you must submit a completed application, an application fee, undergraduate transcripts, and GMAT scores. Admission to the regular MBA program is based on undergraduate GPA and GMAT scores. To be admitted, a minimum 1000 index must be obtained on the formula (GPA x 200) + GMAT total score. GMAT: In addition to the minimum 1000 index, a minimum 20 Verbal and 22 Quantitative GMAT sub-score and a 450 score total are required for graduate admission. Currently, the Analytical Writing Analysis sub-score is not used as an admission criterion.

Students must apply separately for the GlobalMBA program. To apply to the GlobalMBA, students must submit a completed application and fee, undergraduate transcripts, and GMAT scores. The minimum GMAT score for the GlobalMBA is 500. These documents are carefully reviewed and qualified candidates are then invited for personal interviews with the admissions committee. All applications for the GlobalMBA must be submitted by April 1.

FINANCIAL FACTS

Annual tuition (in-state/out-of-state)	$5,567/$19,999
Books and supplies	$900
% of students receiving aid	20
% of first-year students receiving aid	32
% of students receiving loans	17
% of students receiving grants	7
Average award package	$9,195
Average grant	$1,046

ADMISSIONS

Admissions Selectivity Rating	**79**
# of applications received	279
% applicants accepted	51
% acceptees attending	69
Average GMAT	519
Range of GMAT	380-680
Average GPA	3.18
TOEFL Required of International Students?	Yes
Minimum TOEFL (paper)	550
Application fee	$30
International application fee	$30
Regular application deadline	7/1
Regular notification	Rolling
Deferment Available?	Yes
Maximum length of deferment	1 sememster
Transfer students accepted?	Yes
Transfer application policy: Transfer credits accepted on a case by case basis.	
Non-fall admissions?	Yes
Need-blind admissions?	Yes

EMPLOYMENT PROFILE

Career Rating	60*
% grads employed at graduation	90

UNIVERSITY OF NOTRE DAME
MENDOZA COLLEGE OF BUSINESS

GENERAL INFORMATION
Type of school   private
Affiliation   Roman Catholic
Environment   city
Academic calendar   semester

SURVEY SAYS...
Friendly students
Good social scene
Good peer network
Happy students
Smart classrooms
Solid preparation in:
Teamwork
Communication/interpersonal skills

STUDENTS
Enrollment of parent
    institution   11,415
Enrollment of MBA program   324
% male/female   75/25
% out-of-state   93
% minorities   22
% international   15
Average age at entry   26
Average years work experience
    at entry   4.25

ACADEMICS
Academic Experience Rating   90
Student/faculty ratio   15:1
Profs interesting rating   88
Profs accessible rating   97
% female faculty   15
% minority faculty   14
Joint Degrees
MBA/JD: 4 years
MBA/MEng: 2 years
MBA/MS: 2 years
Prominent Alumni
Don Casey, Group Pres., Global
Franchises/ Vistakon; Paul J. Stich,
Pres. & CEO/ Counterpane Internet
Security; Paul Reilly, Chairman &
CEO/Korn Ferry Int'l; Jim Corgel,
General Mgr/IBM eBusiness Svcs.
Hosting.

Academics

Students who enroll in the University of Notre Dame's Mendoza College of Business know what they're getting into. With its storied past, Notre Dame gives MBAs more than just a business education. They get the Golden Dome, Knute Rockne, the Grotto, the Basilica, an education grounded in Catholic values and, of course, some of the biggest football fans in the world. Students say, "Your acceptance letter welcomes you to the Notre Dame Family and means it. I can't imagine a lot of institutions that take such a warm, committed approach to their students. But this is one of the reasons why the alumni are tight and supportive." Professors are dedicated to students; one student reports, "I even have a professor who came in to school on a weekend to answer a question that I had about a subject that he did not teach." And with all this good will, it's no wonder "the school has a lot of energy."

Because of the school's grounding in Catholicism, ethical studies are a component of most of the classes. Students say that "the focus on ethics make sure [they] keep in mind the most important things when they make business decisions." Still, students need not be Catholic to apply or succeed. As one student says, "I have never met a more religiously diverse group of students. I have learned more about world religions over beers at the bars than in any history or theology course that I have ever studied. People are very open to discussing these 'deep' topics."

Students entering the program in May and August of 2005 will experience a new curriculum and modular format. Centered on the themes of thought, action, and values leadership, the curriculum combines rigorous training in the basic business disciplines with an in-depth treatment of business ethics and applied courses and projects that require students to put their knowledge into action. Unique to the curriculum are required courses in ethics, values in decision making, business communications, and integrated problem solving.

Mendoza offers elective concentration tracks in operations management, general management, corporate finance, investments, entrepreneurship, business-to-business marketing, consumer marketing, and consulting. Students largely agree that the "finance faculty is outstanding" but believe that the school should offer "more course offerings in nonprofits, law, and accounting." Others add that the school "could use better courses in technology." Students note that it could "do a better job of getting us up to speed on the technology and software that would be beneficial to us as businesspeople and make us stand out in the workplace."

Though Notre Dame has campuses all over the world and Mendoza offers opportunities to study in China, Belgium and Chile, students wish the school had "more of an international outlook." In addition, in cooperation with Notre Dame's law school, Mendoza also offers a four-year MBA/JD.

Career and Placement

Notre Dame, like many other schools, has suffered from the poor economy, but its career services department has done their best to combat it. According to one student, "There has been a great deal of restructuring in the career services office. It appears to be working to provide more opportunities for the students, but only time will tell." One student says, "Recruiting is impressive, but it is very regional and there aren't many opportunities for people looking to go back to the East Coast as I am. With that said, I have had great success getting a job on the East Coast, thanks to the active alumni (both grad and undergrad networks)."

MARY GOSS, DIRECTOR OF ADMISSIONS
276 MENDOZA COLLEGE OF BUSINESS NOTRE DAME, IN 46556-4656 UNITED STATES
PHONE: 219-631-8488 • FAX: 219-631-8800
E-MAIL: MBA.1@ND.EDU • WEBSITE: WWW.ND.EDU/~MBA

With more than 240 alumni clubs worldwide, Notre Dame's network is among the strongest in the country, and the almost-fanatic pride that graduates take in their school means that most alumni are more than willing to lend a hand. As one student says, alumni are "absolutely outstanding in terms of helping students find what jobs they want and helping them get those jobs." Another student adds, "I have yet to call or e-mail an alum that didn't give a positive response."

Companies that recruit regularly on campus include General Electric, Johnson & Johnson, and IBM. The median base salary for students graduating in 2004 was $80,000. About 41 percent of those graduates ended up working in the Midwest and 59 percent ended up working in finance/consulting.

Student Life and Environment

It turns out that Notre Dame really does inspire a *Rudy*-like devotion in its students, who wax poetic about the trees that "line enormous quads filled with bustling students. Wondrous brick buildings mark the university's growth during the past 150 years. To the south, a modern-day coliseum sits waiting to erupt six Saturdays each fall. And at the center of it all, a magnificent golden dome and a Basilica spire rise above the trees, toward the heavens, communicating Notre Dame's grace and power to the world." Because of the school's reputation and fanatic loyalists, students who end up there have often waited their entire lives to be a part of Notre Dame.

One student also points out that another advantage to a small town is that "on any particular evening out, I am likely to run into half my class. The MBA program is a tight-knit group, and I think we respect one another's abilities and appreciate our unique personalities." No wonder the alumni keep coming back. As one student says, most students at Notre Dame are "honored to be a part of the school and determined to be successful partners in its future."

Admissions

The Notre Dame admissions staff looks for three characteristics in the students they accept: "a demonstrated track record and aptitude for academic success, a track record of professional success, and leadership qualities that show you will be an active participant in the MBA community." Diversity is important to the school, so admissions encourage "you to apply even if your profile is atypical." Despite this, in a class of about 130 students, only about 16 percent are female and 23 percent are minority students (from the United States). The average work experience was 4.75 years, and the middle GPA range was 3.1-3.4. The middle GMAT range was 620 to 710. About 23 percent of students were international in 2003, and 30 different countries were represented.

FINANCIAL FACTS

Annual tuition	$32,820
Fees	$375
Books and supplies	$1,450
Room & board (on/off-campus)	$6,915/$11,685
% of students receiving aid	82
% of first-year students receiving aid	89
% of students receiving loans	58
% of students receiving grants	62
Average award package	$39,750
Average grant	$15,595
Average student loan debt	$43,464

ADMISSIONS

Admissions Selectivity Rating	90
# of applications received	679
% applicants accepted	46
% acceptees attending	41
Average GMAT	657
Range of GMAT	610-700
Average GPA	3.3
TOEFL Required of International Students?	Yes
Minimum TOEFL (paper/computer)	600/250
Application fee	$100
International application fee	$100
Regular application deadline	1/15
Regular notification	2/15
Early decision program?	Yes
ED Deadline/Notification	11/15 / 12/15
Deferment Available?	Yes
Maximum length of deferment	1 year
Non-fall admissions?	Yes
Need-blind admissions?	Yes

APPLICANTS ALSO LOOK AT

Northwestern University, The University of Texas at Austin, University of Michigan, Vanderbilt University.

EMPLOYMENT PROFILE			
Career Rating	86	**Grads employed by field**	**%: avg. salary**
Placement rate (%)	84	Finance	37: $80,000
% grads employed immediately	60	Marketing	15: $82,000
Average starting salary	$80,000	MIS	2: NR
		Operations	2: NR
		Consulting	22: $75,000
		General Management	17: $80,000
		Other	4: NR

UNIVERSITY OF OKLAHOMA
MICHAEL F. PRICE COLLEGE OF BUSINESS

Academics

Students at the Price College of Business at the University of Oklahoma are drawn to "the biggest and best university in the region" because of the reasonable tuition and the perception that "Price is a good school, with a ton of potential, and the support of some heavy-hitters to make it happen." Finance and entrepreneurship are the star attractions at this "small program with lots of one-on-one contact with professors." As one student explains, "The small class size of the program is an asset in that every professor knows who you are and are willing to help you where they can." Another student adds, "The greatest strengths of the Price College lie in the character of the staff at OU. The facilities are nice and [are] getting better, but the desire of the faculty to see us succeed is what's most impressive."

Price works first-year students hard, requiring six core courses from them each semester. Students report that "there's a lot of team and individual work the first year. It's a hard-core lock-step program." While students like the teamwork concept, some complain that the execution is lacking, in large part due to teammates who refuse to pull their own weight. We heard several complaints from students who felt that "the overall academic experience would have been fine except for the group situation. [Students] are forced into groups at the beginning of the year, and typically two of you do all the work, and the three others freeload. I suppose if you are a freeloader, this is a good deal, as you will suffer no ill effects from your freeloading. In fact, you will likely do better than those who do the work; you can study for exams while others are working on projects and papers."

Second-year studies, in contrast to first year, are "easy and relaxed." However, students feel that too many of the second-year electives "are taught at night as part of the part-time program" at a satellite campus in Oklahoma City. The source of this problem, students feel, is the size of the program; one student explains, "Course offerings are too slim because of the small number of students, so holes exist in student training. If someone does get hired at a top-notch firm, they start behind the curve and most of their learning is on the job." On the upside, Price offers "great summer special programs (both nationally and abroad)." Students feel that the school has a promising future. One student writes, "This isn't a bad place, although sometimes it feels like it's building from scratch. Any opportunities you find in this program will be seeds that you'll need to grow on your own. But the dean has a real vision for this program, so it could go places."

Career and Placement

The Michael F. Price College of Business Student Support Center offers Oklahoma business students all the following services: workshops in resume and cover-letter creating; mock interviews, videotaped for review; self-assessment tests and other tools; personal counseling; alumni networking opportunities; an executive speaker series; and the opportunity to participate in mentoring programs. In addition, the school participates in the Southwest MBA Alliance to sponsor job fairs and other recruiting events. The office also helps students find domestic and international internships between the first and second years of the program. Students feel the office "is pretty good" and recognize that it labors under a handicap. One MBA explains, "Recruiters won't make a stop here because the pool of candidates is too small to justify it, and more students won't come here because jobs are too scarce in Oklahoma."

Top employers of Price MBAs include American Airlines, Bank of Oklahoma, ConocoPhillips, Devon Energy, Exxon, Kerr-McGee Corporation, OGE, RiskMetrics, SBC Communication, and TXU.

GINA AMUNDSON, DIRECTOR OF GRADUATE PROGRAMS
1003 ASP AVENUE, PRICE HALL, SUITE 1040, NORMAN, OK 73019-4302 UNITED STATES
PHONE: 405-325-4107 • FAX: 405-325-7753
E-MAIL: GAMUNDSON@OU.EDU • WEBSITE: PRICE.OU.EDU/MBA/

Student Life and Environment

Students report that the University of Oklahoma "has a great atmosphere to work in and a lot of options, when you want to get away from the school life." Most students agree that "Norman is cool, and you are close to Oklahoma City. We have great athletics, and they are a good distraction from studies. Norman is affordable and has a few good bars, although the town dies in the summer."

The MBA program itself, however, has little life of its own. "It's nonexistent," one student writes and adds that "if you don't put it together on your own, there's nothing going on. It's getting better with this year's incoming class, but [there] is no support from the administration for quality-of-life issues (other than the occasional faculty member visiting a get-together)." A good start, one student suggests, would be for the school to "plan extensive social activities for students' spouses and children. Right now the school does not have such activities."

Price students "are driven, friendly, and will amount to something. They are the greatest strength of the program." Each class includes between 30 and 40 full-timers with part-time students filling out the ranks. Price also has a large international population.

Admissions

The University of Oklahoma considers all the following elements of an MBA application: GMAT score (typically at least 600, minimum 50th percentile in math and verbal, and at least 3.5 on the analytical writing section); final 60 hours of undergraduate course work (students typically have at least a 3.2 GPA for this period); a resume (two or more years full-time experience is desired but not required); three letters of recommendation; and the applicant's personal statement of career and educational goals. The admissions committee also considers undergraduate extracurricular involvement and commitment to community service.

FINANCIAL FACTS

Annual tuition (in-state/out-of-state)	$4,342/$12,677
Fees	$2,712
Books and supplies	$1,000
Room & board	$5,960
Average grant	$5,303

ADMISSIONS

Admissions Selectivity Rating	89
# of applications received	118
% applicants accepted	55
% acceptees attending	71
Average GMAT	625
Range of GMAT	590-660
Average GPA	3.45
TOEFL Required of International Students?	Yes
Minimum TOEFL (paper/computer)	550/213
Application fee	$40
International application fee	$90
Regular application deadline	7/1
Regular notification	Rolling
Deferment Available?	Yes
Maximum length of deferment	1 year
Transfer students accepted?	Yes
Transfer application policy: Students may transfer into our PT MBA program from other AACSB accredited institutions.	
Need-blind admissions?	Yes

APPLICANTS ALSO LOOK AT

Oklahoma State University, South Texas College of Law, The University of Texas at Austin.

EMPLOYMENT PROFILE

Career Rating	79	Grads employed by field	%: avg. salary
Placement rate (%)	84	Accounting	14: $58,750
% grads employed immediately	60	Finance	23: $58,750
Average starting salary	$63,292	MIS	23: $68,000
		Consulting	10: $65,000
		General Management	14: $45,000
		Other	16: $62,000

University of Oregon
The Charles H. Lundquist College of Business

GENERAL INFORMATION
Type of school	public
Environment	city
Academic calendar	quarter

SURVEY SAYS...
Friendly students
Happy students
Smart classrooms
Solid preparation in:
Teamwork

STUDENTS
Enrollment of parent institution	20,033
Enrollment of MBA program	109
% male/female	73/27
% out-of-state	36
% minorities	8
% international	30
Average age at entry	27
Average years work experience at entry	3.6

ACADEMICS
Academic Experience Rating	**88**
Student/faculty ratio	4:1
Profs interesting rating	82
Profs accessible rating	87
% female faculty	13
% minority faculty	18

Joint Degrees
MBA/JD (4 years)
MA/MBA in International Studies or Asian Studies: 3 years

Prominent Alumni
Clare Villari, '80, Sr VP/Partner, Wellington Mgmt Co; Christopher Leupold, '89, Managing Director, Merrill Lynch; Young Tai Nam, '90, Exec. Vice Chairman, Korea Stock Exchange.

Academics

Despite its small size and off-the-beaten-path location, the Charles H. Lundquist College of Business MBA program at the University of Oregon is quickly developing a national reputation. Credit lies primarily with two nationally recognized programs. The first, in sports business, provides MBAs with "invaluable connections in the sports industry" through "coursework and opportunities to meet and work with top execs." The other program, in entrepreneurship, thrives thanks to its excellent faculty, who "have propelled this small program into many national top 25 lists over the past three years. This program gives Oregon MBAs unique access to, and preparation for, the top domestic and international business plan competitions." Oregon also offers programs in corporate finance, financial analysis, marketing, MIS, and supply chain management.

No matter what area students choose, they agree that "the greatest strengths of this school are the faculty and small class size. The staff and faculty go out of their way to help students, and the small class size makes them very accessible to each and every student." All 110 MBAs here are full-time students, a situation that fosters a close academic community. This makes it easier for students to face down "a rigorous presentation-skills module that runs for the entire first year" as well as "challenging, team-based projects such as SPP (the Strategic Planning Project), in which students gain experience in planning marketing strategy." Professors earn high marks for "trying very hard to ride the forefront of thought in marketing, strategy, and sustainable business. It is the strength of the institution that the desire is so strong and resources are available to us," vouches one student.

MBAs also benefit from the university at large ("We are encouraged to draw from other schools in the university in order to meet our own needs, which allows great flexibility," writes one student) and "facilities and classroom technology that are highly superior."

Career and Placement

Success in recruitment faces two hurdles at the University of Oregon. First is the small class size, which many companies see as a disincentive to visit campus. Second is the school's relatively out-of-the-way location, which is not ideal for a quick visit. One student explains, "Eugene, Oregon is not easily accessible for business recruiters, but there is nothing that can fix that. It is especially difficult to get companies from outside the northwest to visit the school."

There are other factors, too. One student writes, "In comparative average salary rankings, the Oregon MBA often ranks below other schools for two reasons: 1) Many students interested in nonprofit and competitive sports marketing careers attend the program. 2) Regional unemployment rates have affected salaries in many areas for graduating students." Fortunately, "the Oregon MBA also has a great network of alumni who are willing to work with current students."

All told, 18 employers typically visit campus each year to seek full-time employees; another 7 come looking for summer interns. Top employers include Hewlett-Packard, Intel, Tektronik, ESPN, and Bear Creek. An interesting stat: nearly one in four Oregon MBAs finds his/her first job outside the U.S.

Student Life and Environment

Even if the location isn't always recruiter-friendly, it is absolutely friendly to the MBAs who attend school here. "Located in one of the most beautiful parts of the country," the University of Oregon bestows an extremely high quality of life on its students. "The town and campus are amazing," and beyond both are abundant natural resources in which

Ms. Laura Balaty, Admissions Assistant
300 Peterson Hall, 1208 University of Oregon, Eugene, OR 97403-1208 United States
Phone: 541-346-1462 • Fax: 541-346-0073
E-mail: info@oregonmba.com • Website: www.oregonmba.com

"outdoor activities abound." While "the workload is heavy" in the program, students here usually find time to unwind. One MBA explains, "Life at the U of O is all about having a healthy environment to support your hard work. I put in a good 60+ hours a week on school, but when we have free time, students get together and take advantage of what the area has to offer. For example, I had class all morning, then went for a quick hike to reenergize to study until 8 or 9, and then I'll be off to meet classmates for a beer at a local microbrewery. That's a 10-hour day of studying, but I can avoid burning out." MBAs don't have to worry about driving home from the bars, either, since "students enjoy free public bus transportation, which is more than ample."

MBAs don't even need to leave campus to enjoy themselves. "In the university at large, there are plenty of events to go to," such as lectures, performances, movies, and sporting events. MBAs within the program say they enjoy "great team-building activities, rafting trips, golf outings, and bagel lunches. There are also football games and low-key and informal social events where we interact with fellow students and faculty." The Lundquist facility is homey and comfortable, a "beautiful new building that serves as a hub for the MBA students and others taking business classes. And it has all the latest technology." One MBA sums up, "The outdoor and on-campus activities are endless, which makes it very easy to get a good balance of schoolwork and social interaction."

Because of the small class size, Oregon MBAs "all know each other after only three weeks. It makes the experience much more enjoyable." Broadening the social circle is the fact that "the MBA and JD programs have good and frequent interaction, attending each other's events." The program has a "very strong Asian population," but otherwise "there is little racial diversity." Students are "very friendly [and] are very willing to use and share their experiences for the benefit of the class." Although "everyone is competitive, there are no egos."

Admissions

With a program that is small by design, Oregon allows itself the luxury to hand-pick each student admitted. Students are chosen for their potential in the business world and for their fit with the program. Admissions officers look for those who are eager for experiential learning, who have good team skills, and who are comfortable with complexity and uncertainty. In addition, successful applicants typically have a minimum GMAT score of 600 (and at least a 60th percentile rank on the quantitative section), an undergraduate GPA of at least 3.0, and two years of full-time, post-undergraduate work experience. Prior to enrollment, students must complete one term each of microeconomics and macroeconomics.

FINANCIAL FACTS

Annual tuition (in-state/out-of-state)	$9,868/$14,167
Fees	$1,650
Books and supplies	$876
Room & board (on/off-campus)	$6,255/$9,800
% of students receiving aid	51
% of first-year students receiving aid	58
% of students receiving loans	35
% of students receiving grants	24
Average award package	$23,349
Average grant	$4,250
Average student loan debt	$33,227

ADMISSIONS

Admissions Selectivity Rating	91
# of applications received	188
% applicants accepted	44
% acceptees attending	66
Average GMAT	632
Range of GMAT	600-650
Average GPA	3.2
TOEFL Required of International Students?	Yes
Minimum TOEFL (paper/computer)	600/250
Application fee	$50
International application fee	$50
Regular application deadline	4/15
Regular notification	5/15
Application Deadline/Notification	
Round 1:	12/15 / 1/31
Round 2:	2/15 / 3/31
Round 3:	3/15 / 5/15
Early decision program?	Yes
ED Deadline/Notification	12/15 / 1/31
Deferment Available?	Yes
Maximum length of deferment	1 year
Need-blind admissions?	Yes

APPLICANTS ALSO LOOK AT

Arizona State University, University of Colorado, University of Washington

EMPLOYMENT PROFILE			
Career Rating	80	**Grads employed by field %: avg. salary**	
Placement rate (%)	91	Finance	13: $56,336
# of companies recruiting on-campus	9	Human Resources	1: $46,000
% grads employed immediately	45	Marketing	13: $58,500
Average starting salary	$57,553	Operations	4: $50,333
		Consulting	6: $62,000
		General Management	2: $75,000
		Other	1: $48,000

UNIVERSITY OF OTTAWA
SCHOOL OF MANAGEMENT

Academics

The School of Management at the University of Ottawa "keeps on top of trends and adapts the program to new trends and the changes in global business practices," students report. The school is ideally located to ride the breaking waves of modern business; Ottawa is the self-proclaimed Silicon Valley North, and it is home to many of the nation's telecom and IT companies including Cognos, Inc.; Corel Corporation; Mitel Corporation; Nortel; and Zarlink. Ottawa's MBA program is geared toward these industries and maintains "a high tech focus. Plus, our proximity to the thriving high-tech sector brings in guest speakers who have relevant experiences." Ottawa's focus on international business is also particularly intense, especially when compared with many American programs.

Ottawa's MBA program is organized thematically with clusters of courses emphasizing issues in integrating business functions, international business, strategy, the developing tech-intensive global economy, and providing value to the business community. Highlights of the curriculum include "a one-term team consulting project, in which students help real businesses with business problems and prepare business plans," among other things. One student notes, "In our project, we are working with the ambassador of Thailand to improve economic relations (export and import) between Canada and Thailand. The focus is about closing a deal. It's very real, and that's great." The MBA can be completed in an intensive full-time program (one year) or a part-time program (28–36 months). Either way, coursework consists of a mix of 12-week classes and 6-week modules. The entire program is cohort-based, with no electives and thus no specialization options. In many courses, students have the choice of instruction in English or French.

Students comment, "[Ottawa professors] are extremely interesting," and they observe that "the experience and insight they bring to the classes are invaluable!" Some students warn, "[the professors] have great qualifications on paper but have a hard time engaging [the students]." Generally, MBAs agree that the faculty is "very professional and knowledgeable."

Career and Placement

The student-funded Career Center at the School of Management offers career-planning services to all business undergraduates, graduate students, and alumni of the university. The office's relationship managers conduct workshops and mock interviews, coordinate recruiting events, assist in the search for internships, and maintain extensive online and hard-copy job databases. The office offers all MBAs a 12-month, 3-stage program; students first learn job-search skills and undergo self-assessment, then commence networking and searching for jobs, and finally learn the finer points of business conduct ranging from etiquette to salary negotiation. Students praise the "many career-oriented workshops/events available."

DIANE SARRAZIN, MBA PROGRAM ADMINISTRATOR
136 JEAN-JACQUES LUSSIER, ROOM 252, OTTAWA, ON K1N 6N5 CANADA
PHONE: 613-562-5884 • FAX: 613-562-5912
E-MAIL: MBA@MANAGEMENT.UOTTAWA.CA • WEBSITE: WWW.MANAGEMENT.UOTTAWA.CA/

Student Life and Environment

In a typical year, slightly less than half the graduating MBAs at the University of Ottawa are full-time students; the rest attend part-time. Because full-timers move much more quickly through the program than part-timers, this means that the vast majority of enrollees are part-time students. Many students have schedules similar to this student, who writes, "I work full-time and attend school part-time. I go to class twice a week for three hours (Tuesday and Thursday from 7:00 P.M. to 10:00 P.M.). I show up on time and leave afterwards. When projects [are required], our group gets together at the school to plan the project. Otherwise, we communicate mostly by E-mail. Once in a while, we do a conference bridge that one of the team members has access to at work. We sometimes go out for a beer (usually the same group), but then you don't get home until 11:00 P.M. or midnight, which makes the next day [a very long day]." Such students appreciate that "the part-time MBA program caters to students who work full-time. Classes are scheduled in the evenings, and the course work can be completed in three years, or less, while working full-time."

Full-time students must deal with the academic burden of an accelerated program, yet most still find time to enjoy "the well-organized social activities." Some activities include "an annual Halloween party, a Christmas celebration, a food drive, theater night, movie night, and a skating party." Students explain that "the School of Management also organizes many conferences with CEOs of well-established companies, such as Cognos and Mitel." Ottawa students "come from 18 different countries. The diversity is fantastic and crucial in our global business environment." Students say that they appreciate their "competitive and friendly peers."

Admissions

Applicants to the School of Management MBA program must provide the school with official transcripts covering all previous academic work (demonstrating a 70 percent overall standing of 3.0), GMAT scores (minimum 50th percentile, with a minimum 4.5 score on the analytical writing section), two letters of recommendation, a resume demonstrating at least two years of managerial or professional work experience postdating undergraduate schooling, evidence of proficiency in either English or French, and evidence of mastery of calculus and linear algebra. Students lacking the necessary math competencies may be admitted provisionally and are required to complete the school's "Fundamentals of Quantitative Analysis" course successfully before commencing MBA work.

FINANCIAL FACTS

Annual tuition (in-state/out-of-state)	$11,200/$19,200
Fees	$945
Books and supplies	$960
Room & board (on/off-campus)	$4,625/$5,760
Average grant	$4,800

ADMISSIONS

Admissions Selectivity Rating	85
# of applications received	342
% applicants accepted	55
% acceptees attending	58
Average GMAT	605
Range of GMAT	560-640
Average GPA	3.2
TOEFL Required of International Students?	Yes
Minimum TOEFL (paper/computer)	600/250
Application fee	$48
International application fee	$48
Regular application deadline	3/1
Regular notification	Rolling
Transfer students accepted?	Yes
Transfer application policy: A maximum of 24 credits could be retained for graduate courses in management completed in a Canadian MBA program or AACSB accredited program.	
Need-blind admissions?	Yes

EMPLOYMENT PROFILE

Career Rating	81	Grads employed by field	%
Placement rate (%)	100	Accounting	5
# of companies recruiting on-campus	158	Finance	16
% grads employed immediately	87	Human Resources	11
Average starting salary	$62,500	Marketing	18
		MIS	3
		Operations	24
		General Management	3
		Quantitative	5
		Other	12
		Internet/New Media	3

UNIVERSITY OF THE PACIFIC
EBERHARDT SCHOOL OF BUSINESS

GENERAL INFORMATION

Type of school	private
Environment	city
Academic calendar	semester

SURVEY SAYS...

Friendly students
Cutting edge classes
Smart classrooms
Solid preparation in:
Teamwork
Communication/interpersonal skills
Presentation skills

STUDENTS

Enrollment of parent institution	6,000
Enrollment of MBA program	48
% male/female	75/25
% out-of-state	15
% part-time	25
% minorities	12
% international	27
Average age at entry	26
Average years work experience at entry	1.50

ACADEMICS

Academic Experience Rating	**78**
Student/faculty ratio	8:1
Profs interesting rating	82
Profs accessible rating	75
% female faculty	29
% minority faculty	12

Joint Degrees
MBA/JD: 3-4 years
MBA/Peace Corps: 4.5 years
MBA/PharmD: 4.5 years

Prominent Alumni
A.G. Spanos, Real Estate
Development; David Gerber,
MGM/UA- Film & TV Production;
Dave Brubeck, Jazz Composer/
Musician; Jaime Lee Curtis, Actress;
Chris Isaak, Rock Musician/Actor.

Academics

At the Eberhardt School of Business at the University of the Pacific, a small cohort of MBAs enjoys a surprising range of degree options, including one- and two-year programs, a part-time option for working professionals, and joint-degree programs in law and pharmacology. The school also offers a unique master's international peace corps/MBA, which includes two years of on-campus study and a two-year Peace Corps assignment.

In all programs, "small class sizes that allow professors to engage students in their education" and a "strong emphasis on field experience" distinguish an Eberhardt degree. Field experience opportunities include participation in an annual global business couse that has taken students to South Korea, Singapore, Chile, Malaysia, Spain, Ireland, France, England, Finland, and Estonia.

Eberhardt offers specialization in five areas: MIS, finance, marketing, management, and entrepreneurship. To accommodate working professionals, many classes are held in the evening. Students with a solid foundation in business principles generally opt for the one-year accelerated program; others choose the two-year track, which begins with a year of classes in MIS, accounting, business law, management, quantitative analysis, managerial economics, finance, marketing, and organizational behavior. Classes are taught by professors who "have great experience in different industries, and apply their experiences to the applications of the course." Students appreciate how "the team aspect of business is stressed within the classroom. The students here apply it to all aspects of Pacific. They have made this a great learning experience." They also give the administration a thumbs up, telling us that administrators "have always been helpful in achieving goals, as well as providing solutions to any problems faced in the past. They've always been reliable."

Career and Placement

Eberhardt MBAs receive career assistance through the ESB's Career Services Office, which serves both undergraduates and graduates in business. Services include monthly career development seminars, one-on-one career counseling, e-recruiting tools, and access to alumni and employers. Many here commend the office's "major push on networking and finding a job before you graduate. The ESB Career Services Office is very helpful." A few, however, feel "the school could increase the number of alumni involved with job recruitment, possibly aiding with internships too."

Twenty-five employers visit the Pacific campus to recruit MBAs each year. Another 25 recruit here for summer interns. Employers who most frequently hire Eberhardt MBAs include Boboli International, Deloitte & Touche, E & J Gallo Winery, Ernst & Young, Accenture, Johnson & Johnson, Kraft Foods, Monier Life Tile, Pacific Southwest Containers, Pac West Telecomm, and the U.S. Government.

Student Life and Environment

Both the size and the nature of the Eberhardt MBA contribute to a low-key extracurricular scene. The small student body is subdivided into one-year and two-year students, full-timers and part-timers, and joint-degree/non-joint-degree MBAs. With many classes held at night and many students commuting to campus, there can be a lack of social activity. One MBA comments, "It's easy for students to feel isolated, as it seems we aren't as unified outside school as [we] are in class." The MBA Association does its best, "trying to gather students every Thursday for socializing, wine tasting, movie nights, bar nights, trips, and other community services as a means of helping others and getting

CHRISTOPHER LOZANO, ESB DIRECTOR, STUDENT RECRUITMENT
MBA PROGRAM OFFICE, 3601 PACIFIC AVENUE, STOCKTON, CA 95211 UNITED STATES
PHONE: 800-952-3179 • FAX: 209-946-2586
E-MAIL: MBA@PACIFIC.EDU • WEBSITE: WWW.PACIFIC.EDU/MBA

together." An MBA reports, "About half the MBA population goes to these events. They're usually fun."

The Pacific community at large offers a great deal more, and MBAs are welcome to partake. One student writes, "Within the university, there are many different schools which include pharmacy, education, engineering, and music (to name a few). By being in a diverse environment, business students can meet other students who come from a wide variety of backgrounds." The campus "has a strong Greek influence, as well as lots of clubs and organizations. If anyone wants to get involved, one does not need to look hard." Another agrees, "Overall, I'm having a great experience at Pacific. Clubs provide a great opportunity to get involved in the community and meet other students. The school also has a lacrosse team that I joined and really enjoy." MBAs approve of the beautiful campus, which "is built much like many of the campuses on the East Coast: brick buildings and ivy-covered walls." The campus so closely follows the Ivy League model, in fact, that moviemakers often use it as a stand-in for Harvard or Yale. On campus, "Students have access to many facilities including the Conservatory, Pacific Theatre, an Olympic swimming pool, track, and many others." The only downside: "While the campus is generally a safe place to be, the surrounding area can be dangerous at night. Campus police do a good job of keeping the university safe, but an escort service would be nice."

Eberhardt MBA's tend to be "young and excited, eager sharks waiting to venture into the depths of the unknown [but] with little to no experience in the work field." Their shark-like qualities notwithstanding, students tend to be "very supportive and enthusiastic about the program." A considerable number "come from other countries such as France, Brazil, and the Philippines, and they bring a wide array of experiences to the education."

Admissions

Applicants to Eberhardt must submit official transcripts for all undergraduate, graduate, and professional schools attended; two letters of recommendation (one from an instructor, one from a work supervisor); GMAT scores; a completed application; and an interview. The Admissions Committee studies grade trends and ranks students by formula score, applying the formula [(undergraduate GPA × 200) + GMAT score] and looking for scores of at least 1200. International students must also submit TOEFL scores (minimum 550 paper-and-pencil, 213 computer-based) and a Certification of Finances. Prior to beginning the MBA program, students must have completed the following prerequisite courses: intro microeconomics, intro macroeconomics, probability and statistics, calculus, and computers and information processing.

Career Rating	78	Grads employed by field	%: avg. salary
Placement rate (%)	85	Accounting	14: $38,333
# of companies recruiting on-campus	25	Finance	19: $52,333
% grads employed immediately	52	Marketing	38: $59,250
Average starting salary	$50,000	MIS	5: $62,000
		Operations	5: $60,000
		Communications	5: $46,000
		General Management	5: $45,000
		Other	9: $45,000

FINANCIAL FACTS

Annual tuition	$22,800
Fees	$450
Books and supplies	$2,100
Room & board	$10,500
% of students receiving aid	60
% of first-year students receiving aid	75
% of students receiving loans	75
% of students receiving grants	40
Average award package	$18,000
Average grant	$6,818
Average student loan debt	$27,500

ADMISSIONS

Admissions Selectivity Rating	85
# of applications received	94
% applicants accepted	51
% acceptees attending	52
Average GMAT	587
Range of GMAT	550-620
Average GPA	3.6
TOEFL Required of International Students?	Yes
Minimum TOEFL (paper/computer)	550/213
Application fee	$75
International application fee	$75
Regular application deadline	3/1
Regular notification	Rolling
Deferment Available?	Yes
Maximum length of deferment	1 year
Transfer students accepted?	Yes

Transfer application policy: They may waive all 1st year courses, if they have completed with a B or better from another AACSB accredited college at the UG level. Students may also transfer up to 2 Advanced courses from another AACSB accredited MBA Program.

Non-fall admissions?	Yes
Need-blind admissions?	Yes

APPLICANTS ALSO LOOK AT

California Polytechnic State University, San Luis, California State University—Sacramento, Saint Mary's College of California, Santa Clara University, University of California—Berkeley, University of California—Davis, University of San Francisco.

University of Pittsburgh
Joseph M. Katz Graduate School of Business

Academics

In 1960, the University of Pittsburgh's Joseph M. Katz Graduate School of Business added the country's first one-year, full-time MBA program, which is still the school's signature program. In it, students' brains are crammed with all the knowledge they would normally get from a two-year program in the span of 11 months. Students, especially those with other commitments, love the program. The school experience is "strenuous; you come up to breathe on Fridays, but the week is so busy." Students say that the "program is top-notch in terms of curriculum and pace."

Because the program is relatively small, with only about 200 full-timers in the one- and two-year tracks, students benefit from individual attention of both the faculty and staff of the school. As one student says, "The faculty care about the students much more so than [the] other schools I looked into." Another student adds that "the teachers are exceptional, the dean is energetic, and everyone has a passion to succeed." The attitude of the administration and faculty also rubs off on its students. "Katz has great students that cooperate with each other and help each other whenever they can. It is not cutthroat around here; it is much more collaborative and caring."

The academic schedule for Katz's one-year program is designed for flexibility. The school offers electives during the day and the evening, in addition to some Saturday courses. In this way, students are able to design a schedule that fits their own needs. The first year of the two-year program is mostly core courses (with one flexible option), and an internship is required during the summer.

In addition to the regular concentrations offered at most schools, Katz offers a few "signature programs" that have a multidisciplinary focus. The three areas are the marketing of technology-based products and services, process management and integration, and valuation and corporate finance. The school offers the following dual degrees: MBA/MS-MIS, MBA/MSIE, MBA/MS BioE, MBA/MIB, and the MBA/JD.

Career and Placement

Though students would like to see more companies coming to campus to solicit their employment, a number of big names have hired from the Katz program in the past five years, including Dell, Deloitte Touche Tohmatsu, Eli Lilly, FedEx, IBM, Playtex Products, PricewaterhouseCoopers, Villeroy & Boch, and WhiteStone Technology Ltd. In addition, students proudly proclaim that alumni are "a great resource for the current students."

Even in a difficult economy, employment prospects at Katz don't seem to be dire. Four months after graduation, 84 percent of Katz's 2003 graduates had accepted offers. The average salary for U.S. citizens was $66,000, and the average salary for a non-U.S. citizen was $60,000.

KELLY R. WILSON, ASSISTANT DEAN AND DIRECTOR
276 MERVIS HALL, ROBERTO CLEMENTE DRIVE, PITTSBURGH, PA 15260 UNITED STATES
PHONE: 412-648-1700 • FAX: 412-648-1659
E-MAIL: MBA@KATZ.PITT.EDU • WEBSITE: WWW.KATZ.PITT.EDU

Student Life and Environment

Katz is located in the area known as Oakland, one of Pittsburgh's "most diverse and intense neighborhoods." Students say, "Pittsburgh is a great, student-oriented city with lots of cheap housing and opportunities for students to participate in cultural activities at reduced rates." And if the city isn't giving them everything they want, "the university is large and affords many opportunities for socializing." One student says, "We usually go out and bar hop every couple of weeks as a group. I have made many good friends because of the team activities we do." Katz's one-year program does provide some unusual stresses because so much information is packed into such a short period of time. To combat these stresses, Katz students (like many b-school students) have a weekly drinking appointment that they like to keep. As one student says, "There is a group that goes out every weekend and just relaxes—something that is needed in this type of program." Another student adds that, "socially speaking, the KGSB is excellent at bringing people together. It's good that they finally have a two-year program in which to solidify those relationships."

Admissions

About 50 percent of Katz's approximately 130 students had one or more years of full-time work experience before they sought to further their education; 36 percent were international students and 27 percent were female. The average GMAT score was 635, and the average undergraduate GPA was 3.3. The average age of a Katz student was 27, and about 19 different countries were represented in the MBA student body including Armenia, Jamaica, Latvia, Morocco, and South Korea.

FINANCIAL FACTS

Annual tuition (in-state/out-of-state)	$26,720/$43,126
Fees	$5,160
Books and supplies	$1,050
Room & board	$11,500
Average grant	$10,000

ADMISSIONS

Admissions Selectivity Rating	88
# of applications received	601
% applicants accepted	51
% acceptees attending	48
Average GMAT	635
Average GPA	3.3
TOEFL Required of International Students?	Yes
Minimum TOEFL (paper/computer)	600/250
Application fee	$50
International application fee	$50
Regular application deadline	12/1
Regular notification	2/1
Application Deadline/Notification	
Round 1:	12/1 / 2/1
Round 2:	1/15 / 3/15
Round 3:	3/1 / 4/15
Round 4:	4/15 / 5/15
Transfer students accepted?	Yes
Transfer application policy: matching coursework, accepting up to 17 credits from an AACSB MBA program, provided that credits were not used to complete a previous MBA degree.	
Need-blind admissions?	Yes

EMPLOYMENT PROFILE

Career Rating	82	Grads employed by field	%: avg. salary
Placement rate (%)	81	Accounting	5: $67,500
# of companies recruiting on-campus	118	Finance	28: $71,700
% grads employed immediately	60	Human Resources	5: NR
% grads employed within three months	39	Marketing	19: $67,000
Average starting salary	$70,000	MIS	5: $50,000
		Operations	22: $77,540
		Strategic Planning	5: $66,500
		Consulting	5: $75,000
		General Management	3: $44,000
		Other	3: $111,000

UNIVERSITY OF ROCHESTER
WILLIAM E. SIMON GRADUATE SCHOOL OF BUSINESS ADMINISTRATION

Academics

"The hallmarks of a Simon Graduate School education are its integration around economic principles and its long-term applicability," school representatives tell us, and students concur. One MBA notes, "Particularly consistent is the economics-based approach that returns in every (yes, every single) class. Sending consistent messages to the students is so very important and creates a solid understanding of business processes that is timeless. If you are looking for the most solid, no-nonsense MBA with a great return on investment, this is the school for you." The Simon approach includes a "heavy quantitative emphasis" that fits well with the school's strongest discipline: finance. Brand management and strategy are among Simon Graduate School's other strong areas.

The Simon Graduate School curriculum lays the work on heavy in the first-year core. One student explains, "The academic workload is different in the first year from what it is in the second year. The first year is brutal—constant team assignments, exams, studying, and labs. I spent most of the first year on campus, scared that I wasn't going to learn enough to keep up with my classmates." Accordingly, first year requires "great time management skills. You are assigned so much homework, reading assignments, and team projects, it's impossible to finish everything. In addition, you have to prepare your resume and cover letters and research for summer internship. Not to mention that networking experience is a big part of b-school, and that requires time to contribute to club activities." The second year "is much more relaxed, in that all the time and effort put into learning the concepts in the first year now allows you to understand concepts in class and apply things better. Teamwork is still extensive in the second year but the pressure to perform doesn't feel as great."

Throughout, students get to know their classmates and professors well because of the "warm and friendly climate" fostered by the small size of the program. One MBA reports, "The professors really get to know you with the smaller size of the classes. It isn't uncommon for professors to cold-call, but not in an intimidating manner. With classes small and classmates and professors comfortable with each other, lectures are interesting and entertaining, personal, and friendly. The school encourages an environment where students ask questions throughout the class, and what started as a lecture becomes a discussion. The small size also means that you know your classmates well and you can approach them with pretty much any question, be it about an assignment, career-related, or just a ride to the happy hour."

The Simon Graduate School "offers 14 concentrations ranging from the more broad-based (finance) to the more specialized (e-commerce and health-sciences management).

Career and Placement

The Career Management Center at the Simon Graduate School recognizes that its remote location is a handicap to students' job searches. To address this situation, the school holds annual interview sessions in New York City and participates in several national consortia to sponsor twice-yearly job fairs in New York City and Atlanta. On-campus interviews, as well as speakers, career panels, video interviewing, and alumni programs supplement these efforts. A recent restructuring of the CMC has made it more amenable to the needs of students planning careers in fields other than finance, and it is working to increase on-campus recruiting.

PAMELA A. BLACK-COLTON, ASSISTANT DEAN FOR MBA ADMISSIONS AND ADMINISTRATION
305 SCHLEGEL HALL, ROCHESTER, NY 14627 UNITED STATES
PHONE: 585-275-3533 • FAX: 585-271-3907
E-MAIL: ADMISSIONS@SIMON.ROCHESTER.EDU • WEBSITE: WWW.SIMON.ROCHESTER.EDU

FINANCIAL FACTS

Annual tuition	$34,710
Fees	$897
Books and supplies	$1,510
Room & board	$8,504
% of students receiving grants	65

Employers who most often hire Simon MBAs include American Express, Barclays, Bausch and Lomb, Citigroup, Deloitte Touche, Diageo, Ford, General Electric, Harris RF Communications, J. P. Morgan Chase, Johnson & Johnson, Kraft Foods, M & T Bank, Manning & Napier Advisors, OppenheimerFunds, PAETEC Communications, PricewaterhouseCoopers, Playtex, Reckitt & Benckiser, UBS Financial Services, and Xerox.

Student Life and Environment

"Due to the quarter system, with midterms and finals arriving quickly, there's a very intense workload" at the Simon school, "so most of school life is spent studying and working on team projects." That's especially true during the demanding first year of the program. Even so, "we also have a great social life here, with all sorts of events to go to and interact with peers. They are usually very well attended, too: Simon Games, Flip Cup, happy hours, bowling, and karaoke. Many events are family-oriented. There are also a lot of professional opportunities for students through clubs, special organizations, and speakers." Happy hours are frequent; the MBA Association holds one every other week, and most clubs hold them almost as frequently. Occasional road trips take students to "professional sporting events in Buffalo, theater, and shopping trips to Toronto—that sort of thing."

Hometown Rochester is "a good, midsize city" and "a charming town," but its "winter is ridiculously long, cold, and snowy." The U of R campus "has excellent amenities, and Simon Graduate School has three of its own buildings, constructed in 1991 and 2001," which "are very nice, as is not having to mix with undergraduates (no undergrad business school)." The program has a large international population, whom students welcome with a single caveat: "Many international students have poor language skills, which is a big problem with team projects," some students warn.

Admissions

According to the school's website, the Simon admissions committee "does not apply specific weights to the main criteria, but rather makes evaluations on the cumulative strength of each application as it compares to others received that year. Work experience, undergraduate record, GMAT results, personal recommendations, and required essays provide the basis for evaluation." Verbal skills count; applicants must score a minimum 40th percentile on the GMAT Verbal section, with at least a 3.5 on the Writing Sample. The Simon School is a member of the Consortium for Graduate Study in Management (headquartered in St. Louis) and participates in its programs to recruit minority and disadvantaged students.

ADMISSIONS

Admissions Selectivity Rating	93
# of applications received	912
% applicants accepted	37
% acceptees attending	39
Average GMAT	664
Range of GMAT	620-700
Average GPA	3.4
TOEFL Required of International Students?	Yes
Application fee	$125
International application fee	$125
Regular application deadline	6/1
Regular notification	7/1
Application Deadline/Notification	
Round 1:	12/1 / 2/15
Round 2:	2/1 / 3/15
Round 3:	4/1 / 5/15
Round 4:	6/1 / 7/1
Transfer students accepted?	Yes
Transfer application policy: No more than 9 credit hours, may not be core courses.	
Non-fall admissions?	Yes
Need-blind admissions?	Yes

APPLICANTS ALSO LOOK AT

Carnegie Mellon, Columbia University, Cornell University, New York University, University of Pennsylvania.

EMPLOYMENT PROFILE			
Career Rating	82	**Grads employed by field %: avg. salary**	
Placement rate (%)	88.6	Finance	46: $75,613
% grads employed immediately	66.5	Marketing	7.3: $77,151
Average starting salary	$77,995	Operations	2.4: $57,333
		Consulting	18.5: $88,656
		General Management	6.5: $81,964
		Other	4: $83,000

UNIVERSITY OF SAN FRANCISCO
MASAGUNG GRADUATE SCHOOL OF MANAGEMENT

GENERAL INFORMATION

Type of school	private
Affiliation	Jesuit

SURVEY SAYS...

Students love San Francisco, CA
Friendly students
Solid preparation in:
Teamwork

STUDENTS

Enrollment of parent institution	8,110
Enrollment of MBA program	378
% male/female	56/44
% minorities	30
% international	35
Average age at entry	28
Average years work experience at entry	5

ACADEMICS

Academic Experience Rating	77
Student/faculty ratio	10:1
Profs interesting rating	82
Profs accessible rating	69
% female faculty	20
% minority faculty	25

Joint Degrees

MBA/JD
MBA/MSN
MBA/MAPS (Asian pacific studies)
MBA/MSEM (environmental management)

Prominent Alumni

Gordon Smith, CEO, PG&E; Lip Bu-Tan, Founder, Walden International Investment Group; Mary Callanan, Retired Treasurer for the County/City of San Fran; Angela Alioto, Attorney, Political Leader; Pierre Salinger, Former Press Secretary to the U.S President.

Academics

"You will receive a grounded, broad-based business degree with lots of teamwork experience" at University of San Francisco's Masagung Graduate School of Management, according to students. If you choose to, you can also pursue an emphasis in telecommunications; USF's unique telecom program takes advantage of the school's "strategic location" among the headquarters of many IT and telecom giants. Hometown San Francisco is also a major financial center of the Pacific Coast; it should come as no surprise, then, that the school also boasts solid programs in finance and entrepreneurship. One student writes, "Our greatest strength is the extensive entrepreneur program. We host the business-plan competition, have venture-capital classes, and have instructors who are real entrepreneurs."

Location plays a key role in many of Masagung's successes. Students explain that "the school has close ties to the surrounding business community, which will be helpful after graduation." Because San Francisco is a world-class city, it is a magnet for great minds and great business people, and some of these folks wind up teaching courses at USF.

Masagung instructors "do a good job bringing relevant experience to the classroom. Some are "spectacular" and "very motivating," and "all seem genuinely interested in each student's education. They encourage open discussions, and the use of teams for research projects/presentations is integrated into most classes," according to students. One MBA observes, "Having attended a large public undergraduate institution, I was completely unprepared for the amount of face-time I get with my professors at the USF MBA program. Overall, they make an effort to be accessible and are fantastic instructors. [That's the] best thing about this program." And if a professor fails to meet expectations, students can take comfort in the fact that "USF has a good feedback process among the students independent of the administrative review."

Masagung allows students to develop an emphasis in entrepreneurship, finance, international business, marketing, or telecommunications. They may also choose a broad range of electives to earn a degree in general management. International study tours are available, as is a semester in Beijing. Students may take advantage of the Jesuit Network to earn exchange-student privileges at numerous institutions around the world.

Career and Placement

The USF Career Services Center offers networking opportunities, a resource center, workshops, counseling, and MBA Alumni Society events. Career Forums and the Job and Internship Fair bring approximately 30 recruiting companies to campus each year, including Accenture; Sprint; Wells Fargo; Fair Isaac; Eastman Kodak; and Infoex International, Inc.

Employers most likely to hire Masagung MBAs include Advanced Fibre Communications; Bank of the West; BioMarin Pharmaceutical, Inc.; California Bank and Trust; Charles Schwab; Cisco Systems; EMQ Children & Family Services; Ernst & Young, LLP; Franchise Tax Board; IBM Global Services; Inverito, Inc.; KPMG; The LaRose Group; Lautze & Lautze; Live Capital; Marcus & Millichap; Marsh, Inc.; Mervyns; OPT Derivatives; Pacific Gas and Electric Company; Peat Marwick; Persona, International; Prudential; Salomon Smith Barney; Systron-Donner; Walden International Investment Group; and Wells Capital Management.

MELISSA DELANEY, ACTING DIRECTOR
2130 FULTON STREET, LONE MOUNTAIN, SAN FRANCISCO, CA 94117-1045 UNITED STATES
PHONE: 415-422-2089 • FAX: 415-422-2066
E-MAIL: GRADUATE@USFCA.EDU • WEBSITE: WWW.USFCA.EDU/SOBAM

Student Life and Environment

Like the population of the city that it calls home, "USF students are diverse in cultures and professions. We enjoy an open atmosphere for dialogue among different views and backgrounds, which aids in learning." Students agree that the school has a large international population, "so if you want to learn about the global business, this is the school."

Students also explain that "because the University of San Francisco is a Jesuit private school, students are mostly calm, well-educated, and compassionate. We have many community activities that our school minister organizes." The small student body makes it "easy to make friends who stick with you through the program. We have enjoyable working relationships, and the school atmosphere promotes social interaction in group studies/work and facilitates proper teamwork." Another benefit of the size of the program is that "we don't need to fight for things like parking spaces, computers, or classes as often as students in public schools."

Students look forward to USF's new School of Business and Management facility opening in fall 2004. One student writes, "Our business school is currently constructing a new building for MBA students. It [will] be completed this summer, and we'll have all our classes at smart classrooms, and there will be a lounge area [where] we can study or socialize."

Admissions

Students admitted to the Masagung MBA program are expected to arrive with proficiency in mathematics through college algebra, statistics through hypothesis testing and standard deviation, fundamental accounting, basic computer skills (word processing, spreadsheet functions), and business writing. The school offers foundation courses in all these areas; these courses are waived for students who demonstrate the required skills. Applicants must submit official copies of all undergraduate and graduate transcripts, GMAT scores, TOEFL scores (international students), two letters of recommendation, two personal essays, and a resume. Interviews are encouraged but not required. Students may enter in either the fall or spring semester.

FINANCIAL FACTS

Annual tuition	$23,125
Fees	$444
Books and supplies	$1,250
Room & board (on-campus)	$8,324

ADMISSIONS

Admissions Selectivity Rating	79
# of applications received	381
% applicants accepted	54
% acceptees attending	70
Average GMAT	535
Range of GMAT	450-650
Average GPA	3.1
TOEFL Required of International Students?	Yes
Minimum TOEFL (paper/computer)	600/250
Application fee	$55
International application fee	$65
Regular application deadline	6/1
Regular notification	Rolling
Deferment Available?	Yes
Maximum length of deferment	1 year
Transfer students accepted?	Yes
Transfer application policy: transfer up to 6 credits for students coming from another AACSB accredited program.	
Non-fall admissions?	Yes

APPLICANTS ALSO LOOK AT

Santa Clara University,

EMPLOYMENT PROFILE

Career Rating	64	Grads employed by field	%: avg. salary
Placement rate (%)	40	Finance	14: $72,000
# of companies recruiting on-campus	30	Marketing	39: $70,000
% grads employed immediately	26	MIS	7: $63,000
		Consulting	4: $65,000
		General Management	4: $59,000
		Other	31: $55,000
		Non-profit	1: $52,000

UNIVERSITY OF SCRANTON
KANIA SCHOOL OF MANAGEMENT

GENERAL INFORMATION

Type of school	private
Affiliation	Roman Catholic-Jesuit
Environment	city

SURVEY SAYS...

Smart classrooms
Solid preparation in:
Quantitative skills
Computer skills

STUDENTS

Enrollment of parent institution	4,300
Enrollment of MBA program	99
% male/female	67/33
% part-time	70
% minorities	2
% international	36
Average age at entry	30
Average years work experience at entry	2

ACADEMICS

Academic Experience Rating	**63**
Student/faculty ratio	17:1
Profs interesting rating	81
Profs accessible rating	82
% female faculty	24
% minority faculty	2

Academics

Offering Northeast Pennsylvania's only AACSB-accredited MBA program, the University of Scranton delivers graduate business study that not only "emphasizes a set of skills and perspectives needed to succeed in the increasingly fast-paced, global and technology-oriented business environment" but does so within the ethical framework of a Catholic education. Typical of Jesuit institutions, the University of Scranton expects its professors to dedicate themselves to teaching. Apparently they meet that expectation; students report, "The faculty here is outstanding. Our professors are very accessible outside the classroom to review course material and offer career guidance."

For students with little academic or professional background in business, the Scranton MBA begins with qualifying modules covering basic concepts in statistics, management, information management, finance, accounting, and marketing. Qualified students may skip these modules and proceed directly to 10 extending courses of their choosing, including at least one international course. The extending courses advance the basic functional areas of business: accounting, enterprise management technology, marketing, management, managerial economics, organizational behavior, financial management, management information systems, and operations management.

The Scranton MBA curriculum also allows for four advanced electives, at least one of which must cover material pertaining to international business. Students may fashion a field of specialization by taking no more than four extending courses in one of the following areas: accounting, finance, international business, marketing, operations management, management information systems, and enterprise management technology. Students may also complete a dual specialization by taking four unique courses in each of the two specialization areas. Specialization is not required; students may choose instead to earn a general MBA degree.

To complete the MBA degree, Scranton students must take two mission specific courses. Business Policy, which is designed to "synthesize the knowledge students have gained in every other extending course in the program." In this course, MBAs "develop, present, and defend their own policy recommendations in case studies which require an understanding of all areas of business to make sound judgments." The other required course is Responsibility, Sustainability, and Justice, which reflects upon the relationship between sustainable development, business, and all affected stakeholders.

In recent years, The University of Scranton has entered into a unique relationship with the Beijing International MBA Program held on the campus of Peking University in Beijing. Through their arrangement, Scranton sends professors to teach in China. Professors return to Scranton with new insights about the world's fastest-growing economy, to the benefit of all Scranton MBAs.

Career and Placement

Scranton MBAs receive career and placement services from the school's Office of Career Services, which serves the university at large. The office, "guided by the principles of Jesuit education and aware of the need to impart knowledge that has immediate and long-term value," seeks to "assume the roles of advisor, teacher, and mentor" for MBAs seeking post-graduation employment. Many do not; full-timers are the minority here, and the majority of part-time students are already employed and looking to advance within their companies.

James L. Goonan, Director, Graduate Admissions
The Graduate School, University of Scranton, Scranton, PA 18510-4631 United States
Phone: 570-941-7600 • Fax: 570-941-5995
E-mail: graduateschool@scranton.edu • Website: www.scranton.edu

Student Life and Environment

Scranton's MBA program is a small one, "scheduled specifically for students who work full-time." Approximately seven in ten Scranton MBAs attend part-time. Because many Scranton MBAs are full-time workers/part-time students, the school offers all classes in the early evening and at night; all classes meet once per week.

Due to the demands of their schedules and the infrequency of their visits to campus, part-time students report, "Many of the school-life activities are not available to MBA students, especially those of us who are working professionals." Those who do have the time to enjoy campus life usually take in university sporting events, enroll in interest-based and background-based clubs and organizations, and participate in the frequent spiritual retreats offered by the campus ministry. Hometown Scranton is located in the Pocono Mountains, approximately 125 miles from New York City, Philadelphia, Syracuse, and Trenton. This city of 70,000 is large enough to provide students with valuable internship and practicum opportunities.

Brennan Hall serves as the home to Scranton's business graduates and undergraduates. The facility, completed in 2000, boasts up-to-date computer labs and high-tech classrooms, as well as ample executive meeting rooms. A campus-wide voice, video, and data network allows students Internet access from just about anywhere on campus.

The University of Scranton's MBA program attracts a large international population; approximately one in three students here originates from outside the United States.

Admissions

According to The University of Scranton website, admissions decisions here are based on a combination of four factors: previous academic performance, as indicated by transcripts; GMAT score, used to "measure certain mental abilities which have been found to be indicators of success" in graduate business programs of business; three letters of recommendation; and, when applicable, prior work experience (work experience is not a prerequisite to admission to the program). Of the four factors, previous academic performance and GMAT scores are considered most important. International students whose first language is not English must provide TOEFL scores in addition to academic records, test scores, and letters of recommendation. A minimum score of 550 paper-and-pencil or 213 computer-based is required for unconditional admission to the program. A score of at least 500 paper-and-pencil/173 computer-based allows conditional admission contingent on the completion of an English language proficiency course.

FINANCIAL FACTS

Annual tuition	$14,460
Fees	$3,200
Books and supplies	$1,000
Room & board	$9,200
% of students receiving aid	15
Average award package	$22,860

ADMISSIONS

Admissions Selectivity Rating	63
# of applications received	98
% applicants accepted	88
% acceptees attending	37
Average GMAT	515
Average GPA	3.2
TOEFL Required of International Students?	Yes
Minimum TOEFL (paper/computer)	550/213
Application fee	$50
International application fee	$50
Regular application deadline	Rolling
Regular notification	Rolling
Deferment Available?	Yes
Maximum length of deferment	2 years
Transfer students accepted?	Yes
Transfer application policy: Transfer credits accepted from an AACSB-accredited Jesuit school, otherwise 6 credits maximum accepted.	
Non-fall admissions?	Yes

EMPLOYMENT PROFILE

Career Rating	69
% grads employed immediately	96
Average starting salary	$49,638

UNIVERSITY OF SOUTH CAROLINA
MOORE SCHOOL OF BUSINESS

GENERAL INFORMATION
Type of school	public
Environment	city
Academic calendar	semester

SURVEY SAYS...
Friendly students
Good social scene
Happy students
Solid preparation in:
Teamwork
Doing business in a global economy

STUDENTS
Enrollment of parent institution	26,000
Enrollment of MBA program	251
% male/female	69/31
% out-of-state	68
% part-time	57
% minorities	11
% international	23
Average age at entry	28
Average years work experience at entry	4.1

ACADEMICS
Academic Experience Rating	**81**
Student/faculty ratio	30:1
Profs interesting rating	78
Profs accessible rating	83
% female faculty	17
% minority faculty	2

Joint Degrees
MBA/JD: 3 years
JD/MACC: 3 years
JD/IMBA: 3-4 years
JD/MHR: 3 years
JD/MA Econ: 3 years

Academics

In 2001, the Moore School of Business upgraded its MIBS program to the international master of business administration (IMBA), within which students can choose from three different tracks. Furthering the school's dedication to exploring the global market, all three include some sort of international component. Students say the "international focus of the school is reflected in every course, the international students, and the international internship experience." And students feel that, with a Moore IMBA under their belts, they'll be "well-positioned for the trend of increasing global commerce." Though the transition to the IMBA wasn't always smooth, students happily acknowledge that the program "is a fresh and newly conceived program, and there are still several tasks to be improved in terms of administration. But its freshness helps to add things in the long run. The best part is diversity. IMBA is a program that speaks many languages, and it should be kept that way."

The three different tracks of study offered by the school are Language Track, which focuses on "intense study and immersion in the language and culture of a region;" Global Track, "for those who may not need another language, [this is] a global approach to the culture and economies of the world"; and the acclaimed Vienna Program, a partnership with the Wirtschaftsuniversität Wien, the acclaimed business and economic university in Austria. Though the programs differ substantially from one another in content and concentration, they are all united by one thing: an intensive core curriculum. All students take the same core classes, which are rarely made up of more than 50 students. Because the core curriculum is compressed and students rush off to overseas studies, "first-year life equals study squared (now you know they're doing a good job teaching quantitative methods)."

Languages offered in Language Track include French, German, Italian, Portuguese, and Spanish. Students who choose one of these options pass through a two-year course. For students who opt to learn Arabic, Japanese or Chinese language and culture, a three-year program is available. In this, "students follow the same format as the two-year language tracks, but they live and study for 12 months in Japan or China before they participate in the internship."

In the second year, after completing their internships, students return to the South Carolina campus and take seven electives in order to specialize in a particular field. Concentrations include marketing and brand management, customer relationship management, economic development, corporate accounting and finance, human resources, operations, and information systems. That same year, students are required to take a two-part management class. The first half "focuses on how to manage in multicultural organizations." The second "examines entrepreneurial practices and organizational transformation." According to one student, who returned from studying in Vienna, students are "happy upon returning to find that the professors that came to Vienna were teaching identical classes in South Carolina. I feel that we all share a common experience with many shared professors, which makes our whole class a strong network, and our professors and course work are an essential part of that."

REENA LICHTENFELD, MANAGING DIRECTOR-GRADUATE ADMISSIONS
1705 COLLEGE STREET COLUMBIA, SC 29208 UNITED STATES
PHONE: 803-777-4346 • FAX: 803-777-0414
E-MAIL: GRADADMIT@MOORE.SC.EDU • WEBSITE: WWW.MOORESCHOOL.SC.EDU

Career and Placement

The main complaint Moore students seem to have with their Career Resources Center is that, despite the program's focus on international studies, there are not enough international employment opportunities. Students complain that the center thinks too regionally and "could do more to pull in companies who are looking for the kind of globally minded students they are graduating and propel them all over the world, and not just the Southeast." Another student complains that though the school "runs a partnership program with Vienna, [it won't lift] a finger about a job in Europe."

Many students counter this by saying, "The Career Center goes out of its way to try to help us out. They are very accessible." And companies as diverse as Accenture; Alcoa Fujikura Ltd.; Anheuser-Busch, Inc.; Bali; Bayerische Vereinsbank; Bertelsmann; BMW; Credit Suisse; and Industrial Bank of Japan have all recruited from Moore (among many others).

Student Life and Environment

Located in downtown Colombia, South Carolina, Moore School of Business has a lot going for it. The city is in the middle of an urban revitalization effort, and the downtown, in particular, is proof. "Nightlife is good," one student says. The city's efforts to redevelop are "bringing the younger crowd back into the inner city. The Vista (downtown nightlife area) on the river is very fun."

And if, as one student says, "South Carolina is a different country inside the U.S. and a very peculiar window to American culture," what better place for a school with an international focus? The diversity of the environment is a deciding factor for many students, and "the social scene is wonderful. We have international potlucks, gatherings at Chinese New Year, and Diwali (an Indian Hindu holiday). When I organized a Diwali dinner, 100 out of the 140 students showed up." Students say their fellow IMBAs are "competitive—but in a fun way, not a detrimental way. Classmates are so giving and willing to help each other with class work and in personal situations. I could not imagine fitting in as well and feeling as welcomed anywhere else."

FINANCIAL FACTS

Annual tuition (in-state/out-of-state)	$32,000/$47,000
Books and supplies	$2,000
Room & board	$8,000
% of students receiving aid	72
Average award package	$10,000
Average grant	$10,000
Average student loan debt	$15,000

ADMISSIONS

Admissions Selectivity Rating	84
# of applications received	262
% applicants accepted	68
% acceptees attending	61
Average GMAT	627
Range of GMAT	590-660
Average GPA	3.3
TOEFL Required of International Students?	Yes
Minimum TOEFL (paper/computer)	600/250
Application fee	$40
Regular application deadline	2/1
Regular notification	3/1
Early decision program?	Yes
ED Deadline/Notification	IMBA: 12/1, IMBA Vienna: 10/1 / 01/1
Deferment Available?	Yes
Maximum length of deferment	1 year
Transfer students accepted?	Yes
Transfer application policy: Can transfer up to a maximum of 12 credit hours (4 courses).	
Non-fall admissions?	Yes
Need-blind admissions?	Yes

APPLICANTS ALSO LOOK AT

Duke University, Georgetown University, Thunderbird, Vanderbilt University, Wake Forest University.

EMPLOYMENT PROFILE			
Career Rating	76	**Grads employed by field**	**%: avg. salary**
Placement rate (%)	90	Accounting	19: $63,800
# of companies recruiting on-campus	66	Finance	19: $63,800
% grads employed immediately	45	Human Resources	1: NR
Average starting salary	$61,500	Marketing	19: $58,200
		MIS	7: $62,530
		Operations	11: $61,950
		Consulting	11: $65,700
		General Management	8: $60,225
		Other	5: $65,633

UNIVERSITY OF SOUTH DAKOTA
SCHOOL OF BUSINESS

GENERAL INFORMATION
Type of school	public
Environment	village
Academic calendar	semester

SURVEY SAYS...
Happy students
Smart classrooms
Solid preparation in:
Finance
Teamwork

STUDENTS
Enrollment of parent institution	7,500
Enrollment of MBA program	275
% male/female	50/50
% minorities	2

ACADEMICS
Academic Experience Rating	**67**
Student/faculty ratio	15:1
Profs interesting rating	74
Profs accessible rating	76
Joint Degrees	
MBA/JD: 3-4 years	

Academics

If you're looking for an accredited MBA program in South Dakota, there's only one game in town. It's the MBA program at USD, the only one in the state to receive AACSB International accreditation. That distinction places the USD MBA among the top 10 percent of all business programs in the United States. Students frequently cite the school's "strong reputation," both locally and nationally, when asked why they choose this program over others.

USD's curriculum stresses "decision-making, problem-solving, understanding the role of business in society, and developing the leadership ability and social responsibility" to help its students "progress to positions of executive responsibility," according to university materials. The goal is not only to "develop future executive leadership for business, industry, and government," but also to "encourage those who have an interest in college teaching and an aptitude for an academic career to continue their work at the doctoral level." For the convenience of its students—many of whom work full-time in addition to attending school—USD offers both a part-time and full-time program, with part-time participation available in Vermillion, Rapid City, and at home over the Internet via the Dakota Digital Network.

In spring 2005, USD introduced yet another option for part-timers: Cohort Express, a program designed to combine the convenience of part-time instruction with the benefits of cohort learning. Participants will complete the entire 22-month program with the same peer group, allowing them to develop the same strong long-term relationships and networking contacts that full-time students enjoy. They'll accomplish this without having to increase the amount of time they spend on campus. Cohort Express requires students to attend classes only one evening a week, or, alternatively, for every other weekend. Plus, they'll be able to do so for the same low tuition and fees that other MBAs here pay.

USD MBAs brag that "the professors are terrific [and] the administration has been flawless. They are very friendly and helpful and have made registration easy." They especially appreciate the school's "no-nonsense approach to learning. It is understood that we are all working adults and there is very little fluff." They report that a new b-school facility is in the planning stages.

Career and Placement

USD MBAs receive career and placement services from the Business School Employment Services Office, which coordinates its efforts with the university's Career Development Center. The office provides assistance with job-search strategy, job listings, a weekly e-mail of useful info, on-campus interviews, resume reviews, mock interviews, resume referrals, career counseling, and an electronic resume book. In 2003, the last year for which such figures were available, a job fair cosponsored by the Employment Services Office and the South Dakota Career Planning and Placement Association brought 130 employers to recruit business undergraduates and graduate students. In that same year, the median starting salary for MBAs was approximately $40,500. Employers of USD business students include AFLAC, Aramark, Citibank, New York Life, Northwestern Mutual, and Wells Fargo.

KUMOLI RAMAKRISHNAN, MBA/EXECUTIVE EDUCATION DEAN
414 EAST CLARK, SCHOOL OF BUSINESS, VERMILLION, SD 57069 UNITED STATES
PHONE: 605-677-5232 • FAX: 605-677-5058
E-MAIL: MBA@USD.EDU • WEBSITE: WWW.USD.EDU/MBA

FINANCIAL FACTS

Annual tuition (in-state/out-of-state)	$6,600/$13,000
Books and supplies	$1,000
Average grant	$4,700

ADMISSIONS

Admissions Selectivity Rating	**68**
# of applications received	49
% applicants accepted	92
% acceptees attending	89
Average GMAT	519
Average GPA	3.2
TOEFL Required of International Students?	Yes
Minimum TOEFL (paper/computer)	550/214
Application fee	$35
International application fee	$35
Regular application deadline	6/1
Regular notification	Rolling
Deferment Available?	Yes
Transfer students accepted?	Yes
Transfer application policy: Maximum of 9 credit hours from an AACSB accredited institution may be transferred.	
Non-fall admissions?	Yes
Need-blind admissions?	Yes

Student Life and Environment

Students at USD evince "strong Midwest values and are very caring individuals" who are "personable and understanding of work and home commitments." The student body is split among adults with considerable professional experience and younger students "fresh out of undergraduate school with few years of experience and the idea of having fun prominently on their minds."

USD is small by state-school standards, with a typical full-time enrollment of just under 8,000. The school competes in NCAA Division II athletics and supports a strong arts community active in music and theater, as well as "a wide range of other recreational, cultural, social, and professional activities and organizations." Hometown Vermillion is small and quiet, a typical city of 10,000. The surrounding area is gorgeous and offers plenty of outdoor fun, but more urbane entertainments are in relatively short supply. For those, students head southeast to Sioux City, Iowa, or north to Sioux Falls.

Admissions

Applicants to the MBA program at the University of South Dakota must submit two official transcripts for all prior academic work, GMAT scores, two letters of recommendation, and a completed application. A minimum undergraduate GPA of 2.7 is required. All international applicants must also submit a Statement of Finance form, a certified bank statement or sponsor's letter, and TOEFL scores if their native language is other than English (minimum acceptable score is 550 on the written exam). Applicants must have completed all of the following before beginning the MBA program: principles of micro and macro economics, 6 hours; principles of accounting I & II, 6 hours; business finance, 3 hours; management (principles or organizational theory), 3 hours; business statistics, 3 hours; calculus, 3 to 4 hours; introduction to management information systems, 3 hours; and production and operations management, 3 hours. Equivalent foundation courses are available at USD, but cannot be counted toward the MBA degree. According to printed material from the school, the School of Business reviews applications, then "recommends the admission status of the applicant to the dean of the Graduate School based on the applicant's undergraduate record, GMAT score, and recommendations. Students may be accepted to a University of South Dakota Graduate School degree program with full admission or provisional admission."

EMPLOYMENT PROFILE	
Career Rating	**70**
Placement rate (%)	90
# of companies recruiting on-campus	45
Average starting salary	$40,000

UNIVERSITY OF SOUTHERN CALIFORNIA
MARSHALL SCHOOL OF BUSINESS

Academics

The Marshall School of Business at University of Southern California first made its mark with its groundbreaking entrepreneurship program—the school was the nation's first to institute such a program—but today, Marshall is much more than an entrepreneurial maverick. With solid departments in finance, strategy, marketing, operations, human resources, and accounting, and emphasis in the business of entertainment, as well as innovative programs that introduce global business issues throughout the curriculum, Marshall has catapulted itself to the top ranks of U.S. MBA programs.

Marshall divides each semester into two terms, concentrating course material to the point that "the workload is killer in both quality and quantity," especially during the first-year core curriculum. Even the most experienced students find the material novel and challenging; one writes, "I had 10 years of very strong work experience (strategy consulting) and wasn't really expecting to learn much during my first-year core classes. Was I ever in for a surprise! I feel so much more prepared for a successful business career after only one semester. It's a great feeling of time and money well spent." Core courses are "extremely well-linked. Professors constantly refer to the other courses we are currently in or have taken to show how well all aspects of business are interrelated." Students appreciate that core professors "are nearly all senior faculty members who have won teaching awards and written books. Each of them chose to teach first-year MBAs because of their passion to engage students in the classroom."

Students report that "Marshall has a very international perspective," evidenced by the seven-week PRIME (Pacific Rim Education Program) course that caps off first year. PRIME incorporates case studies, teamwork, lectures, and a 10-day research trip to a Pacific Rim country (Chile, Brazil, China, Japan, Singapore, Thailand, Cuba, or Mexico) to combine expert instruction and on-site, real-time experiential learning. Students agree that "the PRIME class and field trip is a definite highlight at the end of the first year." Students may also opt to participate in the MBA international exchange program, which sends second-year students abroad for a semester.

Marshall offers more than 15 areas of concentration—a wide assortment for a program of its size. Throughout all departments, students brag that "professors are friendly and accessible. They are master teachers. They seem to have more of an interest in teaching versus other professors who seemed more interested in making themselves more known in their fields (experienced as a Wharton undergraduate taking MBA level courses)."

Career and Placement

Students applaud USC for improving Marshall's national rankings. They also recognize that it will take a while for the Career Resource Center to catch up to the school's heightened stature, though the new and more robust career-oriented training/education curriculum is a step in the right direction. One student says, "As a recent addition to the top 20, we still need to get the recruiters to stop by our career center on their way over to Anderson." Notes another MBA, "The administration and Career Resource Center have spent great effort and financial resources to continue to improve the recruiting opportunities at Marshall. I am confident on-campus recruiting opportunities will continue to improve as more companies come to Marshall for recruiting and the economy rebounds in the coming years."

Likely employers of Marshall MBAs (besides private firms and corporations) include federal judges and government and public-interest nonprofits. Private corporations include Agilent Technologies, Amgen, Apple Computers, Bank of America Securities, Cingular Wireless, ConAgra Grocery Products, Deloitte Touche Tohmatsu, Dell, Fox Entertainment,

A. Keith Vaughn, Director of MBA Admissions
Popovich Hall Room 308, Los Angeles, CA 90089-2633 United States
Phone: 213-740-7846 • Fax: 213-749-8520
E-mail: marshallmba@marshall.usc.edu • Website: www.marshall.usc.edu

KPMG, Hewlett-Packard, Ernst & Young, Guidant, Honeywell, Intel, Kraft Foods, Mattel, Nestlé USA, Paramount Pictures, PricewaterhouseCoopers, Procter & Gamble, Raytheon, SBC, Sony Pictures, Teradyne, Toyota, Walt Disney Co., and Wells Fargo.

Student Life and Environment

The school spirit of USC students and alumni is legendary. It's also a lifelong passion, as evidenced by the school's vaunted Trojan Network, a 68,000-strong alumni base that "rabidly works to help students, pulling them into the Trojan family to help them meet the industry players who will eventually connect them with jobs, business partners, clients, and investors." And where better to meet those contacts than at Trojan football games? Students report that "for all home football games, the students sponsor an alumni tailgate, and over 1,000 alumni show up to enjoy each others' company and to network."

Despite the demands of their program, Marshall students find time not only to attend football games but also to get involved with the community. They participate in "Challenge-4-Charity Weekend up at Stanford, which supports Special Olympics. There is something that involves all of us each month [like] parties or gym days with underprivileged kids. Volunteering is very strong here." Professional clubs are also popular, as "there is a club for virtually any interest a student could have, and if for some reason a club doesn't exist, it is very easy for students to create one. Many clubs bring in excellent speakers from both big and small companies to share their experiences, and a few clubs have 'Industry Nights' during which many professionals come to USC to share their experience in a more intimate, roundtable setting." The school is located "in the heart of downtown Los Angeles. However, the majority of graduate business students live off campus, typically about a 20-minute commute. Students have the opportunity to experience a variety of cultures and neighborhoods no matter where they decide to live, ranging from the low-key beach cities (Manhattan Beach, Hermosa Beach) to the entertainment-rich areas (Hollywood)." Like Randy Newman, they love L.A.

Admissions

The Marshall MBA program is "highly selective," and the admissions committee carefully considers all aspects of an application to determine which candidates have "outstanding leadership potential as well as intellectual and interpersonal abilities to contribute to our academic and extracurricular programs." All applicants must submit official academic transcripts, letters of recommendation, a personal statement, GMAT scores, and a resume. Non-English speaking international students must submit TOEFL scores. USC reports that "Marshall is a member of the Consortium for Graduate Study in Management, an alliance of 14 graduate schools of business committed to creating career opportunities for African Americans, Hispanic Americans, and Native Americans. Marshall also hosts an annual Diversity Weekend geared toward prospective minority applicants."

Prominent Alumni

Yang Ho Cho, Chairman and CEO, Korean Air Lines Co., Ltd.; Bradford D. Duea, Pres., Napster Division of Roxio, Inc.; J. Terrence Lanni, Chairman and CEO, MGM MIRAGE; Alison May, CEP and Pres., Red Envelope

FINANCIAL FACTS

Annual tuition	$34,221
Fees	$1,634
Books and supplies	$2,400
Room & board	$14,436

ADMISSIONS

Admissions Selectivity Rating	94
# of applications received	1693
% applicants accepted	37
% acceptees attending	44
Average GMAT	685
Range of GMAT	640-730
Average GPA	3.3
TOEFL Required of International Students?	Yes
Minimum TOEFL (paper/computer)	600/250
Application fee	$125
International application fee	$125
Regular application deadline	4/1
Regular notification	5/17
Application Deadline/Notification	
Round 1:	12/1 / 2/1
Round 2:	1/15 / 3/22
Round 3:	2/15 / 4/19
Round 4:	4/1 / 5/17
Need-blind admissions?	Yes

APPLICANTS ALSO LOOK AT

Columbia University, Duke University, New York University, Stanford University, University of California—Berkeley, University of California—Los Angeles.

EMPLOYMENT PROFILE

Career Rating	85	Grads employed by field	%: avg. salary
Placement rate (%)	78	Finance	35: $74,484
# of companies recruiting on-campus	55	Marketing	31: $74,897
% grads employed immediately	53	MIS	1: $85,000
Average starting salary	$75,029	Operations	3: $88,025
		Strategic Planning	3: $82,400
		Consulting	10: $75,308
		Entrepreneurship	2: $93,500
		General Management	9: $70,692
		Internet/New Media	3: $84,800

UNIVERSITY OF SOUTHERN INDIANA
SCHOOL OF BUSINESS

Academics

The MBA program at the University of Southern Indiana benefits from the huge undergraduate population of business and marketing majors at USI's School of Business. With nearly 2,000 such undergraduates, USI can maintain a much broader range of graduate business offerings than could most schools of its size. The school offers an MBA in general management and a master's of science in accountancy (MSA).

USI's MBA program offers up to 18 hours of foundation courses for students with little or no undergraduate background in business. Students must complete or place out of these courses before turning to the 30-hour core sequence. This system allows part-time students to complete their MBAs within three years and full-timers to complete the degree within two years. The MSA curriculum includes 15 hours of accounting, 3 hours of business law, 3 hours of finance, and 9 hours of electives.

Students report that USI's approach "is very good at giving the student a core basis in everything business-related," but that the program would benefit from "more focus on specialized business areas such as entrepreneurship, global marketing, international business, Internet technology, and other specialized fields of study as opposed to [a] broad scope of [the] MBA program." Some students also believe that the school goes too far to accommodate students whose jobs leave them too busy for intensive study. One MBA observes, "Some classes are 'watered down' for the nontechnical students. For instance, most classes take all calculus-based problems out of the curriculum so that most of the students would not be intimidated. I believe that real-life economic and operations problems require one to develop models and perform standard calculus computations to arrive at an answer."

Students who want to dig deeper will find willing accomplices in the faculty. USI professors "are very knowledgeable in their chosen field. Marketing, finance, and economics professors all do very well with their material." Their "diverse backgrounds and experiences help students to gain a better understanding of all the fields represented in the program." USI's busy MBAs also love "being able to resolve most of administrative issues over the Internet. That's extremely convenient," one student comments. Overall, the students feel they receive "good academic 'bang for the buck,'" and that "you can definitely take pride in this school," according to a survey.

Career and Placement

The Career Counseling Center at USI assists students through assessment testing, personalized counseling, workshops, online job databases, and resume books. The office maintains a library of electronic and print resources pertaining to all aspects of the job search. Students may also access the electronic resources of the entire University of Indiana system. MBAs and MSAs explain that "career placement seems greatly tailored toward accounting majors. It could be more broad." Because most USI MBAs have jobs, which frequently contribute toward the students' tuition, the school places a relatively low priority on career services for its MBA students.

PEGGY HARREL, DIRECTOR OF GRADUATE STUDIES
8600 UNIVERSITY BOULVARD EVANSVILLE, IN 47712 UNITED STATES
PHONE: 812-465-7015 • FAX: 812-464-1956
E-MAIL: GSSR@USI.EDU • WEBSITE: WWW.BUSINESS.USI.EDU

Student Life and Environment

Evansville, with a population of 120,000, is a small industrial city in southern Indiana; about one-third of its jobs are in manufacturing (Toyota is the metro area's biggest employer). The closest large city is Louisville, Kentucky, about 120 miles away; Nashville, Indianapolis, and St. Louis are all within a 200-mile radius. Students appreciate the small-town setting, which they find conducive to study. "Coming from a much larger city, I think Evansville is wonderful. The community is great," one MBA writes.

Students also love the "nice atmosphere on campus and up-to-date facilities." One MBA writes, "There are many things a person can do. The gym facilities are brand new. New buildings are popping up every year. It's a great place [that] has many community builders and activities for students. It is a great campus to just hang out at and get to know people." One student notes, "USI provides a close community for the students who wish to be involved. There is always help and always activities to participate in."

Most students, however, are simply too busy to get involved with campus life. One student explains, "The MBA degree program at USI is designed for working adults. Most of us don't spend much extra time after class unless [it is] necessary." One typical student writes, "I commute one hour to school, work a full-time job as a health-system quality leader, travel two hours one way to sing in a chorus each week, am a cantor, and am very active in my church with my husband. [I also] have a grown daughter who is married with an eight-month-old son and take two to three courses at a time. The amount of time necessary to be an active participant in all of this keeps me from being more active in school activities—other than the MBA program and requirements." Professors recognize "that the MBA student has a tough schedule to juggle" and usually create assignments accordingly.

Admissions

Admission to the School of Business at USI is based primarily on GMAT score and undergraduate transcript. The admissions office also considers leadership potential and work experience. Students may supplement their applications with letters of recommendation, personal statements, and an interview, but none of these are required. According to the school's website, "all candidates for admission to the MBA program must demonstrate proficiency in computer skills. Proficiency may be established by successfully completing college-level course work within five years of admission to the MBA program or by passing a proficiency exam provided through the MBA office."

FINANCIAL FACTS

Annual tuition (in-state/out-of-state)	$3,510/$6,930
Fees	$220
Books and supplies	$850
Room & board (on/off-campus)	$5,480/$7,772
% of students receiving aid	55
% of first-year students receiving aid	77
% of students receiving loans	45
% of students receiving grants	5
Average award package	$6,586
Average grant	$1,567
Average student loan debt	$10,850

ADMISSIONS

Admissions Selectivity Rating	81
# of applications received	65
% applicants accepted	48
% acceptees attending	77
Average GMAT	519
Range of GMAT	430-650
Average GPA	3.41
TOEFL Required of International Students?	Yes
Minimum TOEFL (paper/computer)	550/213
Application fee	$25
International application fee	$25
Regular application deadline	Rolling
Regular notification	Rolling
Transfer students accepted?	Yes
Transfer application policy: Twelve accepted hours can be transferred into the program.	
Non-fall admissions?	Yes
Need-blind admissions?	Yes

EMPLOYMENT PROFILE

Career Rating	73
Placement rate (%)	89
Average starting salary	$56,967

UNIVERSITY OF SOUTHERN MAINE
SCHOOL OF BUSINESS

GENERAL INFORMATION
Type of school	public
Environment	town
Academic calendar	semester

SURVEY SAYS...
Students love Portland, ME
Friendly students
Solid preparation in:
Teamwork

STUDENTS
Enrollment of parent institution	11,089
Enrollment of MBA program	118
% male/female	84/16
% out-of-state	20
% part-time	80
% international	20
Average age at entry	31
Average years work experience at entry	4.60

ACADEMICS
Academic Experience Rating	**70**
Student/faculty ratio	20:1
Profs interesting rating	73
Profs accessible rating	66
% female faculty	25
% minority faculty	5

Joint Degrees
BS/MBA: 5 years
MBA/MS in accounting: 5 years
MBA/MSN in nursing: 3 years
MBA/JD: 4 years

Academics

The MBA program at the University of Southern Maine focuses its attention primarily on students "who wish to advance their careers and contribute to their companies." It serves a largely part-time student body whose members hold full-time jobs in the area and seek a degree that will help them "develop cross-functional business solutions to real-world problems [and] cultivate a broad critical perspective, interpersonal skills, and the analytical tools of management." USM's full-time student body is primarily enrolled in the 3-2 MBA program, which allows undergraduates to earn a bachelor's degree and an MBA in five years.

Part-time students can complete USM's 33-credit sequence in two years, although some take longer. The curriculum consists of nine three-hour core courses and two three-hour electives. "All classes are held in the evening and night" so that working students can attend the MBA program, which students appreciate. One such student writes, "This school is well-located for part-time students and it caters well to them. The administration strongly supports the students." Because of the limited number of electives available, students cannot fashion an area of concentration here, a situation some would like to see addressed. One says, "I work in the financial services industry and would love to be able to come out of USM with a finance concentration MBA."

USM professors "are well integrated into the local business community, opening up several great opportunities for enriching projects." Their quality as classroom instructors varies; "Some seem to teach to the lowest common denominator, but generally they are good to very strong," students tell us. They single out instructors in operations, accounting, and finance for their expertise and "ability to inspire learning in their students." Many agree the b-school facility "needs to be vastly improved," adding that "the school desperately needs a new building of their own with more modern, comfortable facilities."

Career and Placement

USM's website states: "Because many of our students are already employed in management positions, we do not have a formal placement service for MBA or MSA students." The site adds that "opportunities for employment often come to our attention," and these opportunities "are passed on to students for consideration." Students may use the services of the USM Career Services Office, which serves the entire university population. Students may also work with the Office of Graduate Studies, which employs a career advisor to administer career assessments, counsel students in resume building and interviewing skills, and arrange networking opportunities.

Student Life and Environment

Because "the University of Southern Maine is mainly a commuter college," "there is really very little in the way of organized outside activities. We all have a local life outside of school which demands our time." One student observes, "There isn't a whole lot of school spirit and clubs like at other universities. The only club I've heard of for the MBA program is the MBA Association. Unfortunately, any clubs that students are asked to participate in have meetings when many students are in class. That also goes for most networking opportunities that are available." Extracurricular life isn't totally dead, though; according to one MBA, "The school does try to bring students together for occasional special events, and many professors hold off-campus gatherings on the last night of class that provide a good networking opportunity with other students."

ALICE B. CASH, GRADUATE PROGRAMS DIRECTOR
PO BOX 9300, PORTLAND, ME 04104 UNITED STATES
PHONE: 207-780-4184 • FAX: 207-780-4662
E-MAIL: MBA@USM.MAINE.EDU • WEBSITE: WWW.USM.MAINE.EDU/SB

USM's MBA program is a small one, the majority of whose students attend part time. They are "good-natured, intelligent individuals" who are "motivated but not extremely driven in a business sense. They are hard-working and striving for knowledge," creating "a positive learning environment." The mix of "older students with families and substantial professional backgrounds and younger students with less work experience but more recent educational experience" is a "positive mix," students say. They also love that "the academic community is quiet and the scenery is wonderful, very relaxing."

Portland is home to the School of Business' main campus. With a population just under a quarter of a million, Portland is the largest city in Maine. It serves as the state's financial, business, and retail center; its major industries include tourism, telecommunications, technology, light manufacturing, and insurance.

Admissions

All applicants to the MBA program at USM must submit a completed application, two copies of official transcripts for all post-secondary work (including work at USM), GMAT scores, three letters of recommendation, a resume, and a personal essay. In addition, international students must also submit a certificate of finances and, if English is not their first language, TOEFL scores. Fully admitted students must have a formula score of 1,100 under the formula [(undergraduate GPA × 200) + GMAT score] and a minimum GMAT score of 500. The GMAT requirement is waived for students who have completed a terminal degree (e.g. PhD, JD, MD). The admissions office considers rigor of undergraduate field of study, reputation of undergraduate institution, potential, likelihood of enhancing the educational environment at USM, demonstrated leadership, evidence of creativity, and record of accomplishment in business in making its admissions decisions. Prior to commencing the MBA program, all students must complete, or demonstrate competency in, the following 'foundation' areas: managing organizational behavior, IT/MIS, economics, accounting, probability and statistics, finance, marketing, and management science. Students with deficiencies in these areas will be notified at the time of their admission.

FINANCIAL FACTS

Annual tuition (in-state/out-of-state)	$4,122/$11,520
Fees	$534
Books and supplies	$1,000
Room & board (on-campus)	$6,800
Average grant	$1,500

ADMISSIONS

Admissions Selectivity Rating	**76**
# of applications received	56
% applicants accepted	71
% acceptees attending	78
Average GMAT	553
Range of GMAT	510-595
Average GPA	3.2
TOEFL Required of International Students?	Yes
Minimum TOEFL (paper/computer)	550/213
Application fee	$50
International application fee	$50
Regular application deadline	8/1
Regular notification	Rolling
Deferment Available?	Yes
Maximum length of deferment	1 year
Transfer students accepted?	Yes
Transfer application policy: Please see catalog. http://www.usm.maine.edu/catalogs/graduate/	
Non-fall admissions?	Yes
Need-blind admissions?	Yes

UNIVERSITY OF SYDNEY/UNIVERSITY OF NEW SOUTH WALES
AUSTRALIAN GRADUATE SCHOOL OF MANAGEMENT

Academics

Students praise the "well-developed generalist course taught by renowned faculty" at the Australian Graduate School of Management, the b-school affiliate of both the University of Sydney and the University of New South Wales. The school, which is "well-known in the Asian Pacific" (especially at home and in Southeast Asia), has made its mark through its "world-class research." In 2005, the *Financial Times* ranked the school 40th in the world for research output.

AGSM's research institutes include the Center for Corporate Change (CCC), described by the school as "Australia's leading center for the study of organizational transformation." Other institutes include the Center for Research in Finance (which "was set up to collect, store, and analyze data for both pure and applied research in finance and related disciplines"), and the Center for Applied Marketing (which "aims to further marketing knowledge and encourage state-of-the-art marketing practice [and which] sponsors an overseas visitor program to ensure that the latest in international thinking is available to Australian researchers and practitioners").

Research is not AGSM's only asset, however. Professors are not just brilliant, innovative thinkers, they are also "very motivating, approachable, and inspiring, with good teaching style and diverse teaching methods." Students caution that "a couple of them are much better on a one-to-one basis than lecturing to a class, so sometimes you have to make use of their openness," but since most professors are "extremely approachable," this rarely causes problems. Students single out the school's "recognized experts in organizational behavior, organizational design, statistics, and negotiations" for praise.

The AGSM curriculum draws on an "innovative, research-driven knowledge base that provides the framework for management decision-making and development of leadership competencies," according to the school. Students approve, but warn that "grading is on a bell curve," making it tougher than usual for students to earn their accustomed As and Bs. They also warn that "for some reason, qualitative subjects are always graded harder than quantitative ones." In other words, don't expect to cruise through. The workload, we're told, is "heavy, but not all that extreme."

Career and Placement

The Career Center of AGSM offers students the usual potpourri of services: workshops, one-on-one counseling, maintenance of a resume book, self-assessment tools, and networking events. The office also runs the Management Projects Program, which "creates, develops, and facilitates opportunities for AGSM students to work in teams with [senior executives] on issues of strategic importance [to] define and analyze a business issue and make recommendations for action through written and oral presentations." Students tell us that AGSM is most effective in placing students in consultancy positions. In 2004, 60 percent of all graduates reported that their job offers were the result of networking; 20 percent attributed their job offer to contacts made through the Career Center.

Those most likely to employ AGSM MBAs include: Accenture, AT Kearney, Colgate Palmolive, KPMG, Macquarie Bank, McKinsey, and Westpac.

Student Life and Environment

The students at AGSM form "a very close-knit and supportive environment, and everyone is made to feel very welcome. The students are high-achieving but not too competitive." One student explains, "The full-time MBA program is intimate. The class size will vary from 90 to 140 for an incoming class. This means that relationships grow quickly and grow strong. Additionally, there is no undergraduate program, so the facilities are dedicated to the graduate students." Students bring "good breadth and depth of experience, and there are many multicultural students from different backgrounds," all of which enhance the AGSM experience. Some students feel the only component missing is an outreach to students' spouses and children. "Inclusion of families through establishment of a formal network/association to help families survive our 'MBA experience' would be great," students tell us.

Because the school sits on the University of New South Wales campus, it has "several thousand post and undergraduate students and a wide range of clubs and societies to join." MBAs enjoy "various networking opportunities for present students, such as barbecues, cruises, courtyard lunches in the sun, presentations, and contests run by clubs. The school has a commitment to ensuring extra-curricular programs accompany demanding course work." All told, AGSM provides "a relaxed atmosphere that accommodates focused students well." Students also love the "clean and tidy" campus, which has "good technology and plenty of appropriate areas to study."

As for hometown Sydney, well, "How can anyone not like Sydney?" The school is located "close to Sydney CBD and Bondi Beach," and the area offers "wonderful weather [and] lots of sunshine." With a population of four million, Sydney is a major business and cultural center.

Admissions

Applicants to the MBA program must have an undergraduate bachelor's degree and at least two years' full-time professional or managerial work experience postdating their undergraduate degree. Students must score a minimum of 550 on the GMAT (a score of 600+ is preferred; those with lower scores must "excel in all other areas"). Students whose native language is not English must score at least a 600 on the TOEFL. Completed applications must include transcripts, test scores, two letters of recommendation (one from a current or recent employer), a detailed resume, and personal-statement essays. Applications "are processed as they are received, [therefore,] the earlier the application, the longer the period of time available for international students to have their student visas approved—this can take up to six months in extreme cases. An early application helps to ensure a place is still available for you."

FINANCIAL FACTS

Annual tuition	$43,617
Books and supplies	$1,160

ADMISSIONS

Admissions Selectivity Rating	**84**
# of applications received	192
% applicants accepted	63
% acceptees attending	51
Average GMAT	642
Average GPA	3.0
TOEFL Required of International Students?	Yes
Minimum TOEFL (paper/computer)	600/250
Application fee	$78
International application fee	$78
Regular application deadline	10/31
Regular notification	Rolling
Deferment Available?	Yes
Maximum length of deferment	1 year
Need-blind admissions?	Yes

EMPLOYMENT PROFILE

Career Rating	85
Average starting salary	$100,545

UNIVERSITY OF TENNESSEE—KNOXVILLE
COLLEGE OF BUSINESS ADMINISTRATION

GENERAL INFORMATION
Type of school	public
Environment	city
Academic calendar	semester

SURVEY SAYS...
Cutting edge classes
Smart classrooms
Solid preparation in:
Teamwork
Communication/interpersonal skills
Presentation skills

STUDENTS
Enrollment of parent institution	25,474
Enrollment of MBA program	140
% male/female	66/34
% out-of-state	32
% minorities	8
% international	18
Average age at entry	26
Average years work experience at entry	3.5

ACADEMICS
Academic Experience Rating	**87**
Student/faculty ratio	4:1
Profs interesting rating	76
Profs accessible rating	69
% female faculty	18
% minority faculty	9

Joint Degrees
MBA/JD: 4years
MBA/MS in Engineering: 2 years

Prominent Alumni
Ralph Heath, VP & COO, Lockheed Martin Aeronautics; Kiran Patel, CFO, Solectron; Joseph O'Donnell, CEO, Artesyn Technology; Bob Hall, CEO, Jewelry Television by ACN; Scott Parish, CFO, Alcon Entertainment.

Academics

The University of Tennessee's College of Business Administration has recently compressed their full-time program so that it now spans a mere 17 months. The school explains their decision thus: "Although compressed in time, this program maintains all of the quality instruction that has made our graduates attractive to corporate recruiters. At the same time, we understand that students make great sacrifices to attend full-time MBA programs, and we are working to reduce that sacrifice. Unconventional? Sure. Challenging? Absolutely." And students concur, calling the 17-month program one of the school's "greatest strengths."

The other great strength of the program is their integrated core curriculum. UTK was the first MBA program in the country to implement a fully integrated core curriculum, which is taught by a "cross-functional faculty team." The school points out that this resulted in the UT MBA program being ranked number two in the country for return on investment. Students also appreciate this, pointing out that since "classes for first-year students are lock-step," they have the opportunity to "become very familiar with peers."

The list of possible concentrations for students isn't long—finance, logistics and transportation, marketing, operations management, JD/MBA—and an MBA/MS in engineering—but students point out with pride that the logistics and transportation program is top-notch. Students say, "It has professors with real-life experiences." And the school points out that their marketing program is sixth in the country for the teaching of marketing skills, while logistics and transportation is ranked number one for educating future logistics/procurement executives. "So far," one student says, "I have learned volumes and have been exposed to a plethora of different real-world case scenarios. I feel that this has been a fabulous investment."

The extras are what makes the program stand out. The school offers a cultural exchange program in Prague. After-class activities "provide the opportunity to hear speakers or participate in activities that enhance the learning experience," and "professors always make themselves available to the students, sometimes even missing a lunch if time is pressing."

Students wish there was "more of an entrepreneurial focus" and complain that the program "just doesn't spend enough time on finance," but apart from that, they agree that it's a "great school" and that "life overall is good."

Career and Placement

Although it has had something of a rocky past, students say that "career services is really picking up under new direction." The average salary for the class of 2001 was about $72,000. More people ended up in logistics and transportation than in any other area, and students who concentrated in supply-chain management and logistics and transportation typically earned several thousand more than those who studied other areas.

Companies who have recruited on campus include Accenture; Amazon.com; AmSouth Bank; Andersen Consulting; Burke, Inc.; Eli Lilly; FedEx; and Hewlett-Packard (among many others).

DONNA POTTS, DIRECTOR OF ADMISSIONS, MBA PROGRAM
527 STOKELY MANAGEMENT CENTER KNOXVILLE, TN 37996-0552 UNITED STATES
PHONE: 865-974-5033 • FAX: 865-974-3826
E-MAIL: MBA@UTK.EDU • WEBSITE: WWW.MBA.UTK.EDU

Student Life and Environment

Knoxville, Tennessee, was recently ranked the "best place to live in the United States and Canada" among cities with a population of fewer than 1 million. This may have something to do with the fact that it's nestled between the Great Smokey Mountains and the Cumberland Mountains, or that it's about a two-hour drive from five national parks, seven state parks, and seven lakes. It is the largest city in East Tennessee; it's also the third largest in the state. The shelter of the mountain ranges ensures that the climate is relatively temperate, with an annual average temperature of about 60°F. Even students coming from big cities have come to enjoy life in a smaller city. "I am enjoying the pace of life and getting to relive college to a certain degree, but this time I have a plan and more responsibility," one former New Yorker says. And other students report that "students do go out together and enjoy the Knoxville nightlife."

Students say that while the 17-month program keeps them very busy, "there is a good balance between school and social life. I have made great contacts." Much of an MBA's free time, apparently, is consumed by football. "Football season is a very exciting time around here!" one student says. "I only wish that the football team was better the past two years." Though most MBAs enjoy the opportunity to socialize over beers at a tailgate party, some complain that "besides the football games, there really isn't much to do."

Admissions

Of the 80-odd students who will enter each fall, 65 percent are male, 35 percent are female, and 18 percent are international. The average age of an incoming student is 27, and the average undergraduate GPA is 3.34. The average GMAT score is 600, and the average amount of work experience is 3.5 years. About 20 percent of the students had worked for less than one year, but 50 percent had worked for three or more. Students came from China, Ecuador, Germany, India, Italy, Japan, Panama, Russia, and South Korea. About 24 percent had an arts-and-sciences background, and 45 percent were business undergrads.

FINANCIAL FACTS

Annual tuition (in-state/out-of-state)	$5,376/$15,156
Fees	$1,000
Books and supplies	$3,000
Room & board (on/off-campus)	$7,400/$12,500
% of students receiving aid	43
% of first-year students receiving aid	27
% of students receiving grants	14
Average award package	$17,784
Average grant	$8,514

ADMISSIONS

Admissions Selectivity Rating	88
# of applications received	230
% applicants accepted	45
% acceptees attending	62
Average GMAT	600
Range of GMAT	560-640
Average GPA	3.3
TOEFL Required of International Students?	Yes
Minimum TOEFL (paper/computer)	600/250
Application fee	$35
International application fee	$35
Regular application deadline	2/1
Regular notification	Rolling
Need-blind admissions?	Yes

APPLICANTS ALSO LOOK AT

Arizona State University, Penn State University MBA, University of Georgia, Vanderbilt University, Wake Forest University.

EMPLOYMENT PROFILE			
Career Rating	74	Grads employed by field	%: avg. salary
Placement rate (%)	67	Finance	17: $54,300
% grads employed immediately	35	Marketing	22: $52,000
Average starting salary	$55,400	Operations	31: $59,800
		Consulting	6: $60,300
		General Management	20: $53,600
		Other	4: $45,200

THE UNIVERSITY OF TEXAS—ARLINGTON
COLLEGE OF BUSINESS ADMINISTRATION

Academics

In its efforts to meet the needs of its diverse student population, the College of Business Administration at University of Texas at Arlington offers several MBA options. There's the Flexible MBA–often referred to simply as "the MBA" because it is regarded as the default option. The Flexible MBA can be completed part-time or full-time, and it jettisons the conventional lockstep MBA curriculum and cohort learning to maximize convenience. This option is offered only on the Arlington campus. Then there's the Accelerated MBA (also known as the Cohort MBA, because students travel through the program with the same group of peers), with its mini-terms scheduled for the convenience of its part-time-student/full-time-worker student body. The Accelerated MBA is offered only at UTA/Fort Worth. UTA also offers an Online MBA, which can be completed "without ever setting foot on campus," and the school participates in an Executive MBA (EMBA) program in Taipei, Beijing, and Shanghai.

Students in the Flexible MBA program may choose a specialization from among the following: finance, accounting, information systems, international business, marketing research, real estate, human resource management, electronic commerce, and enterprise resource planning. Current students praise the economics department ("the professors are producing advanced research and presenting it in class along with other new research done in the field"), the accounting and operations management department, and the marketing research program, which "is offered only in limited schools across the country."

The Accelerated MBA program receives even more enthusiastic endorsements from students, one tells us, and "There is tremendous value in being in with the same classmates for 2.5 years and who all have industry experience. Through presentations from classmates with experience in the field, I have learned more about the defense industry, the pharmaceutical industry, the health care industry, the banking industry, and manufacturing in general." This "extremely focused" program "is excellent for working adults." Students in the Online MBA programs can earn only general MBAs without concentrations.

In all programs, students love "the overall value, [the] up-to-date technology, [and the] user-friendly registration, enrollment, and work processes." Professors here "are really good and very engaging with the class. They come from all walks of life: Some write their own textbooks, some have owned their own businesses, some are teaching for fun, some have taught forever! Given the strong professional presence of the students, they are always kept on their toes and questioned regarding anything that might not make sense."

Career and Placement

Career Services at UTA include "comprehensive assessment, industry analysis, career exploration and informational interviews, managing in a diverse environment, career-focused academic advising, and internships," the school tells us. In addition, students take a Careers Class that "presents both practical and theoretical perspectives on careers and managing in a changing work environment." Students gripe that "the school still needs to work hard on getting more known companies to visit the campus for recruitment." They also identify alumni connections as an area needing improvement. Employers most likely to hire UTA MBAs include Alcon Laboratories, Sabre Group Holdings, Inc, Nokia, American Airlines, and Bank of America.

Student Life and Environment

UTA's MBA programs are "made for working professionals looking to earn a degree, but not necessarily a second "college experience." Students yearning to meet new friends and embellish another undergraduate experience should look for more personalized

Graduate Business Services
Box 19376, Arlington, TX 76019 United States
Phone: 817-272-3004 • Fax: 817-272-5799
E-mail: gradbizs@uta.edu • Website: www.uta.edu/gradbiz

service at other institutions. To be sure, UTA is a very large, growing institution that offers all the facilities and resources of most major academic institutions at a much lower cost. However, "most students are part-times with full-time jobs, so mingling is not a top priority." The full-timers in the Flexible MBA program are the exception—they do spend considerable time together. They tell us that "life at school is moderately paced, which allows most students to get into other activities apart from academics." One full-time student explains, "There are many opportunities for students to get involved, if they want them. UTA is a school where you have to seek out the opportunities—you will find them if you look. I am very involved on campus on the part of the graduate school. Yet such opportunities are not always advertised and made known to all the students eligible."

All programs at UTA boast impressive diversity stats. One student reports, "The school is extremely diverse; almost any class has a spread of Asians, Africans, Europeans, Middle Easterners, Hindus, and Hispanics." Students in the Flexible MBA program are "a mixed bag. Like any academic program, you have foreign students, students with a lot of work experience, and students who are fresh out of undergrad. It's a very stimulating and rewarding combination." Cohort MBAs are all "industry professionals from the Dallas/Fort Worth area," notes a part-timer. They are all very vocal, intelligent, and engaging in the classroom. I've never had this much fun in a real classroom before. Vacations, gatherings, and celebrations among students is common." Everyone here is "very career-oriented and outgoing. Many students have families and are married."

Students observe that "one of the greatest strengths of UTA is that we are located in a very active business market. This large metroplex allows for many opportunities to go outside the classroom as well as bring in local experts."

Admissions

Admissions officers at UTA consider all of the following: GMAT score, undergraduate GPA and curriculum, work experience, essays (including a 200-word statement of academic intent), and letters of recommendation. Applicants are ranked using the formula [(undergraduate GPA ? 200) + GMAT score], and the average admitted student scores approximately 1,100 (which, of course, means that many admitted students score lower than 1,100). Students whose first language is not English must also submit TOEFL scores (this requirement is waived for students who have earned a postsecondary degree from a U.S. college or university). International students must also provide a bank affidavit and financial statement. To promote diversity within the student body, UTA College of Business Education supports activities sponsored by the McNair Scholar Program and the National Black MBA Association.

FINANCIAL FACTS

Annual tuition (in-state/out-of-state)	$4,944/$13,998
Fees (in-state/out-of-state)	$2,058/$2,253
Books and supplies	$1,000
Room & board (on/off-campus)	$4,800/$6,000
% of students receiving aid	20
% of first-year students receiving aid	22
Average award package	$8,500
Average grant	$1,000
Average student loan debt	$23,475

ADMISSIONS

Admissions Selectivity Rating	**79**
# of applications received	413
% applicants accepted	49
% acceptees attending	39
Average GMAT	546
Range of GMAT	470-620
Average GPA	3.2
TOEFL Required of International Students?	Yes
Minimum TOEFL (paper/computer)	550/213
Application fee	$30
International application fee	$60
Regular application deadline	6/10
Regular notification	Rolling
Early decision program?	Yes
ED Deadline/Notification	Rolling/ 6/15
Deferment Available?	Yes
Maximum length of deferment	1 year
Transfer students accepted?	Yes
Transfer application policy: Maximum number of transferable credits is nine. Grades B or better from an AACSB accredited university.	
Non-fall admissions?	Yes
Need-blind admissions?	Yes

THE UNIVERSITY OF TEXAS—AUSTIN
McCOMBS SCHOOL OF BUSINESS

GENERAL INFORMATION
Type of school   public
Environment   metropolis
Academic calendar   semester

SURVEY SAYS...
Students love Austin, TX
Friendly students
Good peer network
Happy students
Smart classrooms

STUDENTS
Enrollment of parent institution	50,000
Enrollment of MBA program	942
% male/female	80/20
% out-of-state	31
% part-time	24
% minorities	8
% international	26
Average age at entry	28
Average years work experience at entry	5

ACADEMICS
Academic Experience Rating	90
Student/faculty ratio	5:1
Profs interesting rating	88
Profs accessible rating	85
% female faculty	19
% minority faculty	19

Joint Degrees

MBA/JD: 7-4 years
MBA/MA (various programs): 3-5 years

Prominent Alumni

Jim Mulva, President & CEO/Conoco Phillips; William Johnson, Chairman, President & CEO/Heinz; Don Evans, former Secretary of Commerce/U.S. Gov't.; Sara Martinez Tucker, President & CEO/ Hispanic Scholarship Fund; Gerard Arpey, Chairman, President & CEO/American Airlines.

Academics

For a combination of an excellent graduate business program and an equally fine quality of life, it's hard to beat the McCombs School of Business at The University of Texas at Austin. Students here agree that "Austin is a very cool town, Texas is a great state, and UT has a top 20 MBA program." They also praise "an atmosphere that is very collaborative and laid-back, but still professional." Students also love the fact that the larger university is big enough to be strong in many disciplines. Our survey respondents see strengths in such b-school staples as accounting, IT, entrepreneurship, real estate and marketing; they're also enthusiastic about the school's unique offerings in investment management, private equity, and energy finance.

The McCombs curriculum consists of 27 credits of core requirements and a minimum of 33 elective credits. If 15 of those credits are devoted to one of five specific functional areas (accounting, finance, management, information technology, or marketing), then one graduates with a concentration. In addition to concentrations, McCombs offers students the option of a specialization, which is basically a "specifically designed set of courses" within a particular discipline. Teamwork and group projects figure heavily in the McCombs curriculum; observes one student, "The cooperative and team environment is the greatest attribute of McCombs. Most classes require some form of group interaction, which is important to life in the professional world." Students report that "most professors use the methods most appropriate for their specific fields of study; from the case method to class discussion, lectures to problem sets, they use them all as required by the material."

Among McCombs' standout features is the Plus Program, a relatively recent addition to the curriculum spurred on by "the school's commitment to hands-on learning and market-driven education." The Plus Program consists of short programs "ranging from international business tours to professional development seminars." Future MBAs report that the Plus Program "helps us gain real-world experience very quickly." Writes one student, the "program gives students excellent opportunities to improve communications skills and work on real-life projects with local companies outside of the academic schedule."

Career and Placement

According to the school, each year "recruiters from hundreds of the world's leading companies" visit the Ford Career Center to recruit McCombs MBAs. Corporate relationships, including "affiliations with high-tech companies," mean employers are a major presence on campus all year round, not just at recruiting time. This allows students to forge strong relationships with potential employers, which, unsurprisingly, pleases McCombs students quite a bit. Almost all the students in our survey reported satisfaction with McCombs' ability to attract recruiters and to place students in internships and jobs.

Top employers of McCombs MBAs include American Airlines; Capital One; Citibank; Dell; Deloitte Consulting; Exelon; Frito Lay; General Mills; HEB; IBM; Johnson & Johnson; Proctor & Gamble; SBC Communications; Samsung; Standard & Poor's; and Union Bank of Switzerland. About half of all graduates remain in the Southwest; the remaining students scatter pretty evenly around the country and the world for their first post-degree jobs.

TINA MABLEY, DIRECTOR OF ADMISSION, MBA PROGRAMS
ADMISSIONS, MBA PROGRAM OFFICE, 1 UNIVERSITY STATION, B6004, AUSTIN, TX 78712 U.S.
PHONE: 512-471-7612 • FAX: 512-471-4243
E-MAIL: MCCOMBSMBA@MCCOMBS.UTEXAS.EDU • WEBSITE: WWW.MBA.MCCOMBS.UTEXAS.EDU

Student Life and Environment

Like seemingly everyone else who lives in Austin, students love their school's hometown. Explains one student, "It's unlike any other environment. It is not New York City, so it doesn't stress you out, and it's not rural America, so it doesn't bore you to death. If you are outgoing, then this is the place to be. Forbes rated Austin as the best city for singles, and that kind of explains it." Students here laud the "many outdoor activities, like biking, running, hiking, and camping that are available in the city. There's also a big lake that provides a great place to relax during the spring and summer." They also praise the "incredible Tex-Mex food" (the barbecue's not half bad, either) and "the night life on Sixth Street, which is better than just about anywhere." If you like live music, you'll love Austin.

On campus, "social life is excellent" at McCombs, with "a great deal of camaraderie among the students." Student organizations "are very involved and very well run," and extracurricular fun is always close at hand, as "Every Thursday night we have Think and Drinks which allow students to mingle at a bar over a beer or two. It's a work hard, play hard culture." Tailgate parties before football games "are always fantastic, with free food, free drinks, and free fun." Married students happily note that "The Student and Significant Others Group is great for those students who bring a partner. The school has great programs for my spouse as well as for my kids."

"Teamwork and cooperation overshadows intense competition" at McCombs; students' awareness that they are in a top-flight program that can yield good jobs for all of them, and also helps keep competitiveness low. A large portion of the student body originates from outside the United States; writes one American student, "I was amazed at the broad spectrum of countries and nationalities represented. This alone has been a tremendous learning experience."

Admissions

Application to McCombs must be submitted online. Admission is extremely competitive. A completed application must include: a resume detailing work history; personal essays; official copies of transcripts for all post-secondary academic work; letters of recommendation; an official score report for the GMAT; and, for international students whose first language is not English, an official score report for the TOEFL. Programs designed to increase minority and disadvantaged populations at McCombs include Jump Start, "which targets undergraduate seniors who are academically qualified for a top-ranked MBA but lack the required work experience"; Explore McCombs, "a three-day preview of the School for qualified African-American, Hispanic-American, and Native American applicants"; and participation in a number of alliances, associations, and consortia dedicated to the goal.

FINANCIAL FACTS

Annual tuition (in-state/out-of-state)	$5,350/$19,890
Fees (in-state/out-of-state)	$9,267/$10,227
Books and supplies	$1,400
Room & board	$12,566
% of students receiving aid	80
% of first-year students receiving aid	80
% of students receiving loans	80
% of students receiving grants	30
Average award package	$26,000
Average grant	$9,258
Average student loan debt	$31,274

ADMISSIONS

Admissions Selectivity Rating	93
# of applications received	1717
% applicants accepted	41
% acceptees attending	45
Average GMAT	670
Range of GMAT	610-720
Average GPA	3.38
TOEFL Required of International Students?	Yes
Minimum TOEFL (paper/computer)	620/260
Application fee	$125
International application fee	$125
Regular application deadline	4/15
Regular notification	5/1
Deferment Available?	Yes
Maximum length of deferment	1 year
Need-blind admissions?	Yes

APPLICANTS ALSO LOOK AT

Duke University, Harvard University, Northwestern University, University of California—Berkeley, University of Michigan, University of North Carolina at Chapel Hill, University of Pennsylvania.

EMPLOYMENT PROFILE

Career Rating	87	Grads employed by field %: avg. salary	
Placement rate (%)	87	Finance	40: $77,550
% grads employed immediately	62	Marketing	23: $75,773
Average starting salary	$77,403	MIS	3: $76,000
		Operations	6: $67,721
		Consulting	13: $86,003
		General Management	11: $75,858
		Other	4: $76,367

THE UNIVERSITY OF TEXAS—DALLAS

SCHOOL OF MANAGEMENT

GENERAL INFORMATION
Type of school   public
Academic calendar   semester

SURVEY SAYS...
Students love Richardson, TX
Smart classrooms
Solid preparation in:
Teamwork

STUDENTS
Enrollment of parent
  institution   14,092
Enrollment of MBA program   1,365
% male/female   73/27
% out-of-state   4
% part-time   95
% minorities   1
% international   51
Average age at entry   29
Average years work experience
  at entry   5

ACADEMICS
Academic Experience Rating   **73**
Student/faculty ratio   18:1
Profs interesting rating   77
Profs accessible rating   65
% female faculty   16
% minority faculty   5

Academics

Most students attend the University of Texas at Dallas' MBA program on a part-time basis, enrolling in either the professional part-time MBA program (available either on-site or online) or one of a number of executive MBA options. Sixty students each year enter the more competitive cohort full-time MBA program, a relatively new offering at the school (the program was established in 1996).

Full-time students call the cohort MBA "one of the best bang-for-the-buck programs out there," one that benefits from "truly outstanding professors, many of whom have real-world work experience as business leaders. Also, all of them are excited about what they teach, and that enthusiasm rubs off on the students." Part-time students agree that professors are "very good and very knowledgeable," and also appreciate that "the school runs a tight ship." Reports one global leadership executive MBA (GLEMBA) student, "The supportive administrators really help out making the 'chore' of all the paperwork much easier so students can concentrate on learning."

All students follow the same basic curriculum, commencing with a "heavy" 29-credit core: "Some of us would rather be able to pick and choose some courses to have a more customized educational experience." Electives allow students to develop specializations in accounting, innovation and entrepreneurship, finance, international management, managerial economics, marketing management, MIS, operations management, or organization and strategy. Students single out the school's "analytic and quantitative approach to business management, with a full scope of leadership/soft skills" as its greatest curricular strength. Writes one student, "Materials are highly relevant and contemporary, the delivery is high quality and interactive, the assignments build upon the material, and the core courses build on one another." Graduate study is further enhanced by the fact that "UTD is a highly research-oriented school, and we have many professors who are well noted for their excellence in research."

Career and Placement

Students at UTD's School of Management have access to two career-services offices: the SOM Career Management Center (CMC), and the UTD Career Center. The offices coordinate efforts to serve both undergraduates and graduate students in business; the CMC focuses primarily on the needs of graduate students. The CMC coordinates career fairs, company information sessions, and on-campus interviews. The office also maintains online bulletin boards and job databases. Students looking for more are encouraged to use school resources to achieve their goals; writes one MBA, "The administration is wonderful. They helped a group I was in develop, implement, and finance a career fair for MBAs specifically."

Employers most likely to hire UTD MBAs include Alliance Data Systems, Bank of New York, Dell, Deloitte, Ernst & Young, KPMG, Lennox, Nortel, and Sabre Holdings.

Student Life and Environment

UTD's School of Management "recently transitioned into a single on-campus facility" that "has everything we need for the business school." Amenities include "wireless internet, technologically advanced classrooms, plenty of computer labs," "a nice lounge area," breakout rooms, and a 350-seat auditorium. Despite the upgrade, some here are not entirely satisfied; they complain that "the campus is boring. The atmosphere within the buildings is not welcoming, there are few trees around, and there are few places to sit outside and enjoy the day while studying."

DAVID RITCHEY, ASSOCIATE DEAN
SCHOOL OF MANAGEMENT BUILDING, 2601 NORTH FLOYD ROAD, RICHARDSON, TX 75080 U.S.
PHONE: 972-883-2750 • FAX: 972-883-6425
E-MAIL: PMBA@UTDALLAS.EDU • WEBSITE: SOM.UTDALLAS.EDU

Because "the majority of graduate students commute" at UTD, "there is not a strong community" among most MBA students. Reports one part-time student, "The professional MBA program is more geared toward working professionals. Classes are in the evening or on weekends, and the professors are well aware that most of the students are working 40 to 60 hours per week (as well as traveling)." Full-time students are more likely to spend free time on campus. They tell us that "there are a lot of activities going on all the time. There are several student academic and non-academic clubs. Every Friday, the international student services office arranges for the celebration of the culture of a country, with food, song, [and] dance. The school frequently organizes CEO lecture series. The Institute for Excellence in Corporate Governance in the school organizes seminars from time to time where top management people from big corporations come for brainstorming on contemporary business issues. Field trips to companies are organized."

UTD's part-time student body "mostly consists of working, married people, many with children. They are interested in performing well in school, but are not highly competitive for grades. In fact, some just want the degree and don't care about the grades. Most students already have a career path and are attending school to further careers that have been started, so you don't feel that you are competing for jobs with them." In the full-time program, "the atmosphere is very family-like. The batches work together in community outreach programs, form study groups, and have parties at each other's homes." Both programs have substantial international populations who "lend interesting insights and viewpoints."

Admissions

All applicants to UTD business graduate programs must submit the following: an online application; official copies of all post-secondary transcripts; an official score report for the GMAT; three letters of recommendation; and a personal statement/essay. International students whose native language is not English must provide an official score report for the TOEFL in addition to the materials listed above. The UTD admissions office looks most closely at the undergraduate transcript and GMAT scores; letters of recommendation and the essay are also considered important factors. Other aspects of the application are considered but are given less weight in the final decision. Admission to the full-time cohort program is more competitive than is admission to part-time programs. All programs require calculus as a prerequisite.

FINANCIAL FACTS

Annual tuition (in-state/out-of-state)	$1,728/$6,372
Fees (in-state/out-of-state)	$2,990/$3,278
Books and supplies	$1,000
Room & board (on/off-campus)	$6,244/$8,244
% of students receiving aid	52
% of first-year students receiving aid	65
% of students receiving grants	51
Average award package	$13,156
Average grant	$6,267

ADMISSIONS

Admissions Selectivity Rating	**76**
# of applications received	728
% applicants accepted	75
% acceptees attending	68
Average GMAT	572
Range of GMAT	504-627
Average GPA	3.2
TOEFL Required of International Students?	Yes
Minimum TOEFL (paper/computer)	550/215
Application fee	$50
International application fee	$100
Regular application deadline	7/1
Regular notification	8/1
Deferment Available?	Yes
Maximum length of deferment	1 year
Transfer students accepted?	Yes
Transfer application policy: Up to 15 graduate hours may be transferred.	
Non-fall admissions?	Yes
Need-blind admissions?	Yes

EMPLOYMENT PROFILE

Career Rating	**81**
# of companies recruiting on-campus	23
% grads employed immediately	57
Average starting salary	$66,600

THE UNIVERSITY OF TEXAS—PAN AMERICAN
COLLEGE OF BUSINESS ADMINISTRATION

GENERAL INFORMATION
Type of school	public
Environment	town
Academic calendar	semester

SURVEY SAYS...
Students love Edinburg, TX
Friendly students
Cutting edge classes
Happy students
Smart classrooms
Solid preparation in:
Communication/interpersonal skills
Presentation skills

STUDENTS
Enrollment of parent institution	17,500
Enrollment of MBA program	186
% male/female	68/32
% part-time	69
% minorities	75
% international	15
Average age at entry	31
Average years work experience at entry	2

ACADEMICS
Academic Experience Rating	**61**
Student/faculty ratio	27:1
Profs interesting rating	71
Profs accessible rating	65
% female faculty	30

Academics

The College of Business Administration at the University of Texas—Pan American offers both an evening MBA program and an online MBA program. The college and the MBA program are accredited by the American Assembly of Collegiate Schools of Business (AACSB).

UTPA's evening MBA program may be completed on either a full-time or a part-time basis. Full-time students with undergraduate degrees in business may complete the program in as little as 18 months. Part-time students may take up to seven years to earn their degrees. Those lacking an academic background in business are required to commence the program with a sequence of foundation courses that cover principles of accounting, economics, management, marketing, statistics, and finance. All students must complete nine core courses and three electives for a total of 36 course hours of work. Students may choose to write a thesis instead of taking six of the nine hours of required electives; thesis topics are subject to approval from the MBA director. Students in the program praise its emphasis on teamwork and the "good availability of classes at night." Yet they also tell us that the facility housing the program "needs to be renovated."

The online MBA is administered jointly with seven other UT campuses (Arlington, Brownsville, Dallas, El Paso, Permian Basin, San Antonio, and Tyler). The online curriculum consists of 48 course hours. Students with sufficient backgrounds in business may have up to four core courses waived, reducing the number of required hours to 36. Online students must take at least two courses in person at their home campuses; all other courses can be completed at home via computer.

Career and Placement

Because UTPA's MBA program is relatively small, graduate students here share a career services office with business undergraduates. That office, called the Center for Advisement, Recruitment, Internships and Retention (CARIR), provides career counseling services, job-related reference materials, and assistance in internship placements. The office participates in numerous regional and national online job databases, which students may access through their UTPA accounts. CARIR also organizes on-campus recruitment events each semester, although most of the recruitment is geared toward undergraduate students.

JERRY PROCK, DIRECTOR OF MBA PROGRAMS
1201 WEST UNIVERSITY DRIVE, EDINBURG, TX 78541-2999 UNITED STATES
PHONE: 956-381-3313 • FAX: 956-381-2970
E-MAIL: MBAPROG@UTPA.EDU • WEBSITE: WWW.COBA.PANAM.EDU/MBA/INDEX.HTM

Student Life and Environment

UTPA is "a commuter campus" that "is not very eventful for graduate students." Aside from "occasional group meetings," MBAs here spend little time on campus. They attend classes, take care of other school-related obligations, and then head home. For all of the students who commute, the school's "parking facilities could be better."

UTPA is located in Edinburg, Texas, a city of nearly 50,000 in the southernmost section of the state. Edinburg is the county seat of Hidalgo County. The majority population is Hispanic, with most residents of Mexican descent. Education and health care are the area's major employment sectors; retail trade capitalizes on the city's location near the Mexico border.

The "career-minded" students in the program are "varied in nationalities and goals," according to their peers. These "resourceful, energetic, focused, and interesting" future MBAs "are typically employed full time, many with families and major commitments. We are nearly all-night students. Students are disciplined and group-oriented."

Admissions

Applicants to University of Texas—Pan American must submit all the following materials to the Admissions Committee: an application to the UTPA Graduate School; sealed copies of official transcripts for all previously attended post-secondary institutions; a sealed copy of an official GMAT score report. In addition, international students whose first language is not English must submit a sealed copy of an official TOEFL score report. Applicants who receive a score of at least 950 under the formula [(undergraduate GPA for final 60 semester hours of academic work × 200) + GMAT score] have the best chance of gaining admission to the program. Those who fail to meet this benchmark may still be admitted on the basis of "strong supporting documentation," such as letters of recommendation, resume, and "other evidence of potential success based on relevant work and leadership experience."

FINANCIAL FACTS

Annual tuition (in-state/out-of-state)	$2,797/$8,900
Fees (in-state/out-of-state)	$314/$402
Books and supplies	$1,500

ADMISSIONS

Admissions Selectivity Rating	**71**
# of applications received	78
% applicants accepted	47
% acceptees attending	73
Average GMAT	420
Average GPA	3.0
TOEFL Required of International Students?	Yes
Minimum TOEFL (paper/computer)	500/173
Application fee	$35
International application fee	$35
Regular application deadline	8/1
Regular notification	Rolling
Transfer students accepted?	Yes
Transfer application policy: Maximum 4 courses accepted.	
Non-fall admissions?	Yes
Need-blind admissions?	Yes

THE UNIVERSITY OF TEXAS—SAN ANTONIO
COLLEGE OF BUSINESS

GENERAL INFORMATION

Type of school	public
Environment	village
Academic calendar	semester

SURVEY SAYS...

Students love San Antonio, TX
Friendly students
Smart classrooms
Solid preparation in:
Teamwork
Quantitative skills

STUDENTS

Enrollment of parent institution	26,340
Enrollment of MBA program	454
% male/female	51/49
% part-time	72
% minorities	30
% international	29
Average age at entry	29
Average years work experience at entry	4.2

ACADEMICS

Academic Experience Rating	**72**
Student/faculty ratio	26:1
Profs interesting rating	77
Profs accessible rating	72
% female faculty	28
% minority faculty	42

Prominent Alumni

Gilbert Gonzalez, U.S. Dept. of Agriculture Undersecretary for Rural Dev; Ernest Bromley, President & CEO of Bromley & Associates; Susan Evers, General Counsel at USAA; William Morrow, President & Vice Chairman of Grande Communications;

Academics

You can earn your MBA at exactly the speed you choose at the University of Texas at San Antonio, a "self-paced" program geared toward the needs of busy area professionals. "Most students work full-time and take one or two classes a semester (three or six semester credit hours) and finish in approximately two years," according to the school's website. Students may take up to six years to complete the degree. Classes are usually offered on weekday evenings and on weekends.

The UTSA MBA program enjoys a boost from the school's PhD programs in accounting, finance, management and organizational studies, and information technology. Faculty in these areas are active in current research in their fields. In addition, faculty members in economics and real estate also publish frequently. The school also positions itself at the vanguard of business education by seeking new and promising disciplines; it has developed an expertise and an academic program in infrastructure assurance and security. Students here praise their professors, noting that "the majority of professors are PhDs with published work and prior experience in their field. Their real-world experience allows them to relate teachings to real-world situations, which help students assimilate new material." They appreciate how "most of the professors are very interested in making sure that their students learn the material and are very accessible and very willing to help." One MBA reports, "Several professors took time on weekends for additional exam preparation for students." Students also love the relatively low cost of the program. One writes, "The greatest strength of this program is the value when comparing tuition costs to the quality of the education and the resources available."

UTSA offers three basic MBA options: a general MBA, nonthesis; a general MBA with a thesis; and a nonthesis MBA with a concentration. All options require 33 hours of coursework (beyond preparatory core courses), 21 hours of which are devoted to Foundations of Knowledge requirements (advanced courses in accounting, managerial economics, financial management, management and behavior, strategy, marketing, and decision analysis). The thesis option requires an additional six hours of electives and six hours of master's thesis credit. The nonthesis option requires 12 hours of electives. Students may use their electives to concentrate in business economics, finance, health care management, information systems, management accounting, management of technology, management science, marketing management, project management, and taxation.

Career and Placement

UTSA employs a career officer dedicated to providing counseling and placement services to graduate business students. Services include career assessment; one-on-one counseling; library services; online resume books and job postings; resume reviews; mock interviews; internships; career fairs and on-campus recruiting; career skills workshops; and networking events. UTSA MBAs appreciate the efforts but wish for something more; "We need more activities for graduate business students, more networking with alumni, and better companies to come recruit on campus," writes one student. Employers most likely to hire UTSA business graduates include HEB Grocery Company, USAA, and Dell Computers.

Student Life and Environment

UTSA is a school in transition; it "was established as a commuter school," but students note that "the last few years have seen a trend towards more traditional students and programs."

Veronica Ramirez, Supervisor, Graduate Admissions
6900 North Loop, 1604 West, San Antonio, TX 78249-0603 United States
Phone: 210-458-4330 • Fax: 210-458-4332
E-mail: graduatestudies@utsa.edu • Website: business.utsa.edu/graduate/

It is exciting to be on a campus that is becoming a real college campus for the first time. The gym is busy even at 10:00 or 11:00 at night, and it's amazing to see the amount of activity that persists on campus even in the afternoon and evening." Students also report that "the addition of the downtown campus in the urban center has allowed for full-time professionals to more efficiently intermix the professional with the academic lives." Even so, this is hardly a lively extracurricular scene for MBA. One student explains, "Most of the courses are offered after 5:00 P.M., which lends itself to many working, commuting students. In this type of environment, it is sometimes difficult to establish a sense of community." However, approximately one-third of the students in the graduate program attend school on a full-time basis. These students tend to work on campus as research and teaching assistants and are on campus most of the day. The MBA Association does its best; it is "active and aggressive in providing MBA students with access to lectures, etiquette dinners, networking opportunities, resume seminars, [and] job fairs."

UTSA's facilities earn students' praise; MBAs tell us the campus "is beautiful and safe," and that "the business building has excellent learning technology in the classrooms. Also, access to computers and research materials is widely available throughout the campus." Things are so good here that many students identify the lack of a football team as the university's most glaring weakness.

The population of the MBA program at UTSA "is very diverse," although "the predominant type is the full-time employed individual, [typically] married, in [their] late 20s or early 30s, and whose time is at a premium." Students represent "an incredibly diverse mix of professions as well as backgrounds. For example, I had a physicist from MIT and an Air Force Colonel in the same class." says one MBA. The school attracts many internationals; one student writes, "There are people from Asia, the U.S., India, and Mexico."

Admissions

Applicants to the UTSA MBA program are required to provide the school with a completed application form, official copies of transcripts from all colleges and universities attended, official GMAT scores, and a personal statement stating the applicant's career and academic goals. A current resume and two letters of reference are officially optional but are "strongly recommended" by the Admissions Office. Applicants need not have majored in business as undergraduates to gain admission. Students with non-business undergraduate degrees are typically required to complete core courses in accounting, business law, economic theory, business finance, information systems, marketing, and quantitative methods prior to beginning work on the MBA. Students who completed undergraduate work in a business field more than seven years prior to admission may also be required to complete some or all core courses.

FINANCIAL FACTS

Annual tuition (in-state/out-of-state) $5,975/$15,363

ADMISSIONS

Admissions Selectivity Rating	**76**
# of applications received	201
% applicants accepted	74
% acceptees attending	74
Average GMAT	561
Range of GMAT	520-600
Average GPA	3.25
TOEFL Required of International Students?	Yes
Minimum TOEFL (paper/computer)	500/173
Application fee	$45
International application fee	$80
Regular application deadline	7/1
Regular notification	Rolling
Deferment Available?	Yes
Maximum length of deferment	2 terms
Transfer students accepted?	Yes
Transfer application policy: Please refer to current graduate catalog.	
Non-fall admissions?	Yes
Need-blind admissions?	Yes

EMPLOYMENT PROFILE

Career Rating	**61**
# of companies recruiting on-campus	117
Average starting salary	$45,780

THE UNIVERSITY OF TULSA
COLLEGE OF BUSINESS ADMINISTRATION

GENERAL INFORMATION
Type of school	private
Environment	metropolis
Academic calendar	semester

SURVEY SAYS...
Students love Tulsa, OK
Friendly students
Happy students
Smart classrooms

STUDENTS
Enrollment of parent institution	4,172
Enrollment of MBA program	121
% male/female	50/50
% out-of-state	31
% part-time	57
% minorities	18
% international	20
Average age at entry	24
Average years work experience at entry	2

ACADEMICS
Academic Experience Rating	**81**
Student/faculty ratio	5:1
Profs interesting rating	87
Profs accessible rating	88
% female faculty	9
% minority faculty	13

Joint Degrees
MBA/JD: 4-6 years
JD/MTax: 4-6 years
Master of Engineering/Technology
Management: 3 years

Academics

The College of Business Administration at The University of Tulsa (TU) offers a number of options to meet the needs of a wide variety of students. For those in a hurry to get their degrees, UT offers a full-time MBA that can be completed (by those with undergraduate degrees in business) in 18 months. For those who work full-time, the school has a part-time program with classes that meet once a week on evenings. And for those who can't make it to campus, UT has an iMBA (Internet-mediated MBA) that requires only two visits to campus: one for orientation, the other for graduation. Many students love this final option; one iMBA student writes, "In the online MBA program, they continue to develop an understanding of 'best practices' in online education and incorporate new knowledge into the delivery of the program." Plus, "the online program also is taught by the same full-time professors who teach the campus-based courses, so the quality of instruction and level of expertise are high."

For students lacking expertise in some or all fundamental business areas, the UT MBA program commences with 8 basic foundation courses; students may apply for a waiver from any or all of these courses. The remainder of the curriculum consists of a one-hour ethics course plus eight core courses and two electives. Students may use the electives to create a specialization in accounting, taxation, finance, or MIS. MBAs report that "the finance program in risk management is great. It's very challenging and very interesting." They also appreciate how the curriculum "helps students become very comfortable and confident in their presentation and speaking skills." Students also add that "several classes provide the opportunity to express [their] own experiences and ideas, which gives a more practical feel to the material." However, some students complain that "there is too much emphasis on quantitative problems, as opposed to learning to read what the output really means." All MBAs agree, "This is a tough school that cannot be breezed through with ease."

UT is a small program, which translates into "very low student-teacher ratios" and "small class sizes," but it also means that there's a limited availability of class times. "We don't have the choice of taking some classes during the day," students say. "The program is set up for the working adults, not for the few full-timers." Luckily, "the professors at The University of Tulsa are fantastic." One student reasons, "A good professor may teach you concepts, but a great professor will teach you to think. Here at UT, the emphasis is more on understanding than remembering." Plus, "professors are very accessible," fulfilling their roles "not only as teachers, but also as professional coaches."

Career and Placement

The Career Services Office at The University of Tulsa works with all students (undergraduate and graduate) and alumni, while the College of Business provides some supplemental services, including assistance in finding summer internships for MBAs. Students report that the school provides "good networking opportunities." One student attests, "I met the CEO of my company (ConocoPhillips) in one of the business forums." But, still, other students say, "Career services needs to make more contacts and deliver a bigger variety of companies for job fairs and job opportunities." As one student explains, "Currently most of the employers recruiting from UT are local companies or government organizations. The school would increase its stature if it could get more national placements than regional ones." Currently more than 80 percent of UT graduates find jobs in the immediate region; [the majority] of the rest are international students who return home after graduation.

REBECCA HOLLAND, DIRECTOR OF GRADUATE BUSINESS PROGRAMS
BAH 217, 600 SOUTH COLLEGE AVENUE, TULSA, OK 74104-3189 UNITED STATES
PHONE: 918-631-2242 • FAX: 918-631-2142
E-MAIL: GRADUATE-BUSINESS@UTULSA.EDU • WEBSITE: WWW.CBA.UTULSA.EDU

Top employers of UT MBAs include AFN Communications, ALLTEL, Bank of Oklahoma, Citgo, Crosby Group, Datatel, First Omni, IBM, KPMG, MCI Worldcom, Nordam, Williams, and Wiltel (formerly Williams Communications).

Student Life and Environment

The University of Tulsa "is not a party school," because "students have to study 24/7 to survive," students say. For those who can afford to take a breather, "there are a number of clubs at the university" with themes ranging "from the outdoors to sports cars." And if you want to let off some steam, "the new gym facility is wonderful. It includes three basketball courts, an indoor and outdoor track, and the latest in cardio and weight-lifting equipment."

MBAs like that "UT attracts focused, career-minded students who tend to be achievement-oriented without being competitive." MBAs say, "Students are mature enough to invest in relationships and group activities that add educational value," which creates "a warm family atmosphere where students and professors can develop a rapport with one another." The only fly in the ointment is the occasional slacker. It seems the administration "needs to be more selective about who they allow into the MBA program. There are too many students on probation for poor grades," according to some MBAs.

Hometown Tulsa—Oklahoma's second-largest city—is large enough to support an AA baseball team, an arena football franchise, and a motor racing circuit. The city is home to Oral Roberts University, an opera company, a theater, and a performing-arts center.

Admissions

Applicants to the MBA program at UT must provide the school with a completed application, official transcripts for all undergraduate and graduate work, GMAT scores, TOEFL scores (international students only), three letters of recommendation, and a resume. UT offers a GM minority scholarship in an effort to increase the program's diversity.

FINANCIAL FACTS

Annual tuition	$13,230
Books and supplies	$1,000
Room & board (on/off-campus)	$5,886/$6,300
% of students receiving aid	20
Average award package	$15,330
Average grant	$10,080
Average student loan debt	$23,375

ADMISSIONS

Admissions Selectivity Rating	75
# of applications received	85
% applicants accepted	67
% acceptees attending	50
Average GMAT	546
Range of GMAT	450-750
Average GPA	3.44
TOEFL Required of International Students?	Yes
Minimum TOEFL (paper/computer)	575/232
Application fee	$30
International application fee	$30
Regular application deadline	Rolling
Regular notification	Rolling
Deferment Available?	Yes
Maximum length of deferment	1 year
Transfer students accepted?	Yes
Transfer application policy: Up to 6 credit hours may be transferred.	
Non-fall admissions?	Yes
Need-blind admissions?	Yes

APPLICANTS ALSO LOOK AT

Oklahoma State University, University of Oklahoma.

EMPLOYMENT PROFILE

Career Rating	77	Grads employed by field:	
Placement rate (%)	93	Other	5
# of companies recruiting on-campus	122		
% grads employed immediately	75		
Average starting salary	$56,100		

UNIVERSITY OF UTAH
DAVID ECCLES SCHOOL OF BUSINESS

GENERAL INFORMATION
Type of school	public
Environment	metropolis
Academic calendar	semester

SURVEY SAYS...
Students love Salt Lake City, UT
Friendly students
Happy students
Smart classrooms

STUDENTS
Enrollment of parent institution	25,500
Enrollment of MBA program	550
% male/female	69/31
% out-of-state	35
% part-time	66
% minorities	6
% international	13
Average age at entry	28
Average years work experience at entry	4

ACADEMICS
Academic Experience Rating	**85**
Student/faculty ratio	5:1
Profs interesting rating	85
Profs accessible rating	80
% female faculty	28
% minority faculty	16

Joint Degrees
MBA/JD: 3-4 years
MBA/March: 3-4 years

Prominent Alumni
Stephen Covey, Co-Founder, VP, Franklin Covey; Spencer Eccles, Chairman, CEO, First Security Corp.; Senator E. Jake Garn, Former US Senator; J. Willard Marriott, Chairman, CEO, Pres., Marriott Corp.; Geoffrey Wooley, Founding Partner, Dominion Ventures.

Academics

The David Eccles School of Business (DESB) at the University of Utah is an up-and-coming business program that students say is "still figuring out its culture and personality." Currently its strengths lie in accounting, finance, and marketing, but lots of interesting and unusual areas are also developing on the school's Salt Lake City campus. Students report that "DESB has unique offerings, like a nonprofit consulting class (set up by the Net Impact chapter)" and the New Venture Development Center, which capitalizes on developments throughout the university. One student explains, "There are some very exciting opportunities in genetic-based medicine, biotechnologies, medical testing, and medical digital-imaging technologies coming out of this university, and I am working to bring these to market through the New Venture Development Center. It is a fabulous opportunity."

Because Eccles "is still a small program, it is very personalized," which students appreciate. They also like the "class curriculum that provides a strong foundation for business students, yet allows them to tailor a unique program to fit their own wants and needs." The school is also flexible enough to adapt to the schedules of its part-timers; one student writes, "The business school has done a great job implementing a professional-based MBA program for working students."

Students cite many areas of strength at the university. The entrepreneurial program, students say, is "extremely pragmatic with professors that have more than succeeded out in the dog-eat-dog world." Finance professors "approach their responsibility with incredible seriousness, with a challenging program that teaches students the critical eye of analysis [and] shows them how to dig deep to find the critical details that make or break investments. This is so much more than the plug-and-chug model." The marketing program "includes a Nobel Prize nominee." Students say, "These people know their stuff. And if you want to learn, they're willing to take the time and make the effort to teach you, inside and outside of class." Throughout the program, "the faculty and administration at the University of Utah provides a broad mix of people and styles. There are definite thought leaders in each respect and field that are able to teach and do things that make being here a very worthwhile experience," some students note.

Career and Placement

The MBA career services office at Eccles is "very active. They are always having student networking nights and sending out info for new job postings." Students agree that their strengths lie in specialized areas. One student explains, "There are good opportunities to network in accounting and finance, but there is limited on-campus recruiting in investment banking and venture capital. For most careers in accounting and finance, there are many great opportunities for on-campus interviews. I already have a full-time job set up for after graduation. I got [a job] offer early in November, and I would say that more than half of my fellow students are in the same boat. Believe me, that takes off a lot of stress." Some MBAs—especially those in areas that are not optimally served—feel that "Career services is understaffed, making job searching an additional responsibility for the student above and beyond their classes and course work."

Top employers of Eccles MBAs include 3M, Accenture, Deloitte Touche Tohmatsu, eBay, FedEx, GE-OEC Medical Systems, Goldman Sachs, IBM, Ford, Intel, Intermountain Health Care, KPMG, PacifiCorp, PricewaterhouseCoopers, UPS, Wells Fargo, and Zions Bank.

Student Life and Environment

The DESB is housed in a new, up-to-date building in which "almost all classrooms have amphitheater seating with wireless connections and power plugs at each workstation. The professor can show you something in Excel, and you can follow along right there instead of trying to write notes and practice it on your laptop later." One student adds, "The tie-in to technology has been a great asset. All professors use WebCT to post syllabi and course work. I love this easy access to everything." Eccles MBAs agree that "the program technology is cutting-edge. Everyone in my program got a free laptop. They just work it into the tuition, but you keep the laptop at the end of the program, and you have three years of free tech support."

While "the Eccles program allows for a social life, not many students take advantage of it." One professional MBA student explains, "Most everyone in my classes works full-time. Also, many people have families. Therefore, life at school is limited to class time and job searches. There is not a strong sense of community or social connection." Full-timers do enjoy a more well-rounded MBA experience that includes "excellent clubs: the U Venture Fund, the Lassonde New Venture Development Center, the Utah Entrepreneur Center, UTEC, and the Smart Start Mentor program." Eccles also hosts "great guest lecturers. I just got back from a lecture given by Lynn Turner, the former chief accountant of the SEC. There were about 40 of us in a classroom and the discussion was very informal with plenty of time for everyone to get their questions answered," one student says. They also "schedule occasional 'Attitude Adjustment Seminars' where MBA students network with the wider community. Actually, the 'seminars' are just people getting together at a club for a few drinks. Alumni, mentors, faculty, and staff are all invited. The Graduate Business Student Association also sponsors exciting campouts, tailgate parties, and pizza parties."

Students agree that "the Utah community is very friendly, safe, and active. Housing near the school is plentiful and public transportation is new this year but very accessible and helpful."

Admissions

The Eccles admissions department requires applicants to provide the following: an undergraduate transcript demonstrating a GPA of at least 3.0, proof of completion of a college-level statistics course, GMAT scores (minimum score of 50th percentile in math required or college algebra must be retaken), letters of recommendation, personal statements, and a resume. International students whose first language is not English must take the TOEFL and TSE. To increase campus diversity, the school has "several privately donated scholarships reserved for underrepresented groups and to help [them] build the gender, ethnic, and geographic diversity of [their] student body."

FINANCIAL FACTS

Annual tuition (in-state/out-of-state)	$9,042/$20,385
Fees	$337
Books and supplies	$1,500
Room & board (on/off-campus)	$8,000/$11,000
% of students receiving grants	37
Average grant	$12,900

ADMISSIONS

Admissions Selectivity Rating	83
# of applications received	164
% applicants accepted	67
% acceptees attending	50
Average GMAT	617
Range of GMAT	560-720
Average GPA	3.4
TOEFL Required of International Students?	Yes
Minimum TOEFL (paper/computer)	600/250
Application fee	$45
International application fee	$65
Regular application deadline	2/15
Regular notification	4/10
Transfer students accepted?	Yes
Transfer application policy: In special circumstances, up to 9 credit hours may be transferred into the program from another program.	
Need-blind admissions?	Yes

EMPLOYMENT PROFILE

Career Rating	77	Grads employed by field	%: avg. salary
Placement rate (%)	91	Accounting	13: $52,062
% grads employed immediately	54	Finance	11: $40,423
% grads employed within three months	91	Marketing	4: $51,435
Average starting salary	$51,188	Operations	2: $44,482
		Consulting	4: $55,000
		General Management	8: $58,500
		Other	4: $62,500

UNIVERSITY OF VERMONT
SCHOOL OF BUSINESS ADMINISTRATION

GENERAL INFORMATION
Type of school   public
Environment   city
Academic calendar   fall/spring

SURVEY SAYS...
Students love Burlington, VT
Friendly students
Happy students
Smart classrooms

STUDENTS
Enrollment of parent institution	10,940
Enrollment of MBA program	59
% male/female	54/46
% out-of-state	40
% part-time	71
% minorities	5
% international	10
Average age at entry	31
Average years work experience at entry	9

ACADEMICS
Academic Experience Rating	**79**
Student/faculty ratio	3:1
Profs interesting rating	83
Profs accessible rating	72
% female faculty	27

Prominent Alumni
Doug Goldsmith, Rock of Ages, CFO & VP; Elisabeth Robert, VT Teddy Bear, Inc., Pres., CFO & Treasurer; Katherine B. Crosett, Kalex Enterprises, Inc., Principal; Alexander D. Crosett, III, Kalex Enterprises, Inc., Principal.

Academics

"The best—make that 'only'—MBA program in Burlington" is how one student at the UVM School of Business Administration wryly encapsulates his school, but this program has a lot more going for it than just its geographic monopoly. With approximately 70 students in the program, UVM can offer its MBA students all the personal attention they desire. Plus, with a large university (and large university resources) looming in the background, UVM MBAs can benefit from "interaction with other programs." An environmental engineer earning his MBA here, for example, praises his easy access to the Rubenstein School of Environment and Natural Resources and the Gund Institute of Ecological Economics.

UVM offers both full-time and part-time options in the MBA but schedules classes for the convenience of part-timers, most of whom have full-time jobs. Nearly all classes meet twice weekly in 75-minute evening sessions. "The night classes offer more flexibility to those who work," one student explains. The program is divided into two parts: the core level, comprised of six required courses covering business fundamentals (marketing, accounting, organization, finance, business law, and production and operations management); and the advanced level, comprised of six distribution requirements covering six functions, three electives, and an integrative capstone course.

Students praise the UVM faculty for "bringing in current events into the classroom." They also appreciate that "professors are very accessible, willing to help with coursework or networking, and are generally good at encouraging stimulating discussion in the classroom." Administrators are also "readily accessible. In fact, the director of the program offers to talk with every student at course-registration time." There are, of course, drawbacks to all small programs, and UVM is no exception. One student warns, "The frustrating part is the limited number of courses offered each semester. Moreover, many of the courses are offered at the same time, making it impossible to take all the courses you want."

Career and Placement

The Career Services Office at UVM, students tell us, "puts very little effort into graduate placement for careers. The people currently in career services are trying hard, but they are starting from scratch in the graduate area as there is no history of on-campus recruiting. There needs to be!" The office could start, one student suggests, by "offering more networking events. I think that they are trying to improve on this area by putting career counselors in place in the business building. We'll see."

RALPH SWENSON, DIRECTOR OF GRADUATE ADMISSIONS
333 WATERMAN BUILDING, BURLINGTON, VT 05405 UNITED STATES
PHONE: 802-656-0655 • FAX: 802-656-4078 • E-MAIL: MBA@BSAD.UVM.EDU
WEBSITE: WWW.BSAD.UVM.EDU/ACADEMICS/DEGREE+PROGRAMS/MBA/

Student Life and Environment

Students tell us that "there is a big difference between part-time students," who make up about two-thirds of the UVM MBA student body, "and full-time students. Part-timers and older, have full-time jobs and have done little or no prior business coursework. Full-timers are younger, typically have a business-related undergraduate degree, and are unemployed. Full-timers and part-timers mingle well despite being in different life stages. They frequently hang out together outside of school." Part-timers "often work, attend classes at night, and have families to attend to. They burn the candle at both ends—and look like it!" The student body boasts a solid contingent of engineers as well as a sizeable international population.

Full-timers here report "a healthy balance of work and leisure. We work hard but have plenty of valuable diversions, such as snowboarding at nearby mountains." While some feel that "it would be better to have more events for the MBA students so that [they] could network amongst [them]selves as well as potentially other members in the community," most here accept the current situation as the unavoidable result of a tiny MBA program. Students tell us, "Burlington is a great small city with lots to offer, especially the quality and variety of live music and restaurants." Montreal is only a two-hour drive from Burlington; Ottawa, Ontario, and Albany, NY, can be reached in three hours.

Admissions

The admissions committee for the UVM MBA program considers academic record, previous work experience, GMAT scores, writing ability, and letters of recommendation in making its decisions. Applicants must submit official transcripts for all college and graduate work, an official GMAT score report, a resume, a personal essay, and a completed application. The average GMAT score of admitted students is 600; their average undergraduate GPA is 3.2. No student may begin the MBA program without first completing prerequisite courses in macroeconomics, microeconomics, calculus, statistics, and computer usage. Students who have completed undergraduate degrees in business within the last five years may waive the prerequisite courses; others may place out of the classes by passing qualifying examinations.

FINANCIAL FACTS

Annual tuition (in-state/out-of-state)	$9,088/$22,728
Fees	$896
Books and supplies	$400
Room & board (on-campus)	$7,016
Average grant	$2,000

ADMISSIONS

Admissions Selectivity Rating	81
# of applications received	46
% applicants accepted	67
% acceptees attending	74
Average GMAT	586
Range of GMAT	470-720
Average GPA	3.3
TOEFL Required of International Students?	Yes
Minimum TOEFL (paper/computer)	550/213
Application fee	$25
International application fee	$25
Regular application deadline	Rolling
Regular notification	Rolling
Deferment Available?	Yes
Maximum length of deferment	1 year
Non-fall admissions?	Yes
Need-blind admissions?	Yes

APPLICANTS ALSO LOOK AT

Boston College, Boston University, University of Connecticut, University of Massachusetts—Amherst, University of New Hampshire

EMPLOYMENT PROFILE	
Career Rating	60*
# of companies recruiting on-campus	20

UNIVERSITY OF VIRGINIA
DARDEN GRADUATE SCHOOL OF BUSINESS ADMINISTRATION

GENERAL INFORMATION

Type of school	public
Environment	city
Academic calendar	semester

SURVEY SAYS...
Friendly students
Smart classrooms
Solid preparation in:
General management
Teamwork

STUDENTS

Enrollment of parent institution	18,978
Enrollment of MBA program	620
% male/female	79/21
% out-of-state	79
% minorities	13
% international	27
Average age at entry	28
Average years work experience at entry	4

ACADEMICS

Academic Experience Rating	**95**
Profs interesting rating	99
Profs accessible rating	98
% female faculty	18
% minority faculty	4

Joint Degrees
MBA/JD: 4 years
MBA/MA in Asian studies 3 years
MBA/MA in government or foreign affairs: 3 years
MBA/ME: 3 years;
MBA/MSN: 3 years;
MBA/PhD: 4 years

Prominent Alumni
Douglas R. Lebda, Founder and former CEO, Lending Tree, Inc.; Steven S Reinemund, Chairman of the Board and CEO, PepsiCo, Inc.; Lawton Fitt, Secretary of The Royal Academy of Arts, London; George David, Chairman and CEO of United Technologies Corp.; E. Follin Smith, Exec. VP, CFO, CAO Constellation Energy Group.

Academics

Most business schools employ case studies in their curricula, but few incorporate them so integrally or so thoroughly as does the Darden Graduate School of Business Administration at the University of Virginia. The case method, which permeates the entire first-year curriculum, requires both a faculty capable of teaching multidisciplinary approaches to problem-solving, and a student body dedicated enough to spend hours a day preparing, reviewing, and discussing cases outside the classroom. The case method process simulates the function of modern managers in a wide variety of different industries, products, processes and styles of management. Fortunately, Darden has both.

Students agree that the case method is demanding. One student notes, "The learning curve is incredibly steep, and the workload is high, but this gives the best base for learning." Another student observes, "There is no doubt that the workload at Darden, especially during the first semester, is probably the toughest of any business school, but you learn to prioritize, rely on your learning team, and think on your feet in a dynamic classroom environment led by exceptional faculty." Because the case method stresses in-class discussion, "you really learn the importance of being able to articulate your arguments."

First-year studies at Darden are especially grueling. Students have revealed that "all the courses are required, you have no scheduling freedom, and the workload is [a] killer. This boot camp ensures that everyone is equally prepared in all core courses." Fortunately, students now report that "curriculum is changing for the first year, where students will be able to choose electives in the fourth quarter." Indeed, first year students will now be able to choose three first year program electives from eleven options during the fourth quarter. The first year program electives are extensions of the core courses and all relate to preparing students for summer internships. Some students complain that "the course work can be too demanding. At certain times of the year, the volume of work necessary exceeds the hours in the day. You have to learn to prioritize, or you won't succeed." Most, however, say that they "wouldn't change a thing." The second-year curriculum "is more like other schools. You pick all your courses, times, and professors, and the workload is much lighter," one student comments.

Through it all, Darden MBAs benefit from what they perceive to be "the best teaching faculty of any business school. The professors are outstanding, and they are very accessible to students. You simply fire an E-mail, and within a day or two, you have an appointment set up with them." One student notes, "It is amazing how well the faculty runs case discussions, which is the most difficult type of teaching. Not many professors could survive in an atmosphere of constant questions and the need to link together so many diverse approaches to create a better understanding for the class."

Career and Placement

Many Darden MBAs would like to see a wider range of companies recruiting on campus. One student explains, "A lot of banks and financial institutions recruit here; we could use more marketing and general-management type opportunities." The school reports that this issue is being addressed as many new companies from Marketing and General Management industries have joined on-grounds recruiting. Students do however, applaud the "extremely helpful and tight-knit alumni network" earns students' applause. MBAs say, "[The alumni network] is among the greatest strengths of Darden. The alumni are extremely helpful when looking for employment."

The 2004 to 2005 MBA recruiters at Darden included Citigroup Global Corporate & Investment Bank, McKinsey & Company, Lehman Brothers, The Boston Consulting

Dawna Clarke, Director of Admissions
PO Box 6550, Charlottesville, VA 22906 United States
Phone: 434-924-7281 • Fax: 434-243-5033
E-mail: darden@virginia.edu • Website: www.darden.virginia.edu

Group, General Electric Company, Pfizer Inc., Booz Allen Hamilton, Capital One Financial, Bank of America Securities, Bank of America, Cargill, Bain and Company, Booz Allen Hamilton and Bear Sterns and Co.

Student Life and Environment

Life at Darden is dictated in large part by the curriculum. Students warn that "the first year is really tough, and the stress is enormous. There is very little time in the first semester for anything but school and resume [preparation]. Many of us are here from 8:00 A.M. to 10:00 or 11:00 P.M. It eases up in the spring, although at that point, recruiting takes up a lot of time." Most MBAs try to find time for at least a little work break, as the popular "Thursday Night Drinking Club (TNDC). The students are a blast when you get them out. There isn't a ton of weekday socialization for first-years who have learning team at night, but once the weekend comes, watch out."

The emphasis on teamwork builds a strong student community, making the program "like a family. There are always school-related activities going on ranging from the Chili Cookoff to the Latin American Student Association Carnival." Extracurricular clubs abound; students say that "the [Darden Leadership Forum] is superb, inviting phenomenal business executives to speak and raise our awareness of the power of business today," while the student-run Darden Capital Management "manages over $2 million of the school's endowment. It provides a fantastic hands-on learning experience for future asset managers that few other top MBA schools offer. It's been a blast!"

Students love "cosmopolitan" hometown Charlottesville and call it "a great college town." One student says, "I can't think of a better place to spend two years than at Mr. Jefferson's university. [There are] lots of things to do outside of class; great football and ACC basketball." One student adds, "The city is both quaint and refined. If you are into the outdoors, hiking, camping, and seasonal skiing are just 30 minutes away. If you are into food, C'ville has a ton of good restaurants and bars. If you are single, there are tons of other grad students in the law, medicine, and other grad schools, as well as a huge undergrad population. As for family folks, the city is safe and very family-friendly. I am enjoying myself."

Admissions

According to Darden's viewbook, the admissions committee looks for "breadth of perspective, international exposure, and diversity," as well as evidence of motivation, interpersonal skills, and leadership in prospective students. The school points out that over 99 percent of successful applicants have full-time work experience. Applicants must submit academic transcripts, GMAT scores, TOEFL scores (non-native English speakers only), four essays, two letters of recommendation, and a resume. Ideally, all prospects should have a personal interview.

FINANCIAL FACTS

Annual tuition (in-state/out-of-state)	$32,300/$37,300
Books and supplies	$2,318
Room & board	$13,627
% of students receiving aid	86
% of first-year students receiving aid	80
% of students receiving loans	83
% of students receiving grants	52
Average award package	$30,618
Average grant	$14,000
Average student loan debt	$62,291

ADMISSIONS

Admissions Selectivity Rating	94
# of applications received	2,110
% applicants accepted	14
% acceptees attending	40
Average GMAT	680
Range of GMAT	650-710
Average GPA	3.3
TOEFL Required of International Students?	Yes
Minimum TOEFL (paper/computer)	650/280
Application fee	$140
International application fee	$140
Regular application deadline	6/5
Regular notification	8/5
Application Deadline/Notification	
Round 1:	11/4 / 12/4
Round 2:	12/4 / 2/5
Round 3:	1/5 / 3/5
Round 4:	6/5 / 8/5
Deferment Available?	Yes
Maximum length of deferment	On a case by case basis.
Transfer students accepted?	Yes
Transfer application policy: Transfer students are accepted but credits cannot be transferred.	
Need-blind admissions?	Yes

EMPLOYMENT PROFILE

Career Rating	92	Grads employed by field	%
% grads employed immediately	64	Finance	33
% grads employed within three months	84	Marketing	16
Average starting salary	$85,000	Operations	2
		Consulting	6
		General Mangement	25
		Accounting	5

UNIVERSITY OF WASHINGTON
UNIVERSITY OF WASHINGTON BUSINESS SCHOOL

Academics

"If you want to get a job in the Pacific Northwest, the University of Washington is the best place you can go," students at this small, prestigious b-school say. That's especially true for folks looking to remain in Seattle after graduation; UW has a big leg up on the competition there because "there is no other major school in Seattle, where there [are] a number of first-class companies." But it's not just location that gives UW its competitive edge; MBAs explain that "the overall academic experience is great here. We are learning all the classic elements of a b-school education in marketing, finance, and operations. There are also innovative programs, such as the e-business program."

UW's areas of strength are extensive; students praise the programs in accounting, e-business, entrepreneurship, finance, and IT. They also love the "outstanding core faculty," who deliver "a first-year core that is extremely challenging, with a broad exposure to the kind of wide variety of disciplines that any businessperson should know about." MBAs report favorably that "all of the first-year core professors make themselves available for a professor-night dinner once each quarter, where we get to sit down with them, drink wine, and get to know them better. It's a great example of how accessible our faculty are."

Second-year students say that their biggest problem is that the school offers too much value. One student explains, "I wish I could make more time in my second year to take more of the electives. There are more must-have courses from must-have professors than I have room in my schedule. It's almost too bad I have to go back out into the workplace, but then I'm excited to practice what I've learned." The administration earns students' thumbs up because "they run things smoothly. They facilitate integration of speakers, networking events, and other activities with classes very well," and they "are behind students and like to make sure [that] students are having a great experience in b-school. They are [also] open to new ideas and willing to try new things." Administrators are currently at work on remedying the school's chief drawback, which is the facility in which it's housed. One MBA notes, "We need a new building. The building we're in is dated and unattractive. Fortunately, there is a plan to build a new building in the next four or five years."

Career and Placement

The Business Connections Center at the University of Washington Business School connects students to area businesses through its MBA mentor program, which "offers students the opportunity to learn about the way business is practiced today, under the guidance of top executives." The school also sets up "Road Shows," in which UW MBAs travel to major cities (like New York, Los Angeles, San Francisco, and San Diego) to network with alumni and area businesses. Students are generally satisfied with the services provided by the BCC, although a number complained that the office is "a bit understaffed."

Top employers of UW MBAs include Alaska Airlines, Amazon.com, AT&T Wireless, Bank of America, Boeing Company, Booz Allen Hamilton, Cap Gemini Ernst & Young, Deloitte Touche Tohmatsu, GE Capital, Hewlett-Packard, Hitachi Consulting, Intel, Microsoft, Paccar, Phillips Medical Systems, Samsung Electronics, Starbucks, Tektronix, Washington Mutual, and Wells Fargo. Approximately 1 in 10 MBAs begins their post-degree career outside the U.S.

Student Life and Environment

UW MBAs agree that there's "great camaraderie among students" in their program. One student says, "The culture is one where students are friendly and helpful in making sure that no one is left behind. Second-year MBA students here lead review sessions to help the first-year students get through the first quarter of the core. In addition, every student is easily approachable and more than willing to share his or her insights into a particular class, the job search, or even how to handle one's personal life. The culture here has allowed me to make friends for life!" Students also appreciate that their classmates are "smart and ambitious but very down-to-earth," with "strong individual and entrepreneurial mind-sets."

Students are also "very active in clubs and efforts to continue developing the program." The program also enjoys a "strong sense of community involvement through volunteerism and fundraising for charity organizations." For example, "everyone participates in Challenge for Charity! We are the West Coast winner year after year, despite the fact that we are the smallest school." As one student explains, "Life here is balanced. We have a finance club, but we also have a hiking club. The same person who interned at a Venture Capital firm over the summer volunteers with the Special Olympics on weekends." Quite a few students at the university "are also involved in initiatives to study how to better market the school."

Leisure fun is abetted by the many options available in Seattle with "its proximity to great hiking, biking, and skiing" and "great microbrews." There's plenty of socializing within the school, too; for example, students "have a program where [they] invite professors to students' homes for potlucks with other students. Typically 10 to 12 students attend each potluck, which creates a relaxed atmosphere [for students] to get to know the professor." Students add that "every other week, there is a 'TG' in the MBA Lounge with food and a keg. We get a chance to relax at the end of a hard week and party a little bit with our classmates. Some of my classmates have become my best friends, and we often go out together." All in all, "social interaction [is] very strong through formal and informal student gatherings and bar nights."

Admissions

The admissions office at University of Washington says, "We consider a broad spectrum of factors. No one factor is weighed more heavily than others. We also seek a highly diverse class in terms of academic background, work experience, and personal experience. Applicants from nonbusiness backgrounds and unique backgrounds are encouraged to apply." Applicants must submit all undergraduate and graduate transcripts, letters of recommendation, a personal statement, a resume, and GMAT scores; an interview is by invitation. To increase minority representation in the MBA program, "the University of Washington sponsors campus-visit programs and receptions for students from underrepresented minority groups. We have scholarships specifically targeting underrepresented minority candidates."

FINANCIAL FACTS

Annual tuition (in-state/out-of-state)	$14,780/$24,720
Fees	$400
Books and supplies	$1,700
Room & board (on/off-campus)	$9,050/$10,600
% of students receiving aid	78
% of first-year students receiving aid	68
% of students receiving loans	68
% of students receiving grants	46
Average award package	$14,450
Average grant	$8,095
Average student loan debt	$22,430

ADMISSIONS

Admissions Selectivity Rating	93
# of applications received	633
% applicants accepted	41
% acceptees attending	38
Average GMAT	677
Range of GMAT	630-730
Average GPA	3.45
TOEFL Required of International Students?	Yes
Minimum TOEFL (paper/computer)	600/250
Application fee	$65
International application fee	$65
Regular application deadline	1/15
Regular notification	4/1
Application Deadline	
Round 1:	11/15
Round 2:	1/15
Round 3:	3/15
Transfer students accepted?	Yes

Transfer application policy: Transfer applicants should apply as any other new student. The status of a transfer student is determined on a case by case basis, depending on the work completed at another school.

Need-blind admissions?	Yes

APPLICANTS ALSO LOOK AT

Arizona State University, Indiana University, Seattle University, University of California, Berkeley, University of Illinois at Urbana-Champaign, University of North Carolina at Chapel Hill, University of Southern California.

EMPLOYMENT PROFILE

		Grads employed by field	%: avg. salary
Career Rating	90	Finance	20: $68,637
Placement rate (%)	97	Human Resources	1: $68,000
% grads employed immediately	84	Marketing	26: $76,500
Average starting salary	$72,241	Operations	4: $74,125
		Consulting	6: $74,167
		General Management	10: $72,000
		Global Management	1: $82,000

UNIVERSITY OF WISCONSIN—MADISON
SCHOOL OF BUSINESS

GENERAL INFORMATION
Type of school	public
Environment	city
Academic calendar	semester

SURVEY SAYS...
Students love Madison, WI
Friendly students
Happy students
Smart classrooms
Solid preparation in:
Teamwork
Communication/interpersonal skills
Presentation skills

STUDENTS
Enrollment of parent institution	41,588
Enrollment of MBA program	342
% male/female	66/34
% out-of-state	58
% part-time	31
% minorities	13
% international	25
Average age at entry	28
Average years work experience at entry	4.4

ACADEMICS
Academic Experience Rating	**95**
Student/faculty ratio	4:1
Profs interesting rating	87
Profs accessible rating	87
% female faculty	19
% minority faculty	13
Joint Degrees	
MBA/JD: 4 years	

Prominent Alumni
Curt S. Culver, Pres., CEO, Director, and Chairman, MGIC Corp.; David J. Lesar, Chairman, Pres., and CEO, Halliburton Company.

Academics

The MBA program at University of Wisconsin—Madison has always been a solid, affordable choice, but it has set its aim higher in recent years. Students report that "the MBA program is undergoing a significant change in its structure." All students are required to align with an academic center "associated with a field of specialization. These centers maintain alumni contacts and a close connection to the business community, and they allow for outstanding faculty and student preparation for cutting-edge aspects of business management." Students recognize many advantages to the new approach. One student writes, "My specialization, the AC Nielsen Center for Marketing Research, is the best in the field. We had over 10 companies come to campus recruiting interns in the first semester extending multiple offers. I stopped interviewing at three offers. I couldn't be happier with my career prospects and the power of the network I will develop through my center!"

Other forthcoming changes to the program include a transition to a lockstep curriculum in the 2004 to 2005 year; students believe "this new system will allow for more overlap between courses." The future will also bring a facilities upgrade—a $40 million MBA addition to the School of Business is scheduled to open in fall 2007. Even without these changes, students would probably find little to fault at UW—Madison. They praise the school's offerings in arts administration, brand management, entrepreneurship, marketing, real-estate, and supply-chain management. Students also boast that "there are a number of resources for graduate students including the graduate computing lab, graduate advisors, and the academic center. The amount of academic support available to graduate students is impressive."

All MBAs at UW—Madison are a happy lot. And why shouldn't they be, given that "Madison consistently ranks high across all business majors, not to mention many other programs on campus. It is the ability to do many things and do them better than anyone else that sets Madison apart. Many schools excel in academics, while others are in support for students, and some in diversity. In comparison, Madison is at the top of its game across the board."

Career and Placement

Students report that, through MBA Career Services, their peers "have had great success getting interviews, internships, and job offers." Students' job searches are aided by alumni, "who have very strong ties to the school and are very helpful when students approach them," and especially by the directors of the academic centers.

Major employers of UW—Madison MBAs include Abbott Laboratories, Allstate Investments, Best Buy, The Clorox Company, Deloitte Touche Tohmatsu, Freddie Mac, General Electric, General Motors Corporation, W.W. Grainger Corporation, Guidant Corporation, Hewlett-Packard, Honeywell, IBM, Intel Corporation, and Kraft Foods. UW—Madison grads find employment across the country and around the world. About 1 in 10 head west for their first post-graduation jobs; approximately eight percent take jobs outside the United States.

Student Life and Environment

Life in the UW—Madison MBA program offers "a great balance between studying, social life, involvement on campus and in the community, and forward-looking career-networking opportunities," according to students. "Because the school is small, everyone knows everyone else," and "as a result, it's a very close-knit group of people. We hang

BETSY KACIZAK, DIRECTOR OF ADMISSIONS AND FINANCIAL AID
3150 GRAINGER HALL, 975 UNIVERSITY AVENUE, MADISON, WI 53706 UNITED STATES
PHONE: 608-262-4000 • FAX: 608-265-4192
E-MAIL: MBA@BUS.WISC.EDU • WEBSITE: WWW.BUS.WISC.EDU/MBA

out together outside of class a lot, which is great," MBAs say. Though the majority of students are from out of state, few have trouble adjusting to the UW milieu. One sanguine student reports, "We like cheese, bratwurst, beer, and sunny days. We boast a hard-working Midwestern work ethic and yet everyone is happy. I mean, everyone waves, smiles, and says hello."

MBAs observe that "the graduate student organizations have a huge impact on student life at UW. The Graduate Business Association sponsors a weekly happy hour, 'TAPS,' that is well attended," as well as town-hall meetings, community-service projects, lunches with the dean, and social gatherings. UW—Madison has clubs and associations dedicated to nearly every major and interest. MBAs also tell us that UW—Madison is especially accommodating to students with families. One student writes, "My family is hugely important to me. We are absolutely ecstatic to be here at UW—Madison. The Joint Ventures Club has been a key source of family and couples activities for us, and we have made many great friends through the club."

The city of Madison is widely regarded as a great place to live, and UW—Madison MBAs don't diverge from the consensus. They explain that "Madison is a great city for students" because it "gives students a positive, exciting environment in which to learn. There are great public libraries to augment the university's extensive resources. Also, there's a plethora of social and recreational options when students need a break (everything from a beer at the union to sailing on the lakes)." One student observes, "There are a ton of things to do here: sporting/outdoor activities, dance, music, films, theater, bars, and everything in between. Graduate students enjoy the myriad of sporting events at UW, and it is easy to get caught up in the Badger hysteria!" Another student notes, "The advantage of a large university is how much free or cheap stuff is available including the fact that most of the arts organizations in town offer discounted student tickets." The only drawback: "Winters are tough. But spring and fall are spectacular."

Admissions

"The admissions committee looks at all aspects of an applicant's profile including work experience, academic performance, standardized test scores, essays, and letters of recommendation," according to UW—Madison. All applicants must submit transcripts, recent GMAT scores (within the past five years), TOEFL scores (international students), letters of recommendation, essays, and a resume showing a minimum of two years of work experience (exceptional candidates may be admitted with less work experience). The school uses all of the following to increase its population of minority/disadvantaged students: the Consortium for Graduate Study in Management, Minority Fellowship Program, and advanced opportunity fellowships.

FINANCIAL FACTS

Annual tuition (in-state/out-of-state)	$9,776/$25,216
Fees	$612
Books and supplies	$830
Room & board (on-campus)	$9,230
% of students receiving aid	65
% of first-year students receiving aid	50
% of students receiving grants	65
Average award package	$7,749
Average grant	$7,500

ADMISSIONS

Admissions Selectivity Rating	96
# of applications received	524
% applicants accepted	32
% acceptees attending	66
Average GMAT	658
Range of GMAT	620-700
Average GPA	3.38
TOEFL Required of International Students?	Yes
Minimum TOEFL (paper/computer)	600/250
Application fee	$45
International application fee	$45
Regular application deadline	6/1
Regular notification	Rolling
Application Deadline/Notification	
Round 1:	1/13 / 2/17
Round 2:	3/3 / 4/7
Round 3:	4/14 / 5/19
Round 4:	6/1 / 6/20
Early decision program?	Yes
ED Deadline/Notification	11/18 / 12/23
Need-blind admissions?	Yes

Career Rating	86	Grads employed by field	%: avg. salary
Placement rate (%)	82	Finance	38: $75,171
% grads employed immediately	60	Human Resources	2: $68,500
Average starting salary	$72,720	Marketing	22: $73,346
		MIS	2: NR
		Operations	14: $73,483
		Consulting	6: $74,000
		General Management	5: $69,417
		Other	11: $64,604

University of Wisconsin—Whitewater
College of Business and Economics

Academics

Since the early 1900s, University of Wisconsin—Whitewater has been known as "the state business school of Wisconsin," a place where students can receive solid, affordable undergraduate and graduate business degrees at a reasonable cost. Whitewater serves its admirable role with distinction; its accounting department, for example, is widely regarded as one of the most effective in the nation due to its graduates' excellent success rate on the CPA exam. Whitewater also excels in several technology-driven areas. Its Management Computer Systems Program is consistently ranked among the best of its kind by the Association of Information Technology Professionals, while the joint degree offered by the Department of Business Education and the Computer and Network Administration has been repeatedly recognized as a Program of Excellence by the National Association for Career and Technical Education (ACTE).

The Whitewater MBA program offers concentrations in accounting, decision support systems, finance, human resource management, international business, IT management, management, marketing, technology and training, and operations & supply chain management, as well as a master of science in computer information systems and a master of professional accountancy. Students appreciate the breadth of choices as well as the variety of full-time and part-time options the school provides for their convenience. Most students opt for either part-time evening courses (offered at both the Whitewater and Waukesha Center campuses) or distance learning, which is growing increasingly popular despite the fact that distance courses are considerably more expensive. One MBA writes, "I chose UW—Whitewater for the flexible class times and the multiple locations. The school truly understands the demanding schedules of students who work full-time and/or have children." Another adds, "The online program is great because it allows you to complete the entire degree off campus."

Satisfaction rates are high among MBAs, who regard Whitewater as "an excellent school with an excellent administration [that] helps you achieve your academic goals by suggesting classes and providing other valuable assistance." They praise professors who "are extremely knowledgeable, yet easy to interact with on a daily basis, [are] very accessible at all times, [and who] strive to have students participate and work together in groups." Most important, they appreciate how "IT is used very well, the subject matter is always current and relevant, and the skills/techniques are easily transferred into the business environment."

Career and Placement

The Career Services Office at Whitewater provides career counseling and placement services to all undergraduate and graduate students at the university. The office coordinates on-campus interviews, career fairs, online job-search tools, the administration of self-assessment instruments, and advisement in resume creation, interviewing, and job-search strategies. Many students tell us that the quality of the office is not a major concern to them, as their primary goal in attending Whitewater is to improve their status at their current jobs.

DONALD K. ZAHN, ASSOCIATE DEAN
800 WEST MAIN STREET, WHITEWATER, WI 53190 UNITED STATES
PHONE: 262-472-1945 • FAX: 262-472-4863
E-MAIL: ZAHND@UWW.EDU • WEBSITE: WWW.UWW.EDU

Student Life and Environment

The Whitewater MBA program is home to "a diverse student body that includes single, married and international students" who "really bring the global work environment into perspective." There is also "a good mix of full-time and part-time students" as well as "a wide variety of ages and experience from students in their 50s to new undergrads." Teamwork is important here, so it's fortunate that "most students are friendly and work well in teams [and] "most everyone has a great sense of humor and is willing to compromise for the better of group projects."

Because so many students attend part-time, "there really is no 'presence' of graduate student organizations on campus. Most students seem to be interested only in school; there really aren't any graduate student activities offered to students." Full-timers—there are about 80 of them here—note that "you can be involved in a variety of business organizations or the Graduate Student Organization" if you choose to be. One student writes, "I particularly love the assistantship I have on campus because I get to continue to interact with undergraduates and watch them grow as well." The school is in the early stages of planning a new dedicated business facility. The completion of the facility should lead to an uptick in MBA-related extracurricular activity.

Whitewater is a popular vacation destination, especially for boating and fishing enthusiasts. The town is also known as "the hang gliding capital of the Midwest" due to the popularity of the sport here. One student notes, "There is not a great deal of crime in Whitewater. It is isolated and peaceful." Although Whitewater is a small town, its proximity to large cities provides access to valuable internships. Both Milwaukee and Madison are 45 minutes off by car; Chicago is 100 miles to the southeast.

Admissions

To gain admission to the MBA program at Whitewater, students must have either 1) at least a 2.75 GPA for all undergraduate work; 2) at least a 2.90 GPA for the final half of their undergraduate work; 3) 12 credits of graduate work completed successfully at Whitewater; 4) at least a 2.50 GPA for all undergraduate work, a minimum GMAT score of 570, and a minimum of five years of professional experience; 5) a formula score of at least 1000 under the formula [(undergraduate GPA ? 200) + GMAT score]; or 6) a formula score of at least 1050 under the formula [(GPA for last half of undergraduate work ? 200) + GMAT score]. Students who have previously completed graduate work at Whitewater must have a minimum GPA of 3.00 in those classes with no grades of 'I' (Incomplete) or 'P' (Pending). Non-native English speakers must demonstrate proficiency by achieving a minimum TOEFL score of 550.

FINANCIAL FACTS

Annual tuition (in-state/out-of-state)	
	$6,452/$17,088
Books and supplies	$2,400
Room & board (on-campus)	$4,800
Average grant	$500

ADMISSIONS

Admissions Selectivity Rating	**70**
# of applications received	136
% applicants accepted	88
% acceptees attending	92
Average GMAT	523
Range of GMAT	320-720
Average GPA	3.1
TOEFL Required of	
International Students?	Yes
Minimum TOEFL	
(paper/computer)	550/213
Application fee	$45
Regular application deadline	Rolling
Regular notification	Rolling
Deferment Available?	Yes
Maximum length of	
deferment	1 year
Transfer students accepted?	Yes
Transfer application policy: They must meet the same requirements as a non-transfer student. Nine credits may be transferred into the program.	
Non-fall admissions?	Yes

APPLICANTS ALSO LOOK AT

Marquette University, University of Wisconsin—Madison, University of Wisconsin—Milwaukee, University of Wisconsin—Oshkosh, University of Wisconsin-Parkside.

EMPLOYMENT PROFILE	
Career Rating	75
Placement rate (%)	88
# of companies recruiting on-campus	15
Average starting salary	$49,000

VALPARAISO UNIVERSITY
COLLEGE OF BUSINESS ADMINISTRATION

Academics

Although long established as a quality Midwestern university, Valparaiso is a fledgling in the world of MBA programs. The school only began offering the MBA in the 2002–2003 academic year, and as of this writing, you could still count its graduates on your fingers. Yet, despite its nascency, the Valpo MBA has already found ways to distinguish itself from the pack, primarily by incorporating ethical issues throughout the curriculum. The program places a special focus on environmental stewardship; the school points out that "often the most effective and efficient decisions are those that include environmental issues from the beginning. Making decisions that include the wise use and conservation of environmental resources is not only the ethical choice, but also is often the most profitable." Students tell us that "the way they incorporate the business world, technology, ethics, and environmental issues into each and every class adds tremendous value" to the program.

Valpo's MBA program is designed with the needs of part-timers in mind. All courses are offered once a week in the evenings. Terms run only seven weeks (six in the summer); this creates six different junctures during the year when students can begin the program. All this flexibility means students can pace themselves and complete the program in as little or as much time as they want; a full-time student can complete the degree in one year. Students endorse the approach; one MBA writes, "I think [it is a strength] that classes are only seven weeks long because they focus on what you need to know rather than provide too much 'useless' material that [you] will never use. This way you [don't] get too bogged down in any course." Students also appreciate the "small-school atmosphere and the leading-edge business topics. We use current topics from magazines and journals often, and I can apply what I'm learning to my work life."

Students give their professors high marks, and they report that "almost all are doctorate-level professionals. They have good, applicable real-world experience. They are also good 'people' persons who can present material clearly and relate well to students (mainly the students in the workforce). They are passionate about what they do and are always available for questions and/or discussion on different topics." Administrators are similarly highly regarded; students explain that they "are always willing to help" and listen attentively to student feedback, "recognizing that it is important for developing future programs" at Valpo.

Career and Placement

"We need to initiate a placement program" for Valpo MBAs, students say; currently students receive career services through the university's career center, which serves all undergraduates and graduate students. The MBA program offers an elective called "Career Development, Survival, and Success," which focuses on many of the skills usually taught at MBA career services offices: self-assessment and understanding, time management, career development, stress management, balancing work and nonwork issues, perspective and bias, surviving office politics, and personal ethical philosophy and behavior. Many Valpo MBAs explain that they have no need for career services since they are employed and intend to remain with their employer after graduation.

ERIN L. BROWN, PROGRAM COORDINATOR
104 URSCHEL HALL, 1909 CHAPEL DRIVE, VALPARAISO, IN 46383 UNITED STATES
PHONE: 800-599-0840 • FAX: 219-464-5789
E-MAIL: MBA@VALPO.EDU • WEBSITE: WWW.VALPO.EDU/MBA

Student Life and Environment

Valpo MBAs envision a day when their program will draw applicants from around the world, but they admit that that day is still a way off. One student explains, "Since the MBA program is so new, there is no critical mass of people from which to draw a truly diverse group. This will change over time, but for now it impedes a true exchange of ideas." Some MBAs also point out that "there are so many fresh undergrad graduates in the program that the older students are obliged to become perhaps overly facilitating in discussions. The younger students do not yet know how to interact in a truly adult/mature way in class." On the plus side, "because Valparaiso University is semi-religiously affiliated, many of the students come equipped with a strong moral compass. This helps students to comfortably engage in moral/ethical conversations."

For now, "most students are part-time, and the program seems to be oriented toward part-timers, both academically and socially. All classes are in the evening, which means MBA students aren't exposed to other students or professors" within the university. One student says that there "is not much of a social aspect [for] the students in the program (at least not one I have seen)." Another student observes, "More socializing will improve networking and lasting friendships, which is what you need to get jobs." Still, "MBA students get along well, and they do occasionally get together outside class in clusters." Big get-togethers are confined to a couple of events each year; students say, "We do have semi-annual parties with spouses invited to help get to know each other outside of the classroom."

Despite any drawbacks, most MBAs agree that "Valparaiso treats its graduate students so well. Resources are abundant, and there are no problems completing any tasks due to the way the school is set up." Hometown Valparaiso is small, but students brag that it "is extremely vibrant and a great place to live and work." One student says, "I would recommend a visit to anyone looking for a great place to complete their business education." Chicago is about 60 miles to the northwest.

Admissions

Applicants to Valpo's MBA program must submit a completed application with a cover letter (explaining their reasons for pursuing the degree), official copies of all undergraduate and graduate transcripts, GMAT scores, and two letters of recommendation. Professional experience, as demonstrated by a resume, is not required but is taken into consideration. Entering students must be proficient in calculus/finite math and have basic computer skills. Applications are processed on a rolling basis; applicants are typically notified of the school's decision within 10 days of receipt of a completed application.

FINANCIAL FACTS

Annual tuition	$19,760
Fees	$60
Books and supplies	$1,000
Average student loan debt	$11,887

ADMISSIONS

Admissions Selectivity Rating	**86**
# of applications received	46
% applicants accepted	48
% acceptees attending	91
Average GMAT	560
Average GPA	3.3
TOEFL Required of International Students?	Yes
Minimum TOEFL (paper/computer)	575/236
Application fee	$30
International application fee	$50
Regular application deadline	8/15
Regular notification	8/25
Deferment Available?	Yes
Maximum length of deferment	1 year
Transfer students accepted?	Yes
Transfer application policy: Students must meet admissions requirements and be in good standing at their current institution. Up to 6 credit hours may be transferred.	
Non-fall admissions?	Yes
Need-blind admissions?	Yes

VANDERBILT UNIVERSITY
OWEN GRADUATE SCHOOL OF MANAGEMENT

Academics

Over and over in our survey, MBA students at Vanderbilt praise the "great sense of community" at the first-rate Owen Graduate School of Management. Observes one student, "There is competition here and fellow students and faculty do not let you off easily, but they also help you through the challenges. Whether it is helping you prepare for an interview that they are preparing for themselves or tutoring you in finance because you tutored them in marketing, students are there for each other." It's not just the student body immersed in community spirit; the administration and faculty also join in. One MBA writes, "The most striking thing at Vanderbilt is the ability to really get to know your professors and the administration. Every Thursday night, we have a social where students can kick back and relax from the hard work week. Many professors will join us for the event and make the effort to get to know the student body outside of the classroom. Another example: [In 2003-2004], we had a student-led initiative to assist all first-year students who didn't have internships secure one. The professors volunteered to help students by reaching out to their industry contacts and finding positions for qualified first-year students. Their assistance helped us achieve a 99.1 percent internship-placement statistic."

Such personal touches are rarely accompanied by crack research, but Owen is also a leader in a variety of fields, and students benefit from their professors' cutting-edge work. The faculty excels in finance and marketing; e-commerce, operations management, and organizational management are also considered extremely strong. One MBA writes, "The greatest strengths of Owen are the various strong concentrations, along with a well-organized academic calendar. Moreover, if we want, we can take more electives depending on personal special interest." The strength of other Vanderbilt divisions adds further value to Owen; "The fact that Owen offers jointly taught courses with other highly ranked programs in the Vanderbilt system like the law, medical, and engineering schools is a huge advantage to Owen students."

Vandy's curriculum is "very rigorous, with challenging assignments that stimulate intellect and creativity." Lectures "incorporate real-world practices and situations into the courses and try and make the courses fun, which encourages active participation among the students." And the administration, which "works very hard to deliver an outstanding product to the students," is "doing an excellent job redefining the strategy, positioning, and mission of the school and is very flexible to include student requests." Looks like a good thing may soon be getting even better in Music City.

Career and Placement

Owen MBAs praise "the creativity of the Career Management Center to react to the changing needs of the students" and tell [them] that "the Career Management Center has been great in this depressed job market, keeping [them] focused on the job search and pointing the way to great job opportunities." Things weren't always so rosy—students report that "the office has gone through a noticeable change in the last couple of years" and that "the administration increased funding to the Career Management Center to respond to the poor recruiting environment"—but the problems, apparently, are all in the past.

Employers most likely to hire Owen MBAs include American Express, Banc America Securities, Citigroup, Dell Computer, Deloitte Touche Tohmatsu, Deutsche Bank, Eli Lilly, Emerson Electric, Ford Motor Company, Gaylord Entertainment, GE Capital, Harrah's Entertainment, Hewlett-Packard, Home Depot, Honeywell, IBM, Johnson &

MELINDA ALLEN, ASST. DEAN, ADMISSIONS & CAREER MANAGEMENT CTR.
401 21ST AVENUE SOUTH, NASHVILLE, TN 37203 UNITED STATES
PHONE: 615-322-6469 • FAX: 615-343-1175
E-MAIL: ADMISSIONS@OWEN.VANDERBILT.EDU • WEBSITE: OWEN.VANDERBILT.EDU

Johnson, Mattel® Toys, Merrill Lynch, Procter & Gamble, Salomon Smith Barney, Sara Lee Corporation, Southern Company, SunTrust Bank, Unilever, and Wachovia Securities.

Student Life and Environment

Although the MBA curriculum is time-consuming, "at Vanderbilt, you don't only live with books. The community helps you to keep a balanced life, so you also have time to play sports or meet outside the school." As one student put it, "One minute you're doing bond arbitrage, another minute you're playing flag football with the same great people." The school sponsors social events "that allow students to network and take a break from class work" (e.g., Thursday Night kegs), program-based clubs and organizations serve students of every interest and background, and intramural sports are extremely popular. Plus, there are plenty of restaurants and bars (and student housing, dispensing with the need for designated drivers) within walking distance of the campus. "The real dilemma," one student explained, "is choosing where to spend your time."

Students also make time to enjoy hometown Nashville, "an excellent city in that it offers all the entertainment of a big city but all in close proximity to campus." The city "has the best music scene in the country," one MBA who's "not even a huge country music fan," writes, noting that "there's all types of music here because Nashville attracts incredible musicians. The fact that everything is so close together, easy to get to, and cheap makes this a better music city than Los Angeles or New York City." Nashville also offers "good food, great parks, and a surprising number of very good employment opportunities." The city is home to big-league hockey and football teams, as well as a AAA minor-league baseball team.

Owen's facility offers "everything and everyone is in one building," with "full integration of technology in the classrooms and Intranet. Class assignments, syllabi, and grades are all at the school's Blackboard website. All students have a laptop, with full support provided by Vandy's IT department."

Admissions

Vanderbilt bases admissions decisions on all the following factors: "Caliber of undergraduate institution, difficulty of major, quality and duration of prior work experience, professional responsibilities and accomplishments, career advancement, career goals, extracurricular/professional/community involvement, leadership potential, interpersonal skills, communication skills, team orientation, diversity, and cross-cultural awareness/understanding/experience/appreciation." Recruitment efforts aimed at minority/disadvantaged students include a Diversity Weekend, "which is open to all prospective students, but specially targeted to prospective U.S. minority students."

FINANCIAL FACTS

Annual tuition	$31,990
Books and supplies	$1,426
Room & board	$10,700
% of students receiving loans	56
Average award package	$36,887
Average grant	$13,500
Average student loan debt	$68,778

ADMISSIONS

Admissions Selectivity Rating	80
# of applications received	615
% applicants accepted	68
% acceptees attending	42
Average GMAT	622
Range of GMAT	590-650
Average GPA	3.2
TOEFL Required of International Students?	Yes
Minimum TOEFL (paper/computer)	600/250
Application fee	$100
International application fee	$100
Regular application deadline	3/1
Regular notification	3/31
Application Deadline/Notification	
Round 1:	11/30 / 1/31
Round 2:	1/15 / 3/15
Round 3:	3/1 / 3/31
Need-blind admissions?	Yes

APPLICANTS ALSO LOOK AT

Duke University, Emory University, Georgetown University, Indiana University, The University of Texas at Austin, University of North Carolina at Chapel Hill, University of Virginia.

EMPLOYMENT PROFILE

Career Rating	90	Grads employed by field %: avg. salary	
Placement rate (%)	91	Finance	41: $73,441
% grads employed immediately	54	Human Resources	6: $74,111
Average starting salary	$74,311	Marketing	21: $71,488
		Operations	5: $74,500
		Consulting	11: $81,500
		General Management	9: $77,500
		Other	7: $72,091

VILLANOVA UNIVERSITY
COLLEGE OF COMMERCE AND FINANCE

GENERAL INFORMATION
Type of school	private
Affiliation	Roman Catholic
Environment	village
Academic calendar	semester

SURVEY SAYS...
Students love Villanova, PA
Friendly students
Cutting edge classes
Helpful alumni
Happy students
Smart classrooms

STUDENTS
Enrollment of parent institution	10,102
Enrollment of MBA program	495
% male/female	70/30
% out-of-state	3
% part-time	90
% minorities	2
% international	5
Average age at entry	28
Average years work experience at entry	5

ACADEMICS
Academic Experience Rating	**82**
Student/faculty ratio	12:1
Profs interesting rating	89
Profs accessible rating	74

Joint Degrees
MBA/JD: 3-4 years

Academics

Villanova may have the perfect solution for Philly area students who can't decide between a full-time and part-time MBA program. The school's new full-time equivalent (FTE) MBA offers many of the conveniences of a part-time program—including once-a-week evening classes—with the best aspects of a full-time program; namely, cohort-based instruction and a quick return on time invested. Of the former, MBAs say, "The cohort factor is the greatest strength of the FTE program. Because we will be studying together for two years, we are able to develop deeper relationships and make more connections that will aid us both during and after the program."

According to a survey, students had a lot to say about the FTE MBA program. One MBA comments, "The FTE MBA program at Villanova has the best of the best, which is why it is separate from the traditional MBA program. This program has an all-star class of professors and an administration second to none. This is the reason I chose this school." The administration "is trying very hard to make this flagship program world-class," and students are confident that it will succeed soon. The first year (2003 to 2004), they admit, was a somewhat bumpy ride; one student reports, "Classes are often disjointed, as professors work to fit too much into a 15-week semester. Also, we were told that prerequisites in [classes like] accounting and statistics were unnecessary, yet I sit in my accounting class (the first in my career) next to CPAs and financial analysts. The program doesn't allow them to skip such classes, but it also doesn't provide the foundation on which I can build a deeper understanding." Our survey respondents say that "the administration and the faculty try their best to remedy any issues that come up as a result of disorganization," and they are confident that administrators "are taking these issues into account as they plan for next year's cohort."

Villanova also enrolls students full-time in the professional MBA program (approximately 60 students) as well as a conventional part-time evening program. All classes meet in the evening and all "are heavily focused on technology, ethics, and the latest business trends and practices." Part-timers explain that "both the faculty and the administration recognize the challenges of working full-time, going to school, and managing a family life, and they are willing to work with us to ensure that we have the best educational experience possible. However, they do not use the aforementioned challenges as excuses to give us a less rigorous program—they still provide us with challenging courses and demand rigorous academic study." Villanova offers specializations in e-business, finance, health-care administration, international business, MIS, and marketing; students are not required to select a specialization in order to graduate.

Career and Placement

Villanova's Career Services Office provides workshops, recruiting events, online job databases, alumni networking opportunities, and online support for all undergraduate and graduate students at the university. The school combines forces with 10 other area schools to sponsor Talent Finder, a job fair dedicated exclusively to MBAs; most other recruiting events are open to the university at large. Most students agree that Villanova needs to make a greater effort to attract recruiters specifically for MBAs. Employers of Villanova MBAs in 2003 included AIG, American Express, Ernst & Young, Goldman Sachs, Lincoln Financial, Merrill Lynch, Morgan Stanley, Pfizer, PricewaterhouseCoopers, Prudential, and the Vanguard Group.

Ms. Elizabeth Eshleman, Associate Director & Corporate Liaison
800 Lancaster Avenue, Bartley Hall, Suite 1054, Villanova, PA 19085 United States
Phone: 610-519-4336 • Fax: 610-519-6273
E-mail: mba@villanova.edu • Website: www.mba.villanova.edu

Student Life and Environment

All MBA classes at Villanova are held in the evenings for the convenience of students, the vast majority of whom hold full-time jobs. Because of these circumstances, "time spent at school is usually limited to class time and time spent in study groups." MBAs also note that "before class and during breaks; however, it is easy to find classmates socializing either in the cafe on the ground floor or outside the room." Students enjoy a collegial atmosphere, especially in the cohort-based FTE program. One student writes, "The work can be hard, but it's made a little easier by knowing that you have 44 other people going through the exact same thing."

The program's main organization is the MBA Society of Alumni and Students, whose mission "is to leverage the diverse professional and personal experiences and relationship of its members by creating opportunities to network, share information, and continue education. The group plans to fulfill this mission by planning events and other programming meaningful to the MBA community, by disseminating information on a regular basis, and by maintaining a Villanova website that contains valuable information regarding upcoming activities, current events, and a comprehensive Villanova MBA e-mailing list." The MBA Society hosts an annual spring banquet. Keynote speakers have included the CEOs of Rohm-Haas, SAP America, and the Philadelphia Stock Exchange.

Villanova's location, students say, is "absolutely fantastic. The campus is beautiful as is the location of the school relative to Philadelphia." The SEPTA train stops right on campus and provides quick, convenient transport to Philly's downtown area.

Admissions

The primary criteria for admission to Villanova's MBA program include undergraduate record (GPA and quality of course work), GMAT scores, TOEFL scores (international students), quality of essays (two), quality of recommendations (two), and work experience. Work experience is not required of most applicants; the FTE MBA, however, has a prerequisite of three years work experience. In all Villanova MBA programs, the average student has five years of post-undergraduate professional experience. Incoming students are required to have basic computer skills and a working knowledge of calculus. Basic core requirements can be waived for students with undergraduate course work in business; students may also place out of these requirements by passing a challenge exam.

FINANCIAL FACTS

Annual tuition	$18,750
Fees	$30
Books and supplies	$800
Average grant	$32,400

ADMISSIONS

Admissions Selectivity Rating	76
# of applications received	285
% applicants accepted	78
% acceptees attending	67
Average GMAT	583
Range of GMAT	540-620
Average GPA	3.2
TOEFL Required of International Students?	Yes
Minimum TOEFL (paper/computer)	600/250
Application fee	$50
International application fee	$50
Regular application deadline	6/30
Regular notification	Rolling
Deferment Available?	Yes
Maximum length of deferment	1 year
Transfer students accepted?	Yes
Transfer application policy: Up to nine credits from AACSB accredited MBA Programs.	
Non-fall admissions?	Yes
Need-blind admissions?	Yes

APPLICANTS ALSO LOOK AT

Drexel University, Temple University.

EMPLOYMENT PROFILE

Career Rating	60*
# of companies recruiting on-campus	320
% grads employed immediately	95

VIRGINIA POLYTECHNIC INSTITUTE & STATE U.
PAMPLIN COLLEGE OF BUSINESS

GENERAL INFORMATION
Type of school	public
Environment	village

SURVEY SAYS...
Students love Blacksburg, VA
Friendly students
Happy students
Smart classrooms
Solid preparation in:
Teamwork

STUDENTS
Enrollment of parent institution	27,262
Enrollment of MBA program	352
% male/female	78/22
% out-of-state	60
% part-time	69
% minorities	1
% international	51
Average age at entry	26
Average years work experience at entry	3

ACADEMICS
Academic Experience Rating	**86**
Student/faculty ratio	2:1
Profs interesting rating	83
Profs accessible rating	84
% female faculty	25

Joint Degrees
MBA/MIM: 3-4 years

Academics

"It's a combination of everything"—including "an outstanding MBA program with very nice faculty, staff, and students; a beautiful campus where you can do a lot of activities (sports, cultural); and a program small enough to give you personal attention in a school that's big enough to put everything at your fingertips"—that makes the Pamplin MBA at Virginia Tech so appealing to students. MBAs here also love that their program is a "great value" and that the curriculum places an emphasis "particularly on liking what you do and doing what's important to you, and on building not only a career but a life."

Pamplin offers both a full-time and part-time MBA. The curricula for the two are identical; each requires 48 credit hours divided almost evenly among required core courses and electives. The full-time program is cohort-based; the part-time program is not. Full-time students praise the cohort system, which gets them "focused on learning from the other students in the program, in addition to the normal course material." Part-timers enjoy the convenience of their program, which offers classes on six campuses throughout Virginia as well as on the Blacksburg campus. Students in both programs tell us that "the curriculum is much more technical and hands-on as opposed to theoretical" and that "the integration of technology to courses is remarkable." Finance and IT departments both receive high marks. Across departments, professors are described as "very knowledgeable and willing to answer any questions we have, willing to give extra help when required, and available for questions and conversations outside of class." The administration "is active as well, keeping in frequent contact by sending out announcements and asking for feedback from students."

Asked how they would improve their program, most students here suggest tweaks rather than an overhaul. A typical student proposes that "the MBA program would benefit from a larger number of students. There are currently less than 50 first-year MBAs in the full-time program. This can cause problems with some concentrations not being offered due to lack of interest. The program would benefit from having closer to 100 students in each class." The school lists the following available concentrations: corporate financial management, e-business technology, global business, hospitality and tourism management, information systems and technology, investment and financial services management, marketing, organizational leadership, and systems engineering management.

Career and Placement

Pamplin MBAs receive placement help both from the university's Career Services Office and from the MBA-dedicated Career Advising Office, which students call "perhaps the program's greatest strength. Barry O'Donnell is in charge of the program and teaches one-credit courses on career search. It's an incredible program." His office also plans MBA recruitment campaigns, "including MBA Corporate Briefings, posting MBA internships and career opportunities, or gaining access to the MBA Association (MBAA), the professional student organization."

Employers most likely to hire Pamplin MBAs include Black & Decker, Giant Food Stores LLC, Air Products and Chemicals, U.S. General Services Administration (GSA), Eastman Chemical Company, Branch Banking and Trust Company, Freddie Mac, Gildner and Associates, Inc., Cox Communications, J.E. Jamerson and Sons, Bank One, and Toyo Tires.

SUSAN VEST, ENROLLMENT COORDINATOR
1044 PAMPLIN HALL, VIRGINIA TECH, BLACKSBURG, VA 24061 UNITED STATES
PHONE: 540-231-6152 • FAX: 540-231-4487
E-MAIL: MBA_INFO@VT.EDU • WEBSITE: WWW.MBA.VT.EDU

Student Life and Environment

"Because of the large size of VT, there is an abundance of things to get involved with" around the Blacksburg campus, including "lots of outdoor activities" such as hiking, camping, skiing, and whitewater rafting in the nearby mountains. One parent/student notes that the campus itself offers "lots of green spaces where our kids can run and play" and plenty of opportunities to participate in intramural sports and pickup games. Social life among full-time MBAs is "active, partly because there are a lot of bars around here." One writes, "We have a dependable social circle and do many things together like going out on Thursday nights, eating dinner together at our favorite Mexican restaurant, and tailgating before football games." Many students here note that "Virginia Tech is a big football school. Especially in the fall, life around here seems to revolve around the Hokies." The MBA Association is "very active," and many MBAs devote some of their spare time to community service. Overall, as one student sums up, "life at school is really enjoyable; not too stressful, but learning a lot."

VT MBAs include "many students with engineering backgrounds," including a number of international students. One MBA observes, "Our class is very ethnically diverse, with many [students] from India and Asia, but all the different cultures seem to mesh extremely well" and the mix creates "a great learning atmosphere." Students also represent a variety of experience levels; "Many students came straight from undergrad while several others have worked for years and have children," students report. Most importantly, "students generally cooperate with one another and help each other. They don't try to run each other down in competition. There is a good camaraderie among first-year students and second-year students are very helpful to first-years."

Admissions

All applications to the Pamplin MBA program must include a completed application form, official GMAT scores, a resume, and two copies of official transcripts from all postsecondary institutions attended. Students may choose to submit two letters of recommendation, but they are not required. International students whose first language is not English must also submit TOEFL scores. The Admissions Office considers all pieces of the application, with emphasis placed on academic record and preparedness for graduate business work, GMAT scores, professional experience, communication skills, goals, and compatibility with the program. One semester of calculus and two semesters of undergraduate accounting are prerequisite to commencing the MBA program.

FINANCIAL FACTS

Annual tuition (in-state/out-of-state)	$6,186/$10,307
Fees	$1,375
Books and supplies	$10,000
% of students receiving aid	90
% of first-year students receiving aid	75
% of students receiving grants	82
Average award package	$6,000
Average grant	$3,000

ADMISSIONS

Admissions Selectivity Rating	90
# of applications received	182
% applicants accepted	40
% acceptees attending	58
Average GMAT	640
Range of GMAT	620-690
Average GPA	3.0
TOEFL Required of International Students?	Yes
Minimum TOEFL (paper/computer)	550/213
Application fee	$45
International application fee	$45
Regular application deadline	2/1
Regular notification	Rolling
Deferment Available?	Yes
Maximum length of deferment	1 year
Need-blind admissions?	Yes

EMPLOYMENT PROFILE

		Grads employed by field	%: avg. salary
Career Rating	74		
% grads employed immediately	71	Finance	36: $43,000
Average starting salary	$50,997	Marketing	8
		MIS	24: $52,818
		Operations	16
		Consulting	4
		General Management	8
		Other	4

WAKE FOREST UNIVERSITY
BABCOCK GRADUATE SCHOOL OF MANAGEMENT

GENERAL INFORMATION

Type of school	private
Environment	city
Academic calendar	semester

SURVEY SAYS...
Friendly students
Happy students
Smart classrooms
Solid preparation in:
Teamwork

STUDENTS

Enrollment of parent institution	6,444
Enrollment of MBA program	556
% male/female	71/29
% out-of-state	75
% part-time	61
% minorities	13
% international	23
Average age at entry	28
Average years work experience at entry	4

ACADEMICS

Academic Experience Rating	**86**
Student/faculty ratio	10:1
Profs interesting rating	88
Profs accessible rating	90
% female faculty	13
% minority faculty	13

Joint Degrees
MBA/JD: 4 years
MBA/MD: 5 years
MBA/PhD: 5 years
MBA/MS in accounting: 6 years

Prominent Alumni
Charles W. Ergen, Chairman and CEO , EchoStar Corporation; G. Kennedy Thompson, Chairman and CEO, Wachovia Corporation; William G. Taylor, Pres., The Springs Company; James H. Steeg, Executive VP and COO, San Diego Chargers; John K. Medica, SVP and Gen. Mgr., Product Group, Dell Computer.

Academics

The Babcock Graduate School of Management at Wake Forest University excels in the financial concentrations and quantitative analytical skills prized by the banking industry. That should come as no surprise because many of the region's major banks are headquartered in nearby Charlotte. The Babcock MBA program commences with a "lockstep core program that is fully integrated; functional tracks are not offered until the second year," though students are allowed to take two electives in their chosen tracks at the end of their first year. Students have high praise for the core, and they describe it as "an integrated program, not a list of courses. Each class builds directly on the last, across all disciplines. You may have accounting four times in one week and not at all the next because you need to learn certain quantitative skills before you can proceed to the next accounting topic." Throughout the core year, "students work with four-to-five member teams, assigned during orientation. The teams are designed to include students from a range of backgrounds. All of the classes are with these teams, and much of the work is done with these people. This gives students an opportunity to work with others, as [they] will in the workforce. It also gives the school an atmosphere of cooperation."

Both years of the program "can be very challenging" because "the workload is heavy and the expectations are high." Fortunately, "students are always willing to help each other out. Working in teams is an essential part of almost every class. You learn from each others' experiences as much as you do from the professors." Small class sizes "allow for good in class discussions and opportunities to participate, but if you want to blend in and coast through b-school unnoticed, this is not the place. Because it is so small, you really can't get away with being unprepared or not participating. [There is a] big emphasis on class participation; it is a large part of [the] grading system." Babcock professors are "extremely helpful and easy to access. Setting up meetings regarding class material, job hunting, or other career information, has been an excellent way for me to learn about opportunities." Students also love how professors "encourage real-world cases." For example, one student explains, "A professor brought the director of a seminary in from Haiti to use as a case study for cost analysis. Another faculty member included branding a local winery in the class deliverables. These projects allow us to practice working with clients, integrate course materials into existing situations, and actually provide beneficial information to nonprofits or start-ups." Teaching here is highly tech-reliant, so "all students are provided with an IBM ThinkPad laptop computer as part of tuition, and all classrooms are outfitted with integrated computer and audio-visual equipment."

Career and Placement

"The help of the Career Management Center is wonderful," students report. Of course, the down economy of the early 2000s has challenged the office; students explain that "the Career Management Center has had a tough time placing people in full-time and internship positions over the last couple of years." Because "we are in an area with lots of bank headquarters, finance is heavily emphasized, and banks recruit heavily here." Students in these areas are most likely to be happy with career services at Wake. MBAs in operations and IT, on the other hand, feel that "the Career Management Center needs to attract more positions/recruiters." Top employers of Wake MBAs include Alex Lee, Philip Morris, Accenture, Key Bank, Bank of America, BearingPoint, Booz Allen Hamilton, General Electric, Lowe's, Sara Lee, and Wachovia. Nearly two-thirds of Wake MBAs find their first jobs in the South Atlantic region; about 3 in 10 find jobs outside the United States.

Student Life and Environment

Wake's MBA program has students burning the candle at both ends; one MBA explains,

STACY POINDEXTER OWEN, DIRECTOR OF ADMISSIONS
PO BOX 7659, WINSTON-SALEM, NC 27109-7659 UNITED STATES
PHONE: 336-758-5422 • FAX: 336-758-5830
E-MAIL: ADMISSIONS@MBA.WFU.EDU • WEBSITE: WWW.MBA.WFU.EDU

"Classes and homework require approximately 12 hours per day in both years. There are lots of activities, clubs, and opportunities to meet staff, faculty, other students, and local business leaders. We work hard and there is an opportunity to play hard." Another student agrees, "It is extremely challenging to manage all aspects of life here. Academics, clubs, and social opportunities are very time-consuming. It is worth every bit of pressure and time, though. The environment here is one of teamwork and stimulation. Everyone is looking out for each other and is excited to be here, learning new things, and meeting new people."

Babcock "does a great job of presenting opportunities to balance your life. There are many social events outside of academics so that students and spouses/girlfriends/boyfriends can mingle and be social. This is key as the real business world requires a social side to your personality," according to MBAs. Students enjoy such extracurricular options as "happy hours at school on Fridays and tailgates at home football games. Social events often coincide with career-related opportunities, such as cocktails and hors d'oeuvres after a club event involving outside speakers (like alumni and corporate recruiters)." MBAs agree that "this is a very social program," in which, "everyone knows each other since the class size is so small. Thus, whenever we all go out, we all go out. It's great to build strong relationships and networking." The student body includes a large international population; one MBA observes, "Thirty percent of the class is reserved for international students and this has really widened my perceptions. Getting input from a Chinese student about a case set in China is really helpful." Hometown Winston-Salem "is not the most hip, but there are opportunities to go out." Those who love the Southern style of living will be most comfortable here. As one MBA notes, "Even though Winston-Salem is struggling economically, it is a great city to live in, due to its relaxing environment. The Southern culture is pervasive, even to those from outside the South." Two larger cities, Charlotte and Raleigh, are within a one-and-a-half hour drive of campus.

Admissions

Wake Forest's admissions decisions "are influenced by demonstrated potential for management careers through academic achievement, professional experience, and community involvement." The school considers all of the following components of the application: GMAT scores, TOEFL scores (international applicants), undergraduate and graduate transcripts, personal statements, letters of recommendation, resume, and an interview. To recruit minority students, "Babcock offers Diversity Weekend, an event for prospective minority, female, and international candidates, and [the university] participates in the National Black MBA Association and the National Hispanic Society of MBAs Career Forums. Through the Wachovia Scholars Program, Babcock is able to offer scholarships to underrepresented full-time students. These scholarships include a full-tuition waiver, stipend, and an international summer study trip."

FINANCIAL FACTS

Annual tuition	$28,000
Fees	$150
Books and supplies	$1,500
Room & board	$5,600
% of students receiving aid	80
% of first-year students receiving aid	78
% of students receiving loans	54
% of students receiving grants	58
Average award package	$31,001
Average grant	$14,813
Average student loan debt	$52,641

ADMISSIONS

Admissions Selectivity Rating	84
# of applications received	414
% applicants accepted	61
% acceptees attending	46
Average GMAT	630
Range of GMAT	580-660
Average GPA	3.2
TOEFL Required of International Students?	Yes
Minimum TOEFL (paper/computer)	600/250
Application fee	$75
International application fee	$75
Regular application deadline	4/1
Regular notification	Rolling
Early decision program?	Yes
ED Deadline/Notification	11/1 / 12/25
Need-blind admissions?	Yes

APPLICANTS ALSO LOOK AT

Duke University, Emory University, Indiana University, University of North Carolina at Chapel Hill, University of Notre Dame, Vanderbilt University, Washington University in St. Louis.

EMPLOYMENT PROFILE

Career Rating	88	Grads employed by field	%: avg. salary
Placement rate (%)	95	Finance	35: $68,375
% grads employed immediately	73	Marketing	25: $67,222
Average starting salary	$70,135	Operations	19: $73,617
		Consulting	15: $71,625
		General Management	6: $79,500

WASHINGTON UNIVERSITY IN ST. LOUIS
JOHN M. OLIN SCHOOL OF BUSINESS

Academics

The emphasis is on "learning by doing" at the Olin School of Business at Washington University, and it is this focus that draws future business leaders to the venerable St. Louis institution. Key to Olin's approach is its Center for Experiential Learning, which puts aspiring MBAs to work solving the actual problems of actual businesses in the area. Students love the experience, and they report that "the Center for Experiential Learning (CEL) provides students the opportunity to benefit from working with St. Louis companies on consulting projects, entrepreneurial projects, and nonprofit consulting projects. It does a great job recruiting companies to participate in its activities on behalf of Olin students."

Olin MBAs also appreciate the flexibility of their curriculum, which "allows students to tailor the program to their liking, taking electives as early as the first semester." The school facilitates both electives and core courses through a unique hybrid academic calendar that is equal parts semester- and quarter-system; each semester is divided into two "mini-semesters," resulting in a pace more commonly associated with a quarter system. Students appreciate that "mini-semesters enable lots of electives and a broad base of knowledge," but they warn that the timing "is a bit aggressive. It's hard for everything to sink in over such a short term." One student puts a positive spin on the accelerated pace; he explains that "the program itself is streamlined to maximize learning in a minimal amount of time. The professors even coordinate material among the core courses to enhance the process." Most students agree that "it's a killer workload, but it means that [students are] better prepared for electives and summer internships."

Olin excels in strategy "(some strategy professors are at the cutting edge)," finance, operations, and accounting. A global-management studies course, offered through CEL, includes a two-week in-country immersion experience. Students explain that professors are "experienced, on the cutting edge of research, and know what's happening in industry, due to regular consulting assignments." Students add, "[The professors] are great researchers and great teachers, are eager to help students, and are also very involved in our successes. They are great resources both while in school and after graduation." The small size of the Olin program means that student interaction with professors and administrators is frequent. Students report that "the school's administration is extremely receptive to students' feedback. The administration really bends over backwards to serve its customers, the students. The dean has an open-door policy, which makes him quite accessible. He's always interested in listening to students' suggestions and feedback."

Career and Placement

Washington University's Weston Career Resources Center (WCRC) enrolls all Olin MBAs in a first-year, first-semester course called "Managing Your Career Strategies." During this course, students "plan a series of key actions that [they] will engage in throughout [their] MBA education and into [their] first year of post-MBA employment." Students explain that their greatest career contacts come not through the WCRC, but rather through their participation in Olin's Experiential Learning program. Students also praise the alumni network and say that "the alumni are very active, and this is reflected in their support of current students, the endowment of the college, and the average gift given by an alumnus." Alumni provide numerous job leads for current Olin MBAs.

Brad Pearson, Director of MBA Admissions and Financial Aid
Campus Box 1133, One Brookings Drive, St. Louis, MO 63130 United States
Phone: 314-935-7301 • Fax: 314-935-6309
E-mail: mba@olin.wustl.edu • Website: www.olin.wustl.edu

Top employers of Olin MBAs include 3M; Anheuser-Busch; Bank of America; Cisco Systems, Inc.; Citibank; Emerson; ExxonMobil; FedEx; GE Capital; Guidant; Honeywell; IBM Corp.; LG Electronic; Mead Johnson; The Hartford; and Wells Fargo. Nearly one in five graduates find a first job outside the United States; about half remain in the St. Louis region.

Student Life and Environment

Olin has "a great social feel," students say. MBAs also note that "students are at school whether it is the weekend or not. It is a central social hub, and there are days spent in study rooms [or] hanging out in the MBA lounge and courtyard." The Friday Afternoon Club (FAC) is a much-anticipated weekly event, in which, "everyone is invited: students, spouses, significant others, children, faculty, and staff. It's a great time to catch up with people you don't see every day and find out what people are doing over the weekend." The event is sponsored by a different club each week and almost always involves a keg, which pleases students; many students agree, "We work hard and play hard."

Olin's facility is a homey building with "comfortable study spaces, adequate meeting rooms, a kitchen, and access to prepared foods, which make the extensive time in the school tolerable." The computer facilities "got a total makeover in 2003," so now "students have the option of using wireless connections in addition to the traditional PCs that have been available in the past. The wireless LAN provides coverage to all student-accessible public areas such as student lounges, the library, study rooms, May Auditorium, and the Lopata Courtyard." The school also has a Polycom video conferencing system that "is often used by students for interviewing with companies."

Olin students tend to be on the youngish side; they are a "great bunch of fun, intelligent personalities, with a diversity of work and cultural backgrounds. We have a great mix of international and domestic students." They "take their academics seriously, but they are not weighed down by enormous, cutthroat pressure." Many MBAs tell us that school keeps them too busy to enjoy the metropolitan life afforded by their St. Louis location.

Admissions

The Olin admissions office scours applicants' records for evidence of "a history of setting and achieving goals." The school also takes into strong consideration the "quality of previous education, the quality of previous work experience, and the quality of the match between the applicant's stated educational and professional objectives and the MBA program's content." Leadership and community service are seen as leading indicators of fitness for the Olin program. Applicants must submit official copies of all undergraduate and graduate transcripts, GMAT scores, TOEFL scores (where appropriate), two letters of recommendation, a personal statement, and a resume. Olin participates in the Consortium for Graduate Study in Management, which funds fellowships for talented minorities.

Prominent Alumni

Priscilla L. Hill-Ardoin MBA '88, Senior VP, Regulatory Compliance SBC Communicatioms; James H. Hance, Jr. MBA '68, Vice Chairman & CFO, Bank of America; Steven F. Leer, MBA '77, Pres. & CEO, Arch Coal, Inc.; W. Patrick McGinnis MBA '72, Pres. & CEO, Nestle Purina Pet Care; William J. Shaw MBA '72, Pres. & COO, Marriott International.

FINANCIAL FACTS

Annual tuition	$34,500
Fees	$625
Books and supplies	$2,500
Room & board	$25,241
Average award package	$40,334
Average grant	$11,610

ADMISSIONS

Admissions Selectivity Rating	87
# of applications received	692
% applicants accepted	54
% acceptees attending	38
Average GMAT	650
Range of GMAT	610-700
Average GPA	3.2
TOEFL Required of International Students?	Yes
Minimum TOEFL (paper/computer)	590/243
Application fee	$100
International application fee	$100
Regular application deadline	1/7
Regular notification	3/18
Application Deadline/Notification	
Round 1:	11/19 / 1/28
Round 2:	1/7 / 3/18
Round 3:	3/4 / 4/29
Round 4:	5/6 / 6/10
Deferment Available?	Yes
Maximum length of deferment	1 year
Transfer students accepted?	Yes
Transfer application policy: Up to 9 credits from an AACSB-accredited graduate program.	
Need-blind admissions?	Yes

APPLICANTS ALSO LOOK AT

Emory University, Indiana University, Northwestern University, University of Chicago, University of Michigan, University of North Carolina at Chapel Hill, Vanderbilt University.

EMPLOYMENT PROFILE

Career Rating	88	Grads employed by field	%: avg. salary
% grads employed immediately	57	Finance	34: $75,848
Average starting salary	$78,691	Human Resources	3: $61,693
		Marketing	23: $81,819
		Operations	6: $84,417
		Consulting	21: $78,860
		General Management	9: $81,500
		Other	3: $83,000

WEST VIRGINIA UNIVERSITY
COLLEGE OF BUSINESS AND ECONOMICS

GENERAL INFORMATION
Type of school | public
Environment | town
Academic calendar | semester

SURVEY SAYS...
Friendly students
Happy students
Smart classrooms
Solid preparation in:
Teamwork

STUDENTS
Enrollment of parent
  institution | 26,600
Enrollment of MBA program | 219
% male/female | 56/44
% out-of-state | 60
% part-time | 76
% international | 50
Average age at entry | 28
Average years work experience
  at entry | 5.5

ACADEMICS
Academic Experience Rating | 86
Student/faculty ratio | 19:1
Profs interesting rating | 89
Profs accessible rating | 87
% female faculty | 18
% minority faculty | 2

Joint Degrees
MBA/JD: 3 years

Prominent Alumni
John Chambers, CEO, Cisco
Systems; Glen Hiner, CEO, Owens
Corning; Homer Hickam, Author;
Ray Lane, Frm. Pres. & COO,
Oracle; Jerry West, GM, LA Lakers.

Academics

West Virginia University offers two distinct MBA options, each designed for a specific demographic. For young students with little professional experience and a desire to move forward quickly, WVU has designed a full-time MBA program that can be completed in just over a year. For more experienced students with a stronger business background and ongoing professional obligations, WVU offers a part-time executive MBA in eight West Virginia cities.

Both MBA options stress the integral nature of technology in modern business. One student observes, "The greatest strength of this program is the broad use of technology in the classes. I would have rated myself as an advanced user of information technology in my role of managing a number of databases before this class, and yet I have learned so much more and become even more comfortable with technology and common software packages." Although the curricula for the two programs vary, both stress the importance of teamwork and cover all major functions of business study.

The full-time program, located in Morgantown, begins with a pre-professional session designed to polish necessary business skills. It then moves through the curriculum thematically, covering such subjects as business planning, organizational skills, implementation, control, and change. Students "take one class for a period of weeks, and then a different class begins. It's a really great structure that allows you to fully concentrate on the material." The program's emphasis on "practical thinking and experience," MBAs tell us, is helpful. One explains, "I am young and do not have much business and working experience, and the MBA program has done an excellent job of easing me into the business atmosphere while challenging me to go further." Professors "make themselves available to help each student, even into the late hours of the evening, and go above and beyond the call of duty for the WVU MBA students"—another plus.

The part-time EMBA brings students to a satellite classroom, where interactive technology allows them to participate in classes with each other and the professor. Classes are videotaped to accommodate working professionals who miss class due to travel. An MBA tells us that "given the complexity of coordinating things, it is amazing how well everything has worked. Any time you are heavily dependent on technology, you expect a certain amount of inconvenience, but I have been pleasantly surprised at how well-maintained the systems are and how committed the school has been to making sure that we are all comfortable with the learning experience." Students also appreciate that "professors visit the various sites during the classes so that we actually meet them and each site gets to experience being remote and being on-site." They also tell us, "The online support given is outstanding. Anything and everything you need to know can be found by a simple Internet connection." A student complains that "too many group projects are required, meaning that additional travel to a central meeting place (one hour for me) was a common occurrence. Usually 20 to 40 percent of your grade is based upon group efforts. This undercuts a lot of the convenience of the program."

Career and Placement

The College of Business and Economics at WVU has its own dedicated Career Development Center to serve business undergraduates and graduate students. The office provides counseling services, workshops, seminars, and on-campus recruiting events. Students tell us that the office seems geared mostly toward the needs of undergraduates. One writes, "The largest improvement to the program could be made with career services tailored specifically to the MBA students. The MBA program would benefit greatly by

BONNIE ANDERSON, ASSOCIATE DIRECTOR
PO BOX 6027, MORGANTOWN, WV 26506-6027 UNITED STATES
PHONE: 304-293-5408 • FAX: 304-293-2385
E-MAIL: MBA@WVU.EDU • WEBSITE: WWW.BE.WVU.EDU

bringing reputable companies to directly meet with business students. The accounting program at WVU has an excellent relationship with the big four accounting firms. The MBA program should seek to achieve a similar relationship with a selected group of organizations."

Student Life and Environment

WVU is a pretty typical large state university, with plenty of extracurricular options for those who seek them. One student notes, "There are many things that WVU offers as special activities. They offer movies, up-all-night activities, that sort of thing. They also have a lot of shows and performers that come to campus." Football games "are always great," and "keg parties, bar crawls, and burning couches are fairly regular affairs. This is a renowned party school." Most MBAs, though, "do not have as much time to enjoy these activities as [they] did as undergrads." Hometown Morgantown "is the kind of wonderful town that you never tire of. It offers absolutely anything and everything you could want, while still holding true to a small-town atmosphere. You would have to search long and hard to match all that it offers."

It's a different story for EMBAs, whose students are "not very focused on campus life. Most people have non-university centered lives."

WVU MBAs are "a diverse group," with "work experience from a number of industries, government, and health care. Some are managers, directors, or vice presidents, while others are in staff positions. They are all willing to share their experiences and opinions." One student writes, "Even though we are so different in the class, we all pull together and work as a team and learn from each other just as much as we learn in the classes. It has been amazing."

Admissions

Applicants to the MBA program must submit official transcripts for all post-secondary academic work, an official GMAT score report, and a resume. Letters of recommendation and a statement of purpose are optional. All students must have full use of a laptop PC that meets prescribed minimum software, memory, and processor-speed requirements; contact the school or visit the website for details. Applicants to the EMBA program must have at least two years of "significant work experience." For applicants with less than five years experience, GPA and GMAT figure most heavily in the admissions decision. Professional experience, especially managerial experience, is the greater factor for applicants with at least five years of experience.

FINANCIAL FACTS

Annual tuition (in-state/out-of-state)	$8,180/$22,100
Books and supplies	$1,500
Room & board	$6,600

ADMISSIONS

Admissions Selectivity Rating	88
# of applications received	284
% applicants accepted	43
% acceptees attending	84
Average GMAT	570
Range of GMAT	520-650
Average GPA	3.35
TOEFL Required of International Students?	Yes
Minimum TOEFL (paper/computer)	580/237
Application fee	$50
International application fee	$50
Regular application deadline	2/28
Regular notification	3/15
Deferment Available?	Yes
Maximum length of deferment	1 year
Transfer students accepted?	Yes
Transfer application policy: Applicants request transfer credits and the admission committee reviews the request.	
Non-fall admissions?	Yes
Need-blind admissions?	Yes

APPLICANTS ALSO LOOK AT

Marshall University, Penn State University MBA, Syracuse University, Temple University, University of Kentucky, University of Pittsburgh, Virginia Polytechnic Institute and State University.

EMPLOYMENT PROFILE	
Career Rating	72
Placement rate (%)	64
# of companies recruiting on-campus	84
% grads employed immediately	64
Average starting salary	$64,200

WICHITA STATE UNIVERSITY
BARTON SCHOOL OF BUSINESS

GENERAL INFORMATION
Type of school   public
Environment   metropolis
Academic calendar   semesters

SURVEY SAYS...
Students love Wichita, KS
Friendly students
Happy students
Smart classrooms
Solid preparation in:
General management
Teamwork
Presentation skills

STUDENTS
Enrollment of parent
  institution   15,000
Enrollment of MBA program   183
% male/female   64/36
% part-time   76
% minorities   30
Average age at entry   25
Average years work experience
  at entry   2

ACADEMICS
Academic Experience Rating   75
Student/faculty ratio   4:1
Profs interesting rating   69
Profs accessible rating   71
% female faculty   20
% minority faculty   4
Joint Degrees
MBA/MSN in nursing: 3-4 years

Academics

There's one obvious and indisputable reason that students choose the Barton School of Business at Wichita State University: "It's the only accredited program in the city of Wichita, Kansas," as one student says. Thus, it is the most convenient choice for the many full-time worker/part-time student MBAs who attend the school. Yet, convenience is hardly Barton's only virtue. The program "concentrates on general management, with particular attention given to developing an understanding of the organization as an integrated system." It also provides students access to "professors who all have PhDs, and most of whom participate in industry consulting. [This] provides a real edge for dealing with real-world business challenges."

With a large part-time enrollment, Barton "has to be flexible, and it is. [Because] there are so many nontraditional students, they take the time to work with each student individually." This is especially important because classes tend to be large. One MBA observes, "We need smaller class sizes. Forty is too many, and I even had class in a room that was too small for the number enrolled. Because of this, class discussion does not take place, and neither does the learning that's associated with discussion. We need more emphasis on thinking through concepts by doing things like writing papers." Students also feel the school needs a tech upgrade, and they explain that "we don't have enough computers and wi-fi services in classrooms."

While Barton has "many great professors," students must also endure "a couple of bad apples." Experience is a factor; students comment that "there's a large percentage of 'this is the first time I have taught this class' professors. Sometimes they assign too much work, maybe to prove a point, and at other times they haven't had a clue what they were doing." One part-time student adds, "Professors tend to think just because we meet once per week that we have time to do lots of reading. Most students are in two-night classes, work, and have personal responsibilities like families, homes, and pets." Barton MBAs are most positive about the instructors in management; they are least enthused about the accounting faculty and warn that "the professors do not teach in an understandable way." The school offers MBA concentrations in five areas: entrepreneurship, finance, health-care administration, marketing, and operations management. It also offers a master's in accountancy, an MA in economics, and a unique combined MBA/MS in nursing degree.

Barton has research centers devoted to economic development, entrepreneurship, international business advancement, management development, and real estate. All provide services to the Wichita business community and allow participating students to learn while developing valuable contacts.

Career and Placement

Wichita State's Career Development Office maintains a satellite office at Barton's Clinton Hall, although the main office that serves all WSU students remains in Grace Wilkie Hall. The office offers resume and cover letter review, mock interviews, job-search counseling, career counseling, and Crossroads, an online service that allows students to coordinate applications and interviews from their own computers. The CDO also sponsors job fairs for the university at large but none specifically for MBAs.

DOROTHY HARPOOL, DIRECTOR OF MBA PROGRAMS
1845 NORTH FAIRMOUNT, WICHITA, KS 67260-0048 UNITED STATES
PHONE: 316-978-3230 • FAX: 316-978-3767
E-MAIL: MBA@WICHITA.EDU • WEBSITE: WWW.WICHITA.EDU/MBA

Student Life and Environment

WSU's large nontraditional student body is generally too busy to linger long on campus. They flood in during the evenings for class, and if they remain afterward, it is to study in the library or to participate in required team projects. One typical student explains, "I have a full-time career, [and] I attend school in the evenings. Life at school is strictly learning by attending class. I do everything else like homework and group work at home or at the library." Another part-timer adds, "There is no life at school. It is a commuter school."

Barton is home to a number of clubs, enjoyed primarily by full-time students, but also by some particularly ambitious part-timers. These include several national honor societies as well as groups devoted to entrepreneurship, international business, human-resource management, and promotion of free enterprise. One part-time MBA explains, "Our business school organizations are well-organized and the school caters to evening students."

Besides the conventional part-timers and full-timers, Barton also hosts participants in the executive MBA program, open only to those with a minimum of five years full-time work experience. One participant reports that "the EMBA program is very demanding and requires significant dedication. The school helps by handling all registration themselves and providing resources so that students do not have to waste precious time. Annual EMBA gatherings are great places for networking."

Hometown Wichita is a city of approximately 350,000. The birthplace of Pizza Hut, Wichita prides itself as a fertile ground for entrepreneurial innovation. From opera to greyhound racing, Wichita has more to offer than most outsiders would suspect. Students tell us that their campus' West Side location "is very convenient, safe, and offers reasonable parking," and that it also boasts "a great gym facility, good student health care, and an overall friendly atmosphere."

Admissions

A completed application to the Barton School of Business must include GMAT scores (the school considers both overall score and component scores), official transcripts for all post-secondary schools attended, a "personal goals" essay, two letters of reference, and a current resume. The school notes that "the specific content of a student's previous education is less important than evidence that the student has sound scholarship, strong personal motivation, and the ability to develop skills necessary to assume a position of leadership." Barton prefers, but does not require, its applicants to have professional work experience.

FINANCIAL FACTS

Annual tuition (in-state/out-of-state)	$4,128/$11,280
Books and supplies	$1,200
Average grant	$6,000

ADMISSIONS

Admissions Selectivity Rating	**83**
# of applications received	93
% applicants accepted	52
% acceptees attending	100
Average GMAT	542
Average GPA	3.2
TOEFL Required of International Students?	Yes
Minimum TOEFL (paper/computer)	570/230
Application fee	$35
International application fee	$50
Regular application deadline	6/1
Regular notification	6/15
Deferment Available?	Yes
Maximum length of deferment	1 year
Transfer students accepted?	Yes
Transfer application policy: Only AACSB accredited classes may be transferred in.	
Non-fall admissions?	Yes
Need-blind admissions?	Yes

EMPLOYMENT PROFILE	
Career Rating	**70**
Placement rate (%)	90
% grads employed immediately	75
Average starting salary	$55,000

WILLAMETTE UNIVERSITY
ATKINSON GRADUATE SCHOOL OF MANAGEMENT

GENERAL INFORMATION

Type of school	private
Affiliation	Methodist
Environment	city
Academic calendar	semester

SURVEY SAYS...
Friendly students
Smart classrooms
Solid preparation in:
Teamwork

STUDENTS

Enrollment of parent institution	2,500
Enrollment of MBA program	134
% male/female	61/39
% out-of-state	33
% part-time	4
% minorities	13
% international	16
Average age at entry	26
Average years work experience at entry	2

ACADEMICS

Academic Experience Rating	**79**
Student/faculty ratio	9:1
Profs interesting rating	67
Profs accessible rating	73
% female faculty	24

Joint Degrees
MBA/JD: 4 years

Prominent Alumni
Grace Crunican, Director, Seattle Dept. of Transportation; James Fitzhenry, Senior VP, FLIR Systems, Inc.; Thomas Neilsen, Chairman, Neilsen Manufacturing, Inc.; Ann Jackson, Executive Director/CEO, Oregon Hospice Association; James McCluskey, Sr. Managing Dir., Bear Sterns Asset Management, Inc.

Academics

The Atkinson Graduate School of Management at Willamette University offers a distinctive MBA that places an unusual "emphasis on harmonizing private enterprise, not-for-profit, and government with community" to "educate and produce highly intelligent and socially responsible individuals." Although 75 percent of Atkinson graduates pursue careers in business, one in four Atkinson graduates moves on to work in the public or not-for-profit sector. Students tell us that "the school excels in nonprofit management and management in general," and they like the fact that Willamette's MBA is accredited for business (AACSB International) and public administration (NASPAA).

The highlight of the Atkinson program is the PaCE project, a two year long endeavor that first has student teams delivering management services to a real not-for-profit organization and later writing and presenting a complete business plan. One student explains, "The class is split into teams, and each team must create a for-profit business and submit 500 collective hours with a not-for profit business partner. The experience is amazing because the students must create a business plan, apply for and receive a small business loan, market their product or service, and exit the business within 10 months. There is more learning to be had in this project than anything else I have ever had to do."

PaCEI and the core curriculum encompass the first year; the second year is given over to "tremendous electives," with especially distinguished offerings in marketing, finance, economics, and organizational development/HR. Professors "genuinely seem to care about the students, whether we are learning in their classes, are finding internships and employment, or need a place to go for a holiday dinner." Faculty members "know their subject matter extremely well, as most are working as consultants in business, government, or not-for-profit organizations." However, "like most schools, there are strong professors and weak professors. All of our professors are incredibly intelligent, but some of them are better at teaching what they know." Administrators earn high marks; students tell us that they are "very involved in the education process, facilitating and celebrating success while seeking to mitigate or resolve conflicts and problems." MBAs love Atkinson's high tech compatibility, reporting that "all students use laptops in class, and with [their] wireless Web, professors give handouts online during class rather than using paper, assignments are submitted through [their] class tools website, and exams can be taken online with a secure program."

Career and Placement

The Career Services Office at the Atkinson School offers a wide range of services, including career fairs, counseling, online job databases, online resume books, self-assessment tools (e.g., CareerLeader), and workshops in interviewing, networking, and resume-building skills. Students feel the office does a good job with local placement, but that "further expanding the emphasis of the career center beyond our metro area and traditional areas of MBA emphasis is necessary. While there are postings for opportunities around the world, the on-campus efforts do tend to focus on traditional roles (mid-level manager to director positions in finance, marketing, and HR departments throughout the mid to upper Willamette Valley and Pacific Northwest coast)." Top employers of Atkinson MBAs include Bonneville Power Administration, Hewlett-Packard, Hollywood Entertainment, Intel Corporation, and Nike.

Student Life and Environment

Willamette's emphasis on "learning by doing" makes it a popular choice for early-career students. This, and the lack of a work-experience prerequisite for admission, means that the student body is on the young side. One student explains, "Although students are of all ages and have different family types, most students are in their mid 20s and unmarried. However, the school does not come across as unfriendly to children or spouses." Another student adds, "I feel that if you are not young (right out of undergrad), you are going to have a hard time feeling that you fit in with the majority of the student body." Others disagree, telling us that "we have many different people here, so it's easy to find a niche that fits your way of life. Don't like to party? Plenty just like you. Like to party? Great; you'll have many to go out with. For those who like to keep their personal and academic lives separate, that's fine—they aren't treated any differently at school."

MBAs tell us that "all students are involved somehow in an extracurricular activity. The school has all professional associations, including the American Marketing Association, Atkinson Student Association, Public Management Association, and SHRM. There are many activities and opportunities to learn and network." Students also enjoy getting together socially, especially for Thursday Night Out (TNO), "a great opportunity to get together with other students and socialize; and with no classes on Fridays, you can begin to wind down from the week. (Also, no classes on Fridays allows students to take on internships, schedule job interviews, and arrange study groups, all without cutting into your weekend time that you want to spend with family.)" Athletic types will be happy to learn that "there is an intramural team for everybody, and you can easily find companions if you are interested in nonteam activities like cycling or hiking."

Willamette is located in Salem, Oregon, "a location that highly encourages studying. The city is safe, not too small, not too big, and not expensive to live. It also offers easy access to a metropolitan city (Portland is only 45 minutes away), outdoor recreation, natural attractions, and other universities." Students brag that "Willamette is one of the most beautiful campuses in the Northwest. The climate is excellent, the people are friendly, and the staff is excellent."

Admissions

The Atkinson admissions office requires applicants to submit GMAT or GRE scores, official transcripts for all undergraduate and graduate work, a personal statement, an interview, and two letters of recommendation. International students whose native language is not English must score at least a 570 on the paper-based TOEFL or at least a 230 on the computer-based TOEFL. No work experience is required, except for the accelerated program (which requires two years' post-baccalaureate work experience and an undergraduate degree in business). Interviews are encouraged but not required. Willamette offers a strong merit-based scholarship program.

FINANCIAL FACTS

Annual tuition	$20,000
Fees	$50
Books and supplies	$1,200
% of students receiving aid	79
% of first-year students receiving aid	79
% of students receiving loans	70
% of students receiving grants	70
Average award package	$24,368
Average grant	$9,394
Average student loan debt	$31,642

ADMISSIONS

Admissions Selectivity Rating	81
# of applications received	178
% applicants accepted	62
% acceptees attending	55
Average GMAT	585
Range of GMAT	530-640
Average GPA	3.3
TOEFL Required of International Students?	Yes
Minimum TOEFL (paper/computer)	570/230
Application fee	$50
International application fee	$50
Regular application deadline	5/1
Regular notification	Rolling
Deferment Available?	Yes
Maximum length of deferment	1 year
Transfer students accepted?	Yes
Transfer application policy: May transfer up to six credits of MBA course work with the approval of the dean.	
Need-blind admissions?	Yes

APPLICANTS ALSO LOOK AT

Gonzaga University, Oregon State University, Portland State University, Thunderbird, University of Oregon, University of Portland, University of Washington.

EMPLOYMENT PROFILE

Career Rating	71	Grads employed by field:	
% grads employed immediately	46	Accounting	7
Average starting salary	$54,000	Finance	16
		Human Resources	7
		Marketing	18
		Operations	2
		Strategic Planning	2
		Consulting	7
		Entrepreneurship	5
		General Management	16
		Non-profit	20

Worcester Polytechnic Institute

Department of Management

Academics

"WPI's greatest strength is its ability to stay ahead of the curve with respect to technology," students at this small, predominantly part-time MBA program in central Massachusetts tell us. Through "a synergy of technical and business factors and real-life scenarios/case studies," WPI delivers an MBA program whose "focus is in the management of technology, with specialty areas that include IT, tech-based entrepreneurship, tech marketing, operations management, and e-business." As one student puts it, "Technology is here to stay, and WPI has done an excellent job establishing a program that addresses the need for better technical managers."

Computing resources are uniformly first-rate. The school reports that "computing services at WPI include powerful UNIX workstations, high-performance computing, electronic classrooms, a campus-wide high-speed data network, high-speed Internet connections, extensive roaming wireless coverage that lets students with wireless-enabled laptops or PDAs to work unplugged, and a web-based information system."

Not surprisingly—given the technological emphasis—WPI is well set up to accommodate distance learners, and in fact its advanced distance learning network (ADLN) program is extremely popular. Students love "the flexibility of the MBA program catering to online students. I am able to work no matter where my job takes me. I'm currently in London and still working on my MBA." Another ADLN student adds, "The facilities are excellent online and in person. I log in to get class materials, download presentations and documents, and participate in online discussions. I am paired up with a person who is taking the class on-site. I can order books online or in person. I can sign up for classes and get help online. It has been a positive experience. The online program is very well done."

WPI's "challenging but rewarding" curriculum means "it's hard work in each and every class" for MBAs. Academics "frequently mimic work scenarios by incorporating real cases for studies, teamwork, and hands-on experience. The school gives us the skills to work in business by increasing our quantitative and qualitative knowledge. The emphasis on teamwork and the integration of diversity of other student's cultures and professional experiences are also strengths of the program." MBAs feel that "the concepts learned in the classroom allow us to better manage our employees, relate to customers, and do our jobs more effectively. We can bring new knowledge to work right away."

WPI's professors are "excellent, knowledgeable, always accessible, willing to help, and go above and beyond." Students also appreciate how "all the faculty at WPI have strong connections with industry, which allows them to integrate their experiences with lecture."

Career and Placement

The Career Development Center (CDC) serves all WPI students, undergraduate, and graduate; the school has no office dedicated exclusively to its business students. The CDC provides students with self-assessment tools, individual counseling, research materials, workshops, job fairs, online job databases, company visits, and assistance in landing summer internships. According to the CDC website, the school "utilizes state-of-the-art technology that makes [them] accessible from any location worldwide. [They] take exceptional pride in [their] services and staff members and will continue to design products that support career-related goals." Companies most likely to hire WPI MBAs include BAE Systems, EMC, Fidelity, GE, Raytheon, Teradyne, and Textron. Following graduation, 85 percent of WPI MBAs remain in New England; 1 in 20 finds work outside the U.S.

Norm Wilkinson, Director, Graduate Management Programs
100 Institute Road, Worcester, MA 01609 United States
Phone: 508-831-5218 • Fax: 508-831-5720
E-mail: GMP@WPI.EDU • Website: WWW.MGT.WPI.EDU

FINANCIAL FACTS

Annual tuition	$21,977
Fees	$85
Books and supplies	$1,100
Room & board	$8,100
% of students receiving aid	66
% of first-year students receiving aid	33
% of students receiving loans	50
% of students receiving grants	50
Average award package	$4,800
Average grant	$34,140
Average student loan debt	$24,000

ADMISSIONS

Admissions Selectivity Rating	75
# of applications received	46
% applicants accepted	96
% acceptees attending	70
Average GMAT	612
Range of GMAT	570-660
Average GPA	3.3
TOEFL Required of International Students?	Yes
Minimum TOEFL (paper/computer)	550/213
Application fee	$70
International application fee	$70
Regular application deadline	8/1
Regular notification	Rolling
Deferment Available?	Yes
Maximum length of deferment	1 year
Transfer students accepted?	Yes
Transfer application policy: Accepted transfer applicants may transfer in up to 9 prior graduate-level credits toward the WPI MBA.	
Non-fall admissions?	Yes
Need-blind admissions?	Yes

APPLICANTS ALSO LOOK AT

Babson College, Bentley College, Boston University, Northeastern University.

Student Life and Environment

"WPI has tons of programs going on during the week and weekend and is a great place for students to kick back and relax or go out with friends," MBAs tell us, although they also report that the majority—made up of part-time and distance-learning students—spend little time on campus. Those who do stick around after class tell us that "WPI recognizes that students need options and must escape from academics occasionally. As a result, the school offers programs to intrigue the mind or engage the student in something different. Students enjoy meeting new students and doing new and exciting things while at WPI (one student learned to juggle and play the flute in addition to learning about chemistry instruments). There are millions of clubs and intramural sports that students can enjoy as well as opportunities to do independent or team research. The opportunities are plentiful."

Hometown Worcester "is a great city that has much historical charm and is up-and-coming in terms of modern development." The city (population approximately 175,000) is home to nine colleges and universities, and it supports an active arts community and a number of fine restaurants. Boston, New England's largest city, "is only a 45 to 60-minute commute away, and WPI offers transportation to those without cars."

Admissions

WPI's website states: "In keeping with our focus on the management of technology, we look for candidates who have a high likelihood of success in a challenging, technology-focused management program, based on their academic and professional records. Applicants should have the analytic aptitude and academic preparation necessary to complete a technology-oriented management program. This includes a minimum of three semesters of college-level math or two semesters of college-level calculus. Applicants are also required to have an understanding of computer systems." The admissions office requires applicants to provide official transcripts from all previously attended undergraduate and graduate institutions, GMAT scores (GRE acceptable for master of science and certificate programs), TOEFL scores (where appropriate), a personal statement, and three letters of recommendation. The Department of Management "works closely with WPI's Office of Diversity & Women's Programs to recruit qualified minority students" and recruits through NSBE and SWE.

EMPLOYMENT PROFILE

Career Rating	91	Grads employed by field	%: avg. salary
Placement rate (%)	97	Human Resources	3: $65,000
# of companies recruiting on-campus	130	Marketing	6: $97,000
% grads employed immediately	94	MIS	30: $83,000
Average starting salary	$94,360	Operations	15: $102,000
		Consulting	25: $80,000
		Entrepreneurship	15: $110,000
		Internet/New Media	6: $95,000

XAVIER UNIVERSITY
WILLIAMS COLLEGE OF BUSINESS

GENERAL INFORMATION

Type of school	private
Affiliation	Roman Catholic-Jesuit
Environment	metropolis
Academic calendar	semester

SURVEY SAYS...

Students love Cincinnati, OH
Friendly students
Happy students
Smart classrooms
Solid preparation in:
Teamwork
Communication/interpersonal skills

STUDENTS

Enrollment of parent institution	6,668
Enrollment of MBA program	857
% male/female	96/4
% out-of-state	15
% part-time	83
% minorities	3
% international	26
Average age at entry	30
Average years work experience at entry	8

ACADEMICS

Academic Experience Rating	**77**
Student/faculty ratio	16:1
Profs interesting rating	79
Profs accessible rating	75
% female faculty	36
% minority faculty	16

Joint Degrees
MBA/MHA: 3 years
MBA/MSN: 3 years

Prominent Alumni
George Schaefer, Pres./CEO Flfth Third Bancorp; Robert J. Kohlhepp, CEO Cintas Corp.; Ken Lucas, US Congressman; Carlos Alcantara, Pres. of International Penzoil-Quaker State; Lloyd Ward, Pres., US Olympic Committee.

Academics

The MBA programs at Xavier University's Williams College of Business "are geared toward the working professional," so much so, in fact, that one of its MBA programs is called "the working professional's evening MBA." Other programs—the weekend MBA and the executive MBA, for example—all are designed with the busy professional in mind.

Consider the executive MBA program, for example, which students tell us "is very well run; Xavier even relieves all administrative tasks for their XMBA students. They prepare packages and provide the textbooks for each class in the classroom prior to our arrival. Lunch is provided in the lobby of the business school building. Generally speaking, our only task at Xavier is to learn, as opposed to worrying about things such as getting parking permits." Writes one enrollee, "When someone like me is working full-time, raising a family, and trying to further my education at the same time, the assistance and support that Xavier gives is wonderful."

Xavier professors "are aware that students work full-time and are both accommodating and understanding about missing class for a business trip. All they ask is that you keep up with the work and learn what you missed, and to be told of conflicts in advance. They are terrific about sticking to their syllabi so students can schedule business trips around exams and presentations." The faculty is praised as "no nonsense. We learn what's important in today's markets and today's businesses rather than wasting collaborative time hashing out the past. The foundations (or the past) are important to know, but the expectation is that you will read and learn about that to prepare for classroom discussions about the present. I like the format because it makes you think more and challenges the professors to keep learning right alongside the students." Students also brag that "the adjunct professors that the university utilizes are a tremendous asset to the overall knowledge gained at the university. It is essential to the education of any MBA student to be taught by someone who works 40 to 50 hours a week in the subject material that they are teaching."

Xavier offers concentrations in six areas: e-business, finance, general business, international business, management-information systems, and marketing. MBAs warn that "the workload is demanding, but you really get a lot out of the program, and it's a very enjoyable experience."

Career and Placement

In January 2004, the Xavier MBA program introduced Corporate Connections, an office dedicated to assist Williams College of Business MBA students and alumni by providing students with the opportunities to network with employers and with one another, as well as serving as a link between the Williams MBA student population and the corporate community. Many students are here to enhance their positions at their current place of employment, and therefore have no need for the CLDO. Those who are seeking employment tell us that Xavier's greatest asset is its local reputation with employers. One student writes, "It gets great respect within the Cincinnati area. People are very impressed when I say 'I am an MBA student at Xavier.'"

Employers who have visited the campus this year include: Cinergy Corporation, Deloitte Touche Tohmatsu, Kforce, Merrill Lynch, Northwestern Mutual, Novartis, Resources Global Professionals, RLG Associates, State Farm, and US Bank.

Student Life and Environment

Xavier's MBA program serves "mostly working people who come to class then leave. Most have little time to enjoy the campus and its offerings." The few extracurricular activities they participate in include "local activities with local companies, clubs, and lots of networking opportunities." Some students stick around after class to participate in study groups, "then go out together to a restaurant or bar."

Cincinnati "is home to some of the greatest employers around: Proctor & Gamble, Cintas Corporation, Fifth Third Bancorp, General Electric, Kroger, Toyota, and GE. These companies play a key role in speaking on job placement, and direction within the MBA program." The Cincinnati metropolitan region is home to about two million people, large enough to support thriving arts, sports, and commercial scenes.

Xavier University, students report, "has changed for the better over the last 10 years. The university has undergone a number of construction projects that have beautified the campus. I feel as though this has contributed positively to the overall enrollment at the school. More people are selecting Xavier as their school of choice than ever before." Students love the fact that "the school is small, the campus is pretty and well-maintained, and classrooms, student lounges, and restrooms are always very clean." They also appreciate how "everyone is nice to everyone here, no matter their age, color, race, religion, or sex. Everyone is an equal."

Admissions

Applicants to Xavier's MBA programs must submit official copies of all academic transcripts, GMAT scores, and a resume. Students with GMAT scores below 400, or quantitative scores below the 25th percentile, are not considered for admission. Work experience is highly recommended but not required for the full-time and working professional MBA programs; the average applicant has five years work experience. For the executive MBA (XMBA), however, candidates must be employed full-time at the time they enter the program and have a significant managerial and leadership experience in middle and upper levels of corporation.

FINANCIAL FACTS

Annual tuition	$10,800
Books and supplies	$900
% of students receiving grants	14
Average grant	$676

ADMISSIONS

Admissions Selectivity Rating	76
# of applications received	396
% applicants accepted	67
% acceptees attending	71
Average GMAT	540
Range of GMAT	450-660
Average GPA	3.2
TOEFL Required of International Students?	Yes
Minimum TOEFL (paper/computer)	550/213
Application fee	$35
International application fee	$35
Regular application deadline	Rolling
Regular notification	Rolling
Deferment Available?	Yes
Maximum length of deferment	1 year
Transfer students accepted?	Yes
Transfer application policy: 6 hours of core curriculum from AACSB accredited programs only. Up to 18 hours of core curriculum form AACSB accredited Jesuit MBA Network Schools	
Non-fall admissions?	Yes
Need-blind admissions?	Yes

APPLICANTS ALSO LOOK AT

Miami University, Northern Kentucky University, University of Cincinnati,

EMPLOYMENT PROFILE

Career Rating	61	Grads employed by field	%: avg. salary
# of companies recruiting on-campus	115	Accounting	4: $55,000
% grads employed immediately	84	Finance	19: $51,000
Average starting salary	$66,622	Human Resources	8: $35,000
		Marketing	4: $55,000
		MIS	12: $70,000
		Operations	19: $83,000
		Strategic Planning	8: $45,000
		Communications	4: $35,000
		Entrepreneurship	4: $75,000
		Quantitative	4: $55,000
		Other	14: $72,500

YALE UNIVERSITY
SCHOOL OF MANAGEMENT

Academics

Although Yale the institution has been around centuries longer than its business school, the school owes its reputation (and its name) to a businessman named Elihu Yale, who made the school's first large donation in 1717. And ever since Yale's School of Management was founded in 1974, the school has been eager to acknowledge its debt to a captain of industry. The School of Management is well-integrated into the university as a whole, and students say, "being part of one of the world's most renowned universities has given me access to unparalleled intellectual experiences." One student says, "I met Joe Stiglitz (Nobel Prize in Economics) at a globalization conference. On Friday, I am attending a talk by Bill Clinton." And more recently, students have encountered George Soros and New York mayor Michael Bloomberg. Students report that this kind of jam-packed and challenging schedule is exactly what you should expect. Another student says, "So far this week I've prepared and presented the marketing strategy for a new medication to senior execs from two major pharmaceutical companies in a case competition, organized an alumni event in New York to improve networking opportunities, had beers with friends after hockey practice, and attended class with the former CEO of Medtronic where we discussed authentic leadership in modern business. It's been a busy week, and it's only Wednesday night!"

According to most, Yale's "program is very quantitative. It attracts many finance and nonprofit gurus." Some students complain that the first year, which consists entirely of core courses, is "much too theoretical," but others see that as a strength. They say, "we spend our time learning fundamental theory instead of business fads, and while this may not give us an advantage during recruiting, our knowledge will stand the test of time and give us an advantage over the course of our career." The "professors are incredible, especially in finance, strategy, game theory, and statistics." They "make themselves totally available. There are more than enough study sessions and TA office hours to ask questions, and my classmates with more experience in these areas are enthusiastic about helping me get to the same level as themselves."

Yale students can also opt for joint degrees in any of the following areas: an MBA/JD with Yale Law School, an MBA/MEM or MF with Yale School of Forestry and Environmental Studies, an MBA/MPH with Yale School of Public Health, an MBA/MD with Yale School of Medicine, an MBA/MARCH with Yale School of Architecture, an MBA/MFA with Yale School of Drama, an MBA/MDIV or MAR with Yale Divinity School, or an MBA/MSN with Yale School of Nursing. The school also offers an MBA/MA in any of the following areas of international studies: East Asian studies, International Relations, and Russian and East European studies.

Career and Placement

Unlike most schools, Yale has a career-service program that more or less gets the approval of its students. Students call it "extremely supportive," and say it "provides one-on-one attention." Some students qualify this by saying it could work on "attracting firms other than banks and management-consulting firms for recruiting." Students also point out that "being close to NYC and Boston is ideal for short trip to interview and visit for jobs and internships." They also appreciate the internship fund, which "provides summer stipends for students taking unpaid or low-paid internships with 501-C3 nonprofits. It is totally student run!"

ANNE COYLE, DIRECTOR OF ADMISSIONS
135 PROSPECT STREET , PO BOX 208200, NEW HAVEN, CT 06520-8200 UNITED STATES
PHONE: 203-432-5932 • FAX: 203-432-7004
E-MAIL: MBA.ADMISSIONS@YALE.EDU • WEBSITE: WWW.MBA.YALE.EDU

Another strength is the alumni network. One student says, "The alumni network I graduate into will be one where strong connections are felt amongst its members due to the unique close-knit atmosphere the school provides. On top of that, I will have the power of the Yale name to help me in my career pursuits."

Companies that regularly recruit on campus include Bear Stearns, Citigroup, Credit Suisse First Boston, Deutsche Bank AG, Goldman Sachs, American Express, Lehman Brothers, Dupont, J. P. Morgan Chase, Morgan Stanley, Proctor & Gamble, IBM, and Intel Corporation

Student Life and Environment

"Yale goes out of its way to make quality of life important for its students. They definitely encourage a sense of community through weekly happy hours and social events to get peoples' minds off the academic demands. There are fun student groups like the wine club, and many recreational sports groups, like rowing or hockey. Everyone is encouraged to participate, regardless of experience." MBAs don't have Friday classes, "so every Thursday at 4:00, the Social Committee brings in a keg (or two) and everyone hangs out in the courtyard and socializes. On Tuesday nights, a number of SOMers can be found at Anna Liffey's playing in the trivia competition and downing some Guinness. Recently, more than 40 students spent a day touring local wineries together on the 'Wine SIG Party Bus.' There are also plenty of parties, Thursday nights at GPSCY, martinis downtown, symphony, and theater—plenty of social opportunities for those who are interested in getting out of the house."

Apart from their superb skills with a keg, however, Yale's MBAs are also praised for their "incredibly high ethical standards. Students are socially responsible but not in-your-face about it." Students are said to be very "active in the community, offering pro bono consulting services to local nonprofits."

Most students agree, however, that the facilities could stand improvement—they're too old and too cold. Another common gripe involves the long distance to the gym.

Admissions

When selecting the 250-odd students who will eventually make up their class, the admissions board at Yale's SOM "seeks a rich, highly interactive community in which students stimulate each other to grow, both intellectually and professionally. The school looks for students from a broad range of backgrounds and with widely differing experiences." In the class of 2005, the average GMAT score was 703, and the average college GPA was 3.5. The average TOEFL was 654, and the minimum TOEFL score required for admission is a 600 (paper-based).

Prominent Alumni

John Thornton, Former Co-COO & Pres., Goldman Sachs; Nancy Peretsman, EVP & Managing Director, Allen & Company; Indra Nooyi, Pres. & CFO PepsiCo Inc.; Fred Terrell, Managing Partner & CEO, Provender Capital Group; Thomas Krens, Director, Solomon R. Guggenheim Foundation.

FINANCIAL FACTS

Annual tuition	$35,000
Fees	$1,452
Books and supplies	$7,200
Room & board	$12,000
% of students receiving aid	77
% of first-year students receiving aid	80
% of students receiving loans	75
% of students receiving grants	44
Average award package	$26,994
Average grant	$8,494
Average student loan debt	$64,669

ADMISSIONS

Admissions Selectivity Rating	97
# of applications received	1998
% applicants accepted	26
% acceptees attending	42
Average GMAT	696
Range of GMAT	680-730
Average GPA	3.5
TOEFL Required of International Students?	Yes
Minimum TOEFL (paper/computer)	600/250
Application fee	$180
Regular application deadline	3/15
Regular notification	3/19
Application Deadline/Notification	
Round 1:	10/26 / 1/20
Round 2:	1/11 / 3/31
Round 3:	3/15 / 5/19
Deferment Available?	Yes
Maximum length of deferment	1 year
Need-blind admissions?	Yes

EMPLOYMENT PROFILE

Career Rating	90	**Grads employed by field**	**%: avg. salary**
Placement rate (%)	86	Finance	47: $82,277
Average starting salary	$83,700	Marketing	13: $85,463
		Operations	2: $79,483
		Consulting	8: $74,875
		General Management	10: $87,625
		Other	20: $87,482

Part III-B
Business School Data
Listings

Arizona State University West

School of Management

Admissions Contact: MBA Admissions
Address: PO Box 37100, Phoenix, AZ 85069-7100
Phone: 602-543-6201 • **Fax:** 602-543-6249
E-mail: MBAINFO@ASU.EDU
Website: WWW.WEST.ASU.EDU/SOM/MBA

GENERAL INFORMATION

Type of School: Public **Environment:** Metropolis **Academic Calendar:** Semester

STUDENTS

% part-time: 100 **Average age at entry:** 33 **Average years work experience at entry:** 9

ACADEMICS

Student/faculty ratio: 20:1 **% female faculty:** 29 **% minority faculty:** 12 **Dual degree:** MBA and MIM-jointly offered with Thunderbird, 3 years.

FINANCIAL FACTS

% of students receiving aid: 20 **% of first-year students receiving aid:** 5

ADMISSIONS

Admissions Selectivity Rating: 78

# of applications received: 139 **% applicants accepted:** 81 **% acceptees attending:** 71 **GMAT Range (25th to 75th percentile):** 500-700 **Average GMAT:** 590 **Average GPA:** 3.5 **TOEFL required of int'l applicants?** Yes **Minimum TOEFL (paper/computer):** 600/250 **Application Fee:** $50 **Regular Application Deadline:** 6/1 **Regular Notification:** 7/1 **Deferment Available?** Yes **Maximum length of deferment:** 1 year **Transfer Students Accepted?** Yes **Non-fall Admissions?** Yes **Need-Blind Admissions?** Yes **Applicants also look at:** Arizona State University, Northern Arizona University, University of Arizona.

EMPLOYMENT PROFILE

% grads employed immediately: 85
Grads employed by field: ....%
Accounting 6
Finance 15
Human Resources 1
Marketing 20
MIS..6
Operations 24
Strategic Planning 1
Consulting 6
Communications...........................1
General Management 7
Other...10

Arkansas State University

College of Business

Admissions Contact: Dr. Thomas Wheeler, Dean, Graduate School
Address: PO Box 60, State University, AR 72467
Phone: 870-972-3029 • **Fax:** 870-972-3857
E-mail: GRADSCH@CHOCTAW.ASTATE.EDU
Website: BUSINESS.ASTATE.EDU

GENERAL INFORMATION

Type of School: Public **Environment:** Town **Academic Calendar:** Semester

STUDENTS

Enrollment of MBA program: 104

ACADEMICS

Student/faculty ratio: 25:1 **% female faculty:** 24 **% minority faculty:** 1

FINANCIAL FACTS

Tuition (in-state/out-of-state): $1,488/$3,744 **Books and supplies:** $2,100 **Room & board:** $3,500 **Average grant:** $6,427

ADMISSIONS

Admissions Selectivity Rating: 60*

# of applications received: 53 **% applicants accepted:** 85 **% acceptees attending:** 80 **TOEFL required of int'l applicants?** Yes **Minimum TOEFL (paper):** 550 **Regular Application Deadline:** Rolling **Regular Notification:** Rolling

EMPLOYMENT PROFILE

% grads employed immediately: 100

Ashridge (United Kingdom)

Ashridge

Admissions Contact: Ursula Chauvineau, Career & Business Relations Manager
Address: Berkhamsted, Hertfordshire, HP4 1NS England
Phone: 001-44-1442-843491 • **Fax:** 001-44-1442-841209
E-mail: URSULA.CHAUVINEAU@ASHRIDGE.ORG.UK
Website: WWW.ASHRIDGE.COM

GENERAL INFORMATION

Type of School: Private

STUDENTS

% male/female: 83/17 **% part-time:** 49 **% international:** 56 **Average age at entry:** 36 **Average years work experience at entry:** 10

ACADEMICS

% female faculty: 10

FINANCIAL FACTS

Tuition: $56,253 **Books and supplies:** $476 **Room & board (on/off campus):** $15,225/$19,068 **Average award package:** $57,204

ADMISSIONS

Admissions Selectivity Rating: 67

# of applications received: 36 **% applicants accepted:** 75 % **acceptees attending:** 67 **GMAT Range (25th to 75th percentile):** 550-690 **Average GMAT:** 580 **TOEFL required of int'l applicants?** Yes **Regular Application Deadline:** 1/5 **Regular Notification:** 1/5 **Deferment Available?** Yes **Maximum length of deferment:** 1 year **Non-fall Admissions?** Yes

AUGUSTA STATE UNIVERSITY
COLLEGE OF BUSINESS ADMINISTRATION

Admissions Contact: MIYOKO JACKSON, DEGREE PROGRAM SPECIALIST
Address: MBA OFFICE, 2500 WALTON WAY, AUGUSTA, GA 30904-2200
Phone: 706-737-1565 • **Fax:** 706-667-4064
E-mail: MBAINFO@AUG.EDU
Website: WWW.AUG.EDU/COBA/

GENERAL INFORMATION

Type of School: Public **Environment:** Village **Academic Calendar:** Trimester

STUDENTS

Enrollment of parent institution: 6,141 **Enrollment of MBA program:** 125 **% male/female:** 84/16 **% part-time:** 66 **% minorities:** 6 **% international:** 8 **Average age at entry:** 31 **Average years work experience at entry:** 9

ACADEMICS

Student/faculty ratio: 11:1 **% female faculty:** 42

FINANCIAL FACTS

Tuition (in-state/out-of-state): $1,998/$7,974 **Fees (in-state/out-of-state):** $380/$380 **Books and supplies:** $500

ADMISSIONS

Admissions Selectivity Rating: 73

# of applications received: 32 **% applicants accepted:** 75 % **acceptees attending:** 88 **GMAT Range (25th to 75th percentile):** 450-680 **Average GMAT:** 520 **Average GPA:** 3.2 **TOEFL required of int'l applicants?** Yes **Minimum TOEFL (paper/computer):** 500/173 **Application Fee:** $20 **International Application Fee:** $20**Regular Application Deadline:** Rolling **Regular Notification:** Rolling **Deferment Available?** Yes **Maximum length of deferment:** 1 year **Transfer Students Accepted?** Yes **Non-fall Admissions?** Yes

BALL STATE UNIVERSITY
MILLER COLLEGE OF BUSINESS

Admissions Contact: DR. INGA HILL, ASST. TO THE DEAN FOR GRADUATE BUSINESS PROGRAMS
Address: WB 147, MUNCIE, IN 47306
Phone: 765-285-1931 • **Fax:** 765-285-8818
E-mail: MBA@BSU.EDU
Website: WWW.BSU.EDU/MBA

GENERAL INFORMATION

Type of School: Public **Environment:** City **Academic Calendar:** Semester

STUDENTS

Enrollment of parent institution: 18,161 **Enrollment of MBA program:** 197 **% male/female:** 58/42 **% part-time:** 73 **% minorities:** 9 **% international:** 21 **Average age at entry:** 27 **Average years work experience at entry:** 4

ACADEMICS

Student/faculty ratio: 30:1

FINANCIAL FACTS

Tuition (in-state/out-of-state): $7,484/$18,764 **Fees:** $240 **Books and supplies:** $1,400 **Room & board (on/off campus):** $7,314/$7,000

ADMISSIONS

Admissions Selectivity Rating: 76

# of applications received: 39 **% applicants accepted:** 59 % **acceptees attending:** 239 **GMAT Range (25th to 75th percentile):** 440-630 **Average GMAT:** 530 **Average GPA:** 3.28 **TOEFL required of int'l applicants?** Yes **Minimum TOEFL (paper/computer):** 550/213 **Application Fee:** $35 **International Application Fee:** $40 **Regular Application Deadline:** Rolling **Regular Notification:** Rolling **Deferment Available?** Yes **Maximum length of deferment:** 2 years **Transfer Students Accepted?** Yes **Non-fall Admissions?** Yes **Need-Blind Admissions?** Yes **Applicants also look at:** Butler University, Indiana University Kokomo, Indiana University—Purdue University at Fort Wayne, Indiana University—Purdue University Indianapolis.

BOISE STATE UNIVERSITY
COLLEGE OF BUSINESS AND ECONOMICS

Admissions Contact: J. RENEE ANCHUSTEGUI, PROGRAMS ADMINISTRATOR
Address: 1910 UNIVERSITY DRIVE B318, BOISE, ID 83725-1600
Phone: 208-426-1126 • **Fax:** 208-426-1135
E-mail: RANCHUST@BOISESTATE.EDU
Website: COBE.BOISESTATE.EDU/GRADUATE

GENERAL INFORMATION

Type of School: Public **Environment:** City **Academic Calendar:** Semester

STUDENTS

Enrollment of parent institution: 17,883 Enrollment of MBA program: 128 % male/female: 58/42 % out-of-state: 54 % part-time: 72 % minorities: 11 % international: 23 Average age at entry: 32 Average years work experience at entry: 6.6

ACADEMICS

Student/faculty ratio: 30:1 % female faculty: 11 % minority faculty: 5 Prominent Alumni: Jan Packwood, President & COO, Idaho Power Co.; William Glynn, President, Intermountain Gas; Steve Heyl, VP Strategic Planning, Arby's; Norm Schlachter, VP Finance, Micron Technology; Mary Schofield, Controller, Boise Division, Hewlett-Packard.

FINANCIAL FACTS

Tuition (in-state/out-of-state): $4,232/$11,288 Fees: $4,672 Books and supplies: $1,800 Room & board (on/off campus): $6,800/$7,200 % of students receiving grants: 10 Average grant: $17,420

ADMISSIONS

Admissions Selectivity Rating: 75

# of applications received: 146 % applicants accepted: 79 % acceptees attending: 62 GMAT Range (25th to 75th percentile): 470-680 Average GMAT: 576 Average GPA: 3.0 TOEFL required of int'l applicants? Yes Minimum TOEFL (paper/computer): 587/240 Application Fee: $30 International Application Fee: $30 Regular Application Deadline: 7/13 Regular Notification: Rolling Deferment Available? Yes Maximum length of deferment: 1 year Transfer Students Accepted? Yes Non-fall Admissions? Yes Need-Blind Admissions? Yes Applicants also look at: University of Minnesota.

EMPLOYMENT PROFILE

Placement rate (%): 85 % grads employed immediately: 80 Average starting salary: $60,938

BRADLEY UNIVERSITY
FOSTER COLLEGE OF BUSINESS ADMINISTRATION

Admissions Contact: DR. EDWARD SATTLER, DIRECTOR OF GRADUATE PROGRAMS
Address: BAKER HALL, PEORIA, IL 61625
Phone: 309-677-2253 • Fax: 309-677-3374
E-mail: ADE@BRADLEY.EDU
Website: WWW.BRADLEY.EDU/FCBA/INDEX.HTML

GENERAL INFORMATION

Type of School: Private Environment: City Academic Calendar: Semester

FINANCIAL FACTS

Tuition: $8,832 Fees : $15 Books and supplies: $700

ADMISSIONS

Admissions Selectivity Rating: 60*

TOEFL required of int'l applicants? Yes Minimum TOEFL (paper): 500 Application Fee: $50 Regular Application Deadline: Rolling Regular Notification: Rolling Deferment Available? Yes Maximum length of deferment: 1 year Non-fall Admissions? Yes Need-Blind Admissions? Yes

BRYANT UNIVERSITY
SCHOOL OF GRADUATE STUDIES

Admissions Contact: KRISTOPHER SULLIVAN, DIRECTOR OF GRADUATE STUDIES
Address: 1150 DOUGLAS PIKE, SMITHFIELD, RI 02917-1284
Phone: 401-232-6230 • Fax: 401-232-6494
E-mail: GRADPROG@BRYANT.EDU
Website: WWW.BRYANT.EDU

GENERAL INFORMATION

Type of School: Private Environment: Town Academic Calendar: Semester

STUDENTS

Enrollment of parent institution: 3,518 Enrollment of MBA program: 337 % male/female: 49/51 % part-time: 85 % minorities: 6 % international: 18 Average age at entry: 28 Average years work experience at entry: 6

ACADEMICS

Student/faculty ratio: 20:1 % female faculty: 19 % minority faculty: 17 Joint Degrees: MBA with a concentration in computer information systems and MSIS, 66 to 78 credits, 7 years to complete both programs. Prominent Alumni: David M. Beirne, Gen. Partner, Benchmark Capital Partners; William J. Conaty, Sr. VP, General Electric; Robert P. Mead, President, Tyco Engineered Products & Services; Thomas Taylor, President & CEO, Amica Insurance; Kristian P. Moor, Exec. VP, Domestic General Insurance.

FINANCIAL FACTS

Tuition: $11,640 Books and supplies: $1,200 Room & board: $9,000

ADMISSIONS

Admissions Selectivity Rating: 74

# of applications received: 139 % applicants accepted: 63 % acceptees attending: 74 GMAT Range (25th to 75th percentile): 460-550 Average GMAT: 510 Average GPA: 3.1 TOEFL required of int'l applicants? Yes Minimum TOEFL (paper/computer): 580/237 Application Fee: $60 International Application Fee: $80 Regular Application Deadline: 7/15 Regular Notification: Rolling Deferment Available? Yes Maximum length of deferment: 1 year Transfer Students Accepted? Yes Non-fall Admissions? Yes Need-Blind Admissions? Yes Applicants also look at: Babson College, Bentley College, Suffolk University, University of Rhode Island.

CALIFORNIA STATE POLYTECHNIC UNIVERSITY—POMONA
COLLEGE OF BUSINESS ADMINISTRATION

Admissions Contact: ADMINISTRATIVE COORDINATOR
Address: 3801 WEST TEMPLE Avenue., POMONA, CA 91768
Phone: 909-869-3210 • *Fax:* 909-869-4529
E-mail: ADMISSIONS@CSUPOMONA.EDU
Website: WWW.CSUPOMONA.EDU/~MBA/

GENERAL INFORMATION

Type of School: Public **Environment:** City **Academic Calendar:** Quarter

STUDENTS

Enrollment of parent institution: 16,304 **Enrollment of MBA program:** 600 **% male/female:** 55/45 **% minorities:** 20 **Average age at entry:** 32 **Average years work experience at entry:** 10

ACADEMICS

Student/faculty ratio: 15:1

FINANCIAL FACTS

Tuition (in-state/out-of-state): $4,420/$6,100 **Books and supplies:** $3,000 **Room & board (on/off campus):** $5,000/$8,000 **Average grant:** $18,500 **Average student loan debt:** $12,000

ADMISSIONS

Admissions Selectivity Rating: 84

# of applications received: 163 **% applicants accepted:** 30 **% acceptees attending:** 59 **GMAT Range (25th to 75th percentile):** 450-720 **Average GMAT:** 520 **Average GPA:** 3.1 **TOEFL required of int'l applicants?** Yes **Minimum TOEFL (paper/computer):** 580/237 **Application Fee:** $55 **International Application Fee:** $55 **Regular Application Deadline:** Rolling **Regular Notification:** Rolling **Deferment Available?** Yes **Maximum length of deferment:** 1-2 Quarters **Transfer Students Accepted?** Yes **Non-fall Admissions?** Yes

EMPLOYMENT PROFILE

Placement rate (%): 80 **# of companies recruiting on-campus:** 400 **% grads employed immediately:** 75 **Average starting salary:** $52,000

CALIFORNIA STATE UNIVERSITY—BAKERSFIELD
SCHOOL OF BUSINESS AND PUBLIC ADMINISTRATION

Admissions Contact: DEBBIE BLOWERS, EVALUATIONS
Address: 9001 STOCKDALE HIGHWAY, BAKERSFIELD, CA 93311-1099
Phone: 661-664-3036 • *Fax:* 661-664-3389
E-mail: ADMISSIONS@CSUB.EDU
Website: WWW.CSUBAK.EDU/BPA/

GENERAL INFORMATION

Type of School: Public **Environment:** Village **Academic Calendar:** Quarter

STUDENTS

Enrollment of parent institution: 6,700 **Enrollment of MBA program:** 84 **% male/female:** 33/67 **% part-time:** 86 **% minorities:** 25 **% international:** 25 **Average age at entry:** 32

ACADEMICS

Student/faculty ratio: 17:1 **% female faculty:** 10 **% minority faculty:** 10

FINANCIAL FACTS

Tuition (in-state/out-of-state): $2,126/$6,646 **Books and supplies:** $2,200 **Room & board (on/off campus):** $4,950/$7,679

ADMISSIONS

Admissions Selectivity Rating: 87

# of applications received: 80 **% applicants accepted:** 28 **% acceptees attending:** 73 **GMAT Range (25th to 75th percentile):** 490-570 **Average GMAT:** 530 **Average GPA:** 3.3 **TOEFL required of int'l applicants?** Yes **Minimum TOEFL (paper/computer):** 550 **Application Fee:** $55 **Regular Application Deadline:** Rolling **Regular Notification:** Rolling **Non-fall Admissions?** Yes **Need-Blind Admissions?**

EMPLOYMENT PROFILE

% grads employed immediately: 95

CALIFORNIA STATE UNIVERSITY— EAST BAY

COLLEGE OF BUSINESS AND ECONOMICS

Admissions Contact: SUSAN LAKIS, ASSOCIATE DIRECTOR OF ENROLLMENT SVCS
Address: 25800 CARLES BEE BOULEVARD, WARREN HALL, ROOM 200,
  HAYWARD, CA 94542
Phone: 510-885-2784 • *Fax:* 510-885-4059
E-mail: ADMINFO@CSUHAYWARD.EDU
Website: CBEGRAD.CSUHAYWARD.EDU

GENERAL INFORMATION

Type of School: Public Environment: City Academic Calendar:
Quarter

STUDENTS

Enrollment of parent institution: 13,455 Enrollment of MBA program: 438 % male/female: 40/60 % out-of-state: 47 % part-time: 57 % minorities: 21 % international: 47 Average age at entry: 32 Average years work experience at entry: 2

ACADEMICS

Prominent Alumni: Hank Salvo, VP-Controller, Clorox; Jack Acosta, CFO/VP, Portal Software; Louis Navellier, Pres/CEO, Navellier & Assoc, Inc.

FINANCIAL FACTS

Tuition (in-state/out-of-state): $4,256/$15,104 Books and supplies: $1,000 Room & board (on/off campus): $7,235/$8,604 % of students receiving aid: 12 % of first-year students receiving aid: 12 % of students receiving loans: 8 % of students receiving grants: 1 Average award package: $8,906 Average grant: $1,604 Average student loan debt: $25,626

ADMISSIONS

Admissions Selectivity Rating: 72
# of applications received: 290 % applicants accepted: 75 % acceptees attending: 70 GMAT Range (25th to 75th percentile): 475-624 Average GMAT: 530 Average GPA: 3.22 TOEFL required of int'l applicants? Yes Minimum TOEFL (paper/computer): 550/213 Application Fee: $55 International Application Fee: $55 Regular Application Deadline: 6/1 Regular Notification: 6/21 Deferment Available? Yes Maximum length of deferment: one Quarter Non-fall Admissions? Yes Need-Blind Admissions? Applicants also look at: California State University—Sacramento, San Francisco State University, San Jose State University, University of California—Berkeley, University of California—Davis.

EMPLOYMENT PROFILE

Placement rate (%): 99 # of companies recruiting on-campus: 204

CALIFORNIA STATE UNIVERSITY— FRESNO

CRAIG SCHOOL OF BUSINESS

Admissions Contact: DR. MARK KEPPLER, DIRECTOR OF GRADUATE STUDIES
Address: 5245 NORTH BACKER AVENUE, FRESNO, CA 93740
Phone: 559-278-2107 • *Fax:* 559-278-4911
E-mail: NYEEG@CSUFRESNO.EDU
Website: WWW.CRAIGMBA.COM

GENERAL INFORMATION

Type of School: Public Academic Calendar: Semester

STUDENTS

Enrollment of parent institution: 19,000 Enrollment of MBA program: 218 % male/female: 55/45 % out-of-state: 15 % part-time: 64 % minorities: 7 % international: 55 Average age at entry: 29 Average years work experience at entry: 7

ACADEMICS

Student/faculty ratio: 6:1 % female faculty: 33

FINANCIAL FACTS

Books and supplies: $650 Room & Board: $10,700

ADMISSIONS

Admissions Selectivity Rating:83
# of applications received: 148 % applicants accepted: 62 % acceptees attending: 72 GMAT Range (25th to 75th percentile): 560-630 Average GMAT: 593 Average GPA: 3.4 TOEFL required of int'l applicants? Yes Minimum TOEFL (paper/computer): 550/213 Application Fee: $55 International Application Fee: $55 Regular Application Deadline: 3/1 Regular Notification: Rolling Deferment Available? Yes Maximum length of deferment: 1 year Transfer Students Accepted? Yes Non-fall Admissions? Yes Need-Blind Admissions? Yes Applicants also look at: California Polytechnic State University—San Luis, Santa Clara University, University of California—Davis.

CALIFORNIA STATE UNIVERSITY— LOS ANGELES

COLLEGE OF BUSINESS AND ECONOMICS

Admissions Contact: JOAN WOOSLEY, ADMISSIONS OFFICER
Address: 5151 STATE UNIVERSITY DRIVE, LOS ANGELES, CA 90032
Phone: 323-343-3904 • *Fax:* 323-343-6306
E-mail: ADMISSIONS@CALSTATELA.EDU
Website: CBE.CALSTATELA.EDU/

GENERAL INFORMATION

Type of School: Public Environment: City Academic Calendar:
Quarter

STUDENTS

Enrollment of parent institution: 18,849 **Enrollment of MBA program:** 330 **% male/female:** 47/53 **% part-time:** 100 **% minorities:** 50 **Average age at entry:** 31

FINANCIAL FACTS

Tuition (in-state/out-of-state): $1,796/$5,732

ADMISSIONS

Admissions Selectivity Rating: 83

# of applications received: 388 **% applicants accepted:** 43 **% acceptees attending:** 52 **Average GMAT:** 560 **Average GPA:** 3.0 **TOEFL required of int'l applicants?** Yes **Minimum TOEFL (paper/computer):** 550/213 **Application Fee:** $55 **Regular Application Deadline:** 6/15 **Regular Notification:** 1/1 **Non-fall Admissions?** Yes

EMPLOYMENT PROFILE

Placement rate (%): 95

CALIFORNIA STATE UNIVERSITY— NORTHRIDGE
COLLEGE OF BUSINESS AND ECONOMICS

Admissions Contact: RON ANDRADE, ASSISTANT DIRECTOR OF GRADUATE PROGRAMS
Address: 18111 NORDHOFF STREET, NORTHRIDGE, CA 91330-8380
Phone: 818-677-2467 • **Fax:** 818-677-3188
E-mail: MBA@CSUN.EDU
Website: CSUN.EDU/MBA

GENERAL INFORMATION

Type of School: Public **Environment:** City **Academic Calendar:** Semester

STUDENTS

Enrollment of parent institution: 30,000 **Enrollment of MBA program:** 275 **% male/female:** 50/50 **% minorities:** 50 **Average age at entry:** 29 **Average years work experience at entry:** 7

ACADEMICS

Student/faculty ratio: 22:1 **% female faculty:** 18 **% minority faculty:** 6

FINANCIAL FACTS

Tuition: $2,082 **Books and supplies:** $200

ADMISSIONS

Admissions Selectivity Rating: 89

# of applications received: 249 **% applicants accepted:** 30 **% acceptees attending:** 73 **Average GMAT:** 552 **Average GPA:** 3.2 **TOEFL required of int'l applicants?** Yes **Minimum TOEFL (paper/computer):** 550/213 **Application Fee:** $55 **International Application Fee:** $55 **Regular Application Deadline:** 5/1 **Regular Notification:** Rolling **Transfer Students Accepted?** Yes **Non-fall Admissions?** Yes **Need-Blind Admissions?** Yes

EMPLOYMENT PROFILE

% grads employed immediately: 85

CALIFORNIA STATE UNIVERSITY— SACRAMENTO
COLLEGE OF BUSINESS ADMINISTRATION

Admissions Contact: JEANIE ALLAM, GRADUATE PROGRAM ACADEMIC COUNSELOR
Address: 6000 J STREET, SACRAMENTO, CA 95819-6088
Phone: 916-278-6772 • **Fax:** 916-278-4233
E-mail: CBAGRAD@CSUS.EDU
Website: WWW.CSUS.EDU/CBAGRAD/INDEX.HTML

GENERAL INFORMATION

Type of School: Public **Environment:** Metropolis **Academic Calendar:** Semester

STUDENTS

Enrollment of parent institution: 28,375 **Enrollment of MBA program:** 311 **% male/female:** 56/44 **% part-time:** 63 **% minorities:** 49 **% international:** 10 **Average age at entry:** 30 **Average years work experience at entry:** 3

ACADEMICS

Student/faculty ratio: 13:1 **% female faculty:** 28 **Joint Degrees:** Master of Business Administration and Juris Docotrate (MBA/JD)McGeorge School of Law : Full-time; approx 4.5 years needed to complete combined program. **Prominent Alumni:** Dennis Gardemeyer, Executive Vice President/Zuckerman-Hertog; Tom Weborg, Chief Executive Officer/Cucina Holdings; William Keever, President/Vodafone Airtouch; Margo Murray, President, CEO/MMHA The Mangers' Mentors Inc.; Scott Syphax, President, CEO/Nehemiah Corporation.

FINANCIAL FACTS

Tuition (in-state/out-of-state): $3,310/$9,160 **Books and supplies:** $1,700 **Room & board (on/off campus):** $9,400/$8,400

Admissions Selectivity Rating: 81

# of applications received: 247 % applicants accepted: 61 % acceptees attending: 66 GMAT Range (25th to 75th percentile): 420-750 Average GMAT: 575 Average GPA: 3.1 TOEFL required of int'l applicants? Yes Minimum TOEFL (paper/computer): 550/213 Application Fee: $55 International Application Fee: $55 Regular Application Deadline: 4/1 Regular Notification: 5/30

Transfer Students Accepted? Yes Non-fall Admissions? Yes

EMPLOYMENT PROFILE

of companies recruiting on-campus: 36

CANISIUS COLLEGE
RICHARD J. WEHLE SCHOOL OF BUSINESS

Admissions Contact: LAURA MCEWEN, DIRECTOR, GRADUATE BUSINESS PROGRAMS
Address: CANISIUS COLLEGE, 2001 MAIN STREET, BAGEN HALL 201, BUFFALO, NY 14208-1098
Phone: 716-888-2140 • **Fax:** 716-888-2145
E-mail: GRADUBUS@CANISIUS.EDU
Website: WWW.CANISIUS.EDU/MBA

GENERAL INFORMATION

Type of School: Private Affiliation: Roman Catholic-Jesuit Environment: Metropolis Academic Calendar: Semester

STUDENTS

Enrollment of parent institution: 5,038 Enrollment of MBA program: 287 % male/female: 66/34 % part-time: 82 % minorities: 10 % international: 7 Average age at entry: 27 Average years work experience at entry: 6

ACADEMICS

Student/faculty ratio: 19:1 % female faculty: 17 % minority faculty: 4 Joint Degrees: Bachelor and MBA—5 years.

FINANCIAL FACTS

Tuition: $31,932 Books and supplies: $1,000 Room & board: $8,100

ADMISSIONS

Admissions Selectivity Rating: 71

# of applications received: 112 % applicants accepted: 72 % acceptees attending: 78 GMAT Range (25th to 75th percentile): 460-557 Average GMAT: 510 Average GPA: 3.1 TOEFL required of int'l applicants? Yes Minimum TOEFL (paper/computer): 500/200 Application Fee: $25 Regular Application Deadline: Rolling Regular Notification: Rolling Deferment Available? Yes Maximum length of deferment: 1 year Transfer Students Accepted? Yes Non-fall Admissions? Yes Applicants also look at: SUNY—University at Buffalo

EMPLOYMENT PROFILE

Placement rate (%): 86 % grads employed immediately: 86 Average starting salary: $48,900

CENTRAL MICHIGAN UNIVERSITY
COLLEGE OF BUSINESS ADMINISTRATION

Admissions Contact: PAMELA STAMBERSKY, DIRECTOR OF GRADUATE PROGRAMS
Address: 105 WARRINER HALL, MOUNT PLEASANT, MI 48859
Phone: 517-774-3150 • **Fax:** 517-774-2372
E-mail: CBAWORK@CMICH.EDU
Website: WWW.CBA.CMICH.EDU

GENERAL INFORMATION

Type of School: Public Environment: Town Academic Calendar: Semester

STUDENTS

Enrollment of parent institution: 16,613 Enrollment of MBA program: 471 % male/female: 59/41 % part-time: 50 % minorities: 1 % international: 34 Average age at entry: 28

ADMISSIONS

Admissions Selectivity Rating: 60*

# of applications received: 151 % applicants accepted: 80 % Average GPA: TOEFL required of int'l applicants? Yes Minimum TOEFL (paper): 550 Application Fee: $30 International Application Fee: Regular Application Deadline: Rolling Regular Notification: Rolling Deferment Available? Yes

EMPLOYMENT PROFILE

Placement rate (%): 100

CENTRAL MISSOURI STATE UNIVERSITY
HARMON COLLEGE OF BUSINESS ADMINISTRATION

Admissions Contact: LAURIE DELAP, ADMISSIONS EVALUATOR, GRADUATE SCHOOL
Address: WARD EDWARDS 1800, WARRENSBURG, MO 64093
Phone: 660-543-4328 • **Fax:** 660-543-4778
E-mail: DELAP@CMSU1.CMSU.EDU
Website: WWW.CMSU.EDU/GRADUATE

GENERAL INFORMATION

Type of School: Public Environment: Rural Academic Calendar: Semester

STUDENTS

Enrollment of parent institution: 10,313 **Enrollment of MBA program:** 52 % **male/female:** 62/38 % **out-of-state:** 6 % **part-time:** 38 % **minorities:** 22 % **international:** 46 **Average age at entry:** 27

ACADEMICS

Student/faculty ratio: 2:1 % **female faculty:** 29 % **minority faculty:** 1

FINANCIAL FACTS

Tuition (in-state/out-of-state): $5,328/$10,320 **Books and supplies:** $800 **Room & board:** $4,988 % **of students receiving grants:** 50

ADMISSIONS

Admissions Selectivity Rating:70

# of applications received: 98 % **applicants accepted:** 59 % **acceptees attending:** 60 **Average GMAT:** 463 **Average GPA:** 3.2 **TOEFL required of int'l applicants?** Yes **Minimum TOEFL (paper/computer):** 550/213 **Application Fee:** $25 **International Application Fee:** $50 **Regular Application Deadline:** Rolling **Regular Notification:** Rolling **Deferment Available?** Yes **Maximum length of deferment:** 2 Semesters **Transfer Students Accepted?** Yes **Non-fall Admissions?** Yes **Need-Blind Admissions?** Yes **Applicants also look at:** Southeast Missouri State University, Southwest Missouri State University, University of Missouri—Kansas City, Widener University.

EMPLOYMENT PROFILE

of companies recruiting on-campus: 136

CLARION UNIVERSITY
COLLEGE OF BUSINESS ADMINISTRATION

Admissions Contact: Dr. Robert S. Balough, Director of MBA Program
Address: 302 Still Hall, Clarion University, Clarion, PA 16214
Phone: 814-393-2605 • **Fax:** 814-393-1910
E-mail: MBA@CLARION.EDU
Website: WWW.CLARION.EDU/MBA

GENERAL INFORMATION

Type of School: Public **Environment:** Rural **Academic Calendar:** Semester

STUDENTS

Enrollment of parent institution: 6,421 **Enrollment of MBA program:** 43 % **male/female:** 67/33 % **out-of-state:** 5 % **part-time:** 9 % **minorities:** 5 % **international:** 42 **Average age at entry:** 29 **Average years work experience at entry:** 3.28

ACADEMICS

% female faculty: 18 % **minority faculty:** 23

FINANCIAL FACTS

Tuition (in-state/out-of-state): $5,772/$9,236 **Fees (in-state/out-of-state):** $1,557/$1,607 **Books and supplies:** $3,650 **Room & board (on/off campus):** $4,816/$4,000 **Average award package:** $8,710

ADMISSIONS

Admissions Selectivity Rating: 67

# of applications received: 36 % **applicants accepted:** 78 % **acceptees attending:** 64 **Average GMAT:** 490 **Average GPA:** 3.2 **TOEFL required of int'l applicants?** Yes **Minimum TOEFL (paper/computer):** 550/213 **Application Fee:** $30 **International Application Fee:** $30 **Regular Application Deadline:** Rolling **Regular Notification:** Rolling **Deferment Available?** Yes **Maximum length of deferment:** 1 year **Transfer Students Accepted?** Yes **Non-fall Admissions?** Yes **Need-Blind Admissions?** Yes

CLARK ATLANTA UNIVERSITY
SCHOOL OF BUSINESS ADMINISTRATION

Admissions Contact: Crysta L. Bolton, Director of Admissions and Student Affairs
Address: 223 James P. Brawley Drive, Atlanta, GA 30314
Phone: 404-880-8447 • **Fax:** 404-880-6159
E-mail: CBOLTON@CAU.EDU
Website: WWW.CAU.EDU

GENERAL INFORMATION

Type of School: private **Affiliation:** Methodist **Environment:** City

STUDENTS

Enrollment of parent institution: **Enrollment of MBA program:** 120 % **male/female:** 38/62 % **minorities:** 38 % **international:** 7 **Average age at entry:** 29 **Average years work experience at entry:** 5

ACADEMICS

Student/faculty ratio: 11:1 % **female faculty:** 19

FINANCIAL FACTS

Tuition: $16,709 **Fees:** $200 **Books and supplies:** $1,000 **Room & Board:** $5,000 % **of students receiving aid:** 95 % **of first-year students receiving aid:** 95 % **of students receiving loans:** 95 % **of students receiving grants:** 95 **Average award package:** $32,000 **Average grant:** $32,000 **Average student loan debt:** $65,000

ADMISSIONS

Admissions Selectivity Rating: 79

# of applications received: 346 % **applicants accepted:** 26 % **acceptees attending:** 82 **Average GMAT:** 446 **Average GPA:** 2.84 **TOEFL required of int'l applicants?** Yes **Minimum TOEFL (paper/computer):** 175/ **Application Fee:** $40 **International Application Fee:** $55 **Regular Application Deadline:** 3/1 **Regular Notification:** Rolling **Deferment Available?** Yes **Maximum length of deferment:** 2 years **Applicants also look at:** Emory University, Georgia State University

Placement rate (%): 95 # of companies recruiting on-campus: 42 % grads employed immediately: 63 Average starting salary: $84,000

CLEMSON UNIVERSITY
GRADUATE SCHOOL OF BUSINESS AND BEHAVIORAL SCIENCE

Admissions Contact: MBA OFFICE - ADMISSIONS, ASSOCIATE DIRECTOR OF MBA PROGRAMS
Address: 124 SIRRINE HALL, BOX 341315, CLEMSON UNIVERSITY, CLEMSON, SC 29634-1315
Phone: 864-656-3975 • **Fax:** 864-656-0947
E-mail: MBA@CLEMSON.EDU
Website: BUSINESS.CLEMSON.EDU/MBA/

GENERAL INFORMATION

Type of School: Public **Environment:** Rural **Academic Calendar:** Aug -May

STUDENTS

Enrollment of parent institution: 16,900 **Enrollment of MBA program:** 181 **% male/female:** 70/30 **% out-of-state:** 56 **% part-time:** 61 **% minorities:** 6 **% international:** 23 **Average age at entry:** 29 **Average years work experience at entry:** 7

ACADEMICS

Student/faculty ratio: 9:1 **% female faculty:** 21 **% minority faculty:** 2 **Joint Degrees:** Dual degrees are allowed on the master's level. Up to 1/6 of the total hours in both programs combined may be double counted. Dual degrees must be declared by the first semester of graduate school. **Prominent Alumni:** Jane Robelot, Co-Anchor of CBS; J. Strom Thurmond, U.S. Senator (died 2003); Robert H. Brooks, President, Naturally Fresh Foods; Kristie A. Kenney, U.S. Ambassador to Ecuador; Nancy Humphries O'Dell, Co-Anchor of NBC's Access Hollywood.

FINANCIAL FACTS

Tuition (in-state/out-of-state): $8,836/$16,064 **Fees:** $364 **Books and supplies:** $2,000 **Room & board (on/off campus):** $8,804/$7,544 **% of students receiving aid:** 32 **% of first-year students receiving aid:** 48 **% of students receiving loans:** 16

ADMISSIONS

Admissions Selectivity Rating: 85
# of applications received: 173 **% applicants accepted:** 55 **% acceptees attending:** 56 **GMAT Range (25th to 75th percentile):** 590-620 **Average GMAT:** 610 **Average GPA:** 3.3 **TOEFL required of int'l applicants?** Yes **Minimum TOEFL (paper/computer):** 580/237 **Application Fee:** $50 **International Application Fee:** $50 **Regular Application Deadline:** 4/15 **Regular Notification:** 4/30 **Deferment Available?** Yes **Maximum length of deferment:** 1 year **Transfer Students Accepted?** Yes **Non-fall Admissions?** Need-Blind **Admissions?** Yes

# of companies recruiting on-campus: 1373 % grads employed immediately: 84 Average starting salary: $53,000

Grads employed by field:% avg. salary:

Accounting	5	$52,000
Finance	7	$52,000
Human Resources	1	NR
Marketing	13	$53,000
MIS	2	NR
Operations	13	$53,000
Strategic Planning	2	NR
Consulting	4	$54,000
General Management	5	$50,000
Quantitative	1	NR
Other	20	NR

CLEVELAND STATE UNIVERSITY
JAMES J. NANCE COLLEGE OF BUSINESS ADMINISTRATION

Admissions Contact: BRUCE M. GOTTSCHALK, MBA PROGRAMS ADMINISTRATOR
Address: 2121 EUCLID AVENUE, BU 219, CLEVELAND, OH 44115
Phone: 216-687-3730 • **Fax:** 216-687-5311
E-mail: CBACSU@CSUOHIO.EDU
Website: WWW.CSUOHIO.EDU/MBA

GENERAL INFORMATION

Type of School: Public **Environment:** City **Academic Calendar:** Semester

STUDENTS

Enrollment of parent institution: 16,300 **Enrollment of MBA program:** 704 **% male/female:** 65/35 **% out-of-state:** 40 **% part-time:** 78 **% minorities:** 10 **% international:** 35 **Average age at entry:** 28 **Average years work experience at entry:** 5.3

ACADEMICS

Student/faculty ratio: 27:1 **% female faculty:** 22 **% minority faculty:** 15 **Joint Degrees:** JD/MBA 4 years, MBA/MSN 3 years. **Prominent Alumni:** Monte Ahuja, Chairman, President & CEO, Transtar Industries; Michael Berthelot, Chairman & CEO Transtechnolgy Corporation; Ted Hlavaty, Chairman & CEO, Neway Stamping & Manufacturing; Thomas Moore, President, Wolf Group; Kenneth Semelsberger, President, COO& Director, Scott Fetzer, Inc.

FINANCIAL FACTS

Tuition (in-state/out-of-state): $8,592/$16,464 **Books and supplies:** $1,300 **Room & board (on/off campus):** $11,000/$12,000 **% of students receiving aid:** 4 **% of first-year students receiving aid:** 8 **% of students receiving loans:** 28 **Average award package:** $14,000

Admissions Selectivity Rating: 66

# of applications received: 423 % applicants accepted: 79 % acceptees attending: 57 GMAT Range (25th to 75th percentile): 460-590 Average GMAT: 500 Average GPA: 3.14 TOEFL required of int'l applicants? Yes Minimum TOEFL (paper/computer): 525/197 Application Fee: $30 International Application Fee: $30 Regular Application Deadline: 7/1 Regular Notification: Rolling Deferment Available? Yes Maximum length of deferment: 1 year Transfer Students Accepted? Yes Non-fall Admissions? Yes Need-Blind Admissions? Yes Applicants also look at: Case Western Reserve University, John Carroll University, Kent State University, The University of Akron.

EMPLOYMENT PROFILE

Placement rate (%): 90 # of companies recruiting on-campus: 66 % grads employed immediately: 84 Average starting salary: $55,100

Grads employed by field:% avg. salary:

Accounting	11	$54,800
Finance	22	$57,500
Human Resources	3	$51,000
Marketing	18	$54,900
MIS	3	$53,600
Operations	15	$58,300
General Management	6	$56,000
Other	12	$51,000
Non-profit	10:	$47,800

COLORADO STATE UNIVERSITY— DENVER EXECUTIVE MBA
COLLEGE OF BUSINESS EXECUTIVE MBA PROGRAM

Admissions Contact: JIM MCCAMBRIDGE, DIRECTOR OF THE EXECUTIVE MBA PROGRAM
Address: DENVER EXECUTIVE MBA OFFICES, 1445 MARKET STREET, SUITE 208, DENVER, CO 80202
Phone: 303-534-3191 • Fax: 303-534-3194
E-mail: DENVERMBA@BUSINESS.COLOSTATE.EDU
Website: WWW.DENVERMBA.COM

GENERAL INFORMATION

Type of School: Public Academic Calendar: Aug-May

STUDENTS

Enrollment of parent institution: Enrollment of MBA program: 40 % male/female: 100/0 Average age at entry: 38 Average years work experience at entry: 14

ACADEMICS

Student/faculty ratio: 2:1 Joint Degrees: The Executive MBA Program is not a combined program; however, there is DVM/MBA combination degree offered on campus in Fort Collins, Colorado through the College of Veterinary Medicine and the College of Business.

FINANCIAL FACTS

Tuition: $1,113

ADMISSIONS

Admissions Selectivity Rating: 78

# of applications received: 32 % applicants accepted: 75 % acceptees attending: 92 Average GMAT: 572 Average GPA: 3.2 TOEFL required of int'l applicants? Yes Minimum TOEFL (paper/computer): /565 Application Fee: $50 Regular Application Deadline: 7/15 Regular Notification: 8/1 Deferment Available? Yes Maximum length of deferment: 1 year

EMPLOYMENT PROFILE

Placement rate (%): 92

COLORADO STATE UNIVERSITY— DISTANCE MBA PROGRAM
COLLEGE OF BUSINESS DISTANCE MBA PROGRAM

Admissions Contact: SUSAN MEYER, MBA PROGRAMS MARKETING AND RECRUITING
Address: COLLEGE OF BUSINESS, 1275 CAMPUS DELIVERY, FORT COLLINS, CO 80523-1275
Phone: 800-491-4622 • Fax: 970-491-2348
E-mail: BIZINFO@LAMAR.COLOSTATE.EDU
Website: WWW.CSUMBA.COM

GENERAL INFORMATION

Type of School: Public Academic Calendar: Aug-May

STUDENTS

Enrollment of parent institution: Enrollment of MBA program: 300 % male/female: 100/0

ACADEMICS

Student/faculty ratio: 35:1 Joint Degrees: DVM/MBA program is a 5-year program and is a joint program witn the College of Business and the College of Veterinary Medicine.

FINANCIAL FACTS

Tuition (per credit): $498 Books and supplies: $880

ADMISSIONS

Admissions Selectivity Rating: 81

# of applications received: 120 **% applicants accepted:** 75 %
acceptees attending: 90 **Average GMAT:** 612 **Average GPA:** 3.1
TOEFL required of int'l applicants? Yes **Minimum TOEFL (comput-
er):** 565 **Application Fee:** $50 **International Application Fee:** $50
Regular Application Deadline: 7/15 **Regular Notification:** 8/1
Deferment Available? Yes **Maximum length of deferment:** 1 year
Non-fall Admissions? Yes

COLUMBUS STATE UNIVERSITY
D. ABBOTT TURNER COLLEGE OF BUSINESS

Admissions Contact: MS. KATIE THORNTON, GRADUATE ADMISSIONS
Address: 4225 UNIVERSITY Avenue, COLUMBUS, GA 31907
Phone: 706-568-2035 • **Fax:** 706-568-5091
E-mail: ADMISSIONS@COLSTATE.EDU
Website: DATCOB.COLSTATE.EDU/

GENERAL INFORMATION

Type of School: Public **Academic Calendar:** Semester

STUDENTS

Enrollment of parent institution: Enrollment of MBA program: 48 %
male/female: 33/67 **% minorities:** 56

ACADEMICS

Student/faculty ratio: 12:1

FINANCIAL FACTS

Tuition (in-state/out-of-state): $3,500/$14,000 **Fees:** $876 **Books
and supplies:** $1,000 **Average grant:** $3,000

ADMISSIONS

Admissions Selectivity Rating: 85

# of applications received: 33 **% applicants accepted:** 36 %
acceptees attending: 100 **Average GMAT:** 500 **Average GPA:** 3.42
TOEFL required of int'l applicants? Yes **Minimum TOEFL
(paper/computer):** 550/213 **Application Fee:** $25 **International
Application Fee:** $25 **Regular Application Deadline:** 7/20 **Regular
Notification:** Rolling **Transfer Students Accepted?** Yes **Non-fall
Admissions?** Yes **Need-Blind Admissions?** Yes

CREIGHTON UNIVERSITY
COLLEGE OF BUSINESS ADMINISTRATION

Admissions Contact: GAIL HAFER, COORDINATOR OF GRADUATE BUSINESS
PROGRAMS
Address: COLLEGE OF BUSINESS ADMINISTRATION, ROOM 212C, 2500
CALIFORNIA PLAZA, OMAHA, NE 68178
Phone: 402-280-2853 • **Fax:** 402-280-2172
E-mail: COBAGRAD@CREIGHTON.EDU
Website: COBWEB.CREIGHTON.EDU

GENERAL INFORMATION

Type of School: Private **Affiliation:** Roman Catholic **Environment:**
Metropolis

STUDENTS

Enrollment of parent institution: 6,723 **Enrollment of MBA program:** 118 **% male/female:** 58/42 **% part-time:** 84 **% minorities:** 1
% international: 31 **Average age at entry:** 25 **Average years work
experience at entry:** 3

ACADEMICS

Student/faculty ratio: 2:1 **% female faculty:** 10 **Joint Degrees:**
Master of business administration/juris doctor (3 years); master of
business administration/doctor of pharmacy (4 years; master of
business administration/master of international relations (3 years);
master of business administration/master of science-inf.

FINANCIAL FACTS

Tuition: $10,206 **Fees:** $764 **Books and supplies:** $1,600 **Room &
board (on/off campus):** $7,000/$6,000 **% of students receiving aid:**
15 **% of first-year students receiving aid:** 8 **Average award package:** $19,653

ADMISSIONS

Admissions Selectivity Rating: 71

# of applications received: 24 **% applicants accepted:** 96 %
acceptees attending: 78 **Average GMAT:** 570 **Average GPA:** 3.4
TOEFL required of int'l applicants? Yes **Minimum TOEFL
(paper/computer):** 550/213 **Application Fee:** $40 **International
Application Fee:** $40 **Regular Application Deadline:** Rolling
Regular Notification: Rolling **Deferment Available?** Yes **Maximum
length of deferment:** 1 year **Transfer Students Accepted?** Yes **Non-
fall Admissions?** Yes **Applicants also look at:** University of
Nebraska at Omaha.

EMPLOYMENT PROFILE

% grads employed immediately: 90 **% grads employed within
three months:** 29
Grads employed by field: ....%
Other...8

DePaul University
Kellstadt Graduate School of Business

Admissions Contact: Christopher E. Kinsella, Director of Admission
Address: 1 East Jackson Boulevard, Suite 7900, Chicago, IL 60604
Phone: 312-362-8810 • *Fax:* 312-362-6677
E-mail: kgsb@depaul.edu
Website: www.kellstadt.depaul.edu

GENERAL INFORMATION

Type of School: Private **Affiliation:** Roman Catholic **Environment: Academic Calendar:** Quarter

STUDENTS

Enrollment of parent institution: 23,570 **Enrollment of MBA program:** 2,045 **% male/female:** 49/51 **% part-time:** 97 **% minorities:** 1 **% international:** 37 **Average age at entry:** 30 **Average years work experience at entry:** 5.2

ACADEMICS

Student/faculty ratio: 12:1 **% female faculty:** 17 **% minority faculty:** 15 **Joint Degrees:** Master of business administration/doctor of jurisprudence (MBA/JD): Full-time, part-time; 140 total credits required; 2.8 to 3.8 years to complete program. Any of the concentrations listed above can be selected for this combined degree. Prominent Alumni: Jim Jenness, CEO, Kellogg's; Richard Driehaus, President, Driehaus Capital Management; Edward Bosowski, President, USG Corporation; Daniel Ustian, Chairman, President and CEO, Navistar International.

FINANCIAL FACTS

Tuition: $40,200 **Fees:** $35 **Books and supplies:** $2,000 **Room & board (on/off campus):** $13,044/$10,800 **% of students receiving aid:** 30 **% of first-year students receiving aid:** 40 **% of students receiving grants:** 30 **Average award package:** $20,000 **Average grant:** $8,000 **Average student loan debt:** $27,810

ADMISSIONS

Admissions Selectivity Rating: 70

# of applications received: 382 **% applicants accepted:** 91 **% acceptees attending:** 81 **GMAT Range (25th to 75th percentile):** 510-600 **Average GMAT:** 550 **Average GPA:** 3.15 **TOEFL required of int'l applicants?** Yes **Minimum TOEFL (paper/computer):** 550/213 **Application Fee:** $60 **International Application Fee:** $60 **Regular Application Deadline:** 7/1 **Regular Notification:** Rolling **Deferment Available?** Yes **Maximum length of deferment:** 1 year **Transfer Students Accepted?** Yes **Non-fall Admissions?** Yes **Need-Blind Admissions?** Yes **Applicants also look at:** Loyola University Chicago, Northwestern University, University of Chicago.

EMPLOYMENT PROFILE

Placement rate (%): 81 **% grads employed immediately:** 74
Average starting salary: $60,158
Grads employed by field:% avg. salary:

Finance 61 $59,000
Marketing 33 $55,000
Consulting 6 $105,000

Drake University
College of Business and Public Administration

Admissions Contact: Danette Kenne, Director of Graduate Programs
Address: 2507 University Avenue, Aliber Hall, Des Moines, IA 50311
Phone: 515-271-2188 • *Fax:* 515-271-4518
E-mail: cbpa.gradprograms@drake.edu
Website: www.drake.edu/cbpa/grad

GENERAL INFORMATION

Type of School: Private **Academic Calendar:** Semester

STUDENTS

Enrollment of parent institution: 5,221 **Enrollment of MBA program:** 229 **% male/female:** 90/10 **% part-time:** 93 **% minorities:** 2 **% international:** 1 **Average age at entry:** 25

ACADEMICS

Student/faculty ratio: 20:1 **% female faculty:** 10 **Joint Degrees:** MBA/Pharm D 6 years, MPA/JD 3 years, MBA/JD 3 years, MPA/Pharm D 6 years. **Prominent Alumni:** Robert D, Ray, Former Governor State of Iowa; Sherrill Milnes, Opera; Daniel Jorndt, Former Chairman/CEO Walgreen's; Dwight Opperman, Former CEO of West Publishing; Marie Wilson, President of MS Foundation for Women.

FINANCIAL FACTS

Tuition: $8,200 **Fees:** $300 **Books and supplies:** $400

ADMISSIONS

Admissions Selectivity Rating: 63

# of applications received: 61 **% applicants accepted:** 84 **% acceptees attending:** 18 **GMAT Range (25th to 75th percentile):** 460-560 **Average GMAT:** 520 **Average GPA:** 3.19 **TOEFL required of int'l applicants?** Yes **Minimum TOEFL (paper/computer):** 550/213 **Application Fee:** $25 **International Application Fee:** $25 **Regular Application Deadline:** 6/1 **Regular Notification:** Rolling **Deferment Available?** Yes **Maximum length of deferment:** one term **Transfer Students Accepted?** Yes **Non-fall Admissions?** Yes **Need-Blind Admissions?** Yes **Applicants also look at:** Iowa State University, University of Iowa.

EMPLOYMENT PROFILE

Placement rate (%): 100 % grads employed immediately: 100 % grads employed within three months: 94 **Average starting salary:** $56,900

Drexel University
Bennett S. LeBow College of Business

Admissions Contact: Rob Palachick, Director of Graduate Enrollment Services & Operations
Address: 3141 Chestnut Street, Philadelphia, PA 19104
Phone: 215-895-6804 • **Fax:** 215-895-1725
E-mail: RAP36@DREXEL.EDU
Website: WWW.LEBOW.DREXEL.EDU

GENERAL INFORMATION
Type of School: Private **Academic Calendar:** Year

STUDENTS
% male/female: 73/27 % out-of-state: 42 % minorities: 14 % international: 18 **Average age at entry:** 28 **Average years work experience at entry:** 5.5

ACADEMICS
Student/faculty ratio: 16:1 % female faculty: 26 % minority faculty: 15 **Joint Degrees:** Upon Completion of one-year MBA, MS in finance, accounting.

FINANCIAL FACTS
Tuition: $45,000 **Books and supplies:** $12,000 **Average grant:** $15,500

ADMISSIONS
Admissions Selectivity Rating: 84
# of applications received: 80 % applicants accepted: 61 % acceptees attending: 45 GMAT Range (25th to 75th percentile): 570-670 **Average GMAT:** 622 **Average GPA:** 3.4 **TOEFL required of int'l applicants?** Yes **Minimum TOEFL (paper/computer):** 600/250 **Application Fee:** $50 **International Application Fee:** $50 **Regular Application Deadline:** 5/24 **Regular Notification:** Rolling **Early decision program?** Yes **ED deadline /notification:** 10/1; 12/1; 1/1 **Deferment Available?** Yes **Maximum length of deferment:** 12months **Transfer Students Accepted? Non-fall Admissions?** Yes **Need-Blind Admissions?** Yes

EMPLOYMENT PROFILE

% grads employed immediately: 40 **Average starting salary:** $61,000

Grads employed by field:% avg. salary:

Field	%	avg. salary
Finance	33	$68,000
Human Resources	7	$68,000
Marketing	13	$72,500
Operations	13	$62,500
Consulting	7	$50,500
General Management	13	$66,500
Other	7	NR

Eastern Illinois University
Lumpkin College of Business and Applied Sciences

Admissions Contact: Dr. Cheryl Noll, Coordinator, Graduate Business Studies
Address: 600 Lincoln Avenue, 4009 Lumpkin Hall, Charleston, IL 61920-3099
Phone: 217-581-3028 • **Fax:** 217-581-6642
E-mail: MBA@EIU.EDU
Website: WWW.EIU.EDU/~MBA

GENERAL INFORMATION
Type of School: Public **Environment:** Village

STUDENTS
Enrollment of parent institution: 11,000 **Enrollment of MBA program:** 173 % male/female: 68/32 % out-of-state: 2 % part-time: 43 % minorities: 5 % international: 26 **Average age at entry:** 25 **Average years work experience at entry:** 3

ACADEMICS
Student/faculty ratio: 22:1 % female faculty: 33 % minority faculty: 8

FINANCIAL FACTS
Tuition (in-state/out-of-state): $4,125/$12,375 **Fees:** $2,094 **Books and supplies:** $325 **Room & board (on/off campus):** $6,000/$8,000 % of students receiving aid: 17 % of first-year students receiving aid: 22 % of students receiving grants: 17 **Average grant:** $7,000

ADMISSIONS
Admissions Selectivity Rating: 70
# of applications received: 122 % applicants accepted: 75 % acceptees attending: 64 GMAT Range (25th to 75th percentile): 450-550 **Average GMAT:** 507 **Average GPA:** 3.24 **TOEFL required of int'l applicants?** Yes **Minimum TOEFL (paper/computer):** 550/213 **Application Fee:** $30 **International Application Fee:** $30 **Regular Application Deadline:** Rolling **Regular Notification:** Rolling **Deferment Available?** Yes **Maximum length of deferment:** 1 academic year **Transfer Students Accepted?** Yes **Non-fall Admissions?** Yes **Need-Blind Admissions?** Yes

EMPORIA STATE UNIVERSITY
SCHOOL OF BUSINESS

Admissions Contact: LAURA EDDY, DIRECTOR OF ADMISSIONS
Address: EMPORIA STATE UNIVERSITY, CAMPUS BOX 4034, 1200
COMMERCIAL STREET, EMPORIA, KS 66801
Phone: 620-341-5403 • **Fax:** 620-341-5909
E-mail: GRADINFO@EMPORIA.EDU
Website: WWW.EMPORIA.EDU

GENERAL INFORMATION
Type of School: Public

STUDENTS
Enrollment of parent institution: 6,000 **Enrollment of MBA program:** 96 **% male/female:** 57/43 **% out-of-state:** 2 **% part-time:** 33 **% minorities:** 3 **% international:** 32 **Average age at entry:** 28

ACADEMICS
Student/faculty ratio: 5:1 **% female faculty:** 10 **% minority faculty:** 26 **Prominent Alumni:** Donna Jacobs, VP, Nuclear Services, Diablo Corporation; Shawn Keough, PhD, Professor, University of Texas.

FINANCIAL FACTS
Tuition (in-state/out-of-state): $3,516/$9,884 **Books and supplies:** $1,200 **Room & board:** $4,500 **Average grant:** $9,328

ADMISSIONS
Admissions Selectivity Rating: 61

# of applications received: 46 **% applicants accepted:** 98 **% acceptees attending:** 60 **Average GMAT:** 496 **Average GPA:** 3.21 **TOEFL required of int'l applicants?** Yes **Minimum TOEFL (paper/computer):** 550/213 **Application Fee:** $30 **International Application Fee:** $75 **Regular Application Deadline:** Rolling **Regular Notification:** Rolling **Deferment Available?** Yes **Maximum length of deferment:** Contingent **Transfer Students Accepted?** Yes **Non-fall Admissions?** Yes **Need-Blind Admissions?** Yes **Applicants also look at:** Institute of Undergraduate Business Studies.

EMPLOYMENT PROFILE
Placement rate (%): 65

ESCP—EAP EUROPEAN SCHOOL
OF MANAGEMENT
ESCP-EAP EUROPEAN SCHOOL OF MANAGEMENT

Admissions Contact: MICHAEL DROUERE, DIRECTOR OF ADMISSIONS
Address: 79 AVENUE DE LA REPUBLIQUE, PARIS, 75011 FRANCE
Phone: 011-331-4923-2607 • **Fax:** 011-331-4923-2012
E-mail: DROUERE@ESCP-EAP.NET
Website: WWW.ESCP-EAP.NET

GENERAL INFORMATION
Type of School: Public

STUDENTS
Enrollment of parent institution: 3,010 **Enrollment of MBA program:** 172 **% male/female:** 67/33 **% part-time:** 82 **% international:** 86 **Average age at entry:** 33 **Average years work experience at entry:** 7

ACADEMICS
Prominent Alumni: Jean Pierre Raffarin, Prime Minister/France; Micherl Barnier, European Commissioner.

ADMISSIONS
Admissions Selectivity Rating: 89

# of applications received: 450 **% applicants accepted:** 40 **% acceptees attending:** 96 **GMAT Range (25th to 75th percentile):** 570-620 **Average GMAT:** 600

EMPLOYMENT PROFILE
Placement rate (%): 98 **# of companies recruiting on-campus:** 200 **% grads employed immediately:** 60 **Average starting salary:** $55,000

FAIRLEIGH DICKINSON
UNIVERSITY—METROPOLITAN
CAMPUS
SILBERMAN COLLEGE OF BUSINESS

Admissions Contact: THOMAS M. SHEA, UNIV. DIRECTOR OF INTL &
GRADUATE ADMISSIONS
Address: 1000 RIVER ROAD, T-KB1-01, TEANECK, NJ 07666
Phone: 201-692-2563 • **Fax:** 201-692-2560
E-mail: GRAD@FDU.EDU
Website: WWW.FDU.EDU

GENERAL INFORMATION
Type of School: Private **Environment:** Village

STUDENTS
Enrollment of parent institution: 11,381 **Enrollment of MBA program:** 840 **% male/female:** 55/45 **% out-of-state:** 45 **% part-time:** 62 **% minorities:** 42 **% international:** 43 **Average age at entry:** 29

ACADEMICS
Student/faculty ratio: 25:1 **Joint Degrees:** MBA in management/MA in corporate and organizational communications. MBA in human resource management/MA in industrial/organizational psychology. **Prominent Alumni:** Michael King, King World—Television's leading syndicator; Patrick Zenner, Former Pres & CEO, Hoffman-LaRoche, Inc.; Anthony Cuti, Chairman, Pres., CEO, Duane Reade Corp.; George Martin, NFL Giants Captain; John Joyce, CFO, IBM.

FINANCIAL FACTS

Fees: $244 **Books and supplies:** $500 **Room & board:** $6,500 **% of students receiving aid:** 74 **% of students receiving loans:** 38 **% of students receiving grants:** 22 **Average award package:** $2,680 **Average grant:** $2,300

ADMISSIONS

Admissions Selectivity Rating: 66

# of applications received: 521 **% applicants accepted:** 70 **% acceptees attending:** 58 **Average GMAT:** 450 **Average GPA:** 3.5 **TOEFL required of int'l applicants?** Yes **Minimum TOEFL (paper/computer):** 550/213 **Application Fee:** $40 **International Application Fee:** $40 **Regular Application Deadline:** Rolling **Regular Notification:** 8/15 **Deferment Available?** Yes **Maximum length of deferment:** NA **Transfer Students Accepted?** Yes **Non-fall Admissions?** Yes **Need-Blind Admissions?** Yes

EMPLOYMENT PROFILE

# of companies recruiting on-campus: 150 **% grads employed immediately:** 55

FLORIDA INTERNATIONAL UNIVERSITY
ALVAH H. CHAPMAN, JR., GRADUATE SCHOOL OF BUSINESS

Admissions Contact: ELLIE BROWNER, DIRECTOR, ADMISSIONS AND STUDENT SERVICES
Address: 11200 SOUTHWEST 8TH STREET-MARC 210, MIAMI, FL 33199
Phone: 305-348-7398 • **Fax:** 305-348-1221
E-mail: CHAPMAN@FIU.EDU
Website: CHAPMAN.FIU.EDU

GENERAL INFORMATION

Type of School: Public **Environment:** Metropolis

STUDENTS

Enrollment of parent institution: 34,550 **Enrollment of MBA program:** 468 **% male/female:** 62/38 **% out-of-state:** 17 **% part-time:** 89 **% international:** 29 **Average age at entry:** 28 **Average years work experience at entry:** 2.5

ACADEMICS

Student/faculty ratio: 40:1 **% female faculty:** 28 **% minority faculty:** 31 **Prominent Alumni:** Augusto Vidaurreta, Founder, Systems Consulting Group & Adjoined Techn; Carlos Migoya, President, Wachovia/First Union Bank, Miami; Anthony Argiz, Managing Partner, KPMG, LLP; Bob Bell, Founder, Banana Boat and Sea & Ski; Anthony Ronconi, Founder/President, Stratasys, Inc.

FINANCIAL FACTS

Tuition (in-state/out-of-state): $26,000/$30,000 **Books and supplies:** $1,800 **Room & board (on/off campus):** $12,000/$18,000 **% of students receiving aid:** 64 **% of first-year students receiving aid:** 96 **% of students receiving loans:** 36 **% of students receiving grants:** 20 **Average award package:** $11,950 **Average grant:** $2,208

ADMISSIONS

Admissions Selectivity Rating: 85

# of applications received: 602 **% applicants accepted:** 35 **% acceptees attending:** 54 **GMAT Range (25th to 75th percentile):** 480-660 **Average GMAT:** 545 **Average GPA:** 3.32 **TOEFL required of int'l applicants?** Yes **Minimum TOEFL (paper/computer):** 550/213 **Application Fee:** $25 **International Application Fee:** $25 **Regular Application Deadline:** Rolling **Regular Notification:** Rolling **Deferment Available?** Yes **Maximum length of deferment:** 1 year **Transfer Students Accepted?** Yes **Non-fall Admissions?** Yes **Need-Blind Admissions?** Yes **Applicants also look at:** Florida State University—Thunderbird, University of Florida, University of Miami, University of South Carolina.

EMPLOYMENT PROFILE

# of companies recruiting on-campus: 100 **% grads employed immediately:** 6 **Average starting salary:** $66,000

Grads employed by field:% avg. salary:

Finance	1	$25,000
Marketing	4	$52,000
Consulting	1	$85,000
General Management	2	$120,000
Non-profit	1	$25,000

FORDHAM UNIVERSITY
FORDHAM BUSINESS SCHOOL

Admissions Contact: FRANK FLETCHER, DIRECTOR
Address: 33 WEST 60TH STREET, 4TH FLOOR, NEW YORK, NY 10023
Phone: 212-636-6200 • **Fax:** 212-636-7076
E-mail: ADMISSIONSGB@FORDHAM.EDU
Website: WWW.BNET.FORDHAM.EDU

GENERAL INFORMATION

Type of School: Private **Affiliation:** Roman Catholic-Jesuit **Environment:** Metropolis **Academic Calendar:** Trimester

STUDENTS

Enrollment of parent institution: 14,000 **Enrollment of MBA program:** 1,628 **% male/female:** 60/40 **% part-time:** 77 **% minorities:** 15 **% international:** 17 **Average age at entry:** 28 **Average years work experience at entry:** 5.5

ACADEMICS

Student/faculty ratio: 11:1 **% female faculty:** 22 **% minority faculty:** 13 **Joint Degrees:** Joint JD/MBA American Graduate School of International Management "Thunderbird" dual degree - MBA/MIM. **Prominent Alumni:** Nemir Kidar, Founder/President Investcorp Bank; James N. Fernandez, EVP Tiffany and Company; Patricia Fili Kurshel, EVP Time Warner; Frank Petrilli, President, CEO TDWaterhouse;

FINANCIAL FACTS

Tuition: $26,565 **Fees:** $387 **Books and supplies:** $1,600 **Average grant:** $3,000

ADMISSIONS

Admissions Selectivity Rating: 86

# of applications received: 1,005 **% applicants accepted:** 51 % **acceptees attending:** 63 **GMAT Range (25th to 75th percentile):** 540-670 **Average GMAT:** 600 **Average GPA:** 3.17 **TOEFL required of int'l applicants?** Yes **Minimum TOEFL (paper/computer):** 600/250 **Application Fee:** $65 **International Application Fee:** $65 **Regular Application Deadline:** 6/1 **Regular Notification:** Rolling **Deferment Available?** Yes **Maximum length of deferment:** 1 Year **Transfer Students Accepted?** Yes **Non-fall Admissions?** Yes **Need-Blind Admissions?** Yes **Applicants also look at:** Baruch College/City University of New York, Boston University, Columbia University, New York University, Pace University, Rutgers, The State University of New Jersey, St. John's University.

EMPLOYMENT PROFILE

Placement rate (%): 81 **# of companies recruiting on-campus:** 73 **% grads employed immediately:** 58 **Average starting salary:** $76,236

Grads employed by field:% avg. salary:

Accounting	8	$74,750
Finance	32	$78,152
Marketing	23	$76,930
MIS	4	$84,500
Operations	4	$85,200
Strategic Planning	2	$81,212
Consulting	5	$79,227
Communications	7	$70,500
Entrepreneurship	2	$60,000
General Management	4	$70,066
Global Management	2	$81,000
Internet/New Media	5	$64,500
Non-profit	2:	$55,00

GEORGE MASON UNIVERSITY
SCHOOL OF MANAGEMENT

Admissions Contact: CAROL HOSKINS, MBA PROGRAM COORDINATOR
Address: 4400 UNIVERSITY DRIVE, MSN 5A2, ENTERPRISE HALL, ROOM 37, FAIRFAX, VA 22030
Phone: 703-993-2140 • **Fax:** 703-993-1778
E-mail: SOMGRAD@GMU.EDU
Website: WWW.SOM.GMU.EDU

GENERAL INFORMATION

Type of School: Public **Environment:** City **Academic Calendar:** Semester

STUDENTS

Enrollment of MBA program: 92 **% male/female:** 98/2 **% part-time:** 75 **% minorities:** 10 **Average age at entry:** 28 **Average years work experience at entry:** 6

ACADEMICS

Student/faculty ratio: 6:1 **Prominent Alumni:** Michael G. Anzilotti, MBA '83, President/CEO First Virginia Bank; William Page Johnson II, BS Finance '88, The Commissioner for Revenue, City of Fairfax, VA.

FINANCIAL FACTS

Tuition (in-state/out-of-state): $11,205/$21,411 **Fees:** $260 **Books and supplies:** $2,000

ADMISSIONS

Admissions Selectivity Rating: 78

# of applications received: 221 **% applicants accepted:** 71 % **acceptees attending:** 59 **GMAT Range (25th to 75th percentile):** 560-660 **Average GMAT:** 594 **Average GPA:** 3.1 **TOEFL required of int'l applicants?** Yes **Minimum TOEFL (paper/computer):** 600/230 **Application Fee:** $60 **Regular Application Deadline:** 4/1 **Regular Notification:** 4/30 **Deferment Available?** Yes **Maximum length of deferment:** 2 years **Transfer Students Accepted?** Yes **Non-fall Admissions?** Yes

EMPLOYMENT PROFILE

# of companies recruiting on-campus: 190 **% grads employed immediately:** 92
Average starting salary: $70,328

GEORGIA COLLEGE & STATE UNIVERSITY

THE J. WHITNEY BUNTING SCHOOL OF BUSINESS

Admissions Contact: MIKE AUGUSTINE, DIRECTOR OF ADMISSIONS
Address: GC&SU CAMPUS BOX 23, MILLEDGEVILLE, GA 31061
Phone: 478-445-6289 • **Fax:** 478-445-1914
E-mail: LAKESHIA.HARDWICK@GCSU.EDU
Website: WWW.GCSU.EDU

GENERAL INFORMATION

Type of School: Public **Environment:** Village **Academic Calendar:** Semester

STUDENTS

Enrollment of parent institution: 5,465 **Enrollment of MBA program:** 130 **Average age at entry:** 28

ACADEMICS

Student/faculty ratio: 17:1 **% female faculty:** 35 **% minority faculty:** 17

Prominent Alumni: Tony Nicely, GEICO—President and CEO; Alex Gregory, YKK Corporation of America—President and CEO; Mike Garrett, Georgia Power Company—President and CEO.

FINANCIAL FACTS

Tuition (in-state/out-of-state): $3,782/$15,128 **Fees:** $710 **Books and supplies:** $700 **Room & board (on/off campus):** $6,282/$6,850 **Average award package:** $7,005 **Average grant:** $2,336

ADMISSIONS

Admissions Selectivity Rating: 82

# of applications received: 67 **% applicants accepted:** 37 **% acceptees attending:** 88 **GMAT Range (25th to 75th percentile):** 470-560 **Average GMAT:** 488 **Average GPA:** 3.3 **TOEFL required of int'l applicants?** Yes **Minimum TOEFL (paper/computer):** 500/173 **Application Fee:** $25 **Regular Application Deadline:** Rolling **Regular Notification:** Rolling **Deferment Available?** Yes **Maximum length of deferment:** 1 year **Transfer Students Accepted?** Yes **Non-fall Admissions?** Yes

EMPLOYMENT PROFILE

# of companies recruiting on-campus: 46

HENDERSON STATE UNIVERSITY

SCHOOL OF BUSINESS ADMINISTRATION

Admissions Contact: MISSIE BELL, GRADUATE SCHOOL ADMINISTRATIVE ASSISTANT
Address: 1100 HENDERSON STREET, BOX 7802, ARKADELPHIA, AR 71999
Phone: 870-230-5126 • **Fax:** 870-230-5479
E-mail: GRAD@HSU.EDU
Website: WWW.HSU.EDU/SCHOOLOFBUSINESS/

GENERAL INFORMATION

Type of School: Public **Environment:** Rural

STUDENTS

Enrollment of parent institution: 3,754 **Enrollment of MBA program:** 45 **% male/female:** 50/50 **% out-of-state:** 5 **% part-time:** 25 **% minorities:** 10 **% international:** 20

ACADEMICS

Student/faculty ratio: 6:1 **% female faculty:** 38 **Prominent Alumni:** Theresa Brown, Senior Systems Software Analyst; Junious Babbs, Assist. Superintendent of Little Rock School Dist.; Richard Hoover, NASA; Billy Hudson, Professor at Vanderbilt University; Bob Fisher, President of Belmont University.

FINANCIAL FACTS

Tuition (in-state/out-of-state): $2,916/$5,832 **Fees:** $411 **Books and supplies:** Room & board: $3,874

ADMISSIONS

Admissions Selectivity Rating: 61

# of applications received: 19 **% applicants accepted:** 100 **% acceptees attending:** 32 **GMAT Range (25th to 75th percentile):** 390-670 **Average GMAT:** 450 **Average GPA:** 3.0 **TOEFL required of int'l applicants?** Yes **Minimum TOEFL (paper/computer):** 550/213 **Application Fee:** $0 **International Application Fee:** $40 **Regular Application Deadline:** Rolling **Regular Notification:** Rolling **Transfer Students Accepted?** Yes **Non-fall Admissions?** Yes **Need-Blind Admissions?** Yes

EMPLOYMENT PROFILE

Placement rate (%): 100 **# of companies recruiting on-campus:** 125 **% grads employed immediately:** 100

IDAHO STATE UNIVERSITY
COLLEGE OF BUSINESS

Admissions Contact: GORDON B. BROOKS, SR., ASSISTANT DEAN FOR GRADUATE PROGRAMS
Address: BOX 8020, POCATELLO, ID 83209
Phone: 208-282-2504 • *Fax:* 208-236-4367
E-mail: BROOGORD@ISU.EDU
Website: COB.ISU.EDU

GENERAL INFORMATION
Type of School: Public **Environment:** Town **Academic Calendar:** Semester

STUDENTS
Enrollment of parent institution: 13,802 **Enrollment of MBA program:** 158 **% male/female:** 72/28 **% part-time:** 37 **% international:** 22 **Average age at entry:** 32

ACADEMICS
Student/faculty ratio: 23:1 **% female faculty:** 13

FINANCIAL FACTS
Tuition (in-state/out-of-state): $5,040/$12,120 **Books and supplies:** $1,000 **Room & board (on/off campus):** $7,500/$7,500

ADMISSIONS
Admissions Selectivity Rating: 74

# of applications received: 74 **% applicants accepted:** 66 **% acceptees attending:** 69 **GMAT Range (25th to 75th percentile):** 410-650 **Average GMAT:** 514 **Average GPA:** 3.45 **TOEFL required of int'l applicants?** Yes **Minimum TOEFL (paper/computer):** 550/213 **Application Fee:** $35 **Regular Application Deadline:** 6/1 **Regular Notification:** 6/7 **Deferment Available?** Yes **Maximum length of deferment:** 2 yrs **Transfer Students Accepted?** Yes **Non-fall Admissions?** Yes

ILLINOIS STATE UNIVERSITY
COLLEGE OF BUSINESS

Admissions Contact: LEE A. GRAF, MBA PROGRAM DIRECTOR
Address: CAMPUS BOX 5570 / MBA PROGRAM, NORMAL, IL 61790-5570
Phone: 309-438-8388 • *Fax:* 309-438-7255
E-mail: ISUMBA@EXCHANGE.COB.ILSTU.EDU
Website: WWW.MBA.ILSTU.EDU/

GENERAL INFORMATION
Type of School: Public **Environment:** Village **Academic Calendar:** Semester

STUDENTS
Enrollment of parent institution: 20,757 **Enrollment of MBA program:** 199 **% male/female:** 67/33 **% out-of-state:** 29 **% part-time:** 77 **% minorities:** 4 **% international:** 31 **Average age at entry:** 26 **Average years work experience at entry:** 6

ACADEMICS
Student/faculty ratio: 3:1 **% female faculty:** 22 **% minority faculty:** 16 **Joint Degrees:** Master of professional accountancy - 30 hours beyond the undergraduate degree in accounting. **Prominent Alumni:** Ann Baughan, Assistant Vice President, State Farm Insurance; Phil Maughan, Vice President, The Northern Trust Company; Karl Heien, Vice President, Smith Barney Inc.; James C. Tyree, Chair and CEO, Mesirow Financial Group; Marty Lyons, Vice President, Archer Daniels Midland Company.

FINANCIAL FACTS
Tuition (in-state/out-of-state): $2,610/$5,454 **Fees:** $778 **Books and supplies:** $825 **Room & board (on/off campus):** $5,576/$5,834 **% of students receiving aid:** 94 **% of first-year students receiving aid:** 89 **% of students receiving loans:** 53 **% of students receiving grants:** 95 **Average award package:** $14,110 **Average grant:** $6,889 **Average student loan debt:** $20,439

ADMISSIONS
Admissions Selectivity Rating: 72

# of applications received: 50 **% applicants accepted:** 86 **% acceptees attending:** 67 **GMAT Range (25th to 75th percentile):** 500-580 **Average GMAT:** 545 **Average GPA:** 3.46 **TOEFL required of int'l applicants?** Yes **Minimum TOEFL (paper/computer):** 600/250 **Application Fee:** $30 **International Application Fee:** $30 **Regular Application Deadline:** 8/1 **Regular Notification:** 8/15 **Early decision program?** Yes **ED deadline /notification:** 2/1–3/1 **Deferment Available?** Yes **Maximum length of deferment:** 1 year **Transfer Students Accepted?** Yes **Non-fall Admissions?** Yes **Need-Blind Admissions?** Yes

INCAE
GRADUATE PROGRAM

Website: WWW.INCAE.AC.CR

GENERAL INFORMATION
Type of School: Private **Academic Calendar:** Trimester

STUDENTS
Enrollment of parent institution: 441 **Enrollment of MBA program:** 441 **% male/female:** 70/30 **% part-time:** 20 **Average age at entry:** 28

ACADEMICS
Student/faculty ratio: 15:1

FINANCIAL FACTS
Tuition: $11,500 **% of students receiving aid:** 3

ADMISSIONS

Admissions Selectivity Rating: 60*

# of applications received: 530 **% applicants accepted:** 60 % **acceptees attending:** 37 **Application Fee:** $50 **International Application Fee: Regular Application Deadline:** 7/15 **Regular Notification:** Rolling

EMPLOYMENT PROFILE

Placement rate (%): 60 **# of companies recruiting on-campus:** 400 **Average starting salary:** $53,000

INDIANA STATE UNIVERSITY
COLLEGE OF BUSINESS

Admissions Contact: DALE VARBLE, DIRECTOR, MBA PROGRAM
Address: INDIANA STATE UNIVERSITY, TERRE HAUTE, IN 47809
Phone: 812-237-2002 • **Fax:** 812-237-8720
E-mail: MBA@INDSTATE.EDU
Website: WEB.INDSTATE.EDU/SCHBUS/MBA.HTML

GENERAL INFORMATION

Type of School: Public **Environment:** Town **Academic Calendar:** Trimester

STUDENTS

Enrollment of parent institution: 10,800 **Enrollment of MBA program:** 105 **% male/female:** 60/40 **% part-time:** 40 **% minorities:** 3 **% international:** 55 **Average age at entry:** 30 **Average years work experience at entry:** 4

ACADEMICS

Student/faculty ratio: 18:1 **Prominent Alumni:** Paul Lo, Pres.CEO SinoPac.

FINANCIAL FACTS

Tuition (in-state/out-of-state): $2,720/$5,920 **Fees:** $25 **Books and supplies:** $900 **Room & board:** $7,800 **% of students receiving aid:** 30 **% of first-year students receiving aid:** 30 **% of students receiving grants:** 30 **Average award package:** $12,210 **Average grant:** $6,210

ADMISSIONS

Admissions Selectivity Rating: 63

# of applications received: 148 **% applicants accepted:** 88 **GMAT Range (25th to 75th percentile):** 400-750 **Average GMAT:** 530 **Average GPA:** 3.0 **TOEFL required of int'l applicants?** Yes **Minimum TOEFL (paper/computer):** 550/213 **Application Fee:** $35 **International Application Fee:** $35 **Regular Application Deadline:** Rolling **Regular Notification:** Rolling **Deferment Available?** Yes **Maximum length of deferment:** 2 years **Transfer Students Accepted?** Yes **Non-fall Admissions?** Yes **Applicants also look at:** Ball State University, Illinois State University, Indiana University— Kokomo, Indiana University—Purdue University Indianapolis, McMaster University, The University of Texas at Austin.

EMPLOYMENT PROFILE

# of companies recruiting on-campus: 15
Grads employed by field: ....%

Accounting	40
Human Resources	10
Marketing	10
MIS	10
General Management	30

INDIANA UNIVERSITY NORTHWEST
SCHOOL OF BUSINESS AND ECONOMICS

Admissions Contact: JOHN GIBSON, DIRECTOR, UNDERGRADUATE AND GRADUATE PROGRAMS IN BUSINESS
Address: 3400 BROADWAY, GARY, IN 46408-1197
Phone: 219-980-6635 • **Fax:** 219-980-6916
E-mail: JAGIBSON@IUN.EDU
Website: WWW.IUN.EDU/~BUSNW

GENERAL INFORMATION

Type of School: Public **Environment:** City **Academic Calendar:** Semester

STUDENTS

Enrollment of parent institution: 4,000 **Enrollment of MBA program:** 110 **% male/female:** 100/0 **% part-time:** 98 **Average age at entry:** 36

ACADEMICS

Student/faculty ratio: 10:1 **% female faculty:** 26 **% minority faculty:** 37

FINANCIAL FACTS

Tuition (in-state/out-of-state): $4,500/$10,400 **Fees:** $500

ADMISSIONS

Admissions Selectivity Rating: 60*

# of applications received: 215 **% applicants accepted:** 91 % **acceptees attending:** 100 **TOEFL required of int'l applicants?** Yes **Minimum TOEFL (paper/computer):** / **Application Fee:** $25 **International Application Fee:** $55 **Regular Application Deadline:** 1/1 **Early decision program?** Yes **Deferment Available?** Yes **Maximum length of deferment:** 1 year **Transfer Students Accepted?** Yes **Non-fall Admissions?** Yes **Need-Blind Admissions?** Yes

INDIANA UNIVERSITY SOUTH BEND
SCHOOL OF BUSINESS AND ECONOMICS

Admissions Contact: DR. KATHERINE L. JACKSON, ASSISTANT DEAN
Address: IUSB PO BOX 7111, SOUTH BEND, IN 46634-7111
Phone: 574-237-4138 • **Fax:** 574-237-4866
E-mail: GRADBUS@IUSB.EDU
Website: WWW.IUSB.EDU/~GRADBUS

GENERAL INFORMATION
Type of School: Public **Environment:** City **Academic Calendar:** Semester

STUDENTS
Enrollment of parent institution: 7,162 **Enrollment of MBA program:** 182 **% male/female:** 52/48 **% part-time:** 77 **% minorities:** 2 **% international:** 95 **Average age at entry:** 31 **Average years work experience at entry:** 3

ACADEMICS
Student/faculty ratio: 17:1 **% female faculty:** 24 **% minority faculty:** 7

FINANCIAL FACTS
Tuition (in-state/out-of-state): $3,316/$7,918 **Fees:** $390 **Books and supplies:** $600 **Room & board (on/off campus):** $5,000/$8,000

ADMISSIONS
Admissions Selectivity Rating: 63

# of applications received: 36 **% applicants accepted:** 97 **% acceptees attending:** 89 **GMAT Range (25th to 75th percentile):** 410-660 **Average GMAT:** 511 **Average GPA:** 3.0 **TOEFL required of int'l applicants?** Yes **Minimum TOEFL (paper/computer):** 550/213 **Application Fee:** $40 **International Application Fee:** $50 **Regular Application Deadline:** 7/1 **Regular Notification:** Rolling **Deferment Available?** Yes **Maximum length of deferment:** 1 year **Non-fall Admissions?** Yes **Applicants also look at:** University of Notre Dame, Western Michigan University.

INDIANA UNIVERSITY—PURDUE UNIVERSITY AT FORT WAYNE
SCHOOL OF BUSINESS AND MANAGEMENT

Admissions Contact: SANDY FRANKE, SECRETARY, MBA PROGRAM
Address: NEFF 366, 2101 COLISEUM BOULEVARD EAST, FORT WAYNE, IN 46805-1499
Phone: 219-481-6145
E-mail: EMAIL@SCHOOL.EDU
Website: WWW.IPFW.EDU/BMS

GENERAL INFORMATION
Type of School: Public **Environment:** Village **Academic Calendar:** Semester

STUDENTS
Enrollment of parent institution: 10,749 **Enrollment of MBA program:** 191 **% male/female:** 65/35 **% part-time:** 91 **Average age at entry:** 32

ACADEMICS
Student/faculty ratio: 1:1

ADMISSIONS
Admissions Selectivity Rating: 60*

# of applications received: 45 **% applicants accepted:** 91 **% acceptees attending:** 95 **Fee:** $30 **International Application Fee:** **Regular Application Deadline:** 7/1 **Regular Notification:** 1/1

INSTITUTO DE EMPRESA
INSTITUTO DE EMPRESA

Admissions Contact: DAVID STANDEN, ADMISSIONS OFFICER
Address: MARÍA DE MOLINA 11-13-15, MADRID, 28006 SPAIN
Phone: 011-34-91-568-9610 • **Fax:** 011 34 91 568 9710
E-mail: ADMISSIONS@IE.EDU
Website: WWW.IE.EDU

GENERAL INFORMATION
Type of School: Private

STUDENTS
Enrollment of MBA program: 292 **% male/female:** 60/40 **% part-time:** 34 **% minorities:** 26 **% international:** 84 **Average age at entry:** 29 **Average years work experience at entry:** 6.3

ACADEMICS
Student/faculty ratio: 11:1 **Prominent Alumni:** Fernando Barnuevo, J.P. Morgan Chase, Head of Global Investment Mgmt; Pilar de Zulueta, Warner Bros. Southern Europe Director; José María Cámara, President of Sony Music, Spain; Juan PableSan Agustín, Vice President, CEMEX; Isabel Aguilera, COO, NH Hoteles.

FINANCIAL FACTS

Tuition: $33,850 **Books and supplies:** $400 **Average grant:** $17,000

ADMISSIONS

Admissions Selectivity Rating: 99

# of applications received: 2,356 **% applicants accepted:** 14 % **acceptees attending:** 88 **Average GMAT:** 670 **Average GPA:** 3.7 **Application Fee:** $120 **Regular Application Deadline:** Rolling **Regular Notification:** Rolling **Deferment Available?** Yes **Maximum length of deferment:** 2 years **Non-fall Admissions?** Yes **Need-Blind Admissions?** Yes **Applicants also look at:** ESADE, IESE Business School, IMD (International Institute for Management Development), INSEAD

EMPLOYMENT PROFILE

Placement rate (%): 99 **# of companies recruiting on-campus:** 200 **Average starting salary:** $72,730

Grads employed by field: ....%
Finance 17
Human Resources 3
Marketing 10
Operations 3
Strategic Planning 9
Consulting 14
Communications...........................13
Entrepreneurship 8
General Management 7
Global Management 7
Venture Capital 4
Other...5

INSTITUTO TECNOLOGICO Y DE ESTUDIOS SUPERIORES DE MONTERREY (ITESM)
EGADE, MONTERREY CAMPUS

Admissions Contact: ING. LETICIA SIERRA, ACADEMIC SERVICES DIRECTOR
Address: AV. FUNDADORES Y RUFINO TAMAYO, COL. VALLE ORIENTE, SAN PEDRO GARZA GARCÍA,
NL 66269 MEXICO
Phone: 818-625-6204 • *Fax:* 818-625-6208
E-mail: ADMISIONES.EGADE@ITESM.MX
Website: WWW.ITESM.MX

GENERAL INFORMATION

Type of School: Private **Affiliation:** Academic Calendar: Quarter

STUDENTS

Enrollment of parent institution: 19,358 **Enrollment of MBA program:** 597 **% male/female:** 79/21 **% part-time:** 90 **% international:** 66 **Average age at entry:** 28 **Average years work experience at entry:** 5

ACADEMICS

Student/faculty ratio: 14:1 **% female faculty:** 25 **Joint Degrees:** Double degree MBA (1 year more than the regular lenght).
Prominent Alumni: Eugenio Clariond Reyes-Retana, General Director of IMSA Group; Fernando Canales Clariond, Ministery of Economic Affairs, Mexico Government; Jose Antonio Rivero Larrea, President of Administration Board, Autlan Group; Jose Antonio Fernandez Carbajal, General Director of FEMSA Group; Luis Sada Gonzalez, General Director of John Deere Mexico.

FINANCIAL FACTS

Tuition: $17,500 **Books and supplies:** $780 **Room & board (on/off campus):** $7,800/$6,400 **% of students receiving aid:** 26 **% of first-year students receiving aid:** 24 **% of students receiving loans:** 3 **% of students receiving grants:** 23 **Average grant:** $11,375

ADMISSIONS

Admissions Selectivity Rating: 83

# of applications received: 199 **% applicants accepted:** 73 % **acceptees attending:** 74 **Average GMAT:** 615 **Average GPA:** 3.5 **Application Fee:** $100 **International Application Fee:** $100 **Regular Application Deadline:** 5/1 **Regular Notification:** 6/1 **Deferment Available?** Yes **Maximum length of deferment:** 1 year **Transfer Students Accepted?** Yes **Non-fall Admissions?** Yes

EMPLOYMENT PROFILE

Placement rate (%): 90 **# of companies recruiting on-campus:** 90

IOWA STATE UNIVERSITY
COLLEGE OF BUSINESS

Admissions Contact: AMY HUTTER, ASSOCIATE DIRECTOR, MBA STUDENT RECRUITMENT
Address: 1360 GERDIN BUSINESS BUILDING, AMES, IA 50011
Phone: 515-294-8118 • *Fax:* 515-294-2446
E-mail: BUSGRAD@IASTATE.EDU
Website: WWW.BUS.IASTATE.EDU/GRAD/

GENERAL INFORMATION

Type of School: Public **Environment:** Rural **Academic Calendar:** Semester

STUDENTS

Enrollment of parent institution: 26,380 **Enrollment of MBA program:** 226 **% male/female:** 58/42 **% out-of-state:** 17 **% part-time:** 63 **% minorities:** 4 **% international:** 36 **Average age at entry:** 27 **Average years work experience at entry:** 4

ACADEMICS

Student/faculty ratio: 4:1 **% female faculty:** 9 **% minority faculty:** 12 **Joint Degrees:** MBA/MS in statistics, 72 credit hours, 3 years MBA/MS in community and regional planning, 73 credit hours, 3 years.

FINANCIAL FACTS

Tuition (in-state/out-of-state): $7,144/$16,770 **Fees:** $684 **Books and supplies:** $1,000 **Room & board:** $9,800 **% of students receiving aid:** 50 **% of first-year students receiving aid:** 50 **Average award package:** $7,144

ADMISSIONS

Admissions Selectivity Rating: 83

# of applications received: 122 **% applicants accepted:** 57 % **acceptees attending:** 52 **Average GMAT:** 593 **Average GPA:** 3.38 **TOEFL required of int'l applicants?** Yes **Minimum TOEFL (paper/computer):** 590/250 **Application Fee:** $30 **International Application Fee:** $70 **Regular Application Deadline:** Rolling **Regular Notification:** Rolling **Deferment Available?** Yes **Maximum length of deferment:** 1 year **Need-Blind Admissions?** Yes **Applicants also look at:** Drake University, University of Iowa.

EMPLOYMENT PROFILE

Placement rate (%): 95 % grads employed immediately: 73 **Average starting salary:** $47,200

Grads employed by field:% avg. salary:

Accounting	4	$45,000
Finance	12	$50,000
Human Resources	10	$50,300
Marketing	25	$47,000
MIS	5	NR
Operations	15	$52,500
Entrepreneurship	4	NR
General Management	25	$45,200

JACKSON STATE UNIVERSITY
SCHOOL OF BUSINESS

Admissions Contact: JESSE PENNINGTON, DIRECTOR OF GRADUATE PROGRAMS
Address: PO BOX 18660, JACKSON, MI 39217
Phone: 601-432-6315 • Fax: 601-987-4380
E-mail: GADMAPPL@CCAIX.JSUMS.EDU
Website: CCAIX.JSUMS.EDU/BUSINESS/

GENERAL INFORMATION

Type of School: Public **Environment:** City **Academic Calendar:** Semester

STUDENTS

Enrollment of parent institution: 6,292 **Enrollment of MBA program:** 1,104

FINANCIAL FACTS

Tuition (in-state/out-of-state): $2,688/$2,858 **% of students receiving aid:** 8

ADMISSIONS

Admissions Selectivity Rating: 60*

# of applications received: 160 **% applicants accepted:** 77 % **acceptees attending:** 89 **TOEFL required of int'l applicants?** Yes **Minimum TOEFL (paper):** 525 **Application Fee:** $20 **International Application Fee:** **Regular Application Deadline:** Rolling **Regular Notification:** Rolling **Deferment Available?** Yes

EMPLOYMENT PROFILE

of companies recruiting on-campus: 150 **Average starting salary:** $30,000

JAMES MADISON UNIVERSITY
COLLEGE OF BUSINESS

Admissions Contact: KRISTA D. DOFFLEMYER, ADMINISTRATIVE ASSISTANT
Address: ZANE SHOWKER HALL, MSC 0206, ROOM 620, HARRISONBURG, VA 22807
Phone: 540-568-3253 • Fax: 540-568-3587
E-mail: MBA@JMU.EDU
Website: WWW.JMU.EDU/MBA

GENERAL INFORMATION

Type of School: Public **Environment:** Town

STUDENTS

Enrollment of parent institution: 16,108 **Enrollment of MBA program:** 89 **% male/female:** 76/24 **% out-of-state:** 48 **% part-time:** 72 **% minorities:** 4 **% international:** 28 **Average age at entry:** 31 **Average years work experience at entry:** 4

ACADEMICS

Student/faculty ratio: 12:1 **% female faculty:** 25 **% minority faculty:** 6

FINANCIAL FACTS

Tuition (in-state/out-of-state): $5,424/$15,840 **Books and supplies:** $2,000 **% of students receiving aid:** 22 **% of first-year students receiving aid:** 6 **% of students receiving loans:** 5 **% of students receiving grants:** 20

ADMISSIONS

Admissions Selectivity Rating: 76

# of applications received: 35 **% applicants accepted:** 86 % **acceptees attending:** 87 **GMAT Range (25th to 75th percentile):** 520-670 **Average GMAT:** 575 **Average GPA:** 3.2 **TOEFL required of int'l applicants?** Yes **Minimum TOEFL (paper/computer):** 550/230 **Application Fee:** $55 **International Application Fee:** $55 **Regular Application Deadline:** 7/1 **Regular Notification:** Rolling **Deferment Available?** Yes **Maximum length of deferment:** 1 year **Transfer Students Accepted?** Yes

EMPLOYMENT PROFILE

Placement rate (%): 100 # of companies recruiting on-campus: 162 % grads employed immediately: 93 Average starting salary: $75,000

KANSAS STATE UNIVERSITY
COLLEGE OF BUSINESS ADMINISTRATION

Admissions Contact: LYNN WAUGH, GRADUATE STUDIES ASSISTANT
Address: 110 CALVIN HALL, MANHATTAN, KS 66506-0501
Phone: 785-532-7190 • **Fax:** 785-532-7216
E-mail: FLYNN@KSU.EDU
Website: WWW.CBA.KSU.EDU

GENERAL INFORMATION

Type of School: Public **Environment:** Village **Academic Calendar:** Semeters

STUDENTS

Enrollment of parent institution: Enrollment of MBA program: 91 % male/female: 70/30 % out-of-state: 4 % part-time: 18 % minorities: 9 % international: 22 Average age at entry: 24 Average years work experience at entry: 2

ACADEMICS

Student/faculty ratio: 5:1 % female faculty: 22 % minority faculty: 4

FINANCIAL FACTS

Tuition (in-state/out-of-state): $6,855/$19,340 Fees: $666 Books and supplies: $1,000 Room & board (on/off campus): $5,000/$6,000 % of students receiving aid: 18 % of first-year students receiving aid: 12 Average grant: $2,500

ADMISSIONS

Admissions Selectivity Rating: 89

# of applications received: 86 % applicants accepted: 40 % acceptees attending: 100 Average GMAT: 548 Average GPA: 3.4 TOEFL required of int'l applicants? Yes Minimum TOEFL (paper/computer): 550/213 Application Fee: $45 Regular Application Deadline: 3/1 Regular Notification: 6/1 Deferment Available? Yes Maximum length of deferment: 1 year Transfer Students Accepted? Yes Need-Blind Admissions? Yes Applicants also look at: Oklahoma State University, University of Kansas, University of Nebraska-Lincoln, University of Oklahoma, Wichita State University.

EMPLOYMENT PROFILE

Placement rate (%): 65 % grads employed immediately: 65 Average starting salary: $42,000

Grads employed by field:% avg. salary:

Accounting	8	$42,000
Finance	30	$46,000
Human Resources	8	$52,000
Marketing	8	$38,000
MIS	8	$55,000
Consulting	22	$42,000
Communications	8	$57,000
Entrepreneurship	8	$38,000

LA SALLE UNIVERSITY
SCHOOL OF BUSINESS ADMINISTRATION

Admissions Contact: KATHY BAGNELL, DIRECTOR, MARKETING AND GRADUATE ENROLLMENT
Address: 1900 WEST OLNEY AVENUE, PHILADELPHIA, PA 19141
Phone: 215-951-1057 • **Fax:** 215-951-1886
E-mail: EMAIL@SCHOOL.EDU
Website: WWW.LASALLE.EDU/ACADEM/SBA/SBA.HTM

GENERAL INFORMATION

Type of School: Private **Environment:** City **Academic Calendar:** Trimester

STUDENTS

Enrollment of parent institution: 5,408 Enrollment of MBA program: 687 % male/female: 59/41 % part-time: 90 % minorities: 12 % international: 11 Average age at entry: 32

ADMISSIONS

Admissions Selectivity Rating: 60*

# of applications received: 142 % applicants accepted: 85 % acceptees attending: 89 Average GMAT: Average GPA: TOEFL required of int'l applicants? Yes Minimum TOEFL (paper): 550 Application Fee: $30 Regular Application Deadline: 8/14 Regular Notification: Rolling Deferment Available? Yes Non-fall Admissions? Yes

EMPLOYMENT PROFILE

Placement rate (%): 99

LEHIGH UNIVERSITY
COLLEGE OF BUSINESS AND ECONOMICS

Admissions Contact: MARY THERESA TAGLANG, DIRECTOR OF RECRUITMENT AND ADMISSIONS
Address: 621 TAYLOR STREET, BETHLEHEM, PA 18015
Phone: 610-758-5280 • **Fax:** 610-758-5283
E-mail: MBA.ADMISSIONS@LEHIGH.EDU
Website: WWW.LEHIGH.EDU/MBA

GENERAL INFORMATION
Type of School: Private **Environment:** City **Academic Calendar:** Semester

STUDENTS
Enrollment of parent institution: 6,733 **Enrollment of MBA program:** 276 **% male/female:** 60/40 **% part-time:** 82 **% minorities:** 8 **% international:** 40 **Average age at entry:** 30 **Average years work experience at entry:** 7

ACADEMICS
Student/faculty ratio: 6:1 **% female faculty:** 20 **% minority faculty:** 27 **Joint Degrees:** MBA & engineering (MBA & E)—45 credit hours MBA & educational leadership (MBA/MEd.)—45 credit hours.

FINANCIAL FACTS
Tuition: $11,250 **Fees:** $240 **Books and supplies:** $1,300 **Room & Board:** $10,800 **% of students receiving aid:** 8 **% of first-year students receiving aid:** 15 **Average award package:** $24,260 **Average grant:** $11,000

ADMISSIONS
Admissions Selectivity Rating: 84
# of applications received: 246 **% applicants accepted:** 63 **% acceptees attending:** 70 **Average GMAT:** 605 **Average GPA:** 3.2 **TOEFL required of int'l applicants?** Yes **Minimum TOEFL (paper/computer):** 600/250 **Application Fee:** $50 **International Application Fee:** $50 **Regular Application Deadline:** 5/1 **Regular Notification:** Rolling **Deferment Available?** Yes **Maximum length of deferment:** 1 year **Transfer Students Accepted?** Yes **Non-fall Admissions?** Yes **Need-Blind Admissions?** Yes **Applicants also look at:** Institute of Undergraduate Business Studies.

EMPLOYMENT PROFILE
Placement rate (%): 96 **Average starting salary:** $78,047
Grads employed by field:% avg. salary:

Finance	38	$82,000
Marketing	15	$45,000
Operations	8	$102,000
Consulting	8	$55,000
General Management	23	$58,000
Other	8	$65,000

LOUISIANA STATE UNIVERSITY— SHREVEPORT
COLLEGE OF BUSINESS ADMINISTRATION

Admissions Contact: SUSAN WOOD, MBA DIRECTOR
Address: ONE UNIVERSITY PLACE, SHREVEPORT, LA 71115
Phone: 318-797-5213 • **Fax:** 318-797-5017
E-mail: SWOOD@PILOT.LSUS.EDU
Website: WWW.LSUS.EDU/BA/

GENERAL INFORMATION
Type of School: Public **Environment:** City **Academic Calendar:** Semester

STUDENTS
Enrollment of parent institution: 4,237 **Enrollment of MBA program:** 150 **% male/female:** 47/53 **% part-time:** 93 **% minorities:** 10 **% international:** 5

ACADEMICS
Student/faculty ratio: 20:1

FINANCIAL FACTS
Tuition (in-state/out-of-state): $3,245/$9,420 **% of students receiving aid:** 60

ADMISSIONS
Admissions Selectivity Rating: 60*
# of applications received: 70 **% applicants accepted:** 71 **% acceptees attending:** 80 **TOEFL required of int'l applicants?** Yes **Minimum TOEFL (paper):** 550 **Regular Application Deadline:** 7/15 **Regular Notification:** Rolling **Non-fall Admissions?** Yes **Need-Blind Admissions?**

EMPLOYMENT PROFILE
Placement rate (%): 98 **# of companies recruiting on-campus:** 30 **Average starting salary:** $40,000

LOUISIANA TECH UNIVERSITY
COLLEGE OF ADMINISTRATION AND BUSINESS

Admissions Contact: DR. MARC C. CHOPIN, ASSOCIATE DEAN OF GRADUATE STUDIES & RESEARCH
Address: PO BOX 10318, RUSTON, LA 71272
Phone: 318-257-4528 • **Fax:** 318-257-4253
E-mail: GSCHOOL@CAB.LATECH.EDU
Website: WWW.CAB.LATECH.EDU

GENERAL INFORMATION
Type of School: Public **Environment:** Rural **Academic Calendar:** Quarter

STUDENTS

Enrollment of parent institution: 11,175 Enrollment of MBA program: 58 % male/female: 62/38 % part-time: 10 % international: 34

ACADEMICS

Student/faculty ratio: 25:1

FINANCIAL FACTS

Tuition (in-state/out-of-state): $2,652/$3,528 Fees: $40 Books and supplies: $800 Room & board (on/off campus): $3,840

ADMISSIONS

Admissions Selectivity Rating: 75

# of applications received: 57 % applicants accepted: 61 % acceptees attending: 80 GMAT Range (25th to 75th percentile): 450-700 Average GMAT: 500 Average GPA: 3.2 TOEFL required of int'l applicants? Yes Minimum TOEFL (paper/computer): 550/213 Application Fee: $20 International Application Fee: $30 Regular Application Deadline: 8/1 Regular Notification: 1/1 Deferment Available? Yes Maximum length of deferment: 1 year Transfer Students Accepted? Yes Non-fall Admissions? Yes

EMPLOYMENT PROFILE

of companies recruiting on-campus: 258

MARSHALL UNIVERSITY
COLLEGE OF BUSINESS

Admissions Contact: DR. MICHAEL A. NEWSOME, MBA DIRECTOR
Address: CORBY HALL 217, 400 HAL GREER BOULEVARD, HUNTINGTON, WV 25755-2305
Phone: 304-696-2613 • **Fax:** 304-696-3661
Website: LCOB.MARSHALL.EDU/

GENERAL INFORMATION

Type of School: Public Environment: Village Academic Calendar: Semesters

STUDENTS

Enrollment of parent institution: Enrollment of MBA program: 80 % male/female: 40/60 % minorities: 15 % international: 30 Average years work experience at entry: 2

ACADEMICS

Student/faculty ratio: 5:1 % female faculty: 10 % minority faculty: 10

FINANCIAL FACTS

Tuition (in-state/out-of-state): $2,884/$8,158 Fees (in-state/out-of-state): $1,100/$1,250 Books and supplies: $1,000 % of students receiving aid: 50 % of first-year students receiving aid: 50

ADMISSIONS

Admissions Selectivity Rating: 73

# of applications received: 100 % applicants accepted: 84 % acceptees attending: 95 Average GMAT: 530 Average GPA: 3.5 TOEFL required of int'l applicants? Yes Minimum TOEFL (paper/computer): 525/195 Application Fee: $20 International Application Fee: $25 Regular Application Deadline: Rolling Regular Notification: Rolling Transfer Students Accepted? Yes Non-fall Admissions? Yes

EMPLOYMENT PROFILE

of companies recruiting on-campus: 45 % grads employed immediately: 88 Average starting salary: $50,000

Grads employed by field: ....%

Accounting 75

MARYMOUNT UNIVERSITY
SCHOOL OF BUSINESS ADMINISTRATION

Admissions Contact: GRADUATE ADMISSIONS, COORDINATOR
Address: 2807 N. GLEBE ROAD, ARLINGTON, VA 22207
Phone: 703-284-5901 • **Fax:** 703-527-3815
E-mail: GRAD.ADMISSIONS@MARYMOUNT.EDU
Website: WWW.MARYMOUNT.EDU/ACADEMIC/BUSINESS/INDEX.HTML

GENERAL INFORMATION

Type of School: Private Affiliation: Roman Catholic

STUDENTS

Enrollment of MBA program: 267

ACADEMICS

Student/faculty ratio: 13:1

ADMISSIONS

Admissions Selectivity Rating: 72

# of applications received: 90 % applicants accepted: 64 % acceptees attending: 67 Average GMAT: 500 Average GPA: 3 TOEFL required of int'l applicants? Yes Minimum TOEFL (paper): 600 Application Fee: $35 International Application Fee: $35 Regular Application Deadline: Rolling Regular Notification: 8/30 Deferment Available? Yes Maximum length of deferment: 1 year Transfer Students Accepted? Yes Non-fall Admissions? Yes

MCNEESE STATE UNIVERSITY
MBA PROGRAM

Admissions Contact: TAMMY PETTIS, UNIVERSITY ADMISSIONS
Address: PO Box 92495, LAKE CHARLES, LA 70609-2495
Phone: 337-475-5147 • *Fax:* 337-475-5151
E-mail: INFO@MAIL.MCNEESE.EDU
Website: WWW.MCNEESE.EDU/COLLEGES/BUSINESS/MBA

GENERAL INFORMATION

Type of School: Public **Environment:** City **Academic Calendar:** Semester

STUDENTS

Enrollment of parent institution: 8,142 **Enrollment of MBA program:** 95 % **male/female:** 68/32 % **out-of-state:** 3 % **part-time:** 64 % **international:** 33 **Average age at entry:** 30

ACADEMICS

Student/faculty ratio: 16:1 % **female faculty:** 1 % **minority faculty:** 45

FINANCIAL FACTS

Tuition (in-state/out-of-state): $1,987/$3,530 **Books and supplies:** $1,000 **Room & board (on/off campus):** $3,200/$3,600

ADMISSIONS

Admissions Selectivity Rating: 61

# of applications received: 36 % **applicants accepted:** 97 % **acceptees attending:** 51 **GMAT Range (25th to 75th percentile):** 250-630 **Average GMAT:** 460 **Average GPA:** 3.6 **TOEFL required of int'l applicants?** Yes **Minimum TOEFL (paper):** 550 **Application Fee:** $20 **International Application Fee:** $30 **Regular Application Deadline:** Rolling **Regular Notification:** Rolling **Deferment Available?** Yes **Maximum length of deferment:** 1 year **Transfer Students Accepted?** Yes **Non-fall Admissions?** Yes **Need-Blind Admissions?** Yes

ACADEMICS

Student/faculty ratio: 9:1 % **female faculty:** 35 % **minority faculty:** 10 **Prominent Alumni:** John Smale, brand management, P&G (retired); Richard Farmer, CEO & Chairman of Board, Cintas, retired; Michael Armstrong, Chairman, AT&T (former); Art Reimers, Partner Goldman Sachs, retired; Tom Stallkamp, President, Daimler/Chrysler (former).

FINANCIAL FACTS

Tuition (in-state/out-of-state): $6,560/$15,284 **Fees:** $1,382 **Books and supplies:** $1,000 **Room & board:** $6,000 % **of students receiving aid:** 25 % **of first-year students receiving aid:** 80 **Average grant:** $2,000

ADMISSIONS

Admissions Selectivity Rating: 85

# of applications received: 102 % **applicants accepted:** 41 % **acceptees attending:** 74 **GMAT Range (25th to 75th percentile):** 520-580 **Average GMAT:** 552 **Average GPA:** 3.2 **TOEFL required of int'l applicants?** Yes **Minimum TOEFL (paper/computer):** 550/220 **Application Fee:** $35 **International Application Fee:** $35 **Regular Application Deadline:** 3/1 **Regular Notification:** Rolling **Deferment Available?** Yes **Maximum length of deferment:** 2 years **Non-fall Admissions?** Yes **Applicants also look at:** Bowling Green State University, Indiana University, The Ohio State University, University of Cincinnati, University of Dayton.

EMPLOYMENT PROFILE

Placement rate (%): 75 **# of companies recruiting on-campus:** 209 % **grads employed immediately:** 30 **Average starting salary:** $55,167

Grads employed by field:% avg. salary:

Finance	42	$45,000
Marketing	42	$61,670
MIS	16	$52,333

MIAMI UNIVERSITY (OHIO)
RICHARD T. FARMER SCHOOL OF BUSINESS

Admissions Contact: JUDY BARILLE, MBA DIRECTOR
Address: LAWS HALL, OXFORD, OH 45056
Phone: 513-529-6643 • *Fax:* 513-529-2487
E-mail: MIAMIMBA@MUOHIO.EDU
Website: WWW.SBA.MUOHIO.EDU/MBAPROGRAM

GENERAL INFORMATION

Type of School: Public **Environment:** Village **Academic Calendar:** Semesters

STUDENTS

Enrollment of parent institution: 16,000 **Enrollment of MBA program:** 55 % **male/female:** 65/35 % **out-of-state:** 36 % **part-time:** 54 % **minorities:** 4 % **international:** 20 **Average age at entry:** 26 **Average years work experience at entry:** 2

MICHIGAN TECHNOLOGICAL UNIVERSITY
SCHOOL OF BUSINESS AND ECONOMICS

Admissions Contact: NANCY REHLING, DIRECTOR OF ADMISSIONS
Address: ADMISSIONS OFFICE, 1400 TOWNSEND DRIVE, HOUGHTON, MI 49931
Phone: 906-487-2335 • *Fax:* 906-487-2125
E-mail: MTU4U@MTU.EDU
Website: WWW.SBE.MTU.EDU

GENERAL INFORMATION

Type of School: Public

ACADEMICS

Student/faculty ratio: 14:1 **Joint Degrees:** A second degree program is available. This is a 47 credit hour program and is available to students who have earned or are earning another bachelors degree. The second degree in business is in business administration.

ADMISSIONS

Admissions Selectivity Rating: 80

# of applications received: 150 % applicants accepted: 63 % acceptees attending: 68 **Average GMAT:** 570 **Average GPA:** 3.3 **Application Fee:** $40

MIDDLE TENNESSEE STATE UNIVERSITY
JENNINGS A. JONES COLLEGE OF BUSINESS

Admissions Contact: TROY A. FESTERVAND, DIRECTOR, GRADUATE BUSINESS STUDIES
Address: PO BOX 290 BAS N222, MURFREESBORO, TN 37132
Phone: 615-898-2368 • **Fax:** 615-904-8491
E-mail: GBS@MTSU.EDU
Website: WWW.MTSU.EDU/~GRADUATE/PROGRAMS/BUAD.HTM

GENERAL INFORMATION

Type of School: Public **Environment:** Village

STUDENTS

Enrollment of MBA program: 386 % male/female: 77/23 % minorities: 12 **Average age at entry:** 24

ACADEMICS

Student/faculty ratio: 20:1

FINANCIAL FACTS

Tuition (in-state/out-of-state): $2,250/$6,100 **Fees:** $300 **Books and supplies:** $1,000 **Room & board:** $2,500

ADMISSIONS

Admissions Selectivity Rating: 69

# of applications received: 241 % applicants accepted: 83 % acceptees attending: 100 **Average GMAT:** 490 **Average GPA:** 3.2 **TOEFL required of int'l applicants?** Yes **Minimum TOEFL (paper/computer):** 525/197 **Application Fee:** $25 **International Application Fee:** $30 **Regular Application Deadline:** 7/1 **Regular Notification:** 8/1 **Deferment Available?** Yes **Maximum length of deferment:** Varies **Transfer Students Accepted?** Yes **Non-fall Admissions?** Yes

MILLSAPS COLLEGE
ELSE SCHOOL OF MANAGEMENT

Admissions Contact: ANNE MCDONALD, DIRECTOR OF GRADUATE BUSINESS ADMISSIONS
Address: 1701 NORTH STATE STREET, JACKSON, MS 39210
Phone: 601-974-1253 • **Fax:** 601-974-1224
E-mail: MBAMACC@MILLSAPS.EDU
Website: WWW.MILLSAPS.EDU/ESOM

GENERAL INFORMATION

Type of School: Private **Environment:** Metropolis **Academic Calendar:** Semester

STUDENTS

Enrollment of parent institution: 1,374 **Enrollment of MBA program:** 90 % male/female: 62/38 % out-of-state: 30 % part-time: 60 % minorities: 14 % international: 6 **Average age at entry:** 28 **Average years work experience at entry:** 4

ACADEMICS

Student/faculty ratio: 12:1 % female faculty: 39 % minority faculty: 5

FINANCIAL FACTS

Tuition: $19,140 **Fees:** $360 **Books and supplies:** $550 **Room & Board:** $10,000 % of students receiving aid: 85 % of first-year students receiving aid: 100 % of students receiving grants: 90

ADMISSIONS

Admissions Selectivity Rating: 77

# of applications received: 81 % applicants accepted: 75 % acceptees attending: 77 **GMAT Range (25th to 75th percentile):** 510-640 **Average GMAT:** 570 **Average GPA:** 3.4 **TOEFL required of int'l applicants?** Yes **Minimum TOEFL (paper/computer):** 550/230 **Application Fee:** $25 **International Application Fee:** $25 **Regular Application Deadline:** 7/1 **Regular Notification:** 7/15 **Deferment Available?** Yes **Maximum length of deferment:** 1 year **Transfer Students Accepted?** Yes **Non-fall Admissions?** Yes **Need-Blind Admissions?** Yes

EMPLOYMENT PROFILE

Placement rate (%): 100 # of companies recruiting on-campus: 19 % grads employed immediately: 85 **Average starting salary:** $48,300

MINNESOTA STATE UNIVERSITY—MANKATO
COLLEGE OF BUSINESS

Admissions Contact: *LIZ OLMANSON, DEPARTMENT ASSISTANT*
Address: *MSU MBA PROGRAM, 150 MORRIS HALL, MANKATO, MN 56001*
Phone: *507-389-2967* • **Fax:** *507-389-5497*
E-mail: *MBA@MNSU.EDU*
Website: *WWW.COB.MNSU.EDU*

GENERAL INFORMATION
Type of School: Public **Academic Calendar:** Semester

STUDENTS
Enrollment of parent institution: 13,000 **Enrollment of MBA program:** 22 % **male/female:** 67/33 % **out-of-state:** 9 % **part-time:** 10 % **minorities:** 5 % **international:** 5 **Average years work experience at entry:** 4.50

ACADEMICS
Student/faculty ratio: 13:1

FINANCIAL FACTS
Tuition (in-state/out-of-state): $6,830/$9,260 **Fees (in-state/out-of-state):** $473/$8,904 **Books and supplies:** $550 **Room & board:** $9,804 **% of students receiving aid:** 10 **% of first-year students receiving aid:** 10 **Average award package:** $15,000 **Average grant:** $15,000

ADMISSIONS
Admissions Selectivity Rating: 75
# of applications received: 30 **% applicants accepted:** 73 % **acceptees attending:** 100 **Average GMAT:** 521 **Average GPA:** 3.32 **TOEFL required of int'l applicants?** Yes **Application Fee:** $40 **International Application Fee:** $40 **Regular Application Deadline:** 6/1 **Regular Notification:** 6/15 **Deferment Available?** Yes **Transfer Students Accepted?** Yes **Non-fall Admissions?** Yes **Need-Blind Admissions?** Yes

MONTANA STATE UNIVERSITY
COLLEGE OF BUSINESS

Admissions Contact: *MARC A. GIULLIAN, MPAC DIRECTOR*
Address: *338 REID HALL, PO BOX 173040, BOZEMAN, MT 59717-3040*
Phone: *406-994-4681* • **Fax:** *406-994-6206*
E-mail: *MGIULLIAN@MONTANA.EDU*
Website: *WWW.MONTANA.EDU/COB/*

GENERAL INFORMATION
Type of School: Public **Environment:** Town **Academic Calendar:** Semester

STUDENTS
Enrollment of parent institution: **Enrollment of MBA program:** 40 % **male/female:** 25/75 % **part-time:** 8 **Average age at entry:** 25

ACADEMICS
Student/faculty ratio: 20:1 **% female faculty:** 33

FINANCIAL FACTS
Tuition (in-state/out-of-state): $3,080/$8,352 **Fees:** $311 **% of students receiving aid:** 50 **Average grant:** $5,000

ADMISSIONS
Admissions Selectivity Rating: 79
# of applications received: 50 **% applicants accepted:** 62 % **acceptees attending:** 94 **Average GMAT:** 520 **Average GPA:** 3.5 **TOEFL required of int'l applicants?** Yes **Minimum TOEFL (paper):** 550 **Application Fee:** $50 **Regular Application Deadline:** 3/15 **Regular Notification:** Rolling **Deferment Available?** Yes **Maximum length of deferment:** 1 year **Transfer Students Accepted?** Yes **Non-fall Admissions?** Yes

EMPLOYMENT PROFILE
Placement rate (%): 85 **# of companies recruiting on-campus:** 17 **% grads employed immediately:** 75 **Average starting salary:** $38,000

Grads employed by field:% avg. salary:
Accounting ....85 ....$38,000

MONTCLAIR STATE UNIVERSITY
SCHOOL OF BUSINESS

Address: *PARTRIDGE HALL 454, UPPER MONTCLAIR, NJ 07043*
Phone: *973-655-4306* • **Fax:** *973-655-5312*
E-mail: *SBUS@MAIL.MONTCLAIR.EDU*
Website: *WWW.MONTCLAIR.EDU/MBA*

GENERAL INFORMATION
Type of School: Public **Environment:** Village **Academic Calendar:** Year-round

STUDENTS
Enrollment of parent institution: 15,000 **Enrollment of MBA program:** 370 **% part-time:** 7 **Average age at entry:** 26

ACADEMICS
Student/faculty ratio: 25:1 **% female faculty:** 20

FINANCIAL FACTS
Tuition: $10,646 **Books and supplies:** $850 **Room & board:** $8,250

MORGAN STATE UNIVERSITY
EARL GRAVES SCHOOL OF BUSINESS AND MANAGEMENT

Website: WWW.MORGAN.EDU/ACADEMICS/SBM/ACADEMIC/SBM.HTM

GENERAL INFORMATION

Type of School: Public Environment: City Academic Calendar: Semester

STUDENTS

Enrollment of parent institution: 5,900 Enrollment of MBA program: 103 % part-time: 100

ACADEMICS

Student/faculty ratio: 12:1

FINANCIAL FACTS

Room & board: $2,990

ADMISSIONS

Admissions Selectivity Rating: 60*

TOEFL required of int'l applicants? Yes Minimum TOEFL (paper/computer): 600/ Application Fee: $20 Regular Application Deadline: Rolling Regular Notification: Rolling Deferment Available? Yes

EMPLOYMENT PROFILE

Placement rate (%): 86 # of companies recruiting on-campus: 150

MURRAY STATE UNIVERSITY
COLLEGE OF BUSINESS AND PUBLIC AFFAIRS

Admissions Contact: DR. GERRY NKOMBO MUUKA, ASSISTANT DEAN AND MBA DIRECTOR

Address: 109 BUSINESS BUILDING, GRADUATE ADMISSIONS OFFICE, SPARKS HALL, MURRAY, KY 42071

Phone: 270-762-6970 • Fax: 270-762-3482

E-mail: CBPA@MURRAYSTATE.EDU

Website: WWW.MURSUKY.EDU/QACD/CBPA/MBA/INDEX.HTM

GENERAL INFORMATION

Type of School: Public Environment: Village Academic Calendar: Semester

STUDENTS

Enrollment of parent institution: 9,000 Enrollment of MBA program: 160 % part-time: 53 Average age at entry: 31

ACADEMICS

Student/faculty ratio: 20:1

FINANCIAL FACTS

Tuition (in-state/out-of-state): $2,852/$7,980 Room & board: $3,800

ADMISSIONS

Admissions Selectivity Rating: 60*

# of applications received: 121 % applicants accepted: 75 % acceptees attending: 52 TOEFL required of int'l applicants? Yes Minimum TOEFL (paper): 525 Application Fee: $20 Regular Application Deadline: Rolling Regular Notification: Rolling Deferment Available? Yes Transfer Students Accepted? Yes Non-fall Admissions? Yes

EMPLOYMENT PROFILE

of companies recruiting on-campus: 170

NEW JERSEY INSTITUTE OF TECHNOLOGY
SCHOOL OF MANAGEMENT

Admissions Contact: OFFICE OF UNIVERSITY ADMISSIONS, OFFICE OF UNIVERSITY ADMISSIONS

Address: EAST BUILDING - ROOM 100, UNIVERSITY HEIGHTS, NEWARK, NJ 07102

Phone: 973-596-3300 • Fax: 973-596-3461

E-mail: ADMISSIONS@NJIT.EDU

Website: WWW.NJIT.EDU/

GENERAL INFORMATION

Type of School: Public Environment: City Academic Calendar: Semester

STUDENTS

Enrollment of parent institution: 8,249 **Enrollment of MBA program:** 191 % **male/female:** 62/38 % **out-of-state:** 10 % **part-time:** 66 % **minorities:** 9 % **international:** 38 **Average age at entry:** 31 **Average years work experience at entry:** 5

ACADEMICS

Student/faculty ratio: 13:1

FINANCIAL FACTS

Tuition (in-state/out-of-state): $10,390/$14,624 **Fees:** $1,236 **Books and supplies:** $1,200 **Room & board (on/off campus):** $8,242/$10,300 **Average grant:** $12,000

ADMISSIONS

Admissions Selectivity Rating: 78

# of applications received: 178 % **applicants accepted:** 60 % **acceptees attending:** 46 **Average GPA:** 3.5 **TOEFL required of int'l applicants?** Yes **Minimum TOEFL (paper/computer):** 525/213 **Application Fee:** $60 **International Application Fee:** $60 **Regular Application Deadline:** Rolling **Regular Notification:** Rolling **Non-fall Admissions?** Yes

EMPLOYMENT PROFILE

Placement rate (%): 100 **# of companies recruiting on-campus:** 60

NEW YORK UNIVERSITY—EMBA
NEW YORK UNIVERSITY STERN EXECUTIVE MBA PROGRAM

Admissions Contact: PETER TODD, ADMISSIONS COORDINATOR
Address: 44 WEST 4TH STREET, SUITE 10-66, NEW YORK, NY 10012
Phone: 212-998-0789 • **Fax:** 212-995-4222
E-mail: EXECUTIVE@STERN.NYU.EDU
Website: WWW.STERN.NYU.EDU/EXECUTIVE/EMBA

GENERAL INFORMATION

Type of School: Private

STUDENTS

Enrollment of MBA program: 100 % **male/female:** 71/29 % **minorities:** 12 % **international:** 20 **Average age at entry:** 33 **Average years work experience at entry:** 10

ADMISSIONS

Admissions Selectivity Rating: 96

# of applications received: 600 % **applicants accepted:** 25 % **acceptees attending:** 67 **Average GMAT:** 660 **Average GPA:** 3.4 **Application Fee:** $150 **International Application Fee:** $150 **Regular Application Deadline:** 2/27 **Regular Notification:** Rolling **Deferment Available?** Yes **Maximum length of deferment:** 1 year **Non-fall Admissions?** Yes

NICHOLLS STATE UNIVERSITY
COLLEGE OF BUSINESS ADMINISTRATION

Admissions Contact: BECKY LEBLANC-DUROCHER, DIRECTOR OF ADMISSIONS
Address: PO BOX 2004, THIBODAUX, LA 70310
Phone: 877-642-4655 • **Fax:** 985-448-4929
E-mail: ESAI-BL@NICHOLLS.EDU
Website: WWW.NICHOLLS.EDU

GENERAL INFORMATION

Type of School: Public **Environment:** Village **Academic Calendar:** Semester

STUDENTS

Enrollment of parent institution: 7,482 **Enrollment of MBA program:** 116 % **male/female:** 49/51 % **out-of-state:** 1 % **part-time:** 59 % **minorities:** 6 % **international:** 12

ACADEMICS

Student/faculty ratio: 15:1 % **female faculty:** 19 **Prominent Alumni:** Barry Melancon, President, AICPA; John Weimer, Justice, Louisiana Supreme Court; Billy Tauzin, U.S. Representative.

FINANCIAL FACTS

Tuition (in-state/out-of-state): $3,075/$8,523 **Books and supplies:** $2,000 **Room & board:** $4,584 % **of students receiving aid:** 20 **Average grant:** $4,000

ADMISSIONS

Admissions Selectivity Rating: 61

# of applications received: 70 % **applicants accepted:** 99 % **acceptees attending:** 57 **Average GMAT:** 486 **Average GPA:** 3.1 **TOEFL required of int'l applicants?** Yes **Minimum TOEFL (paper/computer):** 550/213 **Application Fee:** $20 **International Application Fee:** $30 **Regular Application Deadline:** 7/1 **Regular Notification:** Rolling **Deferment Available?** Yes **Maximum length of deferment:** 1 Semester **Transfer Students Accepted?** Yes **Non-fall Admissions?** Yes **Need-Blind Admissions?** Yes

NORTH CAROLINA STATE UNIVERSITY
COLLEGE OF MANAGEMENT

Admissions Contact: PAM BOSTIC, MBA PROGRAM DIRECTOR
Address: MBA PROGRAM OFFICE/CAMPUS BOX 7229, RALEIGH, NC 27695-7229
Phone: 919-515-5584 • **Fax:** 919-515-5073
E-mail: MBA@NCSU.EDU
Website: WWW.MBA.NCSU.EDU

GENERAL INFORMATION

Type of School: Public **Environment:** Metropolis

STUDENTS

Enrollment of parent institution: 29,637 Enrollment of MBA program: 363 % male/female: 68/32 % out-of-state: 11 % part-time: 73 % minorities: 9 % international: 27 Average age at entry: 29 Average years work experience at entry: 4.3

ACADEMICS

Student/faculty ratio: 3:1 % female faculty: 19 % minority faculty: 13 **Prominent Alumni:** Tony O'Driscoll, IBM-Senior Learning Strategist; John McCarley, Bowe/Bell & Howell, CIO, V.P. for IT; Eric Gregg, Triangle Tech Journal, Publisher; John Silvestri, Cantor Fitzgerald, V.P. Operations; Sam Matheny, Capital Broadcasting Group, DTV-VP & General Manag.

FINANCIAL FACTS

Tuition (in-state/out-of-state): $8,038/$19,962 Fees: $1,088 Books and supplies: $1,000 % of first-year students receiving aid: 97 Average grant: $14,950 Average student loan debt: $31,108

ADMISSIONS

Admissions Selectivity Rating: 87

# of applications received: 95 % applicants accepted: 58 % acceptees attending: 69 Average GMAT: 617 Average GPA: 3.4 TOEFL required of int'l applicants? Yes Minimum TOEFL (paper/computer): 620/260 Application Fee: $55 International Application Fee: $65 Regular Application Deadline: 3/1 Regular Notification: 4/1 Deferment Available? Yes Maximum length of deferment: 1 year Transfer Students Accepted? Yes Need-Blind Admissions? Yes

EMPLOYMENT PROFILE

% grads employed immediately: 58 Average starting salary: $61,500

NORTH DAKOTA STATE UNIVERSITY
COLLEGE OF BUSINESS ADMINISTRATION

Admissions Contact: MBA DIRECTOR
Website: WWW.NDSU.EDU/CBA/

GENERAL INFORMATION

Type of School: Public Environment: City

STUDENTS

Enrollment of MBA program: 537 % male/female: 60/40 % part-time: 89 % international: 8 Average age at entry: 29

ACADEMICS

Student/faculty ratio: 19:1 Joint Degrees: MBA/JD–105-127 credits (3.5 to 5 years).

FINANCIAL FACTS

Tuition: $7,632 Fees: $25

ADMISSIONS

Admissions Selectivity Rating: 60*

# of applications received: 162 % applicants accepted: 90 % acceptees attending: 80 Average GMAT: Average GPA: TOEFL required of int'l applicants? Yes Minimum TOEFL (paper/computer): 550/ Application Fee: $30 International Application Fee: Regular Application Deadline: Rolling Regular Notification: Rolling Deferment Available? Yes Non-fall Admissions? Yes

EMPLOYMENT PROFILE

Placement rate (%): 95 # of companies recruiting on-campus: 40

NORTHERN ILLINOIS UNIVERSITY
COLLEGE OF BUSINESS MBA PROGRAMS

Admissions Contact: MONA SALMON, ASSISTANT DIRECTOR
Address: BARSEMA 203, DEKALB, IL 60115
Phone: 866-648-6221 • **Fax:** 815-753-1668
E-mail: MBA@NIU.EDU
Website: WWW.COB.NIU.EDU/MBAPROGRAMS

GENERAL INFORMATION

Type of School: Public Environment: Rural

STUDENTS

Enrollment of parent institution: 25,000 Enrollment of MBA program: 528 % male/female: 100/0 % part-time: 99 Average age at entry: 32 Average years work experience at entry: 9

ACADEMICS

Student/faculty ratio: 24:1 % female faculty: 19 % minority faculty: 4

FINANCIAL FACTS

Tuition (in-state/out-of-state): $8,154/$11,538 Books and supplies: $750

ADMISSIONS

Admissions Selectivity Rating: 68

# of applications received: 262 % applicants accepted: 97 % acceptees attending: 70 Average GMAT: 550 Average GPA: 3.2 TOEFL required of int'l applicants? Yes Minimum TOEFL (paper/computer): 550/213 Application Fee: $30 Regular Application Deadline: 6/1 Regular Notification: Rolling Deferment Available? Yes Maximum length of deferment: 2 yearsTransfer Students Accepted? Yes Non-fall Admissions? Yes Need-Blind Admissions? Yes

Northern Kentucky University
College of Business

Admissions Contact: *Bob Salyer, MBA Program Director*
Address: *College of Business, Nunn Drive, Highland Heights, KY 41099*
Phone: *859-572-5165* • **Fax:** *859-572-6177*
E-mail: *MBUSINESS@NKU.EDU*
Website: *WWW.NKU.EDU/~MBUSINESS*

GENERAL INFORMATION

Type of School: Public **Environment:** Metropolis

STUDENTS

Enrollment of parent institution: 11,799 **Enrollment of MBA program:** 192 **% part-time:** 93 **Average age at entry:** 34 **Average years work experience at entry:** 2

ACADEMICS

Student/faculty ratio: 20:1

FINANCIAL FACTS

Tuition (in-state/out-of-state): $2,600/$7,800

ADMISSIONS

Admissions Selectivity Rating: 60*

# of applications received: 61 **% applicants accepted:** 79 **% acceptees attending:** 71 **Average GMAT:** Average GPA: **TOEFL required of int'l applicants?** Yes **Minimum TOEFL (paper):** 550 **Application Fee:** $25 **Regular Application Deadline:** 8/1 **Regular Notification:** Rolling **Deferment Available?** Yes **Transfer Students Accepted?** Yes **Non-fall Admissions?** Yes

EMPLOYMENT PROFILE

Placement rate (%): 92 **# of companies recruiting on-campus:** 40 **% grads employed immediately:** 69 **% grads employed within three months:** 92 **Average starting salary:** $47,627

Oakland University
School of Business Adminstration

Admissions Contact: *Donna D. Free, Coordinator of Graduate Business Programs*
Address: *432 Elliott Hall, Rochester, MI 48309-4493*
Phone: *248-370-3287* • **Fax:** *248-370-4964*
E-mail: *GBP@OAKLAND.EDU*
Website: *WWW.SBA.OAKLAND.EDU*

GENERAL INFORMATION

Type of School: Public **Environment:** Town **Academic Calendar:** Semester

STUDENTS

Enrollment of parent institution: 16,901 **Enrollment of MBA program:** 579 **% male/female:** 66/34 **% out-of-state:** 5 **% part-time:** 95 **% international:** 5 **Average age at entry:** 28 **Average years work experience at entry:** 5

ACADEMICS

Student/faculty ratio: 19:1 **% female faculty:** 16 **% minority faculty:** 5

FINANCIAL FACTS

Tuition (in-state/out-of-state): $5,468/$9,603 **Fees (in-state/out-of-state):** $490/$490 **Books and supplies:** $800 Room & board: $7,170 **Average grant:** $4,500

ADMISSIONS

Admissions Selectivity Rating: 71

# of applications received: 146 **% applicants accepted:** 86 **% acceptees attending:** 79 **Average GMAT:** 537 **Average GPA:** 3.24 **TOEFL required of int'l applicants?** Yes **Minimum TOEFL (paper/computer):** 550/213 **Application Fee:** $50 **International Application Fee:** $50 **Regular Application Deadline:** 8/5 **Regular Notification:** Rolling **Deferment Available?** Yes **Maximum length of deferment:** 1 year **Transfer Students Accepted?** Yes **Non-fall Admissions?** Yes **Need-Blind Admissions?** Yes **Applicants also look at:** Wayne State University.

EMPLOYMENT PROFILE

Placement rate (%): 98 **% grads employed immediately:** 98 **Average starting salary:** $70,000

The Ohio State University
Max M. Fisher College of Business

Admissions Contact: *Alison Merzel, Assistant Director, Graduate Programs Office*
Address: *100 Gerlach Hall, 2108 Neil Avenue, Columbus, OH 43210-1144*
Phone: *614-292-2249* • **Fax:** *614-292-9006*
E-mail: *FISHERGRAD@COB.OSU.EDU*
Website: *FISHER.OSU.EDU/MBA*

GENERAL INFORMATION

Type of School: Public **Academic Calendar:** Quarter

STUDENTS

Enrollment of parent institution: 58,365 **Enrollment of MBA program:** 541 **% male/female:** 77/23 **% out-of-state:** 15 **% part-time:** 51 **% minorities:** 19 **% international:** 32 **Average age at entry:** 27 **Average years work experience at entry:** 4.6

ACADEMICS

Student/faculty ratio: 5:1 % female faculty: 24 % minority faculty: 18 **Joint Degrees:** MBA/JD (four years); MBA/MHA (three years); MBA/MD (five years); MBA/PharmD (five years). **Prominent Alumni:** Mark Goldston, CEO, United Online, Inc.; Lionel Louis Nowell, Sr. VP and Treasurer, Pepsico, Inc.; James O'Brien, Chairman and CEO, Ashland Chemical; Jim Rohr, Chairman and CEO, PNC Bank; Leslie Wexner, Chair, CEO and Founder of Limited Brands.

FINANCIAL FACTS

Tuition (in-state/out-of-state): $14,970/$26,853 **Fees:** $585 **Books and supplies:** $600 **Room & board (on/off campus):** $12,000/$16,000 **% of students receiving aid:** 52 **% of first-year students receiving aid:** 57 **% of students receiving grants:** 45 **Average award package:** $13,200 **Average grant:** $11,500

ADMISSIONS

Admissions Selectivity Rating: 60*

# of applications received: 609 **% applicants accepted:** 56 **% acceptees attending:** 40 **GMAT Range (25th to 75th percentile):** 500-770 **Average GMAT:** 664 **Average GPA:** 3.4 **TOEFL required of int'l applicants?** Yes **Minimum TOEFL (paper/computer):** 600/250 **Application Fee:** $40 **International Application Fee:** $50 **Regular Application Deadline:** Rolling **Regular Notification:** Rolling **Deferment Available?** Yes **Maximum length of deferment:** 1 year **Need-Blind Admissions?** Yes **Applicants also look at:** Case Western Reserve University, Indiana University, Purdue University, University of Michigan, University of North Carolina at Chapel Hill.

EMPLOYMENT PROFILE

Placement rate (%): 98 **% grads employed immediately:** 80 **Average starting salary:** $75,895

Grads employed by field:% avg. salary:

Finance	27	$73,102
Marketing	20	$73,938
Operations	14	$74,250
Consulting	16	$77,290
Entrepreneurship	1	NR
Other	15	$74,000
Internet/New Media	6	$71,000
Non-profit	1:	NR

OHIO UNIVERSITY
COLLEGE OF BUSINESS

Admissions Contact: JAN ROSS, ASSISTANT DIRECTOR, GRADUATE PROGRAM
Address: 514 COPELAND HALL, ATHENS, OH 45701
Phone: 740-593-4320 • **Fax:** 740-593-1388
E-mail: ROSSJ@OHIO.EDU
Website: WWW.COB.OHIOU.EDU/GRAD/

GENERAL INFORMATION

Type of School: Public **Environment:** Rural **Academic Calendar:** Quarters

STUDENTS

Enrollment of parent institution: 19,000 **Enrollment of MBA program:** 105 **% male/female:** 55/45 **% out-of-state:** 50 **% minorities:** 7 **% international:** 20 **Average age at entry:** 25 **Average years work experience at entry:** 2

ACADEMICS

Student/faculty ratio: 10:1 % female faculty: 10 % minority faculty: 10 **Joint Degrees:** MBA/MSp Ad–24 months; MBA/MA International Affairs–24 months.

FINANCIAL FACTS

Tuition (in-state/out-of-state): $10,340/$19,150 **Fees (in-state/out-of-state):** $660/$6,060 **Books and supplies:** $4,700 **Room & board:** $10,000 **% of students receiving aid:** 70 **% of first-year students receiving aid:** 70 **Average award package:** $15,000 **Average grant:** $8,000

ADMISSIONS

Admissions Selectivity Rating: 77

# of applications received: 264 **% applicants accepted:** 64 **% acceptees attending:** 62 **GMAT Range (25th to 75th percentile):** 470-670 **Average GMAT:** 555 **Average GPA:** 3 **TOEFL required of int'l applicants?** Yes **Minimum TOEFL (paper/computer):** 600/250 **Application Fee:** $30 **Regular Application Deadline:** 3/1 **Regular Notification:** 4/1 **Deferment Available?** Yes **Maximum length of deferment:** 1 year **Need-Blind Admissions?** Yes

EMPLOYMENT PROFILE

Placement rate (%): 80

OKLAHOMA CITY UNIVERSITY
MEINDERS SCHOOL OF BUSINESS

Admissions Contact: LESLIE MCKENZIE, M.ED., SENIOR GRADUATE ADMISSION REPRESENTATIVE
Address: 2501 N BLACKWELDER, ANN LACY ADMISSION BUILDING, OKLAHOMA CITY, OK 73106
Phone: 405-208-5351 • **Fax:** 405-208-5356
E-mail: GADMISSIONS@OKCU.EDU
Website: WWW.YOUATOCU.COM

GENERAL INFORMATION

Type of School: Private **Affiliation:** Methodist

STUDENTS

Enrollment of parent institution: 3,695 **Enrollment of MBA program:** 657 **% male/female:** 90/10 **% out-of-state:** 20 **% part-time:** 60 **% minorities:** 30 **Average age at entry:** 28

ACADEMICS

Student/faculty ratio: 13:1 % female faculty: 31 % minority faculty: 33 Joint Degrees: MBA/JD—114 credit hours, (MBA - 30 and JD - 84) MBA/MSN(masters of science in nursing) - 75 credit hours. Prominent Alumni: Michael J. Maples, Former EVP, Worldwide Products, Microsoft; Dennis Dougherty, Intersouth, Founding Partner; Dr. Righard Ng, Pacific Manager, GE; Martha Burger, VP, HR, Treasurer, Chesapeake Energy.

FINANCIAL FACTS

Tuition: $10,872 Fees: $774 Books and supplies: $1,000 Room & board (on/off campus): $3,700/$6,000

ADMISSIONS

Admissions Selectivity Rating: 61

# of applications received: 47 % applicants accepted: 87 % acceptees attending: 54 Average GMAT: Average GPA: 2.88 TOEFL required of int'l applicants? Yes Minimum TOEFL (paper/computer): 550/213 Application Fee: $30 International Application Fee: $70 Regular Application Deadline: Rolling Regular Notification: Rolling Deferment Available? Yes Maximum length of deferment: 1 year Transfer Students Accepted? Yes Non-fall Admissions? Yes Need-Blind Admissions? Yes Applicants also look at: Oklahoma State University, University of Oklahoma.

OKLAHOMA STATE UNIVERSITY
SPEARS SCHOOL OF BUSINESS

Admissions Contact: JANICE ANALLA, ASSISTANT DIRECTOR, MBA PROGRAM
Address: OKLAHOMA STATE UNIVERSITY, 102 GUNDERSEN HALL, STILLWATER, OK 74078-4011
Phone: 405-744-2951 • Fax: 405-744-7474
E-mail: MBA-OSU@OKSTATE.EDU
Website: SPEARS.OKSTATE.EDU/MBA/

GENERAL INFORMATION

Type of School: Public Environment: Town Academic Calendar: Semester

STUDENTS

Enrollment of parent institution: Enrollment of MBA program: 215 % male/female: 71/29 % part-time: 63 % minorities: 1 % international: 43 Average age at entry: 24 Average years work experience at entry: 1

ACADEMICS

Student/faculty ratio: 25:1 Joint Degrees: MBA/MSTM—68 credits (2.5 years) DO/MBA 36 credits (1.5 years/3 Semesters). Prominent Alumni: Tiffany Sewell Howard, Chief Operating Officer, The Charles Machine Works; Dennis Reilley, CEO, Praxaire; Charlie Eitel, Chairman & CEO, Simmons Companies; Don Humphries, VP & Treasurer, Exxon Mobile.

FINANCIAL FACTS

Tuition (in-state/out-of-state): $3,380/$11,570 Fees: $1,662 Books and supplies: $4,290 Room & board: $5,302 Average award package: $4,000 Average grant: $1,000 Average student loan debt: $8,000

ADMISSIONS

Admissions Selectivity Rating: 91

# of applications received: 126 % applicants accepted: 41 % acceptees attending: 48 GMAT Range (25th to 75th percentile): 590-640 Average GMAT: 627 Average GPA: 3.36 TOEFL required of int'l applicants? Yes Minimum TOEFL (paper/computer): 575/ Application Fee: $25 International Application Fee: $50 Regular Application Deadline: 7/1 Regular Notification: Rolling Deferment Available? Yes Maximum length of deferment: 1 year Transfer Students Accepted? Yes Non-fall Admissions? Yes Need-Blind Admissions? Yes Applicants also look at: The University of Tulsa, University of Arkansas—Fayetteville, University of Kansas, University of Oklahoma.

EMPLOYMENT PROFILE

Placement rate (%): 63 % grads employed immediately: 57 Average starting salary: $43,484

Grads employed by field:% avg. salary:

Field	%	avg. salary
Accounting	11	$43,500
Finance	20	$30,875
Marketing	8	$49,426
MIS	2	$55,000
Operations	2	$45,000
Consulting	8	$46,666
General Management	20	$43,900
Quantitative	2	$70,000
Other	17	$49,266
Non-profit	5:	$25,500

OREGON STATE UNIVERSITY
SCHOOL OF BUSINESS ADMINISTRATION

Admissions Contact: DIANE JARVI, MBA PROGRAM COORDINATOR
Address: 200 BEXELL HALL, CORVALLIS, OR 97330
Phone: 541-737-3716 • Fax: 541-737-4890
E-mail: JARVI@BUS.OREGONSTATE.EDU
Website: WWW.BUS.OREGONSTATE.EDU/

GENERAL INFORMATION

Type of School: Public Environment: Town Academic Calendar: Quarter

STUDENTS

Enrollment of parent institution: 19,162 Enrollment of MBA program: 65 % male/female: 55/45 % minorities: 13 Average age at entry: 29 Average years work experience at entry: 3

ACADEMICS

Student/faculty ratio: 3:1 % female faculty: 15 % minority faculty: 18

FINANCIAL FACTS

Tuition (in-state/out-of-state): $9,366/$15,603 Fees: $525 Books and supplies: $1,350 Room & board (on campus): $6,336

ADMISSIONS

Admissions Selectivity Rating: 82

# of applications received: 142 % applicants accepted: 50 % acceptees attending: 65 Average GMAT: 554 Average GPA: 3.23 TOEFL required of int'l applicants? Yes Minimum TOEFL (paper/computer): 575/233 Application Fee: $50 Regular Application Deadline: 3/5 Regular Notification: Rolling Deferment Available? Yes Maximum length of deferment: 99 Transfer Students Accepted? Yes Non-fall Admissions? Yes Need-Blind Admissions? Yes Applicants also look at: Portland State University, University of Oregon.

EMPLOYMENT PROFILE

of companies recruiting on-campus: 200

PACE UNIVERSITY
LUBIN SCHOOL OF BUSINESS

Admissions Contact: JOANNA BRODA, DIRECTOR OF GRADUATE ADMISSION
Address: ONE PACE PLAZA, NEW YORK, NY 10038
Phone: 212-346-1531 • Fax: 212-346-1585
E-mail: GRADNYC@PACE.EDU
Website: WWW.PACE.EDU/LUBIN

GENERAL INFORMATION

Type of School: Private Environment: Metropolis Academic Calendar: Semester

STUDENTS

Enrollment of parent institution: 13,670 Enrollment of MBA program: 1,197 % male/female: 53/47 % out-of-state: 6 % part-time: 81 % minorities: 8 % international: 47 Average age at entry: 29 Average years work experience at entry: 3

ACADEMICS

Student/faculty ratio: 23:1 % female faculty: 18 % minority faculty: 19 Joint Degrees: Master of business administration/doctor of jurisprudence (MBA/JD). Prominent Alumni: Ivan G. Seidenberg, President and CEO Verizon Communications; John R. Danieli, President, CEO, Owner Computer Merchant LTD; Herbert Henkel, Chairman, President & CEO Ingersoll Rand; Mel Karmazin, CEO Sirius Satellite Radio Inc.; Marie J. Toulantis, CEO Barnes and Noble.

FINANCIAL FACTS

Tuition: $27,720 Fees: $460 Books and supplies: $2,930 Room & board (on/off campus): $8,400/$17,980 % of students receiving aid: 54 % of first-year students receiving aid: 63 % of students receiving loans: 30 % of students receiving grants: 33 Average award package: $14,710 Average grant: $5,443 Average student loan debt: $20,963

ADMISSIONS

Admissions Selectivity Rating: 77

# of applications received: 870 % applicants accepted: 49 % acceptees attending: 43 GMAT Range (25th to 75th percentile): 490-570 Average GMAT: 534 Average GPA: 3.21 TOEFL required of int'l applicants? Yes Minimum TOEFL (paper/computer): 570/230 Application Fee: $65 International Application Fee: $65 Regular Application Deadline: 8/1 Regular Notification: Rolling Transfer Students Accepted? Yes Non-fall Admissions? Yes Need-Blind Admissions? Yes

EMPLOYMENT PROFILE

Placement rate (%): 95 # of companies recruiting on-campus: 174 % grads employed immediately: 20 Average starting salary: $54,200

Grads employed by field: ....%

Accounting	14
Finance	32
Human Resources	4
Marketing	18
MIS	9
Consulting	5
General Management	5
Global Management	5
Other	8

PACIFIC LUTHERAN UNIVERSITY
SCHOOL OF BUSINESS

Admissions Contact: ABBY WIGSTROM-CARLSON, DIRECTOR OF GRADUATE STUDIES & EXTERNAL RELATIONS
Address: OFFICE OF ADMISSIONS, TACOMA, WA 98447
Phone: 253-535-7151 • Fax: 253-536-5136
E-mail: BUSINESS@PLU.EDU
Website: WWW.PLU.EDU/~BUSA/MBA

GENERAL INFORMATION

Type of School: Private Affiliation: Lutheran Environment: City

STUDENTS

Enrollment of parent institution: 3,463 Enrollment of MBA program: 70 % male/female: 83/17 % out-of-state: 9 % part-time: 36 % minorities: 7 % international: 21 Average age at entry: 31 Average years work experience at entry: 9

ACADEMICS

Student/faculty ratio: 12:1 % female faculty: 30 % minority faculty: 10

FINANCIAL FACTS

Tuition: $15,522 Books and supplies: $850 Room & board: $6,410 Average grant: $1,219

ADMISSIONS

Admissions Selectivity Rating: 66

# of applications received: 34 % applicants accepted: 94 % acceptees attending: 72 GMAT Range (25th to 75th percentile): 460-590 Average GMAT: 533 Average GPA: 3.25 TOEFL required of int'l applicants? Yes Minimum TOEFL (paper/computer): 550/213 Application Fee: $40 International Application Fee: $40 Regular Application Deadline: Rolling Regular Notification: Rolling Deferment Available? Yes Maximum length of deferment: 1 year Transfer Students Accepted? Yes Non-fall Admissions? Yes Need-Blind Admissions? Yes Applicants also look at: Seattle Pacific University, Seattle University, University of Washington.

EMPLOYMENT PROFILE

Average starting salary: $75,000

PENN STATE UNIVERSITY ONLINE MBA

PENN STATE UNIVERSITY iMBA

Admissions Contact: DUSTY HASSELMAN, PROGRAM SPECIALIST
Address: 207 MITCHELL BUILDING, UNIVERSITY PARK, PA 16802-3601
Phone: 814-898-6527 • Fax: 814-898-6528
E-mail: IMBA@PSU.EDU
Website: WWW.WORLDCAMPUS.PSU.EDU/IMBA

GENERAL INFORMATION

Type of School: Public

STUDENTS

Enrollment of parent institution: 83,177 Enrollment of MBA program: 62 % male/female: 100/0 % out-of-state: 78 % part-time: 100 % international: 10 Average age at entry: 32 Average years work experience at entry: 7.5

ACADEMICS

Student/faculty ratio: 30:1 % female faculty: 23 % minority faculty: 25

FINANCIAL FACTS

Tuition: $23,000

ADMISSIONS

Admissions Selectivity Rating: 85

# of applications received: 124 % applicants accepted: 57 % acceptees attending: 87 Average GMAT: 602 Average GPA: 3.1 TOEFL required of int'l applicants? Yes Minimum TOEFL (paper/computer): 600/250 Application Fee: $75 International Application Fee: $75 Regular Application Deadline: 5/31 Regular Notification: 6/7 Deferment Available? Yes Maximum length of deferment: 1 year Transfer Students Accepted? Yes Need-Blind Admissions? Yes

EMPLOYMENT PROFILE

% grads employed immediately: 100

PENNSYLVANIA STATE UNIVERSITY—HARRISBURG CAMPUS

SCHOOL OF BUSINESS ADMINISTRATION

Admissions Contact: DR. THOMAS STREVELER, DIRECTOR OF ENROLLMENT SERVICES
Address: 777 WEST HARRISBURG PIKE, MIDDLETOWN, PA 17057
Phone: 717-948-6250 • Fax: 717-948-6325
E-mail: HBGADMIT@PSU.EDU
Website: WWW.HBG.PSU.EDU/SBUS

GENERAL INFORMATION

Type of School: Public Environment: Village Academic Calendar: Semester

STUDENTS

Enrollment of parent institution: 3,239 Enrollment of MBA program: 207 % male/female: 64/36 % out-of-state: 5 % part-time: 88 % minorities: 7 % international: 5 Average age at entry: 27 Average years work experience at entry: 3

ACADEMICS

Student/faculty ratio: 12:1

FINANCIAL FACTS

Tuition (in-state/out-of-state): $9,264/$17,592 Books and supplies: $4,170 Average grant: $4,200

ADMISSIONS

Admissions Selectivity Rating: 67

# of applications received: 76 % applicants accepted: 91 % acceptees attending: 90 Average GMAT: 520 Average GPA: 3 TOEFL required of int'l applicants? Yes Minimum TOEFL (paper/computer): 550/213 Application Fee: $50 International Application Fee: $50 Regular Application Deadline: 7/18 Regular Notification: Rolling Deferment Available? Yes Maximum length of deferment: 3 years Transfer Students Accepted? Yes Non-fall Admissions? Yes Need-Blind Admissions? Yes

Placement rate (%): 100 **Average starting salary:** $45,000

QUEEN'S UNIVERSITY
QUEEN'S SCHOOL OF BUSINESS

Admissions Contact: 613-533-2302, PROGRAM MANAGER
Address: GOODES HALL, QUEEN'S UNIVERSITY, SUITE 414, KINGSTON, ON K7L 3N6 CANADA
Phone: 613-533-2302 • **Fax:** 613-533-6281
E-mail: INQUIRY@MBAST.QUEENSU.CA
Website: WWW.MBAST.COM

GENERAL INFORMATION

Type of School: Public **Environment:** City **Academic Calendar:** 12 months

STUDENTS

Enrollment of parent institution: 17,510 **Enrollment of MBA program:** 78 % **male/female:** 78/22 % **minorities:** 5 % **international:** 42 **Average age at entry:** 31 **Average years work experience at entry:** 7

ACADEMICS

Student/faculty ratio: 3:1 **Joint Degrees:** Queen's-Cornell Executive MBA - (dual degree)-17 months part-time. **Prominent Alumni:** Mr. Mel Goodes, Retired Chair & CEO, Warner-Lambert Co.; Mr. Don Carty, Former President & CEO, AMR Corp, & American Airli; Mr. Donald Sobey, Chairman, Empire Corporation; Ms. Cathy Williams, CFO, Shell Canada; Mr. Gord Nixon, President and CEO, RBC Financial Group.

FINANCIAL FACTS

Tuition: $44,354 **Fees:** $639 **Room & board:** $15,000 % **of students receiving aid:** 15 % **of students receiving grants:** 78 **Average grant:** $5,000

ADMISSIONS

Admissions Selectivity Rating: 86

of applications received: 240 % **applicants accepted:** 65 % **acceptees attending:** 47 **GMAT Range (25th to 75th percentile):** 630-700 **Average GMAT:** 675 **Average GPA:** 3.2 **TOEFL required of int'l applicants?** Yes **Minimum TOEFL (paper/computer):** 600/250 **Application Fee:** $100 **Regular Application Deadline:** 1/15 **Regular Notification:** 2/15 **Deferment Available?** Yes **Maximum length of deferment:** 1 year **Non-fall Admissions?** Yes **Need-Blind Admissions?** Yes **Applicants also look at:** Harvard University, Massachusetts Institute of Technology, Stanford University, University of Pennsylvania, University of Toronto, University of Western Ontario, York University.

Placement rate (%): 80 # **of companies recruiting on-campus:** 101 % **grads employed immediately:** 47 **Average starting salary:** $80,000

Grads employed by field:% avg. salary:

	%	avg. salary
Finance	18	$71,625
Human Resources	2	$NR
Marketing	22	$77,000
MIS	2	$NR
Operations	10	$70,500
Consulting	12	$74,600
Entrepreneurship	2	$NR
General Management	10	$NR
Other	22	$86,050

RIDER UNIVERSITY
COLLEGE OF BUSINESS ADMINSTRATION

Admissions Contact: CHRISTINE ZELENAK, DIRECTOR, GRADUATE ADMISSIONS
Address: PJ CIAMBELLI HALL, 2083 LAWRENCEVILLE ROAD, LAWRENCEVILLE, NJ 08648-3099
Phone: 609-896-5036 • **Fax:** 609-895-5680
E-mail: GRADADM@RIDER.EDU
Website: WWW.RIDER.EDU/172_63.HTM

GENERAL INFORMATION

Type of School: Private **Environment:** Village **Academic Calendar:** Semester

STUDENTS

Enrollment of parent institution: 5,509 **Enrollment of MBA program:** 282 % **male/female:** 49/51 % **out-of-state:** 23 % **part-time:** 85 % **minorities:** 5 % **international:** 19 **Average age at entry:** 26 **Average years work experience at entry:** 5

ACADEMICS

Student/faculty ratio: 15:1 % **female faculty:** 24 % **minority faculty:** 26 **Joint Degrees:** BS/BA/MBA; BS/BA/MAcc Each are 5 year programs. **Prominent Alumni:** Dennis Longstreet, Company Group Chairman, Johnson and Johnson; Robert Christie, President and CEO, Thomson Corp.; Bernard V. Vonderschmitt, Chairman of the Board, Xilinx, Inc.; Anne Sweigart, Chair, President and CEO, D & E Communications; Kenneth Burenga, Former President and CEO, Dow Jones & Co..

FINANCIAL FACTS

Tuition: $10,800 **Fees:** $210 **Books and supplies:** $700 **Room & board:** $9,190 % **of students receiving aid:** 21 % **of first-year students receiving aid:** 37 % **of students receiving loans:** 15 % **of students receiving grants:** 8 **Average award package:** $11,448 **Average grant:** $6,122

ADMISSIONS

Admissions Selectivity Rating: 72

# of applications received: 137 **% applicants accepted:** 72 % **acceptees attending:** 85 **GMAT Range (25th to 75th percentile):** 420-560 **Average GMAT:** 500 **Average GPA:** 3.29 **TOEFL required of int'l applicants?** Yes **Minimum TOEFL (paper/computer):** 585/240 **Application Fee:** $45 **International Application Fee:** $45 **Regular Application Deadline:** 8/1 **Deferment Available?** Yes **Maximum length of deferment:** 1 year **Transfer Students Accepted?** Yes **Non-fall Admissions?** Yes **Need-Blind Admissions?** Yes **Applicants also look at:** Drexel University — Professional MBA, Fairleigh Dickinson Univ.—Metropolitan Campus, La Salle University, Monmouth University, Rutgers, The State University of New Jersey, Rutgers, The State University of New Jersey—Camden, Seton Hall University.

EMPLOYMENT PROFILE

# of companies recruiting on-campus: 136

ADMISSIONS

Admissions Selectivity Rating: 74

# of applications received: 228 **% applicants accepted:** 85 % **acceptees attending:** 48 **GMAT Range (25th to 75th percentile):** 510-640 **Average GMAT:** 586 **Average GPA:** 3.22 **TOEFL required of int'l applicants?** Yes **Minimum TOEFL (paper/computer):** 580/237 **Application Fee:** $50 **International Application Fee:** $50 **Regular Application Deadline:** 8/1 **Regular Notification:** Rolling **Deferment Available?** Yes **Maximum length of deferment:** 1 year **Transfer Students Accepted?** Yes **Non-fall Admissions?** Yes **Need-Blind Admissions?** Yes

EMPLOYMENT PROFILE

Grads employed by field: ....%
Operations 6
Other..6

ROCHESTER INSTITUTE OF TECHNOLOGY
COLLEGE OF BUSINESS

Admissions Contact: NANCY WOEBKENBERG, MARKETING MANAGER
Address: 105 LOMB MEMORIAL DRIVE, ROCHESTER, NY 14623
Phone: 585-475-2229 • **Fax:** 585-475-5476
E-mail: GRADINFO@RIT.EDU
Website: WWW.RITMBA.COM

GENERAL INFORMATION

Type of School: Private **Environment:** City **Academic Calendar:** Quarter

STUDENTS

Enrollment of parent institution: 15,334 **Enrollment of MBA program:** 355 **% male/female:** 59/41 **% out-of-state:** 25 **% part-time:** 42 **% minorities:** 5 **% international:** 27 **Average age at entry:** 26 **Average years work experience at entry:** 3.5

ACADEMICS

Student/faculty ratio: 9:1 **% female faculty:** 15 **% minority faculty:** 3 **Prominent Alumni:** Daniel Carp, Chairman & CEO, Eastman Kodak Company; Thomas Curley, President & CEO , Associated Press.

FINANCIAL FACTS

Tuition: $22,965 **Fees:** $357 **Books and supplies:** $1,500 **Room & board:** $6,500 **% of students receiving aid:** 36 **% of first-year students receiving aid:** 41 **% of students receiving grants:** 36 **Average award package:** $7,982 **Average grant:** $7,982

RUTGERS, THE STATE UNIVERSITY OF NEW JERSEY
RUTGERS BUSINESS SCHOOL

Admissions Contact: GLENN S. BERMAN, ASSISTANT DEAN FOR ADMISSIONS
Address: 190 UNIVERSITY AVENUE, NEWARK, NJ 07102-1813
Phone: 973-353-1234 • **Fax:** 973-353-1592
E-mail: ADMIT@BUSINESS.RUTGERS.EDU
Website: BUSINESS.RUTGERS.EDU

GENERAL INFORMATION

Type of School: Public **Academic Calendar:** Trimester

STUDENTS

Enrollment of parent institution: 50,000 **Enrollment of MBA program:** 308 **% male/female:** 57/43 **% out-of-state:** 7 **% part-time:** 78 **% minorities:** 13 **% international:** 20 **Average age at entry:** 27 **Average years work experience at entry:** 4.5

ACADEMICS

Student/faculty ratio: 15:1 **Joint Degrees:** MPH/MBA, MD/MBA, JD/MBA, MS/MBA in biomedical sciences. **Prominent Alumni:** Tom Renyi, Chairman+CEO, Bank of NY; Gary Cohen, President, Becton-Dickinson Medical; Irwin Lerner, CEO, Hoffmann-La Roche; John D. Finnegan, President & CEO, The Chubb Corporation; Ralph Izzo, President & COO, PSE&G.

FINANCIAL FACTS

Tuition (in-state/out-of-state): $14,698/$25,275 **Fees:** $1,268 **Books and supplies:** $3,000

ADMISSIONS

Admissions Selectivity Rating: 88

# of applications received: 331 **% applicants accepted:** 48 % **acceptees attending:** 38 **GMAT Range (25th to 75th percentile):** 610-690 **Average GMAT:** 640 **Average GPA:** 3.2 **TOEFL required of int'l applicants?** Yes **Minimum TOEFL (paper/computer):** 600/250 **Application Fee:** $50 **International Application Fee:** $50 **Regular Application Deadline:** 5/1 **Regular Notification:** Rolling **Deferment Available?** Yes **Maximum length of deferment:** 1 year **Transfer Students Accepted?** Yes **Non-fall Admissions?** Yes **Need-Blind Admissions?** Yes **Applicants also look at:** Baruch College/City University of New York, Columbia University, Fordham University, New York University, Seton Hall University.

EMPLOYMENT PROFILE

Placement rate (%): 88 **# of companies recruiting on-campus:** 50 **% grads employed immediately:** 76 **Average starting salary:** $72,420

SAINT MARY'S UNIVERSITY (CANADA)
SOBEY SCHOOL OF BUSINESS

Admissions Contact: JENNIFER JOHNSON, MBA PROGRAM MANAGER
Address: 923 ROBIE STREET, HALIFAX, NS B3H 3C3 CANADA
Phone: 902-420-5729 • **Fax:** 902-420-5119
E-mail: MBA@SMU.CA
Website: WWW.SMU.CA/MBA

GENERAL INFORMATION

Type of School: Public **Academic Calendar:** Semester

STUDENTS

Enrollment of parent institution: 8,000 **Enrollment of MBA program:** 225 **% male/female:** 44/56 **% out-of-state:** 34 **% part-time:** 42 **% international:** 23 **Average age at entry:** 29 **Average years work experience at entry:** 3.5

ACADEMICS

Student/faculty ratio: 5:1

FINANCIAL FACTS

Tuition: $5,500 **Books and supplies:** $1,000 **% of students receiving aid:** 20 **% of first-year students receiving aid:** 10 **% of students receiving grants:** 20 **Average grant:** $2,500

ADMISSIONS

Admissions Selectivity Rating: 84

# of applications received: 305 **% applicants accepted:** 57 % **acceptees attending:** 59 **Average GMAT:** 600 **Average GPA:** 3.3 **TOEFL required of int'l applicants?** Yes **Minimum TOEFL (paper/computer):** 550/220 **Application Fee:** $35 **International Application Fee:** $35 **Regular Application Deadline:** Rolling **Regular Notification:** Rolling **Deferment Available?** Yes **Maximum length of deferment:** 1 year **Transfer Students Accepted?** Yes **Non-fall Admissions?** Need-Blind Admissions?** Yes

SALISBURY UNIVERSITY
FRANKLIN P. PERDUE SCHOOL OF BUSINESS

Admissions Contact: JANINE VIENNA, MBA DIRECTOR
Address: 1101 CAMDEN AVENUE, SALISBURY, MD 21801-6837
Phone: 410-548-3983 • **Fax:** 410-548-2908
E-mail: JMVIENNA@SALISBURY.EDU
Website: MBA.SALISBURY.EDU

GENERAL INFORMATION

Type of School: Public **Environment:** Town **Academic Calendar:** Semester

STUDENTS

Enrollment of parent institution: 7,000 **Enrollment of MBA program:** 81 **% male/female:** 63/37 **% part-time:** 55 **% minorities:** 1 **% international:** 11 **Average age at entry:** 24 **Average years work experience at entry:** 2

ACADEMICS

Student/faculty ratio: 22:1 **% female faculty:** 10

FINANCIAL FACTS

Tuition (in-state/out-of-state): $7,080/$15,000 **Fees:** $240 **Books and supplies:** $1,000 **Average grant:** $26,592

ADMISSIONS

Admissions Selectivity Rating: 62

# of applications received: 46 **% applicants accepted:** 98 % **acceptees attending:** 87 **Average GMAT:** 490 **Average GPA:** 3.1 **TOEFL required of int'l applicants?** Yes **Minimum TOEFL (paper/computer):** 550/213 **Application Fee:** $45 **International Application Fee:** $45 **Regular Application Deadline:** 3/1 **Regular Notification:** 4/1 **Transfer Students Accepted?** Yes **Non-fall Admissions?** Yes **Need-Blind Admissions?** Yes

SAM HOUSTON STATE UNIVERSITY
COLLEGE OF BUSINESS ADMINISTRATION

Admissions Contact: DR. LEROY ASHORN, COORDINATOR OF GRADUATE STUDIES
Address: PO Box 2056, Huntsville, TX 77341-2056
Phone: 936-294-1239 • *Fax:* 936-294-3612
E-mail: BUSGRAD@SHSU.EDU
Website: COBA.SHSU.EDU/

GENERAL INFORMATION

Type of School: Public Environment: Town

STUDENTS

Enrollment of MBA program: 164 % male/female: 49/51 % part-time: 71 % minorities: 7 % international: 5

FINANCIAL FACTS

Tuition (in-state/out-of-state): $2,301/$7,317

ADMISSIONS

Admissions Selectivity Rating: 61

# of applications received: 58 % applicants accepted: 86 % acceptees attending: 60 GMAT Range (25th to 75th percentile): 460-550 Average GMAT: 504 Average GPA: TOEFL required of int'l applicants? Yes Application Fee: $20 Regular Application Deadline: Rolling Regular Notification: Rolling Transfer Students Accepted? Yes Non-fall Admissions? Yes Need-Blind Admissions? Yes Applicants also look at:

EMPLOYMENT PROFILE

Placement rate (%): 80

SAMFORD UNIVERSITY
SAMFORD UNIVERSITY SCHOOL OF BUSINESS

Admissions Contact: DR. DOUGLAS L. SMITH, DIRECTOR OF GRADUATE STUDIES
Address: DBH 344, SCHOOL OF BUSINESS, 800 LAKESHORE DR., BIRMINGHAM, AL 35229
Phone: 205-726-2040 • *Fax:* 205-726-2464
E-mail: BUSINESS.GRADUATE.STUDIES@SAMFORD.EDU
Website: WWW.SAMFORD.EDU

GENERAL INFORMATION

Type of School: Private Affiliation: Baptist Environment: Town Academic Calendar: Nine-weeks

STUDENTS

Enrollment of parent institution: 4,440 Enrollment of MBA program: 160 % male/female: 100/0 % part-time: 100 Average age at entry: 31 Average years work experience at entry: 7

ACADEMICS

Student/faculty ratio: 12:1 % female faculty: 20 % minority faculty: 10 Joint Degrees: Master of business administration/master of accountancy (MBA/MAcc): part-time; 45-63 total credits required; 18 months to 7 years to complete program. Concentrations in management, accounting.

FINANCIAL FACTS

Tuition: $7,902 Books and supplies: $600

ADMISSIONS

Admissions Selectivity Rating: 72

# of applications received: 80 % applicants accepted: 76 % acceptees attending: 93 GMAT Range (25th to 75th percentile): 470-570 Average GMAT: 515 Average GPA: 3 TOEFL required of int'l applicants? Yes Minimum TOEFL (paper/computer): 550/213 Application Fee: $25 International Application Fee: $25 Regular Application Deadline: Rolling Regular Notification: Rolling Deferment Available? Yes Maximum length of deferment: 1 year Transfer Students Accepted? Yes Non-fall Admissions? Yes Need-Blind Admissions? Yes Applicants also look at: University of Alabama at Birmingham.

EMPLOYMENT PROFILE

Placement rate (%): 100

SAN DIEGO STATE UNIVERSITY
GRADUATE SCHOOL OF BUSINESS

Admissions Contact: S. SCOTT OR S.TEMORES-VALDEZ, MBA PROGRAM COORDINATOR/MSBA PROGRAM COORDINATOR
Address: 5500 CAMPANILE DRIVE, SAN DIEGO, CA 92182-8228
Phone: 619-594-8073 • *Fax:* 619-594-1863
E-mail: SDSUMBA@MAIL.SDSU.EDU
Website: WWW.SDSU.EDU/BUSINESS

GENERAL INFORMATION

Type of School: Public Environment: City Academic Calendar: Semester

STUDENTS

Enrollment of parent institution: 33,670 Enrollment of MBA program: 623 % male/female: 64/36 % out-of-state: 12 % part-time: 46 % minorities: 12 % international: 36 Average age at entry: 28 Average years work experience at entry: 5

ACADEMICS

Student/faculty ratio: 35:1 % female faculty: 14 % minority faculty: 3 Joint Degrees: Master of business administration/master of arts in latin American studies (MBA/MA), 2-4 years. Joint MBA/JD, 4 years to complete.

FINANCIAL FACTS

Tuition (in-state/out-of-state): $3,422/$7,490 Books and supplies: $1,260 Room & board: $8,787

Admissions Selectivity Rating: 88

# of applications received: 740 % applicants accepted: 46 % acceptees attending: 61 GMAT Range (25th to 75th percentile): 560-620 Average GMAT: 602 Average GPA: 3.3 TOEFL required of int'l applicants? Yes Minimum TOEFL (paper/computer): 570/230 Application Fee: $55 International Application Fee: $55 Regular Application Deadline: 4/15 Regular Notification: 5/15 Transfer Students Accepted? Yes Non-fall Admissions? Yes Need-Blind Admissions? Yes Applicants also look at: University of San Diego.

SETON HALL UNIVERSITY
STILLMAN SCHOOL OF BUSINESS

Admissions Contact: JOAN LILJEGREN, DIRECTOR OF GRADUATE ADMISSIONS
Address: GRADUATE ADMISSIONS - STILLMAN SCHOOL OF BUSINESS, 400 SOUTH ORANGE AVENUE, SOUTH ORANGE, NJ 07079-2692
Phone: 973-761-9262 • **Fax:** 973-761-9208
E-mail: STILLMAN@SHU.EDU
Website: WWW.BUSINESS.SHU.EDU

GENERAL INFORMATION

Type of School: Private Affiliation: Roman Catholic Environment: Village Academic Calendar: Semester

STUDENTS

Enrollment of parent institution: 8,293 Enrollment of MBA program: 560 % male/female: 66/34 % part-time: 83 Average age at entry: 26 Average years work experience at entry: 4

ACADEMICS

Student/faculty ratio: 25:1 % female faculty: 21 Joint Degrees: MBA/MS International Business—63/66 credits (3 to 5 years); MBA/JD (open to full-time students only)—115/118 credits (3.5 to 4 years); MBA/MSN—54 credits (2.5 - 5 years); MS International Business/MA Diplomacy & International Relations —57 credits. Prominent Alumni: James O'Brien, Managing Director / Morgan Stanley; Gerald P. Buccino, Chairman and CEO of Buccino & Associates; Michael Wilk, Partner / Ernst & Young; Stephen Lalor, Partner / Ernst & Young; Joseph M. LaMotta, Chairman Emeritus Oppenheimer Capital.

FINANCIAL FACTS

Tuition: $21,810 Fees: $615 Books and supplies: $1,458 Room & Board: $10,200 % of students receiving aid: 28 % of first-year students receiving aid: 38 % of students receiving loans: 25 % of students receiving grants: 8 Average award package: $15,863 Average grant: $11,093 Average student loan debt: $26,501

Admissions Selectivity Rating: 81

# of applications received: 421 % applicants accepted: 56 % acceptees attending: 56 GMAT Range (25th to 75th percentile): 500-700 Average GMAT: 565 Average GPA: 3.3 TOEFL required of int'l applicants? Yes Minimum TOEFL (paper/computer): 550/213 Application Fee: $75 International Application Fee: $100 Regular Application Deadline: 6/1 Regular Notification: Rolling Early decision program? Yes ED deadline /notification: MBA / Sport Mgmt. 4/1/4/15 Deferment Available? Yes Maximum length of deferment: 1 academic year Transfer Students Accepted? Yes Non-fall Admissions? Yes Need-Blind Admissions? Yes Applicants also look at: Boston College, Columbia University, Fairleigh Dickinson Univ.—Metropolitan Campus, Montclair State University, New York University, Pace University, Rutgers—The State University of New Jersey.

EMPLOYMENT PROFILE

of companies recruiting on-campus: 200 % grads employed immediately: 80

SOUTHEASTERN LOUISIANA UNIVERSITY
COLLEGE OF BUSINESS & TECHNOLOGY

Admissions Contact: SANDRA MEYERS, GRADUATE ADMISSIONS ANALYST
Address: SLU 10752, HAMMOND, LA 70402
Phone: 800-222-7358 • **Fax:** 985-549-5632
E-mail: SMEYERS@SELU.EDU
Website: WWW.SELU.EDU/ACADEMICS/BUSINESS

GENERAL INFORMATION

Type of School: Public Environment: Village Academic Calendar: Semester

STUDENTS

Enrollment of parent institution: 15,472 Enrollment of MBA program: 201 % male/female: 56/44 % out-of-state: 4 % part-time: 35 % minorities: 22 % international: 23 Average age at entry: 26

ACADEMICS

Student/faculty ratio: 5:1 % female faculty: 20 % minority faculty: 13 Prominent Alumni: Robin Roberts, ESPN Sportscaster; Russell Carollo, Pulitzer Prize Winner; Harold Jackson, President (Retired) Sunsweet Products; James J. Brady, Former President, National Democratic Party; Carl Barbier, Federal Judge.

FINANCIAL FACTS

Tuition (in-state/out-of-state): $2,986/$6,982 Books and supplies: $1,000 Room & board (on/off campus): $4,290/$7,172 % of students receiving aid: 48 % of first-year students receiving aid: 66 % of students receiving loans: 20 % of students receiving grants: 7 Average award package: $7,216 Average grant: $3,367

Admissions Selectivity Rating: 63

# of applications received: 70 % applicants accepted: 91 %
acceptees attending: 86 GMAT Range (25th to 75th percentile):
450-530 Average GMAT: 490 Average GPA: 3.1 TOEFL required of
int'l applicants? Yes Minimum TOEFL (paper/computer): 525/195
Application Fee: $20 International Application Fee: $30 Regular
Application Deadline: 7/15 Regular Notification: Rolling Deferment
Available? Yes Maximum length of deferment: 1 year Transfer
Students Accepted? Yes Non-fall Admissions? Yes

EMPLOYMENT PROFILE

of companies recruiting on-campus: 150

SOUTHERN ILLINOIS
UNIVERSITY—CARBONDALE
COLLEGE OF BUSINESS ADMNISTRATION

Admissions Contact: DR. DON GRIBBIN, MBA PROGRAM DIRECTOR
Address: REHN HALL 133, 1025 LINCOLN DRIVE, MAIL CODE 4625,
CARBONDALE, IL 62901
Phone: 618-453-3030 • *Fax:* 618-453-7961
E-mail: MBAGP@CBA.SIU.EDU
Website: WWW.CBA.SIU.EDU

GENERAL INFORMATION

Type of School: Public Environment: Town Academic Calendar:
Semester

STUDENTS

Enrollment of parent institution: 21,589 Enrollment of MBA program: 134 % male/female: 61/39 % part-time: 48 % minorities: 10
% international: 10

ACADEMICS

Student/faculty ratio: 12:1 Joint Degrees: MBA/JD, 105 credits, 3 to
4 years; MBA/master of science in agribusiness econmics
(MBA/MS), 51 credits, 1 year to 2.5 years; MBA/master of arts in
communication (MBA/MA), 51 credits, 1 year to 2.5 years.

FINANCIAL FACTS

Tuition (in-state/out-of-state): $5,760/$11,520 Fees: $1,414 Books
and supplies: $840

Admissions Selectivity Rating: 73

# of applications received: 78 % applicants accepted: 69 %
acceptees attending: 63 GMAT Range (25th to 75th percentile):
440-570 Average GMAT: 507 Average GPA: 3.4 TOEFL required of
int'l applicants? Yes Minimum TOEFL (paper/computer): 550/213
Application Fee: $35 International Application Fee: $35 Regular
Application Deadline: 3/15 Regular Notification: 6/1 Deferment
Available? Yes Maximum length of deferment: 1 year Transfer
Students Accepted? Yes Non-fall Admissions? Yes Applicants also
look at: Eastern Illinois University, University of Illinois at Urbana-
Champaign, University of Missouri—Columbia, Western Illinois
University.

EMPLOYMENT PROFILE

of companies recruiting on-campus: 30

SOUTHERN ILLINOIS
UNIVERSITY—EDWARDSVILLE
SCHOOL OF BUSINESS

Admissions Contact: DIANE JONES, ADMISSIONS OFFICER
Address: CAMPUS BOX 1186, EDWARDSVILLE, IL 62026
Phone: 618-650-3840 • *Fax:* 618-650-3979
E-mail: MBA@SIUE.EDU
Website: WWW.SIUE.EDU/BUSINESS

GENERAL INFORMATION

Type of School: Public Environment: Village Academic Calendar: 10
weeks

STUDENTS

Enrollment of parent institution: 13,493 Enrollment of MBA program: 209 % male/female: 52/48 % part-time: 76 % minorities: 5
% international: 9 Average age at entry: 27 Average years work
experience at entry: 5

ACADEMICS

Student/faculty ratio: 9:1 % female faculty: 24 % minority faculty:
3 Prominent Alumni: Fernando G. Aguirre, President & CEO of
Chiquita Brands International; Michael A. Drone, President & CEO of
Drone & Mueller and Assoc.; Ralph Korte, President, Korte
Construction Company; Ann Ficken, General Partner, Edward Jones;
Matthew P. Kulig, President & CEO of Global VeloCity, Inc.

FINANCIAL FACTS

Tuition (in-state/out-of-state): $2,880/$5,760 Fees: $629 Books
and supplies: $1,000 Room & board: $6,610 % of students receiving aid: 35 % of first-year students receiving aid: 4 % of students
receiving loans: 22 % of students receiving grants: 4 Average
award package: $9,123 Average grant: $3,455 Average student
loan debt: $27,091

SOUTHERN METHODIST UNIVERSITY
COX SCHOOL OF BUSINESS

Admissions Contact: ARRION RATHSACK, DIRECTOR, MBA ADMISSIONS
Address: PO BOX 750333, DALLAS, TX 75275
Phone: 214-768-1214 • **Fax:** 214-768-3956
E-mail: MBAINFO@MAIL.COX.SMU.EDU
Website: MBA.COX.SMU.EDU

GENERAL INFORMATION

Type of School: Private **Environment:** Town **Schedule:** Full-time/part-time/evening

STUDENTS

Enrollment of parent institution: 10,000 **Enrollment of MBA program:** 1,008 **% male/female:** 76/24 **% out-of-state:** 51 **% part-time:** 82 **% minorities:** 9 **% international:** 24 **Average age at entry:** 28 **Average years work experience at entry:** 5

ACADEMICS

Student/faculty ratio: 4:1 **% female faculty:** 11 **Joint Degrees:** JD/MBA, 4 years; MA/MBA arts administration, 24 months. **Prominent Alumni:** Thomas W. Horton, Senior VP/CFO - American Airlines; David B. Miller, Managing Director - El Paso Energy; Ruth Ann Marshall, President - MasterCard; James MacNaughton, Managing Director - Rothschild, Inc.; C. Fred Ball, CEO - Bank of Texas.

FINANCIAL FACTS

Tuition: $28,542 **Fees:** $2,662 **Books and supplies:** $2,000 **% of students receiving grants:** 70 **Average grant:** $15,000

ST. CLOUD STATE UNIVERSITY
HERBERGER COLLEGE OF BUSINESS

Admissions Contact: GRADUATE STUDIES OFFICE, GRADUATE ADMISSIONS MANAGER
Address: 720 4TH AVE. SOUTH, AS-121, ST. CLOUD, MN 56301-4498
Phone: 320-308-2112 • **Fax:** 320-308-3986
E-mail: GRADUATESTUDIES@STCLOUDSTATE.EDU
Website: WWW.STCLOUDSTATE.EDU/MBA

GENERAL INFORMATION

Type of School: Public **Academic Calendar:** Semester

STUDENTS

Enrollment of parent institution: 15,000 **Enrollment of MBA program:** 109 **% male/female:** 79/21 **% part-time:** 69 **% minorities:** 38 **Average age at entry:** 28 **Average years work experience at entry:** 5

ACADEMICS

Student/faculty ratio: 25:1 **% female faculty:** 26

FINANCIAL FACTS

Tuition (in-state): $12,492 **Fees:** $449 **Books and supplies:** $1,650

Admissions Selectivity Rating: 73

# of applications received: 129 **% applicants accepted:** 78 %
acceptees attending: 91 **GMAT Range (25th to 75th percentile):**
470-700 **Average GMAT:** 541 **Average GPA:** 3 **TOEFL required of**
int'l applicants? Yes **Minimum TOEFL (paper/computer):** 550/213
Application Fee: $35 **International Application Fee:** $35 **Regular**
Application Deadline: Rolling **Regular Notification:** Rolling
Early decision program? Yes **ED deadline /notification:** 04/15,
06/15/1/1 **Deferment Available?** Yes **Maximum length of defer-**
ment: 2 years **Non-fall Admissions?** Yes

EMPLOYMENT PROFILE

# of companies recruiting on-campus: 130 **Average starting salary:**
$38,000

ST. MARY'S UNIVERSITY OF MINNESOTA
SCHOOL OF GRADUATE & PROFESSIONAL PROGRAMS

Admissions Contact: SARAH LANG, DIRECTOR OF ADMISSIONS
Address: 2500 PARK AVENUE, MINNEAPOLIS, MN 55404-4403
Phone: 612-728-5100 • **Fax:** 612-728-5121
E-mail: TC-ADMISSION@SMUMN.EDU
Website: WWW.SMUMN.EDU/GRADPRO

GENERAL INFORMATION

Type of School: Private **Affiliation:** Roman Catholic **Environment:**
Rural

ACADEMICS

Student/faculty ratio: 12:1

FINANCIAL FACTS

Tuition: $8,520 **Books and supplies:** $500 **Average award package:**
$18,090

ADMISSIONS

Admissions Selectivity Rating: 60*

# of applications received: 104 **% applicants accepted:** 68 **TOEFL**
required of int'l applicants? Yes **Minimum TOEFL (paper/comput-**
er): 550/213 **Application Fee:** $25 **Regular Application Deadline:**
Rolling **Regular Notification:** Rolling **Transfer Students Accepted?**
Yes **Non-fall Admissions?** Yes

STATE UNIVERSITY OF NEW YORK—ALBANY
SCHOOL OF BUSINESS

Admissions Contact: ALBINA Y. GRIGNON, ASSISTANT DEAN
Address: 1400 WASHINGTON AVE. BA 361, ALBANY, NY 12222
Phone: 518-442-4961 • **Fax:** 518-442-4975
E-mail: BUSWEB@ALBANY.EDU
Website: WWW.ALBANY.EDU/BUSINESS

GENERAL INFORMATION

Type of School: Public **Environment:** City **Academic Calendar:**
Sept–May

STUDENTS

Enrollment of parent institution: 17,000 **Enrollment of MBA pro-**
gram: 343 **% male/female:** 61/39 **% out-of-state:** 40 **% part-time:**
77 **% minorities:** 14 **% international:** 35 **Average age at entry:** 28
Average years work experience at entry: 5

ACADEMICS

Student/faculty ratio: 20:1 **% female faculty:** 17 **% minority facul-**
ty: 1 **Joint Degrees:** Master of science nanoscale engineering and
nanotechnology/MBA (2 years). **Prominent Alumni:** Herbert Lurie,
Manag Director, Investment Banking Merrill Ly; Jeffrey Black,
Managing Partner, Accenture; Steve Rotella, President and CEO,
Chase Manhattan Mortgage Corp.; Harold Cramer, VP, Exxon Mobil
Fuels; Richard Fairbanks, Chairman Pinebush Technologies.

FINANCIAL FACTS

Tuition (in-state/out-of-state): $7,100/$11,340 **Fees:** $1,028 **Books**
and supplies: $1,000 **Room & board (on/off campus):**
$9,000/$7,500 **% of students receiving aid:** 60 **% of first-year stu-**
dents receiving aid: 50 **% of students receiving loans:** 75 **% of stu-**
dents receiving grants: 10 **Average award package:** $14,200
Average grant: $18,000 **Average student loan debt:** $20,000

ADMISSIONS

Admissions Selectivity Rating: 78

# of applications received: 329 **% applicants accepted:** 56 %
acceptees attending: 60 **GMAT Range (25th to 75th percentile):**
450-640 **Average GMAT:** 535 **Average GPA:** 3.2 **TOEFL required of**
int'l applicants? Yes **Minimum TOEFL (paper/computer):** 600/250
Application Fee: $60 **Regular Application Deadline:** 4/5 **Regular**
Notification: 6/5 **Deferment Available?** Yes **Maximum length of**
deferment: 1 Year **Transfer Students Accepted?** Yes **Need-Blind**
Admissions? Yes **Applicants also look at:** SUNY—Buffalo.

Placement rate (%): 78 # of companies recruiting on-campus: 25 % grads employed immediately: 60 Average starting salary: $54,900

Grads employed by field:% avg. salary:

Finance	5	$42,000
Human Resources	19	$43,000
Marketing	10	$57,020
MIS	10	$60,000
Consulting	38	$55,000
Non-profit	3:	$43,000

STEPHEN F. AUSTIN STATE UNIVERSITY
COLLEGE OF BUSINESS

Admissions Contact: MICHAEL STROUP, MBA DIRECTOR
Address: PO BOX 13004, SFA STATION, NACOGDOCHES, TX 75962-3004
Phone: 936-468-3101 • *Fax:* 936-468-1560
E-mail: WWW.MBSMITH@SFASU.EDU
Website: WWW.COB.SFASU.EDU

GENERAL INFORMATION
Type of School: Public Environment: Town

STUDENTS
Enrollment of parent institution: 10,000 Enrollment of MBA program: 60 % male/female: 75/25 % out-of-state: 12 % part-time: 55 % minorities: 15 % international: 12 Average age at entry: 26 Average years work experience at entry: 5

ACADEMICS
Student/faculty ratio: 14:1 % female faculty: 50 % minority faculty: 5

FINANCIAL FACTS
Tuition (in-state/out-of-state): $1,692/$5,904 Fees: $610 Books and supplies: $1,000 Room & board (on/off campus): $4,500/$6,000 % of students receiving aid: 10 % of first-year students receiving aid: 10 Average award package: $3,300 Average grant: $3,300

ADMISSIONS
Admissions Selectivity Rating: 65

# of applications received: 23 % applicants accepted: 83 % acceptees attending: 79 GMAT Range (25th to 75th percentile): 360-660 Average GMAT: 492 Average GPA: 3 TOEFL required of int'l applicants? Yes Minimum TOEFL (paper/computer): 550/213 Application Fee: $25 International Application Fee: $50 Regular Application Deadline: 8/15 Regular Notification: 8/15 Deferment Available? Yes Maximum length of deferment: 1 year Transfer Students Accepted? Yes Non-fall Admissions? Yes Need-Blind Admissions? Yes Applicants also look at: Northwestern University, Sam Houston State University, Texas State Univeristy—San Marcos, University of North Texas.

EMPLOYMENT PROFILE
Placement rate (%): 100 % grads employed immediately: 95 Average starting salary: $50,000

Grads employed by field:% avg. salary:

Accounting	35	$48,000
Finance	2	$85,000
Marketing	30	$47,000
General Management	33	$43,000

STEVENS INSTITUTE OF TECHNOLOGY
THE WESLEY J. HOWE SCHOOL OF TECHNOLOGY MANAGEMENT

Admissions Contact: JAMES RUNKLE, ASSISTANT DIRECTOR OF GRADUATE ADMISSIONS
Address: CASTLE POINT ON HUDSON, HOBOKEN, NJ 07030
Phone: 201-433-4733 • *Fax:* 201-216-8044
E-mail: GRADADMISSIONS@STEVENS.EDU
Website: WWW.STEVENS.EDU

GENERAL INFORMATION
Type of School: Private

STUDENTS
Enrollment of parent institution: 2,919 Enrollment of MBA program: 54 % male/female: 89/11 % part-time: 83 % minorities: 33 % international: 44

ACADEMICS
Prominent Alumni: Henry Gantt, Father of Project Management; Alexander Calder, Sculptor; Alfred W. Fielding, Inventor of Bubble Wrap; Lawrence Babbio, Vice Chair and President, Verizon Communications; Charles Stewart Mott, Co-Founder, General Motors.

FINANCIAL FACTS
Tuition: $22,500 Books and supplies: $500 Average grant: $13,500

ADMISSIONS

Admissions Selectivity Rating: 79

# of applications received: 60 % **applicants accepted:** 48 % **acceptees attending:** 66 **Average GMAT:** 520 **Average GPA:** 3.2 **TOEFL required of int'l applicants?** Yes **Minimum TOEFL (paper/computer):** 550/213 **Application Fee:** $55 **International Application Fee:** $55 **Regular Application Deadline:** Rolling **Regular Notification:** Rolling **Deferment Available?** Yes **Maximum length of deferment:** 2 years **Transfer Students Accepted?** Yes **Non-fall Admissions?** Yes **Need-Blind Admissions?** Yes **Applicants also look at:** Columbia University, Fordham University, Lehigh University, New York University, Rutgers—The State University of New Jersey.

EMPLOYMENT PROFILE

# of companies recruiting on-campus: 300

TENNESSEE STATE UNIVERSITY
TENNESSEE STATE UNIVERSITY

Admissions Contact: LISA SMITH, DIRECTOR OF PUBLIC SERVICE
Address: 330 10TH AVENUE NORTH, SUITE K, NASHVILLE, TN 37203
Phone: 615-963-7137 • **Fax:** 615-963-7139
E-mail: LSMITH11@TNSTATE.EDU
Website: WWW.COB.TNSTATE.EDU

GENERAL INFORMATION

Type of School: Public **Environment:** City

STUDENTS

Enrollment of parent institution: Enrollment of MBA program: 250 **Average age at entry:** 28 **Average years work experience at entry:** 4

FINANCIAL FACTS

Tuition (in-state/out-of-state): $3,884/$10,356 **Books and supplies:**

ADMISSIONS

Admissions Selectivity Rating: 72

# of applications received: 39 % **applicants accepted:** 79 % **acceptees attending:** 100 **Average GMAT:** 510 **Average GPA:** 3.2 **TOEFL required of int'l applicants?** Yes **Minimum TOEFL (paper/computer):** 500/ **Application Fee:** $25 **Regular Application Deadline:** 1/1 **Regular Notification:** 1/1 **Deferment Available?** Yes **Maximum length of deferment:** 1 year **Transfer Students Accepted?** Yes **Non-fall Admissions?** Yes **Need-Blind Admissions?** Yes

EMPLOYMENT PROFILE

# of companies recruiting on-campus: 20

TEXAS A & M UNIVERSITY-CORPUS CHRISTI
COLLEGE OF BUSINESS ADMINISTRATION

Admissions Contact: BETSY O'LAVIN, DIRECTOR OF MASTER'S PROGRAMS
Address: 6300 OCEAN DRIVE, CORPUS CHRISTI, TX 78412
Phone: 361-825-2655 • **Fax:** 361-825-2725
E-mail: EOLAVIN@COB.TAMUCC.EDU
Website: WWW.COB.TAMUCC.EDU

GENERAL INFORMATION

Type of School: Public **Environment:** Village **Academic Calendar:** Semester

STUDENTS

Enrollment of parent institution: 6,161 **Enrollment of MBA program:** 150 % **male/female:** 56/44 % **part-time:** 70 % **minorities:** 25 % **international:** 1 **Average age at entry:** 32 **Average years work experience at entry:** 7

FINANCIAL FACTS

Tuition (in-state/out-of-state): $2,878/$9,328

ADMISSIONS

Admissions Selectivity Rating: 65

# of applications received: 45 % **applicants accepted:** 89 % **acceptees attending:** 82 **GMAT Range (25th to 75th percentile):** 410-600 **Average GMAT:** 500 **Average GPA:** 3.1 **TOEFL required of int'l applicants?** Yes **Minimum TOEFL (paper/computer):** 550/213 **Application Fee:** $30 **International Application Fee:** $50 **Regular Application Deadline:** Rolling **Regular Notification:** Rolling **Deferment Available?** Yes **Maximum length of deferment:** 1 year **Transfer Students Accepted?** Yes **Non-fall Admissions?** Yes **Need-Blind Admissions?** Yes

EMPLOYMENT PROFILE

# of companies recruiting on-campus: 250

TRUMAN STATE UNIVERSITY
DIVISION OF BUSINESS AND ACCOUNTANCY

Admissions Contact: DR. JEFF ROMINE, MASTER OF ACCOUNTANCY COORDINATOR
Address: VH 2400, 100 EAST NORMAL, KIRKSVILLE, MO 63501-4221
Phone: 660-785-4378 • **Fax:** 660-785-7471
E-mail: JROMINE@TRUMAN.EDU
Website: WWW.TRUMAN.EDU

GENERAL INFORMATION

Type of School: Public **Environment:** Village **Academic Calendar:** Semester

STUDENTS

Enrollment of parent institution: 6,200 **Enrollment of MBA program:** 16 % **male/female:** 75/25 % **minorities:** 8 % **international:** 13 **Average age at entry:** 23

FINANCIAL FACTS

Tuition (in-state/out-of-state): $4,072/$7,400 **Books and supplies:** $500 % **of students receiving aid:** 63 **Average grant:** $8,000

ADMISSIONS

Admissions Selectivity Rating: 60*

# of applications received: 18 % **applicants accepted:** 78 % **acceptees attending:** 71 **GMAT Range (25th to 75th percentile):** 540-640 **Average GMAT:** 599 **Average GPA:** 3.5 **TOEFL required of int'l applicants?** Yes **Minimum TOEFL (paper):** 560 **Application Fee:** $0 **International Application Fee: Regular Application Deadline:** 6/1 **Regular Notification:** Rolling **Deferment Available?** Yes **Non-fall Admissions?** Yes

EMPLOYMENT PROFILE

Placement rate (%): 100 # of companies recruiting on-campus: 20 % grads employed immediately: 79 **Average starting salary:** $40,000

Grads employed by field:% avg. salary:

Accounting ....100 ......$40,000

UNIVERSITE LAVAL
FACULTÉ DES SCIENCES DE L'ADMINISTRATION

Admissions Contact: BERNARD GARNIER, DIRECTOR, MBA PROGRAMS
Address: PAVILLON PALASIS-PRINCE, QUÉBEC, QC G1K 7P4 CANADA
Phone: 418-656-3080 • **Fax:** 418-656-5216
E-mail: REG@REG.ULAVAL.CA
Website: WWW.FSA.ULAVAL.CA/HTML/FORMATION.HTML

GENERAL INFORMATION

Type of School: Public **Academic Calendar:** Semester

STUDENTS

Enrollment of parent institution: 38,226 **Enrollment of MBA program:** 1,111 % **male/female:** 56/44 % **out-of-state:** 21 % **part-time:** 67 % **international:** 31 **Average age at entry:** 35 **Average years work experience at entry:** 4

ACADEMICS

Student/faculty ratio: 25:1 % **female faculty:** 32

FINANCIAL FACTS

Tuition (in-state/out-of-state): $2,118/$12,272 **Books and supplies:** $3,000 **Room & board:** $2,301 % **of students receiving grants:** 4

ADMISSIONS

Admissions Selectivity Rating: 79

# of applications received: 1,351 % **applicants accepted:** 53 % **acceptees attending:** 49 **Average GPA:** 3.0 **TOEFL required of int'l applicants?** Yes **Minimum TOEFL (paper/computer):** 550/213 **Application Fee:** $30 **International Application Fee:** $30 **Regular Application Deadline:** 2/1 **Regular Notification:** Rolling **Deferment Available?** Yes **Maximum length of deferment:** 1 year **Non-fall Admissions?** Yes

EMPLOYMENT PROFILE

Placement rate (%): 95 **Average starting salary:** $54,302

UNIVERSITY OF ALABAMA IN HUNTSVILLE
COLLEGE OF ADMINISTRATIVE SCIENCE

Admissions Contact: DR. J. DANIEL SHERMAN, ASSOCIATE DEAN
Address: ASB 102, HUNTSVILLE, AL 35899
Phone: 256-824-6024 • **Fax:** 256-890-7571
E-mail: GRADBIZ@UAH.EDU
Website: WWW.UAH.EDU

GENERAL INFORMATION

Type of School: Public **Environment:** City **Academic Calendar:** Semester

STUDENTS

Enrollment of parent institution: **Enrollment of MBA program:** 120 % **male/female:** 58/42 % **minorities:** 14

ACADEMICS

Student/faculty ratio: 5:1 % **female faculty:** 23 % **minority faculty:** 10

FINANCIAL FACTS

Tuition (in-state/out-of-state): $4,500/$9,000 **Books and supplies:** $527

ADMISSIONS

Admissions Selectivity Rating: 76

# of applications received: 95 % **applicants accepted:** 74 % **acceptees attending:** 86 **Average GMAT:** 542 **Average GPA:** 3.4 **TOEFL required of int'l applicants?** Yes **Minimum TOEFL (paper):** 550 **Application Fee:** $35 **International Application Fee: Regular Application Deadline:** 8/1 **Regular Notification:** 1/1 **Transfer Students Accepted?** Yes **Non-fall Admissions?** Yes **Need-Blind Admissions?** Yes

EMPLOYMENT PROFILE

Placement rate (%): 90 % **grads employed immediately:** 80

University of Alaska—Anchorage
College of Business and Public Policy

Admissions Contact: *Al Kastar, Director of Admissions*
Address: *PO Box 141629, Anchorage, AK 99514-1629*
Phone: *907-786-1480 • Fax: 907-786-4888*
E-mail: *ANMBS1@UAA.ALASKA.EDU*
Website: *WWW.CBPP.UAA.ALASKA.EDU*

GENERAL INFORMATION
Type of School: Public **Environment:** City **Academic Calendar:** Sept-May

STUDENTS
Enrollment of MBA program: 66 % **male/female:** 35/65 % **part-time:** 74 % **minorities:** 12 % **international:** 24

ACADEMICS
Student/faculty ratio: 20:1 % **minority faculty:** 22

FINANCIAL FACTS
Tuition (in-state/out-of-state): $3,636/$7,074 **Fees:** $352 **Books and supplies:** $500 **Room & board:** $6,730 **Average grant:** $6,057

ADMISSIONS
Admissions Selectivity Rating: 84
# of applications received: 50 % **applicants accepted:** 36 % **acceptees attending:** 72 **GMAT Range (25th to 75th percentile):** 450-640 **Average GMAT:** 524 **Average GPA:** 3.3 **TOEFL required of int'l applicants?** Yes **Minimum TOEFL (paper):** 550 **Application Fee:** $45 **Regular Application Deadline:** Rolling **Regular Notification:** Rolling **Deferment Available?** Yes **Maximum length of deferment:** One Semester **Transfer Students Accepted?** Yes **Non-fall Admissions?** Yes **Need-Blind Admissions?** Yes

University of Alaska—Fairbanks
School of Management

Admissions Contact: *Nancy Dix, Director*
Address: *PO Box 757480, Fairbanks, AK 99775*
Phone: *907-474-7500 • Fax: 907-474-5379*
E-mail: *ADMISSIONS@UAF.EDU*
Website: *WWW.SOM.UAF.EDU/SOM/MBA.HTM*

GENERAL INFORMATION
Type of School: Public **Environment:** Town

STUDENTS
Enrollment of MBA program: 34 % **male/female:** 50/50 % **minorities:** 30 **Average age at entry:** 30 **Average years work experience at entry:** 7

ACADEMICS
Student/faculty ratio: 3:1 % **female faculty:** 20 % **minority faculty:** 70

FINANCIAL FACTS
Tuition (in-state/out-of-state): $3,996/$8,154 **Books and supplies:** **Average grant:** $16,928 **Average student loan debt:** $12,166

ADMISSIONS
Admissions Selectivity Rating: 71
# of applications received: 9 % **applicants accepted:** 89 % **acceptees attending:** 100 **Average GMAT:** 533 **Average GPA:** 3.43 **TOEFL required of int'l applicants?** Yes **Minimum TOEFL (paper/computer):** 550/213 **Application Fee:** $50 **International Application Fee:** $50 **Regular Application Deadline:** 8/1 **Regular Notification:** 8/1 **Deferment Available?** Yes **Maximum length of deferment:** 1 year **Transfer Students Accepted?** Yes **Non-fall Admissions?** Yes **Need-Blind Admissions?** Yes

University of Arkansas at Little Rock
College of Business

Admissions Contact: *Dr. Ken Glachus, MBA Advisor*
Address: *2801 South University Avenue, Little Rock, AR 72204*
Phone: *501-569-3356 • Fax: 501-569-8898*
Website: *WWW.CBA.UALR.EDU*

GENERAL INFORMATION
Type of School: Public **Environment:** City **Academic Calendar:** Semester

STUDENTS
Enrollment of parent institution: 9,925 **Enrollment of MBA program:** 225 % **male/female:** 58/42 % **out-of-state:** 1 % **part-time:** 87 % **minorities:** 8 % **international:** 15 **Average age at entry:** 29

FINANCIAL FACTS
Tuition: $30,500

ADMISSIONS
Admissions Selectivity Rating: 60*
# of applications received: 87 % **applicants accepted:** 66 % **acceptees attending:** 74 **TOEFL required of int'l applicants?** Yes **Minimum TOEFL (paper):** 550 **Regular Application Deadline:** Rolling **Regular Notification:** Rolling **Deferment Available?** Yes **Applicants also look at:** Babson College, Florida State University, Indiana University South Bend, Rensselaer Polytechnic Institute, University of Florida, University of Pennsylvania, University of Texas.

EMPLOYMENT PROFILE
Placement rate (%): 95 **Average starting salary:** $40,000

University of Baltimore
Merrick School of Business

Admissions Contact: Jeffrey Zavronty, Assistant Director of Admissions
Address: 1420 North Charles Street, Baltimore, MD 21201
Phone: 877-277-5982 • **Fax:** 410-837-4793
E-mail: Admissions@ubmail.ubalt.edu
Website: business.ubalt.edu/graduateprograms/mba.html

GENERAL INFORMATION
Type of School: Public **Environment:** Metropolis **Academic Calendar:** Semester

STUDENTS
Enrollment of parent institution: 4,639 **Enrollment of MBA program:** 506 % male/female: 57/43 % out-of-state: 16 % part-time: 54 % minorities: 18 % international: 33 **Average age at entry:** 29

ACADEMICS
Student/faculty ratio: 15:1 % female faculty: 25 % minority faculty: 34 **Joint Degrees:** MBA/MS in nursing - 66 credits (2 to 7 years); MBA/PhD in nursing - 85 credits (2 to 7 years); MBA/PharmD - 155 credits (2 to 7 years); MBA/JD - 102-123 credits (3 to 7 years).
Prominent Alumni: William Donald Schaeffer, Govenor, State of Maryland; Peter Angelos, Owner, Baltimore Orioles; Joseph Curran, Attorney General, State of Maryland; Vernon Wright, Vice Chairman, MBNA America Bank.

FINANCIAL FACTS
Books and supplies: $900

ADMISSIONS
Admissions Selectivity Rating: 72
# of applications received: 376 % applicants accepted: 62 % acceptees attending: 63 **GMAT Range (25th to 75th percentile):** 470-520 **Average GMAT:** 500 **Average GPA:** 3 **TOEFL required of int'l applicants?** Yes **Minimum TOEFL (paper/computer):** 550/213 **Application Fee:** $30 **International Application Fee:** $30 **Regular Application Deadline:** Rolling **Regular Notification:** Rolling **Deferment Available?** Yes **Maximum length of deferment:** 1 year **Transfer Students Accepted?** Yes **Non-fall Admissions?** Yes **Need-Blind Admissions?** Yes **Applicants also look at:** Loyola College in Maryland, University of Maryland—College Park.

EMPLOYMENT PROFILE
# of companies recruiting on-campus: 120

University of California— Berkeley (MFE)
Haas School of Business

Admissions Contact: Yong No, Assistant Director
Address: MFE Program, S 545 Haas School of Business, #1900, Berkeley, CA 94720-1900
Phone: 510-642-4417 • **Fax:** 510-643-4345
E-mail: MFE@haas.berkeley.edu
Website: www.haas.berkeley.edu/MFE/index.html

GENERAL INFORMATION
Type of School: Public

STUDENTS
Enrollment of parent institution: **Enrollment of MBA program:** 60 % male/female: 78/22 % minorities: 5 **Average age at entry:** 29 **Average years work experience at entry:** 3.7

ACADEMICS
Student/faculty ratio: 3:1

FINANCIAL FACTS
Tuition: $42,000 **Fees:** $2,666 **Books and supplies:** $9,040 **Room & board:** $16,543

ADMISSIONS
Admissions Selectivity Rating: 98
# of applications received: 390 % applicants accepted: 24 % acceptees attending: 64 **Average GMAT:** 699 **Average GPA:** 3.5 **TOEFL required of int'l applicants?** Yes **Minimum TOEFL (paper/computer):** 570/230 **Application Fee:** $175 **International Application Fee:** $175 **Regular Application Deadline:** 3/4 **Regular Notification:** 5/31 **Application Deadline/Notification Round 1:** 10/29 / 1/31 **Round 2:** 12/10 / 03/18 **Round 3:** 1/21 / 5/2 **Round 4:** 3/4 / 5/31 **Non-fall Admissions?** **Need-Blind Admissions?** Yes **Applicants also look at:** Boston University, Carnegie Mellon, Columbia University, Massachusetts Institute of Technology, Stanford University, University of Chicago, University of Michigan.

The University of Chicago GSB—Europe Campus

Admissions Contact: Silvia Rull, Admissions Coordinator
Address: Arago 271, Barcelona, 08007 Spain
Phone: 011-34-93-505-21-54 • **Fax:** 011-34-93-505-21-58
E-mail: barcelona.inquiries@gsb.uchicago.edu
Website: gsb.uchicago.edu/execMBAeurope

GENERAL INFORMATION
Type of School: Private **Academic Calendar:** Quarter

STUDENTS

Enrollment of MBA program: 3,000 % male/female: 76/24 % minorities: 7 % international: 26 Average age at entry: 35 Average years work experience at entry: 12

ACADEMICS

% female faculty: 14 Joint Degrees: MBA/AM area studies in business; MBA/AM international relations and business; JD/MBA law and business; MD/MBA medicine and business; MBA/MPP public policy studies and business; MBA/AM social service administration and business. Prominent Alumni: Philip Purcell, Chairman and CEO of Morgan Stanley; James Kilts, Chairman and CEO of the Gillette Company; Karen Katen, President of Pfizer Pharmaceuticals.

ADMISSIONS

Admissions Selectivity Rating: 60*

Average GMAT: 684 Average GPA: 3.4 Application Fee: $100 Regular Application Deadline: 5/1 Regular Notification: Rolling Deferment Available? Yes Maximum length of deferment: 1 year Transfer Students Accepted? Yes Non-fall Admissions? Yes

EMPLOYMENT PROFILE

Grads employed by field: ....%

Finance	15
Marketing	17
Consulting	15
General Management	37
Other	16

UNIVERSITY OF COLORADO AT COLORADO SPRINGS

GRADUATE SCHOOL OF BUSINESS ADMINISTRATION

Admissions Contact: MAUREEN CATHEY, MBA PROGRAM DIRECTOR
Address: 1420 AUSTIN BLUFFS PARKWAY, COLORADO SPRINGS, CO 80918
Phone: 719-262-3408 • *Fax:* 719-262-3100
E-mail: BUSADVSR@UCCS.EDU
Website: WEB.UCCS.EDU/BUSINESS

GENERAL INFORMATION

Type of School: Public Environment: City Academic Calendar: Semester

STUDENTS

Enrollment of parent institution: 7,407 Enrollment of MBA program: 273 % % part-time: 100 Average age at entry: 29 Average years work experience at entry: 7

ACADEMICS

Student/faculty ratio: 8:1 % female faculty: 15 % minority faculty: 3

FINANCIAL FACTS

Tuition: $8,000

ADMISSIONS

Admissions Selectivity Rating: 70

# of applications received: 79 % applicants accepted: 90 % acceptees attending: 76 GMAT Range (25th to 75th percentile): 490-560 Average GMAT: 540 Average GPA: 3.2 TOEFL required of int'l applicants? Yes Minimum TOEFL (paper/computer): 550/213 Application Fee: $60 International Application Fee: $75 Regular Application Deadline: 6/1 Regular Notification: Rolling Deferment Available? Yes Maximum length of deferment: 1 year Transfer Students Accepted? Yes Non-fall Admissions? Yes Need-Blind Admissions? Yes

UNIVERSITY OF COLORADO AT DENVER

COLLEGE OF BUSINESS AND ADMINISTRATION

Admissions Contact: , GRADUATE ADMISSIONS COORDINATOR
Address: CAMPUS BOX 165, PO BOX 173364, DENVER, CO 80217-3364
Phone: 303-556-5900 • *Fax:* 303-556-5904
E-mail: GRAD.BUSINESS@CUDENVER.EDU.
Website: WWW.BUSINESS.CUDENVER.EDU

GENERAL INFORMATION

Type of School: Public Environment: Metropolis Academic Calendar: Semester

STUDENTS

Enrollment of parent institution: 11,050 Enrollment of MBA program: 1,249 % male/female: 89/11 % out-of-state: 1 % part-time: 71 % minorities: 10 % international: 14 Average age at entry: 25

ACADEMICS

Student/faculty ratio: 35:1

FINANCIAL FACTS

% of students receiving aid: 29 Average grant: $1,000

ADMISSIONS

Admissions Selectivity Rating: 60*

# of applications received: 547 % applicants accepted: 74 % acceptees attending: 64 TOEFL required of int'l applicants? Yes Minimum TOEFL (paper/computer): 525/197 Application Fee: $50 Regular Application Deadline: 6/1 Regular Notification: Rolling Deferment Available? Yes Maximum length of deferment: 1 year Transfer Students Accepted? Yes Non-fall Admissions? Yes Need-Blind Admissions? Yes

EMPLOYMENT PROFILE

Placement rate (%): 97 # of companies recruiting on-campus: 77 % grads employed immediately: 90 Average starting salary: $57,903

UNIVERSITY OF DAYTON
SCHOOL OF BUSINESS AMINISTRATION

Admissions Contact: JANICE GLYNN, DIRECTOR MBA PROGRAM
Address: 300 COLLEGE PARK AVENUE, DAYTON, OH 45469
Phone: 937-229-3733 • **Fax:** 937-229-3882
E-mail: MBA@UDAYTON.EDU
Website: WWW.SBA.UDAYTON.EDU/MBA

GENERAL INFORMATION

Type of School: Private **Affiliation:** Roman Catholic **Environment:** City **Academic Calendar:** Semester

STUDENTS

Enrollment of parent institution: 10,180 **Enrollment of MBA program:** 446 **% male/female:** 54/46 **% part-time:** 79 **% minorities:** 10 **Average age at entry:** 29 **Average years work experience at entry:** 7

ACADEMICS

Student/faculty ratio: 12:1 **% female faculty:** 11 **Joint Degrees:** Joint juris of doctor of law (JD) and master of business administration (MBA) 3-5 years (combined JD and MBA degrees). **Prominent Alumni:** Allen Hill, President and CEO, Dayton Power and Light; Phil Parker, President & CEO, Dayton Area Cham. of Commerce; Mike Turner, US Congressman, OH.

FINANCIAL FACTS

Tuition: $10,494 **Fees:** $75 **Books and supplies:** $600

ADMISSIONS

Admissions Selectivity Rating: 74

# of applications received: 353 **% applicants accepted:** 83 **% acceptees attending:** 80 **Average GMAT:** 560 **Average GPA:** 3.2 **TOEFL required of int'l applicants?** Yes **Minimum TOEFL (paper/computer):** 550/213 **Regular Application Deadline:** Rolling **Regular Notification:** Rolling **Deferment Available?** Yes **Maximum length of deferment:** 1 year **Transfer Students Accepted?** Yes **Non-fall Admissions?** Yes **Need-Blind Admissions?** Yes **Applicants also look at:** Miami University, University of Cincinnati, Wright State University, Xavier University.

EMPLOYMENT PROFILE

# of companies recruiting on-campus: 225 **% grads employed immediately:** 92

UNIVERSITY OF DELAWARE
MBA PROGRAMS—COLLEGE OF BUSINESS AND ECONOMICS

Admissions Contact: RONALD I. SIBERT, DIRECTOR OF MBA PROGRAMS
Address: 103 MBNA AMERICA HALL, NEWARK, DE 19716
Phone: 302-831-2221 • **Fax:** 302-831-3329
E-mail: MBAPROGRAM@UDEL.EDU
Website: WWW.MBA.UDEL.EDU

GENERAL INFORMATION

Type of School: Public **Environment:** Town **Academic Calendar:** Semester

STUDENTS

Enrollment of parent institution: 20,949 **Enrollment of MBA program:** 302 **% male/female:** 49/51 **% out-of-state:** 27 **% part-time:** 76 **% minorities:** 5 **% international:** 50 **Average age at entry:** 27 **Average years work experience at entry:** 4.63

ACADEMICS

Student/faculty ratio: 30:1 **% female faculty:** 14 **% minority faculty:** 3 **Joint Degrees:** MA economics/MBA - 57 credits. **Prominent Alumni:** Hon. Thomas R. Carper, Governor State of DE, Candidate for US Senate; Leonard Quill, CEO & Chairman of the Board, Wilm. Trust Corp.; Howard Cosgrove, Chairman & CEO Conectiv; Dennis Sheehy, Partner, Deloitte and Touche.

FINANCIAL FACTS

Tuition (in-state/out-of-state): $3,610/$7,710 **Fees:** $646 **Books and supplies:** $1,400 **Room & board (on/off campus):** $6,200/$7,200 **% of students receiving aid:** 60 **% of first-year students receiving aid:** 26 **% of students receiving grants:** 18 **Average award package:** $7,440 **Average grant:** $3,940

ADMISSIONS

Admissions Selectivity Rating: 74

# of applications received: 259 **% applicants accepted:** 75 **% acceptees attending:** 65 **GMAT Range (25th to 75th percentile):** 330-750 **Average GMAT:** 555 **Average GPA:** 3.0 **TOEFL required of int'l applicants?** Yes **Minimum TOEFL (paper/computer):** 587/240 **Application Fee:** $50 **Regular Application Deadline:** 5/1 **Regular Notification:** Rolling **Deferment Available?** Yes **Maximum length of deferment:** One academic year **Transfer Students Accepted?** Yes **Non-fall Admissions?** Yes **Need-Blind Admissions?** Yes **Applicants also look at:** Temple University, University of Pennsylvania, Villanova University.

Placement rate (%): 96 % **grads employed immediately:** 59
Average starting salary: $59,568

Grads employed by field:% avg. salary:

Finance ....18 ....$57,000

Human Resources............4 ......$67,000

Marketing ....18 ....$63,250

MIS ....9 ......$49,250

Operations........................10 ....$74,750

Consulting........................18 ....$72,700

General Management ......14 ....$65,667

Other ....9 ......$68,625

UNIVERSITY OF DETROIT MERCY
COLLEGE OF BUSINESS ADMINISTRATION

Admissions Contact: *TYEARA ROUNDS, DIRECTOR OF RECRUITING*
Address: *PO BOX 19900, DETROIT, MI 48219-0900*
Phone: *313-993-1245 • Fax: 313-993-3326*
E-mail: *ADMISSIONS@UDMERCY.EDU*
Website: *WWW.BUSINESS.UDMERCY.EDU*

GENERAL INFORMATION

Type of School: Private **Affiliation:** Roman Catholic **Environment:** City **Academic Calendar:** Semester

STUDENTS

Enrollment of parent institution: 5,571 **Enrollment of MBA program:** 140 % **male/female:** 89/11 % **part-time:** 80 % **minorities:** 23 % **international:** 34 **Average age at entry:** 32 **Average years work experience at entry:** 5

ACADEMICS

Student/faculty ratio: 30:1 % **female faculty:** 17 % **minority faculty:** 13 **Joint Degrees:** JD/MBA 3 years. **Prominent Alumni:** Thomas Angott, Chairman of the Board, C.F. Burger Co.; Thomas Capo, Dollar Thrifty Automotive Group; Armando Cavazos, Pres.& CEO, Credit Union One; James Padilla, Pres. Ford Motor Co.; Emil Simon, Owner, The Rollick Beverage Co.

FINANCIAL FACTS

Tuition: $13,680 **Fees:** $570 **Books and supplies:** $1,200 **Room & board:** $3,584 **Average grant:** $40,000

ADMISSIONS

Admissions Selectivity Rating:73

# of applications received: 141 % **applicants accepted:** 67 % **acceptees attending:** 55 **GMAT Range (25th to 75th percentile):** 450-650 **Average GMAT:** 520 **Average GPA:** 3.35 **Application Fee:** $25 **International Application Fee:** $50 **Regular Application Deadline:** 7/15 **Regular Notification:** 8/1 **Deferment Available?** Yes **Maximum length of deferment:** 2 years **Transfer Students Accepted?** Yes **Non-fall Admissions?** Yes **Applicants also look at:** Oakland University, Wayne State University

# of companies recruiting on-campus: 110 % **grads employed immediately:** 95
Average starting salary: $57,000

UNIVERSITY OF HOUSTON— CLEAR LAKE
SCHOOL OF BUSINESS AND PUBLIC ADMINISTRATION

Admissions Contact: *JANICE SAUERWEIN, ACTING REGISTRAR*
Address: *2700 BAY AREA Boulevard, HOUSTON, TX 77058-1098*
Phone: *281-283-2521 • Fax: 281-283-2530*
E-mail: *ADMISSIONS@CL.UH.EDU*
Website: *WWW.ADMIN.UHCL.EDU/BPA/INDEX.HTML*

GENERAL INFORMATION

Type of School: Public **Environment:** Metropolis **Academic Calendar:** Semester

STUDENTS

Enrollment of parent institution: 7,785 **Enrollment of MBA program:** 470 % **male/female:** 85/15 % **part-time:** 67 % **minorities:** 7 % **international:** 15 **Average age at entry:** 31 **Average years work experience at entry:** 5

ACADEMICS

Student/faculty ratio: 18:1 % **female faculty:** 31 % **minority faculty:** 9 **Joint Degrees:** Master of healthcare administration/MBA—57-78 (3 years).

FINANCIAL FACTS

Tuition (in-state/out-of-state): $3,312/$10,980 **Fees:** $5,004 **Books and supplies:** $1,800 **Room & board:** $12,836 % **of students receiving aid:** 20 **Average award package:** $8,300 **Average grant:** $1,000 **Average student loan debt:** $26,916

ADMISSIONS

Admissions Selectivity Rating:77

# of applications received: 224 % **applicants accepted:** 50 % **acceptees attending:** 59 **GMAT Range (25th to 75th percentile):** 400-680 **Average GMAT:** 508 **Average GPA:** 3.18 **TOEFL required of int'l applicants?** Yes **Minimum TOEFL (paper/computer):** 550/213 **Application Fee:** $35 **International Application Fee:** $75 **Regular Application Deadline:** 8/1 **Regular Notification:** Rolling **Deferment Available?** Yes **Maximum length of deferment:** 1 year **Transfer Students Accepted?** Yes **Non-fall Admissions?** Yes **Need-Blind Admissions?** Yes

EMPLOYMENT PROFILE

# of companies recruiting on-campus: 18

University of Louisiana at Monroe
College of Business Administration

Admissions Contact: Miguel Perez, Coordinator of Assessment and Internal Affairs
Address: 700 University Avenue, Monroe, LA 71209-0100
Phone: 318-342-1100 • **Fax:** 318-342-1101
E-mail: PEREZ@ULM.EDU
Website: ELE.ULM.EDU/MBA/

GENERAL INFORMATION
Type of School: Public **Academic Calendar:** Semester **Enrollment of parent institution:** 10,942 **Enrollment of MBA program:** 78 % **male/female:** 60/40 % **out-of-state:** 14 % **part-time:** 19 % **minorities:** 5 % **international:** 32 **Average age at entry:** 27

ACADEMICS
Student/faculty ratio: 2:1

FINANCIAL FACTS
Tuition (in-state/out-of-state): $1,900/$7,858 **Fees:** $382 **Books and supplies:** $600 **Room & board:** $2,560 **Average grant:** $5,000

ADMISSIONS
Admissions Selectivity Rating: 68
# of applications received: 57 **% applicants accepted:** 79 % **acceptees attending:** 78 **GMAT Range (25th to 75th percentile):** 390-710 **Average GMAT:** 500 **Average GPA:** 3.0 **TOEFL required of int'l applicants?** Yes **Minimum TOEFL (paper/computer):** 480/157 **Application Fee:** $20 **International Application Fee:** $30 **Regular Application Deadline:** 7/1 **Regular Notification:** 7/15 **Deferment Available?** Yes **Maximum length of deferment:** 1 year **Transfer Students Accepted?** Yes **Non-fall Admissions?** Yes

University of Louisville
College of Business and Public Administration

Admissions Contact: Dr. Audrey Kline, Associate Dean for Academic Programs
Address: CBPA Dean's Office, Louisville, KY 40292
Phone: 502-852-6440 • **Fax:** 502-852-7557
E-mail: AUDREY.KLINE@LOUISVILLE.EDU
Website: CBPA.LOUISVILLE.EDU/

GENERAL INFORMATION
Type of School: Public **Environment:** Metropolis **Academic Calendar:** Semester

STUDENTS
Enrollment of parent institution: 21,725 **Enrollment of MBA program:** 493 **% male/female:** 63/37 % **out-of-state:** 48 % **part-time:** 63 % **minorities:** 6 % **international:** 49 **Average age at entry:** 28

ACADEMICS
Student/faculty ratio: 30:1 **% female faculty:** 19 % **minority faculty:** 18 **Joint Degrees:** Master of engineering/master of business administration (ME/MBA)—minimum 3 years to complete the program; juris doctor/master of business administration (JD/MBA)—4 years to complete the program. **Prominent Alumni:** Robert Nardelli, Chief Executive, Home Repair; David Jones, Chairman, Health Insurance; James Patterson, Chairman, Food; Thomas Winsett, CEO, Credit Card Processing; Leonard Hardin, Chairman, Banking.

FINANCIAL FACTS
Tuition (in-state/out-of-state): $6,300/$17,334 **Books and supplies:** $900 **Room & board (on/off campus):** $4,300/$8,400 **Average grant:** $2,000

ADMISSIONS
Admissions Selectivity Rating: 72
# of applications received: 275 **% applicants accepted:** 72 % **acceptees attending:** 125 **GMAT Range (25th to 75th percentile):** 490-690 **Average GMAT:** 517 **Average GPA:** 3.5 **TOEFL required of int'l applicants?** Yes **Minimum TOEFL (paper):** 550 **Application Fee:** $50 **International Application Fee:** $50 **Regular Application Deadline:** Rolling **Regular Notification:** Rolling **Deferment Available?** Yes **Maximum length of deferment:** 2 years **Non-fall Admissions?** Yes

EMPLOYMENT PROFILE
% grads employed within three months: 17

University of Maine
Maine Business School

Admissions Contact: Chris Hockensmith, Assistant to the Director of Graduate Programs
Address: 5723 DP Corbett Business Building, Orono, ME 04469-5723
Phone: 207-581-1973 • **Fax:** 207-581-1930
E-mail: MBA@MAINE.EDU
Website: WWW.UMAINE.EDU/BUSINESS

GENERAL INFORMATION
Type of School: Public **Environment:** Village **Academic Calendar:** Semester

STUDENTS
Enrollment of parent institution: 11,135 **Enrollment of MBA program:** 79 **% male/female:** 66/34 % **out-of-state:** 1 % **part-time:** 58 % **minorities:** 2 % **international:** 17 **Average age at entry:** 34 **Average years work experience at entry:** 5

ADMISSIONS

ACADEMICS

Student/faculty ratio: 4:1 % female faculty: 50

FINANCIAL FACTS

Tuition (in-state/out-of-state): $4,572/$13,032 Fees (in-state/out-of-state): $570/$570 Books and supplies: $700 Room & board (on/off campus): $5,728/$5,728 Average grant: $4,500

ADMISSIONS

Admissions Selectivity Rating: 68

# of applications received: 50 % applicants accepted: 92 % acceptees attending: 72 Average GMAT: 538 Average GPA: 3.21 TOEFL required of int'l applicants? Yes Minimum TOEFL (paper/computer): 550/213 Application Fee: $50 Regular Application Deadline: 6/1 Regular Notification: 7/1 Deferment Available? Yes Maximum length of deferment: 1 year Transfer Students Accepted? Yes Non-fall Admissions? Yes Need-Blind Admissions? Yes

UNIVERSITY OF MANITOBA
I.H. ASPER SCHOOL OF BUSINESS

Admissions Contact: EWA MORPHY, GRADUATE PROGRAM MANAGER
Address: 324 DRAKE CENTER, WINNIPEG, MB R3T 5V4 CANADA
Phone: 204-474-8448 • Fax: 204-474-7544
E-mail: ASPER_GRAD@UMANITOBA.CA
Website: WWW.UMANITOBA.CA/ASPER

GENERAL INFORMATION

Type of School: Public Environment: Village

STUDENTS

Enrollment of parent institution: 27,000 Enrollment of MBA program: 155 % male/female: 65/35 % out-of-state: 6 % part-time: 88 % minorities: 17 % international: 44 Average age at entry: 32 Average years work experience at entry: 8

ACADEMICS

Student/faculty ratio: 30:1 % female faculty: 18 % minority faculty: 32 Prominent Alumni: F. Ross Johnson, Chairman/CEO RJM Group; Robert W. Pollock, Chairman, Drake International; Gerald W. Schwartz, Chair, President and CEO, Onyx Corp.; Martin S. Weinberg, President, CEO Assante Corporation; Bill McCallum, President and CEO, Great-West Life Annuity Insurance.

FINANCIAL FACTS

Tuition: $15,252 Books and supplies: $2,100 Room & board (on/off campus): $5,800/$8,200 Average grant: $4,000

ADMISSIONS

Admissions Selectivity Rating: 86

# of applications received: 115 % applicants accepted: 51 % acceptees attending: 64 Average GMAT: 590 Average GPA: 3.36 TOEFL required of int'l applicants? Yes Minimum TOEFL (paper/computer): 550/213 Application Fee: $75 International Application Fee: $90 Regular Application Deadline: 5/1 Regular Notification: Rolling Transfer Students Accepted? Yes Non-fall Admissions? Yes Need-Blind Admissions?

EMPLOYMENT PROFILE

of companies recruiting on-campus: 90 % grads employed immediately: 70 Average starting salary: $65,000

UNIVERSITY OF MASSACHUSETTS—BOSTON
GRADUATE COLLEGE OF MANAGEMENT

Admissions Contact: WILLIAM KOEHLER, GRADUATE PROGRAM DIRECTOR
Address: 100 MORRISSEY BOULEVARD, MBA OFFICE, BOSTON, MA 02125-3393
Phone: 617-287-7720 • Fax: 617-287-7725
E-mail: MBA@UMB.EDU
Website: WWW.MANAGEMENT.UMB.EDU

GENERAL INFORMATION

Type of School: Public Academic Calendar: Semesters

STUDENTS

Enrollment of parent institution: 13,000 Enrollment of MBA program: 247 % male/female: 35/65 % out-of-state: 34 % part-time: 65 % minorities: 11 % international: 28 Average age at entry: 28 Average years work experience at entry: 5

ACADEMICS

Student/faculty ratio: 13:1 % female faculty: 31 % minority faculty: 31 Prominent Alumni: Thomas M. Menino, Mayor, City of Boston; Joseph Abboud, Fashion Designer; James Kantelis, CEO, Sprague Energy Corp.; Mark Atkins, CEO, Invention Machine; Joseph Kennedy, U.S. Congressman.

FINANCIAL FACTS

Tuition (in-state/out-of-state): $2,590/$9,758 Fees (in-state/out-of-state): $6,322/$9,011 Books and supplies: $900 % of students receiving aid: 45 % of first-year students receiving aid: 40 % of students receiving loans: 22 % of students receiving grants: 23 Average grant: $9,000 Average student loan debt: $20,500

Admissions Selectivity Rating: 87

# of applications received: 237 **% applicants accepted:** 38 % **acceptees attending:** 57 **GMAT Range (25th to 75th percentile):** 515-650 **Average GMAT:** 571 **Average GPA:** 3.25 **TOEFL required of int'l applicants?** Yes **Minimum TOEFL (paper/computer):** 600/250 **Application Fee:** $40 **International Application Fee:** $60 **Regular Application Deadline:** 6/1 **Regular Notification:** 7/1 **Application Deadline/Notification Round 1:** 03/01 / 03/15 **Round 2:** 06/01 / 07/01 **Deferment Available?** Yes **Maximum length of deferment:** 1 Semester **Transfer Students Accepted?** Yes **Non-fall Admissions?** Yes **Need-Blind Admissions?** Yes **Applicants also look at:** Babson College, Bentley College, Boston College, Boston University, Northeastern University, Suffolk University, University of Massachusetts—Amherst

EMPLOYMENT PROFILE

Placement rate (%): 85 **% grads employed immediately:** 75 **Average starting salary:** $71,000

UNIVERSITY OF
MASSACHUSETTS—LOWELL
COLLEGE OF MANAGEMENT

Admissions Contact: DUNCAN G. LABAY, PHD, MANAGEMENT GRADUATE PROGRAMS DIRECTOR
Address: 1 UNIVERSITY AVENUE, LOWELL, MA 01854-2881
Phone: 978-934-2848 • **Fax:** 978-934-4017
E-mail: MBA@UML.EDU
Website: WWW.UML.EDU/COLLEGE/MANAGEMENT/

GENERAL INFORMATION

Type of School: Public **Environment:** City

STUDENTS

Enrollment of parent institution: 12,350 **Enrollment of MBA program:** 322 **% male/female:** 68/32 **% part-time:** 91 **% minorities:** 4 **% international:** 6 **Average age at entry:** 28 **Average years work experience at entry:** 5

ACADEMICS

Student/faculty ratio: 25:1

FINANCIAL FACTS

Tuition (in-state/out-of-state): $1,600/$6,400 **Fees (in-state/out-of-state):** $5,400/$8,000 **Books and supplies:** $1,000 **% of students receiving aid:** 4

Admissions Selectivity Rating: 70

# of applications received: 181 **% applicants accepted:** 83 % **acceptees attending:** 84 **GMAT Range (25th to 75th percentile):** 480-560 **Average GMAT:** 525 **Average GPA:** 3.0 **TOEFL required of int'l applicants?** Yes **Minimum TOEFL (paper/computer):** /230 **Application Fee:** $20 **Regular Application Deadline:** Rolling **Regular Notification:** Rolling **Non-fall Admissions?** Yes

EMPLOYMENT PROFILE

Placement rate (%): 90

UNIVERSITY OF MIAMI
SCHOOL OF BUSINESS ADMINISTRATION

Admissions Contact: SUSAN GERRISH, ASSOCIATE DIRECTOR
Address: PO BOX 248505, CORAL GABLES, FL 33124-6524
Phone: 305-284-4607 • **Fax:** 305-284-1878
E-mail: MBA@MIAMI.EDU
Website: WWW.BUS.MIAMI.EDU/GRAD

GENERAL INFORMATION

Type of School: Private **Environment:** Town **Academic Calendar:** August-May

STUDENTS

Enrollment of parent institution: 15,250 **Enrollment of MBA program:** 302 **% male/female:** 71/29 **% out-of-state:** 15 **% part-time:** 12 **% minorities:** 46 **% international:** 22 **Average age at entry:** 26 **Average years work experience at entry:** 3

ACADEMICS

Student/faculty ratio: 13:1 **% female faculty:** 27 **Joint Degrees:** JD/MBA, can be completed within a period of 3.5 to 4.5 years. Visit website, www.bus.miami.edu/grad to review options.

FINANCIAL FACTS

Tuition: $28,992 **Fees:** $194 **Books and supplies:** $1,200 **Room & board** $8,328 **% of students receiving aid:** 68 **% of first-year students receiving aid:** 69 **% of students receiving loans:** 50 **% of students receiving grants:** 39 **Average award package:** $25,476 **Average grant:** $13,593 **Average student loan debt:** $40,656

ADMISSIONS

Admissions Selectivity Rating: 82

# of applications received: 480 **% applicants accepted:** 61 % **acceptees attending:** 42 **GMAT Range (25th to 75th percentile):** 530-680 **Average GMAT:** 605 **Average GPA:** 3.2 **TOEFL required of int'l applicants?** Yes **Minimum TOEFL (paper/computer):** 550/213 **Application Fee:** $50 **International Application Fee:** $50 **Regular Application Deadline:** Rolling **Regular Notification:** Rolling **Deferment Available?** Yes **Maximum length of deferment:** 1 year **Non-fall Admissions?** Yes **Need-Blind Admissions?** Yes

Placement rate (%): 82 # of companies recruiting on-campus: 70

UNIVERSITY OF MICHIGAN— DEARBORN
SCHOOL OF MANAGEMENT

Admissions Contact: CHRISTINE BRZEZINSKI, GRADUATE ADMISSIONS COORDINATOR
Address: SCHOOL OF MANAGEMENT, 19000 HUBBARD DR., DEARBORN, MI 48126-2638
Phone: 313-593-5460 • **Fax:** 313-271-9838
E-mail: GRADBUSINESS@UMD.UMICH.EDU
Website: WWW.SOM.UMD.UMICH.EDU

GENERAL INFORMATION
Type of School: Public Environment: City Academic Calendar: Semester

STUDENTS
Enrollment of parent institution: 8,152 Enrollment of MBA program: 407 % male/female: 65/35 % part-time: 90 % minorities: 20 Average age at entry: 30 Average years work experience at entry: 5

ACADEMICS
Student/faculty ratio: 30:1 % female faculty: 38 % minority faculty: 25 Joint Degrees: Dual MBA & MSEngineering in industrual engineering. 4-5 years part-time. Dual MBA & master of health services administration.

FINANCIAL FACTS
Tuition (in-state/out-of-state): $10,999/$22,433 Books and supplies: $1,200 Average grant: $1,500

ADMISSIONS
Admissions Selectivity Rating: 78
# of applications received: 98 % applicants accepted: 69 % acceptees attending: 76 Average GMAT: 574 Average GPA: 3.2 TOEFL required of int'l applicants? Yes Minimum TOEFL (paper/computer): 560/220 Application Fee: $60 International Application Fee: $75 Regular Application Deadline: 8/1 Regular Notification: Rolling Deferment Available? Yes Maximum length of deferment: 1 year Transfer Students Accepted? Yes Non-fall Admissions? Yes Need-Blind Admissions? Yes Applicants also look at: Eastern Michigan University, Michigan State University, Oakland University, University of Detroit Mercy, University of Michigan, Wayne State University.

EMPLOYMENT PROFILE
% grads employed immediately: 97

UNIVERSITY OF MINNESOTA DULUTH
LABOVITZ SCHOOL OF BUSINESS AND ECONOMICS

Admissions Contact: CANDY FURO, ASSOCIATE ADMINISTRATOR
Address: 31 LSBE, 412 LIBRARY DRIVE, DULUTH, MN 55812
Phone: 218-726-8986 • **Fax:** 218-726-6789
E-mail: GRAD@D.UMN.EDU
Website: WWW.D.UMN.EDU/SBE/DEGREEPROGS/MBA/

GENERAL INFORMATION
Type of School: Public Environment: Village Academic Calendar: Semester

STUDENTS
Enrollment of parent institution: 10,000 Enrollment of MBA program: 84 % male/female: 50/50 % part-time: 60 % minorities: 5 % international: 10 Average age at entry: 35 Average years work experience at entry: 10

ACADEMICS
Student/faculty ratio: 20:1
Prominent Alumni: Jon Gerlach, CFO; Chris Mahai, President/CEO; Elaine Hansen, Director; Jim Vizanko, CFO.

FINANCIAL FACTS
Tuition: $8,400 Books and supplies: $1,000 Room & board: $6,000 % of students receiving aid: 35 Average grant: $15,000

ADMISSIONS
Admissions Selectivity Rating: 84
# of applications received: 22 % applicants accepted: 68 % acceptees attending: 100 GMAT Range (25th to 75th percentile): 535-640 Average GMAT: 585 Average GPA: 3.39 TOEFL required of int'l applicants? Yes Minimum TOEFL (paper/computer): 550/213 Application Fee: $55 International Application Fee: $75 Regular Application Deadline: 7/15 Regular Notification: 9/1 Application Deadline/Notification Round 1: 7/15 / 8/31 Round 2: 11/1 / 12/31 Round 3: 5/1 / 6/30 Deferment Available? Yes Maximum length of deferment: 1 year Transfer Students Accepted? Yes Non-fall Admissions? Yes Need-Blind Admissions? Yes Applicants also look at: St. Cloud State University, University of Minnesota, University of St. Thomas (Minnesota).

EMPLOYMENT PROFILE
% grads employed immediately: 90

UNIVERSITY OF MISSISSIPPI
SCHOOL OF BUSINESS ADMINSTRATION

Admissions Contact: DR. JOHN HOLLEMAN, DIRECTOR OF MBA
ADMINSTRATRION
Address: 319 CONNER HALL, UNIVERSITY, MS 38677
Phone: 662-915-5483 • *Fax:* 662-915-7968
E-mail: JHOLLEMAN@BUS.OLEMISS.EDU
Website: WWW.MBA.OLEMISS.EDU

GENERAL INFORMATION
Type of School: Public **Environment:** Village **Academic Calendar:** Semester

STUDENTS
Enrollment of parent institution: 13,500 **Enrollment of MBA program:** 96 % **male/female:** 59/41 % **out-of-state:** 41 % **minorities:** 4 % **international:** 8 **Average age at entry:** 26 **Average years work experience at entry:** 2

ACADEMICS
Student/faculty ratio: 30:1 % **female faculty:** 18

FINANCIAL FACTS
Tuition (in-state/out-of-state): $7,094/$15,899 **Books and supplies:** $5,000 **Room & board (on/off campus):** $8,800/$10,000 **Average grant:** $1,469

ADMISSIONS
Admissions Selectivity Rating: 81
# of applications received: 225 % **applicants accepted:** 45 % **acceptees attending:** 55 **GMAT Range (25th to 75th percentile):** 500-610 **Average GMAT:** 550 **Average GPA:** 3 **TOEFL required of int'l applicants?** Yes **Minimum TOEFL (paper):** 600 **Regular Application Deadline:** 4/1 **Regular Notification:** 5/1 **Non-fall Admissions?** Yes **Need-Blind Admissions?** Yes

EMPLOYMENT PROFILE
Placement rate (%): 99 **# of companies recruiting on-campus:** 90 % **grads employed immediately:** 70 **Average starting salary:** $52,500

Grads employed by field: ....%
Accounting 5
Finance 15
Marketing 15
MIS...............................20
Consulting 10
Entrepreneurship 5
General Management 5
Internet/New Media 25

UNIVERSITY OF MISSOURI— KANSAS CITY
HENRY W. BLOCH SCHOOL OF BUSINESS & PUBLIC ADMINISTRATION

Admissions Contact: 816-235-1111, DIRECTOR OF ADMISSIONS
Address: 5100 ROCKHILL ROAD, KANSAS CITY, MO 64110
Phone: 816-235-1111 • *Fax:* 816-235-5544
E-mail: ADMIT@UMKC.EDU
Website: WWW.UMKC.EDU/BLOCH

GENERAL INFORMATION
Type of School: Public **Environment:** Metropolis **Academic Calendar:** Semester

STUDENTS
Enrollment of parent institution: 14,256 **Enrollment of MBA program:** 330 % % **part-time:** 100 **Average age at entry:** 30 **Average years work experience at entry:** 4

ACADEMICS
Student/faculty ratio: 13:1 % **female faculty:** 20 **Joint Degrees:** JD/MBA (4 years) JD/MPA (4 years). **Prominent Alumni:** Kay Waldo Barnes, Mayor, Kansas City, Missouri; Terry Dunn, President and CEO, Dunn Industries; Dave Thomas, Executive Director, Sprint Foundation; Tom Holcom, President, Pioneer Financial Services; Bob Regnier, President, Bank of Blue Valley.

FINANCIAL FACTS
Tuition (in-state/out-of-state): $4,577/$11,808 **Fees:** $358 **Room & board (on/off campus):** $7,930/$7,912 % **of students receiving aid:** 29 % **of students receiving loans:** 24 % **of students receiving grants:** 5 **Average award package:** $11,923 **Average grant:** $5,856 **Average student loan debt:** $11,425

ADMISSIONS
Admissions Selectivity Rating: 70
# of applications received: 158 % **applicants accepted:** 84 % **acceptees attending:** 72 **GMAT Range (25th to 75th percentile):** 470-560 **Average GMAT:** 515 **Average GPA:** 3.23 **TOEFL required of int'l applicants?** Yes **Minimum TOEFL (paper):** 550 **Application Fee:** $35 **International Application Fee:** $50 **Regular Application Deadline:** 5/1 **Regular Notification:** Rolling **Deferment Available?** Yes **Maximum length of deferment:** 1 year **Transfer Students Accepted?** Yes **Non-fall Admissions?** Yes **Need-Blind Admissions?** Yes

EMPLOYMENT PROFILE

# of companies recruiting on-campus: 30 **% grads employed immediately:** 52

Average starting salary: $55,000

Grads employed by field:% avg. salary:

Finance	17	$41,000
Human Resources	4	NR
Marketing	24	$57,000
MIS	10	$51,000
Operations	7	$81,000
Entrepreneurship	7	$43,500
General Management	14	$69,750
Other	10	NR

THE UNIVERSITY OF MONTANA— MISSOULA
SCHOOL OF BUSINESS ADMINISTRATION

Admissions Contact: KATHLEEN SPRITZER, ADMINISTRATIVE OFFICER
Address: SCHOOL OF BUSINESS ADMIN., UNIV. OF MONTANA, MISSOULA, MT 59812
Phone: 406-243-4983 • **Fax:** 406-243-2086
E-mail: KATHLEEN.SPRITZER@BUSINESS.UMT.EDU
Website: WWW.MBA-MACCT.UMT.EDU

GENERAL INFORMATION

Type of School: Public **Environment:** City **Academic Calendar:** Semester

STUDENTS

Enrollment of parent institution: 13,564 **Enrollment of MBA program:** 184 **% male/female:** 46/54 **% part-time:** 47 **% minorities:** 5 **% international:** 10 **Average age at entry:** 29 **Average years work experience at entry:** 2.5

ACADEMICS

Student/faculty ratio: 26:1 **% female faculty:** 31 **% minority faculty:** 1 **Joint Degrees:** JD/MBA, 3 years; MBA/PharmD, 5 years.

FINANCIAL FACTS

Tuition (in-state/out-of-state): $6,150/$14,230 **Books and supplies:** $1,800 **Room & board (on/off campus):** $8,750/ **% of students receiving aid:** 10 **% of students receiving grants:** 10 **Average grant:** $9,000

ADMISSIONS

Admissions Selectivity Rating: 60*

# of applications received: 146 **% applicants accepted:** 75 **% acceptees attending:** 88 **GMAT Range (25th to 75th percentile):** 460-710 **Average GMAT:** 566 **Average GPA:** 3.2 **TOEFL required of int'l applicants?** Yes **Minimum TOEFL (paper/computer):** 580/237 **Application Fee:** $45 **International Application Fee:** $45 **Regular Application Deadline:** 4/15 **Regular Notification:** 5/1 **Deferment Available?** Yes **Maximum length of deferment:** 1 year **Transfer Students Accepted?** Yes **Non-fall Admissions?** Yes **Need-Blind Admissions?** Yes **Applicants also look at:** Idaho State University, Montana State University, University of Oregon, University of Washington, Washington State University.

EMPLOYMENT PROFILE

Placement rate (%): 83 **# of companies recruiting on-campus:** 25 **% grads employed immediately:** 83 **Average starting salary:** $44,031

UNIVERSITY OF NEBRASKA— LINCOLN
COLLEGE OF BUSINESS ADMINISTRATION

Admissions Contact: JUDY SHUTTS, GRADUATE ADVISER
Address: CBA 125, LINCOLN, NE 68588-0405
Phone: 402-472-2338 • **Fax:** 402-472-5180
E-mail: CGRADUATE@UNLNOTES.UNL.EDU
Website: WWW.CBA.UNL.EDU

GENERAL INFORMATION

Type of School: Public **Environment:** City **Academic Calendar:** Semester

STUDENTS

Enrollment of parent institution: 21,792 **Enrollment of MBA program:** 123 **% male/female:** 80/20 **% out-of-state:** 20 **% part-time:** 50 **% minorities:** 2 **% international:** 13 **Average age at entry:** 26 **Average years work experience at entry:** 6

ACADEMICS

Student/faculty ratio: 6:1 **% female faculty:** 19 **% minority faculty:** 12 **Joint Degrees:** MBA/JD (4 years); MBA/Arch (3 years). **Prominent Alumni:** Marsha Lommel, Pres/CEO Madonna Rehabilitation Hospital; Vinod Gupta, Founder/Chairman InfoUSA; David Maurstad, Director, Federal Emergency Mgt Agency (FEMA); Bernard Reznicek, National Directo, Central States Indemnity Co.; William Ruud, Policy Director, State of Idaho.

FINANCIAL FACTS

Tuition (in-state/out-of-state): $4,560/$12,288 **Fees:** $675 **Books and supplies:** $894 **Room & board (on/off campus):** $6,410/$6,600 **% of students receiving aid:** 63 **% of first-year students receiving aid:** 75 **% of students receiving loans:** 18 **% of students receiving grants:** 40 **Average award package:** $15,000 **Average grant:** $2,885

ADMISSIONS

Admissions Selectivity Rating: 80

# of applications received: 70 **% applicants accepted:** 74 **% acceptees attending:** 69 **GMAT Range (25th to 75th percentile):** 550-640 **Average GMAT:** 595 **Average GPA:** 3.48 **TOEFL required of int'l applicants?** Yes **Minimum TOEFL (paper/computer):** 550/213 **Application Fee:** $45 **International Application Fee:** $45 **Regular Application Deadline:** 6/15 **Regular Notification:** Rolling **Transfer Students Accepted?** Yes **Non-fall Admissions?** Yes **Need-Blind Admissions?** Yes **Applicants also look at:** Arizona State University, Creighton University, University of Iowa, University of Kansas, University of Nebraska at Omaha.

EMPLOYMENT PROFILE

Placement rate (%): 37 **% grads employed immediately:** 37 **Average starting salary:** $41,865

Grads employed by field:% avg. salary:

Finance	14	$31,350
Marketing	14	NR
MIS	14	$52,000
Consulting	14	$50,000
General Management	14	$32,000
Other	29	$41,850

UNIVERSITY OF NEVADA—RENO
COLLEGE OF BUSINESS ADMINSTRATION

Admissions Contact: , *ASSOCIATE DIRECTOR OF GRADUATE STUDIES*
Address: *MAILSTOP 326, RENO, NV 89557*
Phone: *775-784-6869* • **Fax:** *775-784-6064*
E-mail: *GRADADMISSIONS@UNR.EDU*
Website: *WWW.COBA.UNR.EDU/MBA/*

GENERAL INFORMATION

Type of School: Public **Environment:** City **Academic Calendar:** Semester

STUDENTS

Enrollment of parent institution: 1,128 **Enrollment of MBA program:** 167 **% part-time:** 74 **Average age at entry:** 29

ACADEMICS

Student/faculty ratio: 30:1

FINANCIAL FACTS

Tuition (in-state/out-of-state): $1,986/$7,094

ADMISSIONS

Admissions Selectivity Rating: 60*

# of applications received: 72 **% applicants accepted:** 93 **% acceptees attending:** 76 **TOEFL required of int'l applicants?** Yes **Minimum TOEFL (paper):** 550 **Application Fee:** $40 **Regular Application Deadline:** 2/1 **Regular Notification:** Rolling **Deferment Available?** Yes **Maximum length of deferment:** 1 year **Non-fall Admissions?** Yes

EMPLOYMENT PROFILE

Average starting salary: $50,000

UNIVERSITY OF NEW HAMPSHIRE
WHITTEMORE SCHOOL OF BUSINESS AND ECONOMICS

Admissions Contact: *GEORGE ABRAHAM, DIRECTOR, GRADUATE AND EXECUTIVE PROGRAMS*
Address: *116 MCCONNELL HALL, 15 COLLEGE ROAD, DURHAM, NH 03824*
Phone: *603-862-1367* • **Fax:** *603-862-4468*
E-mail: *WSBE.GRAD@UNH.EDU*
Website: *WWW.MBA.UNH.EDU*

GENERAL INFORMATION

Type of School: Public **Environment:** Village **Academic Calendar:** Trimester

STUDENTS

Enrollment of parent institution: 14,431 **Enrollment of MBA program:** 241 **% male/female:** 70/30 **% out-of-state:** 55 **% part-time:** 72 **% minorities:** 10 **% international:** 10 **Average age at entry:** 32 **Average years work experience at entry:** 7

ACADEMICS

% female faculty: 20 **Joint Degrees:** Current UNH seniors can apply early admission to the MA in economics and MS accounting program to shorten their length of time in graduate school. **Prominent Alumni:** Dan Burnham, President of Raytheon, Defense; Michael Baldwin, President and COO, Cheesecake Factory; Terry Tracy, Managing Director, Soloman Smith Barney; John Hollowell, President, Colonial Williamsburg; David Cote, Chairman/President/CEO of Honeywell.

FINANCIAL FACTS

Tuition (in-state/out-of-state): $7,510/$18,540 **Fees:** $1,642 **Books and supplies:** $1,500 **Room & board (on/off campus):** $7,080/$8,000

Admissions Selectivity Rating:72

# of applications received: 131 % applicants accepted: 85 % acceptees attending: 67 GMAT Range (25th to 75th percentile): 510-600 Average GMAT: 560 Average GPA: 3.19 TOEFL required of int'l applicants? Yes Minimum TOEFL (paper/computer): 550/213 Application Fee: $60 International Application Fee: $60 Regular Application Deadline: 7/5 Regular Notification: Rolling Early decision program? Yes ED deadline /notification: 4/1/5/15 Deferment Available? Yes Maximum length of deferment: 1 year Transfer Students Accepted? Yes Non-fall Admissions? Yes Need-Blind Admissions? Yes Applicants also look at: Babson College, Bentley College, Boston University, Suffolk University

EMPLOYMENT PROFILE

Placement rate (%): 88 # of companies recruiting on-campus: 60 % grads employed immediately: 85 Average starting salary: $61,623

Grads employed by field:% avg. salary:

Accounting	5	$52,493
Finance	20	$56,700
Marketing	20	$80,000
MIS	15	$82,500
Operations	20	$645,000
General Management	20	$50,000

UNIVERSITY OF NEW ORLEANS
COLLEGE OF BUSINESS ADMINSTRATION

Admissions Contact: ROSLYN SHELEY, DIRECTOR OF ADMISSIONS
Address: ADMIN BUILDING RM 103, NEW ORLEANS, LA 70148
Phone: 504-280-6595 • *Fax:* 504-280-5522
E-mail: ADMISSIONS@UNO.EDU
Website: WWW.UNO.EDU

GENERAL INFORMATION

Type of School: Public Environment: Metropolis Academic Calendar: Semester

STUDENTS

Enrollment of parent institution: 17,360 Enrollment of MBA program: 810 % male/female: 51/49 % out-of-state: 30 % part-time: 46 % minorities: 25 % international: 26 Average age at entry: 30

ACADEMICS

Student/faculty ratio: 24:1

Prominent Alumni: Dr. James Clark, Chairman of the Board, Netscape Communications; Michael Fitzpatrick, CEO, Rohm & Haas; Erving Johnson, Starting Center, Milwaukee Bucks; Mike Kettenring, President & General Manager, Gillett Broadcasting; Dr. Reuben Arminana, President, Sonoma State University.

FINANCIAL FACTS

Tuition (in-state/out-of-state): $3,084/$10,128 Books and supplies: $1,150 Room & board: $4,122 Average grant: $2,697

ADMISSIONS

Admissions Selectivity Rating: 66

# of applications received: 575 % applicants accepted: 67 % acceptees attending: 62 GMAT Range (25th to 75th percentile): 400-510 Average GMAT: 459 Average GPA: 3 TOEFL required of int'l applicants? Yes Minimum TOEFL (paper/computer): 550/213 Application Fee: $20 Regular Application Deadline: 8/28 Regular Notification: 9/1 Deferment Available? Yes Maximum length of deferment: 1 Semester Transfer Students Accepted? Yes Non-fall Admissions? Yes Need-Blind Admissions? Yes

EMPLOYMENT PROFILE

of companies recruiting on-campus: 100

UNIVERSITY OF NORTH CAROLINA AT WILMINGTON
CAMERON SCHOOL OF BUSINESS

Admissions Contact: KATHY ERICKSON, GRADUATE PROGRAMS ADMINISTRATOR
Address: 601 SOUTH COLLEGE ROAD, WILMINGTON, NC 28403-5920
Phone: 910-962-3903 • *Fax:* 910-962-3815
E-mail: GRADSTUDIES@UNCW.EDU
Website: WWW.CSB.UNCWIL.EDU

GENERAL INFORMATION

Type of School: Public Environment: Rural Academic Calendar:

STUDENTS

Enrollment of parent institution: 10,300 Enrollment of MBA program: 120 % male/female: 61/39 % part-time: 100 % minorities: 3 Average age at entry: 31 Average years work experience at entry: 8

ADMISSIONS

Admissions Selectivity Rating: 87

# of applications received: 147 % applicants accepted: 44 % acceptees attending: 92 Average GMAT: 549 Average GPA: 3.5 TOEFL required of int'l applicants? Yes Minimum TOEFL (paper/computer): 500/213 Application Fee: $45 International Application Fee: $45 Regular Application Deadline: 2/1 Regular Notification: Rolling Deferment Available? Yes Maximum length of deferment: 1 year Non-fall Admissions? Yes

EMPLOYMENT PROFILE

Placement rate (%): 100

UNIVERSITY OF NORTH TEXAS
COLLEGE OF BUSINESS ADMINISTRATION

Admissions Contact: DENISE GALUBENSKI OR KONNI STUBBLEFIELD, GRADUATE ACADEMIC ADVISORS
Address: PO Box 311160, DENTON, TX 76203
Phone: 940-369-8977 • *Fax:* 940-369-8978
E-mail: MBA@COBAF.UNT.EDU
Website: WWW.COBA.UNT.EDU

GENERAL INFORMATION
Type of School: Public **Environment:** City **Academic Calendar:** Semester

STUDENTS
Enrollment of parent institution: 31,155 **Enrollment of MBA program:** 515 **% part-time:** 63 **Average age at entry:** 32 **Average years work experience at entry:** 5

ACADEMICS
Student/faculty ratio: 45:1 **% female faculty:** 22 **% minority faculty:** 17 **Joint Degrees:** MBA—operations management science/MS—engineering technology (48 hours); MBA (any professional field)/MS in merchandising (54 hours); MBA (any professional field)/MS in hospitality management (54 hours).

FINANCIAL FACTS
Tuition (in-state/out-of-state): $2,126/$4,448

ADMISSIONS
Admissions Selectivity Rating: 60*

# of applications received: 533 **% applicants accepted:** 55 **Average GMAT:** 527 **TOEFL required of int'l applicants?** Yes **Minimum TOEFL (paper/computer):** 550/213 **Application Fee:** $50 **International Application Fee:** $75 **Regular Application Deadline:** 7/15 **Deferment Available?** Yes **Maximum length of deferment:** Three Semesters **Transfer Students Accepted?** Yes **Non-fall Admissions?** Yes **Need-Blind Admissions?** Yes

UNIVERSITY OF NORTHERN IOWA
COLLEGE OF BUSINESS ADMINISTRATION

Admissions Contact: NANCY L. HOFFMAN, MBA PROGRAM ASSISTANT
Address: COLLEGE OF BUSINESS ADMINISTRATION, CURRIS BUSINESS BUILDING 325, CEDAR FALLS, IA 50613-0123
Phone: 319-273-6243 • *Fax:* 319-273-2922
E-mail: MBA@UNI.EDU
Website: WWW.CBA.UNI.EDU/MBA/

GENERAL INFORMATION
Type of School: Public **Environment:** Town **Academic Calendar:** Trimester

STUDENTS
Enrollment of parent institution: 13,441 **Enrollment of MBA program:** 90 **% male/female:** 100/0 **% part-time:** 97 **% minorities:** 1 **% international:** 1 **Average age at entry:** 34 **Average years work experience at entry:** 5

ACADEMICS
Student/faculty ratio: 25:1 **% female faculty:** 17 **% minority faculty:** 19

FINANCIAL FACTS
Tuition (in-state/out-of-state): $5,488/$13,012 **Fees:** $343 **Books and supplies:** $500 **Room & board (on/off campus):** $4,864/$5,654 **% of students receiving loans:** 27 **% of students receiving grants:** 5 **Average award package:** $10,664 **Average grant:** $12,500 **Average student loan debt:** $5,151

ADMISSIONS
Admissions Selectivity Rating: 83

# of applications received: 65 **% applicants accepted:** 55 **% acceptees attending:** 75 **Average GMAT:** 570 **Average GPA:** 3.3 **TOEFL required of int'l applicants?** Yes **Minimum TOEFL (paper/computer):** 600/250 **Application Fee:** $20 **International Application Fee:** $50 **Regular Application Deadline:** 7/20 **Regular Notification:** Rolling **Deferment Available?** Yes **Maximum length of deferment:** 1 year **Transfer Students Accepted?** Yes **Non-fall Admissions?** **Need-Blind Admissions?** Yes

EMPLOYMENT PROFILE
# of companies recruiting on-campus: 180 **Average starting salary:** $48,400

UNIVERSITY OF PENNSYLVANIA
THE WHARTON SCHOOL GRADUATE DIVISION

Admissions Contact: ROSEMARIA MARTINELLI, DIRECTOR OF ADMISSIONS AND FINANCIAL AID
Address: 420 JON M. HUNTSMAN HALL, 3730 WALNUT STREET, PHILADELPHIA, PA 19104-6340
Phone: 215-898-6183 • *Fax:* 215-898-0120
E-mail: MBA.ADMISSIONS@WHARTON.UPENN.EDU
Website: WWW.WHARTON.UPENN.EDU/MBA

GENERAL INFORMATION
Type of School: Private **Environment:** Metropolis **Academic Calendar:** Semester

STUDENTS
Enrollment of parent institution: 23,236 **Enrollment of MBA program:** 1,702 **% male/female:** 67/33 **% minorities:** 16 **% international:** 40 **Average age at entry:** 29 **Average years work experience at entry:** 6

ACADEMICS

Student/faculty ratio: 5:1 % female faculty: 20 % minority faculty: 11 **Joint Degrees:** MBA/JD; MBA/MD; MBA/DMD-dental; MBA/MSE engineering; communication; MBA/MA, MBA/MA, MBA/MSW; MBA/PhD; MBA/animal health economics training program; MBA/VMD (Vetrinary); MBA/MSN (nursing). **Prominent Alumni:** J.D. Power III, Founder & Chairman, JD Power & Assoc.; Klaus Zumwinkel, Chairman & CEO, Deutsche Post AG; Lewis Platt, Former Chairman, Hewlett-Packard; Arthur D. Wollins, President & CEO, Medtronic, Inc.; Peter S. Lynch, Vice Chairman, Fidelity Management & Research Co.

FINANCIAL FACTS

Tuition: $37,323 **Fees:** $5,900 **Books and supplies:** $2,478 **Room & board (on campus):** $14,200 % of students receiving aid: 87 % of first-year students receiving aid: 60 % of students receiving loans: 60 % of students receiving grants: 40 **Average award package:** $35,000 **Average grant:** $5,000 **Average student loan debt:** $85,000

ADMISSIONS

Admissions Selectivity Rating: 99

# of applications received: 7,215 % applicants accepted: 16 % acceptees attending: 71 GMAT Range (25th to 75th percentile): 660-760 **Average GMAT:** 714 **Average GPA:** 3.5 **TOEFL required of int'l applicants?** Yes **Application Fee:** $200 **International Application Fee:** $200 **Regular Application Deadline:** Regular Notification: Application Deadline/Notification Round 1: 10/16 / 12/23 Round 2: 1/8 / 3/25 Round 3: 3/18 / 5/20 **Deferment Available?** Yes **Maximum length of deferment:** Case-by-case **Need-Blind Admissions?** Yes

EMPLOYMENT PROFILE

Placement rate (%): 93 % grads employed immediately: 74 **Average starting salary:** $115,000
Grads employed by field:% avg. salary:
Consulting.........................21 .... $120,000

UNIVERSITY OF PORTLAND
PAMPLIN SCHOOL OF BUSINESS ADMINISTRATION

Admissions Contact: MELISSA MCCARTHY, MBA PROGRAM COORDINATOR
Address: 5000 N. WILLAMETTE BOULEVARD, PORTLAND, OR 97203
Phone: 503-943-7225 • **Fax:** 503-943-8041
E-mail: MBA-UP@UP.EDU
Website: WWW.UP.EDU

GENERAL INFORMATION

Type of School: Private **Affiliation:** Roman Catholic **Environment:** Metropolis **Academic Calendar:** Semester

STUDENTS

Enrollment of parent institution: 3,000 **Enrollment of MBA program:** 149 % male/female: 60/40 % out-of-state: 25 % part-time: 65 % minorities: 7 % international: 19 **Average age at entry:** 29 **Average years work experience at entry:** 5

ACADEMICS

Student/faculty ratio: 13:1 % female faculty: 20 % minority faculty: 15 **Prominent Alumni:** Dr. Robert B. Pamplin. Jr., Philanthropist / Entreprenuer; Fidele Baccio, Co-Founder Bon Appetit.

FINANCIAL FACTS

Tuition: $24,660 **Books and supplies:** $600 % of students receiving aid: 60 % of first-year students receiving aid: 60% of students receiving grants: 9 **Average award package:** $18,500 **Average grant:** $4,500

ADMISSIONS

Admissions Selectivity Rating: 73

# of applications received: 64 % applicants accepted: 84 % acceptees attending: 70 **Average GMAT:** 560 **Average GPA:** 3.3 **TOEFL required of int'l applicants?** Yes **Minimum TOEFL (paper/computer):** 570/230 **Application Fee:** $50 **International Application Fee:** $50 **Regular Application Deadline:** Rolling **Regular Notification:** Rolling **Deferment Available?** Yes **Maximum length of deferment:** 1 year **Transfer Students Accepted?** Yes **Non-fall Admissions?** Yes **Need-Blind Admissions?** Yes **Applicants also look at:** Portland State University.

EMPLOYMENT PROFILE

of companies recruiting on-campus: 40

UNIVERSITY OF RHODE ISLAND
COLLEGE OF BUSINESS ADMINISTRATION

Admissions Contact: LISA LANCELLOTTA, COORDINATOR, MBA PROGRAMS
Address: LIPPITT RD., BALLENTINE HALL, KINGSTON, RI 02881
Phone: 401-874-5000 • **Fax:** 401-874-4312
E-mail: MBA@ETAL.URI.EDU
Website: WWW.CBA.URI.EDU/GRADUATE/MBA.HTM

GENERAL INFORMATION

Type of School: Public **Environment:** Rural **Academic Calendar:** Semesters

STUDENTS

Enrollment of parent institution: **Enrollment of MBA program:** 244 % male/female: 62/38 % part-time: 91 % minorities: 10 % international: 43 **Average age at entry:** 29

ACADEMICS

Student/faculty ratio: 4:1 **Joint Degrees:** MBA/Pharm.D—7 years; MBA/Marine Affairs—5 years; MA/Engineering—5 years.

FINANCIAL FACTS

Tuition (in-state/out-of-state): $8,676/$24,876 **Fees:** $1,900 **Books and supplies:** $3,500

ADMISSIONS

Admissions Selectivity Rating: 80

# of applications received: 100 **% applicants accepted:** 66 % **acceptees attending:** 86 **Average GMAT:** 578 **Average GPA:** 3 **TOEFL required of int'l applicants?** Yes **Minimum TOEFL (paper/computer):** 575/233 **Application Fee:** $30 **International Application Fee:** $45 **Regular Application Deadline:** 6/1 **Regular Notification:** Rolling **Deferment Available?** Yes **Maximum length of deferment:** 1 year **Transfer Students Accepted?** Yes **Non-fall Admissions?** Yes **Need-Blind Admissions?** Yes **Applicants also look at:** Babson College, Boston College, Boston University, Bryant College, Northeastern University, Suffolk University, University of Connecticut.

EMPLOYMENT PROFILE

Average starting salary: $62,576

UNIVERSITY OF RICHMOND
ROBINS SCHOOL OF BUSINESS

Admissions Contact: DR. RICHARD S. COUGHLAN, ASSOCIATE DEAN FOR GRADUATE AND EXECUTIVE PROGRAMS
Address: MBA OFFICE, ROBINS SCHOOL OF BUSINESS, UNIVERSITY OF RICHMOND, VA 23173
Phone: 804-289-8553 • **Fax:** 804-287-6544
E-mail: MBA@RICHMOND.EDU
Website: ONCAMPUS.RICHMOND.EDU/ACADEMICS/BUSINESS/DEPARTMENTS/MBA/INDEX.HTML

GENERAL INFORMATION

Type of School: Private **Environment:** City **Academic Calendar:** Semester

STUDENTS

Enrollment of parent institution: 4,492 **Enrollment of MBA program:** 147 **% male/female:** 100/0 **% part-time:** 100 **Average age at entry:** 28 **Average years work experience at entry:** 5

ACADEMICS

Student/faculty ratio: 3:1 **% female faculty:** 24 **% minority faculty:** 2 **Joint Degrees:** Juris doctor/master of business administration (3-4 years). **Prominent Alumni:** David Beran, Senior Vice President, Philip Morris USA; Lyn McDermid, Chief Information Officer, Dominion Resources; Lew Boggs, President, Property Investment Advisors; Rex Smith, President & CEO, Bank of Richmond; Mark Hourigan, President, Hourigan Construction.

FINANCIAL FACTS

Tuition: $25,010 **Books and supplies:** $2,300 **Average award package:** $11,450 **Average grant:** $10,028 **Average student loan debt:** $38,900

ADMISSIONS

Admissions Selectivity Rating: 74

# of applications received: 64 **% applicants accepted:** 84 % **acceptees attending:** 69 **GMAT Range (25th to 75th percentile):** 510-620 **Average GMAT:** 579 **Average GPA:** 3.12 **TOEFL required of int'l applicants?** Yes **Minimum TOEFL (paper/computer):** 600/250 **Application Fee:** $50 **International Application Fee:** $50 **Regular Application Deadline:** 5/1 **Regular Notification:** 6/1 **Deferment Available?** Yes **Maximum length of deferment:** 1 Year **Transfer Students Accepted?** Yes **Need-Blind Admissions?** Yes **Applicants also look at:** College of William & Mary, Virginia Commonwealth University.

EMPLOYMENT PROFILE

% grads employed within three months: 100

UNIVERSITY OF SAN DIEGO
SCHOOL OF BUSINESS ADMINISTRATION

Admissions Contact: STEPHEN PULTZ, DIRECTOR OF ADMISSIONS
Address: 5998 ALCALA PARK, SAN DIEGO, CA 92110
Phone: 619-260-4524 • **Fax:** 619-260-4158
E-mail: GRADS@SANDIEGO.EDU
Website: BUSINESS.SANDIEGO.EDU

GENERAL INFORMATION

Type of School: Private **Affiliation:** Roman Catholic **Environment:** Metropolis

STUDENTS

Enrollment of parent institution: 7,262 **Enrollment of MBA program:** 219 **% minorities:** 18 **Average age at entry:** 27 **Average years work experience at entry:** 3

ACADEMICS

Student/faculty ratio: 2:1 **Joint Degrees:** MBA/JD, 5-6 years; MBA/MSN, 3.5 years; MBA/MSIT, 3 years; MBA/MSRE; MBA/MSGL, 3.5 years; IMBA/JD, 4-5 years.

FINANCIAL FACTS

Tuition: $14,850 **Fees:** $126 **Books and supplies:** $1,220

ADMISSIONS

Admissions Selectivity Rating: 82

# of applications received: 177 **% applicants accepted:** 47 % **acceptees attending:** 82 **GMAT Range (25th to 75th percentile):** 500-600 **Average GMAT:** 567 **Average GPA:** 3 **TOEFL required of int'l applicants?** Yes **Minimum TOEFL (paper/computer):** 580/237 **Application Fee:** $45 **International Application Fee:** $45 **Regular Application Deadline:** 5/1 **Regular Notification:** Rolling **Deferment Available?** Yes **Maximum length of deferment:** 1 year **Transfer Students Accepted?** Yes **Non-fall Admissions?** Yes **Applicants also look at:** Pepperdine University, San Diego State University.

University of South Alabama
Mitchell College of Business

Admissions Contact: , Associate Dean
Address: 182 AD, Mobile, AL 36688-0002
Phone: 251-460-6141 • *Fax:* 251-460-6529
Website: WWW.USOUTHAL.EDU/GRADUATEPROGRAMS/BUSINESS.HTML

GENERAL INFORMATION
Type of School: Public Environment: City

STUDENTS
Enrollment of parent institution: 12,300 Enrollment of MBA program: 162 % male/female: 55/45 % part-time: 20 % minorities: 2 % international: 30

ACADEMICS
Student/faculty ratio: 20:1 % female faculty: 21

FINANCIAL FACTS
Tuition (in-state/out-of-state): $1,192/$2,384 Fees: $254 Books and supplies: $1,200

ADMISSIONS
Admissions Selectivity Rating: 71

# of applications received: 70 % applicants accepted: 71 % acceptees attending: 84 Average GMAT: 488 Average GPA: 3.1 TOEFL required of int'l applicants? Yes Minimum TOEFL (paper): 525 Application Fee: $25 International Application Fee: $25 Regular Application Deadline: 8/1 Regular Notification: 1/1 Deferment Available? Yes Maximum length of deferment: text marker Transfer Students Accepted? Yes Non-fall Admissions? Yes Need-Blind Admissions? Yes

EMPLOYMENT PROFILE
Placement rate (%): 93

University of South Florida
College of Business Administration

Admissions Contact: Wendy Baker, Assistant Director of Graduate Studies
Address: 4202 E. Fowler Avenue, BSN 3403, Tampa, FL 33620
Phone: 813-974-8800 • *Fax:* 813-974-7343
E-mail: MBA@COBA.USF.EDU
Website: WWW.COBA.USF.EDU

GENERAL INFORMATION
Type of School: Public Environment: Metropolis Academic Calendar: Fall

STUDENTS
Enrollment of parent institution: 35,117 Enrollment of MBA program: 402 % male/female: 60/40 % out-of-state: 40 % part-time: 61 % minorities: 16 % international: 6 Average age at entry: 27 Average years work experience at entry: 5

ACADEMICS
Student/faculty ratio: 4:1 % female faculty: 11 % minority faculty: 14 Joint Degrees: MBA-Master of Business Administration AND MSM-Master of Science in Management Information Systems 24-60 months.

FINANCIAL FACTS
Tuition (in-state/out-of-state): $5,594/$21,469 Fees: $37 Books and supplies: $700 Average grant: $3,250

ADMISSIONS
Admissions Selectivity Rating: 75

# of applications received: 252 % applicants accepted: 73 % acceptees attending: 61 GMAT Range (25th to 75th percentile): 510-590 Average GMAT: 552 Average GPA: 3.3 TOEFL required of int'l applicants? Yes Minimum TOEFL (paper/computer): 550/213 Application Fee: $30 International Application Fee: Regular Application Deadline: 6/1 Regular Notification: 6/1 Deferment Available? Yes Maximum length of deferment: 1 year Transfer Students Accepted? Yes Non-fall Admissions? Yes Need-Blind Admissions? Yes Applicants also look at: Florida State University, University of Central Florida, University of Florida.

The University of Southern Mississippi
College of Business

Admissions Contact: Gabriel McPhearson, Assistant Director, Graduate Business Programs
Address: Box 5096, Hattiesburg, MS 39406-5096
Phone: 601-266-4653 • *Fax:* 601-266-5814
E-mail: MBA_MPA@CBA.USM.EDU
Website: WWW.USMMBA.USM.EDU

GENERAL INFORMATION
Type of School: Public Environment: Village Academic Calendar: Semester

STUDENTS
Enrollment of parent institution: 15,253 Enrollment of MBA program: 135 % male/female: 68/32 % out-of-state: 32 % part-time: 70 % minorities: 20 % international: 15 Average age at entry: 32

ACADEMICS
Student/faculty ratio: 30:1 % female faculty: 25 % minority faculty: 15 Joint Degrees: MBA/MPH (master of public health) - 69 credits (2 to 6 years).

FINANCIAL FACTS

Tuition: $5,170 **Fees (out-of-state):** $4,878 **Books and supplies:** $1,500 **Room & board (on/off campus):** $5,629/$6,500 **% of students receiving aid:** 75 **% of students receiving grants:** 25 **Average grant:** $8,690

ADMISSIONS

Admissions Selectivity Rating: 73

# of applications received: 134 **% applicants accepted:** 69 **% acceptees attending:** 78 **Average GMAT:** 505 **Average GPA:** 3.26 **TOEFL required of int'l applicants?** Yes **Minimum TOEFL (paper/computer):** 550/213 **Application Fee:** $25 **International Application Fee:** $25 **Regular Application Deadline:** 7/15 **Regular Notification:** Rolling **Deferment Available?** Yes **Maximum length of deferment:** 2 Semesters **Transfer Students Accepted?** Yes **Non-fall Admissions?** Yes **Need-Blind Admissions?** Yes

EMPLOYMENT PROFILE

# of companies recruiting on-campus: 26 **Average starting salary:** $31,300

UNIVERSITY OF STRATHCLYDE— GLASGOW

UNIVERSITY OF STRATHCLYDE GRADUATE SCHOOL OF BUSINESS

Admissions Contact: MEG LAVERY
Address: 199 CATHEDRAL STREET, GLASGOW, G4 0QU
Phone: 141-553-6118 • **Fax:** 141-553-6162
E-mail: ADMISSIONS@GSB.STRATH.AC.UK
Website: WWW.GSB.STRATH.AC.UK

GENERAL INFORMATION

Type of School: Private

STUDENTS

Enrollment of MBA program: 70 **% male/female:** 72/28 **% part-time:** 43 **% minorities:** 65 **% international:** 75 **Average age at entry:** 32 **Average years work experience at entry:** 9

FINANCIAL FACTS

Fees: $31,600 **Room & board (on/off campus):** $13,500/$15,300

ADMISSIONS

Admissions Selectivity Rating: 70

# of applications received: 300 **% applicants accepted:** 82 **% acceptees attending:** 16 **Average GMAT:** 560 **Average GPA:** 3.4 **TOEFL required of int'l applicants?** Yes **Minimum TOEFL (paper/computer):** 600/250 **Regular Application Deadline:** Rolling **Regular Notification:** Rolling **Deferment Available?** Yes **Maximum length of deferment:** 2 years **Non-fall Admissions?** Yes

UNIVERSITY OF SYDNEY/ UNIVERSITY OF NEW SOUTH WALES

AUSTRALIAN GRADUATE SCHOOL OF MANAGEMENT

Admissions Contact: DEBBIE SHIVELY, ADMISSION OFFICE
Address: MBA PROGRAM, AGSM, UNSW SYDNEY NSW, 2052 AUSTRALIA
Phone: 0011-61-2-9931-9412 • **Fax:** 0011-61-2-9931-9231
E-mail: MBA@AGSM.EDU.AU
Website: WWW.AGSM.EDU.AU

GENERAL INFORMATION

Type of School: Public

STUDENTS

Enrollment of MBA program: 226 **% male/female:** 69/31 **% international:** 63 **Average age at entry:** 30 **Average years work experience at entry:** 5

ACADEMICS

Student/faculty ratio: 2:1 **% female faculty:** 24 **Prominent Alumni:** Grant Freeland, Vice-President, Boston Consulting Group; Guido Belgiorno, Managing Director, Transfield Pty Ltd; Ron Sodoma, Senior Vice-President, Bank of America; Tony Kongats, CEO, Cap-XX Pty Ltd; Andrew Roberts, General Manager, Multiplex Constructions.

FINANCIAL FACTS

Tuition (in-state/out-of-state): $34,918/$43,324 **Fees (in-state/out-of-state):** $363/$664 **Books and supplies:** $4,619 **Room & Board:** $11,085 **% of students receiving aid:** 10 **% of first-year students receiving aid:** 20 **% of students receiving grants:** 10 **Average award package:** $225,759 **Average grant:** $13,768

ADMISSIONS

Admissions Selectivity Rating: 60*

# of applications received: 192 **% applicants accepted:** 62 **% acceptees attending:** 51 **GMAT Range (25th to 75th percentile):** 610-710 **Average GMAT:** 642 **Average GPA:** 3.0 **TOEFL required of int'l applicants?** Minimum **TOEFL (paper/computer):** 600/250 **Application Fee:** $75 **International Application Fee:** $75 **Regular Application Deadline:** 9/30 **Regular Notification:** Rolling **Deferment Available?** Yes **Maximum length of deferment:** 1 year

EMPLOYMENT PROFILE

Placement rate (%): 85 **# of companies recruiting on-campus:** 15 **Average starting salary:** $100,545

Grads employed by field:% avg. salary:

Finance	10	...$73,986
Marketing	15	...$89,063
Strategic Planning	13	....$75,754
Consulting	23	..$103,403
Entrepreneurship	12	....$90,542
General Management	6	......$86,487
Other	21	....$85,085

THE UNIVERSITY OF TAMPA
JOHN H. SYKES COLLEGE OF BUSINESS

Admissions Contact: FERNANDO NOLASCO, ASSOCIATE DIRECTOR, GRADUATE STUDIES IN BUSINESS
Address: 401 W. KENNEDY BOULEVARD, TAMPA, FL 33606-1490
Phone: 813-258-7409 • **Fax:** 813-259-5403
E-mail: MBA@UT.EDU
Website: WWW.MBA.UT.EDU

GENERAL INFORMATION
Type of School: Private **Environment:** Metropolis **Academic Calendar:** Semester

STUDENTS
Enrollment of parent institution: 4,879 **Enrollment of MBA program:** 412 **% male/female:** 58/42 **% out-of-state:** 7 **% part-time:** 65 **% minorities:** 11 **% international:** 42 **Average age at entry:** 28 **Average years work experience at entry:** 4

ACADEMICS
Student/faculty ratio: 12:1 **% female faculty:** 38 **Joint Degrees:** MBA/MSTIM, MSN/MBA, BS Chemistry/MBA,. **Prominent Alumni:** Wayne Huizenga, Jr., Dennis Zank, COO, Raymond James; Lyndon Martin, Member, Legislative Assembly, Cayman Islands; Jorgen Adolfsson, Swedish technology entrepreneur.

FINANCIAL FACTS
Tuition: $6,240 **Fees:** $70 **Books and supplies:** $562 **Room & board:** $6,670 **% of students receiving aid:** 55 **% of first-year students receiving aid:** 16 **% of students receiving loans:** 38 **% of students receiving grants:** 27 **Average award package:** $10,872 **Average grant:** $9,604 **Average student loan debt:** $21,603

ADMISSIONS
Admissions Selectivity Rating: 80
# of applications received: 351 **% applicants accepted:** 46 **% acceptees attending:** 69 **GMAT Range (25th to 75th percentile):** 460-540 **Average GMAT:** 520 **Average GPA:** 3.34 **TOEFL required of int'l applicants?** Yes **Minimum TOEFL (paper/computer):** 577/230 **Application Fee:** $35 **International Application Fee:** $35 **Regular Application Deadline:** Rolling **Regular Notification:** Rolling **Deferment Available?** Yes **Maximum length of deferment:** 1 year **Transfer Students Accepted?** Yes **Non-fall Admissions?** Yes **Need-Blind Admissions?** Yes **Applicants also look at:** University of Florida, University of South Florida.

EMPLOYMENT PROFILE
Placement rate (%): 87 **# of companies recruiting on-campus:** 75
Average starting salary: $55,600
Grads employed by field:% avg. salary:

Accounting	10	$50,667
Finance	18	$73,400
Human Resources	3	$75,000
Marketing	13	$43,375
MIS	8	$62,500
Operations	5	$31,500
Consulting	3	NR
General Management	25	$68,187
Other	10	NR
Non-profit	5:	$60,000

UNIVERSITY OF TENNESSEE AT CHATTANOOGA
COLLEGE OF BUSINESS ADMINISTRATION

Admissions Contact: ANDREA EVANS, GRADUATE PROGRAM LIAISON
Address: GRADUATE SCHOOL, DEPARTMENT 5305, 615 MCCALLIE AVENUE, CHATTANOOGA, TN 37403
Phone: 423-425-4667 • **Fax:** 423-425-5223
E-mail: ANDREA-EVANS@UTC.EDU
Website: WWW.UTC.EDU

GENERAL INFORMATION
Type of School: Public **Environment:** City **Academic Calendar:** Semester

STUDENTS
Enrollment of parent institution: 8,528 **Enrollment of MBA program:** 276 **% male/female:** 50/50 **% out-of-state:** 27 **% part-time:** 93 **% minorities:** 10 **% international:** 20 **Average age at entry:** 27 **Average years work experience at entry:** 3

ACADEMICS
Student/faculty ratio: 23:1 **% female faculty:** 46 **% minority faculty:** 15 **Prominent Alumni:** General B. B. Bell, Four-Star General in U.S. Army.

FINANCIAL FACTS
Tuition (in-state/out-of-state): $2,736/$6,867 **Books and supplies:** $1,000 **Room & board (on/off campus):** $6,450/$7,800 **Average grant:** $9,500

ADMISSIONS

Admissions Selectivity Rating: 80

# of applications received: 74 % **applicants accepted:** 41 % **acceptees attending:** 80 **GMAT Range (25th to 75th percentile):** 350-700 **Average GMAT:** 500 **Average GPA:** 3.18 **TOEFL required of int'l applicants?** Yes **Minimum TOEFL (paper/computer):** 550/213 **Application Fee:** $25 **International Application Fee:** $25 **Regular Application Deadline:** Rolling **Regular Notification:** Rolling **Deferment Available?** Yes **Maximum length of deferment:** 5 Years **Transfer Students Accepted?** Yes **Non-fall Admissions?** Yes **Need-Blind Admissions?** Yes **Applicants also look at:** East Tennessee State University, Georgia State University, Middle Tennessee State University, Tennessee Technological University, University of Georgia, University of Tennessee, Vanderbilt University.

EMPLOYMENT PROFILE

Placement rate (%): 95 **# of companies recruiting on-campus:** 35 **% grads employed immediately:** 85

UNIVERSITY OF TENNESSEE AT MARTIN
COLLEGE OF BUSINESS AND PUBLIC AFFAIRS

Admissions Contact: JAMES GREEN, COLLEGE OF BUSINESS & PUBLIC AFFAIRS GRADUATE PROGRAM
Address: 103 BUSINESS ADMINISTRATION BUILDING, MARTIN, TN 38238-5015
Phone: 731-587-7333 • **Fax:** 731-587-7241
E-mail: BAGRAD@UTM.EDU
Website: WWW.UTM.EDU/DEPARTMENTS/SOBA/

GENERAL INFORMATION

Type of School: Public **Environment:** Rural **Academic Calendar:** Semester

STUDENTS

Enrollment of parent institution: Enrollment of MBA program: 200 **% male/female:** 45/55 **% minorities:** 10

ACADEMICS

Student/faculty ratio: 15:1

FINANCIAL FACTS

Tuition (in-state/out-of-state): $3,768/$7,650 **Books and supplies:** $1,000

ADMISSIONS

Admissions Selectivity Rating: 60*

Average GMAT: 504 **Average GPA:** 3.22 **TOEFL required of int'l applicants?** Yes **Minimum TOEFL (paper):** 525 **Application Fee:** $25 **Regular Application Deadline:** Rolling **Regular Notification:** Rolling **Deferment Available?** Yes **Non-fall Admissions?** Yes

EMPLOYMENT PROFILE

Placement rate (%): 99

THE UNIVERSITY OF TEXAS AT EL PASO
COLLEGE OF BUSINESS ADMINISTRATION

Admissions Contact: YOLANDA RUIZ, GRADUATE COORDINATOR
Address: ROOM 102, COLLEGE OF BUSINESS, EL PASO, TX 79968
Phone: 915-747-5174 • **Fax:** 915-747-5147
E-mail: COBA@UTEP.EDU.
Website: WWW.UTEP.EDU/COBA/

GENERAL INFORMATION

Type of School: Public **Environment:** Metropolis **Academic Calendar:** Semester

STUDENTS

Enrollment of parent institution: 14,500 **Enrollment of MBA program:** 245 **% male/female:** 62/38 **% part-time:** 76 **% minorities:** 42 **% international:** 18 **Average age at entry:** 32

ACADEMICS

Joint Degrees: MBA/master in public administration (MBA/MPA), 60-78 credits, 2 to 6 years.

FINANCIAL FACTS

Tuition (in-state/out-of-state): $1,172/$3,035

ADMISSIONS

Admissions Selectivity Rating: 60*

# of applications received: 65 **% applicants accepted:** 30766 **% acceptees attending:** 100 **TOEFL required of int'l applicants?** Yes **Minimum TOEFL (paper):** 600 **Application Fee:** $15 **Regular Application Deadline:** 7/1 **Regular Notification:** Rolling **Non-fall Admissions?** Yes

EMPLOYMENT PROFILE

# of companies recruiting on-campus: 103

THE UNIVERSITY OF TEXAS AT TYLER

SCHOOL OF BUSINESS ADMINISTRATION

Admissions Contact: DR. MARY FISCHER, DIRECTOR OF GRADUATE PROGRAMS IN BUSINESS
Address: 3900 UNIVERSITY BOULEVARD, TYLER, TX 75799
Phone: 903-566-7363 • **Fax:** 903-566-7372
E-mail: GSMITH@MAIL.UTTYL.EDU
Website: WWW.UTTYLER.EDU/CBT/MBA.HTM

GENERAL INFORMATION

Type of School: Public **Environment:** City **Academic Calendar:** Semester

STUDENTS

Enrollment of parent institution: 3,459 **Enrollment of MBA program:** 101 **% male/female:** 59/41 **% part-time:** 98 **% minorities:** 5 **% international:** 5 **Average age at entry:** 32

ACADEMICS

Student/faculty ratio: 15:1

ADMISSIONS

Admissions Selectivity Rating: 60*

TOEFL required of int'l applicants? Yes **Minimum TOEFL (paper):** 550 **Regular Application Deadline:** Rolling **Regular Notification:** Rolling **Deferment Available?** Yes

UNIVERSITY OF TOLEDO

COLLEGE OF BUSINESS ADMINISTRATION

Admissions Contact: DAVID CHATFIELD, DIRECTOR MBA & EMBA PROGRAMS
Address: COLLEGE OF BUSINESS ADMINISTRATION, THE UNIVERSITY OF TOLEDO, TOLEDO, OH 43606-3390
Phone: 419-530-2775 • **Fax:** 419-530-7260
E-mail: MBA@UTOLEDO.EDU
Website: WWW.BUSINESS.UTOLEDO.EDU/

GENERAL INFORMATION

Type of School: Public **Environment:** City **Academic Calendar:** Semester

STUDENTS

Enrollment of parent institution: 19,480 **Enrollment of MBA program:** 342 **% male/female:** 65/35 **% part-time:** 69 **% minorities:** 9 **% international:** 23 **Average age at entry:** 28 **Average years work experience at entry:** 3

ACADEMICS

Student/faculty ratio: 10:1 **% female faculty:** 21 **Joint Degrees:** JD/MBA - 3 years. **Prominent Alumni:** Edward Kinsey, Co-Founder, Ariba, Inc.; Ora Alleman, VP, National City Bank; Michael Durik, Executive VP, The Limited Stores, Inc.; Marvin Herb, CEO Coca-Cola Bottling Company; Julie Higgins, Exective VP, The Trust Company of Toledo.

FINANCIAL FACTS

Tuition (in-state/out-of-state): $8,619/$17,431 **Fees:** $1,064 **Books and supplies:** $1,200 **Room & board (off campus):** $5,830 **Average grant:** $16,116

ADMISSIONS

Admissions Selectivity Rating: 64

# of applications received: 166 **% applicants accepted:** 89 **% acceptees attending:** 54 **Average GMAT:** 510 **Average GPA:** 3.2 **TOEFL required of int'l applicants?** Yes **Minimum TOEFL (paper/computer):** 550/213 **Application Fee:** $40 **International Application Fee:** $40 **Regular Application Deadline:** Rolling **Regular Notification:** Rolling **Deferment Available?** Yes **Maximum length of deferment:** 1 year **Transfer Students Accepted?** Yes **Non-fall Admissions?** Yes **Applicants also look at:** Bowling Green State University, The University of Findlay.

UNIVERSITY OF TORONTO

JOSEPH L. ROTMAN SCHOOL OF MANAGEMENT

Admissions Contact: CHERYL MILLINGTON, DIRECTOR OF MBA RECRUITING AND ADMISSIONS
Address: 105 ST. GEORGE STREET, TORONTO, ON M5S 3E6 CANADA
Phone: 416-978-3499 • **Fax:** 416-978-5812
E-mail: MBA@ROTMAN.UTORONTO.CA
Website: WWW.ROTMAN.UTORONTO.CA

GENERAL INFORMATION

Type of School: Public **Environment:** City **Academic Calendar:** Sept-May

STUDENTS

Enrollment of parent institution: 64,000 **Enrollment of MBA program:** 332 **% male/female:** 73/27 **% part-time:** 19 **% minorities:** 50 **% international:** 40 **Average age at entry:** 28 **Average years work experience at entry:** 5

ACADEMICS

Student/faculty ratio: 7:1 **% female faculty:** 22 **Joint Degrees:** JD/MBA (4 years); BASC/MBA (5 years, 8 months); master of nursing/MBA (4 years); MA Russian & Eastern European studies/MBA (4 years). **Prominent Alumni:** Joseph L. Rotman, Founder & Chairman, Clairvest Group Inc.; Ian Locke, General Partner, Jefferson Partners, Toronto; Don Morrison, CEO, Research In Motion, Waterloo, Ont.

FINANCIAL FACTS

Tuition (in-state/out-of-state): $21,800/$29,800 **Books and supplies:** $800 **Room & board (on/off campus):** $8,000/$10,000 **% of students receiving aid:** 70 **% of first-year students receiving aid:** 70 **% of students receiving loans:** 70 **% of students receiving grants:** 20 **Average grant:** $8,000

ADMISSIONS

Admissions Selectivity Rating: 92

# of applications received: 1,312 **% applicants accepted:** 40 **% acceptees attending:** 52 **GMAT Range (25th to 75th percentile):** 550-720 **Average GMAT:** 640 **Average GPA:** 3.5 **TOEFL required of int'l applicants?** Yes **Minimum TOEFL (paper/computer):** 600/250 **Application Fee:** $150 **International Application Fee:** $150 **Regular Application Deadline:** 4/30 **Regular Notification:** 7/1 **Application Deadline/Notification Round 1:** 1/15 / 3/15 **Round 2:** 4/30 / 7/1 **Early decision program?** Yes **ED deadline/notification:** 1/15 (domestic students only) /3/15 **Deferment Available?** Yes **Maximum length of deferment:** 1 year **Need-Blind Admissions?** Yes **Applicants also look at:** McGill University, Queen's University, University of Western Ontario, York University.

EMPLOYMENT PROFILE

Placement rate (%): 90 **# of companies recruiting on-campus:** 330 **% grads employed immediately:** 69 **Average starting salary:** $83,000

Grads employed by field:% avg. salary:

Finance	53	$80,000
Marketing	8	$65,500
Operations	9	$92,000
Consulting	18	$102,000
General Management	8	$78,000
Other	4	$77,500

UNIVERSITY OF TULSA
THE UNIVERSITY OF TULSA

Admissions Contact: RON COOPER, DIRECTOR, GRADUATE BUSINESS PROGRAMS
Address: 600 SOUTH COLLEGE AVENUE, BAH 217, TULSA, OK 74104-3189
Phone: 918-631-2242 • *Fax:* 918-631-2142
E-mail: GRADUATE-BUSINESS@UTULSA.EDU
Website: WWW.CBA.UTULSA.EDU

GENERAL INFORMATION

Type of School: Private **Affiliation:** Presbyterian

STUDENTS

Enrollment of parent institution: 4,174 **Enrollment of MBA program:** 121 **% male/female:** 46/54 **% out-of-state:** 44 **% part-time:** 57 **% minorities:** 8 **% international:** 31 **Average age at entry:** 25 **Average years work experience at entry:** 3

ACADEMICS

Student/faculty ratio: 5:1 **% female faculty:** 9 **% minority faculty:** 13 **Joint Degrees:** JD/MBA - 25 credit hours of business, 79 credit hours of law. JD/MTAX - 24 credit hours of TAX, 79 credit hours of law. Masters in engineering and technology management (METM)- 18 credit hours of business, 18 credit hours of engineering.

FINANCIAL FACTS

Tuition: $11,340 **Fees:** $54 **Books and supplies:** $1,000 **Room & board (on/off campus):** $9,360/$9,360 **% of students receiving aid:** 81 **% of first-year students receiving aid:** 85 **% of students receiving loans:** 38 **Average award package:** $13,389

ADMISSIONS

Admissions Selectivity Rating: 75

# of applications received: 85 **% applicants accepted:** 79 **% acceptees attending:** 75 **GMAT Range (25th to 75th percentile):** 490-595 **Average GMAT:** 546 **Average GPA:** 3.44 **TOEFL required of int'l applicants?** Yes **Minimum TOEFL (paper/computer):** 575/232 **Application Fee:** $30 **International Application Fee:** $30 **Regular Application Deadline:** Rolling **Regular Notification:** Rolling **Transfer Students Accepted?** Yes **Non-fall Admissions?** Yes **Need-Blind Admissions?** Yes **Applicants also look at:** Oklahoma State University, University of Oklahoma.

EMPLOYMENT PROFILE

# of companies recruiting on-campus: 46 **% grads employed immediately:** 72 **Average starting salary:** $48,964

UNIVERSITY OF WARWICK
WARWICK BUSINESS SCHOOL

Admissions Contact: JO MOUND, MBA MARKETING AND RECRUITMENT TEAM
Address: WARWICK BUSINESS SCHOOL, COVENTRY, CV4 7AL ENGLAND
Phone: 011-44-0-24-7652-4100 • *Fax:* 011-44-0-24-7657-4400
E-mail: WARWICKMBA@WBS.AC.UK
Website: WWW.WBS.AC.UK

GENERAL INFORMATION

Type of School: Public **Academic Calendar:** Trimester

STUDENTS

Enrollment of parent institution: 16,000 **Enrollment of MBA program:** 500 **% male/female:** 80/20 **% part-time:** 85 **% minorities:** 50 **% international:** 77 **Average age at entry:** 32 **Average years work experience at entry:** 9

ACADEMICS

Student/faculty ratio: 12:1

FINANCIAL FACTS

Tuition: $46,665 **Books and supplies:** $2,500 Room & board: $11,000 **Average grant:** $230,000

ADMISSIONS

Admissions Selectivity Rating: 87

# of applications received: 300 **% applicants accepted:** 47 % **acceptees attending:** 51 **GMAT Range (25th to 75th percentile):** 550-680 **Average GMAT:** 623 **Average GPA:** 3 **TOEFL required of int'l applicants?** Yes **Minimum TOEFL (paper/computer):** 620/260 **Application Fee:** $132 **International Application Fee:** $132 **Regular Application Deadline:** Rolling **Regular Notification:** Rolling **Deferment Available?** Yes **Maximum length of deferment:** 1 year **Applicants also look at:** Cranfield University, University of Cambridge, University of London, University of Manchester, University of Oxford.

EMPLOYMENT PROFILE

Placement rate (%): 92 **# of companies recruiting on-campus:** 15

UNIVERSITY OF WEST FLORIDA
COLLEGE OF BUSINESS

Admissions Contact: GRADAUTE ADMISSIONS OFFICE, REGISTRAR OFFICER **Address:** 11000 UNIVERSITY PARKWAY, PENSACOLA, FL 32514 **Phone:** 850-474-2230 • **Fax:** 850-474-3360 **E-mail:** ADMISSIONS@UWF.EDU **Website:** WWW.UWF.EDU/MBA

GENERAL INFORMATION

Type of School: Public **Environment:** City

STUDENTS

Enrollment of MBA program: 190 **% male/female:** 54/46 **% part-time:** 85 **% minorities:** 18 **% international:** 42 **Average age at entry:** 30

ACADEMICS

Student/faculty ratio: 25:1

FINANCIAL FACTS

Tuition (in-state/out-of-state): $6,245/$23,537 **Books and supplies:** $650 **Average grant:** $1,000

ADMISSIONS

Admissions Selectivity Rating: 70

# of applications received: 75 **% applicants accepted:** 71 % **acceptees attending:** 94 **GMAT Range (25th to 75th percentile):** 420-535 **Average GMAT:** 473 **Average GPA:** 3.21 **TOEFL required of int'l applicants?** Yes **Minimum TOEFL (paper/computer):** 550/213 **Application Fee:** $30 **Regular Application Deadline:** 6/1 **Regular Notification:** Rolling **Transfer Students Accepted?** Yes **Non-fall Admissions?** Yes

UNIVERSITY OF WEST GEORGIA
RICHARDS COLLEGE OF BUSINESS

Admissions Contact: JOHN R. WELLS, DIRECTOR, MBA PROGRAM **Address:** 1600 MAPLE STREET, CARROLLTON, GA 30118-3000 **Phone:** 678-839-5032 • **Fax:** 678-839-5040 **E-mail:** JWELLS@WESTGA.EDU **Website:** WWW.WESTGA.EDU

GENERAL INFORMATION

Type of School: Public **Environment:** City **Academic Calendar:** Semester

STUDENTS

Enrollment of parent institution: 10,255 **Enrollment of MBA program:** 66 **% male/female:** 55/45 **% out-of-state:** 8 **% part-time:** 53 **% minorities:** 32 **% international:** 39 **Average age at entry:** 27

ACADEMICS

Student/faculty ratio: 20:1 **% female faculty:** 15 **% minority faculty:** 4

FINANCIAL FACTS

Tuition (in-state/out-of-state): $2,106/$8,370 **Fees:** $489 **Books and supplies:** $1,200 **Room & board (on/off campus):** $4,550/$7,000 **% of students receiving aid:** 24 **% of first-year students receiving aid:** 15 **% of students receiving loans:** 4 **% of students receiving grants:** 4 **Average award package:** $7,893 **Average grant:** $500

ADMISSIONS

Admissions Selectivity Rating: 70

# of applications received: 40 **% applicants accepted:** 88 % **acceptees attending:** 74 **GMAT Range (25th to 75th percentile):** 480-610 **Average GMAT:** 541 **Average GPA:** 3.3 **TOEFL required of int'l applicants?** Yes **Minimum TOEFL (paper/computer):** 550/213 **Application Fee:** $20 **International Application Fee:** $20 **Regular Application Deadline:** 8/3 **Regular Notification:** 8/15 **Deferment Available?** Yes **Maximum length of deferment:** 1 year **Transfer Students Accepted?** Yes **Non-fall Admissions?** Yes

EMPLOYMENT PROFILE

Placement rate (%): 98 **# of companies recruiting on-campus:** 52

UNIVERSITY OF WISCONSIN— EAU CLAIRE

SCHOOL OF BUSINESS

Admissions Contact: Ms. JAN STEWART, *MBA PROGRAM ASSISTANT*
Address: 105 GARFIELD AVENUE, EAU CLAIRE, WI 54702-4004
Phone: 715-836-4733 • *Fax:* 715-836-2409
E-mail: ADMISSIONS@UWEC.EDU
Website: WWW.UWEC.EDU/COB/ACADEMICS/MBA/INDEX.HTM

GENERAL INFORMATION

Type of School: Public Environment: Town Academic Calendar: Semester

STUDENTS

Enrollment of parent institution: 10,500 Enrollment of MBA program: 130 % male/female: 55/45 % out-of-state: 10 % part-time: 90 % minorities: 5 % international: 60 Average age at entry: 29 Average years work experience at entry: 8

ACADEMICS

Student/faculty ratio: 5:1 % female faculty: 30 Joint Degrees: Partner in the University of Wisconsin Internet Consortium MBA Program. Students may combine online courses with on campus courses.

FINANCIAL FACTS

Tuition (in-state/out-of-state): $5,380/$16,014 Books and supplies: $1,000 Room & board (on campus): $3,560

ADMISSIONS

Admissions Selectivity Rating: 60*

Average GMAT: 532 Average GPA: 3.2 TOEFL required of int'l applicants? Yes Minimum TOEFL (paper/computer): 550/213 Application Fee: $45 Regular Application Deadline: Rolling Regular Notification: Rolling Deferment Available? Yes Maximum length of deferment: 1 year Transfer Students Accepted? Yes Non-fall Admissions? Yes Need-Blind Admissions? Yes

EMPLOYMENT PROFILE

Placement rate (%): 100 # of companies recruiting on-campus: 200 % grads employed immediately: 100

Grads employed by field: ....%
Accounting 20
Marketing 20
MIS...10
Operations 10
Entrepreneurship 10
General Management 30

UNIVERSITY OF WISCONSIN— LA CROSSE

COLLEGE OF BUSINESS ADMINISTRATION

Admissions Contact: KATHY KIEFER, *DIRECTOR*
Address: 1725 STATE STREET, LA CROSSE, WI 54601
Phone: 608-785-8067 • *Fax:* 608-785-6695
E-mail: ADMISSIONS@UWLAX.EDU
Website: WWW.UWLAX.EDU

GENERAL INFORMATION

Type of School: Public Academic Calendar: Semester

STUDENTS

Enrollment of parent institution: 8,509 Enrollment of MBA program: 51 % male/female: 63/37 % part-time: 73 % minorities: 4 % international: 7 Average age at entry: 29 Average years work experience at entry: 3

ACADEMICS

Student/faculty ratio: 30:1 % female faculty: 28 % minority faculty: 22

FINANCIAL FACTS

Tuition (in-state/out-of-state): $6,150/$17,252 Books and supplies: $500 Room & board: $4,500 % of students receiving aid: 15

ADMISSIONS

Admissions Selectivity Rating: 72

# of applications received: 35 % applicants accepted: 83 % acceptees attending: 62 Average GMAT: 550 Average GPA: 3.4 TOEFL required of int'l applicants? Yes Minimum TOEFL (paper): 550 Application Fee: $48 Regular Application Deadline: Rolling Regular Notification: Rolling Deferment Available? Yes Maximum length of deferment: Rolling Transfer Students Accepted? Yes Non-fall Admissions? Yes Need-Blind Admissions? Yes

EMPLOYMENT PROFILE

% grads employed immediately: 98

UNIVERSITY OF WISCONSIN— MILWAUKEE

SCHOOL OF BUSINESS ADMINISTRATION

Admissions Contact: SARAH M. SANDIN, *MBA/MS PROGRAM MANAGER*
Address: PO BOX 742, MILWAUKEE, WI 53201-0742
Phone: 414-229-5403 • *Fax:* 414-229-2372
E-mail: UWMBUSMASTERS@UWM.EDU
Website: WWW.UWM.EDU/BUSINESS

GENERAL INFORMATION

Type of School: Public Environment: City Academic Calendar: Semester

STUDENTS

Enrollment of parent institution: 26,084 **Enrollment of MBA program:** 314 **% male/female:** 65/35 **% out-of-state:** 14 **% part-time:** 76 **% minorities:** 13 **% international:** 14 **Average age at entry:** 27 **Average years work experience at entry:** 3

ACADEMICS

Student/faculty ratio: 10:1 **% female faculty:** 27 **% minority faculty:** 4 **Joint Degrees:** Master of human resources and labor relations—2-7 years; master of public administration, non-profit management—2-7 years; MBA/MS nursing—3-7 years. **Prominent Alumni:** Robert Probst, Exec VP, Tamarack Petroleum Co.; Mary Ellen Stanek, Managing Director, Robert Baird & Co; Roger Fitzsimonds, Retired Chairman & CEO, Firstar Corporation; Keith Nosbusch, CEO, Rockwell Automation; Craig Kasten, Chairman & Co-Founder, Doral Dental.

FINANCIAL FACTS

Tuition (in-state/out-of-state): $9,525/$23,961 **Books and supplies:** $800 **Room & board (on/off campus):** $6,500/$6,000 **% of students receiving aid:** 25 **% of first-year students receiving aid:** 47 **% of students receiving loans:** 25 **Average award package:** $11,747 **Average grant:** $4,662

ADMISSIONS

Admissions Selectivity Rating: 74

# of applications received: 197 **% applicants accepted:** 63 **% acceptees attending:** 58 **GMAT Range (25th to 75th percentile):** 470-570 **Average GMAT:** 526 **Average GPA:** 3.14 **TOEFL required of int'l applicants?** Yes **Minimum TOEFL (paper/computer):** 550/213 **Application Fee:** $45 **International Application Fee:** $75 **Regular Application Deadline:** Rolling **Regular Notification:** Rolling **Deferment Available?** Yes **Maximum length of deferment:** 1 year **Transfer Students Accepted?** Yes **Non-fall Admissions?** Yes **Need-Blind Admissions?** Yes **Applicants also look at:** Marquette University, University of Wisconsin—Madison, University of Wisconsin—Whitewater.

EMPLOYMENT PROFILE

Placement rate (%): 85 **# of companies recruiting on-campus:** 80 **% grads employed immediately:** 30 **Average starting salary:** $65,069

Grads employed by field:% avg. salary:

	%	avg. salary
Accounting	20	$77,200
Finance	20	$48,500
Human Resources	2	$54,875
Marketing	13	$79,000
MIS	26	$67,000
Operations	12	$57,500
Strategic Planning	2	$50,000
Consulting	2	$50,000
General Management	3	$54,250

UNIVERSITY OF WISCONSIN— OSHKOSH

COLLEGE OF BUSINESS ADMINSTRATION

Admissions Contact: LYNN GRANCORBITZ, MBA PROGRAM ASSISTANT DIRECTOR AND ADVISOR
Address: 800 ALGOMA BLVD., OSHKOSH, WI 54901
Phone: 800-633-1430 • **Fax:** 920-424-7413
E-mail: MBA@UWOSH.EDU
Website: WWW.UWOSH.EDU/COLLEGES/COBA/ASSETS/GRAD/INDEX.PHP

GENERAL INFORMATION

Type of School: Public **Environment:** Village **Academic Calendar:** Semester

STUDENTS

Enrollment of parent institution: 10,528 **Enrollment of MBA program:** 525 **% male/female:** 40/60 **% out-of-state:** 99 **% part-time:** 95 **% minorities:** 2 **% international:** 3

ACADEMICS

Student/faculty ratio: 11:1

FINANCIAL FACTS

Tuition (in-state/out-of-state): $4,664/$13,622

ADMISSIONS

Admissions Selectivity Rating: 60*

# of applications received: 220 **% applicants accepted:** 91 **% acceptees attending:** 50 **TOEFL required of int'l applicants?** Yes **Minimum TOEFL (paper):** 550 **Application Fee:** $45 **International Application Fee:** Regular **Application Deadline:** 7/1 **Regular Notification:** Rolling **Deferment Available?** Yes **Non-fall Admissions?** Yes **Applicants also look at:** Rensselaer Polytechnic Institute, St. John's University, University of California—Berkeley, University of California—Los Angeles, University of Chicago.

EMPLOYMENT PROFILE

Placement rate (%): 98 **% grads employed immediately:** 98

UNIVERSITY OF WISCONSIN— PARKSIDE

SCHOOL OF BUSINESS AND TECHNOLOGY

Admissions Contact: BRAD PIAZZA, ASSISTANT DEAN
Address: 900 WOOD ROAD, BOX 2000, KENOSHA, WI 53141-2000
Phone: 262-595-2046 • *Fax:* 262-595-2680
E-mail: PIAZZA@UWP.EDU
Website: WWW.UWP.EDU/DEPARTMENTS/BUSINESS

GENERAL INFORMATION

Type of School: Public Environment: City Academic Calendar:
Semester

STUDENTS

Enrollment of parent institution: 5,000 Enrollment of MBA program: 83 % part-time: 90 % international: 1 Average age at entry: 33 Average years work experience at entry: 3

ACADEMICS

Student/faculty ratio: 6:1 % female faculty: 35 % minority faculty: 30

FINANCIAL FACTS

Tuition (in-state/out-of-state): $5,994/$16,604 Fees: $277 Books and supplies: $300

ADMISSIONS

Admissions Selectivity Rating: 61

# of applications received: 28 % applicants accepted: 96 % acceptees attending: 89 GMAT Range (25th to 75th percentile): 330-680 Average GMAT: 460 Average GPA: 3.0 TOEFL required of int'l applicants? Yes Minimum TOEFL (paper/computer): 550/213 Application Fee: $45 International Application Fee: $45 Regular Application Deadline: 8/1 Regular Notification: Rolling Deferment Available? Yes Maximum length of deferment: 1 year Transfer Students Accepted? Yes Non-fall Admissions? Yes Need-Blind Admissions? Yes

UNIVERSITY OF WYOMING

COLLEGE OF BUSINESS

Admissions Contact: TERRI L. RITTENBURG, DIRECTOR OF MBA PROGRAM
Address: PO BOX 3275, LARAMIE, WY 82071
Phone: 307-766-2449 • *Fax:* 307-766-4028
E-mail: MBA@UWYO.EDU
Website: BUSINESS.UWYO.EDU/MBA

GENERAL INFORMATION

Type of School: Public Environment: Town Academic Calendar:
Semester

STUDENTS

Enrollment of parent institution: 11,904 Enrollment of MBA program: 63 % male/female: 64/36 % part-time: 48 % international: 18 Average age at entry: 28

ACADEMICS

Student/faculty ratio: 3:1

FINANCIAL FACTS

Tuition (in-state/out-of-state): $2,988/$8,676 Fees: $246 Books and supplies: $300 Room & board: $6,212 % of students receiving loans: 34

ADMISSIONS

Admissions Selectivity Rating: 60*

Average GMAT: 558 Average GPA: 3.2 TOEFL required of int'l applicants? Yes Minimum TOEFL (paper/computer): 525/197 Application Fee: $40 Regular Application Deadline: 2/1 Regular Notification: Rolling Deferment Available? Yes Maximum length of deferment: 1 year Transfer Students Accepted? Yes Non-fall Admissions? Need-Blind Admissions? Yes

EMPLOYMENT PROFILE

Placement rate (%): 98 # of companies recruiting on-campus: 20 % grads employed immediately: 56 % grads employed within three months: 80 Average starting salary: $38,878

UTAH STATE UNIVERSITY

COLLEGE OF BUSINESS

Admissions Contact: SCHOOL OF GRADUATE STUDIES, ADMISSIONS OFFICER
Address: 0900 OLD MAIN HILL, LOGAN, UT 84322-0900
Phone: 435-797-1189 • *Fax:* 435-797-1192
E-mail: GRADSCH@CC.USU.EDU
Website: WWW.USU.EDU/COB

GENERAL INFORMATION

Type of School: Public Environment: Town Academic Calendar:
Semester

STUDENTS

Enrollment of parent institution: 23,908 Enrollment of MBA program: 197 % male/female: 82/18 % out-of-state: 2 % part-time: 71 % minorities: 1 % international: 3 Average age at entry: 32 Average years work experience at entry: 10

ACADEMICS

Student/faculty ratio: 30:1 % female faculty: 19 % minority faculty: 7 Joint Degrees: International MBA in food and agribusiness (1.5 years). Prominent Alumni: Ron Labrum, Pres & CEO Cardinal Health; Annette Herman, CEO United Healthcare Utah; Kay Toolson, CEO Monaco Coach; Mark James, VP Human Res Honeywell; Michael Kraupp, VP Finance SkyWest Airlines.

Virginia Commonwealth University
School of Business

Admissions Contact: Jana P. McQuaid, Interim Director, Graduate Studies in Business
Address: 1015 Floyd Avenue, PO Box 844000, Richmond, VA 23284-4000
Phone: 804-828-4622 • *Fax:* 804-828-7174
E-mail: GSIB@VCU.EDU
Website: WWW.GSIB.BUS.VCU.EDU

GENERAL INFORMATION

Type of School: Public **Environment:** Metropolis **Academic Calendar:** Semester

STUDENTS

Enrollment of MBA program: 226 **% male/female:** 64/36 **% out-of-state:** 9 **% part-time:** 76 **% minorities:** 13 **% international:** 4 **Average age at entry:** 28 **Average years work experience at entry:** 4.5

ACADEMICS

Student/faculty ratio: 20:1 **% female faculty:** 15 **% minority faculty:** 5 **Joint Degrees:** 5 year BS / master of accountancy (for entering undergraduate students) BS engineering/MBA; PharmD/MBA; MBA/MSIS.

FINANCIAL FACTS

Tuition (in-state/out-of-state): $6,066/$15,904 **Fees (in-state/out-of-state):** $1,324/$1,363 **Books and supplies:** $800 **Average grant:** $8,375 **Average student loan debt:** $9,800

ADMISSIONS

Admissions Selectivity Rating: 75

# of applications received: 290 **% applicants accepted:** 68 **% acceptees attending:** 62 **GMAT Range (25th to 75th percentile):** 460-610 **Average GMAT:** 539 **Average GPA:** 3.1 **TOEFL required of int'l applicants?** Yes **Minimum TOEFL (paper/computer):** 600/250 **Application Fee:** $50 **International Application Fee:** $50 **Regular Application Deadline:** 6/1 **Regular Notification:** 7/1

Early decision program? Yes **ED deadline /notification:** 4/1 / 5/1 **Deferment Available?** Yes **Maximum length of deferment:** 1 year **Transfer Students Accepted?** Yes **Non-fall Admissions?** Yes **Need-Blind Admissions?** Yes **Applicants also look at:** College of William & Mary, James Madison University, University of Richmond.

Wake Forest University— Evening MBA—Charlotte
Babcock Graduate School of Management

Admissions Contact: Leslye Gervasi, Director, MBA Programs-Charlotte
Address: One Morrocroft Center, 6805 Morrison Blvd.-Suite 150, Charlotte, NC 28211
Phone: 704-365-1717 • *Fax:* 704-365-3511
E-mail: CLT.MBA@MBA.WFU.EDU
Website: WWW.MBA.WFU.EDU

GENERAL INFORMATION

Type of School: Private **Academic Calendar:** Semester

STUDENTS

Enrollment of parent institution: 6,444 **Enrollment of MBA program:** 556 **% male/female:** 71/29 **% out-of-state:** 75 **% part-time:** 61 **% minorities:** 13 **% international:** 23 **Average age at entry:** 32 **Average years work experience at entry:** 9

ACADEMICS

Student/faculty ratio: 10:1 **% female faculty:** 13 **% minority faculty:** 13 **Joint Degrees:** JD/MBA (law/MBA), 4 years; MD/MBA (medicine/MBA), 5 years; PhD/MBA (graduate school of arts & sciences/MBA), 5 years; MSA/MBA (master of science in accountancy/MBA), 6 years.

FINANCIAL FACTS

Tuition: $27,000 **% of students receiving aid:** 74 **% of first-year students receiving aid:** 80 **% of students receiving loans:** 70 **Average award package:** $22,680 **Average grant:** $12,250 **Average student loan debt:** $39,277

ADMISSIONS

Admissions Selectivity Rating: 60*

# of applications received: 63 **% applicants accepted:** 79 **% acceptees attending:** 100 **TOEFL required of int'l applicants?** **Application Fee:** $75 **International Application Fee:** $75 **Regular Application Deadline:** Rolling **Regular Notification:** Rolling **Deferment Available?** Yes **Maximum length of deferment:** 1 year **Need-Blind Admissions?** Yes

WAKE FOREST UNIVERSITY— EVENING MBA— WINSTON-SALEM

BABCOCK GRADUATE SCHOOL OF MANAGEMENT

Admissions Contact: JAMIE BARNES, DIRECTOR, EVENING & FAST-TRACK EXECUTIVE PROGRAMS
Address: PO BOX 7368, WINSTON-SALEM, NC 27109-7368
Phone: 336-758-5422 • **Fax:** 336-758-5830
E-mail: ADMISSIONS@MBA.WFU.EDU
Website: WWW.MBA.WFU.EDU

GENERAL INFORMATION

Type of School: Private **Academic Calendar:** Semester

STUDENTS

Enrollment of parent institution: 6,444 **Enrollment of MBA program:** 556 **% male/female:** 71/29 **% out-of-state:** 75 **% part-time:** 61 **% minorities:** 13 **% international:** 23 **Average age at entry:** 32 **Average years work experience at entry:** 9

ACADEMICS

Student/faculty ratio: 10:1 **% female faculty:** 13 **% minority faculty:** 13 **Joint Degrees:** JD/MBA (law/MBA), 4 years; MD/MBA (medicine/MBA), 5 years; PhD/MBA (Graduate School of Arts & Sciences/MBA), 5 years; and MSA/MBA (master of science in accountancy/MBA), 6 years.

FINANCIAL FACTS

Tuition: $27,000 **% of students receiving aid:** 75 **% of first-year students receiving aid:** 77 **% of students receiving loans:** 69 **% of students receiving grants:** 11 **Average award package:** $21,811 **Average grant:** $10,058 **Average student loan debt:** $39,882

ADMISSIONS

Admissions Selectivity Rating: 60*

# of applications received: 63 **% applicants accepted:** 83 **Application Fee:** $75

International Application Fee: $75 **Regular Application Deadline:** Rolling **Regular Notification:** Rolling **Deferment Available?** Yes **Maximum length of deferment:** 1 year **Non-fall Admissions?** **Need-Blind Admissions?** Yes **Applicants also look at:** Duke University, University of North Carolina at Chapel Hill, University of North Carolina at Greensboro.

WAKE FOREST UNIVERSITY— FAST-TRACK EXECUTIVE

BABCOCK GRADUATE SCHOOL OF MANAGEMENT

Admissions Contact: JAMIE BARNES, DIRECTOR, EVENING & FAST-TRACK EXECUTIVE PROGRAMS
Address: PO BOX 7368, WINSTON-SALEM, NC 27109-7368
Phone: 336-758-5422 • **Fax:** 336-758-5830
E-mail: ADMISSIONS@MBA.WFU.EDU
Website: WWW.MBA.WFU.EDU

GENERAL INFORMATION

Type of School: Private **Academic Calendar:** Semester

STUDENTS

Enrollment of parent institution: 6,444 **Enrollment of MBA program:** 556 **% male/female:** 71/29 **% out-of-state:** 75 **% part-time:** 61 **% minorities:** 13 **% international:** 23 **Average age at entry:** 36 **Average years work experience at entry:** 14

ACADEMICS

Student/faculty ratio: 10:1 **% female faculty:** 13 **% minority faculty:** 13 **Joint Degrees:** JD/MBA (law/MBA), 4 years; MD/MBA (medicine/MBA), 5 years; PhD/MBA (Graduate School of Arts & Sciences/MBA), 5 years; and MSA/MBA (master of science in accountancy/MBA), 6 years.

FINANCIAL FACTS

Tuition: $44,625 **% of students receiving aid:** 45 **% of first-year students receiving aid:** 56 **% of students receiving loans:** 44 **% of students receiving grants:** 13 **Average award package:** $24,228 **Average grant:** $10,834 **Average student loan debt:** $40,875

ADMISSIONS

Admissions Selectivity Rating: 60*

# of applications received: 66 **% applicants accepted:** 68 **% acceptees attending:** 100 **Application Fee:** $75 **International Application Fee:** $75 **Regular Application Deadline:** Rolling **Regular Notification:** Rolling **Deferment Available?** Yes **Maximum length of deferment:** 1 year **Need-Blind Admissions?** Yes **Applicants also look at:** Duke University, University of North Carolina at Chapel Hill, University of North Carolina at Greensboro.

WAKE FOREST UNIVERSITY— SATURDAY MBA—CHARLOTTE
BABCOCK GRADUATE SCHOOL OF MANAGEMENT

Admissions Contact: LESLYE GERVASI, DIRECTOR, MBA PROGRAMS—CHARLOTTE
Address: ONE MORROCROFT CENTRE, 6805 MORRISON BLVD., SUITE 150, CHARLOTTE, NC 28211
Phone: 704-365-1717 • *Fax:* 704-365-3511
E-mail: CLT.MBA@MBA.WFU.EDU
Website: WWW.MBA.WFU.EDU

GENERAL INFORMATION
Type of School: Private **Academic Calendar:** Semester

STUDENTS
Enrollment of parent institution: 6,444 **Enrollment of MBA program:** 556 **% male/female:** 71/29 **% out-of-state:** 75 **% part-time:** 61 **% minorities:** 13 **% international:** 23 **Average age at entry:** 29 **Average years work experience at entry:** 7

ACADEMICS
Student/faculty ratio: 10:1 **% female faculty:** 13 **% minority faculty:** 13 **Joint Degrees:** JD/MBA (law/MBA), 4 years; MD/MBA (medicine/MBA), 5 years; PhD/MBA (Graduate School of Arts & Sciences/MBA), 5 years; and MSA/MBA (master of science in accountancy/MBA), 6 years.

FINANCIAL FACTS
Tuition: $27,000 **% of students receiving aid:** 79 **% of first-year students receiving aid:** 83 **% of students receiving loans:** 79 **Average award package:** $18,614

ADMISSIONS
Admissions Selectivity Rating: 60*
# of applications received: 45 **% applicants accepted:** 98 **% acceptees attending:** 84 **Application Fee:** $75 **International Application Fee:** $75 **Regular Application Deadline:** Rolling **Regular Notification:** Rolling **Deferment Available?** Yes **Maximum length of deferment:** 1 year **Non-fall Admissions?** Yes **Need-Blind Admissions?** Yes

WASHINGTON STATE UNIVERSITY
COLLEGE OF BUSINESS AND ECONOMICS

Admissions Contact: CHERYL OLIVER, MBA@WSU.EDU
Address: PO BOX 644744, PULLMAN, WA 99164-4744
Phone: 509-335-7617 • *Fax:* 509-335-4735
E-mail: MBA@WSU.EDU
Website: WWW.CBE.WSU.EDU/GRADUATE

GENERAL INFORMATION
Type of School: Public **Environment:** Village

STUDENTS
Enrollment of parent institution: 18,000 **Enrollment of MBA program:** 82 **% male/female:** 70/30 **% part-time:** 82 **% minorities:** 1

ACADEMICS
Student/faculty ratio: 40:1

FINANCIAL FACTS
Tuition (in-state/out-of-state): $10,000/$19,000 **Fees:** $600 **Books and supplies:** $1,080 **Room & board:** $8,720 **Average grant:** $4,000

ADMISSIONS
Admissions Selectivity Rating: 93
# of applications received: 148 **% applicants accepted:** 29 **% acceptees attending:** 74 **Average GMAT:** 590 **Average GPA:** 3.38 **TOEFL required of int'l applicants?** Yes **Minimum TOEFL (paper/computer):** 580/237 **Application Fee:** $35 **Regular Application Deadline:** 3/1 **Regular Notification:** 4/1 **Need-Blind Admissions?** Yes

WAYNE STATE UNIVERSITY
SCHOOL OF BUSINESS ADMINISTRATION

Admissions Contact: LINDA S. ZADDACH, ASSISTANT DEAN OF STUDENT AFFAIRS
Address: OFFICE OF STUDENT SERVICES, 5201 CASS, ROOM 200, DETROIT, MI 48202
Phone: 313-577-4505 • *Fax:* 313-577-5299
E-mail: L.S.ZADDACH@WAYNE.EDU
Website: WWW.BUSADM.WAYNE.EDU

GENERAL INFORMATION
Type of School: Public **Environment:** Metropolis **Academic Calendar:** Semester

STUDENTS
Enrollment of parent institution: 33,314 **Enrollment of MBA program:** 1,288 **% male/female:** 58/42 **% part-time:** 90 **Average age at entry:** 28

ACADEMICS
Student/faculty ratio: 35:1 **% female faculty:** 5 **% minority faculty:** 5

FINANCIAL FACTS
Tuition (in-state/out-of-state): $6,120/$12,330 **Fees:** $760 **Books and supplies:** $700 **Average grant:** $5,373

ADMISSIONS
Admissions Selectivity Rating: 70
# of applications received: 421 **% applicants accepted:** 71 **% acceptees attending:** 68 **Average GMAT:** 500 **Average GPA:** 3.09 **TOEFL required of int'l applicants?** Yes **Minimum TOEFL (paper/computer):** 550/213 **Application Fee:** $50 **International Application Fee:** $50 **Regular Application Deadline:** 8/1 **Regular Notification:** Rolling **Transfer Students Accepted?** Yes **Non-fall Admissions?** Yes

EMPLOYMENT PROFILE

Placement rate (%): 95 **Average starting salary:** $70,000

WEBER STATE UNIVERSITY
JOHN B. GODDARD SCHOOL OF BUSINESS AND ECONOMICS

Admissions Contact: DR. MARK A. STEVENSON, MBA ENROLLMENT DIRECTOR
Address: 3806 UNIVERSITY CIRCLE, OGDEN, UT 84408-3806
Phone: 801-626-7545 • **Fax:** 801-626-7423
E-mail: MBA@WEBER.EDU
Website: GODDARD.WEBER.EDU/DP/MBA

GENERAL INFORMATION

Type of School: Public **Environment:** Village

STUDENTS

Enrollment of parent institution: 16,800 **Enrollment of MBA program:** 75 **% male/female:** 68/32 **% minorities:** 4 **% international:** 9 **Average age at entry:** 31 **Average years work experience at entry:** 5

ACADEMICS

Student/faculty ratio: 5:1 **% female faculty:** 38

FINANCIAL FACTS

Tuition (in-state/out-of-state): $6,000/$13,000 **Books and supplies:** $2,000 **Average grant:** $3,145

ADMISSIONS

Admissions Selectivity Rating: 79

# of applications received: 63 **% applicants accepted:** 75 **% acceptees attending:** 94 **GMAT Range (25th to 75th percentile):** 530-620 **Average GMAT:** 571 **Average GPA:** 3.4 **TOEFL required of int'l applicants?** Yes **Minimum TOEFL (paper/computer):** 550/213 **Application Fee:** $30 **International Application Fee:** $30 **Regular Application Deadline:** 6/1 **Regular Notification:** Rolling **Deferment Available?** Yes **Maximum length of deferment:** 1 year **Transfer Students Accepted?** Yes **Non-fall Admissions?** Yes **Need-Blind Admissions?** Yes **Applicants also look at:** University of Utah, Utah State University.

EMPLOYMENT PROFILE

Placement rate (%): 9 **# of companies recruiting on-campus:** 326

WESTERN CAROLINA UNIVERSITY
COLLEGE OF BUSINESS

Admissions Contact: PHILIP LITTLE, DIRECTOR OF MBA PROGRAM
Address: 104 FORSYTH BUILDING, 112 FORSYTH BUILDING, CULLOWHEE, NC 28723
Phone: 828-227-3588 • **Fax:** 828-227-7414
E-mail: FDEITZ@EMAIL.WCU.EDU
Website: WWW.WCU.EDU/COB/MBA/

GENERAL INFORMATION

Type of School: Public **Environment:** Rural **Academic Calendar:** Semester

STUDENTS

Enrollment of parent institution: 8,396 **Enrollment of MBA program:** 132 **% male/female:** 62/38 **% part-time:** 59 **% minorities:** 13 **% international:** 33 **Average age at entry:** 29 **Average years work experience at entry:** 7

ACADEMICS

Student/faculty ratio: 3:1 **% female faculty:** 26 **% minority faculty:** 5

FINANCIAL FACTS

Tuition (in-state/out-of-state): $1,723/$11,308 **Fees:** $1,622 **Books and supplies:** $3,000 **Room & board:** $6,800 **% of students receiving aid:** 83 **% of first-year students receiving aid:** 52 **% of students receiving loans:** 40 **% of students receiving grants:** 38 **Average award package:** $11,136 **Average grant:** $4,350 **Average student loan debt:** $23,614

ADMISSIONS

Admissions Selectivity Rating: 61

# of applications received: 63 **% applicants accepted:** 94 **% acceptees attending:** 49 **GMAT Range (25th to 75th percentile):** 440–570 **Average GMAT:** 495 **Average GPA:** 3.02 **TOEFL required of int'l applicants?** Yes **Minimum TOEFL (paper/computer):** 550/213 **Application Fee:** $40 **International Application Fee:** $40 **Regular Application Deadline:** Rolling **Regular Notification:** Rolling **Deferment Available?** Yes **Maximum length of deferment:** 1 year **Transfer Students Accepted?** Yes **Non-fall Admissions?** Yes **Need-Blind Admissions?** Yes **Applicants also look at:** Appalachian State University, University of North Carolina at Charlotte.

WESTERN ILLINOIS UNIVERSITY
COLLEGE OF BUSINESS AND TECHNOLOGY

Admissions Contact: DIRECTOR OF MBA PROGRAM
Address: 1 UNIVERSITY CIRCLE, 115 SHERMAN HALL, MACOMB, IL 61455
Phone: 309-298-3157 • **Fax:** 309-298-3111
E-mail: ADMISSIONS@WIU.EDU
Website: WWW.WIU.EDU/USERS/MICOBTD/

GENERAL INFORMATION
Type of School: Public **Environment:** Village **Academic Calendar:** Semester

STUDENTS
Enrollment of parent institution: 132 **Enrollment of MBA program:** 132 **% male/female:** 58/42 **% out-of-state:** 1 **% part-time:** 37 **% minorities:** 1 **% international:** 15 **Average age at entry:** 24

FINANCIAL FACTS
Tuition (in-state/out-of-state): $4,608/$7,974 **% of students receiving aid:** 34

ADMISSIONS
Admissions Selectivity Rating: 60*
# of applications received: 250 **% applicants accepted:** 50 **% acceptees attending:** 60 **TOEFL required of int'l applicants?** Yes **Minimum TOEFL (paper):** 550 **Regular Application Deadline:** Rolling **Regular Notification:** Rolling **Deferment Available?** Yes **Maximum length of deferment:** 1 **Transfer Students Accepted?** **Non-fall Admissions?** Yes

WESTERN MICHIGAN UNIVERSITY
HAWORTH COLLEGE OF BUSINESS

Admissions Contact: HAL BATES, HCOB ACADEMIC ADVISING AND ADMISSIONS
Address: 2240 SEIBERT ADMINISTRATION BUILDING, KALAMAZOO, MI 49008-5211
Phone: 269-387-5075 • **Fax:** 269-387-5710
E-mail: ASK-WMU@WMICH.EDU
Website: WWW.HCOB.WMICH.EDU

GENERAL INFORMATION
Type of School: Public **Environment:** City **Academic Calendar:** Semester

STUDENTS
Enrollment of parent institution: 27,829 **Enrollment of MBA program:** 366 **% male/female:** 69/31 **% out-of-state:** 2 **% part-time:** 48 **% minorities:** 6 **% international:** 35 **Average age at entry:** 28

ACADEMICS
% female faculty: 28 **% minority faculty:** 22

FINANCIAL FACTS
Tuition (in-state/out-of-state): $6,981/$14,978 **Fees:** $602 **Books and supplies:**
$5,356 **Room & board (on/off campus):** $6,496/$6,824 **Average grant:** $5,376

ADMISSIONS
Admissions Selectivity Rating: 71
# of applications received: 144 **% applicants accepted:** 74 **% acceptees attending:** 39 **Average GMAT:** 550 **Average GPA:** 3.0 **TOEFL required of int'l applicants?** Yes **Minimum TOEFL (paper):** 550 **Application Fee:** $35 **International Application Fee:** $55 **Regular Application Deadline:** 7/1 **Regular Notification:** 8/1 **Deferment Available?** Yes **Maximum length of deferment:** 1 Semester **Non-fall Admissions?** Yes

WESTERN WASHINGTON UNIVERSITY
COLLEGE OF BUSINESS AND ECONOMICS

Admissions Contact: CARRIE J. THURMAN, PROGRAM COORDINATOR
Address: 516 HIGH STREET, PARKS HALL 419, BELLINGHAM, WA 98225-9072
Phone: 360-650-3898 • **Fax:** 360-650-4844
E-mail: MBA@WWU.EDU
Website: WWW.CBE.WWU.EDU/MBA

GENERAL INFORMATION
Type of School: Public **Environment:** Town

STUDENTS
Enrollment of parent institution: 12,500 **Enrollment of MBA program:** 84 **% male/female:** 60/40 **% part-time:** 27 **% minorities:** 8 **Average age at entry:** 30 **Average years work experience at entry:** 7

ACADEMICS
% female faculty: 17

FINANCIAL FACTS
Tuition (in-state/out-of-state): $5,694/$16,221 **Fees:** $543 **Books and supplies:** $1,500

ADMISSIONS
Admissions Selectivity Rating: 75
# of applications received: 126 **% applicants accepted:** 71 **% acceptees attending:** 48 **Average GMAT:** 555 **Average GPA:** 3.3 **TOEFL required of int'l applicants?** Yes **Minimum TOEFL (paper/computer):** 567/227 **Application Fee:** $35 **Regular Application Deadline:** 5/1 **Regular Notification:** 6/1 **Non-fall Admissions?** Yes

WIDENER UNIVERSITY
SCHOOL OF BUSINESS ADMINISTRATION

Admissions Contact: LISA BUSSOM, ASSISTANT DEAN
Address: 1 UNIVERSITY PLACE, CHESTER, PA 19013
Phone: 610-499-4305 • *Fax:* 610-499-4615
E-mail: SBAGRADV@MAIL.WIDENER.EDU
Website: WWW.WIDENER.EDU/SBA

GENERAL INFORMATION
Type of School: Private **Environment:** Town **Academic Calendar:** Semester

STUDENTS
Enrollment of parent institution: 6,265 **Enrollment of MBA program:** 143 **% male/female:** 34/66 **% part-time:** 80 **% minorities:** 24 **Average age at entry:** 30 **Average years work experience at entry:** 7.5

ACADEMICS
Student/faculty ratio: 6:1 **% female faculty:** 33 **% minority faculty:** 2 **Joint Degrees:** MBA/juris doctor (3 years full-time, 4 years part-time), MBA/master of engineering (2 years full-time, 5 years part-time), MBA/doctor of clinical psychology (5 years full-time), MBA in health and medical services administration/doctor of clinical psychology. **Prominent Alumni:** Leslie C. Quick, founder, Quick & Reilly; H. Edward Hanway, CEO, Cigna Corp.; Paul Biederman, Chairman, Mellon Mid-Atlantic; Tiffany Tomasso, VP Sunrise Assisted Living.

FINANCIAL FACTS
Tuition: $11,780 **Fees:** $120 **Books and supplies:** $750 **Room & board (on/off campus):** $8,100/$7,650 **% of students receiving aid:** 31 **% of first-year students receiving aid:** 9 **% of students receiving loans:** 30 **% of students receiving grants:** 5 **Average award package:** $14,750 **Average grant:** $7,074 **Average student loan debt:** $22,510

ADMISSIONS
Admissions Selectivity Rating: 73

# of applications received: 125 **% applicants accepted:** 65 **% acceptees attending:** 75 **GMAT Range (25th to 75th percentile):** 440-530 **Average GMAT:** 488 **Average GPA:** 3.24 **TOEFL required of int'l applicants?** Yes **Minimum TOEFL (paper/computer):** 550/213 **Application Fee:** $25 **International Application Fee:** Regular **Application Deadline:** 8/1 **Regular Notification:** Rolling **Deferment Available?** Yes **Maximum length of deferment:** 1 year **Transfer Students Accepted?** Yes **Non-fall Admissions?** Yes **Need-Blind Admissions?** Yes **Applicants also look at:** Drexel University, La Salle University, Penn State University—Great Valley Campus, Saint Joseph's University, Temple University, University of Delaware, Villanova University.

WILFRID LAURIER UNIVERSITY (CANADA)
WILFRID LAURIER UNIVERSITY

Admissions Contact: SUSAN MANNING FABER, MBA MARKETING COORDINATOR
Address: 75 UNIVERSITY AVENUE WEST, WATERLOO, ON N2L3C5 CANADA
Phone: 519-884-1970 • *Fax:* 519-886-6978
E-mail: WLUMBA@WLU.CA
Website: WWW.WLU.CA/MBA

GENERAL INFORMATION
Type of School: Public

STUDENTS
% male/female: 89/11 **% international:** 2 **Average age at entry:** 30 **Average years work experience at entry:** 7

FINANCIAL FACTS
Tuition: $20,000 **Books and supplies:** $7,000

ADMISSIONS
Admissions Selectivity Rating: 80

# of applications received: 474 **% applicants accepted:** 69 **% acceptees attending:** 65 **Average GMAT:** 592 **Average GPA:** 3.3 **TOEFL required of int'l applicants?** Yes **Minimum TOEFL (paper/computer):** 550/213 **Application Fee:** $100 **International Application Fee:** $100 **Regular Application Deadline:** Regular **Notification:** Deferment Available? Yes **Maximum length of deferment:** 1 year, case by case **Transfer Students Accepted?** Yes **Non-fall Admissions?** Yes **Need-Blind Admissions?** Yes

EMPLOYMENT PROFILE
Placement rate (%): 100 **# of companies recruiting on-campus:** 300 **Average starting salary:** $80,000

WINTHROP UNIVERSITY
COLLEGE OF BUSINESS ADMINISTRATION

Admissions Contact: DIRECTOR OF GRADUATE STUDIES
Address: 209 TILLMAN HALL, ROCK HILL, SC 29733
Phone: 803-323-2204 • *Fax:* 803-323-2292
E-mail: GRADUATESTUDIES@WINTHROP.EDU
Website: CBA.WINTHROP.EDU

GENERAL INFORMATION
Type of School: Public **Environment:** Town **Academic Calendar:** Semester

STUDENTS
Enrollment of parent institution: 5,304 **Enrollment of MBA program:** 250 **% male/female:** 100/0 **% part-time:** 60 **Average age at entry:** 34

FINANCIAL FACTS

Tuition (in-state/out-of-state): $2,370/$4,360

ADMISSIONS

Admissions Selectivity Rating: 60*

TOEFL required of int'l applicants? Yes **Minimum TOEFL (paper):**
550 **Application Fee:** $35 **Regular Application Deadline:** 7/15
Regular Notification: Rolling **Deferment Available?** Yes **Non-fall
Admissions?** Yes

WRIGHT STATE UNIVERSITY
RAJ SOIN COLLEGE OF BUSINESS

Admissions Contact: MICHAEL EVANS, DIRECTOR, MBA PROGRAMS
Address: 110 RIKE HALL, DAYTON, OH 45435-0001
Phone: 937-775-2437 • *Fax:* 937-775-3545
E-mail: MBA_DIRECTOR@WRIGHT.EDU
Website: WWW.WRIGHT.EDU/BUSINESS

GENERAL INFORMATION

Type of School: Public **Environment:** City **Academic Calendar:**
Quarter

STUDENTS

Enrollment of MBA program: 470 **% male/female:** 57/43 **% part-
time:** 32 **Average age at entry:** 31 **Average years work experience
at entry:** 5

ACADEMICS

Student/faculty ratio: 8:1 **% female faculty:** 24 **Joint Degrees:**
MBA/MS Nursing (2 - 5 years); MBA/MS S/A economics (2-5 years).

FINANCIAL FACTS

Tuition (in-state/out-of-state): $10,500/$17,796 **Books and supplies:** $1,300

ADMISSIONS

Admissions Selectivity Rating: 69

# of applications received: 416 **% applicants accepted:** 84 **%
acceptees attending:** 67 **Average GMAT:** 525 **Average GPA:** 3.1
TOEFL required of int'l applicants? Yes **Minimum TOEFL
(paper/computer):** 550/213 **Application Fee:** $25 **Regular
Application Deadline:** 8/1 **Regular Notification:** 8/2 **Deferment
Available?** Yes **Maximum length of deferment:** 4 Quarters **Transfer
Students Accepted?** Yes **Non-fall Admissions?** Yes **Need-Blind
Admissions?** Yes

SCHOOL SAYS

In this section you'll find schools with extended listings describing admissions, curriculum, internships, and much more. This is your chance to get in-depth information on programs that interest you. The Princeton Review charges each school a small fee to be listed, and the editorial responsibility is solely that of the university.

AUBURN UNIVERSITY

AT A GLANCE
What's in it for you? Education, knowledge, and an MBA degree second to none; financial aid and scholarships; location, academic reputation, and opportunities for networking with career advancement—all combine to present a well-earned reputation of quality, opportunity, and results!

CAMPUS AND LOCATION
Auburn University is a comprehensive Land-Grant University (chartered in 1856) located in Auburn, Alabama approximately 100 miles from Atlanta's Hartsfield-Jackson International Airport. Auburn is ideally located 200 miles from the famous white sand beaches of the Gulf of Mexico and approximately the same distance from the beautiful Appalachian Mountains of Georgia, Tennessee, and North Carolina. The area boasts a particularly beautiful campus which features many historic buildings, trees, seasonal flowering plants, clean air and water in a thriving university community. The campus offers many opportunities for cultural diversity, arts, entertainment, nationally-ranked collegiate sports teams, and outdoor recreational activities. A student body of 23,000 students blends well with the area population of 45,000 citizens who represent the area's educated, diverse, and skilled work force.

DEGREES OFFERED
The Auburn MBA program is fully accredited by the AACSB-International (1980) and features an outstanding on-campus full-time MBA degree program which requires completion of 36–39 semester hours over 17 months start-to-finish.
Additionally, non-traditional students who need flexibility have access to the Auburn Distance Learning MBA Program (limited to the U.S., Canada, and U.S. Military bases) which mirrors completely the on-campus academic program. The executive MBA program (with separate healthcare and technology tracks) for managers and executives; and a physicians executive MBA program for medical doctors combine limited campus residencies, an international study trip, and distance learning modes.
In addition to the MBA degree, the Auburn College of Business offers an array of other masters and doctoral degrees including: MS in finance; master of human resources; MS in economics; master of management information systems; master of accountancy; and PhD in management.

PROGRAMS & CURRICULUM
The Auburn MBA degree requires completion of 36–39 semester hours and 17 months start-to-finish. Eight of the 12 MBA curriculum classes are core/required classes; four elective courses may be selected from options across a wide variety of academic areas.
Additionally, Auburn MBA students may choose a dual-degree track and earn a masters degree in engineering or management information systems concurrently with their MBA degree. In two years, students could earn two degrees. Concentrations are available to MBA students who choose electives in areas such as: Economics, finance, health care administration, human resources management, management information systems, management of technology, marketing, production/operations management, sports management, and supply chain management.
The Auburn College of Business is housed in the state-of-the-art Lowder Business Building which offers wireless technologies, dedicated computer labs, video classrooms, and instructional areas optimized for student-instructor interactions with enhanced learning environments.

EXPENSES & FINANCIAL AID
Financial aid is offered to MBA students in the form of graduate research assistantships and graduate fellowships as well as merit-based scholarship awards. Assistantships are awarded on a competitive basis with GMAT scores, previous academic achievement, and skill set/experience being the key criteria.
Expenses:
Alabama resident tuition: $2,305 per semester°
Non-Alabama resident tuition: $6,915 per semester°
Student fees: $300 per semester (approx.)

Books: $400 per semester (approx.)
Room and board: $5,000 per semester (approx.)
°University tuition may be waived for students who are awarded a Graduate Assistantship

FACULTY
Faculty who teach in the Auburn MBA program are all tenure-track and terminally qualified (PhD) in their academic fields. All are accessible and available to students both in class and outside to ensure a productive learning environment and provide guidance to students. Most faculty have previous industry work experience and/or outside consulting experiences which provide real-world balance between theory and practical applications.
The Auburn MBA program invites up to 50 new students to join each year. The recent diverse group is comprised of students from the U.S., Germany, Egypt, Thailand, Turkey, Honduras, Columbia, Brazil, West Bank, India, China, Taiwan, France, Nigeria, and Korea. Approximately one-third have undergraduate degrees in business, one-third with engineering degrees, and one-third in other academic disciplines.
The competitive admissions process values GMAT score, undergraduate GPA/degree/institution attended, resume/work experience/leadership skills, recommendations, and essays in the overall review process. Each applicant is considered on the strength of their overall application, standardized test scores, previous academic achievements, and resume/leadership skills. March 1 is the priority application deadline for fall semester entry.
Required application items:
- 4-year bachelors degree
- E-application to Auburn University Graduate School [www.grad.auburn.edu]
- Payment of graduate school processing fee ($25 U.S. citizens; $50 international students)
- 1-page [paper] MBA application form, www.mba.business.auburn.edu
- Official GMAT score
- Official TOEFL score (minimum 550 pbt; 213 cbt)
- Resume/CV
- 3 recommendations
- 2 essays (questions included with paper MBA application form)
- Official transcripts of all previous college credits
Mail or deliver all items to:
MBA Admissions
College of Business
415 W. Magnolia Avenue, Suite 503
Auburn University
Auburn, Alabama 36849 USA
Telephone: 334-844-4060
Fax: 334-844-2964
E-mail: mbadmis@auburn.edu
Internet: www.mba.business.auburn.edu [click on 'Apply' to access downloadable application form and directions]

ADDITIONAL INFORMATION
A "Leadership Certificate" offers students opportunities to gain experience and insight in developing personal leadership skills. These events and programs are provided at no additional cost to MBA students and include:
- The Blue Ridge Conference on Leadership in Ashville, NC
- Frequent leadership seminars and Visiting Executive roundtable events
- Essays and research papers which compete for scholarship awards

CAREER SERVICES & PLACEMENT
Networking, career services, and placement resources are provided to MBA students as they consider options and connections for MBA internships and full-time career jobs. Several career fairs are conducted on campus and in the Lowder Business Building each year. Additional networking opportunities are offered via the periodic visiting executive program.

BABSON COLLEGE
The Franklin W. Olin Graduate School of Business

AT A GLANCE

Leveraging our world leadership role in entrepreneurial management education, we weave innovation into all that we do. Our students learn how to recognize and define the changes critical to growing businesses in a competitive, global marketplace. Our graduates launch startups or lead global enterprises, driving the inspiration to develop new products, processes, and markets. As BusinessWeek detailed in its 2004 ranking of Babson as the #26 MBA program in the U.S., "Grads who are grounded in the fundamentals but who also have the business-building skills are in high demand these days. That's something that sets Babson College's F.W. Olin Graduate School of Business apart from its peers." Babson is the MBA that delivers.

CAMPUS & LOCATION

Babson College, founded in 1919 by financier and entrepreneur Roger W. Babson, is located on a 450-acre wooded site in Wellesley, Massachusetts, just 12 miles away from Boston. Boston and the surrounding region offer a pleasing and exciting environment rich in art, history, and intellect.

DEGREES OFFERED

Babson offers a master of business administration degree.

PROGRAMS & CURRICULUM

The two-year MBA program is an integrated curriculum stressing innovation, creative problem-solving, and the ability to recognize opportunity. The highlight of the first year is the Babson Consulting Alliance Program, which assigns student teams to year-long projects with local businesses. The second year (30 credit hours) is designed to build upon first-year course work, allowing students to focus their interests with elective courses.

The one-year MBA is an accelerated program that allows students with undergraduate business degrees to complete their MBA in three rigorous full-time semesters. Beginning each May, students enroll in a series of integrated modules during the first semester and then join the second-year MBA students to complete the equivalent of 15 courses in one calendar year. Candidates who work in the Boston area may complete the summer modules full-time, return to work in September, and finish the remainder of the program on a part-time basis in two years.

For working professionals, we offer two programs that allow students the flexibility to continue their career while pursing an MBA. The new fast-track MBA program is a blended learning MBA program that combines Web-based and classroom learning and allows students to earn their MBA in 26 months. The collaborative, team-based learning environment, combined with teaching from world-class faculty, allows you to apply what you learn immediately to your career.

FACILITIES

Babson students have access to an extensive business collection of print, media, and electronic resources. A staff of professionals is available to help students find the information they need and to offer instruction in the use of those databases on which business practitioners rely.

EXPENSES & FINANCIAL AID

Twelve-month academic year cost estimates for 2005-2006 for the two-year MBA program are $44,023 for tuition, $2,525 for books and supplies, and $22,770 for living expenses.

Tuition for the one-year MBA program is $44,023.

Per-credit tuition for the evening MBA program is $953.

The pre-MBA for international students cost $1,000.

Merit programs that award scholarships include Babson fellows, Olin fellows, Babson fellowships for students of color, Olin scholarships, and Babson scholars.

FACULTY

Babson's faculty is an internationally and a professionally diverse group, from areas in Asia, Australia, Europe, North America, and South America and with backgrounds in pharmaceutical, banking, high technology, retailing, and other industries. They are practitioners and scholars, executives and teachers, and researchers and consultants who have lived and worked in international settings.

STUDENTS

Students in the two-year MBA program are, on average, 29 years old and have about five years of work experience. GMAT scores range from 580 to 680. Women make up 27 percent of the class. Students come from such diverse industries as banking and investment institutions to advertising, biotechnology, publishing, telecommunications, and high technology. International students make up 29 percent of MBA enrollment.

ADMISSIONS

Students are admitted to the program based on a careful evaluation of academic records, professional qualifications, GMAT scores, and personal attributes. Interviews are required for admission to full-time MBA programs. The current class's GMAT scores range from 580 to 680, and the average undergraduate GPA is 3.2. International students must submit TOEFL results and official English translations of all academic documents. All candidates should have strong mathematics, computer, economics, and business writing skills.

For more information, applicants should contact:

Office of Graduate Admission

F. W. Olin Graduate School of Business

Babson Park, MA 02157-0310

Telephone: 781-239-4317; 800-488-4512 (toll-free within the U.S.)

Fax: 781-239-4194

E-mail: mbaadmission@babson.edu

Website: www.babson.edu/mba

SPECIAL PROGRAMS

Global business perspectives are not new at Babson. An international concentration is available and requires bilingualism, participation in a global management program, and completion of required and elective international courses. The global management program places students in structured field-consulting projects with corporations in Asia, Australia, Europe, and South America. International electives combine intensive classroom experience with industry-based projects in international settings. International internships, electives, and study-abroad opportunities satisfy the two-year MBA program's cross-cultural requirement and are open to students in all Babson MBA programs.

CAREER SERVICES & PLACEMENT

Made up of a staff of seven professionals, the Center for Career Development offers a career management curriculum that is integrated into first-year course work and is required for all full-time students; an online professional-development survey of work experience and interests, allowing the staff to direct students to internship and employment opportunities; internships offering either stipends or course credit; job fairs; and online alumni and employer databases.

BENTLEY COLLEGE
Elkin B. McCallum Graduate School of Business

AT A GLANCE

The business university education offered by Bentley goes deep and wide to address the complex questions that surface in today's business environment. What are the ethical guidelines that drive an organization's accounting procedures? Does the new customer relationship marketing program violate consumer privacy laws? Can the target audience effectively navigate a company's new software program? Students explore the answers to these and other questions in depth at the McCallum Graduate School.

CAMPUS & LOCATION

Bentley is located in suburban Waltham, Massachusetts, just 10 miles from Boston. Getting to Boston from Bentley is easy. The college runs a free shuttle bus to Harvard Square in Cambridge, where you can take public transportation into the heart of the city.

PROGRAMS & CURRICULUM

Master's in business administration

The MBA program at the McCallum Graduate School of Business prepares its graduates to excel and lead in an information-driven, ever-changing business world. The program develops strong skills in decision-making, communication, leadership, and teamwork. Students gain the depth and breadth of expertise critical to move ahead in their current field or for a career change-at an institution whose resources and focus are fully committed to the study of business.

Master's of science (MS)

In today's global economy, demand is high for professionals with an expertise in virtually every field of business-from capital markets to e-commerce to systems development. Bentley offers specialized master of science (MS) programs that combine in-depth knowledge of the theory and tools critical to each discipline, while also exploring how each specialty relates to other functional areas within an organization.

MS+MBA

This innovative new program is designed for those who wish to become effective leaders in high level knowledge-based organizations with a particular emphasis on state-of-the-art information technology solutions, or consistent and highly appealing user experience. The MS+MBA integrates in-depth knowledge of user needs and/or technology solutions with strong business management skills.

With full-time study, graduates earn two credentials, the MS (ensures technical knowledge and skills) and the day MBA (ensures strategic, organizational, and leadership skills), in the time it previously took to earn the MBA.

FACILITIES

Bentley's business-oriented, high-tech academic centers and learning labs give students hands-on experience with the latest hardware and software in finance, marketing, accounting and languages. Most classes incorporate projects and assignments that make use of the specialized software available in these facilities, allowing students to apply concepts learned in class. The centers and labs, including the Center for Marketing Technology, the Hughey Center for Financial Services, the Accounting Center for Electronic Learning and Business Measurement, and the Design and Usability Testing Center feature the same high-end hardware and software that businesses use today. Many of the labs benefit the corporate community as well, offering consulting and employee education.

EXPENSES & FINANICAL AID

Tuition for the 2005-2006 academic year is $2,733 per three-credit course. Payment for tuition is due by the start of classes each semester and may be paid by check, MasterCard, VISA or Discover. For your convenience, Bentley offers two payment plan options. For additional information on financial aid and scholarship opportunities, please contact our Student Accounts Office at 781-891-2171.

FACULTY

To advance the frontiers of knowledge, foster curricular innovation, enhance teaching, and inform and improve business practice, Bentley professors pursue a rigorous agenda of scholarship and applied research. Much of this work is transdisciplinary, with faculty from the business disciplines and the arts and sciences collaborating with one another, as well as with outside scholars and business leaders.

ADMISSIONS

The McCallum Graduate School of Business seeks highly motivated individuals with outstanding professional and educational credentials who will contribute to the learning experience of other graduate students. Applications for the day MBA program are accepted only for the fall term. Applications for the evening MBA or any MS program are accepted on a rolling basis; students may begin study either in September or January.

For more information, applicants should contact:

Office of Graduate Admissions

McCallum Graduate School of Business

175 Forest Street

Waltham, MA 02452-4705

Telephone: 781-891-2108

Toll-free within the U.S.: 800-442-4723

Fax: 781-891-2472

Website: www.bentley.edu

SPECIAL PROGRAMS

Bentley has continually promoted a commitment to ethics, civic engagement, and social responsibility through teaching, research, and corporate and community relations. These efforts are now being given even stronger emphasis through the Bentley Alliance for Ethics and Social Responsibility (BAESR). A collaborative effort connecting several campus-based centers and initiatives, BAESR's mission is to build on, enhance, and extend the work of the Center for Business Ethics, the Bentley Service-Learning Center, the CyberLaw Center, the Cronin International Center, and the Institute for Women in Leadership. Key campus-wide initiatives include Bentley's diversity efforts, Risk Management Research Program, Institutional Review Board (IRB), Academic Integrity Policy, and the Class Book Program.

BAESR will amplify, enhance, and extend the work of these various centers and initiatives, support and encourage greater awareness of, respect for and commitment to ethics, service, and social responsibility in our research, curricula, and campus culture.

CAREER SERVICES & PLACEMENT

The Miller Center for Career Services at Bentley College helps graduate students learn how to leverage a graduate degree in the job market, fine-tune personal and professional goals, and connect with leading employers in a range of industries. Through the Graduate Student Workshop series, the Miller Center for Career Services offers guidance on a full spectrum of job search topics, including interview preparation, cover letter writing and salary negotiation. The career-counseling staff is well versed in job market trends and able to provide valuable insight on career development issues. The center also offers one-on-one advising with an experienced counselor to help sharpen career development goals. Additionally, the Career Management series offers a structured group of career development workshops customized by academic degree program, class level, and concentration.

BOISE STATE UNIVERSITY
The College of Business and Economics

AT A GLANCE
The Boise State MBA provides the depth of knowledge required for success in our dynamic business world. A strong general MBA curriculum, taught by professors with both PhD degrees and industry experience, gives students the basics. In addition, Boise State MBA students take electives in order to gain expertise in accounting and finance, high-tech marketing, information technology, entrepreneurship, and international business. Students may also focus outside the business curriculum with their electives in such areas as engineering, health science, instructional & performance technology, or public administration. Depth of understanding sets Boise State MBA graduates apart from the pack.

CAMPUS & LOCATION
Boise State University is a metropolitan university reflecting the character of Idaho's capital city-the center of business, government, health care, finance, and technology. The state's largest city and largest university combine to offer students a wealth of both educational opportunities and off-campus experiences not available anywhere else in Idaho.

Nestled along the Boise River, Boise has a pleasant, four-season climate. Rated "most livable" by several national magazines, Boise offers a host of cultural events, recreational opportunities and business ventures. It is one of the premiere locations in the country for those who like the outdoors.

DEGREES OFFERED
The College of Business and Economics at Boise State University offers graduate programs leading to the following degrees: master of business administration (MBA), master of science in accountancy (MSA), master of science in accountancy, taxation (MSAT), master of management information systems (MMIS), and the master of science in management information systems (MSMIS) degrees. Each program is designed to help future business leaders develop and refine the skills needed for success.

The MBA provides a high quality academic program for tomorrow's business leaders. While gaining broad exposure to current topics in finance, marketing, operations management and human resources, students hone their skills in critical thinking, problem solving, strategy formulation, and leadership. MBA students have the option of emphasizing such areas as accountancy/finance, high-tech marketing, entrepreneurship, information technology, public administration, health administration, and engineering.

The MSA provides graduate education for individuals seeking to enhance their professional competence in accountancy. Students advance their previously acquired knowledge and skills through a focus in providing value-added services to their clients and employers.

The MSAT provides focused graduate instruction in advanced taxation issues. The MSAT degree builds upon the student's previously acquired knowledge and provides the skills necessary to provide value-added services in the complex taxation environment.

The MIS degrees provide advanced education for people working in organizations driven by information and information technology. Students obtain a deep, focused understanding of the ways in which information technology and systems support business activities. The MSMIS is a thesis-based program designed to prepare students for research and further study at the doctoral level. The MMIS is a non-thesis program with a focus on professional development.

FACILITIES
Boise State is home to a number of state-of-the art facilities for cultural, entertainment, research, recreation, and sports events that serve a captive audience of nearly 20,000 students as well as the 550,000 people living in the greater Treasure Valley.

Campus recreation facilities include gymnasiums, an outdoor center, climbing gym, racquetball and squash courts, exercise rooms, indoor track, a lap pool, tennis courts, cardiovascular and strength equipment, recreation field, sand volleyball courts, and outdoor basketball courts.

EXPENSES & FINANCIAL AID
Annual tuition and fees for 2004-2005 are $4,971 for full-time Idaho residents and $12,017 for non-residents. Books and supplies cost approximately $800 per semester. On-campus and off-campus housing is available. Contact the University Housing Office for assistance and further information about housing options.

A limited number of graduate assistantships are available. To be eligible, students must be admitted by the application deadline to the MBA, MSA, MSAT or MIS program and attend as full-time students during the academic year(s) of the awards. Graduate Assistant applications can be located on the Boise State Graduate Business Programs web at http://cobe.boisestate.edu/graduate

FACULTY
Boise State University attracts faculty who are dedicated to excellence in teaching, creative in generating new knowledge, and generous in using their expertise to solve problems. In addition to helping students learn, Boise State's faculty assist business, industry, government, and professional groups with educational programs and research and development efforts.

STUDENTS
Boise State University has nearly 20,000 students of which approximately 150 are in the MBA program. Students come from all parts of the world and from diverse academic and professional backgrounds.

Students in Boise State University's MBA program bring a wide variety of work experience. Many Boise State MBA students are professional people, continuing their education while working full-time. This mix of backgrounds promotes the beneficial exchange of quality and excitement of the program.

A recent student profile shows the average student age is 33 years old with an average of over six and one-half years of full-time work experience. Women comprise 47 percent of the student population, and minority students make up 10 percent of the MBA student body.

ADMISSIONS
Each MBA applicant must satisfy the admissions criteria and successfully complete each step within the admissions procedures before a final decision will be made. The admissions committee's responsibility is to review and evaluate each applicant's prior academic performance, leadership experience, professional experience, aptitude for graduate study, general motivation, and managerial attributes based on the admission standards set by the College of Business & Economics for the MBA program. See the website for specific requirements for applying.

CAREER SERVICES & PLACEMENT
Boise State's University Career Placement Center provides career guidance and information through computerized career guidance/information systems and from professional staff. Information and advice on resume and cover letter writing, application procedures, interviewing, and other job-hunting skills are available. A library of career and employer information is also available. Notification of internship and employment opportunities, participation in on-campus interview, and optional establishment of a file of professional references is available to all students during their academic careers.

BRANDEIS UNIVERSITY
Brandeis International Business School

AT A GLANCE

The Brandeis International Business School (IBS) is a pioneering school dedicated to preparing students for the careers of the global economy in international finance, management, and economic policy. We teach state-of-the-art theory, immerse students in international experiences, and connect them to best practice in business and policy.

CAMPUS & LOCATION

Seven major universities and 250,000 students are located in the greater Boston area. You can cross-register among schools and enjoy an extraordinary wealth of activities, clubs, restaurants, and sports targeted to students. Boston is also an important center of finance, technology, and consulting.

DEGREES OFFERED

We have four degree programs offering a wide range of skills for careers:

- MBA international: Managerial and analytical skills for international investments and businesses

- Master of arts in international economics and finance: Analytical and technical skills for business and policy decisions in global markets

- PhD: Advanced preparation in theory, institutions, and empirical analysis

- Master of science in finance: Applied financial theory and analysis for mid-career professionals

PROGRAMS & CURRICULUM

Our courses are highly flexible, offering a choice of concentrations and more than 50 electives—a high proportion of which are new each year, reflecting developments in the world's economy. Global theory and practice are integrated into every course.

EXPENSES & FINANCIAL AID

Tuition for 2005–2006 is $31,532 (or half that for one semester). The same charges apply for study abroad, but students receive a grant to offset the cost of airfare. Students should anticipate a 3 to 5 percent annual increase in tuition costs for future years.

Living expenses for a single individual on an economical budget are around $10,000 to $12,000 for the academic year. Limited housing is available in graduate residence halls for approximately $5,000 for the academic year for a single person.

IBS is aggressively committed to attracting highly qualified students. Relative to other business and professional schools, we offer generous financial aid, awarding more than $2.5 million in scholarships and loans each year.

The school awards both merit-based and need-based aid. Our major merit-based scholarship programs offer awards to nearly one-third of incoming students. Students do not have to apply separately for financial aid. Every applicant, whether from the U.S. or from other countries, is automatically considered for merit-based scholarships, and every student who completes the Statement of Financial Resources in our application is also considered for need-based awards. The school notifies students of financial aid awards upon admission.

Despite our generous aid program, students need to have substantial resources of their own because the Brandeis degree is costly. All master's students will need to finance their living expenses, and nearly all of them pay a significant portion of it.

In addition to aid from Brandeis, students should explore scholarships offered by their employers, government, and other public and private sources. IBS students frequently apply to, and receive support from, the Fulbright, Muskie, Ron Brown, World Bank, Ford, Mandela, Soros and other scholarship programs.

U.S. residents may be also eligible for low-cost federal loans. To apply, complete the Free Application for Federal Student Aid (FAFSA) form and indicate Brandeis University as a recipient (Title IV code 002133). This can be done online at www.fafsa.ed.gov.

FACULTY

Brandeis is known for passionate teaching and academic excellence, and IBS has assembled a faculty that is unusually skilled in teaching, research, and professional practice. Given the school's intimate scale, students often establish close contacts with faculty and participate in their research.

STUDENTS

International to the core, we are truly focused on the global economy. From a course on the global economic environment to advanced electives, the IBS experience is thoroughly international. More than half of our students come from Europe, Asia, Africa, and Latin America—56 countries in all this year—and international experiences are built into our programs in partnership with major foreign schools and companies.

ADMISSIONS

The Graduate Admission Committee has established the following criteria in evaluating applicants to all degree programs:

- Scholastic achievement as evidenced by academic course work, particularly in courses relevant to the program.

- Aptitude for graduate study as evidenced by scores on the Graduate Record Examination (GRE) or the Graduate Management Admission Test (GMAT).

- Motivation, leadership, and maturity as evidenced by work experience.

CAREER SERVICES & PLACEMENT

IBS graduates have an enviable placement record, holding positions in leading corporations and public sector institutions across the globe. Alumni have secured positions at Lehman Brothers, A. T. Kearney, J. P. Morgan Chase, GE Capital, McKinsey & Co., Merrill Lynch, Euromoney, and the World Bank.

The Office of Career Services (OCS) seeks to connect students, alumni, and employers with a range of targeted services and programs. We provide students the tools needed to succeed in their job search, offer alumni tools for their continued career success and opportunities to participate in developing current students' career skills, and enable employers to access well-prepared and highly qualified candidates for job opportunities.

CLAREMONT GRADUATE UNIVERSITY
Peter F. Drucker Graduate School of Management

AT A GLANCE

The Peter F. Drucker and Masatoshi Ito Graduate School of Management, located in beautiful Claremont, California, is a unique management school dedicated to training people to become effective and ethical leaders and managers in whatever industries they serve. This focus stems from our belief that management is a liberal art, a human enterprise encompassing perspectives from the social and behavioral sciences. Named after one of the most prominent management thinkers of the twentieth century, Peter F. Drucker, the Drucker MBA program offers a high quality interactive educational experience: small classes averaging 25 students, and instruction from world-renowned professors. Approximately 70 percent of our classroom instruction is either in discussion or case analysis format, and we incorporate team building in classroom projects and presentations.

CAMPUS & LOCATION

Nestled in the foothills of the San Gabriel Mountains, this charming community is famous for its tree-lined streets, the Claremont Colleges consortium, and charming old town restaurants and shops. Claremont provides the atmosphere of a New England college town within comfortable driving distance of major Southern California attractions.

DEGREES OFFERED & CURRICULUM

The Drucker School offers the MBA degree. We attract students who already exhibit strong leadership and achievement skills or who clearly show the potential to develop such skills. These students typically wish to develop themselves both as individuals and as professional executives fully competent in the complex, globally connected economy. Consistent with Peter F. Drucker's philosophy of management, our school's mission is to study strategically important managerial issues and advance the theory and practice of management through teaching and field-based research that contributes to the betterment of society. This mission influences all aspects of the quantitatively and qualitatively balanced curriculum.

The Drucker MBA curriculum allows the student to sequentially build knowledge and develop professional skills. Core courses or foundation level courses provide candidates with an understanding of the fundamental disciplines of management. Advanced core courses are geared to help students integrate key concepts and skills necessary for strategy or general management. Elective courses allow students to specialize in a particular field of interest.

Our flexible curriculum allows both full-time and part-time students to select an area of emphasis in strategic management, risk management/finance, leadership, marketing, information sciences, and human resources. Students are also able to take courses outside of the management program. Other disciplines are available to through the various schools in the Claremont Graduate University and within the Claremont Colleges consortium.

EXPENSES & FINANCIAL AID

These are all estimated costs and are subject to change.

Tuition: $18,807 full-time (16 units)/ $1,214 per unit. *Fees:* $125 per semester. *Books & Supplies:* $510 per semester. *Average Rent:* $600–$700/ month (We offer on-campus graduate apartments on a first come, first serve basis, as well as off-campus housing resources/assistance.). *Expenses:* Expected expenses for a full-time student are approximately $15,000 per year. This figure is based on 16 units and includes on-campus housing, personal expenses, books, and student fees.

Financial Aid: Merit- and need-based scholarships are available for U.S. and international students alike. Institutional financial aid is based on the applicant's GMAT score, academic qualifications, professional work experience, and let-

ters of recommendation. To be considered, applicants must complete the Application for Institutional Financial Aid, which is included in the admission application, and have all application materials submitted by the appropriate admission and financial aid deadlines. Government loans (FAFSA for U.S. citizens and permanent residents) and international student loans are also available. To be considered for need-based aid—Perkins loan and work-study— applicants must have all their admission application materials and FAFSA application completed by March 2. To be considered for Federal Stafford Loans, these same materials must be completed no later than June 2. Please contact the Office of Student Financing at finaid@cgu.edu or call 909-621-8337.

STUDENT LIFE

Students can participate in clubs, such as the Drucker School Student Association (DSSA), the Management Consulting Association, the Finance and Investment Association, the Marketing Association, Net Impact, Drucker Entrepreneurship Club, and the Drucker International Club. For additional information, visit the following website at http://www.cgu.edu/pages/2191.asp.

ADMISSIONS

We do not require an undergraduate background in business or economics. Nor do we have minimum cut-offs for the GMAT and GPA as we attempt to individualize each student's application by evaluating the whole person. For an application to be complete, applicants must submit the following:

- Application
- Student profile sheet and application for institutional financial aid (if applicable)
- Three letters of recommendation
- Official transcripts from every college/university attended
- Personal statement
- Current resume
- GMAT score
- TOEFL score (for international students)
- $55 application fee
- Interview (by invitation)

Application Deadlines:
- Fall semester (financial aid applicants): February 15
- Fall semester (regular applicants): May 1
- Spring semester (international and financial aid applicants): October 1
- Spring semester (regular applicants): November 15

If applying for financial aid, all documents must be in by the above dates. We offer rolling admissions based on space availability.

CAREER MANAGEMENT

The ultimate objective of any successful career services function within a business school is the successful transition of students out of the classroom and into the working world with job and career opportunities closely aligned with the graduates' interests and capabilities. The career management services provided to students at the Drucker School are designed to provide the tools needed to successfully navigate a course into the working world and beyond. While the department has attracted major U.S. corporations to recruit students— companies such as A.T. Kearney, Accenture, Rain Bird, Deloitte & Touche, Johnson & Johnson, and Mattel—our strength has been in training students to successfully conduct a significant portion of their own job and career search. Students have available to them a ready arsenal of programs, workshops, and company information sessions designed to help them define their short- and long-term objectives and provide significant information about companies, industries, and career paths. We invite you to learn more about our capabilities and programs by visiting our website: http://careers.cgu.edu.

COLUMBIA UNIVERSITY

COLUMBIA
BUSINESS
SCHOOL

THE UNIVERSITY AT A GLANCE

A Columbia Business School MBA gives graduates the edge in a world that demands smart, flexible, effective business leaders. The MBA program fosters an entrepreneurial mind-set aimed at identifying and capturing opportunity—the stuff of which business leaders are made.

Columbia Business School maintains one of the strongest corporate recruiting programs, consistently ranking among the top five favorite hunting groups of corporate recruiters. The school's location and relationships with New York's largest firms and industry leaders create unique opportunities for students. The school boasts a worldwide network of more than 35,000 alumni, some at the highest levels of business.

LOCATION AND ENVIRONMENT

New York City is a major capital of industry, boasting internationally recognized firms in finance and fashion, media and high tech, arts and entertainment, real estate, and manufacturing. With thousands of multinational companies, a diverse real-estate market and the major stock, bond and commodity exchanges, the city is a living laboratory for the Columbia community.

The only Ivy League school in Manhattan, Columbia University provides a traditional, world-renowned academic setting, while offering students access to New York City's array of cultural and social outlets showcasing museums, Broadway shows, professional sports teams, concert halls, and restaurants.

MAJOR AND DEGREES OFFERED

Hailed as one of the most innovative MBA curricula, Columbia Business School's course offerings prepare students to take leadership roles across sectors, while giving them fundamental skills applicable to all disciplines.

Specialized programs such as entrepreneurship, real estate, and social enterprise provide students with the opportunity to focus on cutting-edge issues that are evolving day by day. Dual-degree programs with 11 other graduate programs within the university are also an option for students whose interests span several fields.

In addition to its renowned MBA program, Columbia Business School offers successful business managers and company executives the opportunity to enhance their careers and expand their knowledge through the prestigious executive MBA (EMBA) program.

ACADEMIC PROGRAM

Each entering class is divided into clusters of approximately 60 students who take every course together for the first year of the program and overlap regularly thereafter. A vital reference group, the clusters form a vital reference group throughout the MBA experience. Like the larger school community, clustermates provide a lifetime of friendship, professional advancement, and inspiration.

Upon completion of the core, students may choose from more than 150 elective courses at Columbia Business School and supplement them with more than 4,000 graduate-level classes at 12 of the university's other schools, including the Graduate School of Arts and Sciences, International and Public Affairs, Journalism, Law, and Social Work.

The strength behind the program is the distinguished, innovative faculty that includes the 2001 Nobel Laureate for Economics, Joseph Stiglitz. Columbia's faculty includes Fortune 500 professionals, who excel at showing their students how to apply knowledge to any business challenge.

OFF-CAMPUS OPPORTUNITIES

Because there is no substitute for personal experience in learning about language, culture, and international business, Columbia Business School exchange programs and study trips take place in almost every part of the world. Almost 250 students have spent a semester at one of 23 leading business schools worldwide through the Chazen MBA exchange program. MBA and executive MBA student study tours have explored business practices and innovation firsthand in more than 25 countries.

FACILITIES AND EQUIPMENT

Columbia Business School is housed in the recently renovated Uris Hall, on the upper part of campus, and in Warren Hall. Warren Hall, a light-filled, eight-story building a five-minute walk from Uris, was built in 1999 to provide shared space for Columbia Business School and Columbia Law School. The facilities feature state-of-the-art connectivity throughout, including Express Web Kiosks.

Tuition, Room and Board, and Fees
Tuition for the 2004-2005 academic year: $36,296
Additional fees: $1116
Room & board: $17,820

FINANCIAL AID

Columbia Business School's financial aid program is designed to facilitate the financing of the MBA program and to recognize students who demonstrate exceptional academic achievement.

Financial aid is available in the form of need-based and merit-based scholarships, and federal, institutional, and private low-interest loans. International students are eligible for merit-based fellowships and can also secure loans through the low-interest tuition loan program.

FULL AND PART-TIME FACULTY

The Columbia Business School faculty generates the ideas that others adapt and teach. At the school, students hear concepts directly from the people who developed them. Adjunct and guest lecturers throughout the program then provide insight in how they have implemented those ideas.

Teaching and research at Columbia Business School are oriented to a global economic environment. The 124 full-time faculty members integrate an international component into their academic research and teaching. The faculty members themselves are citizens of the world-more than half have lived or worked abroad, and one-quarter spend several weeks teaching or consulting overseas in any given year.

STUDENT ORGANIZATIONS AND ACTIVITIES

Students have a variety of opportunities outside the classroom to hear from those with seasoned perspectives: hundreds of noted business leaders visit the school each year as lecturers, teachers, and mentors. The Millennium Lecture Series brings to campus such world leaders and heads of state as King Abdullah II of Jordan and Benjamin Netanyahu, former prime minister of Israel, while the Silfen Leadership Series attracts speakers from the highest corporate levels, such as Sanford I. Weill, chairman and CEO of Citigroup Inc.

ADMISSIONS PROCESSES AND REQUIREMENTS

Applicants are evaluated in three categories: professional promise, personal characteristics, and academic credentials. Columbia looks for well-rounded people from diverse economic, social, ethnic, geographic, and professional backgrounds. Ideal applicants have demonstrated leadership, have the ability to work as members of a team, and can contribute to the academic experience of their peers.

Columbia Business School has a rolling admissions process. Applications are reviewed in the order in which they are received and decisions can be rendered at any point during the review period.

Application requirements include 2 references and 4 essays. While interviews are not required, many prospective students are invited to interviews with alumni or current students. Interviews are by invitation only.

DREXEL UNIVERSITY
LeBow College of Business

AT A GLANCE
Recognized by *Financial Times, U.S. News & World Report,* and *Entrepreneur* for superior programs, Drexel University's LeBow College of Business empowers, enriches, and inspires future business leaders through an innovative strategic approach to business education defined by leadership and ethics, industry perspectives, and technological orientation.

CAMPUS & LOCATION
Ranked by *U.S. News and World Report* as a top national doctoral university, Drexel University, located in Philadelphia, is one of the region's premier universities located in the Northeast business corridor, with close proximity to Baltimore; Boston; New York City; and Washington, DC. Philadelphia is an ideal place to earn a graduate business degree as the Philadelphia business region is ranked ninth in the nation for the number of Fortune 500 companies and tenth for new business formations. With its diverse economy, excellent education institutions, and many recreational options, Greater Philadelphia traditionally ranks among the "most livable" metropolitan areas.

DEGREES OFFERED
LeBow College offers a master of business administration, master of science, and doctor of philosophy. One-year, two-year, LeBow evening, accelerated Drexel (LEAD), professional (full-time, part-time), technology, and executive MBA degree programs are available. Depending on the program, classes are offered during the day, in the evenings and weekends, or online. The flexibility of programs enables students to find programs and schedules that best suits their needs.

The professional MBA requires between 48 and 60 quarter credit hours depending on the student's prior academic record. Students take an initial series of integrated foundation courses followed by one or two areas of concentration in accounting, economics, entrepreneurship, financial management, international business, investment management, management information systems, marketing, organization management, production and operations management, taxation, or healthcare systems management.

The one-year MBA maximizes the quality, effectiveness, and rigor of a comprehensive, full-time MBA program in an accelerated time frame and is designed for a select group of highly motivated students. The integrated curriculum explores the following areas: entrepreneurship, international business, leadership, managerial finance, and strategic management.

Students who seek a high degree of specialization can complete the master of science degree in accounting or finance in two years taken independently or in one year after the completion of the one-year MBA. The Drexel executive MBA at LeBow College of Business, ranked among the world's best and first in the nation for career progress by *Financial Times,* is designed for seasoned professionals who are looking to maximize their leadership potential.

PROGRAMS & CURRICULUM
An MBA from Drexel University's LeBow College of Business equips you with an overview of business, complemented by a choice of relevant concentrations and is highly respected throughout the business world and fully accredited by AACSB International (the Association to Advance Collegiate Schools of Business)—the top ranking available to a U.S. business school.

The Drexel MBA curriculum is student-centered and market-driven. Our professors use a variety of teaching methods, including lectures, case studies, and student teams, as well as the latest technology.

FACILITIES
MBA students take classes in the Pearlstein Business Learning Center—one of the nation's most technologically advanced academic business environments. Classes are taught in web-enabled classrooms—simulated corporate boardrooms—equipped with the latest technology.

LeBow College of Business is home to research-learning facilities such as the Baiada Center for Entrepreneurship in Technology, the Sovereign Institute for Strategic Leadership, LeBow Center for Research Excellence, and the LeBow Center for Teaching Excellence.

Drexel's W.W. Hagerty Library's strength lies in its online collection. The library houses 300,000 volumes and electronic resources specializing in business which are remotely fully accessible.

EXPENSES & FINANCIAL AID
Tuition for the professional MBA full-time and part-time is billed on a per credit hour basis. For the 2005–2006 academic year, the cost is $760 per credit hour. Tuition for the one-year MBA for 2004–2005 was $50,000. Merit scholarships and the Drexel alumni-trustee endorsement grant are available for students who are interested in the full-time professional MBA and the one-year MBA. Drexel alumni who are interested in the full-time or part-time professional MBA are eligible for the Drexel grad grant.

FACULTY
Internationally renowned faculty members at Drexel University's LeBow College of Business are among the world's most highly read and respected business educators. Pioneers as well as educators, faculty members incorporate the latest business and technological advances in course delivery. Professors are experts in their fields and have industry knowledge that enables them to blend the academic with the real world. This unique combination of theoretical knowledge and management practice translates into the day-to-day practicality needed for career success. Faculty members maintain strong ties with the regional business community, enhancing the academic experience through guest lectures and special events.

STUDENTS
Students represent widely diverse academic, professional, and international backgrounds, and the student culture is enriched by the variety of their perspectives.

ADMISSIONS
Prospective students can apply online by visiting www.lebow.drexel.edu/apply. All applicants must have received a four-year bachelor's degree from an accredited college or university. Degrees earned abroad will be evaluated and must be deemed equivalent. The admissions committee reviews applications based on undergraduate record, GMAT (Graduate Management Admission Test) score, quality and quantity of professional experience, clarity of career goals, professional references, a statement of purpose, and a professional resume. Students whose native language is not English and who do not hold a bachelor's degree from a U.S. institution are required to take and submit a TOEFL (Test of English as a Foreign Language) score.

CAREER SERVICES & PLACEMENT
LeBow College's Office of MBA Career Services offers students self-assessment resources, job search tools, and organized employer networking activities. Some of the resources include resume writing assistance, interviewing preparation, and negotiation workshops.

INDIAN SCHOOL OF BUSINESS
Kellogg, Wharton, and London Business School

AT A GLANCE

The ISB is about creating business leaders who are ready to take charge. Our post graduate program (PGP) in management offers extraordinary learning opportunities which combine basic business fundamentals with the advanced learning necessary to be successful business leaders. We welcome you to discover ISB.

The ISB is born of a partnership of eminent business leaders, entrepreneurs, and academics from around the world. This corporate-academia partnership has ensured that the content of our programs is relevant, international in perspective, and delivered at world-class standards.

CAMPUS & LOCATION

Spread over a scenic expanse of 250 acres, the ISB campus is situated on the outskirts of Hyderabad, 45 minutes away from the international airport. The campus provides an ideal study environment with air-conditioned lecture theatres, learning resource center, meeting rooms, coffee bars, and restaurant facilities.

EXPERIENCING INDIA

Few countries on earth have the prodigious diversity that India offers. From north to south and east to west, the people, the languages, the customs, the cuisines, and the landscape are astonishingly different. Hyderabad is located centrally in India, a city which is a fusion of the traditional and the modern.

DEGREES OFFERED

The ISB offers a one-year post graduate program in management. The ISB program is unique in that it provides the equivalent of a typical two-year MBA program in one year. It provides the fundamentals of management education along with the flexibility of individual exploration in chosen areas of interest.

POST GRADUATE PROGRAM IN MANAGEMENT

The program starts with the pre-term courses and the rest of the academic year is divided into eight terms. Each term comprises four courses of 20 contact hours each, which add up to 640 contact hours over the entire program. Students have the option of doing two additional electives, taking the contact hours to 680. These contact hours do not include the leadership development program and the Take Charge course, and are broadly comparable to two-year MBA programs in leading business schools around the world.

FACILITIES

ISB offers a wide range of facilities on campus to ensure a students life is hassle free and enriching. The heart of the ISB community is the Academic Center. This is equipped with state-of-the-art-facilities, in particular a broadband communications network that ensures instant global connectivity. ISB students work and live in a wired and wireless environment. Students can interact by computer or video-link with faculty, business leaders, and students anywhere in the world during the course, projects, and research studies. The Learning Resource Center (LRC), towering in the middle of the Academic Center, hosts the library. Aimed at being the most comprehensive business library in Asia, the LRC has an extensive collection of books & databases covering all aspects of management & business and over 1,500 periodicals. The databases that the LRC has subscribed to include ABI-Inform Global, Economist Intelligence Unit, ISI Emerging Market, Prowess and Vans Electronic Library, among others.

EXPENSES & FINANCIAL AID

Estimate of Expenses for 2004-2005 (USD):

Tuition: $27,000

Accommodation expenses: $ 2,350, shared; $3,650 studio

Every student is required to have a laptop computer.

Financial aid is available for the entire program in the form of loans and scholarships. Educational loans covering up to 90 percent of the cost, at discounted rates are offered by various banks subject to meeting their loan requirements. Scholarships are merit-based. The details of terms and requirements of loans are available on the website. The ISB helps loan applicants in the processing and disbursement of the loans.

FACULTY

The ISB has a portfolio faculty model—it aims to achieve an ideal mix of permanent and visiting faculty that will give the students the benefit of international exposure as well as a strong research base. Recently, faculty from Wharton, Kellogg, London Business School, Stanford, Chicago, Duke, and Texas, among others, have taught at the ISB. The origins and distinctive research of our faculty members ensure that our program offers content that is contemporary and global in its perspective.

STUDENTS

The collective profile of 276 students at ISB is as follows: The student body is 19 percent female and 81 percent male. The average age of students is 27, with a range of 21-42 years. 24 percent of students are married, and 76 percent are single. Average work experience is 5 years, with a range of 0-18 years. The number of students with international experience is 68, or 25 percent, with an average of 3.2 years and a range of 0.5-10 years.

ADMISSIONS

The ISB looks for interesting people, from diverse economic, social, ethnic, and geographic backgrounds, who can add to their classmates' experiences. Their common denominators are a record of achievement, demonstrated leadership, and the ability to work as members of a team. We seek applicants who have superior academic credentials and who display intellectual curiosity.

For further information on admissions, please contact:

The Admissions Office

Indian School of Business

The ISB Campus

Gachibowli, Hyderabad 500 019

India

Telephone: +91 (40) 2300 7474

Fax: +91 (40) 2300 7099

E-mail: admissions@isb.edu

Website: www.isb.edu/pgp

CAREER SERVICES & PLACEMENT

The ISB continued its impressive placement record with an outstanding placement season for the second batch of students of the post graduate program in management.

The ISB's comprehensive career development program helped students explore a wide range of career opportunities. Our distinctive focus on lateral placements translated into 221 offers for lateral positions with a noteworthy 81 percent of the class receiving lateral offers. Students enhanced their careers through their interaction with faculty, their peer group, and the career opportunities provided by the school with more than 50 percent of the class of 2003 making career shifts this year.

MARIST COLLEGE

AT A GLANCE

Marist College is a comprehensive liberal arts college with a national reputation for excellence in the use of technology in education. Offering comprehensive graduate, pre-professional, internship, and online opportunities—in addition to an extensive undergraduate curriculum—Marist is distinguished by its location, a 175-acre riverside campus in the heart of the Hudson River Valley; and by a nearly quarter-century of collaborative research and development partnerships with industry leaders such as Marist's neighbor, IBM, that has placed the college at the forefront of computer technology innovations and growth.

The MBA program at Marist is recognized as one of the best business programs in the world. Designed to meet the needs of career-building professionals while being sensitive to the time demands of today's working adults, the MBA program requires a minimum of 30 credits of graduate study in core and elective courses, and offers most courses online as well as on campus. The online MBA attracts students from throughout the United States, Europe, Asia and South America. At Marist, you can expect an outstanding experience among high-caliber peers, as well as lifelong relationships with an influential global network!

RECOGNITION

The Association to Advance Collegiate Schools of Business (AACSB), the premiere accrediting organization for business schools worldwide, has accredited the Marist College School of Management business programs, undergraduate and graduate.

The Princeton Review named Marist one of the "Best 357 Colleges" in the country, and the School of Management one of the "Best 143 Business Schools" in the world. *US News & World Report* consistently places Marist in its top tier. *Barron's* calls Marist one of the nation's 260 best buys in college education. *Yahoo! Internet Life* magazine selected Marist for its list of the 100 most wired campuses in the nation.

CAMPUS & LOCATION

Marist's 175-acre campus overlooks the Hudson River in the heart of the historic Hudson River Valley, midway between New York City and Albany. The college is now home to nearly 6,000 undergraduate and graduate students, from over 40 states and 15 countries. Marist is regionally accredited by the Middle States Association of Colleges and Schools, and Marist was one of the first institutions of higher education in the Hudson Valley to offer a degree program designed specifically for adult students. The college also has learning sites in Fishkill and Goshen, NY, and offers classes as well in Kingston and Monticello, NY.

Very few colleges are located in a region that is itself a world-class center for commerce and the arts, and fewer still capitalize on this opportunity like Marist does. The Hudson River Valley provides Marist with a priceless laboratory for teaching and research, and the college's access to major cities in the northeast provides excellent work and study opportunities with industry and civic leaders, such as AT&T, Computerworld, the EPA, Fox News, Merrill-Lynch, MTV, the Wall Street Journal, and the White House, among others.

DEGREES OFFERED

Marist offers 30 undergraduate majors and eight master's degrees. For adult students, Marist offers the online organizational leadership and communication BS degree completion program. Online graduate offerings include the master's of business administration (MBA), the MA in communication, the master of public administration (MPA), and the MS in information systems, as well as advanced certificates in executive leadership, production management, and information systems.

EXPENSES AND FINANCIAL AID

Marist's part-time adult undergraduate students pay $445 per credit, while the graduate degrees are offered at $562 per credit. Most courses are three credits. Financial aid is available, as well as scholarship and loan opportunities and convenient payment plans.

FACULTY

Marist boasts 182 full-time faculty, as well as 376 part-time faculty. There is a 16:1 student/faculty ratio, and the average class size 20. Many of the Marist faculty members also have professional experience in their field, bringing a real-world perspective to their business and industry acumen.

CAREER SUCCESS

Marist College alumni provide career support and internship opportunities to current students through the college's Center for Career Services, and there are chapters throughout the country to provide opportunities for grads to network professionally and socially. In addition, the Center for Career Services focuses on helping students define their career goals and meet prospective employers through a variety of recruiting programs. They also provide advice for resume building and interviewing skills, and for students interested in pursuing advanced study, they help find postgraduate scholarships and fellowships to fund their study.

Marist has exceptional placement rates in graduate schools, especially in the fields of business, communications, law, medicine, and science. Among the colleges attended by recent grads: Boston College, Columbia, Cornell, Georgetown, New York Medical College, Notre Dame, Oxford, Rutgers Law School, Stanford, Syracuse, and Tufts.

Marist grads also go on to work at many well-known companies. This is a small sample: Bear-Stearns, Deloitte & Touche, Goldman-Sachs, IBM, the Office of the New York State Attorney General, the Internal Revenue Service, U.S. Secret Service, Time-Warner/AOL, MTV Network, Sun America, Simon & Schuster Publishing, and Memorial Sloan-Kettering Cancer Center.

Well-known Marist grads include: Tim Brier, co-founder of Priceline.com; Chris McCann, president of 1-800-FLOWERS.com; Rik Smits, former NBA All-Star for the Indiana Pacers; Ross Mauri, vice-president of e-server development for IBM; Bernadette Grey, who edited *Working Woman Magazine*; Lark-Marie Anton, press secretary to NY Mayor Michael Bloomberg; Bill O'Reilly, successful author and cable news talk show host; Michael McCarthy, vice president at Madison Square Garden Network; Tom Ward, CEO for Maidenform; J.W. Stewart, ESPN news anchor; Margaret O'Rourke, Boston College Law Professor; and Alvin Patrick, producer for MTV Network.

NOVA SOUTHEASTERN UNIVERSITY

The H. Wayne Huizenga School of Business and Entrepreneurship

AT A GLANCE

The H. Wayne Huizenga School of Business and Entrepreneurship is housed in a five-story, state-of-the-art facility on Nova Southeastern University's main campus in Fort Lauderdale, Florida. Named for entrepreneur Carl De Santis, the 261,000 square foot building provides easy access to NSU's extraordinary technological and academic resources, epitomizing the school's growth and innovation. Home to the Entrepreneur Hall of Fame, the venue features distinctive architectural design concepts and a three-story atrium which is frequently utilized to host numerous campus events, lectures, conferences, executive briefings, and professional development seminars for the business community.

CAMPUS AND LOCATION

Our mission is to offer academic programs at times convenient to students, employing innovative delivery systems and rich learning resources on campus and at distance sites.

In addition to its 300-acre main campus, eight student education centers are located throughout the state of Florida, Nevada, and the Caribbean; in addition, over 30 locations have been established worldwide where students can participate in unique educational offerings. Programs are also available in an online format.

The Huizenga School has also tailored delivery of its bachelor's and master's programs to the particular needs of corporations, offering custom degree programs on-site for companies, including: American Express, BellSouth, Citibank, Palm Beach County Sheriff's Office, Royal Caribbean Cruise Lines, Tyco, and Verizon.

EXPENSES AND FINANCIAL AID

Nova Southeastern University offers a comprehensive program of financial aid to assist students in meeting educational expenses. Financial aid is available to help cover direct educational costs such as tuition, fees, and books; as well as indirect educational expenses such as food, clothing, and transportation. To qualify and remain eligible for financial aid, students must be fully admitted into a university program, eligible for continued enrollment, a United States citizen, national or permanent resident, and make satisfactory academic progress toward a stated educational objective in accordance with the university's policy on satisfactory progress for financial aid recipients.

For information on sources of financial aid and for application forms, please contact:

Nova Southeastern University

Office of Student Financial Assistance

3301 College Avenue, Horvitz Administration Building

Fort Lauderdale-Davie, Florida 33314-7796

Broward County: 954-262-3380

Miami-Dade County: 305-940-6447, ext. 7410

Toll Free: 800-806-3680

www.nova.edu/cwis/finaid

FACULTY

Faculty members of the H. Wayne Huizenga School of Business and Entrepreneurship comprise some of the best minds and most dedicated professionals in the industry. Their extensive experience in both the academic and business realms make them sought after as consultants in industry, government, and the nonprofit sector. They bring dynamic, experiential, global perspectives to the classroom and provide the support and guidance necessary for academic success. All faculty members hold a doctoral degree.

PROGRAMS

The H. Wayne Huizenga School of Business and Entrepreneurship at Nova Southeastern University (NSU) is committed to fostering within its students the ability to work as a team, the tools to manage change and become innovative thinkers, and the freedom to cultivate their entrepreneurial spirit. Founded in 1971, the business school is known for its entrepreneurial perspective in both the delivery and content of its educational programs. Students encounter some of the most enriching coursework available in education today. Graduates include successful leaders, managers, and entrepreneurs around the world.

The Huizenga School serves more than 4,500 bachelor's, master's, and doctoral students in a variety of degree programs as well as a wide range of optional academic specializations and concentrations tailored for preparation in meeting the demands of today's workforce. Within the Huizenga School, the Hudson Institute of Entrepreneurship and Executive Education delivers enriching seminars, workshops, and customized executive education programs. The International Institute for Franchise Education has been established to round out the Huizenga's school executive education portfolio.

Administrators and faculty members are keenly attuned to the complicated demands placed on today's employees, mangers, and leaders. Courses are continually refined to incorporate current and relevant practices. Students at the Huizenga School experience some of the most exciting, enriching coursework available anywhere in education today.

Nova Southeastern University is accredited by the Commission on Colleges of the Southern Association of Colleges and Schools (1866 Southern Lane, Decatur, Georgia 30033-4097; Telephone: 404-679-4501) to award bachelor's, master's, educational specialist, and doctoral degrees.

CAREER SERVICES AND PLACEMENT

The Office of Career Services provides career consulting and job search assistance to students and alumni in reaching their chosen goals and career destinations. Services are available to students on an ongoing basis, from the time a student enters the university and throughout their career. Located on the fourth floor of the Alvin Sherman Library at NSU's main campus, the Office of Career Services can be contacted at http://www.nova.edu/career or via telephone at 954-262-7201 or 800-541-6682, ext. 7201 for information on programs, individual counseling with a career consultant, job leads, the Career Track model, e-recruiting, and career selection.

RICE UNIVERSITY
Jesse H. Jones Graduate School of Management

AT A GLANCE
Ranked as the #1 finance program (second in the world) by *The Economist* in 2003, the Rice MBA program at the Jesse H. Jones Graduate School of Management of Rice University has risen quickly from its founding in 1974. The small class size of 180 students provides an intimate, dynamic learning environment in the new state-of-the-art facility. Close connections with the faculty and alumni open a world of opportunities. Houston is home to the second largest concentration of Fortune 500 headquarters. Whether you are interested in staying in Texas, working elsewhere in the U.S., or relocating internationally, you can achieve your goals with a Rice MBA.

Additional information and a full list of media mentions are available through our website at www.jonesgsm.rice.edu.

CAMPUS & LOCATION
Rice University is located on a beautiful wooded 300-acre campus in central Houston, minutes from the downtown business district and the city's world-class theater district. The campus is located across the street from the renowned Texas Medical Center and within walking distance to the museum district, Houston Zoological Gardens, and Hermann Park. The surrounding neighborhood is one of Houston's most attractive. The new light-rail line connects Rice to Downtown, Minute Maid Park (home of the MLB Astros), and Reliant Stadium (home to the NFL Texans).

DEGREES OFFERED
The Jones School focuses all of its energy on graduate business education. Available degrees include the MBA, MBA for executives, MBA/master's in engineering with the George R. Brown College of Engineering at Rice, and MBA/MD in conjunction with Baylor College of Medicine.

FACILITIES
In August 2002, the Jones School occupied its new home of 167,000 square feet. The new building offers three-times the space of Herring Hall (the previous home of the Jones School) and houses everything from the dean's office to the Business Information Center to the Career Planning Center. Wired and wireless technology is in place to assist in research and information gathering.

Additional information and photos of the new facility can be reviewed at www.jonesgsm.rice.edu/jonesgsm/The_New_Building_Home.asp.

EXPENSES & FINANCIAL AID
Application fee: $100

Tuition: $30,900 for the 2005–2006 year. Laptop computer, hardware, and software are included in this price.

Total estimated expenses: approximately $44,700 per year

Financial aid: About 65 percent of each class receives financial aid from the school. We offer a limited amount of aid to international students. An independent association, RICE-TMS, funds minority scholarships for Jones School students.

FACULTY
The Jones School's faculty is consistently recognized for their knowledge, research, teaching ability, and student focus. Each member of the Jones faculty maintains a balance between teaching and research, ensuring that students receive the most current, leading-edge education.

STUDENTS
"Classroom learning is only one aspect of a complete business education. In this era of rapid globalization, change is the only constant, and companies want more than good managers; they want great leaders who can resolve issues with a multidisciplinary approach.

"While many business schools continue to emphasize theory, the Jones School curriculum builds on theory with an experiential learning process we call Action Learning. We're one of two business schools that require all our students to take their classroom knowledge into real business settings.

"We've applied this philosophy of change as the only constant to ourselves as well. After seeking input from our faculty, students, and industry leaders—including top management at major corporations to determine which skills they consider most valuable—we've designed an innovative course of study that provides all you'll need to excel in the global business environment. Our focus on leadership has been widely recognized, including by the *Wall Street Journal*."

—Gilbert R. Whitaker, Jr., Dean

ADMISSIONS
Admission requirements are a bachelor's degree; GMAT (no minimum, average scores are 630–660); TOEFL for international applicants (minimum score of 600); no work experience required of exceptionally qualified students (up to 5 percent of the class) and the average work experience is four to five years. Deferred admission is possible for two years.

Academic background: You must have a four-year undergraduate degree from an accredited college or university if you received your education in the United States. If you are an international applicant, your undergraduate degree must be the equivalent of a U.S. four-year degree. If you have completed a three-year bachelor of commerce (BCom) degree, we also require a two-year master of commerce (MCom) degree. Your undergraduate and graduate GPAs, GMAT scores (or GRE scores if you are applying to the joint MBA/ME degree program or MCAT scores if you are applying to the MBA/MD program), choice of major, electives, course load, and grade patterns are all considered. Interviews are by invitation.

Leadership potential: Your demonstrated leadership and management experiences, both on the job and through extracurricular activities, will help us assess your leadership potential.

Confidential evaluations: Evaluations from employers and/or professors shed perspective on your capabilities, enabling us to assess your qualifications more accurately.

A personal statement: Three essays that articulate your career goals, work experience, and reasons for choosing Rice University's Jones School are a crucial component of your application. Use them to convey intangibles: Why are you pursuing an MBA? How have you benefited from your academic, professional, and personal opportunities? What qualities will you bring to the Jones School, and what will you seek from us?

For contact information, check out www.jonesgsm.rice.edu

CAREER SERVICES & PLACEMENT
According to *The Financial Times* in 2003, the Jones School received the highest ranking among U.S. business schools for Career Progress, defined as "the degree to which alumni have moved up the career ladder three years after graduating. Progression is measured through changes in level of seniority and the size of the company in which they are employed." It was ranked sixth in the world in this category.

ROLLINS COLLEGE

Crummer Graduate School of Business

AT A GLANCE

The Crummer School, located in Orlando, Florida, is known worldwide for its use of technology in the classroom, exceptional faculty, and the success of its graduates. In February 2002, Forbes ranked the Crummer School among the top regional MBA programs nationwide. The MBA program at Rollins College is considered by many as "Florida's Most Prestigious MBA". Each Crummer student is given a notebook computer that is loaded with the latest software, the total price of which is included in tuition. Also included in tuition is an international business trip-a week in Europe visiting firms and getting a real-world perspective on international business from people who live it.

The success of our program is demonstrated by the fact that 98 percent of our graduates are placed!

CAMPUS & LOCATION

As the oldest university in the state of Florida, Rollins College carries a long history of providing excellent liberal arts education. Located in the charming city of Winter Park, the small, private college is just five miles from downtown Orlando, a booming business community.

In addition to the well-known theme park attractions, the Orlando area is home to many international headquarters, including Harris Corporation, AAA, Tupperware, and Lockheed Martin.

DEGREES OFFERED

Rollins College offers the MBA degree in five innovative program formats:

- Accelerated MBA: A one year full-time MBA program for students who have at least three years of full-time work experience

- Early advantage MBA: A two-year MBA program especially designed for students with little or no work experience. Includes many extras including a mentor program, summer internships, and both domestic and global consulting projects

- Executive MBA: A 19-month MBA program for senior level professionals. Classes meet on alternating Fridays and Saturdays

- Professional MBA: A 32-month MBA program offered on weekday evenings for working professionals.

- Saturday MBA: An MBA program that meets just on Saturdays for 19 months and requires students to have at least five years of work experience.

PROGRAMS & CURRICULUM

The Crummer School offers MBA degree in five innovative program formats. Each is designed to provide a general management education with the opportunity to earn a concentration in a chosen business discipline through selection of the elective courses. The Crummer School has a strong focus on entrepreneurial and global issues, offering many popular electives in each area. A popular finance elective course provides students the opportunity to direct the real-world investment decisions of the Crummer/SunTrust Portfolio.

FACILITIES

Rollins College, the first college in Florida, was founded in 1885 by a group of community leaders who envisioned a New England-style liberal arts college for Florida's young adults. Today Rollins occupies a beautiful 67-acre campus on the shores of Lake Virginia in Winter Park, an upscale suburb of Orlando, Florida. Crummer Hall houses all of the MBA classrooms as well as all faculty and administrative offices. The executive-style classrooms feature state-of-the-art projection equipment and LAN access. The career development area is an elegant location for recruiters to interview Crummer students. The building also features two executive style board rooms, student lounge, networked study rooms, executive dining room, and a computer lab.

EXPENSES & FINANCIAL AID

Total tuition is $42,360 ($14,120 a term) for the accelerated MBA Program, $51,360 ($12,840 a term) for the early advantage MBA program, $39,760 ($4,970 a term) for the professional MBA program, $44,000 ($5,500 a term) for the Saturday MBA program, and $52,200 ($6,525 a term) for the executive MBA program. All tuition costs include the notebook computer, and tuition for the EAMBA, AMBA, and EMBA programs includes an international study trip. Please contact the Financial Aid Office for information on how to finance your education and scholarship opportunities.

FACULTY

The Crummer School hires only experienced faculty members with proven track records and doctorate degrees. Because of the integrative nature of the Crummer curriculum, faculty members work closely together to ensure that each class builds upon the others, thereby avoiding a redundancy of material and creating an interdisciplinary approach to education. Class sizes are kept intentionally small so that faculty-student interaction is high. In addition to their teaching experience, faculty members maintain close ties with the business community through consulting work and research. This brings the theoretical material to life in the classroom and encourages immediate application of the course material.

STUDENTS

The Crummer School enrolls 40 AMBA students, 75 EAMBA students, 70 PMBA students, 40 SMBA students, and 40 EMBA students each year. Crummer classes average 25 percent international students (full-time only) and 46 percent women. Approximately one-third of Crummer students have business undergraduate degrees; other disciplines include engineering, humanities, computer science, and the social sciences.

ADMISSIONS

The Crummer School evaluates each candidate on an individual basis, seeking a balance among the various application criteria. Each applicant to the Crummer School is required to submit a formal application, an application fee, a score on the Graduate Management Admission Test (GMAT), all undergraduate and graduate transcripts, and two to three letters of recommendation. A formal interview is also required for all programs. Work experience is evaluated for all but the EAMBA Program. The average full-time student enters the program with a 3.2 undergraduate GPA and a 595 on the GMAT. Average work experience for the AMBA Program is nine years.

Director of Admission

Crummer Graduate School of Business

Rollins College

1000 Holt Avenue-2722

Winter Park, FL 32789-4499

Telephone: 407-646-2405; 800-866-2405 (toll free)

Fax: 407-646-2402

CAREER SERVICES & PLACEMENT

The dedicated and professional career management team prepares students to successfully be recognized as leaders who add value to their organizations and communities. We firmly believe that career management is a developmental process that must be an integral part of your total educational experience. Our goal is to provide the crucial skills enabling you to have "ownership" of your career planning and job search process.

SAINT PETER'S COLLEGE

AT A GLANCE

Saint Peter's College, the Jesuit college of New Jersey, continues to provide academic excellence and personal care. Since 1872, the college has developed various ways of meeting student needs through academic advisement and career services.

DEGREES OFFERED

Students can earn a master of arts degree in administration and supervision or a master of arts: teaching and reading specialist. Each concentration prepares teachers for certification by the State of New Jersey. Programs are offered on a semester basis and classes meet in the late afternoons and evenings. Summer sessions are available also.

For persons who earned their undergraduate degrees in an area other than education and want to be certified to teach nursery through eighth grade or ninth through twelfth grade, the college offers a 26-credit teacher certification program. The program consists of six courses (18 credits) in addition to eight credits in student teaching.

The master of business administration program has five areas of concentration: finance, management, management information systems, marketing, and international business. The finance concentration emphasizes corporate and international finance as well as advanced topics in financial markets and analysis. The international business concentration focuses on the strategies needed for taking a worldwide perspective of business and the various aspects of globalization, an integral part of the mission of many organizations. The concentration in management examines organizational structure and management control to create flexible, adaptive, and efficient organizations. The concentration in management information systems provides a comprehensive overview of components, technologies, services, current issues, and problem-solving techniques present in every business organization. The marketing concentration focuses on marketing planning strategy and research, consumer behavior, and international aspects of marketing. The MBA is 48-credits with a common core of 24 credits. The MBA program runs on a trimester calendar, with courses offered in the evenings and on weekends.

Saint Peter's College offers a 30-credit master of science in accountancy degree program which provides students with the knowledge and skills needed to handle these demands as they enter the 21st century. The program also fulfills anticipated requirements in New Jersey whereby students need 150 credit-hours of education to sit for the CPA exam. Similar to the MBA program, the MS in accountancy runs on a trimester calendar, with courses offered in the evenings and on weekends.

The teacher certification, MBA and MS in accountancy programs can be completed strictly in the evenings or strictly on weekends. Students can also mix and match their class schedule by taking evening and weekend courses.

The master of science in nursing offers two areas of specialization: adult nurse practitioner and case management with a functional concentration in nursing administration. Both options consist of core courses that provide a foundation in graduate study and theoretical and clinical practica. The 37-credit MSN in Case Management is offered on a trimester basis. The 39-credit MSN in Adult Nurse Practitioner is offered on a combined trimester/semester schedule. For nurses who already possess a master's degree in nursing and want to earn a certificate as an adult nurse practitioner, a 25-credit post-master's certificate is offered. Graduate study in nursing is offered exclusively at the Englewood Cliffs campus.

The college also offers an RN to MSN bridge program for registered nurses who hold bachelor's degrees in fields other than nursing. The program consists of one four-credit Bridge course as well as an undergraduate course in statistics and nursing research. In addition, all policies, requirements and procedures for admission into the MSN program apply.

CAMPUS & LOCATION

Graduate programs are available at the Jersey City and Englewood Cliffs campuses conveniently located in northern New Jersey and accessible by all major forms of transportation. The main campus in Jersey City is 12 minutes from Manhattan by PATH train. The branch campus at Englewood Cliffs is one mile north of the George Washington Bridge. Graduate students can also take courses at two offsite locations in South Amboy, New Jersey and at the Jersey City Waterfront.

FACILITIES

Every student has a computer id that permits access to 18 computer labs, our campus network, E-mail and the Internet. All classrooms are wired for computer access. The Blackboard Classroom System makes class material available on line 24/7 and facilitates communication between students and professors.

The Yanitelli Recreational Life Center on the Jersey City Campus has indoor tennis, basketball, racquetball and squash courts, a track, a swimming pool, a sauna, and workout rooms. Student lounges on both campuses offer a bite to eat or drink. The College Store on both campuses sells textbooks as well as various other items. In Jersey City, shuttle service is provided to and from the Journal Square PATH station, and between the campus and the Armory parking lot. At Englewood Cliffs and Saint Peter's Prep, there is ample parking in lots adjacent to the academic buildings.

EXPENSES AND FINANCIAL AID

For 2005–2006, cost is $730 per credit. Loan information, installment planning and tuition deferment information is available in the office of financial aid.

FACULTY

In addition to being dedicated teachers, the faculty members at Saint Peter's hold PhDs from leading universities and are scholars, researchers, and professionals in their fields. These experienced educators use a variety of teaching approaches including lectures, classroom discussions, case studies, team projects, simulation exercises, and independent study. They are supportive of students in their endeavors to balance commitments to study, family, and work.

STUDENTS

The students at Saint Peter's College are parents, employees, spouses and community members who now seek to add a graduate degree to their list of accomplishments. Its graduates are successful business professionals, healthcare professional, teachers, and entrepreneurs, who have used their learning for self-fulfillment, to change careers, or to earn a promotion in their current career.

ADMISSIONS

To be considered for admission, applicants must possess a 4-year baccalaureate degree from an accredited undergraduate institution. A completed application, 3 letters of recommendation, official transcripts from all institutions attended, GRE, GMAT or MAT scores and a personal statement, must be submitted to the Office of Graduate Admissions. International applicant requirements can be found on the Saint Peter's College website.

For more information call the Office of Graduate Admissions and speak with the graduate admissions coordinator at 201-915-9203. Candace Amorino, Graduate Admissions Coordinator

DEGREES

MA in education: Administration & supervision; reading, teaching

MBA: International business, management, management information systems, finance, marketing

MSN: Adult nurse practitioner, case management, RN to MSN bridge program

MS in accountancy

SOUTHERN METHODIST UNIVERSITY
Cox School of Business

PROGRAMS & CURRICULUM

The two-year MBA curriculum is composed of 60 credit hours that include a global experience and a modular curriculum, the Cox School's program builds a strong portfolio of diverse international perspectives and course offerings. Cox MBA students are required to select and complete a concentration in one of the following areas: Accounting, financial consulting, finance (corporate or investments), information technologies and operations management, e-business/telecommunications, general management, strategic leadership, marketing (marketing consulting or product and brand management), and strategy and entrepreneurship.

The American Airlines global leadership program is a mandatory, all travel expenses paid, two-week, travel-abroad course. All first-year students visit one of three regions of the world—Asia, Europe, or Latin America—to meet with business and government leaders. The goal is to allow students to experience how business is conducted globally. In addition, the school's location at the gateway to NAFTA and Latin America is well positioned for enhancing international perspectives.

Cox's distinguished Business Leadership Center (BLC) complements the classroom curriculum throughout the two-year period. The BLC's innovative program is designed to help students develop effective management skills through seminars that center on interpersonal and communication skills, team building, and negotiation skills. Courses are organized by business leaders and taught by outside consultants from some of today's most progressive corporations.

An international exchange program allows select students to experience their international business education firsthand by studying abroad. Cox has relationships with schools in Australia, Belgium, Brazil, China, Denmark, England, France, Germany, Japan, Mexico, Singapore, Spain, and Venezuela.

FACILITIES

Facilities at Cox are some of the most technologically advanced, and include wireless internet access for the over 1,500 students are enrolled in the Cox School working toward BBA, MBA, and executive MBAs. The Cox School of Business complex includes the Joseph Wylie Fincher Memorial Building, the Cary M. Maguire Building, and the Trammell Crow Building. The Fincher Building houses administrative and faculty offices while the Maguire and Crow Buildings house classrooms, computer labs, and student study rooms. Included in the Cox School complex is the Business Information Center (BIC), combining traditional features of a university library with the technological advancements of online databases and other resources.

The James M Collins Executive Education Center is a state-of-the-art teaching and conference facility designed to meet the evolving needs of business executives, managers, and professionals. The Collins Center will house the Cox School's Division of Executive and Management Development and executive MBA Program.

EXPENSES

The estimated cost of tuition and fees for 2005–2006 is $33,650; books and supplies are approximately $2,000. Off-campus housing generally costs between $600 and $1,200 per month.

Merit scholarships are awarded to students each year based on individual merit and achievement. Recipients are selected on the basis of demonstrated academic achievement, managerial experience, and managerial potential. A variety of named scholarships and awards are available. Scholarships are awarded for the entire two-year period, subject to satisfactory academic performance. Approximately 75 percent of Cox MBA students receive some form of merit scholarship. The Cox Distinguished MBA Scholars program awards up to 10 full-tuition scholarships each year to new students.

STUDENTS

Cox MBA students come from all regions of the United States and the world. Each fall, Cox enrolls approximately 100 new students into the full-time MBA program and joint degree program (Juris Doctor). Students have a wide variety of academic disciplines and professional experiences. Cox's small size not only promotes collaboration among students, it also creates a close and supportive environment for students, the faculty, and the staff. The small size also gives students significant opportunities to assume leadership roles in MBA student organizations and advisory groups.

ST. JOHN'S UNIVERSITY
Peter J. Tobin College of Business

AT A GLANCE

For nearly 80 years, St. John's University's Peter J. Tobin College of Business has offered future business leaders a strong foundation in management education with a focus on developing individuals for the most senior corporate positions in the world. The importance that we attach to practical business knowledge and technology, globalization as reflected in our being a first mover among U.S. business schools in establishing a campus abroad, and a deep appreciation for the special ethical challenges of business practice in our contemporary environment enable the college to offer unique opportunities for students who are committed to excellence. These features, combined with our network of over 35,000 alumni worldwide, talented and dedicated faculty, outstanding resources, and commitment to a values-based business education, all make the college unique in providing business leadership skills for life.

CAMPUS & LOCATION

The Peter J. Tobin College of Business (TCB) has three residential campuses in exciting New York City and one campus in Rome, Italy. The park-like Queens and Staten Island campuses are minutes away from Manhattan. The 10-story building that makes up the Manhattan campus stands in the heart of New York's financial center. The campus in Rome, Italy, reflects the broad reach and international focus maintained by The Tobin College of Business.

DEGREES OFFERED

The MBA degree is offered with specializations in accounting, taxation, decision sciences, executive management, finance, financial services, international business, international finance, marketing management, insurance, actuarial sciences, risk management, and computer information systems for managers. Successful completion requires a minimum of 36 credit hours; additional credits may be required, depending on previous course work that has been completed in business and economics. Individual plans of study are developed for each student in consultation with advisers and faculty members in the college. The degree may be completed on either a part-time or full-time basis and includes study in the MBA core, specialization courses, and electives. The master of science (MS) degree is offered in taxation, accounting and in insurance financial management and the management of risk. Advanced professional certificates (APCs) are available to individuals who have completed the MBA degree and are designed to enable such students to accrue additional knowledge or skills in another field or update and enhance skills in their current field. Eighteen credits are required for completion of the APC.

The Rome campus offers the MBA degree in international finance and marketing.

PROGRAMS & CURRICULUM

The Tobin College has a long history of providing a strong educational foundation to individuals who have risen to senior executive positions all over the world. The educational philosophy is grounded in the importance of not only conveying business knowledge and skills but also developing leaders who appreciate the need to think, and often act, globally and who realize and value the role that ethics and social responsibility plays in successful business practice.

The Tobin College is fully accredited by AACSB International—The Association to Advance Collegiate Schools of Business.

FACILITIES

The main library of the university is in St. Augustine Hall, located on the Queens campus. Together with the collections of the Loretto Memorial Library on the Staten Island campus, the Law School Library, the Oakdale Campus Library, the Kathryn and Shelby Cullom Davis Library in Manhattan, and the Rome campus library, the total university library collection numbers 1.7 million volumes and includes more than 6,000 periodic subscriptions. These materials support course offerings as well as students' cultural and recreational interests. The collection includes government documents and audiovisual materials.

EXPENSES & FINANCIAL AID

Tuition in 2003–2004 is $685 per credit. An additional $75 general fee per term is due at the time of registration. A limited number of graduate assistantships are awarded, based on academic merit.

To be considered for on-campus housing, students should submit their request to the Office of Admission. Through the university's housing service, students can find comfortable and convenient off-campus housing in surrounding neighborhoods. All inquiries concerning off-campus housing should be directed to the Office of Student Life at 718-990-6257.

FACULTY

The faculty at the Tobin College of Business is drawn from leading institutions all over the world. Our full-time faculty number 101, and this group is complemented by business practitioners who regularly serve as adjunct instructors or co-teachers.

STUDENTS

With a student enrollment that reflects the cultural diversity present within actual business settings and the very special business center that is Manhattan in close proximity, the Tobin College has succeeded in launching the careers of more than 35,000 business leaders worldwide. Currently, there are over seven hundred students enrolled at the Tobin College Graduate Division. Special opportunities exist for students to network with alumni of the college for the purposes of career information and development and internships.

ADMISSIONS

Admission to Tobin College has become increasingly competitive in recent years, and prospective students are encouraged to begin the process early. All applicants must possess a baccalaureate from an accredited institution or the international equivalent. The candidate should submit, in addition to the $40 nonrefundable application fee, official transcripts from all undergraduate, graduate, and professional schools they attended. In addition, results of the Graduate Management Admission Test (GMAT) taken within the last five years, a resume, letters of recommendation, and a personal statement should be submitted with the application. Details of these requirements may be obtained from the Office of Admissions of the Tobin College or from the college's website. Applicants who do not speak English as their primary language must also submit the results of the TOEFL.

CAREER SERVICES & PLACEMENT

The Career Center's professional placement programs offer a wide variety of services designed to give each graduate student and alumnus the competitive edge. Services and resources include career advisement, on-campus interviews, full-time and part-time employment opportunities, a career resource library, resume preparation and interview techniques, a videotape library, and mock interview sessions. Owing largely to these services and the extensive network of successful alumni, the Tobin College has consistently enjoyed a high rate of job placement for MBA students within three months of graduation, most recently over 80 percent.

UNIVERSITY OF ARKANSAS—FAYETTEVILLE

Sam M. Walton College of Business

AT A GLANCE

The MBA program at the Sam M. Walton College of Business is a 38 credit-hour program, providing a balanced mix of case studies and lectures as well as individual work and team projects in an AACSB International-approved curriculum. Redesigned in 2000, the lock-step program begins around July 1 of each and ends around June 30 of the following year. In addition to a Strategic Retail Alliances concentration, you may also choose such traditional degree concentrations as finance, global business, or entrepreneurship.

CAMPUS & LOCATION

Location, Location, Location: Part of the larger University of Arkansas system, the Walton College is located in Fayetteville, Arkansas. Situated in the heart of the Ozark Mountains, this community of 60,000 residents is situated in the northwestern corner of the state and is a two-hour drive from Tulsa, four hours from Kansas City, and five hours from Dallas and St. Louis. A regional airport offering daily flights to Atlanta, Chicago, Dallas, Memphis, New York, and St. Louis services the area.

PROGRAMS & CURRICULUM

The MBA program at the Sam M. Walton College of Business has a strategic advantage over other MBA programs in the field of retail marketing. Our concentration in Strategic Retail Alliances prepares you like no other program for a successful career in the consumer packaged goods industry in the rapidly growing mass retail sector.

The Right Tools: Through partnerships with AC Nielsen, IRI and Spectra, MBA students at the University of Arkansas gain hands-on experience with the leading market research tools and category management tools in the consumer packaged goods industry, the only MBA program in the U.S. to have all three systems available.

Real-World Experience: Our MBA students tackle real-world issues by taking leadership roles in consulting projects with Fortune 500 firms such as Procter & Gamble, Wal-Mart, FujiFilm, JB Hunt, Alltel Communications, and others.

Retail Focus: The Center for Retailing Excellence is emerging as a leader in supporting research in the issues facing the retailing industry. The CRE annual conference and symposium, "Understanding the Mass Retail Shopper" was attended by over 350 retailing executives, who came to hear speakers such as Bob Flaherty, vice president, Nestlé, and Todd Hale, a senior vice president with AC Nielsen's Homescan Consumer Insights Sales and Service.

The accelerated, one-year MBA program at the Walton College is a 38-credit-hour program, providing a balanced mix of case studies and lectures as well as individual work and team projects in an AACSB International-approved curriculum. In addition to a Strategic Retail Alliances concentration, you may also choose such traditional degree concentrations as finance, global business, or entrepreneurship.

EXPENSES & FINANCIAL AID

Tuition and fees:

- In-state: $324 per enrollment hour

- Out-of-state: $654.50 per enrollment hour

- Fees: $40.57 per enrollment hour

- International Student Service Fee: $55 per semester

Mandatory International Student Health Insurance: $336 fall semester and $474 spring semester

Fayetteville consistently has been selected as one of the best cities in which to live in the United States. The area has a relatively low cost of living; students can expect to pay approximately $11,746 a year for living expenses, including room, board, books, supplies, and personal expenses.

The Sam M. Walton College of Business offers a limited number of graduate assistantships each year. Some graduate assistantships are teaching assistantships, others provide research assistance to faculty, and others are off-site assistantships with local corporations. A limited number of graduate assistantships is available for each master's degree program. The assistantship includes a monthly stipend, tuition (in-state and out-of-state), plus 60 percent of the student's health insurance premiums. International students are eligible for graduate assistantships.

STUDENTS

The University of Arkansas—Fayetteville serves as the major center of liberal and professional education and as the primary land-grant campus for the state. The university offers graduate education leading to the master's degree in more than 82 fields and to the doctoral degree in more than 30 carefully selected areas.

ADMISSIONS

Major factors considered in the admission decision include professional work experience, undergraduate academic record, performance on the Graduate Management Admissions Test (GMAT), letters of recommendation, and the applicant's maturity and motivation as demonstrated in two essays. Applicants with two or more years of professional work experience will be given preference for admission into the full-time program.

Although no specific minimum score requirements have been established for admission, successful applicants are expected to rank in the 80th percentile (580 or higher) on the GMAT and possess a cumulative undergraduate grade point average of 3.4. Applicants whose native language is not English must present satisfactory scores on the TOEFL (550 paper-based or 213 computer-based) or IELTS (6.5).

International applicants, all applicants without an undergraduate business degree, and applicants who completed an undergraduate degree in business more than three years ago should submit their completed application materials by November 15. Admission decisions for early applicants are made by December 15, giving the successful applicant sufficient time to complete the preparatory work prior to matriculation in the summer. Preference in admission and financial aid is given to applicants who submit their application prior to February 15. All applications received after February 15 are processed on a space-available basis. In no case is an applicant admitted after May 15.

Website: www.uark.edu/depts/mba/

CAREER SERVICES & PLACEMENT

Career Connections: The Walton College has a dedicated Career Development Center with a network of alumni in nearly every major local company, including Wal-Mart, Procter & Gamble, JB Hunt, Acxiom, FujiFilm, Kraft Foods, Unilever, Tyson Foods, IBM, and others.

UNIVERSITY OF BRITISH COLUMBIA
Sauder School of Business

SAUDER
School of Business
UNIVERSITY OF BRITISH COLUMBIA

AT A GLANCE
The UBC MBA is a rigorous 15-month program built around a challenging and results-focused curriculum that prepares students for business leadership. Students can choose to either enhance the depth of their specialization or to broaden their skill set through a range of more than 80 elective modules in 14 different subject areas. Central to the UBC MBA is an innovative, award-winning three-month core program integrating seven key business disciplines into one foundation course.

CAMPUS & LOCATION
The University of British Columbia (UBC), located in Vancouver, boasts to be one of Canada's most beautiful university campuses. It was established in 1915 and is the nation's third largest university, with an enrollment of over 38,000 students from around the world. The Sauder School of Business is Canada's premier research business school with internationally renowned faculty who are at the forefront of management thinking.

PROGRAMS & CURRICULUM
The Integrated Core provides an intensive foundation in finance, marketing, accounting, human resources, statistics, managerial economics, and information systems. It is team taught as one comprehensive course to mirror the complexity of the global business environment. Individual subject areas are taught separately and from an integrative perspective to help develop students' understanding of the true multidimensional nature of business. Students develop a broad-based, senior-level strategic approach to business decision making, as well as collaborative and leadership skills.

Following the integrated core, students can enhance their marketability by developing expertise in one of seven areas of specialization: entrepreneurship, finance, information technology management, marketing, organizational development & human resources, strategic management, or supply chain management. Sub-specializations are also offered in e-business and international business. Each specialization consists of required and elective modules.

Students also have the opportunity to apply their knowledge through either a three-month internship with an organization or an industry project supervised by a faculty member related to their area of specialization.

The professional development program (PDP) is dedicated to enhancing students' personal effectiveness through seminars, workshops, guest speakers, discussion groups, networking events, career coaching, and self-directed activities. Valuable skills taught during PDP include time and meeting management, presentation skills, managing multicultural teams, conflict resolution, as well as career management tools.

The UBC MBA program offers students a global perspective through specialized international courses, interaction with the multicultural student body and faculty, and participation in one of the many MBA exchanges. The UBC MBA program exchanges with an impressive list of 24 leading business schools in 21 different countries around the world.

FACILITIES
The Henry Angus Building is the primary home of the Sauder School of Business, although some executive education seminars take place downtown Vancouver at UBC Robson Square.

The David Lam Management Research Library houses a collection of print and electronic materials covering all facets of business management and acts as a resource for students and academic researchers as well as members of the business community.

EXPENSES & FINANCIAL AID
Tuition fees for the 15-month MBA program are $36,000 CAD (subject to change—see www.ubc.ca/mba) for both domestic and international students. Participants can expect to spend another $15,000 to $20,000 CAD for books, materials, and living expenses during the program.

All domestic and international students admissible to the program are eligible for merit-based awards up to full tuition. Application to the UBC MBA serves as application to these awards and it is the applicant's advantage to apply early to be considered for scholarships. UBC MBA students also have access to an institutionally negotiated loan package to financially support their studies.

MBA students are not encouraged to work part-time during the program. However, most students earn an average salary of $3,000 CAD per month during their summer internships. Some students are also asked to provide marking or exam invigilation assistance to business school subjects during their program of studies. A number of performance-based scholarships are available to recognize top students in the MBA program.

FACULTY
The Sauder School of Business has over 100 faculty members with impressive backgrounds and achievements. For a current list of faculty and their academic and research profiles, please visit the website at www.sauder.ubc.ca/faculty/index.cfm.

STUDENTS
Honored by the university's Campus Advisory Board on Student Development for having "a significant positive impact on student life and student development," the UBC MBA program experience fosters a spirit of cooperation and teamwork evident from study groups to social events. Beyond the rich educational experience, the reward is a lifetime network of international friends and business contacts. The business school network links 24,000 alumni in 60 countries around the world.

ADMISSIONS
Applicants must have a four-year bachelor's degree or recognized equivalent from an accredited institution, with a solid academic record and a competitive GMAT score to be eligible for admission to the UBC MBA. Candidates with diverse academic and professional backgrounds are encouraged to apply. Applicants with less than two years of work experience are admitted to the program only under exceptional circumstances. Successful candidates possess managerial and leadership potential, maturity, ambition, drive and a clear sense of purpose, demonstrated by professional experience, extracurricular activities, personal interests, and written submissions.

SPECIAL PROGRAMS
UBC offers a joint LLB/MBA degree, which is a four-year program administered jointly by the business school and the law school. A two-year MBA/MAPPS (master of arts, Asia Pacific policy studies) joint degree is also offered.

CAREER SERVICES & PLACEMENT
The Sauder School of Business Career Center offers personal consultation and a structured program to assist in identifying, developing, and achieving career goals. Program participants complete a Web-based self-assessment test prior to beginning classes to clarify career direction. During the period of study, MBA students receive one-on-one career coaching and skills training in areas such as resume building, personal presentation, business etiquette, interviewing, and networking.

THE UNIVERSITY OF COLORADO AT COLORADO SPRINGS
College of Business & Administration

AT A GLANCE

The University of Colorado at Colorado Springs, along with the College of Business & Administration, was established in 1965. The campus is the fastest growing of the four in the University of Colorado system. The College of Business & Administration awards the bachelor of science in business administration degree and the master of business administration degree (MBA). Students may pursue an MBA either through our on-campus program or via distance learning. Both degree programs are accredited by the AACSB International: The Association to Advance Collegiate Schools of Business. AACSB International is the highest accreditation that a college of business can earn in the United States; only 30 percent of the nation's schools have earned it.

There are many factors that distinguish the UCCS Graduate School of Business Administration from other graduate business programs, but one stands above the rest: our commitment to blending business practice and research into every aspect of our educational programs. As the largest professional college on the campus of the University of Colorado at Colorado Springs and one of only a third of the business schools across the country to receive the prestigious accreditation from AACSB International: The International Association for Management Education, the Graduate School of Business Administration has been helping to prepare students for careers in business since 1965.

CAMPUS & LOCATION

CU—Colorado Springs is located on approximately 514 acres in northeast Colorado Springs, at the foot of Austin Bluffs, a rugged natural cliff formation. The campus provides a spectacular view of the Front Range of the Rockies including Pikes Peak, a 14,100-foot mountain. Inspired by the view from its pinnacle, Katharine Lee Bates wrote *America the Beautiful* in 1893. The campus boasts easy access to Interstate 25, downtown, and recreational areas.

DEGREES OFFERED

You will find that our MBA program offers an educational experience that creates lifetime career value. We not only offer a general MBA but also various specializations and graduate certificates. We offer our MBA in two delivery methods, on-campus and online, with various specializations, thereby offering you the quality and flexibility necessary for you to complete the program successfully and in time. This dual mode of delivery assures that students who begin their MBA with us either on-residence or on distance will finish with us in either format. Also offered is an executive MBA in collaboration with Boulder and Denver graduate programs.

PROGRAMS & CURRICULUM

To earn your MBA at UCCS, you will take a total of 36-48 credit hours of courses, depending on your academic background. These courses may be taken on campus or online. We've divided these hours into three categories:

Preparatory Courses: 12 hours (4 classes)

The preparatory courses are an integral component to the MBA degree curriculum. The concepts in these courses are fundamental to your education.

Core Course: 21 hours (7 classes)

Core Courses make up the heart of the MBA program and cover areas that are directly applicable in today's business world.

Area of Emphasis/Elective Courses: 15 hours (5 classes)

You can develop expertise in a chosen specialization. Maximum flexibility is offered with a choice of 10 possible emphases. The MBA electives enhance your background by allowing you to develop extra breadth for greater cross-functionality or additional depth in your selected area of emphasis.

EXPENSES & FINANCIAL AID

Distance MBA: $1,390 per course plus a $51 technology fee per course (fall 2004); all courses are 3 hours. 36 hours, or 12 courses are required (approximately $18,000 for the whole program). If preparatory courses are needed, total tuition will be higher.

On-campus: $289 per credit hour for Colorado residents, plus fees. 36–48 hours are required. (Approximately $15,000 for the whole program)

On-campus out-of-state: $982 per credit hour for non-residents of Colorado, plus fees. 36–48 hours are required (approximately $39,000 for the entire program).

FACULTY

The MBA faculty members at UCCS are doctoral-qualified academic scholars from preeminent universities. They are leaders in their fields who author and edit peer-reviewed journals and textbooks. Our faculty members are devoted to excellence in teaching. Our faculty demonstrates the entrepreneurial spirit in the classroom by sharing prior business experience, research findings, and current cutting edge issues with students. The academic strength of our professors emphasizes the themes and issues that dominate today's business environment: technology management, global competitiveness, and strategic planning. Our faculty consults for Fortune 500 companies, conduct research in their business specialty, and publish in leading academic journals.

STUDENTS

Student success is paramount to our thinking, teaching, programs, and processes and is the key to our success. We commit to creating quality and value as hallmarks of the college, to living our ideals, to treating others with respect, and to working collaboratively for the best interests of the college and university.

We will establish and maintain mutually beneficial relationships with all of those individuals who and organizations that have an interest in our success.

ADMISSIONS

The two primary factors are prior academic performance and scores on a standardized test. The GMAT is the standardized test that is preferred. There is no minimum score; however, the accepted average is 540–590. LSAT, MCAT, or DAT results are accepted for applicants who hold the corresponding degree. GRE results are accepted if the exam is taken prior to applying to program. There is no minimum GPA; however, the average undergraduate grade point average for admitted MBA students is approximately 3.00.

CAREER SERVICES & PLACEMENT

The College of Business Career & Placement Center was created to provide business students and alumni with assistance in career development by offering the needed resources to be successful. The College of Business Career & Placement Center also provides a link between students and the business community through experience e-recruiting network. This network allows students to post resumes and search for jobs and internships. Employers are able to post open positions and view student resumes.

UNIVERSITY OF IOWA
Henry B. Tippie School of Management

THE UNIVERSITY OF IOWA
TIPPIE SCHOOL OF MANAGEMENT

AT A GLANCE

The University of Iowa's Henry B. Tippie School of Management offers a master of business administration (MBA) degree that consistently ranks in the top 50 MBA programs in the world. There are many characteristics that contribute to the quality of the Tippie MBA including a flexible curriculum and great placement results.

We attract the best and brightest students from around the world to our program. While at Tippie, students enhance their knowledge of business fundamentals and further their professional development. The end result is successful graduates that are tomorrow's business leaders.

LOCATION AND ENVIRONMENT

Iowa City is a diverse, highly cosmopolitan community of 60,000 set in the natural scenic beauty of Iowa's rolling hills and woods. The University of Iowa campus is the heart of Iowa City. The 1,900-acre campus is located along both sides of the Iowa River. The campus community provides a rich variety of activities and resources for students including Big Ten athletics, natural history and art museums, the Center for the Arts, Hancher Auditorium, and the UI hospitals and clinics.

Business programs are housed in the 187,000-square-foot John Pappajohn Business Building and the newly constructed Pomerantz Center. Multimedia capabilities and instructional technology are integrated throughout the classrooms and facilities. In addition to the largest computer laboratory on campus, a wireless LAN provides students access to a full range of technology services. Opening in 2005, the Pomerantz Center provides additional classrooms for MBA students and a full-service Career Center.

DEGREES OFFERED

The Tippie School of Management offers a full-time MBA program on-campus. The MBA program for professionals and managers is offered during the evening in Cedar Rapids, the Quad Cities, Newton, and Des Moines, Iowa. The executive MBA is offered on-campus and in Des Moines, Iowa. A dual MBA/masters in engineering program is offered in cooperation with Iowa State University in Cedar Rapids. International MBA programs are offered in Hong Kong and Beijing. The Tippie College of Business also offers a master of accountancy degree and PhD programs in economics and business. Students may also pursue a dual degree program with the MBA in law, nursing, library science, hospital and health administration, and medicine.

ACADEMIC PROGRAMS

A world-class MBA program improves students' professional and personal lives, intellectually, practically, and ethically. The Tippie MBA's integrated program of quality academics, experiential business applications, and professional development does exactly that. Management education at Tippie is characterized by unmatched academic training, guided experience-based learning, and transforming professional development. Five curricular themes challenge you to stretch your intellectual abilities, inspire you to reach new heights of achievement, and elicit your best efforts in every endeavor.

FACILITIES AND EQUIPMENT

The state-of-the-art facilities of the John Pappajohn Business Building and Pomerantz Center provide an outstanding arena for learning. The Tippie School of Management uses the latest communications and course delivery technology to help your class network effectively.

EXPENSES

The Tippie MBA provides one of the best returns on investment available. This nationally accredited program provides a top-notch education that can help you take your career to the next level.

2005-2006 ACADEMIC YEAR TUITION AND FEES (FULL-TIME MBA PROGRAM)

Annual Tuition

Iowa Residents	$11,970
Non-residents	$21,960

Computer Fees	$215
Health Fees	$182
Student Union, Activities, and Service Fees	$200
Building Fee	$119

Total Tuition and Fees

Iowa Residents	$12.686
Non-residents	$22,676

Housing, textbooks, and personal living costs are approximately $12,000 per year.

Merit-based financial aid is offered to outstanding candidates each year. The criteria for these awards mirror those for admission-academic record, work history, leadership experience, test scores—although only those with the highest qualifications receive offers for aid. Domestic and international applicants are eligible for awards. Awards may consist of a scholarship, a graduate assistantship, or both. Most scholarships vary from $1,000 to $4,000. Graduate assistantships provide a salary of approximately $8,000, a contribution toward health insurance costs, and resident tuition status for non-Iowa residents.

FACULTY

Engaging. Experienced. World-renowned. Tippie MBA faculty combine exemplary teaching and academic research with consulting practices that enhance in-class applications of the latest developments in business. Tippie's faculty realize how critical it is to stay "in-the-know" and on the pulse of emerging business trends and innovative practices. Our teaching combines the latest trends in business management with traditional theories that have withstood the tests of time. It's the best way to send students into the marketplace with a competitive edge.

STUDENT ORGANIZATIONS AND ACTIVITIES

MBA student organizations provide many venues for participation in activities outside the classroom. These organizations offer the opportunity for students to demonstrate leadership involvement and collaboration. Student clubs organize professional development events, career networking opportunities, social events, and many other activities that enhance the Tippie MBA experience.

Tippie MBAs are not passive recipients of education, but active players in determining the type of MBA experience delivered. Student organizations provide the primary venue for participation in activities outside the classroom. These organizations offer the opportunity for students to demonstrate leadership, involvement, and collaboration. Student clubs organize professional development events, career networking opportunities, social events, and many other activities that enhance the Tippie MBA experience.

The entering class in the full-time MBA program averages nearly 4 years of work experience, a GPA of approximately 3.36 (4.0 scale), and a GMAT score of 645.

ADMISSIONS

The Tippie MBA is seeking candidates who have clearly demonstrated the ability to complete a rigorous academic program and the potential for success in a professional environment. The admission review process includes consideration of a number of factors that are all important in our decision: academic background; standardized tests (GMAT and TOEFL); work experience; leadership; and the admissions interview.

CAREER SERVICES & PLACEMENT

Tippie MBA Career Services staff are true partners in helping you achieve your career goals. During your first semester, you refine your resume, prepare a portfolio, pair up with an alumni mentor, and complete your personal marketing plan. Staff members are your advocates, consultants, and marketers. They are your coaches as you practice your interviewing skills and learn to market your most important asset-yourself.

UNIVERSITY OF MASSACHUSETTS—BOSTON

College of Management Graduate Programs

AT A GLANCE

The University of Massachusetts (UMass) Boston boasts nearly 12,000 commuting students in its undergraduate, graduate, and continuing education programs, making it the second-largest campus of the University of Massachusetts system. UMass Boston is a community of scholars who take pride in academic excellence, diversity, research, and service. The fabric of academic research and scholarship is tightly woven into the public and community service needs of Boston and the modern metropolitan center.

The UMass Boston College of Management offers master's level degrees in both business administration (MBA) and accounting (MSA). Drawing students from greater Boston and around the world, our MBA and MSA programs bring together a diverse group of highly talented young professionals from the healthcare, financial services, manufacturing, computer, consulting and education industries, among others.

Numerous student organizations, including the Graduate Student Association, the MBA Association and the MSA Association, provide graduate students of the College of Management with opportunities for professional development, networking and building a sense of community. An extensive alumni network keeps students connected to the College of Management and its resources even after graduation.

CAMPUS & LOCATION

The university is located on a beautiful landscaped peninsula just south of downtown Boston, overlooking Boston Harbor and the Harbor Islands. The university's neighbors are the John F. Kennedy Presidential Library and the Massachusetts State Archives and Commonwealth Museum. The city of Boston itself, with its worldwide standing as a cultural center and its well-earned reputation as America's favorite college town, offers UMass Boston students a wealth of resources for academic and social exploration and entertainment. Everything from Fenway Park to the Museum of Fine Arts is easily accessible from UMass Boston via both public and private transportation.

Floor-to-ceiling windows looking out onto sparkling views of Boston Harbor, stunning atrium spaces, sage-green carpeting—these are some of the first things people may notice in exploring UMass Boston's new 330,000-square-foot Campus Center. Opened in the spring of 2004, the Campus Center serves as a gateway to the university offering a spectacular arrival-point for visitors and creating new opportunities for encounters and activities that enrich the academic experience. All of UMass Boston's student organizations are housed in the new center. Students will also find a food court and dining area, a large contemporary bookstore, academic and career advising offices, a game room, numerous lounges and study areas with wireless and hard-wired internet connections, computer kiosks, a ballroom, an alumni room, and spaces for meetings and conferences. "The One Stop," a streamlined student service center, reduces the time required to conduct registration, billing, and financial aid business.

PROGRAMS & CURRICULUM

The MBA and MSA programs in the College of Management combine strategically focused management curricula with optional specializations that prepare students for specific management responsibilities. Classes are typically taught by experienced full-time faculty with both academic and professional qualifications.

Small class size creates an active learning environment with a great deal of faculty-student interaction. MGT 650, a first-semester course, incorporates the team-building and analytical skills that will be practiced throughout both programs. Many College of Management classes have a major case-study component that provides insight into corporate, nonprofit, and small business issues. Others use projects and simulations to generate involvement and practical experience. Both course work and student resources help students develop the communications, presentation and analytical skills required of contemporary managers.

The College of Management graduate programs are committed to the success of all their students, both academically and professionally, and to providing the individual attention and support that will turn their academic accomplishments into professional reality.

STUDENTS

Our students in the UMass Boston MBA and MSA programs are a diverse mix of professionals from a wide range of professional, geographic, ethnic and cultural backgrounds. Hailing from some 31 states and 57 countries, graduate students in the College of Management are accomplished managers, accountants, educators, healthcare providers, researchers and consultants who seek the knowledge and credentials needed to enhance and advance their careers. They come to us with an average of nearly six years of professional experience.

UNIVERSITY OF ROCHESTER
William E. Simon Graduate School of Business Administration

AT A GLANCE
The William E. Simon Graduate School of Business Administration at the University of Rochester in Rochester, New York, offers an integrated, cross-functional approach to management, which uses economics as both the framework and common language of business and the skills to become an effective leader.

The Simon School has been ranked nationally and internationally among the top 30 schools of business. The school is accredited by the AACSB—the Association of Collegiate Schools of Business International since 1966. Visit us at www.simon.rochester.edu

CAMPUS & LOCATION
The Simon School is situated on the River Campus of the University of Rochester, near the banks of the Genesee River and three miles from downtown Rochester, New York. The park-like setting of the campus provides the perfect environment for quiet study or social activity.

PROGRAMS & CURRICULUM
The Simon School's MBA programs are designed to train individuals to solve management problems as team members in a study-team structure. It is a place where thinkers become leaders. The curriculum emphasizes learning the principles of economics and effective decision-making through a mix of lecture, case study, and project courses. The degree program requires 67 hours (twenty quarter courses) and can be completed in six quarters of full-time study. Four core courses are required in the underlying disciplines of economics, applied statistics, accounting, and computers and information systems. One course must be taken in each of the functional areas of finance, marketing, operations management, and organization theory.

FACILITIES
Schlegel Hall is a four-story classroom and student-services building. The building contains nine case-style classrooms, which seat 35 to 100 students and 21 rooms for group study. Classrooms are equipped with state-of-the-art audiovisual technology to facilitate contemporary educational processes.

The Simon School Computing Center manages delivery of a comprehensive range of computing and communications services to Simon students, faculty, and staff. Located on the fourth floor of Schlegel Hall, the Computing Center is an 8,000-square-foot, state-of-the-art facility, which includes a 3,200-square-foot student lab. The center operates more than 70 networked microcomputers with high-speed Internet access as well as access to laser printing and other output devices. All systems run a collection of popular software for student use. The Simon School has a wireless LAN system which makes Web access even easier.

EXPENSES & FINANCIAL AID
In addition to the $125 application fee, tuition was $1,124 per credit hour or $33,720 per year for 2004–2005. The cost of books and supplies averages $1,400 a year, and living expenses (rent, food supplies, personal expenses, and health insurance) were estimated at less than $10,000 for the 2004–2005 academic year. Both U.S. and international applicants are eligible for merit awards. The deadline for applying for merit-scholarship assistance is February 1 for September applicants and August 1 for January applicants.

FACULTY
The Simon School faculty is known internationally for leading scholarship in management education. There is a long tradition at Simon of coordinating teaching and research, as well as integrating knowledge from all of the functional areas into the curriculum. Faculty accessibility is a specific benefit of a Simon education. Teaching awards for the best teachers are presented annually by each MBA class, and teaching is improved continuously through a formal faculty peer-review. Leading-edge research is intrinsic to teaching the basic scientific principles of management. Many research findings used by the Simon faculty in classroom study have served as foundations for corporate practices in use today. Simon faculty members serve as editors on four major academic journals, and recent studies of research productivity rank them among the top five faculties in the United States.

STUDENTS
Each September approximately 130 students enter the Simon community as members of four cohorts (class teams). Another 50 students join their classmates in January as cohort number five. Each cohort takes all core classes together. September entrants complete the first-year core courses during the fall, winter, and spring quarters; the majority of January entrants complete core courses during the winter, spring, and summer quarters. Within each cohort, students are assigned to a study team of four or five members. Due to the large number of students from outside the United States (40 percent), the study-team structure at the Simon School takes on special significance. Each team always includes representatives from at least two countries.

ADMISSIONS
A Simon School Admissions Committee reads each application individually and evaluates recommendations, teamwork, and communication skills, the nature and scope of prior work experience, the undergraduate academic record, GMAT scores, TOEFL scores as an indicator of English-language skills, evidence of leadership and maturity, and career focus. English language proficiency is critically important for successful interaction in the Simon School's geographically diversified study-team structure. Potential contributions to Simon classmates and to the world's business community are carefully considered. All undergraduate majors are represented in the program.

SPECIAL PROGRAMS
The special orientation program is another way in which Simon strives to instill a thirst for leadership in each student. In addition to welcoming students into the program, the special orientation is an excellent opportunity to jump-start the career planning process. During the two-week special orientation period, students participate in a statistics review workshop, self-assessment exercises, personal selling and communication skills instruction, corporate leadership training, and one-on-one career counseling. The goals of the program include acclimating students to campus life, assessing and building on specific skills, and introducing the valuable programs of the Career Management Center. In addition, students participate in several student-managed modules designed to enhance leadership skills in the areas of team building, training in diversity issues, ethical decision making, and social responsibility.

CAREER SERVICES & PLACEMENT
The Career Management Center's counseling and education staff offers targeted, personalized counseling to assist students in identifying, initiating, and implementing highly effective career plans. Through individual career counseling and engaging industry focused programs, students develop a career-search strategy to capture a rewarding internship and fulfilling full-time position upon graduation.

THE UNIVERSITY OF TAMPA
The John H. Sykes College of Business

JOHN H. SYKES
COLLEGE
OF
BUSINESS
THE UNIVERSITY OF TAMPA

AT A GLANCE
By exploring our MBA program you've recognized that a leading twenty-first-century enterprise requires rethinking of yourself and your career. Technological, environmental, demographic, and political changes are transforming the world, creating new demands for performance. Our goal is to provide you with perspective, skills, mentoring, and lots of opportunities for fully expressing your potential and meeting those demands.

The John H. Sykes College of Business is accredited by AACSB International—The Association to Advance Collegiate Schools of Business. The university is also accredited by the Southern Association of Colleges and Schools to award associate, baccalaureate, and master's degrees.

CAMPUS & LOCATION
The 100-acre University of Tampa campus offers a full-service educational setting that includes a comprehensive library, a broad range of technology and support, an active Career Services and Placement Center, and many student programs.

DEGREES OFFERED
The John H. Sykes College of Business offers the following graduate programs: master of business administration, master of science in accounting, and master of science in technology and innovation management.

The MBA program is delivered in a part-time or full-time schedule and requires between 42.5 and 51.5 credit hours to complete depending upon the undergraduate background. Full-time students can complete the entire program in as little as 16 months in the accelerated full-time day program. Students who work full-time can complete the course work in less than three years in the flex part-time evening program

The MS-TIM program focuses on developing managers to lead the process of innovation in all types of business and takes the global perspective necessary to compete successfully through technology innovation. The program has been extensively benchmarked against similar degrees offered by leading business schools around the world. The courses are specific to technology companies and industry, focused on actual issues that are particularly acute in technology companies. The MS-TIM is offered part-time in the evenings and requires 34 hour hours.

FACILITIES
When it comes to technology, the John H. Sykes College of Business is keeping pace! The new 80,000-square-foot facility boasts more than 1,300 data ports for high-speed networking and access to the Internet. You can log onto the information highway in all 30 classrooms, student break-out rooms, three computer labs, and even in the hallways and vending area. Use these to communicate with your professors, classmates, and students here and around the world.

The Macdonald-Kelce Library provides complete research and study aids in convenient, comfortable and quiet surroundings. UTOPIA, our online catalog provides Web access to Library holdings and links to e-books and databases. Using E-Search, students can remotely access online databases such as Business Source Premier, ABI-INFORM, DISCLOSURE, and Investext. The library staff will assist you in accessing these information sources. You may obtain materials from other area, regional and national libraries through Interlibrary Loan. Also available through UTOPIA are U.S. government documents and many are available both on- and off-campus. Documents include publications such as STATUSA and USA Trade Online. While in the library, you may connect through the library's wireless network.

The Vaughn Center is the new hub of campus life. The first two floors house a multi-cuisine dining facility featuring restaurant-style and fast casual cooking. It's a great place to grab dinner or coffee on the run between your office and class. There is also a convenience store, Barnes & Noble Campus Store, cyber café, game rooms, computer labs, and information desk.

EXPENSES & FINANCIAL AID
Tuition for 2005–2006 is $408 per credit hour. Tuition is payable at registration each semester. In addition, a $35 student services fee is required each term. The cost of books, supplies, health insurance, and personal expenses is additional.

UT graduate assistantships are available each academic year to selected full-time graduate students. Assistantships provide a tuition waiver for up to 9 credit hours per semester, plus a $1,500 stipend. Graduate assistants work 20 hours per week for an academic or administrative office, carry a full course load (at least 8 credit hours), and maintain a 3.0 overall GPA.

FACULTY
All of the MBA faculty members have PhDs. More than half of our graduate faculty has won awards for teaching and professional excellence. Many of our faculty members have owned their own businesses, have helped lead and build major companies, or are engaged in consulting at the highest leadership levels. Faculty members serve on boards and councils throughout the community. They've been quoted in *Fortune, Barron's, The Wall Street Journal*, and in dozens of local, national, and international media.

STUDENTS
Students bring unique cultural practices and perspectives on business, providing an environment in which alternative ideas and ways of thinking are freely exchanged. When international students graduate, they take with them cutting-edge business practices and techniques that make them successful wherever they go. The cultural and educational exchanges that occur at UT provide a perfect training ground for both international and U.S. students.

ADMISSIONS
Admission to UT's MBA program is competitive and is based on a number of factors. Applications are processed on a rolling basis and students are admitted for the fall, spring, or, on a limited basis in the summer sessions. Individual interviews are encouraged but not required. All students admitted to the MBA program must have earned four-year undergraduate degrees. A specific undergraduate degree is not required. A GMAT score of at least 450 or a GRE score of at least 1,000 in verbal and quantitative components and a 3.0 GPA in all previous college work are required.

Students entering the MBA program are expected to be competent in mathematics, have strong communications skills (both written and oral), and be competent with use of computers.

CAREER SERVICES & PLACEMENT
Graduate students can expect individualized attention from the professional staff of the Career Services Center. Typical graduate services include resume critique, design and referral, personal career advising, interview skills refreshers, on-campus company interview opportunities, and informational interviews with other professionals from the greater Tampa Bay area.

UNIVERSITY OF WASHINGTON BUSINESS SCHOOL

AT A GLANCE

More choices. Key connections. A future you define. University of Washington MBA students are immersed in one of the most innovative MBA experiences in the world, built to deliver a personalized education for a career path each student defines for themselves with extensive input. Students begin with first year integrated curriculum that includes tailored development of communication and leadership skills and opportunities for international study and hands-on learning. By doing projects during the school year and internships either with local companies like Microsoft, Amazon.com, and Starbucks, or in places like Thailand or Boston, students connect often with the business community. A unique, individualized approach to career services, a renowned mentor program, and access to 40,000 alumni worldwide provide students with the unparalleled educational flexibility and customized career resources that now distinguish the University of Washington MBA program.

CAMPUS AND LOCATION

Seattle, WA—where Pacific Rim business opportunities meet Pacific Northwest quality of life. The region's dynamic economy is a hotbed for business development across industrial sectors and an ideal laboratory for real-world practice. The UW achieves international recognition in both teaching and research. Since 1975, the university has ranked first among public institutions in the number of federal grants and contracts awarded to its faculty members. Its sixteen schools and colleges provide education to 34,000 students, who can choose from more than 100 academic disciplines and 5,000 courses.

DEGREES OFFERD

The UW Business School offers an undergraduate degree and a full range of graduate degrees. Offerings include:

- BA
- MBA
- Evening MBA
- Executive MBA
- Global MBA
- Technology management MBA
- Master of professional accounting
- PhD

MBA CIRRICULUM

In the first year, the UW MBA program focuses on an integrated study of major business functions — fundamentals in accounting, finance, marketing, ethics, operations management and information systems are woven into modules of varying length. In the spring quarter of year one, students select bridge electives to gain exposure to topics available in year two and develop skills that can be applied in optional summer internships. Year two presents an open-ended opportunity to individualize the program of study. Students can follow a traditional concentration with courses across eleven disciplines or customize a concentration of classes.

EXPENCE

The UW Business School MBA program offers a very good value. Out-of-state tuition is $8,240 per quarter; and Washington residents pay $4,297. Other annual expenses are estimated at about $17,241. Here is a breakdown:

- Room and board: $10,338
- Books, computers, and supplies: $3,000
- Local transportation: $1,260
- Personal expenses: $2,253
- MBA Association dues (for two years): $190
- MBA Club dues: $200

FINANCIAL AID

Financial aid is available from the University of Washington and the UW Business School in the form of loans, work-study, scholarships, and academic employment. All admitted applicants are considered for merit-based scholarships. Once admitted, students may also apply for other business school scholarships. Domestic applicants may obtain federal loan application forms at http://www.fafsa.ed.gov. Visit the UW Office of Student Financial Aid at http://www.washington.edu/students/osfa/ for more information.

FACULTY

The UW Business School philosophy emphasizes a partnership between students and faculty members. Professors at the UW Business School have achieved recognition for both teaching and research. MBAs praise the faculty's active involvement in student learning and their integration of research and teaching. Professors take a personal interest in their students and, in return, they demand a high level of student effort and commitment.

STUDENT BODY

The UW Business School strives to create an environment that is representative of society as a whole—age, racial or ethnic origin, cultural background, activities and accomplishments, goals, life experiences. Class size for each entering MBA cohort at the UW Business School is around 100 students. Students' undergraduate degrees are distributed almost equally among liberal arts, business, engineering, and science. The average student in last year's class was 29 years old and had 5 years of work experience. International students made up about 22 percent of the class and represented 17 different countries. The class that entered in 2005 had an average GPA of 3.45 and an average GMAT score of 677.

ADMISSIONS

The UW Business School believes that personal connections are essential to business education, just as they are to business. Advance counseling is strongly advised for anyone considering an MBA program. The MBA program encourages campus visits to meet face-to-face with admissions staff or attend a reception held in cities nationwide. Each fall, the UW Business School admits up to 150 men and women with the highest potential for achievement in management. The MBA program seeks individuals who have demonstrated high-quality academic work, and who will contribute to the diversity of both the student body and the ranks of professional management. Applicants must:

- Complete the equivalent of a four-year U.S. bachelor's degree from an accredited college or university

- Meet a quantitative analysis requirement and possess minimum English language skills

- Take the GMAT

Apply to each school, college, or department of interest if pursuing a dual degree.

UNIVERSITY OF WESTERN ONTARIO
The Richard Ivey School of Business

AT A GLANCE

The Richard Ivey School of Business offers a full complement of pre-business, undergraduate, MBA, executive MBA, PhD, and executive development programs, all based on the premise that experience is the foundation of true learning.

It begins with Ivey's case-study methodology, grounded in the experience and knowledge of faculty who are consultants to businesses around the globe. Add to this mix the contributions of its students—some of the brightest minds in business today—and you have the reasons why Ivey consistently earns top marks worldwide.

Many schools claim to teach the case-study method, but it is practiced in its truest form by just a few. Only Ivey offers students a learn-by-doing rather than a learn-by-listening approach. Cases present data, information and scenarios that give students the opportunity to step into the shoes of decision-makers and through this approach, students develop the ability to sort through complex information and identify the most effective solutions.

In presenting their ideas in the Ivey classroom, they gain the confidence to deliver ideas clearly, defend and debate with their peers, and develop solutions that are immediately applicable to the business world.

Through challenge and debate, students develop a disciplined approach to solving business problems. This approach is learned in the classroom and proven daily by Ivey's alumni network of more than 17,000 business leaders in 75 countries worldwide. Plus, Ivey is the only Canadian business school with North American, European, and Asian advisory boards, 15 alumni ambassador chapters, and an alumni partnership program designed to connect you with people who will make a difference in your career.

One in four Ivey alumni is a senior executive in companies that span every industry and every continent around the world. That's over 4,000 senior executives who are part of the Ivey network.

Ivey alumni play a role in students' development at the school as well. Through the *Ivey Alumni Partnership Program*, students partner with alumni who in turn share career and business advice. The partnership allows students and alumni to network with new contacts—people who can provide career information that can lead to new career opportunities.

CAMPUS AND LOCATION

Ivey's main North American campus is located at The University of Western Ontario (Western) in London, Canada—approximately halfway between Toronto and Detroit, USA. However, the school has a definite international reach with campuses in Hong Kong and Toronto (Mississauga), and academic links with partner universities in 25 countries.

Ivey holds accreditation from the European Foundation for Management Development, joining the ranks of top tier international business schools that meet the strict quality education standards set by The European Quality Improvement System (EQUIS). Ivey has also been selected by the British government as one of the 50 top schools in the world (based on post-graduate salaries and employment potential), entitling Ivey MBAs automatic access and visas to work in the UK after graduation.

The school's association with Western dates back to 1878 when the university was founded. Western includes 11 other faculties and professional schools, three affiliated colleges, two teaching hospitals, two affiliated research institutes and enrolls more than 25,000 students annually.

DEGREES OFFERED

Ivey offers undergraduate honors business administration (HBA), MBA, executive MBA, PhD, and executive development programs. The Hong Kong campus offers programs in EMBA, MBA and executive development. In addition, Ivey offers many "streams" and concurrent degrees at both the MBA and undergraduate level. At the MBA level, Ivey offers a China business MBA stream, biotech MBA stream, finance MBA stream, CMA/MBA stream, entrepreneurship MBA certificate, and an MBA/law degree. At the undergraduate (HBA) level, Ivey offers concurrent degrees in engineering/business, health science/business, kinesiology/business, law/business, medical sciences/business, and honors science/business.

EXPENSES AND FINANCIAL AID

An Ivey education is an investment in your future. Tuition for the MBA program is as follows:

	First Year	Second Year	Total
Entering fall of 2005	$28,000°	$28,000°	$56,000°
(domestic students)	$28,000°	$28,000°	$56,000°
Entering fall of 2005 (international students)	$30,000°	$30,000°	$60,000°

°subject to UWO Senate approval and subject to change

FACULTY

The Richard Ivey School of Business includes 78 full time professors and 4 lecturers who are experts in their field. Ivey's faculty members are the perfect complement to Ivey learning. Each faculty member brings a unique perspective to the classroom. There are many backgrounds at Ivey, including Canada, the U.S., United Kingdom, France, India, Germany, Belgium, Denmark, Lebanon, China and the Philippines, bringing international education and experience to their areas of expertise.

Our faculty does more than just deliver facts. They are tireless researchers, curious about how business works in the real world. The hallmark of Ivey research is relevance as it's based in the current realities of business. From finance, to organizational behavior, to marketing and global business, research at Ivey has a significant impact on management practice—and the impact is felt in the classroom.

STUDENTS

We actively recruit to attract the highest quality candidates to apply to Ivey. Our goal is to enroll a full class each year. Regretfully, the number of applications exceeds the number of spaces in the program, and Ivey cannot offer admission to each applicant. Admission works on a rolling basis for the MBA program. For more information please visit http://www.ivey.uwo.ca/mba/admissions.htm, http://www.ivey.uwo.ca/emba, http://www.ivey.uwo.ca/hba.

Many candidates may not have enough resources to cover the cost of the MBA program for two years. Ivey has developed the MBA loan program in partnerships with the following Canadian banks: ScotiaBank, Royal Bank, TD Canada Trust, Bank of Montreal and ING Direct to create attractive loan packages for Ivey MBA candidates. For more information please visit http://www.ivey.uwo.ca/mba/finances/loan.htm

CAREER SERVICES

Ivey's Career Management office is the largest international Career Management office at any business school. With 18 staff in London, Hong Kong and Shanghai Career Management is equipped to provide students with personal and diverse consultation and opportunities.

Ivey Career Management has received high accolades from both recruiters and students. In the most recent *Wall Street Journal* business school ranking, the Richard Ivey School of Business was ranked #2 worldwide by recruiters in the management consulting industry.

Ivey draws recruiters from the world's best corporations around the world. Strong corporate relationships, a world-class reputation and an enhanced career management curriculum have resulted in a 44 percent increase in job postings in 2005. All student groups, domestic and international, have increased placement to date this year.

VANDERBILT UNIVERSITY
Owen Graduate School of Management

AT A GLANCE
The Vanderbilt Owen Graduate School of Management is dedicated to setting a new standard in business education. Owen stands apart among leading business schools in providing a rigorous, relevant education that fully prepares graduates for their roles as the ethical leaders of tomorrow—persons who will shape their worlds and our future.

The Vanderbilt MBA program offers an intimate, collaborative environment in which individuals are encouraged to fulfill their potential. Graduates are highly prized by recruiters, who ranked Owen #2 in the 2005 *Wall Street Journal* survey of top regional business schools. The Vanderbilt MBA program is world-class, known internationally for its Top 10 Finance program, as well as one of the strongest human and organizational performance programs in the country.

OUR PROMISE
To students: Here is a place where you'll be challenged to achieve your potential, where you'll find support as you shape your future, discover life-long friends and mentors, and open doors to new possibilities.

To faculty and staff: Here is a place where you can engage, think, reach, teach, influence people, and transform the world around you.

To business: Here is a place where you will find the men and women who have the skills, the drive, and the determination to move your organization forward.

To alumni: Here is a place that you can call home, build business relationships, and inspire those who follow to reach even higher.

CAMPUS AND LOCATION
Nashville is one of the Southeast's most vibrant and livable cities, featuring excellent restaurants, music venues, sporting events, museums, historic sites, mild weather, and a dynamic business climate.

Vanderbilt University was founded in 1873 and enrolls more than 11,000 undergraduate and graduate students throughout its 10 schools. Vanderbilt is located a mile and a half from downtown Nashville on a park-like campus that was designated a national arboretum in 1988.

Vanderbilt Owen Graduate School of Management opened its doors in 1969 to ten students and ten faculty members. Today, as one of the world's leading business schools, Owen retains one of the nation's best student-faculty ratios of 10:1. Owen is known for a spirit of teamwork, challenging academics, and a stimulating research environment.

DEGREES OFFERED
Owen offers MBA, executive MBA, MS finance, and PhD degrees, as well as dual degree programs that allow multidisciplinary study in management and another graduate or professional program such as law or medicine.

ACADEMIC PROGRAMS
All Owen full-time MBA students start with the required courses in "the core"—an intense immersion in the fundamentals of management. Students are required to specify a primary area of concentration in accounting, finance, general management, human and organizational performance, information technology, marketing, operations, or strategy. Students may also pursue an emphasis in brand management, entrepreneurship, environmental management, health care, or international business.

In 2005, Owen will launch an MBA degree with a health care specialization, a groundbreaking program that combines the core business education with real-world health care experience. The school also offers a law and business program, which gives students an opportunity to take interdisciplinary courses at Vanderbilt Law School. The executive MBA program meets on alternate weekends over 21 months, and provides the knowledge and the credentials for mid-career managers and executives to succeed in today's dynamic business environment.

The Vanderbilt master of science in finance degree (MSF) is a nine-month intensive program offering an advanced business degree in quantitative financial analysis.

FACILITIES
The Walker Management Library, ranked by *The Princeton Review* as the #1 b-school library in the U.S., provides world-class research support for students and faculty.

EXPENSES AND FINANCIAL AID
Tuition:
Full-time MBA (2 years): $33,830 per year (2005–2006)
Executive MBA (2 years): $38,450 per year (all-inclusive: books, fees, etc.)
MS finance (1 year): $33,830 per year (2005–2006)

All admitted applicants are considered for merit-based scholarships. Approximately 51 percent of admitted students are offered scholarships, and the average award is $13,423. U.S. citizens and permanent residents are eligible to apply for Federal Stafford Loans and private loan programs. International students may apply for private loans with a U.S. citizen or permanent resident as a co-signer.

FACULTY
Owen faculty members have made an impact on NASDAQ, founded the world's first academic research center dedicated to the study of e-commerce and the Internet, and contributed to advances in many other areas of global business. To shape innovative business managers and insightful leaders, professors combine lectures, discussions, case studies, and group projects with experiential learning opportunities in the business community.

STUDENT BODY
Students come from a wide variety of academic, professional, and personal backgrounds, and from nearly 40 countries. In this tight-knit community, you will find a unique, collegial culture in which students truly flourish, working closely with each other and with faculty, alumni, and the business community to meet and exceed their personal and professional goals. Students share a passion to achieve their goals by working hard, accepting new challenges, and supporting each other through teamwork in the classroom and beyond.

ADMISSIONS
The Admissions Committee evaluates applicants on the basis of academic ability, professional experience, personal qualities, and leadership potential. Applicants offered admission average a 3.3 GPA, 636 GMAT, and five years of post-baccalaureate work experience. http://admissions.owen.edu.

SPECIAL PROGRAMS
Owen hosts information sessions, receptions, and on-campus weekend events, and participates in major recruiting events around the world. We encourage visits to campus, especially when classes are in session.

CAREER SERVICES & PLACEMENT
Owen offers a highly personal approach to career management, ensuring that each student receives individual attention and access to the knowledge, resources, and guidance required to accomplish their career goals. The Career Management Center supports students with counseling, negotiation assistance, industry seminars, on-campus interviews, recruiter feedback, networking trips, and more.

Salaries for Vanderbilt MBAs are highly competitive with other top business schools. The rigorous curriculum, extensive recruiting contacts, global alumni network, and reputation for creating well-rounded managers help propel graduates into successful careers in many different industries, functional areas, and geographic regions. Plus, the relationships built at Owen will support and enhance your career opportunities for years to come.

WILLAMETTE UNIVERSITY
Atkinson Graduate School of Management

THE SCHOOL AT A GLANCE

Willamette University's Atkinson Graduate School of Management offers the only MBA accredited by the two most prestigious organizations governing management education: AACSB International (business) and NASPAA (public administration). The distinctive dual accreditation provides professional recognition and respect in all sectors, and prepares students for careers in entrepreneurial, business, consulting, government, and nonprofit organizations. The school has also been profiled as one of the country's best business schools by *Business Week* and *U.S. News & World Report*.

CAMPUS AND LOCATION

Willamette University is located in Salem, Oregon. Salem is the second largest city in Oregon and has twice been honored as an "All American City." The Salem-Portland I-5 corridor is home to a multitude of businesses (including Northwest legends Nike, Intel, and Tektronix) and hosts a large variety of government and nonprofit organizations. Salem is home to the Oregon State Capitol, many historic sites, 96 city parks, indoor and outdoor concerts featuring international performers, art and wine festivals, bike paths, running trails, and the popular Riverfront Park.

DEGREES OFFERED

Willamette University's Atkinson Graduate School of Management offers the MBA for business, government, and nonprofit management. The Atkinson School MBA is the first and only MBA program accredited for both business (AACSB International) and public administration (NASPAA). Students may also pursue a joint MBA/JD degree through a cooperative agreement with Willamette University's College of Law. Candidates for the MBA/JD joint degree program must apply and be admitted to both the College of Law and the Atkinson School.

ACADEMIC PROGRAMS

The Atkinson School MBA has two program options; the "two-year" MBA program and the "accelerated" option. Both are designed for students with different academic and professional backgrounds.

The distinct experiential and curricular advantages of the Atkinson School MBA make the two-year (21 month) full-time MBA program an excellent choice for early career students pursuing career entry or change, and experienced students pursuing career change or advancement.

The "accelerated" waiver-based option of the Atkinson School MBA is designed for people seeking career change or advancement who have a strong background in the academic study of business as well as professional work experience. Students admitted to the accelerated program focus their studies in the Atkinson School elective curriculum, and complete the Atkinson School MBA in approximately 9 to 15 months of full-time study (or longer as a part-time student).

FACILITIES

Willamette University facilities include two libraries, a wireless computer network, a number of computer labs, state-of-the art classrooms, recreational and fitness facilities, dining centers, a student center, a concert hall, an art museum, student apartments, and more. Atkinson School classrooms are spacious, modern, and facilitate interaction among students and between students and faculty. Atkinson students have 24-hour-a-day wireless access to the Internet, E-mail, and local network software and printing services. The University's Mark O. Hatfield Library and the J.W. Long Law Library support the research needs of Atkinson students. Services include a Management/Economics Librarian who assists students and faculty, electronic databases, books, periodicals, journals, newspapers, specialized materials, and programs that provide access to more than four million books, journals, and library resources.

EXPENSES AND FINANCIAL AID

The budget for full-time Atkinson School students includes the estimated costs of tuition, books, fees, and living expenses (living expenses include room, board, and personal expenses). Estimated

Expenses for 2005-2006:
Tuition: $19,020 **Student Body Fee:** $50 **Books:** $1,200 **Living Expenses:** $7,550 to $11,350

Willamette University offers a variety of programs to make your Atkinson School MBA as affordable as possible. Atkinson students finance their education with the help of loans, scholarships, family resources, income from work, and Tuition Management Systems payment program. Full-time students may be eligible for Atkinson School scholarships. Refer to the website for further information about financial options.

FACULTY

Atkinson faculty are leaders of community and professional organizations; authors of books, articles, and software packages; editors and reviewers of professional journals; entrepreneurs; consultants to business, government, and nonprofit organizations; and members of national and regional boards that make important decisions about management education in America. Their professional experience with current management issues and dedication to teaching make Atkinson an exciting place to learn. One hundred percent of Atkinson faculty members have a doctorate degree. Three endowed faculty chairs (economics and finance, public policy, and international management) provide special resources that enhance teaching innovation and scholarly research.

STUDENTS

The Atkinson student profile is characterized by the same diversity of age and experience that is common to the work environment of most organizations. Students come to the Atkinson School with a variety of academic backgrounds and work experience. The average student is 22 to 28 years of age and has zero to five years of work experience. Forty percent of the students are women; 60 percent are men. Twenty-five percent are international students and 10 percent are minority students. Although generally from the Western U.S., students come from 14 states and 14 countries.

ADMISSIONS

The Atkinson School MBA program is designed for students pursuing career entry, career change or career advancement, and welcomes applicants with extensive work experience as well as recent college graduates.

Admission to the Atkinson School is based on academic ability and managerial potential. Academic ability is evaluated by the applicant's past academic performance, recommendations, and performance on the GMAT or GRE. Managerial potential is evaluated by the applicant's general experience, work experience, motivation, leadership, involvement in organizational or community activities, communication skills, and commitment to attain a graduate management education. Please see the website for details on documentation that is required from potential applicants.

For information, contact:
Admission Office, Atkinson Graduate School of Management
Willamette University
900 State Street
Salem, OR 97301
Telephone: 503-370-6167; Toll Free: 1-866-MBA-AGSM
Fax: 503-370-3011
E-mail: mba-admission@willamette.edu
Internet: www.willamette.edu/mba

CAREER SERVICES & PLACEMENT

The Atkinson School works with students and employers to provide a complete program of services connecting students and alumni with employment opportunities. Career service programs help students develop strategic career management skills, improve job search skills, and obtain internships and employment.

XAVIER UNIVERSITY

AT A GLANCE

The MBA programs are designed for working professionals. Programs challenge committed, career minded students who want to learn and apply skills, insights, and classroom experiences immediately. Three distinct MBA curriculums are offered to meet student needs: the evening program, the weekend program, and the executive MBA program.

CAMPUS AND LOCATION

Xavier University is a private coeducational university located in Cincinnati, Ohio. Xavier's 125-acre campus is located in a residential neighborhood only a short drive from downtown Cincinnati, a diverse, bustling community that *Places Rated Almanac* has called America's 11th most livable city. Cincinnati is accessible, affordable, safe and blessed with small-town charm, big-city excitement, mild weather, and its own famous brand of chili.

The nation's 23rd largest region, Greater Cincinnati is home to 1.9 million people, two professional sports teams, and the headquarters of six Fortune 500 companies. Cincinnati is located on the banks of the Ohio River and at the convergence of three states—Ohio, Kentucky and Indiana.

ACADEMIC PROGRAMS

The curriculum of the MBA program for working professionals consists of five components:

- Foundation skills
- Business and system skills
- Integrated functions
- Matrix course
- Concentrations & electives

These are the basis of an educational experience hallmarked by a high degree of flexibility and responsiveness to the scheduling and developmental needs of students. Courses are offered for two or three credit hours. Three credit hour courses meet for 16 weeks while two credit hour courses meet for seven weeks, thus allowing students the flexibility of completing three classes during the semester, but only attending two nights a week.

AREAS OF INTEREST

- E-business
- Finance
- Business administration (general)
- International business
- Management information systems
- Marketing

EXPENSES AND FINANCIAL AID

Financial needs are integral to selecting the right MBA program. Xavier University provides options to assist students make the financial investment of this degree as easy as possible. Tuition is updated annually in the summer term and is listed on the Xavier website. Options include:

- Graduate School of Business grants
- Graduate assistantships
- Tuition payment plans
- Low-interest loans

FACULTY

University professors and outstanding business professionals provide course instruction to MBA students. Availability is their hallmark, be it in person, electronically, or by phone. Assessment is continual so that courses are cutting edge. Be it guest lecturers, case studies, or computer simulations, MBA students receive an education that will provide them the foundation to achieve goals and successfully master the trends of current business.

STUDENT BODY

The Xavier MBA program serves "working people," though there is a strong contingent of students who attend full time. Extracurricular activities in which students participate include: professional development workshops, networking events, and "Meet the Firm" nights, as well as meeting on campus before or after class for study groups.

Major demographics of the MBA student body for the academic year 2004 are as follows.

- 17 percent of the MBA student body enrolled full time.
- 8 years is the average work experience of the MBA student body.
- 41 percent of the MBA student body earned a bachelor's degree in discipline other than business.
- 530 are the median GMAT score of the MBA student body.
- 35 percent of the MBA student body is female.
- 13 percent of the MBA student body is a minority.
- 26 percent of the MBA student body is international.

ADMISSIONS

The Xavier MBA program office offers seamless admissions. Admission materials may be submitted electronically, via post, or in person. As such, five pieces of information (domestic applicants only) are needed to complete an application. These include an application, a resume, transcripts, GMAT scores, and the $35 application fee. These pieces may be submitted individually.

Additional information can be obtained by contacting the MBA office at (513) 745-3525 or via email at XUMBA@xavier.edu.

CAREER SERVICES & PLACEMENT

The Xavier MBA program offers students and alumni the Professional Development Center (PDC). The PDC's mission is to provide Xavier students and alumni with career transition tools and opportunities that will enable them to develop professionally and advance within their organizations and throughout their professional careers. The PDC offers the following resources: MBA job board, "Meet the Firm" nights, MBA professional networking hour, MBA professional development workshops in interviewing excellence, salary negotiation, career self assessment, networking for life, leadership, and excellence in presenting, EBA executive mentoring program, traditional and virtual career fairs, and leadership training and retreats.

Those who are seeking employment tell us that Xavier's greatest assist is its reputation with employers. One student writes, "It gets great respect within the Cincinnati area. People are very impressed when I say 'I am an MBA student at Xavier.'"

Employers who have visited campus this year include: Ethicon Endo Surgery, State Farm Insurance, Merrill Lynch, Northwest Mutual, Cinergy Corporation, to list a few.

DECODING DEGREES

Many business programs offer a number of degrees, including joint or combined degree programs with other departments (or with other schools) that you can earn along with your MBA. You'll find the abbreviations for these degrees in the individual school profiles, but we thought we'd give you a little help in figuring out exactly what they are.

AGSIM	Master in International Management	IPD	Interdisciplinary Product Development
AM	Social Service Administration	JD	Juris Doctorate
APC	Advanced Professional Certificate	LLB	Bachelor of Law
BA	Bachelor of Arts	MA	Master of Arts
BASC	Bachelor in Engineering	MAB	Master of Agribusiness
BBA	Bachelor of Business Administration	MACC	Master of Accountancy (or Accounting)
BPA	Bachelor of Public Affairs	MAAE	Master of Arts in Applied Economics
BS	Bachelor of Science	MAECON	Master of Arts in Economics
BSB	Bachelor of Science in Business	MAg	Master of Agriculture
BSBA	Bachelor of Science in Business Administration	MAIB	Master of Arts in International Business
CIS	Computer Information Systems (or Sciences)	MAIS	Master of Accounting and Information Systems
DBA	Docctor of Business Administration	MALL	Master of Arts in Language Learning
DDS	Doctor of Dental Surgery	MAPS	Master of Asian Pacific Studies
DMD	Doctor or Dental Medicine	MAR	Master of Arts in Religion
DO	Doctor of Osteopathic Medicine	MARCH	Master of Architecture
DPS	Doctor pf Professional Studies	MAS	Master of Actuarial Science
EdD	Doctor of Education	MBA	Master of Business Administration
EDM	Executive Doctor of Management	MBE	Master of Business Education
EMBA	Executive MBA	MBI	Master of Business Informatics
EMIB	Executive Master of International Business	MBS	Master of Business Studies
EMPA	Executive Master of Public Administration	MD	Doctor of Medicine
EMS	Executive Master of Science	MDIV	Master of Divinity
EMSM	Executive Master of Science in Management	ME	Master of Engineering
EMSMOT	Executive Master of Science in Management of Technology	MECOM	Master of Electronic Commerce
EMST	Executive Master of Science in Taxation	MEd	Master of Educational Leadership/ Master of Education
GDPA	Graduate Diploma in Accounting	MEM	Master of Engineering and Management
GEMBA	Global Executive Master of Business Administration	MEng	Master of Engineering
HRIM	Hotel, Restaurants and Institutional Management	MF	Master of Forestry
		MFA	Master of Fine Arts
IAMBA	Information Age Master of Business Administration	MHA	Master of Health Administration
		MHR	Master of Human Resources
IMBA	International MBA	MHRM	Master of Human Resources Management
		MIA	Master of International Affairs

MIAS	Master of International and Area Studies	MSGFA	Master of Science in Global Financial Analysis
MIB	Master of International Business	MSHA	Master of Science in Health Administration
MIE	Master of Industrial Engineering	MSHFID	Master of Science in Human Factors in Information Design
MILR	Master of Industrial and Labor Relations		
MIM	Master of International Management	MSIAM	Master of Science in Information Age Marketing
MIS	Management Information Systems		
MISM	Master of Information Systems Management	MSIB	Master of Science in International Business
MLAS	Master of Liberal Arts and Science	MSIE	Master of Science in Industrial Engineering
MMIS	Master of Management Information Systems	MSIM	Master of Science in Industrial Management
MMR	Master of Marketing Research	MSIMC	Master of Science in Integrated Marketing Communications
MMS	Master of Management Science		
MNO	Master of Nonprofit Organizations	MSIR	Master of Industrial Relations
MOD	Master of Science in Organizational Development	MSIS	Master of Science in Information Systems
		MSISE	Master of Science in Industrial and Systems Engineering
MPA	Master of Public Administration		
MPACC	Master of Professional Accounting	MSISM	Master of Science in Information Systems Management
MPH	Master of Public Health		
MPIA	Master of Public and International Affairs	MSIT	Master of Science in Information Technology
MPL	Master of Planning	MSITM	Master of Science in Information Technology Management
MPP	Master of Public Policy		
MRED	Master of Real Estate Development	MSM	Master of Science in Management
MS	Master of Science	MSMIS	Master of Science in Management Information Systems
MSA	Master of Science in Accountancy (or Accounting)	MSMOT	Master of Science in Management of Technology
MSAIS	Master of Science in Accounting Information Systems	MSN	Master of Science in Nursing
		MSOD	Master of Science in Organization Development
MSAT	Master of Science in Accountancy, Taxation MSB Master of Science in Business	MSpAd	Master of Sports Administration
		MSRE	Master of Science in Real Estate
MSBA	Master of Science in Business Administration	MSS	Master of Social Science
		MSSA	Master of Science in Social Administration
MSE	Master of Science in Engineering	MST	Master of Science in Taxation
MSEC	Master of Science in Electronic Commerce	MSTM	Master of Science in Telecommunications Management
MSF	Master of Finance		
MSFA	Master of Science in Financial Analysis	MSW	Master of Social Work
MSFS	Master of Sciences in Foreign Services	MTAX	Master of Taxation
MSG	Master of Science in Gerontology	MTLM	Master of Transportation and Logistics Management

NEMBA	National Executive Master of Business Administration
PharmD	Doctor of Pharmacy
PhD	Doctor of Philosophy
SM	Master of Science
TSM	Telecommunications Systems Management
VMD	Doctor of Veterinary Medicine

INDEXES

ALPHABETICAL LIST OF SCHOOLS

S

T

U

V

USA

ALABAMA

ALASKA

ARIZONA

ARKANSAS

CALIFORNIA

ABOUT THE AUTHOR

Nedda Gilbert is a graduate of the University of Pennsylvania and holds a master's degree from Columbia University. She has worked for The Princeton Review since 1985. In 1987, she created The Princeton Review corporate test preparation service, which provides Wall Street firms and premier companies tailored educational programs for their employees. She currently resides in New Jersey.

Manage Student Loan Debt Like A Pro

Upon arriving at your future alma mater as a freshman you will be asked one of the most important, yet most difficult questions of your life, "What do you want to do when you graduate?" For some, the answer to this question was as clear as day from the beginning. However for most, it was a question with an impossible answer. It is a question that all post high school graduates know is peering its ugly head around the corner, and inevitably, has to be answered.

After several days of thinking and mulling over the seemingly endless possibilities, speaking with advisors and conversing amongst friends, the decision is made and the course has been set. With the whisper of one single, simple little phrase, you begin the journey of the rest of your life.

Many of the professions that young people choose these days require a post secondary education of some sort. These specialized positions demand the highest level of skill, concentration, and more importantly, time and money.

Now that you have completed the first step along the path to accomplishing your ultimate goal and received your undergraduate degree, there are many decisions that need to be made, and many things that need to be considered. Taking into account the cost associated with receiving a specialized degree in a field such as medicine, money is on the top of most students' minds. "How will I pay for this? How will I repay my undergraduate loans while still attending school? What will happen when I graduate?"

In 1965, the Federal Government passed *The Higher Education Act*. This legislation was passed to strengthen the educational resources of our colleges and universities. It provides assistance for students wanting to enroll in postsecondary and higher education programs such as medical, law, or business school, and encourages more students to pursue their college and graduate school dreams.

Tuition increases have far outpaced the growth in personal and family income over the past two decades. For this reason, the need for private and federal aid has increased dramatically. As schools have become more expensive to attend, students and parents have been required to increase the amount of borrowing that they need under Federal Programs. As a result, the amount that students and parents have to pay on a monthly basis has also increased.

In order to address this problem and try to ease the financial burden on student borrowers, Congress passed the *Consolidation Loan Program* under the *Higher Education Act in 1986*. With this program, student loan borrowers are able to consolidate their multiple Federal Student Loans into one new Loan, while at the same time, extending their repayment term and locking in a fixed interest rate. By doing this, borrowers are able to lower their monthly payments enabling them to avoid delinquency and default.

THE FEDERAL CONSOLIDATION LOAN PROGRAM

The Federal Consolidation Loan Program is a unique program offered by the Federal Government that provides student loan borrowers with the following benefits:

- Lower monthly loan payments.

- Lock in a fixed interest rate for the life of the loan.

- Ability to merge all of the existing eligible federal loans into one new loan thereby making only one payment per month.

- Maintain their existing in-school deferment option if attending a graduate school and have no prepayment penalties. In-school deferment allows borrowers to postpone their payments while they are enrolled at least half time. While in deferment, all subsidized Stafford loans included in the consolidation will accrue zero interest.

- Availability of several repayment plans, including standard level payments, graduated payments, and income-based payments, allowing borrower to select the plan that best meets his or her needs.

- Potential interest rate reductions or other benefits, depending on the lender.

The Federal Consolidation Loan Program could be in the best interest of many students depending on the interest rates at the current time. There are no additional service fees for setting up a Consolidation Loan.

The eligibility guidelines for the program are very simple. In order to be eligible for a consolidation loan, a borrower must:

- Have outstanding loans made under the Federal Family Education Loan Program (FFELP), Direct, Perkins or Health Professions Student Loan (HPSL) program.

- Be in repayment period (including deferment and forbearance) or grace period.

- If a borrower is in default on their loans, certain rules/requirements apply in order to include these loans in the consolidation. Not all lenders will consolidate defaulted loans.

- Although Federal rules do not require a minimum balance many lenders may set minimum balance requirements. Typical minimums range from $5,000 to $10,000.

Qualifying Loans Under the Program:

Several types of student loans are eligible for Consolidation, including:

- Federal Family Education Loan Program (FFELP)

    Federal Subsidized and Unsubsidized Stafford Loans

    Federal PLUS Loans

    Federal Consolidation Loans

- Direct Loan Program

    Direct Subsidized and Unsubsidized Stafford Loans

    Direct PLUS loans

    Direct Consolidation Loans

- Perkins Loan Program

    Federal Perkins Loans

- Health Profession Student Loans (HPSL)

- Other

    Federal Education Assistance Loans (HEAL)

    Federal Nursing Student Loans (NSL)

CONSOLIDATION, WHEN IS THE RIGHT TIME?

A borrower can consolidate their student loans upon the completion of an undergraduate or graduate degree. As for those planning to attend postsecondary school, there are a few things to consider.

One of the great benefits of a higher education is the entitlement to in-school deferment on all federal loans. A borrower is legally entitled to this deferment even if they consolidate their student loans after they receive their undergraduate degree! The Department of Education states that students considered at least half-time (typically a minimum of six credit hours per semester) are not only eligible, but are legally guaranteed in-school deferment.

If this is the case, what is the benefit to consolidating only a portion of your student loans? All Stafford loans have variable interest rates prior to using the FFEL Consolidation Program. Once your loans have been consolidated the interest rate is locked in for the life of the loan and cannot go any higher. This is the primary and obvious reason to consolidate all eligible Stafford loans while still accumulating student loan debt.

The loans that will be taken out for postsecondary school may maintain their variable interest rates until the program is complete or the course load drops below half time. If the current interest rates are low in comparison to past years, you should secure whatever eligible debt you have incurred at these rates and consolidate the postsecondary school loans later. In fact, the option to roll all loans together or consolidate the remaining loans in a completely separate consolidation is something to be decided later.

The Six Month Grace Period = Opportunity for Big Savings

Most know that they do not necessarily have to begin paying off their student loans until six months after graduation. This six months is called a Grace Period or a period in which recently graduated students are awarded time to decide where they are going to live, find a job, etc. before they are required to make payments on their student loan debt.

Despite popular belief, the grace period typically may be the best time to consolidate student loans. When in a grace period, student loan interest rates are actually over a half of a percent lower than when the required payments begin six months after graduation.

STUDENT LOAN INTEREST RATES

Not all student loan borrowers have the same interest rate when they take advantage of the Consolidation Loan Program. This is not due to personal credit or the lender selected, but rather to government rules. A borrower's interest rate is determined by several factors.

FFELP Consolidation is a federal program and the actual interest rate is determined by a set of rules defined by the U.S. Department of Education. The fixed interest rates are determined by taking the weighted average of all of the loans being consolidated and rounding to the nearest 1/8th of a point.

Rates for Stafford and PLUS loans first disbursed on or after July 1, 1998, are adjusted on July 1 of each year based on the results of the last auction of the three-month Treasury bills before June 1st.

Many mailings and advertisements from Consolidation lenders offer the lowest possible rate and interest rate reductions. It is standard practice for companies to offer 0.25 percent reduction for making automatic EFT payments from a checking account. Many also offer a 1 percent interest rate reduction once a certain number of on-time payments have been received. The actual interest rate that is determined by the U.S. Department of Education is the maximum that a lender can charge and is the same from company to company.

Repayment Options

The Federal Consolidation Loan Program allows borrowers to get the best payoff terms without imposing penalties for early repayment. All Stafford loans are initially on a ten-year payoff plan, leaving many to opt for a nonpayment status such as deferment or forbearance when experiencing a cash flow problem in the short-term. Many borrowers want lower monthly payments, which will lengthen the payoff term. Switching to a longer-term payoff plan provides an immediate increase in short-term cash flow. Since there is no pre-payment penalty with the program, a borrower can make aggressive payments towards the principal at any time.

Most lenders do not require a borrower to accept the longer term associated with the repayment plans, so if they are opposed to it, other options exist. At the borrower's request, the servicer of his/her consolidation can adjust the payment plan to a ten-year payoff schedule. Borrowers are initially set up on the following terms based upon the balance of their Consolidation Loan:

- **10 years** for less than $7,500

- **12 years** for $7,500 to $10,000

- **15 years** for $10,000 to $20,000 ($20,000 balance monthly payment drop from $192 to $110)

- **20 years** for $20,000 to $40,000 ($35,000 balance monthly payment drop from $335 to $191)

- **25 years** for $40,000 to $60,000 ($50,000 balance monthly payment drop from $480 to $234)

- **30 years** for $60,000 and above ($100,000 balance monthly payment drop from $960 to $415)

A borrower may choose from the most suitable of four repayment plans:

- **Standard Repayment**

The monthly payment amount is fixed over the life of the Loan. The most popular plan is the level repayment method. Many borrowers choose this plan because they like the security and simplicity of a fixed monthly payment. However, more importantly, the level repayment plan usually is the least expensive in terms of total interest charges. The latter plans cost more because they slow down the repayment of the principal.

- **Graduated Repayment**

The Graduated Repayment Plan can vary from lender to lender, however many lenders offer more affordable interest only payments with the initial installments. After a certain number of the interest only payments the borrower will begin to pay down on the principle, resulting in higher payments. Other lenders offer pay increases every two years on the loans. The loan is repaid in the same timeframe as the Standard Repayment, but the total interest costs are slightly higher. The purpose of this payment plan is to provide the borrower more disposable income immediately upon beginning repayment.

- Extended Repayment

This plan allows the borrower to repay his/her Federal Consolidation Loans over a 25-year period under a level or graduated repayment schedule. To be eligible, the oldest Federal Stafford (subsidized and unsubsidized), Federal PLUS and/or Federal Consolidation Loan must have been disbursed on or after October 7, 1998 (borrowers who have pre-1998 loans can qualify for extended repayment if they consolidate all of the pre-1998 loans). In addition, the combined outstanding balance on all eligible Loans must be at least $30,000.01.

- Income-sensitive repayment

Initial monthly payments are based on monthly earnings and are adjusted annually, according to changes in income.

A new federal loan allows a borrower to consolidate again and restart a brand new term. While extending the repayment term may increase the overall amount of interest paid over the life of the loan, those who have higher debt often find the longer payoff schedule to be acceptable.

In addition to the choice of plans, the borrower can switch from one repayment plan to another at least once a year. There's no extra cost or penalty. All it takes is a phone call to his/her servicer or lender.

MAKING THE RIGHT DECISION

Now that all of the benefits of the Federal Consolidation Loan Program have been explained in their entirety, it is up to you, the borrower, to make the final decision. Find the company that offers the best explanation of terms, or find the one with the best incentives. Remember, the official interest rate formula is the same everywhere. The decision simply becomes a matter of personal choice. So what are you waiting for? Consolidate your student loans today and save money today!

More expert advice from